Footprint Tibet

Gyurme Dorje
3rd edition

"Tibet's high altitude clearly distinguishes it from its neighbours. However, as the source of many of Asia's great rivers and having immeasurable effect on the regional climate, it cannot easily be ignored. The Tibetan people have a distinct identity. Our language, diet, dress and way of life are unique. Our rich and ancient culture, strongly influenced by Buddhism, has much of value to contribute to the welfare of the world."

HH Dalai Lama, foreword to *Footprint Tibet*, first edition (1996)

❶ **Guge**
The deserted troglodyte citadel of Tsaparang

❷ **Kailash and Manasarovar**
Sacred axis mundi of Hindu and Buddhist cosmology

❸ **Jangtang**
The world's second largest nature reserve

❹ **Mount Everest**
Base camp at the roof of the world

❺ **Sakya**
Legacy of 13th century Sakya and Mongol power

❻ **Gyantse Kumbum**
An elaborate walk-in stupa with chapels arranged in a spiritual hierarchy

❼ **Lhasa**
Bustling metropolis, where modernity collides with world heritage sites

❽ **Mindroling**
Vital monastery of the Nyingma tradition, with outstanding murals and sculptures

❾ **Samye-Chimphu**
The dramatic setting of Tibet's first Buddhist monastery and meditation hermitage

❿ **Pome and Pemako**
A land of virgin forests set against snow peaks and magical lakes

Tibet Highlights

See colour maps at back of book

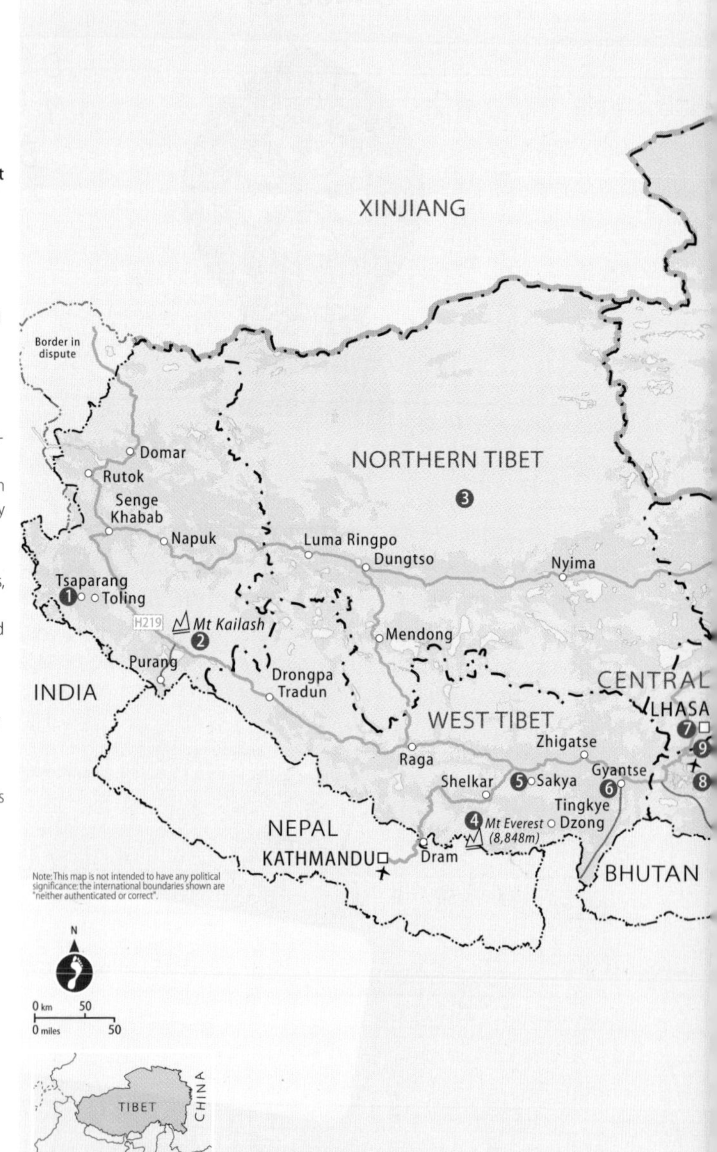

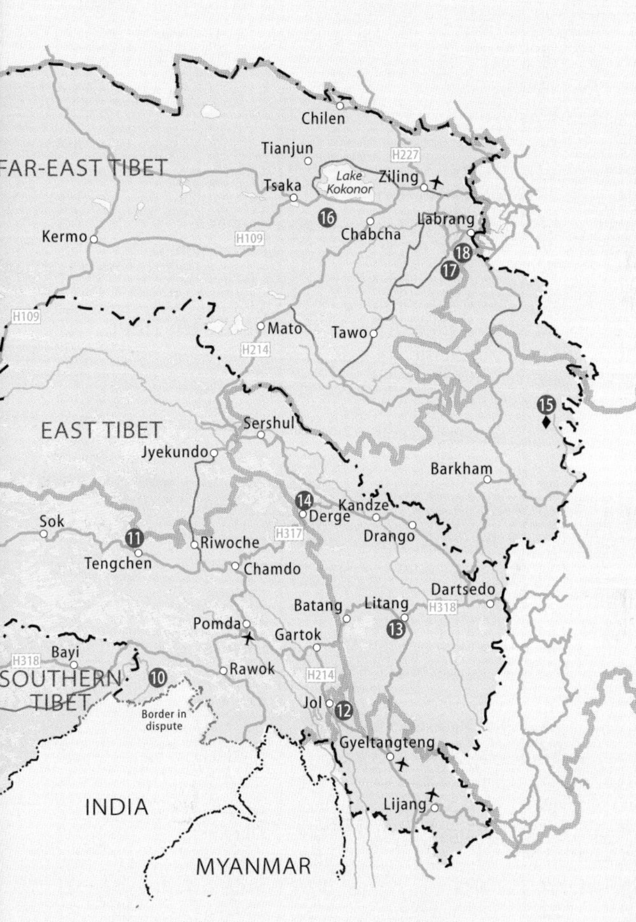

11 Khyungpo Tengchen
Hilltop stronghold of the pre-Buddhist Bon tradition

12 Kawa Karpo
Jagged snow range, a botanists' paradise and focal point for hardy pilgrims

13 Litang
Don't miss the colour and pageantry of the horse festival held here annually, from 1st August

14 Derge
Visit the country's most eclectic and active printing press, a repository of Tibetan literature preserved in woodblock form

15 Dzitsa Degu and Sertso
National parks replete with mineral-tinted lakes and primeval forests – and the only five-star hotel on the Tibetan plateau!

16 Amdo Grasslands
Ride horseback and work with local nomads and monks on the restoration of a revered wall of carved scriptures

17 Repkong
The cultural heart of Amdo, where a distinctively vibrant tradition of Tibetan painting survives

18 Labrang Tashikyil
Large monastic city at the edge of the Tibetan world

Contents

Nomad tent near Ganden

Western Tibet

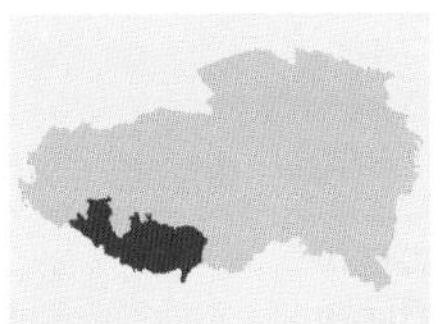

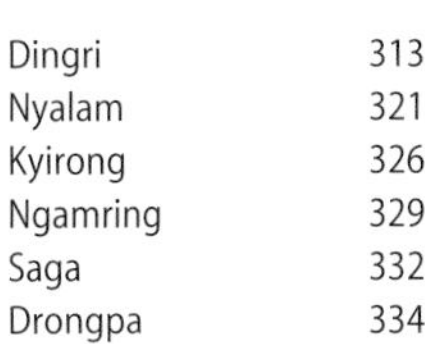

Northern Tibet

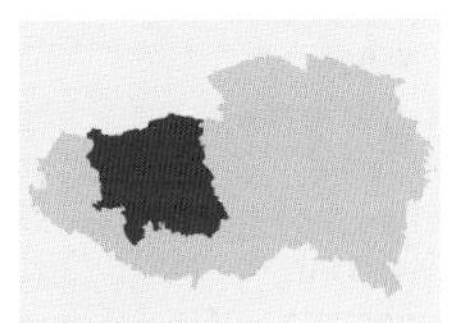

Far West Tibet

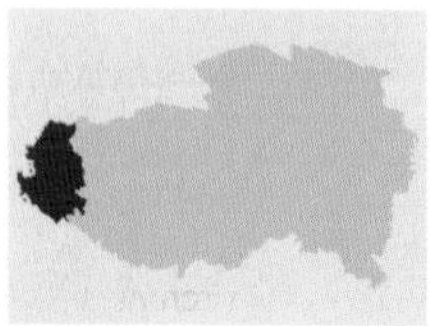

Eastern Tibet

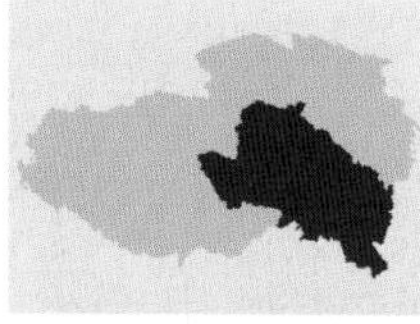

Far East Tibet

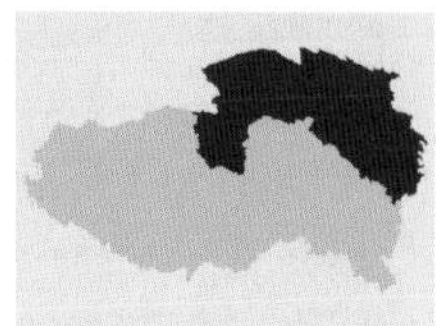

Gateway Cities

Background

Footnotes

Inside front cover

Inside back cover

Power of prayer
Prayer flags fluttering in the breeze on a bridge over Kyi-chu, Lhasa.

A foot in the door

Somewhat astonishingly, there are still some people who think of Tibet as a diminutive entity on the scale of Nepal. But this mountainous bastion of Mahayana Buddhism and custodian of a rich and sophisticated literary heritage which proudly rivals those of India and China, is as vast as Western Europe. The mighty rivers that originate here sustain the lives of billions inhabiting the neighbouring South and East Asian plains: from Karachi to Calcutta, from Dhaka to Saigon, and from Shanghai to Tianjin. It may be sparsely populated, mostly pristine, and economically underdeveloped but click online and you can explore the far-reaching global phenomenon of Tibetan Buddhism, grapple with the thorny issues of human rights and political activism, or even access the virtual world of Tibet that has inspired Hollywood epics and romantic fiction.

Despite the ongoing, unresolved problems arising from Chinese cultural and economic penetration, and over-centralized political control, Tibet is a destination with many attractions for visitors. The mountainous terrain of the plateau presents the ultimate challenge for climbers, trekkers and adventurers. The power places and monasteries, sanctified by centuries of consummate meditation, inspire Buddhist pilgrims from all corners of the earth. The wildlife of the Jangtang grasslands and the diversified flora of the Khampa gorges are a magnet for naturalists. The courage, resolve, and robust humour of the Tibetan people, determined to maintain traditions that often conflict with the values of their colonists, command the respect and concern of an impotent international community who bear witness to their dilemma. For, in the words of a well-known local proverb, Chinese succumb to doubt and Tibetans succumb to hope!

The future of Tibetan culture

According to the 2001 National Census, there are over 10 million people, including almost five million Tibetans, living within the borders of Greater Tibet (Chinese and Muslim immigrants from the east and northeast account for 45 percent of the total population). The people of the plateau are stout-hearted and independently minded, living in complete harmony with their environment. The upper grasslands and watersheds are the preserve of the nomads who live their lives largely without outside interference. By contrast, in some low-lying towns and cities, the palpable tension between indigenous Tibetans and Chinese migrants reflects the courageous resolve of people determined to conserve their cultural heritage, mingled with the pragmatism of others who reluctantly accommodate themselves to alien ways. Here, the central issue of conflict is not modernisation, which all sides appear to espouse, but the quest for cultural identity, economic prosperity and self-determination.

Stereotypes and first hand impressions

So many bizarre and anecdotal accounts of Tibetan journeys have been published that there are few countries that have had to endure more exaggerated stereotyping. The geographical remoteness and rugged

Barkhor
The heart of Lhasa and a good place to buy almost anything

terrain, combined with a self-imposed isolationism and tragically misplaced, conservatism ensured that until recently very few outsiders ever reached the plateau. This has given rise to two contrasting misconceptions: from the westerner's point of view, the plateau was often seen as a Buddhist utopia, aloof from the brutality and turbulence of global conflicts; for the Chinese, Tibet was a barbarous, uneducated land of feudal serfdom. Tibet does have "hidden lands" (*beyul*) or remote valleys, deemed to be more conducive to the practice of Buddhism, but the romantic Hollywood myth of Shangrila, the land where time stands still, is a pretentious fantasy. And mainland Chinese, however well educated, often find it hard to understand that Tibetan culture may credibly have rivalled and in some respects surpassed their own ancient heritage.

Shifting ground

But there are very recent signs that direct contact with Tibet has begun to blur these extreme perspectives. Many western visitors to Tibet are now capable of adopting a more realistic view of the country, while the recent influx of Chinese tourists has begun to awaken a long dormant sense of Buddhist spirituality. There are several Tibetan lamas who now count a large number of Chinese devotees among their following!

Ganden Namgyeling Monastery
A resident at Ganden Namgyeling Monastery freshens up.

1
2
4
5
7
8
10
11

3

6

9

12

1 *Women returning to their village in Lhartse county. The landscape of the Brahmaputra basin here is arid and sandy.* *▸▸ See page 304.*

2 *Pilgrim from Eastern Tibet with beads in her hair, visiting Ganden Namgyeling Monastery.* *▸▸ See page 146.*

3 *Village houses at Chodzom, where the roads from Shelkar and Dingri converge, south of Mount Everest Base Camp.* *▸▸ See page 316.*

4 *Ornate door knocker, typical of Derge metal-craft, on a gate at Tashilhunpo monastery, seat of the Panchen Lamas, Zhigatse.* *▸▸ See page 280.*

5 *Potato chips frying in a brazier in a roadside Lhasa restaurant, one of many small eateries new catering for international visitors.* *▸▸ See page 127.*

6 *Truck carrying travellers and pilgrims from remote areas of Western Tibet to Lhasa. Few public buses travel on these roads.*

7 *A mountain stream near Mount Wangkur, above Ganden Monastery, on the trail followed by pilgrims and trekkers bound for Samye.* *▸▸ See page 148.*

8 *Village boy carrying* dri *milk, a typical pastoral scene in this highland region around Dingri.* *▸▸ See page 314.*

9 *Young monastic pilgrim from East Tibet, outside Jokhang temple.* *▸▸ See page 70.*

10 *Doves hovering around the rooftop of the Potala.* *▸▸ See page 92.*

11 *Monks holding an informal discussion on the roof of the Jokhang Temple. More formal debates can be seen, for example, at the monasteries of Sera Thekchenling (Gelukpa) and Dzongsar Tashi Lhatse (Sakya).* *▸▸ See pages 123 and 498.*

12 *Stone cairn erected by devotees at Pang La pass on the approach to Mount Everest. Marine fossil relics from the prehistoric Tethys Sea abound.* *▸▸ See page 315.*

Sacred mountains

Sacred peaks of snow and ice, bare rock and slate or grass-covered ranges are found throughout the Tibetan plateau. Among them, the most important focal points for Buddhist and Bon pilgrimage are Mount Kailash in Ngari, Mounts Amnye Machen and Nyenpo Yurtse in Golok, Mount Kawa Karpo in Dechen, Mount Zhara Lhatse in Minyak, Mount Dakpa Shelri in Tsari, Mount Bonri in Kongpo, Mount Yarlha Shampo in Yarlung, Mount Nyenchen Tanglha near Lake Namtso Chukmo, and Lapchi Gang along with other perennial snow massifs in the Himalayan range. During the pilgrimage season, these peaks and their secret grottoes, retaining the resonance of the great hermits and meditators of the past, are circumambulated by Tibetans from all parts of the plateau, as well as by devotees from India, Nepal and the West.

Monasteries and palaces

For visitors interested in the Buddhist culture of Tibet, only a few of the great monasteries and palaces of historic importance have survived the ravages of the recent past relatively unscathed, along with a small number of temples which were used as granaries. In Lhasa, there are outstanding works of art to be seen in the Potala and Norbulingka palaces of the Dalai Lamas, in the city temples of Jokhang, Ramoche and Lukhang and in the surrounding monasteries of Drepung and Sera. Other monasteries in far-flung parts of the country, such as Tashilhunpo, Sakya and Labrang, still proudly display some of their original treasured artefacts, as does the renowned xylographic printing press at Derge. Traditional artistic skills, including painting and sculpture, are once again in great demand as local communities throughout the plateau strive to rebuild their historic shrines and temples.

Everest from Pang La Pass

Potala Palace, one-time winter residence of the successive Dalai Lamas

Festivals

The convergence of Tibet's spiritual and secular life can best be seen during the summer and autumn festival season when, throughout the length and breadth of the country, finely dressed crowds assemble to attend or participate in the diverse equestrian events, folk singing and dancing performances, contests of marksmanship and trials of strength, interspersed with the colourful pageantry of sacred dance (*cham*). Commercial travellers vigorously ply their wares from tents, as traditional handicrafts change hands, along with modern goods, weaponry and religious artefacts.

Virgin wilderness

Tibet, like the North and South Poles, has some of the earth's last great uncharted territories. The vibrant blue salt lakes of the Jangtang Plateau are home to migratory birds from Siberia, including the black-necked crane. The deep forested gorges of Kham carry all the great rivers of East and Southeast Asia, while the Yellow River meanders through the northeastern grasslands of Amdo – ancestral home of the nomadic *drokpa*, who live in black yak wool tents, tending their herds of yak and dri. Further west, the Brahmaputra flows along the continental suture through a landscape of high-altitude desert. Vast sand dunes shift along its banks, concealing sheltered lateral valleys, where farming communities (*rongpa*) subsist on highland barley. In the far west are the deserted cave cities of the Sutlej valley and the gorge of the upper Indus.

Buddhist heritage

Among all the Buddhist countries of Asia, the highest developments of Indian Buddhism were preserved in Tibet. This was due partly to geographical proximity, partly to temporal consideration and partly to the aptitude which the Tibetans themselves displayed for the diversity of Indian Buddhist traditions. The sparse population, the slow measured pace of daily life and an almost anarchical disdain for political involvement encouraged the spiritual cultivation of Buddhism to such an extent that it came to permeate the entire culture.

All schools of Buddhism in Tibet maintain the monastic discipline of the *vinaya*, the graduated spiritual practices and philosophical systems based on the sutras, and the esoteric meditative practices associated with the tantras. Different schools developed in different periods of Tibetan history, each derived from distinctive lineages or transmissions of Indian Buddhism, and among them the most influential continue to be the Nyingmapa, the Sakyapa, the Kagyupa and the Gelukpa. Throughout the country there are monasteries representative of all these diverse traditions, each of which can also claim great lamas or spiritual teachers at their head, many of them forming revered lines of incarnate or familial descent. Such are the Dalai and Panchen Lamas, the Karmapas, the Sakya Trichens and the Minling Trichens. Active monasteries, colleges and meditation hermitages representative of all these traditions can be visited throughout the length and breadth of the Tibetan plateau.

Local devotees and tourists in the flagstone courtyard of the Jokhang Temple

Essentials

Footprint features

Planning your trip

Navigating Tibet

Greater Tibet conveniently forms seven geographical zones: Lhasa (the capital), Central Tibet (Kyi-chu Valley), Southern Tibet (Lhokha and Kongpo), Western Tibet (Tsang and Lato), Northern Tibet (Jangtang Plateau), Far West Tibet (Ngari), Eastern Tibet (Kham), and Far East Tibet (Amdo and Gyarong). Our text intentionally follows these traditional boundaries, which still have profound cultural, ethnic and linguistic relevance for Tibetans even though they are partially blurred by the current political division of the plateau into a truncated autonomous region and several autonomous prefectures.

By contrast, the current system of local government, according to which prefectures are subdivided into administrative counties (Tib. dzong, Ch. xian) does broadly reflect Tibetan traditions and aspirations, and therefore provides a suitable template for the whole of the Tibetan plateau. Each geographical zone consists of several administrative counties, each of which is described in turn, highlighting the places of historical and touristic importance, close to the main motor roads, as well as the lesser jeep tracks, trekking routes and more remote sites. Practical information on services, including hotels, restaurants, transport and road conditions has been updated in this edition, but the main emphasis continues to be placed on Tibet's cultural heritage: the monasteries, local history and the spectacular terrain, given that many key destinations offer very little or no choice of accommodation or meals!

Great care has been taken to make a distinction between the names of the counties and the names of the county capitals – something which Chinese cartographers have tended to blur in recent years – much to the chagrin of local communities. For example, the location of Lhasa Airport is actually Rawame in Gongkar County – not Gongkar, as shown on most Chinese maps. This is not, as some have suggested, a distinction between old and new place names. The real names are still used by local people and even appear on Tibetan signboards in the county towns, but they are ignored by outsiders who fall for this exercise in sloppy cartography. How would the citizens of Leeds or Tucson feel if their cities were arbitrarily renamed Yorkshire and Arizona?

Each county is introduced by a heading in English and Tibetan script, and a margin entry indicating the Chinese and Pinyin equivalents, along with population and area statistics derived from the recent national census in 2001. In most cases, a map has been included, showing the accessibility of the main sites and towns.

Wherever possible, the text employs Tibetan place-names, taking the view that it is important to maintain their usage, even in areas where Chinese names are now more commonly employed. For the aid of the traveller who may have difficulty finding Tibetan place-names on Chinese maps or bus station timetables, a concordance of Tibetan and Chinese place-names has been appended (see pages 819-834). Travellers in Tibet will quickly understand that there are widely divergent and bewildering transliterations for Tibetan place-names. I have adopted a standard method of transliteration that corresponds closely to the Tibetan orthography, and have tried to apply this consistently, regardless of local variations in pronunciation. We would expect no less in English. Who would spell Edinburgh as Edinboro or Arkansas as Arkansaw? When the local vernacular suggests a widely different pronunciation, I have added this information in brackets.

The general map of the plateau (see colour maps at back of the book) indicates the traditional boundaries of the various geographical zones as well as the modern prefectural boundaries, but for more detail the reader should refer to the computer-generated maps at the end of the book, which clearly show the county borders and county towns, the major rivers and roads, and the important 5,000-m contour, which broadly divides settled from nomadic communities.

NB Good, accurate maps of Tibet are extremely rare, particularly those combining sound topographic and toponymic information. This guide has drawn on extensive field visits to compile schematic town and county plans which, along with the computer-generated colour maps are all drawn with the most up to date information available.

Where to go

Since the plateau as a whole is as large as Western Europe, it is obviously impossible to go everywhere in the course of a single trip! There are five neighbouring gateway cities offering access to Tibet: Kathmandu in Nepal, Chengdu in Sichuan, Kunming in Yunnan, Lanzhou in Gansu, and Kashgar in Xinjiang, very difficult to enter through but easier as an exit point. Among these, Kathmandu is an important hub for visitors to Central, Southern, Western, and Far West Tibet. Chengdu is the base for visitors to Kham and Gyarong, as well as Central and Southern Tibet. Kunming gives access to Southern Kham and to Central Tibet. Lanzhou is the most convenient embarkation point for Amdo, while Kashgar offers a less frequently travelled route to Northern and Far West Tibet. Information on all these cities, including international air and road connections, may be found in the Gateway Cities chapter (see pages 707-734). **NB** At the time of writing there are positive indications that the Sikkim-Tibet border will soon be opened for international travel, for the first time since the 1950s. This would make Gangtok an important gateway city for Tibet, possibly supplanting Kathmandu as the preferred southern entry point.

Organized and independent travel

Before deciding upon an itinerary, the first step is to decide whether you wish to go as an individual traveller or arrange your travel through a tour operator. The latter option, though more expensive, is the only one which will reliably enable you to visit the so-called 'closed' areas of Eastern. Western, Southern, and Far West Tibet. All arrangements, including international flight connections to any of the five gateway cities, Chinese visas and Tibet travel permits will be made by your tour operator. This does not imply having to take a 'package' tour, as operators are quite used to organizing tours for very small groups or even single travellers.

On the other hand, if you have a low budget, time to spare, great physical endurance, and are able to accept the risk of being unceremoniously ejected from the closed areas of the country, the former option is perfectly feasible. With the formal opening of Kandze prefecture in December 1998 much of the plateau, including those parts of Kham under the jurisdiction of Sichuan and Yunnan provinces and most of Amdo, has been officially designated as 'open' and accessible to the individual traveller. At the time of writing, most of the Tibetan Autonomous Region including Chamdo and Ngari prefectures are still closed, as are parts of Jyekundo prefecture under the authority of Qinghai province and a few counties in the Ngawa prefecture of Sichuan province. In between, there is the grey area of Lhasa and its environs, officially 'open', but in practice highly restricted by the Tibet entry permit requirement. Individual travellers, after obtaining a standard Chinese tourist visa, should first consult the information on the neighbouring gateway cities (see page 733). Of these, access from Lanzhou, Kunming and Chengdu currently offer the best prospects for the FIT traveller.

When to go

April to June and September to November are generally the best and most popular months. The rainy season, though mild in comparison with that of India and Southeast Asia, can bring flash floods and high rivers, which break up the poor road surfaces. Be prepared to trek across landslides in the rainy season. However, the Tibetan plateau, and particularly the south, is not as cold as one tends to imagine. With the exception of high passes and the Jangtang plateau the snow, even in winter, rarely stays on the ground for more than a few hours. The days are generally warm and it is only at night that the temperature can really drop. It is the extreme dryness of the air rather than the cold that characterizes Tibetan weather. Nearly all of the rain falls in July and August, and there is practically no snow below 5,000 m.

The winters are tough, especially in the north. There can be icy winds, and passes are often blocked with snow. Nevertheless, the sun shines continuously and the light is superb. Long distance travel in this period is much more rigorous. However, in the sheltered valleys of Lhasa, Tsetang, Zhigatse and Southern Kham the winter days are mild and beautiful. From December to March the streets of Lhasa are full of weird and wonderful peoples from the four corners of Tibet. In many respects, this is one of the best times of the year to visit.

In general, the west of Tibet tends to be drier, while the east is more subject to the weather patterns of Southeast Asia. During August, especially, the plateau can be very wet, but this is also a very good time of year to visit festival sites. For a listing of festival dates, see page 46.

Tours

The following tours encompass all geographical zones and will assist you in choosing your destination; but they are by no means exclusive. A number of them overlap and it is obviously possible to combine parts of one with another. These recommended routes are also highlighted in the main body of the text, when the relevant geographical zone is described. The right hand column cross-references each stage of the tour to specific pages of the guide, and you will be able to read around these in more detail before planning your route.

NB All except the third entail long overland journeys exceeding 1,000 km.

1 Cultural tour of Central, Southern and Western Tibet

This itinerary is usually the one preferred by first-time visitors to Tibet, in that it combines the main historic palaces and monasteries of Tibet's heartland with a close Himalayan encounter, and relatively comfortable travel and accommodation en route. Starting from the gateway city of Kathmandu in Nepal, you fly to Lhasa and then to the former capitals of Tsetang and Zhigatse, before cutting through the highland region, and back overland to Nepal. Travel is by four-wheel drive or minibus (if you do not visit Everest Base Camp).

Length: 15 days
Best time to visit: Apr-Jun, late Sep-Nov

Alternatively, you can extend the trip by organizing an extension from the Chongye Tombs to Lhodrak and reach Nakartse on the road to Gyantse from the south (see pages 210-227). Another possible extension, into Namling county, crossing the new bridge east of Zhigatse, would enable you to visit the sacred hermitage of Zabulung in northern Shang (see page 262-263).

Day 1	Kathmandu	708	Day 9	Mindroling	176
	Gongkar Airport	62		Overnight: Gyantse	267
	Overnight: Lhasa	59	Day 10	Zhalu Monastery	286
Day 2-6	Lhasa	59		Overnight: Zhigatse	276
Day 7	Lhasa	59	Day 11	Zhigatse	276
	Samye Monastery	179	Day 12	Sakya Monastery	298
	Overnight: Tsetang	189		Overnight: Shelkar	314
Day 8	Chongye Tombs	211	Day 13	Everest Base Camp	317
	Tradruk Temple	201		Overnight: Shelkar	314
	Yumbu Lagang Palace	204	Day 14	Dingri	313
	Overnight: Tsetang	189		Overnight: Dram	324
			Day 15	Return to Kathmandu	708

2 Mount Kailash and Guge Kingdom

This is an itinerary for the hardy adventurer or gritty pilgrim, combining the regions of Western, Northern, and Far West Tibet, and culminating in the circuit of the sacred Mount Kailash and the medieval Guge capitals of Toling and Tsaparang. Travel by a four-wheel drive vehicle.

Length: 25 days
Best time to visit: May-Jul, Sep-Oct

Day 1	Kathmandu	708	Day 11	Tsaparang	385
	Overnight: Dram	324	Day 12	Toling	380
Day 2	Dingri	313	Day 13	Tirthapuri	355
	Overnight: Shelkar	314	Day 14	Darchen	358
Day 3	Dzarongpu Monastery	316	Day 15-18	Mount Kailash trek	359
	Overnight: Everest	315		Manasarovar Lake	369
	Base Camp	317	Day 19-20	Manasarovar Lake	369
Day 4	Overnight: Shelkar	314		Jiu Monastery	372
Day 5	Lhartse	304		Overnight: Purang	358
	Overnight: Ralung Chutsen	311	Day 21	Mayum La Pass	335
Day 6	Tsochen	340	Day 22	Baryang	335
Day 7	Gertse	343	Day 23	Saga	332
Day 8	Gegye	352	Day 24	Nyalam	323
Day 9	Senge Khabab	354	Day 25	Dram	324
Day 10	Tsamda	378		Return to Kathmandu	708

3 Kyi-chu Valley

Around Lhasa, it is possible to explore the Kyi-chu valley of Central Tibet with relatively short travel stages. For those disinclined to undertake a long expedition, this itinerary highlights rural life and the historic monasteries of the Upper Kyi-chu which are close to the capital. Enjoy bathing in the hot springs at Zhoto Tidro. Travel by a four-wheel drive vehicle.

Length: 15 days
Best time to visit: Apr-Oct

Day 1	Kathmandu	708	Day 10	Zhoto Tidro Hermitage	157
	Gongkar Airport	62	Day 11	Drigung Monastery	156
	Overnight: Lhasa	59	Day 12	Uruzhva Temple	153
Day 2-5	Lhasa	59		Katsel	154
Day 6	Yerpa Caves	145		Overnight: Gyama	153
Day 7	Taklung Monastery	150	Day 13	Ganden Monastery	146
Day 8	Reting Monastery	152	Day 14	Lhasa	59
Day 9	Zhoto Tidro Hermitage	157	Day 15	Return to Kathmandu	708

4 Brahmaputra Gorges and the Salween-Mekong Traverse

This combines a tour of the beautiful forested Kongpo region of Southern Tibet with the northern and southern overland routes to and from Chamdo in Kham. **NB** The route is easily reversed. The stretch from Nyangtri to Pasho is often impassable in the rainy season or when the road is broken up by glacial snow-melt. Travel by a four-wheel drive vehicle.

Length: 19 days
Best time to visit: Apr-Jun, late Sep-Oct

Day 1	Kathmandu	708
	Gongkar Airport	62
	Overnight: Lhasa	59
Day 2-3	Lhasa	59
Day 4	Draksum Lake	251
Day 5	Buchu Temple	243
Day 6	Timpei Caves	240
Day 7	Lunang	249
	Po-me	430
Day 9	Pasho	435
Day 10	Chamdo	417
Day 11	Chamdo	417
Day 12	Riwoche	413
Day 13	Riwoche Temple	414
	Overnight: Riwoche	413
Day 14	Tengchen	412
Day 15	Tengchen Monastery	412
Day 16	Sok Dzong	408
Day 17	Nakchu	407
Day 18	Lhasa	59
Day 19	Return to Kathmandu	708

5 Lhasa to Chengdu Overland

This increasingly popular itinerary enables visitors to travel through the 'closed' areas of East Tibet from Lhasa via Chamdo and Derge to Chengdu in Sichuan. There are a number of important monasteries en route, such as those at Chamdo, Derge, Kandze, and Lhagang. **NB** The journey can be rugged and some facilities are poor. It is easily reversed; and the northern route from Lhasa to Chamdo (pages 59 and 417) can be substituted for the southern one shown here. Also, the southern route from Chamdo via Batang and Litang to Dardo (pages 417-489) can be followed instead of going via Derge as shown here. Travel by a four-wheel drive vehicle.

Length: 21 days
Best time to visit: Apr-Jun, late Sep-Oct

Day 1	Kathmandu-Lhasa	708
Day 2-4	Lhasa	59
Day 5	Samye Monastery	179
	Overnight: Tsetang	189
Day 6	Gyatsa	230
Day 7	Menling	237
Day 8	Lunang	249
Day 9	Po-me	430
Day 10	Pasho	435
Day 11	Chamdo	417
Day 12	Chamdo	417
Day 13	Derge	501
Day 14	Derge	501
Day 15	Kandze	532
Day 16	Kandze	532
Day 17	Tawu	538
Day 18	Lhagang Monastery	477
Day 19	Dartsedo	479
Day 20	Wolong Panda Reserve	485
Day 21	Chengdu	722

6 Lhasa to Lanzhou Overland

This route crosses the desolate West Kokonor plateau of the Far East Tibet region, to reach the fabled Kokonor – one of Inner Asia's largest lakes, before travelling through Kumbum, Repkong and Labrang, which are at the cultural heart of Amdo. The Repkong style of painting is particularly renowned. **NB** This itinerary is reversible. Travel by a four-wheel drive vehicle or minibus.

Length: 16 days
Best time to visit: May-Oct

Day 1	Kathmandu-Lhasa	708	Day 11	Ziling	573
Day 2-4	Lhasa	59	Day 12	Kumbum Monastery	576
Day 5	Nakchu	407		Overnight: Ziling	573
Day 6	Amdo	408	Day 13	Repkong	604
Day 7	Toma	550	Day 14	Labrang	668
Day 8	Kermo	552	Day 15	Labrang	668
Day 9	Lake Kokonor	560	Day 16	Lanzhou	730
Day 10	Lake Kokonor	560			

7 Lhasa to Kunming Overland

This truly memorable journey combines the route from Lhasa to Chamdo in Kham with a descent of the Mekong River, bypassing the plunging glaciers of the sacred Mount Kawa Karpo into the rich flowering landscapes of Dechen county and Yunnan. **NB** This itinerary is reversible; and the northern route from Lhasa to Chamdo (pages 406-417) could be substituted for the southern one shown here. It is also possible to go from Markham across the Yangtze to Batang and then southwards into Yunnan via Chaktreng (page 462-473).

Length: 18 days
Best time to visit: Apr-Jun, late Sep-Nov

Day 1	Kathmandu	708	Day 10	Chamdo	417
	Gongkar Airport	62	Day 11	Dzogang	440
	Overnight: Lhasa	59	Day 12	Markham	441
Day 2-4	Lhasa	59	Day 13	Tsakhalho	442
Day 5	Draksum Lake	251	Day 14	Dechen	443
Day 6	Lunang	249	Day 15	Gyeltang	449
Day 7	Po-me	430	Day 16	Lijiang	454
Day 8	Pasho	435	Day 17	Dali	457
Day 9	Chamdo	417	Day 18	Kunming	727

8 Kham and Amdo Overland

Starting in the gateway city of Chengdu and ending in Lanzhou, this is a detailed itinerary combining the grasslands of Kham and Amdo with the Amdo cultural heartland around Kumbum, Repkong, and Labrang. There are many monasteries en route including those at Lhagang, Kandze, Dzokchen, Zhechen, Jyekundo and Zhiwu. **NB** This itinerary is reversible. Travel by a four-wheel drive vehicle or minibus.

Length: 22 days
Best time to visit: May-Oct

Day 1	Hong Kong/Beijing		Day 13	Jyekundo	517
	Overnight: Chengdu	722	Day 14	Mato	631
Day 2	Chengdu	722	Day 15	Mount Amnye Machen	548
Day 3	Wolong Panda Reserve	485		Overnight: Wenchuan	628
Day 4	Dartsedo	479	Day 16	Chabcha	624
Day 5	Lhagang Monastery	477		Overnight: Lake Kokonor	560
Day 6	Tawu	538	Day 17	Ziling	573
Day 7	Kandze	532	Day 18	Kumbum Monastery	576
Day 8	Dzogchen Monastery	505		Overnight: Ziling	573
Day 9	Dzogchen Monastery	505	Day 19	Repkong	604
Day 10	Zhechen Monastery	507	Day 20	Labrang	668
	Overnight: Sershul	510	Day 21	Labrang	668
Day 11	Zhiwu	514	Day 22	Overnight: Lanzhou	730
Day 12	Jyekundo	517			

9 Golok and Gyarong Overland

Length: 21 days
Best time to visit: Apr-Jun, Sep-Oct

This exciting itinerary combines the Labrang, Repkong and Kumbum heartland of Amdo with the nomadic region of Golok and the Jonangpa and Nyingmapa monasteries of the upper Gyarong in Far East Tibet. **NB** It can easily be reversed. Travel by a four-wheel drive vehicle.

Day 1	Hong Kong/Beijing Overnight: Lanzhou	730	Day 12	Dzamtang	648
Day 2	Labrang Monastery	668	Day 13	Dzamtang	648
Day 3	Repkong	604	Day 14	Sertal	645
Day 4	Ziling	573	Day 15	Sertal	645
Day 5	Kumbum Monastery	576	Day 16	Drango	537
	Overnight: Chabcha	624	Day 17	Lhagang Monastery	477
Day 6	Darlag	639	Day 18	Dartsedo	479
Day 7	Tarthang Monastery	640	Day 19	Tsenlha	661
Day 8	Jigdril	640	Day 20	Wolong Panda Reserve	485
Day 9	Ngawa	650	Day 21	Chengdu	722
Day 10	Ngawa	650			
Day 11	Barkham	658			

10 Eastern Kham Overland

Length: 26 days
Best time to visit: May-Jun, late Sep-Oct

This focuses on the gorges and grasslands of eastern Kham (currently in Sichuan). It combines the Chinese Buddhist pilgrimage site of Mount Emei with a number of renowned Nyingmapa, Sakyapa and Gelukpa monasteries. **NB** This can be reversed. Travel by four-wheel drive vehicle.

Day 1	Hong Kong/Beijing Overnight: Chengdu	722	Day 14	Katok Monastery	493
Day 2	Chengdu	722	Day 15	Katok Monastery	493
Day 3	Emei Shan	486	Day 16	Dzongsar Monastery	498
Day 4	Emei Shan	486	Day 17	Derge	501
Day 5	Ya'an	486	Day 18	Derge	501
Day 6	Dartsedo	479	Day 19	Dzogchen Monastery	505
Day 7	Nyachuka	473	Day 20	Dzogchen Monastery	505
Day 8	Litang	465	Day 21	Kandze	532
Day 9	Batang	463	Day 22	Kandze	532
Day 10	Litang	465	Day 23	Lhagang Monastery	477
Day 11	Nyarong	535	Day 24	Dartsedo	479
Day 12	Pelyul Monastery	495	Day 25	Wolong Panda Reserve	485
Day 13	Pelyul Monastery	495	Day 26	Chengdu	722

11 Nature Parks of Amdo

Length: 23 days
Best time to visit: Apr-Oct

The last of these recommended itineraries runs from Chengdu to Lanzhou, passing through the beautiful nature reserves of the Minjiang valley and those of the Amnye Machen range, Drakar Tredzong and Lake Kokonor. The scenery is spectacular and rewarding. **NB** This itinerary can be reversed. Travel by a four-wheel drive vehicle.

Day 1	Hong Kong/Beijing Overnight: Chengdu	722	Day 2	Chengdu	722
			Day 3	Zungchu	692

Day 4	Sertso Park	690	Day 16	Tsogyenrawa	632
Day 5	Dzitsa Degu Park	694	Day 17	Drakar Tredzong	626
Day 6	Dzitsa Degu Park	694	Day 18	Drakar Tredzong	626
Day 7	Dzoge	684	Day 19	Chabcha	624
Day 8	Labrang Monastery	668	Day 20	Lake Kokonor	560
Day 9	Repkong	604	Day 21	Ziling	573
Day 10	Machen	632	Day 22	Kumbum Monastery	576
Day 11	Chuwarna	635		Ziling	573
Day 12-14	Amnye Machen	632	Day 23	Lanzhou	730
Day 15	Machen	632			

International tour operators

A number of overseas operators run tours in the Tibetan area. They vary greatly in price, depending upon the number of days, the number of persons in a group, the remoteness and distance covered by the itinerary, and the package arrangement (ie full board or half-board). Prices are slightly lower than comparable tours of Bhutan, ranging from US$100 per day to over US$200 per day. Tibet travel arrangements may be made by any of the following international operators, some of which have a worldwide client base:

Australia
Peregrine Adventures, 258 Lonsdale St, Melbourne, Victoria 3000, T3-9663-8611, F3-9663-8618, www.peregrine.net.au.

France
Terres d'Aventure, 6 rue Saint Victor, 75005 Paris, T33-153-737773, F33-140-469522, www.terdav.com.

Hong Kong
Abercrombie & Kent, 27th floor Tai Sang Commercial Building, 24-34 Hennessy Rd, Wanchai, T852-28657818, F852-28660556.
China Travel Service, Kowloon Branch, 1st floor Alpha House, 27-33 Nathan Rd, T852-7214481, F852-7216251.

Nepal
Adventure Travel Nepal Ltd, PO Box 272, Lazimpath, Kathmandu, T977-1415995/223328, F977-1414075/419126.
Summit Trekking, Kopundol Height, Lalitpur, PO Box 1406, Kathmandu, T977-1521894, F977-1523737.
Tibet Travels and Tours, PO Box 7246, Tridevi Marg, Kathmandu, T977-1249140, F977-1249986.

UK
KE Adventure Travel, 32 Lake Rd, Keswick, Cumbria, CA 12 5DQ, T44-17687-73966 F44-17687-74693, www.keadventure.com.
Occidor Adventure Tours, 10 Broomcroft Rd, Bognor Regis, West Sussex PO22 7NB, T44-1243-582178, F44-1243-587239.
Steppes East, The Travel House, 51 Castle St, Cirencester, Glos GL7 1QD, T44-1285-651010, www.steppeseast.co.uk. Tailor-made journeys and escorted tours. Contact Steppes East for further information or a copy of the brochure.
Trans Himalaya, 4 Foxcote Gdns, Frome, Somerset BA11 2DS, T44-1373-455518, F44-1373-455594, www.trans-himalaya.com. Organizes travel throughout the Tibetan plateau as well as in Mongolia, China and the Himalayas.

USA
Geographic Expeditions, 2627 Lombard St, San Francisco, CA 94123, T415-9220448, F415-3465535, www.geoex.com.
High Asia, PO Box 2438, Basalt, Colorado, CO 81621, T203-248 3003, www.Highasia.com.
Snow Lion Expeditions, Oquirrh Pl, 350 South 400 East, Suite G2, Salt Lake City, UT 84111, T1-800-809-0034, www.snowlion.com.
Wilderness Travels, 801 Allston Way, Berkeley, Ca 94710, T415-5480420.

NB Listings for local and regional tour operators will be found in the Gateway Cities chapter, and within the directories for specific cities on the Tibetan plateau. Among these some of the best are:

Beiijng

Longmen Travel, A9 Daqudeng Lane, Meishuguan Houjie, T010-64074616, F010-64012180, h_qingcn@yahoo.com.cn.

Chengdu

Tibet Trans Himalaya Expeditions,1 North Shuangqing Rd, Bldg 2, Apartment 2A, T028-82984421, info@trans-himalaya.com.
Khamtrek, 252 Shunji Mansion, T028-86510838, khamtrek@mail.sc.cninfo.net.

Kunming

Yunnan Exploration and Amusement Travel, 1st floor Building B (North Section), 73 Renmin West Rd, Kunming, T0871-5312283, F0871-5312324.

Lanzhou

Gansu Silk Road Travel, 361 Tianshui Ave, Lanzhou, T0931-8414498, F0931-8418457.

Lhasa

Highland Treks and Tours, 13 North Lingkor Rd, T0891-6328808, tibethighland@mail.sc.cninfo.net.
Holyland Adventures, 215 West Dekyi Lam, T/F0891-6834472, holyland@public.ts.xz.cn.
Windhorse Adventure(WHA), 1 North Mirik Lam, T0891-6833009, F0891-6836793, wha@public.ls.xz.cn.

Finding out more

There is no unified tourist organization as such for the Tibetan plateau, since each province under which Tibet is administered has its own Tourism Bureau. Tourism within the Tibetan Autonomous Region is administered by the **Tibet Tourism Bureau (TTB)**, Yuanlin Rd, Lhasa, T0891-34315, F0891-6334632. For information on travel to East Tibet, contact:
Gansu Provincial Tourism Bureau, 209 Tianshui Ave, Lanzhou, T0931-8426847.
Qinghai Provincial Tourism Bureau, 21 Huanghe Rd, T0971-6143711, F0971-8238721.
Sichuan Provincial Tourism Bureau, 180 Renmin Nan Rd, Chengdu, T028-85527478.
Yunnan Provincial Tourism Bureau, Huancheng Nanlou St, Kunming, T0871-3132895.

However, such organizations tend to be highly bureaucratic and for practical information you will have to rely on international tour operators or the domestic travel agencies.

Websites

The following websites will direct readers to publishers and distributors of available

books on Tibet, a short selection of which is given on pages 784-786.
www.wisdompubs.org
www.snowlionpub.com
www.shambhala.org
www.demon.co.uk/wisdom.com
www.rangjungyeshe.com
www.tibetan.review.to
www.tricycle.com

Tibetan Buddhist studies

The following internet lists provide general information and discussion forums on Buddhism from either scholastic or practical perspectives:
www.budhscol.com
www.BuddhaL.com
www.dharmanet.org
www.edharma.com

In addition, there are various websites representing specific Buddhist organizations and schools or monasteries of Tibetan Buddhism.

Nyingmapa sites:
www.dudjomba.org
www.dzogchenmonastery.net
www.rigpa.org www.shechen.12pt.com
www.palyul.org www.nyingma.org and
www.dzogchen.org
Kagyupa sites:
www.karmakagyu.org www.rumtek.org
www.tsurphu.org www.kagyu.org
www.drukpa-kargyud.org and
www.drikung.org
Sakyapa sites:
www.aadz12.ukgateway.net www.sakya.org
www.sakya-ngor.org and
www.mypage.direct.ca/w/wattj (The Sakya Resource Guide)
Gelukpa sites:
www.tsongkhapa.org www.drepung.org
www.fpmt.org www.ganden.org
www.namgyal.org and www.gyudmed.org
NB Information on NGOs which are active inside Tibet may be found below, page 31, under Working and Studying in Tibet.

Tibet information services

Wide-ranging information on Tibetan cultural and political organizations throughout the world may be found at **Tibet Online Resource Gathering**, www.tibet.org. A more comprehensive, through inevitably outdated listing of cultural organizations is also given in **A Handbook of Tibetan Culture**, edited by Graham Coleman and published by Rider (1992). In addition, the following organizations may be contacted in specific countries:

Australia

Tibet Information Service, PO Box 87, Ivanhoe, Victoria, 3079, T03-6634484
Tibetan Studies Bulletin, www.ciolek.com/WWWVL-TibetanStudies.html.

Canada

Canada-Tibet Friendship Society, PO Box 6588, Postal Section A, Toronto, Ontario, M5W 1X4, T0416-5313810.
World Tibet News, McGill, Montreal, listserv@vm1.mcgill.ca (SUB WTN-L).

France

Tibet News, Paris www.tibet.fr.

Germany

Tibet News, www.tibet-initiative.de.

India

Amnye Machen Institute, PO McLeod Ganj, HP, 176219, T0091-1892-21441; www.amnyemachen.org.
Information Office of the Tibetan Government in Exile, Gangchen Kyishong, Dharamsala, HP, 176215, T0091-1892-2457/2598.
Library of Tibetan Works and Archives, Gangchen Kyishong, Dharamsala, HP 176215, T0091-1892-2467.
Tibet House, 1 Institutional Area, Lodhi Rd, New Delhi 110003, T611515.
Tibetan Youth Congress, www.tibetanyouthcongress.org.

Japan

Tibetan Cultural Centre of Japan, 2-31-22, Nerima, Nerima-ku, Tokyo, T03-39915411.

Nepal

Office of Tibet, PO Box 310 Lazimpat, Kathmandu, T11660.

Words and phrases

Pronunciation and spelling
The spelling adopted for the representation of both Tibetan and Sanskrit names in this work is designed with the general reader in mind, rather than the specialist. Exact transliterations have therefore been avoided.
Tibetan Tibetan spellings have been chosen which broadly reflect a modern Central Tibetan pronunciation (not necessarily that of Lhasa). Please note that a final *e* is never silent, but pronounced in the manner of the French *é*. *Ph* is never pronounced like an English *f*, but like a *p* with strong aspiration. Among the important regional variants, the general reader should be aware that in some parts of the country, **ky** or **khy** may be pronounced as *ch*, **gy** as *j*, **b** as *w*, **dr** as *b*, and **ny** as *hmy*. Also suffixes may be elided, and the basic vowel sounds may change, such that **u** becomes *i*, and so forth.
Sanskrit In the absence of diacritics to represent Sanskrit letters, the following simplified conventions have been observed throughout: **palatal c** is rendered as *c* (but to be pronounced as in *Italian ch*); **palatal s** is rendered *sh*, and **retroflex s** as a simple *s*. The names of all deities are given, wherever possible, in their Sanskrit rather than Tibetan forms. For a correspondence between the Sanskrit and Tibetan names see the glossary page 835 and the iconographic guide, page 788.

UK
Tibet Foundation, 1 St James' Market, London SW1Y 4SB, T+44-20-7930-6001, F+44-20-7930-6002, www.tibet-foundation.org.
Tibet House, 1 Culworth St, London NW8 7AF, T0207-7225378, www.tibet.com.
Tibet Information Network, 7 Beck Rd, London E8 4RE, T0208-5335458, www.tibetinfo.net.
The Tibet Society, & Relief Fund of the UK, Unit 9, 139 Fonthill Rd, London, N4 3HF, T0207-2721414, www.tibetsociety.com.

USA
The Milarepa Fund, www.milarepa.org.
Tibet House, 3rd floor 241 E 32nd St, New York, NY 10016, T0212-2135392, www.tibethouse.org.
Tibet Interest List, Indiana, listserv@listserv.indiana.edu.
Tibetan Cultural Centre, 3655 South Snoddy Rd, Bloomington, Indiana 47401, T0812-8558222
China News Digest, New York, www.cnd.org.

Language

English is spoken by very few people in Tibet, and French or German by even fewer! The best language for communication is Tibetan (especially the dialects of To-ke, Tsang-ke, U-ke, Kham-ke and Amdo-ke), and for a selection of useful words and phrases see Footnotes, page 756. Unfortunately, there is no space in this work for a more extensive introduction to the language. For travellers bound for Central Tibet **Andrew Bloomfield** and **Yanki Tsering's Learning Practical Tibetan** (Snow Lion, 1997), which also has a set of audio cassettes is recommended.

In recent decades Chinese has become something of a lingua franca, preferred even by Tibetans from different parts of the plateau when communicating with one another. There have been conscious attempts to reverse this trend by moving towards a universally standard form of Tibetan, but the obstacles are formidable. **NB** On the other hand visitors should know that Tibetans sometimes complain about foreigners addressing them in Chinese, and if one wants to elicit a favourable response there is no substitute for Tibetan. Nor should one forget the minority languages spoken within Tibet: the Qiangic dialects of Gyarong, the Monpa and Lhopa dialects of Lhokha, the Mongolian, Tu, and Salar languages of Amdo, and so forth. For a list of useful works on the Tibetan language see the bibliography on page 786.

Disabled travellers

Apart from the airports and hospitals where wheelchairs can be provided, there are very few hotels on the Tibetan plateau with suitable access facilities for disabled travellers – only a handful of them have elevators and even fewer have ramps! Our advice would be to carry portable equipment (such as wheelchairs) from home, and ensure that a travelling companion is always at hand to assist when climbing steps and staircases. There are no tour operators offering guided tours in Tibet specifically for disabled people, but several international operators and their local agents will ensure that additional support is provided for clients who are disabled.

Gay and lesbian travellers

Although homosexuality still faces much legal opposition and social stigma in Chinese society as a whole, the larger mainland cities do have clubs and bars which function as meeting points. In Tibet, however, public expression of homosexuality is extremely rare. Traditionally there were a few monastic institutions in which homosexuality was not regarded as an infringement of monastic discipline, but there appears to be no contemporary evidence of such practices. Heterosexual services are now widely available in the nightclubs, bars and brothels of many Tibetan towns and cities, and some of these establishments may also cater for homosexuals. Gay or lesbian travellers who make their travel arrangements through international tour operators and local agents should expect to be treated like other clients.

Student travellers

Organizations like **STA** in the UK provide cheap flights to China, and an international student card will give access to slightly cheaper domestic flights, trains and buses within mainland China, but you should not expect such concessions in Tibet, where FIT individual travel is relatively rare and those who do backpack through the country frequently have to pay higher fares for long distance buses than the locals. Nonetheless, Gap year travel for young students has become quite fashionable in Tibet, and the challenge will be to use public transport wherever possible, having obtained the necessary internal travel permits from the police.

Travelling with children

Tibetans are very fond of children, and travellers who take their children to Tibet can expect to make new friends more easily. Airline, rail and bus tickets, as well as services provided by international tour operators and their local agents, can be discounted for children aged 5-15 years of age by as much as 30%. Most children travel well at high altitude and they can be more resilient than their parents. One of my daughters travelled through Amdo (Far East) when she was 4 months old, and reached Everest Base Camp at the age of four, without any difficulties! It is always wise to carry a suitable supply of children's medications, including calpol, liquid paracetemol, rehydration powders and remedies for stomach upsets. If your child has to consult a doctor, the gateway cities and most of the larger towns and cities on the plateau do have hospitals with facilities for treating children, and pharmacies will provide local medication suitable for children. Please also refer to the section on Health, page 52.

Women travellers

Tibet is regarded as one of the safest destinations in Asia for foreign women. Dress sensibly, wearing long skirts, trousers, or the local chuba, when travelling in the countryside. Shorter knee-length skirts may be worn in larger cities like Lhasa and Ziling, during the summer months. Although Khampa men in particular are renowned for their machismo and bravado, there are very few reports of foreign women being sexually harassed, even in the Kham region of Eastern Tibet. Local women are frequently teased and taunted in Tibetan society, but the unwelcome attention paid to western female travellers in South Asia has largely bypassed Tibet, where the sparsely populated terrain provides a greater sense of personal space and dignity.

Working and studying in the country

Most foreigners working in Tibet are employed either in the health or language teaching sectors, in some cases by municipal authorities or academic institutions, and in others by NGOs active within Tibet. There are also a few NGOs that have managed to contribute towards cultural restoration projects. For information on working opportunities with Tibet, the following organizations could be consulted:

Appropriate Technology for Tibetans, 117 Cricklewood Broadway, London NW2 3JG, UK, T+44-208-4508090, F+44-208-4509705.

Asia, Via della Battaglia, 00185, Roma, Italy, T+39-6-44340034, mc8125@mclink.it; Lhasa Office, T+86-891-6820337.

Kham Aid Project, 619 South Olive St, Suite 204, Los Angeles, CA 90014, USA, T+1-213489-7688, F+1-213489-7686, www.khamaid.org.

The Makhad Trust, Wolseley House, Oriel Rd, Cheltenham GL50 1TH, UK T+44-1242-544546, www.makhad.org.

Monasteries in Tibet Fund, 256 S Robertson Blvd, Suite 9379, Beverley Hills, CA 98211, USA.

The Orient Foundation, Queen Anne House, 11 Charlotte St, Bath BA1 2NE, UK, T+44-1225-336010.

Rokpa Trust, Samyeling, Eskdalemuir, Scotland, T+44-13873-73232, www.rokpa.org.

Shalu Association for Tibetan Cultural Heritage, 127 rue de Sevres, Paris 75006, T+33-1-45679503.

Tibet Foundation, 1 St James' Market, London SW1Y 4SB, UK, T+44-20-7930-6001, F+44-20-7930-6002, www.tibet-foundation.org.

Tibet Poverty Alleviation Fund, 5th floor Dargye Hotel, 34 East Lingkhor Lam, Lhasa, T+86-0891-6291966, matthew@tpaf.org.

Tibetan Plateau Ecological Project, 300 Broadway, Suite 28, San Francisco, CA 94133, USA, T+1-415-788-3666 x 132, F+1-415-788-7324, tppei@earthisland.org

Trace Foundation, 31 Perry St, New York City, NY 10014, USA, T+1-212 367-7380, F+1-212 367-7383.

NB Studying the Tibetan language inside Tibet is also possible at institutions such as the Tibet University in Lhasa, the Nationalities Institute in Chengdu, and the Nationalities Institute in Ziling. For details please contact these institutions or their relevant websites. In Lhasa, there is a two-year language course at Tibet University, each year being divided into two semesters. The spring semester starts in March and the autumn semester in August. If you wish to study there, you should write one year ahead for an application form. Long-term student visas can be arranged at overseas Chinese embassies once the formal registration process has been completed. For a list of embassies and consulates, see below, page 33.

Before you travel

Visas and immigration

Visas A valid passport including a standard Chinese entry visa is essential and visas are obtainable from most Chinese embassies and consulates, sometimes on sight of flight tickets and travellers' cheques. In the high season (August/September) confirmation of booking through a domestic Chinese travel agency is often required, and this is all that one needs to travel to those parts of the Tibetan plateau which are officially designated as 'open' to individual travellers. The cost of a standard Chinese tourist visa varies from US$12-120 according to the nationality of the applicant and the type of visa required. Individual visas may be issued for single or double entry, with a validity of one, two, or three months. Group visas may be issued, even for small parties of less than five, for the specific duration of a fixed itinerary (single or double entry). Multiple entry visas are normally issued for business or educational purposes only, ranging in validity from six to 12 months, and are more expensive (US$120-250). Normally three working days are required to process an application from the date of its submission, but express services are also available at a premium.

Permits As of autumn, 2004, there are still some parts of Tibet which are closed to the individual traveller, even with a standard Chinese visa. These include the Tibetan Autonomous Region, parts of Jyekundo prefecture in Qinghai, and the Dzamtang, Ngawa, Trochu, and Chuchen counties of Sichuan province. To visit such "closed" parts of Tibet two or three documents additional to the standard Chinese visa must be obtained. First, all foreigners intending to visit the Tibetan Autonomous Region require an Entry Permit issued by the Tibet Tourism Bureau. Second, for internal travel within any of these "closed" counties, foreigners require an **Alien Travel Permit (ATP)**, issued by the public security bureau responsible for the area to be visited (Lhasa, Zhigatse, Senge Khabab, Chengdu, Barkham and so forth). Third, for destinations in Chamdo prefecture, a **Military Permit** issued by the Southwest Military Command is also essential. Though individual travel is not permitted within these areas without the proper documentation, there are inevitably individuals who still manage to reach Lhasa from Kermo, or Chamdo from Kunming or Chengdu, travelling overland with some degree of risk. New regulations on entry into Tibet from Nepal were introduced in the autumn of 2003. Anyone proposing to enter Tibet from Nepal must now have a group visa issued by the Chinese Embassy in Kathmandu with approval from the Tibet Tourism Bureau in Lhasa (US$43 per person, one full working day required for processing). Any other valid Chinese visa stamps in your passport will be cancelled automatically when this document is issued.

To obtain these permits, it is necessary to make your travel arrangements through a bona fide agency, providing details of age, sex, nationality, passport number, occupation and address, preferably two months before departure. The visa authorization will then be faxed or telexed to the Chinese embassy of your choice, and a standard Chinese visa will be issued. Alternatively, those who enter China with a standard Chinese tourist visa can also make ad hoc arrangements with a local agency in any of the neighbouring gateway cities to obtain an entry permit and ATP and (if required) a military permit before entering

Internal travel: the need for permits

In order to understand these restrictions on internal travel, it is important to keep in mind the political situation in China and Tibet. It took a backward turn in 1989 when martial law was declared in Lhasa for over a year. Although this has been lifted, the military presence close to the capital and in other urban areas is intimidating and tourists are still closely watched. It is important to be aware that the Tibet problem remains unresolved, many Chinese officials still harbour an instinctive xenophobia, and so one must take care not to jeopardise the position of anyone who may help while you are there. The current attitude of the central government to foreign tourists in Tibet is ambivalent. They want the foreign exchange, while knowing full well that many visitors sympathize with the Tibetan cause.

Ostensibly to protect the fragile environment, but actually to bolster security and maximise financial returns, the authorities have forbidden the 'backpacking lone traveller' and insist on supervised group tours at fixed rates, which bear little or no direct relation to the facilities that are provided! Your enjoyment of a journey through closed areas of Tibet will, to a large extent, depend upon your own ability not to be disturbed by repeated requests for fees, permits and even for photography, as well as some exorbitant rates for hotel accommodation. However, with the recent opening of much of Kham and Amdo and the lifting of permit restrictions in those areas, it is hoped that the internal travel permit will gradually be phased out throughout the Tibetan plateau.

the closed areas of the Tibetan plateau. To be safe, it is better to make prior arrangements through a tour operator or travel agent before leaving home.

The ATP specifies every destination and town that you wish to visit and cannot be changed once you have arrived in the intended closed area. Therefore be certain to detail all possible destinations in your request as well as the route(s) you wish to follow.

Chinese embassies and consulates

Australia, 15 Coronation Dr, Yarralumla, ACT 2600, T062-2734780, 2734781. Consulate: 77 Irving Rd, Toorak, Melbourne, Victoria, T03-8220604.
Austria, Meternichgasse 4, 1030 Vienna, T06-753149/7136706.
Belgium, 443-5, Avenue de Tervureen, 1150 Brussels, T02-7713309/7712681.
Canada, 515 St Patrick's St, Ottawa, Ontario KIN 5H3, T0613-2342706/2342682.
France, 11 Ave George V, 75008, Paris, T1-47233677/43367790.
Germany, Karfurtsenallee 12, Bonn 2 (Bad Godesberg), T0228-361095/362350.
Hong Kong, Visa Office, Ministry of Foreign Affairs of the PRC, 5/F Low Block, China Resources Building, 26 Harbour Rd, Wanchai, T5851794/5851700.
Italy, 56 via Bruxelles, 56-00198 Rome, T06-8413458/8413467.
Japan, 3-4-33, Moto-Azabu, Minato-ku, Tokyo, T03-34033380/34033065.
Nepal, Baluwatar, Kathmandu, T412332/415383.
Netherlands, Adriaan Goekooplaan 7, 2517 JX The Hague, T070-3551515/9209.
New Zealand, 2-6 Glenmore St, Wellington, T064-4721383/4721384.
Spain, C/Arturo Soria 113, 28043 Madrid, T01-5194242/3651.
Sweden, Lodovagen 8 115 25, Stockholm, T08-7836739/7830179.
Switzerland, Kalecheggweg 10, 3006 Bern, T031-447333/434593.
UK, 49-51 Portland Pl, London W1N 3AH, T0207-6311430. Consulate: 43 Station Rd,

Edinburgh EH12 7AF, T0131-3164789.
USA, 2300 Connecticut Ave NW, Washington DC 20008, T202-3282500/3282517, F202-3282582. Consulates: 3417 Montrose Boulevard, Houston, Texas 77006; 104 South Michigan Ave, Suite 1200, Chicago, Illinois 60603; 1450 Laguna St, San Francisco, CA 94115; 520 12th Ave, New York, NY 10036.

Foreign embassies

Royal Nepalese Consulate: Gyatso To Lam, Lhasa, T0891-6322881. This is the only foreign embassy on the Tibetan plateau.
US Consulate General, 4 Lingshiguan Rd, Zhongbei, Chengdu, T028-5583992.

Customs

Until 1993 it was essential for all foreign visitors to complete a customs declaration form on arrival and countersign its duplicate on exiting the country, so that the import of luxury electronic goods in particular could be closely monitored. Such controls have since been relaxed for travellers arriving by air, and you may also import four bottles of liquor, two cartons of cigarettes, and 72 rolls of still film or 1,000 m of video film. **NB** 16 mm cameras are not permitted, except when special licenses have been arranged for filming, but high resolution 8 mm and digital cameras are unrestricted.

Foreigners are generally not subject to more than perfunctory baggage checks on entering and leaving Tibet, but in periods of political tension (which are commonplace) controls may be tightened. Certain items such as Dalai Lama photographs, critical literature and Tibetan national flags are sensitive; and the export of antique objects, including religious statues and jewellery, made before 1959 is officially prohibited. Old carpets and household items are more easily taken out, and it is best if some receipt or proof of purchase can be shown. There are shopkeepers in Lhasa who can arrange such receipts for a variety of purchases, regardless of their source!

Vaccinations

Have a check-up with your doctor, if necessary, and arrange your immunizations well in advance. Try ringing a specialist travel clinic if your own doctor is unfamiliar with health in Tibet. You should be protected against typhoid, polio, tetanus and hepatitis A, and for travel in certain remote areas of the Jangtang Plateau, immunization against rabies is also recommended.

Malaria prophylaxis is recommended for visitors to low-lying sub-tropical parts of southern or eastern Tibet, including Metok and Dzayul; but since the particular course of treatment for a specific part of the world can change from time to time, you should seek up to date advice from the **Malaria Reference Laboratory** ⓘ *T0891-600350 (recorded message, premium rate)*, or the **Liverpool School of Tropical Medicine** ⓘ *T0151-7089393*. In the USA, try **Center for Disease Control** ⓘ *Atlanta, T404-3324555*.

Yellow fever vaccination with a certificate is only required if you are coming from infected areas of the world. Vaccination against cholera or smallpox is not necessary, but occasionally immigration officials might ask to see a certificate.

What to take

It is always best to keep luggage to a minimum. A sturdy rucksack or a hybrid backpack/suitcase, rather than a rigid suitcase, covers most eventualities and survives bus boot, roof rack and plane/ship hold with ease. Serious trekkers will need a framed backpack. A complete checklist of items required for long treks or overland journeys is given below under Trekking, pages 49-51.

Everybody has their own list. Obviously what you take depends on your budget and where you are intending to go. Here is a selection of those items most often mentioned by travellers – pick and choose as you wish:

air cushions for slatted seats; an inflatable **travel pillow** for neck support; **strong shoes** (bearing in mind that footwear over 9½ English size, or 42 European size, may be difficult to obtain); a small **first-aid kit** and guide; fully **waterproof top clothing**; **waterproof treatment** for leather footwear; **wax earplugs** (which are almost impossible to find outside large cities) and an airline-type **eye mask** to help you sleep in noisy and poorly curtained hotel rooms; **sandals** (rubber-thong Japanese-type or other which can be worn in showers to avoid athlete's foot); a **polyethylene sheet** 2 m by 1 m to cover possibly infested beds and shelter your luggage; **polyethylene bags** of varying sizes (up to heavy duty rubbish bag size) with ties; a **toilet bag** you can tie round your waist (if you use an **electric shaver**, take a rechargeable type); a **sheet sleeping-bag** and pillow-case or separate pillow-case (they are not changed often in cheap hotels); a 1½-2-m piece of **100% cotton** that can be used as a towel, a bed-sheet, towel, makeshift curtain and wrap; a **mosquito net**; a **straw hat** which can be rolled or flattened and reconstituted after 15 minutes' soaking in water, a **clothes line**; a **nailbrush** (useful for scrubbing dirt off clothes as well as off yourself); a **vacuum flask**; a **water bottle**; a **small dual-voltage immersion heater**; a light nylon waterproof **shopping bag**; a universal bath- and basin-**plug** of the flanged type that will fit any waste-pipe (or improvise one from a sheet of thick rubber); **string**; **velcro**; **electrical insulating tape**; large **penknife** preferably with tin and bottle openers, scissors and corkscrew (the famous Swiss Army range has been repeatedly recommended – for knife sharpening, go to a butcher's shop); **alarm clock** or watch; **candle**; **torch** (flashlight) – especially one that will clip on to a pocket or belt; **pocket mirror**; **pocket calculator**; an **adaptor and flex** to enable you to take power from an electric-light socket. Remember not to throw away spent batteries containing mercury or cadmium; take them home to be disposed of, or recycled properly.

Useful medicaments are given in the Health section (page 52); to these might be added some lip salve with sun protection, and pre-moistened wipes (such as 'Wet Ones'). Always carry toilet paper and natural fabric sticking plasters. Dental floss can be used for backpack repairs, as well as its original purpose. **Contact lens solution** can be difficult to find, especially outside major cities. Ask for it in a chemist/pharmacy, rather than an optician's. Never carry firearms. Their possession could land you in serious trouble.

Insurance

Before you travel make sure the medical and cancellation insurance you take out is adequate. The standard Trailfinders' insurance policy, available through **Trailfinders'** outlets in UK, covers most requirements for travel in Tibet. An additional premium will be payable to cover mountaineering expeditions.

Money

Currency

The national currency is the Yuan (¥) or Renminbi (RMB), popularly called 'kwai'. 10 Jiao (pronounced 'mao') = 1 Yuan and 10 Fen = 1 Jiao. The exchange rate is still approximately US$1 = ¥8.3, despite US efforts to have the currency revalued upwards.

Travellers' cheques and credit cards

In mainland China TCs are accepted and major currency denominations are easily changed in the larger cities, most of which also have ATM machines, which will accept international credit cards. On the Tibetan plateau, credit card cash withdrawals can be made at the **Bank of China** in Lhasa and Ziling for a surcharge of 3%. ATM facilities in Lhasa are now available at certain branches of the Bank of China and the **Agricultural Bank of China**. The larger hotels on the plateau, such as the Lhasa Hotel, Himalaya Hotel, Qinghai Hotel, and Jiuzhaigou International Hotel also provide currency exchange facilities and will accept credit cards.

Exchange

The **Bank of China** has branches in Lhasa, Dram (Zhangmu), Zhigatse, Ziling (Xining), Kermo (Golmud), Dartsedo (Kangding), Gyeltang (Zhongdian), Barkham, and Zungchu (Songpan), which will change travellers' cheques and hard currency. Unofficial money changers prefer US$ cash. **NB** Remember to carry a sufficient amount of RMB for long overland drives or treks. Outside these larger cities, you will not have access to exchange facilities. Even if your tour is pre-arranged, when travelling in remote areas it is always wise to carry extra cash to cover unforeseen contingencies (such as payment of entrance and photographic fees).

Cost of living and travelling

Most commodities available In Tibet are priced slightly higher than they would be in mainland China. Individual travellers will find that food and public transport in the "open" areas of Eastern Tibet (Kham and Amdo) are reasonably inexpensive, somewhere in between the cost of living in India and in Thailand. In "closed" areas of the country, food can still be inexpensive but the cost of hiring suitable vehicles is much higher in those areas where foreigners are discouraged from using public transport. Hotel prices will vary widely from US$2 per bed in some inexpensive guesthouses to over US$160 in upmarket hotels. Since most travellers in Tibet come on prearranged and prepaid itineraries, they will only have to budget for incidental expenses and personal purchases.

Getting there

Air

Flights to the neighbouring gateway cities Since the Tibetan plateau at present has no transcontinental or long-haul flight connections, the air traveller will first have to reach one of the five neighbouring gateway cities: Kathmandu, Chengdu, Kunming, Lanzhou or Kashgar, or else one of the newly emerging gateway cities for long distance air travel: Beijing, Shanghai, Guangzhou, Chongqing or Xi'an. Information on flights to all these gateway cities may be found below (see pages 14-734). Travellers should contact the various airline websites for updated price and schedule information. A direct charter flight operated by **Hainan Airlines** runs occasionally from Hong Kong to Lhasa, but many have found it to be unreliable.

Flights into Tibet The only civilian airports on the Tibetan plateau are currently those at Gongkar near Lhasa, Pomda (Ch Bangda) near Chamdo, Gyeltang (Ch Zhongdian) near Dechen, Dzitsa Degu National Park (Ch. Jiuzhaigou), Ziling (Ch Xining), and Kermo (Ch. Golmud) in Amdo. There are also plans under way to construct new airports at Senge Khabab (Ch Shiquanhe) in Ngari, at Dabpa (Ch Daocheng) to the south of Litang and at Nyangtri in Southern Tibet. **NB** The prices given here are current but subject to frequent change.

Flights to Lhasa **Air China South-west** have connections to Lhasa from Chengdu (1¾ hours) daily at ¥1,270; from Beijing (four hours 50 minutes via Chengdu) daily at ¥2,010; from Kathmandu (55 minutes) on Tuesday and Saturday at US$273

(April-November only), from Ziling (two hours) on Monday, Wednesday, Friday and Sunday at ¥1,360, from Kunming (3¼ hours via Gyeltang) on Wednesday and Saturday at ¥1,810, from Gyeltang (1¾ hours) on Wednesday and Saturday at ¥1,250, from Chongqing (two hours 20 minutes) on Monday, Wednesday and Sunday at ¥1,370, from Xi'an (3¾ hours) on Monday, Wednesday, Friday and Sunday at ¥1,390, from Shanghai (six hours via Xian) on Wednesday and Sunday at ¥2,310, and from Guangzhou (4¾ hours via Chongqing) on Monday at ¥2,100.

Tickets to Lhasa can be obtained from **Air China South-west** offices in Kathmandu (T009771-419770), Hong Kong (T00852-25286898), Chengdu (T008628-86668080), Kunming (T0086-871-3539702), Ziling (T0086971-8133333), Shanghai (T0086-21643333355), Guangzhou (T0086-2086220156), Chongqing (T008623-67853191), or Beijing (T0086-10-66017579, and also from a variety of local ticketing offices in downtown Chengdu which offer discount rates. If you can speak Chinese, try calling T86748781. **NB** Most travellers still find it easier to liase with their travel agent or tour operator prior to departure because flight tickets to Lhasa can only be issued on receipt of a valid Tibet entry permit.

Transport to Lhasa from Gongkar Airport 99 km by bus, minibus, or land cruiser. A newly constructed road bridge will soon link Gongkar Airport with the Kyi-chu south bank highway, via Sinpori Tunnel. When opened in the autumn of 2004 this will reduce the driving distance to only 55 km.

Flights to Chamdo **Air China China South-west** have connections to Pomda Airport near Chamdo from Chengdu on Tuesday, Wednesday, Saturday and Sunday (1 hour 5 minutes) at ¥750, and from Lhasa (55 minutes) on Thursday at ¥720. Permit restrictions apply, and travellers should be prepared: Pomda is reckoned to be the world's highest civilian airport! Tickets from Lhasa may be purchased from Air China Southwest, Nyangdren Rd, T0086-891-6333331.

Flights to Gyeltang (Ch Zhongdian/ Deqin) **Yunnan Airways** operate daily flights from Kunming (55 minutes) at ¥560. **Air China Southwest** operate the same route on Wednesday and Saturday, continuing on to Lhasa before returning via Gyeltang to Kunming.

Flights to Dzitsa Degu (Ch Jiuzhaigou) **Air China South-west** and **Sichuan Airlines** have daily flights from Chengdu to Amdo's world-famous nature reserve at ¥470.

Air Routes into Tibet

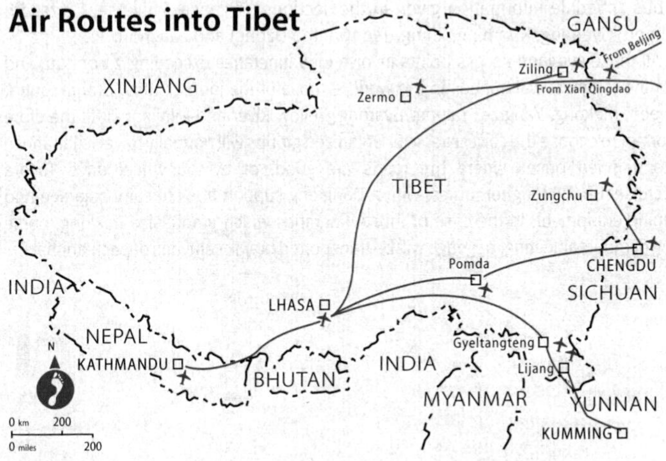

Flights to Ziling (Ch Xining) There are daily flights from Beijing as well as flights from Chengdu (on Tuesday to Sunday inclusive) at ¥1,310 and ¥910 respectively, Guangzhou (on Tuesday, Thursday and Saturday) at ¥1,450, Lhasa (Monday, Wednesday, Friday and Sunday) at ¥1,290, and Urumqi (on Monday-Thursday inclusive and Saturday) at ¥1,030.

Flights to Kermo (Ch Golmud) **China North-west Airlines** have flights from Xi'an (2 hours 55 minutes via Ziling) on Tuesday, Thursday and Saturday at ¥1,200, and from Qingdao (4 hours 50 minutes via Zhengzhou or Ziling) on Tuesday, Friday and Sunday at ¥1,800.

Rail

The only railway on the Tibetan plateau is that running from Ziling to Kermo in Amdo (¥126 per soft-seat, ¥149 per hard-sleeper, and ¥221 per soft-sleeper). There are daily express and local services. A recently announced plan to extend the railway from Kermo to Lhasa (1,120 km) is now being implemented, with an anticipated completion date of 2007. This project, which will cost a staggering US$2.4 billion, entails the construction of 286 bridges and 10 tunnels, one of which will be 1.5 km long, and about 50,000 engineers and labourers are expected to participate. The high altitudes, exceeding 4,545 m above sea level at one point, will require special train engines that can function with little oxygen as well as pressurized cars to keep passengers from suffering altitude sickness. The central government has apparently written off the immense cost of boring ice tunnels through the Kunluns and laying tracks over the permafrost surface of the Jangtang Plateau (which can rise and fall by 1 m from winter to summer), on the grounds that the railway is expected to bring to fruition their long-term political and economic goals, further integrating Tibet with the Chinese mainland. Under these circumstances, Tibetan fears that their culture will be further diluted by a new wave of Chinese migrants coming in by rail are well founded. Sixteen passenger and freight trains will make the journey each day, taking only half the time that it would by road.

The new **Lhasa Railway Station** will soon be constructed near Tashigang to the west of the city.

Road

The main motor roads into Tibet start at Kalpa in the Kinnaur region of India (presently closed), Kathmandu in Nepal, Gangtok in Sikkim (soon to be opened), Kunming via Dali in Yunnan, Chengdu via Ya'an, Wolong or Wenchuan in Sichuan, and Lanzhou via Ziling or Labrang. On some of these overland routes public transport is available. See the bus schedule information given in the sections on Lhasa, Zhigatse, Dartsedo, Chengdu, Gyeltang, Kunming, Ziling, Tso (Ganlho Dzong) and Lanzhou.

All these overland access points involve long itineraries exceeding 2,000 km, and cross the toughest watersheds in the world – those of the Indus, Sutlej, Brahmaputra, Salween, Mekong, Yangtze, Yalung, Gyarong, Yellow River and Minjiang. It is therefore important to choose the correct vehicle. Organized groups will normally travel in Japanese air-conditioned buses where the roads are good, or by four-wheel drive Toyota landcruiser on the tougher routes, with a Dongfeng support truck to carry baggage and camping equipment. In the case of those itineraries which emphasize trekking, horse riding or mountaineering, baggage will be transported by yak caravans or pack-animals.

Touching down

Airport information

At **Gongkar Airport**, transportation to Lhasa or Tsetang is normally provided by the local travel services. Public buses are also available to Lhasa (99 km on old road, 55 km on new road, ¥25-35) and Zhigatse (¥50). Buses depart Lhasa for the airport at 0600, 1300, and 1700; and a daily bus departs Zhigatse for the airport at 1200. Taxis are available to Lhasa or Tsetang (¥100 on average); while at **Pomda Airport**, 4WD taxis are available to Chamdo (120 km, ¥100). The airports at **Gyeltang, Dzitsa Degu, Ziling** and **Kermo** are all relatively close to town. Further airport information may be obtained from **Air China Southwest** ⓘ*Lhasa, T0086-891-6822567*, or at **Gongkar Airport** ⓘ*T0086-891-6182221 ext. 2422.*

Baggage An experienced traveller carries as little luggage as possible. Remember that you are allowed no more than the normal weight (20 kg) and that you may be liable to pay for excess baggage. You should also carry essentials, medication, reading material, cameras, flashlights, and other necessities (eg toilet paper) at all times in your flight bag or, as many prefer, in a lightweight backpack. If you are trekking or undertaking a long overland drive, you may have to supply your own tent and sleeping bag. Bring your own water-bottle, a screw-top cup or jar (for thirst-quenching jasmine tea), and a pocket-knife with bottle opener/corkscrew attachments, as well as a can opener, scissors, sewing kit, and pocket-size screwdriver. A complete checklist of items required for long treks or overland journeys is given below under Trekking, pages 49-51.

Local customs and laws

Clothing

The air temperature in Tibet can change very quickly with a passing cloud or the coming of the night. A flexible system of 'layered' clothing is recommended: thermal underwear, cotton shirts, a warm pullover and windproof jacket and some light rain-gear, as well as a sun-hat and a scarf or face-mask to ward off the dust. For overland travel or trekking, strong but lightweight walking boots should be worn, and gloves, woollen hats, thick socks and hiking poles are all useful. For the hot springs, people may want to bring swimwear. A rucksack is indispensable for trekking and most trekkers prefer to bring their own down jacket and sleeping bag.

Apart from the larger tourist hotels and major cities, no laundry or dry-cleaning service is available. If you wish to avoid the do-it-yourself option, it is sometimes possible to come to a private arrangement for laundry services with local guesthouse attendants.

Conduct

The challenge in Tibet is to remain polite and courteous in social relationships regardless of the difficulties which arise! Remember that loss of self-control is less likely to bring about your desired response. When visiting a monastery or temple, do not smoke, wear a hat, or interrupt prayers and on-going ceremonies. External photography is generally allowed, whereas internal photography of the images and murals inside a temple may be prohibited, or require a fee, normally imposed by the authorities. Always ask before photographing. Bribes are officially frowned upon,

Touching down

Official time Tibetan time is absurdly the same as time in Beijing since a single time zone prevails throughout the regions controlled by China, ie GMT + eight hours. This accounts for the long daylight evenings and dark early mornings. Consequently, the border crossings between Tibet and Nepal or between Xinjiang and Pakistan may be the only places on the ground where travellers experience a sense of jet-lag!

Hours of business Government buildings, banks and offices are open from Monday-Friday (0930-1230, 1530-1800). Saturday (only recently) and Sunday are public holidays, as are the main festivals of the Chinese calendar: New Year's Day (1 January), Tibetan New Year, Chinese New Year (Spring Festival), International Working Women's Day (8 March), International Labour Day (1 May), Youth Day (4 May), Children's Day (1 June), Founding of the Chinese Communist Party (1 July), Army Day (1 August), and National Day (1 October).

Weights and measures Metric – the same as in China. Traditional measurements are also in use. 1 kg = 2 gyama (Ch jin), 1 ha = 15 mu, 1 km = 2 litres, 1 m = 3 chi.

Voltage 220 volts, 50 cycles AC. The current is variable and the hours of operation unpredictable. Carry a range of plug conversion adapters. Rely on battery-operated equipment. A strong flashlight is also essential.

but often accepted when discreetly offered. Small gifts, however, are widely appreciated. Photographs of important lamas from the various Buddhist or Bon traditions are revered throughout the monasteries, villages, and towns of Tibet, but photographs of the Dalai Lama, which may not at present be sold in public outside certain parts of Amdo, should be avoided unless they can be given discreetly in confidence. At the time of arrival or departure, it is customary to exchange white offering scarves (Tib. *katak*), or gifts. See also the sections on Trekking, page 49, and Media, page 58.

Visiting monasteries

When visiting monasteries, you will not usually have to remove shoes, as in India, but do remember to be modestly dressed, to remove your hat, to abstain from smoking, and to proceed around or through sacred shrines in a clockwise manner. Never sit down pointing your feet towards the images of a temple or its inner sanctum. You may feel privileged to bear witness to the revival of this ancient culture, even if distressed by the obvious signs of wanton destruction, mostly dating from the 1960s, and by the apparent lack of activity in some monasteries. This can be balanced at the end of your trip by a visit to neighbouring Kathmandu or Bhutan, where many of Tibet's greatest lamas have actively rebuilt their communities in exile. Independent Bhutan also preserves the ancient spiritual heritage of Tibet intact, having avoided the depredations of the Chinese Cultural Revolution. Nonetheless, in many remote monasteries of East and Far East Tibet you will be heartened by the genuine non-sectarian approach and commitment to the meditative and scholarly life shown by elderly and young monks or nuns alike, with scant material resources.

More difficult is the reintroduction of systematic Buddhist learning and meditation practice. Many of the great Tibetan masters who live in exile have returned home for visits to encourage a Buddhist renaissance; but the authorities often continue to react with suspicion and misunderstanding. This is particularly noticeable in and around Lhasa, where the political indoctrination of monks and nuns continues and a hardline campaign seeks to marginalize the influence of the Dalai Lama, oblivious to the abject failure of past repression. It is clear for all to see that Tibetan hearts and minds support the Dalai Lama in his quest for a genuine autonomy in association with China, which would sustain Tibetan culture in the decades ahead. Yet such repression is by no means confined to Lhasa. Witness the eviction of several thousand committed Tibetan and Chinese Buddhist practitioners from Larung Gar in Sertal in 2001.

Tipping

Tipping is officially frowned upon, but widespread in hotels and travel agencies. Remember to tip your driver in Tibet as well as your guide. In view of the road conditions, the driver will often receive as much as the guide.

Prohibitions and getting out of trouble

Gambling for high stakes at mahjong and prostitution are endemic in modern Tibetan towns and cities where there is a large Chinese military presence. In certain hotels clients will be solicited over the telephone for such services, while in others they will be tacitly provided on the premises. Though technically illegal under Chinese law, the authorities consistently turn a blind eye to prostitution. The publicity given to occasional government-sponsored anti-corruption campaigns seems to have little impact in reality. Travellers are more likely to fall foul of the authorities if they pass through "closed" areas of the country without proper documentation, in which case the police can impose stiff fines and penalties or, more seriously, if they engage directly in overt political activities.

Responsible tourism

Although there are still some who refuse to visit Tibet for political reasons, contacts with the outside world are highly valued because they do act as a conduit for information and provide an immediate experience of life in Tibet that cannot easily be acquired by other means. The argument in favour of engagement is supported by the moderate Dalai Lama, whose envoys were able to revisit Tibet in 2002 and 2003 for the first time in over 20 years, and even by the pro-independence International Campaign for Tibet in Washington D.C. Their recently published travel guidelines advise visitors to espouse religious freedom, to buy from Tibetans, to avoid purchasing antiquities, to protect wildlife and the environment, to hire Tibetan guides wherever possible, and to protect the identities of Tibetan associates.

Safety

In urban areas pickpockets are commonplace, and venues of entertainment, such as karaoke bars, nightclubs and discotheques, can sometimes erupt into flash-points of violence, reminiscent of the Wild West. Foreign visitors should be aware of the risks facing the indigenous population who engage in acts of political dissent; and should not compromise friends or acquaintances. Do not distribute photographs of the Dalai Lama in public places or even upon random request. In general it is best if unwitting visitors make little contact with Tibetans in urban areas; but, as always, what one can or cannot do will depend upon who one knows. Some undercover policemen are themselves among the most affable and gracious hosts when introduced socially by those with the right connections! In general the crime rate in Tibet is low, and you will be received courteously throughout the length and breadth of the country. Some remote village communities may be suspicious of passing strangers, but you are more at risk from the dangerous road conditions than from the country's inhabitants. Overland travel in Tibet remains a pastime for the adventurous.

Police → *To contact the police in any prefectural city, call T110.*

The various branches of the police force, known as the **Public Security Bureau** (Tib Chide Lekhung, Ch Gonganju), monitor traffic, crime, political dissent, and visa extensions. Offices are found in all cities, towns, and lesser townships, but visa extensions are only possible in major cities, such as Lhasa, Zhigatse, Tsetang, Senge Khabab, Kermo, Zungchu, Dartsedo, Gyeltang, Barkham and Ziling. These offices are also responsible for issuing Alien Travel Permits (ATP) for the 'closed' areas of the Tibetan plateau within their jurisdiction.

Getting around

There are few paved roads in Tibet. Most roads are therefore subject to clouds of dust and landslides can cause delays in summer. Public transport is accessible to all travellers in open areas, but in closed areas it is largely reserved for locals, and hitchhiking is discouraged. For this reason alone, truly independent travel over long distances is not easy, and you should ensure that you have adequate transport for your chosen destination in advance – often a four-wheel drive landcruiser with a support truck.

Air and rail

Once inside Tibet, the only domestic air connections are those already mentioned, linking Lhasa with Chamdo, Gyeltang and Ziling, and Ziling with Kermo. This will of course change when the new airports are opened at Senge Khabab, Dabpa, and Nyangtri. The only rail link runs from Lanzhou through the Tsongkha valley to Ziling and on past Lake Kokonor to Kermo. The extension of this line to Lhasa will be completed in 2007.

Road

In view of this limited transport infrastructure, most people are totally dependent on the road network, which is extensive but precarious. The main paved roads on the Tibetan plateau are **Highway 109** from Lanzhou via Ziling and Kermo to Lhasa, the sections of **Highway 213** from Lanzhou via Labrang to Luchu and from Mewa to Chengdu, **Highway 227** from Ziling to Chilen, the sections of **Highway 214** from Ziling via Jyekundo to Nangchen, from Chamdo to Pomda Airport, and Dechen via Gyeltang to Kunming, the sections of **Highway 318** from Chengdu via Dartsedo to Litang, and from Lunang via Lhasa to Takar, the section of **Highway 219** from Senge Khabab to Gar Gunsa, and the section of **Highway 317** from Dartsedo to Derge. Other newly paved roads link Lhasa with Tsetang and Zhigatse, Zungchu with Chengdu, Dzamtang with Barkham and Ziling with Repkong and Machen. However, only short sections of Highway 318 (sometimes euphemistically called the "Friendship Highway") between Zhigatse and Dram on the Nepal border have as yet been paved. The others are all unpaved dirt roads, plagued by palls of dust, ruts left by HVG transport vehicles, and landslides in the rainy season. Roads crossing high passes are periodically snowbound from late October through to March.

The principal means of road transport for local people and independent travellers (in open areas only) is the public bus. Tourists and those travelling through closed areas usually hire a four-wheel drive landcruiser or Japanese bus, along with its driver. Owing to the rugged nature of the terrain, many routes in Tibet are for the adventure traveller only.

Hitchhiking As stated above, hitchhiking is officially prohibited in the Tibetan Autonomous Region, but some drivers will take risks to offer a ride to foreign visitors in order to make a little money. It is useful for potential hitch-hikers to know the districts or prefectures to which TAR number plates refer: A: Lhasa; B: Chamdo, C: Lhokha, D: Zhigatse, E: Nakchu, F: Ngari, G: Nyangtri. The following Sichuan number plates will also be useful for travellers to Kham: A Chengdu, T Ya'an, V Kandze, U Ngawa and W Mili. Useful Yunnan number plates are: A Kunming, L Dali, P Lijiang, and R Dechen. Similarly, the following letters identify Amdo (Qinghai and Gansu) number plates: A Ziling; AB Serkhok; AC Rushar; AO Gonlung; B Tsongkha Khar, Drotsang, Dowi and Kamalok, C: Tsojang (Bongtak Tianjun, Kangtsa, Dabzhi, Chilen, Mongyon and Tongkor); D Malho (Bayan Khar, Jentsa, Repkong and Tsekok), E Tsolho (Trika, Mangra, Kawasumdo, Chabcha and Tsigortang), F Golok (Mato, Machen, Gabde, Darlag, Padma, Jigdril), H Tsonub (Kermo, Mangnai, Tsaidam, Panchen Zhingde and Ulan); P Ganlho (Sangchu, Luchu, Machu, Lintan, Tewo, Drukchu), N Linxia, A Lanzhou.

Cycling Mountain bike cycling is possible in the open areas of the Tibetan plateau, but cyclists who wish to ride through closed areas, even on the road from Lhasa to Kathmandu via Dram, require an Alien Travel Permit. Cycling itineraries can be arranged by the travel services.

Maps

The best English language maps available in Tibet are the **China Tibet Tour Map,** published by the TAR Mapping Bureau in 1993 and the **Map of Mountain Peaks** on the Qinghai-Xizang Plateau, published by the China Cartographic Publishing House in 1989. More detailed maps are available for readers of Tibetan. They include the **Tibetan Language Map of the Ngawa Autonomous Prefecture,** published in Sichuan, the wall-size **Tibetan Language Map of TAR,** published in Lhasa, and the **Map of Tibet and Adjacent Regions,** published by the India-based Amnye Machen Institute in 1996. Some Chinese maps are also useful, especially the **China Road Atlas,** the **Sichuan Road Atlas,** and the **County Atlases of the Tibet Autonomous Region, Qinghai, Sichuan, Gansu and Yunnan,** which all provide distances between points on the motor roads, and the newly published urban street plans of Lhasa, Zhigatse, Barkham Dartsedo, Gyeltang and Ziling.

English language maps available outside Tibet include the **Operational Navigational Charts** (ONC) and the **Joint Operations Graphic Series** (JOG), both published in the United States. The latter were reproduced in Victor Chen's *Tibet Handbook*. These maps are more useful for their topography but they are remarkably weak on place-name data. The map of the TAR (1:2,000,000) published recently by **Gizi Maps** in Budapest (T36-1-326 0717) is currently the best for toponymics. The as yet unpublished digital atlases of Michael Farmer in London and Claude Andre in Paris are awaited with great anticipation since they will take Tibetan cartography to a new level.

As for English language street plans, the **Lhasa City Map**, published in India by the Amnye Machen Institute in 1995 is the most detailed map of the Tibetan capital, and **On this Spot Lhasa**, published by the International Campaign for Tibet in 2001, highlights a number of historically important and politically sensitive sites within the city. The recently published **Mapping the Tibetan World** (Kotan, 2000), which takes much of its format and content from the first edition of this Tibet guide (1996), is generally out of date, but it does include some useful street plans (even if they are heavily sinicized). The US maps and others, including French language maps and the **Cyrillic Karta Mera** series, are all available at **Stanfords** ① *12-14 Long Acre, Covent Garden, London WC2E 9LP, T020-7836 1321, www.stanfords.co.uk.*

Sleeping

Most hotels in Tibet offer twin-share or triple accommodation, and some of them also have single rooms and suites. Guesthouses tend to have more triples and dormitories, but even there a single supplement may be paid to keep beds empty. For further details of the hotels in each city or town, see the relevant Essentials sections. The hotel categories are determined by the price of the average double room, exclusive of local taxes: **AL**: US$140+ (five star), **A**: US$90+ (four star), **B**: US$50+ (three star), **C**: US$30+, **D**: US$20+, **E**: US$6+

Hotels

With the notable exception of Dzitsa Degu (Ch. Jiuzhaigou) in Amdo, which now has five-star facilities, the best hotels available on the Tibetan plateau range from four-star and three-star downwards. By contrast, the neighbouring gateway cities such as Kathmandu, Chengdu, Lanzhou, and Kunming offer the full range of luxury to budget accommodation. Within Lhasa, the better hotels, such as Lhasa Hotel, Himalaya Hotel, Tibet Hotel, and International Grand Hotel, vary in price from US$62 to US$122. Off-season winter discounts amounting to as much as 20% are available. Outside Lhasa, there are also large modern hotels with en suite bathrooms and hot running water in Tsetang and Bayi (Southern Tibet), in Zhigatse, Gyantse and Sakya (Western Tibet), in Senge Khabab (Far West Tibet), in Chamdo, Gyeltang, Dechen, Derge, Kandze, Dartsedo and Jyekundo (East Tibet), and in Ziling, Repkong, Labrang, Barkham, Mewa and Zungchu (Far East Tibet). The typical price range in such establishments will be US$15-70. Many of these towns and cities also have cheaper hotel and guesthouse accommodation for budget groups and independent travellers.

Guesthouses

There are some reasonably clean and well-managed guesthouses in far-flung places such as Purang, Gertse, Tsochen, Saga, Sok Dzong, Tengchen, Dzogang, Markham, Dabpa, Manigango, Zhiwu, Tawu, Chabcha, Mato, Darlag and Ngawa. The traveller should be aware that such guesthouses have shared toilet and bathroom facilities. Bring your own disinfectant and toilet paper! Prices here will range from US$5-10 per bed (or US$10-20 per room). Other guesthouses, some of which are quite large, like the Hebei Hotel in Toling, are poorly maintained, and the shared toilet facilities leave much to be desired. A gas mask would be a useful asset in such establishments. Many smaller townships and villages have traditional Tibetan-style guesthouses – adobe buildings constructed around a walled courtyard. The Farmers' Guesthouse in Lhartse, Pematso Guesthouse in Ba me, the Yak Hotel in Baryang, the Yak Hotel in Old Drongpa, and the Labrang Hotel in Labrang are among the best. A few hotels and guesthouses have also been built adjacent to hot springs, and some of these have hot mineral waters pumped directly into the bathrooms, as at the Health Spa Hotel and the Wenchuan Hotel in Trika (Amdo).

Camping

In smaller places, you can stay in simple roadside transport stations or head out of town to set up a camp (in which case you will also need a stove and cooking utensils). Such transport stations are highly variable and often decidedly unclean, sometimes lacking the most basic facilities. Camping is often preferable.

Eating

Food

The restaurant categories in this book provide a rough guide to upmarket, mid-range and downmarket prices for the independent traveller. 🍴🍴🍴: US$10+, 🍴🍴: US$5+, and 🍴: US$3+. Organized tours in Tibet may include a full package with three meals daily, or a half package with breakfast and dinner only. In Lhasa a minimum package (hotel only) is also available. International cuisine (Continental, Nepalese, Indian etc.) is only offered at a small number of restaurants and hotels in the Lhasa and Dzitsa Degu areas. A few specialist restaurants will offer Tibetan, Peking, Cantonese or Korean dishes. Otherwise the standard cuisine offered in restaurants throughout the Tibetan plateau is either Sichuan or Muslim.

Tibetan cuisine for the most part is pretty basic, the staple consisting of large amounts of *tsampa* (roasted barley flour) and endless bowls of butter tea. Naturally you will have a chance to taste this delicacy during your stay, but it is highly unlikely that you will want to repeat the experience every day! On the other hand, there are some very good dishes to be had, for example the famous *momo*, a steamed meat dumpling which resembles the Chinese *jiaoze*, or Tibetan country-style noodles (*then-thuk*), and whilst you are in Lhasa you can arrange to have traditional Tibetan banquet (18 dishes) including *lasha* (lamb with radish), *gyuma* (black pudding), *thu* (cheesecake), and *dresi* (sweet rice), topped up with copious cups of '*chang*', the local barley wine.

In nomadic areas, the staple diet consists of yak meat and mutton (fresh or dried), supplemented by delicious yoghurt. Cheese also comes in many varieties: hardened cubes which must be carefully sucked to avoid damaging the teeth, moderately soft slivers which are easy to digest and, in East Tibet, an assortment of cheeses similar to cottage cheese or cheddar (Tib Jo-she). Desserts are not generally served but delicious apples, apricots, peaches and walnuts are available in season.

During day trips and long overland journeys, it is sometimes necessary to take a picnic lunch – either supplied by the hotels or the local travel agency. Organized tours, which include camping, will have a cook who can prepare a full campsite meal, or take over the kitchen of a roadside restaurant. In drier regions of West and Far West Tibet, you must carry more tinned provisions, while in the more fertile eastern regions, fresh vegetables are plentiful. To supplement this diet, you may wish to carry instant soups, cheeses, pâtés, biscuits, chocolates, coffee, and so forth, which can be very welcome if the weather suddenly turns nasty, or if you have stomach trouble.

Drink

Beer and soft drinks are generally served with all meals in Tibet, while imported alcohol is available only in the larger restaurants and tourist hotels of Lhasa and Dzitsa Degu. Bottled mineral water can be bought easily in the towns. Tea and thermos bottles of hot water are provided in hotel and guesthouse rooms, and this is probably the most refreshing remedy for the dry and dusty atmosphere prevalent on the Tibetan plateau. Bottled mineral water or boiled water is essential for drinking and indeed for brushing the teeth. Some restaurants will also provide Indian-style sweet milk tea or Nescafé. However, butter tea (soja/poja) or salted black tea (ja-dang) is generally drunk at home. The national alcoholic drinks are chang, a fortified barley ale, and arak, a type of distilled liquor. Dried fermented millet (tomba) is brewed in areas bordering Sikkim and

 Bhutan, while 'Lhasa Beer' (Lhasa Pijiu) and other brands of beer, as well as Chinese spirits, can be purchased throughout the plateau.

Entertainment

Traditional entertainment in Tibet includes secular and religious festivals (see next section), and Tibetan operatic performances. Nowadays, in the larger cities there are also sporting contests, while mahjong and pool are extremely popular, along with the new wave of downtown cinemas, video lounges, computer games, discotheques, nightclubs, bars, karaoke establishments, and seedy massage parlours. Tibetans have a great passion for seasonal outdoor picnics and for the Nang-ma – best described as an evening of traditional music and dance, somewhat reminiscent of the Scottish ceilidh, but in a sophisticated modern nightclub setting. The music on offer here includes live performances of traditional and modern Tibetan songs, interspersed with popular Chinese, Indian or Uighur songs (depending on the area) and interludes of western disco music. Cinemas offer mostly Chinese films and a few foreign movies of the Hollywood or Bollywood variety that have been dubbed or subtitled.

Festivals and events

Festivals

The Tibetan lunar calendar is calculated each year by astrologers from the Mentsikhang in Lhasa and Dharamsala. It is based on a cycle of 60 years, each of which is named after one of 12 animals and one of five elements in combination. For example, 2004 is called the wood monkey year. A calendrical year normally contains 12 months, but the addition of an extra intercalary month for astrological reasons is not uncommon. In general, the Tibetan lunar month runs about two months behind the western calendar. Many festivals are traditionally held throughout the Tibetan calendar – some are nationwide and others applicable to a certain area only. They may also be religious or secular in character. The main horse festival season falls between the fifth and the seventh months of the year (usually July-September), and some are now fixed in relation to the solar calendar, eg Jyekundo Horse Festival, which begins on 25 July, and the Litang Horse Festival, beginning in recent years on 1 August.

Major events in the Tibetan calendar are shown opposite. The next year's calendar is prepared in the late autumn or winter and only then can the dates be matched to the western calendar. In addition, the 10th day of every month is dedicated to Padmasambhava who introduced the highest Buddhist teachings from India in the eighth century. The 25th day of each month is a Dakini Day, associated with the female deities who are the agents of Buddha-activity. The 29th day of each month is dedicated to the wrathful doctrinal protector deities, while the 15th and 30th are associated with the Buddha, and the eighth with the Medicine Buddha.

Public holidays

The dates of traditional festivals vary according to the lunar calendar, whereas most modern Chinese holidays are tied to the solar calendar.

Chinese Public Holidays

1 Jan	New Year's Day
22 Jan	Chinese New Year/Spring Festival
21 Feb	Tibetan New Year
8 Mar	International Working Women's Day
1 May	International Labour Day
4 May	Youth Day
1 Jun	Children's Day

Festival dates, 2005

Lunar Date	Western Date	Event
1st of 1st month	9 Feb (2005)	Losar, Tibetan New Year
8th of 1st month	16 Feb	Monlam, the Great Prayer Festival
15th of 1st month	23 Feb	Day of Offerings
10th of 4th month	18 May	Tsurphu Tsechu Festival
15th of 4th month	23 May	Enlightenment of Buddha
18th of 4th month	26 May	Gyantse Horse Festival
15th of 5th month	22 Jun	Samye Doldhe Festival
15th of 5th month	22 Jun	Local Deities' Day
15th of 5th month	22 Jun	Tashilhunpo Festival
4th of 6th month	21 Jul	Dharmacakra Day
10th of 6th month	7 Jul	Birth of Padmasambhava
15th of 6th month	21 Jul	Ganden Serthang Festival
13-16th of 6th month	19 Jul-22 Jul	Tashilhunpo Monlam
29th of 6th month	4 Aug	Drepung Zhoton (Yoghurt Festival)
1st of 7th month	6 Sep	Zhoton (Yoghurt Festival)
27th of 7th month	19 Sep	Bathing Festival
30th of 7th month	3 Oct	End of Rain Retreat
30th of 7th month	3 Oct	Damzhung Horse Festival
1st of 8th month	4 Oct	Ongkor (Harvest Festival)
22nd of 9th month	23 Nov	Descent from the God Realms
15th of 10th month	15 dec	Palden Lhamo Procession in Barkhor
25th of 10th month	26 Dec	Anniversary of Tsongkhapa
6th of 11th month	5 Jan (2006)	Nine Bad Omens
7th of 11th month	6 Jan	Ten Auspicious Omens

1 Jul	Founding of the Chinese Communist Party
1 Aug	National Army Day
1 Oct	National Day

Shopping

The Tibetans invariably bargain for their purchases and expect foreign visitors to do the same. In the markets, feel free to talk with your hands and pocket calculator! Avoid buying artefacts which have in fact been imported from Nepal. According to government regulations you may not export antiques unless you have obtained a receipt or red seal. Nonetheless, there are galleries in Lhasa which will supply some form of documentation to facilitate the export of antiques in checked baggage.

What to buy

Books Available at outlets of **Xinhua** Bookstores and through private book sellers throughout the country. Very few foreign language publications are available – most texts are in either Chinese or Tibetan, but there are also a number of large-format photographic and art books available with English captions.

Buddhist artefacts For sale in the main market places of Lhasa, Zhigatse, Chamdo, Derge, Dartsedo, Labrang and Kumbum including traditional loose-leaf style woodblock printed books, offering materials (incense, butter lamps, water-offering bowls, libation cups), and ritual instruments, such as bells, vajras, cymbals, shin-bone trumpets (kangling), skull-drums, oboes (gyaling) and horns (radong/dongchen).

Carpets Carpets of various sizes and designs, both modern and traditional, are woven at local carpet factories, and sold at outlets in cities such as Lhasa, Zhigatse, Gyantse and Kandze.

Ceramics and coins It is still possible to find elegant Tibetan ceramic teacups with finely carved metal stands and lids in some of the market stalls, and there are a large number of Japanese and Chinese coins from the Meiji and Guomintang periods that will attract collectors. Old pre-1951 Tibetan paper money is also available.

Clothes The large department stores are good for modern manufactured Chinese clothes, including suits, jackets, shirts, shoes, and especially Mongolian cashmere sweaters. In the open-air markets traditional Tibetan clothing can also be purchased, including male and female chubas, silk shirts or blouses, long multicoloured felt boots with sturdy leather soles, and hats made of brocade, felt or fox-skin. Ready-to-wear monastic robes are also available for itinerant monks and nuns.

Electrical goods The large department stores in cities such as Lhasa, Ziling and Zhigatse carry an assortment of modern Chinese and imported electrical goods, including cameras, mobile phones, DVD equipment, and televisions.

Furniture Wooden cabinets, tables and altar shrines carved and brightly painted with traditional motifs are for sale in cities such as Lhasa and Zhigatse. Most can be exported in sections for assembly. Antique furniture is also available at some galleries.

Jewellery Traditional Tibetan jewellery includes necklaces, rings, earrings, and hair-ornaments, inset with red coral, blue turquoise or yellow amber stones. There are some good outlets in Lhasa but most of the jewellery on sale in the markets is fake or else manufactured in Nepal – particularly the finely worked filigree silver and white metal pieces.

Metalwork The Khampa areas of the east, particularly the Horpo area of Derge and Chamdo, are recognized as having the best metalworking forges and foundries in Tibet. Some of the finest items available include intricately carved amulet boxes, brass stupas, jewellery settings, and of course the traditional Khampa knives with elegantly carved scabbards and hilts, which are almost impossible to export, even in checked baggage, following the events of 9/11.

Musical instruments Apart from the Buddhist accessories mentioned above, there are shops in Lhasa, Zhigatse and the Lhartse areas in particular where traditional Tibetan guitars (dranyen) can be purchased.

Offering scarves Silk and cotton scarves (*katak*), usually white in colour but also red, blue, yellow or green, are sold to pilgrims and devotees for offering in temples or to important teachers, as well as to the public for important secular events, including marriage ceremonies, departures and arrivals.

Paintings Both antique and modern painted scrolls (*tangkas*) sewn in brocade are available from specialist studios in Lhasa. Generally speaking it is better to commission a painted scroll from one of the more reputable artists in order to ensure that the iconography is accurate (see under Lhasa, page 130). Modern paintings are also available at certain galleries in the capital.

Photography Simple print film is commonly available in the larger towns and cities in Tibet, but slide film and digital cards are almost impossible to obtain even in the tourist shops of the major hotels. You are therefore advised to stock up before leaving home. Outdoor photography is free of charge, but be careful not to film sensitive and strategic industrial or military installations. Internal photography in temples and monasteries may be permitted for a fee. Always ask first! Recommended films: for colour prints, Fuji

HR100 or equivalent, and Fuji HR600 for interiors; for colour slides, Kodak chrome 3 ASA 25 and 64, and Kodak Tungsten ASA 160 for interiors; for black and white, Kodak T-max ASA 100, and Kodak Tri-X for interiors. A UV filter or polarizer can help reduce the exposure problem caused by high altitude solar glare in Central and West Tibet. Mornings and late afternoons usually offer the best conditions for filming, and at other times try under-exposure by half a stop. There is some spectacular scenery, but if you go during the wet season make sure to protect film against humidity, and at all times try to protect your equipment from dust. Use a lens hood.

Prayer flags Multicoloured sets of prayer flags of varying sizes printed with mantras and protective animals are sold in all the traditional markets. Cheaper and smaller versions of these are also printed on paper for dispersal on mountain passes.

Statues The best statues for sale in Tibet are the *cire perdu* images of gilded brass and copper manufactured in Patan in Nepal. These are preferred by local Tibetans to the cheaper and less refined yellow brass images that are also available.

Textiles Old Chinese and Tibetan textiles are available through specialist galleries and dealers. Newly hand-made and machine-manufactured brocades and silks can be found in small shops in the Barkhor market of Lhasa, along with multicoloured woven wool aprons from Chedezhol, and regional woollen fabrics of various designs.

Trekking equipment There are now several outlets for specialist trekking equipment in Chengdu. Ziling, Lhasa and Zhigatse, where good quality tents, boots, sleeping bags, down jackets and trousers etc can all be purchased.

Woodwork Intricately carved covers for Tibetan loose-leaf books, along with well fashioned tsampa containers and wooden drinking cups inlaid with silver or pewter are among the best buys. Carved wooden moulds for dough-offerings (*zan-par*) may also be of interest, as are square woodblocks used for printing prayer flags.

Sport and activities

Summer festivals featuring equestrian skills, athletic field events, and dance festivals – both religious and secular – are a major attraction in the grasslands of Eastern Tibet. Modern spectator sports like football and basketball have a certain degree of local popularity, but there will be few opportunities for casual visitors to participate. It has, however, become quite commonplace for travellers to take part in roadside games of pool and strike up unexpected friendships. The main recreational pursuits that attract travellers to Tibet are of course trekking and mountaineering.

Mountaineering

For details of climbing fees and organization in the Himalayas and in the Tibetan Autonomous Region as a whole, refer to an international tour operator, or directly to the **Tibet Mountaineering Association** ⓘ *Lhasa, T0891-6333720, F0891-6336366.* For the Minyak Gangkar, Kawalungring, and Minshan ranges, contact the **Sichuan Mountaineering Association** ⓘ *Chengdu, T028-85588047, F0028-85588042*. For Amnye Machen and the Kunluns, the **Qinghai Mountaineering Association** ⓘ *Ziling, T0971-8238877, F0971-8238933*. and for the Kawa Karpo range, the **Yunnan Mountaineering Association** ⓘ *Kunming, T0871-3164626, F0871-3135246*. The international and local travel agencies listed in this guide can also provide relevant information, as can the head office of the **China Mountaineering Association** ⓘ *9 Tiyuguan Rd, Beijing, T010-67123796, F010-67111629*.

Trekking

The sheer vastness of the Tibetan plateau offers great scope for trekking. Some remote areas are even now only accessible on foot or horseback. Trekking conditions

Himalayan Environment Trust Code of Practice

Campsite Leave it cleaner than you found it.
Deforestation Make no open fires and discourage others from making them for you. Limit use of water heated by firewood in conservation areas (use of dead wood is permitted elsewhere). Choose accommodation where kerosene or fuel-efficient wood-burning stoves are used.
Litter Remove it. Burn or bury paper and carry away non-degradable litter. If you find other people's litter, remove theirs too! Pack food in biodegradable containers. Take all batteries/cells away with you.
Water Keep local water clean. Do not use detergents and pollutants in streams and springs. Where there are no toilets be sure you are at least 30 m away from the water source and bury or cover waste. Do not allow cooks or porters to throw rubbish in nearby streams and rivers.
Plants Do not take cuttings, seeds and roots in areas where this is illegal.
Giving to children encourages begging. **Donations** to a project, health centre or school is more constructive.
Respect **local traditions and cultures**.
Respect **privacy** and ask permission before taking photographs.
Respect **holy places**. Never touch or remove religious objects. Remove shoes before entering temples if required to do so.
Respect local **etiquette**. Dress modestly, particularly when visiting temples and shrines and while walking through villages; loose, lightweight clothes are preferable to shorts, skimpy tops and tight-fitting outfits. Avoid holding hands and kissing in public.

are very different from those in Bhutan and Nepal, where the travel agencies have had many years' experience at organizing treks and where the routes have often been over-trekked. By contrast, trekking in Tibet offers the prospect of an original, fresh experience, and the possibility of mingling with Tibetan pilgrims – since most of the routes are in fact ancient pilgrimage trails. Many well known trekking routes, including those to Mount Kailash, Lake Manasarovar, Mount Everest, Ganden-Samye, Mount Kawa Karpo and Mount Amnye Machen, are described in this book with the relevant chapters. Pilgrimages to Mount Kailash are particularly significant during the water horse year (which coincided with 2002 and will next occur in 2062) and those to Mount Kawa Karpo with the water sheep year (last in 2003 and next in 2063). The best months are April-June and September-November, although even in the rainy season trekking is not always problematic.

On organized treks, tour operators will provide cooking equipment, food, and sometimes tents. In general on such expeditions you will want to travel with the bare minimum of equipment. You don't want to carry anything more than what is essential. Nonetheless, away from Lhasa the travelling is hard, so self-sufficiency is important, and there are a number of required items.

Dietary supplements for trekking First, although organized tours will have a cook to prepare main meals, the dishes will often be basic, especially if you are trekking in West or Far West Tibet, where fresh vegetables are rare. Therefore it is strongly recommended that you bring a small camping stove of your own with a fuel bottle, as well as some freeze dried meals for the sake of variation in diet. You can also prepare your own hot drinks (coffee, cocoa, etc) whenever you want to. You may also like to bring some high protein fruit and nuts or muesli bars as well as chocolate, jerk beef, cheese, pâté, and so forth.

Clothing for trekking Second, because the temperatures on the Tibetan plateau are subject to extreme fluctuations you need to think in terms of 'layered clothing' that you can peel off and put on with ease. The weather will be warm to hot during the day and can be cool to freezing at night, and it is often dusty and windy depending on the location and season. At high altitude, the dry atmosphere stops perspiration so you won't become as dirty as usual and need not wash completely nor change clothes every couple of days. So you do not need to bring more than two or three items of any clothing. **NB** If you intend to take an address book, do leave a duplicate at home in case of loss or water damage, or, better still, open a free yahoo or hotmail account and mail the information to yourself before leaving home.

The following items of clothing are recommended for long treks: good comfortable walking shoes or boots (be sure to wear them in first); Band-Aid/elastoplast for blisters; thick wool socks (at least three pairs); light sandals or canvas shoes; long underwear (silk is good as winds can be icy); sufficient changes of underwear and T-shirts; cotton or woollen shirts (with pockets); wool sweaters (at least two, one to be worn over the other); trousers or jeans (possibly one heavy, one light-weight); a waterproof coat; a down-filled jacket; a sun hat, dark glasses, scarf or cravat (essential); and gloves. In general, Gortex is recommended for both walking boots and trekking clothes.

Trekking equipment Third, some of the following items will be supplied by the tour agency responsible for organizing your trek, but you should ensure that you obtain the others prior to your departure from Lhasa or wherever. Various camping items can be purchased or hired cheaply in Kathmandu, Chengdu, Ziling or Lhasa. Carry your luggage in a backpack or heavy duty travel bag (with strong straps/handles), and keep your immediate necessities in a small knapsack, or shoulder bag (camera bag).

You should bring your own sleeping bag (suitable for all-weather outdoor conditions), an insulation mat, an umbrella, a flashlight (headlamp recommended) and extra alkaline batteries, a water flask and/or thermos bottle, rehydration powders, a small stove (multifuel if possible) and fuel bottle, cooking and eating utensils, a Swiss-type army knife (with bottle and can openers etc), matches (waterproof preferable), a waterproof pouch or belt for money and passport, a medical kit (as outlined below under Health), suntan lotion, and (if possible) your own lightweight tent.

Some remote trekking trails are not well defined, so it is easy to lose the way, and high-altitude rescue is non-existent. It is therefore essential to trek with a reliable local guide. Pack animals can be hired locally for certain treks, as in the Everest region, the Kailash region, the Kongpo region, and the upper Kyi-chu region.

NB When trekking in Tibet, please observe the Himalayan Code of Practice (see box), and be serious about the conservation of the ecology and the environment, even if locals or guides set a bad example.

Suggested routes on the Tibetan Plateau For a listing of recommended travel routes on the Tibetan plateau, see above, pages 20-25. There are also tailor made special interest and itineraries for Buddhist groups, photographers, cyclists, botanists, art historians, musicologists and ethnologists.

Health

Local populations in Tibet are exposed to a range of health risks not encountered in the western world. Many of the diseases are major problems for the local poor and destitute and though the risk to travellers is more remote, they cannot be ignored. Obviously five-star travel is going to carry less risk than back-packing on a minimal budget.

The health care in the region is varied. The best clinics and hospitals are to be found in the larger towns and cities, while remote countryside areas have fewer and more basic amenities. As with all medical care, first impressions count. If a facility is grubby then be wary of the general standard of medicine and hygiene. It's worth contacting your embassy or consulate on arrival and asking where the recommended (ie those used by diplomats) clinics are. Providing embassies with information of your whereabouts can be also useful if a friend/relative gets ill at home and there is a desperate search for you around the globe. You can also ask them about locally recommended medical do's and don'ts. If you do get ill, and you have the opportunity, you should also ask your medical insurer whether they are satisfied that the medical centre or hospital that you have been referred to is of a suitable standard.

Before you go

Ideally, you should see your GP or travel clinic at least six weeks before your departure for general advice on travel risks and vaccinations. Make sure you have travel insurance, get a dental check (especially if you are going to be away for more than a month), know your own blood group and if you suffer a long-term condition such as diabetes or epilepsy make sure someone knows or that you have a Medic Alert bracelet/necklace with this information on it.

Basic vaccinations recommended include **Polio** if none in last 10 years; **Tetanus** again if you haven't had one last 10 years (after five doses you have had enough for life); Diphtheria if none in last 10 years **Typhoid** if nil in last three years; **Hepatitis A** as the disease can be caught easily from food/water.

Special vaccines for Tibet include: **Rabies** (especially for stays of more than one month and if you are visiting rural areas); and **Japanese Encephalitis** may be required for rural travel at certain times of the year (mainly rainy seasons).

There is no malaria risk in Tibet but use mosquito avoidance measures to reduce your risk of Dengue fever when travelling in low-lying counties of southeast Tibet.

Mosquito repellents Remember that DEET (Di-ethyltoluamide) is the gold standard. Apply the repellent every four to six hours but more often if you are sweating heavily. If a non-DEET product is used check who tested it. Validated products (tested at the London School of Hygiene and Tropical Medicine) include Mosiguard, Non-DEET Jungle formula and non-DEET Autan. If you want to use citronella remember that it must be applied very frequently (ie hourly) to be effective. If you are popular target for insect bites or develop lumps quite soon after being bitten, carry an Aspivenin kit. This syringe suction device is available from many chemists and draws out some of the allergic materials and provides quick relief.

The Australians have a great campaign, which has reduced skin cancer. It is called Slip, Slap, Slop. Slip on a shirt, Slap on a hat, Slop on **sun screen.**

Pain killers. Paracetomol or a suitable painkiller can have multiple uses for symptoms but remember that more than eight paracetomol a day can lead to liver failure.

Ciproxin (Ciprofloxacin). A useful antibiotic for some forms of travellers diarrhoea.

First aid kits

Although pre-packaged first aid kits for travellers are available from many camping and outdoor pursuit shops, it is unlikely that you will ever need to use at least half of their contents. If you are visiting very remote areas, for example if you are trekking, it becomes more important to ensure that you have all the necessary items. You may want to bring with you a supply of sticky plasters and corn plasters (Band Aid etc), intestinal treatments such as Imodium, and antihistamine tablets. Flagyl can be bought across the chemist's counter in Nepal whereas, in the UK at least, a doctor's prescription is required. Paracetamol is readily available. Tibet's larger hospitals and medical centres do not seem to have any shortage of sterile, single-use needles, but to be safe you should bring your own supply, the standard 'green' size are the most versatile. If you have any specialized requirements, it is recommended that you bring them with you.

Immodium. A great standby for those diarrhoeas that occur at awkward times (ie before a long coach/train journey or on a trek). It helps stop the flow of diarrhoea and in my view is of more benefit than harm. (It was believed that letting the bacteria or viruses flow out had to be more beneficial. However, with Immodium they still come out, just in a more solid form.)

Pepto-Bismol. Used a lot by Americans for diarrhoea. It certainly relieves symptoms but like Immodium it is not a cure for underlying disease. Be aware that it turns the stool black as well as making it more solid.

MedicAlert. These simple bracelets, or an equivalent, should be carried or worn by anyone with a significant medical condition.

For longer trips involving jungle or mountain treks taking a clean needle pack, clean dental pack and water filtration devices are common-sense measures.

On the road

Diarrhoea and intestinal upset

→ *One study showed that up to 70% of all travellers may suffer during their trip.*

Symptoms Diarrhoea can refer either to loose stools or an increased frequency; both of these can be a nuisance. It should be short lasting but persistence beyond two weeks, with blood or pain, require specialist medical attention.

Cures Ciproxin (Ciprofloxacin) is a useful antibiotic for bacterial traveller's diarrhoea. It can be obtained by private prescription in the UK. You need to take one 500 mg tablet when the diarrhoea starts and if you do not feel better in 24 hours, the diarrhoea is likely to have a non-bacterial cause and may be viral (in which case there is little you can do apart from keep yourself rehydrated and wait for it to settle on its own). The key treatment with all diarrhoeas is rehydration. Try to keep hydrated by taking the right mixture of salt and water. This is available as Oral Rehydration Salts (ORS) in ready-made sachets or can be made up by adding a teaspoon of sugar and a half teaspoon of salt to a litre of clean water. Drink at least one large cup of this drink for each loose stool. You can also use flat carbonated drinks as an alternative. Immodium and Pepto-Bismol provide symptomatic relief.

Prevention The standard advice is to be careful with water and ice for drinking. Ask yourself where the water came from. If you have any doubts then boil it or filter and treat it. There are many filter/treatment devices now available on the market. Food can also transmit disease. Be wary of salads (what were they washed in, who handled them), re-heated foods or food that has been left out in the sun having been cooked earlier in the day. There is a simple adage that says wash it, peel it, boil it or forget it. Also be wary of unpasteurized dairy products, these can transmit a range of diseases from brucellosis (fevers and constipation), to listeria (meningitis) and tuberculosis of the gut (obstruction, constipation, fevers and weight loss).

Altitude sickness

Symptoms Acute mountain sickness can strike from about 3,000 m upwards and in general is more likely to affect those who ascend rapidly (for example by plane) and those who over-exert themselves. Teenagers are particularly prone. On reaching heights above 3,000 m, heart pounding and shortness of breath, especially on exertion, are almost universal and a normal response to the lack of oxygen in the air. Acute mountain sickness takes a few hours or days to come on and presents with headache, lassitude, dizziness, loss of appetite, nausea and vomiting. Insomnia is common and often associated with a suffocating feeling when lying down in bed. You may notice that your breathing tends to wax and wane at night and your face is puffy in the mornings – this is all part of the syndrome.

Cures If the symptoms are mild, the treatment is rest, painkillers (preferably not aspirin-based) for the headaches and anti-sickness pills for vomiting. Should the symptoms be severe and prolonged it is best to descend to a lower altitude immediately and reascend, if necessary, slowly and in stages. The symptoms disappear very quickly with even a few 100 m of descent.

Prevention The best way of preventing acute mountain sickness is a relatively slow ascent. When trekking to high altitude, some time spent walking at medium altitude, getting fit and getting adapted, is beneficial. On arrival at places over 3,000 m a few hours' rest and the avoidance of alcohol, cigarettes and heavy food will go a long way towards preventing acute mountain sickness.

Other problems experienced at high altitude are sunburn, excessively dry air causing skin cracking, sore eyes (it may be wise to leave your contact lenses out) and sore nostrils. Treat the latter with Vaseline. Do not ascend to high altitude if you are suffering from a bad cold or chest infection and certainly not within 24 hours following scuba diving.

Sun protection

Symptoms White Britons are notorious for becoming red in hot countries because they like to stay out longer than everyone else and do not use adequate sun protection. This can lead to sunburn, which is painful and followed by flaking of skin. Aloe vera gel is a good pain reliever for sunburn. Long-term sun damage leads to a loss of elasticity of skin and the development of pre-cancerous lesions. Years later a mild or a very malignant form of cancer may develop. The milder basal cell carcinoma, if detected early, can be treated by cutting it out or freezing it. The much nastier malignant melanoma may have already spread to bone and brain at the time that it is first noticed.

Prevention Sun screen. SPF stands for Sun Protection Factor. It is measured by determining how long a given person takes to 'burn' with and without the sunscreen product on. So, if it takes 10 times longer to burn with the sunscreen product applied, then that product has an SPF of 10. If it only takes twice as long then the SPF is 2. The higher the SPF the greater the protection. However, do not just use higher factors just to stay out in the sun longer. 'Flash frying' (desperate bursts of excessive exposure), as it is called, is known to increase the risks of skin cancer. Follow the Australians' with their Slip, Slap, Slop campaign referred to earlier.

Bites and stings

It is a very rare event indeed for travellers, but if you are unlucky (or careless) enough to be bitten by a venomous snake, spider, scorpion or sea creature, try to identify the creature, without putting yourself in further danger (do not try to catch a live snake). Snake bites in particular are very frightening, but in fact rarely poisonous – even venomous snakes bite without injecting venom. Victims should be taken to a hospital or a doctor without delay. Commercial snake bite and scorpion kits are available, but are usually only useful for the specific types of snake or scorpion. Most serum has to be given intravenously so it is not much good equipping yourself with it unless you are used to making injections into veins. It is best to rely on local practice in these cases, because the particular creatures will be known about locally and appropriate treatment can be given.

Symptoms Fright, swelling, pain and bruising around the bite and soreness of the regional lymph glands, perhaps nausea, vomiting and a fever. Symptoms of serious poisoning would be: numbness and tingling of the face, muscular spasms, convulsions, shortness of breath or a failure of the blood to clot, causing generalized bleeding.

Treatment of snake bite Reassure and comfort the victim frequently. Immobilize the limb by a bandage or a splint and get the person to lie still. Do not slash the bite area and try to suck out the poison because this sort of heroism does more harm than good. If you know how to use a tourniquet in these circumstances, you will not need this advice. If you are not experienced, do not apply a tourniquet.

Precautions Do not walk in snake territory in bare feet or sandals – wear proper shoes or boots. If you encounter a snake stay put until it slithers away and do not investigate a wounded snake. Spiders and scorpions may be found in the more basic hotels, in some sub-Himalayan regions of Nepal and northwest India. If stung, rest and take plenty of fluids and call a doctor. The best precaution is to keep beds away from the walls and look inside your shoes and under the toilet seat every morning.

Ticks and fly larvae

Ticks usually attach themselves to the lower parts of the body often after walking in areas where cattle have grazed. They take a while to attach themselves strongly, but swell up as they start to suck blood. The important thing is to remove them gently, so that they do not leave their head parts in your skin because this can cause a nasty allergic reaction some days later. Do not use petrol, vaseline, lighted cigarettes etc to remove the tick, but, with a pair of tweezers remove the beast gently by gripping it at the attached (head) end and rock it out in very much the same way that a tooth is extracted. Certain tropical flies which lay their eggs under the skin of sheep and cattle also occasionally do the same thing to humans with the unpleasant result that a maggot grows under the skin and pops up as a boil or pimple. The best way to remove these is to cover the boil with oil, vaseline or nail varnish so as to stop the maggot breathing, then to squeeze it out gently the next day.

Hepatitis

Symptoms Hepatitis means inflammation of the liver. Viral causes of the disease can be acquired anywhere in the world. The most obvious symptom is a yellowing of your skin or the whites of your eyes. However, prior to this all that you may notice is itching and tiredness.

Cures Early on, depending on the type of hepatitis, a vaccine or immunoglobulin may reduce the duration of the illness.

Prevention Pre-travel hepatitis A vaccine is the best bet. Hepatitis B (for which there is a vaccine) is spread through blood and unprotected sexual intercourse, both of these can be avoided. Unfortunately there is no vaccine for hepatitis C or the increasing alphabetical list of other Hepatitis viruses.

Dengue fever

Unfortunately there is no vaccine against this and the mosquitoes that carry it bite during the day. You will feel like a mule has kicked you for two to three days, you will then get better for a few days and then feel that the mule has kicked you again. It should all be over in seven to 10 days. Heed all the anti-mosquito measures that you can.

Leptospirosis

Various forms of leptospirosis occur throughout the world, transmitted by a bacterium which is excreted in rodent urine. Fresh water and moist soil harbour the organisms, which enter the body through cuts and scratches. If you suffer from any form of prolonged fever consult a doctor.

Rabies

Remember that rabies is endemic throughout certain parts of the world, so avoid dogs (or any animals) that are behaving strangely. If you are bitten by a domestic or wild animal, do not leave things to chance: scrub the wound with soap and water and/or disinfectant, try to at least determine the animal's ownership, where possible, and seek medical assistance at once. The course of treatment depends on whether you have already been satisfactorily vaccinated against rabies. If you have (this is worthwhile if you are spending lengths of time in developing countries) then some further doses of vaccine are all that is required. If not already vaccinated then anti rabies serum (immunoglobulin) may be required in addition. It is important to finish the course of treatment.

SARS

Each year there is the possibility that avian flu or SARS might rear its head. Check the news reports. If there is a problem in an area you are due to visit you may be advised to have an ordinary flu shot or to seek expert advice.

Sexual health

The range of visible and invisible diseases is awesome. Unprotected sex can spread HIV, Hepatitis B and C, Gonorrhea (green discharge), chlamydia (nothing to see but may cause painful urination and later female infertility), painful recurrent herpes, syphilis and warts, just to name a few. You can cut down the risk by using condoms, a femidom or avoiding sex altogether.

Water

There are a number of ways of purifying water. Dirty water should first be strained through a filter bag and then boiled or treated. Bringing water to a rolling boil at sea level is sufficient to make the water safe for drinking, but at higher altitudes you have to boil the water for a few minutes longer to ensure all microbes are killed. There are sterilising methods that can be used and there are proprietary preparations containing chlorine (eg Puritabs) or iodine (eg Pota Aqua) compounds. Chlorine compounds generally do not kill protozoa (eg Giardia). There are a number of water filters now on the market available in personal and expedition size. They work either on mechanical or chemical principles, or may do both. Make sure you take the spare parts or spare chemicals with you and do not believe everything the manufacturers say.

Further information

Websites

Foreign and Commonwealth Office (FCO) (UK), www.fco.gov.uk This is a key travel advice site, with useful information on the country, people, climate and lists the UK embassies/consulates. The site also promotes the concept of 'Know Before You Go'. And encourages travel insurance and appropriate travel health advice. It has links to the Department of Health travel advice site, see below.

Department of Health Travel Advice (UK), www.doh.gov.uk/traveladvice This excellent site is also available as a free booklet, the T6, from Post Offices. It lists the vaccine advice requirements for each country.

Medic Alert (UK), www.medicalalert.co.uk This is the website of the foundation that produces bracelets and necklaces for those with existing medical problems. Once you have ordered your bracelet/necklace you write your key medical details on paper inside it, so that if you collapse, a medical person can identify you as someone with epilepsy or allergy to peanuts etc.

Blood Care Foundation (UK), www.bloodcare.org.uk The Blood Care Foundation is a Kent-based charity "dedicated to the provision of screened blood and resuscitation fluids in countries where these are not readily available". They will dispatch certified non-infected blood of the right type to your hospital/clinic. The blood is flown in from various centres around the world.

The Health Protection Agency www.hpa.org.uk This site has up to date malaria advice guidelines for travel around the world. It gives specific advice about the right drugs for each location. It also has useful information for those who are pregnant, suffering from epilepsy or planning to travel with children.

World Health Organisation, www.who.int The WHO site has links to the WHO Blue Book on travel advice. This lists the diseases in different regions of the world. It describes vaccination schedules and makes clear which countries have Yellow Fever Vaccination certificate requirements and malarial risk.

Fit for Travel (UK), www.fitfortravel.scot.nhs.uk This site from Scotland provides a quick A-Z of vaccine and travel health advice requirements for each country.

British Travel Health Association (UK), www.btha.org This is the official website of an organization of travel health professionals.

Travel Screening Services (UK), www.travelscreening.co.uk This is the author's website. A private clinic dedicated to integrated travel health. The clinic gives vaccine, travel health advice, email and SMS text vaccine reminders and screens returned travellers for tropical diseases.

Books

The Travellers Good Health Guide by Dr Ted Lankester, ISBN 0-85969-827-0.
Expedition Medicine (The Royal Geographic Society) Editors David Warrell and Sarah Anderson ISBN 1 86197 040-4.
International Travel and Health World Health Organisation Geneva ISBN 92 4 158026 7.
The World's Most Dangerous Places by Robert Young Pelton, Coskun Aral and Wink Dulles ISBN 1-566952-140-9.

Keeping in touch

Communications

Internet

Internet cafés can be found in Lhasa and other large urban areas like Zhigatse and Chamdo, but are not yet as universal as they have become in South and Southeast Asia. Hotels and restaurants will often offer internet facilities. As elsewhere, this has become the most inexpensive form of communication, and the rates are very competitive, averaging ¥10-20 per hour.

Post

Postage stamps for letters and postcards are widely available in county towns, which all have China Post outlets, and in the large tourist hotels. Some hotels also provide post box facilities. To save time, you may prefer to buy postage stamps in Chengdu, Lhasa, Lanzhou, or Kunming at the beginning of your trip. Larger packages should preferably be mailed from one of these provincial capital cities, and EMS express services are available. Postcards cost ¥4.20 (airmail), and aerogrammes ¥5.20. Parcels (maximum 30 kg) sent by surface mail begin at ¥108 to UK and ¥83.50 to USA for a 1 kg parcel; and ¥162 to UK or ¥159 to USA for a 1 kg airmail parcel. EMS rates to United Kingdom are ¥220 for a 500 g letter, and ¥280 for a 500 g packet, and to USA ¥180 and ¥240 respectively. An EMS surcharge of ¥75 is charged for letters or packets that are slightly overweight. When sending mail it is best to have the country of destination written in Chinese. For collecting mail, there is a post restante facility at the Lhasa GPO, but it may be better to use such facilities at the larger hotels such as Lhasa Hotel, Tibet Hotel or Himalaya Hotel. Fax services are also available at most county post offices.

Telephone

IDD calls can be made from **China Mobile** outlets in any county town, and also from major hotels in open areas of the country. DDD calls can be made and received locally in all county towns and most townships, but be prepared for long delays. For a list of area codes see the front dust-jacket. ICC phone cards (used for making both IDD and DDD calls) can be purchased in post offices and China Mobile outlets in denominations of ¥20, ¥50 and ¥100. Mobile phones are increasingly used in Tibet, and dual-band international phones with a roaming facility should connect via the **China Telecom** or **China Unicom GSM** network whenever you are in close proximity to a county town with a China Mobile satellite mast. Pay-as-you-go phone cards are available for pay-as-you-go Chinese mobile phones. Satellite phones can also receive a signal in most locations on the plateau.

The Tibet international dialling code is the same as that of China, 86.

Media

Newspapers are widely available throughout the country, but they are of limited value, even for those who read Tibetan (*Mimang Tsakpar*) or Chinese (*Renmin Ribao*). The only English newspaper is the *China Daily*.

There are local **television** and **radio** broadcasting services in each of the provinces or prefectures into which Tibet is now divided, as well as mainland CCTV Chinese channels, Phoenix TV stations, and certain Star TV channels, broadcast from Hong Kong. **CNN** and **BBC World** are not generally available, except in the best tourist hotels. Lhasa, Qinghai, Kandze and Ngawa television services are all active in programme making. Some productions are voiced over `or subtitled in Tibetan.

Footprint features

Introduction

The holy city of Lhasa (Ch *Lasa Shiqu*) is the historic capital of Tibet, situated on the north bank of the Kyi-chu River, where the valley opens out to its fullest extent. To the north of the city lies an impenetrable 5,200 m range, extending from Mount Gephel Utse (above Drepung in the west) to Mount Dukri Tse (above Pawangka) and Mount Sera Utse (above Sera in the east). To the south, on the far bank of the river, is the Chakyak Karpo range. There are smaller hills in the valley: the most prominent being Marpori ('Red Mountain') on which the Potala Palace is constructed, Chakpori (where Tibet's medical college and temples once stood, now dominated by a radio mast), and Bonpori (surmounted by a Chinese temple dedicated to Ling Gesar). The Kyi-chu River at Lhasa meanders past several island sandbanks, among which Kumalingka ('Thieves' Island'), the best known, and an adjacent island, are now the site of an extensive housing development scheme in neo Sino-Tibetan architectural style. The principal tributaries in the valley, the Dongkar, Lhalu, Nyangdren and Dokde, have all been integrated into the Chera irrigation system.

Recommended itineraries: 1, 3 (also 4-7). See page 20.

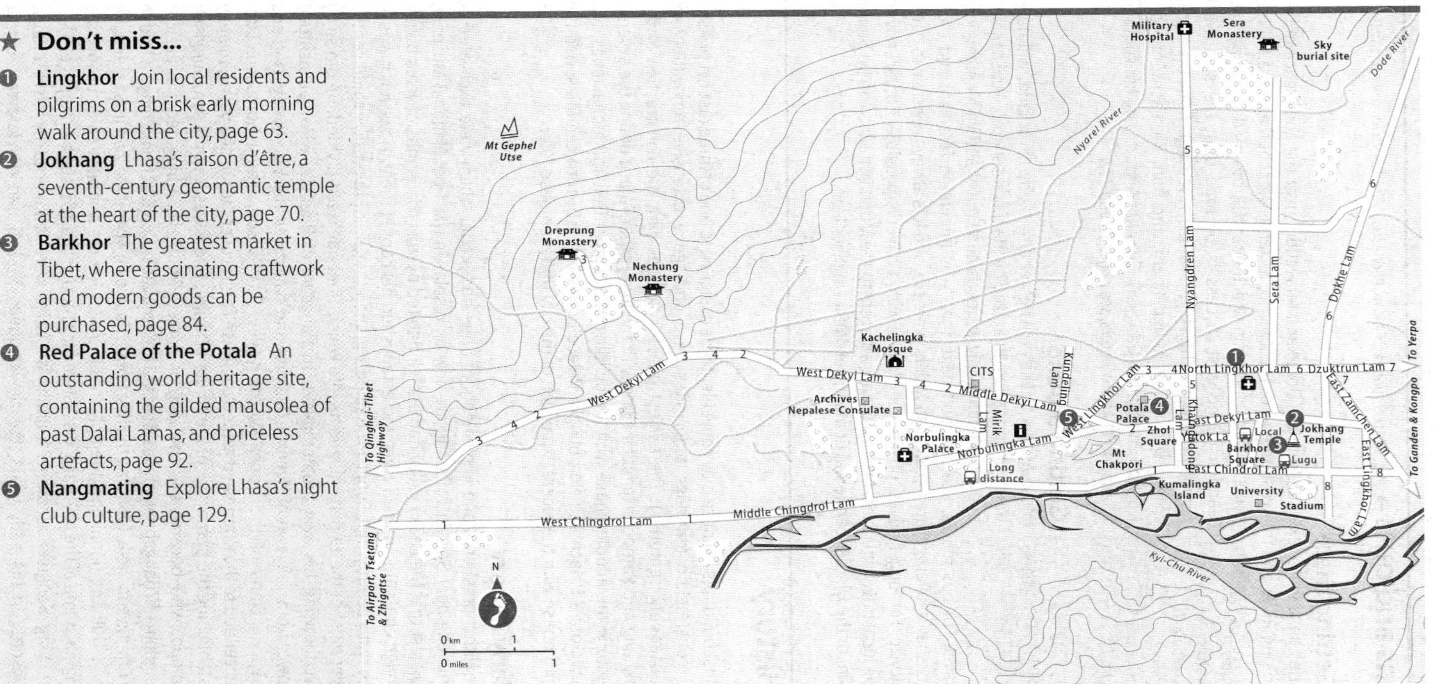

★ Don't miss...

❶ **Lingkhor** Join local residents and pilgrims on a brisk early morning walk around the city, page 63.

❷ **Jokhang** Lhasa's raison d'être, a seventh-century geomantic temple at the heart of the city, page 70.

❸ **Barkhor** The greatest market in Tibet, where fascinating craftwork and modern goods can be purchased, page 84.

❹ **Red Palace of the Potala** An outstanding world heritage site, containing the gilded mausolea of past Dalai Lamas, and priceless artefacts, page 92.

❺ **Nangmating** Explore Lhasa's night club culture, page 129.

Ins and outs → *Pop: 180,000. Altitude: 3,490 m. Phone code: (86)-891. Colour map 3, grid B3.*

Getting there

The Lhasa valley extends from the Dongkar intersection, near the confluence of the Tolung River and the western end of the Kyi-chu, as far as Ngachen and the hill-top ruins of Dechen Dzong, which overlook the roads to Yerpa and Ganden in the east. Access is by road from the southwest (Gongkar Airport, Zhigatse, Gyantse, Tsetang), from the north (Ziling, Damzhung, Yangpachen), and from the east (Chamdo, Kongpo and Meldro Gangkar). Gongkar Airport is 99 km south of Lhasa. *For further details, see pages 36 and 132.*

Area: 664 sq km
Temperature:
Jan: maximum 10°, minimum -8°,
Jul: maximum 25°, minimum 10°
Oxygen: 68%
Rainfall: 1,462 mm of which 90% falls in summer and early autumn (Jul/Sep)

Getting around

Most visitors to Lhasa, whether arriving by air or land, will have their transportation organized by the travel services. Public buses in the city charge only ¥2 for daytime travel and ¥3 for night-time travel. For bus routes, see transport page 132. Taxis (minimum fare ¥10) and cycle rickshaws (average fare ¥5) are also widely available, and it is always possible to hire a bicycle. For longer drives, private vehicle hire with a driver is possible. Contact any of the local travel agencies, the **Taxi Stand**, adjacent to the Moonlight Disco on Do Senge Lam or the **District Car Rental Company** on West Lingkhor Lam.

History

Most buildings in Lhasa may conveniently be assigned to one of three distinct phases of construction (although older sites have undergone extensive renovations in subsequent centuries). The earliest phase coincides with the construction of the Jokhang and Ramoche temples along with the first Potala Palace during the seventh century; the middle phase with the building of the great Gelukpa monasteries, the new Potala Palace and Norbulingka Palace during the 15th-18th centuries; and the third phase with the recent expansion of the city under Chinese rule.

Early history

Neolithic potsherds and implements of bone and stone, which were excavated at Chugong near Sera in 1984 and are now on display in the Tibet National Museum, suggest that the Lhasa valley had been inhabited by man thousands of years before Songtsen Gampo unified Tibet and established his capital there. However, it was in the sixth century that Songtsen Gampo's grandfather, Takri Nyenzik, gained control over most of the 12 petty kingdoms into which Tibet had been divided. He did so by overthrowing his own brother-in-law, Tri Pangsum of Phenyul, who had usurped power from Takyawo of Nyenkar (Meldro) and tyrannized the Wa, Nyang, Non and Tsepong clans of the Upper Kyi-chu valley. Takri's son, Namri Songtsen, later succeeded to the throne and gained complete control over the Kyi-chu valley, thereby establishing the framework of the Tibetan Empire; and it was Namri's son, Songtsen Gampo, who became the first king of unified Tibet. He subjugated the ancient kingdom of Zhangzhung in the west, and then moved his capital from Chingwa Taktse in Chongye to Rasa, founding the first Potala Palace on Mount Marpori in 637, and the Rasa Trulnang (ie Jokhang) temple in 641. Following the temple's construction, the original name of the city, Rasa, was altered to Lhasa or Lhaden (see below, page 71).

King Songtsen Gampo's building activities were influenced by his Buddhist consorts: in his early years, the Newar queen Bhrkuti had the **Jokhang** temple constructed at the centre of a geomantically important network of temples around the country (see page 70). In his later years, the Chinese queen Wencheng constructed the **Ramoche** temple, and his Tibetan queen Monza Tricham founded the temple at **Drak Yerpa**, north of the city. Other significant constructions from that period included the nine storey **Pawangka tower/hermitage**; and the temples of **Meru Nyingba**, **Tsamkhung** and **Drak Lhaluphuk**. Lhasa flourished as the capital of the Tibetan Empire until the assassination of King Relpachen by Langdarma in the ninth century resulted in the fragmentation of the country and the desecration of the sacred sites.

15th-18th centuries

The next major period of development began in 1409 when Tsongkhapa instituted the Great Prayer Festival at the Jokhang temple, and the three great monasteries of the Lhasa region were founded: **Ganden** in 1409, **Drepung** in 1416 and **Sera** in 1419. The Jokhang temple was also renovated and enlarged at this time through the patronage of the kings of the Phakmodru Dynasty. Eventually, in 1642, Lhasa was restored as the capital of Tibet, following the defeat of the armies of the king of Tsang by the Mongolian forces of Gushi Qan. With the latter's assistance, the Fifth Dalai Lama established a theocratic form of government (*chosi nyiden*) which endured until the occupation of Tibet by Communist forces in 1951. The four regency (see page 747) temples of Lhasa were built during this period; but above all, to symbolize the enhanced status of Lhasa, the Fifth Dalai Lama rebuilt the 13-storey **Potala Palace**. Later, in the 18th century the Seventh Dalai Lama began the construction of the summer palace complex at **Norbulingka**.

Until recent decades, there were only three principal routes around Lhasa: the **Nangkhor** (inner circuit) around the Jokhang temple, the **Barkhor** (intermediate circuit) with its many market stalls, and the **Lingkhor** (outer circuit) which skirted the entire city including the Potala Palace. Pilgrims and traders alike would move around the holy city on these circuits, invariably in a clockwise direction. The great religious sites of the city were the focal points of attraction: the Jokhang temple surrounded by its Barkhor shrines, Ramoche and Chakpori, the Potala and Norbulingka palaces, and the outlying monasteries of Drepung, Nechung, Sera and Pawangka. Residential parts of the city and its suburbs also had their distinct names: Rabsel, Hawaling and Telpung-gang to the south and southwest of the Barkhor; Tromzigang, Kyire and Banak Zhol to the north of the Barkhor; Zhol village, nestling below the Potala, Denpak to the northwest of the city, Lhalu, Pelding, and Nyangdreng to the north, Dokde and Tsangrel to the northeast, Ngachen and Changdrong to the east. A number of the modern roads have been named after these places, which by and large survive, although the village of Zhol has now been relocated into apartment blocks behind the Potala at Lhalu.

Modern Lhasa

The third and most recent phase of construction in Lhasa has been carried out under the Chinese occupation, subjecting the city to unrelenting expansion and transformation, its noble buildings obscured by the nondescript concrete tower blocks characteristic of many present day Chinese cities. The best of modern architecture is represented by the Telecommunications Tower Building on Dekyi Lam, the Foreign Trade Building on Chingdrol Lam, and the International Grand Hotel on Mirik Lam. Lhasa currently functions as the capital not of the whole of Tibet, but of the Tibetan Autonomous Region (Tib *Po Rangkyongjong*; Ch *Xizang Zizhiqu*). As such it is responsible for the administration of seven districts: Lhasa has seven counties under its jurisdiction; Lhokha has 12 counties; Nyangtri has seven counties, Zhigatse has 18 counties; Ngari has seven counties; Nakchu has 12 counties; and Chamdo has 14 counties (taking recent administrative changes into account).

Most of the new buildings constructed in Lhasa reflect a cumbersome two-tier or three-tier bureaucracy because the government departments of the TAR, Lhasa District, and Lhasa Municipality have separate offices scattered throughout the city.

However unwelcome this development may be, it cannot be ignored and; indeed, it is the plan of contemporary Lhasa, rather than the traditional pilgrim circuits, that dictates how the visitor will make his or her way to the ancient and medieval sites of historic importance, described in the following pages.

Orientation: the two arterial roads

Most visitors will approach Lhasa from the southwest or north, whether driving the short distance from Gongkar Airport, or the longer overland routes from Nepal via Zhigatse and from Ziling via Kermo and Nakchu. These approach roads converge to the west of the city at Dongkar. Just west of Dongkar, the valley begins to open out into a wide plain and the Potala Palace is visible from afar. A large military HQ has recently been constructed near the intersection, where there's also a large petrol station complex and the Dongkar Restaurant. From Dongkar two roads lead into town: the main avenue, Chingdrol Lam (Ch *Jinzhu Lu*, with its extension Jiangsu Lam) follows the river bank upstream all the way to the east end of the city, and a recently paved extension of Dekyi Lam (Ch *Beijing Lu*) skirts the Lhasa Cement Factory

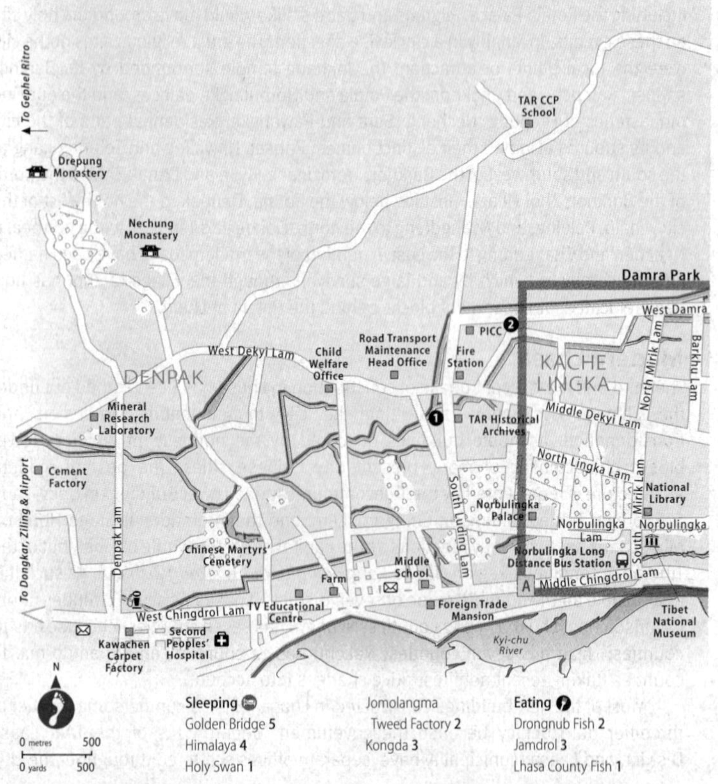

(Ch Sunyitrang) to enter the city through the defile between Chakpori and Marpori hills, formerly the real gateway to the city. Each of those west-east arteries will now be described in turn. Descriptions of other interconnecting roads will be found under Central, West, East, North and South Lhasa.

Chingdrol Lam and Jiangsu Lam

Chingdrol Lam passes through one of the most rapidly developing parts of the city, favoured by the influx of Chinese immigrants who have established their small businesses (shops, restaurants, karaoke bars and massage parlours) to service the army which occupies much of the land in this sector of the city. The road is divided into west, middle and east sections, the last of them extending into Jiangsu Lam (named after the Chinese province of Jiangsu which financed its recent reconstruction).

Starting from **Dongkar**, you pass to the north side of **West Chingdrol lam** (Ch Jinzhu Xi Lu), an engineering and machinery institute, a petrol station, and a large military complex including warehouses, carpentry workshops, the Tolung Dechen Tax Bureau, the Chinese Martyrs' Cemetery, a TV educational centre, small farms, a local police station, the West Suburbs Post Office, Middle School Number Nine, a liquid gas station, the College of Agriculture and Animal Husbandry, and the Military

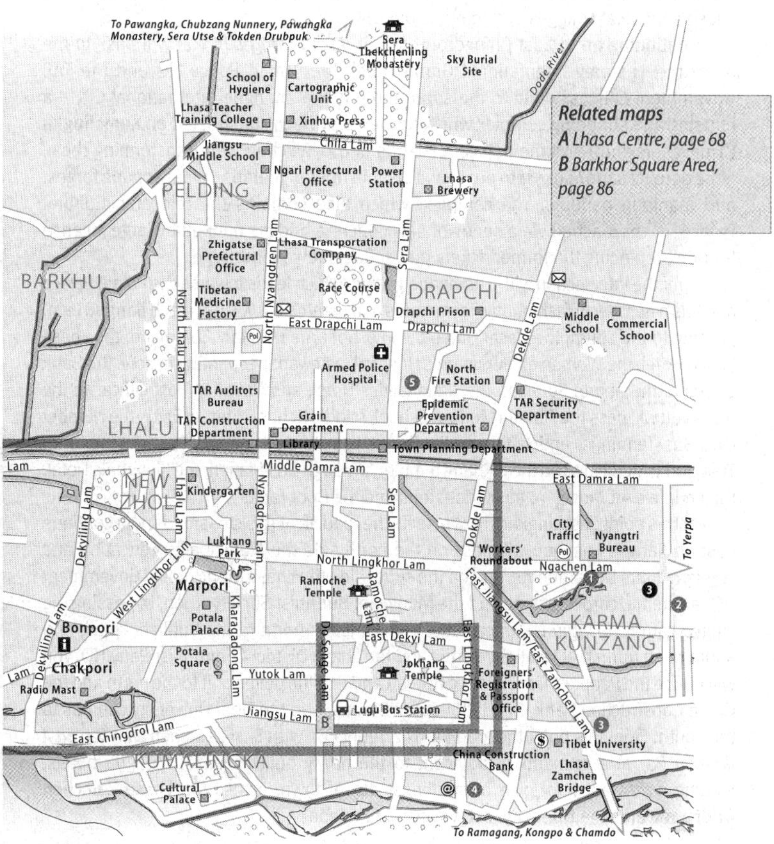

 Publications Office. Looking further north you will see the palls of smoke rising above the yellow buildings of the Lhasa Cement Factory, and behind them, like a cluster of brilliant white grains of rice on the hillside of Gephel Utse, the buildings of **Drepung Monastery**. On the south side of West Chingdrol Lam, towards the river, you will pass a military car repair centre, dysfunctional windmills, the leather factory, a local police station, the Post Office Training School, a local post office, the Lhasa Freight Depot, the Kawachen Carpet Factory, a geological research unit, the Hospital for Skin Diseases (also known as the Second People's Hospital), the Water Department, and the high-rise glass and concrete structure of the new Foreign Trade Mansion.

After the intersection with South Luding Lam, you reach **Middle Chingdrol Lam** (Ch *Jinzhu Zhong Lu*), passing on the north side the TAR Agricultural Machinery Company, the TAR schools of banking, hygiene, and finance, the Municipal Traffic Bureau, and the Long Distance Bus Station. On the south side there is a petrol station, the TAR Environment Bureau, the Municipal Armed Police Unit, and the Bluebird Katak Restaurant, serving one of the best Sichuan hot-pots in Lhasa. A memorial dedicated to the workers who died in the construction of the Ziling-Lhasa highway stands to the east, opposite the junction with Mirik Lam (Ch *Minzu Lu*), on which the Norbulingka Palace and Lhasa Hotel are located (see below, page 105). Ahead you will see the radio and television mast on the summit of Mount Chakpori, where Lhasa's medical colleges and temples once stood.

Continuing on to East Chingdrol Lam (Ch *Jinzhu Dong Lu*), you will pass to the north the 11-storey International Grand Hotel, the Armed Police HQ and the TAR Government Offices, while to the south there is the Zhonghe International City— a housing and shopping complex which has recently been constructed on **Kumalingka** ('Thieves' Island') and the adjacent islands of the Kyi-chu River, transforming these once derelict sandbanks into neat rows of Sino-Tibetan prefabs, metalworking forges, and mahjong parlours. The complex, which also contains the relocated Cultural Palace, is approached via a series of new concrete bridges flanked by large incense burners, replacing the former rickety prayer flag-strewn footbridge.

After the intersection with Kharngadong Lam, which leads towards the Potala Palace and has a number of fashionable restaurants and nightclubs, you will reach **Jiangsu Lam**, passing to the south: the Gesar Hotel, the PLA Tibet Area Military Command, the Lhasa Peace Hotel, the Women and Children's Hospital, a newspaper printing factory, the Bank of China, the Sports Stadium, the Nationalities Hotel, and Hebaling Post Office. To the north you will pass the Tibetan Medical School, Middle School Number Eight, the Number One Bus Terminus, and (after the Do Senge Lam turn-off leading to the Hospital of Traditional Medicine and the Jokhang temple), the Lugu Bus Station, the Xiongbala Hotel, the People's Art Museum, the Kadak Hotel and the Boot Factory.

At this point East Lingkhor Lam bisects the road. If, at this crossroads, you continue east on Jiangsu Lam you will pass on the north side the Municipality Education and Foreign Affairs Departments, and on the south side the Lhasa Municipality Government HQ, a cinema, carpet factory, and the Municipal Buddhist Society. Then, bypassing the Lingyu Lam (Ch *Lingju Lu*) intersection, which leads north to the Sunlight Hotel, and south to an upmarket red-light district and the Lhasa District Communist Party HQ, you will notice the Peoples' Consultative Bureau and a traffic police unit to the north and the China Construction Bank, the National Tax Bureau, and the Tibet University campus to the south. From this point the road forms a T-junction with East Zamchen Lam (Ch *East Jiangsu Rd*) at a roundabout adjacent to the newly built Loga and Kongda hotels, leading northwest into town or southeast out of town, across the **Lhasa Zamchen Bridge** towards the Upper Kyi-chu valley and Kongpo.

Dekyi Lam

Taking this road into Lhasa from Dongkar, you follow a more traditional route, along Dekyi Lam (Ch *Beijing Lu*) which also stretches the entire length of the city and is divided into west, middle and east sections. On **West Dekyi lam** (Ch *Beijing Xi Lu*), you will pass to the south the factories and residential compounds of the Lhasa Cement Factory (Ch *Sunyitrang*), and the Mineral Research Laboratory. After that, passing through Denpak village, you will see, on the hillside immediately above, **Drepung** and **Nechung** Monasteries (see below, pages 110 and 115). Then, to the north of the road you will pass the Lhasa City Engineering and Construction Unit and the TAR Road Transport Maintenance Head Office; while to the south there is a child welfare office and the Purang Border Quarantine Bureau.

Next, you will reach the Luding Lam intersection, at the southeast corner of which there is the TAR Customs Office, a distinctive green-painted building with a prominent clock tower Then, continuing east on to **Middle Dekyi lam** (Ch *Beijing Zhong Lu*) you will pass to the north the TAR Fire Station, the TAR Opera Troupe, the TAR Hygiene Head Office, the TAR Finance Head Office, China Construction Bank, the TAR School of Performing Arts, the Muslim Cemetery Kache Lingka, the TAR Scientific Association, the TAR Civil Administration Buildings, the Tibet Tourism Corporation, Windhorse Adventure Travel, a Bank of China branch (with ATM), two internet bars, a photocopy shop, the TAR Road Planning Department, the TAR Petroleum Company and the Tibet Gaozheng Hotel. In this section, there are also a number of restaurants and bars geared to the tourist market and local government employees (in contrast to those on Chingdrol Lam which largely service the army). They include the Victoria Wine Bar, Tanfulu Chinese Restaurant, Pemaraga Tibetan Restaurant, Meling (Aisharan) Tibetan Restaurant, Yuhuli Bar, Snow Dragon Tibetan Restaurant, Music Kitchen Café, Yeti Café and Notting Hill Bar. Opposite, on the south side, are the TAR Statistics Department, the TAR Insurance Offices, the Bright Pearl Restaurant, the Tibet Hotel, the Xinhua Bookshop, the Hebei Mansion Hotel (with its Holyland Adventure Travel Agency and Mad Yak Restaurant), the Lhokha Prefecture Office, the 52 Beer Bar and the Lhasa Hotel. However, this south side, between the Xinhua Bookshop and the Lhasa Hotel, has now become one of the city's most active red-light districts.

Now the road intersects with **Mirik lam** (Ch *Minzu Lu*), which leads north to Damra Lam (Second Ring Road) and south to Chingdrol Lam. If you continue east from this intersection, you will pass on the north side the TAR Petroleum Company, the Yindu Disco Nightclub, the Tibet Pearl Hotel, the Lhasa Trade Mansion, the Wella Spa Complex, and (after the Barkhu Lam intersection that leads to Lhasa's vast enclosed night market), a local police station, China Mobile, the TAR Telecommunication Tower Building, the Akhu Tonba Bar, the Riverside Fish Restaurant, the Telecommunication Hotel, a large supermarket, and the disused Xing Mao Hotel. Then, after the intersection with Dekyilingka Lam, you will pass the Foreign Trade Company, and the excellent Gyugyu Gyakoling Hotpot Restaurant, adjacent to the Golden Yak Roundabout. Opposite, on the south side are the Chipel Dumra Tibetan Restaurant, the TAR High Court, the TAR Mapping and Survey Department, the Rang Khyimchen Mentang Tibetan Restaurant, the Trungchin Jiyon Hotpot Restaurant, and the Lhasa Petrol Station.

Continuing east on **Middle Dekyi Lam** after the roundabout, you will notice on the north side of the street, the Chorten Karpo Trokyi Restaurant, the Snowgod Palace Tibetan Restaurant, TAR Television and Radio HQ and the Alibaba Restaurant (with the Yiwan Nightclub upstairs). Now the road passes through the valley between Chakpori and Marpori Hills, where a reconstructed stupa gateway (*Drago Kani*) once more dominates the approach to the city. It soon opens out on to the vast and newly constructed Potala Square. On the north side of the square you will see in succession the Lingkhor circuit around the Potala Palace, an upmarket Tibetan restaurant, an antiques gallery, and the entrance to the renowned **Potala Palace** itself, with the 15th-century Zhamarpa Palace in the foreground. To the south, is the enclosed **Zhol Doring** (see below, page 94), and the open expanse of Potala Square (formerly the Cultural Palace Park), where a large rocket-like monument commemorating the founding of the TAR has recently been constructed. On the west side of the square there is an Osark Mountaineering and Trekking Store and a number of Fuji and Kodak photographic shops, with three restaurants upstairs: the Mongolian Mutton Roast Restaurant, the Darpel Tibetan Restaurant, and the Beijing Mutton Restaurant.

If you leave the square and head east on to **East Dekyi lam** (Ch *Beijing Dong Lu*), the road is soon intersected by Kharngadong Lam, after which you will reach an area of recent upmarket redevelopment. Here, on the north side, you will pass the Lhasa Post Office, the Post Hotel, and, after the Nyangdren Lam T-junction which leads to the CAAC Airline Office, the TAR Mineral Bureau, the Trokyi Nangmating Nightclub, the Serkhang Hotel, and the Number Three Bus Terminus. Opposite on the south side are the New Century Hotel, the Le Bailong Supermarket, and the TAR Planning Association. Next, after the Do Senge Lam intersection, you will reach an area where fine old buildings have recently been torn down for redevelopment. Then, to the north you will pass the Municipal Construction Bureau, the Yak Hotel, the Lhasa Kitchen, the Dunya Restaurant, the Ramoche Lam turn-off leading to **Ramoche Temple** (see below, page 88), Shide Tratsang, Meru Tratsang Printery and a local police station. On the corresponding south side are the Kailash Hotel, the Kyichu Hotel, the Green Trekking Company, the Mentsikhang Lam turn-off, the Tromzikhang Market, the Kirey

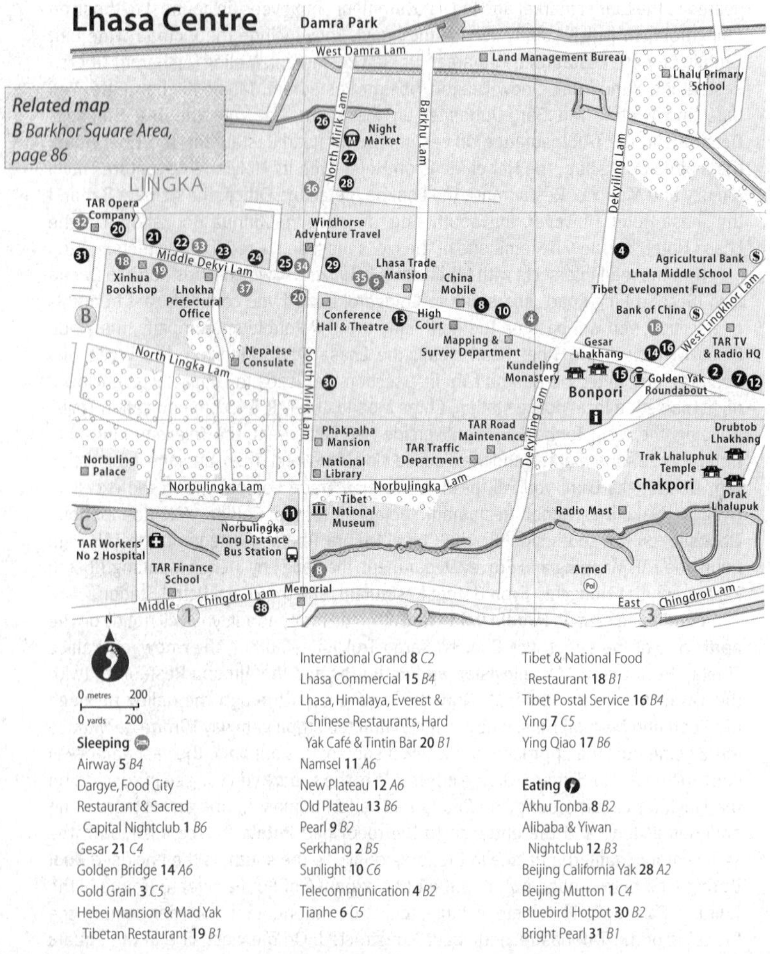

Sleeping
Airway 5 *B4*
Dargye, Food City Restaurant & Sacred Capital Nightclub 1 *B6*
Gesar 21 *C4*
Golden Bridge 14 *A6*
Gold Grain 3 *C5*
Hebei Mansion & Mad Yak Tibetan Restaurant 19 *B1*
International Grand 8 *C2*
Lhasa Commercial 15 *B4*
Lhasa, Himalaya, Everest & Chinese Restaurants, Hard Yak Café & Tintin Bar 20 *B1*
Namsel 11 *A6*
New Plateau 12 *A6*
Old Plateau 13 *B6*
Pearl 9 *B2*
Serkhang 2 *B5*
Sunlight 10 *C6*
Telecommunication 4 *B2*
Tianhe 6 *C5*
Tibet & National Food Restaurant 18 *B1*
Tibet Postal Service 16 *B4*
Ying 7 *C5*
Ying Qiao 17 *B6*

Eating
Akhu Tonba 8 *B2*
Alibaba & Yiwan Nightclub 12 *B3*
Beijing California Yak 28 *A2*
Beijing Mutton 1 *C4*
Bluebird Hotpot 30 *B2*
Bright Pearl 31 *B1*

Hotel, the Gang-gyen Hotel, the Bank of China (for foreign exchange) the Banak Zhol Hotel, and an internet café.Then, after the East Lingkhor Lam intersection which leads south to the Public Security Bureau and East Chingdrol Lam, you will pass the People's City Hospital to the north, and the Municipal Electric Bureau and Foreigners' Registration & Passport Office to the south. At its eastern extremity, the road then forms a T-junction with Lingyu Lam, before connecting with East Zamchen Lam (Ch *Jiangsu Dong Lu*), and heading northwest into town or southeast towards the bridge.

Central Lhasa: orientation and attractions

In downtown Lhasa there are two main north-south streets linking Chingdrol Lam with Dekyi Lam. One of these, **Kharngadong Lam**, leads northwards from the Dekyi Lam intersection to the Airway Hotel and the vegetable market and southwards to the Agricultural Bank of China (with an ATM machine), the Communication Hotel, the TAR Government HQ, the Lhasa Fire Brigade, the Lhasa Department Store, and various fashionable night clubs and restaurants. The other, **Do Senge Lam**, leads north from the Dekyi Lam intersection to the TAR newspaper offices and south to Primary School Number One, a large supermarket, Alotsang Tibetan Restaurant (aka "Pink Curtain"),

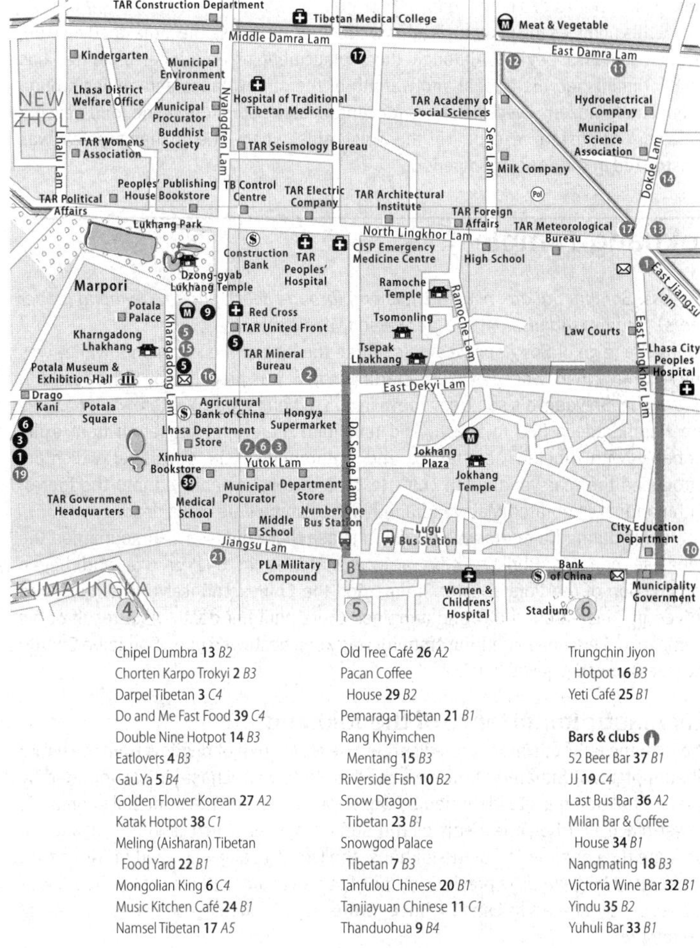

Chipel Dumbra **13** *B2*
Chorten Karpo Trokyi **2** *B3*
Darpel Tibetan **3** *C4*
Do and Me Fast Food **39** *C4*
Double Nine Hotpot **14** *B3*
Eatlovers **4** *B3*
Gau Ya **5** *B4*
Golden Flower Korean **27** *A2*
Katak Hotpot **38** *C1*
Meling (Aisharan) Tibetan Food Yard **22** *B1*
Mongolian King **6** *C4*
Music Kitchen Café **24** *B1*
Namsel Tibetan **17** *A5*
Old Tree Café **26** *A2*
Pacan Coffee House **29** *B2*
Pemaraga Tibetan **21** *B1*
Rang Khyimchen Mentang **15** *B3*
Riverside Fish **10** *B2*
Snow Dragon Tibetan **23** *B1*
Snowgod Palace Tibetan **7** *B3*
Tanfulou Chinese **20** *B1*
Tanjiayuan Chinese **11** *C1*
Thanduohua **9** *B4*
Trungchin Jiyon Hotpot **16** *B3*
Yeti Café **25** *B1*

Bars & clubs
52 Beer Bar **37** *B1*
JJ **19** *C4*
Last Bus Bar **36** *A2*
Milan Bar & Coffee House **34** *B1*
Nangmating **18** *B3*
Victoria Wine Bar **32** *B1*
Yindu **35** *B2*
Yuhuli Bar **33** *B1*

 the Aegean Sea Music Shop, the City Taxi Stand, a discotheque, and the terminus for the Number Three and Number Five buses. » *For listings, see pages 124-134.*

Yutok Lam

From the entrance to the TAR Government HQ on Kharnadsong Lam, **Yutok Lam** (also called Mimang Lam) leads eastwards to the gates of the Jokhang, Tibet's holiest shrine and the true centre of Lhasa. This road has recently been widened and turned into a pedestrian precinct. On the south side are the Xinhua Bookstore, the TAR Procurator's Office, the public baths, the TAR Industrial and Commercial Bureau, a large department store, and the restored 18th-century Yutok Bridge. On the corresponding north side are the Lhasa Department Store, the Ying Hotel, the Lhasa Tianhe Hotel, the Gold Grain Hotel, the TAR Grain Department, and the terminus for the Number Two bus. Then after the Do Senge Lam intersection, you will notice the Lhasa City Cinema on the south side, along with the Barkhor Police Station, the Alotsang No. 2 Tibetan Restaurant and the Friendship Store, while the Moonlight Discotheque, the taxi stand, the terminus for the numbers Three and Five buses, tangka painting shops, jewellery stores and the Hospital of Traditional Medicine (*Mentsikhang*) are all on the north side. Market stalls, many of them occupied by Tibetan traders selling traditional artefacts and tourist trinkets, line both sides of the road.

At this point, as the Jokhang is approached from the west, the radial road network of ancient Lhasa begins. Although the replacement of traditional buildings has greatly diminished the appeal and warmth of the narrow lanes and gullies around which Lhasa citizens lived their lives for centuries, the structure of the road network remains unchanged, except on the west side where the Jokhang plaza was constructed in the 1960-1970 period.

Jokhang Temple ཇོ་ཁང

ⓘ *Maps: Barkhor Square, page 86. Jokhang (ground floor), page 74. Jokhang (upper floors), page 79. Admission: ¥30 per person, ¥90 photopass.*

During the reign of Songtsen Gampo's father, the king of the Kathmandu valley was one Amshuvarman, whose own era, starting in 576, was preceded by Shivadeva and followed by Shivadeva's son Udayadeva in 621. When he was overthrown in 624, his son Narendradeva fled to Lhasa, and remained there until his return from exile, probably with Tibetan assistance, and enthronement in 641, after which he introduced the Matsyendranath cult. He is said to have vanished into the foot of Kathmandu's celebrated Matsyendranath image at the time of his death.

It was during Narendradeva's exile in Lhasa that Songtsen Gampo married the Nepalese princess Bhrikuti, who arrived in Lhasa in 632 or 634 and began construction of the Potala. Later, he married the Chinese princess Wencheng who arrived in Lhasa around 641 and remained there until her death. As a resulf of his marriage to Wencheng, the Tang emperor Gao Zong bestowed upon Songtsen Gampo the title Baowang, 'jewel king'.

Geomantic importance of the Jokhang

The Jokhang is Tibet's most sacred shrine, the focal point of pilgrims from the entire Tibetan plateau. Situated at the heart of the old town of Lhasa, it was founded by Queen Bhrikuti on a site identified by Queen Wencheng as the principal geomantic power-place in Tibet, the heart of the supine ogress which is Tibet. In 638, to facilitate the construction of the Jokhang, the Othang Lake was filled in with earth, transported by goats. The previous name of the town, Rasa ('Place of the Goat') was subsequently altered to Lhasa ('Place of the Deity') following the consecration of the temple.

However, further obstacles had to be eliminated by the construction of 12 outlying geomantic temples before the building of this central temple could be completed. Thus the Jokhang came to form the centre of a grand geomantic scheme, temples erected in three successive rings of four on the body of the 'supine ogress' on her shoulders and hips, elbows and knees, and hands and feet. On the Jokhang's eventual completion in 647, the temple was known as **Rasa Trulnang** ('magical apparition of Rasa'), and also as **Gazhi Trulnang** ('magical apparition endowed with four joys') because its construction was said to have brought happiness to the four classes of the populace.

The main gate of the Jokhang temple faces west towards Nepal in recognition of Queen Bhrikuti who bore the expense of the Jokhang's construction. The original design appears to have had a Newar model, and only later was it said to have been modelled on Vikramashila Monastery in Northwest India. The earliest part of the building, traces of which indicate distinctive Newar influence, is to be seen in the original door-frames of the four ground-floor inner chapels dedicated to Mahakarunika, Amitabha, Shakyamuni, and Maitreya, and those of the second floor at the centre of the north and south wings and the Zhalre Lhakhang of the east wing, as well as the Songtsen Chapel of the west wing. The fact that the Newar queen wished to add a third storey but never did may indicate her premature death. Later, when the third storey was added, the temple was said to represent the three buddha-bodies (*Trikaya*) or three world-systems (*Tridhatu*).

Bhrikuti installed the main images in a pentadic arrangement (five main chapels flanked by *vihara*-like cells) with a square hall: the deity Dipamkara Buddha in the form of Acala in the centre with Amitabha and Maitreya on either side; and Mahakarunika and Shakyamuni Aksobhyavajra on the north and south wings respectively. There were four gates: one in each of the four walls, and 37 columns represented the 37 sections of the Vinaya.

Songtsen Gampo erected the protector shrines, with images of the *naga* kings, Ravana and Kubera, to safeguard the temple from the elements. He also concealed his treasures (*terma*) in important pillars of the Jokhang; perhaps following the age-old Tibetan tradition of concealing wealth at the foundation of buildings or pillars.

Renovations

The Jokhang has undergone continuous renovation since its original establishment. The main phases of renovation are as follows:

Queen Jincheng (eighth century) refurbished the temple, King Senalek Jinyon (eighth-ninth century) cleared the outer courtyard, and King Relpachen (ninth century) built the Meru Nyingba Temple to the rear; while adding certain minor images.

Atisha (11th century) discovered Songtsen Gampo's testament, the *Kachem Kha-kolma*, in the Jokhang; while Zangkar Lotsawa Phakpa Sherab (11th century) enlarged the central inner sanctum and altered the Zhelre Lhakhang.

Gompa Tsultrim Nyingpo (12th century) renovated the other chapels, including the Zhalre Lhakhang murals of the second storey and built the inner circuit (*nangkhor*).

Gade Zangpo and Monlam Dorje of Tsel Gungtang (14th century) renovated the first two storeys of the main hall.

Phakdru Drakpa Gyeltsen (15th century) built the front extension or Outer Jokhang and Tsongkhapa inaugurated the Great Prayer Festival in 1409.

The Fifth Dalai Lama and his four regents including Sangye Gyatso (17th century) added further chapels and halls, replacing the old tiled roof with one of gilded copper.

The Eighth and Eleventh Dalai Lama (18th-19th centuries) and their regents from Tsomonling renovated the chapels and murals.

The Thirteenth Dalai Lama (20th century) repaired the chapels, halls, murals and roofs.

Changkya Qutuqtu and senior monks of Gonlung in Amdo presented the rooftop dharma-wheel motif in gilded copper.

The Fourteenth Dalai Lama (20th century) refurbished the chapels and extended the Labrangteng Palace.

Following the damage of the Cultural Revolution, basic restoration of the site (2,600 sq m) was carried out between between 1972 and 1982, and the temple was reopened in 1979 with only nine monks.

The murals and partition walls of the second storey were removed and replaced during the 1990s.

Layout

The three-storey Inner Jokhang forms a square (82.5 sq m), enclosing the main hall known as *Kyilkhor Thil* which is surrounded by the inner circumambulation pathway (*nangkhor*), beyond which is the great courtyard and the three-storeyed western extension, containing secondary chapels, storerooms, kitchens, toilets and residential quarters. The Meru Nyingba temple adjoins the Jokhang on the east side, while the south and west sides are adjoined by other buildings. This whole building is surrounded by the intermediate circumambulation pathway (*barkhor*); which in turn is surrounded by the old city of Lhasa, with the Potala beyond. The outer walkway (*lingkhor*) on which pilgrims even now circumambulate the entire holy city of Lhasa forms an outer ring road, and much of it has been incorporated into the modern road infrastructure of the city.

Outer Jokhang

In the square in front of the entrance, the Jokhang plaza, formerly known after its flagpole, the Juya Darchen, there is the stump of a willow reputedly planted by Princess Wencheng. It is flanked by two more recent willows and enclosed within a new stone wall. In front of the stump is the pock-marked obelisk of 1794 warning against smallpox, and another inscriptionless stele. In an adjacent enclosure to the north is the 6-m obelisk of 823 with an inscription commemorating the Sino-Tibetan Peace Treaty of 821/822. Outside the entrance, there are scribes who write the names of deceased persons or living petitioners on red paper in gold ink, to be incinerated in the butter lamps of the central inner sanctum.

The **entrance portico** (*Khyamra Gochor*) with six fluted columns is fronted by a courtyard (*dochal*) where pilgrims' prostrations have worn the flagstones smooth. Side murals depict the Four Guardian Kings and the Four Harmonious Brethren. The structure is surmounted by a balcony hidden by a yak-hair curtain, from which dignitaries would observe ceremonies conducted below. The upper north wing of the western extension contains the **Labrangteng Palace**, from which successive Dalai Lamas would watch important ceremonies. It has a grand reception hall; while below are storerooms, and the **Sitar Courtyard**, where living animals would be ransomed from the slaughterhouse as an act of merit. The south wing of the western extension contains the offices of the former Tibetan cabinet. **NB** If the main door is closed, access is gained from a ticket office in the Wood Enclosure (*Shingra*) to the south. Originally known as the "death enclosure", this was where Lhalung Palgyi Dorje assassinated the apostate king Langdarma in 846.

Gyalchen Zhi Lhakhang (Zimgo Chinang Nyiwar) Entering from the left and after passing two large prayer wheels, the pilgrim first sees statues of the Four Guardian Kings backed by 17th- and 19th-century frescoes of *gandharvas* and *nagas*, and flanked by paintings of Samantabhadra's paradise. This antechamber leads through the inner portal.

Kyamra Chenmo (Great Courtyard) The Great Courtyard which measures 1,248 sq m was constructed during the lifetime of Tsongkhapa for the inaugural Great Prayer Festival in 1409. It is in the form of an open atrium, its cloistered walls embellished with large murals which were commissioned in 1648 and restored in the

19th century. Among them, the murals of the west wall depict Gushi Qan, the Fifth Dalai Lama and the Fourth Panchen Lama; and the thousand buddhas of this aeon. The murals of the south wall depict the founding of the three large monasteries around Lhasa, and the life of the Buddha. The west murals above the entrance illustrate the nine aspects of Amitayus, and the meditational deities Guhyasamaja, Cakrasamvara, and Bhairava, as well as Kalacakra. On the north side is the two-storeyed residence of the Dalai Lama, with its gilded roof and window overlooking the courtyard. The nearer roof of the western extension, which can be accessed from the courtyard, overlooks the Jokhang plaza and the Potala to the west.

Starting from the northwest corner of the Great Courtyard, the following chapels and sacred objects are passed:

1) The Chapel of the Three Approaches to Liberation (**Namthar Gosum Lhakhang**), which once held 15th-century images of the Buddhas of the Three Times, the Eight Bodhisattvas and the two gatekeepers, and which is now used exclusively for storage. An interior staircase leads down from the Dalai Lama's private quarters.

2) The Great Throne Platform (**Shugtri Chenmo**), on which successive Dalai Lamas would sit, and which is backed by paintings depicting Shakyamuni, Avalokiteshvara and Manjushri with the Thousand Buddhas.

3) The Chapel of Tara (**Dolma Lhakhang**), containing a restored image of Tara in the form of Cintamanicakra, flanked by White and Green Tara, and backed on the left and right respectively by images of Nyaknyon Sewa Rinchen (who sculpted the original Cintamanicakra image) and Atisha. Its west wall has two-tiered images of the Twenty-one Taras, originally commissioned by the Seventh Dalai Lama, with Shantaraksita, Padmasambhava and Trisong Detsen forming a trio on the north side, along with Tsongkhapa and his foremost students. A long stone altar stands in front of the inner gateway. Outside the door is a stone bearing a handprint, attributed to either Nyaknyon, Drukpa Kunlek or Longdol Lama.

4) The Stone of Tsangnyon Heruka, a replica of which can be seen embedded in one of the northwest columns beyond the entrance to the Chapel of Tara.

5) The **Inner Circumambulation** (*nangkhor*) is lined with prayer-wheels and murals outlined in gold on red background, which depict the Thousand Buddhas and scenes from the *Avadanakalpalata*, interspersed with stupas and relief-images. On the north side are four interconnecting 17th-century chapels which were dedicated respectively to Hayagriva in the form of **Tamdrin Sangdrub**, **Mahakarunika**, **Sarvavidvairocana** and **Shakyamuni Buddha**, but which are all empty at the present time. On the east side there are the Chapel of the Sixteen Elders (**Neten Chudruk Lhakhang**), containing replica images of the Sixteen Elders, which had been originally commissioned in the 17th century by Sangye Gyatso; the Chapel of Padmasambhava's Hundred Thousand Images (**Gurubum Lhakhang**), containing replica images of the peaceful and wrathful aspects of Padmasambhava and the dakini Simhavaktra, which had been commissioned in the 19th century by the Thirteenth Dalai Lama, and the **Sera Dago**, which is a gate connecting the Jokhang with Meru Nyingba temple and the **Dago Rung-khang** kitchen (used during the Great Prayer Festival by the monks of Sera). On the south side there are interconnecting chapels, dedicated to the Eight Medicine Buddhas, the Sixteen Elders, the lineage-holders of the Graduated Path (*lamrim*), and Shakyamuni Buddha. Unfortunately they are all empty at present, as is the three-storeys high assembly hall, once occupied by monks from Ngakpa College at Drepung, and which still offers an excellent rooftop view of the Jokhang. Outside the wall, on the south side is the **Sung Chora** debating courtyard, renovated in 1986, and containing a yellow stone platform where thrones (*shugtri*) for Tsongkhapa, the Dalai Lama, and the Ganden Tripa were formerly set up during the Great Prayer Festival, and where the annual Geshe examinations were held.

During the Great Prayer Festival, the monks of the three main monasteries would be seated in the Great Courtyard – those from Sera in the north, Drepung in the centre, and Ganden in the south. The Dalai Lama would be flanked by Shartse Choje and Jangtse Choje, the hierarchs of the two colleges of Ganden monastery, and the entire ceremony would be supervised by the Ganden Tripa (head of the Gelukpa school) and the Tsokchen Umdze from Drepung.

Inner Jokhang

Ground Floor **Main Gate (Zhung-go)**: embedded in the flagstones in front of the gate is a fossil known as Amolongkha, and a footprint of the Thirteenth Dalai Lama. The gate is ornamented with Derge-crafted metalwork and surrounded by murals depicting Maitreya (left), Je Yabsesum (above), and Dipamkara (right).

Nowadays a metal security gate restricts unauthorised access.

Vestibule The outermost chapels of the vestibule including the Driza Zurphu Ngapa are empty, and one of them now functions as a control room for the electricity supply. The innermost chapels contain images depicting wrathful protector deities, such as Shridevi and Mahakala on the north side; and benign *naga* kings alongside vases of good luck charms on the south side. These protectors are said to have appeared to Songtsen Gampo in a vision during the original construction of the Jokhang, and were charged with its protection.

Kyilkhor Thil (Main Hall) The two-storey main hall is divided into three sections – two with short columns (*kawa thung-thung*) and one with long columns (*kawa ringbo*). Immediately beyond the entrance there are two rows of short transverse columns the southernmost ones bearing tangkas of the Sixteen Elders. Then, in the centre of the hall, are six magnificent replica statues: a 6-m west-facing image of Padmasambhava in the form of Nangsi Zilnon (donated by the late Dilgo Khyentse

Jokhang (Ground floor)

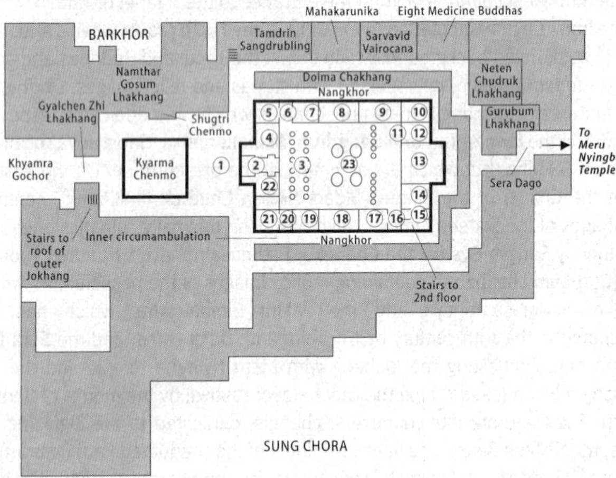

1 Main gate
2 Driza Zurphu Ngapa Nojinkang (N) Lukhang (S)
3 Kyilkhor Thil
4 Lama Lhakhang
5 Amitabha Lhakhang
6 Tagpa Chorten
7 Menlha Lhakhang
8 Mahakarunika
9 Jampa Truze
10 Othang Gyatso Lhakhang
11 Tsongkhapa Lhakhang
12 Amitabha Lhakhang
13 Jowo Shakyamuni Lhakhang
14 Jampa Chokhor Lhakhang
15 Chenrezi Sengedradrok Lhakhang
16 Yungdrung Phuk
17 Jangzik Lhakhang
18 Jampa Chezhi Lhakhang
19 Menlha Lhakhang
20 Sangye Rabdun
21 Tsepak Lhagu Lhakhang
22 Chogyel Yab-yum Lhakhang
23 Nine tall columns

Rinpoche and consecrated by Minling Chung Rinpoche), a smaller west-facing image of Shakyamuni in the form of Thuwang Zangthama, a 4-m west-facing image of Mahakarunika, an enormous 8-m west-facing image of Maitreya in the form of Barzhib Jampa, and two smaller north-facing images of Maitreya known as Miwang Jampa and Lhazang Jampa. These are named respectively after their original commissioners: Barzhib Chukorwa, Miwang Sonam Topgyel and Lhazang Qan. The tall painted columns, which form four groups of nine at the centre of the hall and support the skylight date from the period of Gade Zangpo's restoration (14th century).

An inner row of 12 short columns (*kawa thung-thung*) with six to each side of the Jowo Lhakhang, running transversely in front of the central inner sanctum, probably dates from the seventh century. These are characterized by short bases and round shafts, suggesting an authentic Nepalese design. Five of them (three at the north end and two at the south end) were plastered, probably in the 14th century for protection or reinforcement, by Gade Zangpo and his son.

Within the Main Hall, there are various chapels which the pilgrim will pass through in a clockwise manner, as follows:

West Wing Chapel of the Spiritual Teachers (Lama Lhakhang) This chapel contains a central image of Tsongkhapa, surrounded by his eight pure disciples—four each from U and Tsang provinces. The former are Geshe Jamkarwa Palden Zangpo, Tokden Jangchub Senge, Rinchen Gyeltsen, and Zangkyongwa; while the latter are Tokden Jampal Gyatso, Geshe Sherab Drakpa, Geshe Jampal Tashi and Geshe Palkyong. The images of this chapel have all been restored, apart from the central image of Tsongkhapa, part of which is original.

Chapel of Amitabha (Opame Lhakhang) Outside this long-defunct chapel is the Stupa of Scrutiny (*Tagpa Chorten*), which was originally fashioned by Sakya Pandita in the 13th century, and contained certain terracotta relics of King Songtsen Gampo. Raised on a clay platform beyond the stupa, behind a protective metal grill, are newly sculpted images of Shakyamuni Buddha, Rinchen Zangpo and Barawa Gyeltsen Zangpo.

North Wing Chapel of the Medicine Buddhas (Menlha Lhakhang): This chapel is dedicated to restored images of the Eight Medicine Buddhas. Outside, raised on a protected clay platform are images of Dolchung Korpon and Milarepa.

Chapel of Mahakarunika (Tsangkhung Jangma) Behind the chain metal curtain of this northern inner sanctum, the door of which appears to have an original frame, there is a restored image of the deity Mahakarunika in the form of Rangjon Ngaden. The original image is said to have self-manifested during the lifetime of King Songtsen Gampo, and has always been highly revered throughout Tibet because, according to one legend, the King, his two foreign queens, and the gatekeeper deities Amritakundalin and Hayagriva were all absorbed into it in the form of light. It also contained buddha relics from Bodh Gaya in India which had been brought to Tibet by Akarmatishila, himself revered as an emanation of King Songtsen Gampo. The original image was severely damaged during the Cultural Revolution and part of it was smuggled to Dharamsala. One portion, however, is contained within the new replica. It is one of the four in the Jokhang with a gilded roof. The chapel also contains secondary images of Khasarpani, Tara, Marici, Hayagriva, Lokeshvara, Bhrikuti, Sarasvati and Amritakundalin. Outside the entrance to this chamber are a series of new images depicting (L-R) Phakmodrupa, Tangtong Gyelpo, Padampa Sangye, Virupa and Shakyashri of Kashmir.

Chapel of Bathing Maitreya (Jampa Truze Lhakhang) The principal image is a replica Maitreya with an original impressive aureole, in front of which is an old restored image of Manjughosa. On its left are images of Amitabha, White Tara, Vajrapani, Avalokiteshvara and Manjughosa. On its right is Tsongkhapa flanked by the reliquaries of Ngaripa Tsondu Nyingpo (who sculpted some of the chapel's original images) and

 Ngok Lekpei Sherab. In the centre of the chapel is a stone butter bowl made by Tsongkhapa. Over the door is a replica of an original Mani Stone engraving (which was one of the Jokhang's most precious artefacts). The stone platform outside the door was once used by King Songtsen Gampo and his queens while bathing, and it is said that the actual clay of the Maitreya image in the chapel was mixed with bath water prior to its construction. Outside, along the wall at this point there is a newly sculpted image of Mahakarunika in a glass case, flanked by statues of Lama Zhang and Zhikpo Dudtsi (11th-12th centuries) who devoted much energy to repairing the dykes that protected the Jokhang from the flooding Kyi-chu waters.

Chapel of the Milk Plain Lake (Othang Gyatso Lhakhang) This chapel contains a stone slab, which is said to give access to a subterranean lake below the Jokhang's foundations. An antechamber contains the Treasury of Jowo Shakyamuni which was once supervised by the Chief Sacristan of the temple. Annual offerings were formerly made in this chapel by the Tibetan Government. Now it is mostly blocked off by the Tsongkhapa Lhakhang.

Chapel of Tsongkhapa (Tsongkhapa Lhakhang) A covered elevated platform supports a small image of Tsongkhapa called Nangyen Ngadrama, with Sakya Choje Kunga Tashi and Buton Rinchendrub on the left, and Thakme Zangpo, Sonam Gyeltsen, Dorje Gyeltsen, and the Third Karmapa on the right. The original central image is said to have been made in Tsongkhapa's lifetime, but there are other traditions attributing its miraculous construction to the protector deity Dharmaraja, or alternatively to a later Mongolian emperor. All these images have now been restored and repositioned.

East Wing Chapel of Amitabha (Opak Lhakhang) The entrance to this chapel, known also as the Room where Final Obstacles are Dispelled, is guarded by replica images of Vajrapani and Ucchusmakrodha – replicas – Langdarma's henchmen during the ninth century were unable to shift the former, and the latter is said to have repelled an historically unsubstantiated Chinese invasion following the death of Songtsen Gampo. Note the original sloping Newar door frame with its unpainted patina. Inside is an image of Amitabha, the original of which is said to have corresponded to the king's own vision, flanked on the left by Vajrapani and on the right by Hayagriva, while the Eight Bodhisattvas are on the side walls. Outside the chamber to the south is a stone platform with images of Songtsen Gampo, his two foreign queens, and Guru Saroruhavajra (commissioned by the Thirteenth Dalai Lama).

Foyer of the Jowo Chapel The highly polished wooden floor of the foyer is flanked by two pairs of guardian kings (with wrathful demeanour on the south side and smiling demeanour on the north side). According to one tradition, the original guardians, now destroyed, were attributed to Princess Jincheng, and sculpted with the first fruits of the earth from the construction at Samye. The elaborately decorated high ceilings display a marked Newar influence. A replica image of Padmasambhava, originally sculpted in the 18th century by Orgyan Drodul Lingpa and kept in a glass case, faces the central inner sanctum, exhorting Jowo Shakyamuni to remain within the chapel and not to be spirited away by the *nagas*.

Chapel of Jowo Shakyamuni (Tsamkhang Uma) The central inner sanctum, which is the largest and loftiest chapel of the Jokhang and one of four with a gilded roof, contains Tibet's most revered image – the 1.5 m **Jowo Rinpoche**, representing the Buddha at the age of 12. This image was reputedly made of an alloy of precious metals mixed with jewels by the celestial sculptor Visvakarman in Kapalavastu, and in later times presented to China by the king of Magadha to commemorate the defeat of the Yavanas. Subsequently it was brought to Tibet by Princess Wencheng. One tradition recorded by Tucci states that the original was partially destroyed in 1717 by the Dzungars, the present image being stylistically later. Originally housed in the Ramoche temple, it was later brought to the Jokhang by Wencheng on the death of Songtsen Gampo and interred in a chamber on the south side behind a painting of

Manjughosa. Queen Jincheng subsequently recovered it and installed it as the central image of the Jokhang. Later it was buried in sand after Trisong Detsen's disloyal Bon ministers decided to return it to China and 300 men could not move it. During that period, the temple was converted to a slaughterhouse. Subsequently the image was once again buried in sand by Langdarma who had the gates of the Jokhang illustrated with the picture of a monk drinking wine. The headdress and ear-ornaments (*na-gyen*) originally dated from time of Tsongkhapa but have been recently replaced), and the pearl-studded robe from the time of the Da Ming emperor. The image was undamaged during the Cultural Revolution, during which the temple was used as a military barracks and its outer courtyard as a slaughterhouse.

Entering the inner sanctum, the pilgrim finds the main image seated upon a three-tiered stone platform, flanked by smaller images of Maitreya and Manjughosa. There are ornate silver-plated pillars with dragon motifs supporting an overhead canopy and a silver sphere above the crown, which was donated by a Mongolian Qan. Steps at the south and north sides grant access to the pilgrim, who can then make offerings directly to the image. Behind the Jowo Rinpoche image, there is a copper plaque with an inscription commemorating earlier restorations of the throne-back and the aureole. In front of the plaque is an east-facing image of Dipamkara Buddha called Acala, which stands back-to-back with Jowo Rinpoche, and is claimed to have once been the central image. Facing the latter, at the back of the chapel is a 6-m image of Vairocana in the form of Himamahasagara (Tib *Tubpa Gangchentso*), flanked by the Twelve Bodhisattvas, along with the gatekeepers Vajrapani and Hayagriva – all of which were sculpted by Zangkar Lotsawa (11th century). Other later statues of the inner sanctum depict the Seventh and Thirteenth Dalai Lamas and Tsongkhapa.

Outside the chapel to the south is a raised platform with images of Atisha flanked by Dromtonpa and Ngok Lekpei Sherab. Behind Dromtonpa is a gilded mural depicting Dolma Darlenma, a 'speaking' form of Tara, which received its name after reputedly requesting Sakya Pandita for an offering scarf.

Chapel of Maitreya and Retinue (Jampa Chokhor Lhakhang) This chapel, which has an original seventh-century Newar door-frame, guarded each side by the protectors Brahma and Sakra, contains the replica of a venerable Maitreya image with webbed feet, which is held to have been originally commissioned by King Krikin, consecrated by the previous Buddha Kashyapa, and brought to Tibet from Nepal as part of Princess Bhrikuti's dowry. Although the present statue is a replica, the finely carved aureole may be original. Flanking the main image are restored images of the Eight Taras Who Protect from Fear, and in the northwest corner is a replica of Princess Wencheng's stove.

Outside on a clay platform are images of Amitayus, Dolpopa Sherab Gyeltsen and Four-armed Avalokiteshvara.

Chapel of Simhanada (Chenrezi Sengedradrok Lhakhang) The main image here is of Amitabha, flanked by six emanations of Avalokiteshvara, of which the first left gives the chapel its name. Outside is a 1.5-m stone column with a hole at the top, to which pilgrims press their ears in order to hear the sound of the mythical anga bird at the bottom of Othang Lake.

South Wing Svastika Alcove (Yungdrung Phuk) In the southeast corner beyond the stairs are replica images of Padmakara, Trisong Desten and Shantaraksita, who collectively founded Samye Monastery. The images were originally sculpted to repel a Mongolian army during the 17th-century civil war, and some sources suggest that the image of Shantaraksita was later substituted by another image of Padmasambhava. Next to them is a gilded mural with a protective grill depicting the Medicine Buddha, Bhaisajyaguru. Then, continuing along the south wing, there are newly sculpted images of the Three Deities of Longevity.

North-facing Chapel (Jangzik Lhakhang) This chapel contains a series of recently reconstructed images depicting the retinue of Amitayus according to the Indian tradition of Jetari. Outside are new murals depicting Songtsen Gampo and his two foreign queens with the ministers Gar and Tonmi Sambhota. The original paintings had been commissioned by Monlam Dorje of Tsel Gungtang. In front, on a protected clay platform are statues of the earliest Sakya hierarchs, including Khon Konchok Gyelpo, Sachen Kunga Nyingpo, Jetsun Sonam Tsemo and Jetsun Drakpa Gyeltsen.

Chapel of Four Sibling Maitreyas (Jampa Chezhi Lhakhang) This chapel, which is one of the four with a gilded roof, contains an image of Maitreya, brought from Drepung to replace the now destroyed silver Maitreya that was traditionally escorted around the Barkhor on the 25th day of the first lunar month during the Jampa Dendren ceremony. The original had been cast by Utpala of Kashmir around the time of Langdarma. Other statues in this chapel include: Manjughosa, Khasarpani, Mahakarunika, Vajrasattva and Jambhala, as well as the sacristan Lharje Gewabum, who is said to have rebuilt one of the Kyi-chu dykes. Behind the image of the protector Vighnantaka at the northeast corner of the chapel is a 50-cm gilded goat's head, replacing a reputedly self-arising original. This depicts the legendary Queen of Goats (*Dungtse Ra'i Gyelmo*) who presided over the filling-in of the Othang Lake.

Chapel of Jowo's Concealment (Jowo Besai Lhakhang) This is the chapel in which Princess Wencheng hid the Jowo Rinpoche image inside a cavity behind the buddha-image on the east wall. The main images depict Amitabha and the Eight Medicine Buddhas. The mural of Manjughosa, known as Jampeyang Koyolma, on the outer wall, is said to have spoken to Princess Jincheng, agreeing to move aside so that the statue could be extracted. Flanking the mural are statues of later Sakya hierarchs, including Sakya Pandita Kunga Gyeltsen, Chogyel Phakpa, and Lama Dampa Sonam Gyeltsen.

Chapel of the Seven Generations of Past Buddhas (Sangye Rabdun Lhakhang) This chapel contains replicas of the Seven Generations of Past Buddhas, which were originally cast in bronze, except for one, which is said to have alighted there miraculously from India.

Chapel of the Nine Aspects of Amitayus (Tsepak Lhagu Lhakhang) This chapel depicts the Nine Aspects of Amitayus, deity of longevity. Outside in the alcove, behind a protective wooden balustrade, there is a mural depicting Prajnaparamita, which once had an open eye in the forehead. This painting was originally attributed to King Songtsen Gampo, and according to one tradition, the open eye naturally appeared of its own accord after an old lady miraculously had her sight restored on praying to the image. Another tradition refers to this painting as "open-eyed Avalokitesvara" (*migje chenrezi*). In any case, the present mural is of modern execution. Other murals in this alcove depict the Three Deities of Longevity (*Tselha Namsum*).

West Wing Chapel of the Religious King and Courtiers (Chogyel Yab-Yum Lhakhang) In this royal chapel, King Songtsen Gampo is flanked (on the left) by Gar, Bhrikuti, Nyatri Tsenpo and Trisong Detsen; and (on the right) by Relpachen, Lhatotori, Wencheng and Tonmi Sambhota. Formerly it also contained images of Mongza Tricham, Gungru Gungtsen and Zhang Lonnyi. The room has original offering bowls and lamps. Outside are important murals depicting the foundation of the Jokhang and the events of Songtsen Gampo's reign, including the construction of the first Potala Palace. The procession of Jowo Sakyamuni from China is vividly depicted, as is the casting of Princess Wencheng's ring into the Milk Plain Lake prior to the construction.

Middle Floor (access from southeast corner) Chapel of the Countenance (Zhalre Lhakhang) The chapel immediately above the central inner sanctum was remodelled by Zangkar Lotsawa when the lower chamber was enlarged. Only the westernmost part of the original chamber remains, offering a view of the chapel below, and this is approached by a recently constructed catwalk. The original approach was walled off to prevent pilgrims walking above the inner sanctum, and its original Pala-style murals (probably executed by Zangkar Lotsawa) were replaced as recently as 1991. The remaining east inner wall has a well preserved three-panelled mural, suggesting a synthesis of Tibetan and Pala styles, which predates the Tibeto-Newari style of the 15th century. These interior murals have been attributed to Gompa Tsultrim Nyingpo.

Chapel of the Guru (Guru Lhakhang) The entrance to this chapel has a seventh century tapering door-frame with exquisite wood carvings in Newari style and a lattice gate. It contains replica images of Padmakara in the form of Saroruhavajra, with his two foremost consorts and eight manifestations.

Chapel of Cakrasamvara (Demchok Lhakhang) Here the principal image depicts the meditational deity Cakrasamvara in union with the female consort Vajravarahi.

Chapel of the Graduated Path (Lam-rim Lhakhang) The statues of this chapel, including Lhodrak Drubchen Namka Gyeltsen and Pawangka Dechen Nyingpo have been renovated since 1992. Outside, the badly restored murals of the southern gallery depict Shridevi, Padmakara with his 25 Tibetan disciples and Tsongkhapa.

Chapel of Munindra and Retainers (Tubwang Tsokhor Lhakhang) This chapel has a richly decorated Newar doorway, flanked by two black lion rampants on a red background. The foremost image depicts Shakyamuni, surrounded by Shariputra, Maudgalyayana, and the Eight Bodhisattvas.

Chapel of Munindra (Tubwang Lhakhang) This chapel contains replica images of Munindra with the seven other Medicine Buddhas. A famous image of Hayagriva in the form of Tamdrin Sangdrub has not yet been replaced.

Chapel of the Shakya King (Shakya Gyelpo Lhakhang) This chapel formerly contained a large silver image of Shakyamuni, built by the Seventh Karmapa in 1479, which was removed to the Jokhang after the end of the civil war in the 17th century. It also contained masks and other sacred objects associated with protector deities—but the present images are replicas, and the silver image has not been replaced.

Jokhang (Upper Floors)

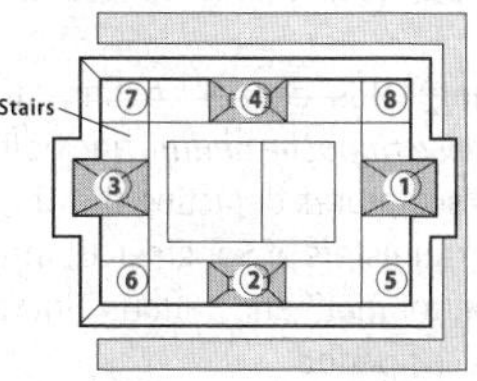

Roof

1 Jowo Gyaphib
2 Jampa Gyaphib
3 Chogyel Gyaphib
4 Tuje Gyaphib
5 Pelhayum Drakmo Lhakhang
6 Tsering Chenga Lhakhang
7 Lhachak Shokhang
8 Neten Chudruk Lhakhang

Stairs to roof

Third Floor

1 Pelachok Dukhang
2 Palden Lhamo Lhakhang
3 Pelha Bedongma Lhakang
4 Lama Lhakhang
5 Tsepak Lhakhang
6 Lolang Lhakhang
7 Neten Chudruk Lhakhang
8 Menlha Deshegye Lhakhang
9 Shakyamuni
10 Tonpa Tsokhor Lhakhang
11 Drelzam
12 Deshegye Lhakhang
13 Tubchen
14 Jowo Utho Lhakhang

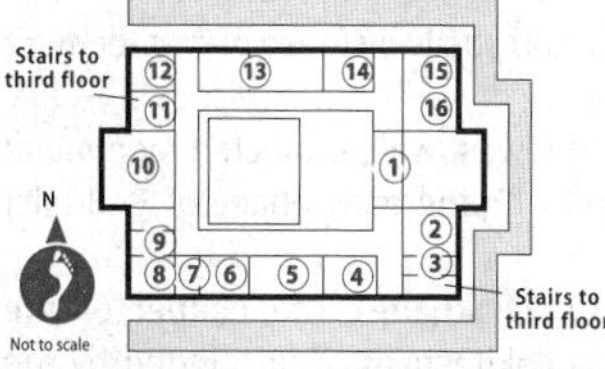

Second Floor

1 Zhalre Lhakhang
2 Guru Lhakhang
3 Demchok Lhakhang
4 Lamrim Lhakang
5 Tubwang Tsokhor
6 Tubwang Lhakhang
7 Shakya Gyelpo
8 Kunga Gonkhang
9 Tachok Lhakang
10 Chogyel Songtsen Lhakhang
11 Thupa Rigdruk Lhakhang
12 Nyento Terabdun
13 Kungarawa Lhakhang
14 Lama Zhang Zimbuk
15 Tsongkhapa Zimbuk
16 Chogyel Zimbuk

Protector Cavern of the Five Aspects of Pehar (Ku-nga Gonkhang) This chapel once contained a revered image of Hayagriva in the form of Tamdrin Sangdrub, flanked by the five kingly aspects of Pehar, Shridevi, Nechung and the gatekeepers Du-tsen and Lu-tsen. The inner recess within the chapel also contained a stuffed image of the protector Cimara. All these originals had been commissioned by the Fifth Dorje Drak Rigzin Pema Wangchuk in the 18th century, and the rituals were maintained until recent times by monks from Dorje Drak. However, the replicas of the present day have all been placed within a glass case in the inner recess, and the rites are conducted in the outer chamber, which is empty except for a few murals depicting the Confession Buddhas and aspects of Tara.

Chapel of the Supreme Horse (Tachok Lhakhang) This chapel contains the restored Seven Precious Insignia of Royal Dominion (*gyelse rinpoche nadun*), including the "supreme horse"; and at its centrepiece there are sculptures depicting the Three Ancestral Kings, flanked by the foreign queens and chief ministers of Songtsen Gampo. Outside in the western gallery the murals depict the parrot motif and various Tibetan translators, kings and lineage-holders of the royal dynastic period.

Chapel of the Religious King (Chogyel Lhakhang) The main shrine of the west wing, is dedicated to King Songtsen Gampo. Note the seventh century door frames. The central image of the king and his two foreign wives was reputedly sculpted by a student of Tangtong Gyelpo named Dungkar Drukdra. (The middle finger of the right hand of the main image is said to be that of Songtsen himself and the image an exact likeness). To the rear are the Seven Generations of Past Buddhas, the originals of which were commissioned by Songtsen Gampo himself, and a series of remarkable wall paintings of mandalas depicting the assemblies of Niladanda, Hevajra, and Vajrabhairava (top left); Bhaisajyaguru, Mahakarunika and Aksobhya (bottom left); Sarvavid Vairocana (concealed behind the central image); Guhyasamaja, Cakrasamvara and Mahacakra Vajrapani (top right); and Amitayus, the Sixteen Elders and Avalokitesvara in the form of Mind at Rest (bottom right). The south wall has further images of Songtsen Gampo with Wencheng and his Tibetan consort.

Among other artefacts on display in this chapel, there was a special gold ring that Princess Wencheng had given to the king, which was only displayed once a year during the Pelha Ritro ceremonies. The ring that is now on display is a new replica, the original having been lost or destroyed. A cabinet resting on a wooden stand in front of the main image still contains an original silver ale-pot, reputedly used by the king himself which may well be of Scythian or Kushan origin, and which is known as 'trungben tagoma". It had been inserted as treasure into the crack of a rock at Yerpa, and later, in the early 15th century, it was extracted by Tsongkhapa and presented to this chapel as an offering. Ale-pot is said to have left its impression in the rock. Some reports also suggest it has been silver-plated in recent centuries. Like the ring, it appears to have been employed only once a year during the Pelha Ritro ceremonies, at which time it is said to have been filled quickly and easily by those of greater merit but slowly by those of feeble merit.

Outside the chapel, the restored murals of the west wall, protected by a metal grill, depict ancient kings and figures associated with the early phase of Buddhist propagation in Tibet.

Chapel of the Six Sages (Thupa Rigdruk Lhakhang) The chapel of the northwest corner is dedicated to Four-armed Avalokiteshvara, surrounded by the Six Sages of the Six Realms. Note the number of murals depicting Amitayus in red on a cream background.

Chapel of the Seven Patriarchs (Nyento Terabdun Lhakhang) This last, east-facing, chapel once contained a central image of Kasyapa, flanked by Ananda, Sanavasika, Upagupta, Dhitika, Kala and Sudarsana, who collectively formed the original succession of the Buddhist monastic order in ancient India. These images have been restored, and the internal murals also depict Amitayus, executed in red line on a gold background. Outside in the gallery there is a wall panel depicting Tsongkhapa, with miniature images of Padmakara and White Tara above his shoulders. Other panels depict kings and lay practitioners associated with the earliest dissemination of Buddhism in Tibet. Also, outside the entrance, there were formerly several large Mani Wheels, one of which has now been restored.

Chapels of Kungarawa (Kungarawa Lhakhang) Heading along the north wing of the middle floor, the pilgrim will pass two south-facing chapels, which were originally dedicated to *yaksa* and *yaksini* protectors, and which in more recent centuries functioned as woodblock and manuscript libraries. Of these the first temporarily houses various new images that have been offered to the Jokhang by private individuals, including the Four Deities of Longevity, Padmakara, Tara, Manjughosa and Mahakarunika. The second has a number of small old images that survived the Cultural Revolution, unlike the library it once contained which was destroyed.

Hermitage of Lama Zhang (Lama Zhang-gi Zimbuk) This chapel was formerly a residence of the illustrious Lama Zhang, and now contains finely sculpted images of Amitabha, Avalokitesvara, and Padmakara. Outside in the northern gallery, the seventh-century frescoes were copied and removed for restoration during the 1980s and replaced in the late 1990s. They now depict narrative scenes illustrating early Tibetan history and the temples and palaces constructed by the early kings.

Hermitage of Tsongkhapa (Tsongkhapa Zimbuk) This room formerly contained images of Tsongkhapa, Hayagriva in the form of Tamdrin Yangsang, and Vajrabhairava in the form of Rapelma— so called because the horns of its bull-head were said to expand in size. Nowadays, the hermitage is closed, dark and empty, but replicas of the Hayagriva and Vajrabhairava images are to be found in the next chapel.

Hermitage of the Religious King (Chogyel Zimbuk) This chapel, distinguished by its round carved wooden door, once contained images of King Songtsen Gampo and his queens which had been sculpted during the Tshalpa era. The present images of the royal family, along with Hayagriva and Vajrabhairava images are all replicas. Outside the murals of the northeast corner have undergone restoration since the late 1990s, and all the original frescoes have been removed, copied and recently replaced.

An impressive line of newly sculpted Confession Buddhas, arrayed transversely along the east wing of the skylight gallery is visible from the second floor. The beam-ends, supported by the columns which rise from the ground floor below, have carved relief images of lion faces, their noses reputedly blunted by Songtsen Gampo's slipping axe and there is a cornice with 100 lion-faced figurines and a single human-faced figurine, which apparently date from the earliest phase of construction.

Top Floor (access from the southeast and northwest corners) All the chapels of the northwest corner and north wing of the top floor are now empty. These include the corner Chapel of the Eight Medicine Buddhas (*Menla Lhakhang*) which once contained silver images of the Eight Medicine Buddhas, commissioned to fulfil the dying wishes of Gushi Qan, as well as a human-size silver image of Vajrapani; the Chapel of the Conqueror Sakyamuni (*Gyelwa Shakya Tubpe Lhakhang*), which once contained images of the Medicine Buddhas surrounded by bodhisattvas and Vaisravana; the Chapel of Sakyamuni and Retainers (*Tonpa Tsokhor Sumgyi Lhakhang*), which contained statues of Munindra flanked by Sariputra, Maudgalyayana, and the eight Main Bodhisattvas; and the Chapel of the Eight Stupas (*Deshek Gyeyi Lhakhang*), which once contained silver stupas symbolising the eight deeds of the Buddha and gilded copper images of the Sixteen Elders. The chapels of the northeast corner and east wing are similarly empty. They include the corner Chapel of the Great Sage (*Tubchen Lhakhang*), which once contained an image of Mahamuni with Sariputra, Maudgalyayana, the eight main bodhisattvas and the two wrathful gatekeepers; the Chapel Above Jowo's Head (*Jowo Uto Lhakhang*), which originally housed the ground floor images of Maitreya and Retainers (*byams-pa chos-'khor*), and later, following

 Zangkar Lotsawa's restoration, held the retainers of Acala, and the five meditational buddhas; and the Turret Office, used by the sacristans of the top floor.

Certain important chapels of the southeast corner and south wing are still functioning. The Chapel of the Shridevi Turret (*Pelhachok Lhakhang*) is a protector chapel formerly supervised by monks from Meru Sarpa Tratsang. Its interior murals, executed in white, red and gold on black background, depict Shridevi, Mahakala, and Bhairava. A door in the southwest corner of this room leads downstairs to the Chapel of Shridevi (*Palden Lhamo Dungkyongma Lhakhang*), containing the replica of a revered peaceful image of the protectress Shridevi; the original face is said to have been painted with blood from King Songtsen Gampo's nose.

In turn, a recess in this chapel gives access to the Chapel of Frog-faced Shridevi (*Pelha Beldongma Lhakhang*), which contains a fearsome natural black stone image of the head of Remati with the face of a frog. This was extracted as treasure by Lama Zhang from Gungtang, and the lower part of its body is stuffed. Despite some damage, the image appears to have survived the Cultural Revolution. A strong odour of wine used to permeate these chapels where the public offered libations to Shridevi, and thousands of rats once swarmed around the offerings of mounds of grain. Each year from the 13th day of the 10th lunar month, the stuffed image of wrathful Shridevi would be escorted to the gallery in front of the turret, where ablutions would be performed. On the following day *tor-ma* offerings would be distributed to the people of Lhasa, and, on the 15th day, in the ceremony called Pelha Ritro which re-enacts the circumambulation of Mount Sumeru by Shridevi, the image would be carried around the skylight gallery of the top floor before being escorted around the Barkhor by monks from Meru Tratsang.

The remaining chapels on the south wing and southwest corner are farely threadbare. They include the Chapel of the Spiritual Teacher (*Lama Lhakhang*), which once contained images of Atisha with his foremost students, a sandalwood model of the Bodhnath Stupa in Nepal, and a precious copy of the *Astasahasrikaprajnaparamita*, inlaid with conch. The Chapel of the Three-dimensional Mandalas (*Lolang Lhakhang*) once housed exquisitely crafted white sandalwood palaces (translated from the sanskirt *vimana*, which is the celestial abode or model palace of a particular meditational deity) of Guhyasamaja, Cakrasamvara and Vajrabhairava, commissioned by Miwang Sonam Topgye in 1732, and now only contains newly sculpted images of the Thousand Buddhas. The Chapel of the Nine Aspects of Amitayus (*Tsepak Lhakhang*) formerly contained a three-dimensional mandala and silver cast images of all the nine aspects of Amitayus, commissioned in 1756 by the Seventh Dalai Lama.

Lastly, the chapels on the west wing are completely empty. They include the Chapel of the Sixteen Elders (*Nechu Lhakhang*), which formerly contained 13th-14th-century clay images of Shakyamuni Buddha flanked by the Sixteen Elders, each of them in a distinctive bas relief grotto, as well as the palace of Bhaisajyaguru, and murals depicting scenes from the *Avatamsakasutra*.

The murals of the south wing, outside the Chapel of the Shridevi Turret, depict Six-armed Mahakala, surrounded by Shridevi and four sylvan mountain spirits (*yaksa*), followed by the Fifth Dalai Lama, Sangye Gyatso and Gushi Qan; and the 12 mountain goddesses. Those of the west wing depict Sukhavati buddha-field, surrounded by images of Amitayus, drawn in black on a soft-tinted copper base. The walls of the north wing depict the Yulokopa buddha-field surrounded by images of Green Tara, drawn in black on a soft green-tinted silver base. The walls of the east wing depict the Potalaka buddha-field, surrounded by images of Vajrasattva, drawn in black on a soft silver base. Despite the recent restoration of these murals, many of them have four or five layers of earlier paint, and the lower layers have yet to be inspected.

The Roof The bright sunlit roofs present a great contrast to the dark smoke-filled chapels of the Jokhang's interior. Among them, the largest gilded roof to the east surmounts the Chapel of Jowo Shakyamuni (**Jowo Gyaphib**). This was donated during the 14th century by Tewmul, the son of Anantamul, king of Yartse, who is regarded as a descendant of Songtsen Gampo. The gilded roof to the south surmounts the head of the Four Sibling Maitreyas (**Jampa Gyaphib**). Its golden lustre is tarnished, reputedly because it had originally been erected on the palace roof of King Gocha and then buried underground for a long period. The gilded roof to the west was donated by the Tibetan government during the lifetime of the Fifth Dalai Lama, and positioned above the chapel containing the likeness of King Songtsen Gampo (**Chogyel Gyaphib**). Lastly, the gilded roof to the north is above the Chapel of Mahakarunika (**Tuje Gyaphib**). It was donated in the late 14th century by Pratimul, the son of king Punimul of Yartse and his minister Palden Drakpa.

The roof also has four corner turrets which function as chapels. The Chapel of the Wrathful Mother Shridevi (**Pelhayum Drakmo Lhakhang**) or southeastern turret once contained a mask and a stuffed image of Remati, reputedly made by the hand of the Fifth Dalai Lama himself. The chapel has been renovated since 1992, and is now open for liturgical rites, though the small prayer flag outside the door which was reputedly "hoisted at a time of good tidings" (**Tamnyen darchar**) by the regent Sonam Chopel when Donyo, the Bonpo king of Beri in Kham, was slain by Gushi Qan during the 17th century no longer stands. The Chapel of the Five Sisters of Longlife (*Tsering Chenga Lhakhang*) or southwest turret contains replica images and thread-crosses of the Five Sisters of Longlife, one of which was commissioned by the Thirteenth Dalai Lama on the advice of the Nyingmapa master Chogyur Dechen Lingpa. Liturgies here were formerly performed by monks from Tshurpu Monastery. The northwest turret once contained charms which control the gods, serpentine water spirits, and the sacred essence of the earth, also a stationery storeroom belonging to the Palace Treasury. Finally, the Chapel of the Sixteen Elders (*Nechu Lhakhang*) or northeast turret once housed an exquisite set of the Sixteen Elders in their grottoes, fashioned of medicinal clay; it also doubled as an office during the Great Prayer Festival. However, neither the northwest nor northeast turrets have yet been restored.

Barkhor radial roads

There are four large prayer-flags situated with the Barkhor ('intermediate circuit') market which surrounds the Jokhang, known respectively as Ganden Darchen in the northeast, Juyag Darchen in the west, Kelzang Darchen in the southwest, and Sharkyaring Darchen in the southeast. The Barkhor market itself is the most active in all Tibet, and it is possible to purchase traditional Tibetan artefacts, religious implements, antiques, modern goods, books, music, clothing, spices, fresh meat and vegetables. Prices are not fixed and you will be expected to bargain.

Working clockwise from the west side, there is a northern lane, called Mentsikhang Lam (or Tengyeling Lam), due east of the Hospital of Traditional Medicine, which leads to East Dekyi Lam and is known for its hotels (Snowland, Shambhala, Pentoc and Tashi Dagye), its restaurants (Snowland, Gangkyi Zakhang, Tibet Kitchen, Amdo Zakhang, Tibet Café and Bar, Base Camp Café, Third Eye, Blue Moon, and Tashi Number One), and its tea houses. Other shops on this tourist street, which is now being pedestrianised, include Snowleopard Carpets, the Boiling Point Internet Bar, Nomad Handicrafts, Yekyil Tours, an efficient drycleaner, and a supplier of outdoor trekking equipment. The regency temple Tengyeling is approached via an alley behind the hospital.

A second road runs northwest from the plaza towards the Tromzikhang market via the butter and meat markets, also giving access to East Dekyi Lam. The popular

 Dhoodgu Hotel is located here. From the Barkhor circuit, the third road, known as Wangdushingka Lam, extends southeast from the southeast corner. The fourth road, known as Waling Lam (or Dunsisung Lam), also leads southeast from the China Construction Bank at the south side towards the nunnery of Ani Tshamkhung, the mosque of Gyel Lhakhang and East Chingdrol Lam. The fifth, known as Rabsel Lam, leads southwest from Makye Ama Restaurant at the southwest corner, slightly east of the Mandala Hotel; and the last Gyedu Lam (or Lugu Lam), leads southwest from the southwest (Dicos Café & Mandala Restaurant) corner of the plaza to the Lugu Bus Station and Chingdrol Lam.

Barkhor buildings and temples

Nangtseshak Jail

This 720-sq m two-storey prison adjoining the north wall of the Jokhang was of great notoriety in the past, but is now disused. In front there is a square, which nowadays functions as a carpet bazaar. The lane entrance to Meru Nyingba temple is located here.

Meru Nyingba Temple

This temple is situated on the northeast side of the Jokhang, and approached from the north arc of the Barkhor. It was one of six temples built by King Relpachen – this one on the site of an earlier temple where Tonmi Sambhota finalized the Tibetan alphabet. It was destroyed by Langdarma and subsequently rebuilt by Atisha to become Gelukpa under the Third Dalai Lama Sonam Gyatso (1543-1589). The oldest existing structure is the Jambhala Lhakhang, the main building being of recent 20th-century construction. The temple is dedicated to doctrinal protectors, especially the diverse forms of Pehar.

Gongkar Chode Branch Temple This Sakya protector shrine is located up a staircase on the right of the lane entrance to Meru Nyingba temple. The central image is of the protector Gonpo Pelgon Dramtso, and was formerly flanked by images of Panjara, Shridevi, and Six-armed Mahakala.

Jambhala Lhakhang This ancient temple lies below the Gongkar Chode branch temple. Originally it was part of King Relpachen's construction. It is only 7.5 m by 7.2 m with a low ceiling, and is said to be where Tonmi Sambhota devised the Tibetan alphabet. Later it became affiliated to Nechung.

The Dukhang (Assembly Hall) This south-facing three-storey complex is approached through a courtyard flanked by a monastic cloister. The main building, constructed by Nechung Khenpo Sakya Ngape in the 19th century, is an extremely active temple. It was renovated in 1986. Mani prayer wheels flank either side of the entrance; the left frescoes depict the protector deity Dorje Drakden, skylight frescoes depict Tsongkhapa then Atisha, each with their foremost students, and Padmasambhava flanked by Shantaraksita and King Trisong Detsen. The central image on the altar is a new Avalokiteshvara, with a large copper Padmasambhava to the right and a sand mandala on the left.

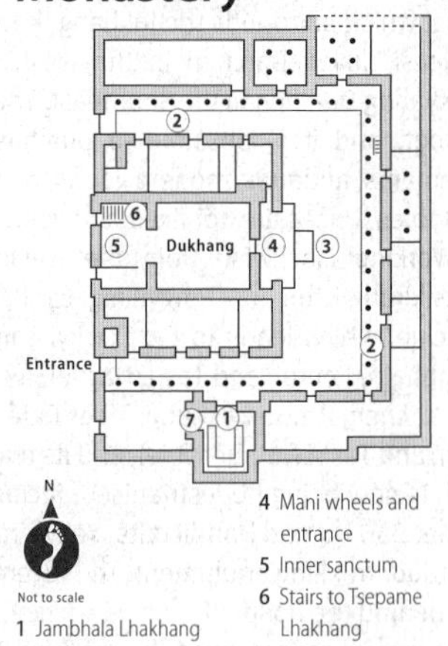

1 Jambhala Lhakhang
2 Monastic cloisters
3 Courtyard
4 Mani wheels and entrance
5 Inner sanctum
6 Stairs to Tsepame Lhakhang
7 Stairs to Gongkar Chode Branch Temple

Lhasa Obelisks

The obelisk or stele is a significant historical monument, constructed to symbolize royal dominion or important political and spiritual events, and often surrounded in four directions by stupas. The obelisks of Lhasa include those in front of the **Jokhang**, namely the legible 3.5-m stele constructed in 823 by King Relpachen to commemorate the peace treaty signed with Tang China, the illegible smallpox stele of 1794, and the inscriptionless stele of the Ming period with animal carvings on its plinth.

In front of the **Potala**, there are four other obelisks: the 3.5-m quadrilingual Kangxi stele of 1721 commemorating the defeat of the Dzungars, and the 4-m quadrilingual Qianlong stele of 1791 commemorating the two defeats of the Gorkhas in 1788 and 1791 respectively, have recently been repositioned in front of the building. Considerably older than these, however, are the **Outer Zhol Obelisk** (*Zhol Chima*) and the **Inner Zhol Obelisk** (*Zhol Nangma*). The former is an 8-m stele constructed by Trisong Detsen in 763 to commemorate the exploits of his General Takdra Lugong whose forces occupied the Chinese capital at Xi'an; and the latter, located below the Potala stairway, commemorates the Fifth Dalai Lama's move from Drepung in the 17th century.

Behind this altar is the **inner sanctum**, containing an image of Padmasambhava in the form of Nangsi Zilnon in the centre flanked by the five aspects of Pehar known as Gyelpo Ku-nga and the gatekeepers Hayagriva and Thoktsen. Frescoes above depict Tsongkhapa, Samantabhadra and the Thirteenth Dalai Lama. The side chapels have images of Dorje Drakden (left) and Shridevi (right).

Upstairs is the **Tsepame Lhakhang** containing 1,000 small images of Amitayus.

The Pawangka Labrang

This three-storey residence of the **Pawangka Rinpoche**, a powerful Gelukpa master who rose to prominence in the early 20th century, is located on the east side of the Barkhor.

Karmashar Lhakhang

This temple is located on the east side of the Barkhor. One of Lhasa's three oracles was based here, the others being at Nechung and Gadong in the Tolung valley. The Karmashar Choje oracle would make one annual prophecy concerning affairs of state on the 30th day of the sixth lunar month after travelling in procession from **Karmashar** to **Sera** monastery accompanied by Cham dancers drawn from the corpse-cutter (*ragyabpa*) and police (*korchagpa*) professions. The prophecy would then be written down and pinned on the door of Karmashar for public inspection.

Ani Tshamkhung Nunnery

ⓘ *Admission fee: ¥15 per person.*

This is one of Lhasa's three nunneries, the others being Drubtob Lhakhang on Chakpori and Chubzang Gonpa at Pawangka. It is located on the left side of Waling Lam, which leads southeast from the Barkhor to the Mosque (*Gyel Lhakhang*). Passing through the perimeter wall, to which the kitchen and living quarters are attached, the yellow two-storey building is located at the rear of the courtyard. The Tshamkhung (meditation hollow) of Songtsen Gampo is downstairs and approached from a small passage on the right side of the building. It contains the chamber where the king meditated in order to avert flooding of the Kyi-chu River. Inside is the meditation hollow – a 1.5 sq m whitewashed earthen well 1.5 m deep and below floor level, which is approached by four steps and surmounted by a glass-framed shrine. A reconstructed black-stone "Ngadrama" image of Songtsen Gampo overlooks the opening and the king's stone seat is positioned in front.

During the first Great Prayer Festival (*Monlam Chenmo*) in 1409 the site was occupied by Drubtob Chenpo Kuchora and his successor Ngari Drubtob Chenpo. The first temple was erected by Tsongkhapa's student Tongten (1389-1445), and the second storey added by Pawangka Rinpoche in the early 20th century.

The nuns of Tshamkhung hold regular fasting or *nyun-ne* ceremonies and are responsible for lighting butter lamps in the Jokhang. Restored between 1982-1984, there are now more than 80 nuns at Tshamkhung. The present **assembly hall**, on the second floor, has a Thousand-armed Avalokiteshvara as its main image – with (right side) Tsongkhapa and his students, Vajrayogini, Aksobhya, Shakyamuni and White Tara; and (left side) Amoghasiddhi, Cakrasamvara, Ling Rinpoche, Pawangka Rinpoche and Green Tara. A large centrally suspended tangka depicts Tsongkhapa with his foremost students.

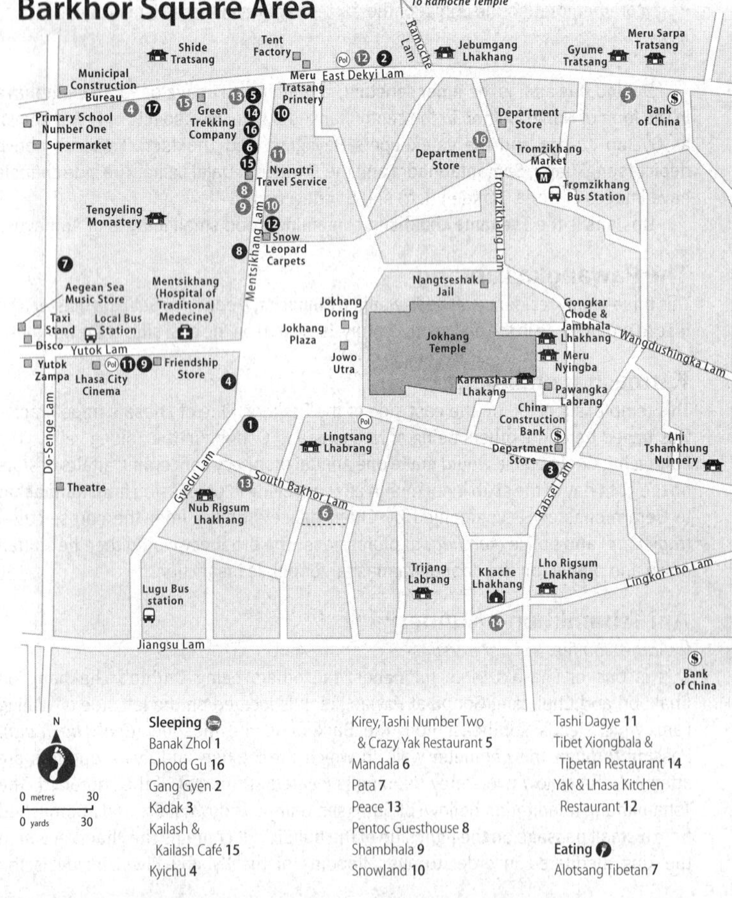

Gyel Lhakhang

Lhasa has around 2,000 Muslims, some descendants of 17th century immigrants from Ladakh and Kashmir, the remainder newly arrived from the Ziling and Linxia regions. At 2,600 sq m, the Gyel Lhakhang is the largest mosque in Lhasa, located at the end of Waling Lam, running from the Sharkyaring flagpole via Ani Tshamkhung. It was constructed in 1716, and subsequently rebuilt twice – in 1793 and 1960. Friday prayers attract over 600 worshippers. The adjacent streets have many Muslim restaurants.

The Small Mosque

Situated due south of the Jokhang and west of Gyel Lhakhang, this mosque buit in the 20th century, has a ground floor bath-house and an upstairs Koranic schoolroom.

Lingtsang Labrang

A two-storey building on the south side of Barkhor Square, with Chinese-style murals and an excellent rooftop view of the Jokhang, this was previously a residence of the late Ling Rinpoche, senior tutor to HH the Fourteenth Dalai Lama.

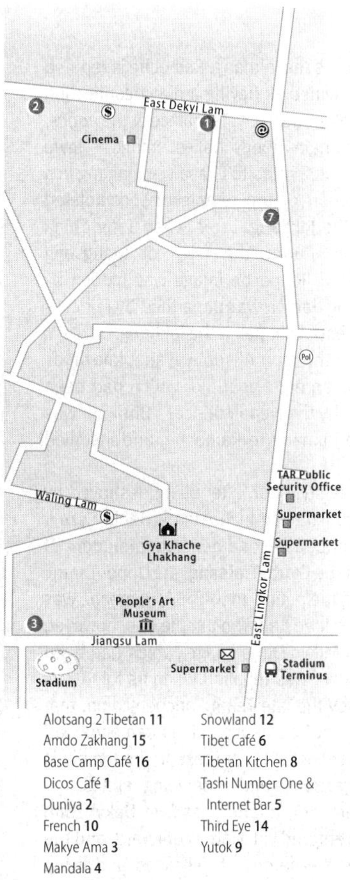

Trijang Labrang

This three-storey building directly south of the Jokhang was once the seat of the late Trijang Rinpoche, the Junior Tutor of HH the Fourteenth Dalai Lama. It is now the headquarters of the Lhasa Cinema Company.

Tonpa

This now dilapidated three-storey building on the south stretch of the Barkhor is said to have once been a residence of Tonmi Sambhota, inventor of the Tibetan script. At present, the building functions as the headquarters of the Barkhor Residents' Committee.

The Mentsikhang (Institute of Tibetan Medicine and Astrology)

The original two-storey Mentsikhang, founded by Dr Khyenrab Norbu in 1916, is opposite the new Lhasa cinema on Yutok Lam. The present multi-storey building slightly to its east functions as the outpatients' department and the offices of the Tibetan Medical and Astrological Research Institute. The penultimate floor until recently housed an exhibition of Tibetan medical artefacts; and the top floor had a shrine dedicated to Yutok Yonten Gonpo, together with Desi Sangye Gyatso and Khyenrab Norbu, as well as a medical tangka exhibition hall.

Yutok Zampa

This renovated ancient bridge 300 m west of the Jokhang, is now contained within the Lhasa Customs Office. Formerly it linked the old city of Lhasa with the suburbs. Named after its 18th-century turquoise-tiled Chinese roof, the bridge is 6.8 m wide and 28.3 m in span; with thick 2-m stone walls that probably date from the seventh century. The bridge has five openings at each end.

The Four Rigsum Lhakhang

These four temples surround the Jokhang in the cardinal directions, each of them containing images of the Lords of the Three Enlightened Families. Among them, the eastern temple, **Shar Rigsum Lhakhang**, was formerly situated opposite the Mosque, the southern one, **Lho Rigsum Lhakhang**, was originally a royal residence and the first building of the Barkhor. Its single-storey chapel is now a private residence. The northern one, the **Jang Rigsum Lhakhang**, once stood opposite the Banakzhol Hotel behind Meru Tratsang, and the western one, the **Nub Rigsum Lhakhang**, was located on a site west of the present Mentsikhang and north of the Yutok Zampa. Of these, only the southern temple survives intact.

Ramoche temple ར་མོ་ཆེ and adjacent tratsangs

Ramoche Temple

ⓘ *Admission: ¥15 per person.*

Location: About 1 km north from Barkhor Square, the temple is on Ramoche Lam across East Dekyi Lam
Maps: Lhasa centre, page 68
Ramoche Temple, page 89

Founded by Princess Wencheng at the same time as the Jokhang, Ramoche is reputed to be the princess's burial site, which she had divined as having a direct connection with the hells or with the subterranean crystal palace of the *nagas*. It originally was built to contain Tibet's holiest image – **Jowo Rinpoche**, which had been transported to Lhasa via Lhagang in a wooden cart. The construction of the temple was completed around the same time as the Jokhang. Later, when Tang China threatened to invade Tibet during the reign of Mangsong Mangtsen (649-676), the Jowo Rinpoche image was hidden by Wencheng in a secret chamber inside the Jokhang; later it was unearthed by Princess Jincheng (post 710) who then installed it in the central chapel of the Jokhang.

As a substitute, an image of Shakyamuni in the form Aksobhyavajra, known as **Jowo Mikyo Dorje**, representing the Buddha as an eight-year old, which had been sculpted by Vishvakarman and brought to Tibet by the Nepali princess Bhrikuti, was taken from the southern inner sanctum of the Jokhang to Ramoche, and installed there as the main image.

Originally, Ramoche was built in the Chinese style but, after being destroyed by fires, the present three-storeyed building was constructed in Tibetan style. In 1474 it was placed under the authority of Kunga Dondrub, a second generation student of Tsongkhapa. It then became the assembly hall of the **Gyuto Tratsang**, the Upper Tantric College of Lhasa and housed 500 monks. During the period 1959-1966, Ramoche was converted into a communist labour training committee hall. The temple has, however, been restored since 1985, and the central Jowo Mikyo Dorje image, which had been severed in two parts during the Cultural Revolution, was repaired when its torso was returned to Tibet, having been found in Beijing by the late Tenth Panchen Lama, that same year. According to some, this image may not be the original, as Ramoche had been damaged by Mongolian incursions in earlier centuries. At present, the temple is once again occupied by the Upper Tantric College monks and undergoing repairs.

Entrance Ramoche is located on Ramoche Lam, a lane near East Dekyi Lam, close by the Tromzikhang market. The temple is entered via a large courtyard, and the ticket office is on the right. Here scribes write the names of deceased and living petitioners in gold ink on red paper, to be offered in the butter lamps of the inner sanctum. The courtyard leads up to an east-facing three-storey gatehouse, containing 10 large fluted columns and two rows of eight Mani Wheels. The upper chambers of the gatehouse contain chapels of later construction and cells for monks.

Khorlam The circumambulatory path around the temple has new rows of Mani Wheels on the south, west and north sides. Outer murals depict the Three Deities of Longevity (*Tselha Namsum*).

Dukhang (Assembly Hall) The assembly hall is approached with the hermitage (*drubkhang*) on the left. This room now functions as a protector chapel, dedicated to Dorje Yudronma, protectress of the Upper Tantric College. The corridor has archaic bas-relief images and beams painted with the Six-Syllabled Mantra, while the right wall has a painting of Dorje Yudronma. By the entrance there is an image of Vajrapani.

The **assembly hall** has a cornice of lion-faced figurines and dakini-faced figurines below the skylight. The central images flank and back the throne of the Dalai Lama. Behind in a glass cabinet are Tsongkhapa with his foremost students: to the left are the First Gyuto Khenpo Kunga Dondrub, Jowo Shakyamuni, Avalokiteshvara, Tara, and then, further left, Guhyasamaja. To the right of the throne are Tsongkhapa, Trijang Rinpoche the Fifth Dalai Lama and Shakyamuni. Against the left wall are images of the three meditational deities Guhyasamaja, Cakrasamvara and Bhairava.

Tsangkhang (Inner Sanctum) Surrounded by an inner circumambulation path (*nangkhor*), the **inner sanctum** is 5.4 by 4.4 m. Here, **Jowo Mikyo Dorje** is seated on a large stone platform, facing west. The entrance is flanked by the Four Guardian Kings. Above the central image are the Seven Generations of Past Buddhas, with the Eight Bodhisattvas to the right and left. The rear wall has images of Tsongkhapa and Maitreya, while the gatekeepers Vajrapani and Hayagriva flank the entrance. Pilgrims have removed plaster from the walls in this chapel, exposing small holes!

Upper Floors The second floor of Ramoche is largely residential; but there is one main chapel containing images of Buddha as King of the *nagas*, surrounded by the Sixteen Elders. An inner sanctum contains images of the Eight Medicine Buddhas and a copy of the *Kangyur*. On the third floor, the front chambers are the Dalai Lama's private apartments, and the rear chamber is a private chapel, enclosed by a wooden balustrade and covered with a gilded roof.

Tsepak Lhakhang

Located south of Ramoche, it has newly sculpted large images of Amitayus, flanked by Shakyamuni and Maitreya. The inner walls have murals depicting the Thirty-five

Ramoche Temple

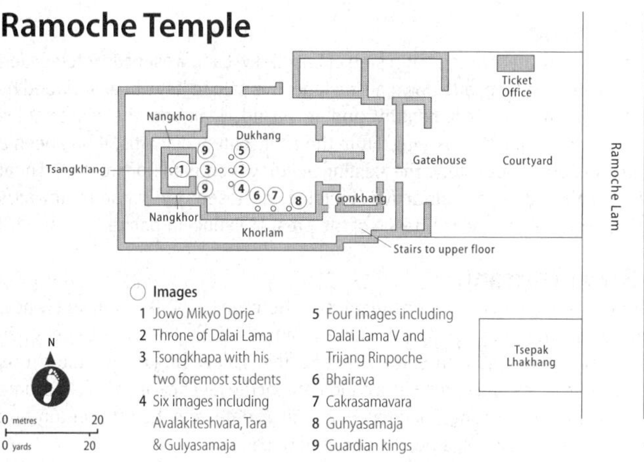

 Confession Buddhas and lineage-holders from all the four major schools of Tibetan Buddhism. In the outer circumambulation path (*korlam*), there are 1,127 wall-painted images of Amitayus, outlined in gold on a red background.

Jebumgang Lhakhang

This temple, located at the junction of Ramoche Lam and East Dekyi Lam, behind the public toilets, is dedicated to Tsongkhapa and it contains 100,000 small images of this master. The building was used as a granary during the Cultural Revolution.

Gyume Tratsang

Gyume Tratsang, the Lower Tantric College of Lhasa, is located on East Dekyi Lam across the street from the Tibet-Gansu Trade Centre and the Kirey Hotel. A number of tantric colleges were established by Tsongkhapa's student Je Sherab Senge (1382-1445), including Se Gyupa (in Tsang), Chumelung (west of Lhasa), and Gyume Tratsang, and those affiliated directly with Tsel Gungtang, Sera, Dechen and Meldro. Among these, the present Gyume complex dates from its reconstruction by Kalon Techen Phagto in the 18th century.

The **ground floor**, approached from the debating courtyard, houses the press for the Lhasa *Kangyur*, and a large assembly hall with an **inner sanctum** (*tsangkhang*) containing new 6-m images of Tsongkhapa and his students. An adjacent protector shrine contains murals of the meditational deities Guhyasamaja, Cakrasamvara and Bhairava, along with the protectors Mahakala, Shridevi, Dharmaraja and Vaishravana.

On the **second floor** of the main temple is the **Dolma Lhakhang**, the images of which include (left to right): Manjughosa, Vajrapani, Tara, Amitayus, Shakyamuni, Tsongkhapa with students, Maitreya in the form of Jampa Chokhorma, Cakrasamvara (with a 'speaking' Tara to the rear), Guhyasamaja, the Thirteenth Dalai Lama, Tsongkhapa, Je Sherab Senge (the founder of Gyume), and Maitreya. New murals on the west wall depict the Eight Aspects of Tara and Vijaya. A balcony attached to the Dolma Lhakhang overlooks the north inner chapel of the ground floor mentioned above.

On the third floor is the **Kangyur Lhakhang** with an old bronze Shakyamuni as its centrepiece, flanked by a set of the *Kangyur* volumes. Its west wall has images of Tsongkhapa and his foremost students. An adjacent **Zhalre Lhakhang** overlooks the 6-m images on the ground floor.

The fourth level contains the private apartments (*zimchung*) of the Dalai Lamas. The Gelukpa tantric study programme at such colleges was known for its austere strictness, and, at Gyume, was accessible only to senior monks from Ganden, Sera and Drepung. Currently there are about 40 monks here.

Shide Tratsang

Shide Tratsang is located on the north side of East Dekyi Lam, west of its intersection with the Mentsikhang Lam, and down a side lane. It is said to have been founded by King Relpachen in the ninth century and is included among the six temples traditionally surrounding the Jokhang. From the 14th century onwards, it has been a dependency of Reting Monastery. The existing building is entered from roof level near the **Reting Labrang** – an attractive building enclosed by gardens towards Tsomonling, which is still the residence of the present Reting Rinpoche.

Meru Sarpa Tratsang

Meru Sarpa Tratsang is located opposite the Kirey Hotel on East Dekyi Lam, but is now occupied by the TAR Theatre Troupe. There is an assembly hall with three small chapels. Formerly affiliated with Shide Tratsang, this college broke away after 1684 and later, after 1912, its preceptor was a candidate for the regency. Its monks became affiliated with **Gyume Tratsang**. The present buildings date from the 19th century and were constructed by Sakya Nga-pe, the abbot of Nechung.

Regency temples of Tengyeling and Tsomonling

The regency temples of Kundeling, Tengyeling, Tsomonling and Tsechokling were constructed during the 17th century after the Fifth Dalai Lama had assumed both spiritual and temporal power. Among these, Tengyeling and Tsomonling are in Inner Lhasa, Kundeling lies to the south of Parmari in the western area of the city, and Tsechokling lies south of the Kyi-chu River.

Tengyeling བསྟན་རྒྱས་གླིང་

Tengyeling is located behind the Mentsikhang in a lane, the entrance of which directly faces the Snowland Hotel. The main assembly hall once contained three eastern chapels, approached by a triple entrance, and an interior western hall; but the compound of the monastery is presently occupied by Tibetan homes and the Lhasa No 1 Middle School. Only the **Protector Chapel (Gonkhang)**, at roof level, is now active. Affiliated with Samye Monastery, it contains reconstructed images of Cimara flanked on the left by Pehar and Padmasambhava, and on the right by Hayagriva and Vajrakumara. Formerly the most important of the regency temples, Tengyeling was the seat of the successive Demo Qutuqtus, who provided three regents of Tibet – the first during the period of the Eighth Dalai Lama from 1757-1777, the second during the period of the Ninth and Tenth Dalai Lamas from 1810 to 1819, and the third from 1886-1895 when he was deposed by the Thirteenth Dalai Lama when he assumed power. When Chao Erh-feng invaded Lhasa in 1910, Tengyeling offered support – for which reason the monastery was later damaged by the Tibetans in 1912, and converted temporarily into a post office. In its place, Meru Sarpa (opposite the Kirey Hotel) was classed as a regency temple.

The residence of the Demo Qutuqtu (**Demo Labrang**) to the north has now been transformed into the Kyichu Hotel on East Dekyi Lam. Slightly west of this building is a new Government Reception Centre, built to receive Tibetans returning from abroad.

Tsomonling ཚོ་སྨོན་གླིང་

Tsomonling (properly pronounced *Tsemonling*) is south of Ramoche. The large courtyard is surrounded on three sides by two-storey monastic cells, which are now occupied by the laity. The building on the north side of the courtyard has two wings: the **Karpo Podrang** in the east and the **Marpo Podrang** in the west. The former is a three-storey building, dating from 1777, which contains the assembly hall, the reliquary chamber of Numun the First and Second Qan, and six chapels (ground floor), the protector chapel (second floor), and the residence of the monastic preceptors (third floor). The latter, dating from the 19th century, contains the assembly hall with reliquaries of Nomun the Third and Fourth Qan, two protector chapels, and a chapel dedicated to the Eight Medicine Buddhas. Tsomonling is the residence of the successive Nomun Qan Qutuqtus, two of whom served as regents: during the period of the Eighth Dalai Lama from 1777-1784, and during the period of the Tenth and Eleventh Dalai Lamas from 1819 until 1844, when the incumbent was exiled to China.

Lingkhor Lam

Named after the traditional pilgrimage circuit around the city of Lhasa and the Potala Palace in particular, this motor route is still frequented by devotees who come from all parts of Tibet to circumambulate the holy city. There are three sections: West Lingkhor Lam, extending northeast from the Golden Yak Roundabout towards Lhalu; North Lingkhor Lam, extending due east behind the Potala Palace and Lukhang Temple as far as the Workers' Roundabout; and East Lingkhor Lam, extending due south from the Roundabout to the riverside. The actual pilgrimage circuit is then completed on present-day Chingdrol Lam and Dekyilngka Lam.

On West Lingkhor Lam, after the Foreign Trade Company and the Gyugyu Gyakoling Hotpot Restaurant on the left, you will pass the Bank of China Head Office, where foreign currency can be exchanged, the Tibet Development Fund, the renowned Lhalu Middle School, China Agricultural Bank, and the TAR Government Reception Vehicle Unit; and on the right, overshadowed by the Potala Palace, the side entrance to the TAR Television and Broadcasting Head Office. There are activity centres for women, children and workers in Lukhang Park.

Turning onto North Lingkhor Lam, you then pass, on the left side of the road, the TAR Political Affairs Head Office, the TAR United Front Department, the People's Publishing House Bookstore, and (after the Nyangdren Lam intersection) the Tuberculosis Control Centre, the TAR Electric Company, the Friendship Guesthouse, the TAR Architectural Survey and Design Institute, the TAR Geology and Mineral HQ, the TAR Office of Foreign Affairs, the terminus for the number six bus, Lhasa City Police HQ, an industrial training school and the Ying Qiao Hotel. On the right side, you will pass the north face of the Potala Palace, the Lukhang Temple and its surrounding park, and (after the Nyangdren Lam intersection), China Construction Bank, the TAR People's Hospital (*Mimang Menkhang*), the Emergency Heath Clinic, the Ramoche Lam turn-off which leads to Ramoche Temple (see page 88), Number Three High School, the TAR Meteorological Bureau and the Telecommunications Building.

Lastly, on East Langkhor Lam you will pass the Dargye Hotel, the Municipal Communist Party HQ, lawcourts, and public security buildings, and (after the Dekyi Lam intersection), the Banak Zhol Gonkhang, the Pata Hotel, the TAR Public Security Bureau, small supermarkets, the Gyel Lhakhang Mosque and the Boot Factory. Crossing Chingdrol Lam and continuing on the last section of East Lingkhor Lam, you will then pass the west Hebaling Post Office, a large supermarket, Middle School Number One, the lane leading to the Postal Training College. small grocery stores, and an internet café, while to the east are the terminus for the number eight bus, small restaurants, a camping store, the TAR Mountaineering Institute, the Himalaya Hotel and (on a lane) the Old Post Hotel.

Potala Palace རྩེ་པོ་ཏ་ལའི་ཕོ་བྲང

ⓘ *Admission: ¥45 per person. Open 0900-1600 except Sun, longer on Wed and Sat. Some rooms closed 1230-1430.*

Location: About 2 km northwest from Barkhor Square, the palace lies outside of the Old City on East Dekyi lam
Maps: Lhasa centre, page 68
Red Palace, Potala, page 97

Aptly named after Mount Potalaka, the sacred mountain abode of the Bodhisattva of Compassion, Avalokiteshvara, the Potala Palace has been identified in different ages as the residence of Tibet's two illustrious and kingly emanations of Avalokiteshvara – Songtsen Gampo during the seventh century and the Fifth Dalai Lama during the 17th century. The building which towers above the city of Lhasa rises from the slopes of Mount Marpori, for which reason it is known locally as **Tse Podrang** ('Summit Palace'). The outer section, known as the **White Palace** has functioned as the traditional seat of government and the winter residence of the Dalai Lamas, while the inner section known as the **Red Palace** contains outstanding temples and the reliquary tombs of eight past Dalai Lamas. In terms of global perception, it is this relic of Tibet's past, present, and future national aspirations which, more than any other, symbolizes the country, like the Great Wall in China or the Vatican in Italy. This 13-storeyed edifice was among the world's tallest buildings prior to the advent of the 20th-century skyscraper, and undoubtedly the grandest building in Tibet. It can be seen from many places – from the outer circumambulatory path (*lingkhor*), from Kumalingka Island, from the adjacent Chakpori Hill, from the Jokhang roofs, to name but some. Wherever one goes in downtown Lhasa, the resplendent golden roofs of the Potala are visible on the skyline.

Ins and outs

Getting there While tourists normally approach from the rear drive-in entrance on the north side of Mount Marpori to avoid the steep climb, the main entrance is from the Eastern Gatehouse above Potala Square on West Dekyi Lam. The outer walls of the Potala form a quadrangle, with fortified gates to the south, east and west, and Mount Marpori to the north. There are watch-towers at the southeast and southwest corners. The auxiliary buildings in front include the Zhamarpa Palace, the Printing Press (*Parkhang*), the Kashag offices and the prison.

The two printing presses are particularly significant: the **Ganden Phuntsoling Parkhang** (southeast corner) is a two-storey 600 sq m structure, contemporary with the White Palace. Its woodblocks which dated from 17th-18th century have been destroyed except for a few which were transferred to the Mentsikhang. The **Gang-gyen Potidengtsunkhang** was constructed during the reign of the Thirteenth Dalai Lama and funded by the 91st Ganden Tripa, whose reliquary is within its grounds. It is a vast six-storey building at the western perimeter wall, containing the Zhol edition of the *Kangyur* and *Tangyur* (second floor). The actual printing room is on the third floor in the **Jampa Lhakhang**, where precious images of Maitreya along with Atisha and Tsongkhapa, Amitayus, King Trisong Detsen, Padmasambhava and White Tara have all been destroyed. The **protector chapel** (*gonkhang*) on the third floor was built only in 1949 but its enormous Bhairava image has also been destroyed. In addition to the woodblocks, the building houses the religious archives of the Tibetan Autonomous Region, and only a small part of this collection has been moved to the new Tibet National Library on Norbulingka Lam.

Traditionally the chapels of the Potala were only open to the public on set days such as the fourth day of the sixth lunar month, and in the fourth lunar month. Now, in the absence of the Dalai Lama, it has the air of a museum, and is accessible six days a week. **NB** pilgrims may enter throughout the day on Wednesday and Saturday so queues will be longer. Also, in the peak seasons (April-October) it is important to book tickets well in advance since visitors can only be admitted at 20-minute intervals in groups of 60.

The Potala

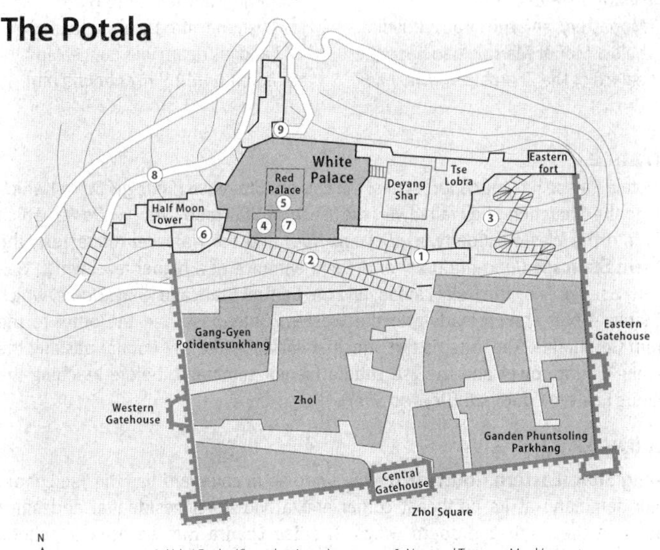

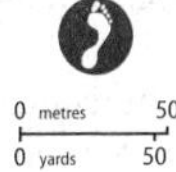

1 U-kyi Do-ke (Central staircase)
2 Nub-kyi Do-ke (Western staircase)
3 Shar-gyi Do-ke (Eastern staircase)
4 Deyang Nub
5 Tsokchen Nub
6 Namgyel Tratsang Monk's quarters
7 Tangka rooms
8 Jang-gi Do-ke (North staircase)
9 Exit to north car park

History of the Potala Palace

Little remains of the original 11-storeyed Potala Palace which King Songtsen Gampo built on Mount Marpori in 637. An illustration of this earlier structure, which was destroyed by lightning in the reign of King Trisong Detsen, is found on the outer wall of the Lamrim Lhakhang in the Red Palace. It appears, however, that the foundations of the present palace date from the earlier period, as do two of the chapels in the Red Palace, namely the Songtsen Nyipuk and the Phakpa Lhakhang (see below, page 98).

When Lhasa was reinstated as the capital of Tibet in the 17th century, after a period of 900 years, during which the seat of government had been successively at Sakya, Tsetang, Rinpung and Zhigatse, one of the first acts to be carried out by the Fifth Dalai Lama was the reconstruction of this national symbol. Prior to its completion, he himself lived at the Ganden Palace in Drepung Monastery, and the largest building below Mount Marpori had been the palace of the Zhamarpas, who had dominated the political life of Lhasa until the defeat of their powerful patrons at Zhigatse in 1641. Nonetheless, the fortress (dzong) of the Kings of Zhigatse is said to have been taken as the prototype or model for the construction of the new Potala Palace.

The Fifth Dalai Lama preserved the original foundations of the seventh-century edifice and had the White Palace built between 1645 and 1653. 7,000 workers and 1,500 artisans were employed on this construction, along with Manchu and Newar artists. The murals of the east wing and the Kangyur Lhakhang were completed in 1648, and the following year he moved from Drepung. The Inner Zhol Obelisk (Doring Nangma) was constructed to commemorate this event.

The central upper part, known as the Red Palace, is mostly attributed to the regent Desi Sangye Gyatso (r 1679-1703) and dated 1690-93. Its interior was finished in 1697. However, the Fifth Dalai Lama died in 1682 and his death was concealed by the regent until 1694, enabling him

Entrance

The Potala Palace has four approaches: the **Eastern Staircase** (*Shar-gyi Do-ke*) which leads to the Sharchen Chok jail tower; the **Western Staircase** (*Nub-kyi Do-ke*) which leads into the Western Courtyard (*Deyang Nub*) and the Namgyel Monastery; the **Northern Staircase** (*Jang-gi Do-ke*) or drive-in entrance at a higher level which was formerly used only by the Dalai Lamas; and the **Central Staircase** (*U-kyi Do-ke*) which bifurcates – one branch leading to the Western Gatehouse and the other to the Eastern Gatehouse. The latter is the principal entrance into the Potala, passing the Taktsang Gormo tower and the Tse Lobdra (senior seminary), before reaching the spacious Eastern Courtyard (*Deyang Shar*).

The White Palace

Deyang Shar (Eastern Courtyard) This 1,500 sq m courtyard has the Tse Lobdra (senior seminary) at its northeast corner and a two-storey residential and office complex in the north and south wings. The **Tse Lobdra** was an eclectic school, founded by the Seventh Dalai Lama (1708-1757), which drew teachers from Mindroling and elsewhere.

The four-storeyed eastern façade of the White Palace overlooks this courtyard, the Dalai Lama's private apartments being in the uppermost gallery. A triple to complete the task without the distraction of political upheavals. There is also an extant Jesuit drawing, dated 1661, which interestingly suggests that two storeys of the Red Palace were actually constructed before his demise. Work on the funerary chapel was carried out between 1692-4, costing 2.1 million taels of silver.

Renovations

Enlargement continued through the 18th century. Then, in 1922, the renovation of the chapels and halls adjacent to the Phakpa Lhakhang was undertaken, along with that of the East Wing of the White Palace, and the Zhol printing press was enlarged. In 1959 the south façade was shelled during the suppression of the Lhasa Uprising, but the damaged porch of the Red Palace and the Potala School (Tse Lobdra) were subsequently restored by the late Tenth Panchen Lama. The most recent renovations have taken place since 1991: the inner walls have been strengthened, the electrical supply stabilized, and extraneous buildings in the foreground of the palace removed to create a large square. Recent indications suggest, however, that these structural changes have not been particularly effective. In August 2001 part of the White Palace's southern facade subsided, probably on account of the excessive number of visitors using the walkways above it (although heavy rainfall might also have contributed). The situation is critical in that the traditional masonry skills employed in the 17th-century construction of the Potala are no longer to be found in Tibet (even in Tsang). The repair was assigned to a Beijing contractor who did little but plant trees to conceal the damaged façade. Repairs were finally completed in 2004. In the meantime visitors to the Potala are obliged to enter and leave by different pathways.

Altogether, the interior area of the 13-storeyed Potala Palace is 130,000 sq m. The building is 118 m high, 366 m from east to west, and 335 m from north to south. There are 1,000 rooms, housing approximately 200,000 images.

wooden ladder (*Sum-ke Go*) leads from the courtyard to the entrance foyer and the main gate. The south wall of the foyer depicts the gold handprints (*chak-je*) of the Thirteenth Dalai Lama and an edict of the Fifth Dalai Lama, proclaiming Desi Sangye Gyatso as his regent. The murals here depict the Four Guardian Kings, the construction of the Mentsikhang on Mount Chakpori, the arrival of Princess Wencheng, and the Jokhang construction.

Ascend the four flights of stairs to the roof of the White Palace, where the private apartments of the Dalai Lamas are located.

Eastern Private Apartments (Nyiwo Shar Ganden Nangsel) The gate leading into the living quarters of the Fourteenth Dalai Lama is marked by tiger-skin maces. The **outer reception room** has an elaborately decorated throne, flanked by portraits of the Thirteenth Dalai Lama and, until recently, the present Fourteenth Dalai Lama. On the northwest wall adjacent to the entrance there is a fine mural depicting the legendary land of Shambhala; and on the southeast wall there is a cracked mural depicting the Mahabodhi Temple at Vajrasana in India. A balcony overlooks the Eastern Courtyard, and there are antechambers on the southeast and southwest corners, which lead into the Dalai Lama's private quarters. These rooms include an **audience chamber** for informal receptions, foreign visitors, and the sealing of official documents. Its altars contain images which include Simhavaktra, and the Three Deities of Longevity (*Tselha Namsum*) and there is an interesting mural illustrating Dhanyakataka, the sacred abode in South India where the *Kalacakra Tantra* was first revealed. A small **Protector Chapel (Gonkhang)** has statues of Six-armed Mahakala, Shridevi, Dorje Drakden, and a table replete with the Dalai Lama's personal ritual implements. The **bedroom/dining room** with its images of the Three Deities of Longevity and Tsongkhapa mural is preserved as it was at the time of the Dalai Lama's departure in 1959. An inner door leads to the bathroom.

Western Private Apartments (Nyiwo Nub Sonam Lekhyil) The living quarters of the previous Dalai Lamas consist of an ornate **reception hall** where audience would be given to the Tibetan cabinet and Manchu ambans, a **bedroom** with murals hand-painted by the Thirteenth Dalai Lama, and an **audience chamber** where government council meetings would be held. This last room contains images of Thubwang Tazurma, Je Tashi Dokarma, Padmasambhava and the Fifth Dalai Lama.

East Main Hall (Tsomchen Shar Sizhi Phuntsok) The East Main Hall is the largest chamber in the White Palace (25.8 m by 27.8 m), with 64 pillars, extending three storeys in height. It was in this hall that each successive Dalai Lama was enthroned, the New Year commemorated, and credentials received from Manchu envoys. The murals depict events from early Tibetan history and the background of the different Dalai Lamas. An inscription in Chinese above the throne reads "May the emancipating service of the Dharma be spread throughout the Universe". The **Golden Urn** from which the names of certain later Dalai and Panchen Lamas were controversially drawn has been removed and is now exhibited in the Tibet National Museum (see below, page 129).

Tangka Rooms Between the White Palace and the Red Palace, there is a yellow building in which the two extant giant appliqué tangkas (*go-ku*) are kept. These were traditionally unfurled from the walls of the Potala at the beginning of the Yoghurt Festival; and since 1994 they have once again been on occasional display at this time of the year. The third tangka was offered to **Batang Monastery** in the early decades of the present century.

Namgyel Monastery and Western Courtyard The Western Courtyard (*Deyang Nub*) serves as a focal point for the **Namgyel Monastery**, which was originally founded at Drepung by the Third Dalai Lama. At the southern perimeter of the courtyard are the monks' cells from which the giant appliqué tangkas were unfurled. The walls of the Namgyel Monastery depict the protector deities and lamas of all the four major lineages.

The Red Palace

Unlike the White Palace which was used for administrative purposes and as a residence, the Red Palace, which looms from the centre of the White Palace, has a spiritual function. Its many temples are interspersed with the eight golden reliquary stupas (*serdung*) containing the embalmed remains of the Fifth Dalai Lama and the Seventh to Thirteenth Dalai Lamas. Four floors extend below the south façade of the Red Palace, but are there only for aesthetic reasons. The north façade is constructed on solid rock. The functional part of the Red Palace has four floors, which are aligned with all but the highest of the storeys of the White Palace.

The **West Main Hall** (*Tsokchen Nub*) is the central structure of the Red Palace. It is surrounded on all four sides by chapels two storeys high, entered from the ground level of the atrium; while the upper three floors have running galleries, reached by a series of ladders and trap-doors. The galleries of the upper two storeys connect on the outward side with a further series of chapels, and inwardly via footbridges with a central pavilion, which is constructed to allow light to filter into the West Main Hall below.

Access to the Red Palace is from the roof of the Potala via an entrance to the fourth floor facing the West Private Apartments (*Nyiwo Nub Sonam Lekhyil*).

Fourth Floor Jamkhang Phuntsok Khyil (east) This chapel contains a large gilded-copper image of Maitreya, which was commissioned by the Eighth Dalai Lama in honour of his relative, the deceased mother of the Sixth Panchen Palden Yeshe. Facing the image is the throne of the Eighth Dalai Lama. The library is positioned on the far wall, containing the *Kangyur*, *Tangyur*, and the *Collected Works of the Fifth Dalai Lama*. Images adjacent to Maitreya include the Fifth Dalai Lama (containing clippings from his own hair), the Three Deities of Longevity (*Tselha Namsum*), the Lords of the Three Enlightened Families (Riksum Gonpo), Acala, Samayatara, Padmasambhava and Kalacakra. A wooden three-dimensional palace (*vimana*) of the meditational deity Kalacakra is kept in the corner. Many old tangkas were destroyed in this chapel by an electrical fire in 1984.

Red Palace (Potala)

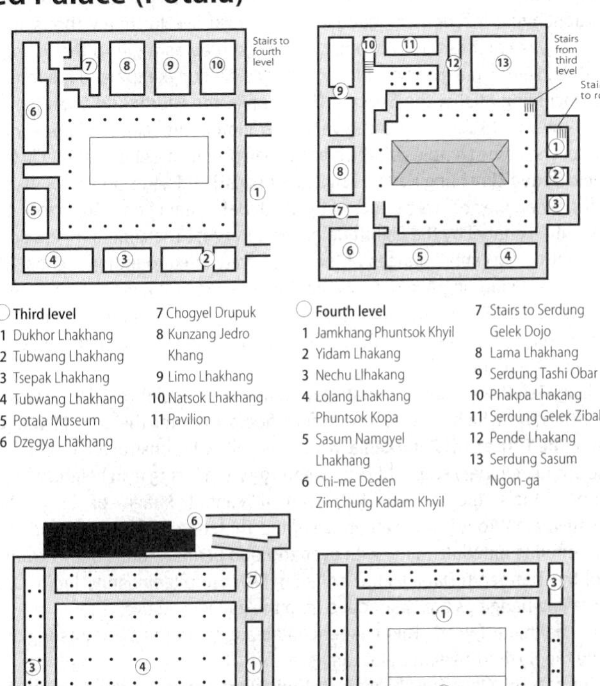

Ground level
1 Lamrim Lhakhang
2 Rigdzin Lhakhang
3 Serdung Dzamling Gyenchik
4 Tsomchen Nub Sizhi Phuntsok
5 Trungrab Lhakhang
6 Exit to north gate
7 Stairs to second level

Second level
1 Running galleries
2 Skylight
3 Stairs to third level

Yidam Lhakhang (east) This chapel once contained the golden reliquary of the Tenth Dalai Lama before its removal to the floor below. In its place the central image depicts the Seventh Dalai Lama, fashioned of medicinal clay and flanked by the various meditational deities, among them Guhyasamaja, Cakrasamvara and Vajrabhairava.

Nechu Lhakhang (east) The main images of this recently reopened narrow chapel are Shakyamuni, flanked by Shariputra, Maudgalyayana, the Sixteen Elders, and Kurukulla. Outside in the gallery, a staircase gives access to the anterior roof of the Red Palace, and visitors are charged ¥10 for the privilege of this panoramic view.

Lolang Lhakhang Phuntsok Kopa (southeast) Originally constructed by Desi Sangye Gyatso, this chapel contains the celebrated three-dimensional mandalas of the meditational deities Guhyasamaja, Cakrasamvara, and Bhairava, which were commissioned in 1749 by the Seventh Dalai Lama, an image of whom is adjacent to the throne; and the murals depict his own life, as well as the ordination of Tibet's first seven trial monks in the eighth century. There are also many small images representative of all four major schools of Tibetan Buddhism.

Sasum Namgyel Lhakhang (south) This former residential chamber was converted into a chapel by the Seventh Dalai Lama whose throne it contains. The west wall has a large silver image of Eleven-faced Avalokiteshvara (285 kg) which was commissioned by the Thirteenth Dalai Lama. A portrait of Emperor Qianlong on the north wall was an enthronement gift to the Eighth Dalai Lama, dated 1762. Beneath it is the quadrilingual inscription "May Emperor Kangxi live for many thousands of years!". This was commissioned in 1722, and presented as a gift to the young the Seventh Dalai Lama. In a glass cabinet are images of Tsongkhapa and his foremost students, including Atisha, the Seventh Dalai Lama, the Fourth and Sixth Panchen Lamas. On the wall to the left is a 120-volume edition of the Manchu *Kangyur*, with trilingual covers, some samples of which have been placed in a glass cabinet in front.

Chi-me Deden Zimchung Kadam Khyil (southwest) This, the largest room on the fourth floor, functioned as a residence of the Sixth Dalai Lama from 1697-1706. It was converted into a chapel by the Eighth Dalai Lama in 1797. The central image depicts Amitayus, with 1,000 small images of the same deity in surrounding niches. Other images include a standing Avalokiteshvara, the masters of the graduated (*lam-rim*) lineage, the Sixteen Elders, the Four Guardian Kings, Tsongkhapa (from China) and the Nyingmapa protectress Ekajati. The murals depict the early Kadampa lineage-holders and Indian kings.

Serdung Gelek Dojo (west) A gateway leads via an enclosed passageway to a staircase, through which one descends four floors to enter the well lit **reliquary chamber of the Thirteenth Dalai Lama**. A viewing gallery is constructed on the fourth floor. The ornate reliquary stupa, built between 1934-1936, is 13 m in height, weighing over 10,000 taels (about 270 kg), with a central image of Eleven-faced Avalokiteshvara. In front is a newer image of the Thirteenth Dalai Lama; and on the altar is an offering mandala made with over 200,000 pearls. Murals depict events in the life of the Thirteenth Dalai Lama, including his 1910 pilgrimage to India. Ornate brocade ceiling hangings are suspended from the galleries above.

Lama Lhakhang (west) This chapel contains a central image of Tsongkhapa, flanked by the Sixth to Twelfth Dalai Lamas.

Serdung Tashi Obar (northwest) The **reliquary chapel of the Seventh Dalai Lama** has a multi-doored entrance. The stupa itself is 9 m in height, with 100,000 precious stones, and flanked by a silver image of the Seventh Dalai Lama, gilded copper images of Maitreya and the Eight Bodhisattvas and a silver reliquary containing remains of Lha Lama Jangchub-o.

Phakpa Lhakhang (north) This is the most revered chapel within the Potala Palace, dating from the original seventh century construction. It houses a **naturally arisen gilded sandalwood image of Avalokiteshvara** which was one of four discovered in Nepal by Akaramatishila in the seventh century, when a sandalwood trunk split open. The triple staircase entrance is surmounted above the door with a trilingual inscription "Wondrous Fruit of the Field of Merit", which was presented by the Manchu Emperor Tongzhi in the 19th century. The central image is flanked by two other standing images representing Tara and Avalokiteshvara. To the left are the Tenth Dalai Lama and Tsongkhapa, while to the right are the Eighth and Ninth Dalai Lamas. Other statues include Kharsapani from Tanak, red sandalwood images of the Eight Bodhisattvas (commissioned by the Fifth Dalai Lama), silver images of the Lords of the Three Enlightened Families, Eleven-faced Avalokiteshvara, and Shakyamuni with the Sixteen Elders.

Inside the cabinet on the left are stone footprints of Padmasambhava (from Gungtang Pass), Tsongkhapa and Nagarjuna; an image of Jetsun Drakpa Gyeltsen called Dzetoma, an image of Panchen Shakyashri (in Tibet from 1204-1214), a jade image of Drogon Chogyel Phakpa Lodro Gyeltsen and an image of Tangtong Gyelpo. To the right of the door, adjacent to a large Vajrapani image, is an old image of Atisha.

Outside, note the bell and the statue of the Sixth Panchen Lama overlooking the approach to this chapel.

Serdung Gelek Zibar (north) This chapel contains the **reliquary stupa of the Thirteenth Dalai Lama**, which was constructed in 1805. The stupa has an inset image of Eleven-faced Avalokiteshvara. Other images include: the Eighth Dalai Lama, Buddha in the form of Tuwang Dudul (commissioned by the Ninth Dalai Lama), and an appliqué tangka depicting Tibet's first king, Nyatri Tsenpo.

Pende Lhakhang (north) This small chapel contains images of the protector deities Chamsing, six-armed Mahakala, and their retainers.

Serdung Sasum Ngon-ga (northeast) This chapel contains the golden **reliquary stupa of the Ninth Dalai Lama**, along with his image in silver, and 114 volumes of the *Kangyur* inscribed in gold, a silver image of Tsongkhapa, and further images of the Sixteen Elders, which were commissioned by the Eighth Dalai Lama.

Third Floor Dukhor Lhakhang (east) The gilded copper three-dimensional palace of the meditational deity Kalacakra (6.2 m in diameter), contained in this chapel, was constructed by Desi Sangye Gyatso. There is also a life-size image of Kalacakra, surrounded by the 172 Kalacakra lineage-holders. On the right are seven religious kings of Tibet and the 25 kings (*khalki*) of Shambhala; as well as a gilt Enlightenment Stupa (*Jangchub Chorten*), eight silver stupas symbolizing the major events of the Buddha's life, and images of Manjughosa, Shridevi, Padmasambhava, and 38 deities in the retinue of Kalacakra. The murals depict Shambhala and the Kalacakra lineages.

Tubwang Lhakhang (southeast) This chapel contains the throne of the Seventh Dalai Lama, and images depicting Shakyamuni, surrounded by the eight standing bodhisattvas, and a manuscript edition of the *Kangyur*.

Tsepak Lhakhang (south) This chapel contains images of the nine aspects of Amitayus; flanked by White Tara and Green Tara. The murals depict the Potala Palace during the late 18th century, as well as the charismatic master Tangtong Gyelpo and the iron bridge constructed by him across the Brahmaputra at Chuwori Chakzam.

Tubwang Lhakhang (southwest) Here the central image is Shakyamuni Buddha, flanked by the Eight Bodhisattvas. There is also a throne of the Seventh Dalai Lama, a manuscript *Kangyur*, and decorations commissioned by the Eighth Dalai Lama.

Potala Museum (west) This exhibition of precious artefacts extracted from other halls and chapels of the palace (admission ¥10) includes excellent tangkas representative of different painting styles.

Dzegya Lhakhang (west) This chapel, constructed by Sangye Gyatso, contains a cubit-sized image of Shakyamuni, fashioned out of medicinal clay, and together with the Sixteen Elders with background scenes depicting the hundred deeds of Shakyamuni.

Chogyel Drupuk (northwest) This hermitage, along with Phakpa Lhakhang mentioned above, is the oldest chamber of the Potala Palace, approached by a ramp which leads into a recessed cavern, supported by one large column which rises through to the floor above and seven smaller columns. There are 28 images in the room. In a niche in the south face of the tall column is an image of the Fifth Dalai Lama, and at its base the stove of King Songtsen Gampo. Of the 28 images, the main deities depicted are Maitreya (1.5 m), Avalokiteshvara (twice), Shaykamuni, Vaishravana and White Tara. Most depict historical personages, such as the youthful clean-shaven Fifth Dalai Lama along with archaic images of Songtsen Gampo, his two foreign queens and Minister Gar Tongtsen (north); King Gungri Gungtsen and Minister Tonmi Sambhota (west); Tsongkhapa, Songtsen Gampo with Queen Mongza Tricham and other members of the royal family (east); and, lastly, Songtsen Gampo with Lama Zhang (south).

Kunzang Jedro Khang (north) This small chapel contains a gilded copper image of Munindra flanked by gilded copper images of Avalokiteshvara, the five meditational buddhas, Padmasambhava and Mahakarunika, which were recently offered to the Potala by the Tibetan businessman Tenpa Dargye.

Lima Lhakhang (north) This adjoining chapel contains a selection of alloy images from Kashmir, India, Turkestan and Nepal, as well as some important ones of Tibetan origin from Reting and Nedong. The larger ones include Tsongkhapa, Amitayus, Six-armed Mahakala and Shridevi.

Natsok Lhakhang (north) The final chapel on the north wing contains a variety of small alloy images of various origins.

Kunzang Chotrinkhang (centre) The pavilion in the centre of the gallery, accessed via a gangplank or catwalk, was originally conceived as a receptacle for offerings to be presented to the reliquary of the Fifth Dalai Lama. Nowadays it functions as a reception hall, tea room and curio shop for visitors.

Second Floor The chapels on the second floor, which overlook the reliquaries of the floor below are closed to the public. However, there are **extraordinary murals** depicting the construction of the Potala Palace and various renowned monasteries, the Great Prayer Festival of Lhasa, and the funeral procession of the Fifth Dalai Lama, whose reliquary stupa is surrounded by gates which are particularly revered by pilgrims.

First Floor West Main Hall (*Tsomchen Nub Sizhi Phuntsok*) At 725 sq m, the West Main Hall is the largest room in the Potala Palace. It has eight tall and 36 short pillars, wrapped in raw silk. The central throne of the Sixth Dalai Lama is surmounted by a plaque, presented by Emperor Qianlong, which carries the legend 'originally pure lotus place'. The 280 sq m murals, dating from the 17th century, depict the Fifth Dalai Lama, the Buddha-field of Mount Potalaka and the Tibetan kings. In the centre of the hall, there is a poorly executed new tapestry depicting the Potala Palace, but note the two other large exquisitely embroidered tapestries depicting the Three Ancestral Religious Kings and the Dalai Lamas, which were presented by Emperor Kangxi. Appliqué tangkas depict Amitabha and the Seven Generations of Past Buddhas, surrounded by the Thirty-five Confession Buddhas (north); the four main Kadampa deities flanked by the Eight Bodhisattvas and Tara who Protects from the Eight Fears (east); the Buddhas of the Three Times surrounded by the Sixteen Elders (south); and the Medicine Buddhas, the Lords of the Three Enlightened Families, and the Seven Generations of Past Buddhas (west).

The four side chapels were originally constructed by Desi Sangye Gyatso:

Lamrim Lhakhang (east) is dedicated to the ancient Indian and Tibetan masters of the 'extensive lineage of conduct' and the 'profound lineage of view', as represented by the Kadampa and Gelukpa schools. In the centre is a gilded silver image of Tsongkhapa, with Asanga (progenitor of the Kadampa) to the right, and Nagarjuna (progenitor of the Gelukpa) to the left. Near the right wall are two Enlightenment Stupas.

Rigdzin Lhakhang (south) is dedicated to the ancient Indian lineage-holders of the Nyingma school and has 20 columns. The central image, weighing 40 kg, depicts Padmakara, flanked by the consorts Mandarava and Yeshe Tshogyel. To the left are gilded silver images of the Eight Awareness-Holders (*Vidyadhara*), who were the teachers of Padmasambhava; and to the right are similar images representing the Eight Manifestations of Padmasambhava. Behind on the east, west, and south walls are the volumes of a *Kangyur* manuscript in gold and black ink.

Serdung Dzamling Gyenchik (west) contains three reliquary stupas, the largest being that of the Fifth Dalai Lama, named **Unique Ornament of the World (Dzamling Gyenchik)**. It extends over 14 m in height, almost to the roof terrace of the fourth storey. Its gold embellishments weigh approximately 3,700 kg, and its jewels are 10 times more valuable. It has a lattice window with a gold image of Eleven-faced Avalokiteshvara. At the western end of the chapel are the reliquaries of the Tenth Dalai Lama (**Khamsum Serdung Gyen-chok**) and the Twelfth Dalai Lama (**Serdung Serjin Obar**), who both died as minors. Behind these lesser reliquaries is a gold manuscript version of the *Kangyur* and *Tangyur* and the Collected Works of Tsongkhapa and his students. The central reliquary is flanked by eight smaller stupas symbolizing the eight major events in the life of the Buddha; and on the east wall there are murals depicting the Fifth Dalai Lama.

Trungrab Lhakhang (north) The images of this chapel illustrate the illustrious past emanations of India and Tibet. At the centre is a solid gold Shakyamuni and a solid silver Fifth Dalai Lama. To the right are King Songtsen Gampo, Dromtonpa, and Tsharchen Losel Gyatso. To the left are the first four Dalai Lamas. In front are the Eight Medicine Buddhas, the Buddhas of the Three Times, the Lords of the Three Enlightened Families and the aspects of Padmasambhava portrayed in the teaching-cycle known as Spontaneously Present Wishes (*Sampa Lhundrub*). Behind is a *Tangyur* manuscript presented to the Seventh Dalai Lama by the Manchus, and a *Kangyur* given by Desi Sangye Gyatso. On the far left is the **reliquary stupa of the Eleventh Dalai Lama** (*Serdung Pende Obar*) with a silver image of King Songtsen Gampo in its lattice window.

From here, the pilgrim exits via the rear (north) gate of the Potala.

Sights around the Potala

Kharngadong Lhakhang

Southeast of the Potala Palace on Karngadong Road is the Kharngadong Lhakhang, which contains ancient carved stone tablets, said to have been removed from the Jokhang.

Dzong-gyab Lukhang Temple

ⓘ *The temple is entered through the Lukhang Park (park admission: ¥2; temple admission: ¥10).*

The excavation of mortar for the construction of the Potala Palace in the 17th century left behind a crater, 270 m by 112 m, which became Lake Lukhang. The small, 40 m wide, island in this lake was once used as a retreat by the Fifth Dalai Lama, and in 1700 a three-storeyed temple dedicated to the *naga* spirits (*Lukhang*) was constructed by Desi Sangye Gyatso and the Sixth Dalai Lama in the Zangdok Pelri style. There, annual offerings were traditionally made by the Tibetan Cabinet (*Kashag*) to appease the *nagas*. Renovations were carried out subsequently by the Eighth Dalai Lama in 1791, by the Thirteenth Dalai Lama in the early decades of this century, and in 1984. In recent years the temple once housed a small Tibetan-language primary school, but this has unfortunately closed following the death of the resident teacher.

Ground Floor The chapel of the ground floor, known as **Meldro Sechen Lhakhang**, has a raised platform supporting images of Nagaraja, riding an elephant and with five snakes above his head and White Tara. The murals of the vestibule depict the buddha-fields of Zangdok Pelri and Abhirati. Behind the chapel there is a closed passageway leading to two rear chambers, one of which contains murals depicting the kings of Shambhala, and the other a series of unidentifiable murals, still covered with yellow ochre from the Cultural Revolution.

Second Floor Here the principal image depicts Shakyamuni Buddha in the form Nagendraraja, with nine snakes above the head symbolizing the nine *naga* kings. Eleven-faced Avalokiteshvara is to the left and the Twenty-one Taras to the right. A 'self-arising' stone image of Padmasambhava sits in front. The murals depict in succession the well known operatic themes of Pema Obar and Drowa Zangmo– the former being based on the life of the great Indian master Padmasambhava and the latter on that of a culture heroine of Mon, birthplace of the Sixth Dalai Lama.

Third Floor The murals of this floor are outstanding, those of the east wall depicting the Eighty-four Mahasiddhas of ancient India, the Twenty-five Disciples of Padmasambhava (*Jewang Nyer-nga*), important Nyingma lineage holders, such as Longchen Rabjampa and Pema Lingpa, and a number of sacred sites, such as Mindroling, Samye and Sakya Monasteries, Gangri Tokar hermitage and Mount Kailash. On the south side is the private apartment of the Dalai Lamas, who would traditionally visit the temple during the fourth month of the lunar calendar. It contains an image of Shakyamuni, and formerly housed a realistic portrait of the Fifth Dalai Lama, which is now kept in Kundeling. The west wall depicts the yogic postures of the Atiyoga meditations – each vignette captioned with the appropriate instructions from Pema Lingpa's *Dzogchen Kunzang Gongdu*. Lastly, the north wall depicts the Hundred Peaceful and Wrathful Deities, the yogic techniques of Anuyoga, after-death scenes, and the protector deities. These magnificent murals which are now in a dilapidated condition have recently been documented by Ian Baker and Thomas Laird in *The Dalai Lama's Secret Temple*.

Drak Lhalupuk and other Chakpori shrines

Opposite the Potala to the southeast is the 3,725 m **Chakpori**, considered sacred to Vajrapani. The slopes of Chakpori contain more than 5,000 rock-carvings, some of which were reputedly carved by Newar sculptors to correspond to the visions of King Songtsen Gampo, who saw images emerge from the hillside during his retreat on the adjacent Mount Marpori.

The east ridge of Chakpori is separated from Mount Marpori by the newly constructed stupas on West Dekyi Lam. Traditionally, this marked the entrance to the city of Lhasa (**Dago Kani**). Beneath the cliffs on the east side are the caves and temple complex of **Drak Lhalupuk**. On the summit a nunnery was constructed in the 15th century by Tangtong Gyelpo, but this was relocated further downhill in 1695 by Desi Sangye Gyatso and Nyingto Yonten Gonpo, who built in its place the **Medical College** (*Menpa Tra-tsang*). A celebrated hilltop temple affiliated with the Medical College, which contained an outstanding coral image of Amitayus made by Tangtong Gyelpo, a pearl image of Mahakarunika and a turquoise image of Tara, was destroyed in 1959 and subsequently replaced by a radio mast. Lhasa Television and Radio still have offices below the west slopes of the hill; while the TAR Television and Radio stations maintain a block of residential apartments—their offices having been relocated to the north side of West Dekyi Lam, next to the Potala.

Drak Lhalupuk ⓘ *Location: About 500 m from the Potala behind Chakpori Hill. Maps: Lhasa centre, page 68. Admission: ¥12 per person.* Follow a dirt road hugging the base of Mount Chakpori's southeast ridge to the **Drak Lhalupuk Cave**, also called Chogyel Zimpuk. Beyond the gateway to the site is the monastic living quarters and the **Karzhung Cave**, containing new religious posters. A flight of stone steps then leads up to the two-storey grotto chapel. On the first floor is the **Tungshak Lhakhang**, containing images of Shakyamuni Buddha, Manjughosa, Tangtong Gyelpo and the Three Deities of Longevity. The murals here depict the Thirty-five Confession Buddhas.

On the second floor is the **Zhalye Lhakhang**, containing the throne of the Dalai Lamas, and the actual **grotto entrance** in its right wall, its entrance marked by large stone butter lamps and an inscribed history of the site and images of Padmasambhava and Amitayus. This original habitation was founded in about 645 by Songtsen Gampo's Tibetan queen Ruyong Gyelmo Tsun, reputedly at a site where the subterranean *nagas* had been detained during the draining of the marsh for the Jokhang's construction. The grotto later came to be associated with Padmasambhava, Nyang Tingzin Zangpo and Phakpa Chegom.

The **oblong cave** measures 27 sq m, its width varying between 4.5 m and 5.5 m. A central column of rock supports the ceiling, which forms a narrow circumambulatory passage around the walls. There are 71 sculptures within the grotto, the earliest of which were sculpted by Newars. Of these, 69 are carved directly into the granite, 47 of them dating from the earliest period, 19 from the 12th/13th century, and three from the 14th/15th century.

Fourteen of those sculptures are on the surfaces of the central column. Its east face has sculpted images of Shakyamuni (1.3 m), with Shariputra and Maudgalyayana, flanked by Maitreya and Avalokiteshvara. The south face depicts Aksobhya Buddha flanked by the bodhisattvas Samantabhadra and Akashagarbha. The west face depicts three medicine buddhas, and the north face Shakyamuni with his two students.

The **south wall of the grotto** has 32 statues in three rows (17, 1, 14). Of these the **top row** has an image of Drubtob Nyima Ze, the yogin who opened and decorated the grotto, along with Yeshe Tsogyel, Dipamkara Buddha and Manjughosa; followed by Longchenpa; Avalokiteshvara with Vajrapani and Amitabha; Ksitigarbha; Shakyamuni with Samantabhadra and Nivaranaviskambhi; Maitreya with Namkei Nyingpo and Yeshe Tsogyel; and Shakyamuni with Yeshe Tsogyel and Tara. The **middle row** has a small Shakyamuni image; and the **lower row** has fine Newar style images of Ksitigarbha, Avalokiteshvara, Maitreya, Samantabhadra, crouching Maitreya, Akashagarbha, Ksitigarbha, Acala, Nivaranaviskambhi, peaceful Vajrapani, Tara, Dolma Rechikma and Tara. Next to the Ksitigarbha image of the lower row is a **clacking stone**, said to have been used by King Songtsen Gampo when communicating with his Chinese consort Wencheng, who was in retreat in the adjacent cave.

The **west wall of the grotto** has six images: Kharsapani, the Buddhas of the Three Times, Mahakala, and Padmasambhava. The northwest corner has a free-standing Shridevi, flanked by Padmasambhava and Vajrapani.

Lastly, the **north wall** has 17 images in two rows, including Amitabha and Shakyamuni (**top row**), and Maitreya (three times), Avalokiteshvara (three times), Nivaranaviskambhi, Tonmi Sambhota, King Songtsen Gampo with his two foreign queens, Minister Gar Tongtsen and Shakyamuni Buddha with his two students (**lower row**).

Neten Lhakhang Adjacent to the grotto is the Neten Lhakhang, a new three-storey yellow building, constructed in 1987 by young people and consequently nicknamed the Youth Monastery. The ground floor is the monastic quarters. The **main chapel on the second floor** has an entrance passage with (on the left) Tsongkhapa and his two foremost students, and (on the right) 11 statues, including two arhats, Shakyamuni,

 Khedrupje and Shakyamuni on the upper row; and Huashang, Dharmatala, and the Four Guardian Kings on the lower row.

The central shrine has a new image of Shakyamuni Buddha with his two main disciples (donated by Dharamsala) and the Sixteen Elders in two rows on either side. There is also a private apartment set aside for the Dalai Lama. The balcony overlooks the Potala Palace and the city. This second floor chapel also has a landing which opens onto the **Gyaza Drubpuk** – the meditation cave of Princess Wencheng. The latter contains a bas-relief 1-m image of Avalokiteshvara, and on the right wall Wencheng's clacking stone cavity. On the left of the landing is another rock face, with a 'self-arising' relief image of Vajrapani.

Drubtob Lhakhang The nunnery of Drubtob Lhakhang, named after Tangtong Gyelpo (1385-1464), stands above and to the right of the Drak Lhalupuk Cave. It is considered a branch of Shugseb Nunnery (see below, page 161). The original site was consecrated by the meditations of Tangtong Gyelpo, and earlier by those of Nyang Tingzin Zangpo. The central image is Tangtong Gyelpo, while the right wall has an image of Yutok Yonten Gonpo and the reliquary stupa of Dr Khyenrab Norbu, founder of the Lhasa Mentsikhang (the Hospital of Traditional Tibetan Medicine). The back wall has paintings of the Three Ancestral Religious Kings and the Medicine Buddha in gold line on a red background.

A large stupa constructed of engraved mani stones is now near completion behind Chakpori hill, accessible from a lane on Dekyilingka Lam. This is a quiet spot frequented by few visitors to Lhasa, and the engravers can be seen daily at work. In the morning many local people come to perform their devotions, making prostrations and circumambulations.

West Lhasa: orientation and attractions

In the western area of the city, there are three north-south streets that connect Chingdrol Lam with Dekyi Lam. Among them, **Luding Lam** leads north from the Dekyi Lam intersection to Damra Lam (Second Ring Road), the TAR Communist Party School and the former TAR Tourism Bureau and guesthouse, and south to the Lhasa County Fish Restaurant, the Quarantine HQ, the TAR Historical Archives, the Animal and Plant Inspection Department, and Chingdrol Lam.

Mirik Lam (Ch *Minzu Lu*) leads north from the Milan Café and Bar at the Dekyi Lam intersection to the imaginatively designed Last Bus Bar and the Old Tree Café which are on the west side, while the Pacan Coffee House, the excellent Beijing California Yak Restaurant, the Golden Flower Korean Restaurant and the Quality Control Bureau are all on the east. Alternatively, turning south from the intersection, you will pass on the east the TAR People's Conference Hall and Theatre, the Bluebird Hotpot Restaurant, Phakpalha Mansion and the Tibet National Library, while to the west are the Lhasa Hotel and North Lingka Lane, which leads to the Royal Nepalese Consulate and the Yarlung Travel Service. Mirik Lam then intersects with Norbulingka Lam, heading west, on which you will soon reach the entrance to Norbulingka Summer Palace. Beyond this intersection, on the east side, you will reach the Tibet National Museum and the 11-storey International Grand Hotel. Opposite on the west side are the Tanjiayuan Chinese Restaurant, the TAR transportation control bureau, the TAR Workers' No 2 Hospital, and the Long Distance Bus Station.

The third of these north-south roads is the recently widened and paved **Dekyilingka Lam**, on the traditional lingkhor circuit, where the former British legation in Lhasa was once located. North of the Dekyi Lam intersection it leads to the Xing Mao Hotel and the Lhalu Primary School on the corner of Damra Lam, while to the south it leads to Kundeling Regency Temple and Chingdrol Lam.

Between North Mirik Lam and North Dekyilingka Lam, **Barghu Lam** also leads north from the Wella Spa to connect with the ring road on Damra Lam. The entrance to Lhasa's night market will be found along here. The covered market, which has become a popular meeting place for younger people, including Tibetans, contains stalls, restaurants and karaoke bars managed by Chinese and Muslim businessmen, and it extends like an airport hanger as far as the other entrance on North Mirik Lam.

Norbulingka Lam is an increasingly important thoroughfare, extending eastwards from the entrance of Norbulingka Palace towards Chakpori Hill. On the north side of the street you will pass the main entrance to the Tibet National Library, a series of impressive car showrooms, a gardening bureau, the People's Daily Tibet Office, the TAR Traffic Department, and the TAR Road Maintenance Bureau, at which point the road is intersected by Dekyilingka Lam (connecting East Chingdrol Lam with Middle Dekyi Lam and West Dumra Lam). Turn north here for Kundeling Monastery and the Gesar Lhakhang on Bonpori Hill, or continue east on Norbulingka Lam to reach the Transport Office Guesthouse and the Tibet Tourism Bureau. Here the road forks – northeast to reach the petrol station at the Golden Yak Roundabout on Middle Dekyi Lam and east to reach the residential apartments of Tibet TV and Radio employees and the Drak Lhaluphuk temple complex on Chakpori Hill. » *For listings, see pages 124-134.*

Gesar Lhakhang

South of Chakpori Hill, on the summit of Parmari, a mountain sacred to the bodhisattva Manjughosa, is the **Gesar Lhakhang**, a Chinese-style temple, which was built in 1792 by the Manchu ambans on behalf of the Qianlong emperor to commemorate the defeat of the Gorkhas. The temple was dedicated to the Chinese god of war and justice Guan Di, who for political reasons was identified with Gesar. A Chinese-inscribed obelisk on the western side is dated 1793.

The temple, under the jurisdiction of Kundeling which lies at its base, comprises a lower **southern courtyard** containing the obelisk and leading to the main temple, and a higher northern chapel known as the **Jamyang Lhakhang.** The **main temple** has a new image of Gesar, backed by 1,000 images of Tara, while the side walls have 1,000 images of Padmasambhava.

Kundeling Regency Temple

Kundeling, one of the four regency temples, is located to the west of the Potala Palace and south of Parmari, on Dekyilingka Lam. The original complex was large and several chapels stood in a pleasant wooded garden. Kundeling's main four-storey temple housed an assembly hall with a ceiling nearly the height of the building. The **main chapel**, dedicated to Tsongkhapa, once contained the reliquary stupas of the successive Tasak Qutuqtus, two of whom served as regents of Tibet – one during the period of the Eighth and Ninth Dalai Lamas between 1791 and 1819, and the other during the period of the Thirteenth Dalai Lama from 1875 to 1886. At present there is a small rebuilt chapel on the site.

Norbulingka Palace ནོར་བུ་གླིང་ཁ

ⓘ *Admission fee: ¥30 per person (Zoo ¥10).*

This 40-ha park is entered from a main gate near the intersection of Norbulingka Lam and South Mirik Lam, south of the Lhasa Hotel and the Nepalese Consulate. The site was developed as the Summer Palace of the Dalai Lamas from the mid-18th century, when the Seventh Dalai Lama selected it on account of a medicinal spring where he would bathe, owing to his frail disposition. Thus the initial **Uyab Podrang** was built, and its site subsequently enlarged in 1755 by the construction of the **Kelzang Podrang.** Later the complex became known as the Summer Palace because the Tibetan government would move here from the Potala on the 18th day of the third lunar month. The Eighth Dalai Lama (1758-1804) expanded the complex, building the debating courtyard, the **Tsokyil Podrang** (marking the location of the original medicinal spring), the **Lu-khang Lho Pavilion**, the **Druzing Podrang** and the adjacent southeast perimeter wall. The Thirteenth Dalai Lama (1876-1933) later upgraded the gardens of the Kelzang and Chensel palaces, developed the Tsokyil Podrang area, and finally in 1930 oversaw the construction of the **Chensel Lingka** in the northwest area of the park. This new complex itself contains three palaces: **Chensel Podrang**, **Kelzang Dekyil Podrang**, and **Chime Tsokyil Podrang**. Finally, the Fourteenth Dalai Lama constructed the new palace or **Takten Migyur Podrang** between 1954-1956.

Norbulingka is divided into three areas: the palaces, the government buildings and the opera grounds, the open air stage and gardens to the east of the complex, adjacent to the entrance, where operatic performances are held during the Yoghurt Festival. Further north and to the west of the Takten Migyur Podrang are the government offices and Lonyenkhang (the former cinema), now occupied by the park attendants, curio shops, and the Cultural Office of Tibet.

The actual palace section contains four integral complexes which are visited by the pilgrim in the following sequence: Kelzang Podrang (southeast), Takten Migyur Podrang (north), Tsokyil Podrang (centre) and Chensel Podrang (northwest).

Kelzang Podrang Complex This three-storey palace is named after the Seventh Dalai Lama, Kelzang Gyatso, who commissioned its construction in 1755. The central feature of the complex is the north-facing reception hall known as **Tshomchen Nyiwo**, entered via a south-facing cloister, which admits bright sunlight into the chamber through its large skylight. The centrepiece is the Dalai Lama's throne, backed by images of Shakyamuni, the Eight Medicine Buddhas and the Sixteen Elders. Murals depict the Lords of the Three Enlightened Families and the Three Ancestral Religious Kings, and there are also 100 appliqué tangkas depicting the Three Deities of Longevity.

On the second floor (approached by stairs at the southwest of the portico) are the following chapels: **Nechu Lhakhang** (north) has images of the Buddha and the Sixteen Elders, the complete works of Tsongkhapa, and murals depicting the Yarlung kings; **Tashi Namrol Lhakhang** (east) is a protector chapel containing images of Six-armed Mahakala, Shridevi, Dharmaraja, Yamantaka and the meditational deities Guhyasamaja, Cakrasamvara and Bhairava. There are two libraries (northwest and northeast) and the private apartments of the Dalai Lamas. The latter include the study room known as **Tosam Gokyil** (southeast), which has murals depicting Shakyamuni, Tsongkhapa's five visions and Manjushri riding a

Norbulingka Palace

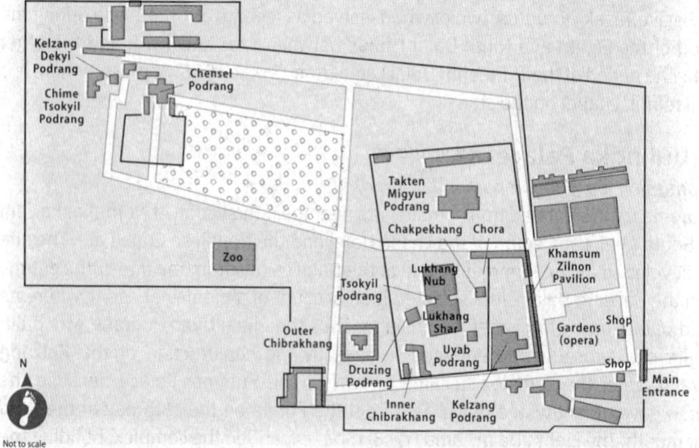

snowlion; the **Reception Hall** with its life-size images of Buddha and Kalacakra and murals depicting the life of the Thirteenth Dalai Lama and his retinue; and the **Cultural Hall** (*Rik-ne Khang*), which functions as a library and has murals depicting Avalokiteshvara, Tsongkhapa's five visions, and the symbol of elemental power and buddha attributes (*namchu wangden*).

The single-storey east-facing **Uyab Lhakhang** is the oldest building in Norbulingka. It is located west of the Kelzang Podrang and was used as a meditation chamber by the Dalai Lamas. Note the simpler construction. The central room contains a golden throne and image of Shakyamuni Buddha, with murals depicting the Three Ancestral Religious Kings, the Sixteen Elders, the Potala Palace, the Jokhang Temple, Reting Monastery and Norbulingka Palace. There is also a small study library (**Chakpe Khang**) and a meditation room (**Nyendzok Khang**).

The two-storey **Khamsum Zilnon** Pavilion, 70 m northeast of the Kelzang Podrang, is built into the grounds of the palace. It was formerly used as a observation point for the Dalai Lamas and their entourage during the Yoghurt Festival. Originally constructed by the Thirteenth Dalai Lama, it was replaced with a more elaborate structure by the Reting regent during the mid-20th century. The chambers of the Dalai Lamas, their tutors and officials are on the second floor.

The south-facing **Chakpekhang**, located north of the Uyab Phodrang, houses metaphysical texts, and its murals depict, among others, Shakyamuni Buddha, the great Buddhist commentators of ancient India known as the 'six ornaments and two supreme ones', Kalacakra, the Sixteen Elders and the Eight Medicine Buddhas. The south-facing **Debating Courtyard** (*Chora*), north of the Chakpekhang, was once reserved for metaphysical discussions between the Dalai Lamas and their tutors.

Takten Migyur Podrang Complex Also known as the New Palace (*Podrang Sarpa*) on account of its recent construction (1954-1956), the Takten Migyur Podrang is an elaborate two-storey building north of the Tsokyil Podrang. The roof is surmounted by the wheel and deer emblem, and the south-facing façade has large glass windows.

Ground Floor Tiger-skin maces symbolizing royal dominion flank the entrance. The **Tshomchen Nelenkhang** in the southeast is a European-style reception room distinguished by a gold image of Manjushri surrounded by gilded copper images of the Eight Medicine Buddhas.

Second Floor The **South Assembly Hall** (*Tshomchen Lhoma Sizhi Dogukyil*) has two entrances on the west side, while the south wall is composed of floor-to-ceiling windows. The north wall has images of Shakyamuni Buddha flanked by Manjushri and Maitreya and a wall-length embroidered frieze depicting the great Indian Buddhist commentators. On the east wall there is an appliqué tangka of Yamantaka, suspended above the splendid throne of the Dalai Lama. The **celebrated murals** of the west, north, and east walls depict 301 scenes from Tibetan civilization – beginning with its legendary origins and continuing down to the period of the Fourteenth Dalai Lama.

The **Zimchung Drodren Semchok-khang** is the name given to the Dalai Lama's private quarters, comprising an anteroom and an inner chamber. The former has an embroidered sofa, above which is an ornate silk appliqué depicting Atisha, Ngok Lekpei Sherab and Dromtonpa, surmounted by the Kadampa protector deities. There is an altar on the north wall with silver images of the Lords of the Three Enlightened Families, and an old Philips gramophone, complete with 78 revolutions per minute records. The **inner chamber** to the east is the bedroom, which has an Indian-style silver altarpiece dedicated to images of Avalokiteshvara, the Three Deities of Longevity and Green Tara. A tangka depicts Tsongkhapa and various Gelukpa masters. Other items of interest include an art deco bed, British plumbing and a Russian radio.

North of the anteroom is another west-facing chamber with a sofa of Indian sandalwood and a shrine containing an image of Shakyamuni Buddha flanked by a silver Vajrayogini and a gilded copper Tsongkhapa. The **Library** (*Zimchung*

 Chakpekhang), in the northwest corner, has a principal image of Manjushri, a throne of the Dalai Lamas, and the murals of its west wall depict the great pilgrimage sites of Indian Buddhism. Inside the library is the **Zimchung Evam Gakyil**, the meditation room of the Dalai Lama, surmounted by paintings of the three meditational deities Guhyasamaja, Cakrasamvara and Bhairava, as well as Padmasambhava flanked by Shantaraksita and King Trisong Detsen. A silver shrine contains images of Guhyasamaja, Mahakala and Manjushri; while a low table supports the three-dimensional celestial palace (*vimana*) of Mahakarunika.

The **North Assembly Hall** (*Ogmin Goden Choling*) is the principal reception room of the New Palace, dominated by its elevated gold throne, backed by gilded copper images of Maitreya flanked by Atisha and Tsongkhapa. The outer murals of the west and east walls depict the 56 episodes of the Buddha's life (above) and the 202 deeds of Tsongkhapa (below). The inner murals of the west wall depict the court of the present Dalai Lama, including the foreign envoys present in Lhasa during the 1940s, while those of the inner east wall depict the entire series of Dalai Lamas. Note that the first four lack the wheel emblem, indicating that they did not exercise the unique fusion of spiritual and temporal power held by their successors. The murals of the south wall depict the legendary abode of Shambhala, the Sixteen Elders, and the Four Guardian Kings.

The **Zimchung Dogu Phuntsok**, entered from the east wall of the North Assembly Hall, functioned as an office and the daytime quarters of the Dalai Lama's mother. It has a white sandalwood shrine complete with sandalwood images of Shakyamuni, the Six Ornaments and Two Supreme Ones of ancient India, Milarepa and Atisha. On the north wall are gold images of Atisha with Ngok Lekpei Sherab and Dromtonpa, while its murals depict Tsongkhapa and his eight main students, with the founders of the major Gelukpa monasteries.

The **Zimchung Jeltrekhang** (southeast corner) where the Dalai Lama would relax with his family members has French furniture, and a white sandalwood shrine, holding images of Shakyamuni Buddha and the Sixteen Elders, which was presented in 1956 by the Mahabodhi Society of India.

Outside this room on a landing, there are murals depicting the omni-directional wheel-shaped geometric poems (*kunzang khorlo*), which cleverly illustrate the names of the Tibetan Kings and the Dalai Lamas. Other murals depict Padmasambhava, flanked by Shantaraksita and King Trisong Detsen, the symbol of elemental power and buddha attributes (*namchu wangden*), the Four Harmonious Brethren (*tunpa punzhi*), the Twenty-five Kulika Kings of Shambhala and the Three Deities of Longevity. Lastly, there is an enigmatic drawing known as Domtson Dampa, which was used to refer obliquely to the great masters of the early phase of Buddhist propagation in Tibet during the persecution of Langdarma. It incorporates a lotus motif, symbolizing Padmasambhava, a book symbolizing Shantaraksita, a sword symbolizing King Trisong Detsen (these three are also identified with the Lords of the Three Enlightened Families), a two-headed duck indicating Shantaraksita and Kamalashila, and a two-headed parrot representing the translators Kawa Peltsek and Chogrolui Gyeltsen.

Tsokyil Podrang Complex The 18th-century recreational complex of Tsokyil Podrang comprises three islands on an artificial lake. Among these, the central island accommodates the **Lhundrub Gyatsel Tsokyil Podrang**, the site of the original medicinal spring used by the Seventh Dalai Lama. The palace was built in Chinese style with a pagoda roof in 1784 by the regent Demo Qutuqtu Delek Gyatso. A boating lake was subsequently added in 1887 by the young the Thirteenth Dalai Lama, and, at the same time, animals were first introduced to Norbulingka Zoo.

The **Lukhang Nub** pavilion was constructed on the north island, also in 1784. Its pagoda roof is supported by several Tibetan-style architectural features including an architrave of *pema* twigs. The shrine is dedicated to Nagaraja, its murals depicting

Ling Gesar and the legendary competition of magical prowess held between Milarepa and the Bonpos at Mount Kailash (see page 359). The **Lukhang Shar** pavilion, east of the lake, houses ritual implements.

West of the lake is the two-storey **Druzing Podrang**, also known as Dekyi Kunga Kyilwei Podrang, which was built by the Eighth Dalai Lama as a library and retreat. The cairn of pebbles made by him can still be seen outside the entrance. The building was renovated in 1982.

On the ground floor, the **assembly hall** (*Tsomchen Chime Gatsel*) contains a wooden image of Avalokiteshvara, which replaces an original Thousand-armed Mahakarunika image now in the White Palace of the Potala. Flanking it are images of Amitayus and a Shakyamuni (in stone from Bodh Gaya), along with the Eight Bodhisattvas. There are also 1,000 small images of Amitayus, and the private library of the Thirteenth Dalai Lama, which has a good collection of medical, historical and Buddhist works, some in Chinese and Mongolian. The library has been properly catalogued by Sertri Rinpoche from Drigung, but its contents have not yet been published. On the **second floor**, the bedroom (northwest) has murals depicting Yamantaka, the Eight Manifestations of Padmasambhava, and the Eight Taras who Protect from the Eight Fears.

An **inner meditation cell** used by the Thirteenth Dalai Lama for Yamantaka meditation has images of Shakyamuni and Tsongkhapa. Further east is an **official chapel** containing images of Padmasambhava, Tsongkhapa with his foremost students, Avalokiteshvara, Manjushri, Amitayus and Shakyamuni, along with a throne surmounted by murals depicting the Five Buddhas of the Enlightened Families.

Chibrakhang The stables (*Chibrakhang*) occupy two buildings to the rear of the Tsokyil Podrang and Kelzang Podrang complexes. Of these, the **Inner Chibrakhang** has murals depicting the rearing of horses. It contains a two-storey building, the upper one being where the Dalai Lamas prepared for outings. The **Outer Chibrakhang** with its stables formerly contained three rusting motor cars, which were the property of the present Dalai Lama – a 1931 Dodge and two 1927 Austins (these have now been removed to the Chensel Podrang); and to its east is an outdoor stage platform, used during the Yoghurt Festival.

Chensel Podrang Complex A pathway leads through the zoo behind these three palace complexes, to the Chensel Podrang, at the northwest extremity of Norbulingka. The main three-storey building was commissioned by the minister Chensel during the early years of the Thirteenth Dalai Lama, and rebuilt by the latter in 1926-1928. A second floor balcony overlooks the courtyard where monks from Drepung would once perform religious dances.

Ground Floor The **Main Audience Hall** (*Tsomchen Nyiwo*) is where monastic ceremonies and *geshe* examinations were once held. The throne is on a raised platform at the north side, with an image of the Thirteenth Dalai Lama to its rear. The side cabinets contain 36 silver statues of the Three Deities of Longevity. Murals depict the 108 deeds of Shakyamuni Buddha and the 80 aspects of Tsongkhapa's career. The central part of this hall now houses a number of interesting and well preserved palanquins used by the previous and present Dalai Lamas. Outside in the vestibule, the horse-drawn carriages of the Dalai Lamas are on display, while the rusting motor cars taken from the Chibrakhang are kept in an adjacent car-port.

Second Floor The study room, known as **Rabsel Paksam Dokyil**, is entered from the west side, its walls decorated by black and white photos taken in 1910 during the Dalai Lama's flight to Calcutta. Also on this floor are the rooms of the Dalai Lama's attendants, and the **Dingjakhang**, a bright south-facing balcony.

Third Floor On the third storey is the **Sizhi Pelbar Assembly Hall**, where the Dalai Lama would give empowerments and private teachings. It contains images of

Thousand-armed Mahakarunika (lifesize) and Thousand-armed Sitatapatra, along with the protector Dorje Drakden. The murals depict the successive Dalai Lamas, from the First to Thirteenth, and the main Gelukpa monasteries. There is an inner meditation chamber called **Tsungdrel Teksum Juggo**.

There are also two smaller palaces within the complex. Some 160 m west of the main Chensel Podrang is the two-storey **Kelzang Dekyi Podrang**, which was constructed between 1926-1928 as an audience hall and later used as a residence. On its ground floor, the **Zimchung Tashi Onang** contains the personal treasury of the Thirteenth Dalai Lama, while on the second floor (entered from the east staircase) there is a **Reception Room** with smaller partitioned chambers to the west. Images include Shakyamuni, Avalokiteshvara and Khedrupje; while the murals include the sacred abodes of Mount Potalaka, Vajrasana, Wutaishan, Tushita and Dhanyakataka.

Further west of this building is the simply constructed **Chime Tsokyil Podrang**, in which the Thirteenth Dalai Lama passed away in 1933, and south of that is the **Usilkhang**, a dilapidated pavilion where the Dalai Lamas would wash their heads.

Khache Lingka The original Muslim quarter of Lhasa is the Khache Lingka, 3 km west of the Potala Palace towards Drepung, entered via a lane opposite the Tibet Hotel. It contains two mosques and a cemetery, the site of which was bequeathed to the Muslim community by the Fifth Dalai Lama and his regent Sangye Gyatso. In 1996 part of the land was leased by a Delhi-based Tibetan businessman who intends to construct a garden hotel. The site is now surrounded by Damra Lam (Second Ring Road) on the north and west, and by North Mirik Lam on the east.

Drepung Monastery འབྲས་སྤུངས་དགོན་པ

ⓘ *Admission: ¥30 per person.*

Location: 8 km northwest of Lhasa on the Gephel Utse ridge above West Dekyi lam
Maps: Lhasa surroundings, page 64

Drepung Monastery was founded in 1416 by Jamyang Choje Tashi Palden (1397-1449), and named after the sacred abode of Shridhanyakataka in South India. Jamyang Choje was one of Tsongkhapa's foremost disciples, and it is known that Tsongkhapa himself taught at the site of the new monastery. The complex developed rapidly with the assistance of the Phakmodru kings, especially Nedong Namka Zangpo, so that by its second year there were 2,000 monks. In the early years of the 16th century, the Second Dalai Lama took possession of the **Ganden Podrang** at Drepung, which was later to become an important centre of political power in Tibet. At the time when the Fifth Dalai Lama assumed spiritual and temporal power in 1641, Drepung had approximately 10,000 affiliated monks, who hailed from 321 different branch monasteries and lived according to nationality in 50-60 different houses, making it the largest monastery in the world. Drepung's influence within the Gelukpa world extended far to the east and northeast through Amdo and Mongolia. The abbot-preceptor of Drepung, known as the **Tripa Khenpo**, was formerly an influential figure within the Tibetan government.

Much of the 20,000 sq m complex at Drepung has survived unscathed, despite repeated plunder inflicted upon it – by King Tsangpa Desi of Zhigatse during the civil war in 1618, by the Mongolians in 1635, Lhazang Qan in 1706 and the Chinese during the recent Cultural Revolution. Many of the surviving buildings date from the 17th-18th century. The monastery reopened in 1980, with a population of approximately 500, most of them young novices, but in recent years the numbers have been considerably reduced in consequence of the active programme of political indoctrination initiated here by resident communist party cadres.

The complex consists of the **Central Assembly Hall** (*Tsokchen Lhakhang*), the **Ganden Palace** (*Ganden Podrang*), and a series of seven colleges (*Tratsang*), each originally under the control of one or other of Jamyang Choje's students, and each containing its own residential units (*Khangtsang*). Four of these colleges (**Ngakpa, Loseling, Deyang**, and **Tashi Gomang**) survive to the present. The other three, Dulwa, Sha-khor, and Tosamling, unfortunately declined during the 18th century. The pilgrim's circumambulatory route around Drepung follows the sequence Ganden Podrang, Assembly Hall, Ngakpa Tratsang, Jamyang Lhakhang, Loseling Tratsang, Tashi Gomang Tratsang and Deyang Tratsang.

Ganden Podrang In 1518 the magnificent residence of **Dokhang Ngonmo** in the southwest corner of Drepung was offered by Miwang Tashi Drakpa of Phakmodru to the Second Dalai Lama, and its name was changed to **Ganden Podrang**. It continued to function as the residence of the successive Dalai Lamas until the Fifth Dalai Lama moved into the newly reconstructed Potala Palace in the late 17th century. Nonetheless, his government continued to refer to itself as Ganden Podrang until 1959.

Left of the entrance gateway is the **Sangak Podrang**, which serves as a protector shrine. The outer chamber contains an image of the Fifth Dalai Lama, the throne of the Dalai Lamas, above which exquisite appliqué tangkas are suspended with glass-cased images of the meditational deities Guhyasamaja, Cakrasamvara, and Bhairava, as well as Tsongkhapa and his foremost students behind. The **inner sanctum** with its distinctive gold on black murals contains images of Dharmaraja, Bhairava, Six-armed Mahakala and Shridevi.

At the northern perimeter of the terrace, is a steep flight of stairs leading to the **main courtyard**, where religious dances were once performed and where the Drepung Yoghurt Festival still begins in summertime. This courtyard is flanked by two-storey residential quarters, which were once occupied by the monks of Namgyel Monastery (before their move to the Potala Palace).

Beyond the courtyard, the lower storey of the palace contains an **Assembly Hall**, which houses Atisha's personal image of 'speaking' Tara (*Dolma Sungjonma*), and other images of Mahakarunika, and the protector deities. A garish but now defaced mural of Mao Zedong survives as a relic of the Cultural Revolution, alongside the directional markers recently put in for the benefit of visitors. The **upper storey** contains the Private Apartments of the Dalai Lamas, which have images of Tsongkhapa with his main students, and an elaborate throne. Attached to the side walls are suspended bookcases containing manuscript volumes of the *Kangyur* and *Tangyur*. Other chambers on this level include the apartments of the late Lamrim Rinpoche, who re-established Drepung during the 1980s, and the library of the Fifth Dalai Lama, which is currently being catalogued. A pathway leads from the rear exit of this building uphill towards Ngakpa Tratsang. Heading in this direction, a side trail soon branches off to the west, leading to a small meditation cave, which has been occupied in recent years by nuns.

Drepung Monastery

Central Assembly Hall (Tsokchen Lhakhang) The 4,500 sq m three-storey central assembly hall is the largest and grandest building in Drepung, rebuilt by Miwang Sonam Topgyel in 1735. Its wide terrace, approached by a flight of 17 steps, overlooks the city of Lhasa and the Kyi-chu valley. The actual entrance is a gateway on the left side of the building.

Ground Floor The main hall on the ground floor (50 m by 36 m) has 182 columns and the two-storey central atrium is well lit from above. On the left side of the hall are the **Lubum Lhakhang**, containing two sunken stupas blessed by the *nagas*, and the silver-plated **reliquary stupas of the Third and Fourth Dalai Lamas**, which are accessible to the public only on the eighth day of the seventh lunar month during the Yoghurt Festival. Beyond the Lubum Lhakhang is the **Lhamo Lhakhang**, containing a picture of the protectress Shridevi painted with blood from the nose of the Fifth Dalai Lama, as well as her three-dimensional celestial palace (*vimana*).

The **main altar** of the Assembly Hall has images of the Sixteen Elders to the far left and right in symmetrical groups of eight. The central group of images and sacred objects comprises the reliquary of the 95th Ganden Tripa, a silver image of Sitatapatra (built in 1951), a gilded copper two-storey high image of Manjughosa in the form of Chokhorma Sungjonma, and other statues of Shakyamuni Buddha, Tsongkhapa Khamsum Zilnon (donated by Longchen Shatra), Thuba Tsultrima, the Thirteenth Dalai Lama, Jamyang Choje Tashi Palden, and the Seventh, Third, Fourth, Fifth, Ninth and Thirteenth Dalai Lamas. The 18th-century murals depict scenes from the *Avandanakalpalata*.

Behind this wall is the **western inner sanctum** known as the **Chapel of the Buddhas of the Three Times** (*Dusum Sangye Lhakhang*), which retains original 15th-century features. Its west wall has images of Hayagriva the gatekeeper, and four standing bodhisattvas, the north wall has silver-plated images of the Buddhas of the Three Times, with smaller gilded copper images of Shakyamuni and his two foremost disciples in front, and the Nine Stupas of Dhanyakataka behind. The east wall has images of Tsongkhapa, four standing bodhisattvas, and the gatekeeper Vajrapani. The reliquary stupa of the late Lamrim Rinpoche has recently been installed inside the hall. Small images of King Songtsen Gampo, his queens and entourage are attached to the columns. Formerly, a Kalacakra ceremony was held in this temple on the 15th day of the third lunar month. East of this chapel is the second or **eastern inner sanctum**, known as the **Miwang Lhakhang**, which contains an 18th-century two-storey high image of Maitreya.

Second Floor The northwest corner of the second storey contains the most venerated chapel in Drepung, known as the **Jampa Tongdrol Lhakhang**. The central 15-m image depicting Maitreya Buddha at the age of eight was constructed by the Phakmodru kings according to the instructions of Tsongkhapa. Its forehead contains buddha relics and a hair from Tsongkhapa's own head, while its throat has a conch shell and its heart contains relics of Kanthaka, the steed of Shakyamuni Buddha. The entrance to this chapel is closed, and access is only gained from the floor above. The Chinese plaque above the chapel entrance was donated by one of the Manchu ambans in 1846.

Also on the second floor is the **Kangyur Lhakhang** which contains three of the 17 *Kangyur* manuscripts and blockprints kept in Drepung: the Litang edition donated by Muji, the king of Jang; the Qing edition donated by the Kangxi Emperor; and a gold-inscribed edition donated by Depa Lobzang Todol as a birthday gift to the Fifth Dalai Lama.

Third Floor The **Zhelre Lhakhang**, from where one can view the head and torso of the sacred Maitreya image below, has a portico where pilgrims prostrate. The chapel also contains over 400 original bronze images. The image used to be further enhanced by a celebrated white conch with a counter-clockwise spiral, which is said to have been buried by Shakyamuni Buddha, rediscovered by Tsongkhapa, and then presented to Jamyang Choje following the construction of Drepung. This was, sadly, stolen by art thieves in 1994. Two reliquaries contain the remains of the Second Dalai Lama and Jamyang Zhepa, while the smaller images in front of Maitreya are, from left to right, Tog-me Zangpo, Tsongkhapa, Seu Rinchen, Tsongkhapa (again) and Jamyang Choje. Eleven other images, including various Dalai and Panchen Lamas, grace the side walls.

The **Dolma Lhakhang** contains three 'self-arising' and 'speaking' 17th-century images of Tara: the Nedong Chime Dolma who protects the water source at Drepung, the Yamdrok Dolma who protects the monastery's wealth and the Gyantse Tsechen Dolma who confers authority on Drepung. The chapel also contains the edition of the Dzamling Yashak *Kangyur*, its 114 volumes inscribed in gold ink with ornately carved sandalwood covers. Other images include: Six-armed Mahakala, and Prajnaparamita whose heart contains an amulet box with a Tsongkhapa tooth relic. At the exit of this chapel is a tangka depicting the Hundred Peaceful and Wrathful Deities.

An adjacent **Printery** contains the *Collected Works of Tsongkhapa*, the *Collected Works of the First and Second Dalai Lamas*, various editions of the *Kangyur*, the *Biography of Atisha*, and the *History of Ganden*, as well as treatises on *vinaya*, grammar and a catalogue of publications.

Roof The Assembly Hall has two gilded roofs, one covering the chapel dedicated to the Buddhas of the Three Times, and the other covering the Jampa Tongdrol chapel. Other rooftop chapels include the **Gyelpo Lhakhang** which has images of the early kings and the Dalai Lamas flanking the central enthroned image of the Fifth Dalai Lama, the **Tsokchen Jowo Khang** which contains a silver Jowo Shakyamuni image flanked by 13 silver stupas, and the **Jampakhang** dedicated to Maitreya.

Jamyang Drubpuk A small meditation cave at the eastern base of the Assembly Hall contains bas-relief images of Tsongkhapa and Jamyang Choje, and an old painting of Tsongkhapa. The rear cave wall backs onto the Assembly Hall.

Jamyang Lhakhang This shrine behind the Assembly Hall and supported by a single pillar has a 'self-arising' image of Manjushri and murals depicting Jamyang Choje and his first disciple, and the Twelve Tenma protectresses. An iron staff substitutes for Jamyang Choje's now lost walking stick with which pilgrims once rubbed their backs to cure rheumatic pains. Adjacent reliquary stupas contain the remains of Lama Umapa of Gadong and Bumdrak Dunpa.

Ngakpa Tratsang This college dedicated to tantric studies is located west of the Central Assembly Hall. It was founded in 1419, originally to admit graduates of the other colleges into tantric studies. Adepts of the Ngakpa Tratsang would subsequently be admitted to the Upper Tantric College (*Gyuto*) or the Lower Tantric College (*Gyume*) in Lhasa. The **assembly hall** (*Dukhang*) which is the later of the two main buildings has images of the Indo-Tibetan *lamrim* lineage-holders, with Tsongkhapa and various Dalai Lamas at the centre. The **Jikje Lhakhang** behind the assembly hall was constructed by Tsongkhapa himself, and houses the sacred image of Bhairava known as 'Chogyel Caktakma' and Dharmaraja holding an iron chain. The image contains the embalmed remains of Ra Lotsawa. The other statues here are of Dorje Drakden, Mahakala, Shridevi, the Fifth Dalai Lama and Tsongkhapa.

Loseling Tratsang The college of dialectics, known as Loseling (1,860 sq m), is southeast of the Central Assembly Hall. The abbot-preceptor of Loseling was highly influential, presiding over 23 residential units (*khangtsang*). The **assembly hall** has 102 columns, and contains numerous volumes of scripture. From left to right the main images and sacred objects are the reliquary stupa of the First Loseling Tripa Legden Rinpoche, the reliquary stupa of the late Kangyur Rinpoche, images of the Fifth, Eighth and Seventh Dalai Lamas, a Bhairava mandala and image of Jamyang Choje, an image of the Fifteen th Ganden Tripa Sonam Drakpa alias Dorje Shukden; images of Tsongkhapa and the Thirteenth Dalai Lama; the throne of Sonam Drakpa; the reliquary stupa of Loseling Dedrub Rinpoche; and images of Tsongkhapa with his foremost students, and Sitatapatra. The niches in the side walls hold 1,000 small images of Amitayus.

There are three inner sanctums. In succession, these are: **Neten Lhakhang** which has images of the Sixteen Elders in three tiers flanking an Enlightenment Stupa; the

Jampa Lhakhang which has a large Maitreya with Shakyamuni Buddha (left), Tsongkhapa (right), and the Thirteenth Dalai Lama (centre), as well as Atisha flanked by Dromtonpa and Ngok Lekpei Sherab; and the **Tubpa Lhakhang** which has a small Shakyamuni image flanked by stupas. The upper level has a **Protector Chapel** accessible only to men. Here, Bhairava is surrounded by the meditational deities Guhyasamaja, Cakrasamvara, and the protector Mahakala.

Tashi Gomang Tratsang East of Loseling, this is the second largest college at Drepung, with 16 residential units (*khangtsang*). Traditionally it housed monks from Amdo, Mongolia and Nakchuka. The **assembly hall** has 102 columns, and images (left to right) of Six-armed Mahakala (twice), the Sixth Dalai Lama, Tsongkhapa (four), Dipamkara Buddha, Avalokiteshvara (twice), the Seventh Dalai Lama, Maitreya, Amitayus, and Jamyang Choje. Distinctive murals depict the 108 episodes in the life of Shakyamuni Buddha.

There are three inner sanctums: **Tsepak Lhakhang** which has images of the Three Deities of Longevity; the **Mikyopa Lhakhang** which has three tiers of images, with Aksobhya at the centre of the top tier, flanked by Shakyamuni and a smaller Aksobhya. The middle tier has Shakyamuni, Avalokiteshvara, Maitreya, and a small Tsongkhapa in front, and on the lowest tier, there are five images of the celebrated Gomang lama Jamyang Zhepa. Lastly the **Dolma Lhakhang** has tiered images of the Twenty-one Taras and the Sixteen Elders. On the second floor is a protector shrine dedicated to Dorje Drakden. Here, the central image is Mahakala, with Bhairava and various local deities.

Deyang Tratsang This, the smallest of the four Tratsang, is dedicated to the Medicine Buddhas. The **assembly hall** has images of Tsongkhapa with his foremost students, Sitatapatra, White and Green Tara, and the Fifth Dalai Lama; while its gatekeepers are the protector deities Dorje Drakden and Shridevi. The **Jowokhang** at the rear of the assembly hall contains an image of Maitreya with Deyang Jangchub Palden and the Seventh Dalai Lama and Tsongkhapa, Shakyamuni, the Third Dalai Lama, the First Rato Tripa Yonten Gyatso, and the Second Deyang Tripa on the right. The monastic kitchen lies east of the assembly hall.

Five Meditation Caves of Jamyang Choje Around Drepung there are five cave hermitages once associated with the monastery's founder. These are: the now destroyed **Nyare Barti Chikhang** (near Ganden Podrang); the enclosed **Warti Shobokhang** (at the western perimeter where water is drawn for the monastery); the aforementioned **Jamyang Drubpuk**; **Wartsokhang** (in the willow garden of Deyang Tratsang); and **Gozhima Shamma** (south of Loseling near Tewu Khangtsang).

Drepung Lingkor There is a one and a half hour pilgrim's circumambulation of Drepung Monastery, which leads west of the perimeter wall and uphill in the direction of Gephel Ritro, before descending in the direction of Nechung. En route the following sacred features can be seen: four 'self-arising' golden fish at Ganden Podrang, Tashi Kangsar, Ngakpa Tratsang and Gungru Khamtsang respectively, a 'self-arising' Green Tara called Dolma Kangchakma, other paintings of Tara at Chiri Rizur, a 'self-arising' Jambhala, a stone throne associated with the Fifth Dalai Lama, and a 'self-arising' stone engraved with the Six-Syllable Mantra of Avalokiteshvara.

Gephel Ritro The hermitage known as Gephel Ritro is three to four hours walk above Drepung Monastery on the Lingkhor. It was founded by Tsepa Drungchen Kunga Dorje in the 14th century. Here, monk herders produce excellent curd, which was formerly reserved for the Dalai Lamas. The ascent from the hermitage to the summit of Gephelri takes another three hours. Juniper offerings are regularly made at the summit, especially on the full moon of the fourth month of the lunar calendar.

Nechung Monastery གནས་ཆུང་དགོན་པ

ⓘ *Admission fee: ¥5.*

Located 1 km southeast of Drepung, Nechung Monastery is the abode of the protector deity Pehar and the seat of the State Oracle of Tibet. Pehar is said to have had legendary associations with Zahor and later, under the name Shingjachen, with the Bhatahor Kingdom of Central Asia. After Bhatahor was subjugated by the Tibetan army under Prince Murub Tsepo, Padmasambhava converted Pehar's five forms to Buddhism, renaming them Gyelpo Ku-nga. The first Tibetan abode of Pehar was at Peharling in Samye. Later a second abode was established at Tsel Gungtang but the image of Pehar in that locale caused havoc, prompting Lama Zhang to expel it by putting it in a casket in the Kyi-chu River. Retrieved from the river at Drepung, the Pehar image escaped from the casket in the form of a dove which flew into a tree at Nechung. This tree is nowadays in the rear left-side chapel, along with an image of Pehar and a photo of the Nechung Oracle.

The first temple at Nechung was constructed in the 12th century; and Pehar since then is said to have periodically left the tree to foretell the future through his medium Dorje Drakden who would possess the Nechung Oracle, making pronouncements on natural disasters, political appointments and so forth. Originally a Nyingmapa establishment, Nechung later developed a close relationship with nearby Drepung; and from the time of the Fifth Dalai Lama its oracles have held highly influential political positions, acting frequently as an intermediary between Pehar and the Dalai Lama.

First and foremost, the oracle was required to undertake a rigorous training in tantric liturgies. Each Great Prayer Festival at Lhasa, the oracle would leave Nechung for Meru Monastery via the Barkhor and appear publicly on the 24th day of the first month of the lunar year to ward off obstacles. When possessed by Dorje Drakden, the oracle would whisper his pronouncements, which would then be interpreted and written down by monk attendants on long blackboards dusted with limestone powder.

The oracle was also generally accessible to the nobility who paid generously for private divinations. In 1904, the medium was faced to abdicate by the Thirteenth Dalai Lama after false predictions concerning the Younghusband Expedition. In 1930 a new medium emerged to confirm the recognition of the new Fourteenth Dalai Lama in 1937. He gave advice during the 1950s concerning the movements of the Dalai Lama and his *geshe* examinations of 1958. The following year, he fled to India with his entourage of six monks. The present incumbent, Lobzang Jikme, was appointed in Dharamsala where he now lives with 20 monks. In 1976 the Drepung monks of Mungod were alarmed by his predictions concerning the well-being of the Dalai Lama.

The buildings of Nechung mostly survived the Cultural Revolution apart from their gilded roofs and embellishments. The complex, nestling within a grove of juniper and fruit trees, is approached via a lane marked by a water tower southeast of Drepung. The **residence of the Nechung Oracle** is located behind the main buildings, while the **School of Buddhist Dialectics** (*Nangten Lobdra*) is down a lane to the left of the main entrance.

Three gates give access to the courtyard. The southern one is always closed, reputedly because Dorje Shugden is said to be waiting constantly outside this gate to usurp power on the departure of Pehar. Murals here depict Pehar and retinue; and there is an inscriptionless obelisk dedicated to Pehar. The three-storey temple at the north end of the courtyard is approached by steps flanked by stone lions and its portico by murals depicting Pehar and Dorje Drakden.

Ground Floor The assembly hall with its dark murals depicting the Deities of the Eight Transmitted Precepts (*Kabgye*) is adjoined by three chapels: among these, the **Jordungkhang** (west) contains the sacred tree stump abode of Pehar's dove emanation, flanked by two Pehar images in peaceful and wrathful guises, along with further images of Padmasambhava and Tsongkhapa; the **Tsenkhang Uma** (centre) has a central image of Shakyamuni with the pedestals of the now destroyed Eight Bodhisattvas. Formerly it also housed the throne of the Nechung Oracle backed by the Kutshab Rinpoche image of Padmasambhava through which Pehar was controlled. Lastly, the **Gon-khang** (east) is dedicated to Remati, and has images of Nyima Zhonu and the Five Aspects of Pehar in the form Kundu Gyelpo. **NB** This last image was regarded as the regent of Nechung in times when no oracle was recognized.

Second Floor There are two chapels on the second floor, the larger of which is the Dalai Lamas' audience room, containing a throne and images of Tsongkhapa, the Fifth Dalai Lama, Shakyamuni Buddha, Maitreya and Avalokiteshvara. The smaller chapel has images of Tsongkhapa and his foremost students, Shakyamuni Buddha, Avalokiteshvara and Tara.

Third Floor Here there is a single chapel with an image of Padmasambhava in the charismatic form of Nangsi Zilnon, which was constructed in 1981. Formerly, the temple also housed the national treasures known as the **Pehar Kordzo**.

North and East Lhasa → *For listings, see pages 124-134.*

North Lhasa: orientation

There are a number of roads leading from Dekyi Lam towards the northern suburbs of the city. These include Lhalu Lam, extending due north from West Lingkhor Lam via Lhalu to Pelding commune; Nyangdren Lam, extending due north from the Post Office on Dekyi Lam to Pawangka and Sera Monastery (see below, page 117); Sera Lam, extending due north from the TAR Foreign Affairs Office on Dekyi Lam towards Drapchi and Sera Monastery and Dokde Lam, extending northeast from the Workers' Roundabout out of town.

On the west side of **Lhalu Lam**, you pass a primary school, the New Zhol village, Lhalu village and Pelding, where there is a quarry and an oxygen production plant. On the east side you pass the TAR Women's Association, the Lhasa District Welfare Office, an experimental kindergarten and the Chamdo Prefectural Office.

On **South Nyangdren Lam**, you pass on the west side the CAAC Airline Office, the TAR Government Personnel Department, a small street market, Lukhang Park side entrance, and (after the Lingkhor Lam intersection), the TAR Quarantine Station, the TAR Veterinary Centre, the TAR Buddhist Society, the Municipal Procurator's Office and the Municipal Environment Bureau. Opposite on the east side of South Nyangdren Lam are the TAR United Front, the TAR Red Cross, several Chinese restaurants including one which specializes in Peking Duck, and (after the Lingkhor Lam intersection) the Tuberculosis Control Centre, the TAR Seismology Bureau, the Fine Art Company, the Nakchu District Office, a computer store and the Inpatients' Hospital of Traditional Medicine. Then, after the intersection with Middle Damra Lam, heading north on **North Nyangdren Lam**, you will pass on the west side the TAR Construction Department, the TAR Auditors' Bureau, the TAR Transport Company, a local police station, the Pharmaceutical Factory of the Hospital of Traditional Medicine, the TAR Gymnastics Association and Gymnasium, the Zhigatse Prefectural Office, the Ngari Prefectural Office, Jiangsu Middle School, Lhasa Teacher Training College and the School of Hygiene. On the corresponding east side are a library, the municipal grain department, a local post office, the entrance to the Tibetan Medical College (*Sorik Lobdra Chenmo*), the Sports and Physical Education School, the Lhasa Transportation Company, Xinhua Press, a cartographic unit and a number of workers' schools. Thereafter, the road leads due north to the Military Hospital and Pawangka, while a detour leads due east to Sera Monastery and the nearby Sky Burial Site.

On **Sera Lam**, you will pass on the west side the terminus for the Number Six bus, the Town Planning Department, the Armed Police Hospital, the TAR Disabled Federation, the Race Course, a fertiliser factory, a hydro-electric power plant and the TAR Construction and Engineering Corporation. On the east side are the Lhasa District Public Security Bureau, the Municipal Milk Company, the TAR Academy of Social Sciences, a meat and vegetable market, a lane leading to the notorious Drapchi Prison and the Lhasa Beer brewery.

On **Dokde Lam**, you pass on the west side the Ying Qiao Hotel, the Municipal Television and Broadcasting HQ, the Municipal Science Association, the Hydroelectric Construction Company, the Epidemic Prevention Department, the North Fire Station, Drapchi Prison, an armed police unit and various electrical or engineering companies in the Drapchi suburbs. On the corresponding east side are the Old Plateau Hotel, the TAR Cultural Bureau, the Ganlho Amdo Office, the TAR Judiciary, the TAR Penal Management Bureau, the TAR Security Department, a local post office, Middle School Number Four, the Commercial School, pharmaceutical companies, motor repair units and agricultural machine suppliers.

A new ring road, known as **Damra Lam** or Second Ring Road (Ch *Erhuang Lu*) has recently been constructed, parallel to Chingdrol Lam and Dekyi Lam in the north of the city. This bypass extends from the Luding Lam intersection, north of the TAR Customs Office as far as the Karma Kunzang suburbs at the east end of the city, and it is also divided into west, middle and east sectors. Heading eastward from the Luding Lam intersection, on West Damra Lam, there is the large Damra Park on the north side, where horse riding is available in the summer, and the PICC Insurance Company offices. On the south side, opposite the park, are the Drongnub Fish Restaurant, the Land Management Bureau, and Lhalu Primary School. Further east, after the intersections with Mirik Lam, Barghu Lam, Dekyilingka Lam, and Lhalu Lam, the ring road is built up on both sides and Middle Damra Lam begins. Here, on the north side, you will pass the TAR Construction Department and the Tibetan Medical College. Finally, the south side of East Damra Lam has the dubious distinction of being Lhasa's newest red-light district, and both the New Plateau Hotel and the Namsel Hotel are located here, alongside the massage parlours and the TAR Water Conservation Bureau.

East Lhasa

Among the outlying easterly parts of the city, which is a rapidly expanding residential area, **Ngachen Lam**, the extension of North Lingkhor Lam, leads out of town towards a power station of the same name and the hilltop ruins of Dechen Dzong. En route, you pass on the north side the Old Plateau Hotel, the city traffic police, the Nyangtri Bureau, the Domestic Satellite Earth Station, which has a revolving observation tower and an armed police auxiliary unit, while to the south side are the Municipal Security Bureau, a pensioners' club, yet another armed police auxiliary unit, the Holy Swan Hotel, the entrance to the affluent suburb of Karma Kunzang, High School Number Two, Middle School Number Three and a flour mill. A side lane leads from here to the Jomolangma Tweed Factory Hotel.

East Zamchen Lam (Ch *Jiangsu Dong Lu*) extends southeast from the Workers' Roundabout across the Kyi-chu River, intersecting Lingyu Lam and Chingdrol Lam. On the east side the most important buildings are the Municipal Cultural Bureau and the Municipal Television Station, followed by the Kongda Hotel and a petrol station, while on the west side there are the Municipal Hygiene Bureau and the Municipal Art Club.

Sera Thekchenling Monastery སེ་ར་ཐེག་ཆེན་གླིང་

At the base of Mount Purbuchok, which forms part of the watershed between the Kyi-chu and the Penpo-chu rivers, Sera Thekchenling was founded in 1419 by Tsongkhapa's disciple Jamchen Choje Sakya Yeshe of Tsel Gungtang (1355-1435). Prior to this foundation, Tsongkhapa and his foremost students had established hermitages in the ridge above (Sera Utse). In time, the monastic community at Sera came to number between 5,000 and 6,000 monks. The complex comprises the Great Assembly Hall (*Tsokchen*), three colleges (previously there were four or five, including Sera To which were gradually amalgamated), and 30 residential units (*khangtsang*). A long driveway divides the complex into eastern and western sectors – the former containing the Great Assembly Hall and the Homdong Kangtsang, and the latter containing the three colleges. The pilgrimage route follows a clockwise circuit in the sequence Sera Me Tratsang, Ngakpa Tratsang, Sera Je Tratsang, Hamdong Khangtsang, Tsokchen Assembly Hall, and Tsongkhapa's hermitage on Mount Phurbuchok. Admission fee: ¥35 per person.

Sera Me Tratsang The Sera Me college, constructed in 1419, covers a large area (1,600 sq m) and has 13 residential units (*khangtsang*). It is the college promoting elementary studies at Sera. Its assembly hall was destroyed by lightning and rebuilt in 1761 by Kunkhyen Jangchub Penpa. It now has eight tall and 62 short columns, with main images of Shakyamuni (in copper) along with Maitreya, Manjushri and Amitayus, as well as Bhaisajyaguru, Tsongkhapa and his students, the Seventh Dalai Lama, Pawangka Rinpoche and various former monastic preceptors of Sera Me.

There are five inner chapels attached to the assembly hall, described here from west to east (ie left to right). Tawok Lhakhang contains an image of Tawok, protector of the east; Je Rinpoche Lhakhang a stupa with an inset image of Tsongkhapa flanked by images of Tsongkhapa and Shakyamuni; Neten Lhakhang, images of the Buddhas of the Three Times flanked by the Sixteen Elders in their mountain grottoes and volumes of the *Prajnaparamita*; Jowokhang once contained the celebrated image of Miwang Jowo Shakyamuni, which has now been replaced with a large new Buddha image, flanked by the Eight Bodhisattvas, and guarded at the gates by Hayagriva and Acala; and lastly, Tsongkha Lhakhang contains amongst others an image of Je Rinpoche together with Atisha, Dromtonpa, the First to Third Dalai Lamas, the Fifth Dalai Lama, Jamchen Shakya Yeshe, Gyeltsen Zangpo, who was the first preceptor of Sera, and Kunkhyen Jangchub Penpa, the founder of the college.

The second floor contains the Nyima Lhakhang which has a central image of Shakyamuni Buddha in the form of Tuwang Tsultrim; and the *Kangyur* Lhakhang, now containing 1,000 small images of Tara since its volumes were destroyed during the Cultural Revolution. The third floor consists of the Dalai Lamas' private apartments.

Ngakpa Tratsang This three-storeyed college building was built in 1419 by Jamchen Choje Shakya Yeshe and refurbished by Lhazang Qan in the early 18th century. It is the smallest of the current three colleges at Sera, focusing, as its name suggests, on tantric studies. The ground floor contains the assembly hall and two inner chapels.

The **assembly hall** has 42 short and four tall columns with elaborately carved capitals. The central image is an original Jamchen Choje Shakya Yeshe wearing a black hat, which was probably presented to Sera by Emperor Yongle (1360-1424) of the Ming Dynasty. Flanking this image are: Maitreya, Gyeltsen Zangpo, who was the first preceptor of Sera, Pawangka Rinpoche, Tsongkhapa with his foremost students, the Thirteenth Dalai Lama, Chokyi Gyeltsen and Sera Je's founder Lodro Rinchen.

As for the two chapels: **Neten Lhakhang** contains images of Shakyamuni Buddha between two sets of the Sixteen Elders, the upper series in Tibetan style and the lower series in Chinese lacquer, which was presented by Emperor Yongle to Jamchen Choje Shakya Yeshe. **Jigje Lhakhang** contains an original 15th-century image of Bhairava, with Mahakala, Dharmaraja, Shridevi and others.

The second storey of the building has the **Tsepame Lhakhang** where the central image of Amitayus is surrounded by the reliquary stupas of Gyeltsen Zangpo and Jetsun Chokyi Gyeltsen, as well as by images of the Eight Medicine Buddhas. The third storey has the Dalai Lamas' private apartments.

Sera Je Tratsang Sera Je is the largest of the three colleges at Sera, covering an area of 1,700 sq m, with 17 residential units (*khangtsang*) which housed mostly immigrant monks from east Tibet and Mongolia. It was founded by Gungyel Lodro Rinchen Senge, a student of Tsongkhapa and Jamchen Choje Shakya Yeshe. The building originally had three storeys, the fourth being added during a period of expansion in the 18th century when the number of columns in the assembly hall was increased to 100. The finely decorated **assembly hall** has murals depicting the deeds of the Buddha, the thrones of the Dalai Lamas and Panchen Lamas and, on its north wall, a series of reliquary stupas, and images of the Eighth and Thirteenth Dalai Lamas, the Second and Ninth Reting Tulkus, and Sera Je's founder, Lodro Rinchen.

The following chapels on the west and north sides of the assembly hall are in sequence: **Dusum Sangye Lhakhang** containing images of the Buddhas of the Three Times and the Eight Bodhisattvas, **Tamdrin Lhakhang** containing the most sacred image of Sera Monastery, **Hayagriva**, sculpted by Lodro Rinchen himself, and enclosed within a gilded copper embossed shrine. The upper left compartment of the shrine contains the **Sera Phur Zhal** dagger, which is traditionally placed on public view only on the 17th day of the 12th lunar month once the Dalai Lama has touched it. The dagger reportedly flew from India to Mount Phurbuchok near Sera and was hidden as treasure (*terma*) at Yerpa before being unearthed by the treasure-finder (*terton*) Darcharuba. The chapel is also bedecked with military regalia befitting a protector shrine room. **Jampa Lhakhang** contains images of Maitreya, Eleven-faced Mahakarunika, and Tsongkhapa with his foremost students, all surrounded by an impressive library. The **Tsongkhapa Lhakhang** contains images of Tsongkhapa with his foremost students, and important lamas of Sera Je as well as Nagarjuna and the other great Buddhist commentators of ancient India and the gatekeepers Hayagriva and Acala. **Jampeyang Lhakhang** (northeast) contains two Manjushri images and one Maitreya image, the central Manjushri in the teaching gesture (*dharmacakramudra*) looking out onto the debating courtyard.

On the second floor, the **Zhelre Lhakhang** (west) permits a view of the sacred Hayagriva image on the floor below, but also contains a small image of Nine-headed Hayagriva, surrounded Padmasambhava, the Fifth Dalai Lama, and the protector deities. On the third floor there is the **Namgyel Lhakhang**; and on the fourth the private apartments of the Dalai Lamas and the preceptors of Sera Je.

The famous **Debating Courtyard** (*Chora*) contains a stone into which 13 syllables A are said to have dissolved once Tsongkhapa had completed his commentary on Madhyamaka philosophy, written in the hermitage above Sera. The seed-syllable A symbolizes the nature of emptiness or the reality underlying all phenomenal appearances. Each afternoon, crowds of monks can be seen debating here in the traditional method, with the antagonist standing and aggressively questioning his seated protagonist.

Hamdong Khangtsang This is one of the principal residential units (*khangtsang*) attached to Sera Je college. Its **assembly hall** has minor images of Tsongkhapa, Chokyi Gyeltsen, Shakyamuni Buddha, and the Three Deities of Longevity. It has two inner chapels: The **Jampakhang** contains a 'speaking' image of Tara, which is said to guard the spring water of Sera, and an image of the late lama Tubten Kunga who renovated Sera before the Cultural Revolution. The **protector chapel** (*Gonkhang*) contains an image of the protector deity Gyelchen Karma Trinle.

Great Assembly Hall (Tsokchen) The four storeyed south-facing **Great Assembly Hall** is the largest building in Sera Monastery (2,000 sq m), with 89 tall and 36 short columns. It was constructed in 1710 by Lhazang Qan. It is entered via a portico with 10 columns. Large appliqué tangkas are suspended from the ceiling along the side walls and there is a central skylight. The main image is that of Jamchen Choje Shakya

 Yeshe, the founder of Sera, with the Fifth, Seventh and Twelfth Dalai Lamas, as well as by a 5-m gilded Maitreya supported by two lions, Tsongkhapa and his foremost students, Chokyi Gyeltsen, Desi Sangye Gyatso and others.

There are three inner chapels, described here in succession: **Jampa Lhakhang** contains a 6-m two-storey image of Maitreya, which is the centrepiece of the building, flanked by the Eight Bodhisattvas and the gatekeepers Hayagriva and Acala. On the south wall is a Yongle eighth-year edition of the *Kangyur* (dated 1410), originally in 108 volumes although three have been lost. This is the oldest extant *Kangyur* printed from woodblocks, and each volume has a cover carved in gold on red lacquer. The **Neten Lhakhang** contains clay images of the Sixteen Elders, each of which encloses an authentic wooden image – the original wooden series having been presented to Sera by the Ming emperor Xuan Zong. Lastly, the **Jigje Lhakhang** contains images of Bhairava and consort with Shridevi and other protectors.

The second floor contains the **Zhelre Lhakhang** (centre), affording a view of the large Maitreya below, with a small Tsongkhapa at the statue heart. The **Tu-je Chenpo Lhakhang** contains a large image of Eleven-faced Avalokiteshvara, which was originally discovered at Pawangka, and which is said to transmit a blessing via a staff from its heart directly to the pilgrim's head. Other images here include Tara and Six-armed Mahakala. The **Shakyamuni Lhakhang** has a statue of Shakyamuni, surrounded by images of various Gelukpa lamas.

The third and fourth floors contain the private apartments of the Dalai Lamas and those of the monastic preceptors of the Great Assembly Hall.

Choding Khang The hermitage of Je Tsongkhapa, known as Choding Khang, is located behind the Great Assembly Hall, on the slopes of Sera Utse Hill. It is entered at roof level via a path adjacent to the painted rock carvings of Tsongkhapa, Jamchen Choje Shakya Yeshe and the protector Dharmaraja. The building replaces the original hermitage, which was destroyed during the Cultural Revolution. Further up the slope is the meditation cave associated with the master, while the hermitages of the Upper Tantric College (*Gyuto*) and Lower Tantric Colleges (*Gyume*) of Lhasa are in front.

Sera Utse Continuing up the trail from Choding Hermitage for one and a half hours, the pilgrim will reach the Sera Utse, a hermitage predating the construction of Sera itself. It consists a two-storey chapel, with monks' quarters which afford a marvellous view of the city of Lhasa, and a protector shrine dedicated to Pehar and Shridevi. An eastward trail leads around the mountain to Ragachok and Phurbuchok in the upper Dode valley; while a westward trail leads to the Tashi Choling hermitage in the Pawangka valley, two and a quarter hours away.

Pawangka Monastery ཕ་བོང་ཁ and adjacent sites

Pawangka is located about 8 km northeast of Lhasa, in a valley on the lower slopes of Mount Dukri to the west of Sera Monastery, and is approached from behind the Lhasa Military Hospital. The original temple was constructed as a tower on the 300-sq m plinth which surmounts an enormous 20-m high granite rock which is said to represent an obelisk upon a turtle. The building is said to have been modelled on Devikoti, a temple in Guwahati, Assam, which in turn had associations with Kusinagara, the sacred place where the Buddha passed away.

Below, at the entrance to the Pawangka valley, is a boulder, painted white with a red border along the top, where the local protector Gonpo Drashe Marpo is said to reside. Above, is a smaller whitewashed monolith – the two being known respectively as the female and male tortoises (*Rubal Pomo*).

The original structures at Pawangka may well predate the Jokhang and Ramoche because King Songtsen Gampo and his queens seem to have gone there on the advice of Shridevi in order to suppress the supine ogress. They constructed a nine-storey palace, known as **Nyangdren Pawangka Podrang**, and there they went into retreat in order to determine the best sites for the construction of their geomantic temples. The Lords of the Three Enlightened Families affirmed their support for this endeavour by leaving 'self-arising' impressions of themselves in stone, which were later placed with the **Rigsum Gonpo Lhakhang**, which the king constructed along with 108 stupas. This temple also contains an original stone inscription of the Six-syllabled Mantra, prepared by Tonmi Sambhota who created the Tibetan alphabet here during a three-year sojourn, following his return from India.

Above the main chapel is the **Gyaza Gonchu Podrang**, the residence of Princess Wencheng. At the eastern extremity of the site is the **Pawang Durtro**, Lhasa's most important burial ground, symbolizing the skull of Cakrasamvara; also the **Tashi Choling** mountain hermitage, the newly reconstructed **Chubzang nunnery**, and the ridge-top **Tokden Drubpuk cave retreat** dedicated to Cakrasamvara.

During the eighth century, King Trisong Detsen and Padmasambhava stayed seven days in the **Tsechu Lhakhang cave** at the base of the site. Tibet's original seven trial monks lived here for some time, but the buildings and stupas were destroyed by Langdarma in 841, causing the protectress Shridevi to advise Lhalung Peldor to kill the apostate king. A two-storey monastery was reconstructed in the 11th century by Potowa's student Drakar, and it housed 200 monks, who gradually rebuilt the 108 stupas. Chogyel Phakpa later carried out further renovations, and the monastery was eventually completed by Khonton Peljor Lhundrub in 1619. A block of stone was brought from Devikota in Kamakhya, Assam, giving Pawangka the name Devikota. The Fifth Dalai Lama added an extra floor in the course of his renovations; so that subsequently the site was visited by all Dalai Lamas when they had obtained their *geshe* degree. The preceptors of Pawangka were later appointed directly by the Tibetan Cabinet (*Kashag*). In the 19th century, the hierarch of Pawangka was the teacher of the late Trijang Rinpoche, senior tutor to the present Dalai Lama.

Pawangka Circumambulation The entire pilgrims' circuit of Pawangka takes approximately one day in summertime, following the sequence: Pawangka, Tashi Choling, Tokden Drubpuk, and Chubzang Nunnery.

A shorter circuit around the base of **Pawangka Rock** begins at the main steps, and runs clockwise. The **east face of the rock** has a cave shrine containing 1-m high images of the Lord of the Three Enlightened Families, Shakyamuni and Acala. The **south face** contains rocks representing the buttocks and sexual organs of the female tortoise; and King Songtsen Gampo's cave retreat (8 m by 12 m) with its original 'self-arising' bas relief image of Shridevi, and other images including the king with his two foreign queens, and Padmasambhava, flanked by Shantaraksita and King Trisong Detsen. The **west face** has a shrine dedicated to Ganden Tripa Tenpa Rabgyel who passed away here.

Nyangdren Pawangka Podrang The present complex is a three-storey circular building, the remains of King Songtsen Gampo's original tower, which is approached from the north by a series of steps. The other three sides are sheer rock faces. The interior floor plan is semi-circular, except for the northern section which is square. Repairs were made to this surviving structure in the 1980s; and 18 of the 108 stupas have now been rebuilt. The ground floor contains storerooms but no chapels, while the second floor contains the assembly hall (*tsokhang*), the protector chapel (*gonkhang*), and the four-pillared chapel (*Kabzhima Lhakhang*).

Among these, the **assembly hall** contains a central reliquary stupa, with an original Shakyamuni in its inner sanctum, flanked by (left side) a 'self-arising' statue of Jowo Lokeshvara that had been transported from Gyama, the birthplace of King Songtsen Gampo; and (right side) a 'self-arising' image called Chubzang Doku Chenrezi which had been brought from Chubzang; and (below in front) another

 Shakyamuni image, returned recently from Beijing. On the north wall of the assembly hall (adjacent to the protector chapel entrance) are, in succession, images of Shantaraksita, the Fifth Dalai Lama, King Songtsen Gampo with his foreign queens, and the Thirteenth Dalai Lama. On the west wall are Padmasambhava flanked by Shantaraksita and King Trisong Detsen, while on the east (next to the window) are old tangkas with the throne of the late the Tenth Panchen Lama below.

The **protector chapel**, entered from the east side of the assembly hall, contains the following newly constructed images: Dorje Yudronma, Vaishravana, Dharmaraja, Guhyasamaja, Cakrasamvara, Bhairava, Magzorma, Gonpo Taksha Marpo (the local protector) and Lhamo Duzorma.

The **four-pillared chapel**, entered from the left of the assembly hall, has new images of Tonmi Sambhota, the kings Lhatotori Nyentsen, Trisong Detsen, Songtsen Gampo and Relpachen, Minister Gar Tongtsen, Khonton Peljor Lhundrub, Reting Trichen, Tenpa Rabgyel and Lhatsun Rinpoche. On the roof is the private apartment of the Dalai Lamas, containing images of Cakrasamvara, Tara, Atisha, Tsongkhapa with his foremost students and Avalokiteshvara.

Rigsum Gonpo Lhakhang The Rigsum Gonpo Lhakhang, located southeast of the main building, was founded by King Songtsen Gampo. Beyond its entrance courtyard and within the portico to the left, in a glass case, is a stone slab (with the Six-syllable Mantra of Avalokiteshvara) reputedly carved by Tonmi Sambhota in person. The left wall contains new images of Tsongkhapa with his foremost students, Shakyamuni, and Eleven-faced Avalokiteshvara. Beyond is an **inner sanctum** containing murals of Thousand-armed Avalokiteshvara and Cakrasamvara, with the throne of the Dalai Lamas and the highly venerated 'self-arising' images of the Lords of the Three Enlightened Families, mentioned above which are of archaic design and were probably embellished by Newar craftsmen in the seventh century.

Adjacent to the entrance is a small shrine containing one of Cakrasamvara's three stone eyes (the others are at Tokden, above, and at Gari nunnery west of Pawangka). Northwest of this chapel is a newly constructed white reliquary; while north of the main building is a shrine containing 'self-arising' images of Tara (left) and Bhaisajyaguru (right). Below this shrine is a single-storey hermitage where Tsongkhapa stayed for one year in retreat.

Gyaza Gonchu Podrang Uphill from Rigsum Gonpo Lhakhang is the yellow chapel of the Gyaza Gonchu Podrang. The ground floor contains the **Zikpa Lhakhang**, which commemorates Tsongkhapa's five visions (*Zikpa Ngaden*), and contains new 2-m images of Tsongkhapa with his foremost students, murals of Vajrapani and Manjushri, and images of Tiger-riding Mahakala and Hayagriva. A side chamber to the left has new images of the Eight Medicine Buddhas and some old tangkas.

Upstairs is the main chapel, dedicated to Princess Wencheng, with images of Tara, Shakyamuni Buddha, Tsongkhapa with his students and King Songtsen Gampo with his foreign queens.

Lhatsun Labrang To the right (east) of the Gyaza Gonchu Podrang is the ruined Lhatsun Labrang; along with the ruined Tsongkha Lhakhang and the Karthog Lhakhang Khapa. The Lhatsun Labrang is entered through a south-facing courtyard, and at its rear, approached through a 1-m high passage is one of the meditation caves of King Songtsen Gampo. To the west of the complex is a whitewashed rock carving of the Arapacana mantra of the Bodhisattva Manjushri.

Upper White Rock To the north of the Lhatsun Labrang is the rocky abode of the protector of Pawangka – a 15-m high boulder, symbolizing the male tortoise, which was formerly separated by King Songtsen Gampo's 108 stupas in order to prevent their meeting, which was predicted to presage various national disasters. The rock was formerly linked to Pawangka by a heavy iron chain, which was destroyed by Langdarma along with the upper six storeys of the original tower. Left of the upper monolith and halfway up Mount Dukri are the **Sepuk meditation caves**, which contain 'self-arising' images of the Twenty-one Taras.

Tashi Choling Hermitage The Tashi Choling hermitage is on the slopes above the carnel ground, and is accessible by a pathway leading uphill from the Lhatsun Labrang. A two-storey building stands at the north side of the courtyard with a backdrop of ruins below. On the right is a shrine containing original images of the Three Deities of Longevity, and smaller images of Shakyamuni, Bhaisajyaguru and the previous Pawangka Rinpoche among others. The central pillar has a finely carved head of Hayagriva.

Tokden Drubpuk About 45 minutes' walk above Pawangka, this hermitage comprises three caves, the main one containing one of Cakrasamvara's three eyes carved in stone, and a 'self-arising' spring, dedicated to Vajravarahi. It was a former retreat of the previous Pawangka Rinpoche, while one of the lesser caves was that of his disciple Tokden Gyaluk.

Chubzang Nunnery Chubzang Nunnery is located at the floor of a ravine, 30 minutes' walk southeast of Tashi Choling. The complex contains an enclosed debating courtyard and an assembly hall, with an entrance courtyard and kitchen. The **inner sanctum** of the assembly hall contains two sets of statues of Tsongkhapa with his foremost students. At present there are over 130 Gelukpa nuns at Chubzang.

South Lhasa: orientation and attractions

The south bank of the Kyi-chu River has, until very recently, been relatively undeveloped. Most buildings belong to the military, and there are also a number of outlying farming villages such as Dekyi Khangsar, Zhapa, Nupa and Gepho. The road from the bridge has now been paved as far as Drib, where the reconstructed regency temple of Tsekchokling is located, and plans are afoot to construct a new paved road along the south bank of the Kyi-chu, which will eventually link up with the new road from Gongkar Airport.

Tsechokling Regency Temple བརྩེ་མཆོག་གླིང་

Tsechokling, classed as one of the four regency temples, is located on the south bank of the Kyi-chu in Drib village. Constructed in 1782 by Yeshe Gyeltsen, tutor of the Eighth Dalai Lama, the main building (700 sq m) formerly contained a set of the Nartang *Kangyur* and a copper image of Tsongkhapa. It never actually provided a regent, but has survived the Cultural Revolution and is now under the guidance of Tsechok Rinpoche.

Ramagang སྐར་ཆུང་ར་མ་སྒང་

The temple of Ramagang, in the extreme southwest of the Lhasa valley, was constructed during the reign of King Relpachen, in traditional design, with a central temple and obelisk surrounded by four stupas in the cardinal directions. Nothing survives of this structure at the present day, although the stupas were photographed by Hugh Richardson in the 1940s.

Sleeping

Central Lhasa *p69, map p68*
B New Century Hotel (Xin Shiji Binguan), 155 Middle Dekyi lam, T6349415, 6334895, F6333354. Has 80 rooms (with minibar and elevator service), standard rooms at ¥498 and suites at ¥1,280, with in-house shop, and night club featuring a Tibetan dance performance.
B Tibet Xiongbala Hotel (Xizang Xiongbala Binguan), 28 Jiangsu lam, T6338888, F6331777. Centrally located 3 star hotel with 83 rooms (attached bath) – deluxe standard ¥518, single ¥368, Tibetan-style suite ¥1,888, and deluxe suite ¥2,388. Has 3 restaurants including an excellent Tibetan Restaurant, coffee shop, business centre, and massage parlour.
C Airway Hotel, 12 East Kharngadong Rd, T6833442, F6333438. Centrally located, but known for its poor service, with 60 rooms (attached bath) – standard twin ¥350, Chinese-style suite ¥580, Tibetan-style suite ¥780. Has restaurant, business centre, ticketing service, tea-house, hairdresser, and KTV.
C Dargye Hotel (Dargye Dronkhang), 34 East Lingkhor lam, T6337777, F6328999. A Khampa owned 5-storey hotel, located at the junction of East Lingkhor lam and North Lingkhor lam, with comfortable rooms (attached bath) – standard ¥400, suite ¥1,200, and Tibetan-style suite ¥1,800. Has Food City restaurants on 2nd floor, business centre, lobby bar, Sacred Capital Nightclub, sauna, health centre, and garden.
C Dhood Gu Hotel (Tib Dogu Dronkhang, Ch Duongu Binguan), 19 Shasarsu Lam, Tromzikhang, T/F6322555. A popular and centrally located hotel under Nepalese management, with traditionally decorated rooms (attached bath) – standard double/ single ¥332, deluxe double/twin ¥498, triple ¥374, Potala view room ¥664, deluxe suite ¥1,038, Has business centre and restaurant.
C Gold Grain Hotel (Sernye Dronkang/ Jingu Fandian), 14 Yutok lam, T6329713, F6330367. Central, with 139 rooms (attached bathroom), which are well sunlit on south side – double ¥380, luxury standard ¥350, luxury suite ¥518, single ¥220, triple ¥100, economy ¥120. Has elevators, Chinese restaurant, dining room, disco, OK, and IDD payphones in lobby.
C Kyichu Hotel, 149 East Dekyi lam, T6338824, F6320234. Well located on East Dekyi lam, with pleasant rooms (attached showers), the preferred base of many expat workers – double ¥260, single ¥180, triple ¥260; also business centre, curio shop, and Nepalese restaurant.
C Lhasa Commercial Hotel (Lhasa Tsong-le Dronkhang), 8 East Kharngadong lam, T6325888, F6325493. A centrally located hotel with 35 rooms (attached bath) – standard ¥320, suite ¥680, deluxe suite ¥880. Has lounge, western café, Sunshine Tea-house, ticketing facility, shopping centre and hairdresser.
C Serkhang Hotel, 25 Middle Dekyi lam, T6362888, F6336860. A fairly new hotel under Amdowa management, 79 standard rooms ¥260, singles ¥320, and suites ¥600; also Chinese restaurant, teahouse, Mahjong Parlour.
C Shambhala Hotel (Shambhala Sol Dronkhang), 1 Mentsikhang lam, T6323888, F6323577. Fairly new central hotel with 70 rooms (attached bath) – standard ¥400, single ¥480, deluxe ¥1,200. Has Western and Chinese restaurants, business centre and sauna.
C Snowland Hotel, 4 Mentsikhang lam, T6323687. Located opposite the Mentsikhang on the northwest corner of the Jokhang Plaza, with 30 rooms (some with attached bath) – double ¥260, deluxe ¥360, economy double ¥80, triple ¥30 per bed, dormitory ¥25 per bed. Has the excellent Snowland Restaurant, serving Indian, Tibetan and Western cuisine, bicycle rental and business services.
C Telecommunication Hotel (Lhasa Logtrin Dronkhang), Middle Dekyi lam, T6810538. A new hotel adjacent to the Telecommunciation Tower Building, with a variety of rooms (en suite) – standard ¥320, single ¥320, triple, ¥480, suite ¥480. Has its own travel service.
C Tianhe Hotel, 5 Yutok lam, T6338138. A new hotel located near the TAR Government Buildings. Standard rooms ¥318, single ¥318, deluxe standard ¥380, and deluxe suite ¥568.
C Tibet Postal Service Hotel (Bojong Draksi Arkhang), Middle Dekyi lam, T6821999, F6813999. Newly opened, central, 80 rooms (standard ¥380, Tibetan and Chinese style suites ¥880), restaurants, IDD telephone.

For an explanation of the sleeping and eating price codes used in this guide, see inside the front cover. Other relevant information is found in Essentials pages 44-46.

C Yak Hotel, 100 East Dekyi lam, T6323496, F6336906. Located close to Ramoche on East Dekyi lam, with 74 rooms (some with attached bath) – double ¥260, triple ¥150. Has well recommended Lhasa Kitchen and Duniya restaurants, IDD calls in room, business services, bicycle rental, ticketing and guiding services.

C Ying Hotel (Ying Binguan), Yutok lam, T6324255. Centrally located with double suites ¥300 and 4-bed rooms ¥200.

D Gang-gyen Hotel, East Dekyi lam, T6337666. Double (attached bath) ¥180, triple (no attached bath) ¥120.

D Kailash Hotel, 151 East Dekyi lam, T6322220, 6340904. A fairly new hotel on East Dekyi lam. Has standard rooms at ¥220, Tibetan-style suite ¥320, standard suite ¥260, and singles ¥160, with popular restaurant.

D Lhasa Peace Hotel (Heiping Fandian), 10 Jiangsu lam, T6330888, F6348612. With 38 standard double rooms at ¥180-240, 4 singles at ¥180, and 2 suites at ¥450, and Chinese restaurant, teahouse and laundry service.

D Mandala Hotel, 31 South Barkhor lam, T6338940, 6324783, F6324787. New hotel with outstanding location on the Barkhor, 36 rooms (some with attached bath) – double ¥240, single ¥200, triple ¥280. Good restaurant and rooftop tea-house, but no telephones in rooms.

D Pata Hotel, East Lingkhor lam, T6338419. A poor hotel, conveniently located behind the Jokhang – double (with attached bath) ¥180, triple (without attached bath) ¥90.

D Tibet Mountains and Rivers Hotel, 29 East Dekyi lam, T6348686, F6336555. With 85 rooms, including standard twin rooms at ¥160, economy standard rooms at ¥80, and deluxe suites at ¥400, with internet café, music tea garden, dance performances, business centre and multi-function hall.

E Banak Zhol Hotel, East Dekyi lam, T6323829. A well-known hotel for backpackers and budget travellers, with 103 rooms – deluxe double (attached bath) ¥100, deluxe Tibetan-style double (attached shower) ¥80, economy double (no attached bath) ¥60, economy single (no attached bath) ¥30, 4-bed room (no attached bath) ¥100. Has the well-liked Kailash Cafe, free laundry and storage service, bicycle rental, and the Potala Folk Travel agency.

E Kirey Hotel, East Dekyi lam, T6323462. For backpackers and budget travellers, has 266 beds – double ¥100 (attached bath), single ¥50 (no attached bath), triple ¥60 (no attached bath), double ¥50 (no attached bath). Has Tashi Number Two and Crazy Yak restaurants, but the communal toilet facilities have been criticised.

E Pentoc Guesthouse, East Mentsikhang lam, T/F6330700/ 86326686. Conveniently located but poor hotel, catering to backpackers, on Mentsikhang lam – double ¥65, triple ¥75, single ¥40, 4-bed ¥100. Has hot showers, video lounge, IDD service, in house travel agency, and mountain bike rental

E Tashi Dagye Hotel, Mentsikhang lam, T6325804. Seedy but inexpensive – double ¥100, triple ¥75. Has Nepalese restaurant, but the hotel is disliked by the many backpackers who are obliged to stay here when they visit Lhasa on cheap packages from Chengdu.

West Lhasa *p104, map p64*

A International Grand Hotel (Guoche Dajiudian), South Mirik lam, T6832888, F6820888. A new 4 star hotel located in the eleven storey Post and Commercial Mansion—standard twin ¥750, business twin or single ¥1,118, standard suite ¥1,868, executive suite ¥2,488, Tibetan suite ¥2,188, with in-house tea-rooms, restaurants, beauty parlour, karaoke etc. Excellent rooms, but designed with windows that cannot open.

A Lhasa Hotel (Lhasa Fandian), 1 South Mirik lam, T6832221, F6834117. A somewhat over-rated 4-star hotel, with 450 rooms (attached bath) and piped oxygen – deluxe rooms (north block) ¥1,010, standard rooms (south and central blocks) ¥778, Tibetan-style rooms ¥1,183, larger suites ¥1,568- ¥2,219, presidential suite ¥8,888. 4 main restaurants (Himalayan for Tibetan and Nepalese dishes, Sichuan for Chinese dishes, Everest for western buffet, and the Hard Yak Café for à la carte western meals), also has swimming pool, Tin Tin Bar, 1 Minzu Lu Coffee Shop, karaoke bar, business centre, tour agency, gift shop, hairdressing and beauty salon, Hilsa Health and Recreation Centre, medical consultations (including Tibetan traditional medicine), CNN and in-house movies.

A Pearl Garden Hotel (Mingzhu Huayuan Jiudian), formerly known as the Grand Hotel, 67 Middle Dekyi lam, T6816666, F6826088. A 3-star hotel, often reserved for government conferences, with 531 rooms (attached bath) – deluxe suite ¥872, deluxe standard room ¥460, triple ¥258, economy room ¥280, and one suite at ¥1,600, with oxygen, beauty salon, hairdresser, shops, business centre, and an in-house Chinese restaurant with a seating capacity of 1200.

A **Tibet Hotel**, 64 Middle Dekyi Rd, T6834966, F6836787. A 3/ 4 star hotel with 258 rooms (attached bath), in the new VIP Building, which are currently the best in Lhasa – single and deluxe twin ¥988, business suite ¥2,800, king deluxe suite ¥8,888. The older building to the front has standard twins and singles ¥880, and deluxe suites at ¥2,800. 10 restaurants, including Western Food Restaurant, National Food Restaurant, Sunshine Banquet Hall, and Garden Bar. Has business and shopping centres, beauty salon, KTV, sauna, massage, travel agency, and discotheque. Rooms have BBC World.

C **Hebei Dasha**, 54 Middle Dekyi lam, T6820999, F6837777. With 68 standard rooms at ¥340, 3 single rooms at ¥348, 4 business-style standard rooms at ¥348, 4 Tibetan-style standard rooms at ¥368, and 6 deluxe suites at ¥1,880 (40% discount available), and beauty salon, hair salon, sauna, health & leisure centre, business centre and conference hall.

East Lhasa *p117, map p64*

A **Himalaya Hotel**, 6 East Lingkhor Rd, Lhasa, T6321111, F6332675. A ¾ star hotel located near the river and within easy walking distance of the Barkhor, it has 132 excellent bedrooms (attached bath) – superior twin ¥859, superior single ¥525, standard twin ¥ 430, triple ¥505, superior suite ¥1,174, deluxe suite ¥1,527, super deluxe suite ¥1,794. Shengdi Chinese Restaurant and Yak Café (both in need of improvement), Shambhala Ballroom, business centre, 4th floor travel agency, foreign exchange facility, shopping arcade, beauty parlour and hairdressing salon, sauna and massage service, and Tibetan restaurants.

B **Old Post Hotel**, 5 Lane One, East Lingkhor Road, T6348888. With 38 rooms including 26 standard rooms at ¥480, 12 triples at ¥580, 6 suites at ¥800-980, with in-house Chinese and Tibetan cuisine, and Tibetan cultural shows.

C **Holy Swan Hotel (Lhaja Trungtrung Dronkhang, Shangtian Fandian)**, 3-3 Ngachen lam, T6326999, F6364555. Located in a quite residential area of East Lhasa, with 80 rooms (attached bath), including 64 standard twin rooms at ¥280, 5 singles at ¥320, 2 triples at ¥300, and 4 suites (range: ¥600-1,088), with 3 restaurants, teahouse, business and shopping centre, KTV, sauna and hairdresser.

C **Kadak Hotel**, Jiangsu lam, T6337771. Has 68 rooms (some with attached bath), superior ¥350. Has business services, travel agency, bicycle rental, dining room, disco and KTV.

C **Sunlight Hotel**, 27 Linyu lam, T6322064, F6335675. With 98 rooms (refurbished rooms have attached baths) – standard ¥260, suite ¥380, deluxe suite ¥680, economy ¥220. Has various ethnic restaurants and KTV.

E **Jomolangma Tweed Factory Hotel (Jomolangma Baltak Zotra Dronkhang)**, Ngachen Lane, T6333568. Located in a quiet narrow lane in East Lhasa – single/ double ¥50, standard ¥45, single (without bath) ¥20, single (without WC) ¥15, 6-bed ¥60.

E **Kongda Hotel**, East Zamchen lam. A new poorly designed hotel – double ¥120, single ¥60-80.

North Lhasa *p116, map p64*

C **Namsel Hotel**, East Damra lam, T6326662, F6326882. A reasonably good hotel but located in remote red-light district of North Lhasa – standard ¥260, deluxe suite ¥380, economy ¥80, and triple (no attached bath) ¥25 per bed. Has restaurants, business facilities, and 24-hr sauna, KTV service.

D **Golden Bridge Hotel**, 40 Sera lam, T6362816. 62 rooms (range: ¥140-240), with Tibetan-style conference hall and business centre.

D **New Plateau Hotel (Sato Dronkhang**, East Damra lam, T6327814. Recently relocated in this red-light district from its former location at the Workers Roundabout – standard ¥180, single ¥120, double ¥100, triple ¥96.

D **Norda Kangsang Hotel**, 68 Sera lam, T6381717, F6381735. A Tibetan-style hotel, with a noisy street front and 31 rooms – standard doubles at ¥240 and singles at ¥140, with multi-cuisine restaurant, Tibetan shop, conference hall, nightclub and café.

E **Friendship Guesthouse (Dzadrok Nelenkhang)**, North Lingkhor lam, T6824615. Has standard twin rooms at ¥80.

E **Old Plateau (Gaoyuan) Hotel**, North Lingkhor lam, T6324916. Is dilapidated and to be avoided at all cost.

E **Tashi Mandala Guesthouse**, Sera lam (Tuanjie Xinchun), T6326556. Has standard twin rooms at ¥50-60 per bed, and triples at ¥20 per bed, with popular in-house restaurant offering both Tibetan and Chinese cuisine.

Eating

Central Lhasa *p69, map p68*

¥¥¥ **Beijing Mutton Restaurant**, West Potala Square. An expensive but well located Muslim-style restaurant, specializing in lamb dishes.

¥¥¥ **Chorten Karpo Trokyi Restaurant** , Middle Dekyi Lam. Good Tibetan food, slightly overpriced.

¥¥¥ **Darpel Tibetan Restaurant**, West Potala Square. Upmarket location, good Tibetan food.

¥¥¥ **Dunya Restaurant**, 100 East Dekyi Lam, T0891-6333374. A popular venue for expats and well-to-do locals, under Dutch management, specializing in Continental and Nepalese cuisine. Salads are recommended. Authentic bar and excellent jazz music.

¥¥¥ **Eatlovers Restaurant**, North Dekyilingka Lam. Has an interesting bakery and Continental menu, with some Nepalese dishes. Good food, but slow service.

¥¥¥ **Food City Restaurant**, Dargye Hotel, 34 East Lingkhor Lam. Expensive Chinese fare.

¥¥¥ **Gau Ya Restaurant**, Kharngadong Lam. Offers the best Peking Duck in town.

¥¥¥ **Kyichu Hotel Restaurant**, West Dekyi Lam. Serves good Nepalese and some continental dishes. Popular with expats, many of whom are based at this hotel.

¥¥¥ **Mongolian King Restaurant (Sokpo Lugsha Tsomo)**, West Potala Square, T0891-6829149. Upmarket location, specializing in Mongolian-style hotpot and BBQ.

¥¥¥ **Snowgod Palace Tibetan Restaurant** , Middle Dekyi Lam. Poor quality Tibetan food and service.

¥¥¥ **Tibetan Restaurant**, Xiongbala Hotel, 28 Jiangsu Lam, T0891-6338888. Excellent Tibetan cuisine, with traditional Tibetan ambience, but slow service.

¥¥ **Akhu Tonba Restauant**, West Barkhor Lam. A popular Khampa haunt, cheap Tibetan fare.

¥¥ **Dicos Café**, West Barkhor Lam, T0891-6326892. Good location for fast food and burgers, overlooking the Jokhang Plaza, but in decline under new management.

¥¥ **Crazy Yak**, located in Kirey Hotel, East Dekyi Lam. Specializes in evening Tibetan banquets, and local opera performances for tourists.

¥¥ **Gau Ya Restaurant**, South Nyangdren Lam. Opposite Air China offices, inexpensive Peking Duck on offer.

¥¥ **Makye Ama Restaurant**, South Barkhor Lam. A reasonably good Tibetan restaurant, geared to the tourist market, and located in a historically important downtown haunt of the Sixth Dalai Lama. Also serves Nepalese dishes.

¥¥ **Mandala Hotel Restaurant**, South Barkhor Lam, T0891-6329645. Nepalese and Tibetan cuisine. Slow service.

¥¥ **Mandala Restaurant**, Barkhor Square. Large dining space, specializing in Nepalese and Indian cuisine, some continental favourites.

¥¥ **Snowland Restaurant**, Mentsikhang Lam, T0891-6337323. A hugely popular restaurant in Lhasa for local Tibetans, visitors, tourists, and expats. Serves Tibetan, Indian, and Continental dishes, with rapid, friendly service, simple but warm atmosphere, reasonably priced.

¥¥ **Tcheu Tang French Restaurant**,13 Mentsikhang Lam, T0891-6345227. Under Tibetan and French management (temporarily closed for reconstruction).

¥¥ **Tibet Café and Bar**, Mentsikhang Lam. Offers Thai, Korean and Tibetan food at reasonable prices.

¥¥ **Yutok Restaurant**, Yutok Lam, T0891-6330931. Good Tibetan food, but slow service.

¥ **Alotsang Tibetan Restaurant**, Do Senge Lam. Also known as the "pink curtain". Serves average Tibetan cuisine.

¥ **Alotsang 2 Tibetan Restaurant**, Yutok Lam, T0891-6330210. A new branch of backpackers' favourite Tibetan restauant.

¥ **Amdo Zakhang**, Mentsikhang Lam. Specializes, as one would expect, in dishes from Far East Tibet. Good value for money.

¥ **Kailash Café**, 143 East Dekyi Lam. T0891-6346288, located near the Banakzhol Hotel. Cheap Nepalese and Tibetan cuisines, popular with backpackers.

¥ **Lhasa Kitchen**, located in Yak Hotel, East Dekyi Lam. Good value for money, average Tibetan cuisine.

¥ **Tashi Number One**, Mentsikhang Lam. For apple pie and some western cuisine. Run-down but still a backpackers' favourite.

¥ **Tashi Restaurant Number Two**, in Kirey Hotel, T0891-6323462. Cheap Tibetan food, run-down and frequented by backpackers.

¥ **Thanduohua**, South Nyangdren Lam. Excellent and inexpensive Sichuan dishes.

¥ **Third Eye Restaurant**, Mentsikhang Lam.

Offers some western fare for backpackers.

Tibet Kitchen, Mentsikhang Lam. Recommended by locals and by backpackers, cheap and wholesome Tibetan fare.

West Lhasa *p104, map p64*

Beijing California Yak Restaurant, North Mirik Lam, T0891-6830300. Expensive but excellent speciality hotpot and yak steak restaurant. Popular with local businessmen.

Bluebird Hotpot (Qingniao Huoguo), South Mirik Lam, T0891-6815601. A very popular and now relocated upmarket Sichuan hotpot restaurant. Reservations required.

Chinese Restaurant, Lhasa Hotel, 1 South Mirik Lam. Overpriced Sichuan fare, with slow service.

Everest Restaurant, Lhasa Hotel, 1 South Mirik Lam. Buffet style restaurant, catering to tour groups. Some continental dishes as well as Chinese dishes on offer.

Golden Flower Korean Restaurant, North Mirik Lam, T0891-6819998. An elegant Korean BBQ restaurant, with waitresses in Korean dress, but expensive.

Hard Yak Cafe, Lhasa Hotel, 1 South Mirik Lam. Offers Continental and Asian favourites. Average quality, and well overpriced. Room service available for hotel guests.

Himalaya Restaurant, Lhasa Hotel, 1 South Mirik Lam. An expensive Tibetan restaurant, offering classical Tibetan music in the evenings during the tourist season.

Katak Restaurant (Qing Niao Hada) West Chingdrol Lam. One of the best upmarket Sichuan hotpot restaurants in Lhasa, formerly known as the Bluebird, and now refurbished under new management.

National Food Restaurant, Tibet Hotel, 64 Middle Dekyi Lam. Expensive and deluxe, but good quality restaurant, specializing in a variety of regional Chinese cuisines.

Riverside Fish Restaurant (Shuijing Gong) 180 Middle Dekyi Lam, T0891-6333885. Cantonese cuisine and seafood. Imported lobster is popular but very expensive.

Tanjiayuan Chinese Restaurant, South Mirik Lam, T0891-6820212. An upmarket Sichuan restaurant, of good quality.

Alibaba Restaurant , Middle Dekyi Lam. For Muslim and Chinese dishes.

Bright Pearl Restaurant, Middle Dekyi Lam, near the Tibet Hotel. Sichuan cuisine.

Chipel Dumra Restaurant (Mingchun Yuan Canting), Middle Dekyi Lam, T0891-6839339. Opposite the Pearl Hotel. Reasonably priced Tibetan and Sichuan cuisine.

Double Nine Hotpot (Jiujiu Huoguo) , Middle Dekyi Lam, T0891-6819599. Currently the most popular of Sichuan hotpot restaurants, competitively priced with good service, located next to the main branch of the Bank of China.

Lhasa County Fish Restaurant (Sixiang Yuzhuang) , South Luding Lam, T0891-6816259. Serves local fish. Tibetans generally do not eat fish, and so this is a restaurant catering almost exclusively to Chinese businessmen and tourists.

Mad Yak Tibetan Restaurant, Hebei Mansion Hotel, Middle Dekyi Lam, T0891-6814955. Occasionally hosts evening performances of Tibetan opera for tourists.

Meling (Aisharan) Tibetan Food Yard, 83 Middle Dekyi Lam, T0891-6825125. Good service and reasonable Tibetan fare, through slightly overpriced.

Pemaraga Tibetan Restaurant, Middle Dekyi Lam. A popular local restaurant, with an excellent Tibetan chef.

Rang Khyimchen Mentang , Middle Dekyi Lam. Home-style Tibetan cuisine. Slightly overpriced.

Snow Dragon Tibetan Restaurant (Xuelong Canting), Middle Dekyi Lam, T0891-6834699. Managed by Zhigatse CITS, and featuring Tibetan opera performances in the evenings.

Tanfulou Chinese Restaurant , Middle Dekyi Lam, T0891-6810020. Recently opened, specializing in Sichuan dishes.

Trungchin Jiyon Hotpot Restaurant Middle Dekyi Lam, alongside the Yak Roundabout almost opposite the Double Nine Hotpot. A less expensive and smaller Sichuan hotpot restaurant.

Yeti Café, 206-10 Middle Dekyi Lam, T0891-6815755. Slightly overpriced Tibetan cuisine, but popular with both locals and tourists.

North and East Lhasa *p116, map p64*

Drongnub Fish Restaurant, West Damra Lam, T0891-6811490. Spacious location, with its own fresh fish ponds, catering mostly for Chinese clients.

🍴🍴🍴 **Shengdi Chinese Restaurant**, Himalaya Hotel, 6 East Lingkhor Lam, T0891-6321111. Expensive Cantonese and Sichuan dishes.
🍴🍴🍴 **Sunlight Hotel Restaurant**, 27 Linyu Lam, T0891-6322064. Overpriced Tibetan and Chinese regional cuisine, in diverse ethnic setting.
🍴🍴 **Holy Swan Restaurant**, Holy Swan Hotel, 3 Ngachen Lam, T0891-6326999. Slightly overpriced Tibetan and Sichuan cuisine.
🍴🍴 **Jamdrol Restaurant**, Karma Kunzang, T0891-6336093. An out-of-the way family-run Tibetan restaurant, catering almost exclusively to TTC tour groups.
🍴 **Namsel Tibetan Restaurant**, Namsel Hotel, East Damra Lam, T0891-6326662. Offers inexpensive Tibetan fare.

Cafés

Base Camp Café, Mentsikhang Lam. Popular with backpacking tourists.
Music Kitchen Café, Middle Dekyi Lam. T0891-6812980. Another late night venue.
Old Tree Café, upmarket location on North Mirik Lam.
Pacan Coffee House, North Mirik Lam, T0891-6830405. Also serves snacks and light refreshments.
Tibet Café and Bar, Mentsikhang Lam. Popular tourist café.

Bars and clubs

Modern upmarket bars are mostly in the west of the city.
52 Beer Bar, T0891-6831020. Located next to red-light district on Middle Dekyi Lam.
Duniya Bar, East Dekyi Lam. Very popular, authentic bar, with good music (jazz, blues etc).
Last Bus Bar, North Mirik Lam. Imaginative design, popular haunt for some tour guides.
Milan Bar and Coffee House, North Mirik Lam. A popular haunt for local businessmen.
Tintin Bar, in the Lhasa Hotel. Expensive and losing clientele.
Victoria Wine Bar, Middle Dekyi Lam, T0891-13989002338.
Yuhuli Bar, Middle Dekyi Lam, T0891-6831668. Under Chinese management.

Below are some of the best Tibetan nightclubs (*nangmating*), where modern and traditional Tibetan songs are performed live, along with popular Chinese numbers. Opening hours 2100-late. There is also a fashion show on Kharngadong Lam.
Sacred Capital Nightclub, in the Dargye Hotel on East Lingkhor Lam, Trokyi Nangmating, next to the Serkhang Hotel on East Dekyi Lam.
Yiwan Nightclub, above Alibaba Restaurant on Middle Dekyi Lam.
Nangmating, located in a lane behind Double Nine Hotpot.

The best discos are the **Yindu** on Middle Dekyi Lam, and **JJ Discotheque** on West Potala Square.

Entertainment

Lhasa has many varied forms of entertainment. Locals devote much time to picnics, parties, and board games, especially Mahjong and Karam. The drinking songs of Lhasa are particularly renowned.

Cinema

The main **Lhasa City Cinema** is located on Yutok Lam. But there are also a profusion of KTV (karaoke) outlets and video parlours throughout the city.

Museums

The **Tibet National Museum** on South Mirik Lam, is a grand building with 5 exhibition halls and expensive souvenir shops, which opened in 2000. Admission costs are ¥30 per person and audio tours are available in English, Tibetan, Chinese and Japanese. Exhibits cover the paleolithic and neolithic periods as well as historical and geographical overviews, Tibetan Buddhism, and household artefacts. There are some outstanding pieces in the collection, but the visitor should beware of official propaganda in the historical section.

The **Tibet National Library** located on the corner of South Mirik Lam and Norbulingka Lam, includes both Tibetan and Chinese literature, with very few secondary sources. Though extensive, there is space for only a small portion of the collection, most of which is still housed in the Potala Archives.

The **TAR Historical Archives**, located behind the Customs Office on West Dekyi Lam, T0891-6824184/0891-6824823, has a fascinating collection of documents, some of which date from the era of Chogyel Phakpa. Other museums such as the **Potala Museum and Exhibition Hall** on Middle Dekyi Lam, and the **Peoples' Art Museum** on the corner of East Chingdrol Lam and Do Senge Lam have little to offer in contrast to the magnificence of the city's temples, monasteries, and palaces.

Music

Traditional Tibetan music may also be heard at the **Himalayan Restaurant** in *Lhasa Hotel*, and the **Snow Dragon Tibetan Restaurant** on Middle Dekyi Lam, and the **Crazy Yak Restaurant** on East Dekyi Lam, as well as in some of the smaller downtown restaurants.

Opera

Classical Tibetan operas are performed at the **TAR Kyormolung Operatic Company**, the **TAR Academy of Performing Arts**, the **Lhasa City Academy of Performing Arts**, and in **Norbulingka Park** during the **Yoghurt Festival** in summer (see below, Festivals).

Shopping

Books, maps, cards and newspapers

Peoples' Publishing House Bookstore, on North Lingkhor Lam.
Xinhua Bookshop, Middle Dekyi Lam, next to Tibet Hotel. Has a wide range of Tibetan cultural publications.
Xinhua Bookstore, on Yutok Lam, the branch on South Barkhor Lam.

Department stores and supermarkets

Lhasa Department Store, on the corner of Yutok Lam and Kharngadong Lam. The largest, modern store, where electrical goods, clothing, children's toys and other goods can be purchased.

Other major supermarkets include **Le Bailong**, opposite the Post Hotel on East Dekyi Lam. Small self-service supermarkets can now be found in a number of central locations on Chingdrol Lam, East Lingkhor Lam and Do Senge Lam, many stocking imported products from Nepal and India as well as mainland China. The Barkhor also has a number of department stores, including a 2-storey shopping complex with escalator access. Chinese textiles, clothing, household utensils, and electrical goods are available here.

Handicrafts

The traditional **market** of Lhasa is around the Jokhang temple in the Barkhor and its radial road system. Tibetan handicrafts may be found here, including textiles, carpets, jewellery, metalwork, leather goods, photographs, and religious artefacts, including paintings, incense and books. Antiques are available, but can only be exported with discretion. Bargaining here is the norm and, as a visitor, you should strive to reduce the proposed price by as much as 50%.

Handicrafts are also available from:
Curio Shop at the Kyichu Hotel.
Friendship Store, and other antique shops on Yutok Lam.
Nomad Handicrafts, Mentsikhang Lam.
Tibet Tashidelek Handmade Carpets & Arts, 41 Middle Dekyi Lam, T0891-6826213.

Also more expensive shops in the Lhasa Hotel and the Himalaya Hotel.
Norlha Shop, North Barkhor Lam, T0891-633075. Fine Buddhist statues, recommended, not least because they also insert a consecrated core into their images.
Tashi Dagye Studio of master artist Nyima Wangdu, on East Barkhor Lam, T0891-13908905315. In particular, the best new tangka paintings are available.
Tent Factory, off East Dekyi Lam. Contact for Tibetan tents and tent fabrics.

For traditional Tibetan furniture, there are outlets near South Nyangdren Lam.

For new carpets, contact the **Carpet Factory**, Jiangsu Lam, the **Kawachen Carpet** factory, West Chingdrol Lam, the **Tibet Potala Carpet Factory**, T0891-6826459, in Denpak below Drepung, or the **Snow Leopard Carpet Showroom**, Mentsikhang Lam, T0891-6321481. The **Boot Factory** on East Chingdrol Lam is also worth visiting.

NB Most shops will accept only RMB currency, and a few will be happy to receive payment in US dollars. Unofficial currency exchange facilities are instantly available; and the main branch of the Bank of China is not too far distant on West Lingkhor Lam.

Music

The best outlet for Tibetan and Chinese VCDs, DVDs and audio cassettes is **Aegean Sea Music Store**, on Do Senge Lam.

Open markets

There are interesting open air markets on Yutok Lam to the west of the Jokhang plaza (for curios), at Tromzikhang in the Barkhor area, at the Lukhang Park Gate on South Nyangdren Lam, and on Kharngadong Rd, near the Potala (for vegetables, meat, clothing and household artefacts). Lhasa's main Night Market has 2 entrances, one on Barghu Lam and the other on North Mirik Lam. It has become the most popular meeting place for younger Tibetans in the evenings.

Photography

Print film and processing are available at photographic shops on West Potala Square, East Dekyi Lam, and Kharngadong Lam; both slide and print film may be available at Lhasa Hotel, though you are advised to carry all your film supplies from home. Digital cards are unavailable at present, outside the digital camera section of the Lhasa Department Store. Print film can easily be developed in Lhasa (1 hr service, ¥26 for a roll of 36).

Stamps and postcards

Stamps are available at GPO, on the corner of East Dekyi Lam and Kharngadong Lam; and also at the reception counters or shops in the major hotels. Postcards can also be purchased at the GPO (¥4 for 10 cards).

Textiles

Friendship Store, on Yutok Lam, and the shops around the Barkhor offer traditional fabrics including brocade silk, and traditional ready-to-wear Tibetan clothing.

Trekking and camping equipment

Osark, on W Potala Square, Green Trekking on East Dekyi Lam, and other outlets on Mentsikhang Lam, and near the Himalaya Hotel on East Lingkor Lam.

Activities and tours

Gymnasium

On North Nyangdren Lam.

Health clubs

Hilsa Recreation and Health Club, Lhasa Hotel, on South Mirik Lam.
Himalaya Hotel, sauna.

Race course

On North Nyangdren Lam.

Sports stadium

On East Lingkhor Lam.

Tour companies

Many hotels have their own affiliated travel agencies, but the following are the best in Lhasa:

Asia Dragon Tour Corporation (Yarlung Travel Service), 3 Mirik Lam, T0891-6835181, F0891-6835182.
China Tibet Qomolungma Travel (CTQT), Rm 1112, Lhasa Hotel, 1 Mirik Lam, T0891-6836863, F0891-6836861.
China Youth Travel Service (CYTS), Rm 1103, Lhasa Hotel, 1 Mirik Lam, T0891-6824173, F0891-6823329.
Golden Bridge Travel Service (GBT), Lhasa Branch, 13 Mirik Lam, T0891-6823828, F0891-6825832.
Highland Treks and Tours, 13 North Lingkor Lam, T0891-6328808, tibethighland@mail.sc.cninfo.net.
Holyland Adventures, 215 Middle Dekyi Lam, T/F0891-6834472, holyland@public.ts.xz.cn.
Lhasa Hotel Tour Department, 1 Mirik Lam, T0891-6824509, F0891-6834117.

Lhasa Travel Service, Sunlight Hotel, 27 Linyu Lam, T0891-6335196, F0891-6335675.
Nyangtri Travel Service, Pentoc Guesthouse, Mentsikhang Lam, T/F0891-6330700.
Shigatse Travels, Yak/Snowland hotels, T0891-6330489, F0891-6330482.
Snow Pigeon Travel Service, 59 Middle Dekyi Lam, T0891-6830888, F0891-6830888.
Tibet Air International Travel Service, 14 Kharngadong Lam, T0891-6333331, F0891-6333330.
Tibet Century Travel Service, 64 Middle Dekyi Lam, T0891-6836887, F0891-6834966.
Tibet Friendship Travel Service, North Nyangdren Lam, T0891-6334534, F0891-6334533.
Tibet International Sports Travel (TIST), Himalaya Hotel, 6 East Lingkhor Lam, T0891-6331421/0891-6334082, F0891-6334855.
Tibet Kailash Travel, Lhasa Office, Yuanlin Lam, T/F0891-6832598.
Tibet Mountaineering Association (TMA), 8 East Lingkhor Lam, T0891-6333720, F0891-6336366.
Tibet Potala Folk Travel Service, 36 Jiangsu Lam, T0891-6323430, F0891-6331357.
Tibet Tourist Corporation (TTC) also known as **China International Travel Service** – Lhasa Branch (CITS), Middle Dekyi Lam, T0891-6836626, F0891-6836315.
Tibet Yungdrung Adventure, New Century Hotel, 155 East Dekyi Lam, T0891-6349410, F0891-6336496.
Windhorse Adventure (WHA), 1 North Mirik Lam, T0891-6833009, F0891-6836793.

Transport

Air

Lhasa is connected via Gongkar Airport (99 km on old road, 55 km on new road) to **Chengdu** and **Beijing** (daily flights), **Kathmandu** (Tue/Thu/Sat), **Chamdo** (Sun), **Gyeltang** and **Kunming** (Wed/Sat), **Ziling** (Mon/Wed/Fri/Sun), **Shanghai** (Wed/Sun), **Xi'an** (Mon/Wed/Fri/Sun), **Guangzhou** (Mon), and **Chongqing** (Mon/Wed/Sun).

Bus

Local There are currently 13 routes around Lhasa: **96. Terminus-West Petrol Station** (via Bank of China, Lhalu, Middle School Number Two, Prefectural Traffic HQ and Ximing Hotel); **97. Terminus-Barghu Market** (via Agricultural and Nomad Bureau, City Peoples' Hospital, Tromsikhang, CAAC Ticket Office, Xue-er and Xue-yi Villages and Jangchub Chumik); **99. Terminus-City Food and Oil Company** (via Dongjiao Settlement, High School Number Two, and Tibet Gangchen Language School); **101. Lugu Terminus-Leather Factory** (via Chingdrol lam); **102. Disco Bus Terminus-Tolung Dechen** (via Norbulingka and the Peoples' Hospital); **103. Disco Bus Terminus-Cement Factory** (via Meru Temple, International Hotel, Traffic Police, Nechung PSB); **104. Disco Bus Terminus-Military Hospital** (via Inspectorate, Peoples Hospital, Tromsikhang, CAAC Ticket Office, No Five Bus Terminus, Geology Department, and Vehicle Control Unit); **105. Disco Bus Terminus- International City** (via Yutok lam and Ngachen Power Station); **106. Ramoche- Drapchi** (via North Lingkhor lam and Dokde lam); **107. Terminus-West Petrol Station** (via Katak Hotel, Lugu, Post and Commence Building, and Farm); **108. Sports Stadium-Taktse** (via Lugu, Lhasa Zamchen, Tsel Gungtang, and Pelting); **109. Zhonghe International City-Karma Kunzang** (via Prefectural Bus Station, CAAC Ticket Office, Tromsikhang, and City Peoples' Hospital); **111. Lhasa Beer Factory-Western Farming Corporation** (via Military Hospital, Irrigation Bureau, Golden Bridge Hotel, Ramoche, Golden Horse Roundabout, Lukhang, Golden Yak Roundabout, China Telecom, Lhasa Hotel, Customs Building, and Military Command Bayi School). Fares: ¥2 (daytime), ¥3 (evening).

Long distance Long distance travel by public bus is uncomfortable, irregular, and slow except on paved roads, which are still few in number. There are 3 long distance bus stations: the main Norbulingka Bus Station on West Chingdrol Lam (see block), the Lugu Bus Station (for Nyemo, Lhundrub and Tsetang), and the Tromzikhang Bus Station (for Nakchu and Kermo).

Norbulingka Bus Station Fares

There are daily departures to all major destinations within TAR and Qinghai.

Destination	Distance	Fares
Chushul	36 km	¥8 (S)
Gongkar	104 km	¥15 (S)
Chidezhol	121 km	¥19 (S)
Dranang	144 km	¥20 (S)
Tsetang	191 km	¥27 (S)
Nyemo	107 km	¥20 (S)
Rinpung	153 km	¥27 (S)
Tadruka	192 km	¥35 (S)
Zhigatse (direct)	281 km	¥40 (S)
Gyantse	264 km	¥38 (S)
Phari	427 km	¥57 (S)
Dromo	473 km	¥88 (S)
Lhartse	567 km	¥70 (S)
Senge Tsangpo	1,818 km	¥516 (S)
Dingri	642 km	¥88 (S)
Nyalam	794 km	¥109 (S)
Dram	824 km	¥113 (S)
Damzhung	162 km	¥46 (D)
Nakchu	326 km	¥46 (S); 82 (D)
Draknak	464 km	¥55 (S); 102 (D)
Yanshiping	653 km	¥72 (S); ¥152 (D)
Marchudram Babtsuk	745 km	¥92 (S); ¥182 (D)
Kermo	1,165 km	¥152(S); ¥262 (D)
Ziling	1,947 km	¥202 (S); ¥340 (D)
Lanzhou	2,227 km	¥232 (S); ¥380 (D)
Linxia	2,409 km	¥242 (S); ¥392 (D)
Gyamda	279 km	¥105 (S)
Bayi	371 km	¥120 (S)
Nyangtri	406 km	¥135 (S)
Tramog	639 km	N/A
Chamdo	1,121 km	¥230 (S)
Pomda Airport	950 km	from Chamdo only
Jomda	1,348 km	from Chamdo only
Drichu Zampa	1,436 km	from Chamdo only
Chengdu	2,415 km	¥352 (S); ¥502 (D)
Chongqing	2,415 km	¥560 (D)

NB S = standard bus, D = deluxe bus.

Cycle rickshaw

Widely available. The price range is ¥4-10 for destinations within the city.

Hitchhiking

Hitchhiking is officially discouraged, but not impossible for the adventurous and experienced traveller.

Taxi

Taxis are easily flagged down in the street or found at the taxi stand on the corner of Yutok Lam and Do Senge Lam. The fares are fixed for all destinations within the city ¥10 (daytime), ¥15-20 (night). Fares to suburban destinations are negotiable.

Directory

Airline offices
Air China, South Nyangdren Lam, near Potala Palace, T6333331.

Banks
Bank of China, Main Branch, West Lingkhor Lam, T6344954, has ATM machine and will issue local currency through credit card transactions. There are also smaller outlets on East Dekyi Lam, between Kirey and Banakzhol Hotels, and on Middle Dekyi Lam. Limited exchange facilities are also available at Lhasa Hotel, Tibet Hotel, and Himalaya Hotel. Larger hotels will accept credit card payments. Money changers in Barkhor will accept and change US dollars into RMB at a rate slightly above that of the banks. The **Agricultural Bank of China** on Kharngadong Lam, T6338462, also has an ATM machine.

Embassies and consulates
Royal Nepalese Consulate, Upper Gyatso Lam, near Norbulingka, T0891-6822881, issues 15-day or 30-day tourist visas for Nepal within 24 hrs.

Hospitals
TAR Peoples' Hospital, North Lingkhor Lam, T0891-6322200 (emergency department). **TAR No 2 Hospital**, Upper Gyatso Lam, T0891-6822115 (emergency department). **Lhasa City Peoples Hospital**, T0891-6323811 (emergency department). The Italian-run **CISP Emergency Medicine Centre**, in TAR Peoples' Hospital, 7 North Lingkhor Lam, T0891-6321059, F0891-6321049; and the **Swiss Red Cross**, 4 Nyangdren Lam, T0891-6320175. The **Hospital of Traditional Tibetan Medicine** (Mentsikhang) has its outpatients department and the affiliated department of calendrical astrology on Yutok Lam, while its pharmaceutical factory and inpatients department are located on Nyangdren Lam, near the Institute of Tibetan Medicine (Sorik Lobdra Chenmo).

Internet
Outside the major hotels and GPO which all provide internet access, try **Boiling Point Internet Bar**, Mentsikhang Lam, **Internet Café** (2 outlets) on Middle Dekyi Lam, near the Lhasa Hotel, **Internet Café** on the corner of East Dekyi Lam and East Lingkhor Lam, and **Internet Bar**, East Lingkhor Lam, opposite the Himalaya Hotel. Price range ¥10-20 per hr.

Post offices
Postal facilities, including EMS express delivery, are available at the **GPO**, the local post offices on Chingdrol Lam and Dekyi Lam, and also through major hotels. The GPO also has its own packing service.

Telephones
All the major hotels and even some of the smaller hotels now have fax and IDD telephone services. ICC phone cards are available for IDD calls at post offices including the **GPO** on East Dekyi Lam, and the **Telecommunication Tower Building** on West Dekyi Lam. "136" pay-as-you-go cards for Chinese mobile phones are also available from China Mobile in the Telecommunication Tower Building. Reverse charge calls can be received at the GPO telephone centre (dial 0086-891-685553). DDD calls can be made from many small shops and outlets throughout the city.

Tourist offices
Tibet Tourism Bureau (TTB), Norbulingka Lam, T0891-6834315/0891-6333635, F0891-6834632. **Lhasa City Foreign Affairs Tourism Bureau**, T0891-6323632.

Useful information
Local directory enquiries T114. **National directory enquiries** T113. **Weather forecast** T0891-6324111. **Lhasa City Public Security Bureau** T110. **Lhasa City Foreigners' Permit Registration Office**, East Lingkhor Lam, T0891-6323170. **TAR Foreigners' Passport Registration Office**, T0891-6324528. **TAR Foreign Affairs Office**, on West Lingkhor Lam, T0891-6824992. **Lhasa City Police**, near Academy of Social Sciences.

Central Tibet (U)

Footprint features

Introduction

The fertile Kyi-chu Valley in which the city of Lhasa is located is one of the more densely populated parts of Tibet. The valley extends from the river's glacial sources in the northern snow ranges of Nyenchen Tanglha, which form a watershed between the Salween and Brahmaputra, as far as its southern confluence with the Brahmaputra (Tib Yarlung Tsangpo) at Chushul. Upper Kyi-chu includes the districts of Tolung, Phenyul, Lungsho, Dri and Meldro, which lie to the northwest and northeast of Lhasa, while the valley downstream from Lhasa is known as Lower Kyi-chu. Currently, the entire Kyi-chu area is divided into six counties administered from Lhasa, namely: Tolung Dechen, Damzhung, Taktse, Lhundrub, Meldro, and Chushul.

Recommended itineraries: 3 (also 4, 6). **See page 20.**

★ Don't miss...

❶ **Tsurphu** Stronghold of the Karmapas, the oldest incarnating lineage in Tibet, page 139.

❷ **Namtso Chukmo** Trek through the watershed Nyenchen Tangla range and along the shores of the tidal lake Namtso, gateway to the wilderness of northern Tibet, page 143.

❸ **Ganden** Amphitheatre setting of the first Gelukpa monastery, founded in 1409 by Tsongkhapa, page 146. Trek from here to Samye on the royal route followed by former Dalai Lamas, page 148.

❹ **Zhoto Tidro and Drigung** Explore the sacred caves, nunnery and revered charnel ground, bathe in medicinal hot springs, page 157.

❺ **Nyetang Dolma Lhakhang** An 11th-century temple founded by the Bengali master Atisha, containing precious relics and orginal images, page 159.

Tolung Dechen County

སྟོད་ལུང་བདེ་ཆེན

→ *Population: 40,570. Area: 2,926 sq km. Colour map 3, grid B2.* 堆龙德庆县

The recently repaved and reopened Lhasa-Ziling Highway leads northwest from the Dongkar intersection, west of Lhasa, and follows the east bank of the Tolung-chu upstream via Tolung Dechen to Yangpachen (77 km). Here, the northern route to Zhigatse branches off to the southwest, following the Lhorong-chu tributary upstream and across Zhugu La pass into Tsang (see below, page 259), while the highway turns northeast for Damzhung (85 km from Yangpachen). In 2007, the new railway line from Kermo will run parallel to this latter road to reach the new railhead west of Tashigang.

The Tolung valley has for centuries been the stronghold of the Karma Kagyu school in Central Tibet owing to the presence there of three great monasteries: ***Tsurphu, Nenang****, and* ***Yangpachen****. The present county capital of* ***Tolung Dechen*** *is located at* ***Namka Ngozhi****, a rapidly developing town 1 km beyond the Dongkar intersection.*

Lower Tolung

Gadong Monastery དགའ་གདོང་དགོན་པ

Standing on the slopes above Namka Ngozhi, this Kadampa monastery was founded by Zingpo Sherapa in the 11th century. It subsequently became the seat of an important oracle, and there is a meditation cave where Tsongkhapa had visions of Manjughosa. A trail leads from the monastery to the summit of Gephel Utse, above Drepung, from where there is also a trekking route into Phenyul.

Kyormolung Monastery སྐྱོར་མོ་ལུང་དགོན་པ

If you continue on the Chushul road from Dongkar (rather than taking the Ziling highway), you will immediately cross the Dongkar Bridge. An unpaved track to the right leads up the west bank of the Tolung-chu for 7 km to Kyormolung. Founded by the Kadampa Vinaya master Balti Wangchuk Tsultrim (1129-1215), it was later associated with Tsongkhapa and three Gelukpa colleges were established. The fine masonry and murals of the main temple have survived the ravages of recent decades. From Kyormolung there are also trekking routes to Nam and Chushul.

Zhongwa Lhachu ཞོང་པ་ལྷ་ཆུ

Near Kyormolung is the sacred site of Zhongwa Lhachu, where there is a natural spring, said to have been brought forth by Padmasambhava's magical prowess. The staff of Padmasambhava was formerly kept in the chapel constructed by Balti Rinpoche, and the spring itself is said to offer visions of the Eight Manifestations of Padmasambhava.

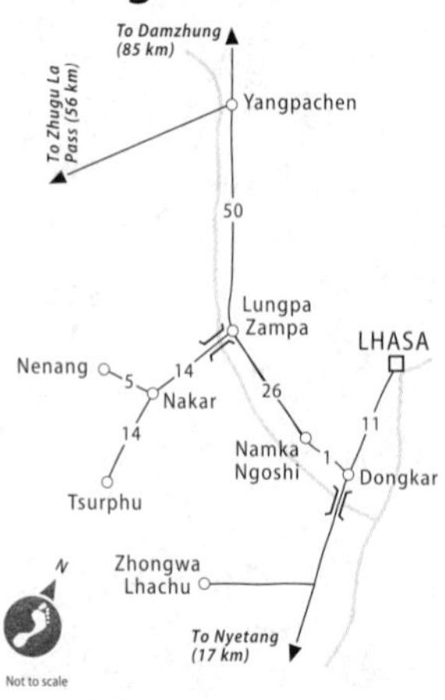

Upper Tolung

Nenang Monastery གནས་ནང་དགོན་པ

Following the Ziling highway from Tolung Dechen on the east bank of the Tolung-chu for 26 km (to kilometre road marker 3,853), you cross the river via the **Lungpa Zampa** bridge (ignoring an earlier bridge of similar iron construction), and enter the Drowolung valley where both Tsurphu (28 km) and Nenang (19 km) monasteries are located. The valley begins at Gurum township, and divides after 8 km, the southern trail leading via Nampa village and Nampa La pass to Chushul, and the western road to **Nakar** from where the Tsurphu and Nenang paths diverge. A signpost by the roadside marks the way to **Nenang**, on the far side of the ridge above Nakar. The monastery was founded by the First Zhamarpa Tokden Drakpa Senge in 1333, and it later became the seat of the successive incarnations of the First Pawo Chowang Lhundrub (1440-1503), the most renowned of whom was the historian the Second Pawo Tsuklak Trengwa (1504-1566). The previous Tenth Pawo Rinpoche (b 1912) recently passed away in India, where he had lived for a number of years. His reincarnation, a child from Nangchen in Kham was recognized by the present Karmapa. He presides over a community of 50 monks, but is at present obliged to live in Lhasa. The principal temples at Nenang are the **Lhakhang Chenmo**, which is currently under reconstruction, and the **Jampa Lhakhang**. At present, the latter functions as the assembly hall. The lower storey houses the throne of Pawo Rinpoche and the library, along with an inner sanctum dedicated to Maitreya, which contains gilded clay images of the Buddhas of the Three Times, Padmasambhava, the Fifth Pawo Rinpoche, Tsongkhapa, Trisong Detsen, Milarepa, Marpa, the Tenth Pawo Rinpoche, and the Sixteenth Karmapa. Murals to the rear depict Vajradhara, Karmapa, Marpa, and Tsongkhapa, while those of the side walls depict the lineages of the Karmapas and the Pawo Rinpoches. There is a large gilded stupa reliquary containing the ashes of the Tenth Pawo Rinpoche, flanked by two smaller ones containing relics of the Sixteenth Karmapa and the Fifth Pawo. On the second floor, there is a gallery and a series of tangkas depicting protector deities such as Shridevi, and murals of Nenang Monastery itself. The residence of the present incumbent is on the third floor.

Tsurphu Monastery མཚུར་ཕུ་

→ *Altitude: 4,300 m, Colour map 3, grid B2.*

ⓘ *Admission: ¥20.*

Continuing along the main pathway from Nakar, which follows the Tsurphu Phu-chu upstream for 14 km, you reach Tsurphu Monastery, the seat of the Karmapa, and one of the two main strongholds of the Karma Kagyu school in Tibet (the other being at Karma Gon in Lhato, see below, page 422). As you approach the monastery you will pass on the left the dilapidated summer palace of the Karmapas, surmounted by a satellite dish.

The Site The temples, palaces, and monastic colleges of Tsurphu were severely damaged during the 1960s, following the flight of the Sixteenth Karmapa to India, but rebuilding has progressed steadily since 1983-1984, largely through the efforts of the late Drupon Dechen Rinpoche and the good auspices of the Hawaian-based Tsurphu Foundation. At present there are 300 affiliated monks. As you drive into the courtyard, to the left you will observe the terraced slope on which the appliqué scrolls of Tsurphu were once hung during religious festivals. An obelisk stands within the courtyard, reputedly erected by King Relpachen to commemorate the building of the ninth-century Changbu Lhakhang at Tsurphu. Turning to face the main buildings, on the left is the Zhipa Tratsang, in the middle is the Karmapa Palace (Labrang) also known as the 'lower citadel of Dharma' (Chogar Ogma), and to the right is the Zuri Tratsang. To the rear is located the recently renovated assembly hall known as Jamyang Lhakhang Chenmo which has massive 4-m thick walls, alongside a new Reliquary Chapel (Serdung Lhakhang). Still higher up the hillside stands the reconstructed palace of the regent of Tsurphu, known as Gyeltsab Podrang Chokhang or 'upper citadel of Dharma' (Chogar

History of Tsurphu

Tsurphu was founded in 1187 by the Karmapa I Dusum Khyenpa (1100-1193) who hailed from the Trehor region of Kham, and was one of the principal followers of Gampopa. The construction marked the site of the ninth-century ruins Changbu Lhakhang, where he had received a vision of the Cakrasamvara mandala. As the founder of the Karma Kagyu school, renowned for its ascetic discipline and yogic prowess, Dusum Khyenpa is also credited with the inception of the *tulku* institution, which later came to dominate Tibet's spiritual and political life during the middle ages. It was he who clearly predicted the circumstances of his subsequent rebirth, and his successor, Karma Pakshi (1204-1283) became the first formal incarnation (*tulku*) to be recognized in Tibet.

Karma Pakshi built the main temple in 1263. It housed an image of the Buddha called Dzamling-gyen, which was said to contain original relics. Since that time altogether 17 Karmapa incarnations have occupied Tsurphu Monastery, some, such as Rangjung Dorje, renowned for their profound spiritual insights, and others such as Chodrak Gyatso and Mikyo Dorje for their vast scholarship. During the age of the Mongolian Qans and Ming Emperors, the Karma Kagyu school flourished, and when Sakya's power was eclipsed, it became the most influential force in Tibetan political life under the successive dynasties of Phakmodru, Rinpung and Tsang. During this period (16th-early 17th century), when the capital of Tibet was located in Tsetang and Zhigatse, it was the Karma Kagyu school based in Tsurphu and Yangpachen which held sway throughout the Lhasa region. However, the defeat of the Tsangpa kings by the Mongolian armies of Gushi Qan in 1642 at the culmination of a prolonged civil war left the school isolated and cut off from its political power base, enabling the Fifth Dalai Lama to establish the Gelukpa theocracy at Lhasa, which persisted until the Chinese occupation of Tibet. Since 1959, when the previous Sixteenth Karmapa established his residence at Rumtek in Sikkim, the Karma Kargyu school has developed an extensive network of Buddhist organizations and centres throughout the world.

Gongma). The regent, Gyeltsab Rinpoche, would preside over Tsurphu during the interregnum following the death of one Karmapa and the investiture of the next. The first to assume this role was the First Gyeltsab Goshi Peljor Dondrub (1427-1489) who installed the Seventh Karmapa Chodrak Gyatso (1454-1506), and from the time of the Tenth Karmapa Choying Dorje (1604-1674), who offered the site to the Sixth Gyeltsab (1659-1698), the successive Gyeltsab Rinpoches have occupied this building. The present regent, Twelfth Gyeltsab (b 1960), lives at Rumtek in Sikkim.

Among these buildings, the **Zhipa Tratsang** was the first to be restored. The upper storey contains a series of five protector shrine rooms, dedicated respectively to Mahakala in the form of Bernakchen, to Shridevi, Vaishravana along with Tseringma, Dorje Drolo and Vajrakila. Outside on the verandah are a number of macabre stuffed animals, suspended from the ceiling.

To the east of the Zhipa Tratsang, is the reconstructed **Karmapa Labrang,** containing in its upper storey the residence of the present incumbent, the Seventeenth Karmapa Orgyen Trinle Dorje (b 1985), who has been recognised by both the Fourteenth Dalai Lama and the Chinese government. Despite his young age the Karmapa fled to India at the end of 1999 in order to pursue his Buddhist studies under suitably qualified masters of the Karmapa tradition. His chambers may be visited

The Seventeen Karmapas

Karmapa I	Dusum Khyenpa (1110-1193)	Karmapa X	Choying Dorje (1604-1674)
Karmapa II	Karma Pakshi (1204-1283)	Karmapa XI	Yeshe Dorje (1677-1702)
Karmapa III	Rangjung Dorje (1284-1339)	Karmapa XII	Jangchub Dorje (1703-1732)
Karmapa IV	Rolpei Dorje (1340-1383)	Karmapa XIII	Dudul Dorje (1733-1797)
Karmapa V	Dezhin Shekpa (1384-1415)	Karmapa XIV	Tekchok Dorje (1798-1868)
Karmapa VI	Tongwa Donden (1416-1453)	Karmapa XV	Khakhyab Dorje (1871-1922)
Karmapa VII	Chodrak Gyatso (1454-1506)	Karmapa XVI	Rikpei Dorje (1921-1981)
Karmapa VIII	Mikyo Dorje (1507-1554)	Karmapa XVII	Orgyen Trinle Dorje (b 1985)
Karmapa IX	Wangchuk Dorje (1556-1603)		

nowadays, but no photography is permitted. The lower throne room has fine murals in Chinese style which depict the Sixteen Elders, and its images include those of Marpa, Milarepa, and Gampopa, along with the First, Second and Sixteenth Karmapas. There is also an interesting mural depicting the traditional plan of Tsurphu.

Behind an adjacent general store, a steep incline leads uphill to the renovated **Jamyang Lhakhang Chenmo**. This massive fortress once contained Tsurphu's most highly venerated image: an enormous 20-m bronze-cast statue of Shakyamuni Buddha, known as the 'Ornament of the World' (Dzamling-gyen), which had been commissioned by Karma Pakshi in the 13th century, but was blasted to pieces during the Cultural Revolution. Only a small fragment of the original bronze statue survives on display here. In its place an 18-m gilded copper replica was installed in 1997, flanked by images of Shariputra, Maudgalyayana, and the Eight Bodhisattvas. Visitors can see a handprint left by the young Seventeenth Karmapa in the masonry. Nearby is a new reliquary chapel known as **Serdung Lhakhang**, which contains the mortal remains of the late Drupon Dechen Rinpoche, alongside central images of Padmasambhava and the previous Sixteenth Karmapa, and a thousand small peripheral images of Shakyamuni.

Further east is the partially restored **Zuri Tratsang**, an upper chamber which contains the room used by Situ Rinpoche on his recent visit to Tsurphu from India. Here, there are documents describing the account of his discovery of the new Karmapa in 1992.

Further uphill and behind this entire complex are the reconstructed buildings of the independently functioning **Gyeltsab Podrang**, which includes a vast assembly hall, where the monks under the authority of Gyeltsab Rinpoche convene. The original five-storey structure dates from 17th century.

The precipitous cliffs above Tsurphu contain the hermitage known as **Drubdra Samtenling**, and to its left is the hermitage of **Pema Khyung Dzong**, once frequented by Karma Pakshi and the Third Karmapa Rangjung Dorje (1284-1339). Higher up is the cave where Karma Pakshi made a meditative retreat in darkness (*muntsam*), and a number of smaller hermitages. There is a pilgrim's circuit around Tsurphu, which takes about three hours, starting west of the perimeter wall and encompassing the Tsurphu burial ground to the north and the cliff-side hermitages mentioned above.

Trekking There are three trekking routes from Tsurphu: north via the 5,300-m Lhasar La pass to the Lhorong-chu valley and Yangpachen (three or four days); south via Nampa La pass to Chushul (two or three days); and southwest via the Tsurphu La pass to Nyemo in Tsang (two or three days).

Tupten Yangpachen Monastery ཐུབ་བསྟན་ཡངས་པ་ཅན་དགོན་པ

From Lungpa Zampa (see above page 139), the Ziling Highway continues north, following the east bank of the Tolung-chu to Yangpachen, via the township of Mar and the old Dechen Dzong. The town of Yangpachen is the site of a geothermal power plant and hothouses which supply vegetables to the Lhasa area. There is a small hospital, a petrol station, an army compound, and a few Sichuan-style restaurants.

Yangpachen monastery is located 14 km along the turn-off for Zhugu La pass (5,300 m) and Zhigatse. It was founded in 1490 by Mu Rabjampa Thujepel on the advice of the Fourth Zhamarpa Chokyi Drakpa (1453-1524), with funds provided by Donyo Dorje of Rinpung. Since that time it has been the main residence of Chokyi Drakpa's subsequent incarnations, the Zhamarpa hierarchs, who wear a red hat in contrast to the black hat worn by the Karmapa. The Zhamarpas held sway in Upper Tolung until 1792 when the status of the Tenth Zhamarpa (1742-1792) was annulled by the Tibetan government, following his alliance with the Gorkha invasion force in an attempted restoration of Kagyu power. The woodblock edition of Golotsawa's *Blue Annals* was removed from the library at Yangpachen and transferred to Kundeling in Lhasa at that time.

The monastery has been under reconstruction since 1986, and in **Pelkor Gonkhang** there is an original image of the protector, Six-armed Mahakala. The present incumbent, the Thirteenth Zhamarpa (b 1952), lives in India and Nepal.

From Yangpachen, the northern route to Zhigatse follows the Lhorong-chu upstream to Zhugu La pass for 56 km, and then descends into the Upper Nyemo and Oyuk districts of Tsang (see below, page 258). To the south of the road, near Yangra, the Kagyu nunnery of **Dorjeling** is once again active.

Damzhung County འདམ་གཞུང

→ *Population: 39,0312. Area: 8,094 sq km. Colour map 3, grid A2.* 当雄县

The Lhasa-Ziling highway leading northeast via Yangpachen opens out into Damzhung county, the capital of which is located at Damchuka. To the north, the road skirts the ***Nyenchen Tanglha*** *range (7,088 m), abode of the protector deity of the same name, which divides the Upper Kyi-chu region from the Jangtang Plateau and the Salween. The Dam-chu and Nyingdrong-chu rivers, which have their sources near Damzhung flow southeast to converge with the Reting Tsangpo at Phodo before flowing down through Meldro and Taktse counties to Lhasa.*

Damzhung

The town has sprung up as an important staging post on the highway for freight trucks and buses. There are a number of roadside restaurants, serving Tibetan, Sichuan, and Muslim food, among which Chamdo Zakhang and Amdo Zakhang are both clean; and in the government compound approached via a bridge to the rear, there is the public security bureau, a cinema, and the large **Damzhung Guesthouse** T0891-6112093, which has singles at ¥110 and doubles at ¥120.

After Damzhung, the highway continues northeast for a further 27 km to **Chorten Rang-go** in Umatang, which lies just beyond the county border, before cutting through the Nyenchen Tanglha range to enter the Salween River system. This point is marked by a series of eight roadside stupas, symbolizing the eight major events in the life of Shakyamuni Buddha. There is also a trekking route from here, which descends into the upper Reting Tsangpo valley.

Namtso Chukmo Lake གནམ་མཚོ་ → *Colour map 3, grid A1*

A newly paved road cuts across country from a turn-off southwest of Damzhung, passes via the cliff-hanging **Jangra Monastery** of the Gelukpa school, and after 25 km crosses the Lhachen La pass (5,150 m). On the 49-km descent from the pass there are spectacular views of the tidal **Namtso Chukmo lake**, which is 70 km long and 30 km wide, making it the second largest saltwater lake on the Tibetan plateau (after Kokonor). The average altitude is 4,718 m, and the landscape is dominated by the snow peak of Nyenchen Tanglha to the southwest.

Namtso township, near the eastern corner of the lake has a small guesthouse and pack animals, which are hired out to those taking the pilgrimage circuit around the lake. The full circuit takes about 18 days on foot, and it is possible to drive only as far as **Tashidor**, a cave hermitage near the bird sanctuary, marked by two lofty sheer rock towers. The overall distance from Damzhung to Tashidor is 74 km. The hermitage caves, which are said to have particular associations with Padmasambhava and his consort Yeshe Tsogyel, were frequented by many great lamas of the past, including the Third Karmapa Rangjung Dorje. Nowadays, they are occupied by occasional hermits of the Nyingma and Kagyu schools. A newly constructed cave temple is maintained by three nuns and two monks, under the supervision of Lama Donga Trinle Ozer, who lived here for 10 years, and Ngawang Tupten Lama who is in charge of the rebuilding. The temple follows the Nyingma tradition, holding Konchok Chidu ceremonies on the 10th day of the lunar month, and Dudjom Troma ceremonies on the 25th. The **bird sanctuary** itself teems with migratory flocks from April to November, and you may glimpse the rare black-necked crane. Following the construction of the new paved road from Damzhung, a higher standard tourist lodge, the Namtso Hotel, has recently been built at Tashidor.

Lake Namtso Chukmo

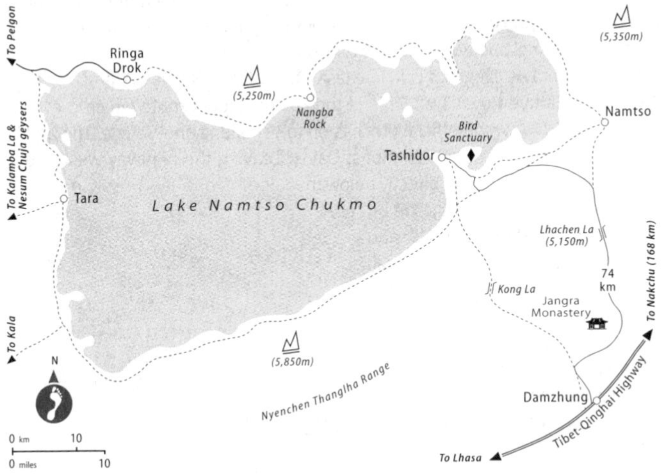

There is a short 2-3 hour pilgrimage circuit of the Tashidor promontory with its long mani-stone wall, passing near the shore; but the longer 18-day circuit of the lake requires careful preparation. Moving anticlockwise (in the Bon manner), on the north shore, a detour leads along a 10-km headland known as Doring, where the hermitage of the ancient Bon scholar Tong-gyang Tuchen of Zhang-zhung was once located and where there are significant ruins, recently documented by John Bellezza. At **Nyingdo**, further west, there are extensive ruins of an ancient Bon monastery. The north promontory of **Nangba Rock** will be reached on the eighth day of the circuit. The ruins of the Bonpo Tachok Gonpa are accessible from here. **Ringa Drok** near the northwest corner will be reached on the 10th day, and **Tara** on the west shore on the 12th.

From Ringa Drok, there is a motorable road to Pelgon; and from Tara, there is another 12-day wilderness trek leading southwards via Kalamba La pass (5,240 m) and the **Nesum Chuja geysers** (which freeze in winter) to Zabulung in North Shang (see below, page 263).

Taktse County སྟག་རྩེ

→ *Population: 25,662. Area: 1,354 sq km. Colour map 3, grid B3.* 达孜县

Taktse county extends from the north of Lhasa Zamchen bridge as far as Lamo on the south bank of the Kyi-chu, and Logon on the north bank and includes two very important sites: the caves of Drak Yerpa and Ganden Monastery, both situated northeast of Lhasa. The county capital is nowadays located at Taktse or Dechen Dzong, 21 km distant from Lhasa, and from here there is a short trekking route to Samye via Gokar La.

Tsel Gungtang ཚལ་གུང་ཐང

The residence of Lama Zhang, the 11th century founder of the Tselpa Kagyu school and caretaker of the Jokhang, was formerly situated 10 km east from Lhasa and south of the present Lhasa-Kongpo highway. The complex included a Kumbum stupa, two early temples, a residential building, and a later Tsuklakhang. Some of these structures have recently been undergoing restoration.

Dechen Dzong བདེ་ཆེན་རྫོང

The county capital, located near the hilltop ruins of Dechen Dzong, which once guarded the approaches to Lhasa from the north, contains a small guesthouse and a Gelukpa temple, known as **Samdrubling**, which was preserved as a granary during the 1960s, and therefore has kept some of its original frescoes undamaged. Alongside it is a newly constructed Jamkhang, containing a three-storey high image of Maitreya. The number eight bus runs from East Lingkhor Lam in Lhasa via Pelting to Dechen Dzong.

The Taktse-Samye Royal Trek This is the old palanquin route which previous Dalai Lamas would follow on official procession to Yemalung and Samye. The trail is wide and still cobbled in certain sections. **Day 1:** Leaving the highway west of the county town at km marker 4611, directly below the ruined dzong, it is possible to drive as far as Shingjang village (3,830 m) on an unpaved road. Pack animals and guides are available here. The trail ascends slowly, following a tributary of the Kyi-chu to the west and bypassing well irrigated barley fields. Fording the river before Jangsu village, it then climbs steeply towards the south through a side valley to emerge on a high grassland ridge frequented by nomads. A fine

History of Drak Yerpa

King Songtsen Gampo and his two foreign queens are said to have meditated here in the **Peu Marsergyi Lhakhang**, where they discovered 'self-arising' symbols of buddha-body, speech and mind, and in the **Chogyel Puk**. Later, Padmasambhava concealed many *terma* objects around Yerpa, including the celebrated ritual dagger of Sera (**Sera Phurzhal**), which was eventually rediscovered by the treasure-finder Darcharuba at Sewalung. Padmasambhava also passed some seven months in retreat in the **Dawa Puk**, which is regarded as one of his three foremost places of spiritual attainment (*drub-ne*). In the ninth century Lhalung Pelgyi Dorje stayed at Yerpa in solitary meditation, both prior to and after his assassination of the apostate king Langdarma.

Then, following the later phase of Buddhist propagation in Tibet, Yerpa came to greater prominence under Kadampa influence: Lu-me founded 108 temples on the hillside, including a **Vairocana Lhakhang**. Marton Chokyi Jungne founded the **Jampa Lhakhang**, and Atisha passed three years here, constructing with the aid of his foremost disciples, the **Kyormo Lhakhang** and the **Chokhang**.

riverside camp (4,800 m) is located below the snow-lined ridge of Gokar La in a wide elevated valley, near a crumbling stone throne, which was once used by previous Dalai Lamas. **Day 2**: Crossing the river, the trail soon climbs sharply over a number of switchbacks to reach the pass (5,100 m). There are excellent panoramas – northeast to the Kyi-chu valley and southwest towards the Brahmaputra. The still well-defined track then descends gradually through boulder strewn moraine before entering a nomadic pasture and a forested ravine, where small meadows are available for camping (4,000 m). **Day 3**: The trail continues downstream through thickening forest and rosebushes to emerge at Nyingong village (3,870 m), behind the Yemalung ridge. Here tractors are available for hire as far as Samye.

Dromto འབྲོམ་སྟོད

Dromto township, situated on the north side of the Taktse Zampa bridge, which spans the Kyi-chu upstream from Taktse, is surmounted by a stupa, marking the meditation hermitage of the Kadampa master Nyen Lotsawa Darmatra (11th century). Two roads diverge here on the north side of the bridge: left to Drak Yerpa and right to Phenyul and Jang (see below, pages 149-153).

Drak Yerpa: the Caves of Mystic Realization བྲག་ཡེར་པ

It takes about two hours to drive to the caves of Drak Yerpa, northeast of Lhasa, either via the Taktse Zampa bridge or via Kawa and Yerpa Da villages on the more direct route from Lhasa (16 km). Following the Yerpa-chu tributary of the Kyi-chu upstream, and past a reservoir, you will arrive at this historic complex of caves and temples, some of which date from the earliest period of Buddhism in Tibet. The amphitheatre ridge of Yerpa and some of its larger caves are visible in the distance from afar the Lhasa-Kongpo road on the south bank of the Kyi-chu. The highest point on the ridge is the peak of **Yerpa Lhari**, abode of the local deity, at the extreme northeast end of the ridge.

The Site The caves are approached via the ruined 11th-century Kadampa monastery of **Yerpa Drubde**, situated some 100 m below the dark cavernous grottoes of the white cliffs.

Among the many caves and ruined shrines, the following (described from west to east) are most important: **Tendrel Drubpuk** associated with Atisha and his Kadampa followers; **Chakna Dorje Puk**, containing a 'self-arising' stone image of Vajrapani; **Jampa Lhakhang**, the largest cave, which once contained a celebrated 13th-century image of Maitreya along with the Eight Bodhisattvas, and below which are relief images of the Lords of the Three Enlightened Families; **Drubtob Puk**, dedicated to the Eighty-four Great Accomplished Masters (*mahasiddha*) of ancient India; **Chogyel Puk**, where King Songtsen Gampo meditated in the seventh century and which once contained images of the King and the protectress Shridevi; **Dawa Puk**, containing a sculpted image of Padmasambhava, a 'self-arising' image of Ekajati and stone footprints of Padmasambhava and his student Lhalung Pelgyi Dorje; **Lhalung Puk**, where Lhalung Peldor hid for some years during the period of Langdarma's persecution; and **Neten Lhakhang**, which was constructed by Lu-me in 1011 and formerly contained images of Shakyamuni Buddha surrounded by the Sixteen Elders. Below this last shrine is the stone throne used by Atisha and a burial ground. Atisha's hermitage, the ruins of which can still be seen, had 300 monks as recently as the 19th century, when it served as the summer residence for the Upper Tantric College of Lhasa (ie Ramoche). A reconstructed temple at Drak Yerpa, containing images of Shakyamuni, Avalokiteshvara and Padmasambhava was recently demolished by the hardline Lhasa authorities on the grounds that it had not been built on one of the historically recognized sites!

Ganden Namgyeling དགའ་ལྡན་རྣམ་རྒྱལ་གླིང་ → *Colour map 3, grid B4.*

ⓘ *Admission: ¥30.*

Situated 45 km east of Lhasa, the monastery of Ganden Namgyeling was founded in 1409 by Tsongkhapa on the Gokpori ridge of Mount Wangkur, overlooking the south bank of the river and the Phenyul valley beyond. It is approached via a turn-off at a village 39 km from Lhasa (road markers 1,529 and 4,591) and from there by a zigzagging dirt road for a further 6 km. Buses leave the Barkhor in Lhasa each morning for the two-hour journey to Ganden (¥10).

Named after the paradise of Maitreya, Ganden was the first and leading Gelukpa monastery, constructed by Tsongkhapa himself. The site, where he himself had meditated, was known to have had ancient associations with King Songtsen Gampo and his queens as **Mount Wangkur** was named after a coronation ceremony performed at the birth of the king, and the adjacent **Mount Tsunmo Dingri** was named after the queens' favourite picnic ground. The sacred Jowo Rinpoche image of Lhasa is said to have indicated the significance of the site to Tsongkhapa, who founded the monastery in 1409 and the Chikhorkhang in 1415. The Assembly Hall (Tsokchen) was built in 1417, and the two colleges of Ganden known as Jangtse (North Point) and Shartse (East Point) were respectively founded by two of his closest disciples – Namka Pelzangpo and Neten Rongyelwa. A tantric college (Gyudra) was also established by another of his students, Je Sherab Senge.

Following the death of Tsongkhapa in 1419, the succession passed first to Gyeltsabje and later to Khedrupje. In this way, the Ganden Tripa (throne-holder of Ganden) came to preside over the Gelukpa school, each generally holding office for seven years (although originally longer periods of office were observed).

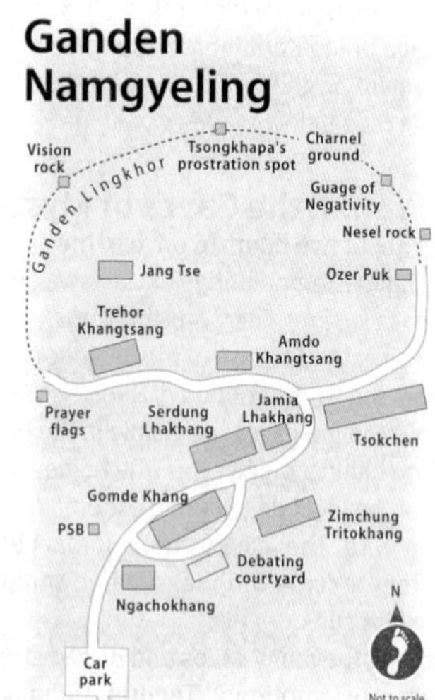

Formerly there were over 3,000 monks at Ganden, but following the brutal destruction of the complex during the Cultural Revolution (more severe than at any of the other five large Gelukpa establishments), the number was reduced to about 300. Then, since 1997 many of the remaining senior monks were forced to retire to their village homes or face the prospect of exile in India, following an authoritarian clamp-down on their activities. However, the Xinhua News Agency reported in 1998 that buildings covering an area of 11,000 sq m had been renovated at Ganden, 41 kg of gold had been utilized to regild the roofs, and murals 1,660 sq m in area had been restored over the previous four years, all at a cost of US$3 million!

Ngachokhang This small temple, located to the right of the trail after the bus stop, is where Tsongkhapa instructed his students. The main chamber has images of Tsongkhapa, flanked by his two foremost students, while the extremely active protector chapel to its left (out of bounds to women) has images of Shridevi, Mahakala, Dharmaraja, and Bhairava. Upstairs are the Dalai Lamas' private apartments and throne.

Serdung Lhakhang Passing the debating courtyard and the meditation hermitage (**Gomde Khang**) on the right, the pilgrim reaches the restored **Serdung Lhakhang**, a red-painted building with a large white stupa. On the ground floor there is an interior courtyard and a Dharmaraja chapel. The main chamber or **Yangpachen Chapel** is on the second floor, containing the restored golden reliquary of Tsongkhapa (*serdung*), known as Tongwa Donden ('Meaningful to Behold'). Constructed in 1629, the chapel is named after a stone to the rear of the golden reliquary, which is said to have flown miraculously from Shravasti (Yangpachen) in India. The present silver stupa replaces the original, destroyed in 1959, which had been gilded by Gushi Qan's grandson and covered with a felt and sandalwood tent by Dzungarwa Tsering Dondrup in 1717. A few relics and skull fragments of Tsongkhapa were retrieved and have been placed within the restored stupa, and a cabinet to the left contains the master's celebrated tooth relic, in a small stupa casket, as well as his begging bowl, tea cup and vajra. The tooth relic is used in the making of barley impressions for consecrating miniature terracotta images (*tsha-tsha*), or for distribution to the faithful. Large images of Tsongkhapa and his foremost students stand in front of the stupa. Left of the entrance is the main Assembly Hall, the side chapels of which contain images representing the Buddhas of the Three Times, and 1,000 small images of Tsongkhapa.

Jampa Lhakhang A small chapel dedicated to Maitreya has recently been reconstructed to the rear of the Serdung Lhakhang.

Tsokchen Further uphill and to the right of the Jampa Lhakhang is the restored Assembly Hall (Tsokchen), which has images of Tsongkhapa flanked by his two foremost students and the Sixteen Elders, as well as some well crafted murals. The inner sanctum, known as the **Sertrikhang,** contains the throne of Tsongkhapa and the successive Ganden Tripas, flanked by the volumes of the Kangyur and backed by two sets of statues depicting Tsongkhapa with his two foremost students. The throne is a replica of a 15th-century original made by Newar craftsmen. Upstairs, the **Chapel of the Countenance** (Zhalrekhang) offers a view of the images and throne contained in the inner sanctum below.

Zimchung Tritokhang Adjacent to the Tsokchen and to the right is the Official Residence of the Ganden Tripa, known as **Zimchung Tritokhang**. The upper storey contains images of Tsongkhapa and his foremost students, with a full set of the Kangyur stacked on the wall behind. A throne used by the Ganden Tripa is at the far end of the room. On the ground floor, there are four chapels: among them, the **Demchok Lhakhang** contains an awesome image of Cakrasamvara, flanked by others representing

 Gyeltsabje, Mahakala, and Vajrayogini (closed to women). The **Dzomchen Lhakhang** contains images of Tsongkhapa and students, flanked by recent lamas Pawangka Rinpoche and Trijang Rinpoche. The **Nyangde Lhakhang** is the simple chamber where Tsongkhapa passed away in 1419, and the **Gyelwa Lhakhang** is a private apartment reserved for visiting Dalai Lamas. It contains images of Tsongkhapa, the Tenth Panchen Lama, and the Thirty-five Confession Buddhas.

Amdo Khangtsang and Trehor Khangtsang Following the track uphill to the left the pilgrim passes in succession the **Amdo Khangtsang** and the **Trehor Khangtsang**. The former has brocade hangings depicting the Thirty-five Confession Buddhas and Sixteen Elders, with an image of the protectress Machen Pomra and the eye of Dharmaraja (kept in a cabinet). The latter has images of Tsongkhapa with his two foremost students.

North Point College (Jangtse) One of the two original colleges of Ganden, much publicity surrounded the recent rebuilding of North Point. However it appears that several columns are already beginning to crack and the building has been declared unsafe for habitation.

Pilgrim's Circuit of Ganden The pilgrim's circumambulatory route follows a one hour Lingkhor around the hilltop, starting from a prominent group of prayer-flags. On the way the pilgrim will pass 'self-arising' imprints of Phadampa Sangye, the Sixteen Elders, Dharmaraja, Tsongkhapa's hat, the Lords of the Three Enlightened Families, and so forth. Then, passing the **Vision Rock** (said to induce supernatural visions when viewed through a hole made by a fist), the pilgrim reaches the highest point on the circuit, **Tsongkhapa's prostration spot**, and then descends to the burial ground (*durtro*) and the narrow cleft called **Gauge of Negativity** (which is said to measure the extent of the pilgrim's negativity). Thereafter, the pilgrim will pass the rock impressions of Tsongkhapa and his students (said to have been made by Tsongkhapa's own fingernails), and other impressions representing Simhavaktra, Dharmaraja's tongue, and a nectar-dripping rock. Next comes Tsongkhapa's hermitage (**Ozer Puk**), containing 'self-arising' and 'speaking' images of Shridevi, Shakyamuni, Amitayus, and Tsongkhapa himself, surmounted by Atisha and Dromtonpa. Further uphill is another Dharmaraja shrine. Lastly, the pilgrim visits the black cone-shaped **Nesel Rock**, on which pilgrims lay their stomachs while spitting or even vomiting out disease!

The Ganden-Samye Trek This a tough 4-5 day trek, traversing two high passes, fast-flowing mountain streams and magnificent, forested valleys, which are virtually uninhabited in their upper reaches. The trek can start from the clearing in front of Ganden Monastery (4,005 m) or from Trubzhi village (where porters and guides are available for hire) in the lower valley to the west of Mount Wangkur. **Day 1**: After acclimatising at Ganden, a poorly defined trail leads uphill to the saddle on Mount Wangkur (4,510 m) before undulating and following the ridge down to Hebu village in the valley below (some distance upstream from Trubzhi). Crossing the river, it ascends a gully to the southwest, passing through uneven marshland to reach the nomad campsite at Yamado (4,230 m). **Day 2**: The trail follows the Yamakyil route between Lugpu and Towa Nagpo hills, climbing steeply through rhododendron slopes to cross a ridge, a moraine field, and a glacial stream on the slow ascent to Zhukar La pass (4,960 m). The descent from the pass follows the contour of the ridge on a well defined path down to the valley floor, where a fast-flowing river is forded, close to a nomad campsite (4,770 m). **Day 3**: Climbing over uneven marshland and passing a small lake to the east, the almost indiscernible trail forks, southeast to cross Kampa La (5,010 m) or southwest to cross Chedur La (4,920 m). Taking the latter, which is the shorter route, the trail bypasses small lakes on both sides of the Chedur La before plunging sharply through a narrow but thickly forested ravine to reach a suitable meadow campsite. **Day 4**: After fording a river and following its east bank downstream, the trail crosses a creek by a small wooden bridge before the valley begins to widen above Chanda village (4,020 m). Below the cliff hermitage of Yemalung (see below, page 188), there is a wide meadow, where a camp can be prepared. Alternatively, continue downhill on an easy trail to Nyingong village (3,870 m) where tractors are available for hire as far as Samye.

Lhundrub County ལྷུན་གྲུབ 林周县

→ *Population: 55,342. Area: 6,795 sq km. Colour map 3, grid A4.*

The districts of Phenyul and Jang which lie to the north of Lhasa include the valley of the Lha-chu or Phenpo-chu, which rises near Yangpachen and flows southeast to converge with the Kyi-chu opposite Ganden Monastery, and the 'northern region' (Jang) of the Pa-chu and Reting Tsangpo, which converge with the Kyi-chu further upstream at Phodo Dzong, the old administrative capital. These two river systems are divided by the Chak La pass (5,300 m). The new county capital is located at Ganden Chungkor, 55 km from Lhasa.

Ins and outs

There are three points of access from the south: via the paved Lhasa-Kongpo road and Taktse Zampa bridge, via Drigung and Phodo Dzong; or via the unpaved road from Sera Monastery, Dokde and Yerpa. There are also trekking routes leading into Phenyul: from Lhasa via Pempogo La pass; from Tolung via Mount Gephelri ridge; and from Damzhung into Jang. Culturally, this region of Tibet has had strong associations with both the Kadampa school (especially at Reting, Nalendra, and Langtang), and with the Kagyu school (at Taklung). The Kadampa establishments were in later centuries absorbed by the Gelukpa and Sakya schools.

Phenyul འཕན་ཡུལ

Logon ལོ་དགོན

After crossing the Taktse Zampa bridge and entering Phenyul, the first site of note is Logon Monastery. Located on the northwest bank of the Kyi-chu, 20 km northeast of the bridge, Logon was founded by the Kadampa master Chengawa Tsultrim Bar (1038-1103) and maintained by his illustrious student Jayulpa. Later it was adopted by the Gelukpas and became the seat of the incarnate master Lo Sempa Chenpo.

Ganden Chungkor

The new county capital (3,720 m) is located at the widest and most fertile part of the Phenyul valley, just north of the monastery of Ganden Chungkor, which has preserved some original murals. The town has three guesthouses, managed by the local Communist Party, the Transportation Bureau, and the Grain Department respectively, and of these the Party offers the best accommodation (¥200 per room). There are small roadside restaurants and shops, an open market, a primary school, a military camp, and a Bureau for Nomadic Affairs. At the main intersection, roads lead east (to Lhasa), south (to Nalendra and Langtang), west (the old trail to Taklung via Tak La) and north to Phodo Dzong (via Chak La). Buses make the 3-4 hour journey to Lhasa each morning.

Langtang Monastery གླང་ཐང་དགོན་པ

Located some 6 km southwest of Ganden Chungkor, on a track which crosses the Phenpo-chu (and continues over Pempogo La pass to Lhasa), the Kadampa monastery of Langtang was founded in 1093 by Langritangpa Dorje Senge (1054-1123). At its height there were over 2,000 monks, but in later centuries its status greatly diminished and it was absorbed by the Sakya school. More recently, many of its buildings were incorporated into a local farming commune, leaving intact only one protector temple and an assembly hall, which contains Langtangpa's revered 'speaking image' of Tara, and a newly sculpted image of Maitreya. Below are the ruins of the Lhakhang Chenmo and a Kadam stupa containing Langtangpa's own relics.

Nalendra Monastery དཔལ་ན་ལེན་དྲ

Located 12 km west of Langtang near the south bank of the Phenpo-chu, Nalendra Monastery was founded in 1435 by the renowned scholar Rongton Chenpo Mawei Senge (1367-1449), and later absorbed by the Sakyapa, who recognized him as one of the 'six jewels of Tibet'. The ruins at Nalendra are extensive, and in the renovated assembly hall, which has some finely executed murals, there is a depiction of the monastery as it once appeared. Rising above a large Enlightenment Stupa in the foreground are the college, the debating garden, the lama's residence, the retreat hermitage, and some nine residential buildings, one of which has been refurbished. This is the Trehor Khangtsang, containing images of the Buddhas of the Three Times, the master Jampal Lekshe and the latter's reliquary stupa. The late Khenpo Tsultrim Gyeltsen of the Lhasa Mentsikhang has been responsible for rebuilding Nalendra and re-establishing in particular the hermitage and college. The latter, which doubles as an assembly hall is located near the top of the hill, next to the debating garden, and it contains as its centrepiece an image of Rongtonpa, with two side chapels dedicated to the Thousand Buddhas and to the protector deities Ekajati, Pehar, Panjaranatha, Shridevi and Cimara. The inner sanctum contains stone footprints of Rongtonpa, a large image of Shakyamuni, flanked by the Eight Bodhisattvas, and an Enlightenment Stupa. Unfortunately the chapels have recently been subjected to art thieves and disturbed by local unrest. Following the death of Khenpo Tsultrim Gyeltsen in 2002, his cremated remains were interred in a reliquary stupa, which can be visited here today.

Shara Bumpa ཤར་འབུམ་པ

The large Kadam dome-shaped stupa known as Shara Bumpa is located north of the county capital and west of Kusha village on the road to Langma and the Chak La pass. It was constructed by Sharapa Yonten Drak (1070-1141), and is revered by pilgrims who believe that circumambulating it cures blindness.

Jang བྱང

Taklung Monastery སྟག་ལུང་དགོན་པ

Driving north from Ganden Chungkor, the paved road bypasses the old Lhundrub Dzong, Rinchen Tang, and the village of Langma before leaving the Phenyul valley. Here it rises to cross Chak La pass (5,300 m) before dropping sharply towards Taklung (4,084 m) in the upper Pha-chu valley, 120 km from Lhasa. Nomadic camps can be seen on high pastures.

The Kagyu monastery of Taklung was founded by Taklung Tangpa Tashipel

(1142-1210) in 1180 on a location previously inhabited by the Kadampa lama Potowa. Taklung Tangpa Tashipel was one of the foremost students of Phakmodrupa Dorje Gyelpo, renowned for his austere observation of monastic discipline. Through his efforts and those of his nephew Kuyalwa and the latter's successor Sangye Yarjon, the monastic population of Taklung eventually expanded to 7,000, and it survived the Mongolian incursions of General Dorta Nakpo unscathed. The main temple, the Tsuklakhang, was completed in 1228. An eastern branch of Taklung was also established by the fourth preceptor, Sangye On, at Riwoche in Kham (see page 414), and this eventually came to eclipse the mother monastery in its importance. Mangalaguru, the fifth preceptor, continued to develop this original seat, but from the 16th century onwards, Gelukpa influence at Taklung became pronounced, as the hierarchs of Sera and Drepung sought to control the appointment of its teachers and the instalment of its incarnate lamas.

The monastery is not visible from the main road, but lies along a track to the west of the Pha-chu River, below a mountain which is said to have a rock near its summit inscribed with a 'self-arising' seed-syllable A, symbolic of the emptiness underlying all phenomena. A nectar stream, descending from that seed-syllable, flows down towards the Pha-chu. At the end of the approach road, three buildings are visible across the stream and above the ruins on the left side: **Jampa Lhakhang**, dedicated to Maitreya, the **Reliquary Lhakhang** which contains the remains of the three enormous stupas which once held the relics of Taklung's three founders, Taklung Tangpa Tashipel, Kuyalwa and Sangye Yarjon, and the **Dargyeling Temple**, containing a large image of Aksobhya Buddha and a side chapel which functions as a protector shrine. The protector deities favoured here are Genyen, Nyenchen Tanglha, and Tseringma.

Looking downhill to the right of the road, the residence of Taklung Tsetrul, the incarnate lama of Taklung, has now been obscured within a cluster of village houses at Koru. Further uphill are the ruins of the great **Tsuklakhang** (the Jokhang of Taklung), the monastic kitchen, and finally, the reconstructed **Assembly Hall** (Zhelrekhang), which contains images of Taklung Tangpa Tashipel and Tangtong Gyelpo, as well as frescoes depicting the meditational deity Cakrasamvara, surrounded by the Taklung lineage-holders.

Sili Gotsang Hermitage སི་ལི་རྒོད་ཚང་

Continuing downstream from Taklung, you drive past a sheer cliff on the left, on top of which the Sili Gotsang Hermitage (4,330 m) is located, adorned with prayer flags. This retreat was founded by Taklung Tangpa Tashipel in the 12th century and used also by the great Drukpa Kagyu master Gotsangpa (1189-1258). It has recently been renovated by the monks of Taklung, and contains in addition to the hermitages a protector shrine dedicated to Mahakala.

Also on the left side of the road, is a Tashi Gomang-style stupa with multiple apertures, originally constructed by the Tibetan Government to mark the place where the Kyi-chu waters first flow southwards in the direction of Lhasa.

Phodo Dzong

Following the Pha-chu downstream to Phodo Dzong, 70 km distant from Ganden Chungkor, you will pass on the right a strikingly conical mountain peak which forms the backdrop to the town. Three rivers converge at Phodo Dzong, the Pha-chu flowing from Taklung, the Phodo Lha-chu flowing from the Damzhung area, and the Reting (or Miggi) Tsangpo flowing from the north of Reting. The old town, surmounted by a ruined fort (dzong), lies between the Pha-chu and the Phodo Lha-chu, and the remains of an old iron-chain bridge, attributed to Tangtong Gyelpo, can still be seen. Alongside them, a modern concrete bridge spans the Phodo Lha-chu, leading to the former county capital, Lhundrub township, on the north bank, and giving access to the Reting valley. Another large metal suspension bridge crosses the Reting Tsangpo from Lhundrub township, leading to the east bank of the Kyi-chu. Below the town, the swelling waters of the Kyi-chu, formed by this confluence, enter the valley of **Lungsho**, which extends southeast as far as Drigung, and once contained important 11th century Kadampa temples, such as Tsongdu and Gyel Lhakhang.

Reting Monastery རྭ་སྒྲེང་དགོན་པ་ → *Altitude: 4,100 m. Colour map 3, grid A4.*

ⓘ *Admission: ¥20.*

The road follows the Reting Tsangpo upstream from Phodo Dzong for 47 km through the beautiful Miggi valley to arrive at Reting. En route, at Chamda village there is a turn-off for Damzhung, 76 km distant on the Lhasa-Nakchu highway.

Reting Monastery situated 4,100 m, amidst a remarkable juniper wood on the lower slopes of **Mount Gangi Rarwa**. The monastery was constructed in 1056 by Dromtonpa, the foremost Tibetan student of the great Bengali Buddhist master Atisha, two years after the latter had passed away at Nyetang, south of Lhasa. Here Dromtonpa established the principal seat of his **Kadampa school**, and, according to legend, 20,000 juniper trees and springs emerged from the hairs of his head.

His successors Neljorpa Chenpo and Potowa expanded the monastery after Dromtonpa's death in 1064; but the Mongolian armies of Dorta pillaged the site in 1240. Later, in the 14th century, Tsongkhapa visited Reting and experienced a vision of Atisha, which inspired him to compose his celebrated *Great Treatise on the Graduated Path to Enlightenment (Lamrim Chenmo)*. From the time of the Seventh Dalai Lama, the abbots of Reting became eligible to serve as regents of Tibet, which they did from 1845-1855, and 1933-1947. The present incumbent, the Sixth Reting, was born in 1997 and was recently recognized by the authorities.

Amid the ruins of Reting, which was badly damaged in the 1960s, it is hard to grasp the former splendour of the buildings. To the extreme west of the hillside there once stood the five-storeyed **Reting Labrang**, the palace of Reting Rinpoche, flanked by stupas. In the centre, stood the **Assembly Hall** (*du-khang*), or **Chokhang Chenmo**, containing a highly revered solid gold image of the meditational deity Jowo Manjuvajra, 45 cm in height, which was the principal meditative object of Atisha, said to have been naturally formed from the union of the primordial buddha Vajradhara and his consort. The hall also once contained a 'speaking image' of Tara and a stupa known as Tashi Pelbar. Only part of this magnificent building has been reconstructed in recent years, and the image of Manjuvarja is still the most venerated object of offering.

To the left of the building is a consecrated spring; and to its right there was formerly the residence of Dromton and a chamber containing his teaching throne. Immediately above the Assembly Hall was the residence of Tsongkhapa, where he composed the *Lamrim Chenmo* and where a lifelike (Ngadrama) image of Atisha was formerly housed. The residence of Tsongkhapa's teacher Remdawa was situated higher still. On the upper east slopes of the hillside, there is an active nunnery known as **Samtenling**. Dromtonpa's meditation cave is in a hill top restored chapel Drak Senge ridge, adjacent to a shrine dedicated to the local deity **Garwa Nagpa**. Outside the cave are a sacred spring, the life-supporting tree of Dromtonpa, and a willow tree embodying Mahakala.

Other hermitages located on the ridge contain the remains of Dromtonpa's stone seat, from which Tsongkhapa later delivered his *Foundation of All Excellence*; while adjacent stone thrones have been adorned with images of Atisha, Dromtonpa and Maitreya. A red-painted rock on the same ridge indicates the residence of Chingkawa, the protective divinity of Reting, which Atisha himself has brought from Nalanda in India.

Below the monastery, in the 'plain of boulders' (**Pawang Tang**), there is a large rock, known as Khandro Bumdzong, which is revered as the abode of the female deity Guhyajnana.

Lamo Monastery ལ་མོ་དགོན་པ

Located 49 km northeast of Lhasa near the Taktse-Meldro road, Lamo Monastery (1109) was one of the earliest shrines built by Lu-me following his return to Central Tibet, when he initiated the later phase of Buddhist propagation.

Meldro Gungkar County
མལ་གྲོ་གུང་དཀར

→ *Population: 41,064. Area: 4,679 sq km. Colour map 2, grid B4.* 墨竹工卡县

Meldro county, administered from the town of Meldro Gungkar, 67 km east of Lhasa, extends from the Gyamazhing Valley, due east of Lamo in the south, as far as Drigung in the north. The capital ***Meldro Gungkar****, which has a small guesthouse and roadside restaurants, stands at the confluence of the Kyi-chu and Meldro Phu-chu rivers, controlling the northern approaches to Drigung and Lungsho valleys, and the eastern approaches to the forested region of Kongpo. The most important sites within the county are: Gyama, birthplace of King Songtsen Gampo; Uru Katsel, a seventh-century geomantic temple; Tangkya Lhakhang on the north bank of the Kyi-chu; Uruzhva Lhakhang, an ancient ninth-century Nyingma temple; Drigung Til Monastery, and Zhoto Tidro hermitage.*

Gyama རྒྱ་མ

The turn-off for the Gyamazhing valley is 58 km northeast of Lhasa and 10 km southwest of Meldro Gungkar, at the village of **Ngonda**. In the lower reaches of this valley is the reconstructed temple of **Gyelpo Gungkar**, containing images of Songtsen Gampo and his two foreign queens, which is said to commemorate the birth of the king at nearby Nenakok.

Further up the valley, you will pass in succession the former Kadampa monasteries of Dumburi, Gyama Trikhang, and Rinchen Gang. Among these, the monastery of **Dumburi**, founded in the 12th century by Dumburipa Dawa Gyeltsen above Nenakok, is still in ruins. **Gyama Tri-khang**, founded by Sangye Onton, the monastic preceptor of neighbouring Rinchen Gang, has an assembly hall with two chapels which survived the Cultural Revolution. The principal image depicting Mahakarunika is new, but there are original murals. One of its four earthen stupas (originally consecrated by Gyar Gomchenpo Tsultrim Senge in the 12th century) still stands. Lastly, **Rinchen Gang**, which was founded in 1181 by Gyar Gomchenpo Zhonu Drakpa and expanded by his nephew Sangye Onton, has a reconstructed temple with an old statue of Sangye Onton and a number of new frescoes and relief images. The monastery had past connections with the Kashmiri Pandita Shakyashri and later came under the influence of the Sakyapa tradition.

Gyama-On and Gyama-Samye Treks There is a 4-5 day trek crossing Tseb La (5,180 m) and Kampa La (5,010 m) passes to Samye, which is considerably easier than the trek from

Ganden; and a longer and less travelled trail from Gyama to On. The two routes diverge after Kampa La. **Day 1**: Driving from Lhasa, the first campsite will be pitched at the clearing of **Basotang** (3,750 m) in the upper reaches of the Gyama valley. **Day 2**: The trail crosses a boulder-strewn river and climbs on to the grassy Damzhung ridge, before descending to ford the river (preferably on horseback). Climbing steeply through forest on the far bank, it then emerges in a clearing at **Chutokha** (4,250 m), near a nomadic encampment. **Day 3**: Climbing from Chutoka, the trail crosses a saddle and enters a tapering ravine, heading towards the **Namgyel Gang** campsite (4,750 m), which occupies the higher and drier ground frequented by nomads, near the glacier at the valley's head. **Day 4**: Climbing steeply into a saddle and thence to the blustery **Tseb La** pass (5,180 m), you then descend into a sheltered valley and a side trail leads downhill (westwards) to Dechen Dzong. Continuing southwards, across the defile towards the distant snowline, the trail soon rises again to reach **Kampa La** pass (5,010 m). Here, on the precipitous descent, it forks: southwest to Nyingdrong and **Samye**, and northwest via Tongdrung La to **On**. The former has already been described (see above). If you take the latter route, you will descend sharply into a lakeland basin frequented by wild geese, and camp overnight at **Tremongpa** (4,850 m). **Day 5**: The trail zigzags uphill from the Tremongpa basin on an uneven surface to cross **Tongdruk La** (5,070 m), from where a subsidiary track heads northeast to Gyama. The main trail crosses a marsh, where herds of gazelle can be seen galloping gracefully across the rough terrain, and then forks: yaks and other pack animals take a circuitous route, while trekkers descend more precipitously through high thickets of purple and pink azelias into the deep ravine formed by the headwaters of the On-chu to reach the campsite at **Onphu Taktsang** (4,500 m; see below, page 196). **Day 6**: Below Taktsang the trail criss-crosses the On-chu, as it descends gradually through more azaleas, bypassing a shrine dedicated to local deities (yul-lha), to reach a riverside camp above **Akhor** (4,180 m). **Day 7**: The final stretch is a three-hour descent by road to Akhor village and the trailhead at Dida, from where vehicles can drive via **Keru Lhakhang** to **Tsetang** (see below, page 189).

Katsel དབུ་རུ་བཀའ་ཚལ

Situated north of the confluence of the Kyi-chu and Meldro Phu-chu rivers, Katsel was originally one of the four district-controlling geomantic temples, specifically constructed by King Songtsen Gampo on the right shoulder of the supine ogress who represented the rigour of the Tibetan terrain. The antiquity of the **Tukdam Tsuklakhang** at Katsel, with its unusual sloping walls, has been remarked upon by Hugh Richardson, who visited the site during the 1940s. Subsequent temples were added to the complex from the time of Padmasambhava onwards, and the monastery was later adopted by the Drigungpas.

The main building at Katsel has been reconstructed in three storeys, the lowest of which has three successive chapels. Of these, the **innermost chapel** contains central images of the Buddhas of the Three Times; and side images of Green Tara and Drigung Rinchen Phuntsok, as well as a stupa in which the latter's relics are preserved. The **middle chapel** contains a library, including the volumes of the Kangyur and Tangyur.

The **second storey** contains images of the Three Deities of Longevity, Amitayus, White Tara and Vijaya, in the inner sanctum, and other images of Tsongkhapa, Shakyamuni, Drigungpa Jikten Gonpo, and Mahakarunika along the left wall. In the far left corner there is an appliqué depicting the protectress Tseringma; while adjacent to the door are the volumes of the Collected Works of Ratna Lingpa and the Biography of Drigung Rinchen Phuntsok.

The **third storey** has a large chapel with fine murals depicting the lamas of the Drigungpa lineage, flanked by tangkas of Padmasambhava, Lama Chodpa, Machik Labdron, and Shakyamuni Buddha, and surmounted by more tangkas depicting Padmasambhava, Shantaraksita, and King Trisong Detsen. The inner wall has images of the Drigung protectress Apchi in her peaceful and wrathful forms, as well as Dorje

Yudronma, Pehar in the form Tukyi Gyelpo, and Cimara, along with tangkas depicting Vajrasattva, Apchi and Mahakala.

Tangkya Lhakhang ཐང་སྐྱ་ལྷ་ཁང

Located in the village of Tangkya on the north bank of the Kyi-chu, and accessible via a bridge a few kilometres north of Katsel, this geomantic temple was originally constructed in the seventh century by King Songtsen Gampo, and later restored by Lu-me during the 12th-century. Further shrines were later added to the complex, including the 12th century temple built to house the remains of the Nyingma lama Zhikpo Dudtsi (1149-1199). Subsequently, the temple came under the influence of other traditions: the Taklung Kagyupa, the Jonangpa, and the Gelukpa, before being absorbed by the Namgyel Monastery of the Potala Palace. The present temple appears to contain three original clay images, extracted from one of the earlier (long destroyed) structures, and some bronze Kadam-style stupas.

Drigung Township

About 25 km north of Meldro Gungkar, the ruins of the Drigung Dzongsar castle brood over the confluence of the Kyi-chu and Zhorong Tsangpo, marking the point where the former abruptly changes course. The Zhorong Tsangpo is the principal southwest flowing tributary of the Kyi-chu, which has its source above the nomad encampment of **Tantuk Sumdo**. A turn-off leaves the main riverside road (which continues following the Kyi-chu upstream as far as Phodo Dzong) for Drigung township (**Drigung qu**), which is located on a promontory between the Zhorong Tsangpo and the Mangra-chu. Here there are small shops and a simple guesthouse.

Zha Lhakhang དབུ་རུ་ཞྭའི་ལྷ་ཁང

Zha Lhakhang is located on the south bank of the Mangra-chu, about 1.5 km upstream from Drigung township. It is a small temple of considerable historic significance for two reasons. Firstly, there are original ninth-century obelisks flanking the entrance gate, which have inscriptions proclaiming the royal rewards and estates granted to Nyangben Tingzin Zangpo, the childhood friend of King Trisong Detsen, who helped ensure the succession of the latter's son Senalek Jinyon in 798. The obelisk on the left is in good condition, while the one on the right is fragmented. It was Nyangben who persuaded Trisong Detsen to invite Vimalamitra, the Buddhist master of the Dzogchen esoteric instructions (*mengakde*), from India, and who then became the principal recipient of these teachings in Tibet. Vimalamitra concealed the teachings at Zhva Lhakhang in the early ninth century until they were rediscovered in the 11th century by the temple caretaker Dangma Lhundrub Namgyel, from which time their transmission has continued unbroken until the present. The second reason for the importance of this site is that the temple complex was restored during the 14th century by the great Nyingmapa master Longchen Rabjampa who fully comprehended its earlier significance for the Dzogchen tradition. Later in the 18th century the site came under the influence of Sera Monastery and was reconstructed by the Seventh Dalai Lama.

The original chapels of the temple, including the shrine dedicated to the Eight Manifestations of Padmasambhava (**Guru Tsengye Lhakhang**) were destroyed during the Cultural Revolution. The restored building is on two levels, the lower storey containing three chapels, and the upper storey a single chamber. Downstairs, the chapel to the left is still bare, the chapel to the right contains images of Padmasambhava along with the three important protectors of the Dzogchen teachings, namely Dorje Lekpa, Ekajati and Rahula, and a *torma* offering shrine. The rear chapel, in the form of an open-air gallery, contains the reconstructed **Tramen Chorten**, under which Longchen Rabjampa interred the sacraments of the Damsi demons at the time of his 14th-century renovations. The upper shrine, used as an assembly hall, contains a solitary image of Longchen

 Rabjampa. Further restoration has recently been undertaken here by Lama Rigzin Gyatso from Nyarong in Kham. To the left and right of the courtyard in front of the temple are the monastic residential buildings (*tratsang*), and behind the left wing there is another newly reconstructed stupa. The **Zangyak Drak** hillside to the left contains a meditation cave associated with the temple's founder Nyangben Tingzin Zangpo, and the **Karpo Drak** peak to the right has caves associated with both Padmasambhava and Dangma Lhundrub Namgyel.

Drigung Til Monastery འབྲི་གུང་མཐིལ་དགོན་པ

→ *Altitude: 4,280 m. Colour map 3, grid A5.*

ⓘ *Admission: ¥20.*

The Monastery of Drigung Til is around 40 km northeast of Drigung township in the upper reaches of the Zhorong Tsangpo valley. Some 10 km along this road there is Yangri Gonpa of the Sakya tradition, where a small temple has recently been rebuilt following the evacuation of an adjacent military base. After climbing steadily for a further 24 km, the road forks just before the township of Menpa, north for Zhoto Tidro and east to Drigung. The monastery is 4 km beyond Menpa, on the slopes of a steep cliff overlooking the valley. The name Drigung ('back of the *dri*') refers to the distinctive contour of the cliff and its ridge, which resembles the back of a *dri* 'female yak'.

There are more than 50 buildings scattered across the upper slopes of the ridge, but three central temples act as a focal point for the entire complex. The **Assembly Hall** (*dukhang*) contains exquisite images of Vajradhara and Shakyamuni Buddha, as well as Padmasambhava in the form of Nangsi Zilnon, Drigung Jikten Gonpo, the founder of the monastery, and Rinchen Phuntsok, who presided over its greatest development. In the centre of the hall are further images depicting Jikten Gonpo and his two immediate successors, Sherab Jungne and Drakpa Jungne, who are collectively known here as Yabsesum.

The other important temples are connected by an open air gallery. Among them, the **Serkhang** to the right of the gallery contains the reliquary stupa, stone footprint and conch of Jikten Gonpo, along with images of Manjughosa, Jikten Gonpo (twice), Ksitigarbha, the protectress Apchi in her peaceful and wrathful forms, and the thrones of the Chetsang and Chungtsang incarnations.

The **Dzamling Gyen** Temple to the left of the gallery contains the reliquaries of Drigung Rinchen Phuntsok, Dorje Rinchen, and the yogin Bachung Rinpoche, who passed away in 1989 after devoting many years to Drigung's reconstruction. Towards the northeast of the ridge, there is a **Protector Chapel** (*gonkhang*) containing images of the protectress Apchi, and a hermitage, once frequented by Jikten Gonpo, and more recently by Bachung Rinpoche. It contains another stone footprint of Jikten Gonpo, along with a clay image of Tara, and tangkas depicting Shakyamuni and Tara.

The ruins of the residence (*labrang*) of the Drigung Chetsang and Chungtsang incarnations have not as yet been renovated, but there are active meditation hermitages (*drubkhang*) scattered across the hillside. To the northwest of the ridge is the famed **Drigung Charnel Ground** (*Drigung Durtro*) to which the dead will be brought from far-off districts of Central Tibet, Kongpo and Nakchuka for sky burial. The circle of stones on which the corpses are dismembered, some 12 m in diameter, is said to represent the mandala of Cakrasamvara. Around the ground are stupas and a third stone footprint of Jikten Gonpo. On the left are two recently constructed chapels, one containing murals of the Hundred Peaceful and Wrathful Deities (which appear to the deceased during the intermediate state after death and before rebirth), and the other containing the shaven hair of the dead. The pilgrim's circumambulation route encompasses the main temples, hermitages and burial ground of Drigung.

Beyond Drigung Til, there are trekking routes which lead through the uppermost reaches of the Zhorong Tsangpo valley to Reting (6-7 days), as well as into the Nyangchu district of Kongpo and the Nyiphu district of Pome (see below, page 430).

History of Drigung Til

The Drigungpa is one of the eight schools derived from the teachings of Phakmodrupa Dorje Gyelpo (1110-1170), whose seat was established at Densatil, northeast of Tsetang (see below, page 227). In 1167, a hermitage was founded at Drigung Til by Minyak Gomring, a disciple of Phakmodrupa, and in 1179, one of Phakmodrupa's most senior disciples, named Jikten Gonpo (1143-1217), inaugurated the monastery. Drigung Til acquired a high reputation for its excellence in meditation, and during the 13th century even rivalled Sakya in its political influence until its destruction by the Mongols in 1290. Following its rebuilding, the monastery once again acquired great wealth, but ceased to play a political role in the affairs of Tibet. The Drigung Kagyu tradition has several connections with that of the Nyingmapa, particularly the tradition of Longchen Rabjampa, who during the 14th century was a highly influential figure in the Drigung region. The high point of its development is considered to be in the 16th century, during the period of Drigung Rinchen Phuntsok, who is also considered to be a Nyingmapa lineage holder. In recent centuries the Drigungpa have had two important incarnate lamas, the Chetsang and the Chungtsang; and in 1959 there were over 500 monks.

Zhoto Tidro Hermitage གཞོ་སྟོད་ཏི་སྒྲོ

The hermitage of Zhoto Tidro (also known as Terdrom) is located about 13 km from the Menpa turn-off, in the side valley of the Rep-chu, to the north of the main Zhorong Tsongpo gorge. The approach to the hermitage (Altitude: 4,500 m) follows a narrow but drivable track up a precipitous cliff above the Rep-chu River and comes to a halt at a vantage point overlooking a gorge, replete with aromatic herbs and containing a medicinal hot spring (**Chutsen Chugang**) and an important nunnery. Two guesthouses have been constructed beside the hot springs, which offer relaxing bathing facilities. One is run by the nunnery ⓣ *T095828-60650, slightly superior through very basic accommodation, ¥180 per room and ¥60 per bed, supplies towels and bathrobes*, and the other by TTC, Lhasa.

History In 772 when King Trisong Detsen offered his queen Yeshe Tsogyel to Padmasambhava, hostile Bonpo nobles forced the master and his new consort to flee the royal court for the sanctuary of the limestone caves and hot springs of Zhoto Tidro. Padmasambhava concealed a number of treasures (*terma*) in the **Kiri Yangdzong** cave above Tidro, which were discovered centuries later by Dorje Lingpa, Drigung Rinchen Phuntsok and others. Yeshe Tsogyel herself remained in meditation at Tidro for many years, which is why the original nunnery was constructed at this particular site. The earliest buildings appear to date from the Kadampa period, but reconstruction has taken place on a number of occasions, the most recent being after the Cultural Revolution. The nunnery, at present housing more than 130 nuns, is headed by the elderly Khandro-la, a veritable emanation of Yeshe Tsogyel, and in its temple there are splendid images of Padmasambhava, his two consorts, and eight manifestations, as well as Shakyamuni Buddha, and a Drigungpa throne.

Tidro Pilgrimage

Starting from the **hot springs**, the hardy traveller may follow the pilgrim's route to the Padmasambhava caves high in the mountains above Tidro. The full circuit will take 10-12 hours. Immediately below the springs, there is a 15-m long subterranean channel through which the river passes. Legend says that Padmasambhava himself created the tunnel in order to drain a lake inhabited by malignant water spirits by throwing his *vajra* at the ridge above, and the mark of the *vajra* can still be seen in the rocks at the tunnel entrance. He then created the hot springs for the benefit of future practitioners. The average temperature of the springs is 40°C, and they are known to contain sulphur, limestone, bitumen, coal and other minerals which, over a one-week stay, can reputedly alleviate gastric disorders, tumours, paralysis, rheumatism, dermatitis, and general debility according to a publication of the Meldro Gungkar Mentsikhang.

The **inner circumambulation** (*nangkor*) leads from the hot springs and the nunnery towards a west ridge which is reached by crossing a bridge over the river. The trail then ascends steeply, reaching hermits' caves and a small chapel affiliated to the nunnery, before crossing Norbu La pass (5,180 m). Here it plunges into another valley before rising to a sky burial ground and the ridge from which the **Kiri Yangdzong** cave (5,060 m) is accessible by traversing a limestone rock face with natural hand and footholds. This immense cavern contains active hermitages and important meditation caves, the most significant being the **Tsogyel Sangpuk**, where Yeshe Tsogyel received the empowerments and teachings of the Innermost Spirituality of the Dakinis (*Khandro Nyingtig*) from Padmasambhava, and subsequently passed many years in retreat. The ceiling of this hermitage, which is reached by a 15-m wooden ladder from the cavern floor, is covered with sheets of ice.

The circuit is completed by descending the limestone face and the scree slopes below to enter a gorge containing the ruined hermitage of Drigung Rinchen Phuntsok (**Drong-ngur Monastery**). From here, the path leads back to the hot springs. There is also an **outer circumambulation** (*chikor*), which encircles the entire Tidro and Drigung region, by taking a northeast valley from Drong-ngur to cross Keleb La pass.

Chushul County ཆུ་ཤུལ

→ *Population: 32,540. Area: 1,482 sq km. Colour map 2, grid B4.* 曲水县

The valley of the Lower Kyi-chu extends from Lhasa southwards, and includes important sites on both banks of the river, as far as its confluence at Takar with the Brahmaputra, which is spanned by the ***Chushul Zamchen*** *bridge. On the south bank of the Brahmaputra opposite the Chushul confluence is the sacred Mount Chuwori (see below, page 166). Four main roads diverge at Takar: due west to Zhigatse via Nyemo and northeast to Lhasa (both on the north bank of the Brahmaputra), and southwest to Gyantse via Gampa La and Lake Yamdrok, or due east to Gongkar Airport and Tsetang (both on the south bank of the Brahmaputra). The distance from Lhasa to Chushul is 36 km on an excellent paved road, and a further 8 km to the bridge at Takar.*

The West Bank of the Lower Kyi-chu

Tashigang བཀྲ་ཤིས་སྒང

Following the paved Lhasa-Chushul highway southwest from the Dongkar intersection, you will pass a number of recently constructed military and industrial complexes, including chemical and petroleum processing plants, two PLA training centres, and a palatial PLA HQ building. After 15 km, you will reach on the left the turn-off for Tashigang, a Sakya monastery under the guidance of Bero Khyentse Rinpoche. The assembly hall (*dukhang*) has an image of Sakya Pandita, flanked by images of Shakyamuni, Avalokiteshvara, and Mahakala. Skylight murals depict the Sixteen Elders, Shakyamuni, Tara, and Atisha. Above the throne of the Dalai Lama, there is a 17th-century tangka depicting Bhaisajyaguru, the Buddha of Medicine. The protector shrine is located upstairs. Currently, there are about 30 monks at Tashigang.

Nyetang Dolma Lhakhang ཉེ་ཐང་སྒྲོལ་མ་ལྷ་ཁང → *Colour map 3, grid B2.*

ⓘ *Admission: ¥10.*

Located 17 km southwest of Dongkar on the right side of the highway, a short distance after passing a large painted relief image of Shakyamuni on the rock face, this celebrated temple dates from the time of the great Bengali master Atisha, who passed away at Nyetang in 1054. The temple is said to have survived the Cultural Revolution virtually unscathed owing to the intervention of Chou En Lai at the expressed request of the Government of East Pakistan (now Bangladesh). An adjacent 15th-century Gelukpa Monastery, known as Dewachen, was destroyed at that time. From the outside, the temple appears to be insignificant, but the sacred artefacts contained within it testify to the importance of the Kadampa tradition in 11th-13th century Tibet. At present there are only nine monks at Nyetang, and they are mostly affiliated with nearby Tashigang.

A double gateway leads through a courtyard (with a protector chapel on the left) to a covered terrace, where there are 11th-century images of the Four Guardian Kings, and two sunken stupas containing the robes of Atisha and his disciple Dromtonpa. In the extreme left and right corners of the terrace there are large prayer wheels, while the murals inset between the chapel doors depict Atisha with his two foremost students, Dromtonpa and Ngok Lekpei Sherab, as well as Shakyamuni, Maitreya, and Manjughosa.

There are three interconnecting chapels, entered from the door to the left and exited by the door to the right. The first, known as the **Namgyel Lhakhang**, contains a large Victory Stupa (Namgyel Chorten), flanked on the left and right by smaller Kadam-style stupas containing relics of Naropa, among which is the 3-m high **Naropa Dungten** holding the precious skull of Naropa, along with Atisha's books and begging bowl. In front of the stupas are small 500-cm high images of the Eight Medicine Buddhas with a clay representation of Atisha at the centre. Images on the left wall depict Tara, Avalokiteshvara, and Amitayus.

The second chapel, known as the **Dolma Lhakhang**, contains 17th-century bronze images of the Twenty-One Taras, which are stacked in two tiers, occupying three walls of the chamber. The central images in the **upper tier** represent Shakyamuni (dated 1288), White Tara (a 'speaking image'), Serlingpa Dharmkirti, who was the teacher of Atisha, and the Thirteenth Dalai Lama. Other images of the Buddhas of the Five Families (Pancajina), dating from 11th century, are in the upper right corner. In the **lower tier**, the central objects of offering preserved inside a glass cabinet include a conch shell from Nalanda, an image of Thousand-armed Mahakarunika, a stupa containing Serlingpa's remains, a small image of Shakyamuni brought by Atisha from India, and a tangka depicting Six-armed Mahakala, which is said to have been painted with the blood from Atisha's nose. An original 'speaking image' of Tara, which Atisha himself revered as an object of meditation, disappeared from the cabinet during the Cultural Revolution, but is said to have been preserved secretly at Norbulingka by the late Tenth Panchen Lama, and has recently been replaced within the cabinet. Other sacred objects in this chapel include a round urn containing Atisha's bone relics, a bronze 13th-century image of Avalokiteshvara Karsapani from India, and, until its theft by international art thieves in 1992, an image of Maitreya known as Atsa Jampa, which was reputedly spared the wrath of the Mongolians by uttering the exclamation 'atsa' ('ouch!').

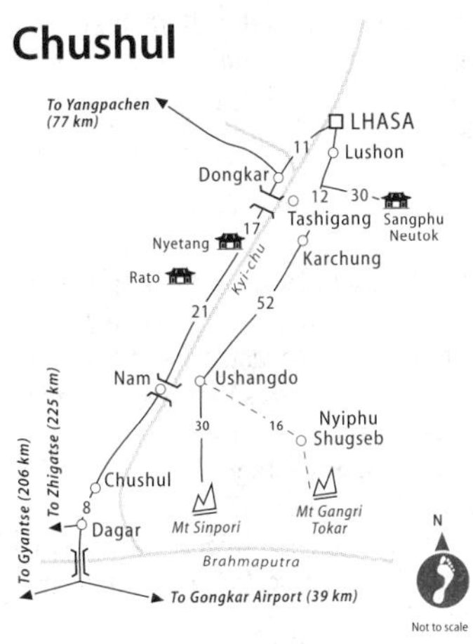

Lastly, the **Tsepak Lhakhang** contains large 12th-century images of the Buddhas of the Three Times and the Eight Bodhisattvas. Among these, the central image is of the Buddha of the Present in the form of Amitayus, fashioned by Dromtonpa from the funerary ashes of Atisha. The stupa containing his remaining ashes has been removed to nearby Tashigang. In the centre of the chapel is the backrest of Atisha's clay throne, with an attached image of Atisha himself, said to have been made in his own lifetime. The inner gates of this last chapel are guarded by large images of the gatekeepers Vajrapani (east) and Hayagriva (west).

The **upper storey** contains the Dalai Lamas' private apartments. The chamber to the left contains a golden throne (*sertri*), backed by statues of Tsongkhapa and his two foremost students, and its walls have photographs of the late Tenth Panchen Lama. The room to the right has a central throne, backed by another set of Tsongkhapa and his students, alongside the Three Deities of Longevity.

The **Protector Chapel** (*Gonkhang*), located to the left of the courtyard, contains images of Nechung Chokyong, flanked by Six-armed Mahakala and Shridevi. It also has photographs of the present Rato Rinpoche and Rato Chung Rinpoche.

Rato Monastery ར་སྟོད་དགོན་པ

Located at Rato village in a side valley, some 5 km behind Nyetang Dolma Lhakhang, Rato Monastery was founded in the 11th century by Taktsangpa and had later associations with the Kadampa master Ngok Loden Sherab and Tsongkhapa. Noted for the study of Buddhist logic and metaphysics, the monastery had about 400 monks at the height of its development. The principal incarnate lamas of Rato are all in exile, living in India, Germany, and the United States; and there are at the moment no more than 90 monks.

The **Assembly Hall** (Dukhang) at Rato has central images of Tsongkhapa with his foremost disciples, and an image of Tara, said to have been the personal property of Atisha. Behind these along the rear wall are images of Shakyamuni Buddha and Atisha, flanked by the Kadampa lamas Luchok Dorjechang, Ngok Loden Sherab, Manga Draksang, Chokla Ozer, Ngok Lekpei Sherab and Yonten Phuntsok.

Behind, within the **inner sanctum** (tsangkhung) is an image of Tsongkhapa, replacing the former magnificent images of the Buddhas of the Three Times and the Eight Bodhisattvas. The extant murals of the assembly hall appear to date from the 17th-18th century. These depict protector deities, such as Dharmaraja and Tsedrekpa; bodhisattvas such as Tara, Manjughosa, Avalokiteshvara, Vajrapani, and Sitapatatra; the lamas of the Lamrim lineage, and the Buddhas of confession and medicine.

Among the other reconstructed temples at Rato: the **Nyitri Lhakhang** contains a protector shrine and the Dalai Lama's private apartments in its upper storeys, the **Jamkhang** contains a large Maitreya, and the **Rinchen Ritro Hermitage** has associations with Longdol Lama. In the mountains to the north there are also meditation caves belonging to Rato Monastery.

Chushul ཆུ་ཤུལ

The highway from Lhasa to Chushul continues southwest from Nyetang Dolma Lhakhang, passing through the village of Nam, where Lhasa's only orphanage was recently established by Semo Dechen, daughter of the late Dilgo Khyentse Rinpoche. A motorable trail leads inland from here to the original Drukpa Kagyu Monastery of **Druk Jangchub Choling**, which was founded before Ralung Monastery (see page 266) by Tsangpa Gyare in 1189. Further south, the main road reaches the village of Jang, opposite which a new bridge has been constructed across the Kyi-chu, leading to Shugseb Nunnery (see below, page 161). The local **Jang Monastery** is a focal point for pilgrims from Lhasa during the celebrations of the fourth lunar month.

Continuing south from Jang, the road soon reaches the new bridge spanning the Kyi-chu, which from autumn 2004 will carry traffic across to the entrance to the **Sinpori Tunnel**, on the new road to Gongkar Airport.

The county town of **Chushul** has grown considerably in recent years, owing to its position near the intersection of the four main roads of Central, Western and Southern Tibet. Much of the construction here has been provided by the Chinese province of Jiangsu. The town has a large two-storey guesthouse, schools, a number of public buildings and many private shops. South of town there is the headquarters of the Chinese Navy in Tibet, a bizarre building with a gateway surmounted by a speedboat. Further southeast at **Takar**, the actual intersection, there is an overt military presence charged with the protection of the strategically important Chushul Zamchen bridge. Formerly, a suspension bridge made by Tangtong Gyelpo spanned the Brahmaputra slightly downstream from here, but it was damaged in the mid-20th century.

The East Bank of the Lower Kyi-chu

Karchung Ramagang སྐར་ཆུང་ར་མ་སྒང

From the military compound at Drib near the regency temple of Tsechokling on the south bank of the Kyi-chu opposite Lhasa, a newly constructed road follows the river downstream in a southwest direction. Ramagang, the site of **Sangda Karchung Monastery**, is located slightly inland from Lushon village about 12 km along this road. The monastery was founded by King Senalek Jinyon (r 798-813), who erected an inscribed obelisk and stupas in each of the temple's four directions, along the design of Samye Monastery. Drepung is visible across the river from the ruins of Sangda Karchung.

Sangphu Neutok Monastery གསང་ཕུ་ནེའུ་ཐོག་གི་ཆོས་གྲྭ

Located about 30 km south and inland from Lushon village, on the upper slopes of a side valley which forks to the left, Sangphu Neutok Monastery was founded in 1073 by Ngok Lekpei Sherab and developed by his nephew, Ngok Loden Sherab. These scholar translators were close disciples of Atisha. Originally there were two Kadampa colleges here, known as Lingto and Lingme. Under the guidance of Chapa Chokyi Senge (1109-1169) the monastery eventually gained renown for its eclectic approach to the study of Buddhist philosophy, and it became a mixed institution with seven Sakyapa and four Gelukpa colleges. The meditation caves of Yakde Panchen and Rongton Sheja Kunzi were located on the upper slopes; while lower down by the river at Sangda, some 16 km distant, the reliquary of Ngok Loden Sherab were formerly preserved. In recent centuries the monastery declined but it was restored by the Thirteenth Dalai Lama prior to its more recent destruction during the Cultural Revolution.

Ushangdo Peme Tashi Gephel འུ་ཤང་རྡོ་དཔེ་མེད་བཀྲ་ཤིས་དགེ་འཕེལ

Following the Kyi-chu downstream from Sangda for approximately 52 km, via the villages of Sheldrong, Namgyel Gang, and Tshena Sha, a side valley leads across the plain of Nyinda (sometimes called Shuntse) to the ruins of Ushangdo Temple. This area is also accessible from Jang on the west bank, via the new Kyi-chu suspension bridge.

The nine-storey temple of Ushangdo was the greatest construction project undertaken by the Tibetan king Relpachen. It is said to have been a pagoda-style building with a blue turquoise Chinese-style roof. The lower floors were used by the king and his ministers, the middle floors by the Indian panditas and their Tibetan translators, and the upper three storeys contained images. The building appears not to have survived Langdarma's persecution; but a small temple with a remarkable Jowo Shakyamuni image was later constructed on the site. Unfortunately, today only its ruins are visible.

Nyiphu Shugseb Nunnery སྙི་ཕུ་ཤུག་གསེབ

Shugseb is located 16 km above Ushangdo in the uplands of Nyiphu. The site was originally consecrated by the yogini Machik Labron (1055-1149), who meditated in the caves of Shugseb, but the first retreat centre was actually established here by Gyargom

 Tsultrim Senge (1144-1204), a student of Phakmodrupa, and founder of the Shugseb Kagyu order. From the 14th century onwards, Shugseb has been an important centre for nuns of the Nyingma school, owing to the teaching of Longchen Rabjampa at nearby Gangri Tokar; and the female incarnation of Shugseb, the Shugseb Jetsunma, ranks as one the highest female incarnations in the whole of Tibet.

There are currently 250 nuns living in huts around the restored temple of Shugseb. Downstairs, there is a new image of Padmasambhava (with an original miniature representative image at its heart), flanked by Vajrasattva, Tara, Longchenpa, Jigme Lingpa, and Jetsunma. Upstairs the chapel is dedicated to Machik Labron, and there is a library of seminal Nyingmapa works, alongside the residence of Jetsunma. From Shugseb there are three- to four-day trekking routes, east to Dorje Drak and south to Sinpori.

Gangri Tokar གངས་རི་ཐོད་དཀར

The ridge of Mount Gangri Tokar (5,336 m) is about one hour's hiking distance above Shugseb Nunnery. From the perspective of pure sacred vision, the site is said to represent the contours of the female deity Vajravarahi. The great Nyingma master Longchen Rabjampa (1308-1363) arrived here at the invitation of his protectress Dorje Yudronma. Here, in the cave hermitage of **Orgyan Dzong** and its inner sanctum, called **Dawa Chushel Puk**, he meditated, edited his *terma* revelations (entitled Kandro Yangtig, Zabmo Yangtig, and Lama Yangtig); and composed his great treatises including the Seven Treasuries (Dzodun) and the Three Trilogies (Korsum Namsum).

In 1993 a temple was constructed around the cave. It contains an image of Longchenpa, and murals depicting the three Dzogchen protectors, Jigme Lingpa, Longchenpa, Rigzin Dupa, Yumka Dechen Gyelmo, Palchen Dupa, Dorje Yudronma, and Hayagriva. The stumps of two juniper trees (abodes of the protectors Rahula and Dorje Yudronma) are visible outside the entrance, alongside a recently replanted juniper. An upper temple, constructed in 1983, has images of the Three Deities of Long Life and of Dorje Drolo. Surrounding the cave are the three talismanic rocks into which four protectors were respectively absorbed during Longchenpa's sojourn: Rahula's to the north, Ekajati's and Dorje Lekpa's to the east and Dorje Yudronma's to the south. Beyond these to the north and south there are two springs, symbolic of Vajravarahi's breasts, and below them two sky burial grounds, emblematic of her legs. Then, further uphill, towards the summit of the ridge that symbolises Vajravarahi's head, there are further meditation caves including the **Melong Puk** hermitage of Melong Dorje, **Samten Puk**, **Dewa Puk**, and **Shar Zimpuk**, the last and most remote being especially favoured for the practice of the highest Dzogchen teachings, known as All-surpassing Realization (*thogal*).

Riwo Tsenga རི་བོ་རྩེ་ལྔ

Southwest of Gangri Tokar is the five-peaked ridge known as Riwotsenga, which is named after the celebrated Buddhist range of Wutaishan in China. There are a number of meditation caves here, including the Zangyak Namka Dzong, the Guru Drupuk and Lharing Longchen Drak.

Sinpori སྲིན་པོ་རི

Mount Sinpori lies 30 km south of Ushangdo, on a promontory between the Kyi-chu and Brahmaputra rivers, east of the confluence. This barren desert-like terrain once contained an important 13th-century Sakya temple which had been constructed by the Bengali scholar Vibhuticandra on the advice of Panchen Shakyashri. The temple was dedicated to and housed a 'speaking image' of Cakrasamvara.

Sinpori is also accessible by ferry from Chushul, by trekking from Shugseb via Leuchung, or walking from Dorje Drak on the north bank of the Brahmaputra. Following the completion of the new airport road from Lhasa to Gongkar, a tunnel now leads traffic through Mount Sinpori and across a new suspension bridge to **Gongkar Airport** on the south bank of the Brahmaputra.

Southern Tibet (Lhokha and Kongpo)

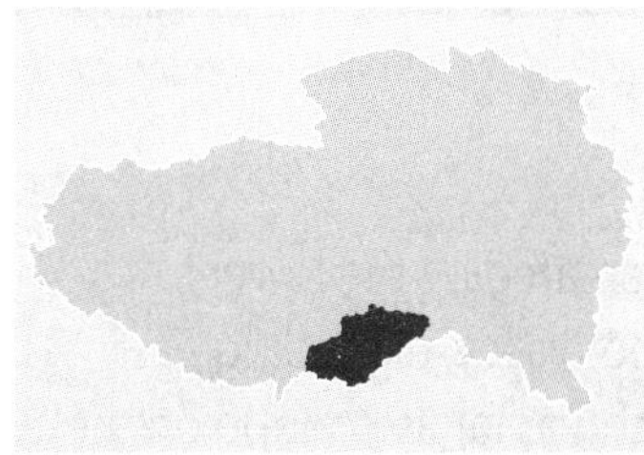

Footprint features

Introduction

Southern Tibet is the region demarcated by the lower Brahmaputra (Tib Yarlung Tsangpo) valley, extending east from its confluence with the Kyi-chu as far as Kongpo on the borders of Powo and Pemako, where it turns through narrow gorges and flows southwest into India. The region includes the lateral valleys adjoining the Brahmaputra on both its north and south banks, and the valleys of its tributaries, which flow south through the Himalayas into East Bhutan and Arunachal Pradesh to converge with this great river in West Bengal or Assam. This vast region, revered as the cradle of Tibetan civilization, is currently divided into 16 counties, four of which are administered from Bayi (Gyamda, Nyangtri, Nang, and Menling), and the remainder from Tsetang, the capital of the Lhokha district (Gongkar, Dranang, Nedong, Chongye, Tso-me, Lhodrak, Nakartse, Zangri, Chusum, Lhuntse, Tsona and Gyatsa). The distance from Lhasa to Gongkar Airport is 55 km (on the new road via the Sinpori Tunnel) or 99 km (on the old road via Takar), and to Tsetang 186 km.

Recommended itineraries: 1 and 4 (also 7). See page 20.

★ Don't miss...

❶ **Gongkar Dorjeden, Dratang and Mindroling** Original mural paintings can be seen in these temples, which were used as granaries during the Cultural Revolution, page 166.

❷ **Chimphu Hermitage** Climb above Samye Monastery to the Zangdok Pelri Rock at Chimphu, an active meditation hermitage, where you will receive a special welcome, page 186.

❸ **Yarlung and Chongye** Step back in time to explore Tibet's early history: the first geomantic temple at Tradruk, page 201, the first palace at Yumbu Lagang, page 204, and the tombs of the kings near Chongye, page 210.

❹ **Kongpo** In this forested enclave you can hike around the shores of the turquoise lake Draksum, page 207, or visit the magnificent three-storey temple at Lamaling where its founder Lama Chonyi even now resides, and the nearby geomantic temple of Buchu, page 243.

❺ **Mt Namchak Barwa** Cross the Brahmaputra by coracle or ferry to view this snow pinnacle at the eastern extremity of the Himalaya, from Padmasambhava's hermitage at Thim Guru Druphuk, page 241.

Gongkar County གོང་དཀར

→ *Population: 46,077. Area: 2,532 sq km. Colour map 3, grid C3.* 贡嘎县

Gongkar county is located on the banks of the Brahmaputra at a point where the river valley is at its widest, which is why ***Gongkar Airport*** *(the civilian airport serving Lhasa) was constructed there in the late 1970s. A second runway and terminal facilities were completed in 1994. The airport lies to the west of* ***Rawa-me,*** *the county capital at the entrance to the Namrab valley; 55 km from Lhasa (on the new road) and 87 km from Tsetang. The borders of Gongkar county extend from the sacred Mount Chuwori opposite Chushul, southwards to Gampa La pass (4,794 m), which is the gateway to Lake Yamdrok and West Tibet, and eastwards as far as the Dol valley on the south bank of the Brahmaputra and Dorje Drak monastery on the north bank. It therefore includes the southern valleys of Gongkar, Namrab and Drib, as well as the northern valleys of Leuchung and Trango.*

Mount Chuwori ཆུ་བོ་རི

The sacred mountain of Chuwori which broods over the sandbanks around the confluence of the Kyi-chu and Brahmaputra rivers is considered to be one of the most auspicious places for meditation practice in Tibet. In the past, the mountain had 108 springs and 108 hermitages dating from the time of King Trisong Detsen in the eighth century. Padmasambhava had a hermitage near the summit at **Namkading**, and it is said that 108 of his yogin followers attained the body of light here at Chuwori. Later, during the 12th century, new hermitages were constructed by the Nyingmapa lama Taton Joye, the First Karmapa Dusum Khyenpa, and Tsangpa Gya-re, and in the 13th century by the Second Dorje Drak Rigzin Lekdenje.

On the lower slopes of the mountain, the monastery of **Chakzam Chuwori** was founded by Tangtong Gyelpo, opposite the celebrated iron suspension bridge which he constructed across the Brahmaputra to Yolri Gong near Chushul which was (damaged in the early decades of the previous century, and has now been replaced by the Chushul Zamchen bridge). At the south end of the old suspension bridge, there was also a Kumbum stupa, containing an image and relics of Tangtong Gyelpo himself.

The monastery of **Pema Wangchuk** was located on a northwest spur of Mount Chuwori; and on the east side, near the Tsechu ('water of life') Spring where pilgrims still flock, there was once an active Nyingmapa monastery called **Tsechu Kopa** or Tsechuling, founded by Menlungpa Lochok Dorje. This site is currently being rebuilt; and pilgrims continue to make the four-hour circuit of the mountain via Phab La (4,250 m).

Gampa La Pass སྒམ་པ་ལ

The approach to Gampa La pass (4,794 m) offers spectacular views of the **Nojin Gangzang** snow ranges and the turquoise **Yamdrok Yutso Lake**. It is 28 km from the south end of the Chushul Zamchen bridge and the switchback road winds its way up from Samar, past deep barren gorges, which are evidence of the Brahmaputra tectonic fault line. Near the pass, which is decorated with colourful prayer flags, there is a turn-off to the right, leading to a hydroelectric installation. For the route from Gampa La to Nakartse, see below, page 224.

Gongkar Valley གོང་དཀར

Driving east from the southern end of the Chushul Zamchen bridge for 26 km, you will see on the left the hilltop ruins and restored buildings of **Gongkar Dzong**, from which this entire region was ruled until the 1950s.

Gongkar Chode Just beyond this hilltop promontory, at the entrance to the Gongkar valley, there is an important monastery called **Gongkar Chode** or Gongkar Dorjeden, which was founded in 1464 by Dorjedenpa Kunga Namgyel of the Sakya School. Here there are still important murals typical of the free-flowing Khyenri school of painting, which were the original work of Jamyang Khyentse Wangchuk (b 1524). The 64-pillared **assembly hall** (*dukhang*) has new images depicting (L-R): Sakya Pandita, Tara, Dorjedenpa and Padmasambhava, along with a sand mandala, which is housed in a glass case. On the throne in front of these images is a photograph of Sakya Trizin, the current throneholder of Sakya, who lives at Rajpur in India. The murals of the assembly hall depicting the Twelve Deeds of Shakyamuni Buddha are relatively new, but there are original Khyenri style murals of the Five Founders of Sakya (Gongma Nga) and Dampa Sonam Gyeltsen flanking the entrance to the central inner sanctum. There are four chapels in the main hall: those on the left are dedicated to the Eight Manifestations of Padmasambhava and the protector Panjaranatha. The latter contains exquisite gold-on-black painted murals of Mahakala in the form of Panjaranatha (Gonpo Gur) and his retinue, the preferred protectors of the Sakya tradition. The walls of the circumambulatory walkway around the **central inner sanctum** have original murals depicting the thousand buddhas of this aeon. The original three-storey high image of Shakyamuni which once graced the inner sanctum has been replaced, but at the heart of the replica is the authentic skull of the Indian master Gayadhara in a glass case. Statues representing the Seven Generations of Past Buddhas have been positioned high on the adjacent walls around the central image. On the right of the assembly hall there is a further chapel containing Khyenri-style murals of the Buddhas of the Three Times.

Upstairs on the second floor, there is a **Gonkhang** (protector chapel) dedicated to Panjaranatha, a **Kangyur Lhakhang**, and two impressive chapels: one is a former **residence of Dorjedenpa** with exquisite Khyenri murals depicting the plan of the original monastery and the accomplished master Virupa interrupting the setting of the sun, as well as images of the Three Deities of Longevity, Tangtong Gyelpo and Dorjedenpa, also a series of tangkas depicting the Eight Manifestations of Padmasambhava. The other is the **Kyedor Lhakhang**, which contains a central image of Hevajra in a glass case, and some exceptional murals typical of the Khyenri style. These depict the main meditational deities of the Sakyapa school. From left to right they include: Vaishravana, Shriheruka, Vajrakila, Vajrapani, Black Yamari, Vajrabhairava, Red Yamari (above door), Guhyasamaja Manjuvajra, Guhyasamaja Aksobhyavajra, Kalacakra, Buddhasamayoga (above door, damaged), Hevajra, Catuhvajrapitha, Hevajra, Cakrasamvara, Vajrasattva, Mahamaya, Buddhakapala, Vajrapani, Cakrasamvara, and Yaksa Vajradamara with his entourage (above the entrance).

Directly opposite the Kyedor Lhakhang, there is yet another chapel, dedicated to the Sixteen Elders. Outside, in the **gallery**, there are fine murals depicting the Six Ornaments and Two Supreme Ones of ancient India, and motifs of geometric poetry.

On the third floor the **Lama Lhakhang** is dedicated to the monastery's founder, containing the reliquary stupa of Dorjedenpa Kunga Namgyel, flanked by images of Vajradhara and Sakya Pandita. Restoration work funded by the Paris-based Shalu Association has strengthened the supporting pillars and stabilized the entire building. The rooftop **Lamrim Lhakhang** has not yet been rebuilt. Formerly, there were other buildings at Gongkar Chode, including a towering **Jamkhang**, a distinctive three-storeyed **Lamdre Lhakhang** and four colleges, which are all in a bad state of disrepair.

Dechen Chockhor Following the road inland from Gongkar Chode for 5 km, you will reach Dechen Chokhor, a 13th-century hermitage and monastery of the Drukpa Kagyu school, located on the slopes 150 m above the road. One small chapel has been rebuilt amid the ruins. Further inland there are one- to two-day trekking routes from Gongkar valley to Lake Yamdrok via the Dra La pass (5,342 m) and Chilung. It is also possible to drive by 4WD around the lake.

Namrab Valley རྣམ་རབ

Continuing east on the main road below Gongkar Chode, a further 10 km will bring you to **Gongkar Airport** and the entrance to the Namrab valley. Gongkar Airport Hotel, T0893-6182171, within the airport complex, has single and double rooms at ¥350, but the facilities are quite basic and most passengers will prefer to commute from Lhasa, Tsetang and even Zhigatse on the day of their flight. There are popular and clean Tibetan and Chinese restaurants outside the gate to the airport, serving mo-mo, Siuchuan-style beef-filled pancakes, butter tea and sweet tea; there's even a small supermarket.

Rawa-me

The Sakyapa monastery of **Tubten Rawa-me** ⓘ *T0893-7392159*, founded by Rawalepa (1138-1210) is situated within the town. It is in a state of disrepair, and has a prominent TV antenna on the roof. By the roadside in Rawa-me, the county town, there are a number of small Tibetan and Chinese restaurants and tea shops.

Some 5 km inland from Rawa-me in the Kyishong township area is the Sakya monastery of **Dakpo Tratsang**, founded by Tashi Namgyel (1398-1459), a disciple of the illustrious Rongton Sheja Kunzik. There is a large renovated assembly hall with some original murals and new images of Sakya Pandita, Tashi Namgyel and Gorampa Sonam Senge. The adjacent protector shrine is dedicated to the deity Pangboche.

Further inland and 150 m up a remote hillside is **Zhung Trezhing**, a hermitage frequented by Ngokton Choku Dorje (1036-1102), a close disciple of Marpa Lotsawa. After he passed away there, his nephew Ngok Kunga Dorje (1157-1234) founded the Trezhing monastery, where a distinct Kagyu lineage (apart from those derived from Milarepa and Gampopa) was maintained. In the past Marpa's skull was preserved here in a reliquary stupa.

Drib Valley གྲིབ

The main road east from Gongkar Airport to Tsetang passes through the township of Chedezhol, at the entrance to the Dol or Drib valley after 17 km. Here there is an active cottage industry engaged in the production of colourful striped ladies' aprons (*pangden*). The ruins of **Chedezhol Dzong** can be seen on a ridge to the east.

Dungpu Chokhor About 4 km inland is the monastery of Dungpu Chokhor, originally founded by Drapa Ngonshe in the 11th century; and later absorbed by the Sakyapas in the 15th century. The **Assembly Hall** has some excellent old frescoes, depicting Mahakala in the form of Panjaranatha with other protectors, and the Twelve Deeds of Shakyamuni Buddha, as well as important Sakya meditational deities headed by Hevajra, the Five Founders of Sakya, and (under the skylight) the lamas of the Lamdre lineage. The **inner sanctum** has an original 'speaking' Tara image, adorned with coral, which was once owned by the Indian master Candragomin, as well as images of Khecari, the Sixteen Elders in their grottoes, and the Eight Bodhisattvas. There are side chapels containing a printery (left) and a Vairocana image surrounded by Taras (right). Upstairs is a protector chapel with Panjaranatha as its centrepiece, and a chamber where HH the Fourteenth Dalai Lama stayed during his flight from Lhasa to India in 1959. Outside in the courtyard, an **ancient temple** attributed to Drapa Ngonshe (see page 173) contains images of the Buddhas of the

Five Families, Padmasambhava, Hayagriva and Vajrapani, and murals depicting the Dzogchen lineage of the Nyingma tradition and Drapa Ngonshe himself. An adjacent Mani Wheel chapel has a vestibule with murals of the Kagyu lineage.

About 3 km further inland and in a side valley east of Khyimzhi village is the monastery of **Sungrabling**, which was originally founded as a Sakya establishment by Nyakton Sonam Zangpo in the 14th century and later absorbed by the Gelukpa.

Trekking Further up the Drib valley, via the township of Namgyel Zhol and Drib La pass, there are three- to four-day trekking routes to the north shores of Lake Yamdrok.

Dorje Drak Monastery ཐུབ་བསྟན་རྡོ་རྗེ་བྲག

The celebrated Nyingma monastery of Tubten Dorje Drak maintains the *terma* tradition of the Nyingma school known as the Northern Treasures (*Jangter*), which was founded by the First Rigdzin Godemchen Ngodrub Gyeltsen (1337-1409). In 1632 the monastery relocated from Tsang to its present tranquil setting on the north bank of the Brahmaputra, when the young Third Rigdzin Ngagiwangpo and his guardian Jangdak Tashi Topgyel were forced to flee the wrath of the kings of Tsang. Their successor, the erudite Fourth Rigdzin Pema Trinle (b. 1641) greatly enlarged the monastery before his untimely death at the hands of the zealous Dzungar Mongolians, who sacked the monastery in 1717. Later, during the 1960s the monastery was once again obliterated. Nonetheless it has been gradually restored in recent years through the efforts of the present incarnation of Dordrak Rigdzin, who lives in Lhasa, and those of Kelzang Chojor and the local community.

Accessible by ferry from Chedezhol (50 mins) the monastery is located at the base of a vajra-shaped rock on the north bank of the Brahmaputra.

Getting there The monastery is mainly accessible by ferry and yak-skin coracle from Chedezhol on the south bank of the Brahmaputra. However, there is also a four-day trekking route from Lhasa to Dorje Drak via Drib, Trangto La (4,977 m), Trangto township and Phushar. When the new road through the Sinpori Tunnel to Gongkar Airport opened in summer 2004, access will also be possible by road along the north bank of the river.

Assembly Hall The reconstructed assembly hall (*tshokchen*) has painted scrolls depicting the Hundred Peaceful and Wrathful Deities, and murals of the Eight Manifestations of Padmasambhava, the thousand buddhas of this aeon and lineage-holders of all traditions. There are three thrones, the central one reserved for Dordrak Rigdzin himself, and the others for Taklung Tsetrul Rinpoche (who resides in exile in Simla and Ladakh), and Chubzang Rinpoche. In the **inner sanctum** the central clay image is of Shakyamuni (replacing a gilded copper three-storey high original), flanked by Shariputra and Maudgalyayana, with Padmasambhava in the form of Rigdzin Tukdrub on the left and Pema Trinle on the right. The Eight Bodhisattvas grace the side walls, while the gates are guarded by Hayagriva and Acala. A side chapel functions as the protector shrine, containing images of Cimara, Rahula, Six-armed Mahakala, Takkiraja, Ekajati, Shinje Chidak and Dorje Lekpa.

The **oldest chapel** to the right (in which no women are allowed) once contained images of the 'three roots' (guru, meditational deity and dakini) of the Dorje Drak tradition; but now it functions as a storeroom, containing an old 'self-arising' stone image of Two-armed Avalokiteshvara, a collection of relics retrieved from images destroyed in the 1960s, a copy of the Derge edition of the *Nyingma Gyudbum*, and a number of other precious objects: the vajra and bell of the Fourth Rigdzin Pema Trinle, a treasure chest (*terdrom*), and part of Milarepa's staff. There is also an interesting 3-D plan of how the monastery once looked. Prior to the Dzungar army's destruction of Dorje Drak in 1717, this ancient chapel had been renowned for its enormous columns and skull-painted gates.

Upstairs Upstairs, the main chapel has images (L-R) of Dorje Drolo, Tangtong Gyelpo, Longchenpa, Ngari Panchen Pema Wangyel and the Three Deities of Long Life. The restored private apartments of Dordrak Rigdzin and Taklung Tsetrul are also on this level, as is the **Library,** which is entered by another staircase on the right of the courtyard. It contains images of Pema Trinle and Padmasambhava, the reliquary of Gyelse Rinpoche, and the anthologies of the *Kangyur*, *Tangyur*, *Nyingma Gyudbum*, and *Longchen Dzodun*.

Kora A pilgrims' circuit leads around the 'vajra rock' to the hermitage of **Dorje Drak Utse**, passing en route rock paintings and sacred footprints. The hermitage of the Drukpa Kagyu master Lingje Repa is nearby at **Napu Cholung**.

Dranang County གྲ་ནང

➔ Population: 36,652. Area: 1,426 sq km. Colour map 3, grid C3. 扎囊县

*Dranang county, with its administrative capital at **Dratang**, is made up of a series of lateral valleys adjoining the Brahmaputra valley, both north and south of the river. These include the Drakyul, Zurkhar and Drakmar valleys on the north bank, and the Dranang and Drachi on the south bank. The distance from Chedezhol to Dratang along the main Gongkar-Tsetang highway is 23 km.*

Drakyul Valley སྒྲགས་ཡུལ

The cave complexes of **Drak Yangdzong** and **Dzong Kumbum**, are a maze of interconnecting limestone passages and natural caverns, full of bizarre rock formations, stalagmites and stalactites.

Ins and outs

Drakyul is most easily approached by ferry from **Yangkyar**, a hydroelectric station 3 km west of Dranang on the Gongkar-Tsetang highway; or alternatively via the Dorje Drak ferry from Chedezhol. The trail begins at **Drakda**, birthplace of Nubchen Sangye Yeshe, 4 km from the north ferry station, where the Drak-chu flows into the Brahmaputra. **NB** Alternative routes are also possible: trekking via Dorje Drak and Phushar (two days); trekking from Samye via Zurkhar (one day); or even from Lhasa via Trango La pass (four days) and from Taktse (four days).

Tsogyel Latso

From the ferrry station you should first visit the Tsogyel Latso in Drakda village (4 km distant). This is an oracle lake revered as the life-supporting talisman of Yeshe Tsogyel, and is said to reveal the secrets of past and future events in its waters. Opposite, on the north shore, is **Kazhima Lhakhang**, an undestroyed branch of Samye Monastery, containing images of Padmasambhava, Vajrayogini, and Yeshe Tsogyel herself.

Ngadrak

Then, proceed to **Ngadrak**, a Karma Kagyu monastery on the west bank of the Drak-chu, some 6 km further inland. This large establishment, under the authority of Nenang, comprises an assembly hall adjoined by five chapels and a monastic residential area, where the caretakers of the Drakyul caves can be found. Two kilometres further north from Ngadrak is **Pema Dzong**, a relatively intact fortress dating originally from the 14th century.

Drak Yangdzong caves

The Drakyul caretakers will help you reach **Drak Yangdzong** via the **Chusi Nunnery** (it is 20 km and will take five hours), which is still largely in a ruinous state. The three main caves, all south-facing, are reached by climbing a white limestone cliff named Shinje Rolpei Podrang. Carved reliefs of Padmasambhava, Shakyamuni Buddha, Milarepa, animal figures are visible near the cave entrances. A strong flashlight is essential.

The first cave, **Shinje Drup-ne Zho**, is a vast cavern, 100 sq m in area, with walls 15 m high and 10 m wide. The cave is at present occupied by hermits from Dorje Drak, but the paintings of the interior chapel depict the Mindroling lineage. The main images are of Padmasambhava in the form of Nangsi Zilnon, flanked by his consorts Mandarava and Yeshe Tsogyel.

The second cave, **Shinje Rolpei Drub-ne**, further west, is reached by a ladder and a narrow tunnel with a rope pulley, which emerges into a deep cavern by way of a sandalwood ladder. Here are the Guru Drupuk, with its divinely shaped rocks representing Maitreya and other deities, and the **Guru Sangwa Drupuk** – the foremost goal of the Drakyul pilgrimage, where Padmasambhava passed three years in retreat.

The third cave, called **Jago Rangjung Drupuk** (or Nego Sarpa), 40 m further west, is 8 m wide, 50 m deep, and in places over 10 m high. The amazing limestone formations inside are held to be part of a 'hidden land' (*beyul*) full of nectar, which was revealed for the first time in the 17th century by the Fourth Rigdzin Pema Trinle of Dorje Drak. The **Shiwa-tsel burial ground** is located higher up the hillside to the west.

Dzong Kumbum caves

The **Dzong Kumbum** cave complex (4,800 m) lies about 10 km above Ngadrak. As at Drak Yangdzong, the approach to the cave is decorated with rock carvings. The entrance is 30 m high, and it is 35 m deep, with five labyrinthine tunnels behind – all of them associated with Padmasambhava.

Dranang Valley གྲ་ནང

The Dranang valley is well endowed with an unusual variety of interesting sites, both prehistoric and Buddhist, for which reason it is renowned as the abode of the '13 saints of Dranang' (Dranang Kyebu Dampa Chuksum), who include illustrious figures such as Drapa Ngonshe, Tsangpa Gya-re, Orgyen Lingpa, Longchen Rabjampa, and Terdak Lingpa. If you wish to spend some time in this district, you can either stay at the small guesthouse in Dratang, the county capital, or commute from Tsetang, 47 km further east.

Dratang Monastery → *Colour map 3, grid C3.*

ⓘ *Admission: ¥20.*

A short 2 km-drive inland from Dratang town on the west fork of the track leads to Dratang Monastery, an important conservation site for Tibet's artistic heritage.

History The temple complex was founded in 1081 by Drapa Ngonshe, a native of Dranang valley and one of the 13 saints associated with it, and completed in 1093 by his nephews.

Hidden Lands

The cave complexes are revered as Padmasambhava's foremost pilgrimage place of buddha-body in Central Tibet. From the perspective of the pilgrim's pure sacred vision the landscape assumes the attributes of diverse deities. These caves have been renowned since the time of Padmasambhava, when 55 of his disciples are said to have attained the body of light after meditating here. Padmasambhava himself frequented these caves, along with his consort Yeshe Tsogyel, whose birthplace, **Sewalung** in Karchen, is lower down in Drakyul. Other major disciples of Padmasambhava associated with the valley and its natural hermitages were Nubchen Sangye Yeshe and Nanam Dorje Dudjom. Later in the 13th century, the Dzogchen master Melong Dorje occupied the **Ngarpuk** cave in upper Drakyul; but the caves have always been remote from ordinary human habitation. It is said that even now there are 'hidden lands' (*beyul*) at Drakyul, inaccessible to all but the fortunate.

The complex was later absorbed by the Sakyapas in the 14th-15th century, damaged by the Dzungar armies in the 18th, repaired in the 1920s and 1930s by Reting Rinpoche, regent of Tibet from 1922-1941, and once again severely damaged by the Chinese in the 1960s. Nonetheless, despite these vicissitudes, the ground floor of the main building has preserved a series of frescoes which are unique in Tibet, in that they are said to represent an important synthesis of the Pala Indian style and Central Asian style (Tucci: 1949).

The Complex Like Samye, the main temples of Dratang are surrounded by an outlying elliptical wall (the only surviving one of three original concentric walls around the complex). No images survive at Dratang. The 20-pillared **assembly hall** and protector shrine to its left are empty, except for late murals from the Sakyapa period. The images of Kadampa lineage holders which were once here are now kept at Mindroling (see page 176).

A triple gateway adorned with paintings of the Four Guardian Kings and various bodhisattvas leads to the **inner sanctum** to the west. The corridor murals depict the life of Shakyamuni and the careers of major bodhisattvas such as Amitayus and Avalokiteshvara. The eight-pillared inner sanctum itself once contained a large 3.4-m image of the Buddha as Thubpa Jangchub Chenpo, flanked by the Eight Bodhisattvas, but these have all been destroyed. The murals have survived – those on the south, north and west walls dating from the 11th century, and those of the east extremities of the north and south walls (near the gates) from the later Sakyapa period. There are around 10 groups of early paintings, depicting Buddha figures surrounded by large throngs of bodhisattvas; the stylistic features of physiognomy, clothing, jewellery and ornamentation all suggesting non-Tibetan influences, both Indian Pala, and Central Asian Khotanese. The best preserved are those of the west wall, where the stylistic line and vibrant colours can be seen to their best advantage.

Adjoining the main temple there were formerly three other chapels. Among them, the Neten Lhakhang and Dolma Lhakhang have not yet been rebuilt, but the **Tuje Lhakhang** to the right, which is dedicated to Mahakarunika, has been restored, as has the **Gonkhang**. The latter is approached via a flight of stairs on the left outer wall of the main temple. It contains images of Padmasambhava, the protector Zhanglon and a sacred yak, where physicians from the Mentsikhang in Lhasa make annual offerings. Behind it there is a **Kyedor Lhakhang**, with fine gold-on-black murals depicting Drapa Ngonshe and the Sakyapa protector deities, and images which

Drapa Ngonshe and Tibet's Medical Tradition

Drapa Ngonshe was particularly renowned throughout Tibet as the discoverer (in 1038) of the *Four Medical Tantras* (*Gyud-zhi*), said to have been drawn from Indian sources by Vairocana and concealed at Samye in the eighth century. These texts form the basis of the entire Tibetan medical tradition. However, Drapa Ngonshe is also credited with the construction of 128 Buddhist temples and shrines throughout Central and Southern Tibet, among which the Dratang Monastery was the most significant. An eclectic spiritual teacher, who had associations with the Nyingma, Zhiche and Kadampa schools, he established Dratang as a pre-eminent centre for the study of tantra among the New Translation Schools (Sarmapa).

include the meditational deity Hevajra. A temple dedicated to the **Buddhas of the Three Times** has been constructed on the third floor with the agency of the Paris-based Shalu Foundation in order to prevent further leaks and damp from threatening the 11th-century murals of the ground floor below. Its circumambulatory walkway has murals depicting the thousand buddhas of this aeon. Originally there was a temple here dedicated to the Thirteen Great Spiritual Teachers of Dranang. The **Kunrig Lhakhang** of the fourth floor has not yet been reconstructed, and there's a fine view of the Jampaling complex in the distance from the open roof top.

Jampaling

Located on the slopes about 3 km to the east of Dratang, and reached via the east fork on the inland track, is the Gelukpa monastery of Jampaling, founded in 1472 by Tonmi Lhundrub Tashi, a descendant of Tonmi Sambhota. There were formerly nine buildings in the complex, all of which were partially or completely destroyed in the 1960s. The 13-storey stupa of Jampaling, known as **Kumbum Tongdrol Chenmo**, was once the largest of its type in Tibet, exceeding the great stupa at Gyantse (see below, page 265), but constructed in a similar multi-chapel style. The murals were the work of Jamyang Khyentse Wangchuk, founder of the free-flowing Khyenri style of painting, existing examples of which can still be seen at Gongkar Chode (see above, page 167).

Reconstruction proceeds at a slow pace here, but the **Maitreya Temple (Jampa Lhakhang)** has been rebuilt on its original site northeast of the stupa. The rear wall of its assembly hall contains some old murals which survive from the earlier structure. Among the other buildings, the 18-m **Tangka Wall** is in a good state of preservation, as is the **Jungden Monastery** of the Sakya school, 200 m east of the temple. The monastic college, the Jampaling Labrang, and the unusual series of shops formerly on the site run by Bhutanese and Nepalese traders have been eradicated.

Serkong Tombs

Located in a side valley, about 11 km west of Dratang Monastery, are the 11 trapezoid stupa-shaped tumuli of Serkong. The largest tumulus which is in the northeast is 20 m high at the front and 7 m high at the rear, with sides 96 m long, rear 87 m, and front 92 m. To its left there is an excavated tomb. Four chambers were dug into the bedrock of the hill below the tumulus: an entrance passage, an entrance cavity, a tomb chamber, and an extension chamber where the deceased's personal effects would be interred. The tombs here are probably contemporary with those of Chongye (where the Yarlung Dynasty kings were buried), the Nang Dzong tombs further east (see page 233). The Serkong tombs appear to have been plundered after the collapse of the Yarlung Dynasty, and later in the 18th century by the Dzungar armies.

The vast ruins of **Pema Choling Nunnery** extend for some 5,000 sq m across the hillside above Serkong. Only the lowest storey of the assembly hall survives.

Riwo Namgyel Monastery

Driving the short 15-km distance from Dratang to Dingpoche in upper Dranang valley, you will have the chance to visit other places of interest en route. The Gelukpa monastery of **Riwo Namgyel** is located on the east slopes of the valley (3,900 m), about 6 km above the village of **Gyurme** where Tsangpa Gya-re was born. The monastery was founded around 1470 by Gonten Gyelpo, and developed into an extensive site (11,000 sq m) with over 60 monks. Later it was absorbed by the Namgyel Monastery of the Potala Palace in Lhasa. The severely damaged assembly hall has recently undergone restoration.

Gyeling Tsokpa Monastery

ⓘ *About 8 km south of Dratang and beyond Gyurme village, the road passes through Gyeling township, where Gyeling Tsokpa monastery is located.*

This eclectic establishment was founded in 1224 by students of the Kashmiri Panchen Shakyashri, and in the 15th century was adopted as a residence by Go Lotsawa Zhonupel, author of *The Blue Annals*.

The three-storey temple is surrounded by a wall and moat, with the lowest storey functioning as a basement. The **second storey** contains the assembly hall and three chapels forming an inner sanctum. Of these, the central **Jokhang** contains old murals showing Shakyamuni Buddha, Avalokiteshvara, Amitayus and the Four Guardian Kings. The side chapels are used as protector shrines, and the entrance to the assembly hall has murals depicting the progenitors of the Nyingma lineage in Tibet: Padmasambhava, Shantaraksita, King Trisong Detsen, and the Twenty-five Disciples (Jewang Nyernga). The main relics of the monastery, including old tangkas and a small 'self-arising' statue of Shakyashri, have been removed to the **Gatsel Puk** hermitage, 4 km higher up the ridge, where there is also a new temple containing images associated with the *Longchen Nyingtig* tradition.

Nyingdo Monastery

ⓘ *Following a westerly trail which begins about 5 km south of Gyeling township, you will reach Peldrong township, where there are 10 plundered neolithic tombs, and from where the Nyingmapa monastery of Nyingdo is accessible.*

This Mindroling branch monastery was originally constructed by Rinchen Lingpa in the 13th century and developed by his successor Nyingdo Tamched Khyenpa (1217-1277). The most important object in this monastery (which is now being rebuilt) is a talismanic pillar from Khyungpo in the upper Salween region of East Tibet, said to offer protection from pestilence, drought and hail.

Dingpoche Monastery

ⓘ *The road continues south from Nyingdo, via Rinchengang (or Raldrigang). Following with trekking route northeast to Mindroling in the Drachi valley (28 km), you will reach Kyilru township, where there is a yellow-walled temple, recently renovated. From Kyilru, there is a trail to the west, leading via Dekyiling village to Dingpoche.*

This monastery was founded in 1567 by Rinchen Pelzang, a student of Pema Karpo (1526-1592) on the summit of a secluded flat spur; and yet it has not escaped destruction over the course of its history – whether at the hands of the Dzungars in the 18th century, or by the Chinese more recently. The four-storey temple, said to represent the mandala of the deity Cakrasamvara, once contained large images of Shakyamuni and his two foremost disciples.

Amid the ruins, some rebuilding has taken place since 1984: there is a new assembly hall (*dukhang*), a new **Jokhang** (with images of Jowo Shakyamuni, White

Tara and Rinchen Pelzang), a new **Guru Lhakhang** (with images of Padmasambhava and his two main consorts), and a **Gonkhang** (with images of Four-armed Mahakala, Shridevi and Dingpoche Chokyong). The **courtyard** (*Chora*) to the south of the complex contains a series of meditation cells (*chokhung*), dug into the ground and covered with blue and white tent canopies, which are used even now for solitary retreat. A rebuilt Victory Stupa (Namgyel Chorten) lies outside the perimeter wall to the southwest, and a partially destroyed Enlightenment Stupa (Jangchub Chorten) is in the southeast corner.

At the hermitage of **Dra Yugang Drak** in the cliffs above Dingpoche, there is a Padmasambhava cave, where, in the 14th century, Orgyen Lingpa discovered a number of *terma*-texts that no longer exist. Later, Minling Trichen Terdak Lingpa stayed here in retreat and constructed an image of Padmasambhava; but the complex was badly damaged in the 1960s.

Yarje Lhakhang

Southwest of Kyilru township and Dekyiling village, the jeep road continues to Yarje Lhakhang, the birthplace of the renowned treasure-finder Orgyen Lingpa, which structurally survived the persecution of the 1960s, and contains new images of Padmasambhava and Avalokiteshvara in the form of Simhanada ('Lion's Roar'). There is also a wall painting that depicts Yarje Orgyen Lingpa himself.

Derong Nunnery

Continuing south from Kyilru and southeast of Dingpoche, you will reach the village of Tashiling and, on the slopes above, the nunnery of **Derong** (also written as Drophu Todrong). Below the nunnery is a ruined house, reputed to be the birthplace of Longchen Rabjampa (1308-1364), the most illustrious of all Nyingmapa masters in Tibet. The buildings are currently undergoing reconstruction.

Dargye Choling Monastery

The last site of interest in the upper Dranang valley is the ruined Nyingmapa monastery of Dargye Choling, about 4 km southwest of Dingpoche. Founded by Natsok Rangdrol and developed by Sangdak Trinle Lhundrub during the 17th century, it was the precursor of Mindroling Monastery in the neighbouring Drachi valley. Sangdak's son, Minling Trichen Terdak Lingpa, was born here in 1646.

Drachi Valley གྲ་ཕྱི

There are two entrances to the Drachi valley from the main Gongkar-Tsetang highway, the first 3 km due east of Dratang, on the west bank of the Drachi-chu, and the second a further 5 km to the east on the east bank. The valley is broad but infertile, for which reason there are fewer habitations here than in neighbouring Dranang. Two sites of great importance stand out: Tsongdu Tsokpa in lower Drachi and Mindroling in upper Drachi. There are also three clusters of ancient burial sites which were recently discovered in the valley.

Tsongdu Tsokpa Monastery

Located 250 m inland on the east approach road, the large Sakyapa monastery of Tsongdu Tsokpa mostly survived the ravages of the 1960s because, like other Sakya monasteries in this part of Southern Tibet, it was used as a granary during the Cultural Revolution. Originally a Kadampa establishment founded by Lu-me, the later Sakya foundation is attributed to the Kashmiri pandita Shakyashri, who, during the 13th century, set up four Buddhist groups in Tibet, known as the Tsokpa Zhi. Other teachers have also had associations with this site, notably Khyungpo

 Neljor Tsultrim Gonpo of the Shangpa Kagyu school (12th century) and Go Lotsawa Zhonupel (15th century).

The main temple, formerly four storeys high but now only three, is entered by a staircase, which leads to the middle floor. No trace remains of the clay image of Shakyashri and the heart of Khyungpo Neljor, which were once preserved here. Few old paintings remain which appear to date from the 19th century. Among them the most interesting are the representations of Two-armed Avalokiteshvara at the entrance, the skylight murals depicting the Eight Medicine Buddhas and the Eight Manifestations of Padmasambhava, and the Thousand Buddhas and Eight Bodhisattvas in the inner sanctum.

Orgyen Mindroling Monastery ཨོ་རྒྱན་སྨིན་གྲོལ་གླིང

→ *Colour map 3, grid C3.*

ⓘ *T0893-7581518. Admission: ¥20. Mindroling is about 8 km inland on the west approach road to upper Drachi, above the village of Mondrub.*

This, the largest Nyingmapa monastery in Central Tibet (100,000 sq m), was founded in 1670 by Terdak Lingpa Gyurme Dorje on the site where, in the 11th century, Lu-me Tsultrim Sherab had built the Kadampa chapel of Tarpaling. Terdak Lingpa thus became the first Minling Trichen (throneholder of Mindroling), a position held by his familial descendants until the mid-19th century, after which the succession passed to the familial descendants of his incarnation. The present throneholder, the Twelfth Minling Trichen Kunzang Wangyel, who is the acting head of the Nyingma school in exile, lives at the Mindroling branch monastery in Dehra Dun, India. Mindroling's extensive buildings were severely damaged by the Dzungar armies in the 18th century, and subsequently by the Chinese. Nonetheless, reconstruction has been continuing in recent decades through the efforts of the late Minling Chung Rinpoche Ngawang Chodrak (1908-1980) and Kusho Jampal, and there is much of interest to see.

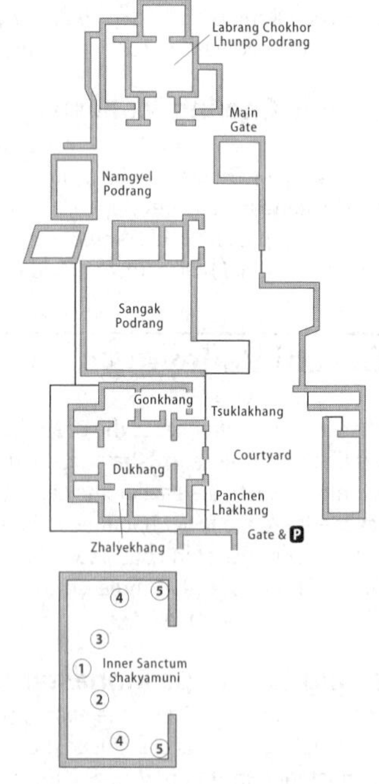

1 Shakyamuni Buddha
2 Shariputra
3 Maudgalyayana
4 Eight Standing Bodhisattvas
5 Two Gatekeepers

The Courtyard There are two gates leading into the courtyard of the former monastic citadel – the main gate on the northeast side and the second gate on the southeast, where vehicles are parked. To enter via the main gate, walk around the residential compound on the southeast wing. Inside the courtyard (from left to right) are: the east-facing **Tsuklakhang** with its impressive masonry façade, the north-facing **Drubcho Sangak Podrang**, the east-facing **Namgyel Podrang** (which was restored in 1944 but is once again in ruins, having been destroyed during the Cultural Revolution), and the south-facing **Labrang Chokhor Lhunpo Podrang**, which is still in ruins and about to lose its

Throneholders of Orgyen Mindroling

Minling Trichen I	Terdak Lingpa Gyurme Dorje (1646-1714)
Minling Trichen II	Pema Gyurme Gyatso (1686-1717)
Minling Trichen III	Gyelse Rinchen Namgyel (1694-1760)
Minling Trichen IV	Gyurme Pema Tendzin
Minling Trichen V	Trinle Namgyel
Minling Trichen VI	Pema Wangyel
Minling Trichen VII	Gyurme Sangye Kunga
Minling Trichen VIII	Trichen Yizhin Wangyel
Minling Trichen IX	Dechen Chodrub [aka Minling Chung Khenpo]
Minling Trichen X	Kunga Tendzin [son of Terdak Lingpa's incarnation, Rangrik Dorje]
Minling Trichen XI	Dondrub Wangyel [the latter's son]
Minling Trichen XII	Kunzang Wangyel, Dandrub's son (b 1931)

remaining murals unless current restoration plans are actually implemented. To the west of the complex, outside the courtyard, there is the recently restored **Kumbum Tongdrol Chenmo** stupa – the 13-storey original had been constructed by Terdak Lingpa himself, but it was completely destroyed during the 1960s. On the east wing of the courtyard are the monastic quarters and guesthouse.

Tsuklakhang Lowest Level The 3½-storey **Tsuklakhang** is entered by a staircase and a vestibule decorated with fine murals of the Four Guardian Kings, the Wheel of Rebirth and an inventory of the building. The assembly hall, which has adjoining chapels on three sides, contains old bronze images of Vajradhara, flanked by the holders of the Lam-rim lineage, reflecting the Kadampa origin of Mindroling, which were originally housed at Dratang (see above, page 171). Its murals depicting Amitayus are original but damaged. Among the side chapels, on the south wing the **Panchen Lhakhang** contains images of Padmasambhava in the form of Nangsi Zilnon, along with Longchen Rabjampa, Terdak Lingpa, and 1,000 miniature images of Padmasambhava. The adjacent **Dungkhang Alcove** houses a set of fine old Kadam-style stupas, the silver reliquary of the Ninth Minling Trichen Dechen Chodrub, a clay image of Terdak Lingpa, and images of the Eight Manifestations of Padmasambhava. On the north side of the hall is the **Gonkhang** (protector shrine) which formerly contained a central image of Mahottara Heruka (Chemchok Heruka), and now contains wrathful protectors. The large **inner sanctum** on the west has original murals and a 4-m Shakyamuni image, flanked by his two foremost disciples, and the Eight Bodhisattvas. These are among the most exquisite original images in Tibet, predating the Cultural Revolution. The gates are guarded by Vajrapani and Hayagriva.

Second Level On the second floor, the main chapel is the **Tersar Lhakhang** on the southeast side. It formerly contained three-dimensional mandalas of the cycles entitled *Wrathful Deities of the Magical Net (Mayajala)*, and the *Gathering of the Sugatas of the Eight Transmitted Precepts (Kabgye Deshek Dupa)*, as well as deities corresponding to the new *terma* revelations of Terdak Lingpa, the silver reliquary of the Tenth Minling Trichen Kunga Tendzin, and the Nartang *Kangyur*. There is a collection of sacred objects preserved here: a part of Guru Chowang's wrist bone with a natural buddha image growing out of it, a painting of Terdak Lingpa consecrated with his own hand and footprints in gold, an image consecrated by Terdak Lingpa in person, the reliquary stupa and walking stick of the late Minling Chung Rinpoche, the imprint in stone of the hoof of Terdak Lingpa's horse, and precious images discovered by the treasure-finders Guru Chowang, Jigme Lingpa, Dorje Lingpa and others. These objects are all securely locked behind a metal grill to deter would-be art thieves, who plundered nearby Yumbu Lagang in 2000. There is also a set of the *Nyingma Gyudbum*, published in India by the late Dilgo Khyentse Rinpoche.

To the right of this chapel is the **Jetsun Migyur Peldron Lhakhang.** It once contained the silver reliquary of Terdak Lingpa's daughter. Beyond it are the rooms of the monastic steward and caretaker. Facing the Tersar Lhakhang is the **Neten Lhakhang** (now empty).

On the left side, in the **Pema Wangyel Lhakhang**, there used to be reliquaries including that of the Sixth Minling Trichen Pema Wangyel. It presently houses images depicting Padmasambhava, Santaraksita, King Trisong Detsen and Terdak Lingpa himself, as well as various scriptures including the Indian edition of the *Nyingma Kama*. Adjacent to that is the **Lhakhang Onangkyil**, which once held reliquaries including the silver stupa of the Seventh Minling Trichen Gyurme Sangye Kunga. To its left are two smaller chapels, **Changlochen** and **Silweitsal,** while the **Zhelyekhang** on the west side of this floor offers a view of Shakyamuni in the inner sanctum below. It also contains the auspicious vases (*yang-bum*) of the monastery.

Third level The highest chapels are those on the third floor and above. Among them, the **Lhakhang Dewachen** is the hermitage of Lochen Dharmashri, containing a lifelike statue of the learned brother of Terdak Lingpa. the **Lama Lhakhang** contains a central image of the primordial Buddha Samantabhadra in union with his consort Samantabhadri and **outstanding murals**, which depict the entire Nyingmapa lineages, from ancient India until the 18th century. The murals are now protected by glass casing, which makes photography rather difficult.

Drubcho Sangak Podrang On the north side of the courtyard, the **Drubcho Sangak Podrang**, which was used in the 1960s as a granary, contains some original murals, although its most important image, Four-armed Avalokiteshvara, no longer exists. On its outer walls, however, a famous fresco has been preserved of Padmasambhava, which is said to have spoken to Terdak Lingpa, requesting him to remain in the world to help living beings and not pass away into the light body.

The lowest floor has been well renovated in recent years. Its central image depicts Terdak Lingpa, and the throne is that of the Minling Trichen. The floor surface of the hall is used for the construction of large sand-mandalas during the fourth month of the lunar calendar. Within the inner sanctum are large 4-m images of Padmasambhava, Shantaraksita and King Trisong Detsen, flanked by the Eight Manifestations of Padmasambhava.

Kumbum Tongdrol Chenmo The new gomang-style stupa (a multi-chapelled walk-in stupa), constructed in 2000 by Kusho Jampal, now dominates the skyline on the approach to Mindroling. It contains a three-storey high Maitreya image, and is itself surrounded by seven smaller stupas, indicative of the deeds of Shakyamuni. Images of Amitabha and Avalokiteshvara stand on the upper floors.

Trekking Retreat hermitages connected with Mindroling are located higher up the valley; and there are trekking routes – one day to Dargye Choling in upper Dranang and four days to Chongye in the east.

Namseling Manor

Following the Gongkar-Tsetang highway east from the entrance to Drachi valley, you reach the Samye ferry crossing after 5 km. Inland from here is the little visited but elegant 15th-century manor house of Namseling. This seven-storey building is a rare example of the Tibetan noble fiefs, hardly any of which survived the Cultural Revolution. Now the first storey has been restored, with the second to sixth to be completed in coming years. There are plans to establish a centre for weaving and pottery here.

Jing Okar Drak

On the Gongkar-Tsetang highway, 22 km east of Drachi valley entrance, there is a turn-off which leads to Okar Drak in Jing. The meditation caves here have associations with Padmasambhava and the Dzogchen master Dzeng Dharmabodhi (1052-1169). Later, *termas* were discovered here by Dorje Lingpa (1346-1405) and Terdak Lingpa of Mindroling.

Zurkhar Valley → *Colour map 3, grid C3*

Ins and outs

The ferry crossing to Samye is 13 km east of Dratang and 39 km west of Tsetang. The complex has a parking area and a small guesthouse, with outside toilets (¥15 per bed). There are no fixed departure times and the crossing takes 1-1½ hours, zigzagging to avoid sandbanks. FIT travellers are generally charged ¥10 for the ferry crossing (locals pay less), From the jetty on the north bank at Zurkhardo there are buses and trucks available to transport pilgrims and tourists to the monastery, about 9 km further east. Tourists pay ¥10 (locals pay ¥3). However, tour parties reserving a whole boat can be charged as much as ¥400 for a combined boat/bus return ticket. **NB** Nowadays, Samye can be approached more quickly from Tsetang via the Nyago Zamchen bridge and the new 50-km road that has recently been constructed on the north bank of the Brahmaputra. There are also trekking routes from Taktse, Ganden, and Gyama (see above) to the east of Lhasa.

Zurkhardo

From the village of Zurkhardo there is an inland route via Nekar and Kharu villages to **Dongakling**, a 15th-century monastery founded by Tsongkhapa's disciple Jangsem Kunga Zangpo, whose mummified remains are preserved in the monastery's inner sanctum.

Taking the road to Samye from the ferry, you will shortly pass on the left side a series of five resplendent white stupas, which stand out at intervals against the sandy rocks. These are the **Stupas of Zurkhardo**, reputedly constructed by Shantaraksita to commemorate the place where King Trisong Detsen first met Padmasambhava. These stupas, which symbolize the Buddhas of the Five Families, are in an archaic style, their plinth and *bumpa* surmounted by a tall spire and *bindu*. They are visible from a long way off on the south bank of the Brahmaputra. Zurkhardo has a clean and pleasant guesthouse.

Samye Monastery བསམ་ཡས་ཆོས་གྲྭ → *Colour map 3, grid C4*

History

Tibet's first monastery was constructed most probably between 775 and 779, although there are other sources suggesting alternative dates, eg 763 (Tang Annals) and 787-799 (Buton). King Trisong Detsen, revered by Tibetans as an emanation of Manjushri, acceded to the throne at the age of 13, and with the assistance of Ba Trizhi he invited Shantaraksita of Zahor, who presided over Vikramashila monastery, to formally establish Buddhist monasticism in Tibet. Buddhist geomantic temples had been constructed in Tibet by King Songtsen Gampo and his queens some 130 years earlier; but the hostility of Bonpo aristocratic families had curbed the formal institutions of the Buddhist religion. So it was that when Trisong Detsen directly confronted this arcane opposition to Buddhism, he invited Padmasambhava of Oddiyana (modern Swat) to subdue the hostile elemental forces of Tibet and make them amenable or subservient to Buddhism. Padmasambhava traversed the entire plateau, transforming negative forces into Buddhist protectors, and introducing the highest tantras and teachings to his fortunate disciples. On the summit of Mount Hepori (see below, page 185), east of Samye, he crushed the local demons and consecrated the site for the construction of Tibet's first monastery.

The preceptors of Samye Monastery were held in high esteem, both socially and politically, throughout Tibet from the eighth until the late 10th century. But following the disintegration of the Yarlung Dynasty and the introduction of the second phase of Buddhist propagation, the site gradually came under the influence of other non-Nyingma traditions: the Kadampas, during the period of Ra Lotsawa, the Sakyapas during and after the period of Lama Dampa Sonam Gyeltshen (14th-16th century), and the Gelukpas under the rule of the Dalai Lamas. Samye thus became a symbol of Tibet's national identity, in which Nyingma, Sakya and Gelukpa schools have all had strong interests.

Sadly, the original buildings are no longer intact, having been damaged by civil war (11th century), fires (mid 17th century and 1826), earthquakes (1816) and the Cultural Revolution (1960s). Yet, the Tibetans have always endeavoured to rebuild and enhance the complex after each round of destruction. Notable renovations were carried out by Ra Lotsawa (11th century), Sonam Gyeltsen (14th century), the Seventh Dalai Lama (1770), the Tibetan government (1849), and the late Tenth Panchen Lama (1986 onwards). During the Cultural Revolution, the village was encouraged to encroach upon the temple, and even in the late 1980s pigs and other farm animals could be seen wandering through the sacred shrines. The current policy is to redefine the area of the monastery by pushing back the village.

Khamsum Sangkhang Ling

Driving into Samye, you pass on the right the edifice of Khamsum Sang-khang Ling, which is the only extant temple among the three built outside the perimeter wall by

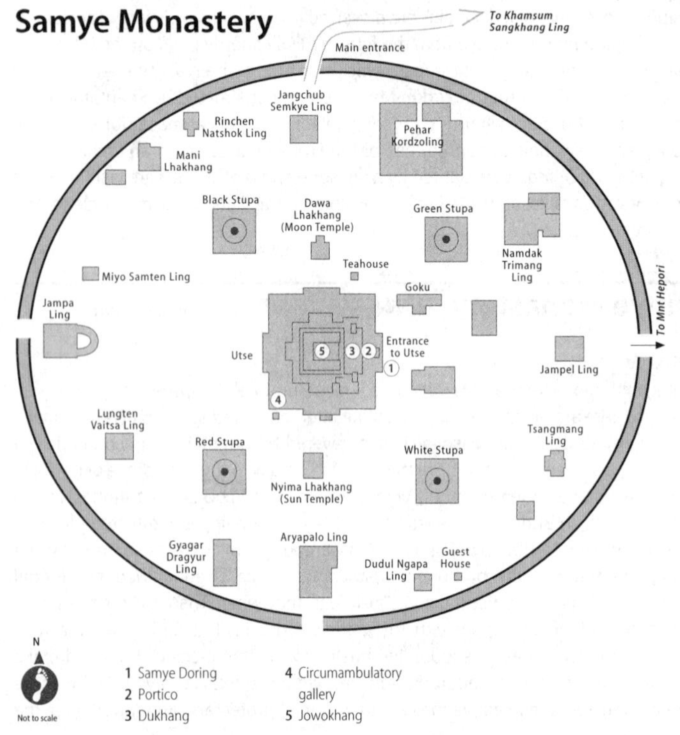

King Trisong Detsen's three queens. This is a four-storey building, which was reconstructed by Reting Rinpoche during the 1940s. It contains interesting murals. The high-ceilinged assembly hall occupies two floors. Its inner sanctum has paintings of the Sixteen Elders and, in its circumambulatory corridor, of Shakyamuni Buddha. On the third floor, there are murals depicting the 1849 reconstruction of Samye, as well as Padmasambhava, Shakyamuni Buddha, Amitabha and others. An unusually well-lit chapel on the fourth floor contains the protector shrine, with finely carved beams and columns, as well as original murals of Shakyamuni, Amitabha, Amitayus and the protectors. One of the best camp sites at Samye is located in a meadow to the southwest of this building.

Perimeter Wall and Stupas

The road into Samye passes round the Khamsum Sangkhang Ling, skirting the reconstructed perimeter wall, distinctively crowned with a succession of 1,008 small stupas. The wall, which is now oval-shaped (the original having had a zigzag design), is over 1 km in circumference, 3-4 m high, and over 1 m thick. There are four gates: one in each of the intermediate sectors (northeast, southeast, southwest and northwest) of the perimeter wall, each leading to the central Utse temple via an enormous 40-50-m high stupa. All four stupas have been recently reconstructed: the green one to the northeast, the red one to the southwest, the black one to the northwest, and the white one to the southeast. The main gate lies to the northeast, and it is through this that the bus or truck from the ferry will enter. Inside the perimeter wall, there are two pilgrims' circuits, an outer route encompassing all the secondary temples, and an inner route that circles the Utse temple at the centre.

Samye Utse

The east-facing Utse temple has four storeys, the second of which also has a terrace at a lower level than its entrance. Each of the three lower storeys are 5-6 m high. Traditionally, the three lowest storeys and their interiors are said to have been fashioned by craftsmen from neighbouring Buddhist lands: the lowest in Indian style, the second in Chinese style, and the third in Khotanese style. Another opinion, perhaps based on the appearance of the Utse following its later renovation, suggests that the first is in Tibetan style, the second in Chinese style, and the third in Indian style. Today, these stylistic features are not self-evident, although one can observe elements of Chinese Buddhist architecture in the beams and columns of the second floor, and Central Asian features in the dress and inwardly sloping postures of the new images on the third floor.

To the left of the entrance is a 5-m stone obelisk, the **Samye Doring**, dating from the original construction, which proclaims Buddhism as the state religion of Tibet. Pairs of ancient stone lions and elephants flank the entrance; and above, in the portico, there is a large eighth-century bronze bell which the king's Tibetan queen Poyong Gyelmotsun donated at the time of the original construction. This is one of three bells still existing from the period of the Yarlung Dynasty – the others being in the Jokhang of Lhasa, and at Tradruk (see below, page 201).

Entering through the portico ⓘ *admission fee: ¥25 per person*, with its inscriptions documenting the history of the monastery and murals depicting the Four Guardian Kings, there is a circumambulatory gallery complete with prayer wheels. Murals here depict the Thirty-five Confession Buddhas, the land of Shambhala, and the renovation work of 1849.

First Floor The inner building has three main doors, one leading to the central assembly hall (*dukhang*), a second to the Avalokiteshvara chapel in the south wing and a third to the protector shrine in the north wing. Entering the large **Assembly Hall** (actually by a small door to the left of its main gate), there are rows of monks' seats running from east to west. The images to the left depict in succession: Tangtong Gyelpo, Buton Rinchendrub, Kamalashila, Vimalamitra, Yudra Nyingpo and Longchen Rabjampa, flanked by two smaller images of Jigme Lingpa (south wall), and Vairocana, Shantaraksita, Padmasambhava, Trisong Detsen and Songtsen Gampo (west wall). Among these, the first five are new and of poor quality, replacing much finer images that were recently removed for no apparent reason. The Padmasambhava image replaces an outstanding original, which is said to have "resembled him in person" (Ngadrama). The Dalai Lama's throne occupies the centre of the hall. The images on the right depict Atisha, flanked by his Kadampa students Dromtonpa and Ngok Lekpei Sherab, the three celebrated emanations of Manjushri Longchen Rabjampa, Tsongkhapa and Sakya Pandita, and (towards the exit) the founders of the Kagyu lineage: Marpa, Milarepa and Gampopa.

The assembly hall leads into the inner sanctum or **Jowokhang** via three tall gates, symbolizing the three approaches to liberation: emptiness, signlessness, and aspirationlessness. Here, there is an inner circumambulatory corridor, with interesting murals depicting the past and final lives of Shakyamuni Buddha. The walls of the inner sanctum are more than 2 m thick, and the ceiling has wonderful painted mandalas. The principal image is a 4-m Shakyamuni in the form of Jowo Jangchub Chenpo, flanked by 10 standing bodhisattvas (ie the standard set of eight plus Trailokyavijaya on the left and Vimalakirti on the right), and the gatekeepers Hayagriva and Acala. Part of the central image is original, and the peripheral figures were sculpted by Chonyi Rinpoche and Semo Dechen of Lamaling. In 1999, new crown ornaments were presented to the central image by Semo Chime, the daughter of the late Dilgo Khyentse Rinpoche, who arrived from Bhutan with a team of skilled artists to restore the murals on the first and third floors. On the left, next to Shakyamuni, is Padmasambhava in the wrathful form of Nangsi Zilnon. Many books, including the *Kangyur* and

Samye Utse

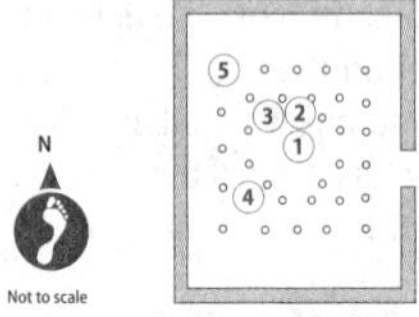

Fourth Floor
1 Central pillar
2 Kalacakra
3 Four pillars
4 Sixteen pillars
5 Twenty one pillars

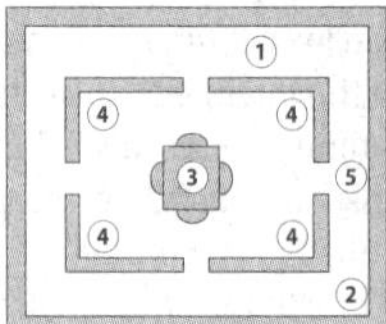

Third Floor
1 Circumambulatory corridor with frescoes
2 Stairs
3 Sarvavid Vairocana
4 Bodhisattvas
5 Entrance door

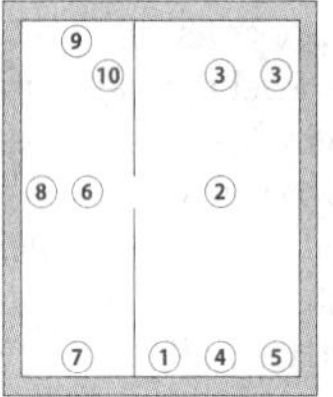

Second Floor
1 Stairs
2 Open gallery
3 Amitayus and Protector Chapels
4 Dalai Lama rooms
5 Relic chamber
6 Main hall
7 Shantaraksita
8 Nangsi Zilnon
9 King Trisong Detsen
10 Secret passage

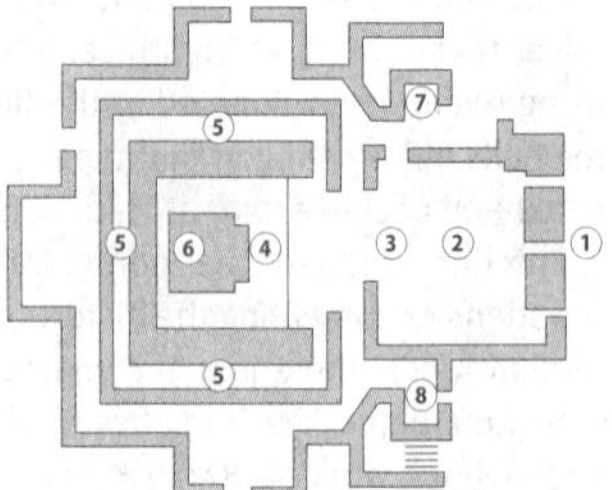

Ground Floor
1 Portico
2 Dukhang
3 Dalai Lama's throne
4 Jowokhang
5 Nangkhor
6 Jowo Jangchub Chenpo
7 Gonkhang
8 Chenrezi Chaktong Chentong Lhakhang

Tangyur, fill the rear wall, and in the outer right corner is a throne for the Dalai Lama, backed by a tangka of Kalacakra.

The **Protector Chapel** (*Gonkhang*) is entered through a door on the right side of the assembly hall. It contains (from left to right) images of: Ekajati, Mahakala in the form of Panjaranatha (Gonpo Gur) and Vajrakumara (west wall); Peldon Masung Gyelpo, Cimara and Shridevi (north wall); and the retinue of Panjaranatha (east wall). A large stuffed snake and assorted weaponry are also kept in this room.

On the south wing of the Assembly Hall, entered by a separate east-facing gate, is the chapel dedicated to Thousand-armed Avalokiteshvara, known as **Chenrezi Chaktong Chentong Lhakhang**. Built in the 14th century by the revered Sakyapa lama Sonam Gyeltsen in memory of his deceased mother, it contains an enormous Avalokiteshvara image. On the south wall is an incomplete series of relief images depicting the Eight Manifestations of Padmasambhava, as well as Milarepa, Atisha, and Green Tara. In the northeast corner, there is a glass case containing some mortal remains of Jangsem Kunga Zangpo (see above, page 179).

Second Floor The second floor is reached by a staircase to the left of the main entrance and a low terrace, where the monks' quarters are located. There is an open gallery with remarkable murals, 92 m in length, which depict the history of Tibet, from the Yarlung period and the life of Padmasambhava, through the Sakya and Phakmodru periods, to the accession of the Fifth Dalai Lama and his successors. Notice the striking depictions of the white-bearded Terdak Lingpa and the Mongol king Gushi Qan. There are also scenes depicting athletic contests and sports.

In the northeast corner there are two chapels, the one to the left is an active protector shrine, and the other dedicated to the Nine Aspects of Amitayus.

In the southeast corner, a passageway leads into the **private apartments of the Dalai Lama**. Here there are interesting murals showing Samye as it used to be. There is also a relic chamber, where the most precious objects of the monastery are now housed some of them kept securely under lock and key. These include: an image of Padmasambhava in the form of Guru Saroruhavajra which was discovered by Nyangrel, the skull of Shantaraksita, a turquoise buddha retrieved from the kingdom of Bhatahor, a turquoise amulet containing hairs of Padmasambhava, the imprint in stone of Padmasambhava's left foot at Gungtang La (the right one being in the Phakpa Lhakhang of the Potala Palace), the staff of Vairocana, a meteorite vajra, and a vajra from the ancient perimeter wall. The caretaker here distributes yellow silk neck-cords, printed with the seal of Padmasambhava.

The spacious **main hall**, whose roof exhibits some Chinese architectural features, contains large gilded copper images of Shantaraksita (south), Padmasambhava in the form of Nangsi Zilnon (west) and King Trisong Detsen (north). Flanking Padmasambhava are smaller images of Amitayus, Padmasambhava's tiger-riding form Dorje Drolo (donated by Semo Dechen of Lamaling), an old image of Jigme Lingpa and Shakyamuni. To the right of the entrance there is a secret passage, where Vairocana is said to have hidden in order to escape the wrath of Queen Tsepong.

Third Floor The reconstructed third floor is reached by a staircase on the left side of the second storey. There is a circumambulatory corridor with gates on each of its four sides. The outer walls of the corridor depict the Twenty-five Disciples of Padmasambhava (Jewang Nyernga), recently repainted in Bhutanese style, and above these there are lattices through which the outer satellite temples of Samye are visible. The inner walls of the corridor depict the buddhas: Aksobhya (east), Ratnasambhava (south), Amitabha (west), and Amoghasiddhi (north).

Entering via the east door, the central image is that of the four-faced Sarvavid Vairocana (Kunrik Nampa Nangze), flanked by Vairocana and Vimalamitra on the left and Padmasambhava and Shantaraksita on the right. Each of the four doors is guarded by two gatekeepers (Hayagriva and Acala), and in each of the corners formed by the doors there are sets of the standing bodhisattvas, distinctively robed and sloping inward, in the Central Asian manner.

Fourth Floor The highest floor of the Utse temple is reached by a step-ladder on the west side of the third floor and a passageway which leads around to the entrance on the east. There is a central image of Kalacakra, along with an image of Padmasambhava and a protector deity, subduing malevolent forces. The central pillar of juniper wood (formerly sandalwood) acts as the life-axis of the building. Surrounding it are three rows of columns: the innermost with four pillars symbolizes the Four Guardian Kings, the second with 16 pillars symbolizes the Sixteen Elders, and the third with 21 pillars symbolizes the Twenty-one Taras. The splendid gilded roofs, which were fully restored in 1989, can be seen from the south bank of the Brahmaputra many miles away.

Outer Temples

Restoration has begun on the outer temples in the complex. These include the four temples of the cardinal directions: Jampel Ling (east), Aryapalo or Tamdrin Ling (south), Jampa Ling (west), and Jangchub Semkye Ling (north). There are eight temples in the intermediate directions: Namdak Trimang Ling (northeast) and Tsangmang Ling (southeast); Gyagar Dragyur Ling (southwest) and Dudul Ngapa Ling (southeast); Lungten Vaitsa Ling (southwest) and Miyo Samten Ling (northwest); and Rinchen Natshok Ling (northwest) and Pehar Kordzoling (northeast). The Dawa Lhakhang lies to the north of the Utse while the Nyima Lhakhang (south of Utse) has yet to be restored. According to the traditional colour symbolism, the temples to the east were white, those to the south yellow, those to the west red, and those to the north black or dark green. In the current phase of reconstruction, these distinctions are not apparent.

The Eastern Temples The temple of **Jampel Ling**, dedicated to Manjughosa, is currently undergoing restoration. There are murals depicting Manjughosa and the thousand buddhas of this aeon and a large Mani Wheel. During the 1980s it served as a commune office.

The satellite temple to its northeast, **Namdak Trimang Ling**, was formerly the residence of Shantaraksita and the Vinaya college. Within its inner sanctum were images of the Buddhas of the Three Times. To the southeast of Jampel Ling, **Tsangmang Ling** formerly contained the printing press of Samye monastery.

Other buildings on the east side include the remains of the stone platform to the northeast of the Utse, once used for displaying appliqué tangkas at festival times, a throne used by the late Tenth Panchen Lama when he visited Samye in the 1980s, and the Monastery Hotel, shops and restaurant on the west side.

The Southern Temples The temple of **Aryapalo**, dedicated to Hayagriva, which originally predated the Utse, has already been restored. It is a two-storey building, entered from the south. The ground floor temple contains images of Hayagriva in the form of Pema Karpo (east), Lokeshvara, Chenrezi Semnyi Ngalso, and Four-armed Avalokiteshvara (north), and in a west side chapel there are images of the Three Ancestral Religious Kings (Chogyel Namsum), Avalokiteshvara and Manjushri. The centrepiece of the upper storey is an image of Padmasambhava.

Among its peripheral temples, **Gyagar Dragyur Ling** in the southwest is located in a beautiful courtyard, with west and east cloistered galleries depicting the Indian panditas and Tibetan translators of the eighth century. It was here, at the same time that the Buddhist translation programme was established by King Trisong Detsen. Inside the chapel are images of Avalokiteshvara in the form of Simhanada, and the

Indian yogin Padampa Sangye. In front is an appliqué frieze depicting the Eight Manifestations of Padmasambhava. **Upstairs** there are images of Padmasambhava flanked by the kings Songtsen Gampo and Trisong Detsen. To the left are images of the Indian panditas, including the Six Ornaments, the Two Supreme Ones and Jinamitra; while to the right are the Tibetan translators, including Nubchen Sangye Yeshe, Vairocana, Zhang Yeshede, Kawa Paltsek, Chokrolui Gyeltsen, Khonlui Wangpo Sungwa and Jnanendraraksita.

The temple of **Dudul Ngapa Ling** to the southeast of Aryapalo temple was formerly a tantric chapel, and has been converted into a new monastic college for Buddhist studies. There are small privately-owned guesthouses and tea shops in the village on the south side of the complex.

The Western Temples The temple of **Jampa Ling**, dedicated to Maitreya, was where the Chinese monks resided during the eighth century; and it was the venue of the Great Debate between Kamalashila and Hoshang Mo-ho-yen (see below). The inner sanctum is semi-circular, corresponding to the shape of the western continent in Indian cosmology; its murals depict Maitreya and Shakyamuni, and there are new images – a large Padmasambhava with Maitreya to its rear.

Its peripheral temple to the southwest, **Lungten Vaitsa Ling**, dedicated to the translator Vairocana, has some extant murals depicting Shakyamuni Buddha and the translator. **Miyo Samten Ling**, which lies to the northwest, was a meditation hall used by Chinese monks in the eighth century.

The Northern Temples The temple of **Jangchub Semkye Ling**, dedicated to Prajnaparamita, was used for storing timber in the recent past, but has now undergone renovation. It contains a large image of Shakyamuni, flanked by Padmasambhava, Shantaraksita and King Trisong Detsen on the left and three founders of Sakya on the right. The Forty-two Peaceful Deities encircle this cluster, and to the rear there is a stone, said to have been brought there from the Sitavana burial ground in India. To its northwest is the peripheral temple, **Rinchen Natshok Ling**, a small chapel with images of the Buddhas of the Three Times, flanked by 12 aspects of Tara, several images of Dorje Drolo, and murals depicting Shakyamuni. Then, to the northeast is the renowned temple of **Pehar Kordzoling**, where Samye's ancient Sanskrit texts were stored in the care of the protector deity Pehar. A turquoise image of this deity, also known as Shingjachen, was brought to Samye from Bhatahor in Turkestan following a successful military campaign in the early ninth century. Downstairs in the reconstructed temple there is the fearsome Shakhang, containing a talismanic leather mask, called Sebak Muchung, which was believed to come alive. Upstairs there is the Gonkhang, containing images of Cimara, Pehar and other protectors, and the *Kangyur* Lhakhang, which sadly lacks its Sanskrit library, but has images of Vajrakila, Padmasambhava and Shridevi. Nowadays, there is a **small tea house** in the village on the north side of the complex.

Sun and Moon Temples The clinic south of the Utse was formerly the **Nyima Lhakhang** or Sun Temple. This shrine was dedicated to the Yaksa Cimara and is therefore sometimes called **Tseumar Chok**. The **Dawa Lhakhang**, north of the Utse, is a particularly archaic structure, with murals depicting the Thousand Buddhas.

Hepori

Mount Hepori is approached to the east of Samye Utse, beyond the government buildings of Samye town. This hill, which offers an incredible bird's eye view of the Samye complex, is revered as one of the four sacred hills of Central Tibet (along with Chakpori at Lhasa, Chuwori at Chushul, and Zodang Gongpori at Tsetang). It was from here that Padmasambhava bound the local divinities of the region under an oath of allegiance to Buddhism. On the summit of Hepori is a rebuilt **Lhasangkang**, or Temple for the Smoke Offering to the Local Deities, and to its northeast is a Padmasambhava meditation cave. On its slopes there were once reliquary stupas, containing the remains of Shantaraksita (east), and those of three of the greatest eighth century translators Kawa Peltsek (north), Zhang Yeshede (south ridge), and Chokrolui Gyeltsen (south end). Some of these have recently been restored. The trek to the summit of Hepori takes less than an hour.

The Monastery Hotel, to the east of the Utse temple, is the best accommodation at Samye. It has double and single rooms (¥100), and triples (¥150). The best rooms are on the third floor, and there are communal showers. Downstairs there is a good Tibetan-style restaurant (menu in English), serving noodle dishes and dumplings (¥6), and sweet or butter tea. Other smaller hotels and restaurants can be found outside the perimeter wall on the east side of the complex.

Chimphu Caves མཆིམས་ཕུ

→ *Colour map 3, grid B4*

The upper valley, Chimphu, forms a natural amphitheatre, its west and east ridges divided by the waters of a sacred stream. To the southeast, there is the **Chimphu Utse nunnery**, which has a large newly constructed temple containing images of Hayagriva (left); Jowo Shakyamuni, Padmasambhava, and Four-armed Avalokiteshvara (centre); and Vajrasattva Yabyum, Ekajati, Gonpo Maning, Rahula, Dorje Lekpa and Nyenchen Thanglha (right).

Currently there are over 100 hermits at Chimphu, the majority from East Tibet. Most of the caves, which are accessible from this temple to the northwest, are clustered around the 15-m high Zangdok Pelri rock.

Ins and outs

The Chimphu hermitage is located about 16 km northeast of Samye in the upper part of the nearby Chimyul valley. Pilgrims begin the five-hour walk to the caves before sunrise, but it is also possible to hire a truck or a tractor at Samye village, which will take you to a clearing around 30 minutes' walking distance below the Chimphu Utse Temple.

Taking the right path from the north end of Samye, you will cross the local irrigation canal and the Samye River before turning left into the Chim valley. Passing the deserted villages of Chimda, you then climb steeply through a wooded grove full of aromatic herbs until you reach a stupa.

Caves on the ascent

At the base of the Zangdok Pelri rock is the **Sangwa Metok Cave**, where in the 18th century Jigme Lingpa received the visions of Longchen Rabjampa which inspired him to reveal the Longchen Nyingtig, and compose the *Yonten Dzo*. Outside is an image of Manjushri carved in the rock, it is said by Padmasambhava's own hand. Nearby is the **Lower Cave of Nyangben Tingdzin Zangpo (Nyangpuk Ogma)**, where both Nyangben and King Trisong Detsen stayed in retreat, the **Meditation Cave of Yeshe Tsogyel (Tsogyel Drubpuk)**, and a rock bearing an impression of Padmasambhava's hat and Yeshe Tsogyel's foot.

The trail divides into upper and lower branches at the 12-m long **Guruta Rock**, where there is an enormous Padmasambhava footprint. On its lower side is the **Upper Cave of Nyangben Tingdzin Zangpo (Nyangpuk Gongma)**, where the *Vima Nyingtig* was concealed by Nyangben in the ninth century and later mastered by Longchen Rabjampa in the 14th. Further west there is a small burial ground, and above the rocks there are further hermitages – those of Ma Rinchen Chok, Shubu Pelzang, and the **Tamdrin Puk**, where Gyelwa Choyang propitiated Hayagriva.

The Establishment of Buddhism in Tibet

Padmasambhava's labour in subjugating the local demons on Mount Hepori paved the way for the establishment of Buddhist monasticism in Tibet. King Trisong Detsen, at Shantaraksita's suggestion, ensured that the complex was modelled on the plan of **Odantapuri Monastery** (modern Bihar Shariff), where the buildings themselves represented the Buddhist cosmological order (with Mount Sumeru in the centre, surrounded by four continents and eight subcontinents, sun and moon, all within a perimeter wall known as the Cakravala). This construction would therefore come to symbolize the establishment of a new Buddhist world order in Tibet. Men were engaged in this unprecedented building project by day, and spirits by night. Hence the monastery's full name: **Glorious Inconceivable Temple of Unchanging Spontaneous Presence** (*Pel Samye Migyur Lhundrub Tsuklakhang*).

King Trisong Detsen then established an integrated programme for the translation of the Buddhist classics into Tibetan, bringing together teams of Indian scholars (*pandita*) and Tibetan translators (*lotsawa*). He and a celebrated group of 24 subjects received instruction on the highest tantras from Padmasambhava in particular, but also from Vimalamitra, Buddhaguhya and others, and through their meditations they attained the supreme realizations and accomplishments of Buddhist practice. In addition, Shantaraksita was requested to preside over the ordination of Tibet's first seven trial monks Ba Trizhi (Srighosa), Ba Selnang (Jnanendra), Pagor Vairocana (Vairocanaraksita), Ngenlam Gyelwa Choyang, Khonlui Wangpo Sungwa (Nagendraraksita), Ma Rinchen Chok and Lasum Gyelwei Jangchub.

In 792 a debate was held between Kamalashila, an Indian proponent of the graduated path to buddhahood, which emphasizes the performance of virtuous deeds, and Hoshang Mo-ho-yen, a Chinese proponent of the instantaneous path to buddhahood, with its emphasis on meditation and inaction. Kamalashila emerged as the victor, but it is clear from Nubchen's treatise *Samten Migdron* that both views were integrated within the overall path to buddhahood. It was in these ways that the king established the future of Buddhism in Tibet.

Drakmar Keutsang cave → *Altitude: 4,300 m*

About 100 m above the Zangdok Pelri rock is the most important of all the caves at Chimphu, the Drakmar Keutsang. This is revered as the primary pilgrimage place of buddha-speech in Central Tibet, and it was here Padmasambhava first gave teachings on the eight meditational deities known as Drubpa Kabgye to his eight main disciples, including the king Trisong Detsen. A two-storey temple has been constructed around the cave, which is at the rear on the ground level. On the altar in the temple there are new images of Padmasambhava, surrounded by his two foremost consorts and eight manifestations. Formerly the most precious objects here were the Jema Atron image of Padmasambhava which had been fashioned by Vairocana and Tami Gontson, and the image of Prajnaparamita which belonged to King Trisong Detsen. The present cave contains an image of Padmasambhava, a blue Vajravarahi and a Jowo image, the sight of which is said to equal the vision of Padmasambhava in person.

The Drakmar Keutsang is renowned for another reason, in that it was here that Padmasambhava temporarily resuscitated the dead Princess Pemasel and taught her

Cimara, The Red Protector: Judgement Night

Tseumar Chok was the abode of Cimara, the red protector of Samye who took over Pehar's role after the latter had been transferred to Nechung near Drepung (see above, page 115). In an awe-inspiring room adjacent to the protector shrine, which was opened once a year, Cimara would by night dispense the judgement of the dead upon evil-doers, chopping them to shreds on a wooden block. The monks of Samye were often, it is said, aware of the thudding sound of the chopping and the stench of blood which filled the air during the night. This wooden block required replacement once a year.

the Kandro Nyingtig for the first time. The place where this resurrection occurred is a flagstone bearing the imprint of her body in front of the cave entrance, known as the **Pemasel Durtro**. Pilgrims are rubbed vigorously on the back and shoulders with a stone reputedly brought from the Shitavana burial ground in India.

Above the ground level, there is a terrace offering spectacular views of the Brahmaputra valley below, and in the west side of the upper chamber there is a 4-m tunnel leading to the **Meditation Cave of Vairocana (Bairo Drubpuk)**. This cave contains images of the translator Vairocana and Longchen Rabjampa.

Ridge-top caves

There are some cave hermitages at the top of the Chimphu ridge, including the **Longchen Gurkarpuk**, associated with Padmasambhava and Trisong Detsen's chief minister, the **Tsogyel Zimpuk**, associated with Yeshe Tsogyel, the cave used by his Nepalese consort Atsara Sale, the **Longchen Puk** and associated with Longchen Rabjampa, and on the far side of the ridge, the **Chimphu Drigugu**, where Padmasambhava stayed in retreat and Vimalamitra concealed the Vima Nyingtig texts. High up on the northeast ridge of Chimphu is **Rimochen**, a site associated with Longchen Rabjampa.

Caves on the descent

On the descent from the Drakmar Keutsang, the trail passes a hermitage containing the reliquary of Gonjo Rinpoche from Kham, and the **Reliquary of Longchen Rabjampa** (*Longchen Dungten*), who passed away at Chimphu in 1363. The site is marked by a commemorative obelisk and inscription. There is a water-of-life spring (*tshe-chu*) by the trail, and on the descent from there, a hermitage with a stupa consecrated by the Third Karmapa Rangjung Dorje in the 14th century and another once frequented by Nubchen Sangye Yeshe. From here the trail leads down to the Chimphu Utse nunnery and the road back to Samye or to Lo at the mouth of the Chim River.

Drakmar Drinzang བྲག་དམར་མགྲིན་བཟང

Following the Drakmar valley 6 km north from Samye through Yugar and Samphu village, on the west bank of the Drakmar-chu, you will arrive at Drinzang, the birthplace of King Trisong Detsen. This was once the country residence of his parents, King Tride Tsukten and Queen Nanamza. A reconstructed temple housing images of the religious kings can be seen here. The house where the king was born once had red and white sandalwood trees growing in its courtyard, but only ruins now remain.

Yemalung Hermitage གཡའ་མ་ལུང

About 16 km further inland from Drakmar Drinzang, on an east fork in the road above Nyingong village (3,870 m), you will reach the remote hermitage of Yemalung. The trail begins in the plain below the hermitage, alongside the crumbling remains of a stone throne, once used by visiting Dalai Lamas. Crossing a wooden bridge, the trail ascends through thick rosebushes and honeysuckle on a series of switchbacks, which periodically offer fine views of Mount Hepori in the distance to the south. The first cave on the route is one where Padmasambhava stayed only one day (at present inhabited by a monk from Shang Zabulung). Climbing steeply to a small clearing where a prayer-flag strewn stupa is circumambulated by pilgrims, a narrow trail leads west towards an old burial ground, and a sacred spring that emerged when Padmasambhava conferred a long-life empowerment on King Trisong Detsen, There is also a narrow rock tunnel called **Bardo Trang** which pilgrims crawl through to test their degree of preparation for the intermediate state after death! The cliff-top **cave hermitage** of Padmasambhava (4,200 m) contains a new image of the master himself, and rocks marked with his foot and handprints. The meditation cave where his disciple Vairocana stayed four years in retreat is located in the slopes above. A temple known as **Drupuk Lhakhang** has been constructed around the main cave. It contains the throne of Terdak Lingpa of Mindroling who discovered the *terma* text entitled Innermost Spirituality of the Awareness Holder (Rikdzin Tuktik) at Yemalung in 1663. The adjacent **Guru Lhakhang** has images of Padmasambhava in the form of Nangsi Zilnon, Four-armed Avalokiteshvara and Shakyamuni, while on its roof there is the fractured base of an older bronze image, destroyed during the Cultural Revolution. Further east is the **Dukhang,** which functions as a small assembly hall for the nine hermits who currently live here. It contains images of Padmasambhava, Shakyamuni and Terdak Lingpa in a glass case, with three Victory Stupas to the right, and tangkas depicting the Eight Manifestations of Padmasambhava and the Twenty-four Disciples (Jewang Nyernga). Still further to the east is the **Gonkhang,** containing the foremost Dzogchen protectors: Rahula, Ekajati and Dorje Lekpa, alongside Padmasambhava. Above this complex there is the reconstructed hermitage of the Fifth Dalai Lama.

Trekking From Nyingong, below Yemalung, there are 3-4-day trekking routes across Gokar La pass to Taktse; and across Zhukar La to Ganden (see above).

Nedong County སྣེའུ་གདོང 乃东县

Tsetang is one of Tibet's largest cities, and the capital of the Lhokha prefecture of the Tibetan Autonomous Region, exercising direct control over the affairs of 13 counties: Gongkar, Tranang, Nedong, Chongye, Tso-me, Lhodrak, Nakartse, Zangri, Chusum, Lhuntse, Tsona, Gyatsa, and Nang. Tsetang is also the capital of ***Nedong*** *county, which is named after the seat of the Phakmodru Dynasty that functioned as the capital of the whole of Tibet from 1349 until its eclipse by the Rinpung fiefdom in 1435.*

The area around Tsetang is regarded as the cradle of Tibetan civilization, in that the Zodang Gongpori caves above the town are said to be the place where the Tibetan race originated. Further south in the Yarlung valley kingship was established and agriculture introduced. The first palace is at Yumbu Lagang and the first Buddhist temple at Tradruk. *» For Sleeping, Eating and other listings, see pages 196-199.*

Tsetang རྩེད་ཐང

Ins and outs → *Population: 40,000. Altitude: 3,510 m. Phone code: 86-893. Colour map 3, grid C4.*

Getting there The distance from Tsetang to Lhasa is 186 km, to Gongkar Airport 87 km and to Dranang 47 km. The county of Nedong extends on the north bank of the

Brahmaputra from Do Valley in the west as far as On Valley in the east; and runs the entire length of the Yarlung Valley (72 km) from Jasa and Sheldrak in the northwest as far as Mount Yarlha Shampo. See Transport, page 198, for further details.

Getting around There are two main roads which intersect at the Horse Roundabout in downtown Tsetang. The road west from the crossroads (Kalzang Lam) leads to Gongkar and Lhasa, while the east road (Gyatsa Lam) Gyatsa and Menling, the north road leads to the Brahmaputra River bank and the old On Valley ferry crossing, while the south road (Nedong Lam) goes to Chongye and Tsona. The Yarlung River (Yarlha Shampo-chu) flows due northwards on the west side of the intersection, and is spanned by four bridges – on the Kalzang Lam, on Yingxong Lam, one (the old Namo Zampa) on Chongye Lam, and one further south.

Approaching the city from the Gongkar/Lhasa direction, the triangular peak of **Mount Zodang Gongpori** is visible long before the buildings are seen nestling below it. At the entrance to the city, on the right side of **Kalzang Lam**, there is a petrol station. A turn-off on the right, **Tsentang Lam,** bypasses the city centre, leading to the southwest and on to Sheldrak and Chongye. Continue east on Kalzang Lam where both sides of the road are occupied by vehicle repair depots and down-market karaoke bars. After passing the Tsetang People's Arts Hall on the left, you will reach the intersection with **Hubei Lam** on the right. Down this road there are many new shops, a law court, Primary School Number Three, the Snow Pigeon Hotel, and a sports stadium. Returning to the intersection and continuing east on Kalzang Lam, you soon cross the Yarlung Bridge, and two hospitals will appear on the left, followed by the Mirik Hotel. A number of small hotels are passed on the right – the Norsi, the Dawo and the Gangjong, followed by the long distance bus station and China Mobile. At this point Kalzang Lam intersects with the Horse Roundabout. Turning left at the roundabout, beyond the Mirik Hotel, you will reach the vegetable, butter and meat markets, where there are small tea shops, and the meteorological bureau.

Turning right at the roundabout into **Nedong Lam**, you will pass, on the left side, the Agricultural Bank of China, the Xinhua Bookstore, a turn-off (Ba-re Lam) that leads into the old Tibetan quarter, a large department store, a carpet and souvenir store, the Post Office Hotel, the Post Office, and the Lhokha Prefecture CCP offices. On the opposite side of the road, you will pass grocery and electrical shops, some of which are run by Hui Moslems from Ziling area, the Pende Arkhang Chenmo Restaurant, Middle School Number One, and the Agricultural and Nomadic Bureau Hotel, which is located at the intersection with a new road (leading to the Water Department and a red light district). Continuing south on Nedong Lam, on the left you will pass the Yarlha Shampo Hotel, the Foreign Affairs Police, a law court, the Gesar Restaurant, the Lhokha Army Unit, a dance hall and the Nedong County Government Offices. Opposite on the right are the Lhokha Government Guesthouse, the Agricultural Bank, the Tsetang Hotel, the Agricultural Bank (another branch) and the high-rise Gold Crane Hotel.

At this point **Yinxong Lam** intersects on the right (leading to the Lhokha

Nedong County

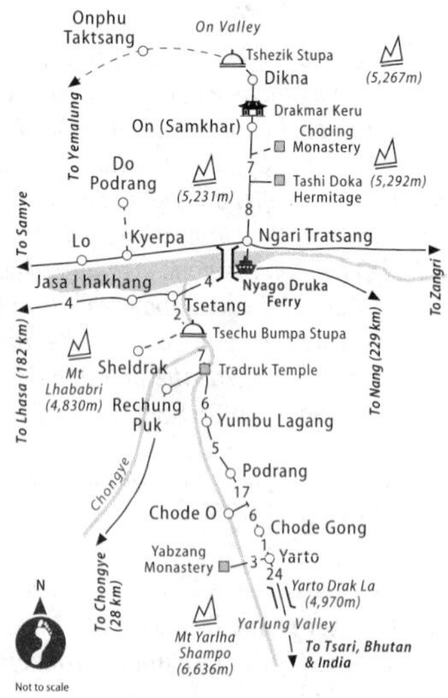

Tsetang: Playground of the Monkey and Ogress

Tsetang means 'playground' – a reference to its importance as the place where a monkey emanation of Avalokiteshvara frolicked in the company of an ogress, thereby fathering the six progenitors of the original Tibet clans (see page 738). The monkey thus symbolizes the compassion of the bodhisattvas and the ogress the destructive or violent aspect of the Tibetan character. Legend associates **Mount Zodang Gongpori** behind Tsetang with the location of the monkey's cave.

Propaganda Office, the Lhokha Tax Bureau, the Construction Bank, the Snow Pigeon Hotel, and various security offices). Continuing south on Nedong Lam, you will pass on the left the Nedong Tax Bureau, the Nedong Post Office, the Agricultural Bank and a military barracks. On the right there is the Lhokha Cultural Bureau, a carpet factory, the small Nedong Guesthouse, and Middle School Number Two.

If, at the Horse Roundabout, you drive due east, onto **Gyatsa Lam** you will reach on the right side a turn-off leading to the monasteries and houses of the old town: **Tsetang Monastery**, **Ngachopa Tratsang**, **Trebuling Monastery** and **Sangak Samtenling Nunnery**. On the left, you will pass the Grain Department Guesthouse, Primary School Number One, the trade department and commercial buildings, before eventually reaching the Nyago Zamchen Bridge that spans the Brahmaputra.

If you follow Ba-re Lam into the open-air market from Nedong Lam, you will find rows of stalls selling cheap Chinese household articles, clothing and shoes. A few stalls have traditional Tibetan items: tangkas, books and religious artefacts. Behind these stalls there is a square, where the Bank of China, a cinema and dance hall are located. Turning left in front of the bank and first right, you will enter the old Tibetan quarter, where the monasteries mentioned above are located. See Transport, page 198, for further details.

History

Mount Lhababri on the west side of the valley is regarded as the place where the first Tibetan king of the Yarlung Dynasty, Nyatri Tsenpo arrived from the heavens (or from India) to rule among men. He occupied the fortress of **Yumbu Lagang** to the south of Tsetang, and his descendants introduced agriculture into the valley at a place called **Zortang** (which some identify as a plot of land at Lharu below Yumbu Lagang, and others with one to the north of town near the metereological bureau.

After Songtsen Gampo unified Tibet in the seventh century and moved his capital to Lhasa, the Tsetang area gradually declined in its importance. But in 1349, **Nedong**, which is now a suburb of Tsetang, became the capital of the Phakmodrupa Dynasty which ruled Tibet until the end of the 15th century. It was during this period that the important monasteries of Tsetang were originally constructed by Tai Situ Jangchub Gyeltsen and his successors. Furthermore, Tsongkhapa was ordained at **Bentsang Monastery** (Tse Tsokpa), which had been founded by Shakyashri in the early part of the 13th century.

Later, during the 18th century, the Seventh Dalai Lama encouraged the development of the Gelukpa school in the Tsetang area, in consequence of which Tsetang Monastery was transformed into **Ganden Chokhorling**, and the **Sangak Samtenling** nunnery was established.

Sights

Tsetang Monastery Located near the entrance to the old Tibetan quarter, Tsetang Monastery was originally a Kagyu site, founded in 1351 by Tai Situ Jangchub Gyeltsen of the Phakmodrupa Dynasty. As such, it held allegiance to Densatil as its mother monastery (see below, page 227). Later, in the mid-18th century, during the lifetime of the Seventh Dalai Lama Kelzang Gyatso, the Kagyu buildings were dismantled and a Gelukpa monastery named **Ganden Chokhorling** erected to replace it. It was refurbished took place from 1900-1912, but in the 1960s only the outer shell was spared and used for salt storage. The assembly hall (*dukhang*), which is maintained by only a handful of monks, has an inner sanctum containing large images of Tsongkhapa with his foremost students, which can be observed from a skylight in the upper storey. There are some original murals within the hall. Nearby, the residential *labrang* has an attached debating courtyard.

Ngachopa Monastery Located slightly to the east of Tsetang Monastery, this one-time Kagyu monastery was also constructed by Tai Situ Jangchub Gyeltsen in the 14th century. Later, in the 17th century, it was absorbed by the Gelukpas, and its assembly hall is known to have contained fine images of Shakyamuni, Amitabha and Maitreya. The complex was severely damaged during the Dzungar occupation of the 18th century and later in the 1960s, but recently a new temple has been built to the rear of the assembly hall. It contains impressive images of the Buddhas of the Three Times, while a nearby protector chapel has Vajrabhairava as its centrepiece. Currently there are around 30 monks at Ngachopa.

Trebuling Monastery Trebuling Monastery is located northeast of Ngachopa within the Shannan Diesel Factory compound. Its assembly hall (*tsokchen*) and residential building still stand. However, the sacred images of Tara and Shakyamuni in the form of Thupa Ngadrama which it once housed have not survived.

Sangak Samtenling Nunnery This active nunnery, located on the slopes of Mount Zodang Gongpori above Tsetang monastery, was originally a 14th-century Sakyapa establishment of the Tsarpa sub-school. It was founded on a former meditation site of Lama Dampa Sonam Gyeltsen and his student Yarlung Senge Gyeltsen. From the mid-18th century, however, it came under the influence of the Gelukpas, and a new foundation was established by Kyerong Ngawang Drakpa. Some of its sacred relics were salvaged during the 1960s. The main image within the assembly hall is a reputedly seventh-century Mahakarunika, flanked by Tara, Tsongkhapa and

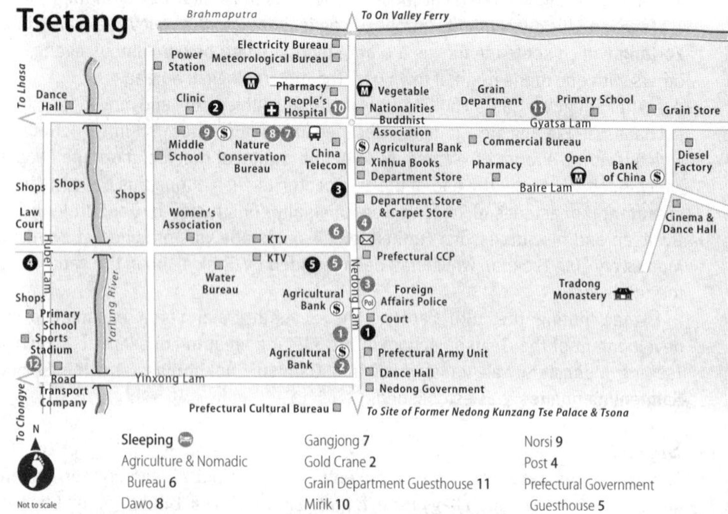

Tangtong Gyelpo, with the Sixteen Elders and Thirty-five Confession Buddhas behind in their individual stucco grottoes. Rear chapels contain further images of Kyenrong Ngawang Drakpa flanked by Avalokiteshvara, in the form of Simhanada, and Manjughosa; and of Tsongkhapa with his foremost students, along with Atisha and Tangtong Gyelpo. Nowadays there are about 70 nuns at Sangak Samtenling.

Museums The **Tsetang Museum**, founded in 1994, has an impressive collection of artefacts but poor security which resulted in an unfortunate theft in February 1996.

Excursions

Zodang Gongpori Mount Zodang Gongpori is one of the four sacred hills of Central Tibet, renowned for its remote cave (4,060 m), where the monkey emanation of Avalokiteshvara is said to have impregnated a demonic ogress, thereby giving rise to the six ancient Tibetan clans. The cave (4,060 m) is located some two hours trekking distance above Sangak Samtenling below a cairn, perched precipitously 500 m above the Yarlung Valley. Within the cave is a naturally produced rock image of the monkey, and there are paintings of simian figures on the southeast wall. Legend holds that a 'hidden land' (*beyul*) is contained inside Mount Zodang Gongpori, its entrance (*bego*) being on the east side of the mountain. The trail continues from the cairn to the summit of Zodang Gongpori (4,360 m), some two hours distant. Another two-day pilgrims' trek leads around the mountain, via the monkey cave, Gonpo La pass (4,750 m), and Tubpa Serlingpa Cave, which once functioned as a retreat centre for Ngachopa Monastery. On the 15th day of the fourth lunar month, pilgrims undertake an even more extensive route, encompassing Tsetang, Luchung, Tradruk and Bentsang.

Nyago Chakzam Bridge Five large stone supports are all that remain of the 14th-century iron bridge, which provided a vital link between Tsetang and the On valley until the present century. With a span of 150-250 m this was one of the celebrated engineer, Tangtong Gyelpo's greatest construction projects. The ruins on the south bank have long been regarded as a shrine to his memory. Nowadays a modern suspension bridge has been constructed at Nyago, carrying vehicles to the north bank of the Brahmaputra, from where Samye and the On valley are both accessible.

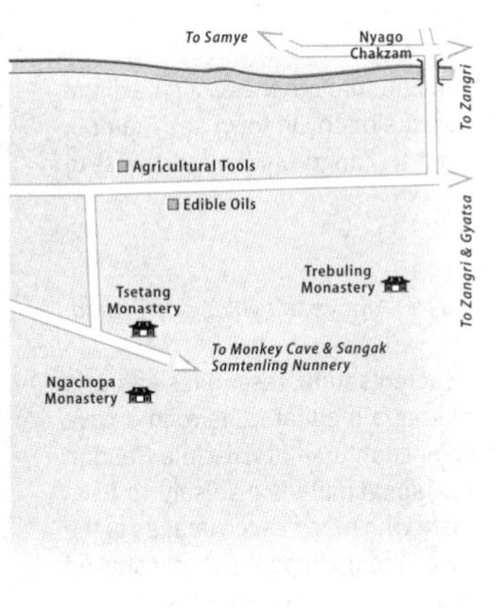

Snow Pigeon **12**
Tsetang **1**
Yarlha Shampo **3**

Eating
Dadong Hai **4**
Fu Li Lai **3**
Gesar **1**
Lhasa Tibet Kitchen **2**
Sichuan **5**

Nedong Kunzang Tse Palace Once located in the extreme south of Tsetang, west of the main road, this 15th-century Tibetan capital no longer exists. Behind the Dzong there was the **Tse Tsokpa Monastery**, established by Shakyashri in the 13th century. Later, it became known as **Bentsang Monastery**, and as such it survived intact until the 1960s. This was where Orgyen Lingpa's sacred relics were stored from which pills were compounded by the Thirteenth Dalai Lama in person. The greatest treasures of Bentsang were removed for safe-keeping to Tradruk, especially the Chinese appliqué Buddha, dating from the Ming Dynasty, and the Padmapani made of 29,000 pearls.

Jasa Lhakhang Some 3-4 km west of Tsetang on the Gongkar/Lhasa highway, there is a turn-off for Jasa Lhakhang. An original ninth-century temple on this site, containing a great image of Vairocana Buddha, was reputedly commissioned by Pelkortsen, grandson of King Langdarma and ruler of Tsang. Later, in the 11th century, reconstruction work was undertaken by the local lords Yuchen and Jasa Lhachen, who founded a Kadampa temple. During the period of Sakya ascendancy, this in turn was absorbed by the Sakyapas. The present site contains a small shrine, rebuilt in 1988. The Pema Shelpuk cave of Sheldrak (see below, page 199) is visible high on the southeast ridge from Jasa.

Do Valley རྡོ

From the village of Lo, where the Chim River enters the Brahmaputra, east of Samye, there is a new motor road which follows the river bank eastwards to Kyerpa, and from there inland to Do Podrang in the Do valley. At Lowo Dongteng, there was formerly a stupa dedicated to Tashi Obar, a deity in the retinue of Cimara.

On Valley འོན → *Colour map 3, grid B4*

Until the construction of the Nyago Zamchen Bridge and the new road to Samye along the north bank of the Brahmaputra, the On valley had to be approached by a seven-hour trek from Kyerpa at the entrance to the Do valley, or by ferry from the old **Nyago Druka** on the south bank. This region has recently become very accessible. The On valley extends north from the hilltop ruins of Ngari Tratsang at its entrance to the Padmasambhava cave of Onphu Taktsang in its upper reaches. In the middle of the valley, there is the hermitage of Tashi Doka, Choding Monastery and Drakmar Keru Lhakhang.

Ngari Tratsang

The ruins of Ngari Tratsang conspicuously stand guard on a hilltop promontory over the entrance to the On valley from the south. This was a Gelukpa monastery, constructed in 1541 by the Second Dalai Lama Gendun Gyatso, for the training of monks from Far West Tibet. It once contained relics which the Tibetan army had plundered from Central Asia back in the eighth century.

From the bridge, there are jeep roads leading inland through the east side of the On-chu valley to Tashi Doka (8 km), through the west side to On town and Tramdo, and along the north bank of the Brahmaputra, east to Zangri (45 km) and west to Samye (41 km).

Tashi Doka Hermitage

ⓘ *The hermitage of Tashi Doka is around 8 km inland, above the village of Trimon, and to the east of the On-chu River.*

This site, endowed with mountain willows and a sacred spring, resembles an oasis amid the surrounding barren hills. In 1415, Tsongkhapa meditated here, in a cave hermitage (*zimpuk*) higher up the slopes, and first encountered his disciple Gendun Drub, the future First Dalai Lama. While in retreat, Tsongkhapa is also said to have been approached by a celestial sculptor named Tashi who made seven images of the master in a single day. Hence the name Tashi Doka. Tsongkhapa reputedly shaved his head seven times in the course of this one day to provide relics for the statues. Within the cave there are some original images of Tsongkhapa, and a large stupa acts as a landmark outside. Down below, the main temple contains images of Tsongkhapa with his foremost students, flanked by the Fifth and Second Dalai Lamas, with Lodro

Zangpo of Zhigatse to the left. The throne has a portrait of the previous, Thirteenth Dalai Lama. The inner sanctum contains images representing the Buddhas of the Three Times, and it has side chapels dedicated to the Sixteen Elders and the Four Guardian Kings. Upstairs there is a small chapel containing the reliquary of a lama from Sera, who was responsible for rebuilding the hermitage until his death in 2000. The site is traditionally maintained by monks affiliated with nearby Ngari Tratsang.

Choding Monastery

ⓘ The extensive ruins of Choding Monastery (4,150 m), which has not yet been renovated, lie on the slopes above Gyelzang village, about 18 km north of Tashi Doka.

This monastery was founded by four disciples of Dampa Sedrakpa in the 12th century, and named by Lama Zhang. It therefore had Nyingmapa and Tselpa Kagyu affiliations, but in the late 15th century it was absorbed by the Gelukpa, after which it became the most powerful institution in the On valley. One of its incarnate lamas, the Fourteenth Gyese Rinpoche Jigme Yeshe Drakpa, was appointed regent of Tibet between 1728-1735.

On Township (On Qu)

Driving inland from the bridge on the dirt road which follows the west side of the valley, you will reach the town of On (3,600 m) after 15 km. An alternative route leads west from Ruka Sumpa on the Tashi Doka-Gyelzang road, to cross the On-chu by a small bridge that leads into the town. There are shops and a very small guesthouse here.

Drakmar Keru Temple

ⓘ Drakmar Keru Temple is located at Ruka Dangpo, a hamlet about 2 km north of On on the west bank of the On-chu.

Epigraphic and documentary evidence attribute the foundation of this temple to King Tride Tsukten, the father of Trisong Detsen, who reigned from 704-755, and is believed to have established altogether five temples to house Buddhist texts bequeathed by the Indian masters Buddhaguhya and Buddhashanti. The site comprises the original *Dukhang*, which was rebuilt as recently as 1957, and two side chapels to the right, known as the Namnang Lhakhang and the Karchung Lhakhang, which both had associations with Atisha (11th century). The buildings are surrounded by a perimeter wall and entered through an east-facing gate, which has a commemorative inscription outside.

The central **Assembly Hall (Dukhang)** of the main building has murals depicting aspects of Padmasambhava and predating the Cultural Revolution. This leads into the high-vaulted **inner sanctum (Jokhang)**, which appears to be of early eighth century construction—its antiquity is suggested by the architecture of its walls, ceiling beams and columns, and the regal motifs of its capitals. The chapel is unusually high – 6.5 m in contrast to its 8.8 m width and 7.6 m depth; suggesting, as Roberto Vitali has argued in *Early Temples of Central Tibet*, that it was first built to contain the massive Buddha image within it. Altogether the chapel contains 13 highly significant images, depicting Jowo Shakyamuni, flanked by the Eight Bodhisattvas and the gatekeepers Hayagriva and Vajrapani, with the royal patrons King Tride Tsukten and his Chinese queen Jincheng in the left corner. Jowo Shakyamuni has a compassionate but stern visage and a massively thick chest, and the surrounding bodhisattvas are well-proportioned and elegant with fine elongated facial features and distinctive shoulder-drapery. According to Vitali, the central image suggests a Khotanese influence while the peripheral figures may well date from the second phase of building, carried out by Dro Trisumje, a chief minister of King Relpachen, in the ninth century. The extant murals of the inner sanctum were repainted in the 1950s, and the rear wall behind the central image supports stacks of Tibetan texts, including liturgies associated with Tara and the Sixteen Elders. Apparently, the chapel was filled with salt during the Cultural Revolution, which ensured that its precious contents remained intact.

To the right of the main building, there is the **Namnang Lhakhang**, containing new replica images of Vairocana Buddha and Atisha, and beyond it is the **Karchung Lhakhang**, where Atisha reputedly resided for six months in the 11th century. It houses the Karchung Chorten, the foundation of which is attributed to Atisha himself, and a set of murals depicting Atisha flanked by his foremost students. The central mural replaces an original, said to have been painted with blood from Atisha's own nose. To the extreme right of this complex, there is a residential area where the caretaker monks, affiliated with Dorje Drak Monastery, now live.

Tshezik Stupa

North of On, the dirt road leads to **Dikna** township (26 km) and **Chabtang** village, where five interconnected stupas can be seen, upon an L-shaped platform. These were constructed by Lama Zhang during the 12th century, and are now in a state of disrepair. A branch of Lhalung Monastery (see below, page 222) was also once located on the summit of Mount Utse Teng (4,600 m) nearby. Heading north from Chabtang, the On valley then divides into three branches, one of which leads southwest to Do Podrang in Do valley, the second slightly northwest to Onphu Taktsang, and the third north to Balo on the Meldro-Gyamda highway.

Onphu Taktsang

ⓘ *Taking the northwest trail from Chabtang, follow the power lines as far as Tramdo, beyond which point it becomes too difficult for tractors, and then trek 30 mins to Akhor. The cave hermitages are 6 hrs' trekking distance uphill from Akhor, passing en route the destroyed nunnery of Ganden Lhatse and the last cultivated farmland of the valley. To reach the caves, one has to ford the On-chu, which can be a hazardous process in summertime! There is a trekking route from here to Gyama (see above, page 251).*

Among the many tiger lairs frequented by Padmasambhava in his meditations, three are pre-eminent: Onphu Taktsang in Lhokha, Paro Taktsang in Bhutan, and Rongme Karmo Taktsang in Derge. Yeshe Tsogyel twice visited Onphu Taktsang in the course of her life to flee from an unwanted suitor and to receive the Vajrakila empowerments from Padmasambhava. In addition to the Nyingmapa, the site also once had strong associations for the no longer existing Taktsangpa Kagyu school (founded 1405). The hermitage of Taktsang Gonpa was destroyed in the Cultural Revolution, and the daughter of the late Taktsang Rinpoche now lives in nearby Dikna. The forested hillside at Onphu Taktsang is said to resemble Zangdokpelri, the glorious copper-coloured mountain of Padmasambhava; and on the approach there is a stone impression of the great master's riding horse. There are three caves, two of which are marked with prayer flags. The lower cave (*drupuk ogma*), now occupied intermittently by students of Lama Chonyi from Lamaling in Kongpo, is that of Padmasambhva himself (an impression of his head may be seen in the rock behind the altar). The middle cave (*drupuk kyilma*), where Yeshe Tsogyel once lived, is on the high ridge to the south, approached via a zigzag pathway, but the upper cave (*drupuk gongma*) to the rear of the mountain is hard to locate nowadays.

Sleeping

Tsetang *p189, map p192*

B Gold Crane Hotel, Nedong Lam. A new high-rise building south of Tsetang Hotel, which, at the time of writing, has not yet received permission to accept foreign guests.

B Snow Pigeon Hotel (Purong Karpo Dronkhang), 1 Hubei Lam, T0893-7828888, F0893-7827777. A new 3-star hotel, with 65 excellent rooms – currently the best in town – doubles at ¥260, singles at ¥880 or ¥1,080, and suites at ¥1,880. All rooms have attached bathrooms, most with showers and a few with basins. There are 2 restaurants downstairs – one Chinese and the other (accessed from outside) serving Tibetan cuisine. On the 2nd floor there is a bar, games room and beauty/massage parlour. The curio shop on the ground floor is uninteresting, but the hotel also has a specialist foot massage facility, located outside the shop.

B**Tsetang Hotel (Zedong Hotel)**, 21 Nedong Lam, T0893-7821668, F0893-7821688. A 3-star hotel with 118 comfortable rooms (en suite bathrooms), in the original 4-storey building. A new annex has recently been constructed to the west of this complex and a roadside extension will soon be completed (for upmarket and budget travellers respectively): standard rooms at ¥523 or ¥423 (low season), and deluxe suites at ¥1,245 or ¥996 (low season). The solar-heated water supply is most effective after 2000, Has good Chinese restaurant (full meal plan ¥324, breakfast ¥108), under the careful management of Mr Sonam Tendzin, with souvenir and gift shop (inflated prices, accepts credit cards), foyer bar and games room, hairdressing and massage service, business centre with email facilities, oxygen bottles, dance hall, and large rooms available for special functions.

C**Lhokha Government Guesthouse**, Nedong Lam. Has clean superior rooms on top floor (min. ¥70 per bed).

C**Post Hotel**, Nedong Lam.

C**Yarlha Shampo Dajudian**, Nedong Lam. Has not yet received permission to accept foreign guests.

D**Agricultural and Nomadic Bureau Hotel**, Nedong Lam.

E**Dawo Hotel**, Kalzang Lam.

E**Gangjong Hotel**, Kalzang Lam.

E**Mirik Hotel**, Horse Roundabout. Cheap and centrally located.

E**Norsi Hotel**, Kalzang Lam.

Eating

Tsetang *p189, map p192*

Cantonese Restaurant, Tsetang Hotel, Nedong Lam. Specializes in overpriced but excellent Cantonese dishes.

Chinese Restaurant, Snow Pigeon Hotel, 1 Hubei Lam. Offers expensive Chinese cuisine in a variety of styles.

Fu Li Lai Restaurant (Tib. Pende Arkhang Chenmo, 7 Nedong Lam. Best Sichuan cuisine in town.

Tibetan Restaurant, Snow Pigeon Hotel, 1 Hubei Lam. Good quality Tibetan food, Tibetan decor.

Gesar Restaurant, Nedong Lam. Bar and Tibetan cuisine.

Lhasa Tibet Kitchen, Kalzang Lam. Inexpensive and wholesome. Offers a wide range of authentic Tibetan dishes.

There are several smaller restaurants in the city centre, serving Tibetan dumplings (momo), noodle soup (thukpa); and simple Sichuan dishes.

Entertainment

Tsetang *p189, map p192*

Cinema

Tsetang Cinema, located on the Town Square, near the Bank of China.

Music

Tibetan operas and traditional music are occasionally performed at concerts in the Tsetang Hotel (enquire at reception). There are discotheques, karaoke bars and video parlour facilities, up-market near Tsetang Hotel and down-market near the truck stops on Kalzang Lam and the old Town Square.

Shopping

Tsetang *p189, map p192*

Bookshops

Xinhua Bookstore, upstairs, near roundabout on east side of Nedong Lam.

Handicrafts

There are expensive souvenir gift shops in the Tsetang and Snow Pigeon hotels, and more competitively priced artefacts including carpets, religious accessories and leather goods are available on the east side of Nedong Lam, near the roundabout. Cheaper alternatives are to be found in the open markets, north of the Mirik Hotel, and on Ba-re

For an explanation of the sleeping and eating price codes used in this guide, see inside the front cover. Other relevant information is found in Essentials pages 44-46.

Lam, but Tsetang is generally not regarded as a good outlet for Tibetan handicrafts.

Modern goods

There is a large department store, near the roundabout on Nedong Lam, and several smaller shops selling mineral water, beer, tinned foods, clothing and electrical goods. Almost all the shops will accept only RMB currency, and rarely accept payment in US dollars. It is best to change currency in Lhasa before reaching Tsetang, but the Bank of China can reputedly assist in emergencies. The open-air market near the old city is well worth a visit, although unique products and antiques are hard to find. Imported liquor and cigarettes are available at the shop in the Tsetang Hotel.

Photography

Print film and processing are available at Tsetang Hotel gift shop, and at photographic shops, especially Muslim-owned electrical stores on the west side of Nedong Lam, near crossroads.

Stamps

Stamps are available at Nedong Post Office, and the Prefectural Post Office, both on Nedong Lam. Alternative, try the lobby and shops of the Snow Pigeon or Tsetang hotels.

Activities and tours

Tsetang *p189, map p192*

Sport

The sports stadium is located on Hubei Lam.

Tour companies

Tsetang Hotel Travel Company, 21 Nedong Lam, T0893-7821796, F0893-7821688.
Lhokha Tourism Bureau, 9 Nedong Lam, T0893-7821675, F0893-7821552.
Shannan CITS, 18 Nedong Lam, T0893-7821169, F0893-7821832.
Tsetang Sports Travel, 15 Nedong Lam, T0893-7821952.
Lhokha Tourism Trade Company, 7 Nedong Lam, T0893-7821128, F0893-7821128.

Transport

Tsetang *p189, map p192*

Most visitors to Tsetang, whether arriving by air or land, will have their transportation organized by the travel services.

Air

Tsetang is connected via Gongkar Airport (87 km due west) to: **Chengdu** and **Beijing** (daily flights), **Kathmandu** on Tue, Thu and Sat in the tourist season and Sat only in the off-season, **Chamdo** on Thu, **Ziling** on Mon, Wed, Fri and Sun, **Kunming** (via Gyeltang) on Wed and Sat, **Chongqing** on Mon, Wed and Sun, **Xi'an** on Mon, Wed, Fri and Sun, **Shanghai** on Wed and Sun, and **Guangzhou** on Mon.

Bus

Long distance Travel by public bus is common. The bus station for Lhasa is located near the Horse Roundabout (last bus departs around 1600). Public mini-buses also run through the Yarlung valley as far as Tradruk and Yumbu Lagang, and can be flagged down en route (¥1-2).

Car/jeep

Long distance Car and jeep transportation is more easily available from Lhasa, but also through the local travel services or the Tsetang Road Transport Company, located behind the Tsetang Hotel, on the Chongye side road.

Directory

Tsetang *p189, map p192*

Banks Bank of China, Town Square, near old Tibetan quarter. Agricultural Bank of China, Nedong Lam. Construction Bank, Yinxong lam. As yet there is no foreign exchange facility in the banks of Tsetang, apart from a desk at the Tsetang Hotel. **Hospitals** Tsetang Peoples Hospital, west of crossroads on north side of Kalzang Lam. Tsetang Hospital of Traditional Medicine, west of crossroads on Kalzang Lam. **Internet** Internet café facilities are available at the Tsetang and Snow Pigeon hotels and at other locations on Nedong Lam. **Post offices** Nedong Post Office,

opposite Tsetang Hotel on Nedong Lam. **Prefectural Post Office**, opposite Lhokha Government Guesthouse on Nedong Lam.
Telephone IDD calls can be made from **China Mobile**, which is located at the intersection of Kalzang Lam and Nedong Lam, from the rooms and lobby of the Snow Pigeon Hotel, or in the business centre/reception of the Tsetang Hotel. ICC cards are available at China mobile.
Useful addresses Police & public security: **Tsetang Foreign Affairs Public Security Bureau**, Nedong Lam, opposite Tsetang Hotel, are responsible for inspection of travel permits and are known to fine transgressors heavily.

Yarlung Valley ཡར་ལུང

*The 72-km long Yarlung valley, which gave its name to the ancient line of Tibetan kings and is sometimes called the cradle of Tibetan civilization, is rich in interesting temples, monasteries, castles, caves, stupas and peaks. Three power places (*ne-sum*), Sheldrak, Tradruk and Yumbu Lagang (or Rechung Puk); and three stupa receptacles (*ten-sum*), Takchen Bumpa, Gontang Bumpa, and Tsechu Bumpa are particularly important.*

The Lower Yarlung Valley

Sheldrak Caves → *Colour map 3, grid C4*

ⓘ *To reach Sheldrak from Tsetang, take the Chongye road and turn off onto a dirt track on the right before the Tsechu Bumpa Stupa. Jeeps can negotiate this track, which follows a Yarlung tributary upstream for 4-5 km, and tractors can reach the village of Sekhang Zhika which lies at the top of the ridge. From here, it is a tough 3-hr trek to the cave. If you walk all the way from Tsechu Bumpa Stupa, it will take 5-6 hrs.*

There are three important caves in the Pema Tsekri range, which dominates the west entrance to the Yarlung valley: the east-facing **Sheldrak Drubpuk** is the first of Padmasambhava's meditation caves in Tibet, from where the indigenous hostile forces and demons were bound under on oath of allegiance to Buddhism. The northeast-facing **Tsogyel Sangpuk**, or secret meditation cave of Yeshe Tsogyel, is identified by a distant prayer flag to the south of the main cave; and the west-facing **Pema Shelpuk** is the celebrated *terma*-site where Orgyen Lingpa revealed the seminal text entitled *Life and Liberation of Padmasambhava (Pema Katang)*. It is accessible from the Sheldrak Monastery or more directly by traversing a somewhat dangerous ridge above the main cave. The last of these caves is also visible from Jasa to the west of Tsetang.

Sheldrak Monastery

Above the village of **Sekhang Zhika** is a burial ground, marked by a stupa consecrated to Hayagriva. The pathway then follows the ridge to the right, leading up to **Sheldrak Monastery**. This restored temple (the original was apparently dedicated to the 14th century treasure-finder Sangye Lingpa) has six monks. It contains images of Padmasambhava with his two foremost consorts, the Eight Manifestations of Padmasambhava, and the Third Karmapa Rangjung Dorje. There are photographs depicting the Longchen Nyingtig assemblage of deities.

Sheldrak Drubpuk Cave

Continuing uphill to the right, the path crosses a sacred spring (*drubchu*) and climbs steeply for 100 m via a rock-hewn stairway to the **Sheldrak Drubpuk Cave**

 (4,550 m). The cave, which is itself at the base of a rock pinnacle called **Kritkita Dzong**, offers through its window a bird's eye view of the contours of the Yarlung valley below: Tradruk, Rechung Puk, Yumbu Lagang and Mount Yarlha Shampo are all visible at a glance.

The Sheldrak Drubpuk cave is one of the most revered pilgrimage places on the Tibetan plateau, symbolizing Padmasambhava's buddha attributes. As such, it is classed alongside Drak Yangdzong symbolizing buddha-body, Chimphu Drakmar Keutsang symbolizing buddha-speech, Lhodrak Kharchu Chakpurchen, symbolizing buddha-mind, and Monka Nering Senge Dzong in Bhutan symbolizing buddha-activities. Thirty-five mantra-adept followers of Padmasambhava were associated with Sheldrak during the eighth to ninth century, and later masters such as Orgyen Lingpa and Terdak Lingpa discovered *termas* in the nearby Pema Shelpuk cave.

The original **'speaking' image of Padmasambhava**, which once graced the cave, has been relocated at Tradruk Monastery, and the altar now has newly constructed images of the Great Master flanked by his two foremost consorts. The rock surface of the west wall has natural impressions representing Avalokiteshvara, The Twenty-five Disciples of Padmasambhava, the Boudhnath Stupa in Nepal, and a crescent moon of the third day of the month.

Northwest of the cave is the **sacred spring** which one of Padmasambhava's disciples, named Nyak Jananakumara, is said to have brought forth from dry rock. Below the cave entrance there is a reconstructed two-storey temple, with complete images of the Eight Manifestations of Padmasambhava on each level. This is where the caretaker of Sheldrak lives.

Tsechu Bumpa Stupa

Just south of the turn-off for Sheldrak on the main Tsetang-Chongye road, there is the reconstructed Tsechu Bumpa stupa – one of the three sacred stupas of Yarlung. Circumambulation of this stupa has long marked the beginning or end of the Sheldrak pilgrimage. This stupa is said to have at its core a rock-crystal Buddha image from India, which was presented to King Trisong Detsen by the translator Chokrolui Gyelsten. Others believe it to contain the armour of King Songtsen Gampo himself. On full moon days the stupa is said to exude the water of life (*tsechu*). The site is marked by a large collection of mani stones.

Tsentang Yui Lhakhang

East of the Tsechu Bumpa Stupa, at the village of **Khartok**, are the ruins of the Tsentang Yui Lhakhang, a temple which has been attributed to Queen Jincheng, or alternatively to one of Songtsen Gampo's queens. The temple once had distinctive blue glazed turquoise roof tiles, which would corroborate the reports of its Chinese origin. During the 15th century, it was an important centre for the development of dialectics in the Sakya school. Nearby, at **Tsentang Gozhi**, the first king of ancient Tibet, Nyatri Tsenpo, is said to have made contact with his Bon subjects after descending from the heavens at **Lhababri**. And since 1984, some 233 earth and stone mound tombs have been discovered in the vicinity of Tsentang.

Mount Lhababri

At the southern extremity of the Pema Tsekpa range, below Sheldrak, there are three hills, the highest of which is Lhababri. This so-called 'hill of divine descent' is where Tibet's first king Nyatri Tsenpo is said to have alighted from the heavens – although there are early historical accounts (eg that of Nelpa Pandita), which claim the king to have been a descendant of the Licchavi king Rupati (Tib Magyapa). The king was carried shoulder-high as if on a sedan chair (*nyatri*) to Yumbu Lagang, where the first palace of the Yarlung kings was constructed.

Tradruk Temple ཁྲ་འབྲུག་ལྷ་ཁང་ → *Colour map 3, grid C4.*

ⓘ *Admission: ¥25.*

History Tradruk temple is the earliest of Tibet's great geomantic temples apart from the Jokhang (some sources even claim it predates the latter). It was reputedly constructed by King Songtsen Gampo on the left shoulder of the supine ogress, symbolizing the rigours of the Tibetan terrain (see page 742). The name Tradruk suggests that a 'falcon' (*tra*) emanated by the power of Songtsen Gampo's meditations overwhelmed a local 'dragon' (*druk*) divinity to facilitate the temple's construction. Later, the site was venerated as one of the three royal temples of Tibet by the kings Trisong Detsen and Mune Tsepo. During that period, offering ceremonies pertaining to the Vinaya and Abhidharma were performed at Tradruk. Plundered during the persecution of Langdarma, the site was renovated and expanded in 1351, and later by the Fifth Dalai Lama, who added the golden roof, and the Seventh Dalai Lama. By the late 18th century, Tradruk had 21 temples. The assembly hall and many of the chapels were obliterated during the Cultural Revolution, but the newly reconstructed buildings were finally reconsecrated in 1988.

Lower Floor Chapels As you approach the entrance, which still has its splendid original timbers intact, there is a **Mani Lhakhang** on the right, containing a large Mani Wheel, and a two-storey building on the left, where Songtsen Gampo is said to have resided during the construction of Tradruk. The portico of the complex no longer has its ancient bell – one of three which dated from the Yarlung period (the others are at Samye and the Jokhang – see above, pages 179 and 70). An intermediate pilgrim's circuit (*barkor*) is accessible from the courtyard beyond the portico. Continuing into the main temple, the **Tsuklakhang**, the plan of which is reminiscent of the Jokhang, you will find the assembly hall surrounded by a series of 12 chapels. From left to right, these comprise: the Ngakpa Lhakhang (west), the Gonkhang (north) and the Tuje Lhakhang (north), the Rabten Lhakhang (north), the Sangye Lhakhang (north), the Chogyel Lhakhang (east), the Dolma Lhakhang Tashi Jamnyom (east), the Tuje Lhakhang (east), the Tsepak Lhakhang (south), the Menlha Lhakhang (south), the Orgyen Lhakhang (south) and the Tongdrol Lhakhang (west).

Among these, the most important is the inner sanctum – the **Dolma Tashi Jamnyom Lhakhang**. This is the original Songtsen Gampo geomantic temple – once containing natural stone images of the Buddhas of the Five Families from Mount Zodang Gongpori, and a standing image of Tara, known as Dolma Shesema ('Tara who consumes her offerings'). Following reconstruction here, the original Dolma Sheshema was inserted into the heart of a new replica.

Tradruk Temple

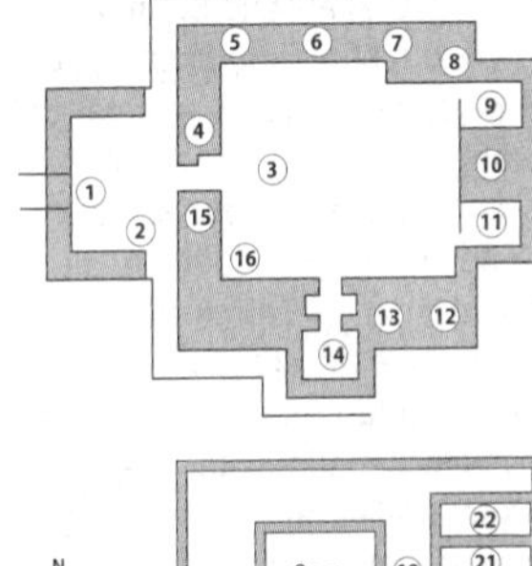

Ground Floor
1 Entrance Portico
2 Mani Lhakhang
3 Tsuklakhang
4 Ngakpa Lhakhang
5 Gonkhang
6 Tuje Lhakhang
7 Rabten Lhakhang
8 Sangye Lhakhang
9 Chogyel Lhakhang
10 Dolma Tashi Jamnyom Lhakhang
11 Tuje Lhakhang
12 Tsepak Lhakhang
13 Menlha Lhakhang
14 Orgyen Lhakhang
15 Tongdral Lhakhang
16 Stairs

Upper Floor
17 Monastic Kitchen
18 Protector Chapel
19 Drubtob Lhakhang
20 Outer Chamber
21 Middle Chamber
22 Inner Chamber

New clay images of the Buddhas of the Five Families similarly replace the original stone statues, the fragments of which have been inserted into their respective replicas as a consecratory core. These are flanked by the Eight Bodhisattvas, and the gatekeepers.

To the left of the inner sanctum, the **Chogyel Lhakhang** contains new images depicting King Songtsen Gampo, his two foreign queens and chief ministers. To the right of the inner sanctum is the **Tuje Lhakhang**, containing an old image of Thousand-armed Mahakarunika flanked by Manjughosa and Vajrapani. In the corner is a stove reputedly used by Queen Wencheng in person.

Among the chapels of the west wing, the **Ngapa Lhakhang** contains images of the Fifth Dalai Lama flanked by other Gelukpa and Kadampa masters, the **Tongdrol Lhakhang** depicts Tsongkhapa surrounded by his major disciples, and the **Gonkhang** has images of Mahakala and his retainers. Among the chapels of the north wing, both the **Tuje Lhakhang** and the **Rabten** Lhakhang contain images of the Eleven-headed Thousand-armed Mahakarunika; while the **Sangye Lhakhang** has Shakyamuni with Shariputra and Maudgalyayana. Among the chapels on the south wing, the **Tsepak Lhakhang** has images of Amitayus flanked by White Tara and Vijaya; and the **Menlha Lhakhang** has images of all the Eight Medicine Buddhas, with Bhaisajyaguru at the centre. Lastly, the **Orgyen Lhakhang** has an outer chamber with images of Amitayus and Mahakala, and an inner chamber with Padmasambhava with his consorts Mandarava and Yeshe Tsogyel, and his eight manifestations.

The newly painted and finely executed murals of the north wall illustrate scenes from the past lives of Shakyamuni Buddha, following the *Avadanakalpalata*; while those of the south wall depict the Eight Manifestations of Padmasambhava, the Peaceful and Wrathful Deities, the Eight Transmitted Precepts (*Kabgye*), and Padmsambhava according to the *Sampa Lhundrub* liturgy.

Upper Floor Chapels Ascending to the second floor, on the right side there is a monastic kitchen and a **protector chapel** with images of Mahakala and Brahma. The main chapel is the **Drubtob Lhakhang** at the rear, which has three chambers. The outermost chamber is empty. The **middle chamber** is protected by a secure metal grill to deter potential art thieves. It contains the remnants of a set of the Eighty-four Mahasiddhas (from whom the chapel derives its name), the 16 volumes of the *Shatasahasrikaprajnaparamita*, an exquisite tangka depicting Padmapani, made of 29,000 pearls, which had been originally housed at Bentsang/Tse Tsokpa monastery (now destroyed, see above, page 193), and a large appliqué tangka of the Buddha clad in red robes against a blue background, which may perhaps date from the Ming period, but is reputedly one of three in Tibet made by Wencheng (the others are kept in the Reliquary Stupa of the Fifth Dalai Lama in the Potala Palace and in the Maitreya Lhakhang at Zhigatse). There is some speculation that the Padmapani tangka may be a forgery, and that the original was misappropriated during the 10 years that it remained in the possession of the Cultural Relics Bureau.

The **innermost chamber** contains on the rear wall the wonderful original Padmasambhava image which had been salvaged from Sheldrak cave, flanked by new images of his foremost consorts and old tangkas depicting Longchen Rabjampa, and other figures all within an intricately carved wooden altar of recent construction. To the right there is a series of rare appliqué tangkas, which had also been retrieved from Bentsang. These depict Avalokiteshvara and Naropa, among others.

Outer temples There are four places of interest outside the temple proper: the **Neten Lhakhang** (west), dedicated to the Sixteen Elders, where there were formerly images of Songtsen Gampo and Padmasambhava; the **Sangak Podrang** (south) where monks from Mindroling have performed tantric rituals since the 17th century; the **Guru Lhakhang** (southeast), and the site of the now destroyed **Namgyel**

Lhakhang (north), a branch of Bentsang Monastery (see above, page 193) where Tsongkhapa received monastic ordination in the 14th century.

Getting there Located on the east side of the Yarlung valley, only 7 km south of Tsetang on a newly paved road surface, Tradruk temple nowadays lies within Tradruk village to the south side of the Tsetang-Podrang road. Public buses run to Tradruk regularly from the Horse Roundabout in Tsetang (¥1-2).

Rechung Puk

ⓘ *The hermitage of Rechung Puk is approached via a turn-off on the right, 3 km south of Tradruk. It takes less than 1 hr to trek uphill to the site from the road below.*

This famous Kagyupa hermitage sits on top of the **Mila Tse** spur which overlooks the bifurcation of the Yarlung and Chongye valleys. This is the retreat of Milarepa's illustrious disciple Rechungpa Dorje Drak (1083-1161) of Loro, who, following the example of his teacher, practised asceticism and meditation here. The site thus became known as Rechung Puk. Later, in 1488, while residing at Rechung Puk, the yogin Tsangnyon Heruka, whose actual name was Sangye Gyeltsen, composed the *Life of Milarepa* and the *Hundred Thousand Songs of Milarepa*, which have since become classic texts of Tibetan Buddhism, well known throughout the world.

Formerly there were 1,000 monks at Rechung Puk, and some rebuilding has taken place since the destruction of the 1960s. The temple contains images of Padmasambhava flanked by his foremost consorts, and Tsangnyon Heruka. Rechungpa's cave to its rear contains his stone seat and new images of Marpa, Milarepa and Rechungpa. The highly esteemed sculpture of Tsangnyon Heruka, which once graced this cave, no longer exists; but there are rock footprints attributed to Milarepa, Rechungpa, the First Karmapa, and also to Tsangnyon Heruka himself. A new assembly hall (*dukhang*) and retreat centre (*drubkhang*) have been constructed above the cave. At the top of the ridge is the ruined base of the **Mila Tse Watchtower**, dating from the Phakmodrupa period.

Gongtang Bumpa Stupa

At the foot of the Mila Tse spur on its west side is the 6-m Gongtang Stupa, one of the three major stupas of the Yarlung valley. This stupa is said to have been built on the advice of Vairocana, the eighth century translator, who resolved a boundary dispute between the rulers of Nedong and Chongye while he was meditating in a nearby cave. The stupa therefore has come to define the entrance to the Chongye valley. A new temple to the west contains images of Hayagriva, with Padmasambhava and Lhodrak Longka Geling on either side.

Bairo Puk

Slightly south of the Gongtang Bumpa Stupa at the east side of the approach to Chongye valley, there is a meditation cave associated with the great translator Vairocana, one of the foremost disciples of Padmasambhava and Dzogchen lineage-holder. Nowadays, it contains only the copper base of its former image, but there is a more enduring rock handprint of Vairocana, and some rock-inscriptions. Heading south from here, you will enter the Chongye and Tso-me counties of Southern Tibet, see below, pages 210 and 215.

Riwo Choling Monastery

East of Tsharu village, which lies to the south of Tradruk, are the vast ruins of the Gelukpa monastery of Riwo Choling, originally founded by Tsongkhapa's student, the First Panchen Lama, Khedrup Je in the 15th century. The monks of Riwo Choling have long acted as caretakers of the Yumbu Lagang Palace.

Yumbu Lagang ཡུམ་བུ་བླ་སྒང

→ *Colour map 3, grid C4.*

ⓘ *Admission fee: ¥25 per person. Photographic fee: ¥40 (¥450 for video cameras). Yumbu Lagang Palace is located 6 km south of Tradruk and 3 km after the turn-off for Rechung Puk (see above), at the point where the paved road from Tsetang comes to an abrupt end. There are inexpensive public buses (¥2) and 2-seater taxis (¥60) making the journey here from Tsetang. At the base of the hill, there is a newly established souvenir and refreshments shop for tourists, and it is possible for tourists to ride horses uphill for a small fee.*

History The resplendent hilltop Yumbu Lagang is reputedly a reconstruction of Tibet's oldest building. Some sources state that when Nyatri Tsenpo emerged as the first king of Tibet in 247 or 127 BC he was escorted to Mount Tashitseri, the 'talismanic hill' (**Lagang**) of 'tamarisk' (**Ombu**), by his Bon followers, and there the first palace, Yumbu Lagang, was established on its summit. This is also suggested by the theme of the murals depicted inside on the second floor of the building. Later, the palace appears to have been refurbished by Lhatotori Nyentsen, the 28th king (b 374 CE). In 433 or 446 CE, Buddhist texts including the *Karandavyuhasutra*, are said to have miraculously fallen upon the palace roof, heralding the first appearance of Buddhism in Tibet. In Nelpa Pandita's *History*, however, it suggests that the Indian scholar Buddharaksita arrived in Tibet with these texts, and deposited them there for the sake of posterity. Known as the 'awesome secret' (*nyenpo sangwa*), the texts, were not understood until Songtsen Gampo embraced Buddhism, five reigns later. According to the injunctions of the King (Gyelpo Katang), Lhatotori Nyentsen's tomb is located within the ridge above Yumbu Lagang. Extensions to the palace were added in subsequent centuries: the two lower chapels by Songtsen Gampo, and the gold roof by the Fifth Dalai Lama. These ancient structures were obliterated during the Cultural Revolution.

The present building dates only from 1982. The three-storey tower is 11 m high, and its sides measure 4.6 m and 3.5 m. Its two lower floors are entered from behind the shrines of their adjoining chapels, and the third floor by a ladder from the roof terrace. At its apex, the central pillar (*tsokshing*) of the tower is decorated with *kataks* and sacred threads, and on each side there is an observation window.

The site The **ante-chamber to the lower chapel** has murals depicting the mystical visions of Tsongkhapa. Then, inside the **lower chapel** (originally constructed by King Songtsen Gampo) there is a central image of Buddha Shakyamuni in the form of Jowo Norbu Sampel. This image is flanked by regal statues: Nyatri Tsenpo on the left and Songtsen Gampo on the right. Further images on the left are Tonmi Sambhota, Trisong Detsen, and Lhatotori Nyentsen; and on the right are Relpachen, Namde Osung, and Minister Gar Tongtsen.

The **second floor chapel** is entered from an open terrace. Inside there is a gallery around which pilgrims walk to observe its fascinating murals and images, as well as those of the Buddha and the kings below. Here, behind a security grill, there is a new gilded sandalwood image of Lokeshvara (replacing an original stolen by art thieves in 1999 which was likened to the famous sandalwood Lokeshvara in the Potala), as well as others depicting Amitayus, Shakyamuni, and Padmasambhava flanked by Shantaraksita and Trisong Detsen.

The murals are particularly relevant. **On the left** are depicted: Nyatri Tsenpo's descent from the heavens at Mount Lhababri and his arrival at Yumbu Lagang; the descent of the 'awesome secret' on the palace roof during the reign of Lhatotori Nyentsen, the arrival of Padmasambhava in the Sheldrak cave, and the Twenty-one Taras. **On the right** are the Eight Manifestations of Padmasambhava, and Shakyamuni with the Sixteen Elders, while beside the door are the protectors Shridevi and Yarlha Shampo.

Zortang

Below Yumbu Lagang to the northwest is Zortang, the first cultivated field in Tibet. Farmers even now ensure a good harvest by sprinkling soil from here onto their own fields. The temple of **Lharu Menlha**, containing images of the Eight Medicine Buddhas, was formerly built near this field.

The Upper Yarlung Valley

Podrang Township and Takchen Bumpa Stupa

Five kilometres south of Yumbu Lagang is **Podrang**, described as the oldest inhabited village in Tibet. Here there is a turn-off on the left, leading northeast, eventually to Eyul. Along this road in Shang-yang commune, are the 119 stupas known as **Gyatsagye**, dating from the 17th century, and on a nearby slope the 6-7-m high **Takchen Bumpa Stupa**, which is one of the three major stupas of Yarlung (see above, page 199). This stupa is named after Sadaprarudita (Tib Taktu Ngu), a bodhisattva figure who appears in the *Prajnaparamita* literature, and whose 'constantly weeping' left eye is said to be preserved within it. The construction dates from the Kadampa period and is attributed to one Geshe Korchen (12th century). Adjacent to the stupa, there is a small Drukpa Kagyu monastery named **Takchen Bumoche**.

Chode O and Chode Gong

ⓘ *After Podrang the Yarlung valley begins to narrow. A futher 17 km south, there is the side valley in which Chode O (Lower Chode) monastery is located, and after 6 km more, the road passes through Chode Gong (Upper Chode) monastery in Yarto township.*

Chode O was founded by the Fifth Dalai Lama and expanded by the Seventh Dalai Lama. Its assembly hall has three floors, the middle one containing the principal images of Shakyamuni with his foremost disciples, the Sixteen Elders and Eight Medicine Buddhas.

Chode Gong is an older institution, founded by Ra Lotsawa during the 11th century and developed later by the Gelukpas. Its four-storey temple has an assembly hall and inner sanctum dedicated to Tsongkhapa and his students, as well as the Thirteenth Dalai Lama, the Buddhas of the Three Times and the Eight Bodhisattvas.

Yabzang Monastery

At Yarto township, 1 km after Chode Gong, there is a further bifurcation – one track leading southeast, and the other west for 3 km to Yabzang monastery. **Yabzang**, founded by Gyurme Long in 1206, was the seat of the small Yabzang Kagyu school, founded by the latter's teacher Geden Yeshe Chenye, himself a disciple of Phakmodrupa. The site is largely in ruins at the present. Its approach has a ramp reminiscent of the Potala at Lhasa.

Mount Yarlha Shampo

Some 24 km beyond Yarto, the road crosses Yarto Drak La pass (4,970 m). The main peak, abode of the protector **Yarlha Shampo** (6,636 m) lies southwest from here. At this watershed pass, the Yarlung valley comes to an end and the road passes via Nyel valley (Lhuntse county) into Tsari (see below, page 234) and via Droshul valley (Tsona county) to the Bhutanese and Indian borders.

Lhuntse County ལྷུན་རྩེ

→ *Population: 32,306. Area: 5,991 sq km. Colour map 2, grid C4.* 隆子县

The county of Lhuntse extends from the watershed at Yarto Drak La pass, through the valleys of the Nyel-chu and Jar-chu, as far as their confluence with the Tsari-chu. Together these rivers (along with the Loro-chu in Tsona county) form the headwaters of the ***Subansiri*** *(Tib Shipasha-chu), a major south-flowing tributary of the Brahmaputra, which enters the Indian state of Arunachal Pradesh (Tib Monyul Tsona), immediately after the confluence. The road from Tsetang to Yarto Drak La pass is 61 km from where it continues to* ***Kyitang****, the capital of Lhuntse county, a further 80 km. Kyitang lies 21 km east of the main Tsetang-Tsona frontier road.*

In the east of the county, 108 km from Lhuntse by motor road, is Sangak Choling, one of the three main gateways to Tsari, the sacred mountain of Southern Tibet which attracts pilgrims from all over the country (see below, page 234).

Upper Nyel Valley (Nyelto) གཉལ་སྟོད

Following the main road south from Tsetang across Yarto Drak La pass, there is a turn-off on the left after 10 km (at marker 194) for Chumdo Gyang and Eyul. Crossing Shopotak La pass (5,001 m), after a further 23 km you will enter the upper reaches of the **Nyel** valley. The Gelukpa monastery of **Gateng** is passed on the descent from the pass after 15 km, and then, at **Shobo Shar** village, another turn-off to the left leads to **Shopo** township in Upper Nyel. The routes from Shopo to Jarto (Upper Jaryul) and Sangak Choling will be described below.

Continuing on the main Tsetang-Tsona highway for a further 4 km (Tsona lies 90 km to the south), you will arrive at the **Kyitang turn-off**, again on the left. The road to the right leads on to Tsona, via Ritang town and monastery. Taking the left road, which follows the Nyel valley, after 21 km you will reach Kyitang.

Kyitang

The administrative capital of the county, the town is largely comprised of government buildings and military compounds; but there are some monasteries of interest in the Kyitang area, especially **Chi-le Gonpa** of the Kagyu school, near the old Lhuntse Dzong and **Trakor Monastery**, which are both located to the west of Kyitang, as well as **Tebura Monastery** to the northwest, and **Shangtse (Yangtse) Monastery** near Lower Nyel (Nyel-me) to the northeast.

Lhuntse County

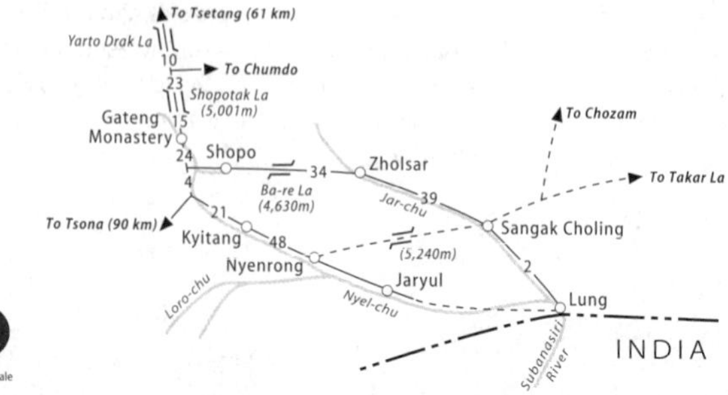

A motor road continues for 48 km from Kyitang down the Nyel-chu valley via **Zhingpa** township as far as **Jaryul** township, which lies east of the Nyel-chu's confluence with the Loro-chu. The Loro-chu valley is nowadays administered by Tsona county (see below, page 208).

Trekking

From Nyenrong on this road, there is a three-day trekking route via Le La pass (5,240 m), Khyimpu and Jar-me to Sangak Choling, which is the gateway to Tsari in the northeast.

An alternative more difficult trek follows the Nyel-chu downstream from this confluence with the Loro-chu, to a second confluence with the Jar-chu at **Lung**. The rapids form a deep gorge which must be crossed and recrossed by a precarious bridge and ladder! The village of **Dron** is the last Tibetan village on the Nyel/Loro-chu, and further downstream the territory is occupied by tribal Assamese Lopas. Many of Dron's villagers are engaged in guiding pilgrims to Tsari, which is still 10 trekking days to the east from this point. At Lung, the combined headwaters of the Subansiri flow south into India.

NB There is a strong military presence at Lung. The border is disputed, and travel restrictions apply. From Lung there is a jeep road leading through Jar-me (Lower Jaryul) to Sangak Choling, 33 km to northwest.

Upper Jaryul Valley (Jarto) བྱར་སྟོད

From **Shopo** in Upper Nyel (1 km east of the main Tsetang-Tsona highway, see above), a jeep road crosses the Ba-re La watershed (4,630 m) between the Nyel and Jarto valleys to **Zholsar** township (34 km). En route, you should stop to visit **Dzongka Chode** monastery, which has a collection of old Buddhist texts. From Zholsar, the road follows the narrow Jarto valley downstream and southeast to **Sangak Choling**, 39 km distant.

Trekking

There are two trekking routes which diverge from this road: a one-day trek from **Shoposang** (opposite the ruins of Tengtse monastery) which leads southwest via the Mo La pass (5,400 m) to Lower Nyel (Nyel-me); and another, five-day, trek from **Pejorling**, which leads north via the Kharpo-chu valley to **Chozam**, the northern gateway to the Tsari pilgrimage in Nang county (see below, page 236). It is also possible to make a four-day trek from **Chumdo Gyang**, following the Eyul road, and then diverging from it to cross the Pu La watershed pass to Zholsar, via Drongzhu, Kyekye, Tengchung and Phudrok in Jarto.

Sangak Choling

The monastery of Sangak Choling was founded in 1515 by Pema Karpo of the Drukpa Kagyu school (1527-1592); and expanded by his successor the Fifth Drukchen Paksam Wangpo (1593-1641). This is one of the main gateways to the Tsari pilgrimage circuit, which lies only a two-day trek to the east. The Drukpa Kagyu school had a particular affinity with Tsari, in that it was Tsangpa Gya-re, the founder of the principal Drukpa monasteries in West and Central Tibet who first opened Tsari as a place of pilgrimage.

Sangak Choling, destroyed in the 1960s, has been under reconstruction since 1986, and now stands on a hillside above a town of the same name. The main temple has a central Shakyamuni image.

Tsari Pilgrimage To reach the pilgrim's circuit from Sangak Choling, it is necessary to trek via Cha La pass (5,060 m). Begin by following the Kyu-chu gorge upstream through a glacial valley. After 12 km the road divides, the northeast track leading to

Takar La and the lesser circuit, and the north track leading to **Chozam** on the higher circuit. Traditionally, the latter, which is also known as the 'circumambulation of the ravines of Tsari' was undertaken only once every 12 years. For a description of the Tsari pilgrimage routes, see the section on Nang county page 236.

Lower Jaryul Valley (Jarme) བྱར་སྨད

Below Sangak Choling, the jeep road continues for 25 km, following the Jar-chu downstream to its confluence with the Nyel/Loro-chu at Lung. Arunachal Pradesh (India) lies a short distance to the south. The border is sealed and it is not possible to enter India.

Tsona County མཚོ་སྣ

→ *Population: 15,171. Area: 5,698 sq km. Colour map 2, grid C4.* 错那县

Tsona county is the modern name for ***Monyul****, the vast region to the east of Lhodrak and south of Lhuntse bordering on Bhutan and Arunachal Pradesh. At present, it includes the Drushul valley and the headwaters of the Tawang-chu, as far south as the sacred* terma *site of Shawuk Tago, as well as the adjacent valleys of the Loro Karpo-chu and Loro Nakpo-chu, which are tributaries of the* ***Subansiri*** *(Tib Shipasha-chu). Traditionally, Monyul has also included Tawang and neighbouring parts of what is now the Indian state of Arunachal Pradesh, as well as Bhutan itself, which in the Tibetan language is often called Southern Monyul.*

History

This region is the land of the Monpa people (see page 759); and although parts of it have long been culturally within the Tibetan orbit, it was not brought under direct rule from Lhasa until the 17th century, around the time when a series of unsuccessful military campaigns were also conducted against the Drukpa theocracy of Bhutan. During the 17th century the Sixth Dalai Lama Tsangyang Gyatso was born at **Orgyen Ling** in Monyul. From then on, Monyul was recognized as having 32 districts: four in Lekpo, six in Pangchen, eight in Dakpa, three in Lawok, six in Drangang, four in Rongnang and one in Shawuk Hrojangdak. The present county capital is located at **Zholshar**, 198 km due south of Tsetang.

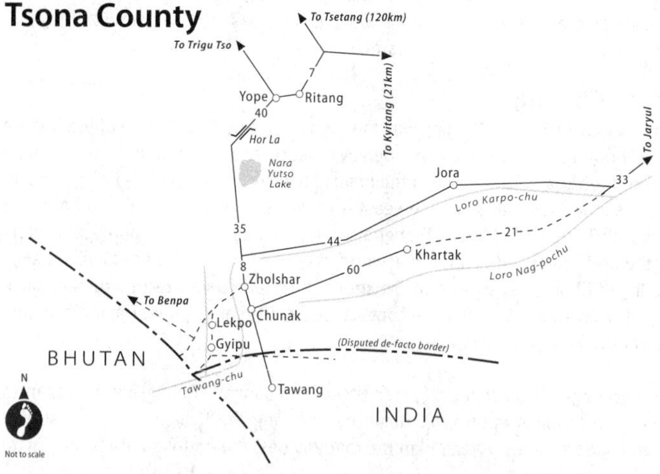

Upper Tawang Valley

At **Ritang** in Upper Nyel, 28 km from Kyitang, there is a reconstructed monastery containing bas-relief carvings which have been restored through the good auspices of the Shalu Association in Paris. Some 13th-14th century murals are also said to have survived here.

After leaving Ritang, the main road from Tsetang to Tsona runs due west. A turn-off on the right at **Yope** leads northwest towards Trigu Tso and Tso-me (see page 215), but the main road cuts southwest through the Nangme-chu valley (a tributary of the Nyel-chu). Then, after crossing Hor La pass (40 km from Ritang), the road turns abruptly due south, passing on the left the large **Nara Yutso Lake**. Further south, at the small **Nyapa Tso** lake, there is a turn-off northeast for the Loro valley (35 km from Hor La pass). A further 8 km beyond this turn-off, you will reach Zholshar, the county capital, located in the upper reaches of the Tawang-chu valley.

Zholshar

Zholshar (Tsona) is a particularly sensitive town, since the road from here leads directly downstream to **Tawang**, a frontier town with a monastery allied to Drepung in Lhasa, but now firmly on the Indian side of the disputed border.

Shawuk Tago

The most important site on the Tibetan side of the border is undoubtedly Shawuk Tago, which lies on the western ridge of the valley, just north of the border. This is a sacred meditation cave associated with Padmasambhava, where the Dzogchen master Melong Dorje later meditated during the 13th century, and where in 1680 Terdak Lingpa unearthed his *terma* text entitled *Great Compassionate One as the Universal Gathering of the Sugatas (Tuje Chenpo Deshek Kundu).*

Drushul Valley

Drushul, situated north and west of Zholshar, is the name of the long gorge of the Nyashang-chu River, a major tributary of the Tawang-chu, with which converges at the Indo-Bhutanese border, south of Tawang. Drushul is renowned as the birthplace and residence of the Nyingma master and treasure-finder Ratna Lingpa (1403-1478). It was here at **Dokhar Lhundrub Podrang** that he compiled his celebrated edition of the *Collected Tantras of the Nyingmapa (Nyingma Gyudbum).*

Trekking

There is a six-day trekking route from Zholshar to Me La pass, on the Northeast Bhutanese border, which follows the Nyashang-chu River downstream through Drushul valley. En route you pass through **Mishi** village and **Dokhar** township, a beautifully forested area situated deep in the gorge. Here, there are eight peaks and eight rivers symbolizing the attributes of the Eight Medicine Buddhas. The trail then cuts southwest across the Chak La pass (4,920 m), to enter the moist **Khechu** valley, with its alpine conifer forests. This valley leads west to **Benpa** township in Lhodrak (a further three days, see page 218), and a southerly trail leads via the Yombu-chu and Me La pass to **Shinbe** in Bhutan.

An alternative seven-day trek from Zholshar (Tsona) crosses into the Nyashang-chu valley via the Po La (4,540 m), and descends through **Lekpo** township and its environs to **Gyipu** (73 km and the East Bhutanese border at **Jangpu** (17 km).

Loro Karpo-chu Valley

Loro valley is the birthplace of the renowned Rechungpa Dorje Drak, one of Milarepa's two foremost disciples. It is possible to drive through the Loro Karpo-chu valley from Zholshar (Tsona), northeast to **Jora** township (52 km), and thence on to Jaryul. Alternatively, the trek from Zholshar to Jora can be undertaken in three easy days. En route, you pass through **Gersum**, Nyala La (5,175 m; the watershed between the Tawang-chu and Loro Karpo-chu), and **Loroto** village. From Jora there is a further three-day trekking pathway north to Lhuntse in the Nyel-chu valley.

Loro Nakpo-chu Valley

Drive south from Zholshar to **Chunak** and thence northeast to **Khartak** (60 km), following the Loro Nakpo-chu downstream. A three-day trek from Khartak to Jaryul township in Lhuntse county descends through the river's narrow gorge to its confluence with the Loro Karpo-chu, west of **Tritongmon Monastery** (21 km). From this point, it is 33 km to **Jaryul** township, from where transport is available to Lhuntse.

Chongye County འཕྱོང་རྒྱས

→ *Population: 17,505. Area: 827 sq km. Colour map 3, grid C4.* 穷结县

The valley of Chongye, southwest of Yarlung, was the ancient capital of the Tibetan kings until Songtsen Gampo consolidated his newly unified kingdom at Lhasa in the seventh century. Subsequently, it became the royal burial ground par excellence. The valley extends from its confluence with the Yarlung Shampo-chu below Rechung Puk as far as the Chongye River's source in Chugo township. The modern county capital, ***Chongye****, lies at the heart of the Chongye valley, 28 km from Tsetang; but the county also includes the outlying townships of Cho and Gyelmen in its lateral valleys to the west.*

Getting there

The motor road to Chongye, leaves Tsetang, heading south on Tsentang Lam past a Chinese military barracks and cemetery. This complex was headquarters of the Chinese military operation during the Sino-Indian border war of 1962. It then cuts south to Tsechu Bumpa, where the Sheldrak pilgrimage begins (see above, page 199). Beyond **Gongtang Bumpa** (see above, page 203), the recently paved road enters the Chongye valley, following the Chongye River upstream. At **Bena** there is a turn-off on the right, which leads to Cho township, the birthplace of Nyak Jananakumara, one of the foremost disciples of Padmasambhava, who attained his meditative realizations at Sheldrak cave (see above, page 199). The main road continues south through **Ju** township, where the principal site is Tangpoche monastery.

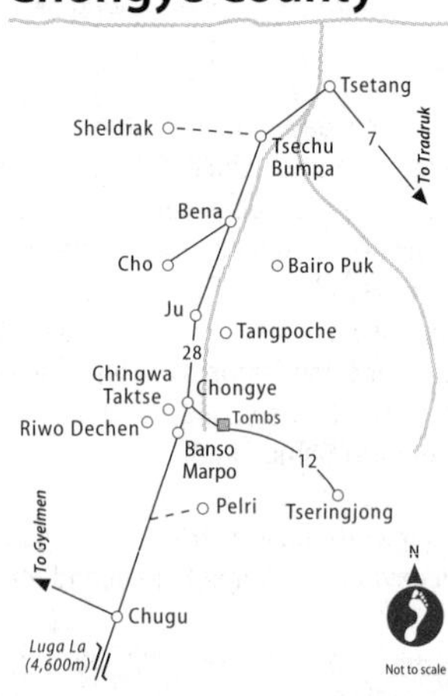

Bonpo Tomb Culture

The funeral custom of earth-burial is rare in Central Tibet, where burial ground dismemberment (sky burial) is the norm for ordinary people and cremation or embalming preferred for important lamas. Nonetheless, during the Yarlung period, when Bonpo tomb culture was at its most influential (see page 739), the Tibetan kings were traditionally interred in colossal tumuli, along with their worldly wealth (and in the earliest cases with their retainers, buried alive). After the collapse of the Yarlung Dynasty, the custom of burying kings in tombs came to an end. During the 1980s a number of other tomb sites have been excavated in Southern Tibet in the lateral valleys of the Brahmaputra, such as Dranang, Yarlung and Nang, but, however large, none appear to have the grandeur and historic significance of the Chongye tombs.

Tangpoche (Solnak Tang) ཐང་པོ་ཆེ

The yellow buildings of **Tangpoche Monastery**, also known formally as Solnak Tang, are located to the east of the valley, not far from Bairo Puk (see above, page 203). This Kadampa institution was founded in 1017 by a group of Lu-me's followers known as the 'seven and a half monks' (*bande-mi che-dang-gye*), who included Drumer Tsultrim Jungne, one of the 10 men of Utsang responsible for revitalizing the monastic ordination in Central Tibet at that time. Shortly afterwards, it became the residence of the Kadampa spiritual benefactor Khuton Tsondru Yungdrung (1011-1075), who invited Atisha to visit the monastery. It subsequently developed as an important centre for the study of Buddhist philosophy; and formerly contained a number of precious relics, including a black Prajnaparamita image, nicknamed Zilpachen ('lustrous'), and an image of Atisha. Tangpoche was gradually absorbed by the Gelukpas, following Tsongkhapa's visit here in the 14th century. The present assembly hall's murals, dated 1915, commissioned by the Thirteenth Dalai Lama; and there are some small images and ancient tangkas.

Chongye Town འཕྱོང་རྒྱས

Although the county capital is a town of greater antiquity than Lhasa, and even in the early 1990s was regarded as a sleepy backwater, it has within the last few years been rapidly reconstructed. From afar (Dungkhar or Pelri) Chongye now has the air of a small Chinese town with its high rise concrete buildings. Three roads intersect at the main square – the Tsetang road from the north, the southwest track through the old village to Riwo Dechen monastery, and the southeast road to the Tombs, Dungkhar, and Tso-me county.

There are restaurant and simple guesthouse facilities, although most visitors will prefer to stay at Tsetang and commute. There are also small roadside shops, selling groceries and household utensils, and a stone carving factory, where local agate is turned into ornaments and bowls.

Chingwa Taktse Castle འཕྱིང་བ་སྟག་རྩེ་རྫོང

Located to the southwest, on the Chingwari ridge above the town, this ruined edifice was the ancient residence of the Yarlung kings, and the centre of their power prior to the construction of Lhasa. Behind it was the fiefdom of the Chongye Depa, the hereditary lord of Chongye, who claimed to originate from the Zahor region of Northwest India and had a well-established Nyingmapa background. It was into this family, as the son of Miwang Dudul Rapten, that the Fifth Dalai Lama was born in 1617. A chapel in the old fortress (dzong) commemorated this event.

Riwo Dechen Monastery རི་བོ་བདེ་ཆེན་དགོན་པ

On the slopes below Chingwa Taktse Castle, you will see the ruins and reconstructed buildings of Riwo Dechen monastery. The Tomb of Songtsen Gampo provides an excellent vantage point for viewing this complex and the ruined castle on the ridge above. Riwo Dechen was founded during the 15th century by the Gelukpa lama Lowo Pelzang, a student of Khedrubje Gelek Pelzangpo (1385-1438), one of Tsongkhapa's foremost disciples who was retrospectively recognized as the First Panchen Lama. Although the original buildings are in ruins, a new monastery has been constructed alongside the original, and there are over 100 monks. The main Maitreya temple was consecrated in 1985.

The Tombs of the Kings

→ *Colour map 3, grid C4.*

ⓘ *Admission fee: ¥30 per person. Photographic fee: ¥75 (¥750 for video cameras).*
A short distance to the south of Chongye town and east of the Chongye River, are the tombs of the greatest kings of the Yarlung Dynasty. Tumuli of 16 kings have been identified in the Chingwardo and Dungkhar valleys. Another two, those of the 28th king Lhatotori Nyen-tsen and the 30th Drong-nyen Deu, are also said to be situated in Chongye valley, respectively below the ruins of Chingwa Taktse Castle and at Zhangdar, further north.

History

While there are various conflicting descriptions of the tombs at Chongye, the following account is derived from the chronicle in Jigme Lingpa's *Collection of Tales (Tamtsok)*, an 18th-century essay based on earlier sources, such as the *Gar Karchag* and *Tentsik Gyatso*, and composed by a native of Chongye, who happens to have been one of Tibet's greatest and most incisive writers of all time.

The tombs of the earliest legendary and prehistoric kings are no longer visible. The first seven kings, from Nyatri Tsenpo to Sibtri Tsenpo, are said to have ascended to the heavens at the time of their demise by means of a sky-cord (*mu*). The eighth and ninth kings (known as the 'two celestial kings of Teng') are said to have been interred at Ya and Dza; the 10th to 16th (known as the 'six earthly kings of Lek') were interred at Yapangtsam; and the 17th to 24th (known as the 'eight middle kings of De') were buried at Chuwo'i Zhung. None of these sites have been identified as yet, their tombs having 'vanished like snow falling on a lake'. Subsequent kings were buried in the plain of **Chinyul Darmotang** (at Chongye), where there are many unidentified mounds of earth, perhaps

Chongye Tombs

Not to scale

Sleeping
1 Government Compound Guesthouse

Eating
1 Restaurants

Chinwardo Valley
1 Banso Marpo
2 Banso Dozher Hralpo
3 Banso Lharichen
4 Banso Lhari Tsuknam
5 Banso of Prince Jangsa Lha-on
6 Banso Lhari Dempo
7 Banso Gyelchen Trulzhi
8 Banso of King Langdarma
9 Banso of Prince Namde Osung
10 Banso Trulri Truknang

Dunghar Valley
11 Banso of Trinyen Zungtsen
12 Banso of King Takri Nyentsen
13 Banso Gungri Sokpolek
14 Banso Gungri Gungje
15 Banso Gyangri Gyangdem
16 Banso of King Mutik Tsepo

containing the tombs of the 'five linking kings of Tsen'. The last of these, the 28th king Lhatotori Nyentsen is said to be interred within Chingwa Taktse Castle.

Nowadays, there are 16 identifiable tombs – 10 in the Chingwardo valley, and six in the adjacent Dungkhar valley. Some of these are on the slopes of Mulari hill, which divides these two valleys. Songtsen Gampo's immediate ancestors and descendants are all interred here.

Chongye/Chingwardo tombs

Banso Marpo or **Muri Mukpo** Among the 10 tombs of the Chongye/Chingwardo valley, the largest (1) is that of Tibet's unifying 33rd king, Songtsen Gampo. This enormous tomb is 13.4 m high with its sides each measuring 129 m. Literary sources describe in detail the vast treasures and entire chapels contained within it. Yet there are other traditions claiming that Songtsen Gampo vanished into light at the time of his passing, into either the Jowo Rinpoche image or the Rangjung Ngaden image of the Jokhang in Lhasa!

On the summit of the tomb, offering a bird's eye view of the entire Chongye valley, there is a reconstructed 13th-century temple, originally attributed to the Nyingmapa lama Menlungpa Shakya-o. The temple is entered through an outer annex with a **Mani Lhakhang** on the right (murals here depict the primordial Buddha Samantabhadra in union with Samantabhadri). Beyond an inner courtyard, the **chapel** contains images of Songtsen Gampo, flanked by his two foreign queens and chief ministers. The **inner sanctum** has images (left to right) of: Amitayus, the Buddhas of the Three Times, and Padmasambhava in the form of Nangsi Zilnon. The gatekeepers are Vajrapani and Hayagriva. The murals depict the Thirty-five Buddhas of Confession (left) and the Eight Manifestations of Padmasambhava (right). Other temples that once formed part of this complex have not yet been restored.

The other nine tombs on the Chongye/Chingwardo side of the valley are visible from the summit of Songtsen Gampo's tomb. As described by Jigme Lingpa, these comprise:

Banso Dozher Hralpo (2), the mausoleum of the 35th king, Mangsong Mang-tsen (left of Songtsen Gampo's tomb).

Banso Lharichen (3), the mausoleum of the 36th king, Dusong Mangpoje, also known as Trulgyi Gyelpo (right of Mangsong Mangtsen's tomb).

Banso Lhari Tsuknam (4), the mausoleum of the 37th king, Tride Tsukten Me Aktsom (on the slopes of Mulari, left of Dusong Mangpoje's tomb).

Banso (5) of Prince Jangsa Lha-on (in front of Tride Tsukten Me Aktsom's tomb).

Banso Lhari Dempo (6), the mausoleum of the 39th king, Mune Tsepo (right of Tride Tsukten Me Aktsom's tomb).

Temple at Chongye Banso

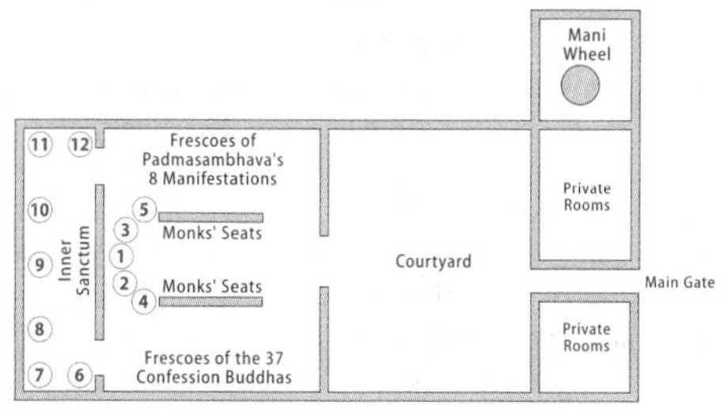

Steps to road

Not to scale

Images

1 Songtsen Gampo
2 Bhrikuti
3 Wencheng
4 Tonmi Sambhota
5 Lonpo Gar
6 Acala Vajrapani
7 Amitayus
8 Dipamkara Buddha
9 Shakyamuni Buddha
10 Maitreya Buddha
11 Padmasambhava
12 Hayagriva

Banso Gyelchen Trulzhi (7), the mausoleum of the 41st king, Tri Relpachen in front of Dusong Mangpoje's tomb, with an inscribed obelisk in the foreground. The obelisk has been recently been enclosed within a small building to offer some protection from the elements. Jigme Lingpa adds that this tomb has also been wrongly attributed to Dengtri, the son of Senalek Jinyon.

Banso (8) of the 42nd and last king, Langdarma (between those of Dusong Mangpoje and Relpachen).

Banso (9) of prince Namde Osung (behind Dusong Mangpoje's tomb).

Banso Trulri Truknang (10), the mausoleum of the 38th king, Trisong Detsen (behind and to right of Tride Tsukten Me Aktsom's tomb, on the left slopes of Mulari, adjacent to Dungkhar valley). **NB** Local reports suggest this tomb is on the far side of Mulari. The ancient obelisk marking it has been missing since the 18th century. Jigme Lingpa notes that it was removed by farmers.

Dungkhar Valley Tombs

In the adjacent Lower Dungkhar valley, there are six further identified tombs:

Banso (11) of the 29th king, Trinyen Zungtsen.

Banso (12) of the 31st king, Takri Nyentsen (right of Trinyen Zungtsen's tomb).

Banso Gungri Sokpolek (13), mausoleum of the 32nd king, Namri Songtsen (left of Trinyen Zungtsen's tomb).

Banso Gungri Gungje (14), mausoleum of the 34th king, Gungri Gungtsen (left of Namri Songtsen's tomb).

Banso Gyangri Gyangdem (15), mausoleum of prince Murub Tsepo (west side of valley).

Banso (16) of the 40th king, Mutik Tsepo also called Senalek Jinyon (nearby Murub Tsepo's tomb, although some say it is in front of Dusong Mangpoje's tomb).

Tseringjong Nunnery ཚེ་རིང་ལྗོངས

The Dungkhar valley where the last six tombs are located was also the abode of Jigme Lingpa, the great Nyingmapa yogin (1729-1798), who established his hermitage above Dungkhar village, 12 km from Chongye. It was from this hermitage that his Longchen Nyingtig tradition spread throughout Tibet. Since the 19th century, Tseringjong ① *T0893-7905219*, has been an active nunnery for practitioners of the Longchen Nyingtig. There are now 24 nuns at Tseringjong, which was reconstructed in 1985. The meditative spirit which gave rise to this powerful hermitage is still apparent today.

Approaching the temple from the road, there is a Mani Wall to the right, with stones depicting the Thirty-five Buddhas of Confession, and a sacred spring to the left. Then, passing a tree and teaching throne of Jigme Lingpa's on the left, and another tree reputedly grown from the hair of Jigme Lingpa on the right, the building is entered by a door next to the kitchen.

An antechamber then leads into the temple proper (door on right). The central images depict Padmasambhava flanked by Shantaraksita and Trisong Detsen. Behind these images against the rear wall are further images, depicting Longchen Rabjampa and Jigme Lingpa among others. In front, there is a throne, and on the left wall (next to the door) an image of the protectress Dorje Yudronma. A printed set of the Lhasa *Kangyur* sits against the right wall. Within the **inner sanctum**, there is a very precious silver reliquary containing the remains of Jigme Lingpa, flanked by images of Longchen Rabjampa (left) and Jigme Lingpa (right). Uphill from here, there is a small **protector chapel,** containing fine newly sculpted clay images of the Dzogchen protectors Rahula, Ekajati and Dorje Lekpa.

Pelri Tekchenling Monastery དཔལ་རི་ཐེག་ཆེན་གླིང

Located in a northeast side valley, and approached via a turn-off to the left a few kilometres upstream from Songtsen Gampo's tomb is the monastery of Pelri

Tekchokling. The original temple was founded in the 15th century by Sonam Tobgyel, lord of Chongye. It subsequently became the residence of the Nyingmapa *terton* Sheab Ozer (1517-1584), but it is most renowned as the birthplace of Jigme Lingpa. The reconstructed main temple contains murals depicting the Eight Manifestations of Padmasambhava, as well as the lineage of Longchen Rabjampa and Sherab Ozer. The ruined building where Jigme Lingpa was born is currently marked by a whitewashed stone.

Gyelmen Chen-ye Lhakhang རྒྱལ་སྨན་སྤྱན་ གཡས་ལྷ་ཁང

Heading up the Chongye valley, before the steep ascent to Lugu La pass begins, there is a turn-off on the right (west), leading to Gyelmen township. Here, the most important site is the **Chen-ye Lhakhang**, a Kadampa centre renowned for its monastic discipline, which was initially established by Geshe Drapa, and later absorbed by the Gelukpa school. The most precious relic here was the right eye of Shariputra, foremost student of Shakyamuni Buddha, after which the temple was called 'right-eye temple' (Chen-ye Lhakhang).

The main road continues uphill through **Chugo** township, near the source of the Chongye-chu River, bypassing a newly constructed dam and an artificial lake. Over the last three years traffic on this road has had to negotiate many detours, making it slow and hard to traverse, but the surface should soon be fully restored and bridges reopened when the construction is completed. The high **Lugu La** pass (4,600 m), which forms the watershed between the north-flowing tributaries of the Brahmaputra, and the Lhodrak region to the south, offers fantastic views of the nomadic grasslands and lakeland terrain around Trigu Lake.

Tso-me County མཚོ་སྨད

→ *Population: 13,554. Area: 6,075 sq km. Colour map 2, grid C4.* 措美县

From Lugu La pass (4,600 m), the road leads southwest to Trigu Lake and the Tamzhol valley of East Lhodrak. This region is nowadays called Tso-me, and administered from its county capital at ***Tamzhol****. The distance from Chongye to Tamzhol is 83 km. At the northwest shore of Trigu Lake, south of the pass,* ***Chaktse Trigu*** *township lies in a vast exposed lakeland plain. Almost every building has a windmill attached. The township is an important intersection, since roads lead from here northwest towards Lake Yamdrok (motorable for 34 km); southeast to Ritang (76 km) near Lhuntse, and southwest to Tso-me (46 km).*

Tso-me County

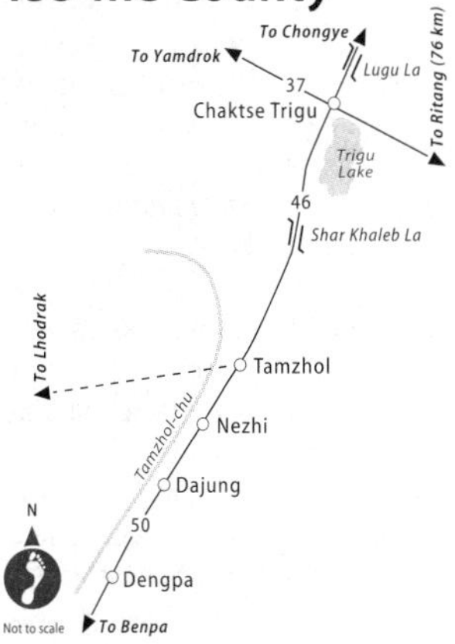

Trigu Lake གྲི་གུ་མཚོ

The bird sanctuary of Trigu Lake is located in a pristine nomad pasture-lands with hot springs near its northwest corner and fertile yak pastures all around this well-drained area. The motion and subtle colour tones of its waters are said to portend good and bad auspices; and, like neighbouring Lake Yamdrok, it has a talismanic connection with the well-being of the Tibetan nation. Prosperity is considered directly proportionate to the rise in its water level. The sacred snow peak of Yarlha Shampo is often visible in the distance to the northeast of the lake – its silhouette reflected in the clear waters – and in the winter months when the lake freezes over, village children can be seen skating and tobogganing on its surface near the southwest corner.

The 50-km drive from Trigu to Tamzhol in Tso-me county is one of the most memorable in Southern Tibet. The road cuts southwest away from the lake shore, and ascends Shar Khaleb La pass (5,129 m). In the autumn months the pass can be almost snowbound, girded by distant snow peaks on all sides, while in summer, the descent exposes a remarkable canyon where the bare red hillsides are severely contorted and eroded, like those around Tsaparang in Far West Tibet (see page 385). To the west, you can see the peaks of Chungkha Mori (5,220 m), Droktri Sharma (5,837 m) and Zholchen Chenri (6,166 m), which are part of the tectonic upheavals which shaped this landscape and form a well-defined watershed between the north and south flowing tributaries of the Brahmaputra. The descent into Tamzhol leads through lateral valleys to the ruined monasteries of Rimon and Tashi Choling.

Tamzhol (Tso-me) Town

The town of **Tso-me** is dramatically set within the eroded gorge of the Tamzhol-chu (sometimes known as Lhodrak Shar-chu), which rises from the watershed at Shar Khaleb, and surges southwest through the East Lhodrak region to converge with the Kuru-chu (Lhodrak Nub-chu) below Kharchu (see below, page 219).

Trekking From Tso-me, the main road leads downstream to Benpa and Khomting Lhakhang (84 km); but it is also possible to undertake a four-day trek to Lhodrak (Dowa Dzong), via Zholra valley, Menzang La pass and Shera La pass.

Mawochok Monastery སྨ་བོ་ལྕོགས

Revered as one of the supreme places for meditation in Tibet since the time of Padmasambhava, the distinctive Mawochok ridge known as **Drakmar Dorje Tsenga** ('five-fold indestructible peak of red rock') dominates the town of Tso-me from the northeast. The site is said to derive its power from the three mountain abodes of the three main bodhisattvas, Avalokiteshvara, Manjushri and Vajrapani, which lie immediately to the south.

History The monastery was the seat of Nyangrel Nyima Ozer (1136-1204), a revered incarnation of King Trisong Detsen who, along with Guru Chowang and Rigdzin Godemchen, is regarded as one of the three supreme treasure-finders (*terton*) of Tibet. As a child, he meditated at the base of Mawochok mountain and received the name Nyima Ozer in a vision. Thereafter, he established his residence on the ridge above, and the monastery developed. The original buildings were destroyed in the 1960s, along with most of Mawochok's treasures, including a famous set of images depicting the three bodhisattvas (Avalokiteshvara, Manjushri, and Vajrapani), King Trisong Detsen's own master copy of the *Gathering of the Eight Transmitted Precepts* (a text rediscovered by Nyangrel himself), and a large bronze stupa.

Main temple A motorable switchback track leads uphill to Mawachok, passing through rough terrain and moraine-covered escarpments. Approaching the main temple from the east, there are three buildings to its left: a **protector shrine**, dedicated to Six-armed Mahakala, and two enormous stupa reliquaries, known as **Tukten Chorten** and **Tashi Obar**, which are greatly revered. They contain the relics of Nyangrel and his son Drogon Namka Pelwa. Among these, Nyangrel's own stupa is said to have been consecrated by the Kashmiri pandita Shakyashri, who was invited to Mawochok in 1204 for the funeral ceremonies.

The **main temple** is entered from the east, although the main images and its two inner sanctums are to the north. Inside, in the northwest corner, next to a wooden prostration board, there are **amazing murals** depicting the life of Nyangrel himself. On the east wall is a copy of the Derge version of the *Kangyur*. The main images are of Padmasambhava and Nyangrel. In the first **inner sanctum**, there is a new image of Vairocana, alongside old images of Nyangrel and his son Drogon Namka Pelwa. The second inner sanctum contains (L-R): old images of Amitayus and Manjushri (in gilded copper), new images of Avalokiteshvara and peaceful Vajrapani, and old images of Amitayus and Vajrasattva, along with an old volume of the *Astasahasrikaprajnaparamita*. The small **assembly hall** has an image of Padmasambhava, a photo offset copy of the Rinchen Terdzo and a central throne, which bears a photograph of the present Mawachok Rinpoche (Chozang Tendzin Gyatso), who lives in Tsetang. The monastery is maintained by 23 monks, under the guidance of Yeshe Tsering, himself a student of the late Dudjom Rinpoche.

Pilgrimage Circuit The pilgrims' circuit around the mountain top encompasses Nyangrel's sacred spring and meditation cave, as well as a burial ground, and rock impressions of snowlions and Eleven-faced Avalokiteshvara. Nearby are the three sacred peaks of the three bodhisattvas: Vajrapani on the left, Avalokiteshvara in the centre and Manjushri on the right. Further to the south are the mountains of Benpa in lower Tamzhol and, beyond, the high Himalayas on the Bhutan-Tibet border.

The best **accommodation** in town is to be found at the Nyiwo Dronkhang, which occupies the second floor of a new concrete building, with shops and restaurants on the floor below. There is also an older guesthouse compound, which caters mostly to truckers. The town has a general store, a cinema, and an expanding Chinese population.

Nezhi Zhitro Lhakhang གནས་གཞི་ཞི་ཁྲོ་ལྷ་ཁང

A few kilometres below the county town, following the Tamzhol-chu downstream, the road passes a ruined watchtower and Phakmodrupa's earthen stupa of **Na'okyok** on the far bank of the river. After Letang village, the road crosses the river to the west bank and descends to **Nezhi** township. Here, you can visit **Nezhi Zhitro Lhakhang**, the residence of the descendants of the Nyingmapa *terton* Guru Chowang (1212-1270), where the images are dedicated to the latter's particular *terma* tradition. Guru Chowang, like Nyangrel, is one of the supreme *terton* of the Nyingma school and, again like Nyangrel, hailed from the Lhodrak region of Southern Tibet. As a young man, he received the bodhicitta vows from Sakya Pandita here in 1229. Formerly the golden reliquary of Guru Chowang was housed here.

The temple Inside the reconstructed temple, which is entered from the east side, the central images are of Padmasambhava and his two foremost consorts. In the far northwest corner there is a large image of Guru Chowang, and by the central pillars tangkas depicting the assemblies of the Hundred Peaceful and Wrathful Deities. There are **two inner sanctums**: the one to the west is dedicated to the Eight Deities of the Transmitted Precepts, who are the wrathful meditational deities of the Nyingma school, in the form revealed by Guru Chowang's own *terma* revelation, entitled *Kabgye Sangwa Yongdzok*. The second to the north was formerly dedicated to the peaceful deities but now contains images of the Buddhas of the Three Times, flanked by Atisha and the Eight Bodhisattvas. Hayagriva and Vajrapani guard its gates.

Watchtowers The road continues southwest from Nezhi, through **Dajung** and **Lu-me**, passing en route a riverside Padmasambhava cave. Below Lu-me, clusters of 15-20-m high **watchtowers** are frequently to be seen. The construction of such defensive towers is well known in other border areas of the Tibetan plateau, including Gyarong. The road then winds its way downstream to **Darma Dzong** (in Dengpa township), before climbing high above the river to enter Benpa township.

Lhodrak County ལྷོ་བྲག

→ *Population: 18,513. Area: 4,027 sq km. Colour map 2, grid C3.* 洛扎县

Traditionally the Lhodrak region of Southern Tibet included both the Kuru-chu (Lhodrak Nub-chu) and the Tamzhol-chu (Lhodrak Shar-chu) river valleys, which respectively extend southwest and southeast to converge below Kharchu, north of the Bhutanese border. Currently, Lhodrak is divided between Tso-me and Lhodrak counties, the latter comprising the upper reaches of the Kuru-chu, from Monda La pass as far as Kharchu; and the lower reaches of the Tamzhol-chu, from its Benpa-chu confluence as far as Kharchu.

The entire county lies to the south of the Brahmaputra watershed, and yet north of the Himalayan massif. This geographically confined but stunningly beautiful region has long been one of great historic importance, where vital traditions of both the Nyingma and Kagyu schools have flourished, acting as a cultural bridge between Tibet and East Bhutan.

*The county capital is located at **Dowa Dzong** on the Zhung-chu tributary of the Kuru-chu. The distance from Tamzhol to Khomting Lhakhang is 84 km, and the distance from Dowa Dzong to Khomting Lhakhang is 67 km.*

***NB** The rapid rivers of Lhodrak are best traversed in spring, early summer and autumn. During the rainy season flash flooding can seriously disrupt itineraries.*

Benpa Township འབེན་པ

Benpa township is located on the west-flowing Benpa-chu tributary of the Tamzhol River. The valley formed by the Benpa-chu connects with the Khechu and Drushul valleys of Tsona county (see above, page 208) via the Ngamogong La pass.

Benpa Drukrel Lhakhang once contained a large gilded copper image of Padmasambhava. Also, 1 km upstream from Benpa township, is the Kagyu monastery of **Benpa Chakdor**, named after its large image of the bodhisattva Vajrapani (Tib Chakdor). The assembly hall contains stone footprints of Milarepa, the First Karmapa, and Gotsangpa. Within the temple to its rear there are renovated images of Vajrapani, flanked by Marpa and Padmasambhava.

The main road from Benpa to Khomting Lhakhang (34 km) leads via **Drak Sinmo Barje** (also called Sengeri), where the clawmarks of the ogress of the rocks, who gave birth to the Tibetan race (see page 738) can be seen on the cliff face. From Pelri there is a side valley leading to Pode La pass (4,965 m) on the Bhutanese border. This leads to **Monka Nering Senge Dzong**, in Bhutan – the foremost hermitage of Padmasambhava symbolizing buddha-activities.

Lhodrak County

Khomting Lhakhang མཁོ་མཐིང་ལྷ་ཁང

Lhakhang Township Lhakhang overlooks the confluence of the Kuru-chu and Tamzhol rivers. It was once an important trading post between East Bhutan, Lhasa and Tsetang. There is a pleasant guesthouse, general store and outside pool tables.

The Temple This geomantic temple, which stands in the middle of Lhakhang township, is one of the border-taming (*thadul*) series of temples constructed by Songtsen Gampo during the seventh century: specifically located on the left elbow of the supine ogress, who represents the rigours of the Tibetan terrain (see page 742).

It is a yellow building with a shingled roof, surrounded by four large trees, planted by Guru Chowang in the 13th century. It once contained a renowned image of Four-faced Sarvavid Vairocana, who embodies all the Buddhas of the Five Families, flanked by the Eight Bodhisattvas. The face representing Amoghasiddhi is said to have been made by King Songtsen Gampo in person. It was within this image that Nyangrel Nyima Ozer (12th century) discovered his *terma* texts entitled *Gathering of the Sugatas of the Eight Transmitted Precepts (Kabgye Deshek Dupa)*. Nothing remains of these images apart from their plinths, but the painted columns and the 19th-century murals above the door depicting the three bodhisattvas, Avalokiteshvara, Manjushri and Vajrapani, are exquisite. This temple urgently requires funds for structural repairs and restoration. Upstairs, in the **Tsedak Gonkhang**, there are some small original images and black-on-gold murals of the protectors.

South to Bhutan

Below Khomting Lhakhang, a two-hour trail to the left leads below Chakpurchen towards the **Kharchu Pelgyi Pukring** cave, where in the 15th century Ratna Lingpa discovered *terma* concealed by Namkei Nyingpo. Opposite the cave is the cliff-top **Senge Zangpo Dzong**, where a temple associated with the Dzogchen lineage-holders Melong Dorje (1243-1303) and Rigdzin Kumaradza (1266-1343) can be seen. On the west bank of the river (reached by crossing the bridge over the Kuru-chu/Lhodrak Nub-chu below Khomting Lhakhang), there is the **Tselam Pelri**, where caves of both the Nyingma and Drigung Kagyu tradition are found. This road leads south to **Ngotong Zampa** bridge on the Bhutan border.

Kharchu Monastery མཁར་ཆུ་དགོན་པ

ⓘ *To reach Kharchu follow the path uphill from the Lhakhang Guesthouse and turn right, behind the military barracks. The trail bifurcates after 15 mins. Take the left track, and ascend to a 2nd bifurcation after 1 hr at a rock-painted image of Jambhala, god of wealth, and bear right. This will lead after a further arduous 1 hr to the summit.*

Situated two hours' walking distance above Khomting Lhakhang, on a spacious hilltop alpine meadow is **Kharchu Monastery**, the seat of Namkei Nyingpo Rinpoche of the Nyingma school. The monastery lies above a semi-nomadic camp, where the dwellings are yak wool tents covering adobe and stone walls, with picturesque flower gardens.

Built on a promontory overlooking the deep forested gorge of Chakpurchen, where Padmasambhava's supreme hermitage symbolizing buddha-mind is located, the site has long been associated with some of the greatest figures of the Nyingma and Kagyu traditions: Namkei Nyingpo, Vairocana and Yeshe Tsogyel (among Padmasambhava's 25 disciples), Shelkar Dorje Tsodron, Gotsangpa, Nyangrel Nyima Ozer, Guru Chowang, Melong Dorje and Drukchen Pema Karpo, the last two of whom founded respectively the main temple and the monastery. From the time of the Fifth Dalai Lama, the monastery has been the seat of the reincarnations of Namkei Nyingpo.

The rebuilt two-storey temple has (downstairs) an **assembly hall** containing new large images of Padmasambhava and Aksobhya Buddha, along with Marpa and Milarepa. The exquisite murals depict the lineage holders of both the Nyingma and Kagyu schools. **Upstairs**, there is a skylight offering a splendid view of the images and murals below, and the *labrang* residence containing the throne of the present Namkei Nyingpo Rinpoche, who currently resides at Bumtang in Bhutan. The complex also includes a kitchen and residential area for monks, a large stupa, a sky-burial site, and a 2-m high water-powered Mani Wheel. This monastery has one of the most idyllic settings in Tibet, and its lofty isolation can best be seen from a high point on the road to Senge township on the west bank of the Kuru-chu River (see below).

Chakpurchen Cave

Padmasambhava's supreme cave of buddha-mind is reached by a steep, forested trail below the hermitages next to the stupa at Kharchu. En route the pilgrim's circuit takes in the **Lhamo Kharchen** hermitage of Phakmodrupa, the **Khandro Dora** platform, the **Chakpurchen Cave**, and the meditation caves of Namkei Nyingpo. The three-storey hermitage of **Lhamo Kharchen**, containing rock footprints of Phakmodrupa, is reached along this trail, across the Kha-chu River by means of an old wooden bridge. Back on the near side of the bridge a trail then climbs uphill to the **Khandro Dora**, where there is an inscribed stone obelisk, and then plunges abruptly to **Chakpurchen Cave**.

The cave entrance is approached by means of a perilously unstable wooden bridge. Inside the cave is a multi-storey wooden hermitage of the Kagyu school, from the top of which there is a long dark passageway zigzagging toward the cave of buddha-mind, shaped like Padmasambhava's own body. (Tradition holds that he created this meditation cavern by tunnelling directly into the mountain, and remained there in dark retreat for seven years.) The cave contains a natural rock impression of Padmasambhava's iron dagger (*chakpur*), hence the name of the cave. Lastly, the meditation caves of Namkei Nyingpo are reached to the left of Chakpurchen.

Sekhar Gutok སྲས་མཁར་དགུ་ཐོག

ⓘ *Sekhar Gutok is located in the township of Se, 35 km northwest of Khomting Lhakhang, in the valley of the Se-chu, an east-flowing tributary of the Kuru-chu (Lhodrak Nub-chu). Access by vehicle is extremely difficult during the rainy season (Jul-Aug), when the road is susceptible to severe mud avalanches.*

This most revered site of the Kagyu school in Tibet comprises the residence of Marpa Chokyi Wangchuk (1012-1096) at Drowolung and the nine-storey tower constructed as an ascetic penance by his foremost disciple Milarepa (1040-1123; or 1052-1135).

Senge The road from Khomting Lhakhang crosses both the Tamzhol-chu and the Kuru-chu in quick succession and then climbs northeast, past a hydroelectric station and large military complex, to reach **Senge** township at the top of the ridge. The views of the Kuru-chu gorge to Bhutan in the south are fantastic from this vantage point. Nearby is the **Senge Drupuk** cave, which has associations with Padmasambhava, Yeshe Tsogyel and Milarepa. The town has guesthouse facilities, but is there basically to service the army.

The main road then descends to recross the Kuru-chu at **Sinmo Zampa** bridge. After 8 km, it divides – the east fork leading to Lhodrak Dzong and the west to Se. Take the latter. At **Gosung Nangma** a trail on the right leads off to Drubtso Pemaling (see below). The main road leads southwest to Se, passing on the left side the **Menchu hot spring** (an important health spa).

Sekhar Gutok The nine-storeyed tower of Sekhar Gutok was constructed as a great act of penance by Milarepa on behalf of Darma Dode, the son of Marpa. For adherents of the Kagyu school, and the Tibetan population as a whole, this single building and the manner of its construction encapsulate the self-sacrifice and renunciation required for success on the Buddhist spiritual path. The **tower** still stands, its distinctive gilded pagoda-style roof temporarily replaced with a simple flat roof, while the restorers await the necessary funds for its refurbishment. At least three of the nine floors contain original murals. From the ground floor upwards the nine storeys comprise: (1) the chamber of Dagmema (Marpa's wife), (2-3) empty chambers, (4) Marpa's retreat, containing some old tangkas, (5) Vajrasattva Chapel, containing an original Vajrasattva image, (6) Kagyu Chapel, containing images (L-R) of Darma Dode, Milarepa, Marpa, Gampopa and Dakmema, (7) Guru Chapel, with images of Padmakara flanked by Mandarava and Yeshe Tsogyel, (8) the Buddhas of the Three Times, and (9) Vajradhara. Fearless pilgrims can sometimes be seen crawling along a narrow ledge outside the highest storey of the tower, thereby ensuring that they will have the good karma to repay their mother's kindness in this very lifetime!

The adjacent two-storey **temple**, which once housed 100 monks, still contains some original images of the Karmapas, and precious relics such as the skull fragment of Dagmema (wife of Marpa). The impressive Gonkhang on the ground floor has original images of the protectors: Ksetrapala, Bernakchen, Six-armed Mahakala, and Shridevi, and within its inner sanctum there is a large image of Shakyamuni flanked by Milarepa and Gampopa. The principal image on the second floor is Padmasambhava in the form of Nangsi Zilnon.

Drowolung Monastery གྲོ་བོ་ལུང་དགོན་པ

The residence of Marpa Chokyi Wangchuk at Drowolung, near Sekhar Gutok, is the original Kagyu foundation in Tibet. It was here that Marpa engaged in the translation of the texts which he had brought from India, and transmitted his teachings and realizations to the four 'great pillars' who were his foremost disciples: Ngok Choku Dorje, Tsurton Wangi Dorje, Meton Tsonpo and Milarepa. The ruined **Podrang Marpa** residence once contained Marpa's reliquary, and images of Marpa and his son Darma Dode. Behind this building is the retreat centre (*drubkhang*) and to its left is the stone throne of the First Karmapa. A hillside stupa marks the way to the cave hermitage, where the grottoes of Marpa, Milarepa and Gampopa are all discernible. Simple guesthouse facilities and groceries are available.

Trekking There is also a trekking route to Sekhar Gutok from Senge township via the Khana La and Rolpa La passes.

There is another three to four hours' trek from Sekhar Gutok to the remote cave of **Taknya Lungten Puk**, where Milarepa undertook his first one-year retreat. Guides from Sekhar can show the way. Marpa's birthplace at **Zhe** lies two to three hours' walking distance north of Sekhar at the foot of Mount Tashi Denga. Trekking routes also lead south to Namgung La pass and southwest to Monla Karchung La pass, both on the Bhutanese border.

Drubtso Pemaling སྒྲུབ་མཚོ་པདྨ་གླིང

This glacial lake nestling in the shadows of the Kulha Kangri Himalayan massif (7,554 m) was consecrated by Padmasambhava as one of the main places for meditation in Tibet.

Padmasambhava's meditation cave is located on the slopes of **Mount Damchen Gara Nakpo**, overlooking the magical turquoise-coloured lake. The trail to the cave follows a precipitous track, leading firstly down to the lake-shore ruins of **Pemaling Monastery**, which was founded by Pema Lingpa (1450-1521). Here, there was once a renowned image of Vajrapani, as well as smaller images of Padmasambhava, Phakmodrupa and the First Karmapa. The cave where Padmasambhava subdued the demon Gara Nakpo through his meditative powers, lies one hour above the ruins (there is one restored building where pilgrims stay), and is surrounded by glaciers on three sides. The nearby **Lhachu** waterfall is said to be the entrance to a 'hidden land' (*beyul*) within Mount Kulha Kangri. The lake is said to emit mystical or atmospheric apparitions and sounds resembling the cries of a seal. The lake also forms part of the

 8-9-day Kulha Kangri pilgrimage circuit, which can only be undertaken by crossing into Bhutan.

Getting there There are three points of access to the lake: a relatively easy 5-6 hours' trek from Sekhar Gutok to Drubtso Pemaling, via Gosum Nangma and Chupak; a harder 7-8 hours' trek from Sekhar Gutok via Tuk and Rongpo La pass (5,050 m); and a nine-hour trek from Lhalung via Drum La pass (5,135 m). A trail southwest from Tuk on the second of these treks also leads to Langdo and the main trade route to the Bumtang district of Bhutan (via Mongla Karchung La pass).

Dowa Dzong ཌོ་བ་རྫོང་

➔ *Government buildings: the PSB, Post Office and government compound are located to the left of the road, adjacent to the square.*

The road from Sekhar Gutok to Dowa Dzong, the capital of Lhodrak county, follows the Kuru-chu upstream for 32 km (or 67 km from Khomting Lhakhang). En route it passes through **Karpo** township, where there is a small shop/restaurant next to a freight truck checkpoint. Before entering town, the valley widens and the ruined fortress of **Dowa Dzong** is visible above the road on the left. The town has an increasing number of Chinese immigrants.

There is a three-storey guesthouse with restaurant facilities. On the main street, north of the square, there are several karaoke bars and shops. The Bank of China is located to the right of the road, adjacent to the square.

Lhalung Monastery ལྷ་ལུང་དགོན་པ

This fascinating monastery is located to the west of Dowa Dzong, on the north bank of the Kuru-chu. Although it is the principal seat of the Lhodrak Sungtrul and Lhodrak Tuk-se incarnations, following in the *terma* tradition of Pema Lingpa (1450-1521), it has also had earlier associations with the Karma Kagyu school and later connections with the Gelukpa. The original foundation is attributed to Lhalung Pelgyi Dorje, the ninth-century assassin of Langdarma who hailed from this part of Southern Tibet. Later, in 1154, the First Karmapa Dusum Khyenpa developed the site into a monastery, and from the 17th century onwards the buildings were occupied by the Lhodrak incarnations of the Nyingma school, with the approval of the Fifth Dalai Lama and the Tibetan government.

The present buildings largely date from the period of the Third Lhodrak Sungtrul Tsultrim Dorje (1598-1669) and they were later expanded by the Eighth Lhodrak Sungtrul Kunzang Tenpei Nyima (1763-1817). Formerly the monastery had a grand appearance, its perimeter wall surrounded by 108 stupas and 108 willow trees (which have since been destroyed).

The Temple Beyond the entrance courtyard, the assembly hall has a Zhitro Lhakhang to its right, and to the rear a Gonkhang and the *labrang* residence of Lhodrak Tuk-se. On the hills to the northeast is a nunnery founded by Longchen Rabjampa.

The **ground floor** of the **Assembly Hall** once housed important 8-m high clay images of the Seven Generations of Past Buddhas (Sangye Rabdun), along with other images of the first seven holders of the Pema Lingpa lineage, and the Three Deities of Longevity (Tselha Namsum). These and the tangkas painted by Lhodrak Tuk-se Gyurme Dorje (b 1641) no longer exist. There is a new image of Padmasambhava against the north wall, and on the west, some damaged murals depicting his life and those of Pema Lingpa and Pawo Tsuklak Trengwa. The decorated pillars have archaic features, but the supporting beams are in need of urgent repair. In the centre of the hall are the thrones of the Lhodrak Sungtrul and Lhodrak Tuk-se incarnations, both of whom are currently in Bhutan. There is also an inner sanctum containing images of the Buddhas of the Three Times. Formerly it housed the reliquary stupa of Lhodrak Tuk-se.

The **second storey** has a central window overlooking the lower hall, surrounded by a gallery from which various chapels extend. On the south side, next to the staircase, there is an oblong room with an image of Pema Lingpa and old **frescoes** of historic importance depicting in three successive panels the lives of Nyangrel Nyima Ozer, Pema Lingpa, and Guru Chowang – the three greatest figures of the Lhodrak region. Adjacent to the door are further murals depicting the deities of the Barchad Lamsel, and above the door is Hayagriva. On the west side, the **protector shrine room** has an image made personally by Tilopa, and on the north side there are two chapels: the first houses the foremost objects of the monastery in a glass case. These include an image of Pema Lingpa, a stupa containing the heart of Lhalung Pelgyi Dorje, the vajra of Jatson Nyingpo, stone footprints of Guru Chowang aged eight and 13, and original images of Amitayus in union with his consort. The second contains the reliquary of the Tenth Lhodrak Sungtrul. On the east side, there is a chapel containing the life-supporting stone (lado) of Guru Chowang.

The **third storey** is approached by a staircase at the southwest corner. The three chapels of the south side respectively contain an image of Shridevi (protector of the Drukpa Kagyu school), the *Kangyur* Library, and a set of new tangkas (formerly images of the Sixteen Elders). On the west side there is a single chapel containing a Padmasambhava image and a talismanic stone associated with Guru Chowang's mother. On the east side the corresponding chapel has images (L-R) of Longchenpa, Vajrakila and Pema Lingpa. Finally, on the north side there are three chapels dedicated to Pema Lingpa, one of which has a stupa and another some interesting murals. An edict on the virtues of dietetics and hygiene, which the first Qing Emperor presented to the Fifth Dalai Lama, was bequeathed to the monastery during the tenure of the first Lhodrak Tuk-se, but it is not currently on display.

In the reconstructed **Zhitro Lhakhang** to the east of the assembly hall there are new images on the north wall representing Garab Dorje, Srisimha, Padmasambhava, Yeshe Tsogyel and Pema Lingpa. On the west and east walls respectively there are relief images of the Hundred Peaceful and Wrathful Deities according to the revelation of Pema Lingpa, each in their respective grottoes. Behind the assembly hall, in the **Gonkhang**, where the Eighth Lhodrak Sungtrul had a meditative vision of Padmasambhava, is a 'speaking' image of Padmasambhava in the form of Guru Saroruhavajra, with a teardrop trickling from its eyes. Upstairs is the residence named **Orgyen Zimpuk**.

Further east from the Gonkhang is the **Mani Ratna Labrang** or residence of the Lhodrak Tuk-se incarnations. It contains the throne and stone footprint of Lhodrak Tuk-se, aged seven, with a mat used only by the Karmapas, and a sealed meditation recess. There are also three talismanic stones, stone footprints of Padmasambhava and Pawo Tsuklak Trengwa, and murals depicting the Twenty-one Taras and the Thousand Buddhas. Outside in the courtyard is a stone *udumbara* lotus.

Layak Guru Lhakhang ལ་ཡག་གུ་རུ་ལྷ་ཁང་

West of Lhalung in Monda township is the temple of **Layak Dzara Guru Lhakhang**, also called **Samdrub Dewachenpo**, which was constructed in the 13th century by Guru Chowang. Formerly this temple contained a Jowo image discovered by Guru Chowang in person, along with relics and a painting of this master. The original temple, styled after the ramparts of Nalanda monastery in India, is illustrated in the Lhalung frescoes. It is not yet possible to determine whether the 1949 reconstruction bears any resemblance to the original, since the temple is firmly locked and still used as a granary. The rear annex is now a private residence. Southwest of Layak at **Negon** there is a reconstructed branch of this monastery.

From **Monda** the road climbs northwest to ascend Monda La pass (5,266 m), the watershed between the lakeland plateau to the north and the south-flowing rivers of Lhodrak. The view of **Kulha Kangri** from Monda La is unrivalled. Beyond the pass is the **Monda Kangri** (6,425 m). The distance from Monda township to Nakartse is 102 km, and to Lhasa, 256 km. South of the watershed, there is a trail leading west of Monda across the Trel La pass, leading to Khangmar county in West Tibet.

Nakartse County སྣ་དཀར་རྩེ

→ *Population: 33,694. Area: 7,660 sq km. Colour map 2, grid C3.* 浪卡子县

The county of Nakartse is a vast high altitude depression containing the two largest lakes in Southern Tibet: Phuma Yutso and Yamdrok Yutso. Along with Trigu Lake (see above, page 215), these form a natural barrier between the Brahmaputra valley to the north and the watershed passes of Lhodrak to the south. The county also acts as a major road link between Central Tibet (U), to the north of Gampa La pass, and West Tibet (Tsang), to the west of Nojin Ganzang range and Khari La pass (5,045 m). It has for centuries therefore been a vital trading link between Lhasa and Bhutan, Sikkim, Nepal and West Tibet. The county capital is located at Nakartse, 154 km from Lhasa, 118 km from Gyantse, and 102 km from Lhodrak.

Phuma Yutso Lake ཕུ་མ་གཡུ་མཚོ

From Monda La pass, the sound of Lhodrak's rushing rivers is left behind, and the road to Nakartse descends into the awesome tranquillity of the lakeland plains to the north. It skirts the east shore of Phuma Yutso (5,040 m), a superb turquoise-coloured lake with three small islands in a vast but sparsely populated high-altitude setting. Apart from seasonal nomadic groups, herds of yak and fierce mastiffs, there are only three lakeside villages: **Tu** in the east (on the main road), **Talma** in the south, and **Phuma Jangtang** in the west.

Trekking Tu, Tulma and Phuma Jangtang are linked by a trekking route that encircles the lake in 8-9 days. Locals undertake this pilgrimage circuit in the springtime, culminating at the Nyingma monastery of **Sengegon** near the northeast end of the lake. Strange mists and lights are often seen reflected on its surface. Perennial snow peaks grace the northwest horizon, the nearest being Gyetong Soksum (6,244 m) and Jangzang Lhomo (6,324 m), with **Nojin Gangzang** (7,191 m) in the far distance. There is a trekking route from the northwest corner of the lake via Chanda La pass, to Ralung monastery in Tsang (see page 266).

Beyond the Ye La pass at the northeast extremity of the lake, the road enters a slightly lower tundra plain, where the rivers drain north into Lake Yamdrok Yutso. Here, large flocks of sheep and goats can be seen grazing, and large villages dot the landscape: notably **Ling** to the east and **Zhamda** on the motor road. The impressive Drakla Gonpa overlooks the village of Zhamda from the strategic heights of an adjacent hillside. It is an active branch of Dorje Drak, with 20 resident Nyingmapa monks under the guidance of Namdrol Dongak Tendzin Dorje.

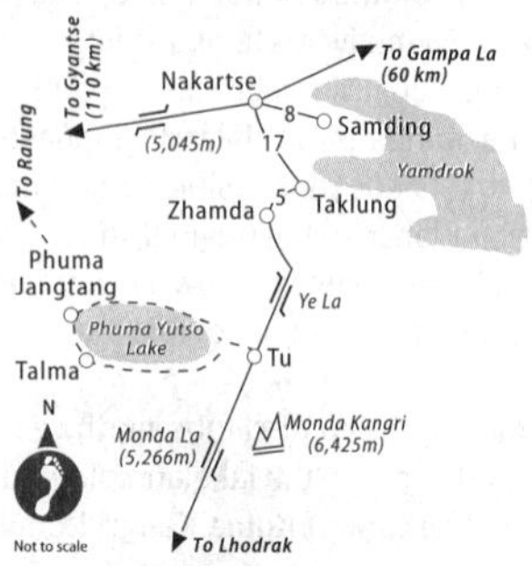

Lho Taklung ལྷོ་སྟག་ལུང

→ *Simple accommodation is available in the government guesthouse and the primary school compound.*

The township of Taklung (or Lho Taklung) lies a few kilometres north of Zhamda village, near the southeast shore of Lake Yamdrok Yutso. At

4,450 m, this is the largest market town between Gyantse and Lhodrak, and the site of an important summer trade fair, attended sometimes by Bhutanese merchants from Bumtang, as well as native Tibetans from Tsang and Southern Tibet. From here, there are trekking routes along the southern shore of Yamdrok Yutso to Docho township, and from there to Dramda township on the east shore.

Sights The town has two principal monasteries and a ruined dzong. The hilltop **Taklung Monastery**, at present unrestored, is a major branch of Dorje Drak (see above, page 150), maintaining the tradition of the Northern Treasures. Its incarnate lama, Taklung Tsetrul Rinpoche now lives in Simla and Ladakh.

The Sakyapa monastery of **Tarling Chode** lies below the hill, within the township. This is the one-time residence of Taktsang Lotsawa, a vociferous 14th-century debating opponent of Tsongkhapa. There are two main buildings separated by a courtyard. The **Assembly Hall**, which retains exquisite wall paintings dating from the 15th to 19th centuries, has a large image of Padmasambhava, backing on to a protector shrine where the main image is of Panjaranatha (Gonpo Gur). Its **inner sanctum** contains the reliquary of Taktsang Lotsawa, images of the Buddhas of the Three Times, three unusual red sandalwood mandalas in Newar style, and Hevajra murals.

The second building has a **Mani Lhakhang**, and a two-storey **Guru Lhakhang**, containing a giant image of Padmasambhava in the form of Nangsi Zilnon, surrounded by his eight manifestations in their respective grottoes. On the adjacent wall is an image of Ekajati, protectress of mantra. The upper floor, entered by a staircase behind the Mani Lhakhang offers a close-up view of Nangsi Zilnon's charismatic face.

Yamdrok Yutso Lake ཡར་འབྲོག་གཡུ་མཚོ

The sacred lake of Yamdrok Yutso (4,408 m) is revered as a talisman, supporting the life-spirit of the Tibetan nation. It is said that should its waters dry, Tibet will no longer be habitable. By far the largest lake in South Tibet (754 sq km), the pincer-shaped Yamdrok Yutso has nine islands, one of which houses a monastery and a Padmasambhava stone footprint. Within its hook-shaped western peninsula, there is another entire lake, **Dremtso** and beyond its southeast extremity yet another, named **Pagyutso**. There are good motorable dirt roads skirting the north and west shores of

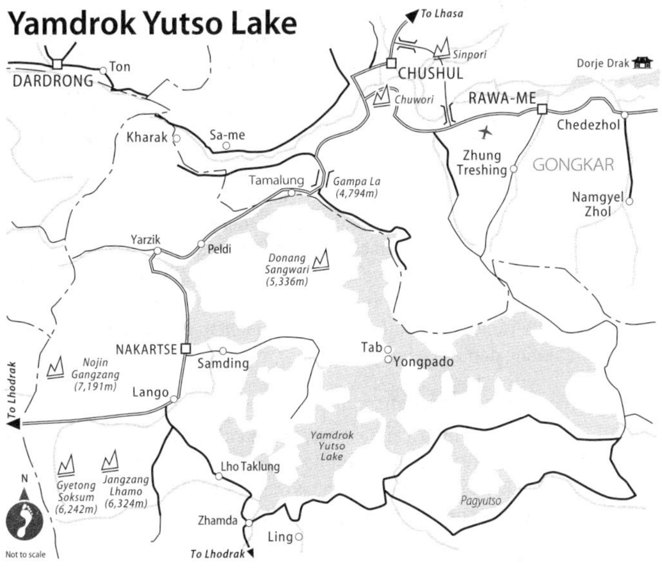

the lake, and motorable or trekking routes which complete the circuit. The Yamdrok region is traditionally famous for its salty dried meat and, more recently, for its fishing.

The main highway from Lhasa to Gyantse descends to the northern lakeshore from Gampa La pass (4,794 m) where the visitor from Lhasa or Tsetang will enjoy the unforgettable vista of its pincer-shaped expanse of turquoise water, with the mysterious **Mount Donang Sangwari** (5,340 m) on the peninsula beyond, and the snow peaks of **Nojin Gangzang** (7,191 m) in the distance. On the descent, you will pass a hydroelectric power station, which has been criticized for depleting the waters of the sacred lake, and reach the shore at **Tamalung**, from which there is a ferry crossing to the peninsula. Now, the highway runs southwest to **Peldi Dzong** and around the **Yarzik** inlet, where a trekking route leads west to **Rampa** township and Ringpung valley in Tsang (see page 264). It then continues due south as far as **Nakartse**, via Dablung, where another ferry crossing leads to the peninsula. Thereafter, it cuts away from the lake to **Lango**, and ascends towards the **Khari La** pass (5,045 m) – a defile between the formidable roadside glaciers of Nojin Gangzang (north) and Jangzang Lhomo, which also marks the border between South Tibet (Lhokha) and West Tibet (Tsang). Just before Lango, the road to Lhodrak turns off the Gyantse highway on the left, leading southeast towards Lho Taklung and Zhamda (see above).

Trekking There is a seven-day trekking circuit around the Yamdrok peninsula, beginning and ending at **Nakartse**, via Samding Monastery, Sharwa (south of Dremtso Lake), Ngardrak township (northeast of Dremtso) and Mekpa (northwest of the peninsula). En route, you can visit the sacred **Mount Donang Sangwari**, where there are Padmasambhava and Yeshe Tsogyel caves, and which offers outstanding views of the snow peaks of Southern and Central Tibet from its summit.

A second four-day trek leads eastward from the Tamalung ferry to **Dramda** on the east shore of the lake, from where there are further trekking options to Yarlung, Chongye and Trigu Lake.

A third trekking route crosses the peninsula, via the **Tamalung** ferry on the north shore as far as Tab, and then traverses the main body of the lake to the southern shore, via **Yongpado** island monastery. From here the townships of the nomadic pasture, including Ling and Docho, to the south of the lake can be reached.

Nakartse སྣ་དཀར་རྩེ

The county town of Nakartse, situated on the Lhasa-Gyantse highway, has grown in recent years on the basis of the wool trade and its status as a transit point for freight trucks and passenger buses. A wool-processing factory has been constructed here. The Chinese population influx is evident in the number of Chinese-owned shops and Sichuan-style eateries. On the ridge above the town is the rebuilt **Nakartse Monastery**, and the ruins of the old dzong, birthplace of the Fifth Dalai Lama's mother.

Mianyang Hotel, has the best rooms in town at ¥35 ber bed and triples (¥150). Post Office Guesthouse, has simple accommodation (range ¥15-25 per bed). There are a number of Sichuan restaurants, including the Tian Fu and the excellent Lhasa Tibetan Restaurant, popular with travellers, truckers, locals and Chinese alike, serving noodles, momo, rice dishes, Tibetan butter tea, and sweet Indian-style tea. On the main road, the Yamdrok Restaurant is also frequented by truckers, public bus passengers and touring parties.

Samding Monastery བསམ་སྡིང་དགོན་པ

This influential monastery, 8 km east of Nakartse, commands the isthmus between the Yamdrok Yutso Lake arm and Dremtso. Founded in the 12th century by Khetsun Zhonudrub, Samding has since the 14th century been a bastion of the Bodongpa school, derived from Bodongpa Chokle Namgyel (1306-1386). The abbess of Samding, Samding Dorje Phagmo, has long been revered as the highest female incarnation in

Tibet. In 1716 she is renowned for having transformed her nun followers into sows in order to thwart the wrath of the Dzungar armies! The present incarnation lives in Lhasa.

Zangri County ཟངས་རི

→ *Population: 15,672. Area: 2,469 sq km. Colour map 3, grid B4.*

*The county of Zangri lies downstream from Tsetang on both banks of the Brahmaputra. On the south bank it extends for some 35 km as far as Rong township, including the villages situated between the Yarlung and Eyul (Si-chu) valleys. On the north bank it extends from the village of Jang below Densatil monastery (16 km east of Ngari Tratsang) as far as Mount Ode Gungyel (6,998 m), including the valleys of Zangri, Olka and Dzingchi. The present district capital is at **Zangri**.*

Rong and Densatil Monastery གདན་ས་མཐིལ་དགོན་པ

Rong → *Colour map 3, B5*

Rong township, approximately 35 km from Tsetang, lies on the south bank of Brahmaputra. Here are the ruins of **Langkor Dzong** and the partially preserved temple of **Chagar Monastery**, which was founded by the Third Dalai Lama in 1577, with the assistance of Sonam Rabten, king of neighbouring Lhagyari. There is a fine but simple Tibetan restaurant at the crossroads in Rong, serving noodles, momo, fresh butter tea and chang.

Ins and outs

To reach Densatil, a recently constructed bridge leads traffic across to the north bank of the Brahmaputra, from a turn-off west of Rong township. (Formerly, one had to take **Lukhang Druka ferry** across to the north shore). After 1 km the road forks – west to Jang and east to Zangri. Take the former road, following the Brahmaputra upstream to **Jang**, which lies at the entrance to the concave valley of Densatil. From here there is a steep three-hour climb to the monastery. A slightly longer four-hour climb is possible from a point further upstream, approaching the monastery from the rear side of Mount Drakri Karpo, via a zigzagging track which almost reaches the summit before cutting around to enter the valley from the west side at a point higher than the monastery itself. The first route is preferable, in that it offers the shade and refreshing streams of the woodlands, whereas the latter is dry and dusty. Either of these access points can also be reached on foot from Ngari Tratsang north of Tsetang.

Unfortunately a hardline and doctrinaire attitude towards outsiders prevails in Zangri. Camping may be preferable to the unwelcoming guesthouse facilities here.

Zangri & Chusum

History

Located amid a juniper and rhododendron woodland with a sheltered amphitheatre near the summit of **Mount Drakri Karpo**, is the Kagyu monastery of Densatil (4,750 m). Founded in 1158 by Phakmodrupa Dorje Gyelpo (1110-1170), this monastery became one of the most influential in Tibet, giving rise to eight diverse branches of the Kagyu school – the Drigungpa, Taklungpa, and Drukpa foremost among them. Between 1349 and 1435 or 1478, the Phakmodrupa family ruled Tibet from their castle at Nedong, near Tsetang (see page 193), and their ancestral monastery at Densatil acquired great wealth and precious religious artefacts. The main temple, **Tsuklakhang Marpo**, once contained 18 exquisitely engraved silver-plated reliquaries containing the relics of the past lineage-holders of Densatil, and six gold pendants. Little evidence of this grandeur remains at the present day.

The site

Approaching the monastery from the west, below the meditation hermitages, the road follows the contours of the ridge to reach what remains of the complex. Adjacent to the kitchen, there is a small temple containing a copy of the *Kangyur*, and fine old images of Vajravidarana, Cakrasamvara and Vajravarahi. A ladder leads up to the next level, where to the left there is a chapel built on the site of Phakmodrupa's straw meditation hut (**Chilpei Khangpa**), and to the right a chapel containing an image of Vajravarahi and a stone footprint of Phakmodrupa. Behind these chapels are the massive red walls of the ruined **Tsuklakhang Marpo**.

Take the pilgrims' circuit around the temple, and see the large elegantly carved **Mani Wall** on the east side. From the ridge to the west of the monastery there are wonderful views of the Brahmaputra valley – both upstream towards Tsetang and downstream towards Gyatsa.

Zangri

Retracing the jeep road from Jang towards the ferry, take the left fork to **Zangri**, the county capital. This is a relatively prosperous town, with wide streets and walled orchards. The grand mansion house of the noble lords of Zangri, named **Samdrub Podrang**, still stands here. Entering town from the west, you will first pass on the left the armed police unit, the post office, a number of small shops and the county government buildings. On the opposite side are the grain and oil department, China Telecom, a bank and a textile store, after which a side road branches northwards towards the river. Continuing east along Main Street on the right you will pass the police station, the Government Guesthouse, the Tax Bureau, the PLA camp, a hospital and primary school. Opposite on the left are the law court, a basketball court, restaurants, bars, a dance hall, and the Zangri Middle School. At this point the road curves northwards towards the river, heading out of town in the direction of Zangri Kharmar.

Zangri Kharmar Temple ཟངས་རི་མཁར་དམར་ལྷ་ཁང

About 8 km east of town, on a 50-m high red rock promontory above the Zangri-Olka road, there is the reconstructed temple and cave hermitage of **Zangri Kharmar,** which was once the residence of Tibet's renowned 11th century female yogini Machik Labdron. The **Cave Hermitage of Machik**, approached via a flight of stone steps cut into the rock, overlooks the Brahmaputra. It contains 1,000 small icons depicting Machik Labdron, flanking the central images of Padmasambhava and Machik herself. Relics housed here include a "life-supporting" pillar, imbued with the vitality of 100,000 dakinis, and a slipper once worn by Machik.

On the summit of the rock there is a temple complex of later construction, with a series of stupas outside the walls. The ground floor of this **Zangri Kharmar Lhakhang** contains images of Tsongkhapa and his foremost students. The upper storey, approached through a courtyard and staircase, houses (L-R): a portrait of a recent incarnation of Machik Labdron, statues of Machik with her father, brother and son, and Karma Chak-me of Riwoche in Kham (who maintained her lineage in the 17th century), a central image of the deity Prajnaparamita, and further statues of Machik with her Indian teacher Phadampa Sangye, Tara and Karmapa Rangjung Dorje, who (in the 14th century) redacted her Chodyul cycle of practices.

Mount Ode Gungyel འོད་དེ་གུང་རྒྱལ

From Zangri, the road continues northeast, following the north bank of the Brahmaputra, as far as the power station of Olka Lokhang. Here, it leaves the river, which, from this point onwards, flows rapidly through a narrow gorge no more than 200 m wide. Mount Palungri/Draklho Kyizhung (5,730 m) slopes down to the south river bank, as does the sacred **Mount Ode Gungyel** (6,998 m) on the north bank. The latter is the abode of the mountain deity of the same name, regarded as the father of Mount Nyenchen Tanglha (see page 142), and revered by Buddhist and Bon pilgrims alike. Tibet's second mortal king, Pude Gungyel, a folk hero who discovered base metals and agriculture, was named after this protector deity. There are seven hot springs in the area, known for their curative properties, including Cholokha, which was once reserved for the use of the visiting Dalai Lama and his entourage.

Olka Takste Dzong འོལ་ཁ་སྟག་རྩེ

The township of Olka, 20 km inland from the power station, lies at the bifurcation of two valleys. It is dominated by the ruins of Olka Takste Dzong, which the Dzungar Mongolians pillaged in the 18th century. The motor road runs north following the fertile **Dzingchi** valley (4,020 m), but soon comes to an end.

Trekking A four-day trek leads via Dzingchi township, rolling grasslands, and Magon La pass (4,820 m) to **Rutok Gonpa** (on the Meldro-Gyamda road). The other track runs northeast into the more arid **Olka** valley, from which there is a four-day trek, via the Gyelung La pass (5,180 m), to Chokhorgyel and Lhamo Latso oracle lake (see below, page 232).

Dzingchi Monastery This ancient monastery was founded in the 10th century at the inception of the later diffusion of Buddhism in Tibet by Garmiton Yonten Yungdrung, a student of Lachen Gongpa Rabsel, who maintained the monastic ordination in Amdo during the interregnum following Langdarma's persecution. The renowned Maitreya of Dzingchi, which dated from the original foundation, was restored in the late 14th century by Tsongkhapa. His student, Gyeltsabje Darma Rinchen, who became the first throne-holder of Ganden and first head of the Gelukpa school, also frequented Dzingchi, and his subsequent incarnations continued to reside there. Taranatha's silver reliquary was kept in the Maitreya temple for almost 300 years until its destruction during the Cultural Revolution. The temple has not yet been renovated; a smaller Maitreya Lhakhang now stands to its rear, alongside a new assembly hall and *labrang* residence.

Dzingchi township There are no shops or guesthouses here. A ruined three-storey stone mansion, regarded as the birthplace of the Eleventh Dalai Lama, is located towards the south of the township, below the monastery.

Garpuk This Padmasambhava meditation cave is situated in the hills east of Dzingchi, but may also be reached from Samtenling in Olka. In later centuries, Gampopa and Tsongkhapa both spent time meditating in the cave, which is once again being used for formal three-year retreats.

Olka Cholung Monastery Located 1½ hours' trekking distance from Olka Taktse, Cholung (4,120 m) is the original Gelukpa hermitage, founded by Tsongkhapa in 1393 on the northern slopes of Mount Ode Gungyel. The Ozerpuk cave where he meditated with the eight disciples of Olka is located above the monastery, and contains stone footprints attributed to the master himself. An impressive reconstructed assembly hall contains images of Tsongkhapa with his eight disciples, and the protector deity Ode Gungyel. Cholung has a simple pilgrims' guesthouse, and food is available. Slightly further east at **Chuzang** (4,100 m), there is another Tsongkhapa hermitage with two reconstructed chapels. These contain stone imprints of the master's feet and hands, and an image of Amitayus, surrounded by many small terracotta tsha-tsha, which were reputedly made by Tsongkhapa.

Olka Samtenling Monastery This ruined hermitage has been associated at different times with the Kagyupa followers of Gampopa and the Gelukpa followers of Tsongkhapa.

Chusum County ཆུ་གསུམ

→ *Population: 15,657. Area: 2,332 sq km. Colour map 3, grid C6.* 曲松县

Chusum county is the modern name for the ancient principality of ***Eyul Lhagyari****, whose inhabitants have long claimed descent from King Songtsen Gampo. This broad valley is formed by the arid gorge of the Si-chu River, which rises near the Podrang La pass (5,030 m) and flows northwest to enter the Brahmaputra downstream from Rong. The county capital is located at* ***Eyul Lhagyari*** *(Chusum), 59 km from Tsetang, and 24 km from Rong, on a turn-off to the left side of the road. Notice the distinctive yellow markings on the traditional buildings of Eyul, its ruined palace, monastery and farm houses. Iron ore mining is an important industry here.*

The ascent from Chusum to Podrang La follows a gradual gradient along an unusually straight road. At **Shakjang** township (8 km from Eyul Lhagyari), there is a turn-off on the right leading to Tozik, **Eyul Chumdo Gyang** (36 km) and from there to Lhuntse county (see above, page 206). Beyond Shakjang, the valley widens to 2 km and the gorge deepens to 70 m. There are cave habitations on the eroded upper ridges; and it was here at **Zarmolung**, in a former Padmasambhava meditation cave called Khyungchen Dingwei Drak, that the Nyingmapa yogini Jomo Menmo (1248-1283) received the visionary *terma* text entitled *Gathering of All the Secrets of the Dakinis (Khandro Sangwa Kundu)*. The distance from Shakjang to the pass is 61 km; and from there to Gyatsa, a further 27 km. Slightly south of the county town, and located on a prominent hill-top ridge, **Tashi Chodzong Mansion**, the former residence of the kings of Lhagyari, is nowadays a two-storey building, preserving some original architectural features.

Gyatsa County རྒྱ་ཚ

→ *Population: 17,740. Area: 3,727 sq km. Colour map 3, grid B6.* 加查县

Gyatsa county lies at the heart of West Dakpo, a region of Southern Tibet renowned for its walnuts and apricots. On the south side of the Brahmaputra, it extends along the highway from Podrang La pass downhill through Lhasol township to the riverside at Dzam, and thence downstream via Drumpa and Lingda to Pamda (55 km). The county capital is located at ***Drumpa****, alongside the Dakpo Tratsang Monastery. A trekking route leads southeast from here, via Loklen (Darmar) township and Ke La pass, to Sangak Choling, the gateway to Tsari. On the north bank of the Brahmaputra, the county also includes the townships of Ngarab and Gyatsa, which are reached via a modern suspension bridge. A motorable track follows the Terpulung-chu valley upstream, to Chokhorgyel monastery in Metoktang (35 km). From here, it is a four-hour trek to Lhamo Latso, Tibet's celebrated oracle lake, in whose waters visions* *portending the rebirth of Dalai Lamas can be seen. From Gyatsa township, yet another route leads southeast via Lung (20 km), to Daklha Gampo monastery, on the lower reaches of the Gyabpurong-chu.*

West Dakpo

Dakpo Tratsang Monastery

Dakpo Tratsang, also known as **Dakpo Shedrubling**, was original a Karma Kargyu monastery belonging to the Zhamarpas. In 1589, the Sixth Zhamarpa Chokyi Wangchuk (1584-1635) was enthroned here. Later in the 17th century, this establishment, like many other Karma Kagyu monasteries in Tibet, was converted to the Gelukpa tradition by Mongolian force of arms. Many of the original buildings including the main temple have survived intact, and there is a recently restored debating courtyard. Accommodation and food are available here or at the guesthouse in **Drumpa**, the county town, which lies alongside the monastery.

Chokhorgyel Monastery

A 35-km drive from Gyatsa township (3,250 m) on the north bank of the Brahmaputra (across the suspension bridge east of Drumpa) passes through the valley of the Terpulung-chu. This road has recently undergone restoration. Half way up this valley, at **Tselgyu** (4,070 m), there is an attractive village of stone houses with thatched and shingled roofs. The marshland of its upper reaches, known as the **Plain of Flowers (Metoktang)**, abounds with a rich diversity of flora and vegetation: rhododendrons, poplars, willows, walnuts, apricots and medicinal herbs, including the highly valued caterpillar fungus (Cordiceps sinensis; Tib yartsa gunbu).

At **Chokhorgyel** (4,500 m), the headwaters are hemmed in by three peaks, abodes of the protector deities Zhidag (north), Shridevi (south), and Begtse (east), and three valleys diverge: the northwest route across Gyelung La pass and Loyul to Rutok (seven days via Emando, Belitang, Dzala, Beri, Shimala, Tsimarpo and Tsatsitang), or to Olka (three days trekking distance); the northeast route to Lhamo Latso Lake (four hours) and the southern route to Gyatsa.

The ruins of **Chokhorgyel Monastery** are extensive, including the large Jampa Lhakhang, the Tsuklakhang and two colleges. The foundation dates from 1509, when the Second Dalai Lama Gendun Gyatso (1476-1542) had a hermitage and meditation cave here. The Dalai Lamas subsequently constructed the Tiktse Podrang residence at the base of the northern peak, and would spend time here in the course of their visionary pilgrimages from Olka to Lhamo Latso Lake. Only a small assembly hall has recently been rebuilt to accommodate the 15 or so monks who are nowadays in residence. It contains a likeness of the Second Dalai Lama, with Maitreya in its inner sanctum and Remati alongside Vajrabhairava in the protector chapel. An obelisk outside the gates of the monastery, inscribed with the site's local history, was erected by the Thirteenth Dalai Lama during the early years of the 20th century.

Gyatsa County

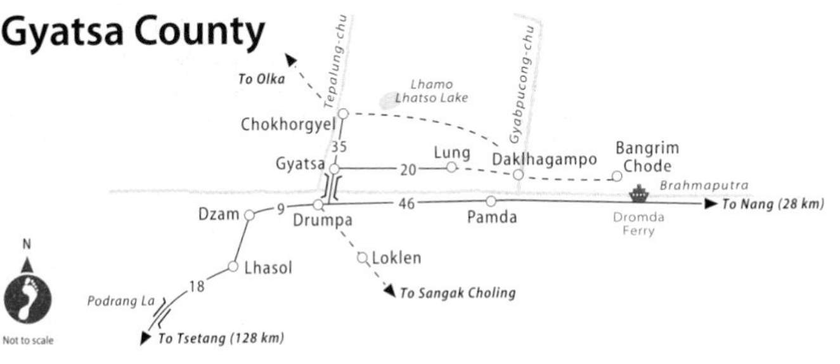

Lhamo Latso Lake ལྷ་མོ་བླ་མཚོ

To reach the oracle lake from Chokhorgyel, it is necessary to trek uphill for four hours to a ridge before descending another 2-3 hours to the lake shore; and it takes a further one hour to circumambulate the lake. Acclimatization is essential before attempting the climb. The trail initially passes below the ruins of **Nyingsaka Monastery** and, crossing a stream, turns north at the base of **Mount Lhamonying** (abode of the protector Begtse). A sharp ascent leads, often through snow-covered ground, to an amphitheatre-shaped ridge (5,300 m), and an ancient stone throne of the Dalai Lamas, dramatically overlooking the visionary lake, 150 m below.

Lhamo Latso Lake is considered sacred to Remati (Tib. Gyelmo Makzorma), a form of the protectress Shridevi, and it is revered as the life-supporting talisman (*la-ne*) of the Dalai Lamas. Visions portending the circumstances of the rebirth of future Dalai and Panchen Lamas are observed in its sacred waters. For example, in 1933, the regent Reting Rinpoche had a vision of the present Dalai Lama's birthplace and circumstances in Amdo. There is a pilgrims' circuit around the shores of the lake and at the eastern extremity prayer flags and a small shrine now rise above the ruined chapel of Remati.

Trekking A 4-5-day trekking route from the north end of the lake also leads down into the Gyabpurong-chu valley, through the villages of Ba and Che, to reach Daklha Gampo monastery.

Daklha Gampo Monastery དྭགས་ལྷ་སྒམ་པོ་དགོན་པ

The Kagyu monastery of **Daklha Gampo** lies on a ridge to the northeast of the eight-peaked Daklha Gampo mountain range, in the lower reaches of the Gyabpurong-chu valley. The distinctively contorted pinnacles of this range stand as an prominent landmark from the highway on the opposite bank of the Brahmaputra.

Getting there To reach the monastery drive east from Gyatsa township for 20 km, hugging the river road as far as **Lung**. From here, there is a six-hour trek to the monastery, via the villages of Rukhag Nyipa and Ngakhang; but the trail is hard to find without the assistance of a local guide from Lung. Alternatively, there is a two-day trek from **Bangrim Chode** monastery further east, accessible via the Dromda ferry on the Brahmaputra.

The complex was founded in 1121 by Gampopa Dakpo Lharje (1079-1153), on a site previously sanctified as a geomantic power place ('head of the ogress') by King Songtsen Gampo and transformed into a repository of *terma* by Padmasambhava. Gampopa came to meditate at the nearby **Namkading** after receiving the teachings and transmissions of the Kagyu lineage from Milarepa. He established three early chapels, **Jakhyil**, **Gomde Zimkhang** and **Chokhang Nyingma**; and gave instructions to his foremost students, who became the fountainheads of their great Kagyu lineages, Phakmodrupa Dorje Gyelpo, the First Karmapa Dusum Khyenpa and Seltong Shogom. They acquired their realizations in the many meditation caverns dotted across the range. Daklha Gampo is therefore revered as the primary Kagyu monastery for the teaching and practice of Mahamudra in Tibet, and it was carefully developed by the successive generations of Gampopa's familial lineage, such as Gampo Tsultrim Nyingpo, and those of his incarnation lineage, such as Gampopa Tashi Namgyel (1512-1587). In 1718 the Dzungar armies sacked the monastery, but it was soon rebuilt and its national influence restored. A few chapels have been renovated following the more recent depredations of the 1960s, including original images of Avalokiteshvara and Cakrasamvara.

This region of Dakpo is also the birthplace of Karma Lingpa – one of Tibet's greatest treasure-finders (*terton*). During the 14th century he unearthed, at Mount Gampodar within the Daklha Gampo range, the *terma* of Padmasambhava, which has received most worldwide acclaim: *The Tibetan Book of the Dead (Bardo Thodol Chenmo)*, a part of the cycle known as *Zhitro Gongpa Rangdrol.*

Nang County ནང་རྫོང

→ *Population: 14,425. Area: 6,477 sq km. Colour map 2, grid B5.* 朗县

Nang county is the name given to the present administrative division of East Dakpo, the principal gateway to the sacred mountain of Tsari, and the region through which the Brahmaputra River cuts its way through an unnavigable 33 km horseshoe-shaped gorge as it flows towards Longpo and Kongpo. The county extends along the main Tsetang-Menling highway for 79 km, from Dromda Druka ferry in the west (46 km from Gyatsa), as far as Zhu in the east. Both banks of the river are characterized here by windswept sandbanks interspersed by small oases of walnut and apricot. The county capital is located at ***Lang*** *(Nang Dzong) where the gorge begins, 28 km east of Dromda. The north-flowing Kurab-chu, Lapu-chu and Kyemtong-chu tributaries all offer trekking access to Tsari region in the south. By contrast, on the north bank of the Brahmaputra, the only major valley is Arnaktang.*

Kurab-chu Valley

On the south bank of the Brahmaputra, beginning from **Dromda Druka**, there is a trekking route to Sangak Choling, the southwest gateway to Tsari. The route follows the Kurab-chu tributary upstream via **Ganden Rabten** (7 km), Kurab Namgyel (5 km), and Sinmonang, before bifurcating. Take the east track, crossing the watershed passes of Gongmo La pass (5,298 m) and Kharpo La (5,001 m). **Ganden Rabten Monastery** is a branch of Ganden Phuntsoling near Lhasa. At **Kurab Namgyel** you can see the hilltop ruins of the dzong from which the whole Tsari was once administered.

Trungkhang

Back on the highway, at **Trungkhang Druka** (5 km east of Dromda), there is a ferry crossing to **Lhenga** on the north bank of the Brahmaputra. The birthplace of the Thirteenth Dalai Lama (1876-1933) lies 4 km east of Lhenga at **Trungkhang**. The former residence of Tibet's previous spiritual and temporal leader is sealed at present.

Lang → *Colour map 2, grid B5*

The small county town of **Lang** (Nang Dzong) is a riverside settlement, which has grown up along the Brahmaputra's sharp bend. Guesthouse and simple restaurant facilities are available.

From here, there are three routes: the riverside highway to Nye and Dungkar (33 km), the short cut to Nye via Kongpo Nga La pass (4,400 m); and the inland route, following the Lapu-chu valley upstream to **Latok** township (18 km).

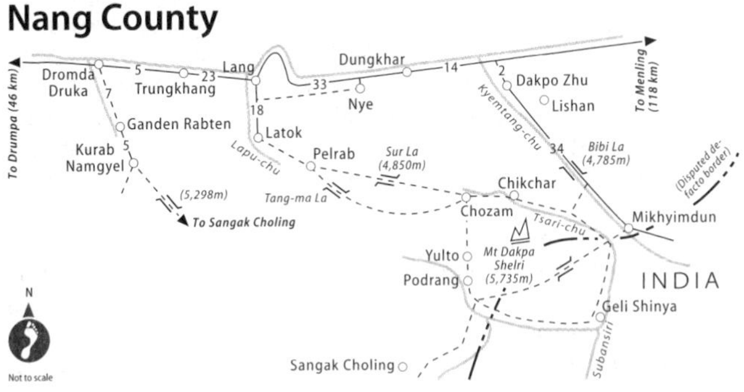

Taking the last of these routes, there is a scenic two-day trek to **Chozam**, the main gateway to Tsari. En route, you pass through the small logging villages of Bara and Pelrab, after which the trail bifurcates: the east track leading alongside the beautiful forested alpine lake of **Tso Bunang** and across Sur La pass (4,850 m) to Chozam; and the west track crossing the Tangma La pass to **Chorten Namu** and then to Chozam.

Dungkar

Both the riverside highway and the Kongpo Nga La short cut lead from Lang to Nye village and Dungkar township. A ferry leads across to **Dungkar monastery**, the seat of Tibet's celebrated contemporary historian, the late Dungkar Lobzang Trinle.

Dakpo Zhu

Some 14 km east of Dungkar, there is a turn-off, which leaves the highway at the entrance of the Kyemtong-chu valley. Following this road for a further 2 km, you will arrive at **Dakpo Zhu**, a one-time haunt of the Nyingmapa yogin Dzeng Dharmabodhi (1052-1136).

Kyemtong-chu Valley → *Colour map 2, grid B5*

The main motorable pilgrimage route to Tsari follows the Kyemtong-chu valley upstream, and across the Bibi La pass (4,785 m) to Chozam and **Mikhyimdun**. North of Kyemdrong township on the east bank of the Kyemtong-chu, at **Lishan**, there is a large recently discovered archaeological site (815,000 sq km), including 184 tombs which have been dated to 700 CE. Above Kyemdrong township, there are trails leading up the valley through Shelrika towards Mount Dakpa Shelri. However, the road to Tsari, motorable for 34 km, cuts southwest to leave the valley. It passes through a deep shrub-filled gorge to level out at an alpine riverside meadow near **Sumbatse**, and then ascends through conifer and rhododendron forest to cross the Bibi La. Lush meadows give way to stunning forests on the descent into **Mikhyimdun** (Tsari township).

Tsari ཙ་རི

Mount Dakpa Shelri (5,735 m) and its environs in Tsari form one of Tibet's most revered pilgrimage circuits – generally ranking alongside those of Mount Kailiash and Mount Amnye Machen. For the Kagyu school in particular, Tsari is classed along with Mount Kailash and Lapchi Gang as one of the three essential power places of the meditational deity Cakrasamvara. Two of Cakrasamvara's 24 power-places mentioned in the *Root Tantra of Cakrasamvara* are said to be in Tsari, Caritra and Devikota.

This holy place of Mount Dakpa Shelri is described as having four gateways, associated with the four bodhisattvas: Manjushri (east), Vajrapani (south), Tara (west) and Avalokiteshvara (north). During the earliest phase of Buddhist propagation in Tibet, Padmasambhava and Vimalamitra (8th-9th century) are said to have entered through the southern gate, and made Tsari a repository of *terma*. Kambalapada and Bhusuku (10th-11th century) entered via the eastern gate. Tsangpa Gya-re Yeshe Dorje (1161-1211) entered through the western gate at the third attempt; and lastly Sonam Gyeltsen of Ralung entered via the northern gate. The four gateways may be identified respectively with Geli Shinya (south), Mikhyimdun (east), Sangak Choling/Podrang Yutso (west), and Chikchar (north).

The main impetus for the opening of the Tsari region as a sanctuary for meditation and focal point of pilgrimage came from Phakmodrupa Dorje Gyelpo (1110-1170), who on the advice of Gampopa, encouraged his students to go there. The major sites have therefore come to be associated with Tsangpa Gya-re and his Drukpa

Kagyu followers, and to a lesser extent with the Drigung and Karma Kagyu schools. As explained in the *Guidebook to Tsari*, by the Eighth Drukchen Chokyi Nangwa (1768-1822), there are three distinct focal points in Tsari: **Mount Dakpa Shelri**, **Lake Tsokar**, and **Mount Tsari Sarma Tashijong**, which are likened to the parts of a symbolic vajra: the western prong, the central knob, and the eastern prong. Among these, the first two come within the **Old Tsari (Tsari Nyingma)** pilgrimage route, and the last within the **New Tsari (Tsari Sarpa)** pilgrimage route.

Tsari Nyingma

Chikchar Located on a beautifully forested mountain ridge above Chozam, **Chikchar** marks the beginning of all the pilgrimage circuits around Mount Dakpa Shelri. The blue and yellow mountain poppies (Meconopsis) which are well known throughout the higher elevations of East Tibet here. And it was here, near the sacred snow peak, that in the 12th century Tsangpa Gya-re had a vision of the Cakrasamvara entourage and consecrated the area. In the 13th century, after the arrival of Sonam Gyeltsen of Ralung and many hermits who left the neighbouring districts of Dakpo and Kongpo to avoid an epidemic, Drukpa Kagyu monasteries were founded within the Chikchar valley at Densa Pangmo, Uripangmo, and Gopangmo. The most important building, however, was the **Dorje Phakmo Lhakhang**, founded between 1567-1574 by Drukchen Pema Karpo (1527-1592) at Bodo or Bokhung Zhungdo, where Tsangpa Gya-re had previously had a vision of the deity Simhavaktra becoming absorbed into the rocks. Northwest of Chikchar, at **Dotsen Tsuklakhang**, there were stones representing the sexual organs of Cakrasamvara and his consort Vajravarahi, which became a focal point of pilgrimage for childless couples. Formerly, no pilgrims were allowed to ride their horses beyond Chikchar, but a jeep road now extends down the Tsari-chu valley towards **Lo Mikhyimdun** (Tsari township) on the present Indian frontier.

Lo Mikhyimdun and Lake Tsari Tsokar Pilgrims following the longest pilgrimage in former times would trek to **Lo Mikhyimdun**, and from there continue downstream to the Subansiri confluence. Below **Chikchar**, the Tsari-chu enters a narrow gorge, and around **Poso Sumdo** the landscape abounds in rhododendrons, hemlock and juniper. (A trail from here leads across Bibi La pass to Kyemtong, see above, page 234.) The border township of **Lo Mikhyimdun** is now the site of an army garrison; and the local population is more than half tribal Lhopa. Cultivated fields of barley and potatoes are found beyond this point. From here, there is an essential two-day trek to the sacred lake of Tsari Tsokar, further east.

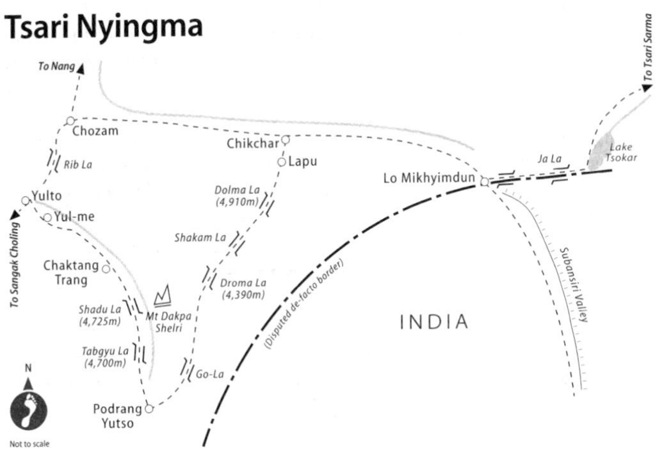

Tsari Nyingma Pilgrimage

The Tsari Nyingma pilgrimage around Mount Dakpa Shelri has three distinct routes. The longest and most arduous, known as Tsari Rongkor, took 10-15 days. It became an official pilgrimage at the behest of the Tibetan Government, and was held once every 12 years in a monkey year to commemorate the date of Tsangpa Gya-re's original opening of Tsari. Sometimes 100,000 people would participate. The shorter routes would be followed between April and September of any year. The Thirteenth Dalai Lama undertook the Tsari pilgrimage in person. Unfortunately, the route passed through Lhopa tribal territory in the south, and the government was often obliged to send an armed escort, notwithstanding oaths of fealty sworn by the natives. The route follows the Tsari-chu downstream from Chozam and Chikchar, via Mikhyimdun and on to its confluence with the Subansiri (*Tib Shipasha*) at Geli Shinya. It then follows this river upstream to its confluence with the Yulme-chu, before cutting northwest through the Yul-me valley to Yulto and Chozam. On the map the route therefore follows a diamond shape. At the present day it is impossible to complete the whole circuit since its southern tropical sections lie within the Indian territory of Arunachal Pradesh across a disputed frontier. The major sacred sites, which are all in the north, can still be visited, however, taking the lesser pilgrimage circuit via the Dolma La pass.

Tsari Tsokar is a stunningly beautiful milky lake, surrounded by glaciers and forested shorelines. It was opened for meditation and pilgrimage by the Third and Fourth Karmapa Rangjung Dorjes (1284-1339 and 1340-1383), and the slopes around its shores harbour meditation grottoes such as the **Khyungtsang Puk**.

The Inner Pilgrimage Circuit (Kyilkhor) This seven-day trek, which is still followed at the present day, is best undertaken between July-September. In spring and autumn, the passes may be closed by snow. The route ascends the Chikchar valley to **Lapu**, location of Kambalapada's Lawapuk cave and the abode of the protectress Dorje Yudronma. Higher up there is the hermitage of the Fifth Drukchen Paksam Wangpo (1593-1641). It then crosses the **Dolma La** pass (4,910 m) to the talismanic lake of Cakrasamvara, the **Demchok Latso** and the **Miphak Gonpo** ravine. No female pilgrims were traditionally allowed to venture beyond the pass. Ascending the glacial Shakam La pass (4,910 m), skirting en route a lake sacred to Avalokiteshvara, the trail then continues southwest, to Droma La (4,390 m) and Go La passes, before reaching **Podrang**, high above the east bank of the Yulme-chu River. Here is the most sacred of Tsari's many lakes, the **Podrang Yutso**, revered as the talismanic lake of Vajravarahi, where Tsangpa Gya-re and Gotsangpa both meditated. The latter's hermitage is above the lake, at **Namkapuk**, on the slopes of Mount Khandro Doi Lhakhang.

From Podrang the route turns sharply north, following the Yulme-chu upstream. It crosses Tabgyu La pass (4,700 m) to enter the **Taktsang** ravine (4,025 m), and the Shadu La pass (4,725 m). Just beyond, at **Kaladungtso Lake**, there is the hermitage of the yogin Dungtso Repa.

The trail then descends into the **Domtsang** ravine, from which point women may again participate in the pilgrimage, and passing through **Chaktang Trang**, it reaches in succession the villages of **Yul-me** (3,500 m) and **Yulto** (4,025 m). This is the stronghold of the Drigung Kagyu school at Tsari, and there is a temple dedicated to Vajravarahi.

From Yulto, there is a trek southwest across the Takar La (5,090 m) and the Kyu valley to Sangak Choling (see above, page 207). The main trail, however, turns northeast to reach the **Chozam** plain, via either the Dorje Drak La or Rib La pass.

Chozam, a village of shingled stone houses, marks the end of the Tsari pilgrimage, and there are access points from here to the main highway in Dakpo, Kurab Namgyel, Lang, and Zhu. The lush plains of **Senguti**, which extend for some 10 km below Chozam and alongside the meandering headwaters of the Tsari-chu, abound in silver firs, primulas, rhododendrons, honeysuckle, and other plants.

Tsari Sarma

Tsari Sarma is the name given to the sacred wildlife sanctuary around the headwaters of the Nelung Phu-chu, which flows northeast to join the Brahmaputra in Menling county. There are three points of access: a six-day trek from Kyemtong via the Lang La pass (4,815 m), Nepar village, and the upper reaches of the Nelung Phu-chu; a four-day trek from Nelung township on the highway in Menling county; or a shorter trek from Lake Tsari Tsokar (see above) via the Langtsang La pass and Langong.

The sanctuary of **Tsari Sarma** was founded by Rigdzin Kumaradza (1266-1343), a lineage-holder of the Nyingmapa school and the principal teacher of Longchen Rabjampa. Until recent times, the prohibition on hunting in this region was strictly enforced, and there was an abundance of wildlife: pheasants, deer, wild sheep, musk deer, wolves and foxes. The three-day pilgrimage around Tsari Sarma starts from **Tashijong** village, passing the sacred lakes of **Yutso Sarma** and **Tsonyam Sarma**, abode of secret dakinis. To the south, the Lo La pass leads across the Assamese Himalayas (Pachakshiri) into the Indian state of Arunachal Pradesh. The border remains firmly closed to outsiders.

Menling County སྨན་གླིང

→ *Population: 17,106. Area: 8,718 sq km. Colour map 2, grid B5.* 米林县

*Menling county is the name currently given to the old districts of **Longpo** and **Lower Kongpo**, south of the Brahmaputra. It extends for 195 km, from a small estuary 13 km east of Dakpo Zhu, as far as Pe township in Lower Kongpo, where the Brahmaputra is channelled through a mighty gorge between Mounts Namchak Barwa and Gyala Pelri at the eastern extremity of the Himalayas. At this point, the river changes its eastern course completely, first to the north and then abruptly to the southwest. The county capital is located at **Dungdor**; now encorporated within Nyangtri (rather than Lhokha) prefecture. From here Tsetang lies 368 km due west, and Lhasa 550 km (via Bayi and Gyamda). The successive lateral valleys extending south from the Brahmaputra towards the Indian border are home to the tribal Monpa and Lhopa populations.*

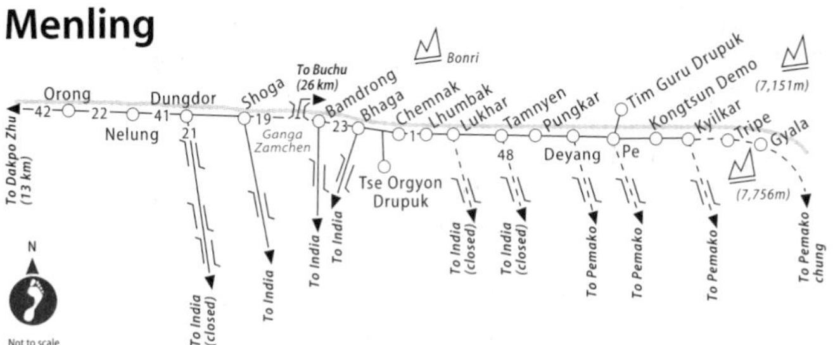

Orong and Nelung → *Colour map 2, grid C2*

The highway from East Dakpo enters Longpo 13 km east of Dakpo Zhu and after 42 km reaches Orong township in Orong valley. There are a number of sites in Longpo connected with the Nyingmapa *terton* Sangye Lingpa of Kongpo (1340-1396), who, throughout his life, also maintained close connections with the Karma Kagyu tradition. At **Jagoshong**, he discovered *terma* concerning Mahakarunika and the Extraction of Elixirs (*chulen*). In the Orong area, at **Orsho Lungdrom**, he unearthed a precious gemstone called 'tiger-meat god'; and in the **Nelung** township area, 22 km further east, the site at Drongsar where he first encountered the Fourth Karmapa Rolpei Dorje is still revered. You can trek from Nelung to Tsari Sarma (see above).

Tashi Rabden

On the north bank of the Brahmaputra, the main place of interest is the Tashi Rabden Monastery, in the Tashi Rabden Phu-chu valley, which once housed 130 monks. There are also further treasure-sites associated with Sangye Lingpa – at **Longpo Kada Trang** and **Longpo Jangde Bumpa**. On the south bank, opposite the confluence of the Tashi Rabden-chu, is the Yulsum Phu-chu valley, which once marked the western extremity of Kongpo.

Dungdor (Menling Dzong)

Dungdor, the county capital, is located 41 km downstream from Nelung. The climate is warm and humid; and the countryside quite thickly forested with conifers and junipers.

Here, there is a government guesthouse, pleasantly constructed of wood, and hot water for washing is available in an outhouse. Sichuan restaurants, Chinese shops, Tibetan market stalls and karaoke bars provide some fascination for the Lhopa tribal visitors.

Inland from Dungdor, there is a military road following the Neyul Phu-chu upstream for 21 km to **Lago Zampa bridge**, and thence to the Neyul Dom La and Dungkar La passes, which lead across the closed border into India.

Further east, at **Shoga**, there is a stone footprint of Padmasambhava and a ruined stupa, which once rotated at the sound of the Vajra Guru mantra. From here, another trail follows the Shoga Phu-chu upstream to Shoga La pass and the Indian border; and at Gangka, 19 km east of Dungdor, the large **Gangka Zamchen** suspension bridge carries traffic over to the north bank of the Brahmaputra. This bridge is also rumoured to have a military underpass, ensuring that access to the frontier cannot be cut off.

Lower Kongpo

If you cross the Gangka Zamchen bridge to the north bank, you will reach the area of Middle Kongpo and Upper Kongpo (see below, pages 243-251). Continuing, instead, on the south bank, where the road rapidly deteriorates, you will bypass the lateral valleys of **Bamdrong** and **Bhaga**, which respectively lead a short distance to Lado La and Bhaga La passes on the Indian border. The latter route has an important military installation, and an extremely well-lit and well-maintained military road.

Tse Orgyen Drupuk

ⓘ *After the military installations of Bhaga and before reaching the township of Chemnak (Chabnak), there is a turn-off on the right, which leads southwest and close to the Indian border.*

Driving along the south bank from Gangka Zamchen bridge, notice on the opposite bank, the large estuary of the Nyang-chu, which flows into the Brahmaputra from the north, alongside the town of Nyangtri, and in the shadows of the sacred mountain, Kongpo Bonri. In the hills high above Chemnak, is the meditation cave of **Tse Orgyen Drupuk**.

At this site in the eighth century, Padmasambhava gave a longevity-empowerment to an old woman who was the only one able to reach the cave and receive the empowerment. The juniper tree next to the cave is said to have sprung from his *khatvanga*. Inside the cave is a 'self-arising' Padmasambhava image in stone and a nectar-producing rock. Older people from Chemnak claim to have seen nectar coming out of the rock. On the altar lies a new brass image of Padmasambhava.

On the ascent to the cave there are several decaying stupas and a sacred stone reputedly shaped like a dying person on all fours prostrating before a lama, with two vultures in attendance, one on either side. Once there was also a temple dedicated to Amitayus, named **Lungtok Chime Lhakhang**, where a stupa made of blood from Padmasambhava's nose (**Shangtrak Chorten**) was preserved.

Chemnak (Chabnak) Monastery

ⓘ *Chemnak township lies 23 km east of the Gangka Zamchen bridge. It is also possible to reach it by coracle from Karma (Tsela Dzong) on the northern bank of the Brahmaputra below Drime Kunden.*

The Gelukpa monastery of Chemnak, also called **Demo Chemnak**, is an imposing building with a shingle roof, situated on a wooded ridge above the road. The temple was restored in 1983. An antechamber has fine murals depicting the Four Guardian Kings and the protectors: Six-armed Mahakala, Bhairava, Dharmaraja and Shukden. Within the main **assembly hall**, there are 21 tangkas and a series of murals depicting the Thirty-five Buddhas of Confession. The main images, behind the throne, are of Maitreya, flanked by a 'speaking' image also of Maitreya, and Tsongkhapa with his foremost students, and two forms of Avalokiteshvara. Along the left wall are images of Padmasambhava with Shantaraksita and King Trisong Detsen; while the right wall has a very large image of Padmasambhava in the form of Nangsi Zilnon. The **inner sanctum** contains 1,000 small images of Tsongkhapa. The imagery reflects the eclectic nature of the community at Chemnak, who include followers of the late Dudjom Rinpoche, head of the Nyingma school, among their numbers.

Chemnak to Pe

About 1 km east of Chemnak, there is a coracle ferry at **Lhumbak** village; and further east, at **Luzhar**, a dirt track leads down to a cable ferry across the Brahmaputra. Both of these crossings offer access to important sites on the north bank, such as Mount Bonri, Demo Chemkar monastery, Menri, Chu Jowo, and Nyangtri (see below, page 242). Inland from the ferry crossing on the south bank, a trail follows the Luzhar phu-chu upstream to Luzhar La pass and the Indian border.

After Luzhar, the road passes through **Tamnyen** township, where glacial streams burst forth from Tamnyen La pass on the Indian border to play havoc with the motorable surface. At **Pungkar**, there is a small general store, and rudimentary guesthouse facilities. Then, approaching **Deyang**, where flash seasonal flooding again is a serious hazard, there is a trail leading up to Deyang La on the border. Finally, at **Pe** township, 48 km from Chemnak, there is a Chinese compound, with medical facilities, a small guesthouse and some supplies. Better to camp near the Tibetan village of Pe, where there are excellent campsites, offering wonderful majestic views of **Mount Namchak Barwa** (7,756 m), until 1992 the world's highest unclimbed peak. Here, the Brahmaputra narrows to only 100 m; and there are ferry boats crossing to Timpei on the north bank.

Black flayed hide and mosquitoes

Padmasambhava encountered Yamsha Nakpo (Black Flayed Hide) at Chaktak Bumpu. According to the Guru's biography, when the demon blocked his passage by placing one foot firmly on Mount Dozhong La and the other on Mount Gyela Pelri, the Guru clapped his hands in astonishment, making the sound "Chaktak Bumbu". He promptly turned into a fish which swam upstream and then turned into a bird. Yamsha Nakpo turned into a bird of prey and went in swift pursuit, but the Guru evaded capture by vanishing into the cave-wall (hence the name of the cave). The demon could not follow. Padmasambhava remained in meditation in the cave for three years, three months and three days until he could manifest signs of spiritual accomplishment. He then pierced the cave-wall with his ritual dagger, stabbing the demon in the process. The stab-mark can still be seen above the altar.

Local informants further explain that Padmasambhava also tamed the wild beasts of Tim Guru Drupuk, including many of the birds which attacked men, and instead permitted the relatively minor irritation of midges and mosquitoes which still thrive here!

Tim Guru Drupuk

Above the village of **Timpei** in Yulsum district on the north bank of the Brahmaputra and dominated to the southeast by Mount Namchak Barwa are the celebrated caves where Padmasambhava and his students practised meditation in the eighth century. If you look across the river outside the main cave, you will see a group of prayer-flags marking the site called **Chaktak Bumbu**. This is where Padmasambhava reputedly encountered the demon Yamsha Nakpo (Black Flayed Hide).

The cave hermitage of **Tim Guru Drubpuk**, rebuilt under the guidance of Nakpo Zilnon Rinpoche of Buchu in Kongpo, is approached via a steep flight of steps. An **ante-chamber** contains a verandah and three large prayer wheels. Inside the temple, which is cared for by the old Khampa ladies of Timpei village, the **chapel** has a single column supported by a Tibetan-style capital (*zhu*). The window on the right offers incredible views of Mount Nakchak Barwa. Tangkas, including two of the Peaceful and Wrathful Deities, adorn the walls, and on the left there is the entrance to the **cave** – an inner recess, containing three images of Padmasambhava, concealed images of Mandarava and Yeshe Tsogyel, and in the centre of the floor an as yet unopened *terma* repository. The aperture in the cave wall forming the shape of a ritual dagger is above the *terma* rock.

As well as Padmasambhava, several of his most important students are said to have occupied other caves higher up the hillside. There are eight caves altogether, those of Padmasambhava, Namkei Nyingpo, Yeshe Tsogyel, Tamdrin Tulku, Chung Tulku, Vairotsana, Guru Drakpo and Senge Dongma, while the last is called Tsalung Jangsa (the place where yogic exercises were practised).

From Tim Guru Drubpuk, there is a three-day trekking route via Sekundo and Nyima La pass to **Dongpatral** near Lunang on the Kongpo to Po-me highway. There are abundant different species of flowers along this route.

Kongtsun Demo

On the south bank of the Brahmaputra, the motorable road continues beyond Pe for a few kilometres as far as **Kyilkar**, passing beyond the approach to Dozhong La pass (4,115 m) and towards Mount Namchak Barwa. This is the district called **Yulsum Trenadong** ('defile where three regions of Puwo, Kongpo and Pemako converge'). It marks the beginning of the Brahmaputra rapids. Here, Padmasambhava is said to have subdued one of the 12 subterranean goddesses (Tenma Chunyi) of Tibet, and nearby there is a cave known as **Trekar Drupuk** where Padmasambhava stayed in meditation.

The name Kongtsun Demo has also been identified as the secret name for the deity Dorje Pokham Kyong. According to various descriptions she is either black or cherry-brown in colour with gold and turquoise head ornaments, and holds a vessel of blood or a divination arrow and chest. She rides a garuda, or a horse with a turquoise mane.

The site at the present time shows few signs of repair. There is a small pilgrims' resthouse consisting of a single room, beside which a large prayer flag has been erected.

Mount Namchak Barwa

The Pepung La pass above Pungkar, the Dozhong La pass (4,115 m) above Pe township, and the Nam La pass (5,225 m) above Kyilkar all give access to the hidden valley of **Pemako** in Metok county (see below, page 433).

The motorable road on the south bank of the Brahmaputra comes to an end at Kyilkar, but a three-day trekking route continues on to **Gyala**, via Tripe, which is the base camp for **Mount Namchak Barwa** (7,756 m), and Lungpe. The **Nambulung** valley before Tripe also leads to Mount Namchak Barwa, and it is revered as an abode of the epic hero Ling Gesar. This mountain is the highest peak of the East Himalayas; and it has a towering snow pinnacle shaped like a ritual dagger (*phurba*), for which reason it is known as 'blazing meteorite' (*namchak barwa*) the best ritual daggers are made of meteorite! Sanctified as a repository of *terma* – some of which were discovered by Sangye Lingpa (1340-1396) and others by Dudul Dorje (1615-1672), the mountain remained unclimbed until a Japanese expedition, astonishingly, scaled its slender snow pinnacle in 1992.

Gyala Shinje Badong

Gyala village is situated on a plain above the river which entails a tough climb up the Tsalung cliff-face. The white sands of the river bank below Gyala offer an attractive camp site. Here the river is navigable, and on the far bank, at **Gyala Shinje Badong**, there is the **Dampa Chokhang** temple, dedicated to Yama Dharmaraja, the 'lord of death' (Tib Shinje Chogyel), which contains an image of Padmasambhava. Alongside the derelict temple there are five rocks shaped like banners with water streaming down between them. Behind the waterfalls, a rock image of Yama in either black or white form is visible during the spring and autumn when the river level is at its lowest. Here, the *terton* Sangye Lingpa discovered his Yamantaka texts, entitled *Yamantaka Lord of Life (Shinje Tsedak)*.

The cave and its adjacent temple can be reached by dug-out log boat. From the north bank, at **Pe Nub** village, the two-day Bonpo pilgrimage circuit of Mount Gyala Pelri (7,151 m) begins.

The Brahmaputra Gorges

During the winter when the Brahmaputra is at its lowest level it is possible to undertake the extremely difficult five-day trek to **Pemakochung**, following the course of the surging rapids through one of the world's deepest gorges, formed by the Namchak Barwa and Gyala Pelri massifs, which are only 21 km apart. Within a contorted stretch of 45 km, the river plunges 3,000 m to the Pemako foothills and the Indian plains beyond.

The trail passes the hot springs of Kenda-chu, the Gotsangpa Drupuk, the Nyuksang cliff, and the Senge Dzong cliff. Before Pemakochung, the trail hugs the river bank (winter access only), and passes the **Kinthup Falls**. At Pemakochung itself, there is a small Nyingmapa monastery. Two days further trekking downstream is the

Drakpuk Kawasum Cave, repository of the key and gateway to the 'hidden valley' of Pemako. Beyond this point, the virtually impenetrable trail follows the river's course as it is propelled north via a series of mighty cascades, including the **Rainbow Falls**, discovered by Kingdon-Ward in 1924. On 8 November 1998, Ian Baker led an expedition sponsored by the National Geographic Society through the gorge, which established that the Rainbow Falls plunged 25 m and that further on through a virtually impenetrable 8-km stretch of twisting gorge there is another 30-35-m waterfall which they named the Hidden Falls. Here the Brahmaputra torrent narrows to only 20 m. The gorge contains subtropical flora, pine, spruce, hemlock, rhododendron, craggy fir and species of fauna such as the takin, which are also found in neighbouring Bhutan. The region is sparsely inhabited by Lhopa people. Crossing Sordem La and Karma La passes (2,560 m), the trail eventually reaches **Tongdem**, where the river converges with the Parlung Tsangpo (also called Po Tsangpo) in Po-me county (see below, page 430). **NB** The Hidden Falls can also be reached on a six-day trek from Po-me county, following the Rong-chu to its confluence with the Parlung Tsangpo. This trail starts at Pelung, and passes through Yuman, Tsachu, Sekundo, Payul and Tsodi.

Nyangtri County ཉང་ཁྲི

→ *Population: 31,901. Area: 9,634. Colour map 2, grid B6. From Lhasa to Bayi via Gyamda the distance is 476 km; from Bayi to Nyangtri 19 km; and from Bayi to Po-me 226 km.* 林芝县

Kongpo is the name given to the Nyang-chu River valley and the area of the Brahmaputra into which it flows, extending from the high Mamzhong La pass (5,000 m) west of Gyamda to Menling in the southwest and the massive snow peaks of Namchak Barwa and Gyala Pelri in the southeast. It may for practical purposes be divided into three areas: ***Lower Kongpo*** *includes the sites on the south bank of the Brahmaputra, from Menling to Pemakochung, which have already been described.* ***Middle Kongpo*** *includes the sites on the north bank of the Brahmaputra and the Nyang-chu River and its estuary below Bepa; and* ***Upper Kongpo*** *includes the upper reaches of the Nyang-chu from Bepa to Mamzhong La and Kongpo Bar La passes. Middle Kongpo corresponds to present day Nyangtri county, and Upper Kongpo to Gyamda county.* ▸▸ *For Sleeping, Eating and other listings, see page 249-250.*

History

The capital of Nyangtri county (nowadays mispronounced Nyingtri and mis-spelt Nyingchi) is located at the burgeoning city of **Bayi**, 19 km north of the Nyang-chu's confluence with the Brahmaputra. As its name suggests, Bayi (1 August, ie Chinese Army Day) was originally a military base, which has undergone rapid development and is now the preferred settlement for Chinese immigrants, since, at a mere 2,910 m, it is considerably lower than Lhasa and has a pleasant climate. Bayi is also the capital of the Nyangtri Prefecture, which includes the seven counties of Menling, Nyangtri, Gyamda, Nang, Metok, Po-me and Dzayul. From Dungdor in Menling to Bayi via the Gangka Zamchen bridge the distance is 74 km.

Nyangtri County

Middle Kongpo

Buchu Tergyi Lhakhang བུ་ཆུ་གསེར་གྱི་ལྷ་ཁང

Driving across Gangka Zamchen bridge from Dungdor in Menling county, Buchu township, on the west side of the Nyang-chu estuary, will be reached after 26 km.

The golden roof of **Buchu Tergyi Lhakhang** is visible from afar, on the east side of the 3 km-wide estuary at Nyangtri, and on the south bank of the Brahmaputra, near Chemnak. This is the most ancient Buddhist shrine in Kongpo and one of four 'border taming' temples (Tadul Lhakhang) built by King Songtsen Gampo in the seventh century. It was constructed according to geomantic theory on the right elbow of the ogress who represented the Tibetan landscape. Originally therefore the temple was associated with the Nyingma tradition. By the 17th century, however, three schools of Buddhism had developed a strong presence in Buchu valley, namely the Drukpa Kagyu at Do Chorten, the Nyingmapa at Dechenteng and the Gelukpa at Buchu Tergyi Lhakhang itself. Later, the temple was formally adopted by the Gelukpa in the time of the regent Demo Rinpoche (r 1886-1895). However, there have only been eight monks based at Buchu in recent years.

The temple has two storeys, surmounted by a golden roof. On the lower level, it formerly contained images of the Eight Manifestations of Padmasambhava and upstairs were eight images of Amitayus. These latter have not yet been restored, and of the eight manifestations, only the lower part of the large Padmasambhava survives with mantra-core (*zungjuk*) intact.

The outer structure of the building was protected in the 1960s when it was used as a granary. Around the outer walls are 50 prayer wheels. Within the gates, there is a courtyard with a small flower garden and an incense burner. An **antechamber** contains inscriptions on the left and right entrances, outlining the history of the temple, and murals depicting Shridevi and Dorje Lekpa (left), Damchen Karnak, Kongtsun Demo, and the Wheel of Rebirth (right), and the Four Guardian Kings (front). On the right side there is also a large prayer wheel.

Beyond the antechamber, there are two main halls. The two-pillared **outer hall** contains the volumes of the *Kangyur* and *Tangyur*, a large Maitreya with smaller images of Amitabha and White Tara to the left, and a magnificent but rarely seen image of Padmasambhava in the standing form called Pema Totrengtsal to the right, along with Shakyamuni and his foremost students. The protectors Dorje Lekpa and Kongtsun Demo grace the side walls. The entrance to the inner hall is flanked by two Gelukpa reliquary stupas, and a glass case to the left contains a number of important relics, including the 'life-supporting stone' (*lado*) of the oath-bound protector of the temple, which has a hole, reputedly pierced in former times by Padmasambhava's ritual dagger; and a 'self-arising' *terma* stone (*rangjung terdo*), dating from the era of King Songtsen Gampo, which also has a hole in the middle and is now used for holding butter-lamp offerings.

The **inner hall** contains images of Padmasambhava, Shantaraksita and King Trisong Detsen to the rear, flanked by 1,000 small images of Shakyamuni Buddha, with Songtsen Gampo and Mahakarunika in front. Alongside Mahakarunika, there is a revered stone footprint of Padmasambhava one of three which he is said to have left in Kongpo (the other two are kept in Lamaling). In the right corner, adjacent to the door, there is a finely decorated *torma*-offering shrine.

The **upper storey**, approached from a staircase in the inner circumambulatory walkway, contains a representation of Mount Potalaka, the celestial paradise of Avalokiteshvara.

Lamaling (Zangdok Pelri Monastery)

Behind Buchu on the ridge of a low-lying hill called **Norburi** is Lamaling, the main seat of the late Dudjom Rinpoche (1904-1987), former head of the Nyingma school. The original temple was built on the hilltop in Zangdok Pelri style, but destroyed by an earthquake in 1930. The second, 20 sq m and smaller in size, was then constructed on the tableland below. When the earlier temple was destroyed, the 'life-supporting' stone (*lado*) of Buchu reputedly moved and this was seen as an omen. Then, when Dudjom Rinpoche performed certain ceremonies outside the new building, a three-horned goat is said to have appeared, wandered up and down, and vanished into a stone, which can still be seen in front of the ruined temple. The new temple was destroyed during the 60s, but for a small image of Mahottara Heruka. In 1987, the ruined walls still bore the fingerprints of Dudjom Rinpoche's son Dorje Pasang, who was killed at that time.

A Dorje Trolo stupa was erected to the west of the ruined temple walls in 1987; and in 1989, restoration began in earnest under the supervision of Dudjom Rinpoche's daughter Semo Dechen and her husband, Chonyi Rinpoche. An exquisite **Zangdok Pelri Temple** and garden complex has since been constructed on the hillside, and a motorable road now links Lamaling with the Buchu valley below. The new images of Lamaling represent the best metal casting tradition of the artisans from Chamdo who assisted Chonyi Rinpoche. The octagonal east-facing building has, unusually, floors and stairs of finely polished wood, and shoes are not permitted inside. On the lowest level there are images of Padmakara, flanked by Mandarava and Yeshe Tsogyel. A stone footprint of Padmasambhava is positioned on the altar, and to the left there is an image of Guru Drakpo. The second level is dedicated to Four-armed Avalokiteshvara, and has a throne bearing a large photograph of the late Dudjom Rinpoche and yet another stone footprint of Padmasambhava. The third level is dedicated to the Buddha Amitabha.

Outside to the north of the garden, there is a new **Shakyamuni Lhakhang**. Its outer chapel, which functions as an assembly hall, has a small image of the Buddha flanked by his foremost students alongside Vajrasattva, and murals depicting the Vajrakila and Troma Nagmo cycles revealed by Dudjom Lingpa in the 19th century. An extremely large Shakyamuni fills the inner chapel. The **residence of Chonyi Rinpoche**, to the south of the complex, is surrounded by a fine flower garden and orchard, frequented by tame antelope. Uphill to the west, there is a new **Dorje Drolo Temple**, containing a small library.

Dechenteng Monastery

Southwest of Lamaling in the direction of Drime Kunden, and separated from it by a small evergreen forest is a branch monastery of Mindroling, called **Dechenteng**. The site was donated by Mindroling to the late Dudjom Rinpoche, and was used by him on one occasion as the venue for an important series of empowerments (Rinchen Terdzo). As in the case of Lamaling, the original structure was destroyed by the 1930 earthquake, and then replaced by a smaller building. At present the site is overgrown by incarvelia flowers and walnut trees.

Chokhorling Monastery

Southwest of Lamaling and below the abode of Drime Kunden are the ruins of two monasteries bearing the name of Chokhorling; one is Nyingma; the other, known as **Ganden Chokhorling**, is a branch of Sera. The latter, a 19th-century temple founded by Nyiden Loyang, had 100 monks. Huge tangkas were once hung out from the temple walls during religious dance performances. Now its ruined walls have magnificent frescoes of the Buddhas of the Three Times and a Wheel of Rebirth, which have survived despite their exposure to the elements.

Drime Kunden Hermitage

Above Chokhorling is a beautiful waterfall concealing the Kongpo retreat of the legendary compassionate prince Vasantara (Drime Kunden).

On the ascent to the waterfall and hermitage, you pass many important sites. The rocks and groves are identified with major events in the life of Drime Kunden. Ascending from Chokhorling one first passes his protector shrine, a bank of rhododendron flowers, and a series of his footprints, handprints and knee-prints in stone. Higher up the hillside, there is a spring, the water of which he brought forth when Ma Khandro offered him ale to drink. The water is said to benefit the eyesight, a reference to the legend that Drime Kunden's own sight was restored after he had offered up his own eyes. The waterfall itself is said to benefit bathers to the extent of an empowerment ceremony received by 108 monks. Above the waterfall is the hermitage of Drime Kunden's wife, Tsampo Mendrel Tsema. It contains a dakinis' dancing platform and a cave where pregnant women go to find omens. If the cave closes behind them, remedies have to be applied to avoid stillbirth or miscarriage or perhaps the mother's death.

In the **main hermitage** is a footprint of Drime Kunden covered by a stone. It also contains a tangka of White Tara which, when regarded purely without clinging to illusions, enables one to see the deity rather than the tangka. During each fourth month a fasting ceremony is held here. Opposite this hermitage is the residence of the protector, Chokyong Jarok Dongchen, and a 'self-arising' rock shaped like the kalantaka bird which would bring messages from Drime Kunden's parents. Above the hermitage, the circumambulation of the Pabri mountain (4,350 m) is said to have the same blessing as 10 million recitations of the Vajra Guru mantra.

In a clearing, on the descent, is a stupa below which there is a footprint and imprint of the seat where Drime Kunden would teach birds and wild beasts. The tree above the seat served as a canopy at that time. Nearby there are also the elbow-prints and handprints of his wife, who waited for him during this final teaching.

From Chokhorling and Drime Kunden, the road leads down to the village of **Karma**, near the ruins of **Tsela Dzong** (2,955 m), and the main road to Dungdor in Menling county. From Karma, there is also a coracle ferry to Chukhor on the east side of the Nyang-chu estuary, and to Chemnak on the south bank of the Brahmaputra.

Bayi → *Phone code: 86-894. Colour map 2, grid B6.*

Following the road from Buchu along the west bank of the Nyang-chu for 29 km, you will reach Bayi. The village of **Drakchi**, which once occupied this strategic site, has been completely absorbed by the recent urban development. The current population, largely Chinese, exceeds 30,000. Here, the **Bayi Zamchen** bridge spans the Nyang-chu River. » *For listings, see pages 249-250.*

Ins and outs

Approaching the city from the south, before the bridge, you will pass the College of Agriculture and Animal Husbandry (Zhingdrok Lobdra) on the left. This complex contains the Oasis Hotel. A temple founded by the late historian, Dungkar Lobzang Trinle is located nearby, alongside Number One Middle School.

Crossing the long bridge over the Nyang-chu, you soon reach the crossroads on **Guangdong Lam,** dominated by the Post Hotel. Turn left for Lhasa, right for the red-light district (which appears to occupy almost one quarter of the city), or straight ahead for the city centre.

The **roundabout** from which four main roads diverge lies at the commercial heart of the city. The Main Bus Station, the four-storey Government Hotel and the

Drime Kunden: The Compassionate Prince

Prince Vasantara (Drime Kunden), as recounted in a sutra and in a later opera bearing his name, was an emanation of Avalokiteshvara sent into exile by his father for giving a precious gemstone to an enemy. In the course of his wanderings, Drime Kunden reputedly lived for 12 years in a hermitage behind the waterfall, formed of his own tears. When Drime Kunden first arrived in Kongpo a yogin emerged from the woods and asked where he had come from. He replied that he had been sent there by his father. The yogin recognized him and asked him to stay.

As a bodhisattva, he tamed the wild tigers and bears which previously ate stray humans and instilled respect for human life into them. After 12 years he gave his final teaching to the beasts, saying that as long as they were to practise loving kindness and compassion his presence or absence would make no difference.

Bank of China are all located in the southwest sector of the roundabout. China Telecom, China Unicom, China Post, and the Agricultural Bank of China are all in the eastern sector, while the Clock Tower overlooks the downtown area from the northern sector of the roundabout.

Heading **northeast** from the roundabout, you will reach a supermarket and the Post Hotel intersection on Guangdong Lam. Heading **southwest** from the Bus Station corner you will reach the Khangpuyan Hotel and the seedy part of town. Heading **southeast** from the Bank of China you will reach the law court, Primary School Number Two, the Bowling & Sauna Complex, the Television Station, the Cultural Palace, and various government buildings. Heading due **north** from the Clock Tower, past electrical shops and department stores, you will reach the open market on the left, a turn-off on the right that leads to the city hospitals, and the main Lhasa-Nyangtri highway. Here, you may turn left for Lhasa (476 km), passing the Communist Party offices, Primary School Number One, the Prefectural Government Buildings, and a military camp; or right for the Foreign Trade Bureau, the New Nyangtri Hotel, the Textile Factory, the Forestry Department, and the road to Nyangtri (19 km).

Excursions

A short distance east of Bayi town is **Mount Pelri**, a sacred peak from whose summit Padmasambhava reputedly dried up a lake covering the valley below to ensure the region's future habitation. Pilgrims circumambulate the mountain in two to three hours, paying their respects to Padmasambhava's rock handprint, kneeprint, as well as a stupa dedicated to Phakmodrupa Dorje Gyelpo.

Nyangtri → *Colour map2, grid B6*

The township of Nyangtri is situated below Bonri, the sacred Bon mountain of Kongpo, at the east estuary of the Nyang-chu River, 19 km south of Bayi. The streets of Nyangtri form a T-junction: the main road to Po-me and Chamdo, turning east to ascend the Serkhyem La pass, and the south road following the riverside to Luding, and then following the Brahmaputra downstream on the north bank. Towards the northwest of town, at **Kushuk Drong** ⓘ *admission fee: ¥20 per person*, there is a 2,000-year-old juniper tree, sacred to the Bonpo, which is protected within a walled enclosure.

The government buildings, public security bureau, small guesthouses, China Post and China Telecom are all situated north of the main intersection. The Bus

Station is located towards the south end of town, as are the Agricultural Bank and the People's Hospital. Nearby, there are small restaurants and teashops.

Sigyel Gonchen

The Bon monastery of Sigyel Gonchen, approached via a turn-off to the left below Nyangtri, is a major pilgrimage attraction for the Bonpo adherents of Khyungpo Tengchen and Hor. Founded in the 14th century by Kuchok Rikpa Druk-se, it once housed 100 monks.

Taktse Yungdrungling Monastery

The motor road passes through Taktse township, above which is another Bon monastery known as Yungdrungling. Originally founded by a Bonpo from Amdo named Dongom Tenpa Lhundrub, it has recently undergone limited reconstruction, and is popular with Bonpo pilgrims from Ngawa and other parts of Amdo. There are precious relics housed here, including a tooth relic of Shenrab Miwoche, founder of the Bon religion.

Mijik Tri Durtro

ⓘ *Admission fee: ¥20 per person.*

This Bonpo burial ground, believed to contain the tumulus of Tibet's first mortal king, Drigum Tsenpo, lies a short distance north of Luding at the confluence of the Nyang-chu and Brahmaputra rivers. Bon literary sources refer to this tomb as **Gyangto Labub**, and there are many dire prophecies pertaining to its subsidence, as it appears over time to have moved closer to the river bank! From Luding there is a ferry crossing to the south bank of the river; and slightly further, at Drena (on the north bank), there is the place where King Drigum Tsenpo's funeral was conducted, in the shadows of **Mount Lhari Gyangto**. At Yungdrung Dzin village, there is a ninth-century obelisk, with an inscription recounting the affinity which King Drigum Tsenpo's sons had with the local divinity of Mount Lhari Gyangto.

Chu Jowo Temple

Slightly east of the confluence, on the north bank of the Brahmaputra, stands the temple of Chu Jowo. This contains a relief image of Jowo Rinpoche in the guise of Four-armed Avalokiteshvara. In this form, Jowo Rinpoche, Tibet's most sacred image contained in the Lhasa Jokhang, is said to have appeared in the Brahmaputra River, honouring a pledge he had made to Kongpo Ben, a devout shoemaker from Kongpo while on a previous pilgrimage to Lhasa. Before returning to Lhasa, Jowo Rinpoche vanished into a stone, taking on the form of the relief image which is revered today. The place where the image is said to have appeared in the river is close to the present temple. The site was restored through local patronage in 1985.

Mount Bonri

Mount Bonri is the highest of the three sacred Bon peaks on the north bank of the Brahmaputra (Muri is further west and Mount Lhari Gyangto southwest). Bonpo pilgrims from all parts of Tibet circumnambulate the slopes of Bonri, particularly during the winter months. Starting at Menri township (41 km from Nyangtri), where there are guesthouse facilities and shops, the three-day trek passes to the left of the Demo valley. Here are the ruins of **Demo Chemkar** monastery, a Gelukpa monastery, which was once the residence of Tibet's regent Demo Tupten Jigme (r 1810-1817). The route towards Bonri La (4,540 m) passes many sites associated with Shenrab and his epic struggle against the demon Kyapa Lagring; as well as the sacred tree, **Sembon Dungshing**, which has been revered as a cemetery for babies since its consecration by Kuchok Ripa Druk-se in 1330. The summit is said to have a stone footprint of Tibet's first king Nyatri Tsenpo. The descent from the pass leads via Zhabchin Dong and Darbong to Nyangtri.

Chinese Karaoke and Tibetan Nangma

Walking through the streets of any town or city in Tibet during the evening, look out for the neon lights flashing above a darkened doorway, and you will have found the local karaoke parlour. Often the legend OK boldly pulsates above the entrance. There are upmarket and downmarket sorts, but two things are certain: they all offer easy access for sexual encounters and this popular Asian pastime has with remarkable pervasiveness taken hold even in the most remote places in Tibet since 1991. The large expensive establishments often have spacious dance floors, fluorescent strobe lighting, multicoloured smoke effects, and disco or live Chinese pop and dance music interspersed with the actual karaoke. The disco formation dance known as "thirty-six" (*Ch sansi-liu*), in which a large group of dancers pirouette in unison is always popular. The big moment comes when some budding impresario orders and pays for a requested song, and then takes the floor, microphone in hand to croon the latest number from Taipei, Hong Kong or mainland China, or perhaps a long-standing favourite. A good turn is rewarded by generous applause and the gift of a scented artificial flower. Tibetans often surpass the Chinese immigrants in their renditions of these Chinese songs, and couples take to the dance floor, accompanying the soloist.

The karaoke repertoire includes a few pleasant duets; but, alas, hardly any Tibetan music. Some speculate that the plain-clothed public security policemen intentionally run the show, and it is true that in this environment many of them become the most congenial of drinking companions. Sometimes in the small hours of the morning, the Tibetans will switch off the big wall screen, and take the microphone to sing impromptu Tibetan songs. Everyone will join in, including the secret policemen and their girlfriends! However, in larger cities, like Lhasa and Bayi where there is a strong military presence, the popularity of karaoke is increasingly being eclipsed by overt prostitution, which has become a significant industry in downtown areas.

In the absence of Tibetan karaoke, the last few years have also seen the flourishing of the upmarket Nangma – a sophisticated type of Tibetan nightclub, where traditional song and dance assume a modern ambience.

Drinking is an important element of this popular culture, and in remote country areas, some groups of revellers will often carry crates of green-bottled beer into the bar. A bucket of cold water may be placed on the floor for refridgeration! As the evening wears on, even the most secret of policemen will loosen up and reveal all! On the other hand, drunkenness can lead to flashpoints of violence; and macho Khampa men may be quick on the draw with their long ornate knives. Brawling between rival groups has been known to close down certain establishments not long after their opening.

Apart from the clubs, small towns also have a number of exceedingly boring Chinese video parlours, and a large number of pool tables or even electronic gambling machines.

Rong-chu Valley

After Nyangtri, the paved highway comes to an end, and a motorable dirt road climbs for 32 km, cutting across the **Serkhyem La** pass (4,515 m) in a series of switchbacks, to enter the valley of the north-flowing **Rong-chu**. This wide and forested valley, which is renowned for its poppies, giant rhubarb and other diverse species of flora, can also be reached by trekking from Tim Guru Drupuk via the Nyima La (see above, page 240). From Serkhyem La pass to Tongjuk township the distance is 46 km. En route you pass through a logging centre at **Lunang**, and **Chu Nyima**, the traditional border between Kongpo and Powo regions.

Lunang

The township of Lunang (3,240 m) is the best place to spend the night between Bayi and Po-me. The idyllic valley of the upper Rong-chu is spacious and open to the south, offering tantalizing views of Mount Namchak Barwa when the skies are clear. The township itself has one main street, running from west to east. The Lunang Hotel is on the south side of the street, opposite the Agricultural Bank and the Forestry Guesthouse. There are small Tibetan-style restaurants, and Sichuan dishes are available at the excellent restaurant in the Lunang Hotel. For a detailed description of the route from here to Chamdo in East Tibet via Powo and Pasho, see below, page 430.

Bepa

The road north from Bayi follows the Nyang-chu upstream, passing large well-established military camps and installations on both sides of the road. The rushing waters of the Nyang-chu, flanked by beautiful conifer forests on both banks, ranks among the most memorable sights in Tibet. Pristine streams surge down to swell the river, among them the Zha-chu and Nezhi-chu, which converge at **Nezhi**. At **Bepa** township, 58 km from Bayi, you reach the border between Nyangtri and Gyamda counties, and from there enter into Upper Kongpo.

Sleeping

Bayi *p245*

C **New Century Hotel (Xin Shiji Fandian)**, Zhuhai lam, T0894-5885388, F0894-5887229. 40 standard rooms at ¥330, 12 singles at ¥330, and 2 suites at ¥888, with business centre and restaurant which are currenly being decorated.

C **New Nyangtri Hotel (Lingzhi Binguan)**, Nyangtri lam, T0894-5873040/ 5821300, F0894-5991105. The best in town, deluxe twin rooms at ¥388, deluxe singles at ¥588, deluxe suites at ¥888-¥988, ordinary suites at ¥488, triples at ¥268, and economy rooms at ¥198.

C **Nyangtri Education Hotel (Lingtri Jiao Yu Fandian)**, Guangdong lam, T0894-5889858, F0894-5885039, has 28 standard twin rooms at ¥288, 2 singles at ¥288, 3 suites at ¥490, and 1 triple at ¥338, with in-house Chinese restaurant, travel agency, and massage service.

C **Oasis Hotel (Luzhou Binguan)**, Menling lam, T 0894-5821300. 71 rooms at ¥360, with cafeteria and hot showers.

C **Post Hotel (You Zheng Binguan)**, Guangdong lam, T0894- 5889666, F0894-5889797. Good value, comfortable and clean, with 54 standard twin rooms (attached bath) at ¥268, deluxe suites at ¥498, and economy rooms at ¥48, with six small dining rooms and one banquet hall.(buffet breakfast Y20 per person), and Sunlight Teahouse on 5th floor.

D **Khangpuyan Hotel (Khangpuyan Dronkhang)**, Goyo Marlam. New and comfortable, with twin rooms at ¥168, singles at ¥228, suites at ¥188, deluxe rooms at ¥488, economy rooms at ¥138, and various categories of common room (¥50-¥75).

For an explanation of the sleeping and eating price codes used in this guide, see inside the front cover. Other relevant information is found in Essentials pages 44-46.

E **Government Guesthouse (Zhengfu Zhaodaisuo)**, Lhasa lam. Much older. The best rooms are ¥95.

E **Government Hotel (Zhengfu Binguan)**, next to the Main Bus Station, T0894-5823577. A 4-storeyed building with adequate but noisy accommodation.

Lunang *p249*

E **Lunang Hotel (Lunang Binguan)**, has standard twin rooms at ¥100.

Cheaper accommodation is available at the following:

Forestry Guesthouse (Nagtso Dzalangkhang).

Lunang Dzakhok Hotel (Lunang Dzakhok Dronkhang), T0894-5892502.

Powo Guesthouse.

Eating

Bayi *p245*

Khalden Ngotselkhang, opposite the Bank of China. Sichuan and hotpot dishes.

Yak Head Tibetan Restaurant (Yakgo Bo-zekhang), adjacent to the Po-me Bus Station. Tibetan cuisine.

Muslim Restaurant, opposite the Post Hotel. Muslim dishes.

There are a number of smaller Sichuan restaurants on Guangdong Lam, fronted by waitresses who seductively and competitively flaunt their cuisine. Other upmarket restaurants and coffee shops can also be found near the roundabout.

Lunang *p249*

Hramzhi Trulso Momo Restaurant, outside the Lunang Hotel.

Powo Tibetan Restaurant, outside the Lunang Hotel

Entertainment

Bayi *p245*

The only entertainment in town appears to be prostitution- not surprising in that the town was originally conceived as a military camp!

Shopping

Bayi *p245*

Handicrafts Woollen goods and Kongpo-style tunics are available at the department stores, near the roundabout, and also at the Textile Factory on Nyangtri Lam.

Modern goods Electrical goods are generally available in the area near the Clock Tower, and in the open market to the northwest.

Photography Print film and processing are available at Kodak and Fuji outlets, near the China Telecom Building.

Stamps Stamps are available at China Post, near the roundabout.

Transport

Bayi *p245*

Bus

The Main Bus Station, for Lhasa, Tsetang, and other long distance destinations is located at the roundabout. Mini-buses leave daily for **Lhasa** at 1030 (¥100). The Po-me Bus Station is located north of the Clock Tower, opposite the Old Government Guesthouse. There are daily departures for **Po-me** at 0930-1030 (¥100 per person, ¥600 for a reserved minibus).

Directory

Bayi *p245*

Banks Bank of China, at roundabout. Agricultural Bank of China, at roundabout. Construction Bank, near Post Hotel. As yet there is no foreign exchange facility. Post office China Post, at roundabout, has EMS service. **Hospitals** Old City Hospital, north of Clock Tower. Bayi Hospital of Traditional Medicine, off Nyangtri Lam. Womens' Hospital, north of Old City Hospital. **Internet** Internet facilities are available at the New Nyangtri Hotel and at China Telecom. **Telephone** IDD calls can be made from China Telecom, which is located at the roundabout, or in the business centre/reception of the New Nyangtri Hotel and the Post Hotel. ICC cards are available at China Telecom.

Lunang *p249*

Banks Agricultural Bank of China, adjacent to the local government buildings. **Post office** China Post, adjacent to the Lunang Hotel.

Gyamda County རྒྱ་མདའ

➔ *Population: 24,160. Area: 12,593 sq km. Colour map 2, grid B5.* 工布江达县

This is an area of stunning natural beauty: verdant alpine forests and clear running streams abound, and there are incredible lakes, epitomized by the island lake of ***Draksum Tso****. Upper Kongpo extends from the* ***Nangsel Zampa*** *bridge where the Nyang-chu River merges with its Drak-chu tributary, northwest of Bepa township, as far as the* ***Mamzhong La pass*** *(5,000 m), which forms the watershed between the Meldro and Nyang-chu rivers. The county capital is* ***Ngapo Zampa*** *(Kongpo Gyamda), 127 km north of Bayi, and 206 km northeast of Lhasa. Other feeder rivers swell the river's current, notably the Banang-chu (which flows north through Drongsar township), and the Pe-chu (which flows northeast through Gyazhing township).*

▸▸ *For Sleeping, Eating and other listings, see page 254.*

Upper Kongpo

Pangri Jokpo Hermitage

Driving north from Bepa township, you will notice on the right the 15-m high stone towers, which are found in many parts of Upper Kongpo. At Nangsel Zampa bridge, 21 km from Bepa, the valley of the Drak-chu abuts the Nyang-chu valley from the northeast. Turn right along a dirt track before crossing the bridge, and you will shortly reach the path leading to the ridge-top Pangri Jokpo hermitage.

A steep two hours' climb through barley fields, shrubs and forested slopes brings you to a clearing below this isolated tranquil retreat, founded by the *terton* Jatson Nyingpo (1585-1656). The hermitage, which for many years has been tended by two elderly female hermits from Nangchen, contains a **Mani Lhakhang** and the **main temple**, built against the rock walls. The temple is exceptionally well lit through its northwest-facing glass windows, and the views it offers of the Nyang-chu valley below are reminiscent of Swiss or Austrian landscapes. The temple has both outer and inner chapels. The former contains images of Padmasambhava, Guru Drakpo, and Simhavaktra – a trio renowned as the Union of All Rare and Precious Things (Konchok Chidu), described in *terma* texts revealed by Jatson Nyingpo himself. The liturgies of these texts are popular throughout both the Nyingma and Kagyu traditions. Alongside these images, to the right is a bas-relief image of Jatson Nyingpo, with a longevity-arrow (*dadar*), which is claimed to have been his personal possession. *Prajnaparamita* texts and small images of Padmasambhava are in the background. The **inner chapel** contains images of Ling Gesar (in peaceful and wrathful forms), Avalokiteshvara (twice) and Shakyamuni Buddha. An **inner sanctum** contains 1,000 small images of Padmasambhava.

Jatson Nyingpo passed away here. His birthplace at **Waru Nam-tsul** is on the opposite side of the valley.

Gyamda County

Lake Draksum Tso

Returning to the Nangsel Zampa bridge, cross over, and take the right turn-off (on the north bank of the Drak-chu River). This newly paved road leads to **Zhoka** township (20 km), near the ruins of the old Zhoka Dzong. En route, you will pass on the left **Len** village, noted for its

12-cornered tapering towers. According to one tradition, these are ancient fortifications, similar in function to those of Lhodrak (see above, page 218) and Gyarong (see page 655), and are said to have been made by demons headed by Ling Gesar's enemy Dud Achung Gyelpo in the remote past. Others sources suggest, however, that they were used for trapping birds of prey, which would dive into the towers in pursuit of their baited quarry.

At **Zhoka**, there is a hydroelectric power station and a small market. Two roads diverge here, the north route leading to **Drukla** township, following the Drukla-chu upstream, and the east route, following the Draksum-chu upstream to the lake which is its source. Take the latter, and cross the **Zhoka Zampa** bridge. The road now passes through a disused but somewhat surreal complex of telecommunication and remote tracking systems (one motorable trail leads through a perimeter fence directly towards a hewn-out mountainside bunker!).

Continue to follow the river upstream for 18 km to **Tsomjuk**, where a bridge crosses it at the point where it leads out of the lake. At **Jepa**, on the south side of the lake, the road ends at a chalet-style guesthouse, complete with dining room, karaoke, dance floor and other amenities favoured by Chinese holiday-makers. The complex, which has no hot running water and a poor electrical supply, is owned by the local Tsomgo Tourist Bureau. There is a plan to upgrade the facilities here within the next year. Camping is also possible nearby, and in summer there are large appliqué Tibetan tents dotting this idyllic meadow. Below you have a wonderful view of the jade-green lake, 16 km long by 3 km wide, girded by steep forested slopes, and with the Tsodzong Island (3,600 m) positioned like a pearl at its centre. The flat-bottomed ferry resembles a surfboard, which is drawn across to the island by an overhead cable. Recently, motor boats and speed boats have also been introduced to the lake by the local tourist authority, which caters mainly for visitors from China.

Tsodzong Island The temple on Tsodzong Island is the birthplace of the *terton* Sangye Lingpa (1340-1396), although there are earlier associations with Padmasambhava and King Trisong Detsen. In the early years of the 20th century, the complex was refurbished by the late Dudjom Rinpoche (1904-1987); and more recently by Konchok Tsering following its destruction during the 1960s. The present reconstruction was encouraged by Dudjom Rinpoche's daughter, Semo Dechen, and her husband Chonyi Rinpoche of Lamaling. The senior caretaker, Neten, passed away in 2000. Along with the surviving junior caretaker Atsang, he was a practitioner of the Dudjom lineage.

The main image of the temple depicts Guru Drakpo. Its head was originally brought to the island by Sangye Lingpa, riding a tigress which left its paw marks on the rocks to the west of the island. Other images depict Padmasambhava, Shakyamuni Buddha, Avalokiteshvara and the protectress Kongtsun Demo. There is also a 'self-manifesting' stone letter A, as described in Jatson Nyingpo's own *terma*. The caretakers' house holds other treasures: a royal seal of King Songtsen Gampo, the bowls used by Sangye Lingpa and the late Dudjom Rinpoche, and a precious manuscript said to be in Jatson Nyingpo's own handwriting.

The pilgrims' circuit of the island begins with this temple, and then moves clockwise, passing the hermitage of Dudjom Rinpoche, a rock from the Shitavana burial ground, the body imprint of Ling Gesar, the stone paw of the tigress, the stone prints of Sangye Lingpa (**all on west side**); the 'life-supporting' tree (*lashing*) of the demon Dud Achung Gyelpo which was cut down by Gesar's golden axe, a treasury belonging to the Karmapa, a tree associated with Ma Khandro, the consort of Drime Kunden (see above, page 245) which has leaves naturally inscribed with seed-syllables and animal year-signs (**all on north side**); a stone snake which has associations with Ling Gesar, and the Tashi Obar stupa, under which is a nectar stream (**all on east side**). Finally, a white stone represents the mistress of the lake, Tsomen Gyelmo (**south side**).

Beyond the far shore of the lake, there are four prominent snow peaks: Mount Ama Jomo Taktse (5,963 m) to the northwest, Mount Namla Karpo (6,750 m) to the north, Mount Naphu Gomri (5,663 m) to the northeast and Mount Darchenri to the east. These sites also have associations with Ling Gesar.

Pilgrims' circuit There is a two-day pilgrims' circuit around the lake, starting from the bridge of **Tsomjuk** and passing by the ruined Gelukpa monastery of **Pibang**, the Vajravarahi cave, the two glacial feeder rivers on the lake's east side (Ortse-chu and Nangu-chu), the ruined Kagyupa monastery of **Darchenri**, and **Tsomgo** township, at the head of the lake. Near the **Jepa** campsite on the south side, there is another glacial feeder river, known as the Penam-chu.

Returning to Zhoka, if you take the north turn-off, you will reach **Drukla** township after 15 km. Here there are more ancient defence towers and the ruins of the **Drukla Monastery**. A trekking route leads further north, for 105 km to join the old Lhasa-Chamdo caravan highway near Lake Artsa (see below, page 427).

Ngapo Zampa (Gyamda Town)

➔ *Altitude: 3,200 m. Colour map 2, grid B5.*

Returning to Nangsel Zampa bridge, turn right and follow the main highway west along the course of the Nyang-chu. After 40 km, you will pass the **Sharlung Zampa** bridge at Sharlung township, where the Banang-chu tributary flows into the Nyang-chu from the south. There is a side road from here leading south to **Drongsar**.

About 8 km further along the main highway, you will reach the county capital, known as **Ngapo Zampa** (Kongpo Gyamda). This is a small town containing one main street reached via bridges at its west and east ends.

Above the town is the monastery of **Neu Dechen Gon**, associated with the late Dudjom Rinpoche's teachings on Vajrakila. In a nearby mountain hermitage are the **Tselha Namsum** meditation caves, associated with the female yogini Machik Labdron.

Gyamda Township and the Chamdo Caravan Trail

About 23 km northwest of Ngapo Zampa, the road passes through Gyamda township, formerly known as **Gyamda Dzong**. From here, there is a four-day trek following the headwaters of the Nyang-chu through **Nyangpo** district and across Tro La pass (4,890 m) to **Artsa**, where a motorable dirt road leads northwest to Nakchu and southeast down the Yi'ong Tsangpo valley. This latter route follows the old caravan trail from Lhasa to Chamdo (see below, page 406), which commenced at Gyamda Dzong.

Nyang-chu Headwaters

Beyond Gyamda township, the terrain becomes slightly more arid. The highway soon reaches **Chimda** (17 km), where Padmasambhava's student Nyak Jananakumara once fled from violent assailants and where, later, in the 14th century, Sangye Lingpa discovered *terma* pertaining to the cycles of wrathful mantras. Continuing uphill from there, you will reach **Gyazhing** township after 44 km, and eventually, after a further 63 km, the watershed pass of **Mamzhong La** (5,000 m). Near the pass, 13 km after Gyazhing, the road diverges from the main river. (A trekking trail leads upstream to Azhang Kongla pass and thence to Dakpo.) From the watershed, which is sometimes confused with a neighbouring pass named Kongpo Bar La, the distance to Lhasa via Meldro Gungkar and Taktse counties is 149 km.

Prayer Flags

In Tibet, any prominent place exposed to the wind may be adorned with multicoloured prayer flags (*darchok*), permitting the natural power of the wind to distribute the blessings of their inscribed prayers as they flap to and fro, for which reason they are known also as 'wind horses' (*lungta*). Domestic rooftops and monastery compounds often have large poles to which these flags are attached, and renewed annually on the third day after the Tibetan New Year. Similarly, most mountain passes (*la-tse*) are marked by cairns of stones (some inscribed with mantras), to which sets of prayer flags are attached. Wherever public buses or private jeeps cross over a major pass, the passengers will invariably disembark to add a stone to the cairn, or tie a newly prepared set of prayer flags and burn incense as an offering to the spirit of the mountain, who would have been tamed and appointed protector of Buddhism by Padmasambhava back in the eighth century. Some will cast paper prayer-flags into the air from the bus window, cheerfully shouting in the ancient paean: "Kyi-kyi so-so! May the gods be victorious!" (*lha-gyel-lo*).

A single set of cotton prayer flags is arranged in this order: blue, white, red, green and yellow, respectively symbolizing the five elements: space, water, fire, air and earth. In each corner of the flag there may be a protective animal: garuda (top left), dragon (top right), tiger (bottom left), and lion (bottom right), while the mantra-syllables forming the main part of the inscription may vary according to the preferred meditational deity of the devotee. Those of the three bodhisattvas, Avalokiteshvara, Manjughosa, and Vajrapani are commonplace, as are the mantras of the female bodhisattva Tara, who protects travellers from the dangers of the road.

Sleeping

Ngapo Zampa *p253*

D **Grain Department Guesthouse** (Drurik Lekhung Dronkhang), located on the south side of the main street, west of the petrol station. The best, with rooms at ¥25 per bed.

E **Gyamda Dzong Guesthouse**, located on the north side of the main street, west of the Bus Station. Has cheaper and noisier rooms at ¥12 per bed.

E **Post Office Guesthouse** (Yigzam Dronkhang), located on the north side of the main street, west of the Bus Station. Slightly better equipped, with rooms also at ¥12 per bed.

Eating

Ngapo Zampa *p253*

There are a number of rather good and inexpensive Sichuan restaurants.

For an explanation of the sleeping and eating price codes used in this guide, see inside the front cover. Other relevant information is found in Essentials pages 44-46.

Western Tibet (Tsang and Lato)

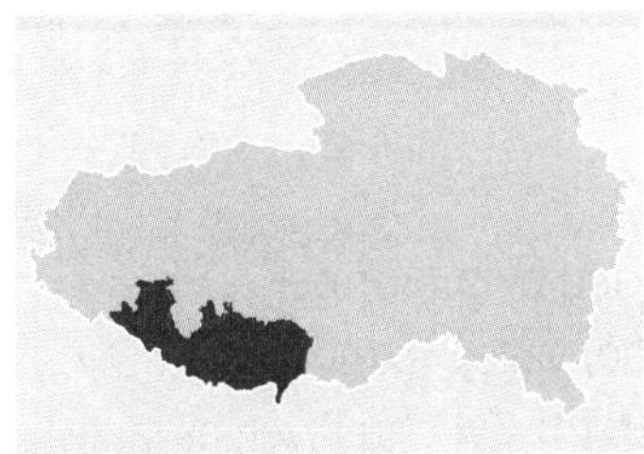

Footprint features

Introduction

Western Tibet is the region bounded by the Upper Brahmaputra (Tib Yarlung Tsangpo) valley, extending upstream from its confluence with the Kyi-chu River, as far as the headwaters in Drongpa county (east of Mount Kailash). Separated on the south from Nepal, Sikkim and West Bhutan by the high Himalayan range, and on the north from the Jangtang Plateau by the Gangtise and Nyenchen Tanglha ranges, this region includes the traditional provinces of **Tsang** and **Lato**. It embraces the lateral valleys adjoining the Brahmaputra on both its north and south banks, the valleys of the south-flowing Gangetic tributaries which traverse Nepal, and those of the south-flowing Brahmaputra tributaries which cross Sikkim and West Bhutan.

The prefectural capital is Zhigatse, 281 km from Lhasa via Nyemo and Chakdam, 348 km via Gampa La pass and Gyantse, and 338 km via Yangpachen and Zhugu La pass.

Recommended itineraries: 1, 2. **See page 20.**

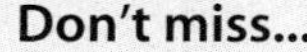

★ Don't miss...

1. **Yungdrungling** Explore one of the largest Bon monasteries in Tibet, page 261.
2. **Gyantse** An attractive old trading town and repository of wonderful 15th-century Newar art, page 267.
3. **Zhalu** An imperial temple with unusual murals, where the Tibetan Buddhist canon was compiled, page 286.
4. **Sakya** The great library in the inner sanctum of Lhakhang Chenmo is a vast collection of manuscripts, which have been gathering dust for centuries, page 297.
5. **Everest and Chowo Oyuk** Trek for three days from Dingri to Dzarongpu nunnery near Everest Base Camp, hiking in full view of the towering range, page 315.

Nyemo County སྙེ་མོ

→ *Population: 29,739. Area: 2,077 sq km. Colour map 2, grid B3.* 尼木县

*The county of **Nyemo** extends from the upper reaches of the Lhorong-chu in the north, across the watershed formed by the snow peaks of **Jomo Gangtse** (7,048 m) and **Kumalungpa Gangri** (5,858 m), and through the fertile valleys of the Nyemo Ma-chu and its tributaries, the Zhu-chu and Phakpu-chu. The county capital is located at **Dardrong**, where the Nyemo Ma-chu and Zhu-chu rivers converge.*

Getting there There are two motorable routes into Dardrong: one from Markyang township (50 km) on the northern Lhasa-Zhigatse highway and another from Ton township (25 km) on the central Lhasa-Zhigatse highway.

Trekking Nyemo is a wonderful area for trekking in close proximity to Lhasa. There is a trail from **Dorjeling nunnery** near Yangpachen (see above, page 142), which follows the Lhorong-chu upstream via Gyedar and Yangyi , before crossing the Zhagong La pass into the Upper Zhu valley. Another trek from Tsurphu monastery links up with that trail at Gyedar; and a third leads from Nakar, south of Tsurphu, to Angang township in the Lower Zhu valley (see above).

Of all these, the easiest point of access is via the central highway. Driving west from Chushul, you continue on the north bank of the Brahmaputra, passing the **Chushul Zamchen** bridgehead at **Takar** (8 km), followed by **Yamtsen Monastery**, and the townships of **Sa-me** (25 km) and **Ton** (30 km), the last of which is regarded as the birthplace of Tonmi Sambhota. There are small roadside refreshment stalls on this route, and a local cottage industry which makes incence. **NB** A new bridge is currently under construction between Ton and Sa-me. On completion, it will carry traffic across the Brahmaputra on a new south bank road to Zhigatse. There are also plans for a secondary road from here through to Khari La pass on the old Lhasa-Gyantse highway.

The turn-off for **Dardrong** at the mouth of the Nyemo Ma-chu is 20 km west of Ton. Dardrong itself is located 5 km inland. There are several small roadside restaurants at the intersection, where public buses and tour groups stop over. However these are likely to close when the new south bank road is completed.

Nyemo Ma-chu valley

From **Dardrong**, a jeep track follows the Nyemo Ma-chu upstream for 50 km to **Markyang** on the northern Lhasa-Zhigatse highway. En route, you will pass through **Lhundrubgang** in Zangri township, which was once the base of an important Tibetan opera troupe. Following its amalgamation with the Jago troupe in neighbouring Zhu valley, it became renowned throughout Tibet as the **Nyemowa Opera Troupe**. Further upstream at **Jekhar** in Dragor (Pagor) township, where the Phakpu-chu converges with the Nyemo Ma-chu, there is the birthplace of **Vairotsana**, the greatest native of Nyemo, a foremost student of Padmasambhava, who ranks

The Brahmaputra/Yarlung Tsangpo River

The **Brahmaputra** is one of Asia's major rivers, extending 2,900 km from its source in Far West Tibet to its confluence with the Ganges in India. There are three head-streams: **Kabji**, **Angsi**, and **Tachok Khabab**, the last of which rises in the Jemayungdrung glacier 60 km southeast of Lake Manasarovar. From their convergence these headwaters, known initially as the **Tachok Tsangpo** and later as the **Yarlung Tsangpo**, flow east for 1,127 km along the tectonic suture line. Then, after being forcibly channelled south through the awe-inspiring gorges between Mount Namchak Barwa and Mount Gyala Pelri, the river enters the Arunachal Pradesh province of India where it is known as the **Dihang**. In Assam it is joined by several Himalayan streams: the Lohit, Dibang, Subansiri, Kameng, Bhareli, Dhansiri, Manas, Champamati, Saralbhanga and Sankosh. Lastly, in the Duars, it is joined by the Tista, before finally converging with the Ganges north of Goalundo Ghat.

In its upper reaches the river is navigable for 644 km from Lhartse eastwards, and there are coracles crossing the river at 3,962 m.

The flora along the banks of the Upper Brahmaputra is confined to shrubs, interspersed with dwarf willow and poplar trees. The true forests begin growing only in the mid-reaches, in **Dakpo** and **Kongpo**, where the climate is moister and warmer. In the southeast, around **Po-me** and **Pemako** expanses of thick, coniferous forest covers the mountaint slopes. Conifers with an undergrowth of rhododendron grow at 3,000-4,000 m; hemlock, spruce, and larch at 2,500-3,000 m; pine trees at 1,500-2,500 m; and tropical monsoon forest below 1,500 m.

among Tibet's finest translators of the eighth century. His footprint, impressed in rock at the age of eight, is preserved there as an object of veneration.

At Markyang on the northern highway, you can turn southwest for **Oyuk** valley (see below, page 260) or northwest, heading across the high **Zhugu La** pass (5,454 m) with its stupendous views of the Jomo Gangtse snows. Yangpachen in the Upper Tolung valley lies 56 km beyond Zhugu La pass. If you take the Oyuk road, after 7 km you will pass through **Senshang** township. From here there is a long and arduous trekking route to **Lake Namtso** via the Kyangu La pass (5,769 m) and Putserteng hamlet.

Nyemo Zhu valley

From Dardrong, another trail follows the fertile Zhu-chu valley upstream to Angang township (19 km). Here are the ruins of **Zhu Kungarawa**, an 11th-century Kadampa monastery founded by Ngok Lotsawa. At **Jago**, northeast of Mount Gangri Pelkye (5,894 m), there is the former home of Nyemo's second opera troupe, prior to its amalgamation with the Lhundrubgang troupe (see above). From here there is a trekking route to Nakar near Tsurphu monastery (see above, page 258). Another trekking route leads from **Sagang** in the Upper Zhu valley across Zhagong La pass to Gyedar, where the trails divide for Yangpachen and Tsurphu.

Namling County རྣམ་གླིང་

→ *Population: 73,134. Area: 9,695 sq km. Colour map 2, grid B2.* 南木林县

Namling is the current administrative name given to the valleys of ***Oyuk*****,** ***Tobgyel*****,** *and* ***Shang*****,** *which all have long and illustrious associations with both Buddhism and Bon. Through these valleys respectively flow the Nang-gung-chu, Tobpu-chu, and Shang-chu rivers, with their various tributaries, which rise amid the southern slopes of the Nyenchen Tanglha range to the north, and flow southwards to converge with the Brahmaputra.*

Getting there The northern and central Lhasa-Zhigatse highways meet at **Trakdruka** on the south bank of the Brahmaputra, opposite Lower Oyuk. The former winds its way from Senshang across the Do-ngu La pass (4,846 m) to Oyuk township and thence to **Trakdruka Bridge** (65 km). The latter follows the north bank of the Brahmaputra upstream from Nyemo, via Dzongkar to the **Nub Khulung Zamchen** bridge in Lower Oyuk, after which it runs along the south bank to Tradruka (75 km). The Tobgyel and Shang valleys are both accessible from the south bank of the river, the former at **Drakchik** ferry (19 km west of Tradruka) and the latter at Tama Bridge (58 km west of Tradruka). The county capital is located at **Ringon** in the Shang valley.

Oyuk Valley → *Colour map 2, grid B2*

Dingma Monastery

Descending from the Do-ngu La pass into Upper Oyuk, the northern Lhasa-Zhigatse highway enters the Nang-gung-chu valley. Below Rinchenling, 27 km after the pass, the Mang-chu tributary converges with the Nang-gung-chu at Domtang village. A trekking route to **Zabulung** in Upper Shang (see below, page 263) follows the **Mang-chu valley** northwest via Rikdzom and Mangra township, and across the Mang La pass. Near the entrance to this valley you can see on a hill the remains of the ancient 11th-century Kadampa monastery of **Dingma**, founded by Ram Dingma Deshek Jungne, a student of the Geshe Potowa (1031-1105). Nearby at **Lukdong** there is also a meditation hermitage associated with Padmasambhava.

Namling

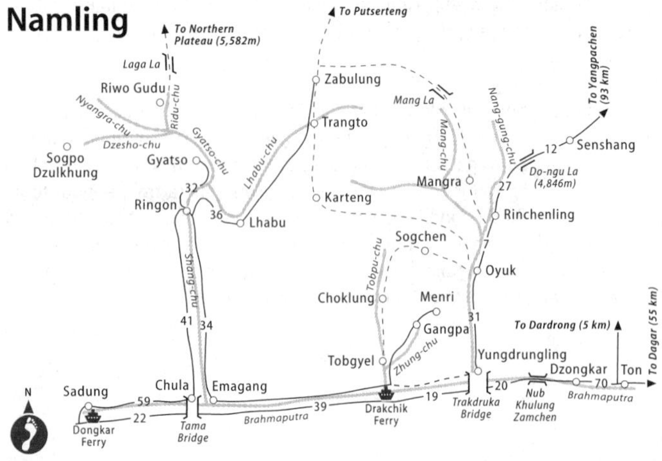

Oyuk Gongon Lhakhang

Oyuk township (Taktse) lies 7 km below the confluence of the Nang-gung-chu and Mang-chu rivers.

The principal shrine is the **Gongon Lhakhang**, which was reputedly constructed by King Songtsen Gampo as one of a series of peripheral geomantic temples. Some even classify it among the 'border-taming' temples. Later in the eighth century, the temple was frequented by Padmasambhava and his students, among them Namkei Nyingpo and King Trisong Detsen. The latter's personal weapons were once housed here. There are guesthouse facilities here.

Trekking From Oyuk township, there are three-day trekking routes, which lead southwest via Sogchen township into the valley of the Tobpu-chu, or into that of its eastern tributary, where **Menri Monastery** is located (see below, page 262). A dirt road passable by jeeps also leads northwest to Karteng and the Shang Lhabu-chu valley (see below, page 262).

Oyuk Jara Gon

At **Jarasa** in Lower Oyuk, there is the abode or castle (Kukhar) of the protector deity Dorje Lekpa: guardian of the Dzogchen teachings. Here, at the hermitage called **Oyuk Chigong** or Oyuk Jara Gon, the great meditation master Chetsun Senge Wangchuk (10th-11th century) remained in retreat, and received the teachings of the *Innermost Spirituality of Vimalamitra (Bima Nyingthig)* in a vision from Vimalamitra. Some of these teachings he concealed and others he imparted to his foremost student, Zhangton (1097-1167). Eventually he passed into rainbow light at the age of 125! There are graphic descriptions in Tibetan literature of how Zhangton was assisted by the protector Dorje Lekpa in his efforts to rediscover the concealed teachings of the *Innermost Spirituality of Vimalamitra*. Later, in the 19th century, when Jamyang Khyentse Wangpo was on pilgrimage here from East Tibet, he recollected the teachings he had received in a past life (as Chetsun Senge Wangchuk) and incorporated them into the teaching cycle now known as the *Innermost Spirituality of Chetsun (Chetsun Nyingthig)*.

Moving on Passing due south through the villages of Nubmalung and Tashigang, the road eventually reaches the Brahmaputra crossing at Tradruka Bridge, 31 km south of Oyuk township. There are small roadside Sichuan and Tibetan restaurants on the south bank.

Yungdrungling Monastery

Located above the east bank of the Nang-gung-chu near its confluence with the Brahmaputra, this is one of the most influential Bon monasteries in recent Tibetan history. Founded during the 19th century by Nangton Dawa Gyeltsen on the ridge of the holy Bon mountain, **Olha Gyel**. The complex had 700 monks prior to its destruction in 1959, but now there are scarcely more than 50. Amid the former ruins of its assembly hall, residential buildings, hermitages and colleges, a number of temples and chapels have been reconstructed. The **Tongrol Lhakhang** contains the reconstructed reliquary of the monastery's founder, and murals depicting the Bonpo lineage-holders and ritual mandalas. The whole complex is clearly visible from the motor road on the south bank of the Brahmaputra, but in the summer months it is impossible for vehicles to ford the Nang-gung-chu. The detour on foot takes two hours (round trip).

Tobgyel Valley → *Colour map 2, grid B2*

Following the Tobpu-chu upstream from its confluence with the Brahmaputra opposite Drakchik Ferry, at **Tobgyel** township (Magada) the valley divides: the west branch following the Tobpu-chu upstream to Tshar, Choklung, the Gelukpa monastery of **Drungzhi** and **Sogchen**. The east branch follows the Zhung-chu upstream, via Gangpa into a Bon stronghold, where the monasteries of Ensakha, Kharna and Menri are located.

Getting there The entrance to the **Tobgyel** valley may be approached by coracle from the **Drakchik** ferry (19 km west of Tradruka) on the south bank of the Brahmaputra, or by trekking – either along the north bank from Yungdrungling in Lower Oyuk, or via the Tobpu-chu headwaters from Oyuk township and Sogchen.

Ensakha and Kharna Monasteries

The Bon monastery of **Ensakha** was founded in Lower Topgyel by Druje Yungdrung Lama in 1072. Following its devastation by floods in 1386, the Bon community moved to Menri. Ensakha was eventually reconstructed and continued to function as a small monastery until recent times. Further upstream are the **Kharna-ri** caves, where Bonpo meditators and hermits have practised for centuries, and where a new monastery was founded in 1838 by Sherab Yungdrung.

Menri Monastery

The Bonpo monastery of **Menri**, higher up the slopes of the Zhung-chu valley, was established in 1405 by Nya-me Sherab Gyeltsen, following the destruction by floods of its precursor, Ensakha monastery. This event is said to have been predicted by Shenrab Miwoche, legendary founder of the Bon religion. For centuries Menri functioned as the most important Bon teaching centre in the country, attracting monks from Tengchen, Ngawa and Gyarong. Prior to its destruction in 1959 there were 350 monks at Menri; but now there are about 50. The ruins are extensive: formerly there were four colleges, a school of dialectics, and a large assembly hall. The oldest building is the **Red Meditation Hermitage (Drubkhang Marpo)**, constructed by the monastery's founder.

Shang Valley

Getting there The Shang valley may be approached from the south bank of the Brahmaputra, either via the newly constructed **Tama Bridge** (58 km west of Tradruka), or the **Dongkar ferry** (80 km west of Tradruka). The bridge carries traffic across to **Emagang** on the west bank of the Shang-chu river estuary; and the ferry passengers alight further west at **Sadung**, from where the road leads downstream to Chula on the west bank of the Shang-chu. Both roads into Shang are motorable, the west bank as far as Gyatso township (73 km) and the east bank as far as Lhabu (70 km) and Trangto. (There is also a jeep trail from Oyuk township via Karteng to Trangto, and another from Lower Tobgyel to Emagang.) A bridge spans the river at **Ringon**, the county capital, and above Takna the two main branches of the Shang-chu River diverge: the valley of the Gyatso-chu extending northwest and that of the Shang Lhabu-chu extending east and northeast.

Emagang Shangda Palchen

In Lower Shang, the most important site is **Shangda Palchen**, the seat of the Zur family in Emagang township. Here, near the village of **Trampa**, the successive generations of the Zur family made their hermitages and securely established the transmission of the *Nyingmapa Oral Teachings* (*kama*) during the 10th century, in the aftermath of the interregnum following Langdarma's persecution. This family lineage originated with Zur Shakya Jungne (10th-11th century), his nephew Zurchungpa Sherab Drak (1014-1074), and the latter's son Zur Drophukpa Shakya

Senge (1074-1135), whose students carried the Nyingmapa teachings throughout Tibet. The detailed accounts of their lives are among the most vivid biographical passages of Nyingmapa literature. When the Sakyapas became the dominant force in Tibetan political life during the 13th century, they maintained a close rapport with the Zurs, encouraging Zur Zangpopel to produce the Nyingmapa anthology of tantras. Later Zurchen Choying Rangdrol (1604-1669) established a close connection with the Fifth Dalai Lama.

Ringon (Namling)

Four roads intersect at **Ringon**, the county capital of Namling: the two southern routes to Dojo and Emagang and the northern routes to Gyatso and Lhabu. The cliff-hanging monastery of **Ganden Chokhorling** at Ringon has, in recent centuries, been the largest monastery in Shang, shared by both the Gelukpa and Sakyapa schools. Above the monastery are the ruins of **Ringon Taktse Dzong** fortress. Another small monastery, **Dechen Rabgye Gonpa**, is associated with the Panchen Lamas.

Gyatso-chu Valley

The motor road continues on the west bank of the river upstream from Ringon. Below Luya, the Shang Lhabu River branches to the east. Heading northwest along the course of the Gyatso-chu tributary, you will reach Gyatso township after 32 km. Here the Dzesho , Nyangra and Ridu headwaters of the Gyamtso-chu converge. Of these, the Ridu-chu leads to the **Riwo Gudu** or **Drak Gyawo** hermitage of the master Zurchung Sherab Drak, and the Dzesho-chu to the limestone cave complex of **Sogpo Dzulkhung** hermitage. In the latter, there is a Padmasambhava cave containing the impression of the master's penis in rock. From **Ridu**, the Laga La pass (5,582 m) leads through the Nyenchen Tanglha range north towards the Jangtang lakes.

Zhang Zhang Dorjeden

Located 5 km east of Ringon, on the south bank of the Shang-chu, this is one of the best known of the 108 monasteries reputedly established by Khyungpo Neljor, founder of the Shangpa Kagyu school. It was here that this master passed away and was interred in a gold and silver reliquary.

Zabulung

Padmasambhava is said to have consecrated five entire valleys for Buddhist practice in each of the four cardinal directions and one at their centre. **Zabulung** valley lies in the middle of this grand design, and as such is the most revered pilgrimage place in the province of Tsang. Located northeast of Ratang (Lhabu), Karteng and Trangto, in the Shang Lhabu-chu valley, this site is renowned for its spectacular **hot springs** and the **Shang Zabulung Monastery**, where there is a meditation cave associated with Padmasambhava and his consort Yeshe Tsogyel. Throughout history, important Nyingmapa *tertons* have undergone profound spiritual experiences here: Dorje Lingpa (1346-1405) and Lhatsun Namka Jigme (b 1597) among them.

Getting there The round trip from Ringon can be undertaken in a single day on the rough motorable road. The best accommodation is available at the county hotel in Ringon.

Trekking A trekking route continues northeast following the Shang Lhabu-chu upstream to the nomadic areas of **Lhabupu**, **Serka**, and eventually to **Putserteng**.

Rinpung County རིན་སྤུངས

→ *Population: 30,838. Area: 1,885 sq km. Colour map 2, grid B3.* 仁布县

*Rarely visited by outsiders nowadays, **Rinpung** in Rong Valley was once the citadel of the Rinpung princes who ruled Tibet from 1435 until 1565. The county is located on the south bank of the Brahmaputra; extending from the currently unused **Shangpa Bridge**, downstream as far as the **Nub Khulung Zamchen bridge** and **Samda** (west of Kharak). Most settlements are to be found in the lateral valley of the **Rong-chu**, which rises at **Yarzik** in Pelde township on the extreme northwest tip of Lake Yamdrok and flows into the Brahmaputra at **Shangpa** (Rinpung township); but the county also includes the valleys of the Yakde-chu and the Bartang-chu; as well as the valley of the southwest-flowing Men-chu, the principal tributary of the Rong-chu. The county capital is located at **Jamchen Zhol** in the Rong-chu valley, 31 km southwest of the Nub Khulung Zamchen bridge.*

Rinpung Dzong

This fortress town is located on a ridge overlooking the west bank of the Rong-chu River. The ruined fortress or **Dzong** of **Ringpung** is further inland on a ridge to the west of the river. It overlooks a large village of around 100 houses.

The Rinpung princes first came to prominence during the reign of the Phakmodrupa king Drakpa Gyeltsen (1374-1440), who appointed **Namka Gyeltsen** as Lord of the Rinpung estates and Governor of Sakya and Chumik.

In 1435, his relation **Rinpung Norbu Zangpo** seized power from Phakmodru, gradually bringing to an end the influence of this aristocratic house of Nedong (see above). Finally in 1478 his son **Donyo Dorje** inflicted a decisive defeat on the kings of Phakmodru; and founded Yangpachen, the seat of the Zhamarpas of the Karma Kargyu school. The family's power was eventually eclipsed in 1565 by **Zhingzhakpa Tseten Dorje** of the Samdrubtse fiefdom at Zhigatse.

Getting there The paved road into the county town branches off the Lhasa-Zhigatse road just east of the Shangpa Bridge.

Rong Jamchen Chode

The road continues inland, following the Rong-chu upstream, past a hydroelectric power station, to **Jamchen Zhol**, the county capital. The most important site is the three-storey **Rong Jamchen Chode** – a Sakyapa monastery which later also acquired Gelukpa associations – originally founded by Zhonu Gyelchok in 1367. The Rinpungpa prince Norbu Zangpo donated an enormous 10-m high Maitreya image. In the early decades of the previous century there are said to have been 1,500 Gelukpa

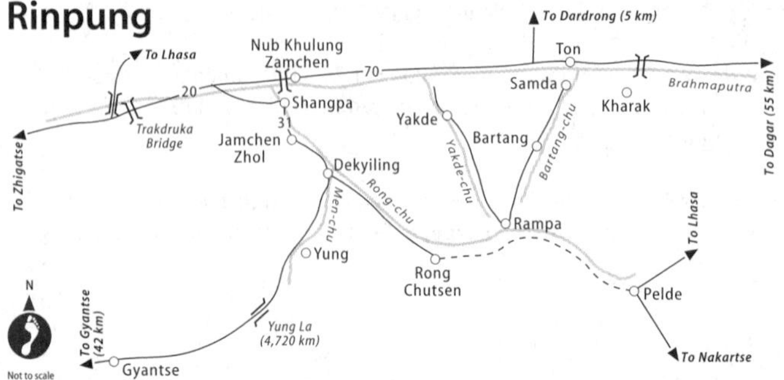

and Sakyapa monks based here. The present reconstructed assembly hall lies below the ruins of the original complex.

There is a government compound with shops and spartan guesthouse facilities, and a military barracks.

Dekyiling

From Jamchen Zhol a branch road continues to follow the river upstream as far as **Dekyiling**, where the Men-chu tributary flows into the Rong-chu from the southwest. This motorable route follows the Men-chu upstream and across the Yung La pass (4,720 m) to **Gyantse** (42 km). In this valley you can visit the college of **Dreyul Kyemotsel**, founded in 1449 by Rinpungpa Kunzang, who was a patron of the Sakyapa lamas Sangyepel and Gorampa Sonam Senge (1429-1489).

Also, 10 km up the valley near Kyi-shong is **Khambulung**, where Jangdak Tashi Topgyel of the Northern Treasures (Jangter) tradition (b 1557) discovered certain *terma* revelations. The **Ngurmik Drolma Lhakhang** once contained a celebrated image of Tara, which is now housed at Tashilhunpo in Zhigatse (see below, page 280). About 7 km further south is the **Gongra Lhundrubding**; also known as **Gongra Ngeden Dorje Ling**, an important Nyingmapa centre, where the Anuyoga texts were transmitted by Gongra Lochen Zhenpen Dorje (1594-1654).

Rong Chutsen Hot Spring and Rampa

The small hot spring known as **Dumpa Chutsen** is located at Chutsen village, just before the Rong-chu valley forms a narrow gorge. Within the gorge at **Rampa** is the hermitage of Padmasambhava's eighth-century disciple, **Nanam Dorje Dujom**. The trail continues southeast to **Yarzik** on the shore of Lake Yamdrok (see above, page 225).

Yakde and Bartang valleys

From Rampa, there are two side valleys branching northeast which lead to the Brahmaputra via Yakde and Bartang respectively. **Yakde** is the birthplace of Yakde Panchen Khyenrab Gyatso (1299-1378), a foremost student of the Third Karmapa, Rangjung Dorje, who also had associations with the Sakyapa school.

Gyantse County རྒྱལ་རྩེ

→ *Population: 61,839. Area: 3,595 sq km. Colour map 2, grid B3.* 江孜县

*The fertile valley of the **Nyang-chu** River, which is the principal tributary of the Brahmaputra in Tsang, rivals the Kyi-chu valley of Central Tibet in its importance as a prosperous farming region and centre of population. The valley is divided into upper and lower reaches; **Upper Nyang**, corresponding to present day Gyantse county, and **Lower Nyang** to Panam county. Upper Nyang therefore extends from the watershed of*

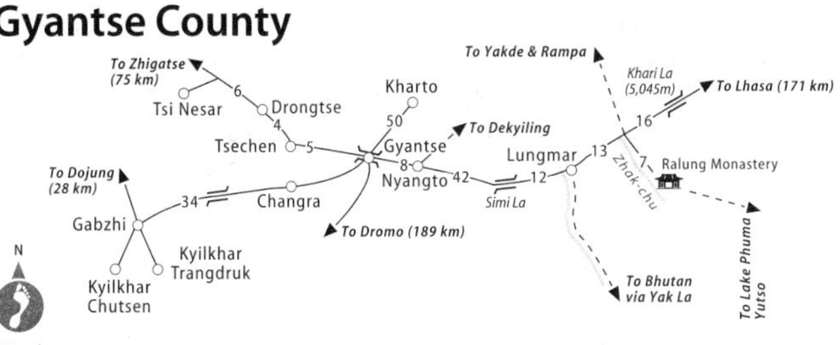

Hierarchs of the Drukpa Kagyu School

Drukchen I (1161-1211)	Tsangpa Gya-re	Drukchen VII (1718-1766)	Trin-le Shingta
Drukchen II (1426-1476)	Choje Kunga Peljor	Drukchen VIII	Kunzik Chokyi Nangwa (1767-1822)
Drukchen III (1477-1523)	Jamyang Chodrak	Drukchen IX	Jigme Migyur Wangyel (1823-1883)
Drukchen IV (1527-1592)	Pema Karpo	Drukchen X	Mipam Chokyi Wangpo (1884-1930)
Drukchen V (1593-1641)	Paksam Wangpo	Drukchen XI	Tendzin Khyenrab Gelek Wangpo (1931-1960)
Drukchen VI (1641-1717)	Mipam Wangpo	Drukchen XII	Jigme Pema Wangchen (b 1963)

the Khari La pass as far as the town of Gyantse, and includes the peripheral valleys formed by the tributaries Nyeru Tsangpo, Luchu, and Narong Dung-chu.

The county capital is at ***Gyantse****, a strategic intersection of great historic importance, 91 km east of Khari La pass (262 km from Lhasa), 86 km southeast of Zhigatse, and 189 km northeast of Dromo.* ▸▸ *For Sleeping, Eating and other listings, see pages 274-275.*

Ralung ར་ལུང་དགོན་པ

Ralung Monastery, the principal seat of the **Drukpa Kagyu** school in Tibet, is located in a spectacularly dramatic setting below the snow peaks and glaciers of Nojin Gangzang (7,191 m), Jangzang Lhamo (6,324 m) and Gyetong Soksum (6,244 m).

To the right of the massive ruined ramparts of the great **Tsuklakhang** (which formerly contained large images of Amitayus and Lingje Repa), more modest temples have recently been reconstructed. Among them, the new **Assembly Hall** contains Tsangpa Gya-re's original reliquary and an interesting photograph of Ralung taken prior to the Cultural Revolution. Its upper two storeys have not yet been rebuilt. In 1999, art thieves stole 42 statues from here, before being apprehended at Tsetang. The **Guru Lhakhang**, dedicated to Padmasambhava, contains the reliquary stupa of Pema Karpo, which had been concealed underground in the 1960s and subsequently retrieved. The **Mutik Lhakhang** is now spartan, but it once contained an impressive pearl mandala of Cakrasamvara. The small single-pillared **Gonkhang** is dedicated to Jarok, Six-armed Mahakala, Shridevi and protectors of the Drukpa Kagyu school. Other rooms include the library (**Pedzokhang**) and the *Kangyur* Reading Room (**Kangyur Donsa**), which has fine murals of the Drukpa lineage, and functions as a residence for the monastery's 15 monks. Beyond this complex are the ruins of the **Ralung Kumbum** stupa and the cave hermitage attached to the monastery, which has always been renowned for its ascetic and meditative approach.

Ins and outs The turn-off for Ralung is signposted above Ralung village, 16 km after Khari La pass (5,045 m) on the left (south) side of the Lhasa-Gyantse highway (75 km from Gyantse). Access is also possible by trekking from Lake Phuma Yutso (see above, page 224) or from Yakde and Rampa (see above, page 265). From the turn-off, the trail follows the **Zhak-chu valley** for 7 km to reach the monastery.

Founded by Tsangpa Gya-re (1126-1216) in 1180, on a site consecrated with the name Ralung by his own master Lingje Repa (1128-1188), the monastery quickly supplanted **Druk Monastery** (see above, page 266) as the foremost seat of the Drukpa Kagyu school in Tibet. It was maintained originally by the so-called 'nine hierarchs named

Senge', and subsequently by the successive incarnations of Tsangpa Gya-re, among whom the most renowned was the writer and historian Drukchen Pema Karpo (1527-1592). The present incarnation, the 12th, resides in India. During the 17th century, Zhabdrung Ngawang Namgyel (1594-1651) fled from Ralung to establish a Drukpa theocracy in **Bhutan**, where his successors were invested with both spiritual and temporal power until the dawn of the 20th century.

Some 21 km below the Ralung turn-off, the highway passes through **Lungmar** township at the entrance to the valley of the **Nyeru Tsangpo**, which leads directly upstream to Yak La pass on the frontier of the Bhutanese district of Gasa. Lungmar is one of the most impoverished areas of Tsang, its lower reaches now filled by a large artificial lake, which has formed since the completion of a hydroelectric dam here in 1998. The highway climbs from Lungmar, skirting the northern shore of this lake to cross Simi La pass (4,380 m) after 12 km, en route for Gyantse. After Nyangto township, it is joined 8 km before reaching the town by the road from Dekyiling on the east (see above, page 265).

Gyantse → *Colour map 2, grid B3*

Gyantse was once considered to be Tibet's third largest town after Lhasa and Zhigatse, but nowadays its status has undoubtedly diminished. In size it is now surpassed by Tsetang, Senge Khabab, Bayi, Nakchu, Chamdo, Derge, Gyeltang, Kandze, Dartsedo, Jyekundo, Chabcha and Barkham, among others. Nonetheless Gyantse has preserved much of its old-world atmosphere, and Tibetan rural life continues here, virtually unchanged, against a backdrop of magnificent 14th-15th century fortresses and temples. However, the pace is expected is pick up rapidly when the long anticipated reopening of the Sikkim-Tibet border for international traffic is announced. The hilltop fortress commands a strategic view of all

Gyantse

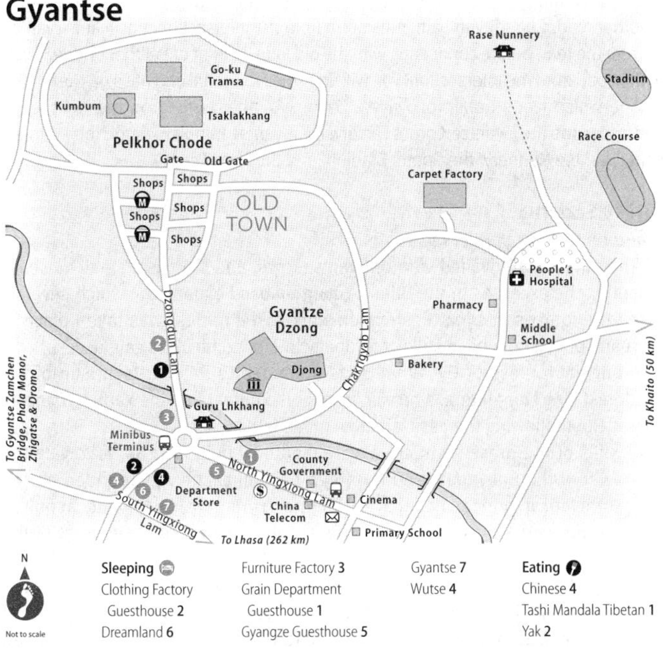

Sleeping
Clothing Factory Guesthouse 2
Dreamland 6
Furniture Factory 3
Grain Department Guesthouse 1
Gyangze Guesthouse 5
Gyantse 7
Wutse 4

Eating
Chinese 4
Tashi Mandala Tibetan 1
Yak 2

approaching roads: from Zhigatse in the northwest, Simi La pass (and Lhasa) in the southeast, and Dromo on the Sikkim frontier in the southwest. For centuries it has dominated the wool and timber trade routes from Nepal, Sikkim and Bhutan.

Orientation

Four routes intersect at a crossroads to the south of town: **Lhasa Lam** leads southeast in the direction of Lhasa (262 km) and northwest into the old town, while **Sharchok Lam** leads northeast towards the new suburbs and Kharto township (50 km), and **Nubchok Lam** leads south across the Gyantse Zamchen bridge, before dividing on the west bank of the Nyang-chu— northwest for Zhigatse and south for Dromo. On Lhasa Lam, beside the bridge, there is a PLA camp, which is identified as the site of Younghusband's former camp at Gyantse.

Turning from Lhasa Lam into **New Dzongdun Lam**, you will pass on the right **South Yingxiong Lam** (where the Gyantse Hotel and a pharmacy are located), followed by the smaller Wutse Hotel on the left and the Dreamland Hotel on the right. There are a number of small Chinese and Muslim restaurants alongside the hotels, some of which have English menus; and the Mandala Tibetan Restaurant is also popular.

Reaching the main downtown intersection, turn east into **North Yingxiong Lam**. On the right you will pass a large department store, the Gyangze Guesthouse, Construction Bank, China Post and China Telecom, while opposite on the left you will pass the Grain Department Guesthouse, the Municipality Government Buildings, the Bus Station and a cinema.

Returning to the intersection, turn west into **Old Dzongdun Lam**, which runs in front of **Gyantse Dzong** to approach the vast walls enclosing **Pelkhor Chode.** Here on the left you will pass the Furniture Factory Guesthouse, a school, and (after the canal) the Clothing Factory Guesthouse, a number of small shops and the vegetable market. On the right side there is the newly constructed **Guru Lhakhang**, and a number of shops selling groceries, electrical goods and traditional wares (Gyantse was once renowned for its Tibetan carpets). To the east of this main street, an older parallel lane runs between cramped village houses towards the original gates of Pelkhor Chode.

Another road, **Chakrigyab Lam**, runs north from the intersection, encircling Gyantse Dzong from the rear, before connecting with the old lane, in front of Pelkhor Chode. If you follow this road from the intersection, you will first cross the canal and pass on the left the steep lane which leads uphill to Gyantse Dzong. Another turning on the right leads northeast towards the Gyantse Carpet Factory, the Gyantse Middle School, the People's Hospital, Gyantse Nunnery, the Sports Stadium and the Race Track.

Gyantse Dzong

ⓘ *Admission fee: ¥25 per person.*

The hilltop offers an unrivalled view of Gyantse town, and there is a small museum documenting the excesses of the British **Younghusband** expedition, which severely damaged the fortress in 1904. Restoration work at the fortress has taken place in recent years, but visitors have still occasionally found it difficult to gain access.

The original fortress of Gyel-khar-tse is attributed to **Pelkhor-tsen**, son of the anti-Buddhist king Langdarma, who vainly sought to perpetuate the Yarlung Dynasty from West Tibet following the assassination of his father.

The walls of the present structure were reputedly built in 1268, following the rise to power of the Sakyapas, and in 1365 a palatial castle was founded on the hilltop by the local prince, **Phakpa Pelzangpo** (1318-1370), who had acquired influence at the court in Sakya through his reputation as a brave general in the southern military campaigns conducted by his Sakyapa overlords, and at Zhalu, where in 1350 he entered into a marriage alliance with the lords of Zhalu. As dowry he was granted the fiefdom of Changra, west of Gyantse, and he invited the great Buddhist master **Buton Rinchendrub of Zhalu** to reside in a temple which he had constructed there. In 1365, in addition to the Gyantse Castle, he also founded the **Tsechen Chode** (Shambu Tsegu) castle and temple complex at the entrance to the Gyantse valley and adopted it as his principal seat. The incarnation of Buton, Drubchen Kunga Lodro, also resided there.

Later, in the 14th century, when Phakpa Pelzangpo's son, **Kunga Phakpa**, expanded the Gyantse complex, the royal residence was moved into Gyantse itself. During this period when the power of Sakya and its Mongolian patrons was being eclipsed by the Phakmodrupa Dynasty at Nedong, the princes of Gyantse were able to maintain considerable independence and exerted great influence in both camps.

The first hilltop temple, known as **Sampel Rinchenling**, was built next to the castle by Prince Kunga Phakpa (1357-1412). Its ruined walls still contain extant 14th century murals – some executed in an authentic Newari style, and others in the Gyantse Tibetan style, which evolved from it.

Pelkhor Chode Temple Complex དཔལ་འཁོར་ཆོས་སྡེ

ⓘ *T0892-8172105. Admission fee: ¥30 per person.*

The great monastic complex of Gyantse is known as **Pelkhor Chode** after the name of Langdarma's son Pelkhor-tsen who is said to have lived here in the ninth century. The main temple, the **Tsuklakhang** was built by **Prince Rabten Kunzang Phak** between 1418-1425. Reflecting the eclectic spiritual background of his ancestors who had long been affiliated to both the Sakyapa and Zhalupa schools, the prince sought to establish an ecumenical community, and he was aided in this task by Khedrupje Gelek Pelzangpo (1385-1438), the foremost student of Tsongkhapa and retrospectively recognized as the first Panchen Lama.

Within the high perimeter walls, other buildings were gradually established: the great **Kumbum** stupa was completed in 1427; followed by an increasing number of colleges which by the end of 17th century numbered 16: representing the Sakyapa, Zhalupa and Gelukpa schools.

At the beginning of the 19th century, there were 18 colleges, the Karma Kagyu and Drukpa Kagyu schools also being represented. However, the **Pelcho Khenpo** or preceptor who presided over the whole monastery and had administrative powers in Gyantse town, was Gelukpa. Only two of these outlying college buildings are now extant; and they contain little of interest. At present there are only 70 monks here.

The northeast corner of the enclosure wall comprises the **Goku Tramsa**, on which large appliqué tangkas would be displayed during the Gyantse festival (fourth month of the lunar calendar). Commissioned by the prince Rabten Kunzang Phak between 1418 and 1419, these enormous hangings depict Shakyamuni Buddha flanked by his two foremost students, as well as Maitreya, Manjushri and others.

The Main Temple The main temple (Tsuklakhang), which survives intact, contains important 15th-century murals and images.

Ground Floor The Ground Floor, entered via a portico with new images of the Four Guardian Kings, has a protector shrine (**Gonkhang**) on the left, between the stairs and the main assembly hall entrance. This is a strongly atmospheric chapel, in which the images represent the main Sakya protectors: Panjaranatha (Gonpo Gur), Six-armed Mahakala, Shridevi and Ekajati. The terrifying frescoes depict charnel ground scenes in bold colours. Inside the 48-pillared assembly hall, there are a few original paintings and sculptures from the 15th century, which reveal a distinctive Tibetan style.

The **main hall**, where the monastic community gathers, still has 15th-century murals, which have been blackened and not yet restored. It would be worthwhile carrying a flashlight here.

The **inner sanctum** (north), which is surrounded by a corridor painted with scenes from the *Sutra of the Auspicious Aeon (Bhadrakalpikasutra)*, contains enormous

Gyantse Kumbum, The Stupa of 100,000 Deities

The principal deities of the 75 chapels are outlined as follows; for a detailed description, please consult *The Great Stupa of Gyantse* by F Ricca and E Lo Bue.

First Storey Here staircases in each of the four cardinal directions, lead to the temples of the second storey. The principal entrance is on the south side.

Second Storey 20 chapels (of which one constitutes the staircase). These depict the deities of the *Kriyatantras* in the following clockwise sequence: 1 (south centre) Mahamuni with Bhaisajyaguru and Suparikirtinamasriraja; 2 (south) Marici; 3 (south) Bhutadamara Vajrapani; 4 (west) Krodha Bhurkumkuta/ Ucchusmakrodha; 5 (west) Aparajita Sitapatatra; 6 (west central) Amitayus in Sukhavati; 7 (west) Parnasabari; 8 (west) Hayagriva; 9 (north) Acala; 10 (north) Mahavidya/ Grahamatrika Kurukulla; 11 (north central) Dipamkara Buddha; 12 (north) Vasudhara; 13 (north) Vyaghravahana Mahakala; 14 (east) Mahabala; 15 (east) Dhvajagra; 16 (east central) Maitreya in Tusita; 17 (east) Vaishravana; 18 (east) Four Guardian Kings (staircase to third storey); 19 (south) Panjaranatha Mahakala; and 20 (south) Usnisavijaya.

Third Storey 16 chapels, depicting the deities of the *Kriyatantras* and *Caryatantras*, in the following clockwise sequence: 1 (south) Vadisimha Manjughosa; 2 (south) Avalokiteshvara Jaganatha; 3 (south) Amitayus; 4 (south) Khadiravani Tara; 5 (west) Avalokiteshvara Simhanada; 6 (west) Avalokiteshvara Amoghapasha; 7 (west) Black Hayagriva; 8 (west) Kurukulla; 9 (north) Manjughosa; 10 (north) Vajravidarana; 11 (north) Vimalosnisa; 12 (north) White Tara; 13 (east) Samantabhadra; 14 (east) Vajrapani; 15 (east) Aksobhya Buddha; 16 (east) Five Protective Dharanis (Pancaraksa murals; ascending staircase).

Fourth Storey 20 chapels, depicting the deities of the *Yogatantras*, in the following clockwise sequence: 1 (south) Vajravalanalarka; 2 (south) Vajrasattva; 3 (south central)

images of the Buddhas of the Three Times, the central Shakyamuni flanked additionally by standing images of Manjughosa and Maitreya.

To the left (west), there is the **Vajradhatu Chapel (Dorje Ying Lhakhang)** containing a central clay image of Sarvavid Vairocana, surrounded by the other four meditational buddhas and 20 peripheral figures. There is also a gold-inscribed manuscript version of the *Kangyur* dated 1431 – one volume of which is currently on display.

To the right (east) is the **Royal Chapel (Chogyel Lhakhang)**, containing exquisite clay images of the ancient kings Songtsen Gampo, Trisong Detsen and Tri Ralpachen. The latter also contains images of Atisha, Kamalashila, Padmasambhava, Shantarakhsita, Manjushri, Eleven-faced Avalokiteshvara, Vajrapani and Shakyashri of Kashmir. The large Maitreya in the centre of the chapel appears to have been added later when the Gelukpa tradition became the dominant school at Gyantse (no mention of it is made in the Nyang Chojung inventory). A recessed chamber on the south wall of this chapel contains the **Silver Reliquary of Prince Rabten Kunzang Phak**, the temple's founder, and many volumes of canonical texts. There are also small images of Amitabha, Shakyamuni, Khedrupje, the Fourth Panchen Lama and the Fifth Dalai Lama.

Upper Floor The upper floor has five chapels which open out on to a central gallery. The staircase is located at the southwest corner of the antechamber. To the left (west) is the **'Path and its Fruition' Temple (Lamdre Lhakhang)**, containing clay images of the lineage-holders of the Sakyapa school, from Vajradhara, Nairatmya, and Virupa onwards. In the centre of the chapel is a three-dimensional mandala

Amitayus (with Paramadya mandalas); 4 (south) Vajrasattva; 5 (south) Jvalana; 6 (west) Prajnaparamita; 7 (west) Vairocana; 8 (west central) Ratnasambhava; 9 (west) Jnanasattva Manjushri; 10 (west) Vajrasattva; 11 (north) Vajrapani; 12 (north) Jvalanalarka; 13 (north central) Amoghasiddhi; 14 (north) Sarvavid Vairocana; 15 (north) Amitayus; 16 (east) Buddhardharmaraja; 17 (east) Buddhavishvarupa; 18 (east central) Aksobhya; 19 (east) Buddhasurya; 20 (east) ascending staircase and murals depicting the Eight Stupas.

Fifth Storey 12 chapels, depicting lineage-holders, in the following clockwise order: 1 (south) Atisha and his Kadampa followers; 2 (south) Buton Rinchendrub and his Zhalupa followers; 3 (south) Virupa and the *Lamdre* lineage of Sakya; 4 (west) Togme Zangpo and his Kadampa followers; 5 (west) Phadampa Sangye and his Chodyul and Zhiche followers; 6 (west) Tilopa and his Kagyupa followers; 7 (north) Dolpopa Sherab Gyeltsen and his Jonangpa followers; 8 (north) King Songtsen Gampo and the royal family; 9 (east) Shantarakshita, Padmasambhava and Kamalashila, with a select group of translators; 10 (east) Padmasambhava with his consorts Mandarava and Yeshe Tsogyel; 11 (east) Shakyashri and his followers; 12 (east) ascending staircase; murals of the Dashakrodha kings.

Sixth Storey (the 'Bowl' or **Bum-pa)** 4 chapels, depicting *Yogatantra* deities in the following clockwise order: 1 (south) Vajrasana Shakyamuni; 2 (west) Shakyasimha Buddha; 3 (north) Prajnaparamita; 4 (east) Vairocana.

Seventh Storey (Lower 'Spire' or ***Harmika*)** 1 chapel depicting the 10 mandalas of the *Father Class of Unsurpassed Yogatantras*.

Eighth Storey (Upper 'Spire' or ***Harmika*)** 1 chapel depicting the 11 mandalas of the *Mother Class of Unsurpassed Yogatantras*.

Ninth Storey (the 'Pinnacle' or **Bindu)** 1 chapel with a gilded-copper image of Vajradhara Buddha, flanked by the masters of the *Kalacakra* but backed by garish new murals.

palace of the deity Cakrasamvara. Exquisite murals depict the yogic activities of the Eighty-four Mahasiddhas of ancient India. Next, the **Maitreya Chapel** contains bronze images of Indian or Newari origin, the most sacred being a small image of Tara.

In front (north), the **Tsongkhapa Chapel** contains images of Tsongkhapa, the Seventh Dalai Lama, Shakyamuni, Buton Rinchendrub, Sakya Pandita, Padmasambhava, and Sakyapa lamas of the Lamdre lineage.

To the right (east), the **Neten Lhakhang** is dedicated to the Sixteen Elders, each image in Chinese style being set within a grotto. There are also images of the Five Aspects of Manjushri and the Four Guardian Kings.

Lastly, on the Upper Floor, just before the stairs there is a second **Neten Lhakhang** chapel dedicated to the Sixteen Elders (east) containing images of Shakyamuni flanked by his two foremost students and backed by the Sixteen Elders in their individual grottoes.

Top Floor The **Uppermost Floor** has a single chapel, the **Zhalyekhang**, containing 15 magnificent wall-painted mandalas, each 8 m in diameter. They are all associated with the foremost meditational deities of the Unsurpassed Yogatantras (Anuttaryogatantras): Kalacakra, Guhyasamaja, Cakrasamvara, Hevajra, Yamantaka and others. There are also images depicting Jowo Shakyamuni, Maitreya, Manjushri, Tsongkhapa with his students, Amitayus, Tara, Sitatapatra and Padmasambhava. The chapel also contains a fascinating black and white framed photograph showing Pelkhor Chode in its former grandeur.

Gyantse Kumbum

ⓘ *Admission: ¥10.*

The great octagonal stupa of Gyantse – one of Tibet's outstanding artistic achievements – was built and decorated between 1427-1439 by Prince Rabten Kunzang Phak in the style known as Tashi Gomang or Kumbum, which combines a terraced stupa exterior with multi-layered interior chapels. Rising 35 m high, the stupa is said to have 108 gates, nine storeys (including the base) and 75 chapels. One tradition identifies the 108 gates with the nine storeys (representing space) multiplied by the 12 astrological signs (representing time). Within the 75 chapels, the images form a progressive hierarchy of three-dimensional mandalas, as outlined in

Gyantse Kumbum

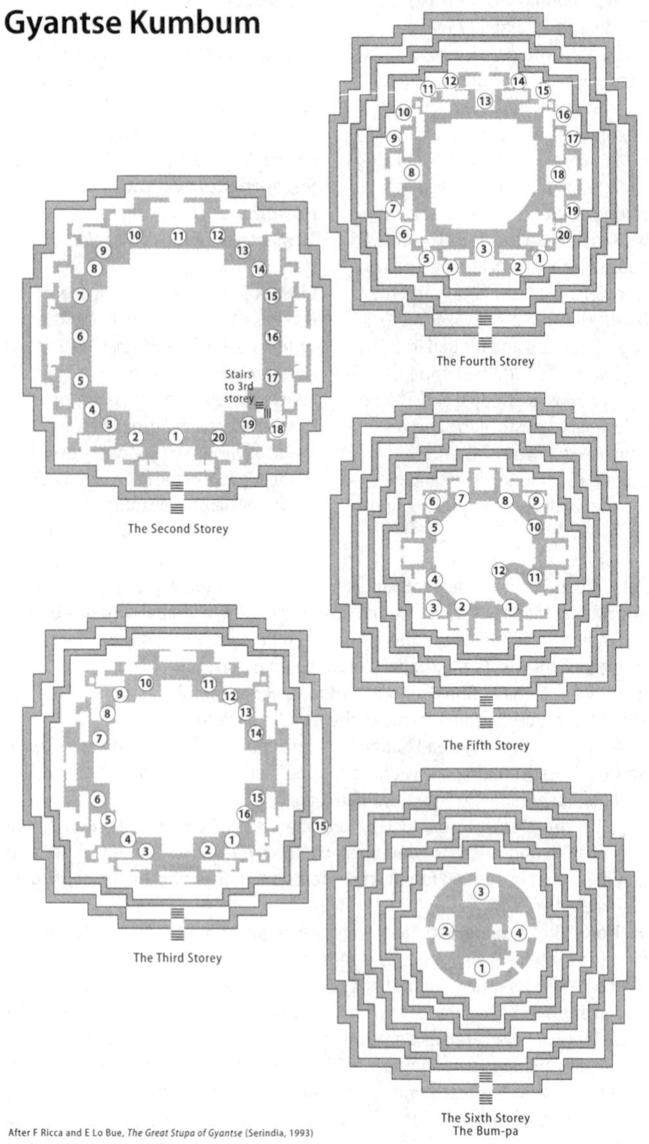

After F Ricca and E Lo Bue, *The Great Stupa of Gyantse* (Serindia, 1993)

the Sakyapa compilation known as the Drubtob Gyatsa, ensuring that the stupa encapsulates within it the entire spiritual path and successive stages of the tantras. For diagram and key to chapels see box, page 270.

Phala Manor

The restored Phala Manor with its spacious courtyard is located across the Nyang-chu, some 2 km beyond the intersection on the west bank. This is the residence of the Phala Family, one of whose recent members acted as a Lord Chamberlain to the present Dalai Lama during his early years. The restoration provides a showpiece for official propaganda against feudal exploitation.

Tsechen Monastery

Crossing the **Gyantse Zamchen** bridge, turn right (northwest) in the direction of Zhigatse. Formerly in the 15th century the princes of Gyantse constructed a fine bridge, surmounted with a decorative stupa gateway, across the Nyang-chu, but no trace of it remains. Even the town has been rebuilt in recent decades following its devastation by floods in the 1950s. From here there are excellent views of the town and its fortress. Continuing northwest, you soon pass, after 5 km, the hilltop ruins of **Tsechen (Shambu Tsegu)**, the seat of the incarnation of Buton Rinchendrub, known as Kunga Lodro, which was founded by Gyantse's first Prince Phakpa Pelzangpo (1318-1370). It was here that the kings of Gyantse resided until the expansion of the town in the early 15th century. Later, the Sakyapa master Rendawa Zhonu Lodro Zhonu (1349-1412), who was Tsongkhapa's principal teacher, resided here. Now only a handful of monks are in residence. The walk from town will take over one hour, but it may be possible to hire a horse-drawn cart on the outskirts of town.

Drongtse Monastery

About 14 km north of Tsechen, overlooking the highway, is the renovated assembly hall of **Drongtse Monastery**, a Gelukpa institution founded in 1442 by the ascetic yogin Rinchen Gyatso, in accordance with a prophecy of Tsongkhapa. Later, Drongtse was adopted as a branch of Tashilhunpo. The ancient colleges for the study of the sutras and tantras have not been rebuilt, but the yellow **Assembly Hall** was reconstructed in the 1980s. It contains a renovated image of Shakyamuni, and (in its upper storey) old images of Manjushri and Maitreya. Behind the monastery is a small chapel containing rock-carved images of Amitayus, Padmasambhava, Tara and other deities.

Tsi Nesar

In a side valley 100 m to the left of the highway, 6 km north of Drongtse, are the reconstructed buildings of **Tsi Nesar**, an ancient geomantic temple (ie a peripheral temple of the 'district-controlling' or 'border-taming' class) attributed to King Songtsen Gampo. No trace remains of its precious murals and images, which reputedly dated back to the 12th century. An adjacent eighth-century temple constructed by King Trisong Detsen to house an image of Prajnaparamita, which was consecrated by Padmasambhava, has also been destroyed.

Kyilkhar Caverns

The **Six Tunnels of Kyilkhar** (Kyilkhar Trangdruk) is an elaborate complex of limestone grottoes, which is associated with Padmasambhava and his consorts. It can be circumambulated by pilgrims in a single day.

A large outer cavern known as the **Assembly Hall** (Dukhang) serves as an antechamber, leading into the **Guru Lhakhang** cave (left side) where there are relief images of Padmasambhava and a stone footprint of Yeshe Tsogyel, aged eight. Adjacent to it is the **Gonkhang** cavern, where protector rituals would be performed. A long 10-m tunnel extends from this antechamber towards an inner recess at the rear of the Dukhang. This is the **meditation cave of Yeshe Tsogyel**; and within it a tunnel leads, via a ladder and suspended rope, to the **Eighteen Tunnels of the Intermediate State** (Bardo Trangchen Chobgye) and the slippery **Elephant's Stomach Tunnel** (Langchen Tropa). Returning to the Dukhang, opposite the entrance to the cave of Yeshe Tsogyel is the **Cave of Mandarava**. Throughout the complex there are many natural rocks forming sacred images discerned by those of pure vision.

Getting there Cross the Gyantse Zamchen bridge and turn right towards Zhigatse. After 1 km, a dirt road on the left leads to **Changra** township. From here, a 34-km drive southwest crosses Namru La pass to reach **Gabzhi** in Kyilkhar township. An alternative 46-km route is also possible from Panam, via **Dojung** (see below). The valley diverges at Gabzhi. The southwest branch, marked by the **Kyilkhar hot springs** and a stupa built by Tibet's eighth-century physician Yutok Yonten Gonpo, leads to **Se** township (see page 298). Take the southeast branch to the caverns.

Sleeping

Gyantse *p265, map p267*

C **Gyantse Hotel**, 6 South Yingxiong Lam, T0892-8172231, F0892-8172366. A 2-star hotel with 120 comfortable rooms (en suite), including doubles at ¥441, singles at ¥441, triples at ¥526, suites at ¥935, and deluxe suites at ¥1,386. Discounts are available in the low season. There is a choice of Tibetan and Western (Chinese) style rooms. The hotel, which is under the skilful management of Mr Lhundrub Tsering, has 4 floors, no elevator, and a reliable solar heated water supply, most effective after 2000, a good Chinese restaurant (full meal plan ¥288, breakfast ¥92), IDD facility in lobby, souvenir and gift shop, foyer bar and games room.

D **Dreamland Hotel**, South Yinxiong Lam. A simple Chinese-run establishment.

D **Wutse Hotel**, South Yinxiong Lam. Under same management as the Wutse Hotel in Zhigatse.

E **Clothing Factory Guesthouse**, Old Dzongdun Lam. Has triples, and cold running water.

E **Furniture Factory Guesthouse**, Old Dzongdun Lam. Has Tibetan-style rooms and dormitory accommodation (¥25 per bed), but cold water only.

E **Grain Department Guesthouse**, North Yingxiong Lam. Dormitory accommodation.

E **Gyangze Guesthouse**, North Yingxiong Lam. Dormitory accommodation.

Eating

Gyantse *p265, map p267*

¥¥ **Sichuan Restaurant**, North Yinxiong Lam. Serves average Sichuan dishes at reasonable prices.

¥¥ **Tibetan & Chinese Restaurant**, Gyantse Hotel. The best and most expensive Chinese food in town is available here.

¥ **Chinese Restaurant**, New Dzongdun Lam. Has English menu for backpackers.

¥ **Clothing Factory Restaurant**, Old Dzongdun Lam. Serves simple and wholesome Tibetan dumplings (*momo*) and noodles (*thukpa*).

¥ **Tashi Mandala Tibetan Restaurant**, upstairs on Old Dzongdun Lam. Tibetan and Chinese food with some continental dishes are on offer here, but like entering a time warp, the establishment has the murals and heady ambience of 1960s hippy restaurants in Kathmandu.

¥ **Yak Restaurant**, Old Dzongdun Lam. For fresh Tibetan bread, try the bakery on Chakrigyab Lam.

Entertainment

Gyantse *p265, map p267*

Outside the horse festival season, the only forms of entertainment are pool and karaoke.

Festivals and events

Gyantse *p265, map p267*

The Gyantse horse festival and archery contest is one of the oldest in this part of Tibet, having

For an explanation of the sleeping and eating price codes used in this guide, see inside the front cover. Other relevant information is found in Essentials pages 44-46.

been introduced by Prince Rapten Kunzang Phak in 1408. It lasts for 5 days, beginning on the 15th day of the 4th month of the lunar calendar **(23rd May 2005)**.

Shopping

Gyantse *p265, map p267*

Handicrafts
There is a souvenir gift shop in the Gyantse Hotel.
Carpet Factory, or stores on Old Dzongdun Lam, near the entrance to Pelkhor Chode. For Tibetan textiles, carpets, handicrafts and religious artefacts.

Modern goods
There is a department store at the intersection, and other general stores on the east side of Old Dzongdun Lam, selling modern Chinese goods: clothing, tinned foods, and basic electrical supplies. **NB** Shops will accept only RMB currency. It is best to change currency in Lhasa before reaching Gyantse.

Transport

Gyantse *p265, map p267*
Most visitors to Gyantse will have their transport organized by the travel services.

Bus
Long distance Travel by public bus is possible from either Lhasa or Zhigatse. The bus station for Lhasa (¥38) is located on North Yingxiong Lam. Mini-buses depart for Zhigatse (¥25) outside the Furniture Factory Hotel.

Car/jeep
Long distance Car and jeep transportation is easily available from Lhasa or Zhigatse.

Directory

Gyantse *p265, map p267*
Banks Construction Bank, North Yingxiong Lam. **Chemists** There is a pharmacy opposite the hospital and another opposite the Gyantse Hotel. **Hospitals** Gyantse People's Hospital, north of Chakrigyab Lam. **Tour companies** CITS, Gyantse Branch, based at Gyantse Hotel. **Useful addresses** Police and public security: Gyantse City Police and Public Security Bureau, south of crossroads, near Gyantse Hotel.

Panam County པ་སྣམ

→ *Population: 41,684. Area: 2,410 sq km. Colour map 2, grid B2.* 白朗县

*The county of **Panam** is a prosperous farming belt, extending from Jangto township on the east bank of the Nyang-chu, downstream as far as Gadong township (20 km), and from **Sharchok Zampa bridge**, following the Gyelkhar Zhung-chu tributary upstream to **Dojung** and **Wangden** townships (28 km).*

*The county capital is located at **Gadong**, on the west bank of the Nyang-chu, 47 km southeast of Zhigatse and 39 km northwest of Gyantse (or in local terms 16 km west of Jangto and 4 km south of Norbu Khyungtse). Jangto and the Gyelkhar Zhung-chu valley are all traditionally part of **Upper Nyang**; while **Lower Nyang** is said to begin from Norbu Khyungtse and extends as far as Zhigatse.*

This relatively low-lying area, which can be subjected to severe flooding in the

Panam County

rainy season, has been targeted in recent years for Chinese settlement. For a time there were protracted negotiations with the European Union Development Fund for aid to implement a massive programme of agricultural development and irrigation. There are fears that the plan which has not yet been implemented, will further endanger the delicate ecosystem and promote the well-being of the immigrants rather than the locals.

Pokhang Monastery

Located above Jangto township on the east bank of the Nyang-chu, this temple was founded in 1213 by Jangchub Pelzangpo, a student of the Kashmiri pandita Shakyashri. Formerly, it contained the robe, bowl and shoes of Shakyashri.

Nyangto-kyi Phuk

Above Pokhang, is **Nyangto-kyi Phuk**, a hermitage affiliated to Zhalu which was once responsible for training adepts in yogic practices, such as the 'inner heat' (*tummo*) and the 'control of vital energy' (*lungom*). Accomplished masters from this hermitage would sometimes participate in the **Yuldruk Barkor cross-country run**: a seemingly impossible two-week marathon tour of Utsang and Lhokha, starting and ending in Zhalu, which was instituted on a 12-yearly basis (pig year) by Buton Rinchendrub in the 13th century and later adopted by the Tibetan government.

Wangden

The Gyelkhar Zhung-chu valley, in which Wangden is located, contains 22 small villages and three monasteries. This area has long been famous for carpet weaving. The rugs of Wangden, which have highly distinctive designs and colour combinations, and a 'warp-faced' backing, were in great demand throughout the Tibetan plateau, and special carpets were commissioned for the use of the Fifth Dalai Lama and the monks who participated in the annual Great Prayer Festival of Lhasa. Efforts are now being made to revive the weaving tradition of the impoverished Wangden valley.

Zhigatse County གཞིས་ཀ་རྩེ

➔ *Population: 93,910. Area: 2,678 sq km. Colour map 2, grid B2.* 日喀则县

Zhigatse City ➔ *For listings, see pages 291-294.*

Zhigatse, commanding the confluence of the Nyang-chu and Brahmaputra rivers, is still regarded as Tibet's second largest city, but this title may even now be a nominal one, in view of the recent rapid development of other cities in East Tibet, such as Chamdo, Gyeltang, Dartsedo and Barkham. The city is slightly higher than Lhasa, at 3,860 m; with an oxygen content of 67% and average annual temperatures are 16° in mid-summer and -5° in mid-winter.

At present, Zhigatse is the capital of the **Zhigatse** prefecture of the Tibetan Autonomous Region, responsible for the administration of 19 counties.

The distance from Zhigatse to Lhasa is 348 km via Gampa La pass and Gyantse, 281 km via Nyemo, or 338 km via Yangpachen and Zhugu La pass.

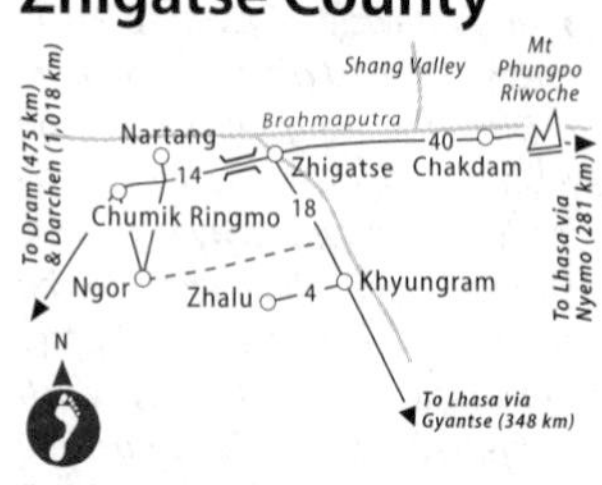

From Zhigatse to Dram (Ch Zhangmu) on the Nepalese border the distance is 475 km; and to Darchen at Mount Kailash in Far West Tibet the distance is 1,018 km.

History

Originally known as the **Samdrubtse Estate (Zhika Samdrubtse)** it was until the 16th century far less significant than the other great sites of the Nyang-chu valley and its environs: **Zur Sangakling**, **Zhalu**, **Nartang**, **Ngor** and **Gyantse**. Further southwest lay **Sakya**, the capital of Tibet from 1268 to 1365. During the 14th-15th century the estate became a fiefdom of the Phakmodrupa kings; and after the usurpation of power by the Rinpungpa princes it was developed as a royal residence. **Tashilhunpo Monastery** was founded under their auspices in 1447 by the First Dalai Lama Gendun Drupa.

Yet, the princes of Zhigatse became powerful patrons of the Karma Kagyu school, particularly following the foundation of the Zhamarpa's residence at Yangpachen (see above, page 142).

In 1565, the power of the Rinpungpas was itself usurped by **Karma Tseten (Zhingshakpa Tseten Dorje)** of the **Nyak** family. He made Zhigatse the **capital of Tibet**. In religious affairs, he adopted a sectarian position, which favoured the Karma Kagyu school at the expense of the others. When he persecuted the Northern Treasures (Jangter) community of the Nyingmapa, he is said to have been ritually slain in 1599 by Jangdak Tashi Topgyel. Unfortunately this made little difference, since the son who succeeded him, **Karma Tensung Wangpo**, maintained the same policy. He forged an alliance with the Chogthu Mongolians and captured Lhasa and Phenyul in 1605.

On his death (1611), he was succeeded by his son, **Karma Phuntsok Namgyel** who, in 1613, established a new 15-point legal system for Tibet. His imposing **castle** at Zhigatse is said to have been a prototype for the Potala palace at Lhasa. In 1616 he forced Zhabdrung Ngawang Namgyel to flee Ralung Monastery for Bhutan, and following the latter's establishment there of a theocratic Drukpa state, the kings of Tsang engaged in a series of unsuccessful military campaigns against Bhutan. In 1618 he also established a Karma Kagyu Monastery, known as **Tashi Zilnon**, on the hill above Tashilhunpo, and once again sent Mongolian armies against Lhasa.

Following his death in 1621, he was succeeded by his son, **Karma Tenkyong Wangpo** (1604-1642). During this period (1626) Zhigatse was visited by Jesuit missionaries. From 1635-1642 much of Tibet was plunged into civil war, the power of the Tsangpa kings of Zhigatse and their Chogthu allies being challenged by the Gelukpas of Lhasa, who were backed by the powerful Mongolian armies of Gushi Qan. Mongolian forces sacked Zhigatse in 1635, and eventually occupied the city in 1642, slaying Karma Tenkyong. From this point on until the present, Lhasa has functioned as the capital of Tibet.

Though deprived of its primary political power, Zhigatse continued to flourish as the seat of government in **Tsang** and as the residence of the **Panchen Lamas**. It became an important trading centre. Goods imported from India included ironware, cotton, dyes, spices and sugar; from China they included porcelain, tea and figs; from Ladakh came dried fruits and turquoise, while various grains and yak products came from within Tibet. The old hilltop castle was damaged by the Dzungar armies in 1717, and finally ruined after the communist suppression of 1959.

Orientation

There are four approaches into town: the southern route from **Gyantse**, the eastern route from **Nyemo**, the western route from **Lhartse**, and the north-western route from the outlying areas of **Dongkar**, **Tanak** and **Phuntsoling**. Of these, the southern approach offers the most dramatic views of Tashilhunpo's red masonry and resplendent golden roofs against the stark background of **Dolmari Hill**, and in the distance, beyond the haze of the Brahmaputra, the darker higher peaks of the **Gangtise** watershed range. **NB** Some of the main streets have recently been renamed.

Chingdrol Lam (now called Shanghai Lam)

A petrol station on the left side of this approach road marks the beginning of town, after which the dirt road gives way first to cobbles and then to the paved surface of South Chingdrol Lam (Ch. Jiefang Nan Lu). Here, in the southern suburbs (Lho), the road initially passes a military cemetery and another petrol station on the left, with a meteorological observatory on the right. At this point it intersects with **Highway 318**

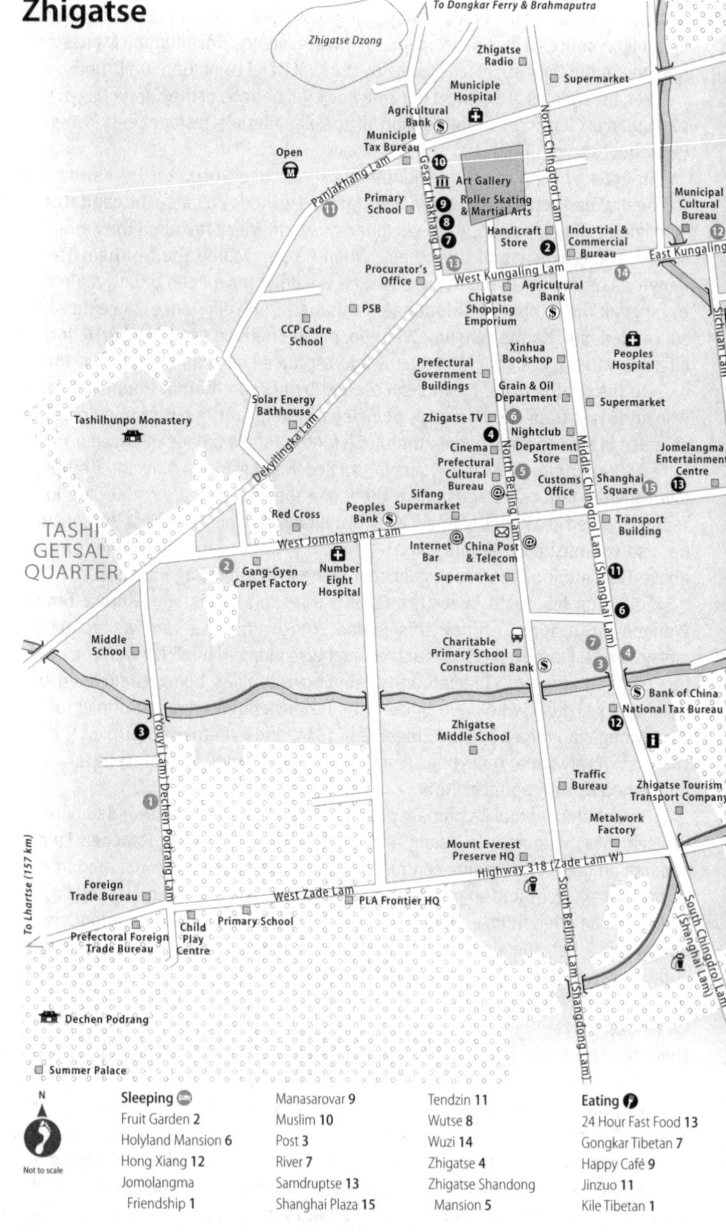

(the so-called China-Nepal Friendship Highway) which leads east out of town towards Lhasa, and west towards Lhartse (passing the Mount Everest Reserve HQ, the Stadium, the Summer Palace and the Foreign Trade Bureau).

Continuing north on **Middle Chingdrol Lam** (Ch. Jiefang Zhong Lu), you will pass on the right Zhigatse Tourism Bureau, the Bank of China, the Zhigatse Hotel, the Xing Yue Restauant, the Jinzuo Restaurant and the Transport Building. Opposite,on the left are the National Tax Bureau, the Post Hotel and the River Hotel.

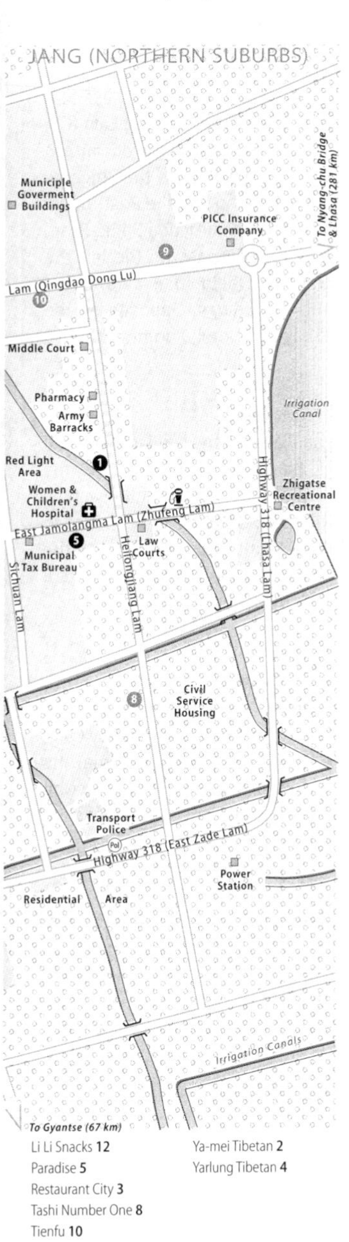

Arriving at a major intersection, turn right on to **East Jomolangma Lam** (now called East Zhufeng Lam) for Shanghai Square, the Jomolangma Entertainment Centre, the Immunization Centre, the Women and Children's Hospital, the Paradise Restaurant, the Law Courts and the Municipal Tax Bureau. Or turn left onto **West Jomalangma Lam** (West Zhufeng Lam) for the Customs Office, China Post and Telecom, Zhigatse TV, the People's Bank, Number Eight Hospital, the Red Cross, the Gang-gyen Carpet Factory, the Fruit Garden Hotel, and the new square in front of Tashilhunpo Monastery.

Returning to the main road, if you continue due north on **Middle Chingdrol Lam**, you will pass on the left large glass-fronted department stores, a palatial karaoke nightclub, the Grain and Oil Department, the Xinhua Bookstore and the Agricultural Bank. Opposite on the right, you will notice a supermarket, the People's Hospital and the Hospital of Tibetan Medicine.

Now you will reach another intersection. Turn left onto **West Kungaling Lam** (Ch. Qingdao Xi) for the Zhigatse Shopping Emporium, the Samdruptse Hotel, and the downtown market. Alternatively, turn right onto **East Kungaling Lam** (Ch. Qingdao Dong Lu) for the Industrial and Commercial Bureau, the Nationalities Bureau of Religious Affairs, the Committee for Returning Overseas Tibetans, the Municipal Cultural Bureau, the Hongxiang Hotel, the Municipal Government Buildings and PICC Insurance (all on the left) or the Veterinary Hospital, the Wuzi Hotel, the Prefectural Science Committee and the Muslim Hotel (all on the right). Thereafter, East Kungaling Lam crosses the Nyang-chu Bridge to connect with Highway 318 to Lhasa.

Continuing on to **North Chingdrol Lam** (Ch. Jiefang Bei Lu), you will pass a supermarket and carpet factory on the right and the Ya Mei Tibetan Restaurant, Zhigatse Radio and a primary school on the left. This is a traditional residential area, occupied by the second, third and fourth Dronglhan (urban districts), and the road soon comes to an end at a T-junction. Turn left for the Dongkar ferry, passing through the northern suburbs (Jang).

Beijing Lam (now called Shandong Lam)

Beijing Lam is the second longest road in the city, running parallel to Chingdrol Lam. **South Beijing Lam** (Ch. Beijing Nan Lu) is quiet and suburban, giving access to a teachers' training college and a welfare centre. By contrast, **North Beijing Lam** (Ch. Beijing Bei Lu) is the commercial heart of the city, leading directly to the downtown market (or first Dronglhan). Heading north, on the left you will pass the Zhigatse Middle School, the Charitable Primary School, the Bus Station and the Post Office. Opposite, on the right, there are the traffic bureau and the Construction Bank. Then, after the intersection with West Jomolangma Lam, you will pass on the left the Prefectural Cultural Bureau, the cinema, the Yarlung Tibetan Restaurant, the Zhigatse TV Station and the Prefectural Government Buildings. Opposite on the right there are the Shandong Mansion Hotel, the Holyland Hotel, and the Zhigatse Shopping Emporium.

Dekyilingka Lam and Dechen Podrang Lam

Turning west at the junction of North Beijing Lam and West Kungaling Lam, you will reach **Dekyilingka Lam**, a pedestrian precinct that runs southwest towards Tashilhunpo Monastery, via the Procurator's Office, the Prefectural Public Security Bureau, the Cadre School, and a solar energy bath-house. Opposite the entrance to Tashilhunpo, **Dechen Podrang Lam** (also called Youyi Lam), leads due south to the **Summer Palace of the Panchen Lamas**, while the houses of the old quarter of **Tashi Getsal** are clustered around the base of **Dolmari** on the right, beyond the monastery.

Gesar Lhakhang Lam

Turning right at the Samdruptse Hotel, you will enter **Gesar Lhakhang Lam**, which extends north towards the ruins of Zhigatse Dzong. On the right side you will pass the Gongkar Tibetan Restaurant, Tashi Number One Tibetan Restaurant, the Happy Café, the Agricultural Bank, and the Tienfu Restaurant. A roller-skating rink and martial arts training centre lies to the rear of these buildings. On the left side are the Number One Primary School and the Municipal Tax Bureau. At the north end, the street opens out into a wide intersection, alongside the open market.

Panjakhang Lam

The open-air market, below the ruined fortress of **Zhigatse Dzong**, is one of the best outside the Barkhor in Lhasa, and traditional artefacts of value can occasionally be found amongst the tourist trinkets. The privately run Tendzin Hotel overlooks the market. North and west of the market, and below the Zhigatse Dzong you pass into a residential area of town houses and craft metal workers. Another road leads northeast of the Dzong towards the **Dongkar ferry**.

Tashilhunpo Monastery བཀྲ་ཤིས་ལྷུན་པོ་དགོན་པ

ⓘ *T0892-8821960. Admission: ¥30.*

History Tashilhunpo, the seat of the Panchen Lamas, was founded in 1447 by **the First Dalai Lama, Gendun Drub**, on the slopes of Dolmari, west of the fortress of Zhigatse Dzong. The original building (the assembly hall known as **Kelzang Lhakhang**) was built above a sacred sky-burial site, the stone slab of which is still to be seen on the floor within. An adjacent chamber, the **Tongwa Donden Lhakhang**, containing the silver reliquaries of the First Dalai Lama Gendun Drub, the Second and Third Panchen Lamas, dates from 1478.

In 1618 a Karma Kagyu monastery known as **Tashi Zilnon** ('suppressor of Tashilhunpo') was constructed on the higher slopes of Dolmari by Karma Phuntsok Namgyel, but no traces of it are now to be seen. The assembly hall of Tashilhunpo and its connecting chapels were refurbished and enlarged following the Civil War by the Fifth Dalai Lama and his teacher the Fourth Panchen Lama.

A **Kudung Lhakhang**, containing the reliquary of the Fourth Panchen Lama was built in 1662; and the splendid **Labrang Gyeltsen Tonpo** residence of the Panchen Lamas dates from the period of the Sixth Panchen Lama (1738-1780).

The **Namgyel Lhakhang** and the massive **Jamkhang Chenmo**, containing the world's largest gilded copper image (26 m high), were subsequently added to the west of the complex by the Ninth Panchen Lama (1883-1937). Formerly, the site also contained five distinct gold-roofed mausolea enshrining the relics of the Fifth to Ninth Panchen Lamas, but these were annihilated during the 1960s.

The late Tenth Panchen Lama (1938-1989) towards the end of his life commissioned a new colossal mausoleum named **Dungten Tashi Namgyel** on the north side of the assembly hall courtyard. Within it he personally reinterred the mortal remains of his five predecessors, side by side. The most recent construction at Tashilhunpo is the new mausoleum, the **Dungten Sisum Namgyel**, which was built to house his own relics, following his untimely death in 1989.

Around the assembly hall there were formerly four colleges: **Shartse** teaching general subjects, **Ngakpa** teaching the tantras, **Tosamling** teaching dialectics, and **Kyilkang**. Of these **Ngakpa** has now been relocated to the front of the assembly hall; while **Kyilkhang** has assumed the combined functions of the other defunct colleges, particularly dialectics.

One of Tibet's most influential monasteries, Tashilhunpo's many branches extend from **Yong He Gong** in Beijing and **Chengde** in Manchuria to **Gyantse**, and in more recent years to **Karnataka** state in South India.

Orientation Tashilhunpo Monastery is counted among the six largest Gelukpa monasteries in Tibet, formerly at its peak housing 4,700 monks. The ticket office is located to the east of the Main Gate (open mornings and afternoons on weekdays and mornings only at weekends); and there is a bookshop to the right of the entrance courtyard. Like Labrang Tashikyil and Kumbum Jampaling Monastery in Amdo, Tashilhunpo has the appearance of a monastic city. There is a 3-km pilgrimage circuit

Tashilhunpo Monastery

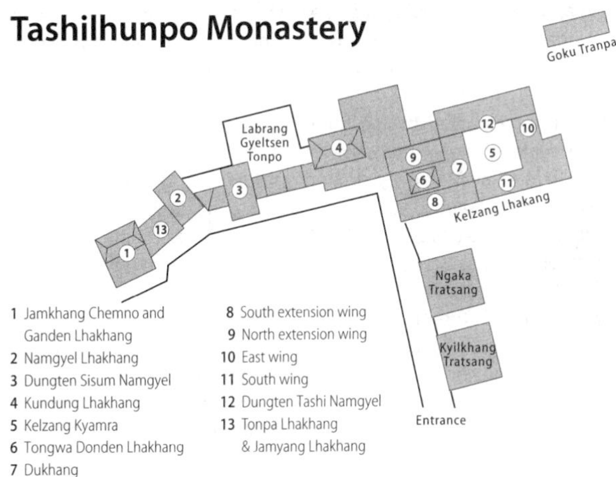

The succession of Panchen Lamas

Panchen Lama I	Khedrub Je Gelek Pelzangpo (1385-1483)
Panchen Lama II	Sonam Chokyi Langpo (1438-1504)
Panchen Lama III	Ensapa Lobzang Dobdrub (1505-1566)
Panchen Lama IV	Lobzang Chokyi Gyeltsen (1567-1662)
Panchen Lama V	Lobzang Yeshe (1663-1737)
Panchen Lama VI	Palden Yeshe (1738-1780)
Panchen Lama VII	Tenpei Nyima (1782-1854)
Panchen Lama VIII	Tenpei Wangchuk (1855-1882)
Panchen Lama IX	Chokyi Nyima (1883-1937)
Panchen Lama X	Trinle Lhundrub Chokyi Gyeltsen (1938-1989)
Panchen Lama XI	Gendun Chokyi Nyima (b 1989)

(*lingkor*) around the complex, including the Dolmari ridge to the rear, and the buildings should ideally be visited in a clockwise sequence, from west to east. Insist on following the correct route if your local tour guide tries to lead you through in reverse! The main buildings are therefore to be visited in the following sequence:

Jamkhang Chenmo This tall building to the west of the complex houses the world's largest gilded copper image, 26 m in height. Constructed during the First World War, this massive **Maitreya**, embodying loving kindness, contains 6,700 teals of gold and 150 metric tons of copper, and within it an enormous juniper tree from **Reting** monastery functions as a life-supporting axis (*sok-zhing*). The body of the image is encrusted with ornaments and precious stones, and its overwhelming visage exudes an aura of calm benevolence. The surrounding murals of the chapel depict 1,000 Maitreyas, drawn in gold line on a red background.

Other murals near the entrance depict the three Kadampa teachers, Atisha, Dromtonpa and Ngok Lekpei Sherab; as well as the triad of meditational deities, Guhyasamaja, Cakrasamvara and Bhairava. Fifteen other small chapels extend throughout the lower and upper floors, and among these special mention should be made of the **Zhelre Lhakhang** and **Utrok Lhakhang**, from which Maitreya's face and crown respectively are seen at close quarters. The **Ganden Lhakhang**, which faces the entrance to the Jamkhang Chenmo, contains 1,000 images of Tsongkhapa.

Tonpa Lhakhang and Jamyang Lhakhang The next complex contains two temples with a common entrance. On the left there is a chapel dedicated to Shakyamuni Buddha, while the one on the right shows various aspects of Manjughosa.

Namgyel Lhakhang Constructed by the Ninth Panchen Lama (1883-1937), the Namgyel Lhakhang contains large impressive images of Tsongkhapa and his two foremost students, flanked by Maitreya and Manjushri. In recent years it has been used as a school of dialectics, and is sometimes closed to the public. The impact of this and the previous chapel is understandably dwarfed by the awesome majesty of Maitreya in the previous chapel.

Dungten Sisum Namgyel The next chapel is the Dungten Sisum Namgyel mausoleum of the late Tenth Panchen Lama, who passed away in suspicious circumstances in 1987. Some 500 kg of gold was donated for the construction of this enormous bejewelled reliquary, which contains his embalmed remains and was consecrated in 1994. A statue representing the Tenth Panchen Lama is seated in front of the mausoleum.

Kudung Lhakhang East of the Dungten Sisum Namgyel, and connected to it via a second floor walkway, is the red-walled gold-roofed chapel containing the silver reliquary of the Fourth Panchen Lobzang Chokyi Gyeltsen (1567-1662). He was the teacher of the Fifth Dalai Lama and the first to have the title Panchen Erdeni Embodiment of Buddha Amitabha conferred on him. His predecessors were retrospectively recognized as such. The importance of this reliquary is manifested by the fact that among all the mausolea of Tashilhunpo, only this one was left standing during the Cultural Revolution. The 11-m high reliquary stupa contains an image of the Fourth Panchen Lama in its niche, and in front are images of the deities symbolizing longevity: Amitayus, White Tara and Vijaya. The murals are still blackened by kitchen smoke from the 1960s, but the courtyard has a fine bell.

Labrang Gyeltsen Tonpo The residence of the Panchen Lamas, which was founded by Gendun Drubpa in 1447, and developed and refurbished by the Sixth Panchen Lama Palden Yeshe (1738-1780), is a three-storey white building, located slightly east and to the rear of the Dungten Sisum Namgyel and the Kudung Lhakhang. It contains a series of seven interconnecting red-painted chapels along its front façade. More recent renovations were carried out between 1976-1978.

From west to east (left to right) the outer chapels are as follows: **Gyanak Lhakhang** was built by the Sixth Panchen Lama in honour of the Qianlong Emperor, who was his disciple, and it contains images of Vajradhara, Bhaisajyaguru, Tsongkhapa and Tara. **Lhendzom Zimpuk** is the chamber where the Panchen Lamas would receive official visitors including the Manchu amban. It contains two thrones and a series of 17 appliqué tangkas depicting the previous lives of the Panchen Lama, which were commissioned in Hangzhou by the Ninth Panchen Lama.

Chime Peldrub Lhakhang is dedicated to Amitayus, flanked by Shakyamuni and Manjughosa. The chapel also contains a full set of the *Kangyur* and *Tangyur*. The next chamber, **Dzegya Gonkhang**, approached via a staircase, contains an image of the protectress Chamsing.

The **Puntsok Kunkyil Lhakhang** contains images of Tsongkhapa and his foremost students. **Kuntu Lhakhang** contains an assemblage of smaller images. Lastly, **Yulo Dolma Lhakhang** contains images of the 21 forms of Tara. Upstairs in the front wing of the Labrang is the chamber where the late Tenth Panchen Lama's embalmed remains lay within a glass shrine from 1989 until the construction of his mausoleum was completed in 1994.

Kelzang Tsuklakhang The Courtyard The large flagstone courtyard known as **Kelzang Khyamra** is east of the Kudung Lhakhang and approached via a high-walled lane. Notice the tall prayer-flag pole (Dukar Khorlo Darchen) which is refurbished each New Year and is said to have talismanic properties. The courtyard is where religious dances would be performed. On its west wing is the **Kelzang Tsuklakhang** and on the north is the colossal new mausoleum constructed in recent years to hold the relics of past Panchen Lamas. An additional two-storey complex of chapels flanks the east wing of the courtyard.

West Wing of the Courtyard: the Assembly Hall Turning to the west wing, the Kelzang Tsuklakhang is a three-storey complex. The outer walls have murals depicting the thousand buddhas of the auspicious aeon (Bhadrakalpa), each with its own verse inscription taken from the *Bhadrakalpika-sutra*.

The downstairs **Assembly Hall (Dukhang)** is the oldest structure at Tashilhunpo, founded in 1447 by the First Dalai Lama and completed in 1459. Measuring approximately 274 m by 46 m, its interior is supported by 48 columns. It was constructed above a **sky-burial slab**, which is still visible on the floor between the high rows of seats. Alongside the massive throne of the Panchen Lama, there are main images of Maitreya in the form of Ajita flanked by Avalokiteshvara and

Manjughosa, and a series of images attached to the pillars, depicting the deities of longevity Amitayus, White Tara and Vijaya, as well as peaceful and wrathful forms of Avalokiteshvara. Appliqué tangkas made in Hangzhou depict 17 past incarnations of the Panchen Lama.

The dark **inner sanctum** contains two chapels: the **Dolma Lhakhang** containing a Newari sculpted image of Cintamanicakra Tara, flanked by Green Tara (twice), Amitayus and Je Sherab Senge; and the **Jowo Lhakhang**, containing images of Shakyamuni flanked by his foremost students, the Eight Bodhisattvas, and two additional images of Manjughosa. Attached to the pillars in the latter chapel are images of the First Dalai Lama and the Fourth Panchen Lama.

South Extension Wing of the Assembly Hall Above the Assembly Hall, the two-storey south extension wing of the Kelzang Tsuklakhang contains seven chapels, three of which are downstairs and four upstairs. In clockwise sequence (east to west), the former comprise: the **Ngonga Lhakhang**, containing a central Kadam-style stupa; the **Gyanak Lhakhang**, containing a silver image of Jowo Shakyamuni, flanked by the Sixteen Elders and the Ninth Panchen Lama; and the **Rinchen Lhakhang**, containing a natural Chinese bronze image of Maitreya, flanked by Vajradhara, Tara and Avalokiteshvara.

A staircase leads from here to the upper storey, where the four chapels are as follows: the **Ngurmik Lhakhang**, containing a miraculous Tara image of Indian origin which was brought to Tibet at the request of Ngurmikpa Darma Nyingpo in the 12th century; the **Pandrub Lhakhang**, containing a silver image of the Fourth Panchen Lama flanked by Sitatapatra and Eleven-faced Mahakarunika; the **Gadong Lhakhang**, containing a large bronze image of Maitreya, which was commissioned by the Fourth Panchen Lama; and the **Natsok Lhakhang**, containing images representative of the diverse Buddhist traditions, with Tsongkhapa and his foremost students at the centre. From here, a staircase leads down to the ground level and through a passageway to the north wing of the Tsuklakhang complex.

North Extension Wing of the Assembly Hall Above the Assembly Hall, the two-storeyed north extension gallery of the Kelzang Tsuklakhang contains three chapels on its lower level and two on its higher level (each of the last two being approached via a separate staircase).

From west to east these comprise: (upstairs) the **Dribsel Lhakhang**, containing an image of Maitreya; (downstairs) the **Gonkhang**, containing images of the dharma protectors Bhairava flanked by six-armed Mahakala, Dharmaraja, and Shridevi; (downstairs) the **Zhelre Lhakhang**, which offers a view of the head and shoulders of Maitreya in the Assembly Hall below, flanked by smaller exquisite images of Manjushri and Avalokiteshvara which were sculpted personally by the Sixth Panchen Lama; (upstairs) the **Kunzik Dukhang**, containing images of Shakyamuni, his foremost disciples and the Sixteen Elders, as well as an active shrine dedicated to the protectress Shridevi in a recess to the right; (downstairs) an oblong-shaped **Zhelrekhang**, offering an excellent view of Shakyamuni with the inner sanctum of the Assembly Hall below, and housing a mandala of the Medicine Buddha and tangkas which depict the Six Ornaments and Two Supreme Ones of ancient India; and, lastly (upstairs),the **Tongwa Donden Lhakhang**, containing eight stupas among which are the precious reliquaries of the First Dalai Lama, the Second and Third Panchen Lamas, and a stone footprint of the celebrated Nyingma lama Guru Chowang (see above, pages 177 and 217).

East and South Wings of the Courtyard On the east and south wings of the courtyard, there is a further series of 11 chapels connected by L-shaped galleries on two levels, those on the lower floor having been constructed by the Fourth Panchen Lama and those on the upper floor by the Fifth Panchen Lama.

Clockwise (from northeast to southeast and southeast to southwest), the former comprise: the **Jowokhang**, containing Jowo Shakyamuni surrounded by the thousand buddhas of the auspicious aeon; the **Nguldung Lhakhang**, containing an image of Vajradhara and a central silver stupa donated by Gushi Qan; the **Parkhang** (Printery), housing the extant **Nartang** woodblocks for a complete set of the *Kangyur* and a partial set of the *Tangyur*; the **Jokhang**; the **Dolma Lhakhang**; and, finally, the **Ganden Lhakhang**, the last of which contains a central image of Tsongkhapa.

The chapels of the upper floor (again clockwise) comprise: the **Tsepak Lhakhang**, dedicated to Amitayus; the **Kangyur Lhakhang**, with images of Shakyamuni and his foremost disciples, where monks congregate each morning to recite texts from the *Kangyur*, the Buddhist Canon which is kept here; the **Dechen Lhakhang**, containing images of Amitabha flanked by Maitreya and Manjushri; the **Ganden Lhakhang**, containing images of Tsongkhapa flanked by the Fifth Dalai Lama, the Sixth and Eighth Panchen Lamas, and the Indian and Tibetan lineage-holders of the Lamas' tradition; and, finally, the **Tingye Dolma Lhakhang**, containing a fire-protecting image of Tara, attributed to Shakyashri, the Pandita of Kashmir (1145-1243).

North Wing of the Courtyard On the north wing of the courtyard there is an impressively large mausoleum, named **Dungten Tashi Namgyel**, which was consecrated in 1988 by the late Tenth Panchen Lama to replace the five older reliquary buildings destroyed during the Cultural Revolution. It houses an enormous reliquary stupa containing, side by side, the mortal remains of the Fifth to Ninth Panchen Lamas. The sum of US$7.75 million is said to have been spent on the construction of this and the Dungten Sisum Namgyel mausoleum mentioned above. Within this chapel a staircase leads up several flights of stairs to a temple that surmounts the reliquary stupa. It contains lifelike statues of the Fifth to Ninth Panchen Lamas.

Ngakpa Tratsang South of the entrance to the **Kelzang Khyamra** courtyard, a passageway leads downhill, back towards the gates of Tashilhunpo. Some distance below the main buildings there is a **Jampeyang Lhakhang**, dedicated to Manjughosa, while the reconstructed **Ngakpa Tratsang** is located to the right of the main path (as you exit). It has a flight of stairs leading up to the assembly hall, where there are images of Tsongkhapa, flanked by his two foremost disciples and the Fourth Panchen Lama. Next to the central throne, there is a canopied mandala of the deity Yamari. Liturgical rituals are performed here each morning.

Kyilkhang Tratsang This college, dedicated to formal debate and the study of dialectics, has an assembly hall containing images which include Shakyamuni Buddha, the First Dalai Lama, Tsongkhapa, and the Fourth Panchen Lama. The **inner sanctum** contains images of Shakyamuni flanked by his two foremost students, the Eight Bodhisattvas and Sixteen Elders, and with a small image of the Ninth Panchen Lama in front. Upstairs the **Gonkhang** is dedicated to the protectress Chamsing.

Goku Trampa Northeast of Tashilhunpo Monastery is the nine-storey tangka wall known as **Goku Trampa**, where a 40-m appliqué depicting the Buddhas of the Three Times is ceremonially displayed during the winter and summer prayer festivals.

Dechen Phodrang Outside the monastery grounds, and on a branch road to the southwest (see above, page 282) is the **Summer Palace of the Panchen Lamas**, which was constructed between 1956-1959 to replace the former summer residence. The building is not at present open to the public, except on national public holidays.

Zhalu Monastery ཞྭ་ལུ་དགོན་པ

Getting there Some 18 km southeast of Zhigatse (or 49 km from Gyantse), at Khyungram in Gyatso township, there is a turn-off on the right, which leads 4 km to Zhalu Monastery.

Gyengong Lhakhang → *Colour map 2, grid B2.*

ⓘ *Admission: ¥30.*

Approaching Zhalu from the turn-off at Khyungram, about 18 km southeast of Zhigatse (or 68 km from Gyantse), you will pass on the right the smaller two-storey **Gyengong Lhakhang**, said to be the first temple built in Tibet at the beginning of the Later Diffusion of Buddhism in 997. Its founder was Loton Dorje Wangchuk, a disciple of Lachen Gongpa Rabsel, and teacher of Jetsun Sherab Jungne. The main image here is of Dorje Rabtenma, a form of the protectress Shridevi; and it was here in the 13th century that the Sakya Pandita received ordination as a Buddhist monk. The restored protector chapel lies to the left of the entrance, and outside there is a stone basin, which was reputedly used by Sakya Pandita following his ordination. Nowadays, pilgrims are aware of a curious mushroom growing from one of the entrance pillars and protected by a glass covering. It is said to have miraculously appeared there at the very moment when Gyengong's present incarnate lama was born in India!

Serkhang Tramo Temple

The **Serkhang Tramo** temple of Zhalu (3,890 m), which stands within a walled enclosure at Zhalu village, was built originally in 1040 by Jetsun Sherab Jungne of Zhangzhung, and renovated in 1290 and 1333 by Gonpopel, Drakpa Gyeltsen and Buton Rinchendrub with funds provided by the Mongolian emperor Oljadu (1265-1307). This east-facing building has a striking Chinese-style roof, made of yellow and green glazed 'turquoise' tiles with porcelain relief carvings, and its interior murals reveal an important synthesis of Pala, Newari, Tibetan and Chinese forms, suggesting that the art of Zhalu became the precursor for the later Gyantse style.

Entering the courtyard, there is a monastic residential compound on the north wing (upstairs), where Zhalu's 65 monks now live. Formerly, there were 3,800 monks at the highpoint of the complex's development. Most belonged to the **Zhalupa** school, a minor but highly influential Buddhist tradition, founded on the basis of the Sakya and Kadam teachings by the 14th-century encyclopaedist Buton Rinchendrub, who edited 227 manuscript volumes of the Tibetan Buddhist Canon here.

The **Serkhang Tramo** itself has been entered via a northeast extension area since the original east gateway was sealed by the construction of a **Protector Temple** or **Gonkhang** annex in the early 14th century.

Ground Floor The temple has three storeys, the ground floor containing an assembly hall (Tsokhang) with seven adjoining chapels and a pilgrim's circuit (*khorlam*). An empty chapel is located immediately to the west (right) of the entrance, and the murals of the east wall are currently undergoing restoration.

To the east (left) of the entrance is the **Protector Temple**, the **Gonkhang**, a 14th-century T-shaped chapel dedicated to Vaishravana, which incorporates within it sections of the original 11th-century walls. The murals here interestingly juxtapose the East-Indian Pala style paintings of the original building with the work of the celebrated Newar artist **Anige** (1245-1306), who developed his distinctive 'western style' at the Yuan capital in Dadu (modern Beijing).

Continuing past the Protector Temple, you will reach the entrance to the **pilgrims' circuit**, decorated with extraordinary vivid and detailed murals of the 100 deeds of Shakyamuni Buddha, which represent the Anige school. Each band of painting has its unique inscription, taken from texts such as the *Jatakamala* and the *Ratnakuta* sutras, which describe the deeds of the Buddha. Here the influence is predominantly Newar, interspersed with a few figures suggestive of Chinese or Central Asian styles. Three small chapels are entered from the pilgrims' circuit, on the south, west and north sides; but of these, only the last has well preserved murals, depicting Avalokiteshvara and Hayagriva among others.

Exiting from this passageway, the four central chapels are then approached. The **Segoma Lhakhang** (south) which once housed the renowned **Zhalu Library** contains a fragmented *Kangyur* and wall paintings of the Buddhas of the Five Families in Newari style. The **Lhakhang Lhoma** (west) contains painted *tsha-tsha* (attributed to Atisha), a copy of the *Kangyur* (which was recently recollated), and a statue of Buton Rinchendrub. A glass cabinet here also contains the sealed ritual vase of the Indian master Virupa, known as **Bumchu Nyongdrol**, which was brought to Tibet by Gayadhara. This is opened once every 12 years, enabling pilgrims to partake of its sacred waters. Alongside it is a leather pouch containing a sandalwood mandala in 108 pieces (which is said to confer liberation when worn as an amulet) and a "self-sounding" conch-shell. The **Lhakhang Jangma** (west) contains restored images depicting Vairocana, flanked by the Eight Bodhisattvas, Hayagriva and Vajrapani. Lastly, the generally closed **Gosum Lhakhang** (north) contains a number of damaged images and quite well preserved Newar-style murals.

Middle and Upper Floors Ascending to the middle floor, there is a **chapel dedicated to Prajnaparamita**, which was renovated in the 14th century. It has a circumambulatory passageway (Yumchenmo Khorlam) with fascinating murals, which illustrate the synthesis of Newar and Yuan styles developed by Anige and his followers, among whom the Tibetan artist Chimpa Sonambum is identified by name. The chapel itself has been used as a storage chamber for religious dance masks and costumes. A restoration programme was recently started here through the generosity of Italian benefactors.

The upper floor has four chapels, dating from the restoration work undertaken by Kunga Dondrub and Buton Rinchendrub in the 14th century.

Among these, the **Deden Lhakhang** (west) contains faded 4-m mandalas of the Yogatantras and a number of images, including the most precious relic of Zhalu Monastery: a self-originated **black stone image of Avalokiteshvara Kharsapani**, with a natural Vajrabhairava image at its rear side. There are also many fine Indian and Kashmiri bronze images, some of which are associated with the pandita Shakyashri. The gilded copper stupas contain relics of Atisha and Buton Rinchendrub. The other images are also notable: a large austere figure of Buton Rinchendrub, the Eight Medicine Buddhas, Maitreya, Amitayus, Padmasambhava, Vajrasattva and Vajrapani. Formerly, there were eight imperial edicts here dating from the time of **Chogyel Phakpa**.

The **Tsepame Lhakhang** (north) contains a central image of Amitayus surrounded by 1,000 small peripheral images. There is also a mandala of Sarvavid Vairocana, and more than 20 other images, including fine bronzes. Amulets which confer "liberation by wearing" (*takdrol*) are on sale in this chapel.

The **Tangyur Lhakhang** (east) where Buton's manuscript version of the *Tangyur* was housed before its destruction, has mandalas of Maitreya, and a circumambulatory passageway with murals depicting Avalokiteshvara and the eight stupas, which suggest a later Tibetan development of the Anige style.

Lastly, the **Neten Lhakhang** (south) contains mandalas of Paramadya, Vajradhatu, Vajrashekhara and Trailokyavijaya; an image of Kalacakra, and statues of Buton Rinchendrub and his disciple Rinchen Namgyel. It was in this one-time residence that Buton repaired the Tibetan Buddhist Canon and composed the 26 volumes of his Collected Works, a complete set of which are still on display here. An inscribed stone plaque is said to date from the temple's original foundation in 1040. The outer walls of this chapel depict the life of Buton, an allegorical chart on the taming of mental excitement and sluggishness in the course of the meditation known as calm abiding (*satipathana*), and an astronomical chart, which reflects one of Buton's own particular interests.

Ripuk Retreat

This cave hermitage (4,010 m), situated about one hour's trekking distance in the hills above, is affiliated to Zhalu. The hermitage was developed by Buton on a site that had originally been sanctified for retreat by Atisha during the late 10th century. Pilgrims still partake of the waters of a sacred spring, which was produced through Atisha's yogic powers. Ripuk over the centuries acquired renown as a centre for meditative retreat, and at its height there were two assembly halls, housing over 300 monks. It contains a restored stupa called **Tongdrol Chenmo**, which Buton Rinchendrub dedicated on behalf of his deceased mother, as well as a restored image of Buton himself.

South of Zhalu in the mountains is **Tarpaling**, the residence of Buton's teacher Tarpa Lotsawa. There is also a two-day trek south-westwards to Ngor Monastery via the passes of Showa La (4,100 m) and Chak La (4,470 m).

Zur Sangakling

Within Chakdam township to the east of Zhigatse, and opposite the estuary of the Shang River (see above, page 262), there is an area of great importance to the Nyingma school of Tibetan Buddhism. This is **Zur Ukpalung**, the seat of Zurpoche Sakya Jungne, who preserved and propagated the Nyingma teachings following Langdarma's persecution and the subsequent interregnum. It is located in **Phaktangma** district and, although the site no longer exists, the impact of the Zur family's activities in this retreat centre over five centuries should not be underestimated. At the village of **Zur Sangakling**, where a temple was restored in 1421, the ritual dagger (*phurba*) of the Zur family was formerly preserved.

Upstream, closer to Zhigatse, the road passes the derelict site of **Thubten Serdokchen**, the residence of Zilungpa Sakya Chokden, which was founded in 1469 as a school of dialectics.

Phungpo Riwoche

Downstream from **Phaktangma** district, on the south bank of the Brahmaputra is **Mount Phungpo Riwoche**, one of the 'four sacred mountains of Tibet'. Padmasambhava passed time here in the **Yupuk** cave retreat, and later in the 10th-11th centuries it was an important site for the Dzogchen lineage since the master Nyang Jangchub Dra attained the rainbow body here. Subsequently the mountain became a favourite haunt of Yungtonpa Dorjepel (1284-1365). Also, at Yupuk, in the hermitage of Padmasambhava, the treasure-finder Dumpa Gyazhangtrom discovered Yamantaka *terma*, and Dorje Lingpa (1346-1405) discovered an image of Vajrasattva.

Nartang Monastery

Nartang Monastery (3,900 m) is located 14 km west of Zhigatse and just to the north of Highway 318, which links Tibet with Nepal. This prominent Kadampa monastery was founded in 1153 by Tumton Lodro Drakpa, a disciple of Sharapa, on a site where Atisha had prophesized the Sixteen Elders would make a unique appearance in Tibet, just as they had at Mount Wutaishan in China. According to legend, Atisha passed through en route for Central Tibet from Guge, and observed a distant rock shaped like an elephant's trunk (*nar*) arising from the plain (*tang*), for which reason the site was given the name Nartang. The original complex ranked with Reting in Central Tibet as one of the most important of all Kadampa establishments. During the 15th century, the First Dalai Lama gave his first teaching here before going on to found Tashilhunpo Monastery in Zhigatse. The complex was subsequently maintained by the laity through the 16th and early 17th centuries, until the Fourth Panchen brought it within the Gelukpa fold, under the influence of Tashilhunpo. Later, with the support of Miwang Sonam Topgyel, Nartang acquired particular renown for its library of wood-blocks (Parkhang).

The high ruined walls of Nartang are extensive, and three small temples have been rebuilt. Among them, the reconstructed **assembly hall**, approached via a portico decorated with murals of the Guardian Kings of the Four Directions, contains images of the Buddhas of the Three Times, and new murals which are currently being completed by artists from Tashilhunpo. Formerly the main image was a form of Tara known as Chumik Drolma. There are four **inner sanctums**: The first (far left) is a small chapel with a central statue of the late Tenth Panchen Lama, surrounded by diverse bodhisattva figures, the second **(left)** has images of the Fourth Panchen Lama, flanked by two attendants, the third (**centre)** has a central glass case containing an image of Tsongkhapa behind which are images of Shakyamuni Buddha flanked by Shariputra, Maudgalyayana and the standing bodhisattvas, while the fourth **(right)** has images of the protector deities Bhairava, Pehar, Vaishravana and Shridevi. Upstairs there is a **reliquary chamber** containing small images, mani stones, and the sacred footprint of Lama Kyoton Monlam Tsultrim of Narthang, along with a tablet depicting Shakyamuni Buddha surrounded by the Sixteen Elders, which was discovered as *terma* by Gotsangpa in nearby Namling county. There is also a photograph of the bearded incumbent Eleventh Lama Narchen (who once presided over the Ngakpa Dratsang in Tashilhunpo and is now in Lhasa). In an adjacent chapel his photograph can also be seen, alongside that of his predecessor, the Tenth Narchen.

To the left of the courtyard, the new **Parkhang** contains an image of Shakyamuni Buddha and 8,000 precious wood-blocks, which are remnants of the original Nartang Canon. The original 180-pillared Parkhang to its rear, now in ruins, once housed 112,000 wood-blocks, including a renowned compilation of the Buddhist canon, the *Kangyur* and *Tangyur*, which was carved here between 1730-1742 at the behest of Miwang Sonam Topgyel, the then ruler of Tibet. Other fragments of this collection, including the only remaining wood-block out of a series of eight depicting the Sixteen Elders, are now preserved at Tashilhunpo.

Behind the assembly hall is the restored **Nechu Lhakhang**, which has a small courtyard with a stupa and prayer wheels, leading to a single chamber. Alongside small images of Tsongkhapa, Avalokiteshvara, Shakyamuni and Pehar, it contains a 1,200 year old stone tablet depicting the Sixteen Elders, into which the Elders themselves had been absorbed at the time of their appearance in Tibet. The tablet was concealed in a well during the Cultural Revolution, and subsequently repainted. For this reason, this chapel is the most revered in Nartang.

In front of the complex are the remains of the **Tashi Gomang Stupa**, constructed during the 15th century, which formerly held the mortal remains of 13 of Nartang's 20 monastic preceptors (*khyenrab*), including the illustrious logician Chomden Rikpei Reldri. The stupa was destroyed during the Cultural Revolution. Currently the monastery has only 40 monks. North of Nartang in the mountains is the **Jangchen Ritro** hermitage, where monks affiliated to Nartang would spend time in retreat.

Ngor Evam Chokden Monastery

Southwest of the Nartang turn-off, the highway passes north of **Chumik Ringmo**, where Chogyel Phakpa held a conclave concerning the Sakya hegemony of Tibet in 1277. The local monastery, near modern Dzong Luguri, was destroyed by floods in the 15th century.

Ngor Evam Chokden (4,240 m) was founded in 1429 by Ngorchen Kunga Zangpo (1382-1444) of the Sakya school. The monastery became an important independent bastion of the Lamdre teachings, and developed its own branches throughout Tibet, as far as Jyekundo and Derge in Kham.

Tibetan carpets

Tibetan carpets are traditionally made on tall free-standing looms, on which pre-dyed woollen weft is threaded through a cotton warp and around a horizontal rod. The loops thus formed are then cut in half with a knife, which forms the pile and releases the rod. This so-called cut-loop method facilitates speedy production, in contrast to the slowly crafted Persian carpet (in which thousands of individual knots are tied). The density of the carpet is determined by the number of knots or loops per square inch, and the use of a wooden mallet to beat down each row. Most Tibetan carpets have had a fairly low density (40-80 knots or loops per sq inch), and it was only in the early 1980s that the first 100-knot carpets were made by the Tibetan refugees Mr Topgyel and Mr Tseten Gyurme based in Nepal. After cutting, the carpets are trimmed and washed.

Traditionally Tibetan carpet-making was a cottage industry, which developed in the Khampa Dzong area south of Gyantse, and the carpets produced even now in the Gyantse area are renowned. Many motifs are found, including dragons, flowers, medallions, birds, tiger-skins, and various natural scenes. There are 36 natural pigments in use; and these are now supplemented by a variety of chemical dyes. The size varies considerably; from the small square cushion-sized mats and single bed-sized rugs (*ka-den*), to the large floor-sized carpets (*sa-den*). There are production outlets for Tibetan carpets in Gyantse, Zhigatse and Lhasa; and in East Tibet, at Kandze, where there are local variations in design including the renowned rainbow border. Some of the best Tibetan carpets in both traditional and modern designs are now made, however, by Tibetan refugees living in Nepal and India.

Prior to its destruction in the Cultural Revolution, Ngor was renowned for its Sanskrit library and Newar-style murals. There were once five residences (*labrang*), two assembly halls (*dukhang*), and 18 colleges (*shedra*), with 600 monks residing here. In recent years, one assembly hall (Tsuklakhang) and two residential buildings, the Luding Labrang and the Khangsar Labrang, have been rebuilt, along with one of the colleges. However, the important residences of Pende Rinpoche (Pende Labrang) and Tartse Khen Rinpoche (Tartse Labrang) have not yet been restored.

Approaching the hill-top complex from Berong, you will first encounter a row of renovated stupas, which formerly contained valuable mandala paintings, now preserved, documented and published in Japan. The **college**, which currently houses 57 monks, is adjacent to the car park. Uphill from here are the assembly hall and the restored residential buildings. Among them, the **Tsuklakhang** is an uninspiring building where 33 monks congregate, and the **Khangsar Labrang** to its south contains the reliquary stupa of Lama Tubten Nyenpa Rinpoche, who passed away in 1987. His reincarnation now studies at the Lingtsang settlement near Clement Town in India. Behind these buildings is the impressively restored **Luding Labrang**, which comprises two temples: The **smaller** of the two contains a central image of Shakyamuni Buddha, flanked by 1,000 small icons depicting himself, and another 1,000 depicting Ngorchen Kunga Zangpo, founder of the monastery. Other images on display here include Ngorchen Kunga Zangpo, Ngakchang Kunga Rinchen, the Seventh Dalai Lama and Khenpo Khangsar. A small protector chapel contains images of Panjaranatha, Shridevi and Chamsing. The **larger temple** has a central image of Ngorchen Kunga Zangpo, in front of which is his original teaching throne. The rear portion of the throne is said to contain 1,000 printed scrolls of the incantation of Vijaya, deity of longevity. Stacked along the sidewalls are printed copies of the Derge *Kangyur* and the Derge *Tangyur*. The murals depict (L-R): the protectors of the Ngorpa tradition, the Seven Generations of Past Buddhas, the Three Deities of Longevity, the meditational deities Guhyasamaja, Cakrasamvara and Vajrabhairava, Sarvavid Vairocana, Acala, Vajrasattva, the Sixteen Elders, the Five Founders of Sakya and the Twelve Deeds of Shakyamuni. Upstairs, next to a small protector chapel, there is the **Lamrim Lama Lhakhang**, where the surviving treasures of Ngor are housed behind a metal security grill. These include precious statues of Ngorchen Kunga Zangpo and Shakyamuni Buddha – the latter inset with an impressive talismanic turquoise, and important possessions of Chogyel Phakpa, including the gong which he used to convene the conclave at nearby Chumik Ringmo following his return from China, a gold-inscribed manuscript of the *Prajnaparamita Sutra*, similar to the one housed at Sakya, which he used on the same occasion, and his personal bowl. Other relics here include remains of the Buddha Kashyapa, the tooth of the bodhisattva Dharmodgata, a dragon's egg, the tusks of a seal, a boot once worn by the Fifth Dalai Lama, a utensil of Gayadhara, a speaking image of Tara, a large ritual dagger of meteorite, and a small image of Shakyamuni, which had been unearthed as treasure. The wooden gates of this temple with their intricate metalwork were offered to Ngor by King Tenpa Tsering of Derge in the 18th century, and have been compared with the gates of the Derge Parkhang itself.

Getting there A jeep track leaves the highway a few kilometres before **Gangchen Monastery**, and leads southeast via Chumik Ringmo to **Berong** village, from which Ngor Monastery is easily accessible. Another track runs due south from Nartang via **Lajung** to Berong. **NB** These routes are well signposted but they may be impassable in summer, when seasonal streams can flood the dirt-road surfaces.

Southwest of Berong are the cave hermitages of Ngorchen Kunga Zangpo, one of which contains his stone footprint. **Berong** village below Ngor may also be reached by trekking from Jamchu on the Zhigatse-Gyantse road via the Dzirak-chu or Zha-chu valleys; and another trek leads up the Dzirak-chu valley from Chumik to Chushar, and thence across Dug-nga La pass, into the Shab valley (see below, page 297).

Sleeping

Zhigatse City *p276, map p278*

B **Hotel Manasarovar**, 20 East Kungaling lam (Qingdao Dong Lu), T0892-8839999, www.hotelmanasarovartibet.com. Currently the best in town, 3-star with 78 elegantly furnished rooms (attached bathrooms, a/c, IDD, oxygen system, fully stocked minibar). Twins and singles at ¥480, suites at ¥1,380, and economy twin rooms at ¥280 and triples (shared bathrooms) at ¥320. Restaurant has Tibetan, Chinese and western cuisine; Jazz Café Bar next door. Lobby shops, hairdresser and massage parlour.

B **Zhigatse Hotel (Rikaze Hotel)**, 13 Middle Chingdrol lam (or Shanghai Zhong Lu), T0892-8822550. An older 3-star hotel, under the management of Mr Wangla, with 123 comfortable and recently upgraded rooms (attached bath), including doubles at ¥460, singles at ¥460, suites at ¥980, Tibetan-style rooms at ¥460, triples at ¥480, and a presidential suite at ¥1,540. It has a solar heated water supply, an improving Chinese restaurant, souvenir and gift shop, bar, IDD facility, sauna and massage service, dance hall, fitness room, and function rooms.

B **Zhigatse Shangdong Mansion**, 5 North Beijing lam (or Shandong lam), T0892-8826138/59, F0892-8826124. A 3-star hotel, with a/c, and 110 rooms, including doubles

For an explanation of the sleeping and eating price codes used in this guide, see inside the front cover. Other relevant information is found in Essentials pages 44-46.

at ¥588, singles at ¥518, suites at ¥1,580, and suites at ¥2,580. IDD facilities are available, and there are Chinese restaurants, a sauna and KTV, beauty salon, gym, nightclub, billiard room and conference rooms.

C **Holyland Mansion**, 3 North Beijing lam, T0892-8822922. New hotel with 93 rooms (attached bath, 24-hr hot water, IDD), including doubles at ¥360, suites at ¥780, and deluxe suites at ¥1,180. There are Sichuan, Guangdong and Tibetan restaurants, a shopping centre, teahouse, and business centre.

C **Samdruptse Hotel**, 2 West Kungaling lam, T0892-8822252, F0892-8821135. 80 rooms, standard rooms at Y160-280, suites, singles and economy rooms, with restaurant, sauna, IDD, business centre and KTV. The hotel is close to the downtown market.

C **Wutse Hotel**, South Heilongjiang lam, T0892-8838999/666, F0892-8838666-8886. A three-storeyed 3-star hotel. Standard twins at ¥320, singles at ¥260, suites at ¥580, and triples at ¥360. Rooms have attached bath (poor hot water supply), and IDD facility. Two restauraunts (Chinese and Tibetan cuisine), and adjacent nightclub, which can lead to sleepless nights.

D **Fruit Garden Hotel**, West Jomolangma lam (or Zhufeng Xi Lu), T0892-8822282. Basic accommodation opposite Tashilhunpo Monastery, with simple dormitory style rooms (Y 20-30 per bed).

D **Hong Xiang Hotel**, East Kungaling lam (Qingdao Dong Lu), T0892-8825988/8823888, F0892-8826666. 60 standard and economy rooms with restaurant, entertainment centre, and barber shop.

D **Jomolangma Friendship Hotel (Zhufeng Zhoudaizuo)**, 8 Dechen Podrang lam (or Youyi lu), T0892-8821929, F0892-8822984. Between Tashilhunpo and the Summer Palace, with 30 rooms (some with attached bath). Standard twins at ¥238, suites at ¥388, triples at ¥288, and 4-bed dorms at ¥30 per bed. Frequented mostly by backpackers.

D **Telecom Hotel (Dianxin Binguan)**, 3 East Kungaling lam (Qingdao Dong lu), T0892-8823888, F0892-8826666. 40 rooms at ¥140, 20 deluxe rooms at ¥200, and 4 singles at ¥200, and Chinese restaurant.

E **Darewa Hotel**, 9 Middle Jomolangma lam (Zhufeng Zhonglu), T/F 0892-8999228. 35 standard rooms at ¥150, 15 rooms at ¥120, 5 triples at ¥150, and a Chinese restaurant.

E **Tendzin Hotel**, Panjakhang lam, T0892-8822018. The backpackers' favourite, with 20 dormitory rooms at ¥20-25 per bed, and a limited number of superior rooms. Tibetan-run and centrally located, opposite open air market. Showers are available for two hours in the evenings, but impossible to escape the incessant barking of dogs at night.

Eating

Zhigatse City *p276, map p278*

TTT **Meihua Chinese Restaurant**, Zhigatse Shandong Hotel, Middle Beijing Lam (or Shandong Zhong Lu). Good quality but overpriced Chinese cuisine.

TTT **Paradise Restaurant**, South Jomolangma Lam (Zhufeng Nan Lu), is the best in town. Expensive but excellent Sichuan and Guangdong cuisine.

TT **Chinese Restaurant**, Wutse Hotel. Good but bland Chinese cuisine.

TT **Chinese Restaurant**, Zhigatse Hotel. Good service and improving menu.

TT **Jazz Café Bar**, East Kungaling Lam (Qingdao Doing Lu). Has light meals and snacks, good ambience.

TT **Mandala Restaurant**, Middle Chingdrol Lam (Shanghai Lu). Offers Nepalese and continental dishes.

TT **Tibetan & Chinese Restaurant**, Hotel Manasarovar, East Kungaling Lam (Qingdao Doing Lu). The Chinese food here is excellent.

TT **Xing Yue Restaurant**, Middle Chingdrol Lam (Shanghai Zhong Lu). Has the best value for quality Chinese food in town, including hotpot options.

T **Gongkar Tibetan Restaurant**, Gesar Lhakhang Lam. Serves average Tibetan cuisine.

T **Happy Cafe**, Gesar Lhakhang Lam. For light snacks.

T **Kile Tibetan Restaurant**, Heilongjiang Lam. Has the best Tibetan dumplings in town, and possibly in Tsang! Excellent value for money.

T **Li Li Snacks**, Middle Chingdrol Lam (Shanghai Zhong Lu), opposite the Bank of China. A very popular breakfast bar, serving Chinese dumplings, rice porridge etc.

T **Tashi Number One**, Gesar Lhakhang Lam. Standard fare to nostalgic 1960s drop-outs.

T **Tienfu Chinese Restaurant**, Gesar Lhakhang Lam. Cheap Sichuan dishes available.

Bars and clubs

Zhigatse City *p276, map p278*
For nightlife, on Middle Chingdrol Lam (Shanghai Zhong Lu), there are discotheques, upmarket karaoke cabarets, low-market karaoke bars, and video parlour facilities. On East Jomolangma Lam (Zhufeng Dong Lu) there are several 88 Hostess Bars, and Sichuan Lam is a concentrated red light area.

Entertainment

Zhigatse City *p276, map p278*
The roller-skating rink and martial arts centre on Gesar Lhakhang Lam may be an attraction. The Sports Stadium is located in the southwest of the city.

Cinema
Zhigatse has 2 cinemas: 1 in North Beijing Lam, adjacent to the Government Buildings and the People's Cinema, towards the north of town, east of the market.

Festivals and events

Zhigatse City *p276, map p278*
For the dates of traditional Tibetan festivals, see above, Essentials, page 46. Tashilhunpo's main festival is held on the 15th day of the 5th lunar month (**22 Jun 2005**).

Shopping

Zhigatse City *p276, map p278*
Handicrafts There are souvenir and gift shops in the larger hotels.
Gang-gyen Carpet Factory, 9 West Jomolangma Lam, T0892-8822733, F0892-8826192, southeast of the Tashilhunpo entrance. Has a wide selection of carpets in various traditional and modern designs (price range: US$50-800). Credit card payment and shipping facilities are also available.

For metalwork, jewellery, and traditional religious or household artefacts, try the open-air market.
Modern goods There are large glass-fronted department stores in Middle Chingdrol Lam, and North Beijing Lam, selling textiles, groceries, and electrical goods. Also, for groceries, try the Sifang Supermarket, located on the north side of West Jomolangma Lam, or the smaller supermarket, next to the Internet Bar on Middle Beijing Lam. Smaller grocery and electrical stores are also to be found. The shops will generally accept only RMB currency, and rarely accept payment in US dollars.
Photography Print film and processing are available at the department stores, and smaller electrical shops in town.
Stamps **Post Office**, on West Jomolangma Lam, or at the reception counters of the major hotels. Stamps available.

Transport

Zhigatse City *p276, map p278*
Permits and onward travel arrangements Most visitors to Zhigatse, whether arriving via Lhasa, Dram (Zhangmu) or Mount Kailash, will have their transportation and travel documents organized by the travel services. However, the Zhigatse Prefectural Public Security Bureau on Dekyilingka Lam does offer a permit service for individual travellers who wish to visit "open" areas en route for Nepal or Lhasa (¥50 per person, minimum group size 3-5, validity 5 days).

Air
Zhigatse air-strip, located in Jangdong township, 45 km east of town, on the central Lhasa highway, is not open to civilian traffic. The distance from Zhigatse to Gongkar Airport is 264 km due east. There are flights to **Chengdu** and **Beijing** (daily), **Kathmandu** on Tue, Thu and Sat in the tourist season and Sat only in the off-season, **Chamdo** on Thu, **Ziling** on Mon, Wed, Fri and Sun, **Kunming** (via Gyeltang) on Wed and Sat, **Chongqing** on Mon, Wed and Sun, **Xi'an** on Mon, Wed, Fri and Sun, **Shanghai** on Wed and Sun, and **Guangzhou** on Mon.

Bus
The main public bus station is located on the corner of Middle Chingdrol Lam and West Jomolangma Lam. S = standard bus, D = deluxe bus. **Lhasa** 0830, 0930, 1030,1130 (¥31). **Gyantse** all day (¥15) (S). **Khangmar** all day (¥45) (S). **Dromo (Yadong)** 0830 (¥80). **Namling** all day (¥15) (S). **Lhartse** 0830 (¥25). **Sakya** 0830, 0930 (¥42) (D), ¥22

(S). **Gampa** all day (¥75) (S). **Kyirong** 0830 (Mon, Wed, Fri) (¥180). **Namring** 0830 (¥45). Saga 2/3 a week (¥130).

Car/jeep

Long distance car and jeep hire is available through Zhigatse Tourism Bureau on Middle Chingdrol Lam, and chartered minibuses may be available through the Zhigatse Transport Company (T0892-8822948).

Taxi and rickshaws

In town, taxis, cycle rickshaws and auto-rickshaws are all available. The fare range is ¥5-¥10 within the town, but expect to pay more for trips to outlying areas.

Directory

Zhigatse City *p276, map p278*
Banks The Bank of China, adjacent to the Zhigatse Hotel has a foreign exchange facility, as does the reception desk at the Zhigatse Hotel. Other banks, including the Agricultural Bank on North Beijing Lam, are not yet able to assist. It may be simpler to change currency in Lhasa or Dram (Ch Zhangmu) before reaching Zhigatse, and not depend upon the local banks or money changers. **Bank of China**, on Middle Chingdrol Lam, adjacent to Zhigatse Hotel. **Hospitals** **People's Hospital**, Middle Chingdrol Lam. **Zhigatse Hospital of Tibetan Medicine**, Middle Chingdrol Lam. **Internet** Internet access is available in the China Telecom Building (¥15 per hr) on Middle Beijing Lam (Shandong Zhong Lu), and at a small café opposite the Shandong Mansion Hotel on North Beijing Lam (¥20 per hr). IDD calls can be made from China Telecom, using ICC cards, which are sold here. **Post office** China Post and Telecom, West Jomolangma Lam, at junction with North Beijing Lam. **Tour companies** Zhigatse CITS, 15 Middle Chingdrol Lam, T0892-8822516, F0892-8821900. **Useful addresses** Police & public security: Zhigatse City Police and Public Security Bureau, Dekyilingka Lam, east of Tashilhunpo Monastery.

Zhetongmon County
བཞད་མཐོང་སྨོན

→ *Population: 41,247. Area: 8,722 sq km. Colour map 2, grid B2.* 谢通门县

The county of Zhetongmon, reached from Zhigatse via the Dongkar cable ferry to the north of town, is composed of three major lateral valleys on the north bank of the Brahmaputra. These are: ***Tanak****, the valley of the Tanakpu-chu and its Namoche-chu tributary which supply Zhigatse with much of its electricity;* ***Zhe****, the valley of the Rong-chu and Zhe-chu rivers; and the upper headwaters of the* ***Mu Tsangpo*** *valley, comprising the Langna-chu and Gya-me-chu. The county capital is located at* ***Zhe Geding****, 138 km northwest of Zhigatse.*

Tanak

From **Dongkar** and **Zhudrong** villages on the north bank of the Brahmaputra, take the west track which follows the river upstream. The **Upper Dongkar** valley is largely inhabited by nomads, but it does contain a productive coal mine. Continuing upstream, you will pass the villages of Chonyi, Tangpe, and Gede, before reaching the entrance to the **Tanak** valley at **Darmar**. Leave the Brahmaputra here and head into the valley.

Above Tashiding on the east bank of the Tanakpu-chu, there is a one-hour trek to **Dolma Puk**, the cave hermitage of the Nyingmapa teacher Tanak Dolmawa Samdrup Dorje (1295-1376). It was here that this renowned master transmitted the oral teachings of the Nyingma school, including the Mahayoga and Anuyoga texts, to his own son Sangye Rinchen (1350-1431), and student Zurham Shakya Jungne. It was here and in the nearby hermitages of **Namkading** and **Lagungo**, that Sangye Rinchen in his turn passed the teachings on to Zhangton Namka Dorje and he to his own student Rikdzin Yudruk Dorje. Samdrub Dorje's birthplace lies further upstream at **Nesar**.

At **Nyuk**, a village known for its terracotta pottery, there is the hermitage and nunnery of **Orgyen Guru**, associated with Padmasambhava. The Dzogchen master Kumaradza passed one winter season in retreat here during the 13th century, and in the 15th century it was here that the Second Rigdzin Lekdenje of the Jangter tradition conferred the Anuyoga teachings.

Across the Tanakpu-chu River, on the west bank is the **Tongchu Power Station**, which supplies Zhigatse town. Further upstream is **Tupten Namgyel**, an illustrious Sakya monastery founded in 1478 by Gorampa Sonam Senge. At **Tanakpu** township there is the **Bur Chutsen** hot springs, known for their medicinal properties (T0892-8332320). Trails lead from the upper reaches of the Tanak valley, via the Kyipogo La pass, to **Shang** in the northeast and, via the Namoche-chu valley and Lungzang La to **Kyaring Tso Lake** on the Jangtang plateau.

Zhe Valley

Getting there The broad 100 sq km Zhe valley, in which the county capital **Zhe Geding** is located, may be reached from **Darmar** at the entrance to Tanak by following the Brahmaputra further upstream via Orgyen, Rungma and Kharu villages; or from **Tupten Namgyel Monastery** via a side valley and the Ji La pass (5,500 m). The plain is drained by the Rong-chu in the west, the Zhe-chu in the centre and the Do-chu in the east.

Heading inland from **Kharu** up the **Do-chu** valley, you will reach the Bon monastery of **Ser Darding**, where a small temple has been rebuilt. The ruined assembly hall was sacked by the Dzungar armies in the 18th century and more recently by the red guards.

Zhe Geding has guesthouse and restaurant facilities in the government compound, as well as an open air market, a post office and a tea shop. A track leads north out of town across a bridge to the renovated monastery of **Zhe Tratang Chenpo**, where there are some original murals. In the southwest of the county, there is **Zhe Ngulchu Chodzong**, the residence of Gyalse Tokme Zangpo (1295-1359) who wrote an influential teaching in verse on the compassionate bodhisattva ideal.

Trekking Heading inland from Chabka township, **Namoche** village is located beyond the head of the Do-chu valley, nestling below the snows of **Mount Zhe Lapu**

Zhetongmon County

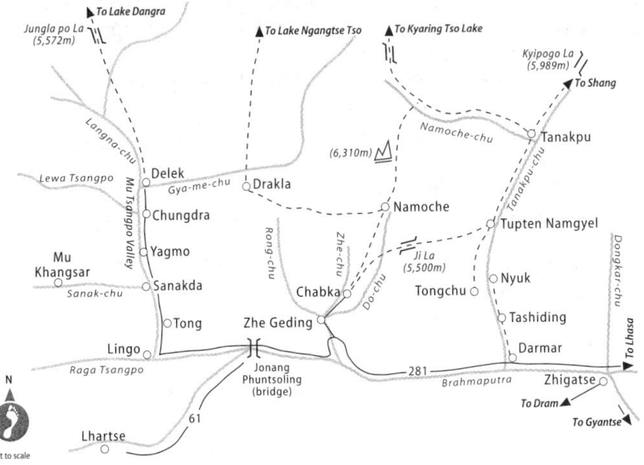

Gangri (6,310 m). A trail from here follows the Namoche River downstream to its confluence with the Tanakpu-chu; and an arduous 17-day trekking route can be undertaken via Khampalho village and Drakla township to **Lake Ngangtse Tso** in the Jangtang Northern Plateau (see below, page 340).

Upper Mu Valley

The **Mu valley**, extending through dramatic gorges towards the Nyenchen Tanglha range, has long been an important caravan route for traders. The lower reaches of the valley may be reached from **Zhe** by following the Brahmaputra upstream, or more easily via the motorable bridge at **Phuntsoling** (see below, page 305). The village of Lingo stands at the arid confluence of the Mu-chu and Raga Tsangpo rivers. Entering the gorge of the **Mu-chu**, there are many rock carvings and paintings to be seen. Above **Tong**, the river banks are terraced and cultivated.

At **Sanakda,** where the Sanak-chu converges with the Mu-chu, a trail leads west to **Mu Khangsar**. The ritual dagger discovered as *terma* by Darcharuwa was kept at **Mu-se**, before being transferred to Sera Monastery in Lhasa (see page 117). The main trail continues north via **Yagmo** and **Chungdra,** where the Lewa Tsangpo converges from the west, and **Delek** township where the Gya-me-chu and Langna-chu headwaters come together. En route, you can detour to visit the ruins of **Lelung Monastery,** which has both Bonpo and Buddhist associations; and, in the upper reaches, the monastery of **Takmolingka,** which was founded by Muchen Konchok Gyeltsen of Ngor in 1436.

Trekking It is possible to undertake a demanding 30-day trek through the gorges of the Mu valley, following the well travelled yak caravan route across Janglapo La pass (5,572 m) to the Bon pilgrimage sites of **Lake Dangra** in the Jangtang Plateau (see below, page 345).

Sakya County ས་སྐྱ

➔ *Population: 44,819. Area: 6,661 sq km. Colour map 2, grid C2.* 萨迦县

*The county of **Sakya** comprises the lateral valleys of the **Shab-chu** and the **Trum-chu,** which flow northwest to converge with the Brahmaputra respectively at **Rungma** and **Lhartse**. Highway 318 from Zhigatse to Nepal crosses the Shab-chu at **Shab Geding,** 60 km from Zhigatse; and a motorable track extends southeast through the long Shab valley for 35 km as far as **Se** township. Beyond Se, there are trekking trails which lead via the remote upper reaches of this valley to **Gampa** county on the Sikkim border. The shorter **Trum-chu** valley, extending from the **Sakya Zampa** bridge as far as **Drongu La** pass, is motorable for its entire length. The route continues beyond the pass via **Mabja** to **Tingkye** county (106 km from the bridge), from where branch roads diverge: west to **Shelkar** (123 km), east to **Gampa** (129 km), and south to **Drentang** in the **Bum-chu** (**Arun**) valley on the East Nepal border (87 km).*

*The administrative county capital is located at **Sakya** in the Trum-chu valley, 21 km upstream from the Sakya Zampa bridge.* ➔ *For Sleeping, Eating and other listings, see pages 303-304.*

Sakya: the 'Pale Earth' religious complex

Before arriving at Lhartse a side road turns south off the main highway to the town and monastery of Sakya. After 21 km driving up the valley of the river Trum one reaches the monolithic structure of the Great Sakya Temple. The massive windowless walls, up to 35 m high are 100 m long and form a square citadel enclosing a temple and monastic complex. Its formidable presence is accentuated by its dark grey colour and its protruding rain spouts carved as mythological gargoyles. It rises above fields to the west and south, a village to the east in front of its main gate and past a slope which runs north, down to the river. Above the river on the far bank rises a jumble of houses and ruins surrounding a second complex of temples and living quarters. This array of houses is about a kilometre in length and is striking in appearance since all buildings are painted with a grey/blue wash embellished with red, white and blue stripes below the roof line and windows. The earth of the ridge behind and for some distance around is pale grey in colour, giving Sakya its name (Tib "sa" = earth; "kya" = pale).

These two areas on either side of the river demarcate the two main monastic institutions of Sakya. The South Monastery (Chode Lho) within the great walled citadel is called the Great Temple (Lhakhang Chenmo) and it emphasized the study of the Buddhist sutras, while the North Monastery (Chode Jang) taught the esoteric Buddhist practices of tantra.

Shab Valley → *Colour map 2, grid B2*

Heading west from Zhigatse across the Zamshar bridge, the dirt surface of Highway 318 cuts southwest to cross the **Tak La Nub pass** (3,960 m), which forms a watershed between the Dzirak-chu and Shab-chu (Re-chu) rivers. The recently rebuilt **Gangchen Monastery** soon comes into view to the north of the road. Having left the fertile Nyang-chu valley behind, the terrain becomes increasingly dry and dusty – a condition that is only occasionally alleviated by short sections of paved road in the vicinity of the county towns and townships.

Tropu Jamchen Chode Monastery

Located east of **Shab Geding**, and in a gorge north of the highway, this ruined but important monastery was founded in the mid-12th century by Rinpoche Gyeltsa, a student of Phakmodrupa, and developed by his own student Jampapel, otherwise known as Tropu Lotsawa (1173-1225). He studied Sanskrit in Nepal, and was instrumental in inviting many Indian panditas to Tropu, notably Shakyashri of Kashmir, Mitrayogi, and Buddhashri. He had a large 80-cubit image of Maitreya constructed there, and a large Kumbum-style stupa was added later in the 15th century. The lineage became known as the Tropu Kagyu; its most renowned adherent being Buton Rinchendrub of Zhalu (see above, page 286).

Shab Geding

Shab Geding was formerly the residence of the preceptors of Sakya. A ruined fortress is prominent on the hillside to the north of the road. Here, the highway crosses the river via the **Shab Geding Zampa bridge**; and all vehicles will pass through a traffic inspection barrier. ▸▸ *For listings, see pages 303-304.*

Qubilai Qan's Mongolian Tribute

The Mongolian armies conquered almost the whole of Asia and eventually extended their rule into Europe as far as Hungary. The Mongolian qans ruled an empire which, at its greatest extent, was among the largest in the history of mankind. Their 'patron-priest' relationship with the throne-holders of Sakya reflects the unique rapport established by Sakya Pandita and his nephew at the Mongolian court. It was they who foresaw that only by such a means could Tibet avoid the tragic fate of Xixia and other kingdoms which had pointlessly attempted to resist the advance of the Mongolian armies by military means.

The model established by the Sakyapas was later adopted by the Tsangpa and Gelukpa rulers of Tibet, and it has in recent times been used by China as one of the main historical justifications for their occupation of Tibet. Qubilai Qan's relationship with Drogon Chogyel Phakpa, and the tributes which they mutually offered at that time are now cited as proof that Qubilai 'ruled over Tibet'. The implication that China has ruled Tibet ever since could, it has been suggested, by the same logic be made against Hungary or any other country conquered by the Mongolians, who racially are quite distinct from the Chinese! At the present day, Outer Mongolia is an independent nation. Inner Mongolia belongs to China, and its Chinese immigrant population now outnumbers the original Mongol inhabitants, despite its 'autonomous' status.

Se Township and the Upper Shab-chu Valley

From Shab Geding, there are side roads leading north towards **Rungma** on the Brahmaputra and south to **Se** township in the **Shab** valley. Taking the latter route, you can drive through **Tsesum** and as far as Se. An alternative two-day trekking route leads from Ngor Monastery to Se via Duk-ngal La pass (4,550 m) and Rabdeling.

Three hours' trekking above Se, brings you to the fortified monastery of **Se Rinchentse**, and the nearby birthplace of Remdawa Lodro Zhonu, a renowned master of the Sakya school who was Tsongkhapa's main teacher. Little but ruins remain, though the site does contain a sacred spring (associated with Padmasambhava) and a hilltop shrine dedicated to the local deity Pen-je.

Trekking From Se township, there is a four-day trek via **Lazhung** to **Sakya**; and from **Mula**, further southeast in the **Shab** valley, there is another four-day trek via the **Gye-chu** valley, **Yago** and **Gurma** to **Gampa** county (see below, page 311). Alternatively, if you continue to trek upstream along the course of the Shab-chu, at **Netsi**, the valley divides: the left branch following the Tradong-chu source, and the right following the Chusum-chu, both of which lead in the direction of South **Khangmar** county (see below, page 308).

Trom-chu Valley

Sakya Monastery ས་སྐྱ་དགོན་པ → *Colour map 2, grid B1*

The Sakya tradition is one of the four main Buddhist schools in Tibet. It was from here that the whole of Tibet was governed during the period of the **Sakyapa hegemony** (1268-1365), and even now there are buildings of historic importance to be seen, which were spared the destruction of the Cultural Revolution.

Getting there From Shab Geding township, Highway 318 continues westward to cross **Tso La pass** (4,410 m), which acts as a watershed between the Shab-chu and Trum-chu rivers. On the long descent from this pass, the **Sakya Zampa** bridge is visible in the distance. Leave the highway after crossing the bridge (67 km from Shab Geding) and turn south into the valley of the Trum-chu and follow this river upstream to **Sakya** township (21 km). The great monastery of Sakya is located 3 km to the left (east) of the township on a side road.

The Five Patriarchs of Sakya The **Khon** family had been influential in Tibet since the eighth century, when **Khon Luiwangpo Sungwa** ranked among the foremost translators of Buddhist Sanskrit texts. Subsequently, during the 11th century, **Khon Konchok Gyelpo** (1034-1102) moved from Southern to Western Tibet, where he studied with Drokmi Lotsawa – a foremost translator and mystic who had also taught Marpa. Drokmi himself had studied with many great Indian masters such as Gayadhara and Virupa, from whom he had received the lineage of the Hevajra Tantra. In 1073, Khon Konchok Gyelpo founded the temple of **Gorum Zimchi Karpo** on the north bank of the Trum-chu River, which eventually became the heart of the complex known as **North Sakya (Chode Jang)**. The foremost images of the Gorum Temple were a bronze Manjughosa in the form of Jamyang Zi-o Barwa and the leather mask known as Gorum Sebakma, which was kept in the Protector Chapel (Gonkhang). This temple is now destroyed, and the whereabouts of its precious relics are unknown.

The son of Khon Konchok Gyelpo was **Sachen Kunga Nyingpo** (1092-1158), who is revered as the first patriarch of Sakya. He studied with Zhangton Chobar, a second-generation student of Drokmi's, and was able to codify the Sakya teachings known as the Lamdre, the 'Path and its Fruit', as well as the Two Revised Texts of the Hevajra Tantra (*Tak-nyi*). Two of Sachen Kunga Nyingpo's four sons, **Sonam Tsemo** (1142-1182) and **Drakpa Gyeltsen** (1147-1216) also became renowned patriarchs of Sakya; and throughout this period the vast complex of North Sakya was developed into 108 temples. Among these, the most important extant or renovated structures are: the **Tantric College (Ngakpa Tratsang)**, the **Dolma Lhakhang** (with a bronze Tara containing the relics of Bari Lotsawa), the **Victory Stupa** containing the relics of Khon Konchok Gyelpo, the **Demchok Lhakhang** (dedicated to Cakrasamvara), the **Mukchung Gonkhang**, the **Yutok Lhakhang**, the **Zhitok Labrang** (containing a number of reliquaries), the **Dolma Lhakhang**, the **West Protector Chapel (Gonkhang Nub)** which contained images of the Chamdrel protectors, and the **Zurkhang Tsuklakhang**, containing an image of Drakpa Gyeltsen named Dzetoma.

The fourth patriarch of Sakya was **Sakya Pandita Kunga Gyeltsen** (1182-1251), a grandson of Sachen Kunga Nyingpo, who was universally regarded as the greatest lama and most prolific scholar of his age. He was invited by Godan Qan to the Mongolian royal court in 1244, and remained there until his death in 1251, the same year in which the Qan himself passed away.

Drogon Chogyel Phakpa (1235-1280), also known as Lodro Gyeltsen, was the last of the so-called 'five patriarchs of Sakya' (Sakya Gongma Nga). As the nephew and heir of Sakya Pandita, he accompanied his uncle to Mongolia, and later was appointed as the personal mentor and advisor to Godan's successor **Qubilai Qan** (1216-1294). Drogon Chogyel Phakpa is credited with the invention of the first Mongolian script, known as Hor-yig, which is still used by the Tu peoples of Northeast Tibet for ceremonial purposes. With Mongolian support, he became the first effective ruler of Tibet since the fragmentation of the Yarlung Dynasty during the ninth century. He established a network of Sakya temples and monasteries throughout the remote parts of East Tibet, particularly around Dzongsar, Derge, Jyekundo, Kandze and Minyak, and he received the title Rinchen Chogyel, 'precious spiritual ruler'. To set the seal on his assumption of power, he oversaw the building of the Great Temple on the south bank of the Trum-chu. This imposing **Lhakhang Chenmo**, predating the building of its outer walls, was begun in 1268 at his behest, with funds provided by Qubilai Qan, who by this time had become the Emperor of China. The construction was eventually completed in 1276 by the regent Shakya Zangpo. Its contents will be described below (see page 300).

In the first half of the 14th century, as a result of Chogyel Phakpa's system of dividing the large monastic structures into smaller units led by their own spiritual preceptors, the then throne-holder **Kunga Lodro Gyeltsen** divided the ruling Khon family into four houses (*labrang*), each of which would take turns to provide the throne-holder. However, by the 15th century two of these houses failed to produce heirs and the rivalries between two brothers of the Ducho Labrang eventually further reduced their number. Power was consequently divided between the two houses of **Dolma Podrang** and **Phuntsok Podrang**, who over succeeding centuries provided the throne-holder in rotation. Two chapels in the upper storey of the **Lhakhang Chenmo** were built by the early throne-holders of these families and named after their illustrious houses.

Meanwhile, by 1354 the political power of the Sakyapas in Tibet had diminished, both as a result of internal feuding and in consequence of the collapse of the Mongolian Yuan Dynasty in China. The political vacuum was filled by the Phakmodrupa family, who were based at Tsetang and favoured the Kagyu tradition.

The unique familial succession of Sakya, nonetheless, continued down to the present day, and its throne-holders are even now revered as important spiritual and regal figures in the Tibetan world. The present throne-holder of the **Dolma Podrang** house, HH Sakya Trizin (b 1945), is the 42nd in line (or 44th if Khon Konchok Gyelpo and Bari Lotsawa are included) and he resides at Rajpur in North India. He has an outstanding command of English and lucidly communicates the philosophical perspective and tradition of the Sakya school throughout the world.

Sakya Sub-schools In the first half of the 15th century, **Ngorchen Kunga Zangpo** (1382-1457) founded the Ngor sub-school, and, later, in the first half of the 16th century, **Tsarchen Losal Gyatso** (1502-1556) founded the Tsarpa sub-school. The former established a number of important branches in Jyekundo and Derge districts of Kham.

The Temples of North Sakya The temples on the north bank of the Trum-chu were built first. Among these the Gorum Temple to the northeast was the oldest, built in 1073 by Khon Konchok Gyelpo. The Utse Nyingba, Utse Sarpa, and Manjughosa temples were constructed successively by Sachen Kunga Nyingpo, Choje Drakpa Gyeltsen and Sakya Pandita Kunga Gyeltsen around the meditation cave of Sachen. Most of these original temples were destroyed during the 1960s, but there are a number of lesser chapels and residential buildings which are well worth visiting. Some of these have been enumerated above. The **Four-Storey Palace (Zhitok Podrang)** and the **Blissful Abode of Secret Mantra (Sangak Dechenling)** are particularly memorable. Aware of the importance of the ancient complex of North Sakya, the monastic preceptors of the present day spend much of their time here.

The Temples of South Sakya ⓘ *Admission ¥45 for foreign nationals and ¥35 for domestic visitors (opening hours 1000-1200; afternoon limited access)*. On the south bank of the Trum-chu, dominating the surrounding college buildings and palaces, is the impressive citadel known as the **Lhakhang Chenmo**. At present there are five rooms open to the public, four of which house images and reliquary stupas containing the mortal remains of Sakya's past throne-holders, including some of the original five patriarchs (Gongma Nga). The fifth contains manuscript fragments and images retrieved from the ruins of the older temples close to the patch of pale earth on the north bank.

The main entrance faces east and is offset from the central axis of the outer gateway. The building is over two storeys high, and has an inner courtyard giving access to the main temples.

The Upper Chapels The upper chapels are approached via a flight of stairs accessed from the portico of the inner gateway. Among them, the **Phuntsok Podrang Lhakhang** is, as its name suggests, the chapel associated with the ruling house of Phuntsok Podrang. It contains fine murals and statues, the principal image depicting Manjughosa. There are also statues of the past lineage-holders and reliquary stupas containing the tombs of early throne-holders associated with this branch of the family line.

On the east side is the **Dolma Podrang Lhakhang**, containing five reliquary stupas of important throne-holders hailing from this branch of the family. The altar has images depicting the Three Deities of Longevity, with White Tara foremost among them.

On the northeast corner, there is a locked chamber containing Sakya's precious collection of Sanskrit palm-leaf manuscripts. Other precious artefacts, including the porcelain collection formerly housed in the main temple, are now kept securely upstairs on this wing, and in the adjacent **Lama Lhakhang**, there are some fine old murals.

The Lower Chapels On the south (left) side of the inner courtyard is the **Phurba Drubkhang**, a large well lit chamber in which Vajrakila rituals are performed, and which has a number of bookcases, positioned between images of Shakyamuni Buddha and Manjushri. All these contents were retrieved from the rubble of the temples of North Sakya, following the destruction of the Cultural Revolution. On the left wall is the wrathful figure of Havajra in union with the female consort Nairatmya. This is the deity involved in the main tantra practised in the Sakya tradition. It was Drokmi Lotsawa who first translated the text into Tibetan, and it thereafter became the main meditational practice of Khon Konchok Gyelpo.

On the north (right) side of the inner courtyard, is the **Nguldung Lhakhang**, which has as its inner sanctum, the **Lhakhang Jangma**. The former houses 11 silver reliquary stupas containing the remains of past throne-holders of Sakya, with that of Ngakchang Kunga Rinchen foremost among them. The 12-pillared **Lhakhang Jangma** has six reliquary stupas containing the remains of important past abbots of Sakya who did not belong to the familial line; and in addition, a series of outstanding wall-painted mandalas, including those of Sarvavid Vairocana and Mayajala.

Assembly Hall (Dukhang)

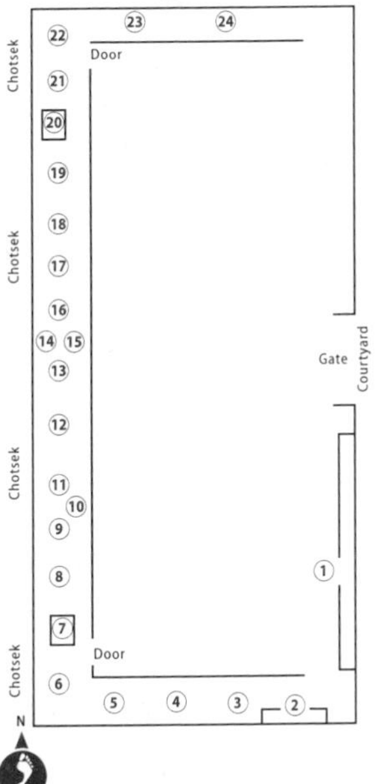

The Assembly Hall (Dukhang) Facing the entrance inside the courtyard is the enormous Assembly Hall (Dukhang). This is nowadays the most significant of the temples at Sakya. Its walls are 3.5 m thick and up to 16 m high. The roof is supported by 40 huge wooden columns made from entire tree trunks. Among these, the four central columns near the entrance are about 2 m in circumference. The northwest pillar, known as **Sechen Kawa**, was a gift from Qubilai Qan. It was moved by hand from Drentang. The southeast pillar, known as **Takmo Kawa** ('tigress pillar'), is said to have been transported from India by a large tigress whose skin, 6 m long, was tied to the column. The one to the southwest, known as **Drongpo Kawa**, is said to have been brought by a wild yak who wept tears at a pass on the way, thus giving rise to a miraculous spring. Lastly, the northeast pillar, known as

The biggest book in the world?

Near the far northwest corner of Sakya's Great Library is what could be the largest book in the world. It is a fully illuminated manuscript in gold lettering of the "*Sutra of the Perfection of Discrimination Awareness in One Hundred Thousand Fascicles*" (*Prajnaparamitasutra*). It lies in a special rack and its pages, in traditional single leaf format, are approximately 1.75 m wide by 0.75 m deep and the book is 0.5 m thick bound between two huge cover planks.

Nakpo Trakdzak Kawa ('pillar bleeding black blood'), is named after a serpent spirit (*naga*) who reputedly wept black blood when it was cut down. The trunk is said to cure diseases when a nail is driven into it.

Around the three walls facing the entrance are a superb series of larger than life-size images, many of them refinely cast. Made at different times and showing a variety of different styles and influences, they mostly depict Shakyamuni Buddha, and contain the relics of the main masters of the Sakya tradition. This is not usually found in Tibetan temples.

Passing clockwise along the southeast, south, west and north walls in succession from the eastern door, you will notice the following images and precious objects: **Southeast Wall**: a gold manuscript edition of the *Kangyur* commissioned by Chogyel Phakpa (1); **South Wall**: a gold manuscript edition of the *Kangyur* commissioned by Yumchok Tendzin Wangmo (2); a cast image of Shakyamuni Buddha (Tubwang Totsema) containing the relics of Shakya Zangpo (3); an image of Shakyamuni Buddha with a hair-ringlet made of white conch, containing the relics of Sharpa Rinchen Gyeltsen (4); images of Avalokiteshvara and Padmasambhava (5); **West Wall**: an image of Shakyamuni Buddha containing the relics of Sakya Pandita (6); the reliquary stupa of Trichen Ngawang Tutob, previous throneholder of Sakya (7); a cast 'speaking' image of Shakyamuni Buddha, named Tuwang Sungjon Tatsema, commissioned by Sachen Kunga Nyingpo (8); a cast image of Shakyamuni Buddha named Lhachen Pelbar, which contains the relics of Chogyel Phakpa (9); the renowned white conch-shell of Sakya, kept in a glass case (10); a cast image of standing Tara which was brought to Tibet by Atisha (11); a cast image of Tara containing the Jamyang Tsogyelma image on which Sakya Pandita meditated when he defeated a Hindu zealot in debate at Kyirong (12); the main image of the temple – a cast Shakyamuni Buddha named Tuchen Totsema, which was commissioned by Drogon Chogyel Phakpa (13); images of the 37 deities of the Sarvavid Vairocanatantra in the foreground (14); a large throne named Zhuktri Tarchikma which the first three patriarchs of Sakya once used, and a smaller throne in front used by the monastic preceptors of Sakya (15); three white-robed images depicting the first three patriarchs of Sakya (16); an image of Manjughosa named Jamyang Metubma, containing the relics of Tekchen Chokyi Lama (17); a cast image of Maitreya named Jamgon Totsema, containing the relics of Jetsun Pejung (18); a cast image of Vajradhara containing the relics of Dharmatala (19); a reliquary stupa named Chodong Dzamling Osel, containing the relics of Trichen Tutob Wangchuk (20); a clay image of Shakyamuni Buddha named Tuwang Totsema, containing the relics of the minister Anglen (21); a cast image of Manjughosa named Jamyang Chokhorma, containing the relics of Sharpa Dukhorwa (22); and **North Wall**: a cast image of Shakyamuni, containing the relics of Sabzang Mati Panchen (23); a cast image of Jowo Aram, containing the relics of Gangkarwa Rinchenpel (24).

Of these objects, the White Conch is revered as the most sacred object in the temple. It was given to Drogon Chogyel Phakpa by Emperor Qubilai Qan, and is regarded as the remains of the Buddha from a previous existence when born as a shellfish. It existed at the time of the present Shakyamuni Buddha, and was used by him in antiquity before being transported from India to China, and thence to Tibet. You may have to persist in order to be shown it!

The **murals** of the upper gallery depict the lamas of the Lamdre lineage; those of the south wall the Hundred Deeds of Shakyamuni Buddha; those of the west wall the life of Drogon Chogyel Phakpa; and those of the north wall the five original patriarchs of Sakya. On the ceiling are hundreds of mandalas representing the outer and inner tantras of the New Translation Schools.

Under these statues in a series of glass cases to the right of the central shrine are objects of art from the Emperors of Mongolia and China that no doubt represent a small part of the treasures of tribute or offerings made to the Sakya masters before the ravages of the Cultural Revolution. **NB** Many of these objects have been removed to a more secure location upstairs.

The Great Library It is well worth asking your guide to show you the library (Chotsek or 'Pendzokhang'). To do so you may have to pay something extra (anything from ¥1 to ¥5). However once this is done you will be led behind the line of statues to a vast collection of Buddhist texts towering to the ceiling that have been gathering dust for centuries. They are stacked two storeys or eight stacks high in racks, made up of 'pigeon holes' in more than 60 sections, the length of the whole Assembly Hall. There in the gloom are thousands of texts the extent of which are only seen with a strong torch. It brings to mind what a portion of the great library of Alexandria must have been like.

Sakya town → *Colour map 2, grid B1*

The town and villages of Sakya are very poor, as is much of Tibet these days, and it is not unusual to be vigorously pursued by gangs of children begging you for money. Do give whatever you can manage but do not give away large amounts randomly just because one child may be more appealing. It is always good to make a donation in the main shrines by placing it on the altar or on Offering Mandalas that usually hold some donations from prior visitors. This will benefit the whole monastery. In town there are a number of small Tibetan restaurants and tea houses, three small guesthouses, a post office and a bus station.

Mabja and the Upper Bum-chu (Arun) River valley

A dirt road continues south from Sakya to leave the Trum-chu River valley via the **Drongu La pass**, for Mabja in the upper reaches of the **Bum-chu (Arun)** valley. **Tingkye** county lies further south (see below, page 311), some 85 km from Sakya township; and there is also a four-day trekking route to **Kharda** and the east face of **Mount Everest** (see below, page 315).

Sleeping

Shab Geding *p297*

E **Zhigatse Guesthouse**, next to the barrier. Has 4-bed dorms at ¥10 per bed.

Sakya town *p303*

C **Manasarovar Hotel**, West Kelsang Lam, T0892-8242222. Best rooms in town. Doubles ¥380, economy 220-280.

E **Sakya Monastery Guesthouse**, is popular with backpackers, offering dormitory accommodation in the range ¥15-20 per bed.

E **Sakya Tibetan Hotel**, basic with dorm-style rooms at ¥10-15 per bed. No electricity, no running water, and open air toilets.

NB Those seeking more comfortable accommodation are advised to continue on to Lhartse, or to camp out.

For an explanation of the sleeping and eating price codes used in this guide, see inside the front cover. Other relevant information is found in Essentials pages 44-46.

Eating

Sakya town *p303*

Mandala Restaurant, the best in town, offering mo-mo, noodles, and meat with rice (range: ¥7-15 per plate), run by a learned former monk from Sakya.

Sakya Monastery Restaurant, attached to the Monastery Guesthouse.

Sichuan Flavour Restaurant, the best Chinese cuisine in town

Tashi Lhatse Restaurant, also offers simple Tibetan fare.

Transport

Sakya town *p303*

Bus

There are 2 buses each day linking **Zhigatse** with Sakya, departing Zhigatse bus station at 0830 and 0930, and retuning in the afternoon. Price: ¥42 (deluxe) and ¥22 (standard).

Lhartse County ལྷ་རྩེ 拉孜县

→ *Population: 44,625. Area: 41,701 sq km. Colour map 2, grid B2.*

*Lhartse county, traditionally known as **Nyingri** district, is located on the south bank of the Brahmaputra, east of the Shab-chu valley. It extends upstream from **Phuntsoling** at the confluence of the **Raga Tsangpo** (Dokzhung Tsangpo) and Brahmaputra, as far as the county capital at **Chushar**, where the **Chushar**, **Mangkar**, and **Trum-chu** rivers all flow into the Brahmaputra. **Chushar** straddles three important motor roads: east to **Zhigatse** via Chutsen and Lepu (157 km), south to **Dram** (Ch Zhangmu) on the Nepal border via Shekar and Dingri (315 km), and west to **Ngamring** (60 km), the gateway to Mount Kailash in Far West Tibet.* ▸▸ *For Sleeping, Eating and other listings, see page 307.*

Bodong Monastery བོ་དོང་དགོན་པ

About 16 km west of **Shab Geding**, there is a turn-off on the north side of the Highway 318, leading to **Tashigang** (14 km) and **Jonang Phuntsoling** (20 km). The **Monastery of Bodong E**, located near Tashigang, was founded by Geshe Mudrapachenpo in 1049. It subsequently became the residence of Tibet's great grammarian Pang Lotsawa Lodro Tenpa (1276-1342) and of Bodong Panchen Cho-le Namgyel (1375-1451). The latter was the prolific writer of some 100 volumes of treatises on sutra, tantra and traditional sciences including poetics and monastic discipline. The temple at Bodong, which gave rise to an independent Buddhist lineage in Tibet, once contained a revered image made from the ashes of Bodong Panchen himself. At **Nyenyo Jagoshong**, further north, there was once a peripheral 'border-taming temple', attributed to King Songtsen Gampo, containing an image of Vaishravana.

Jonang Phuntsoling ཇོ་ནང་ཕུན་ཚོགས་གླིང

Jonang Phuntsoling was formerly the stronghold of the Jonangpa school, which since the 17th century has been confined to remote areas of Dzamtang and Ngawa in Southern Amdo (see below, page 650), following the closure of their mother monastery and its transformation into a Gelukpa establishment. The original foundation is attributed to **Kunpangpa Tu-je Tsondru** (1243-1313), a lineage-holder of Yumo Mikyo Dorje who received the Kalacakra teachings from the Kashmiri pandita Somanatha in the 11th

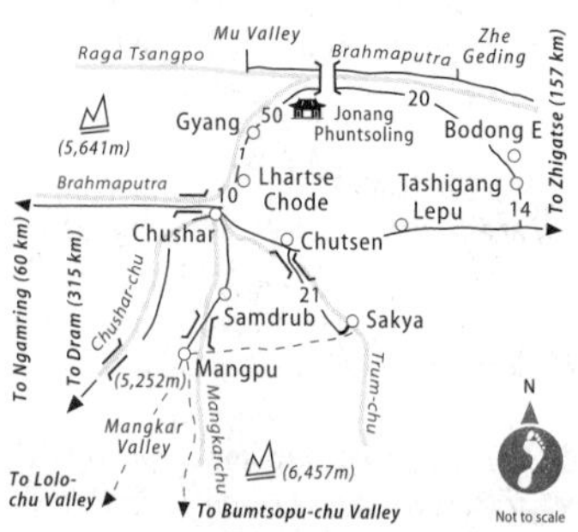

century, and founded the school, renowned for its philosophical exposition of 'extraneous emptiness' (*zhentong*). This is the view that all the attributes of Buddhahood are extraneously empty of mundane impurities and defilements, but not intrinsically empty in a nihilistic sense, their experience thereby transcending all notions of existence and non-existence.

The most important figure connected with this school was **Dolpopa Sherab Gyeltsen** (1292-1361), a prolific commentator on the combined sutra and tantra traditions including the Kalacakra Tantra. He refined the philosophical exposition of 'extraneous emptiness' and expanded the monastery. In particular, near his own hermitage, which lies below a Padmasambhava meditation cave on **Mount Jomo Nagyel** (5,744 m), he built the Kumbum-style stupa named **Tongdrol Chenmo** in the side valley of **Jonang**, a two hour walk from the monastery along a pleasant trail amid sand dunes. This 20-m high stupa is almost of the same dimensions as the Kumbum at Gyantse. It is octagonal in shape and has seven storeys. The extant murals are said to reflect the provincial **Lato** style, which represents an early synthesis of Nepalese **Newar** and indigenous Tibetan elements, incorporating fewer Chinese-inspired elements than the paintings of Zhalu or Gyantse. Unfortunately, the main figures have been recently overpainted with bright colours, leaving only small surrounding areas of the faded original artwork. **NB** The stupa is generally locked, and the caretaker may be found in a nearby nunnery on an adjacent hill (40 minutes' hiking distance).

The main monastery at Phuntsoling and the Kumbum were subsequently expanded by **Taranatha** (1575-1634), with funds provided by the kings of Tsang; and given the name **Takten Phuntsoling**. Following the civil war, the monastery was absorbed by the Gelukpa school and its name was altered to **Ganden Phuntsoling** during the lifetime of Taranatha's fifth incarnation.

The red buildings of the monastery presently stand within **Phuntsoling village**. The main four-storey temple has an inner sanctum containing images of Aksobhya Buddha, flanked by the Eight Bodhisattvas, and some excellent old murals. The library containing gold-inscribed texts on black or indigo paper is no longer extant; though some of its woodblocks have been preserved at Derge in Kham, and elsewhere. In 1998 the monastery was closed and its monks evicted following the failure of an indoctrination programme. The hilltop **residence of Taranatha** is in ruins; whereas the **Tangka Wall (goku)** and **Mani Stone Wall** have survived. A protector shrine dedicated to Bektse, named **Drakram Gonkhang**, was founded nearby by Bodong Rinchentse.

Getting there **Phuntsoling** township is located at the confluence of the Brahmaputra and Raga Tsangpo (Dokzhung Tsangpo) rivers, 50 km from **Shab Geding** on a branch road to the northwest of Highway 318, and 61 km from **Chushar** via another road which follows the Brahmaputra downstream to the confluence. A weak suspension bridge spans the river here, immediately above the defunct **Phuntsoling Chakzam**, which was constructed by Tibet's famous bridge-builder Tangtong Gyelpo during the 15th century. The area is dominated by an enormous shimmering white sand dune to the west.

Gyang

The district traditionally known as **Gyang** or **Drampa** lies 50 km southwest of **Phuntsoling**, to the east of the Lhartse plain. Here in the seventh century, King Songtsen Gampo founded one of his primary geomantic temples, the **Drampagyang Lhakhang**, which once contained a celebrated image of Vairocana Buddha, but is now in ruins.

At neighbouring **Gyang Yonpolung**, there are the ruins of a small Nyingmapa temple below meditation caves associated with Padmasambhava, Yeshe Tsogyel and Namkei Nyingpo. It was here that, during the 14th century, the treasure-finder Zangpo Drakpa discovered the popular liturgical text known as the 'Seven Chapters' (*Leu Dunma*). This text included an inventory, which paved the way for Rigdzin Godemchen's revelation of the **Northern Treasures** (Jangter) at **Zangzang Lhadrak** (see below, page 331) in 1366.

Further northwest, and on the other side of the Chushar-Phuntsoling road, is the destroyed Kumbum-style stupa of **Gyang Bumpoche**, built by the Sakyapa Sonam Tashi (1352-1417) and Thangtong Gyalpo (1385-1464), and decorated in the **Lato** style of painting.

From the 17th century onwards, this area was developed by the Panchen Lamas, who had a summer palace constructed nearby, and made lavish donations to the temple and the stupa.

Lhartse Chode and Gayadhara Lhakhang

The Gelukpa monastery of **Lhartse Chode** ⓘ *T0892-832297*, is located 10 km north of **Chushar**, the modern county capital of Lhartse. Behind the monastery on a hill are the ruins of the old **Lhartse Dzong**, and to the east are the buildings of old Lhartse village. Formerly there were 1,000 monks in this institution, which dates originally to the 13th century. The assembly hall contains some 17th-century murals, and restoration work is continuing.

Below the ruined fortress is the **Gayadhara Lhakhang**, which was built around the cave hermitage of Drokmi Lotsawa (993-1050) and his contemporary, the Kashmiri pandita Gayadhara. These figures were the teachers of Khon Konchok Gyelpo who founded the original Gorum Temple at Sakya in 1073, giving birth to the Sakyapa school.

Chushar Town → *Colour map 2, grid B1*

Some 10 km south of Lhartse Chode and the old Lhartse village, is **Chushar**, the county capital of modern Lhartse (4,050 m). The town is an important staging post on the roads from **Zhigatse, Dram (Zhangmu)** on the Nepal border, and **Mount Kailash** in Far West Tibet. Three river valleys extend upstream to the south: the Trum-chu, which leads via the **Zhichen Chutsen hot springs** to **Sakya** (see above, page 296); the Mangkar-chu which leads to the **Mangkar** hermitages; and the Chushar, which leads across **Gyatso La** pass (5,252 m) on the main highway, eventually reaching **Shelkar** at the confluence of the **Bum-chu (Arun)** river and its **Lolo-chu** tributary. The distance from **Chushar** to **Shelkar** is 75 km. The dirt road for **Ngamring** and **Mount Kailash** branches off the highway after an occasionally manned police checkpoint at the small **Chushar Zampa** bridge and then crosses the Brahmaputra via the **Lhartse Chakzam** suspension bridge. **Mount Yakri** (5,641 m) dominates the road on the far bank of the river.

Until recently **Chushar** was a small 'one horse' Tibetan town, with one main government shop down a side street, three guesthouses, a post office, a grocery store, a cinema and one petrol pump consisting of a rubber hose protruding from the broken window of an oil-stained mud hut. The petrol station had been a popular meeting point! It lay opposite the two small Sichuan and Muslim restaurants in town. In 1993 Chushar underwent a radical transformation when it was inundated with Chinese immigrants who held permits for shops on the main high street. This coincided with the opening of a modern Chinese petrol station at the east end of town and the construction of the Lhartse Chakzam bridge across the Brahmaputra. The main street has now begun to take on the characteristics of thousands of other small Chinese towns.

Heading into town from Sakya or Zhigatse, you will pass the Tibetan Farmers' Adventure Hotel, the police station, the traffic police, the petrol station, the Friendship Restaurant, and vehicle repair shops on the right, while opposite on the left there are the tax bureau, the bus station, a new office block, China Post and Telecom, a bath-house, massage parlour and the Weiwu Café. At this point the open market intersects main street on both sides. Continuing westwards, you will then pass the Rongcheng Restaurant, the Namtso Hotel, the Holyland Restaurant, the Lhartse Hotel and the Grain Department Guesthouse on the right, with the Chengdu Restaurant and various small shops on the left. Here one can pick up any last minute purchases, such as three-minute noodles or Chinese beer, for the journey across the

Northern Plateau. Beyond the next intersecting lane, there are a number of small shops, restaurants and village houses on both sides of the street before you reach the Chushar Zampa and the police checkpoint.

Mangkar valley

The track to **Mangkar** leaves Chushar via the street running due south between the post office and the cinema. Take the east track at the next intersection, and head south to **Samdrub** and **Mangpu**, deep in the Mangkar gorge. The snow peaks of **Lhago Gangri** (6,457 m) dominate its upper reaches. From **Mangpu**, a trekking trail leads to the right into the Mangkar valley, where there are said to be 13 great meditation caves. Among these, the cave hermitage of Tsarchen Losal Gyatso (1502-1567), founder of the Tsarpa sub-school of the Sakyapa tradition, lies within the **Monastery of Tubten Gepel**, and his tomb is located at the nearby monastery of **Dar Drongmoche**. Ma Rinchen Chok, one of Padmasambhava's 25 disciples, was born in middle Mangkar.

In the upper reaches are the ruins of **Ganden Dargyeling**, a Gelukpa monastery, and various meditation caves associated with Drokmi Lotsawa, who transmitted the Sakyapa teachings here to Khon Konchok Gyelpo. These include: the **Osel Dawa Puk**, where Drokmi meditated; the **Dragyur Puk**, where he translated Sanskrit texts; and the **Sungak Lamdre Puk** where he received the transmission of the 'Path and its Fruit' (Lamdre). At nearby **Mugulung hermitage**, Drokmi gave teachings to Marpa Lotsawa of the Kagyu school and Zurpoche Shakya Jungne of the Nyingma school.

Trekking From Mangkar, there is a three-day trekking route to Sakya via **Drumchok**, a shorter trek southwest to the Lolo-chu valley, and yet another due south to the Bumtsopu-chu valley.

Sleeping

Chushar Town *p306*

E **Namtso Hotel (Tianhu Binguan)**, T0892-8322838. Has twin rooms (no running hot water) at ¥90; and some economy rooms at ¥15-50 per bed. Also Rongcheng Chinese Restaurant.

E **Farmers' Adventure Hotel**, T0892-832333, F0892-8322336. Has clean twin rooms at ¥70. Traditional Tibetan countryside ambience, shared bathroom facilities, Tibetan dining area off reception.

E **Grain Department Guesthouse**, has even more basic amenities!

E **Lhartse Hotel**, has twin rooms at ¥90 (shared toilet facilities and no running water), and an average restaurant that is popular with drivers.

Eating

Chushar Town *p306*

ǂǂ **Chengdu Restaurant**, Sichuan cuisine.

ǂǂ **Rongcheng Restaurant**, Namtso Hotel. The best Chinese food in town.

ǂ **Friendship Restaurant**, opposite China Post and Telecom, has wholesome Tibetan meals (rice, meat, noodles, vegetables).

ǂǂ **Holyland Restaurant**, general Chinese and some Tibetan dishes.

ǂ **Weiwu café**, for tea and snacks.

Transport

Chushar Town *p306*

Bus

Buses depart regularly for **Zhigatse** (¥35 or ¥25), but it is somewhat more difficult for foreigners to travel on to Dingri and Dram without alien travel permits and pre-arranged transportation, because there are well-manned checkpoints to negotiate. A better option would be to take the bus to Senge Khabab, on the northern route to Mount Kailash, which has no checkpoints, and to apply for Ngari permits on arrival there.

For an explanation of the sleeping and eating price codes used in this guide, see inside the front cover. Other relevant information is found in Essentials pages 44-46.

Khangmar County ཁང་དམར

→ *Population: 19,603. Area: 5,172 sq km. Colour map 2, grid C2.* 康马县

*Khangmar county includes the valleys of the **Drumpayu-chu** and **Nyeru-chu** rivers, which flow due north from their Himalayan watersheds to converge with the **Nyang-chu**, at **Nenying** and **Lungmar** respectively. The main highway from Gyantse to **Dromo** (Ch Yadong) on the Bhutan and Sikkim borders passes through the **Drumpayu** valley; and from the **Nyeru** valley, there are mountain passes leading directly into the **Gasa** district of **North Bhutan**.*

*The county capital is located at **Khangmar** (Nyangchu), 48 km south of Gyantse. At **Kala** township (44 km further south), there is a security checkpost which monitors all traffic heading towards the border. **Nenying** and **Yemar** temples are sites of historic importance located in Khangmar county.*

Nenying Monastery

In the lower valley of the Drumpayu-chu, 15 km south of Gyantse, you can visit the monastery of **Nenying**, which was founded in the late 11th century by Jampel Sangwa of Samye. Over subsequent centuries, Nenying was developed eclectically by the Bodongpa and the Gelukpa traditions, amongst others. The renovated assembly hall contains a large new image of Tsongkhapa, and further north there is an old temple, probably surviving from the original complex, which contains faded murals of the Pala style, reminiscent of those at Gyantse Dzong. Nenying is currently administered from **Sapugang** township, 11 km further south, where there are interesting coloured rock carvings.

Gamru

At Sapugang, the road crosses to the east bank of the **Drumpayu-chu**, and 1 km further south, at **Darmar**, there is a trail turning southwest from the main highway. This trail follows the **Gamrupu-chu** upstream, through a wide side valley, to **Gamru** township. Above Gamru, the trail eventually crosses the **Drulung La pass**, which forms a watershed between the **Tradong** source of the **Shab-chu** and the **Drumpayu-chu** rivers.

Khangmar

The county capital is located 18 km south of **Darmar**, in a sheltered side valley close to the highway. The government buildings have guesthouse and dining facilities; but the PSB vigilantly inspect passers-by to ensure that those heading south towards the sensitive Sikkim and Bhutanese borders have bona fide travel permits. **NB** Permits are easier to obtain for this county as of 2004, in anticipation of the opening of the Sikkim-Tibet border.

Nyerulung

From **Khangmar**, a motorable side road leads southeast to cross the Nelung La pass and enter **Nyeru** township in the Nyeru Tsangpo valley. Trekking routes from here follow the valley downstream to **Lungmar** and **Ralung Monastery** (see above, page 266), or northeast across country to **Phuma Yutso Lake** and **Lhodrak** (see page 218). There are also trails into the **Gasa** district of **North Bhutan** via the **Yak La pass** (east of Lake Drumpa Yutso) and via **Wakye La pass** above the source of the Nyeru-chu. **NB** These passes are only accessible to local Bhutanese traders who ply their wares in Dromo county.

Yemar

Yemar Temple, located 12 km south of **Khangmar** and just to the north of **Salu** township, on a ridge above the highway, is a deserted but extremely important temple, where life-size images survive from the 11th century. Its foundation is attributed to one Lharje Chojang, considered to be a previous emanation of the Kashmiri pandita Shakyashri, who himself visited the site in 1204. The temple has three chapels surrounded by a perimeter wall and an inner circumambulatory path. The **central chapel** (north) is dedicated to the Buddha Amoghadarshin, flanked by six forms of Maitreya; the **West chapel** (left) to Amitayus, flanked by 16 standing bodhisattvas, and the **East chapel** (right) contains a relief sculpture depicting the Buddha's **Subjugation of Mara**. The Italian Tibetologist Professor Tucci has compared the images of Yemar (Iwang) with those of **Tsi Nesar**, **Kyangpu**, and **Dratang**, which are no longer extant, and concluded that the garments and facial features suggest an early Tibetan synthesis of Indian **Pala** and **Khotanese** Central Asian styles. Restoration work at Yemar is on-going. The internal renovation of the West chapel and the East chapel has now been completed, and the old perimeter wall, surmounted by 108 stupas, has been rebuilt. Restoration of the central chapel has not yet been carried out, and no decision has been made as to whether monks will once again be permitted to reside there.

Kala

The highway continues south from **Yemar**, passing through **Samada** township, where the ruined **Kyangpu** temple is located, and **Mangdza**, from where a side trail follows the Drumpayu-chu to its source and the Yak La pass to Bhutan. At **Mangdza**, the main road leaves the valley and enters the **Kala plain**. 34 km south of Yemar at Kala township, the highway skirts the northeast shore of **Lake Kalatso**. Here there is an important police checkpoint, which can only be passed by if they are prepared to undertake a cross country trek around **Lake Kalatso** to the west, or via **Lapchi Gonpa** to the east. A motorable branch road leads west from Kala to **Gampa** county (110 km). From **Lapchi Gonpa**, a difficult trek leads to **Gasa** in Bhutan.

Dromo County གྲོ་མོ

→ *Population: 11,528. Area: 3,968 sq km. Colour map 2, grid C2.* 亚东县

Dromo county is a stunningly beautiful area, comprising the valley of the ***Amo-chu*** *(or Dromo Machu) River, also known in neighbouring Sikkim as the* ***Chumbi valley****, and the parallel valleys of its more westerly tributaries: the* ***Tangkarpu-chu*** *and* ***Khambuma-chu****. These three rivers all converge at* ***Sharsingma****, the county capital of Dromo (Ch Yadong), before flowing into the* ***Ha*** *(Lhade) district of West Bhutan. The terrain varies dramatically: north of the Tang La pass (4,639 m), which marks the Himalayan watershed, the landscape of the Tibetan plateau is barren; but offering amazing views of the snow peaks of* ***Jomolhari*** *on the Bhutanese border, and* ***Longpo Gyeldong*** *on the Sikkimese border. Further south, the roads plunge through lush gorges, where alpine forest and flowers abound.* ***Sharsingma*** *(2,865 m) is 160 km south of* ***Khangmar****, 18 km northwest of* ***Dorin*** *in North Bhutan, and 16 km northeast of* ***Dzaleb La pass*** *(4,386 m), on the Sikkimese frontier.*

Himalayan Watershed

From **Kala**, the highway skirts the west shore of **Lake Dochentso**, and continues south, passing through **Guru**, where Younghusband's British Expeditionary Force engaged the Tibetan army in 1904. At **Duna** township, 40 km south of the Kala checkpoint, there is a trekking route northwest to the Butang-chu valley, a tributary of the **Khambuma-chu**. The main road gradually ascends **Tang La**, the Himalayan watershed pass (4,639 m), from which the snow peaks of **Jomolhari** (7,314 m) and **Longpo Gyeldong** (7,128 m) are clearly visible, the former only 8 km distant. The pass is crossed 22 km south of Duna.

Phari Dzong

Below the **Tang La pass**, the highway enters the valley of the **Amo-chu** (Chumbi), and continues gently downhill to **Phari Dzong** (4,360 m), 9 km distant. Phari township is a bustling market town located on an exposed 'sow-shaped' hilltop and was often given the dubious distinction of being the dirtiest town in Asia! It strategically overlooks the trading route via **Tremo La pass** to **Paro** in West Bhutan, and the various westerly trails which penetrate the **Dongkya** range to enter Sikkim. From here, there are two motor roads to **Sharsingma** (Yadong), one via the **Khambuma-chu** valley and the other via the **Dromo** valley.

Khambuma Valley

Drive northwest from Phari for 22 km and you reach **Tengkar** in the upper Khambuma-chu valley. From here, **Khambu Monastery** and its 12 medicinal hot springs are in close proximity. The glacial waters of this alpine valley, hemmed in by the Dongkya Sikkim range and the Himalayas, are highly revered.

Trekking Trekking routes lead from the Khambuma valley into Northeast Sikkim, ie from **Khambu-to** via the **Tso La pass**, and from **Khambu-me** via the **Chimkipu** valley. Further south, the Khambuma-chu merges with the Tangkarpu-chu, and thereafter with the Dromo Amo-chu at **Sharsingma** (Yadong).

Dromo Valley

The fertile Dromo valley, which yields an abundance of buckwheat, barley, and potatoes, is divided into three sectors: **Dromo-to** township , where the river flows through gentle alpine meadows, bypassing the Bon settlements of **Zhulung**, **Sharmang** and **Nubmang**; **Sharsingma** (Yadong), a relatively low-lying town (2,865 m) where the three rivers converge; and **Dromo-me** where flowering plants and conifer forests abound.

Logging is the main industry; and the gorges still are relatively rich in wildlife, including pheasants, the Tibetan snowcock, and even the Himalayan black bear with its characteristic white V-shaped markings. The capital, **Sharsingma**, is 46 km south of **Phari Dzong**. It is a hospitable town, despite the security concerns entailed by its proximity to the border. Indian-style sweet tea and Himalayan-style fermented millet (tongba) are popular beverages in this part of the country. **NB** Permits can now be obtained for Sharsingma, in anticipation of the long-awaited cross-border agreement with India in neighbouring Sikkim.

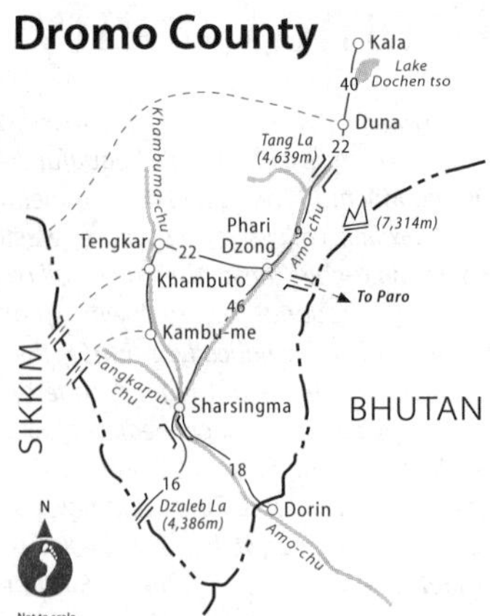

The town has guesthouse and restaurant facilities, in addition to schools, a bank, a post office, and hydro-electric station.

Crossing the **Dromo Zamchen** bridge the highway leads southwest and steeply uphill from Sharsingma through rhododendron forests to the **Natho La** and **Dzaleb La** passes on the Sikkim border.

Gampa County གམ་པ

→ *Population: 9,320. Area: 3,979 sq km. Colour map 2, grid C2.* 岗巴县

*Gampa county is the region covered by the headwaters of the **Yeru Tsangpo**, which rises north of the snow peaks of the Tibet-Sikkim Himalayas: **Mount Lonpo Gyeldong** (7,128 m), **Mount Lhachen Zangdrak** (6,889 m), and **Mount Tarchen Drokri** (6,830 m) at the eastern extremity of the **Chorten Nyima La** (see below, page 312). The Yeru Tsangpo meanders west into Tingkye county, where it converges with the Bum-chu (Arun) before flowing south into East Nepal. Also included in Gampa county are the side valleys of its major tributary: the **Kholchu Tsangpo**, which flows south to its confluence west of Dargye village; and those of the latter's minor tributaries, the **Jemalung-chu** and **Gye-chu**, which converge at Gyelung.*

*The county capital is located at **Gampazhol**, 110 km west of Kala (on the Gyantse-Dromo road), and 95 km northwest of Drakang (below Duna on the Gyantse-Dromo road). Access is also possible by undertaking a four-day trek from **Badur** in the Shab valley (see above, page 297) to **Gampa Dzong** via Yakgo La pass, Gye-chu valley, Gurma village, and Dargye township.*

Gampa Dzong

This impressive old fortress, which was frequently photographed by British Everest Expeditions during the early decades of the last century, overlooks the new county town, where the Chinese bureaucrats have something of a hardline reputation. The main focal point of pilgrimage in this county is the **Chorten Nyima** hermitage (see below, page 312) on the south border of **Gampa** and **Tingkye** counties. The hermitage can be approached by a motorable track from **Gampa Dzong**, via **Mende** (Gampa township), and **Dranglung** village.

Tingkye County གཏིང་སྐྱེས

→ *Population: 18,015. Area: 4,900 sq km. Colour map 2, grid C1.* 定结县

*Tingkye county comprises the lower valley of the **Bum-chu (Arun)** River, from the point below **Tsogo** where it flows due south to enter East Nepal via **Drentang** township, and the valleys of its major tributaries: the **Yeru Tsangpo** and **Chenlung-chu** (the latter flowing into the Yeru Tsangpo via the Bumtsopu-chu). The county capital, **Tingkye Dzong**, is located above the confluence of the **Bum-chu** and **Yeru Tsangpo**, at a strategic intersection. The distance from Tingkye Dzong to Sakya is 85 km, to Shelkar 134 km, and to Gampa Dzong 129 km.*

Lower Bum-chu Valley

From **Jigkyob Zampa** bridge, located 31 km north of **Tingkye Dzong**, 92 km east of Shelkar, and 54 km south of Sakya, there is a four-day trekking route to **Kharda** in the Lower Bum-chu valley. Passing south of the confluence of the Bum-chu and Yeru Tsangpo, the trail skirts on the east the snow peak of **Mount Nyarori** (6,724 m) in the Ama Dribma range, which acts as a watershed between these rivers. Continuing on the east bank of the river, it then cuts through several lateral ravines, via **Kharkung**, and ascends the Chokchu La pass, offering wonderful views of **Mount Makalu** (8,470 m).

Descending to the confluence of the Trakar-chu with the Bum-chu above **Chugo**, the trail subsequently crosses the Bum-chu by bridge to the west bank, and heads south through alpine forest for **Kharda**, the gateway to the **Khangzhung** east face of **Mount Everest**, and the Kharda glacier (see below, page 318).

Below Kharda, a difficult trail heads down the west bank of the Bum-chu to **Drentang** township, joining the main road from **Tingkye** and **Zar** (45 km). South of Drentang, the river flows into Nepal, where it is known as the **Arun**. A major dam is to be constructed in the deep **Arun** gorges of east Nepal.

Lake Tsomo Dramling

Southeast of Chenlung township, there is a sacred lake known as **Tsomo Dramling**, where pilgrims undertake a circumambulation, starting from **Tashitse** on the southwest shore and passing through Dotra on the northeast shore.

Zar Monastery

In the county capital, **Tingkye Dzong**, there is an important petrol station, and various amenities geared to service the army, which has a large base in town. From here, the motor road follows the Yeru Tsangpo upstream for 42 km to **Zar** bypassing Chushar across the river. At **Pukhu**, north of **Zar**, there is a small rebuilt Kagyu monastery.

Zar township, with its ruined fortress and monastery, lies on a ridge below **Mount Gang Langchen**, which is 'shaped like the head of an elephant'. The monastery, which belongs to the Gelukpa school, has two renovated buildings, including a three-storey assembly hall. On the slopes of Mount Gang Langchen there are meditation caves and lakes associated with Padmasambhava, Yeshe Tsogyel and Yutok Yonten Gonpo.

Getting there Above **Zar**, the road divides, the southerly track leading across **Nye La pass** to **Dekyi** and **Drentang** on the Nepal border (45 km); and the easterly road to **Tingkye** township. Below **Tashi Rabka** on the former, there are also trekking routes into Nepal via the **Rabka La pass** (4,972 m) and the **Yangmagang La pass** (5,182 m).

Chorten Nyima

Chorten Nyima is regarded at the gateway to the hidden land of Sikkim (Drejong), the heart of which lies within the folds of Mount Kangchendzonga. It is an extremely active pilgrimage centre, and there is a nuns' retreat hermitage to the west. The three cliff-top stupas, which are the focal point of pilgrimage, are attributed to Namkei Nyingpo and Yeshe Tsogyel, students of Padmasambhava, who himself meditated here.

The largest of the stupas, known as **Rangjung Shelgyi Chorten**, contains a crystal stupa which reputedly fell from the sky. Additionally, there are three sky-burial sites, consecrated originally by Padmasambhava and Namkei Nyingpo, and medicinal springs renowned for possessing the 'eight attributes of pure water'. These are now utilized as the source of the fabled Chorten Nyima Mineral Water, which is

Gampa & Tingkye Counties

bottled and marketed inside Tibet! The **assembly hall** in its upper storey contains images of Hayagriva and Manjughosa, as well as a small 'self-arising' ritual dagger (*phurba*) engraved with an image of Hayagriva.

The **Tamdrin Lhakhang** contains the meditation cave of Padmasambhava, and relics such as the Guru's stone footprint and a bronze image of Jowo Shakyamuni. The site can also be approached from **Gampa Dzong**, via **Dranglung** (see above, page 311).

Getting there Driving east from Zar, after 26 km you will reach the prosperous farming village of **Muk**. Take the left turn at the next intersection, 1 km beyond Muk (the right leads to **Gye Gonpa** and **Jewo Gonpa** in the Gen-chu valley). Then, leave the main Tingkye-Gampa road at the subsequent junction, 8 km further on, turning right to head due south. A river bed trail leads directly to the snow peaks of the **Chorten Nyima range**, nestling on the frontier between Sikkim and Nepal. The world's third highest peak **Mount Kangchendzonga** (8,585 m) lies further south. The range has 13 peaks, the highest being **Mount Chorten Nyima** (6,927 m) itself. Glacial streams rise within the range, heading south to converge with the **Tista** River in Sikkim.

Dingri County དིང་རི

→ *Population: 45,638. Area: 14,156 sq km. Colour map 2, grid C1.* 定日县

*The westernmost parts of Tsang province are traditionally known as **Lato**, the 'highland' region of Tibet; and this vast area is divided into North Lato and South Lato. The former comprises the upper reaches of the Brahmaputra and Raga Tsangpo, corresponding to present day Ngamring, Saga, and Drongpa counties, and the latter comprises the Bum-chu (Arun), Matsang Tsangpo (Sunkosi), and Kyirong Tsangpo (Trishuli) valleys, corresponding to present day Dingri, Nyalam and Kyirong counties. In recent decades, the whole of South Lato, along with neighbouring Tingkye county, has been incorporated into the vast Jomolangma National Nature Reserve (area 33,819 sq km).*

*Among these, Dingri county occupies the upper reaches of the **Bum-chu (Arun) River**, and the lateral valleys formed by its tributaries, the foremost of which are: the Lolo-chu, Shel-chu, Rongpu-chu, Trakar-chu, Kharda-chu, Ra-chu Tsangpo, and Langkor Gya-chu. It also includes the valleys of the **Rongshar Tsangpo** and **Lapchi Gang Tsangpo**, which*

Dingri County

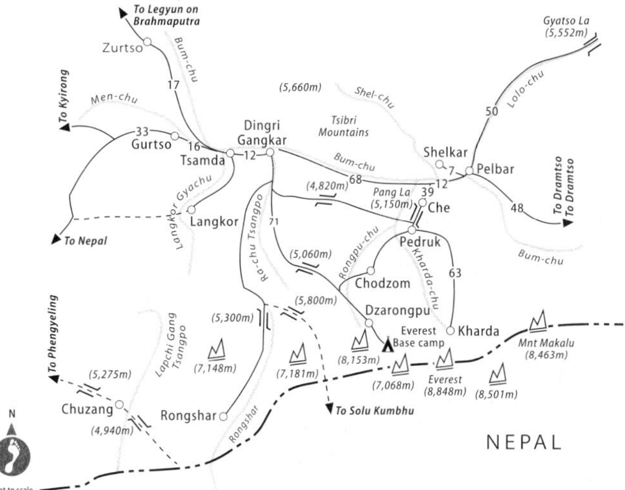

*flow southwest into Nepal to join the **Sunkosi River**. The county is bordered on the south by the formidable barrier of the high Himalayan range, including **Mount Everest** (Jomolangma/Jomo Gangkar), **Makalu**, and **Cho Oyo** (Jowo Oyuk).*

*The county capital is located at **Shelkar**, 75 km from **Chushar** in Lhartse, 123 km from **Tingkye**, and 240 km from **Dram** (Zhangmu) on the Tibet-Nepal border.*
▸▸ *For Sleeping, Eating and other listings see pages 320-321.*

Shelkar

The heavily rutted Highway 318 runs southwest from Lhartse, across the high **Gyatso La pass** (5,220 m), and then descends steeply into the barren Lato plains, following the Lolo-chu downstream. On the descent, the Everest range can be seen in the distance, and the **Lolo hot springs** are visible by the roadside, 38 km below the pass.

Below **Pelbar** (4,350 m), 12 km further on, a turn-off on the right leads into **Shelkar**, following the **Shel-chu** tributary upstream (7 km). The ruined fortress and monastery are prominent on the upper slopes of **Mount Shelkar Dorje Dzong**, overlooking the town. The area headquarters of the **Jomolangma Nature Reserve** is located here. Since its inception in 1989 it has assumed some responsibility for the maintenance and ecology of the entire Everest region.

Shelkar Chode Monastery, founded originally in 1266 by the Kagyu lama Sindeu Rinchen, has been a Gelukpa monastery since the 17th century. There were formerly some 300 monks here, and an active branch of the monastery has been established in Boudha, Nepal. The restored **assembly hall** contains images of Tsongkhapa and his foremost students, alongside Padmasambhava and Vajradhara.

A motorable road leads up the **Shel-chu valley** from Shelkar as far as **Gemar** township (50 km), on the north side of the **Tsibri** range. Pilgrims can sometimes be seen approaching as they circumambulate the sacred Tsibri mountain in a clockwise direction.

Tsibri

The **Tsibri** mountain range, true to its name, resembles a series of protruding ribs (*tsibma*). During the 11th century, the remote crags of Tsibri were inhabited by Padampa Sangye, the Indian master who introduced the lineages of **Chod** and **Zhije** into Tibet. Subsequently, Gotsangpa Gonpopel (1189-1258) of the Drukpa Kagyu school founded his hermitage on the southeast cliff-face. His own student, Yangonpa Gyeltsenpel (1213-1258) was born locally at **Lhadrong**; and his successors effectively established many Drukpa foundations around the mountain.

In the present century, a series of 11 retreat hermitages was established around the mountain by Tsibri Tripon Lama who came here from Central Tibet in 1934. Among them were **Dingpoche**, **Langtso** and **Tashi Tongmon**. Some of these sites are functioning at the present time. However, the large **Nerang Printery** which he also founded to the southwest of Tsibri no longer exists.

The nuns of **Nabtra**, the Nyingmapa monastery on the northeast side of Tsibri, under the guidance of Nabtra Rinpoche, were renowned for their meditative excellence and expertise in the traditions of Mindroling and Longchen Nyingtig. The previous Nabtra Rinpoche was a *mantrin* of great status; his present incarnation now lives in Nepal. Pilgrims often undertake the five-day circuit of **Tsibri** mountain on foot via Khangsar, **Nakhok, Ngonga, Pangleb** and **Tsakor**. Further north from Tsibri is the watershed range dividing South Lato from North Lato. **Mount Drakri** (5,871 m) is the highest of these peaks.

Lake Tingmo Tso

Below Shelkar, the highway from Lhartse intersects the roads leading east to Tingkye and west to the Nepal border. Taking the Tingkye road, after about 48 km you will reach **Dramtso** township on the north shore of **Lake Tingmo Tso. Tsogo** township lies south of the lake and on the south bank of the Bum-chu.

Everest Range

Bounded on the east by the deep gorge of the **Bum-chu (Arun) River** and on the west by that of the **Matsang Tsangpo (Sunkosi)** are some of the world's highest mountains of the East Himalayan range, forming a natural barrier between Tibet and Nepal. Clustered together in close proximity, these comprise: **Makalu** (8,463 m), **Lhotse** (8,501 m), **Everest**, known locally as Jomolangma or Jomo Gangkar (8,848 m), **Bumo Ritse** (7,068 m), **Jowo Oyuk** (8,153 m), **Jowo Guru** or Menlungtse (7,181 m), and **Jowo Tseringma** or Gauri Shangkar (7,148 m). There are tremendous trekking opportunities in the environs of each of these peaks, and those around **Mount Everest** are particularly well known.

On the Tibet side, **Mount Everest** may be approached from the north face at **Dzarongpu**, or the East **Kangzhung face** at **Kharda** or Karma. A motorable dirt road that was originally constructed for the 1960 Chinese expedition to Everest leaves the highway on the left (south) 12 km after **Pelbar** and 5 km after the **police checkpoint,** where all passports will be inspected. Take this turn-off, where a sign indicates that the distance to Everest Base Camp is 100 km, and soon you will reach the village of Che (4,390 m), where the Jomolangma Nature Reserve begins and permits for Everest Base Camp are checked. A trekking fee ⓘ *¥65 per person*, is payable here, along with a high vehicle tariff (¥500-700). The switchback trail then ascends **Pang La pass** (5,090 m), where the high Himalayan range comes abruptly into view. Then, on the descent into **Pedruk** (4,210 m), an agricultural valley 39 km to the south, there is a cart track which branches off to the west, crossing **Lamar La pass** (4,820 m) for **Dingri Gangkar** (2-3 days trekking).

Everest Region

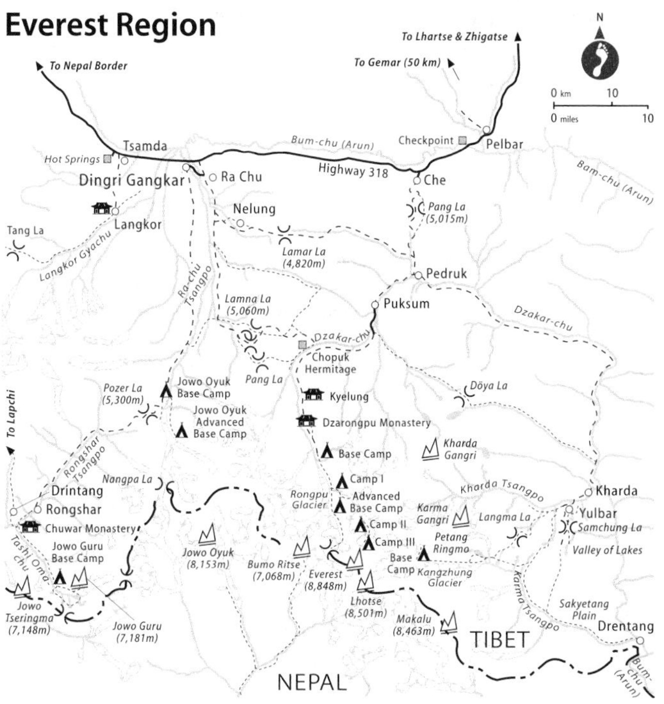

Everest

For 13 years after it was found to be the highest mountain in the world, **Peak XV** had no European name. In 1865 the then Surveyor-General of India suggested that it be named after his predecessor, Sir George Everest, the man responsible for the remarkable Great Trigonometrical Survey which ultimately determined its height. Everest himself, while honoured, was privately unhappy, as it was official policy that mountains be given their local vernacular name. However, an exception was made and the name stuck.

Everest has been climbed many times and by many routes since 1953. The route taken by Hunt's expedition is the 'Ordinary Route', disparagingly called the 'Yak' route by Sherpas. The first Chinese expeditions to reach the summit from the north side did so in 1960 and 1975. We shall never know if the British mountaineers Mallory and Irvine preceded them in 1924, when they perished on the mountain. Following his achievement on Annapurna's South Face, Chris Bonington led two expeditions to tackle Everest's Southwest Face and, with Dougal Haston, succeeded in reaching the summit in 1975. In 1970 Yuichiro Muira tried to ski down the Lhotse Face from the South Col, spent most of it airborne and out of control and ended unconscious on the edge of a crevasse! Rheinhold Messner and Alison Hargreaves have climbed it without oxygen. Peter Hillary followed in his father's footsteps and stood on the summit in 1990. In April 1988, two teams of Japanese met on top, having scaled the North and South Faces. There to record the event was a television crew!

On 29 September 1992 a 'GPS' survey using signals from satellites determined the height of Everest as 8846.1 m. Although this is 2 m lower than believed previously, Everest is still higher than K2, despite claims to the contrary made in the New York Times in March 1987. In April 1993 the team that first climbed Everest trekked to the Base Camp for a 40th anniversary reunion – to find 1,500 other climbers waiting their turn to go to the top of the world.

Upper Dzakar-chu Valley (Dzarongpu)

Two roads diverge at **Pedruk**, the 63-km east track leading to **Kharda** (see below, page 312) and the west track to **Dzarongpu**. Take the latter, and continue up the **Dzakar-chu** valley to **Paksum** (4,210 m) and **Chodzom** (4,510 m).

Above Chodzom is the deserted Nyingmapa hermitage of **Chopuk**, which is built into the limestone cliffs to the west of the road. Here, a 71-km motorable cart track (three days' trekking) branches off to cross **Lamna La pass** (5,060 m) and descend through the **Rachu Tsangpo** valley to **Dingri Gangkar**. The main road continues south, via Kyelung, to reach **Dzarongpu Monastery** (4,980 m). The drive from Pedruk (50 km) will take about two hours. » *For listings, see pages 320-321.*

Dzarongpu Monastery

Communities of nuns affiliated with the Nyingmapa tradition of Mindroling have been living in the Dzarongpu area since the late 18th century. The complex was revitalized at the beginning of the 20th century by the First Trulzhik Ngawang Tendzin Norbu (d 1940) who constructed a temple named **Do-ngak Choling**. Branch monasteries were also established across the **Nangpa La pass** in the **Shar Khumbu** region of East Nepal (see below, page 319). At the high point of its development, the Dzarongpu area (meaning "upper reaches of the Dza valley") had over 500 monks and nuns.

Early British mountaineering expeditions have provided invaluable documentary evidence concerning the monastery's development and Trulzhik Rinpoche's activities. The recently renovated **assembly hall** contains an image of this master, whose present incarnation lives in Nepal, alongside an image of Terdak Lingpa, founder of Mindroling. In addition to the liturgical texts of the Mindroling cycle, the Longchen Nyingtig is also an important spiritual practice for the 30 monks and nuns who live here. Additional rebuilt chapels include the **Kangyur Lhakhang** and the **Zhitro Lhakhang**. A hermitage affiliated with the monastery is also located above a nearby rockslide and alongside a Padmasambhava meditation grotto. Here are the ruins of **Sherabling Nunnery** and a residence built by the previous Trulzhik Rinpoche.

Rongpu Face

Above Dzarongpu Monastery, the trail continues up to the **Everest Base Camp** (5,150 m), located in a sheltered spot below the moraine slopes leading up to the **Central Rongpu Glacier**. Memorial plaques, including one dedicated to Mallory, stand alongside a traditional Tibetan stupa. The views of the north face of Everest from this vantage point are particularly fine. However a liaison office has been established here by the Tibet Mountaineering Association with the intention of extracting a US$100 fee per day for each tourist hiking above 5,500 m! A trail skirts the east side of the glacier and crosses a creek to reach the **Advanced Base Camp** (5,460 m), from which mountaineering ascents of the north face and the northeast ridge can be made. **Camp I** is located at 5,400 m, **Camp II** at 5,940 m, and **Camp III** at 6,300 m.

NB Trekking above the Everest Base Camp should only be undertaken by those who have fully acclimatized and are properly prepared for high altitudes.

Everest

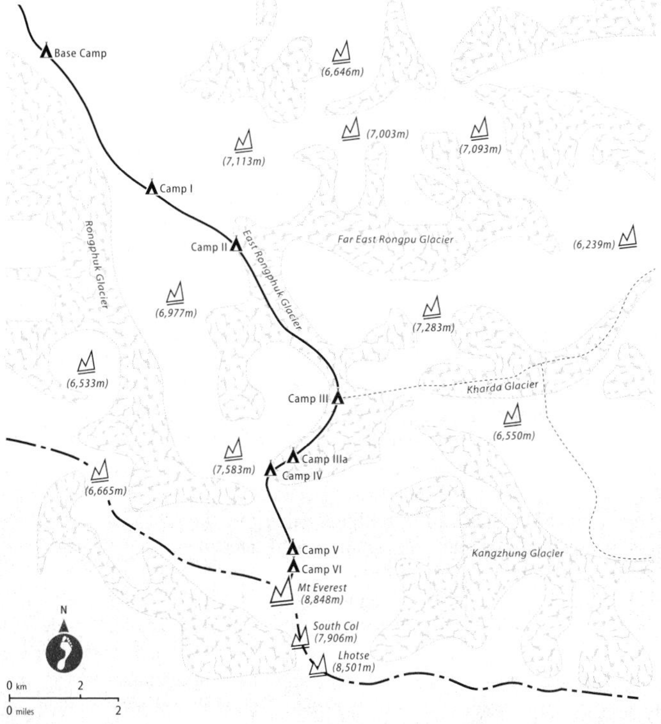

 Nonetheless it is possible to reach Camp III without resorting to professional mountaineering equipment.

Kangzhung Face

Taking the motorable cart track that leads east from **Pedruk** village, you will reach **Kharda** after 63 km. The track follows the lower reaches of the **Dzakar-chu** downstream to its confluence with the **Bum-chu (Arun)**, before following the latter downstream through the gorge to **Kharda** township (see above, page 312).

An alternative route to Kharda from Everest Base Camp entails four days' trekking via Doya La pass (5,124 m) and Chongpu valley. Situated on an elevated ridge above the Bum-chu gorge, **Kharda** (3,690 m) is a forested, fertile and heavily populated area. At Kharda there is a small guesthouse, several shops, a clinic, a school and a government compound.

Follow the Kharda Tsangpo upstream to **Yulbar**, where the four-day trek to the **Kangzhung face** via Langma La pass (5,350 m) begins. The view from the pass of Makalu's jagged peaks is particularly impressive.

Head into the **Karma Tsangpo** valley, where there are further stunning views of Makalu; and then continue climbing towards its source, to reach the **Kangzhung Face Base Camp** in Petang Ringmo meadow. Here, the campsite offers dramatic close-up views of Mount Everest and Mount Lhotse. A 5,950-m ridge further to the west provides even closer views of all three of these 8,000-m peaks – Everest being only 5 km distant.

Another four-day trek follows the **Karma Tsangpo** downstream towards its confluence with the **Bum-chu**, crossing Samchung La pass (4,600 m), and passing through a valley containing 13 glacial lakes of varied pristine hues, and the **Sakyetang plain**. The low-lying confluence (2,300 m), close to **Drentang** on the East Nepal border, abounds in subtropical vegetation and flora. From here, you can follow the Bum-chu upstream towards Tingkye or Shelkar.

Dingri Gangkar

Dingri Gangkar (4,360 m) lies on the slopes of a ridge, overlooking the Everest range, at the heart of the wide 80-km plain formed by the **Bum-chu (Arun) River**. Two major tributaries converge with the Bum-chu at Dingri: the **Rachu Tsangpo**, which rises near Dzarongpu below Mount Everest and the **Langkor Gyachu**, which rises above Rongshar.

For centuries the town has dominated the trade routes linking Tibet with **Shar Khumbu** in East Nepal via the Nangpa La pass (two days' trekking), and **Kodari** via the Nyalam Tong La pass (182 km). Trekking routes also lead north across the plain to Zangzang and Chung Riwoche in **North Lato**.

During the late 18th century when the Tibetan government requested the assistance of Emperor Qianlong's Chinese army to repel the Gorkha invasions of Tibet, a fortress was constructed on the hill above the town. Along with many other fortifications from that period which cover the plain as far as **Gurtso**, it now lies in ruins.

The town itself has in recent decades been rebuilt in cramped conditions to accommodate the military camp, which lies to the south of the highway. The village houses lie to the south of the army camp in close proximity, although only the camp has functional electricity (the locals have been informed that their smoke-filled dwellings should be connected to the grid within the next two years). From the rooftops there are memorable views of the entire Everest range – particularly clear during full moon nights.

Heading into town from Shelkar, immediately after crossing a bridge that spans the Rachu Tsangpo, you will pass on the right (north) the Snow Leopard Hotel, which has a Mount Everest observation telescope. Then you will reach the turn-off on the left that leads into the township. The Army Guesthouse, a small restaurant and a general store can all be reached along this lane, at the end of which there are further excellent views of the snow range, below the hillside village houses. Continuing on the highway itself, you will pass the Himalaya Hotel, the Lao Dingri Hotpot, the Everest View Hotel and the Amdo Hotel and Restaurant, all on the right, with the Himalaya Restaurant and a number of small teashops on the left. The highway then crosses a second bridge on the way out of town.

The distance from **Shelkar** to **Dingri** is 68 km, and from **Dingri** to **Dram** on the Nepal border 182 km. Motorable cart trails (which are also trekking routes) extend from Dingri southwards to **Jowo Oyuk Base Camp** and **Rongshar** via **Pozer La** (5,300 m), and southeast for 71 km to **Dzarongpu** near Everest Base Camp, via Lamna La (5,060 m) and Lamar La (4,820 m). ▸▸ *For listings, see pages 320-321.*

Dingri Langkor

Drive west from Dingri along the highway for 12 km as far as **Tsamda**, where there is a hot spring bathing facility ⓘ *¥10 per person*, and an excellent Amdo Restaurant. From here there is a motorable cart road leading to **Langkor Monastery**. Avoid driving in the summer months when the **Langkor Gyachu River** bursts its banks. Otherwise hire a horse and cart from Dingri Gangkar. Langkor village and monastery are located inland from the highway on a south-facing ridge, in full view of **Mount Jowo Oyuk**.

This ranks among the most important pilgrimage places of the entire Lato region, in that it was here in 1097 that the Indian yogin Phadampa Sangye founded a hermitage and disseminated the teachings of Chod and Zhije in Tibet for the first time. His foremost Tibetan student was the yogini Machik Labdron (on whom see above, page 773). Here, Phadampa Sangye delivered a memorable teaching on ethics and conduct to the people of Dingri, entitled *Hundred Verses of Admonition to the People of Dingri* (*Dingri Gyatsa*).

A festival is held here each year on the 14th day of the sixth month of the lunar calendar. The **temple** is located within the village of **Langkor**. The track follows the contour of the hillside, passing a medicinal spring said to have been brought forth by Padmasambhava. The temple, which retains its original pillar and beam structure, contains images of Phadampa Sangye and Tangtong Gyelpo, and partially faded murals depicting Padmasambhava and Milarepa. Adjacent cave hermitages are associated with Padmasambhava, Phadampa Sangye and Machik Labdron.

Trekking A three-day trek from **Langkor** also leads to **Nyalam** via the **Tong La pass**. This was the traditional trading route between Dingri and Central Nepal prior to the construction of the motor road.

Rongshar

The beautiful **Rongshar** valley, southwest of Dingri, is the sacred abode of the 11th century yogin Milarepa, and at the same time a botanist's paradise, nestling below the high snow peaks of **Jowo Tseringma** (Gauri Shangkar) and **Jowo Guru** (Menlungtse). To reach Rongshar, head due south from Dingri on a cart road in the direction of the **Nangpa La pass** (5,800 m), which eventually leads into the **Shar Khumbu** area of East Nepal. **Tsamgye** (Rongshar township) is one day's drive or at least four days' trekking from Dingri.

Passing through the villages of Penak, Shator-me, and Shator-to, the trails divide at **Kyarak** (38 km) near the Jowo Oyuk base camp. For Nangpa La, which remains closed to foreigners, cross over to the east bank of the **Kyarak-chu** and trek due south via the Jowo Oyuk advanced base camp. **Mount Jowo Oyuk** (Cho Oyu) 8,153 m, looms to the south. For Rongshar, a further 47 km from Kyarak, remain on the west bank of the river, and head southwest towards **Pozer La** pass (5,300 m). Having crossed this pass and entered the **Rongshar Tsangpo** valley, the barren landscape gives way to junipers and rhododendrons (4,650 m), and the road soon plunges down, following the course of the rushing river to **Taktsang** (4,030 m), where side valleys branch off to

Salung (northwest) and **Zhung** (southeast). There is a profusion of large fragrant white rose bushes.

On the descent to **Tsamgye** (3,380 m), **Mount Jowo Tseringma** (7,148 m) comes into view, dominating the valley from the south. Avoid the bureaucrats here, and continue downstream to **Chuwar Monastery** (3,250 m), dramatically situated above the confluence of the **Rongshar Tsangpo** and **Tashi Oma-chu**. The gorge of the latter leads east to **Mount Jowo Guru** (7,181 m).

Many sites in this region have associations with Milarepa, who lived in the remote hermitages of the Rongshar valley for many years, eventually passing away at Dri-che Cave in Chuwar. The cave and the ruins of the Nepalese-style **Chuwar Monastery,** which was founded by the Tenth Karmapa in 1630 and later absorbed by the Gelukpas, have long been the focal points of pilgrimage in the valley. Nothing remains of the monastery, but for irreparably damaged images of the Buddha's retainers in its inner sanctum. Downstream from **Drubden**, where there are cave hermitages of both Milarepa and Gampopa, the Rongshar Tsangpo enters Nepal (2,750 m), where it flows into the **Bhotkosi**, a major tributary of the **Sunkosi River**. Another trail climbs 400 m from Drubden to **Drintang** (3,630 m) and the **Drakmar caves**, where Milarepa taught his disciple Rechungpa. Here the cave hermitages directly face the snow-capped Mount Jowo Tseringma.

Jowo Guru Base Camp

From Chuwar, a trekking route follows the Tashi Oma-chu upstream, via Milarepa's Domphuk cave, to the base camp (4,570 m) of **Mount Jowo Guru**, and the four sacred lakes which lie above.

Lapchi Gang

From **Drintang** in lower Rongshar, another trekking route leads via Trode and north across Gangchen La pass (4,940 m) into the forested valley of **Lapchi Gang**. The snow peaks of this revered valley are regarded as the abodes of the meditational deities Cakrasamvara, Vajrapani, Manjughosa and Avalokiteshvara. Here, the **Lapchi Gang Tsangpo** flows parallel with the Rongshar Tsangpo, crossing the Tibet-Nepal border.

There are a number of 11th-century hermitages associated with Milarepa in the upper and lower reaches, including the **Dudul Cave, Bepa Gong Cave** and **Se Cave**, which are classed among his 'four great meditation caves'. The pagoda-roofed monastery, known as **Chura Gepheling**, is situated above the confluence of the east and west tributaries of the Lapchi Gang Tsangpo. The **assembly hall** contains a venerated image of Milarepa, reputedly made by Rechungpa from his master's nosebleed, and a stone said to be the master's life-supporting talisman (*lado*).

Ascending the valley of the west tributary, you pass through **Chuzang**, where Milarepa subdued a hostile demon who sought to obstruct the opening of the Lapchi Gang hermitages to Buddhist practitioners. **Jamgang La pass** (5,275 m) at the head of the valley leads across the watershed to **Pengyeling Monastery** on the Dingri-Nyalam stretch of the Nepal highway.

Sleeping

Pelbar *p314*

Everest Hotel, T0892-8262775. Under the management of Mr Ngawang Dorje, most travellers will stay here rather than at the old guesthouse in Shelkar. It has 51 poorly maintained rooms (with attached bathrooms but no running water and limited electricity) priced outrageously at ¥340. The hotel restaurant, located in an outbuilding, is very good, friendly and pleasantly decorated.

For an explanation of the sleeping and eating price codes used in this guide, see inside the front cover. Other relevant information is found in Essentials pages 44-46.

There are also 2 transport station guesthouses at the Shelkar turn-off, offering cheap dormitory accommodation.

Shelkar *p314*
D Simple barracks-style guesthouse with a good Chinese restaurant. Foreigners may now be discouraged from staying here.

The town has a high altitude post office, grocery stores and a bookshop.

Pedruk *p315*
E At Pedruk, which is the administrative township for the Everest Region, there are 2 small guesthouses, the **Geje Serling Hotel** and the **Jomolangma Pelbar Hotel**, which both have dormitory rooms (outside toilets) at ¥10 per bed, and offer meals at ¥10-15 per dish.

There are also a number of well-stocked general stores.

Upper Dzakar-chu Valley *p316*
Paksum
E **Jomolangma Guesthouse and Restaurant**, good, but slightly overpriced.

Chodzom
There are rooms in the local school compound, but slightly better family accommodation is also available (¥10 per bed) with meals included for ¥6 and thermoses of sweet tea for ¥5.

Dzarongpu Monastery *p316*
E The monastery has a recently constructed guesthouse with triples at ¥40 per bed, and 4-bed dormitories at ¥25 per bed. An alternatve option is the large enclosed camping space below the stupa.

Dingri Gangkar *p318*
E **Snow Leopard Hotel (Sazig Dronkhang)**, T0892-8262268, offers the best accommodation in town with 27 comfortable Tibetan-style rooms (no attached bathroom, outside toilets, Tibetan restaurant) at ¥60 per bed and ¥120 per room. The hotel, which has a Mt Everest Observation Telescope at the south end of its compound, is under the same management as the Everest Hotel at Pelbar.
E **Amdo Hotel and Restaurant** (with outside toilets and hot shower room), has double, triple and 4-bed rooms at ¥20-25 per bed.
E **Everest View Hotel**, is locally-run and slightly more spacious.
E **Himalaya Hotel** (with outside toilets and a restaurant) has double rooms at ¥20-30.

Eating

Pelbar
Everest Hotel Restaurant, offers wholesome Chinese and Tibetan cuisine.

Dzarongpu Monastery *p316*
Alongside the parking area, there is a small shop and a seasonal restaurant offering meals at ¥10.

Dingri Gangkar *p318*
Amdo Restaurant, specializes in mo-mo and mutton dishes.
Himalaya Restaurant, offers wholesome Tibetan cuisine (¥5-20 per dish).
Lao Dingri Hotpot, for fiery Sichuan hotpot.

Nyalam County གཉའ་ལམ

→ *Population: 13,994. Area: 5,57 sq km. Colour map 1, grid C5.* 聂拉木县

Nyalam county comprises the townships of ***Menpu*** *and* ***Zurtso*** *around the headwaters of the* ***Bum-chu River****, and those of* ***Tsangdong, Tsongdu,*** *and* ***Dram*** *in the* ***Matsang Tsangpo (Sunkosi)*** *valley. Highway 318 from Lhasa traverses the Great Himalayan range at* ***Yakrushong La pass*** *(5,200 m), also known nowadays as* ***Nyalam Tong La,*** *and then precariously follows the course of the* ***Matsang Tsangpo*** *downstream to the Tibetan customs barrier at* ***Dram (Zhangmu/Khasa),*** *and the* ***Friendship Bridge*** *on the Nepal border. This is currently Tibet's most important land border with the outside world. The trading community of* ***Dram*** *are said to be among the most prosperous people in all Tibet.*

*The county capital is located at **Tsongdu**, 30 km north of the border, and 152 km from **Dingri**. The **Arniko Highway** which runs from **Kodari** to **Kathmandu** (122 km) via **Barabise** was constructed by the Chinese in 1960s.* ▸▸ *For Sleeping, Eating and other listings, see pages 325-326.*

Bum-chu (Arun River) Headwaters

From **Dingri**, the highway cuts northwest to **Gurtso** (28 km), where the **Men-chu river** joins the **Bum-chu**. The township of **Zurtso** is located 17 km further north near the source of the Bum-chu, and a drivable by jeep track leads via Zurtso to **Legyun** and **Taktse** on the Brahmaputra in North Lato.

Gurtso has a military camp with spartan guesthouse facilities, and a vital road maintenance depot, responsible for clearing snowfall from the high Himalayan passes to the south. The highway follows the **Men-chu** upstream (southwest) from Gurtso, passing Menpu township and **Menkhab-to** village, where ruined 18th-century fortifications can be seen.

After 33 km (road marker 614), the road divides: the west route leading to **Kyirong** and Far West Tibet (see below, page 350). Striking views of **Mount Shishapangma** (8,012 m), the highest peak entirely inside Tibetan territory, dominate the west horizon.

Himalayan Passes

The highway cuts through the Himalayan range via the Lalung La pass (5,124 m) and the Yakrushong La pass (5,150 m), which are crossed in quick succession. The latter is sometimes known as **Nyalam Tong La** ('pass from which Nyalam is visible'), although the original Tong La pass lies further east on the traditional Dingri-Nyalam trade route. Pilgrims stop at the second pass to raise prayer flags, burn incense, scatter 'wind-horse' paper inscriptions and build cairns. This is the last contact with the Tibetan plateau. Below the passes, the road descends steeply into the valley of the **Matsang Tsangpo** (Sunkosi River). Trails to the east lead directly to **Langkor** and **Dingri** via the Tong La.

Mount Shishapangma

There are three approaches to the spectacular snow peaks of **Shishapangma** (Goshainathan), which at 8,012 m was the last of the world's 8,000 m peaks to be climbed. The northern base camp is accessible from **Serlung** on the Kyirong road (see below, page 326), the eastern side from a turn-off 32 km south of the **Yakrushong La pass**, and the southern base camp from the county capital at Tsongdu by trekking upstream through the **Tsongdupu-chu valley**.

Descending into the upper reaches of the Matsang Tsangpo valley, the **eastern approach** leaves the highway at km marker 5318, and reaches **Ngora** (4,340 m) after 11 km. Here there are small terraced barley fields and a Nyingmapa village monastery. From Ngora, the trail climbs to the sacred **Kong-tso Lake**, in close proximity to the icefalls of Mount Shishapangma and Pholha Gangchen, and then crosses **Kongtso La pass** (5,180 m) to reach **Shingdip** (4,480 m) in the Tsongdupu-chu valley. The trek takes two days, and from Shingdip, where the trail connects with the southern

approach, it is possible to head upstream for the south base camp of Shishapangma or descend to Tsongdu.

The **southern approach** to Shishapangma is easier in that no passes are crossed en route. The trail begins at **Tsongdu Gonpa**, following the south bank of the Tsongdupu-chu upstream and bypassing another trail that detours to the scenic **Dara-tso Lake**. There are suitable campsites at **Drakpochen** meadow (4,050 m) and Shingdip en route for the south base camp (4,920 m). The snow range of the Jugal Himal is visible to the south, but Shishapangma itself does not come into view without trekking in the direction of the advanced base camp (5,150 m). The round trip from Tsongdu takes 4-5 days.

Pengyeling Monastery

At **Tsangdong** township, also known as **Nesar**, 40 km below Yakrushong La on the highway, the climate changes as the dryness of the plateau is replaced by the warmer moist air of the Indian subcontinent. A trail to the east leads to **Lapchi Gang** via Tashigang, where there is a police checkpoint.

The temple of **Pengyeling** ⓘ *admission: ¥10*, lies 4 km south of Tsangdong. The temple is built around the sacred **Namkading Cave** of Milarepa, which overlooks the approach to the hidden valley of **Lapchi Gang**. The buildings are invisible from the motor road (at road marker 5335), some 3 km below the highway, and above the west bank of the **Matsang Tsangpo**. An antechamber contains on its side walls a detailed description of the pilgrimage sites associated with Milarepa in the locality of Pengyeling and Lapchi. The **Namkading Cave** contains rock impressions of Milarepa's seated meditation posture and handprint – the latter having appeared in the rock when Milarepa assisted his student Rechungpa prop up the low ceiling with a boulder. Images include Milarepa, Tsongkhapa, and the protectress Shridevi, whose mule also reputedly left a footprint in the stone when she appeared in a vision to Milarepa.

The **main temple**, to the east of the cave entrance contains an assembly hall with a principal image of Padmasambhava, and fine frescoes depicting Shakyamuni, Milarepa and Marpa. The caretaker of Pengyeling lives above and behind the temple where there are smaller caves associated with Rechungpa and the protector deities of the Gelukpa tradition. This one-time Kagyu temple complex has been affiliated to the Gelukpa monastery of Sera since the late 17th century.

Tsongdu

Tsongdu, the county capital of Nyalam (3,750 m), lies 11 km south of **Pengyeling**, deep within the gorge of the **Matsang Tsangpo** at the point where both the river and the road cut through the Himalayan range. **Mount Dorje Lakpa** (6,990 m) rises above the town to the west. For centuries this has been the main trading post between Tibet and Nepal. The valley of the **Tsongdupu-chu** tributary runs northwest towards the southern base camp of Mount Shishipangma, and the Bod-chu tributary joins the Matsang Tsangpo from the east below the town.

Crossing a suspension bride that spans the Matsang Tsangpo at the entrance to town, there is a police checkpoint on the left, where travel permits and vehicle licences are inspected. Then, turning into the main street, you will pass on the right (west) Tsongdu Gonpa, where the southern approach to Mount Shishapangma begins, followed by a middle school, a hospital, the Nongiyale Hostel, the Nyalam County Hostel, the local government buildings, and the Heyi Yuan Restaurant (which also offers hot showers). Opposite on the left (east) are the jail, the Ngaden Restaurant, the Zatsang Guesthouse, the Xifeng Store, the Agricultural Bank, the Nepalese Restaurant, further government buildings, the Electric Company, and the Snowland Nyalam Hotel.

Dram (Zhangmu)

Below Nyalam, the road plunges through the **Matsang Tsangpo** gorge, hugging a precipice above the rapids. There are spectacular waterfalls on both sides of the gorge. About 12 km below Nyalam, there is the 54-bed Chusham Hotel, which is well located in a tranquil part of the valley near the **Chusham hot springs**, but often lacking in electricity.

The border town of **Dram** (Ch **Zhangmu**; Nepali **Khasa**) lies 31 km below Nyalam at an average altitude of 2,300 m. Just above the entrance to town there is yet another police checkpoint where travel documents are inspected – particularly those of incoming travellers. The sprawling town extends down the hillside for over 4 km through a series of switchback bends. In the rainy season (July-September) motor vehicles are sometimes unable to reach the town from either Nyalam or from the **Friendship Bridge** on the Nepal border owing to landslides, which are a constant hazard to the local population. Nonetheless, the people of Dram tend to be among the wealthiest in Tibet. Black market trading in assorted commodities, gold and currency is rife.

In the upper part of town you will pass China Post & Telecom, and the Sunlight Hotel on the left (east) with the Bank of China on the right (west). Steep flights of steps provide short cuts for pedestrians and heavily loaded porters seeking to avoid the switchbacks. In the middle part of town there are many small Chinese-owned hairdressers, karaoke bars, and shops selling electrical goods, as well as cheap imports from Nepal and India. The Himalayan Lodge is located here on the right (west) and the Tashi Hotel is directly opposite on the left (east). Then, continuing into the lower part of town, you will pass the Snowland Tea House and the Gang-gyen Hotel on the left (east) with the **New Monastery** (Gonpa Sarpa), the Tenxanghe Hotel, the Bank of China, a massage parlour, and the Frebol Hotel on the left (west). Immediately south of the Frebol Hotel, the road is blocked by the Chinese Customs and Immigration Post.

At the border

The customs and immigration posts open at 1000 Beijing time, and by the time you have gone through all formalities and driven or walked the 8 km downhill to the actual frontier on the **Friendship Bridge** (Dzadrok Zampa), the Nepalese customs will be on the point of opening at 0930 Nepal time (some two hours difference). Foreign tourists and travellers generally have to endure only a casual inspection at the customs post (baggage will be scanned), although any pre-1959 antiques can be confiscated if found. Entry procedures at this border crossing are more complicated. Those arriving from Nepal will have to show a valid Tibet entry permit. Until recently a minimum of five names had to be inscribed on it, and a fee was charged for cancelling bogus names from the list. However, from 2002 onwards, permits have been issued to smaller parties. To reach the Friendship Bridge (Dzadrok Zampa/ Youyi Qiao) on the actual border, there is an 8-km series of switchbacks to be traversed, either on foot (in which case porters are available at ¥55 or by truck/auto-rickshaw at ¥57. However, foreigners can sometimes be charged higher rates for these services. The inconveniences of this land border may be alleviated in the near future if the proposed construction of a cable car service between the Customs Post and the Friendship Bridge is completed on schedule.

Kodari

Visitors arriving at Kodari should have a valid visa for Nepal, obtainable from any Nepalese embassy or consulate, including the one in Lhasa. Visas can also be issued at the border (price US$30-50, validity 60 days), assuming you have a passport-size photograph to hand. The current exchange rate (January 2004) is US$1 = Nepali Rs 73. Accommodation is available in Kodari at the simple Lakshmi Lodge (Rs 35 per bed), and there are buses to Kathmandu via Barabise (seven hours, Rs 200 per person). A taxi service to Kathmandu and Tribhuvan Airport is also available (Rs 1,100).

Arniko Highway

The **Arniko Highway** connects Kodari with **Kathmandu**, 112 km to the southwest. There are numerous police checkpoints and the administration of impromptu fines can be a lengthy affair. The overall journey will take about six or seven hours.

The quiet village of **Tatopani**, which takes its name from the local hot springs, is located 3 km downstream from Kodari. The road continues through Tatopani, following the Matsang Tsangpo, here known as the Sunkosi River, downstream for 24 km on the scenic stretch to **Barabise**. It traverses ancient, deep cut gorges, which are especially vulnerable to **landslides** during and after the monsoon. At Barabise, a densely populated town of little interest located at the Sunkosi's confluence with the Bhot Kosi, there are several basic guesthouses and restaurants. Further south, the highway passes through **Lamosangu**, a quieter village with a few shops and a simple guesthouse, and just before the village of **Baliphi**, there is a turn-off for **Jiri** and the trekking routes of Eastern Nepal. After a further 16 km, the road descends to its lowest point at **Dolalghat**, where the Sunkosi and Indravati have their confluence.

Thereafter, you begin to climb again for the first time since crossing the Himalayan passes, as the road winds its way through the picturesque **Panchkal** Valley. A patchwork of fields dominates the valley floor while innumerable minute terraced fields cover the slopes. Ascending for 29 km, you eventually reach the hill station of **Dhulikhel** (1,585 m) on the eastern rim of the Kathmandu valley. **Dhulikhel** is an established village with a history of settlement that goes back to its days as a stopover on the India-Tibet trade route. Its people are predominantly Newari. For those who wish to admire the southern Himalayan panoramas, in a quiet setting away from Kathmandu, Dhulikhel along with **Nagarkot**, is one of the best options. There is excellent top range accommodation available at the Himalayan Horizon Sun-n-Snow and the Dhulikhel Mountain Resort, mid-range accommodation at the Himalayan Mountain Resort and the Royal East Inn, and budget accommodation at the Dhulikhel Lodge, the Peace Paradise and the Nawranga, among others.

There is a pleasant trail from Dhulikhel to **Namobuddha** (Tib Tagmo Lujin), via Kavre Banjyang and the Tamang village of Phulbari, which Tibetan pilgrims invariably follow. Namobuddha is one of Nepal's holiest Buddhist sites and commemorates the supreme compassion of the Buddha in his legendary self-sacrifice to a starving tigress at Panauti. The hilltop is dominated by a large stupa (Dharma Dhatu), and to one side is a small monastery, built by Trangu Rinpoche. From Dhulikhel, the Arniko Highway descends to **Banepa**, before passing just to the south of **Bhaktapur** and **Thimi** in the Kathmandu valley, only 30 km distant.

Sleeping

Tsongdu *p323*

E **Snowland Nyalam Hotel**, T0827-2111-2250. Under the management of Mr Tashi Dondrub, this is by far the best in town, with double rooms at ¥80 and beds at ¥40. The hotel has a restaurant and a trekking service for Shishapangma base camp and other destinations.

Dram *p324*

C **Frebol Hotel (Zhangmu Quxiang/ Dram Chushang)**, T0892-8742221. Has the best accommodation in town, with doubles at ¥450. The Chinese-style restaurant is mediocre. Curiously, this 5-storey hotel has its reception office on the top floor, which is at road level, and its restaurant on the lowest floor. Electricity is erratic (though candles are provided) and the rooms are sometimes damp.

E **Gang-gyen Hotel**, T0892-8742188. Has dormitory accommodation at ¥30-40 per bed (best rooms on 6th floor).

E **Himalayan Lodge**, remains the backpackers' favourite.

For an explanation of the sleeping and eating price codes used in this guide, see inside the front cover. Other relevant information is found in Essentials pages 44-46.

D Pema Hotel, T0892-8742098, higher up the hillside, has doubles at ¥200.

Eating

Tsongdu *p323*
Nepalese Restaurant, among the various eateries offers an excellent alternative to Sichuan cuisine.

Dram *p324*
There are many small roadside restaurants in town serving Sichuan, Tibetan and pretty good Nepalese cuisine.
Gang-gyen Restaurant, adjacent to Qixingjiao Chinese Restaurant.
Lhasa Tibetan Restaurant, in the middle part of town, offers local dishes.
Qixingjiao Chinese Restaurant, in the lower part of town.
Tashi Delek Restaurant, in the middle part of town, offers local dishes.

Directory

Dram *p324*
Banks The main branch of the Bank of China is located in the upper part of town, but it now conveniently has a sub-branch next to the Frebol Hotel. The many blackmarket money-changers who hover around the hotels and banks will offer a slightly better exchange rate for the US dollar and also convert Chinese RMB into Nepali Rupees. **Post offices** The Post & Telecom Office is located in the upper end of town. DDD and sporadic IDD facilities are available at telephone booths in both the upper and lower parts of town.

Kyirong County སྐྱིད་གྲོང

→ *Population: 11,664. Area: 8,869 sq km. Colour map 1k grid C5.* 吉隆县

*Kyirong county in **South Lato** occupies the valleys of the **Kyirong Tsangpo River** (Trishuli) and its tributaries as well as the adjacent **Gungtang-chu** headwaters and the basin of **Lake Pelkhu Tso**. To the south straddling the Tibet/Nepal border lie the mighty snow peaks of the Himalayan range: Ganesh Himal (7,406 m), Langtang (7,232 m) and Shishapangma (8,012 m). Further north there are trails crossing the high watershed passes into North Lato, and the Brahmaputra valley. The Kyirong gorge and valley form one of Tibet's most beautiful picturesque alpine regions; and it boasts sites of historic importance, connected with King Songtsen Gampo, Padmasambhava, Milarepa, and Sakya Pandita, among others. The county capital is located at **Dzongka**, 127 km east of the turn-off on the Gurtso/Nyalam road (see below), 103 km south of Saga, and 75 km north of Rizur Zampa on the Nepal border.*

Serlung to Shishapangma

On the Gurtso-Nyalam road, which connects with the Arniko Highway to Kathmandu, there is a turn-off below **Lalung La pass**, north of the Himalayan range, which cuts westwards, following the **Nakdo-chu** tributary of the **Men-chu** (itself a source of the Bum-chu) upstream to **Serlung** (4,630 m). Just before reaching Serlung, where pack animals can be hired, a turn-off on the left leads south for 15 km to

Kyirong County

Shishapangma base camp (4,850 m). The Tibet Mountaineering Association maintains a toll gate here, charging entry fees for both tourists and vehicles. This is a motorable approach road, which was constructed for the 1964 Chinese expedition, and it extends slightly beyond the base camp. From the roadhead, there is a four-hour trek to the advanced north base camp (5,270 m), and a further five hour climb to reach the best viewing point for the **Yambugangla glacier** on the north side of **Shishapangma** (8,012 m).

Lake Pelkhu Tso

After Serlung, the main road passes through the desolate plain of **Digur Tang**, with its enormous sand dunes and the closely neighbouring snow peaks of Shishapangma (8,012 m) and **Langtang** (7,232 m) to the south. Leaving the Bum-chu basin, it then descends into the depression of **Pelkhu Tso** (4,600 m), a cobalt blue lake into which the glacial streams of the Da-chu and Lha-chu drain.

Below the cliffs on the east shore is the cave hermitage of Milarepa, known as **Laphu Pemadzong**. The road, however, skirts the south shore of the lake and then turns abruptly north, following the west shoreline. In the afternoons this terrain is exposed to strong biting winds, reminiscent of those in the Dingri plains. Reaching the base of **Jakhyung La pass** (5,180 m), also known as Ma La, the road forks. Take the right turn, which leads north into **Saga** county (69 km), via a small lake called **Tso Drolung**; or cross the pass (left) to reach the county capital at **Dzongka**.

Trekking Trekking routes also skirt the north shore of the lake to reach **Gongmo**, from where the trail crosses **Shakyel La pass**, to reach Trepa and township on the Brahmaputra. **Drakna Druka** is an important ferry crossing on the Brahmaputra; and trails lead downstream from here to Lhartse or upstream to Tango and Saga county.

Dzongka

Dzongka, the county capital, lies 34 km below **Jakhyung La pass**, overlooking the confluence of the **Kyirong Tsangpo** and its main tributary, the **Zarong-chu**. There is a trail following the latter upstream and across Tagya La pass to Achen and the Brahmaputra.

Owing to its mild climate and location, Dzongka thrived over the centuries as an important centre for Nepalese trade. Most of the ancient perimeter walls were destroyed by the Gorkha armies of the 18th century; but a significant portion of the southwest section survives even now. Within this enclosure is the Gelukpa monastery of **Ganden Palgyeling** which has some original murals and sculptures. Further north are the new buildings of Dzongka – the government compound and the commercial quarter, where there are distinctly unhygienic guesthouse facilities. The once inhabited cave settlement of **Lhamog Gonpa** is located on a hill promontory above the town.

Upper Kyirong Gorge

If you take the south road from Dzongka, following the **Kyirong Tsangpo** downstream, you will reach the township of Kyirong after 68 km. At **Orma** village the river valley narrows into a spectacular 35-km gorge devoid of settlements. Side valleys occasionally extend east or west from the gorge. At Gun, a trail leads east to **Tsalung**, the birthplace of Milarepa in Gunda district (4,300 m). Further south, at Longda, a trail leads west from the gorge to the ruined **Drakar Monastery**. Above it the important cave hermitage of Milarepa, known as **Drakar Taso** (3,600 m), contains wood-carved images of Padmasambhava, Milarepa and Maitreya.

The main road continues its descent of the gorge to **Drotang** (3,320 m), from where another trail leads west to Kyangpa Monastery and Milarepa's cave hermitage at **Kyangpa Namka Dzong**. Mount Riwo Pelbar is visible to the southwest. The Kyirong gorge eventually opens out at **Ragma** (3,000 m), where there are cultivated fields.

Stabbing at shadows

In the 13th century, Sakya Pandita visited Phakpa Wati Lhakhang, and it was here that he defeated the Hindu master Haranandin in debate. In order to subdue the intruder he requested help from the Nyingmapa yogin Darcharuwa, who had discovered a renowned ritual dagger (*kila*) at Yerpa and acquired extraordinary yogic prowess. Legend recounts that when Haranandin flew into the sky, 'flapping his hands like wings', Dracharuwa stabbed his shadow with the ritual dagger, causing him to fall to the ground, 'like a bird struck by a stone'! Subsequently no non-Buddhist masters from India sought to propagate their views inside Tibet.

Lower Kyirong Valley

The **Ragma** valley, extending eastwards from the Kyirong Tsangpo, contains the **Jangchub Dzong** cave hermitage of Milarepa and **Riwo Pelbar Monastery** with its nearby Padmasambhava power place. The main Kyirong valley, forested and alpine in character, descends through Magal, Garu Monastery, and Pangzhing village, before reaching the heart of Kyirong.

Jamtrin Temple Jamtrin Gegye Lhakhang, northeast of Kyirong township, is one of the four geomantic 'further taming temples' (*yangdul lhakhang*) founded by King Songtsen Gampo during the seventh century. The four-storey temple in an unusual pagoda design is said to be located on the right foot of the supine ogress.

Phakpa Wati Lhakhang The most historically significant building in the township of Kyirong (2,774 m) is the four-storeyed Phakpa Wati Lhakhang. This Nepalese pagoda-style temple once contained the renowned Phakpa Wati image of standing Lokeshvara, the bodhisattva of compassion. According to legend, King Songtsen Gampo during the seventh century despatched the incarnate monk Akarmatishila to Nepal, where in a forest in the Indo-Nepalese borderland, he found a sandalwood tree-trunk, which had split open in four segments to reveal the four 'self-arising' images of Lokeshvara. Known collectively as the 'four sublime brothers' (Phakpa Chezhi) these are: Phakpa Lokeshvara (the most sacred image in the Potala Palace) Phakpa Ukhang (whereabouts unknown); Phakpa Jamali (in Nepal); and Phakpa Wati. This last image was originally brought to Lhasa with the others, but expelled to Kyirong by Bonpo ministers during the eighth century. There it remained, in the Phakpa Wati Lhakhang until 1656 when it was transported back to Lhasa for safekeeping. The temple has outer murals depicting the great monasteries of Lhasa.

Jadur Bonpo Monastery

The important Bonpo site known as Jadur, near Yangchu Tangkar village outside Kyirong township, is a focal point for Bonpo pilgrims heading in the direction of Mount Kailash. A festival is held here during the fourth month of the lunar calendar.

Samtenling Monastery

Accessible by a full day trek from Kyirong township via Neshar, Samtenling Gonpa is the largest monastery of the valley. Originally a Kagyu site, frequented by the yogin Repa Zhiwa, it was later converted to the Gelukpa school in the 17th century, following the defeat of the Tsangpa kings in the civil war, and thereafter regarded as a branch of Shelkar Chode. The large complex of ruined buildings at Samtenling testifies to the monastery's former grandeur, and the snow peaks of Langtang and Ganesh Himal form a memorable backdrop. A flourishing branch of Kyirong Samtenling was established at Boudha in Kathmandu during the early 1960s.

Kyirong-Nepal

Two roads diverge south of Kyirong township, the westerly one following the **Kyirong Tsangpo** downstream to the Nepal border (29 km) – passing through **Khimbuk** village, **Rizur Zampa** bridge (spanning the Lende Khola-chu), and **Rashuwa Dzong**. On the Nepal side, the road passes through Syabunbesi and Dunche, before reaching Trishuli and Kathmandu. **NB** There is a new Sino-Nepalese project to upgrade this road and open it to commerce and international tourism as an easier alternative to the Nyalam-Barabise road. The easterly road is motorable only as far as **Langchu**, and thereafter it becomes a trekking route, passing through Dra, Kharbang, and Sa-le, before fording the border stream at **Chusumdo**. On the Nepalese side, it continues on to Sadang Kadu and the Langtang National Park. Without crossing the border, you can follow another trail eastwards to the Laga La glacier (west of Mount Shishapangma).

Gungtang

The **Gungtang** valleys, which form part of the **Gandaki** headwaters, are more remote than that of Kyirong, located on a side road suitable for jeeps 187 km from Saga and 216 km from Dzongka. This road crosses the celebrated **Gungtang La pass** (also known as Jang La), from which Padmasambhava entered Tibet during the eighth century. Stone footprints of Padmasambhava from the rocks of Gungtang La are kept in the Phakpa Lhakhang of the Potala Palace and at Samye Monastery. A trekking route also leads more directly from Dzongka to Chang and from there into the heart of Gungtang.

The southern approaches from Nepal are more rugged – traversing the passes of Gya La, Lachen La, Lachung La and Monla Drakchen. The main settlements of Gungtang are Rud, Nying, Nyam and **Chang** – the last of which has a medicinal hot spring. **Okla Gonpa** is the principal monastery.

Ngamring County ངམ་རིང

→ Population: 45,220. Area: 17,804 sq km. Colour map 1, grid C6. 昂仁县

The region of North Lato comprises the counties of ***Ngamring*, *Saga*** *and* ***Drongpa***, *which occupy the upper reaches of the Brahmaputra, and those of its major tributaries, including the* ***Raga Tsangpo*** *and* ***Rikyu Tsangpo***. *Among these, Ngamring county, sometimes referred to as the gateway to Mount Kailash and Far West Tibet, is the barren area which divides the Raga Tsangpo and the Brahmaputra. The main road runs northwest from Lhartse, crossing the Brahmaputra via the Lhartse Chakzam bridge or the Drapu ferry, to enter the county. It then passes through Gekha and Zangzang townships to rejoin the river at Saga. The most important historical sites are located at* ***Chung Riwoche*** *and* ***Zangzang Lhadrak***. *The county capital of* ***Ngamring*** *is located to the northeast of Gekha on a turn-off, 60 km from Lhartse, and 240 km from Saga.*

Ngamring County

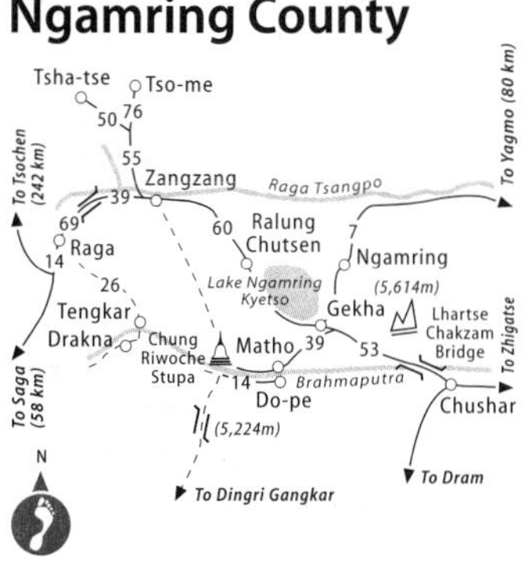

Gekha and Ngamring

After crossing the Brahmaputra at **Lhartse Chakzam** bridge, the recent construction of which has put an end to the adventures of the ferry crossing, the road ascends a rocky river valley, with **Mount Yakri** (Yakpo Gangri, 5,614 m) to the northeast and the bright blue waters of **Lake Langtso** to the south. A longer valley then leads up to **Gekha** township, 53 km from Lhartse. Gekha lies at the southeast corner of **Lake Ngamring Kye-tso**, and has a road transport station, with simple accommodation (¥20 per bed), and dining facilities. The county capital, **Ngamring** is a growing town, located on a side road 7 km northeast of Gekha, on the northeast shore of the lake. There are excellent views of the lake from the road. In town, the main site is **Ngamring Monastery**, an original 13th-century Sakyapa foundation, which was partially converted to the Gelukpa school in the 17th century. Exposed to strong winds blowing across the lake, Ngamring's claim to fame is that it is regarded as the home of Tibetan opera, in that Tangtong Gyelpo, the founder of Tibetan opera, hailed from this area.

Ammenities The town has a recently constructed county hotel, along with several small Chinese restaurants and the usual nightlife.

Dokzhung Tsangpo valley

From Ngamring there is a branch road which follows the **Dokzhung Tsangpo** section of the Raga Tsangpo downstream towards Lingo at its arid confluence with the Mu-chu in Zhetongmon county (see page 296). This drivable trail by jeep passes through **Chowok** (Mekhang) township after 57 km, and terminates at **Yagmo** township after a further 23 km.

Chung Riwoche Kumbum

Some 500 m before reaching Gekha township on the drive from Lhartse, there is a seemingly insignificant dirt track leading left (southwest), which crosses the low ranges dividing the Raga Tsangpo from the Brahmaputra. At **Matho**, 39 km from that turn-off, an iron bridge spans the Brahmaputra, carrying vehicles across to **Do-pe** township, which is some 36 km away on the south bank. A further 14 km drive will bring you into view of the magnificent Chung Riwoche stupa across the river on the north bank. The overall distance from Matho to Chung Riwoche is therefore about 50 km, on a difficult road. A narrow iron bridge spans the river here, alongside an original iron-chain footbridge attributed to Tangtong Gyelpo. **NB** Wide-bodied Dongfeng trucks are unable to cross the bridge, which is nonetheless motorable for landcruisers.

The stupa of **Chung Riwoche** overlooks the Brahmaputra from its vantage point at the base of **Mount Pal Riwoche** and the ruins of Chung Riwoche Monastery. It was constructed during the period 1449-1456, and had associations with both the Sakyapa school and Tangtong Gyelpo's own Chakzampa tradition. The design and extant murals are reminiscent of similar stupas at Jonang Phuntsoling and Gyang Bumpoche (see above, pages 304 and 306). According to the biography of Tangtong Gyelpo, it is largely the work of local artists of the so-called **Lato style**, which derives from the art of **Zhalu** but exhibits a more naive brushstroke and line technique than the cosmopolitan style of the **Gyantse Kumbum** (see page 270).

The stupa has eight storeys and a basement with its own interior circumambulatory walkway. The rectangular chapels on the second to fifth floors are contained within the terraced steps (*bangrim*) of the stupa, while the circular chapels of the sixth and seventh are in the bulbous dome (*bumpa*). The eighth floor is in the form of an open circular roof terrace, surmounted by a recently restored bell. The extant wall-painted mandalas are representative of the Sakyapa school.

Trekking Chung Riwoche can also be approached on the north bank of the Brahmaputra on a poor but safer motorable road from **Matho** and **Nyinkhar**, or by trekking from **Zangzang** via Choka. A more ambitious seven-day trek from South Lato follows the old trade route from **Dingri Gangkar** (see above, page 318). It crosses the **Bum-chu (Arun)** River and Khangsar village, before traversing the watershed **Me La** pass (5,224 m), which offers distant views of **Mount Drakri** (5,871 m) and **Mount Bulhari** (6,040 m) to the east. A second pass, **Kure La** (5,498 m) is then crossed, and on the descent the trail passes west of **Yulchen** township before reaching the south bank of the Brahmaputra at Chung Riwoche. Trails also follow the river banks upstream from Chung Riwoche to **Drakna** township in Kyirong county (see above page 327).

Ralung Chutsen

If one continues northwest from Gekha on the main route, a hot spring known as **Ralung Chutsen** comes into view on the right side of the road a few kilometres past the northwest shore of Ngamring Kyetso lake. Here there is a hot spring bathing house with simple guest rooms; and, if you arrive in the late afternoon, is a reasonable place to stop for the night. Apart from the guest rooms there are good grass-covered campsites. The baths themselves consist of square stone pools inside private rooms with large skylights open to the stars (if you bathe in the evening). The elderly Tibetans who manage it will flush the existing water away and replace it with fresh water if you ask politely. A small fee is charged per person whether you stay in a tent or in a room. A stop here is preferable to **Raga** which is two hours or so further on. **NB** If you stay at the hot springs and intend travelling on the **northern route to Mount Kailash**, it is important to leave early the next day in order to reach **Tsochen** county before nightfall.

Zangzang Lhadrak

The district of Zangzang is renowned as the birthplace of **Rigdzin Godemchen** (1337-1408), the renowned treasure-finder (*terton*) of the Nyingmapa school, who discovered and revealed the **Northern Treasures** (Jangter). On the 60-km drive from Gekha to Zangzang township, **Mount Trazang** is passed to the southwest of the road, as you cross the switchback Gar-la pass (4,700 m). The master's birthplace is at Toyor Nakpo, northeast of this mountain, on the summit of which he unearthed the keys to his treasure-texts in April 1366. Almost two months later, in the nearby cave of **Zangzang Lhadrak**, he discovered the 500 seminal works of the Northern Treasures tradition in a blue treasure-chest with five compartments. The tradition which he founded spread throughout remote areas of Ladakh and South Tibet, as far as Dartsedo in Kham; and these original sites continue even now to be revered focal points of pilgrimage for adherents of this lineage.

Descend from the pass through wide grasslands into the new town of **Zangzang** (4,520 m), which has a somewhat drab and bleak appearance. The best accommodation here is at the Zangzang Hotel, T0892-8312458, which has twin rooms with large windows at ¥70 (¥35 per bed), with no attached bathrooms. Upstairs there is the surprisingly good Sato Gyepa Sichuan Hotpot Restaurant. Other guesthouses in the township, including the Kungyi Nelenkhang, are more basic (¥15-25 per bed). There are also small Tibetan restaurants, among which the Tashi Bo-ze is probably the best. Some drivers will not stop here, preferring to continue on to **Raga**, 122 km beyond Zangzang.

Jangtang routes from Zangzang

A few kilometres northwest of Zangzang township on the main road, there is a turn-off which heads due north in the direction of the **Jangtang Plateau**. Following this trail passable by jeep, after **Kang-lhe** village, the road leaves the Raga Tsangpo basin and crosses the watershed into the Jangtang lakeland. Some 55 km from the turn-off, the trail divides, one branch following the **Taklung-chu** northwest for 50 km to **Tsha-tse** township, on the southeast shore of **Lake Zhuru-tso**; and the other heading north for 76 km along the valley of the **Tatok Tsangpo**, to **Tso-me** township. Arduous trekking routes from these two townships skirt the east shore of the large lake **Dangra Yutso**, as far as **Ombu** on the north shore. From there, a jeep road leads 167 km to join the main Amdo-Gertse road at **Nyima** (see below, page 345).

Upper Raga Tsangpo

The main road from Zangzang to Saga runs west, following the south bank of the Raga Tsangpo upstream. After 39 km it crosses **Gye La pass** (4,770 m), and then, at **Gyedo** village, there is a turn-off on the right (north) for the lakes **Chudrang-tso** and **Amchok-tso**. A second higher pass is then crossed (4,890 m).

Raga township (4,800 m) lies on the main road, 69 km beyond the pass and near the source of the Raga Tsangpo. It is merely a cluster of mud-walled compounds used as rest rooms for truckers, including the Lhato Guesthouse and Restaurant, which has 10 rooms (¥15-25 per bed). A dirt trail suitable for jeeps leads south for 26 km to **Tengkar** on the Brahmaputra, from where it is possible to trek to **Drakna** township and **Pelkhu Lake** (see below, page 327).

Raga's importance lies in the fact that it is the closest settlement to one of West Tibet's most important road junctions. Some 14 km after Raga, the main road splits in two: the northern branch heading into the Jangtang Plateau for **Tsochen** (242 km), and thence to **Gertse**, **Gegye** and **Senge Khabab**; and the southern branch rejoining the Brahmaputra at **Saga** (58 km), and following it upstream to its source in Drongpa county. The former is sometimes known as the **northern route to Mount Kailash** and the latter as the **southern route to Mount Kailash**. In this text, the southern route will be described first, since it remains within the **North Lato** district of West Tibet as far as Drongpa.

Saga County ས་དགའ

→ *Population: 12,058. Area: 13,374 sq km. Colour map 1, grid C5.* 萨嘎县

*Saga county in **North Lato** is the region occupied by the upper Brahmaputra and its tributaries: the **Rukyok Tsangpo** and **Kyibuk Tsangpo**. The county capital is located at **Kyakyaru** (Ch. Saga), 58 km from the Raga junction on the North Lato or Lhartse road, 105 km from Dzongka on the South Lato or Dram road, and 146 km from Drongpa on the southern route to Mount Kailash.* » *For Sleeping, Eating and other listings, see pages 333-334.*

Tengkar

A jeep track leads 26 km south from Raga to **Tengkar** township on the north bank of the Brahmaputra. Downstream from here (and still on the north bank) are the villages of Sharu, Salung and Taktse, the last of which has a hot spring. Fording the Brahmaputra at Tengkar, a trail continues from **Drakna** township on the south bank to Lake Pelkhu and Dzongka (see above, page 326).

Kyakyaru

Descending from Raga into the Brahmaputra valley, the main road soon leads to a major military checkpoint, where all passports and travel documents are inspected. Even Lhasa and Zhigatse residents require special border access permits to continue at this point. The town of Kyakyaru is located just beyond the checkpoint.

Kyakyaru (4,290 m) straddles the **Dargye Tsangpo** above its confluence with the Brahmaputra, 14 km west of old **Kyakya** village and 58 km southwest of the Raga road junction. The river is crossed here via the **Saga Chakzam** bridge. The town is strategically located at the intersection of three motor routes: the Lhartse road from the east, the Dzongka road from the south, and the Purang and Drongpa road from the west. The town has grown in recent years to service an important Chinese military garrison, which functions as the headquarters of the border patrol force, monitoring the entire length of the Tibeto-Nepalese frontier as far west as the Indo-Nepalese border. Soldiers from the garrison also are likely to have target practice near the centre of town; so don't be surprised if you hear machine gun fire at any time of the day. As you leave town heading west they may give a friendly wave from the low side of the road while they shoot bullets over your head at targets placed on the slope above. There is little of interest here in Saga, so rest well! On the southern route to Mount Kailash, Kyakyaru is the last town with IDD telephone connections and reasonable shopping facilities.

Dzongka and Zhungru roads

A few kilometres south of Kyakyaru, the road reaches the **Kyakya Druka** ferry, leading to the south bank of the Brahmaputra. Heading south on this jeep road, after 37 km there is a turn-off on the right (west), which leads to **Zhungru** township. The main road continues due south for a further 32 km, after which it again divides, the right (west) branch leading to **Dzongka** (34 km) in Kyirong county, and the left (east) branch leading around the southern shores of **Lake Pelkhu** to join the Dram (Zhangmu) highway. Take the latter route if you wish to reach Nepal quickly and avoid the Lhartse detour.

If you take the **Zhungru** turn-off, you will reach the township of Trhango after 75 km. Trhango lies close to the south bank of the Brahmaputra, and it is also the roadhead for the renowned Gungtang La (Jang La) pass through which Padmasambhava first entered Tibet in the eighth century. A ferry crossing, **Zhungru Druka**, links Pudrak, Zhungru and other villages on the north bank with those on the south bank, including Trhango and Rila.

Dargyeling

The **southern route to Mount Kailash** and Purang leaves Kyakyaru, crossing the **Saga La** pass (4,650 m) and following the **Dargye Tsangpo** upstream in a northwest direction. After **Garshok**, it reaches the township of **Dargyeling**, 26 km from the county town. Further upstream, the road passes the confluence of the combined waters of the **Rukyok Tsangpo** and **Kyibuk Tsangpo**, before following the **Men-chu** tributary of the Brahmaputra, via Lhaktsang, and across another pass (4,740 m) into Drongpa county. The valleys are rugged with little vegetation. The distance from Dargyeling to Drongpa Tradun (Old Drongpa) is 119 km.

Sleeping

Kyakyaru *p332*

NB It is important to reach Kyakyaru as early as possible in order to obtain the best accommodation in town.

D Karda Hotel, has the best and cleanest rooms in town, with twins at ¥180.

E Saga Guesthouse, T0802-2192. A Tibetan-style adobe building, arranged around a courtyard, with dormitory-style rooms at ¥50 per bed.

E Sheru Hotel, also has basic accommodation (¥25 per bed)

E Transport Station, also has dormitory accommodation at ¥45 per bed.

E Yak Hotel, has simple rooms at ¥25 per bed.

For an explanation of the sleeping and eating price codes used in this guide, see inside the front cover. Other relevant information is found in Essentials pages 44-46.

Eating

Kyakyaru *p332*

Karda Restaurant, in Karda Hotel, has the best Chinese food in town. Popular with locals and the military, as well as Kailash-bound travellers and pilgrims.

Trokyi Tibetan Restaurant, has the best Tibetan cuisine.

Directory

Kyakyaru *p332*

A short walk down the main road leads past local shops with IDD telephone facilities, a supermarket, and small Sichuan-style restaurants. The adjoining street has government buildings, a hospital, post office, and the offices of China Mobile.

Drongpa County འབྲོང་པ

→ *Population: 18,037. Area: 28,940 sq km. Colour map 1, grid C5.* 仲巴县

Drongpa county is the region around the source of the Brahmaputra River, which in its uppermost reaches is known as the ***Tachok Tsangpo****. To the south lies the Nepalese enclave of* ***Lowo Matang*** *(Mustang) and the glacial sources of the Brahmaputra. To the north are some of the great Jangtang lakes – Ngangla Ringtso, Taro-tso, and the Drangyer saltfields. The main road following the course of the Brahmaputra through Drongpa county is the* ***southern route to Mount Kailash****, rich in nomadic grassland pastures. The county capital, known as New Drongpa, is located 22 km west of* ***Drongpa Tradun****, 167 km from Kyakyaru in Saga and 224 km from Mayum La pass, which divides West Tibet from the Ngari region of Far West Tibet.* ▸▸ *For Sleeping, Eating and other listings, see page 336.*

Drongpa Tradun

The road leading from the Men-chu valley of Saga county into Drongpa initially passes through vast sand dunes, and for a large part of the distance stays close to the north bank of the Brahmaputra. From the pass on the border that separates these two counties, there are fine views of **Mount Longpo Gangri** (7,095 m) to the northeast and the Himalayan ranges (Mustang Himal and Gautam Himal) to the south. The road thereafter deteriorates considerably, making travel much slower than before.

The Drongpa river valley, formed by the combined waters of the **Tsa-chu** and **Yur-chu**, is a broad delta of sand and low-lying scrub. The waters of the river flow south into the Brahmaputra. One of King Songtsen Gampo's geomantic temples of the 'further-taming' (*yangdul*) class, named **Jang Traduntse**, is located on a hill-top promontory in this valley, on the 'right knee' of the supine ogress. It contains a large statue of Padmasambhava. The town of Drongpa Tradun, also known as Old Drongpa lies below the temple. It was from here and from neighbouring **Zhungru** that Tibetan traders and lamas would traditionally make their way into **Lowo Matang** (Mustang), via the **Lektse Tsongra** market and the **Chu'arok** river valley.

Old Drongpa

Like Kyakyaru, Old **Drongpa** was developed originally as a military base, and it was once the main check post for illegal traffic (such as hitchhiking tourists). It had no restaurant save a public kitchen where local people could come and pick up a bowl of rice and

Drongpa County

greasy gruel. It was located on the south side of a wind-swept sand dune and was singularly uninviting. Then, abruptly, in 1993, the town was moved some kilometres west! That is, at least the military garrison and administrative buildings moved, leaving a semi-ghost town on the old site, which is inhabited mostly by local Tibetans. Nonetheless, there are simple guesthouse and restaurant facilities here, which cater mostly for truckers and tour parties heading for Ngari.

New Drongpa

The present county capital, known as New Drongpa, is easy to miss, in that it is concealed some distance away from the main road on the far west side of the Drongpa river valley, 22 km from Drongpa Tradun. Look out for the turn-off some 8-10 km west of the new bridge and just before the road enters the Brahmaputra gorge. However, since there is little of interest in New Drongpa, if it is not late you are advised to press on.

Baryang

From Drongpa, the main road continues to follow the Brahmaputra valley upstream, ever closer to its source. After a further 57 km, the road crosses **Soge La pass** (4,725 m), and descends 36 km to the small township of **Gacho**. Some nine km beyond Gacho, after crossing some of the large sand dunes, there is a small hamlet of Tibetan houses, known locally as **Dutu**. Located on the eastern side of a rocky ridge on the south side of the road it is the focus for a number of families who graze their animals on the rich surrounding pastures. Nomads pitch their tents here, and there is a fine water supply nearby. From this point on, increasing herds of healthy of yaks and goats are to be seen on both sides of the road. The next main settlement is **Baryang** (4,350 m), 14 km after Gacho; but since the township has little of interest, it may be better to camp.

Horpa

The road crosses the **Neu Tsangpo River** at **Horpa**, 30 km west of Baryang. This river eventually flows into the Brahmaputra below Baryang. A new bridge has recently been constructed here. Formerly the crossing was dangerous and vehicles were often trapped midstream. Whether the whole **southern route to Mount Kailash** is open or not may still depend largely on this one crossing if the bridge is damaged by flash floods in summer. If the river has to be forded, and the weather is fine you should attempt to make the crossing as early as possible in the day, before the snow melt has swollen the river. If it has been raining it may be necessary to wait for assistance to arrive. It is always sensible to make this crossing together with other vehicles. Once across, the road continues through sandy grasslands.

Lungkar

From Horpa, a side road leaves the Brahmaputra valley to follow the **Neu Tsangpo** upstream. Crossing the high **Me La** watershed, it descends into the Jangtang Plateau after 58 km. It then bypasses **Ribzhi** village on the east shore of Lake Balungtso, and after a further 105 km it comes to a halt at **Lungkar** township on the southwest shore of **Lake Tarotso**. Recently Lungkar has been given an enhanced status as the capital of a new county bearing its own name (Ch Longe'er). There are old trade routes heading north from here to the **Drangyer saltfield** and the vast lake **Ngangra Ringtso**.

Mayum La pass

From Horpa, the main road continues to follow the north bank of the Brahmaputra upstream to **Satsam** (50 km) and, then, after crossing to the south bank, traces the course of the **Mayum Tsangpo** feeder river towards the **Mayum La pass** (4,980 m), which marks the frontier between West Tibet and Far West Tibet. The distance from Satsam to the pass is 50 km. The road across Mayum La may be impassable if it has been raining heavily. It is often practical to camp out at **Ngari Punsum** before the pass and negotiate it in the morning while the earth may be frozen. It is a long, gradual pass that consists largely of marshy soil. Herds of wild ass (kyang) and antelope may occasionally be seen grazing here. Near the top there is a newly established army camp and a military checkpoint, where all passports and travel documents will be inspected. Once over the pass, the road to **Barga** and **Mount Kailash** is straightforward.

On the northeast side of the **Ganglungri** range, which divides Drongpa county from the **Simikot** region of Northwest Nepal, there are the glaciers of **Jema Yungdrung, Ngangser** and **Gyama Langdzom** which are included among the sources of the Brahmaputra.

Sleeping

Old Drongpa *p334*

E **Gangjong Tibet Hotel**, has a few rooms (¥25 per bed).with no courtyard or outside toilets, but it does have a good homestyle restaurant.

E **Tashi Hotel**, has poor accommodation (¥25 per bed).

E **Yak Hotel**, has spacious Tibetan style 4-bed dormitories (¥25 per bed, ¥100 per room), with outdoor toilets and a large courtyard.

New Drongpa *p335*

E **Government Guesthouse**, is the best available with dormitories at ¥30 per bed.

E **Mandala Hotel**, at the east end of town has inferior accommodation (¥25 per bed).

Baryang *p335*

E **Dekyi Dronkhang**, is a small family-run guesthouse, with a friendly atmosphere (at ¥25 per bed). The family kitchen can be used as a restaurant.

E **Tashi Hotel**, has dormitory accommodation at ¥30 per bed.

E **Yak Hotel**, the largest in the township, a comfortable Tibetan courtyard-style guesthouse (at ¥25 per bed), popular with Kailash-bound pilgrims in summertime.

Eating

Baryang *p335*

Amdo Restaurant, offers lamb dishes – Qinghai and Muslim specialities.

Shandong Restaurant, has bland but wholesome Chinese cuisine.

Sichuan Restaurant, the best Chinese restaurant here.

Tsonub Restaurant, offers homestyle Tibetan cuisine.

For an explanation of the sleeping and eating price codes used in this guide, see inside the front cover. Other relevant information is found in Essentials pages 44-46.

Northern Tibet (Jangtang Plateau)

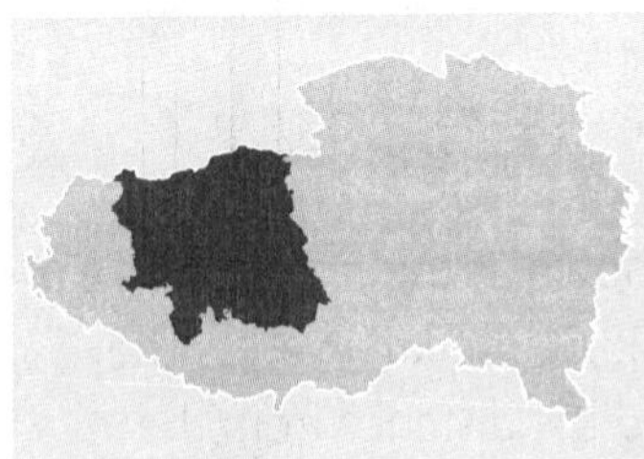

Footprint features

Introduction

The northern plateau of Tibet, known as the Jangtang, is a vast lakeland wilderness, over 438,000 sq km in area. The average elevation is 4,500 m, and the distance from the easternmost parts which adjoin Nakchu and Amdo counties to Lake Pang-gong in the far west exceeds 1,300 km. The northern limits of the plateau are demarcated by the Kunlun Mountains and the southern edge by the Gangtise and Nyenchen Tanglha ranges. The basin of the upper Indus lies to the west, and those of the upper Salween and Yangtze are to the east and northeast. In general the western parts of the plateau are higher than the eastern parts.

The Jangtang plateau is mostly contained within the Tibetan Autonomous Region, although the extreme northeast parts currently fall within Qinghai province. Four counties form its heart: among them are **Tsochen** and **Gertse** counties in Ngari prefecture, through which the northern route from Raga to Mount Kailash passes; and **Shentsa** and **Palgon** in Nakchu prefecture, which link the Lhasa-Ziling highway with Far West Tibet.

Recommended itineraries: 2, 6. **See page 20.**

★ Don't miss...

1. **Gertse County** Unrivalled panoramic views of the northern grasslands, page 343.
2. **Aru Lake** The best area for wildlife observation in the Jangtang plateau, page 344.
3. **Dangra Yutso** A fabled lake which is a focal point for Bon culture, page 345.
4. **Tsonyi** 'Twin Lakes' is a remote trailhead for wildlife observation at Yibuk Tsaka and for exploration of the 6,000-m peaks of the Kunlun range, page 346.

Background

Geography of the Jangtang

The Jangtang plateau itself has no external drainage, but it is dotted with brackish salt lakes, some of which were once part of the Yangtze and Salween basins, and others remnants of the Neo-Tethys Sea. Most of these are at elevations of 4,500-5,000 m; and among them the largest include **Namtso** and **Serling** (both 81 km across), **Dangra Yutso** (64 km long), **Ngangla Ringmo**, and **Lake Pang-gang** (48 km by 113 km). It is clear that these lakes are relics of once significantly larger bodies of water, the traces of which can be observed in the relief of the ancient shorelines. Certain lakes have become salt swamps, while others are connected by small streams.

The internal river network is largely undeveloped – the longest being the **Tsakya Tsangpo** which drains into Lake Serling. In winter, the rivers freeze to the bottom, thus confining drainage to the summer months. These processes and frost weathering have lead to the formation of colossal accumulations of friable material, which has levelled the relief. Due to the winnowing of fine particles, the coarser gravel-pebble material is gradually compacted and polished, forming a shiny mantle that is subject to no further deflation. In addition, the thickness of certain salt swamps is so great that they form entire beds which have acquired unique and strange shapes – pyramids, spheres and cones.

Flora of the Jangtang

At least 53 species of plants grow in the stony tundra landscape of the Jangtang. These belong to the genus of the Gramineae, Compositae and Cruciferae. The **northern** portion of the **plateau** and the **Eastern Kunluns** are more desertified. On the better drained areas there are creeping shrubs of teresken, acantholiumn, capsella, astragalus, thermopsis, sage and saussurea. Along the shores of certain lakes with internal drainage grow sedges and in poorly drained swampy areas Tibetan cobresia. In ravines sheltered from the winds there are poa, sheep's fescue and reaumurea.

In the **southern** and **south-eastern** parts of the **Jangtang** where the precipitation marginally increases, the alpine steppes encourage the growth of poa, sheep's fescue, feather grass and quack grass; also sandwort, delphinium, sage, astragalus and saussurea. Juniper grows sparsely on the shores of Lake Namtso.

Overall, there are a few creeping shrubs capable of growing in the salty Jangtang soils: caragana, myricaria, ephedra, and tansy among them, but extensive areas of salt swamp are completely devoid of vegetation cover.

Jangtang Nature Reserve → *Colour map 6, grid C2*

In 1993 the northernmost parts of the Jangtang were declared as the world's second largest nature reserve (300,000 sq km), exceeded only by the ice-caps of the Greenland National Park. Here roam the much depleted herds of wild ungulates (wild yak, wild ass, blue sheep, argali, gazelle and antelope); and the plateau's remaining large predators (snow leopard, wolf, lynx and brown bear). The ubiquitous pika predominates at the bottom of the food chain.

Tsochen County མཚོ་ཆེན

→ *Population: 11,791. Area: 35,887 sq km. Colour map 6, grid C1.* 措勤县

Tsochen county on the **northern route to Mount Kailash** is a nomadic region with road access to Gertse and Amdo in the north, and to Ngamring or Saga in the south. The county capital is located at **Mendong**, near the northwest shore of Lake Tashi Namtso. The distance from the capital to Raga is 242 km, and to Gertse 260 km.

South of Mendong

Heading north into the Jangtang Plateau from Raga on a long, straight deeply potholed road, a concrete bridge is crossed. Down the slope to the right of the road at this point there is a large geothermal area. If the water table is high enough geysers spout forth every few minutes or so. One shoots steaming water over 15 m high. At one time it is said that there were over 100 geysers here, and there is a small renovated bath house. The road skirts a small lake and then passes along the full length of **Lake Takyel-tso** (4,950 m), which is teeming with fish.

Snaking its way north up long valleys, the road crosses over two main passes— the first of which is the watershed (5,280 m). The second pass (4,890 m) leads on to the Jangtang plateau, offering a vista of ever-changing scenery. Snow-capped peaks, among them **Mount Sanglung** (6,174 m), rise far to the west through the occasional huddle of wind-whipped road maintenance depots or small Tibetan hamlets nestled against the leeward side of a stony ridge. The lake **Gyesar-tso** lies to the south of Mount Sanglung.

Late in the long day the road descends into the broad sandy plains of the **Yutra Tsangpo** valley – a river which drains into the small **Lake Lungkar-tso** to the southeast. Drivers must be careful to follow recent tracks since they can be led into treacherous quicksands. Some 35 km before Mendong, the county town of Tsochen, there is a turn-off on the left (west) which leads 14 km to **Kyangtreng** township, on the shore of **Lake Kering-tso**. The main road continues north, crossing the **Tsochen Tsangpo** to reach the capital around dusk.

Mendong

Mendong (4,650 m) is a small town on the banks of the Tsochen Tsangpo river, situated near the northwest corner of the large Lake Tashi Namtso. It consists of one main street, with restaurants, shops and assorted government buildings.

Tsitri

A motorable side road from Tsochen leads 50 km to Tsitri township, northeast of **Lake Tashi Namtso**. There are a number of small hamlets in this nomadic pastureland, interspersed between smaller lakes, such as Ngangkok-tso.

Tsochen Mendong Gonpa

The most important monastery in Tsochen county is the Kagyu monastery of Tsochen Mendong Gonpa which lies east of Mendong by the banks of the Tsochen Tsangpo, in the nomadic area known as **Chokchu-me**. The mountain to the west is well known even now for its abundance of medicinal herbs. It is a branch of Tsurphu, founded by the students of the charismatic local lama, **Karma Ngedon Tengye** (1820-1889), whose embalmed remains were entombed here in a reliquary temple (**Kudung Lhakhang**). In the early decades of the previous century assembly halls, a protector shrine, **Mani Lhakhang**, and nunnery were added, and at its height there were approximately 100 monks and nuns residing nearby. The monastery developed under the supervision of a succession of drubpon ("masters of meditative attainment", ie meditation teachers) trained at Tsurphu,

Tsochen County

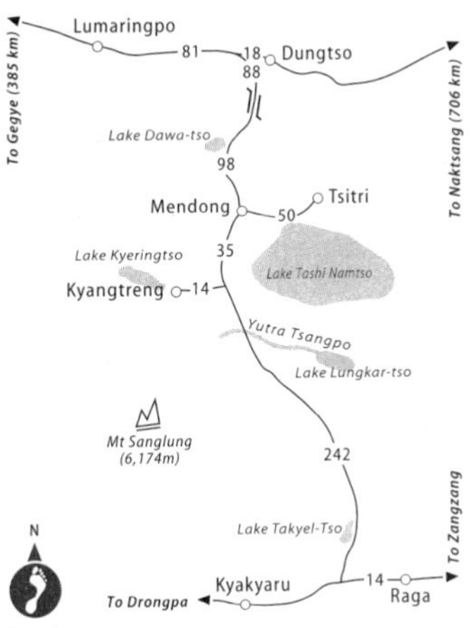

and following its destruction during the Cultural Revolution has been under reconstruction since 1984, due to the efforts of the late Lama Sherab. At present there are 20 monks here.

The main **assembly hall** (*dukhang*) consists of an antechamber where the monks congregate and an inner chapel with a large reliquary stupa of Lama Sherab and some old tangkas in the gallery. The images to the rear are (L-R): Milarepa, Padmasambhava, Gampopa, Shakyamuni, and Shridevi (twice). The smaller temple (**lhakhang**), which has a **Gonkhang** dedicated to Bernakchen in its upper storey, contains a smaller reliquary stupa of Lama Sherab, and 1,000 miniature Shakyamuni images.

Other reconstructed monasteries in the area include the **Tsochen Jomo Gonpa**, where there are 17 Kagyupa nuns, and the **Penda Lhakhang**, which is ministered by four monks and nuns, also of the Kagyu school.

North of Mendong

Continuing on the northern route to Mount Kailash from Mendong, the trip now changes from a rugged journey to an arduous expedition. Crossing **Norchung La pass** (4,590 m) after 43 km, it soon reaches the shore of the wide **Lake Dawa-tso**, around which are clusters of nomad tents. This is a traditional grazing land for herds of yaks, goats and sheep. You may notice well-made cairns of rock up to 2 m high. They are actually hollow and, if undamaged, hold cooking and camping equipment for a family of nomads who will have left it there the previous year before setting out for their winter dwelling. The goods will remain untouched until they return. After driving along the northeast shoreline, the road climbs through a narrow valley (4,830 m) to emerge on the lush marshy plain of **Dawazhung**. Here there is an abundance of wildlife. Wild geese, storks and many other types of waterfowl share the area with yaks and gazelles as well as the occasional lammergeier. The Kagyu monastery of **Burkar Gon**, located in Dawazhung township, was founded in 1920 by Karma Sherab Ozer. Currently there are 35 monks and nuns residing here.

The road crosses the high 5,000 m **Norgo La** pass, 98 km north of Mendong. After **Tsetraloma**, an important bridge-crossing where there are basic guesthouse and restaurant facilities, it runs through a narrow valley girded on the north by a snow-peaked range and then sweeps down 72 km into a vast salt plain, where it spreads out into dozens of tracks. These eventually veer west for 16 km, and, near **Dungtso** (4,400 m), meet up with the main Jangtang lateral road which links Amdo county in the east with the Far West Tibet. The raw force of the late noon sun blasts the landscape into a bleached monochrome over a featureless terrain. The town of Lumaringpo, capital of Gertse county, lies 81 km west of this road junction.

Sleeping

Mendong *p341*

E **Plateau Hotel (Sato Dronkhang/ Gaoyuan Lushe)**, T0892-2612442. The best option here, with twin and single rooms at ¥100 (no hot running water). A new economy guesthouse complex will soon be opened in the same compound, with rooms at ¥30 per bed.

Bank Guest House, a poorer alternative to the adjacent Plateau Hotel.

Tanug Guesthouse, at the entrance to the town, a poorer alternative to the Plateau Hotel.

Eating

Mendong *p341*

Chengdu Huaitai Restaurant, T0897-2612256. Specializes in Sichuan cuisine.

Friendship Restaurant, offers Tibetan food.

Linxia Restaurant, on the opposite side of the street to the Chengdu Huaitai

For an explanation of the sleeping and eating price codes used in this guide, see inside the front cover. Other relevant information is found in Essentials pages 44-46.

Restaurant. Offers Muslim cuisine.
Markham Restaurant, near the Linxia Restaurant. Khampa cuisine.

The town also has a number of reasonably well-stocked general stores.

Gertse County སྒེར་རྩེ

➔ *Population: 17,169. Area: 97,771 sq km. Colour map 6, grid C1.* 改则县

Gertse is a large, desolate county bordering Drongpa in the south, Gegye in the west, and the Kunlun Mountains in the north. The capital is located at Lumaringpo, 260 km from Mendong in Tsochen county, 836 km from Draknak (Amdo) in the upper Salween basin, and 385 km from Napuk (Gegye) in the upper Indus valley. According to both oral tradition and archival sources, some 300 years ago there were seven villages of Kham, known as Teryik Drongdun, which migrated en masse to settle in the Gertse region. The very name Gertse is said to have been borrowed from their original neighbourhood, and many distinctive customs have been retained along with their unusual dialect.

East of Lumaringpo

Near Dungtso township where the roads from Tsochen and Amdo converge, you can head east in the direction of Nyima and Shentsa counties or west for Gegye on the northern route to Mount Kailash. Taking the latter route, you will pass **Lake Dungtso** to the north side of the road. The Karma Kagyu monastery of **Lowo Dechen Gon** can be visited nearby. Reconstructed in 1988-1993, it was originally founded at the site of an ancient meditation cave complex, on the slopes of hill resembling the protector Mahakala in the form of Bernakchen. Within the township the Gelukpa temple known as **Dungtso Lhakhang** has only two monk attendants. After 81 km Lumaringpo, the county capital, suddenly appears in the distance beyond a conical, solitary hillock. It lies in the middle of nowhere; another one-street town.

Lumaringpo

Lumaringpo (4,245 m) is larger than Mendong and it is the foremost administrative centre for the nomads of the Jangtang plateau. Its main street is bisected north-south by a number of lanes, down one of which, to the south, is the post office and the town hall. To the north of town there is a set of the eight stupas, symbolizing the deeds of Shakyamuni Buddha, and a long wall of mani stones, adorned with yak and goat horns. At the east end of the town is the hospital and dispensary (often strangely empty), the telecommunications centre and the larger official guesthouses. At the other end of town, a few hundred metres away, is the quarter occupied by Tibetan itinerants. This features the busiest and liveliest area of town: namely the pool halls, electric games parlours, 'chang' drinking houses, and gambling dens. Around here the traders from Kham, East Tibet, pitch their tents and sell all kinds of goods. The cheap truck stops are also to be found at this end of town.

Gertse County

Mikmar

There are side roads extending from Lumaringpo into remote parts of the

 Jangtang plateau. One leads due south for 100 km to **Mikmar** township, nestling between lakes Tsatso and Lakor-tso. From there, an old trade and trekking route runs further southwards, following the **Dobrong Tsangpo** valley into **Drongpa** county (see above, page 334). In this locality the most important monastery is Mikmar Gonpa, revered in oral tradition as the right eye of Lake Manasarovar. This monastery, which belongs to the Nyingma school, was founded by Orgyan Chopel, a student of Zhabkar Tsokdruk Rangdrol, at the site of a meditation hermitage which had been frequented over the centuries by Gangri Lhatsen, Padmasambhava, Tsangpa Gyare, Gotsangpa, and others. Formerly the monastery contained images of Shakyamuni, Longchen Rabjampa, Jowo Yizhin Norbu and Avalokiteshvara, all fashioned of East Indian bronze, as well as an image of Padmasambhava made of medicinal clay, and 21 lineage-holders of gilded copper. Following its destruction during the Cultural Revolution, reconstruction slowly began in 1985 and there are now some 16 monks at Mikmar Gonpa.

Another road leads northwards from Lumaringpo for 35 km to **Khangtok** township in the **Mikpa Tsangpo** valley, and thence for 154 km to the remote outpost of **Lugu** by the shore of **Lake Drakpo-tso**, where the Karma Kagyu temple known as Gonpa Luma once stood.

Gertse Drakgyam Gon

At Khangtok, this Kagyu monastery, also known as Karma Drubgyu Tendar Chokhorling, was founded in 1950 by Lama Karma Yonten (1926-1988) and rebuilt in 1989. It comprises a meditation hermitage, established by Lama Tsegon of Tsurphu, and an eight-pillared temple containing gilded copper images of Jowo Shakyamuni, Vajrapani and Vajradhara as well as copies of the *Rinchen Terdzo* and the Collected Works of both Mipham Rinpoche and Karmapa Khakhyab Dorje. Above the monastery in the uplands of Drakgyam valley there is the meditation cave known as **Tsenper Phuk**.

There are several 6,000 m peaks in the region to the east of Lugu, bordering Shentsa county. Trekking routes also run from Lugu through the lakeland region bordering the Kunlun Mountains, and thence out of Tibet into Xinjiang. The northern parts of Gertse county are occupied by the Jangtang Nature Reserve (see above, page 340). The best area for wildlife observation is reputedly the **Aru Lake basin** (34°N, 82.5°E) and the environs of **Memar** and **Ngamong Lakes** (34.5°N, 82°E) which are located near the West Kunlun range. Getting there: to reach the Aru basin drive northwest from Lumaringpo via Khangtok, Lakar La pass and Gyatso hamlet. **NB** Motorable trails in these remote northern areas can still be snow-bound in May.

The **northern route to Mount Kailash** runs northwest from Lumaringpo, passing Oma township after 90 km. **Lake Tarab-tso** lies beyond, on the border of Gertse and Gegye counties. The town of **Napuk** is 295 km from Oma, in the upper Indus valley.

Sleeping

Lumaringpo *p343*

D **Gertse Hotel**, T0897-2652197, opposite the hospital. Has comfortable twin rooms (with a/c but no hot running water) at ¥160 (¥80 per bed), and ¥120 (¥60 per bed) for rooms without a/c.

E **Gertse Guesthouse**, an adjacent building to the Gertse Hotel in the hotel compound. Twins at ¥90 ((¥45 per bed) and 4-bed dorms at (¥35 per bed).

Eating

Lumaringpo *p343*

Chong Wei Sichuan Restaurant, opposite the Gertse Hotel. Does surprisingly good stir-fries.

Drung Ching Sichuan Restaurant, next door to the Gertse Hotel. Popular.

The town has a number of shops where general supplies and even some fresh vegetables can be purchased. IDD calls can be made from China Post and Telecom Office.

Shentsa County ཤན་རྩ

→ *Population: 16,596. Area: 205,202 sq km. Colour map 6, grid C2.* 申扎县

From **Dungtso** where the Tsochen and Gertse roads intersect, head eastwards across the length of the Jangtang plateau towards the Lhasa-Ziling highway, passing through Shentsa and Palgon counties. Until recently **Shentsa** was by far the largest of the Jangtang counties, extending from the present day Xinjiang and Qinghai provincial borders in the north to the Brahmaputra watershed in the south. As such the county was larger than the United Kingdom! But now it has been subdivided into Nyima county and Shentsa proper, governed from Naktsang. In this region there are 67 lakes, including some of Tibet's largest: Serling, Dangra Yutso, Ngangtse-tso, Kering-tso, Taktse-tse and Uru-tso. In the northeast there are a number of 6,000 m peaks including **Purok Gangri** (6,482 m) and **Norlha Gangri** (6,136 m), not to mention the Kunlun Mountains on the Xinjiang border further north. The entire northern region forms part of the Jangtang Nature Reserve. Ten large salt fields testify to the importance of this region for the traditional trading commodity of the Jangtang plateau. The county capital of Shentsa is located at **Naktsang** (Shentsa), 805 km from Lumaringpo in Gertse county, and 232 km from Palgon. However, owing to the vastness of this sparsely populated region, there is a second administrative centre at **Tsonyi** (Twin Lakes) in the north. The distance from Naktsang (Shentsa) to Tsonyi is 442 km.

Ins and outs

Driving eastwards from Dungtso, the road reaches **Kyewa** township in the valley of the **Boktsang Tsangpo** after 244 km, and then passes south of Lake Taktse-tso for 78 km to **Nyima** county town. Here, there is a turn-off which leaves the main road, heading southwest for 167 km via Kanglung to **Ombu** township on the northern shore of **Lake Dangra Yutso**.

Dangra Yutso Lake → *Colour map 1, grid C2*

The shores of Dangra Yutso sustained a relatively large population in ancient times. Research by John Bellezza documents a number of ruined hamlets, fortifications and megaliths in its environs. The entire Dangra region is sacred to the Bonpo, and at Ombu itself there is a small Bonpo temple and hermitage complex, known as Ombu Zhangzhung Gon, which is affiliated to Menri Gonpa. Bonpo pilgrims come from afar to circumambulate the lake, most following their preferred anti-clockwise route. The trek takes 11 days (carry all essential supplies and camping equipment). Three days into the trek, the trail passes through an area rich in wildlife and thence to the impressive **Serzhing Monastery**, beyond the southwest corner of the lake. This is revered as one of the most important ancient Bon monasteries in Tibet, although today it is largely in ruins. On the fifth day the trail passes through the **Tango Tsangpo** valley in view of the glaciers of **Mount Tangori** (6,450 m), frequented largely by Bon hermits (and a few Nyingmapa). At **Tso-me** township in this valley, there is a motorable route to **Zangzang**, and a 14-day trek through the **Mu-chu** valley to **Phuntsoling**.

Continuing on the circuit of the lake, on the 10th day the trail reaches **Orgyen**

 Gonpa – a small rebuilt Bonpo monastery with a cave temple containing a rock handprint of Shenrab Miwoche, founder of the Bon religion. Nearby at **Khyungdzong**, there was once an important Bonpo *terma* site and hermitage, as well as a seventh-century castle belonging to the kings of Zhangzhung. There is also a trail leading due east from here to **Gyakok** township, on the shore of Lake Ngangtse-tso, and eventually to **Drowa** township.

Naktsang

To reach the county capital from Ombu, return to the turn-off at **Nyima** county town on the main Gertse-Amdo road, and continue driving eastwards, along the north shore of the enormous **Lake Serling**. Cross the **Tsakya Tsangpo** near its confluence with the lake, and after 204 km, you will reach a major intersection, where side roads branch off both to the north and south. The former leads to **Tsonyi** district. Taking the latter, the road cuts southwest via Zhung-me township to **Naktsang**, 180 km distant. This is the largest settlement within the county, located southeast of the elongated lake Kering-tso, and there are simple but spartan guesthouse facilities. During the 17th century, Naktsang was the focus of a military campaign directed against the nomadic traditions of the Jangtang by the Mongolian governor Ganden Tsewang. An ancient trade and pilgrimage route leads from here southwards, through Batsa township into the **Shang** valley of Tsang (page 262).

Tsonyi

Head northwest from Dayul on the lateral highway to **Tsonyi** (262 km). There are excellent areas further west for wildlife observation - particularly around the **Yibuk Tsaka** salt basin and the **Rongma** hotsprings (33°N, 86.8°E).

Palgon County དཔལ་དགོན

→ *Population: 33,065. Area: 99,112 sq km. Colour map 6, grid B3.* 班戈县

Palgon county in the hinterland of **Lake Namtso Chukmo** is relatively close to the Lhasa-Ziling highway. The circuit of this amazing lake and its ancient Bon sites documented by John Bellezza have already been mentioned (see above, pages 143-144). In addition, there are 46 lesser lakes and 21 rivers, of which the **Tsakya Tsangpo**, draining into Lake Serling, is the longest.

If you approach the county capital, **Namru**, from the north, you should take the turn-off at **Dayul** which leads to Shentsa, and then after 10 km cut southeast in the direction of Namru, 62 km distant. Here there is simple transport station accommodation.

A jeep track leads directly south from Namru to Lake Namtso Chukmo, passing through the townships of **Poche** (52 km) and **Dechen** (65 km); and from Dechen due west to **Shelyer** along the Bo-chu valley (52 km). Another jeep track heads from Namru directly east for 226 km to join the Lhasa-Ziling highway. Alternatively, from Dayul on the main road to Amdo county, the distance is 211 km. In the north, the Jangtang Nature Reserve occupies the part of Palgon County adjacent to the Qinghai border.

Far West Tibet (Ngari)

Footprint features

Introduction

The vast region of Far West Tibet, known as Ngari, in Tibetan (Ch Ali), is, like the neighbouring Jangtang plateau, one of the least populated parts of the country. Access to this region is still only possible through a long overland journey from the bordering countries of Nepal and India (the latter closed to non-Indian nationals), or from Pakistan and Kazakhstan via the Xinjiang Autonomous Region (East Turkestan). Within Tibet, the region may be approached via the northern route (Amdo or Tsochen and Gertse), or the southern route (Saga and Drongpa). At the heart of the region is sacred Mount Kailash, the focal point for most visitors, renowned for its spiritual magnetism and natural beauty. Furthermore, within the canyons and valleys of the upper Sutlej River are numerous ruins of ancient cities that once comprised the kingdom of Guge. A number of temples are still intact and contain exquisite murals and decorative motifs, some dating back more than 1,000 years. Close to the Indian border, this area has only recently been opened to western travellers and is well worth including in an itinerary. The whole Ngari region has been earmarked for tourism development and access will eventually by possible by air once the new airport is open at Senge Khabab.

In the description which follows, the northern route to Kailash passing through the counties of the upper Indus will be described first, followed by the southern route from Tsang, the western route through Guge, and the north-western route through Xinjiang.

Recommended itinerary: 2. See page 20.

★ Don't miss...

1. **Tirthapuri** Camp by the upper Sutlej and bathe in the wonderful sulphur pools at Tirthapuri Hotsprings, page 355.
2. **Pilgrimage trekking** Spend six days circumambulating the sacred Mount Kailash and Lake Manasarovar, in the company of Tibetan and Indian pilgrims, page 359.
3. **Khyunglung Ngulkhar** Ancient troglodyte capital of the fabled Bon kingdom of Zhangzhung, page 379.
4. **Roof of the world** Above Toling, a breathtaking 170 degree Himalayan panorama extends in an arc from the peaks of Western Nepal to the mountains of Zangskar and Ladakh, page 381.
5. **Guge** It's worth spending three days here to explore the 11th-century temples of Toling, page 381, and the deserted citadel of Tsaparang, page 385, along with the more recently documented sites of Dungkar and Piyang, where there are magnificent murals, page 391.

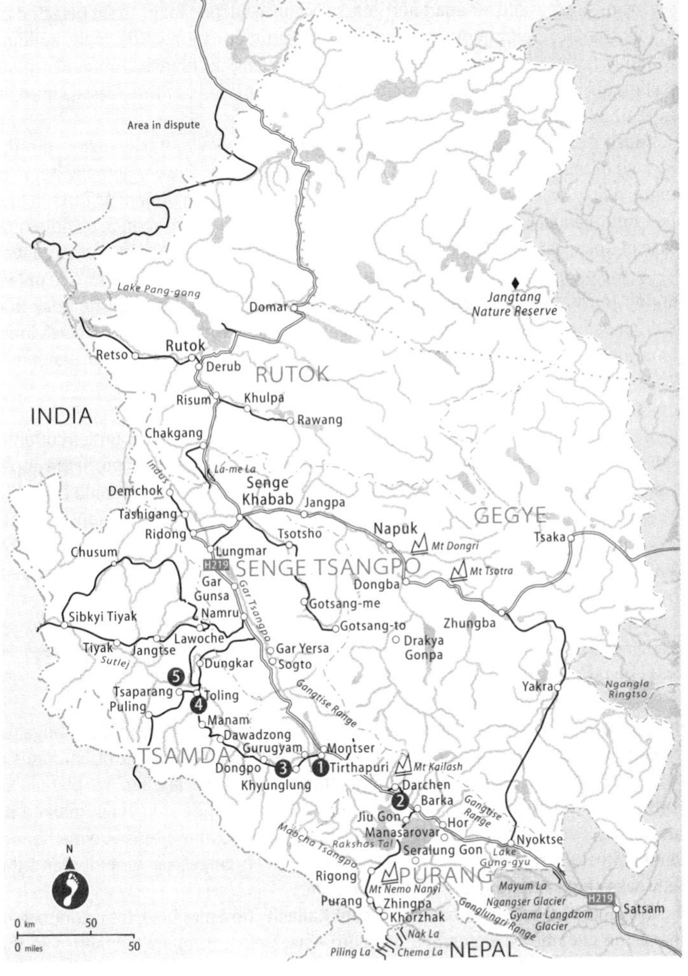

Background

Traditionally, the region of Ngari is said to have comprised three districts (Ngari Korsum): the district of **Maryul** including **Rutok**, **Ladakh**, and **Zangkar**, the district of **Guge**, corresponding to the heartland of the ancient Zhangzhung kingdom, and the district of **Purang**. However, Tibetan influence in Central Asia was particularly strong during the periods of the Zhangzhung and Yarlung dynasties and some claim the three districts of Ngari were much larger.

Ins and outs

The journey across the great Northern Plain into Far West Tibet passes through a land where the lifestyle remains close to what it has been for centuries. The landscapes and vistas are vast, treeless and sparsely inhabited but exhilarating, like a moonscape. Lone groups of nomads dwelling in low, black tents tend flocks of sheep and goats as well as herds of the ubiquitous yak (the 'grunting ox', according to its Latin name).

Towns are few and far apart and generally consist of one main street bisected by another, neither being more than a few hundred metres long. The main building invariably is the local government complex, including a Chinese communist party meeting hall, and there are few facilities to meet the needs of the average intrepid traveller, let alone a tourist.

Much of the journey consists of little more than parallel tracks across the flat expanse of the plateau. The distances to be covered each day entail many hours of bumpy riding. Transport is usually prearranged through international or Tibetan tour operators because permit restrictions still apply in Ngari. For information on obtaining these permits, see Essentials page 32. It is likely that you will travel in a small convoy led by one or more four-wheel drive Toyota landcruisers accompanied by one or two support trucks carrying food, baggage and fuel. It will be the pace of the truck that determines how quickly the distances can be covered. Although this involves long, somewhat gruelling days, the faster the grand scope of the Northern Plateau is traversed the more time can be spent near the sacred Mount Kailash.

The geographical zone of Far West Tibet comprises five of the seven counties currently under the administration of Ngari prefecture: **Gegye** and **Senge Tsangpo**, in the upper Indus valley, **Rutok** county in the Aksai Chin and Northern Plateau, **Tsamda** county in the upper Sutlej valley, and **Purang** county where the Karnali and Brahmaputra rivers have their sources to the south and west of Mount Kailash. The other two (Gertse and Tsochen), which geographically belong to the Jangtang, have already been described. The prefectural capital is **Senge Khabab** (Ch Shiquanhe).

Land and environment

The region is demarcated by the Himalayas in the south, and the Gangtise Range (or Trans-Himalayan Range) in the north. The **Gangtise** Range (5,500-6,000 m) forms a watershed between the upper Brahmaputra River and the landlocked plateau of Northern Tibet (Jangtang). The northern and southern slopes are gentle, marked by flat peaks, low elevations relative to the Tibet plateau, and intensive weathering, whereas the western slopes are broken by the deep gorges of the Indus and the heavily eroded sandstone canyons of the Sutlej.

The unique 6,714-m pinnacle of **Mount Kailash** (Tib Gang Ti-se/Gang Rinpoche), lies at the geographic watershed of South Asia. Before it, a few kilometres to the

Khampa traders of Ngari

The vast region is strikingly reminiscent of the wide open spaces of the American Wild West, an image also borne out by the inhabitants. The nomads bear a strong physical resemblance to North American Indians, such as the Navaho. In the towns tall Khampa traders from East Tibet are like `macho' cowboys. They swagger about, gold teeth flashing behind a wide knowing smile, long hair wound in red or black braid embellished with a large gold and turquoise earring, their feet balanced on high-heeled riding boots or showing through holes in Chinese canvas trainers, and wearing a bulky gown or `chuba' (Tibet's national costume) tied loosely round the waist with a fat money belt from which dangles a long knife in a silver scabbard. They stand outside their tented shops on the edge of town selling everything from batteries to baseball hats, from music cassettes to motor spare parts. There is a similar sense of lawlessness to the cowboy west in this land that is free of any visible boundaries. It makes the accounts by previous travellers to Tibet of robbers raiding the caravans of traders and pilgrims all too real.

Brian Beresford

south, are two lakes, **Mapham Yutso** (Manasarovar) and **Lakngar** (Rakshas Tal), shaped respectively like the sun and the moon. The sources of four major rivers rise from this geomantic crown and flow in the four cardinal directions: the **Indus** (north), **Brahmaputra** (east), **Karnali** (south) and **Sutlej** (west). It is for this reason and because of the unique beauty of the region that Mount Kailash has been looked upon as a sacred realm – a goal of pilgrimage by peoples from Tibet, India and other parts of Asia for thousands of years.

Further north, the **Nganglung Gangri** range (elevation 5,700-6,300 m) separates the upper Indus from the Jangtang plateau. The highest peak is **Ngari Gangri** (6,348 m), and the range is less rugged than the Himalayas, with more rounded and weathered hills.

Climate

Ngari is marked by the greatest extremes of dryness and the lowest temperatures. In Senge Khabab (4,280 m) the annual rainfall is less than 100 mm and the mean January temperature -12°. In recent years, however, the climate has become more inconsistent. During the Indian monsoon from late June to mid-September heavy rains often reach as far as the northern slopes of the Gangtise range, causing rivers to become impassable and increasing erosion. Deforestation of the Himalayas is thought to be the main cause.

Flora and fauna

The landscape is barren, reminiscent of the Jangtang steppes north of the Gangtise range, but there are some variations in flora. Here juniper grows, along with barberry and honeysuckle.

The region between the source of the Brahmaputra and Mount Kailash abounds with wildlife, especially after the rainy season of July and August. Apart from the herds of **yak** there are large herds of **wild ass** (*kyang*), a large and vividly marked creature which gallops away from the road when disturbed. You have to be quick to take photographs. More common throughout Far West Tibet are the Tibetan **gazelle** (Tib *gowa*; *Procapra picticaudata*) and **Hodgson's antelope** (Tib *tso*; *Pantholops hodgsoni*). The former is small and similar to the wild chamois of the European Alps.

The Upper Indus Valley

The Indus is 2,900 km in length, encompassing a drainage area of 1,165,500 sq km (of which 453,248 sq km are within the mountain area). The annual flow is 207 billion cu m. The actual source of the Indus is the stream known in Tibet as the Senge Khabab or Jang Senge Khabab ("northern source from the lion-shaped rock"). This source lies to the north of Mount Kailash at 5,500 m in a remote valley within the Sengto district of Gegye county. In its uppermost reaches the river which emerges from this glacial source is called the Senge Tsangpo. It flows northwest for about 320 km through Drakya Gonpa, Dongpa, and Napuk townships of Gegye county, and then west to Senge Tsangpo, where it converges with the Langchu Tsangpo and the Gar Tsangpo, before cutting northwest through Tashigang and Demchok. Here, the river leaves Tibet, crossing into India at about 4,570 m. The river volume in Tibet is mainly snow-fed, but thereafter it passes through Ladakh, Baltistan, and the alluvial plains of Pakistan, where it provides the life support for millions of people. Over 5,000 years ago its waters sustained the Indus Valley Civilization, one of the earliest settlements of mankind. Major tributaries include the Zangskar, Shyok, Shigar, Gilgit, Astor, Kabul, and the five Punjab rivers.

The latter is larger, distinguished by its long, slightly curved horns and white rump. Other animals commonly seen are the **marmot** (*chiwa*), which resembles a brown, furry football with legs, and the **abra**, a small Tibetan rodent like a gerbil that lives in large colonies of burrows in healthy grasslands.

Huge flocks of migrating birds can also be seen throughout the late summer, making their way south over the Himalayas to India for the winter. In addition there are indigenous birds such as the graceful **Brahmany geese** which have golden-coloured bodies and a black head, and which mate for life. They have become the subject of numerous love songs and poems in Tibet. It is well known that if one should die or be killed, the mate will pine and grieve until it too passes away.

Gegye County དགེ་རྒྱས

→ *Population: 12,834. Area: 54,885 sq km. Colour map 1, grid A2.* 革吉县

Gegye county on the **northern route to Mount Kailash** *extends from Lake Tarab-tso, on the edge of the Jangtang plateau, as far as Dongpa and Napuk in the upper Indus valley. The capital is located at* **Napuk**, *383 km from Lumaringpo in Gertse, and 112 km from Senge Khabab.*

Tsaka

Driving west from **Oma** township in Gertse county, the road passes south of **Lake Tarab-tso**, and climbs steadily for 94 km to **Tsaka** (Ch Yanba), where there are commercial salt fields and a small **guesthouse** ⓘ *¥15-30 per bed*. At Tsaka, the Karma Kagyu monastery of **Tashi Choling** was founded in 1894 by Kunga

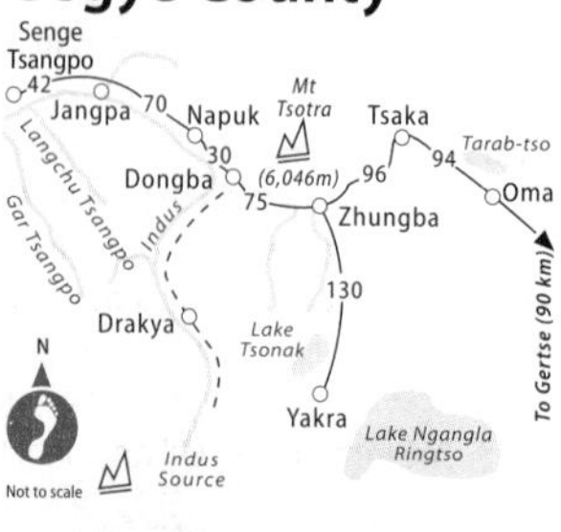

Tashi Rinpoche (1858-1918). All its precious artefacts were destroyed during the Cultural Revolution, and restoration is proceeding slowly. There are now 23 monks and nuns in residence.

Zhungba

The road then cuts southwest through a shallow gorge and climbs again for 96 km to **Zhungba** township on the Shang-chu River, passing **Lake Nyer-tso** to the west. A side road passable by jeep leads south from Zhungba to **Yakra** (130 km) on the southeast shore of **Lake Tsonak**, and from here there is a trekking route to the large lake **Ngangla Ringtso** on the border of Drongpa county (see page 334). In Zhungba, there are two small reconstructed Kagyu temples, known as **Shang Lukhang** and **Kyawo Lhakhang**.

Dongba

The main road from Zhungba cuts northwest, with **Mount Tsotra** (6,046 m) to the right, crossing high passes, including the Jangtang-Indus watershed (5,100 m). After 75 km, it reaches **Dongba** township, descending into the valley of the upper Indus. There is a small Kagyu monastery, **Drirapuk Gon**, here, ministered by only three monks.

During the latter half of the 17th century a nomadic group of approximately 50 families under the leadership of Behu Agya was forced to leave its ancestral homeland in the Nangchen region of Kham, and they moved westwards, eventually to occupy the three pasturelands of **Kongchen**, **Seng-to** and **Senge-me** in Dongba in the upper Indus basin. In return for military assistance against Ladakh, the Tibetan government and their Mongolian allies formally appointed Behu Agya as the chieftain (pon) of this locality, inhabited by more than 100 nomadic groups. His descendants maintained this hereditary succession, known as the Dongba Pon, through to the mid-20th century.

A motorable branch road follows the river upstream to the larger **Drakya Gonpa** and the broad **Yalung Selung** range (6,105 m), with access to Mount Kailash.

Drakya Drubgyu Tengyeling

This monastery was founded near Seng-to in the Upper Indus valley during the 19th century by the Fourteenth Karmapa Tekchok Dorje (1797-1868) at the behest of its patron Ponmo Sonamtso, the estranged wife of the chieftain of Drongpa. Formerly it contained an image of the Eighth Karmapa Mikyo Dorje, fashioned of Chinese bronze, a bronze image of Manjughosa which was once the property of the Sixth Karmapa, a gold and silver image of the Fifteenth Karmapa which was personally donated by the late Sixteenth Karmapa, Rikpei Dorje, and many other treasures. The monastery, which administered to the spiritual needs of the nomadic community, was utterly destroyed in 1968. The present restored temple dating from 1986-1988 contains assorted clay images of the Karma Kagyu lineage, and there are now 20 monks.

The main motorable route continues northwest from Dongba, following the Indus gorge downstream to **Napuk** (4.450 m), the county capital of Gegye, only 30 km distant. **Mount Dongri** (5,825 m), a major landmark, lies to the east as the town is approached.

Napuk → *Colour map 1, grid A2*

The present county capital is a completely new town, in a poor location at the base of a cliff where the prevailing winds create a semi-permanent sand storm. Such is the 'skill' of the latter-day geomancers who created it! This very bleak town, which was set up mainly to control the nomads, will be reached in the late afternoon if you have left Lumaringpo early in the morning. The road now is quite straightforward and the average speed can be increased accordingly. It may be best to continue on to **Senge Khabab**, the prefectural capital.

To reach Senge Khabab from Gegye, continue following the Indus downstream towards **Jangpa** (70 km) and (then, on) for 42 km to the prefectural capital. ▸▸ *For listings, see pages 356-358.*

Senge Tsangpo སེང་གེ་གཙང་པོ

→ *Population: 12,422. Area: 11,802 sq km. Colour map 1, grid A2.* 噶尔县

Senge Tsangpo county, formerly known as Gar, straddles the confluences of the Indus River and two of its tributaries: the Langchu Tsangpo, which converges at Senge Khabab town, and the Gar Tsangpo, which converges south of Tashigang. The town, which is both the prefectural and county capital, is located 112 km from Napuk in Gegye, 127 km from Rutok, 255 km from Toling, and 428 km from Purang. ▸▸ *For Sleeping, eating and other listings, see pages 356-358.*

Senge Khabab → *Colour map 1, grid A2*

The **northern route to Mount Kailash** continues following the upper Indus valley through **Jangpa** village (70 km beyond Gegye) and on to **Senge Khabab** (42 km from Jangpa), which is by far the largest town in the entire region. It is a new Chinese-built town, named after the source of the **Indus River** (Tib Senge Khabab, Ch Shiquanhe), which has its confluence with the **Langchu Tsangpo** here. The traditional capital of the Ngari region was Gartok, a nomadic encampment 49 km distant in the Gar Tsangpo valley (see below, page 355).

After the long, arduous journey across the desert expanse of the Northern Plateau, the bright neon lights and asphalt streets of Senge Khabab assume a somewhat surreal appearance. An unusual sand barrage protects the town from the strong sandstorms that blow in from the southeast. The town has high-rise buildings, restaurants, general stores, nightclubs and an industrial cement plant. This is a welcome opportunity to spend one or two days washing clothes etc while preparing for the last, most important, stage of the journey to Mount Kailash. One should also check or obtain **permits** for Tsaparang, Toling and Mount Kailash from the police and the cultural relics bureau.

There are four roads which diverge at the capital: one leading northeast to Gegye and Gertse (see page 352 and page 343), another (Highway 219) leading due north to Rutok (see below, page 393), a third (the recently paved section of Highway 219) leading west to the confluence of the Indus with the Gar Tsangpo, and a fourth which leads southeast to Tsotsho township.

From Senge Khabab you can go directly to Mount Kailash on the new road in a single day. Otherwise you may break the journey at Montser.

Langchu Tsangpo Valley → *Colour map 1, grid A2*

A side road driveable by jeep leads southeast from Senge Khabab, following the **Langchu Tsangpo** upstream. After 40 km it reaches its terminus at **Tsotsho** township, where the local chieftain had a hereditary status dating back to the appointment of his ancestor Jurik Chingwadur by the 17th-century Mongolian governor Ganden Tsewang in return for military assistance. An ancient trekking route leads from Tsotsho into the upper reaches of this valley to **Gotsang-me** and **Gotsang-to**.

Tashigang and Demchok

→ *Colour map 1, grid A1*

Taking the old southern road from Senge Khabab, you will reach the confluence of

Senge Tsangpo County

the Indus with the Gar Tsangpo at **Ridong** after about 30 km. From here the road to Mount Kailash follows the Gar Tsangpo upstream (southeast), while a side road passable by jeep continues northwest following the course of the Indus downstream to **Tashigang** (21 km). Here, in a dramatic riverside location, is the monastery of Tashigang Gonpa, which was originally founded by the Drukpa Kagyu lama Taktsangwa of Ladakh, but converted by force to the Gelukpa school by the Mongolian army during the 17th century when Ganden Tsewang placed it under the authority of Sera Je college in Lhasa. Nonetheless, there are extant murals at Tashigang indicative of its original Drukpa Kagyu heritage. The pot-holed surface of this side road continues on through the upper Indus gorge to reach **Demchok** and the Indian frontier (closed to tourists), where the river flows into Ladakh.

Gar Tsangpo Valley → *Colour map 1, grid A2*

The new paved road, leading west from Senge Khabab is the main **northern route to Mount Kailash**, which follows the Gar Tsangpo upstream. Driving is fast on this excellent surface, passing through **Lungmar** and **Gar Gunsa**, the ancient winter capital of Ngari district, 49 km from Senge Khabab.

On old maps Gar Gunsa is referred to as Gartok. Following the military campaign of the Mongolian general Ganden Tsewang in Ngari against the invading forces of the king of Ladakh (circa 1681), the region was secured under the authority of the Fifth Dalai Lama. Gar Gunsa then became the seat of a viceroy appointed by the central government in Lhasa to whom all foreign travellers were supposed to apply for travel permission. It lay on one of the main caravan routes. Today it is nearly impossible to see where it once was situated. All that remains are mounds of rubble.

Further south, the road passes through **Namru** after 23 km, where there is an important turn-off leading to Toling, 144 km distant, in the upper Sutlej valley (see below, pages 380 and page 385). Namru was formerly the seat of the Namru Chieftain (Namru Pon), a rank initially conferred on Hor Dodrak, chieftain of the Hor troops who migrated from Namru near Lake Namtso, after being mustered by the Mongolian governor Ganden Tsewang in 1679. Five km after Namru, the paved road comes to an abrupt end. There are plans for the army to extend it all the way to Mayum La pass and to Purang. Continuing along the Gar Tsangpo valley on the old dirt road, you will soon reach **Gar Yersa**, the ancient summer capital of the Ngari viceroy, and **Sogto** village.

After Sogto, the road crosses a watershed, leaving the source of the Gar Tsangpo behind, and following the southwest side of the **Gangtise** range into a wide sandy valley which forms part of the upper Sutlej basin. This road can be quite treacherous in the rainy season because it follows a poorly cut track along the sandy floor of the river valley. Bumpy ruts cut through the sandy surface, causing vehicles to lurch. Sections of the road also ford streams and rivers whose depth can be deceptive. However an experienced driver should be familiar with the hazards and cover the journey safely. Eventually the road reaches the new township of **Montser**, 203 km from Senge Khabab.

Montser → *Colour map 1, grid B2*

Montser (4,380 m) is a small coal mining town with little of redeeming interest. There are no streets to speak of, nor a town centre, just housing compounds and open space. So you will have to enquire where the truck stops are. There are at least two truck stops in Montser, which is usually reached at dusk. The small **Dunchu Lhakhang** of the Gelukpa school has only six monks.

Tirthapuri → *Colour map 1, grid A2*

Before setting out from Montser on the road to Darchen, you can take a detour to visit the hot springs, picnic ground and pilgrimage site of **Tirthapuri**. It is about 6 km southwest of Montser. Here is a cave associated with Padmasambhava, the Indian master who established Buddhism in Tibet in the eighth century and his Tibetan consort Yeshe Tsogyel. You may prefer just to spend a short time here and return after the circuits of Mount Kailash and Lake Manasarovar. Tirthapuri is one of the traditional pilgrimage sites visited after Mount Kailash (for a detailed description, see below, page 372).

Gurugyam Monastery → *Colour map 1, grid A2*

Getting there The road to **Khyunglung**, which leaves the Tirthapuri road 8 km south of Montser, passes southwest through a broad agricultural valley dotted with single family compounds. The Bon Monastery of **Gurugyam Dongak Drakgyeling** (4,240 m) is located about 15 km from the turn-off, at the western limit of this valley. Camp here!

This is one of the most important Bonpo monasteries in Far West Tibet, founded in 1936 by Khyungtrul Yungdrung Gyeltsen Pelzangpo below the Yungdrung Rinchen Barwa meditation cave, where the revered Bon masters of Zhangzhung, Gyerchen Drenpa Namka, Tsewang Rigzin and Pema Tongdrol had meditated in antiquity. Today it has a strong connection to the main Bonpo settlement at **Dolanji** in North India where many of its monks gathered after the Chinese invasion and have successfully re-established the Bon tradition in exile. Gurugyam was rebuilt in 1989-1991 from walled ruins and is one of the finest examples of a Bon monastery in the Ngari prefecture, rebuilt under the direction of the ninth successive master of Gurugyam (the Ninth Tsawei Rinpoche).

The **Yungdrung Rinchen Barwa** cave hermitage, situated in the cliffs above, is particularly associated with the Bonpo master **Gyerchen Drenpa Namka**, who lived and meditated here for centuries, according to the Bon chronicles. He was also renowned as a great doctor – his mortar and pestle for grinding herbs and medications can still be seen beside the pathway leading up to his room. A steep climb leads through a series of staircases and tunnels before reaching Drenpa Namka's meditation cave, cut deep into the cliff above the temple. Inside the cave there is a palpable sense of sanctity amidst a remarkable wealth of religious objects, which include the reliquaries of the previous eight masters of Gurugyam.

The other major temple associated with Drenpa Namka is a box-like shrine on the top of a canyon directly to the east. Inside is a statue of the master himself, which was decapitated by the Chinese and has now been given a new head by devotees. Unfortunately the replacement is two or three times larger than normal – obviously the devotion exceeded any sense of the conventional!

A few hundred metres east of Gurugyam, there is an even older site, known as **Zhangzhung Gonpa**, which is located at a prominent square mound surrounded by a number of collapsed stupas. This is reckoned to have been active during the same era as Khyunglung.

Khyunglung From Gurugyam, you can also make an expedition to the ruins of one of Tibet's earliest cities, known as **Khyunglung** ('Garuda Valley'). Dating back to 2,000 BC or even earlier it was established by the first kings of Zhangzhung, the original name for Far West Tibet, and it continued to be occupied for 3,000 years. For a description of Khyunglung (which is in Tsamda county), see below, page 379.

Sleeping

Napuk *p353*

D **Gegye Shanghai Hotel**, T0897-2632455. 15 rooms, which are the best in town – standard twin rooms at ¥90, suites at ¥160, and deluxe suites at ¥240.

E **Grain Department Guesthouse**, dormitory accommodation at ¥25 per bed.

If these guesthouses are full, camp against a sheltered bluff, 2 km out of town. Perfectly adequate for the few hours rest that one needs, this bluff is formed by an uninhabited complex of buildings, originally made for the

Muslim construction workers who were brought down from Xinjiang province.

Senge Khabab *p354*

C **Ali Post Hotel** (Ngari Daksi Arkhang), T0897-2828888. Currently has the best rooms in town (a/c and attached bathrooms with hot running water) – standard twin rooms at ¥320, triples at ¥280, suites at ¥500, and deluxe suites at ¥580.

C **Shanxi Hotel** (formerly known as the Ali Hotel), T0897-2822370, F0897-2821487. Has deluxe twin rooms at ¥320, deluxe doubles with attached bath at ¥688, and cheaper rooms from ¥100.

C **Telecom Hotel** (Dianxing Fandian), T0897-2822998. Has doubles and singles at ¥400, and suites at ¥600.

C **Ying Hotel**, T0897-2821354. Has twin rooms (evening showers only) at ¥270, economy rooms at ¥170, and dormitory beds at ¥35-60.

E **Mu Kunsang Guesthouse**, T0897-2823055. Has poor accommodation, without toilets (range: ¥30-¥100 per bed).

E **Shing Shui Guesthouse**, located behind the Ali Post Hotel. Has 40 simpler rooms, at ¥40 per bed.

NB If you try to camp out at Senge Khabab, the police can arrest you and fine you the price of a night's stay at one of the expensive hotels.

Montser *p355*

Montser Guesthouse, to the east of the township. Has 8 very basic rooms, with beds, mattresses, and a quilted sheet (¥ 15 per bed).

Eating

Napuk *p353*

Lhasa Tibetan Restaurant, offers the best Tibetan cuisine in town.

There are also small Sichuan-style restaurants, a Muslim restaurant, and the Gangjong Tibetan Restaurant, opposite the entrance to the Gegye Shanghai Hotel.

Senge Khabab *p354*

Ali Post Hotel and the **Shanxi Hotel**, restaurant meals are expensive and reasonably good.

The Dringar Toktse Restaurant (Qing Xiang Lou), T0897-2825578. Serves Muslim, Amdowa and Tu cuisine, is next to the Ali Post Hotel.

Jingmaowei Commercial Trade Restaurant, opposite the Shanxi Hotel, T0897-2826489. Among the cheaper local Sichuan-style restaurants.

The Lhasa Tibetan Restaurant, located next to the Ying Hotel.

Montser *p355*

There are small seasonal Tibetan and Sichuan restaurants, but only the guesthouse restaurant remains open throughout the year.

Entertainment

Senge Khabab *p354*

Nothing of note by day, but the bizarre nightlife includes karaoke bars, massage parlours, discotheques, nightclubs, and a casino.

Shopping

Senge Khabab *p354*

Department Store at the town crossroads allows the purchase of food and other supplies.

There are several other small general stores.

Activities and tours

Senge Khabab *p354*

Tibet Kailash Travel, T0897-321400/21799, F0897-321496, organize travel throughout Ngari, including the routes from Simikot in Nepal and Kashgar in Xinjiang.

Transport

Napuk *p353*

Bus

Public buses connect Napuk with **Senge Khabab** (¥50) and **Lhasa** (¥726).

Senge Khabab *p354*

Air

The airport is likely to transform the situation here when it opens. In the meantime all transportation is by road.

Bus

Bus station, T0897-7876591. There is a bus service on alternate days to and from **Lhasa** (range ¥660-786) operated by **Tibetan Antelope Travel** (T0897-2822226), but foreigners are not usually permitted to travel by public bus through the checkpoints in Zhigatse prefecture. Buses also run on alternate days to **Yecheng** in Xinjiang via Rutok and **Darmar** (range: ¥200-410).

There are occasional minibuses on the route between Senge Khabab and **Purang** (¥400).

Taxi

Taxis and auto-rickshaws are available within the town (fare range: ¥5-10).

Directory

Senge Khabab *p354*

Banks Foreign currency (especially US dollars) can be changed at the Bank of China only. No TCs or credit cards will be accepted. **Hospitals** In town there is a modern hospital, which also dispenses Tibetan medicine. **Telephones** IDD and DDD calls can be made from China Post and Telecom (opening hours: 0930-1330 and 1630-1830).

Purang County སྤུ་ཧྲེང

→ *Population: 7,845. Area: 11,641 sq km. Colour map 1, grid B3.* 普兰县

Purang county is the heart of Far West Tibet, where the four great rivers of South Asia diverge from their glacial sources around Mount Kailash. It is the goal of the great pilgrimage routes which approach this sacred mountain from the north (Gegye or Xinjiang), from the west (Kinnaur in India), from the south (Almora in India and Simikot in Nepal), and from the east (Drongpa). The county capital is located at **Purang**, *known as Taklakot in Nepali, which lies 104 km south of Barka township, in the valley of the Karnali River (Tib Mabcha Tsangpo). The distance from here to Senge Khabab, the prefectural capital, is 428 km, to Drongpa in Tsang 487 km, and to Toling in the upper Sutlej valley 434 km.*

Before leaving Montser you may decide to take a detour to visit Tirthapuri and Gurugyam Monastery (in Senge Tsangpo county) and Khyunglung (in Tsamda county). Otherwise drive directly to Darchen. The 68-km road from Montser to **Darchen**, *where the circuit of Mount Kailash begins, follows the Gangtise or Trans-Himalayan Range directly down (southeast) to the* **Barka** *Plain between Mount Kailash and the two lakes.* ⓘ *The Kailash Nature Reserve charges foreigners ¥50 per person to enter the area. Tickets will be issued in Darchen itself (if you approach from Toling or Senge Khabab), or at the Barka checkpoint (if you approach from Mayum La or Purang).*

Darchen → *Colour map 1, grid B2*

Darchen (4,575 m), more properly known and still signposted as Lhara, was formerly an important sheep station for the nomads and their flocks. Until the late 1980s it still consisted of only two permanent buildings. One survived the mass destruction of religious shrines during the Cultural Revolution since it was said to have belonged to the Bhutanese government through the Drukpa Kagyu tradition, which still claimed jurisdiction over it. Resembling a temple, it is coloured in red ochre and serves as a shelter for Tibetan pilgrims. The second building was created in the 1980s to accommodate the first wave of pilgrims from India, and therefore known

as the IP (Indian Pilgrim) Guest House. In 1995 a medical centre and dispensary (the Tibetan Medical and Astro Institute) was inaugurated. Sponsored by Swiss Tibetan benefactors it has since become a centre for training doctors in traditional medicine and for dispensing medicine and treatment for the various illnesses that afflict the local nomadic community. More recently, Mount Kailash has become a popular destination for tourists and trekkers, and Darchen has correspondingly changed out of all recognition. Sleaze, garbage and prostitution are the hallmarks of this once tranquil pilgrims' trailhead. Consequently many visitors and pilgrimage groups now prefer to camp further west at Darpoche or to stay at Jiu Gonpa beside Lake Manasarovar (see below, page 369), and send their guide on ahead to make the final preparations for the circuit of the sacred mountain.

Mount Kailash གངས་རིན་པོ་ཆེ

→ *Colour map 1, grid B2*

For most travellers to Far West Tibet the prime focus of their journey is the sacred peak of Mount Kailash (6,714 m). This extraordinary mountain is regarded as the 'heart of the world', the 'axis mundi', the centre of Asia, by Buddhists, Hindus, Jains and followers of other spiritual traditions. Of all the special destinations for the traveller to reach, Mount Kailash is surely one of the most sublime and sacred. Its geographical position as the watershed of South Asia is unique and it is this which gives it a cosmic geomantic power. From its slopes flow four great rivers in the four cardinal directions – the Indus north, the Brahmaputra east, the Karnali south into the Ganges, and the Sutlej west. ▸▸ *For Sleeping, Eating and other listings, see page 380.*

Before Mount Kailash lie the twin lakes of **Manasarovar** (4,600 m) and **Rakshas Tal** (4,584 m), shaped respectively like the sun and moon, and which are said to have associations respectively with the forces of light and dark. Further south, just on the edge of the Tibetan plateau and near the Himalayas is another snow-capped peak, **Mount Nemo Nanyi** (Gurlamandhata; 7,728 m), which is one of the highest inside Tibet. Its three peaks and four ridges form a swastika, an ancient symbol of the infinity of the universe.

Mount Kailash itself is known in the Tibetan language as **Gang Ti-se** and informally as **Gang Rinpoche** ('Precious Snow Mountain'), and in Chinese as **Gang Rinboqe Feng**. Though only 6,714 m high, it stands quite alone like a great white sentinel guarding the main routes into Tibet from India and Nepal in the south and west.

Traditionally a pilgrim undertakes the 52-km trekking circuit or circumambulation (*khorlam*) around Mount Kailash commencing at **Darchen** (4,575 m) and crossing the 5,630-m **Dolma La pass** on the second day of the three-day walk. This is followed by a trek of the same duration around the beautiful turquoise **Lake Mansarovar**. The journey is then completed with a rest and camp at the hot springs and geysers of **Tirthapuri**, a few hours' drive away and especially associated with Padmasambhava. All along the pilgrimage route are places of historical and spiritual interest. **NB** The most important year for the circuit of Mount Kailash is considered to be the water horse year of the Tibetan calendar, which coincided with 2002, and will next coincide with 2062. It is believed that a circuit undertaken during that year carries the merit of 12 conventional circuits of the sacred mountain!

The Rigour of the Routes to Mount Kailash

Although Mount Kailash and its environs are of exceptional natural beauty, until the new airport at Senge Khabab opens, it can still only be reached via lengthy and often arduous travel along one of several motorable routes into the region.

Despite the bureaucratic restrictions imposed on visitors, facilities for the foreign

A pilgrim's view of Mount Kailash

The approach to Darchen from Montser, passing eastwards along the southern ridge of the Gangtise range, offers a spectacular panoramic view where the most striking feature is the snow massif of **Mount Nemo Nanyi** (7,728 m), one of Tibet's highest mountains, known in Nepali as Mount Gurlamandhata. It lies to the southeast of **Lake Rakshas Tal**. Do not be deceived into thinking this is Mount Kailash! The sacred mountain remains hidden for most of the journey. Mountain after mountain seem to be possible contenders until, finally, it rises above all those before it; a giant snow-capped pyramid when viewed from the west; majestically standing aloof from all those lesser peaks that surround it. Now these neighbouring mountains really do seem to bow down before its magnificence!

As one moves closer, its form seems to change with every mile passed; from a pyramid, to a breast, to a dome. Now one observes clearly how it rises alone, unique among mountains. Its dominance of the entire landscape is unlike anything in the mighty Himalayas. Its 6,714 m is not touched or even glanced at by any mountain near it. As Darchen comes closer its form becomes rounded and the extraordinary black markings on its faces cut into the form of a universal cross or eternal swastika through its snow-capped mass. It is not of this mundane world because it now makes even the Himalayas seem ordinary. It grew up through the depths of the great ocean, the **Tethys Sea**, some 50 million years ago. The **Great Himalayas** on the other hand are one of the newest ranges on the planet, arbitrarily wrenched out of the Asian landmass as it met the tectonic plate of the Indian subcontinent, buckling skyward from the massive forces unleashed below the surface some 20 million years ago.

Mount Kailash's very whiteness and convex south face, like a mirror, is said to reflect the sun's rays out, beyond the confines of the planet. Like a giant crystal, its three faceted sides encompass a trinity that rises glittering at the nexus of the Hindu and Buddhist planetary universe. From the stark duality of its white sheen and black mystery etched into its every face – the inner and outer, splits the triad of its faces, complete and self-contained. Grudgingly through the valleys and folds of the land it then manifests into four, the great rivers of the world flowing in the four cardinal directions: the sacred rivers which are the sources of civilizations and knowledge: north the **Indus**, spawning the earliest, the Indus Valley civilization; east, the **Brahmaputra** feeding the mystics of Tibet before cutting through the eastern Himalayas and cascading down into Bengal and the source of the great philosophy and knowledge of ancient India; south via the **Karnali** into the **Ganges**, India's life-blood and the well-spring of its spiritual inspiration and ongoing timeless presence; and west, along the **Sutlej**, little known but in fact the link with the mystics of the Indian Himalayas and the sustainer of the richness of life in the northwest of India. Thus the mountain would appear, just on its own to a viewer from afar.

Brian Beresford

traveller are sparse and the way itself, from whichever direction, is rugged and often tiring. Local food is basic and needs to be supplemented and a large degree of self-reliance and fortitude is essential. Furthermore, the sacred Mount Kailash has never easily allowed visitors into its sanctum, but with fortitude, patience and a pure, constant intention to reach and circle its snow-capped peak, one will succeed. For all these reasons, the journey to and through Far West Tibet requires the appropriate preparation, both logistically and mentally.

The traveller who is prepared to undergo the rigours of this journey will come into contact with a way of life that has undergone little change for centuries, and experience the wonder of a unique wilderness and culture largely untouched by the modern world. Therefore, despite all drawbacks and hardships, to participate in a pilgrimage to Mount Kailash or simply to travel in this unique and stunningly beautiful and unpolluted natural environment can be one of life's most rewarding experiences.

Five Routes to Mount Kailash

There are four main approaches, each of which roughly follows one of four great river valleys, located in the four cardinal directions of the mountain. In addition, there is a fifth traditional route reserved for Indian pilgrims. Yet another, the route from Simla and Kinnaur along the Hindustan Highway into Tsamda county is still closed for political reasons.

Northern Plateau Route

1,981 km from Lhasa; 1,500 km from Lhartse: **1** Lhartse-Raga (241 km); **2** Raga-Tsochen (242 km); **3** Tsochen-Gertse (260 km); **4** Gertse-Gegye (370 km); **5** Gegye-Senge Khabab (112 km); **6** Senge Khabab-Montser (207 km); **7** Montser-Darchen (68 km).

Mount Kailash & Lake Manasarovar

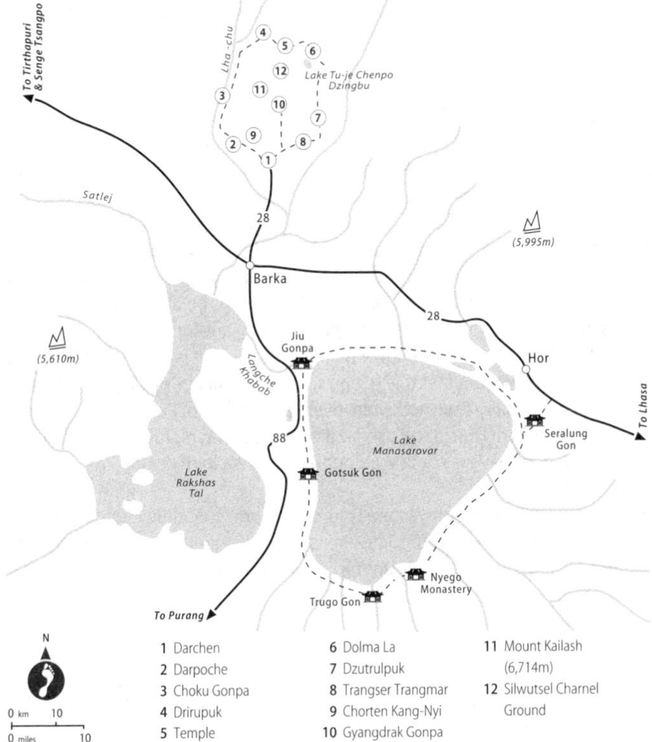

Departing from Lhartse on the Lhasa-Dram highway, the northern route traverses the Jangtang Plateau to **Senge Khabab**, the prefectural capital of Far West Tibet (Ngari) in the upper Indus valley, and then cuts south to **Mount Kailash** directly or via Tsamda, where the great sites of **Tsaparang** and **Toling** can be visited. Until the 1990s this was the only legitimate route open to foreign travellers, and of the four main routes it is still the most commonly used since it remains open throughout the year.

Southern Brahmaputra Route

1,338 km from Lhasa; 857 km from Lhartse: **1** Lhartse-Saga (293 km); **2** Saga-Old Drongpa (145 km); **3** Old Drongpa-Barka (397 km); and **4** Barka-Darchen (22 km). **Or** 993 km from Kathmandu: **1** Kathmandu-Dram (122 km); **2** Dram-Dzongka (204 km); **3** Dzongka-Kyakyaru (103 km); **4** Kyakyaru-Old Drongpa (145 km); **5** Old Drongpa-Barka (397 km); and **6** Barka-Darchen (22 km).

Departing from Kathmandu via Dram and Kyirong, or from Lhartse via Ngamring, this route follows the course of the Brahmaputra upstream through Saga and Drongpa counties. The road is harder to traverse from late June until early September due to snow-melt, or during the monsoon when heavy rainfall swells the several rivers which need to be forded.

This southern road is the most direct route to Mount Kailash, closely following the valley of the upper **Brahmaputra** upstream and across the watershed. Those setting out from Lhasa will drive to Saga via Lhartse and Ngamring, while those starting in Nepal will do likewise, driving via Dram and Kyirong.

Northwestern Xinjiang Route

1,641 km from Kashgar: **1** Kashgar-Yarkand/Yecheng (249 km); **2** Yarkand-Mazar (249 km); **3** Mazar-Tserang Daban (456 km); **4** Tserang Daban-Domar (172 km); **5** Domar-Rutok (123 km); 6. Rutok-Senge Khabab (117 km); **7** Senge Khabab-Montser (207 km); and **8** Montser-Darchen (68 km).

Departing from **Hunza** in Pakistan via the Karakorum highway, from Bishkek in Kyrghyzstan, or from **Almaty** in Kazakhstan, this route effectively begins at **Kashgar** in the Xinjiang Autonomous Region, north of Tibet. Kashgar can also be reached by air from Beijing.

Leaving Kashgar, the road skirts the northern frontiers of Pakistan, Kashmir and Ladakh in Northwest India, cutting across the disputed territory known as the **Aksai Chin**, for which reason it has been strictly off-limits for foreign travellers. The Aksai Chin is a large region claimed by India, and it can sometimes be difficult or impossible to obtain the necessary permits to leave Kashgar, particularly for individual travellers. On the other hand if flying from Urumqi or Beijing to Kashgar it is possible to make all arrangements for permits to enter this region with an Urumqi or Beijing-based travel agent. If you enter China from Pakistan over the Kunjerab Pass and along the Karakoram Highway from Hunza to Kashgar it becomes a memorable and economic journey. Remember however to obtain a double entry visa for Pakistan if you wish to exit via the same way.

NB At present, this northwestern route is more commonly undertaken in reverse, to exit from Far West Tibet into Pakistan or Kyrgyzstan. Nonetheless, the tourist authorities of Far West Tibet are trying to have the approach from Kashgar officially opened.

West Nepal Route

1 Simikot-Darapani (trekking); **2** Darapani-Sali Khola (trekking); **3** Sali Khola-Muchu (trekking); **4** Muchu-Yari (trekking); **5** Yari-Sip (trekking) **6** Sip-Nara La-Hilsa (trekking)-Purang (driving, 28 km); **7** Purang-Darchen (driving, 126 km).

Over recent years it has been possible to travel on this route under the auspices of certain trekking and travel agencies in Kathmandu, but is somewhat expensive, and permit restrictions apply both on the Nepal and Tibet sides of the border. It begins with a flight from Kathmandu via Nepalganj to **Simikot**, a small village nestling on the spur of a mountain. An intense six-day trek following the **Karnali** valley takes one over the **Nara La** pass (4,570 m) before crossing the Tibet border at Hilsa and driving via Zher to **Purang**. This ancient town at the base of Mount Nemo Nanyi (Gurlamandhata) has been the focus for Nepalese traders and pilgrims from India for thousands of years. One can then travel by bus, truck, or pre-arranged landcruiser for a half-day to Darchen at the base of Mount Kailash. **NB** It is also possible to hire a helicopter from Nepalganj or Simikot to Hilsa, in which case this route actually offers the shortest and quickest approach to Mount Kailash. Acclimatisation can be a problem for those flying in to Hilsa by helicopter.

Indian Pilgrim Route

880 km from Delhi: **1** Delhi-Almora (395 km); **2** Almora-Bhirinaga (68 km); **3** Bhirinaga-Dardu La pass (78 km); **4** Dardu La pass-Garyang (157 km); **5** Garyang-Jang La pass (38 km); **6** Jang La pass-Purang (18 km); **7** Purang-Darchen (126 km).

This was first reopened in 1980, a remarkable act resulting from the first international agreement between India and China since the Sino-Indian border war of 1962. Thus it was the Hindu pilgrims who were the first to make their way to Mount Kailash since the Cultural Revolution. Until 1980 even local Tibetans had been forbidden to circumambulate or visit the sacred mountain.

Today the Indian pilgrimage is organized as a lottery by the Delhi government. Each year 5,000-10,000 Hindus apply from all parts of India. Approximately 1,000 are selected by lottery, and after medical examinations and fitness tests, they depart from Delhi via Almora and Bhirnag, travelling in groups of 30-40, for 10 days commencing in June/July. After five days' trekking they cross the **Jang La** (Lipulekh) pass where they are exchanged with the outgoing group and met by Chinese tour guides, before being driven to **Purang** and Darchen. Following a rest day, they journey to Mount Kailash where half commence the circuit of the mountain while the other half go to Lake Manasarovar. After three days they switch around before beginning their journey home three days later. Recently, Indian pilgrims who have taken no part in this selection process have also been visiting Mount Kailash in ever-increasing numbers via **Dram** in Nepal, where specialist tour operators await their arrival.

The pilgrims must bring all their supplies with them from India. However, most are ill-prepared in terms of equipment and clothing. Many arrive clad in light cotton clothes and flimsy canvas sneakers, usually topped by a woollen balaclava or plastic rainhat. Despite this, their strong and genuine devotion carries them through the experience. For Hindus, Mount Kailash is the abode of Shiva, the God of Destruction, and it has been one of the most sacred pilgrimage destinations for over 5,000 years.

The Circumambulation of Mount Kailash

Preparation

Darchen is the starting and completion point for the general circuit of the sacred mountain. It is wise to spend at least a day acclimatising and making final preparations. **NB** It is possible to store extra baggage at the Ngari PSB Gangtise Guesthouse.

Weather Observe the weather conditions and ask those who have made the trek in the past few days what conditions you are likely to encounter. The weather will determine to a large extent the amount of baggage you need. Do not be concerned with a change of clothes for each day. Extra pairs of socks and underwear are the most that are needed. Do not forget a good raincoat and parka all-weather jacket, even if the sky is clear blue. Strong walking shoes are essential.

Acclimatization By the time you arrive in Darchen (4,575 m) you should be reasonably acclimatized to the altitude (it is said that over 3,660 m it takes from 10 days to three weeks for the blood count to adjust to less oxygen). Remember the Dolma La pass is not far under 5,700 m: plan to carry as little extra weight as possible.

Porter Arrange for a Tibetan porter or yak to carry your baggage in Darchen. The price ranges from around ¥45 for a yak, the same for a yak-herder or porter and ¥50 for a horse per day. This can be done by approaching likely-looking people or by making arrangements through the guesthouse manager. If you have arranged your travel through an agency everything will be handled by your tour guide.

Provisions **Water** It is said that one should drink around four litres of liquid a day to replace the fluid lost through perspiration at high altitude. So it is important to carry sufficient bottles of mineral water, or to stock up whenever you come across a spring or fresh stream. Dehydration leading to digestive problems is always possible at high altitude. Arrange to carry a good-sized water bottle with you and drink from it throughout the day. Orange or fruit flavour powders such as 'Tang' are good to mix in the water.

Food You need to plan the food to take. Each day the body burns a lot of energy so you need to start with a substantial breakfast of carbohydrates and glucose. Muesli, granola, and porridge oats are all beneficial. Do not hold back on sugar or glucose either. A large mug or two of tea, coffee or cocoa is vital. Carry at least six grenola-type bars (two a day) for moments when you feel your energy flagging. Glucose tablets are also helpful. In the evening you need to make up a thick soup or dehydrated stew and hot tea or chocolate.

Apparatus Your luggage should include a stove, fuel and cooking utensils as well as cleaning soap and scourer. Also candles, matches, torches, batteries, ground sheet, sleeping bag and tent if you want to sleep outside the pilgrim shelters. All these items should be provided when trekking with a commercial operator.

Gyangdrak Gonpa

Gyangdrak Gonpa (5,010 m) is an easy trek from Darchen and can be done whilst waiting for porters etc. It is a Drigung Kagyu monastery in the central approach valley of Mount Kailash, which was originally founded some 800 years ago by the Drigung retreat administrator Drubtob Guya Gangpa, and has been rebuilt since 1983. This is said to be the actual place where the founding master of the Bon tradition, Shenrab Miwoche, stayed when he came to Tibet several thousand years ago and imparted the first Bon ritual practices. It is said that he was only able to teach basic rituals relating to the pacification of the spirits who control mountains and environment. The more advanced Bon teachings of Dzogchen arose much later. The ruins of the Drigung hermitage of **Selung** (4,940 m) lie beyond Gyangdrak. Both these sites are located within the inner circuit (*nangkor*) of Mount Kailash and towards its south face. The inner circuit, which bypasses two glacial lakes of different colours, is usually undertaken only by those who have already made 12 circuits on the standard outer route!

The outer circuit: Day One, Darchen to Drirapuk → *(22.5 km)*

Leave as soon as possible after breakfast. The trail follows along the western spur of the foothills before reaching a cairn of prayer stones where it turns north into the great western valley. Descending to the valley floor at Serzhong, you will soon reach **Chorten Kang-nyi**, the "two-legged" stupa, which acts as a gateway to the **Lha-chu** valley beyond. This stupa was blown up in the 1960s and rebuilt in 1987: it was the first Buddhist structure on the circuit to be replaced. A few hundred metres east of this, and above the trail is **Darpoche** (4,660 m).

This "great flagpole" is taken down and redecorated on the full moon day of the Buddha's Enlightenment Festival (around May/June each year). Hundreds of Tibetan pilgrims come for this event, which marks the beginning of the pilgrimage season since the Dolma La pass is blocked by snow until April.

Above the shallow depression of **Darpoche** is a large flat ledge of red rock. On its surface, alongside a footprint of the Buddha, many prayers and mantras are carved. It was here that the Buddha came with 500 disciples from India. They were said to have flown there over the Himalayas by means of their supernatural powers. The view from this place looks down upon a wide flat expanse of the valley floor. Steep cliffs rise high on either side. The **Lha-chu** ('Divine River') flows down from the valley ahead and pours out onto the gentle slope of the **Barka Plain**, flowing into the waters of the **Rakshas Tal** ('Demonic Lake') in the far distance. On the valley floor are ruins of 13 stupas, dynamited in the 1960s. **NB** It is currently possible to drive from Darchen to this valley and start trekking here if time is limited.

A footbridge now crosses the river and above it, nestling in the cliff face is the rebuilt Kagyu monastry of **Choku Gonpa** (4,770 m), which was originally founded by Nyepo Drubtob in accordance with a prophesy of Gotsangpa. The central image representing Amitabha, the buddha-body of actual reality (*dharmakaya*), is contained in a glass case alongside Naropa's conch and teapot. Do not be surprised if the attendant monk here is uncooperative. Photos are strictly forbidden of the shrines. In 1991 a gang of art thieves from Nepal, working for western art dealers, broke into the shrine and stole 16 ancient statues. Two of the gang were caught and admitted they were stealing to order, using photos taken by 'tourists' the previous year. This helps one to understand the cool reception one often receives in such places. If time permits a walk over the bridge to Choku Gonpa is worth including in the trek. The view of the south face of the mountain, if clear, is striking. Below the monastery, but not discernible, is the **Langchen Bepuk** ('Hidden Elephant Cave') where Padmasambhava stayed and meditated when he came to Mount Kailash.

One can climb down from the Buddha's Platform directly to the trail below, or return to Chorten Kang-nyi and rejoin the circuit. The trail now continues up the Lha-chu valley. The path is not steep but climbs steadily. The red escarpments of the eastern wall tower above the valley obscuring the peak from view. After some time you pass the **Three Pinnacles of Longevity** above the opposite cliff face. They represent the Three Deities of Longevity: Amitayus, White Tara and Vijaya. Above the trail the western cliffs become smooth and form what seems to be a giant seat, known as the saddle of Ling Gesar. Rising higher to the east is the rock formation regarded by Hindus as the monkey god Hanuman in prayer to the mountain. Buddhists call it the **"Torma-offering of Padmasambhava"**.

After two hours you come upon a grassy plain populated by marmots. Rivulets of pure sweet water cross the trail. There is a rock in the middle of this spot, which is associated with **Mahakala**, one of the main Buddhist protectors. In summer a small tented restaurant and tea house caters to the needs of passing pilgrims. Now the valley begins to turn east and, as though gazing down from the heavens, directly above is the western face of Mount Kailash, a triangular facet of rock dripping with great drops of overhanging snow. This is a face of the mountain rarely seen in photos, yet it has a power and beauty of its own.

From this turn in the valley it is another two hours at least before reaching **Drirapuk** (4,920 m). At this point the going is not so easy and, if it is late afternoon or near sunset, each step seems a race against time. If your yaks and porters have not gone ahead (unlikely by now) you may prefer to camp along this northeastern part of the valley. But it is best to proceed on and up.

NB Once Drirapuk is in sight it is important to keep to the trail. Do not be hasty. It actually passes your destination on the far side of the Lha-chu. Unless you are prepared to remove shoes and socks and chance a wade through the river (which can be risky when the water is high) it is better to keep walking past Drirapuk and you will find a bridge which crosses the river over two spans. Many pilgrims drowned here before it was built in 1986. Now follow the trail down the opposite bank and traverse a second bridge of one span which crosses a tributary from the valley north. A short distance away is the Indian Pilgrims' Rest House at Drirapuk (4,920 m).

Drirapuk Temple This is further up the hill behind the rest house. It encloses a retreat cave associated with the great yogin Gotsangpa. Drirapuk ('Cave of the Female Yak Horn') is so named because its walls bear the indentations of a dri's horn. Gotsangpa, who stayed here from 1213 to 1217 was a disciple of one of Milarepa's disciples and is known as the author of the first history and guide book of Mount Kailash.

The north face The location here presents one with a spectacular view of the great north face of the mountain. Unlike the south face which has a smooth slope, usually covered in snow apart from the unique vertical striations down its centre, the north face is a near-vertical sheer cliff some 1,520 m high consisting of jet black rock. In only a few places does the snow cling to it, creating extraordinary oval panels like massive eyes sited within long mask-like bands of horizontal strata, all framed by the near-circular dome of the peak which itself is flanked by two symmetrical mountains. It is as though the gods rent the mountain with a cosmic sword and then swept the rubble of the shattered half into two tidy piles.

The 'pile' to the right is the mountain associated with the bodhisattva **Vajrapani**, the one to the left, the peak associated with **Avalokiteshvara** and beyond that a third is known as the mountain of **Manjughosa**. These three patron bodhisattvas of Tibet respectively embody enlightened power, compassion and discriminative awareness.

The view of the north face is equally spectacular at midnight (in the moonlight) as at midday.

Day Two: Drirapuk to Dzutrulpuk → *(22.9 km)*

This day is the climax of the pilgrimage. The **Dolma La pass** lies 6.4 km ahead but 762 m above Drirapuk, and the ascent will take about four hours. Physically it is the most arduous day. Breakfast early and set off as the sun's rays break over the ridges above. After the footbridge, the trail rises up a rocky slope. Take this gently but steadily. It soon reaches a level walk. The peak of Mount Kailash rises to the right and can now be seen linked to a long spur which joins the eastern ridge. This is the top edge of the glacial valley from which the Lha-chu flows.

Silwutsel charnel ground The trail continues to meander leveling and then up short staircases. At one point it passes by a large pile of discarded clothes, utensils and personal items including hair and teeth. This is the Silwutsel charnel ground, the place of death. Named after a famous cremation ground near Bodh Gaya in India. Tibetan pilgrims discard an item of their possessions here. It represents the renouncing of attachment to worldly objects and to this life. Without such an understanding death remains a moment to fear.

Just above Silwutsel is a knoll over which all loose rocks have been piled up into small cairns. This place linked to Vajrayogini, a dakini who inhabits fearsome places such as charnel grounds. She is the consort of the wrathful meditational deity Cakrasamvara (Khorlo Demchok), who is said to preside over Mount Kailash.

Dolma La All along the path from here are special places connected to the history and mythology of the mountain. The air becomes more rarefied and it is essential to

Milarepa and Mount Kailash

For Buddhists Milarepa's influence in the history of Mount Kailash is most important. Although the Buddha himself was said to have flown there with 500 saints by means of their miraculous powers, the mountain had been the most sacred place for followers of the Bon religion for hundreds of years. It was to Mount Kailash that the founder of Bon, Shenrab Miwoche, first came and taught in Tibet perhaps several thousand years before Christ (his dates are imprecise). Even after Padmasambhava Buddhism and Indian masters became established in Tibet, Mount Kailash continued to be venerated especially by the Bonpos. This changed when Milarepa became a mendicant master and began teaching a small band of disciples. He travelled to Mount Kailash on the basis of a prophecy of the Buddha which states that "this mountain at the navel of the world ... like a crystal stupa is the abode of Cakrasamvara, a great place of accomplished yogins ... nowhere is more marvellous or wonderful ...".

When he arrived there Milarepa met a powerful Bonpo master called **Naro Bonchung** who presided over Mount Kailash and Lake Manasarovar. Each disputed the other's authority and they agreed to resolve this in a competition of their magical powers. First they tested each other at Lake Manasarovar. Naro Bonchung stood astride the lake in one step. Milarepa spread his body over the whole surface and then balanced its waters on his finger. Not satisfied, they went to the mountain and circumambulated it in opposite directions. They met at Dolma La pass and thus began a series of feats of strength, power and magic which still left the contest unresolved.

Naro Bonchung then suggested the first to the summit after dawn on the full moon day would be the victor. Before sunrise Naro Bonchung appeared in the sky flying on his drum to the top. Despite the concern of his disciples Milarepa did not appear to be worried. Naro's ascent had ceased and he was just flying around on his drum at the same level. Then, as the rays of the sun first struck the top Milarepa joined them and was instantly transported to the summit. Naro the shaman was shocked and fell from his drum. It dropped from the sky and tumbled down the south face of Kailash gouging out a vertical line of pits and crevices. The Bonpo conceded defeat and was given jurisdiction over a neighbouring mountain called Bonri to the east.

From that contest by Milarepa until today the mountain has been influenced primarily by Buddhist adherents of Cakrasamvara, the wrathful meditational deity, who is the Buddhist tantric aspect of Great Compassion. At the same time Mount Kailash remains a major pilgrimage for Tibetan Bonpos whose custom is to circle it anticlockwise and who revere the Dalai Lama as strongly as other Tibetans. For Hindu pilgrims from India, Mount Kailash is the abode of Shiva, the Lord of Destruction and one of the triumvirate which includes Brahma and Vishnu. Jains too have traditionally made pilgrimage to Mount Kailash.

take short rests, breathing deeply, before continuing. Shortly after passing a small azure pool below the trail it turns right and begins the ascent to the **Dolma La** ('Pass of Tara'). Now it's only possible to walk a few metres before stopping, gulping in air, before covering the next short distance. At last you reach the 5,630-m pass and are able to sit down and take in the meaning of that moment. At the pass is a large boulder into which 21 emanations of Tara are said to have been absorbed during Gotsangpa's sojourn here. The boulder is festooned with prayer flags, and the whole area has an atmosphere of great festivity. Tibetans leave momentos of themselves such as a tooth, a lock of hair or even a personal snapshot, at the pass.

Dolma La to Dzutrulpuk After perhaps 30 minutes and a warm drink you will descend a steep, rock-strewn path to the valley below. Just below the pass are the milky green waters of the **Tu-je Chenpo Dzingbu** (Skt. Gaurikund), the "pool of great compassion', where Hindu pilgrims should bathe. Take great care now because it is easy to sprain your ankle or worse. You must negotiate steep staircases down to a snowfield. The only way down is to jump from boulder to boulder across a large rockfall. On the ridge above is a formation known as the **Lekyi Ta-re** ('Axe of Karma'), as though one's previous actions, if ignored, may, at any moment ripen in an accident, suffering or death.

A final steep descending staircase brings you to the **Lham-chu** valley floor, about one hour from the pass. From here it is still four hours' trekking to the day's final destination with no shelter in between. It is better to remain on the right hand side of the river, the west bank, even though parts of the trail seem easier on the east bank. If not, you may get trapped and unable to re-cross it. The walk now becomes very pleasant and relaxing (as long as the weather is clear and there is no howling gale). The path follows the gentle slope of the valley over grassy fields and clear brooks for several kilometres before it narrows and turns further south to merge with another valley before reaching **Dzutrulpuk**, the 'Miracle Cave' of Milarepa (4,690 m).

Day Three: Dzutrulpuk to Darchen → *(11.3 km)*

Stay in the rest house and spend the next morning exploring the caves and visiting the temple and shrine that has been built around Milarepa's cave. The original 13th-century temple no longer exists, and the present building dates only from 1983.

Milarepa's cave The main temple encloses Milarepa's cave which is capped by a large slab of rock, said to carry the impression on its underside of the shape of Milarepa's shoulders and upper back. This was formed when he forced the huge rock higher to make the cave more roomy. Unfortunately it now was too high and draughty. So the top of the slab (which is encased inside a mud wall) holds imprints of his feet and hands where he pressed down on the rock to make it lower and just right!

You may sit within the cave, where the central image depicts Milarepa himself. A torch is useful. There are stone footprints of Padmasambhava, Yeshe Tsogyal, Ling Gesar and his horse arrayed on the altar within the cave. In the main temple there are tangkas depicting the Drigung lineage and a central image of Amitabha, flanked by Avalokiteshvara and Padmasambhava. It is appropriate to make an offering either by placing money on the altar or giving it to a temple attendant. They may then offer you blessed relics which look like large white pills. These are made from deposits gathered during the cleaning of the rock roof of the shrine. Do not assume that they are freely given. Photography may not be allowed inside the cave, but the caretakers will accept money for one of their own polaroid photographs, which you may take away.

Outside the temple a few metres to the south is a huge hexagonal boulder. It stands upright as though placed there by hand. It once stood alone but has been half encircled by a stone wall built in the late 1980s. This wall now is beginning to collapse. It is said that Naro Bonchung hurled this boulder at Milarepa in the midst of their contest of magical powers. Milarepa caught it and placed it down gently, just above his meditation cave.

Surrounding the boulder and the temple complex are dozens of stacks of Mani Stones, rocks carved with prayers and quotations from the scriptures. Hardly a stone

Blessed objects from the Lake

Apart from the numerous abra rodent colonies between Hor and Seralung, lapping the northeast shoreline are strange **egg-shaped bundles of lake grass**. They occur nowhere else, which is enough to confer on them sacred status. Devotees take one or two for their blessings. Also along this stretch it is possible to find small **stones of black jet**. These are treasured for their association with the Karmapas. The shoreline sand changes continuously. Along a short stretch just south of Seralung it is made of five-coloured grains: black, white, red, yellow and greenish-blue. If you find such sands, they are of special value. Moreover one often finds the dried-out bodies of fish, which are highly treasured for their medicinal properties and are said to ease the pains of childbirth if just a small piece is eaten.

Brian Beresford

remains untouched. Hundreds of thousands of prayers cover the valley's slope. They continue in heaps up to a vertical cliff face. Along its base there are strata into which retreat caves have been created. One imagines Milarepa's disciples meditating here, following his example by living off soup made from the abundant nettles that grow all about. Many of the caves contain meditation platforms, self-contained by dry stone walls that divide them from their cooking partitions and entrance areas. It is well worth the short climb up to these caves before beginning the final stage of the trek.

The return to Darchen The walk back to Darchen is easy and the exit from the valley can be reached within three short hours. Just as the valley allows the river to flow out into the Barka plain, the walls become steep and the trail passes through multicoloured strata of rock changing from red to yellow, from black to purple. This section is known as the **Trangser Trangmar** ('Gold and Red Cliffs'). The trail now turns right as it skirts the base of the foothills before finally returning to Darchen. This very last section is drivable, and pre-arranged vehicles may meet trekking parties at the point where the final descent begins.

NB There are many more sites of lesser significance on the three-day circuit of Mount Kailash, but those just described are all that an average pilgrim would be able to absorb in the short time available.

Circumambulation of Lake Manasarovar

After completing the circuit of Mount Kailash, the next day you can embark on the circuit of **Lake Manasarovar**. The Tibetan names for the lake are **Mapham Yutso** and **Tso Madropa**, the later being a translation of a secondary Sanskrit name, **Anavatapta**. From Darchen drive 22 km to Barka township, at the crossroads.

Barka is a small administrative base for the people living in the environs of Mount Kailash and the lakes. All travel documents and passports will be inspected at a checkpoint here, where the roads from Senge Khabab, Drongpa and Purang all converge. There are small tented restaurants and even overnight accommodation is available as a last resort.

Day One

To reach the starting point for the circuit of Lake Manasarovar, take the eastern road from Barka, which leads 28 km to **Hor** township (4,560 m) on the road to Drongpa. Hor

Lakes Manasarovar and Rakshas Tal

Below the sacred Mount Kailash, there is the contrast and balance inherent in the two majestic lakes. Here the symbiosis is complete. One, **Lake Manasarovar** ("Lake Conceived from the Mind of God") is a disc of turquoise brilliance, passive, at peace, whole in its very nature and presence. Shimmering blue at 4,572 m, it is one of the highest bodies of pure water on the surface of the earth. Its waters are not just fresh, they are pure beyond conventional scientific confirmation, remaining pure for at least six years. Upon its surface the great dome of Mount Kailash is reflected for much of the year. In the winter it then freezes over as great ice sheets explode like voices from the underworld. It is alive, sustaining a teeming richness of trout, carp and huge freshwater dolphins. Migrating birds from Europe, Central Asia and Siberia rest here on their journeys south to the Indian subcontinent.

A short distance down the riverbed of the **Langchen Khabab**, which is the source of the Sutlej River, leads one to the dark and stormy shores of Lake **Rakshas Tal**, some 15 m lower and totally disconnected from Lake Manasarovar. Shaped like the crescent moon it embodies the forces of the night, the dark and unknown side of the psyche, yet is essential for the wholeness of life. Without the cool mystery of the night and the presence of the lunar phases sunrise could not sustain the fullness of life. Life would be consumed by the solitary brilliance of the sun.

Brian Beresford

is a haphazard collection of mud-walled houses and assorted compounds, located slightly inland from the northeast corner of the lake. There are a few small shops here, including hairdressers and the Holy Lake Shop, selling groceries and extra provisions. Opposite the Holy Lake Shop, there are two small guesthouses – the **Yangtso Hotel** ⓘ *basic dormitory-style rooms, ¥30 per bed*, and an unnamed **Dronkhang** ⓘ *rooms at ¥15 per bed*. Barrack-style accommodation is also available at the **Army Guesthouse** ⓘ *¥35 per bed*. There is a small Chinese Restaurant, opposite the Dronkhang, which has its own grocery store in front.

From Hor, drive on to **Seralung Gon**, the so-called eastern gateway to the lake. The rebuilt compound here replaces a Drigung Kagyu monastery that originally was sited a few hundred metres up the valley behind. Overnight accommodation may possibly be available here. Camping is the alternative.

Day Two

The trek now covers some 22.5 km to reach **Trugo Gon**, a monastery at the southern gateway to the lake. Although level, the sandy trail becomes arduous by the day's end. For the first few kilometres you should keep to the shoreline but then the trail cuts across a sandy headland, heading towards the bridge that crosses the **Trak Tsangpo** River. Wildlife abounds and herds of wild ass (*kyang*) graze on the valley floor. Soon Trugo Gon comes into view. The distance is deceptive for now, no matter how much ground one seems to cover, it never appears to be any closer. It is best not to look ahead and instead to enjoy the grassy fields full of flowers and mosses. Eventually, the track passes the ruins of **Nyego Monastery** at the lake's edge. It once was associated with Atisha, the Indian master who revived Buddhism in 11th century Tibet. Trugo Gon is now a simple one-hour walk away.

The grandest lightshow on earth

The area around the source of the **Brahmaputra** is undeniably beautiful. Parallel to the road, the Tibetan plateau rolls south to the white jagged wall of the Himalayas. At dusk, as wisps of smoke drift above the black silhouettes of the nomads' tents, the herds of yak lumber back home to camp, spurned on by hoots and whistles from the yak-herders and their sons. The folds in the hills turn a deep indigo while the snow teeth of the Himalayas, now cobalt blue in the eastward shadowlands, gleam with gold caps across the horizon as the sun sets, giving its last caress of the day to these crown jewels of Asia.

It sets, slipping away in the west and, if one turns toward the east a miraculous sign seems to hint at the sun's rise the next day – high in the sky above, vast rays of pink and red light streak across the deep blue stratosphere to converge on a now-vacant point in the distant east. It is the grandest lightshow on the planet; the shadows of peaks hundreds of miles away in the west are cast through the heavens, parallel to infinity but appearing to converge as the viewer perceives their perspective played out on a cosmic plane. This unique, awesome display may be seen just after sunset when few clouds remain, depending upon the conditions, along much of the Upper Brahmaputra, as well as at Lake Manasarovar and perhaps most vividly at Toling in the Upper Sutlej.

Brian Beresford

Day Three

Trugo Gon is the most active monastery around Lake Manasarovar. Originally Drukpa Kagyu, the monastery has long been affiliated to Shepeling at Purang (see below, page 374), and its inner sanctum contains images of the Buddhas of the Three Times. The complex is currently supervised by a reincarnate Gelukpa monk from Amdo named Lama Lobzang, who has been training younger monks over a number of years and has successfully established a **pilgrims' guest house** ⓘ *¥25 per bed*, nearby with a stupa outside the entrance.

Trugo Gon is also a location where Nepalese Brahmins come to make ritual ablutions in the lake waters. They trek up from the Limi valley in Northwest Nepal, following the trail across Labtse La pass through the Himalayas. Most are very poor and only visit the lake. The main date for them is the full moon in August during the monsoon when the rain and wind are numbingly cold. These thin, frail men recite mantras and prayers building up the strength to walk naked into the lake and immerse themselves completely before rushing out to huddle around a small fire.

From Trugo Gon you follow the shoreline for most of the day. Before the southwest corner, however, be prepared to encounter swarms of mosquitoes or midges. It may be necessary to cover your mouth, nose and ears with a cloth or scarf for this section. Having turned north, the western shoreline becomes a low cliff face. Some four or five hours from Trugo, you will observe caves with blackened ceilings that once were inhabited. Above them is the rebuilt Gelukpa monastery of **Gotsuk Gon**, the original foundation of which is attributed to Gotsangpa and Kyapgon Jinpa Norbu. An elderly lama and a few monks reside here. It is well worth the climb since there is a superb view of the lake from its roof.

Continue following the shoreline and the trail will turn left, pointing almost directly to the peak of Mount Kailash in the distance. Again the trail swings north towards the Tseti Guesthouse, where some Indian pilgrims stop overnight. It is said that some of Mahatma Gandhi's ashes were brought here and cast into the lake's waters. You can stop here since the road is nearby, or continue on to Jiu Monastery, the appropriate destination for the day, almost four hours from Gotsuk Gon.

Jiu Gonpa

Jiu Gonpa ('Sparrow Monastery') at the lake's western gateway sits atop a conical outcrop of red rock. Originally founded by the Drukpa Kagyu lama Kyapgon Gangriwa, inside there is a small shrine and cave where Padmasambhava meditated with his consort Yeshe Tsogyel before leaving this world. Various revered objects are to be found inside the cave, such as the granite rocks with clear imprints of Padmasambhava's hands and feet. Above the cave there is a small temple, with an image of Padmasambhava and the reliquary stupa of Lama Tsewang, who was responsible for rebuilding the complex during the 1980s. The spiritual practices followed here combine the *termas* of the Dudjom Tersar tradition and those of Jatson Nyingpo with Drukpa Kagyu liturgies. Above the temple there is a small protector chapel.

At Jiu Gon there is the **source of the Sutlej River**, known as the Ganga-chu or Langchen Khabab. When the fortunes of Tibet are low, it is almost dry, as is the present situation. The only water that remains is the brackish cusp of hot springs behind Jiu Gonpa, where a **glass-roofed bathhouse** ⓘ *admission ¥20*, has been constructed. The Tibetans have also created several open-air stone baths where you can wash yourself and your clothes in the clean hot water.

At this point, the circuit of the lake can be completed in about 10 hours, passing the remote cliff-side hermitage of **Serkyi Jakyib** and **Langna Gonpa**, above the northern shore. Alternatively, transportation can be pre-arranged to rendezvous at either Trugo Gon or Jiu Gon, from where you may either drive out of Ngari prefecture or continue on to Tirthapuri, traditionally the third and final destination of the pilgrimage. ▸▸ *For listings, see page 380.*

Tirthapuri: the Cave of Padmasambhava

→ *Colour map 1, grid B2*

Concluding the pilgrimage is a visit to **Tirthapuri** (4,330 m), where sacred hot springs and a geyser emerge above the embankment of the Sutlej River. In the upper reaches, enclosed by a temple, there is a small cave where Padmasambhava meditated with his consort Yeshe Tsogyel. It contains two granite stones in which indentations of their footprints are clearly present, and a hole through which Padmasambhava is said to have extracted the consciousness of a demonic ogress, who previously inhabited the cave. The original temple was constructed by the Nyingma lama Gonchen Chonyi Zangpo of Dorje Drak, and it once contained images of Padmasambhava flanked by Amitabha and Shakyamuni. In recent times the building has been maintained by Drigung Kagyu monks. Internal photography is forbidden.

The surrounding landscape consists mainly of red and white earth. Around the cave are dozens of unusual rock formations, almost all of which have become imbued with religious significance. Events from the lives of the buddhas and bodhisattvas are associated with and recounted at each place, in accordance with the Tibetan concept of 'sacred outlook'. The entire pilgrim's circuit takes about one hour, bypassing a cremation area, medicinal holes, the temple enclosure, a hole for testing the degree of one's positive and negative past actions, a series of mani stone walls, and the hot springs themselves.

The hot springs at Tirthapuri are clean for bathing and two small public pools with pleasant temperatures have been excavated. The larger pool nearer the cave complex is too hot for bathing, but local pilgrims and invalids draw off its curative waters. In the past there was a geyser that erupted every few minutes spraying water 6 m or so into the air. The water table must be lowering because this has not happened since the late 1980s. From one of the blowholes, however, small white flecks or 'pills' of lime can be found. Tibetans strain the water for these and use them for medicinal purposes, since they are said to have a consecrated power to cure disease.

At Tirthapuri, the Sutlej flows past grassy paddocks that are ideal for picnics or camping. The tranquillity of the place is an attraction for most Tibetan pilgrims who come here to rest and relax after the intensity of their Mount Kailash and Lake Manasarovar circuits. The pilgrim now has the opportunity to confirm and assimilate the experiences of the previous days. The spaciousness and blessings here provide a means for uniting the power and majesty of Kailash with the peace and beauty of Lake Manasarovar. In this way the pilgrimage is completed.

Tachok Khabab Source

Heading east from Hor township, you drive southeast for 92 km to reach the village of Nyoktse on the north shore of **Lake Gung-gyu**, and then continue climbing for 40 km to reach the **Mayum La** pass (4,980 m). Here you will leave Ngari for the Brahmaputra valley, en route for Central Tibet. The source of the Brahmaputra, known as the **Pakshu** or **Tachok Khabab**, lies on the far side of the pass, in the glaciers of the **Ganglungri** range (see above, page 336). This area can also be approached by trekking from **Trak La** pass (5,300 m) to the south of **Seralung Monastery**.

Mabcha Tsangpo Valley

The **Mabcha Khabab**, rising near Shiri Langdor northwest of **Mount Nanda Devi** (7,815 m), on the Tibetan side of the Indo-Tibetan border, is a major source of the **Karnali** River. It flows southeast from its source to **Rigong** township, where it becomes known as the Mabcha Tsangpo (Karnali). The motor road from Barka which cuts through the isthmus between Lake Manasarovar and Lake Rakshas Tal enters the valley of the Mabcha Tsangpo at Rigong, and then continues downstream to Purang, the county capital, 104 km from Barka.

Purang → *Colour map 1, grid B2*

Driving south from Barka through the isthmus between lakes Manasarovar and Rakshas Tal, after crossing Gurla La pass (4,600 m) and passing in close proximity to Mount Nemo Nanyi, you will reach the ancient township of **Purang** (Ch Bulan), 104 km distant, which the Nepalis and Indians call **Taklakot** (a corruption of the Tibetan **Takla Khar**). Purang (3,900 m) is the administrative base for the Kailash region and traditionally it has been the focus for pilgrims from India coming via **Almora** and the **Jang La** pass (Lipulekh; 5,090 m). Purang lies on the Mabcha Tsangpo, the Tibetan tributary of the Karnali, which rises in the peacock-shaped rocks of the **Mabcha Khabab** ('Peacock Source'), near Shiri Langdor, south of lake **Rakshas Tal**. South of Purang, the river, now known as the **Mabcha Tsangpo** ('Peacock River') flows through the villages of **Khorzhak**, and **Zher**, before crossing the Tibetan-Nepal frontier at Hilsa. In Nepal, it initially flows through the valleys of **Limi** and **Omlho**, before the deep Karnali gorge begins. ▸▸ *For listings, see page 380.*

Purang is a fascinating trading station close to the Tibetan borders with India and Nepal. It was here that most of the early travellers from India reached Tibet and make their first contact with the Tibetan authorities. It has been a capital of the kingdoms of Far West Tibet since the early 10th century, although the troglodyte dwellings here were inhabited at a much earlier period. This was where **Sudhana** (Chogyel Norzang), a previous incarnation of Shakyamuni Buddha, reputedly lived. His exploits are recounted extensively in the *Gandhavyuhasutra*, a section of the voluminous *Avatamsakasutra*, which describes the events in a bodhisattva's life exemplifying the development of great compassion and the awakening of enlightened mind (*bodhicitta*). One of the most popular of Tibetan operas enacts the life of Chogyel Norzang.

The Ruins of Shepeling Monastery

Rising above the town of Purang is a high, steeply sloping ridge capped with a large complex of ruins (4,160 m). Before the Chinese invasion this was the residence of the regional administrator as well as the temple and monastic complex for several hundred monks. In those days it was referred to as the 'Dzong' or fortress of **Shepeling**. Such buildings in commanding positions were once common throughout Tibet. The main monastery was of the Gelukpa school but there was also an adjacent Sakya monastery.

To walk up and explore the ruins gives one an excellent view, taking in the northern slopes of the Himalayas from Nepal to India and the **Jang La** pass as well as the whole southern face of **Mount Nemo Nanyi**. It takes just over an hour from the cave dwellings to reach the top.

Cave dwellings and Tsegu Gonpa

From the road on the east bank of the Karnali River you can cross a suspension bridge to the west side where, in the cliff above the Tibetan traders' houses, there are ancient cave dwellings. Remarkably many are still inhabited. This was probably the original town of **Purang** and it may date back several thousand years to the time when cave cities were created across Asia. It is likely that it was in such cave cities man first lived in secure settlements instead of following a nomadic lifestyle.

At the western end of the caves is an ancient temple cut into the cliff. It is known as **Tsegu Gonpa** ('Nine-Storey Monastery') and includes many terraced levels going up the cliff. It can be reached by steps, ladders and platforms hanging off the wall. In the lower levels there is the residence of the family who look after the temple. Be polite as you approach and wait to be asked to enter. You will have to walk through the house, which itself is fascinating, and then be led up to the temples above. The walls are covered in highly polished murals that are unique in style. They have been darkened from the smoke of lamps over hundreds of years. It is helpful to bring a torch with you.

The temple belongs now to the Drigung Kagyu and Gelukpa schools, yet it may even predate the founding of these schools of Buddhism.

Trading markets

At Purang one can still see how many of the Tibetan border towns were used as trading posts for the nomadic produce of the **Jangtang**, such as wool and salt which would be bartered for the rice and palm sugar of Nepal and the Indian plains. This centuries-old trade continues here today. Below the cave dwellings a trading camp forms over the summer and early autumn months when large encampments of Nepalese appear. Those in front of the caves come for the salt and rice trade. Sheep and goats are loaded up with a double backpack holding up to 30 kg of produce before they make their way over the trail on a three-week journey to the Indo-Nepalese Terai.

Tanga Follow the path past the caves and soon you'll reach the busy trading camp, known as Tanga. This larger camp below the Shepeling ruins consists of streets of temporary one-room residences over which the traders sling tarpaulins for the roof. The prohibition against permanent roofs is said to date back to a 1904 treaty between Tibet and Britain! This is a fascinating glimpse of a bustling bazaar that has been barely touched by time. The Nepalese bring every kind of practical item, from cooking utensils to cotton cloth and manufactured goods from India, to sell or trade for the wool and salt brought by the Northern Plateau nomads. The wool bales, resembling giant doughnuts, are carried by yaks and, once sold, are undone into long skeins which are stretched down the alleyways and prepared for transport south.

The Chinese authorities today let this small trade continue (although Indians are now excluded) probably because the traders barely eke out an existence from it.

Khorzhak Temple and Village → *Colour map 1, grid B2*

ⓘ *T0897-2822740.*

About 30 km further down the Karnali river valley, the rough motorable road passes through the small village of **Korzhak** (Ch *Korqag*), or Kojarnath as it is known in Nepal. Literally, this name indicates a sacred place where a 'retinue' or 'a venerable object and its surroundings' (*khor*) is 'placed' (*zhak*). According to authoritative sources, the venerable object that was once 'placed' here was a silver image of Jowo Manjuvajra, a modern replica of which can be seen in the Yilhun Lhakhang, From the few existing photos of the Khorzhak image it appears to have represented the Pala style of Indian Buddhist art. All that remains of the original image today is part of its lotus flower base. Another tradition reports that when the temple was first constructed this image spoke aloud, indicating that it wished to be placed directly upon an amolingka fossil embedded in the ground, saying "I have wandered (*khor*) to this place and here I shall settle (*chags*)!" Yet, other literary sources suggest that the temple is named after its founder, King Kho-re, a fifth generation descendant of the last Tibetan king Langdarma.

The village is situated on a beautiful bend in the Karnali River (3,790 m) and is dominated by the large red wall of the **Khorzhak Temple** complex which faces the river with an enormous inscription of Avalokiteshvara's six-syllable mantra: OM MANI PADME HUM. Khorzhak was originally founded in 996 by King Khor-re and its central image was installed shortly thereafter by Prince Lha-de of Purang. A Kadampa institution, associated with the great translator Rinchen Zangpo, it came under the control of Sakya and since the 14th century it has been considered a branch of Ngor. Nowadays only two of the 32 temples which once formed this complex still stand – these are the two oldest and most important – the Yilhun Lhakhang and the Tashi Tsekpei Lhakhang.

Among them, the **Yilhun Lhakhang** has outer and inner gates with a spacious courtyard, and old side murals on the approach to the inner sanctum. The foremost image was of silver, depicting Jowo Shakyamuni in the form Manjuvajra. Later in the 13th century, silver images of Avalokiteshvara and peaceful Vajrapani were placed alongside it by King Namgonde and his consort Jabum Gyelmo. The temple has been damaged and reconstructed several times over the centuries, most recently following the Cultural Revolution, and there are currently some 17 monks. The central silver images, which were destroyed, have been replaced – only the base of the central image and the legs of Avalokiteshvara are original. There are additional smaller images of Padmasambhava and Rinchen Zangpo to the left, with an old image of Tara and the head of an old Maitreya image to the right. The murals here depict the Sakya lineage.

The **Tashi Tsekpei Lhakhang** is an old flagstoned temple, slightly smaller in size, with eight pillars. It was originally founded by Rinchen Zangpo, the great translator, and it now functions as an assembly hall and protector chapel. The entrance gate is of wood, carved in a Nepalese design representing the hundred deeds of Shakyamuni. The vestibule has murals of the Four Guardian Kings. Inside, in the hall there are stuffed animals suspended from the beams, and the plinths of two damaged stupas, which were originally constructed by Rinchen Zangpo. The murals of the gallery are old, depicting the Sakya lineage, as well as Atisha and Rinchen Zangpo, while those of the hall are new, poorly executed and uninteresting. There are five chapels adjoining the main hall here: Among them, the Yumchenmo Chapel on the left has some old murals, depicting Dorje Yudronma, the protectress

Ganges and Karnali Rivers

The **Ganges**, sacred river of India, flows for 2,510 km from its sources to its confluence with the Brahmaputra in Bengal. There are five headwaters, namely: the Bhagirathi, Alaknanda, Mandakini, Dhauliganga, and Pindar, that all rise in **Uttarakand** in India, not in Tibet. Of these the two main sources, Alakanda and Bhagirathi, originate at an elevation of about 3,050 m in an icy cavern below **Gangotri Glacier**. **Gaumukh**, 21 km southeast of Gangotri is often cited as the Ganges' actual source.

However, in close proximity to these, a major source of the **Karnali**, one of Ganges' main tributaries, does rise in Tibet, to the south of **Lake Rakshas Tal**. It flows through **Purang** to cut southeast of **Mount Nemo Nanyi** (Gurlamandhata) and enter Northwest Nepal. There it converges with other tributaries of the Karnali, and flows into India, where, as the **Gogra**, it eventually converges with the Ganges at **Patna**.

of Rinchen Zangpo, and Prajnaparamita. The clay images here are all new, sculpted by an Amdo artisan and sponsored by the Italian NGO Asia. Next, the Dolma Lhakhang contains old murals depicting the 21 Taras. Formerly a library of manuscripts was housed on its upper level. The central Jampa Lhakhang has old murals that are indiscernible, but for one depicting Rinchen Zangpo. The Gonkhang on the right is dedicated to Panjaranatha, and the Tonpa Lhakhang contains murals depicting Padmasambhava and the deeds of Shakyamuni.

There is one other locked temple at Khorzhak, containing assorted manuscripts and woodblocks, and side chapels with old murals.

Ritual masked dances

On certain special days of the month monks from the region come here to perform a day-long series of ritual masked dances. They still use many of the costumes and masks made before 1959. Local maidens who are betrothed come out on such occasions and display their family jewellery and fine clothes. This usually takes place in September or after the harvest in early October. Enquire at the Peacock Guest House to see whether any festivals are coming up.

Trekking

Providing you have the right permits and visas, you can trek from Purang out of Tibet. There are various trails: via **Zhingpa** township and **Jang La** pass (18 km) into India, if you are an Indian pilgrim, via **Zher** and **Nara La** pass into Nepal if you are of any other foreign nationality, and via Piling La, Chema La, or Nara La into Nepal if you are Nepalese. If you lack such travel documents, you will be placed under arrest and sent back to Tibet.

Foreign travellers entering Nepal here will complete immigration and customs formalities in Purang, and then drive via Korzhak to **Zher** (3,780 m), some 40 km to the southeast, in the company of a military escort. A final perfunctory baggage inspection may be made at the Zher Army Camp, after which it will be necessary to walk down to the bridge at Hilsa.

Crossing to the south bank of the Karnali at Hilsa, the trail now enters Nepal. There is a landing area for helicopters at Hilsa, and pre-arranged flights to Simikot and Nepalganj are possible. Otherwise, be prepared for a five- or six-day trek. The trail climbs steeply from Hilsa to **Nara La** pass (4,570 m), before descending to **Sip** and the green meadows of **Yari** (3,670 m) in the Karnali valley. Passports and trekking permits will be inspected here by the Nepalese police, and from this point on to Simikot you have to be accompanied by a Nepalese liaison officer. The trail continues to undulate through the Karnali valley via Tumkot and **Muchu**, where a second passport inspection is made. There are interesting temples dedicated to Avalokiteshvara in this region, and the predominant cultural influence is still Shepeling Monastery in Purang. Passing over to the north bank by a suspension bridge, the trail drops into the river gorge above **Yangkar** (2,900 m) and crosses the **Sali Khola** tributary to reach **Kermi** (2,790 m) and the police checkpoint at **Darapani** ((2,350 m). The trek eventually ends at **Simikot** (2,870 m), from where flights are available to Kathmandu via Nepalganj.

The alternative is to begin the return journey from Purang via Guge, Saga or one of the other routes described above. If you haven't yet been to Guge and have the time, it is a very worthwhile side-trip on the way back to Senge Khabab.

Sleeping

Darchen *p358*
Darchen Township Guesthouse will be open from summer 2004 onwards and for a time it should provide the best accommodation here. Camping facilities are available in the guesthouse compounds, but the expense, environment and lack of sanitation leave much to be desired. Better to camp at Darpoche.
Kunga Guesthouse, smaller than Ngari possible Gangtise Guesthouse, has simpler rooms at ¥100 per bed.
Ngari PSB Gangtise Guesthouse, T0897-2822728. Large guesthouse, which expanded from the **IP Guesthouse**, is the best in town, with reasonably clean and well insulated rooms at ¥120 per bed. There are Portakabin toilets outside, as well as a traditional adobe toilet. The guesthouse restaurant can provide food or cooking facilities for trekking groups who have their own cook.

Jiu Gonpa *p372*
There are 2 very simple guesthouses in the village below the monastery (¥25 per bed). The larger of the two has a large dining room, and a small shop. However, it is much better to stay at the new Indian Pilgrims' Guesthouse, beside the lakeshore, which has very clean and pleasant rooms at ¥120 per bed. The names of the devout Hindu sponsors of this complex are inscribed on the outer walls of the building.

Purang *p373*
E **Longfeng Hotel**, located next to the Peacock Hotel. New, comfortable and clean (shared toilet facilities), with triples at ¥120. Foreigners are not yet permitted to stay here.
E **Peacock Hotel**, T0806-2362. In the government compound, has carpeted rooms, but no running water – doubles at ¥120 and single suites at ¥280.
E **Grain Department Guesthouse**, T0806-2215. Has carpeted rooms, doubles at ¥100.
E **Pulan Indian Pilgrim Guest House**, is a cheaper alternative, which is simple but comfortable, with individual bungalows and well prepared Chinese meals.

Eating

Darchen *p358*
There are a few seasonal restaurants, among which the one signposted **Shop and Eating** is probably the most popular.

Purang *p373*
¶¶ **Peafowl Restaurant**, best Chinese in town.
¶ **Samdrub Restaurant** , Tibetan cuisine, reasonably good.
There are a number of Chinese and Muslim restaurants in town. You could try the **Chao Da Jiu Ja**, the **Thousand Years** or the **Fairy Crowd**.

Shopping

Darchen *p358*
Just outside the main compound of the Ngari PSB Gangtise Guesthouse, there are shops selling souvenirs, canned food, and the ever-present green-bottled beer, as well as tea, butter, tsampa, powdered milk, biscuits, and instant noodles. The seasonal campsite at Darchen also brings traders who sell tinned meat, kerosene, and even some fruit and vegetables. Most supplies, however, should be purchased at Senge Khabab,

Purang or Lhartse, depending on your route to Mt Kailash.

Directory

Darchen *p358*
Medical services The Swiss Medical Clinic, administered by one Dakpo Namgyel. There is also a recently built local township clinic. **Permits** Permits will be inspected in Darchen prior to the trek.

Purang *p373*
Banks Foreign exchange facilities are available at the Bank of China for Indian, Nepalese and other foreign nationals.
Telephones DDD and possibly IDD calls can be made from the China Post and Telecom building.

Tsamda County རྩ་མདའ

→ Population: 5,702. Area: 28,033 sq km. Colour map 1, grid B1.

Tsamda county is the current name for the region w札达县ce was known as the **Guge** *kingdom. It extends along the banks of the upper* **Sutlej** *from Khyunglung, southwest of Montser, as far as the Indian border, where the river flows into Kinnaur below the Sibkyi La pass. The valley of the* **Rashok Tsangpo**, *which gives access to Southern Ladakh and Spiti also lies within Tsamda, as does the valley of the* **Gyaza Kar-chu**, *through which the Uttarakashi district of Uttar Pradesh can be reached. The county capital is located at* **Toling**, *180 km from Senge Khabab (via Namru), and 443 km from Purang. The new county name, Tsamda, is a contraction of* **Tsa** *(parang) and* **Da** *(wa-dzong), which are two of the most important sites within the upper Sutlej valley.*

The Tsamda area is characterized by the striking complex of canyons cutting through the red sandstone composite of what was once an ocean floor, all descending into the upper Sutlej River. For much of the year these canyon tributaries are dry, only becoming impassable or hazardous in the monsoon. Those south of the Sutlej, such as the Manam Tsangpo, Dapa-chu, and Tophu-chu, rise in the Himalayas near the Indian border, which is heavily patrolled. The north is bounded by the Gar Tsangpo valley and southern slopes of the Gangtise Range.

Tsamda County

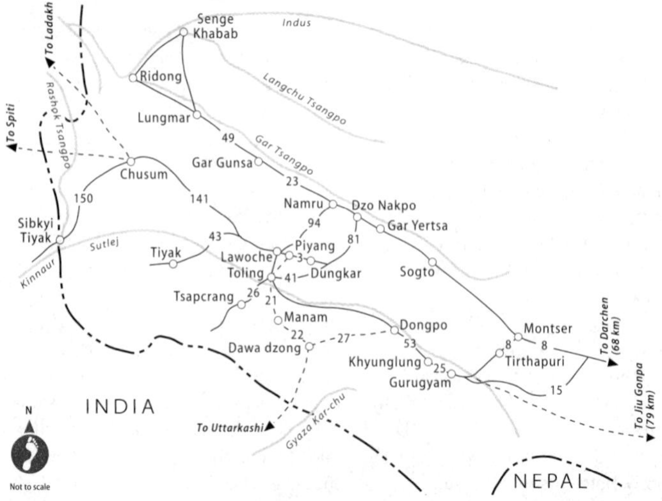

History

It was in this region of Far West Tibet that Tibetans appear to have first established permanently inhabited cities. At that time, in the antiquity of the pre-Christian era, the kingdom was known as **Zhangzhung**. From Bon chronicles that have recently come to light, the Far West area was known (reputedly as far back as 2,800 BC!) as the 'heartland', in contrast to Central Tibet, which was known as the 'outlying' area, and the regions of Kham and Amdo, which were termed the 'gateway' lands. However Tibet was not a unified country at that time – the vast distances and geography being more conducive to the development of independent semi-feudal states. The Bon kingdom of Zhangzhung was not actually absorbed into a unified Tibetan state until the conquests of King Songtsen Gampo were successfully completed later in the seventh century.

Later, following the assassination of Langdarma, the last king of unified Tibet in 841, and the consequent collapse of the Tibetan empire, unsuccessful attempts were made to re-establish the monarchy by Langdarma's son Namde Osung (840-893) and his grandson Pelkortsen (881-910). But they were thwarted by internal rebellions. The latter's son Nyima Gon fled to Ngari, where he founded Purang in 912. His son Tashi Gon established the Guge kingdom, and his son in turn was the illustrious King Yeshe-o (947-1024), who sponsored the literary and temple building activities of the great translator Rinchen Zangpo (958-1055). After the Indian master Atisha came to Guge, Buddhism was further revitalized and the kingdom flourished.

Khyunglung Ngulkhar: the capital of Zhangzhung

→ *Colour map 1, grid B2*

Getting there From **Montser** township on the main Senge Khabab-Darchen road, take the trail which cuts south for 8 km to the **Tirthapuri** hot springs (see above, page 372) on the banks of the Sutlej. An alternative trekking route from **Jiu Gonpa** on the shore of Lake Manasarovar follows the Sutlej downstream from its source near Lake Rakshas Tal for 79 km via Gyanyima Dzong to reach Tirthapuri.

The road cuts westward from Tirthapuri, at first passing through a broad agricultural valley dotted with single family compounds. Camp at the Bonpo monastery of **Gurugyam** (see above, page 356), about 15 km from Montser at the western limit of the valley. Thereafter the trail follows the Sutlej downstream into Tsamda county. Continue on this trail, via the Gerikyung camping ground, to **Khyunglung**.

NB Since you must cross two passes above the steep cliffs on the north bank of the Sutlej and then descend back down to the river before fording to the south bank, it is preferable to arrange the hire of horses and yaks before setting off from Gurugyam. Ensure that your local guide is allowed to cross this county border (since some local Tibetans may not be able to do so without first obtaining a special permit).

Khyunglung

The ruins of Tibet's earliest inhabited city are located on the northern bank of the Sutlej at the western end of the Khyunglung valley, approximately 25 km southwest of Tirthapuri. First noted by Professor Tucci in 1932 as a "troglydite settlement", it is a vast cave city sprawling over lesser valleys and canyons which, at its peak, must have held a population of 2,000-3,000 people. In 1988, on the basis of recently discovered chronicles, Professor Namkai Norbu confirmed this as the location where the earliest kings of Zhangzhung such as Limichar had established their dynasty in antiquity.

On reaching the entrance of this valley, you will pass the small village of Khyunglung after approximately 5 km, and from there it is another 2 km to the western end of the valley, where you can camp near an outcrop of white limestone facing the broad complex of caves on the far bank of the river. A suspension bridge below the white limestone traverses the Sutlej at its narrowest point and leads left to the cave city. To the right another pathway leads towards a hot springs and a series of white and blue lime terraces.

The cave city itself extends 1 km along a red cliff. The centre of the complex is reached via a valley at the western end of the city. This leads up past myriad cave dwellings cut into the conical formations of the red sandstone aggregate, to reach the ruins of the actual **Ngulkhar**, or the 'Silver Castle' of the kings. Here the multi-storeyed rooms are finely hewn from the earth, and there is evidence of outer wooden structures that would have made them very imposing. Below the king's residence, the city consists of pathways and tunnels winding past walls and cave habitations that cover every serviceable slope.

There is little evidence of anything related to Buddhism or even to the Bon tradition so that one has the sense of walking amidst the ruins of one of the world's oldest cultures.

Dawadzong མདའ་པ་རྫོང → *Colour map 1, grid B1*

From Khyunglung the trail continues on the south side of the Sutlej at some distance from the river, reaching the Gelukpa monastery of **Dongpo Gon** after 53 km (three days). Dongpo Gon was once a large monastery, its foundation being attributed to Khewang Jamyang Shinti, but at present there are very few monks here. **Dawadzong** lies 27 km further west on the Dawa-chu tributary, where there is a fabled landscape of natural pyramid formations. The ridge-top Gelukpa monastery known as **Dawa Gon**, the foundation of which is also attributed to Khewang Jamyang Shinti, comprises an assembly hall, a Maitreya Temple (Jamkhang) and a *Labrang*. For a vivid description of this area, see Lama Govinda's account in *The Way of the White Clouds*.

Manam Tsangpo Valley → *Colour map 1, grid B1*

The trail continues from Dawadzong in the direction of the county capital, crossing the **Manam Tsangpo** river after 22 km. Here at **Manam Gonpa**, there is an enormous complex of ruins dating back to the period of King Lha Lama Jangchub-o (984-1078), which even now holds an untold number of precious works of art, buried beneath the rubble. It is said that a community of 208 households was initially established here by the king, and to accommodate the venerable master Atisha between 1037 and 1041 he constructed two temples – the Jangchub Geneling and the Jampapel Lhakhang, both of which are now in ruins. Four other temples were later added to the complex by King Laga in the 13th century. A further trek of 21 km from Manam will bring you to Toling, capital of Tsamda county, on the left bank of the Sutlej.

Toling མཐོ་ལྡིང → *Colour map 1, grid B1*

The county capital of Tsamda, known as Toling or Toding, may be reached by two main motorable routes which turn south off the Senge Khabab-Darchen highway to cross the watershed leading into the Sutlej valley. ▸▸ *For Sleeping, Eating and other listings, see pages 393-393.*

Ins and outs

Turn off the paved section of the highway at Namru, 23 km southeast of Gar Gunsa (see above, page 355), and the second further turning south on the dirt section of the highway at Dzo Nakpo, where the Bauer Army Camp is also located. The latter road (122 km) crosses three passes, and 41 km before reaching Toling there is a turn-off on the right, that leads west for 13 km to Dungkar where spectacular caves have recently been discovered (see below, page 392). Taking the former road from Namru, which is only open during the short summer season, you will cross two watershed passes, including Ayi La (5,500 m), before reaching the crossroads of **Lawoche** after 94 km. Here there are four possible routes: one driving northwest via Chusum (141 km) to Sibkyi Tiyak on the Kinnaur frontier (150 km); a second leading west to **Jangtse** and Tiyak townships (48 km); a third leading east to Piyang and Dungkar (13 km) and a fourth heading southeast through deeply eroded canyons for 50 km to Toling in the Sutlej valley.

Taking the last of these roads, you will soon see far down below in the valley floor the capital of the ancient kingdom of Guge. From various vantage points on the descent into Toling (3,650 m), there are some of the most spectacular views in Tibet. The vast sweep of the Himalayas is discernible, as the range turns northwest from Nepal and along the Indian border as far as Ladakh and Kashmir, spanning several hundred kilometres. One of the marvels of this vista is the awareness that one is apparently looking down on the Himalayas. It gives one the real sense of Tibet as the roof of the world. The dome-shaped snow-cap of Mount Nanda Devi is particularly prominent. The final descent into the Sutlej gorge is equally memorable. Visible through billowing clouds of dust from passing vehicles are bizarre contorted and eroded shapes, reminiscent of a gothic cathedral, that rise from the steep canyon walls.

The Temples of Toling

History

The temples and religious buildings of **Toling** are the most significant in Far West Tibet. They were constructed under the guidance of the great Tibetan translator **Rinchen Zangpo** around 1014-1025, although some sources suggest an earlier date (996). During his lifetime he is said to have built 108 temples throughout Far West Tibet and Ladakh, and although few still exist, those at Toling (along with Tsaparang) are considered to be the finest examples of the **Guge style** of Buddhist art. Even though the city was subsequently replaced as a political centre of power by the citadel of Tsaparang, where the later kings of Guge established their capital, slightly closer to the Indo-Tibetan trade routes, the importance of the Toling temples for the cultural heritage of Ngari remain unsurpassed.

It was primarily due to the influence of Rinchen Zangpo that Toling became the main religious centre of the Guge kingdom prior to the visit of the great Indian master **Atisha** (982-1054) in 1042. The great translator was himself the monastic preceptor of Toling at the time of Atisha's arrival. Yet, without the support of the King of Guge, **Yeshe-o** (947-1024), the impact of these two great masters on Tibetan Buddhism would have been far less significant. The king was a devout patron of Rinchen Zangpo's activities, and he himself founded important monasteries at Toling and at Tabo in Spiti. According to a legend recounted in the Biography of Atisha, he sacrificed everything over several years, culminating in his own life, to invite the illustrious and peerless pandita Atisha to Tibet. After refusing several requests made by the Tibetan translators and scholars studying at Vikramashila and Odantapuri monasteries in North India, Atisha finally agreed to travel when he heard of the death of the king. Yeshe-o had been captured by invading troops from Qarloq who demanded ransom. When his nephew Jangchub-o (984-1078) came to see him the king responded by saying, "I am an old man. My life now is short. Use the ransom to invite and assist Atisha to come to Tibet". Consequently, when Atisha arrived in Guge he was amazed to see Buddhism flourishing. Historical sources suggest, however, that the actual victim was not the king but rather his other nephew, Prince Ode (995-1037), who was captured and killed following an unsuccessful campaign against neighbouring Brusha (modern Gilgit).

Atisha must have been impressed with the architectural style of the Toling temples which were based upon the Kashmiri style and the Pala/Sena style of Bengal, his homeland in Northeast India. An effort had also been made to incorporate Indian elements found in Samye, Tibet's first monastery. The interiors were solidly embellished with paintings in the contemporary Indian and Nepalese styles, following formal conventions that within a few centuries were to be obliterated by the Muslim invasions of India. This artistic tradition, that has come to be known as the Guge style, provides a unique link to the Buddhist art of North India that today can only be found in a few other temples exemplary of Rinchen Zangpo's work in Ladakh (at **Alchi**) and Spiti (at **Tabo**) during the early 11th century.

The site

The Toling complex originally comprised six major buildings. The entrance was from the east where today is a run-down concrete town hall. Clockwise from here within the compound were the **Neten Temple** containing images of the 16 Elders; the **Mani Dungchyur Lhakhang**; the **Assembly Hall (Dukhang)**, still intact and commonly known as the Red Temple due to the colour of its outside walls; the **Mandala Chapel of Yeshe-o** (Kyilkhor Lhakhang or Gyatsa Lhakhang), at the west end of the compound; the **Lhakhang Karpo** (White Temple), and the **Serkhang**, the actual Golden Temple (a three-storeyed temple, founded in 1067-1071 by Prince Zhiwa-o, and now destroyed, which formerly had exquisite images and murals depicting the assembled deities of the Kriyatantras and the Unsurpassed Yogatantras). The best and most detailed work on the complex at Toling in English is undoubtedly Roberto Vitali's *Records of Tho-ling* (High Asia, 1999).

NB It is absolutely essential to bring with you a strong flashlight in order to see the paintings clearly.

The Dukhang (Assembly Hall or Red Temple)

This is the largest temple at Toling, formally known as Pal Peme Lhundrub Tsuklakhang, and it was once used by the monastic assembly for gatherings, discourses and collective ritual practices. Formerly it had some 36 pillars, and its foremost images depicted the Buddhas of the Three Times in gilded copper. Distinguished by its red-washed outer walls, inside it contains the largest and earliest display of Indian and Guge painting at Toling (c 13th-14th centuries, though some scholars cite the period of restoration as during the 15th-16th centuries). The highly organic form of the decorative embellishments such as the flora which entwine each of the figures shows the overriding influence to be Indian/Kashmiri with a hint of Nepalese style. The artists must still have held the principles transmitted to them from the Kashmiri masters brought into Tibet by Rinchen Zangpo a century or two earlier.

The vestibule has primitive representations of the Four Guardian Kings, and cosmological charts, while inside the gate the adjacent murals depict protector deities of the Kadampa and Gelukpa traditions. The ceiling has decorative wooden panels, painted in a distinctive Kashmiri style.

Along the left-hand wall are floor-to-ceiling rows of deities entwined in wreath-like borders each interweaving into a whole organic complex across the entire space. Nearly all the deities are peaceful in form and many are in blissful union with their consorts (symbolizing the integration of skilful means and emptiness). In succession they include Sarvavid Vairocana, Vajrasattva, and Guhyasamaja, followed by historical figures: King Yeshe-o, and Atisha flanked by his foremost students. These paintings were heavily coated with mud and dust on account of the temple's neglect, but they have now been partially cleaned.

The rear wall (west) held the main shrines and altars beneath a large statue of the Buddha (added long after the original construction). Within the inner pilgrim's walkway (*korlam*), which passes along the left, back and right sides of the altar, there is a series of paintings depicting the life of the Buddha. Nearly all are miniatures, which include individualistic details of rural and domestic life. The colours are still vivid and the expressions specific to each figure depicted in the paintings. Also included are stories from the early kings of Guge and the development of Buddhism in Tibet.

The right (north) wall of the temple was once similar to its opposite wall but has been seriously damaged. The principal murals here depict Rinchen Zangpo, Cakrasamvara and Hevajra. A basic shrine now provides the focus for the temple with a few images and framed photos on it. In the early 1980s this was full of extremely precious images that had been donated during the period of 'relaxation' of the early 1980s. It also then held over a dozen other statues and sacred images that had been released from storage by the authorities for reconsecration. In the early 1990s it is alleged that a gang of art thieves based in Kathmandu stole everything, having sent photos around the world to determine the highest bidder. For this reason, the Tibetan people may object strongly to the photography of such objects today.

Lhakhang Karpo (The White Temple)

Nearly opposite the red-walled Assembly Hall there is an unimpressive, squat portico leading into what appears to be a shabby windowless block. This portico, although painted, is wooden, framed by two stout, short pillars and probably 500 years old. It opens into a long rectangular temple with a pebble-stone floor and lines of 42 thin pillars supporting a multi-panelled, multi-decorated ceiling, and culminating in a large recent image of Shakyamuni Buddha. Positioned high along the inner wall are the plinths of the destroyed Eight Medicine Buddhas – only one of which has recently been replaced. A small statue of Rinchen Zangpo sits in front of Shakyamuni.

Along the left and right walls are murals depicting a series of the main male and female bodhisattva deities. Over 3 m high, some of them are represented within a formal aureole, others within a celestial palace, and yet others in a natural landscape setting of mountains and forests. Arrayed along the left (west) wall is a pantheon of the male deities, and along the opposite wall are the female deities. Unfortunately most of the male deities have been seriously affected by water seepage. Those that remain however, such as Sarvavid Vairocana, Mahakarunika, Vajrapani and Manjughosa are sublime examples of the Guge art form.

Of greater value still is the intact wall depicting the female deities: they begin near the door, with a depiction of the life of the Buddha, above a graphic frieze illustrating life in the world and, with the surface peeled back, in the underworld, bringing to mind images from Hieronymous Bosch. The line of female deities includes Vijaya, ensurer of long life, wrathful White Tara, an opponent to life's inner dangers; Bhuvatrayacalanatara, 'earth mother' and protector from dangers in forest, jungles and wild lands, Sarasvati the muse of music and poetry, Red Tara the protector from earthquakes and natural disasters, Mahaprajnaparamita the 'Great Mother' of discriminative awareness, bestower of intelligence and knowledge, and Green Tara the compassionate bestower of protection out of good actions.

Created in the 16th century they depict the major pantheon of peaceful and semi-wrathful deities that are central to the renaissance of Buddhism in Tibet as expressed by the Kadampa tradition, whose founder Rinchen Zangpo features at the head of the line of female deities, and by the Gelukpa tradition – Tsongkhapa's verses of praise to "The Foundation of Good Qualities" (Yon-ten Shi-gyur-ma) are inscribed below the entire freeze. Prior to the Chinese invasion Toling had 400 Gelukpa monks, most of whom later found sanctuary in India. Nowadays there are fewer than 30 monks here.

Serkhang Chorten

As stated above, the original Serkhang Temple has been destroyed, and only one of its peripheral Serkhang stupas has recently been restored to the east of the monastery.

Hermitages above Toling

Along the cliff walls of the canyons above Toling one can see the caves and now crumbling walls of what once were retreat quarters for the monks. These can be

Mandala Chapel of King Yeshe-O

The most impressive building at Toling is at the western focal point of the entire complex. The walled remains of King Yeshe-o's Mandala Chapel are unlike any seen elsewhere in Tibet. Superficially it resembles many other ruins from the Cultural Revolution and although there is an entrance from the east, the central shrine itself is accessed through a gap in the southeast inner wall. One enters a square hall with secondary chapels opening off from the middle of each wall. Around the mud-streaked walls of the central and secondary shrines are aureoles in relief, spaced equally about 2 m apart above 1 m-high pedestals which once must have supported life-size images of deities. At first there appears to be no main shrine, that is until one begins to imagine the object which all these figures face, and one's gaze moves from the vivid blue sky above the walls to the mounds of earth and mud on the ground below. There in the rubble it is just possible to make out the shape of a broad lotus with a pedestal at its heart situated in the centre of the inner shrine.

At this point, one is, in fact, standing in the midst of the central sphere of a life-sized three-dimensional mandala, which in most circumstances would only be represented in two dimensions on a mural or scroll painting. A large statue of the main tantric deity would have been on the lotus pedestal, facing east, embellished with gold, precious jewels, ornaments and robes, probably surrounded by four or eight secondary figures on the petals of the lotus. Initiates and devotees would have been led into this inner sanctum in a state of reverence and wonder, awed by the beauty, balance and harmony of this extraordinary display which would have been illuminated by soft light cascading from the windows in the bell-tower directly above the central deity. The figures on the surrounding walls would have been gilded and painted and the walls themselves no doubt embellished with buddhas, bodhisattvas and tantric deities along similar lines to those in the Dukhang (Red Temple) or the White Temple at Tsaparang (see below page 387). The mandala itself was that of Vajradhatu or Vairocana, the main tantra practised by Rinchen Zangpo and one which encompasses and synthesizes many of the other *Yogatantras*.

The central hall is encircled by a series of shrines and chapels (similar

reached by road by turning left off the main route to Toling and climbing up through the canyons. Once on top an entire new complex opens out, for along each ridge to the south is a series of temples and caves hardly seen by outsiders. Once they were reached by climbing through man-made tunnels and staircases cut into the cliff face. Paths zigzagged up to the top from where one was also afforded a vast panoramic view of the upper Sutlej valley. It may still be possible to reach the peak directly above Toling provided that you carry a shovel for cutting steps and a rope for safety.

Routes to Uttarakashi and Chamoli

In addition to the two motorable routes into Toling from the Senge Khabab-Darchen road, the county capital can also be approached by trekking from Tirthapuri and Dawadzong (see above, page 355 and page 380). Another road driveable by jeep leads out of town to the west, passing through Tsaparang (26 km) and Puling (56 km). From Puling there are trekking routes to **Uttarakashi** in North India via Tajak La pass, and to **Chamoli** via Dronyi La pass (currently closed).

to those in the Jokhang in Lhasa), facing inwards and today mainly filled with dirt and rubble through which here and there protrude torsos and remnants of what once were objects of profound faith and devotion. In the centre of the west wall of this hall is a tall shrine that once held a 5-m standing figure of Avalokiteshvara. There follows a series of rooms which now contain the relief remains of two-dimensional mandalas.

According to literary sources, the central chapel was dedicated to Vairocana (Namnang Lhakhang), and it was surrounded by 18 other chapels, the names and foremost images of which are as follows (clockwise sequence): 1) Dudul Lhakhang (immediately in front, Shakyamuni Buddha); 2) Jikje Lhakhang (Vajrabhairava); 3) Atsara Lhakhang; 4) Tashi-o Lhakhang (Shakyamuni); 5) Menla Lhakhang (Eight Medicine Buddhas); 6) Tu-je Lhakhang (Eleven-faced Avalokiteshvara); 7) Dolma Lhakhang (White Tara); 8) Gyelma Riknga (Buddhas of the Five Families); 9) Sungma Lhakhang (Vajrabhairava, Dharmaraja and so forth); 10) Jampa Kerzheng Lhakhang (Maitreya); 11) Chakdor Lhakhang (Vajrapani); 12) Yum Lhakhang (Green Tara); 13) Jampa Ngalso Lhakhang (Maitreya); 14) Je Lhakhang (Tsongkhapa and students; obviously installed later!); 15) Tsepame Lhakhang (Amitayus); 16) Kangyur Lhakhang; 17) Tangyur Lhakhang; and 18) Jamyang Lhakhang (Manjughosa).

Towering above each of the four corners of the temple complex are the only stupas of the Indian *prasada* style in existence. They are also uncommon in being made up of terracotta units, since most Tibetan stupas are made from mud and stone. Within each are chambers that contain pages from Buddhist manuscripts and hundreds of thousands of small, palm-pressed votive images known as **Tsa-tsa**. Despite being only around 10 cm in size, the attention to detail is remarkable, including not only a perfect figure of the deity but a depiction of the appropriate mantra or tiny stupas in the background. Such objects are added to the `core' of any large stupa in order to enhance its sanctity and power.

These Tsa-tsa can also be found spilling out from the broken shell of many of the stupas that stand in rows of 108 outside the Toling complex on land adjacent to the cliffs above the Sutlej river. Sadly in the last few years even these have begun to be destroyed, or given enhanced help in their collapse by local people wishing to gain more land.

Tsaparang → *Colour map 1, grid B1*

History

The Guge kingdom appears to have endured hard times during the period of the Sakyapa hegemony in Tibet (13th-14th centuries) – its northern and southern enclaves functioned quite separately at this time. Then, following the collapse of the power of the Sakya and the rise of the Phagmodrupa dynasty in Central Tibet, the kingdom was revitalised at Manam by King Namgyelde (1368-1439) and by his son Puntsokde (1409-1480). The latter established a new capital at Tsaparang in the Sutlej valley, where he founded the lower Loteng Monastery and the upper Dreteng Monastery, along with a labyrinth of tunnels and passageways, hewed out of the mountainside. During this time the Ngor sub-school of Sakya, the Drigung Kagyu school and the Gelukpa school were most influential – the last of these eventually coming to prominence through the efforts of Ngawang Drakpa, a senior disciple of Tsongkhapa. The great period of temple building at Tsaparang coincided with the reigns of Lobzang

 Rabten (late 15th century) and King Jikten Wangchuk (mid-16th century).

Less than a century later, in 1624 the first European to reach Tibet, a Portuguese Jesuit based in Goa named Antonio del Andrade, arrived at Tsaparang. At this time the kingdom had less than 50 years to endure before its total collapse. It has sometimes been said that because the king favoured Andrade and allowed him to build a church jealousies arose on the part of the Buddhist lamas and officials who then conspired with the ruler of Ladakh to bring about the kingdom's untimely end. However, according to local historical knowledge, the downfall of the kingdom of Guge is far more dramatic. Why the city was never re-inhabited has always remained something of a mystery.

Apparently relationships between the rulers of the three kingdoms gradually deteriorated over the centuries. This was especially true in the case of the kings of Ladakh/Rutok. Battles had been fought between these rulers from the north and their cousins in the south at both Guge and Purang. Over 40 years after the Jesuit was recalled to India in 1685 a youthful king in his early 20s was forced to confront armies from the north. Deeply loved by his subjects, his own forces were able to repel the aggressors repeatedly. It became clear to the king of Ladakh that he could only succeed with help from outside forces. Thus the supposedly Buddhist king of Ladakh paid for the assistance of Muslim tribal mercenaries.

With this additional strength his army soon laid siege to the city, encircling the population of several thousand in Tsaparang town around the base of the citadel. With their army decimated the people had no protection. The Ladakhi ruler then threatened to slaughter 50 people a day until the young king capitulated. From the heights of the royal citadel, impregnable and secure with its own secret water source, the King volunteered to renounce his position and depart from the realm saying that he would devote himself to the anonymity of a monastic life. He promised never to lay claim to the throne in the future on the condition that his subjects be spared their lives and that his queen and family, along with the ministers of court be guaranteed free and safe passage out of the land. To the relief of the people of Tsaparang the invaders agreed to these conditions.

The young king, his queen and their children as well as the ministers and commanders of the army descended from the heights of the citadel, bypassing a huge siege tower that was being built up the side of the 170-m high cliffs. They presented themselves to the invaders and were all immediately bound and taken prisoner. The young king and his family were slaughtered immediately in full view of the population. Members of the court, ministers and generals were led down the hillside where they were all beheaded, their bodies tossed into the ravine below. The heads were then impaled upon spears and poles, forming a circle around the entire town. In this way a Muslim army repeated its ruthless techniques of war, ensuring that the 'infidels' immediately departed and never returned. A tragic testimony to this episode still exists in a secret cave, located deep in the ravine, where the headless torsos of the ministers were laid to rest over 300 years ago.

From the 1680s until the first half of the 20th century, Tsaparang was a ruin intact in time, virtually untouched except for the removal of the valuable timbers for new accommodation. Its major temples such as the **White**, **Red**, **Vajrabhairava** and **Demchok** temples, were intact when Professor Tucci visited in 1932 and still later when Lama Govinda and Li Gotami documented them in 1948-1949. However the ravages of the Cultural Revolution swept through in the 1960s and wrecked the finely detailed surroundings of the statues, broke open their hearts and reduced the main figures to rubble. It was as though the apparent physicality of the statues presented a greater threat to the new, abstract ideology of communism for the masses than plain two-dimensional murals. Today the ruins of Tsaparang, because they were already vacant when the Chinese invaded and thus were only lightly affected by the Cultural Revolution, are one of the finest examples of early historical ruins in Tibet, and now deemed part of the 'great artistic and historical treasures of ancient China'.

Citadel of Tsaparang

To reach **Tsaparang**, 26 km west from Toling, it is best to leave before sunrise. Exploring this vast ruin takes all day. In the lower reaches of the city there are four main temples. The wall paintings and statues display some of the earliest examples of Tantric Buddhist art in existence. High above these temples is the citadel of the kings. One must climb up through a secret tunnel cut into the interior of the hillside to reach the top of this natural fortress, which was the residence of Puntsokde and the later kings of Guge. All that now remains intact is a small temple known as the **Demchok Mandala**. It has exquisite tantric murals inside.

The entire complex is located around a spur in the canyons south of the Sutlej. Like Khyunglung further east and upstream, Tsaparang lies on one of the main trade routes linking India and Kashmir in the west with Central Tibet in the east or the Silk Road in the north. At its height Tsaparang was a bustling city and home to perhaps several thousand people, giving rest and support to caravans of traders, as well as refuge and religious knowledge to members of the monastic community. The diversity of the population is vividly depicted in murals of the construction and consecration of the Red Temple.

On the approach to the citadel, the surviving red-walled temples of **Loteng Monastery** are visible on the far side of the infamous ravine. This complex, surrounded by a perimeter wall, was founded by King Puntsokde as a summer residence for the royal family of Guge. There is a fort higher up the slopes, and all around are the remains of 15th-century stupas, some of them still filled with miniature terracotta images (*tsa-tsa*).

Dolma Lhakhang

After passing through the ticket office manned by the Cultural Relics Bureau, and the newly-built gate at the base of the city's slopes, the bulk of the Lhakhang Karpo looms immediately to the right. Climbing a flight of stone steps to the left, you will first reach the **Dolma Lhakhang**, a small chapel dedicated to White Tara, which was built around the late 16th century, as a private chapel for the Regent of Tsaparang. It follows the style of the Vajrabhairava Temple (see below) with the figures gilded and the remaining colours limited to black and red. Most of the paintings are heavily coated in black soot from smoke and may even have been scorched by fire, but the murals of the side walls depicting three aspects of the meditational deity Guyhasamaja, and two aspects of Avalokiteshvara stand out. On the altar there is a new statue of White Tara, while the rear wall features a central image of the Buddha seated with his right hand in the gesture of calling the earth as a witness to his past merits (bhumisparshamudra). His main disciples, Shariputra and Maudgalyayana stand on the throne with him. On either side are two important masters of the Lam-rim teachings: Tsongkhapa, on the left and Atisha, on the right. These murals are seriously ruined and stylistically flat, lifeless and uninspiring.

Lhakhang Karpo (The White Temple)

Climbing to the right from the Dolma Lhakhang, a few steps higher you will reach a porch in front of the entrance to the **Lhakhang Karpo**, which was founded by King Jikten Wangchuk during the mid-16th century. You enter, stepping down the dusty floor of a high-ceilinged hall, diffused with a soft white light that lingers on the particles of dust, covering the room with a silvery glow. The silence is total and yet it feels as though you are being watched. You begin to explore the corners of gloom and just as you turn around your gaze is met by a ferocious set of eyes above a snarling mouth and fangs, over 3 m high, protecting either side of the doorway. These would have been forms of Hayagriva and Acala.

Now as your eyes adjust you can begin to make out the extraordinary contents of this temple. Around the walls were once larger than life-size statues of the Eight

 Bodhisattvas, flanking the central image of Maitreya. Each was seated upon a 1-m high pedestal that is individually appropriate to each deity. All once were framed in elaborate terracotta aureoles that were easily broken in the 1960s. The finest record we have is the photographic archive of Li Gotama and Lama Govinda, dated 1948-1949.

On the background walls there is a series of painted panels stretching from floor to ceiling. Each is unique in its content and proportions. Some are merit-gaining repetitive images of hundreds or thousands of buddhas; others consist of a series of vignettes depicting the lives of the tantric masters, including one or two incomplete panels that reveal the means by which they were made; yet others include detailed large images of Thousand-armed Avalokiteshvara and other deities. Among the prominent historical murals are those depicting Tsongkhapa and Atisha, with their foremost students, Jetsun Sherab of Zhalu and King Yeshe-o.

The main feature of the statues (and paintings) is that they are executed in a highly distinctive style found nowhere else in Tibet. The work certainly appears to have been influenced by India, if not actually supervised by Indian master artists from Kashmir or Bengal. The torsos are elongated, the robing of the figures is loose, the ornamentation and crowns are unlike the later form of deities in Tibetan art; and perhaps most of all, the rendering of the background wall design is flexible and varied within the confines of its purpose, to an extent that is paralleled only in the temples at **Alchi**, Ladakh, in a slightly more rigid form.

Sadly all the three-dimensional figures, in addition to the destroyed aureoles, have been broken in one way or another. Usually each had its heart ripped open, revealing little more than the sacred prayers of consecration and the life-pole which rises through the centre of the figure giving it strength and symbolic life. Most also had their arms and hands, which were once displaying mudras, broken or torn off. Despite this destruction the statues retained a kind of dignity which today has been ruined by the botched attempt at restoration. Mud has been slapped into the cavities and smeared over the facial gashes without any skill in such a way that now, with the addition of gold enamel paint, many of the figures appear to be afflicted by some disease.

The ceiling of the temple is composed of panels painted with individual decorative motifs, which are generally illustrative of Guge art. At the altar end of the temple which once held a large statue of the Buddha there is a magnificent wooden skylight. Fashioned of painted beams forming a hollow square, it gradually reduces in size at 45 degree turns, making a small tower which allows a shaft of light to enter and illuminate the shrine. On its sidewalls the chapel has pedestals upon which still sit figures in armour. These are likely to be some of the religious kings of Guge and Yarlung. Painted on the lower walls are episodes from the life of the Buddha.

NB Photography inside the temples is forbidden and you are likely to be shadowed by a zealous Tibetan guide.

Lhakhang Marpo (The Red Temple)

Directly above the White Temple, up some steep steps is the **Lhakhang Marpo** (Red Temple), which was founded by Queen Dondrubma, consort of King Lobzang Rabten in the late 15th century. The acacia doors are original, either carved in Kashmir or under the guidance of Kashmiri artisans in Tsaparang. Each has three panels containing the Sanskrit seed syllables of the mantra of great compassion OM MA-NI PAD-ME HUM. The door frame has weather-beaten figures of kings and bodhisattvas. The only other comparable door lintels are found in the inner sanctums of the Jokhang in Lhasa.

The doors open onto a tall hallway filled with piles of rubble in the centre merging with a broken stupa to the right. The back wall where the central shrine once stood is vacant except for the upper decorative tendrils that held offering gods and goddesses surrounding the 3-m high central figure of Dipamkara. To either side of the altar the deep blue hue rear walls have deities seated on lotus platforms. A few of the figures still remain. They comprise some of the Thirty-five Confession Buddhas. The rubble in the centre of the room once was a throne supporting an image of Shakyamuni Buddha and was probably added some time after the completion of the temple. The stupa to the right was also a later addition and appears to be in the Kadam-style associated with Atisha.

The most outstanding feature of the Red Temple is the series of murals which rise from 60 cm above the floor to the ceiling. They comprise two levels. The lower 60 cm consists of a frieze while the remaining upper area contains a series of images which, together with their thrones and the surrounding aureoles, are approximately 4 m high. Both the frieze and the deities are rendered in the highly decorative form of the Guge style, covered in a high gloss varnish that perhaps has helped preserve their deep, rich colours.

The **frieze**, commencing on the north wall to the right of the altar, depicts episodes from the life story of the Buddha. Each story is contained in a panel of flat colour. The temptation of the malevolent forces and the Buddha's enlightenment are two of the most outstanding. Copies made by Lama Govinda are supposed to exist in the Prince of Wales Museum, Bombay. On the rear wall (east) there is a set of the eight stupas symbolizing the major acts of the Buddha. These are followed by the emblems of a universal emperor as incorporated in the mandala offering of the material world. On the right side of the door is a remarkable depiction of the construction of the Red Temple, and the dignitaries attending its inaugural consecration. Animals and humans are shown carrying wood and building materials; musicians and dancers celebrate the festivities; dignitaries from both Tibet and foreign lands dressed in their respective costumes are seated in ranks; ministers, generals, relatives and close family members sit in line before the king, who is flanked by his queens, princesses and princes; all turning in devotion to the radiant central image of Dipamkara to whom the temple is dedicated. Dipamkara himself is flanked on the far side by rows of monks, teachers and illustrious monastic preceptors.

The magnificent paintings above the frieze on the sidewalls are the Buddhas of the Five Families and the Medicine Buddhas. On the rear wall are the well known figures of Padmasambhava, Avalokiteshvara, Green Tara and a protector flanking either side of the doorway. To the right of the door are Manjughosa, White Tara, and Vijaya. All are seated on individually elaborate thrones and literally melting into the swirling decorative elements characteristic of the Guge style.

Dorje Jigje Lhakhang (Vajrabhairava Temple)

Just a few metres in front of the Red Temple's courtyard is a small protector chapel known as the Vajrabhairava shrine. This, together with the **Neten Lhakhang** below it, was created at a later date than either the White or Red temples. Both are distinctly decorated in accordance with the pantheon of the Gelukpa tradition. On the altar, now vacant, once stood a large wrathful image of Vajrabhairava, the bull-headed tantric emanation of Manjughosa. This is most likely the deity that Lama Govinda saw from the skylight in 1948, the photo appearing in The Way of the White Clouds.

On the walls of the shrine are images of deities from the Unsurpassed Yogatantras, such as Cakrasamvara, Hevajra, Guhyasamaja; Green Tara and the protectors near the door: Mahakala, Shridevi, Dharmaraja, and others. The figures on the walls to the side of the altar are of Tsongkhapa and Atisha along with their closest disciples. All are interspersed with miniature paintings of the mahasiddhas and lineage masters. The extraordinary feature of this entire room is that all the paintings are reduced to a range of black, red and pure gold colours. Every figure has been covered in gold leaf and the ornaments embossed in relief. Moreover the crowns and rendition of the jewels is strikingly real in the style peculiar to Guge. The overall effect is one of light and richness despite the fact that the paintings are heavily covered with centuries of candle soot and dust. This combination of gold and grime is like the radiance of a jewel penetrating the gloom of fog at dusk.

Caves and jails The lower slopes of Tsaparang are covered with pathways, staircases, tall mud walls and caves cut into the soft sandstone. Some of the caves were small shrines and still have paintings and charcoal drawings of the Buddha and other figures. Some are repositories for **tsa-tsa** votive images, others have meditation cells sculpted into their walls, and one niche formerly contained a free-standing Vajrabhairava image. Slightly higher there is a cave nowadays identified as the royal kitchen, its walls and ceiling blackened by charcoal. Then, about halfway up the lower slope is a huge cave cut into the heart of the hillside, which curves down for at least 15-20 m like a large well. Surprisingly it was used as a jail or detention pit for men. Another for women was also excavated.

The siege wall Near the top of the slope is a strange windowless structure of dressed granite, the only one of its kind. Between 3-5 m high it is rectangular, about 15 m wide and sited at the foot of the cliff. This was the base of a huge siege tower built by the invading Muslim army who destroyed the kingdom on behalf of the King of Ladakh at the beginning of the 18th century. It seems improbable that the tower would have reached a height of over 150 m, but perhaps it helped convince the king, safe in the citadel, to give himself up to the invaders.

Citadel of the Kings

Above the siege tower there are a number of caves and tunnels. The one on the extreme right is the entrance to a staircase that twists and turns upwards through the interior of the citadel. The way is lit every now and then by shafts of light or windows offering a view from the top of a sheer cliff down to the dry river valley. The height of the citadel is 170 m from the top of the slope. The exit opens out onto a complex of collapsing walls and pathways that covers the top from edge to edge. Along the western edge runs a pathway protected by a low wall.

At the far end (south) the ridge narrows and becomes totally impassable. Here the cliff has caved in; once there was a narrow road that allowed horses access to the top. The first structure to the south is a large open corral with attached stables. Next to it is a deep well which provided water from an aqueduct through a tunnel to the south. Walking back to the entrance one passes the high walls of what once was the assembly hall of Dreteng Monastery before reaching the only intact building, a square red-walled temple known as the **Demchok Mandala**. Directly beneath this is a cave with dusty murals of wrathful deities. The lower torso of a statue remains. This was a shrine of the protector Mahakala.

Demchok Mandala Shrine

Built as late as the 16th century this small shrine was probably created under the personal instructions of the king and his spiritual mentor. The walls are covered from floor to ceiling in a precise arrangement of deities, corresponding to the mandalas of the Unsurpassed Yogatantras. Each of the roof panels has one of the peaceful symbols of the Buddhist doctrine, such as the wheel, the lotus, the three jewels, the eternal knot and the vajra.

The temple takes its name from a miniature three-dimensional mandala that once stood in the now vacant space in the centre of the room. It was dedicated to Cakrasamvara, considered by Buddhists to reside at Mount Kailash. It once held 32 miniature figures of the peripheral deities and was about 2.5 m in diameter. All that remains now are some of the outer walls and the lotus petal floor of the mandala. It was partially intact when Govinda saw it in 1948 and it is widely believed that Prof Tucci removed most of the figurines of deities and dakinis in 1932.

The bands of figures on the walls begin at the base with a frieze depicting the charnel grounds where Indian yogins would meditate on death and confront ghosts or spirits. These places of terrifying events are vividly rendered, replete with corpses, beasts, demons, yogins, birds of prey, and atmospheric jungle. Traditionally there were eight great cemeteries in India. Above these is a frieze depicting the dakinis, the messengers of buddha-activity, embodying emptiness. Next is the broad band of tantric deities.

Each wall has five main figures, representing the central figure of the mandala and those of the four cardinal directions. On the left (south) wall are the aspects of Cakrasamvara himself, on the rear (west) wall the forms of Guhyasamaja, on the right (north) side are the aspects of Hevajra, and on the rear walls on either side of the door the protector Mahakala as well as labelled images of the king, his retainers, and contemporary masters. Above the main deities, there is a long frieze depicting the mahasiddhas and important lamas from the Tibetan lineages.

The rendering of these deities is superb in its refinement of the torsos, the power and dynamism of the wrathful figures (Cakrasamvara and Hevajra) and the sublime gentleness of the peaceful figures (Guhyasamaja). The ornaments and decorative elements in the fabric are as fine as the designs of a master jeweller. The pigments of the colours are still fresh and are not overwhelmed by an excess of gilding. Overall the content of this small temple amply rewards one for undertaking the rigours of the journey.

Outside the Demchok Mandala and adjacent to it is a newly built rest room where beer and soft drinks are served! This is said to have been rebuilt at the site of the Guge queen's chambers.

Winter Palace

Along the path toward the north end of the citadel is the entrance to the King's **Winter Grotto**. This comprises a series of seven rooms branching off a central hallway dug from the very heart of the mountain approximately 12 m below the surface. Access is down a nearly vertical tunnel with an iron railing for support. The warmth of the earth sheltered the king and his retinue from the bitter cold of winter. Secret tunnels led to a water supply and could be used to make an escape in the event of danger. Windows are cut through the outside wall, providing light to the interior and a breathtaking view of the valley below.

From the northernmost ramparts one has a vertigo-inducing view down the cliff face to the complex of buildings and temples spread around the lower slopes. Stupas stand on the spurs of ridges and across the small stream to the east is another large stupa in an Indian style, as at Toling. The Sutlej valley's gorge cuts the broad vista from east to west and far in the distance under the bleached blue midday sky are the snow-dusted peaks of the Gangtise Range.

Dungkar and Piyang

→ *Colour map 1, grid B1*

In 1992-1993 much publicity was given to a series of painted caves, located north from Toling at the small village of **Dungkar** and some 3 km away amidst the ruins of **Piyang**.

Ins and outs

There are three roads leading from Toling to the Dungkar/ Piyang valley. The first is the old road to Senge Khabab. Turn off after 50 km at Lawoche and head east across a pass to reach Piyang (10 km). The second is a rough tractor trail, which leads directly north for 38 km from Toling to connect with the former road in the upper Piyang valley. The third is the new road from Toling to Dzo Nakpo. Turn off after 41 km and head west to Dungkar (13 km). Approaching the complex from the Piyang or Dungkar side, the valley opens out into green pastures, and there are two small villages. Records suggest that there were some 4,000 caves in the valley that were once inhabited, and nowadays there are reckoned to be around 2,000 that survive at the Piyanga and Dungkar ends of the valley. Some of these have been elaborately painted, and there are also extant temples. Each of the two sites has its own caretaker to whom passes and admission tickets purchased at the Cultural Relics Bureau in Toling have to be shown. **NB** It may not always be easy to locate these caretakers on arrival.

Dungkar

The oldest temple at Dungkar is attributed to Princess Lhei Metok, daughter of King Yeshe-o (10th century), but the building that is most prominent nowadays is **Tashi Choling**, which was constructed for Tsongkhapa's student Ngawang Drakpa in the 15th century. More interesting are three of the older cave temples, which may possibly contain the earliest murals in Far West Tibet. One of these has nine large painted mandalas, a second contains a thousand bass relief images of Tara, and a third has a thousand similar images of Shakyamuni Buddha, with two reliquary stupas containing embalmed remains of past masters.

The first thing that strikes you is the similarity of the paintings with those of the early art at the caves of **Dunhuang** at the eastern edge of the Silk Route. The figures have elongated torsos and sit on semi-spherical lotuses like those in the Dunhuang mandalas. The most distinctive feature is the manner in which the spaces surrounding the mandalas are incorporated. Instead of the precise decorative patterns of the Guge style there are hosts of flying *apsara*, or offering goddesses. Their diaphanous gowns waft around them in soft breezes in a similar way to 10th-century figures at Dunhuang. Even the colour of the murals is similar – a light blue overall, featuring pastel colours. Perhaps these works were created by Indian painters on their way to the cities of the Silk Route 1,000 years ago.

Other caves nearby which have not been locked up also contain paintings, although seriously damaged by age and weathering.

Piyang

Some 3 km from Dungkar, at the far end of the valley are the extensive ruins of Piyang (more properly written at Piwang). The oldest building here was the **Karsak Lhakhang**, attributed to King Yeshe-o. The monastery at Piyang is affiliated to the Sakyapa tradition, and the complex is known to have had extensive royal patronage. King Puntsokde, builder of Tsaparang, was crowned here in 1424. There are also interesting cave paintings at Piyang, some of them depicting the Lamdre lineage holders of the Sakya school, but the restored temple has unfortunately lost its original murals. These sites, visited by Schlagenweit and Tucci in the 19th and 20th centuries respectively, may well reveal further treasures if they are properly explored, and without doubt throughout the upper Sutlej valley there are other important sites waiting to be discovered. In 1998-1999, for example, Chinese archaeologists discovered 26 ancient tombs and a pit for sacrificial horses, which have been carbon dated to the pre-Christian period of the ancient Zhangzhung kingdom.

Roads to Kinnaur, Spiti and Ladakh

Driving north from Toling, via the **Lawoche** intersection, you will reach **Chusum** township after 141 km, and **Sibkyi Tiyak** in the Sutlej gorge after 150 km. Here there is the currently closed Indian border, across which lies the ethnic Tibetan region of **Kinnaur** (Tib Kunu). In Kinnaur, the Hindustan Highway leads through Kalpa to Simla in Himachal Pradesh. Within Chusum township there are six small reconstructed Gelukpa temples or monasteries, each of which now has only a handful of monks. Among them, **Barchok Puntsok Rabten Gon** was reputedly founded before 1600 by Khepo Lekpel.

The traditional trade route to Kinnaur is a caravan trail, leading directly from **Jangtse** township to **Tiyak** in the Sutlej valley and thence to Sibkyi Tiyak. Tiyak is renowned as the birthplace of Lha Lama Yeshe-o (b. 958), and there are 12 reconstructed temples or monasteries of which nine are Kagyupa, two Gelukpa and two Nyingmapa. Among them, **Ranyi Lhakhang** was reputedly founded by Rinchen Zangpo and now follows the Kagyu tradition, **Lhakpak Lhakhang** represents the Nyingma school, and **Nuwa Gon** the Gelukpa.

Trekking

From Chusum there is also another trekking route which leaves the Sutlej basin, crossing into the valley of the **Rushok Tsangpo**. Here there are two trails, one following the river downstream via Sumdo to **Tabo**, across the Indian border at Spiti, Himachal Pradesh; and the other following the river upstream via Khayungshing La pass into Southern **Ladakh**.

Sleeping

Toling *p380*

D **Guge Hotel**, T08071-2268. Run down and should be avoided if possible. The rooms here are expensive at ¥240 (¥120 per bed).
D **Hebei Hotel**, currently has the best rooms in town (carpeted and double- glazed), with doubles at ¥180 (¥90 per bed). Unfortunately the toilets are outside and in a foul condition.
E **Telecom Hotel**, also has some good rooms, doubles at ¥140 (¥70 per bed).

NB None of the hotels in Toling have reliable running water systems, and none have indoor toilet facilities.

Eating

Toling *p380*

Hollywood Teahouse, outside the Guge Hotel. Tibetan dishes.
Jian Nan, outside the Guge Hotel. Sichuan cuisine.
Workers' Restaurant, the best in town for Sichuan cuisine.
Yum Shan, outside the Guge Hotel. Sichuan cuisine.

There are also a number of bars (including Your Best Friend Bar) and nightclubs in town, as one would expect to find in a military garrison.

Directory

Toling *p380*

Hospital County Hospital T0897-2106.
Permits Special permits are required from the local branch of the Cultural Relics Bureau in town if you wish to visit Toling Monastery, the complex at Tsaparang, or the cave temples of Dungkar and Piyang. A nominal fee is charged for this service. However you (or your tour operator) will also have to pay for the site admission tickets (¥80 for Toling, ¥105 for Tsaparang, and ¥90 for the Dungkar/ Piyang complex). These admission tickets are issued on arrival at Toling Monastery or Tsaparang, but they have to be prepaid in Toling for Dungkar and Piyang. **NB** Such permits are in addition to the police ATP permits which you will have already obtained in Lhasa or Senge Khabab.
Telephones DDD and possibly IDD calls can be made from the **China Post** and **Telecom** building.

Rutok County རུ་ཐོག

日土县

→ *Population: 7,310. Area: 68,609 sq km. Colour map 1, grid A2.*

The county of Rutok in the extreme northwest of Tibet borders the Xinjiang Autonomous Region and Ladakh. Geographically it forms part of the Northern Plateau (Jangtang) in the sense that its rivers drain internally into lakes, such as the long tapering ***Lake Pang-gong****, which lies half inside Tibet and half inside Ladakh. None of its waterways drain into the Indus basin, which lies just a short distance to the south. The county capital is located at* ***Rutok****, 127 km from Senge Khabab and 1,239 km from Kashgar in Xinjiang.* ▸▸ *For Sleeping, Eating and other listings, see page 397.*

Maga Tsangpo Valley → *Colour map 1, grid A2*

The road from **Senge Khabab**, the prefectural capital of Far West Tibet to Kashgar in Xinjiang province passes through Rutok county. It crosses **La-me La** pass after 31 km, leaving the Indus basin to descend into the valley of the **Maga Tsangpo**. The township of **Chakgang** is 26 km below the pass, and from there to **Risum** township it is a further 30 km. At Risum there are remarkable prehistoric rock carvings (see below, page 395) and Tselung Lhakhang, a small Gelukpa temple. From here, a motorable side road leads eastwards, following a tributary of the Maga Tsangpo upstream to Khulpa and **Rawang** (60 km), where there are a number of small salt lakes, and the small Tsa'u Mani Lhakhang of the Gelukpa school.

The main road from Risum continues to follow the Maga Tsangpo downstream for 30 km, as far as **Derub**, where a turn-off cuts northwest for Rutok, the county capital, 10 km distant. The river itself flows immediately into Lake Pang-gong.

Rutok → *Colour map 1, grid A1*

In the ninth century Namde Osung, the younger Buddhist son of the apostate king Langdarma, fled Central Tibet and established Buddhism in Far West Tibet. He divided Ngari into three regions at **Guge**, **Rutok** and **Purang**, giving authority to rule to each of his three sons and their descendants. Thus **Rutok** became the capital of the kings of northern Ngari. Over 500 years later political rivalries saw **Rutok** join with **Ladakh** to lay waste the kingdom of **Guge**, and wage war against the kingdom of **Purang**.

Today the newly built town of Rutok is basically a Chinese military garrison of harsh concrete buildings and satellite dishes. Located in a slight depression, its two main thoroughfares hold a few small groups of laconic soldiers in their ill-fitting green uniforms. Apart from the army, the residents of this sleepy town seem to be mainly Tibetan as well as a few Muslim traders from Xinjiang. Dust-covered Tibetan children with spiky uncut hair and ragged clothes are sometimes the only people one sees in the three broad and dusty avenues of the town. At Rutok, the hilltop citadel of **Lhundrub Choding Gon** was founded jointly by the charismatic yogin Drukpa Kunlek and the Gelukpa master Yonten Gyatso. Following the campaigns of the Mongolian general Ganden Tsewang against Ladakh in the late 17th century, the eclectic traditions of Rutok, which also had a Sakyapa presence, were overruled and the monastery was handed over to the authority of Sera Je college in Lhasa.

A road leads due west from Rutok for 65 km to **Retso** township, giving access to a traditional trade route via **Lake Mendong-tso** and across the Chugu La and Kharmar La passes into **Ladakh**.

Pang-gong Lake → *Colour map 1, grid A1*

The long (113 km) **Lake Pang-gong**, located north of Rutok, straddles the Indo-Tibetan border and eager Chinese officials boast that it is patrolled by the highest navy in the world! They also say that the waters at the Tibetan end are fresh and potable while those at the Ladakh end are saline. Be that as it may, the region surrounding the lake is renowned for its wildlife. Herds of asiatic wild ass graze along its shore line and massive flocks of migrating birds rest here on the way from Siberia south to India. In the late summer and autumn seasons thousands of birds can be seen. Muslim fishermen from **Xinjiang** are often seen paddling out from the shore on large inner tubes to net the fish that abound in the lake. Tibetan Buddhists generally never go fishing. The

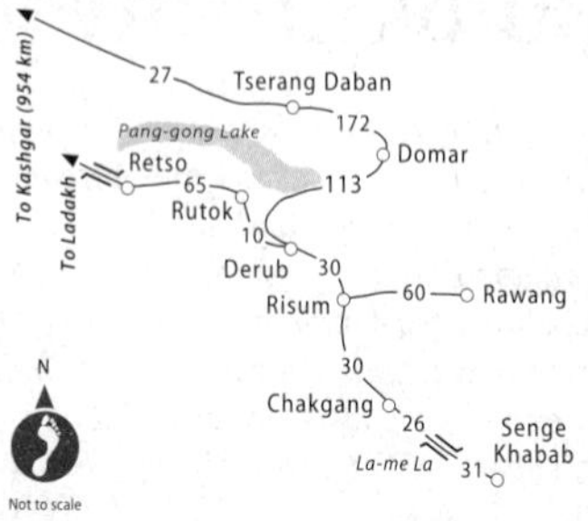

The Rutok prehistoric rock carvings

About 40 km south from **Rutok** at **Risum** hamlet, the road crosses a low culvert and turns left around the corner of a cliff facing flat wet lands from which fresh springs bubble forth. On the cliff to the left of the road one suddenly comes across a mass of ancient carvings chiselled into the surface of the red and black schist rocks. These remarkable images were discovered only in 1985 by the Lhasa Cultural Relics Institute and are extremely important for the insight they give into the key elements in the ancient nomadic way of life. Some rubbings and reproductions are currently on display in the *Lhasa Museum*.

Included are stylized figures of deer, sheep, yak, antelope, wolf or dog, fish and men. Most are rendered in outline only and in many panels the figures are realistically portrayed rearing up or galloping. Their physicality is accented by spiral swirls and elaborate curving branches on the body, antlers or tail. Birds are also present although they are eagle-like, and yet in the midst of what seems a shower of sparks. In this way they reflect the features of the mythical Garuda, a half-man half-eagle that flies in the midst of a blazing fire eliminating all negativity. There are also abstract carvings of strange bicellular forms, evoking the cosmic egg, one of the images found in the Bon philosophy for the origin of existence.

These rock carvings are among the most significant prehistoric images in Tibet. Petroglyphs in the same style have been unearthed inside burial mounds on the steppes of Central Asia, and more recently at other sites within the Jangtang plateau.

On the main road there are two distinct groups of petroglyphs at the location known as **Rimotang**, 1.5 km southeast of **Risum**. After crossing the culvert the first is a few hundred metres on the left. The second is about a hundred metres further on. The figures are cut into a dark red-coloured schist or granite. Some were defaced recently by devout Buddhists carving mantras over portions of the petroglyphs. This Buddhist graffitti is most abundant at **Rimotang**. The location is alongside a broad lush valley which may be a reason why the images are located here. It is ideal for the nomads to graze their animals while en route. Directly beneath the rock face is a small, natural spring.

Another set is located 32 km west of **Rutok** town, on the north bank of the Chulung River and is known as **Luri Langkar**. They are similar to those of **Rimotang** and are spread over six panels less than 4 m above ground.

One final group known as **Karke Sang** lies 159 km northeast of Rutok and about 25 km south of **Domar township**. They are sited in a cave and along a ridge west of the **Karke Sang cave**. Downstream one can see evidence of a more intensively cultivated landscape.

surrounding area is a natural habitat for various types of wild animals, which is why there are now plans to establish a wild game hunting park, with a sliding scale of rates according to the rarity of the animal killed, along the lines of the Balung hunting park in Qinghai province (see below, page 554).

Domar

Rejoining the highway at Derub, 10 km southeast of Rutok, you can continue driving northwards to **Domar** township, 113 km distant in the Northern Plateau. At the outset, the road follows the eastern shoreline of Lake Pang-gong, and the landscape along this stretch is breathtaking in its beauty. The extreme clarity of the atmosphere gives the strange, multicoloured earth of the hills, cliffs and plains a surreal visionary quality. Have your camera ready to take some memorable landscape photos.

The drive to Domar (4,350 m) from Rutok takes only half a day. The surrounding terrain, as the name suggests, is deep red in colour. The township, a bleak settlement with a military garrison, must be the last outpost for a soldier coming from remote mainland China. One could not get posted to a more distant location than here! It is also at the edge of the **Aksai Chin**, a disputed region claimed by India, who belatedly discovered a Chinese road traversing the middle of the territory in the 1960s. The Tibetan settlement of concrete buildings and nomadic tents is located at the southern end of the township. Some 100 m left of the road, are three stupas and a pile of mani stones which local devotees circumambulate. North of the Tibetan settlement, the road crosses a river, only 10 m wide, and forks: left for the Xinjiang border, and right for the military barracks. The military presence at the garrison is small, although many convoys appear to pass through. They own the only telephone in town, linked to Rutok and Hong Liu Tan in Xinjiang, and it may be used by them alone.

Xinjiang Border

From Domar township, the road continues up the Domar valley, crossing a major pass (5,250 m), and then turns right to cross the Aksai Chin and leave the Northern Plateau of Tibet for Xinjiang province. The last settlements on Tibetan territory are at **Sumzhi** and **Tserang Daban** transport station, 172 km from Domar, where it is possible to stay overnight. Just beyond Sumzhi on this road, there is a high 5,050-m pass which local drivers wisely treat with caution. Tserang Daban has no military garrison, but there is a transport station, which is set 50 m off the road and therefore inappropriate for potential hitch-hikers. Its concrete sheds have rickety beds and very dirty blankets. Yak-dung stoves are provided, along with hot water and dry instant noodles (¥60). It takes at least half a day to reach the bleak outpost of Tserang Daban from Domar, and the actual border, which is unguarded, lies 36 km further north.

Khotan and Mazar

The road from the Tibet-Xinjiang border to Kashgar initially continues passing through the largely uninhabited Aksai Chin. Very occasionally, Tibetan nomads can be seen leading their herds of yak and sometimes two-humped camels across the plateau. Alongside the highway are many forms of flora which are unique to the region. A number of these plants have highly prized medicinal properties, considered to be especially efficacious in the Tibetan pharmacopoeia. Some five hours further on, the road passes through the military garrison of **Da Hong Liu Tang** (4,200 m), situated at the lower edge of the Aksai Chin plateau, where the climate is significantly milder. Simple, clean accommodation is available in the barracks. Da Hong Liu Tan is situated in a deep brown valley, from where the road begins its descent into the Western Kunlun Mountains through deep gorges and across rushing rivers.

Some two to three hours after Da Hong Liu Tan, you will reach the turn-off for **Mazar** (3,700 m), and it is possible to spend the night here. Mazar, 456 km from Tserang Daban, is a ghost town of long concrete compounds and if you are heading directly to Kashgar, it may be preferable to keep going and camp out somewhere near fresh water. Nowadays, Mazar is also the starting point for treks into the Karakorums (see below, page 777) on the Pakistan border, particularly the Base Camp for the ascent of K2, the world's second highest peak. K2 is not, however, visible from the highway.

On the descent through the **Western Kunluns**, the road crosses three passes (between 3,000 and 4,000 m), from the last of which there is a dramatic view of the Taklamakhan Desert. Leaving the Kunlun foothills, the landscape dramatically changes. The high altitude environment of the Tibetan plateau and the Aksai Chin is suddenly left behind, as sand dunes, camels, fruit orchards, and the Islamic culture of the Uighur people come into view. How little cultural exchange there has been in this border area over recent centuries!

The road then descends into the valley of the **Karakax River**, where a detour cuts through to **Khotan** at the southern extremity of the Taklamakhan Desert on the Silk Route. Perhaps as sparsely populated as the Arabian Desert, Khotan is a region comprised of barren wastelands and ethereal blue lakes, which are among the last remnants of the Ice Age. As they melted and formed rivers flowing north through the Kunlun range they once fed the renowned Khotanese Buddhist civilization. The merchants and scholars of Khotan travelled along this route to India and China, trading in Chinese silk and other commodities, or studying and translating the Sanskrit Buddhist scriptures, several hundred years before Buddhism was established in Tibet. However, as the great rivers from Tibet's Northern Plateau dried up, the Khotanese civilization collapsed. It was buried under the desert sands until European explorers uncovered its traces at the turn of the 20th century.

Modern Khotan is two hours' drive from Karghilik, and is famous for its carpets, jade and hand-made silk. Virtually nothing remains of its ancient Buddhist ruins (which were documented by Stein), but the markets and oases are of interest. Excursions to the fringe of the Taklamakhan Desert can be arranged here.

Descending from the Karakax valley into the Yarkand River basin, the road soon reaches the checkpoint at **Karghilik** (Ch. Yecheng), 249 km from Mazar. Karghilik is a sprawling town, which has become the main centre for Chinese immigration into Western Xinjiang. Extensive irrigation in this region has transformed huge areas of the desert. Normally one will arrive soon after lunchtime and, after a short stop for food, continue onto Kashgar, a further 249 km.

About one hour's drive north from Karghilik, you will reach the ancient town of **Yarkand**, which still has important historical significance for the Uighur people, despite the destruction of its old city during the Cultural Revolution. Of its ancient buildings, all that remains is the grand gate of the old palace, the central mosque, and the royal cemetery. These can easily be visited in one hour.

The remote gateway city of **Kashgar** lies some 200 km north of Yarkand, and can be reached in three hours. On the approach to the city, the Pamirs are glimpsed in the distance. For onward connections from Kashgar see below.

Sleeping

Rutok *p394*
There is a truck station with overnight accommodation (¥40 per bed). Electric ring heaters, blankets, hot water bottles and televisions are supplied.

Domar *p395*
E **Domar Military Garrison**, has clean rooms (¥45 per room), excellent canteen food and nearby outdoor toilet facilities.
E **Domar Transport Station**, has basic accommodation (¥25 per room) and is well located for hitch-hiking.

Khotan *p396*
E **Hetien Yin Binguan**, T202-2203. Has doubles at ¥90 and dormitory accommodation at ¥20 per bed.
C **Hotan Hotel** (Hetian Wai Binguan), T202-3564. Currently the best in town, with doubles and triples at ¥280 and dormitory accommodation at ¥40 per bed.
E **Jiaotong Binguan**, T203-2700. Has comfortable doubles at ¥120.
E **Xingfu Lushe** (Happy Hotel), has simple rooms at ¥30 per bed.

Karghilik *p397*
D **Jiaotong Binguan**, T728-5540. Has doubles rooms at ¥160.
E **Mountaineering Hotel** (Dengshan Binguan), has dormitory accommodation at ¥35 per bed.

Yarkand *p397*

D Shache Binguan, T851-2365. Foreigners are obliged to stay here; overpriced rooms at ¥160.

Eating

Rutok *p394*

Shou Tue Chinese Restaurant, lakeside restaurant offering fresh fish on the menu.

Domar *p395*

Domar transport station, on the left side of the road and a small Tibetan café serving noodles, tsampa, and hot drinks.

At the Xinjiang border and military barracks junction, a small restaurant sells freshly prepared Chinese food.

Khotan *p396*

Chinese transport station, after 4 hrs, where truckers stop for lunch, small, stir-fry dishes are available (¥30).

Transport

Khotan *p396*

Air

Khotan has 4 direct flights per week to **Urumqi**.

Bus

Public buses are available to **Kashgar**, **Urumqi** and intermediate destinations.

Karghilik *p397*

Bus

Public buses run frequently between Karghilik and **Kashgar** (¥23).

Eastern Tibet (Kham)

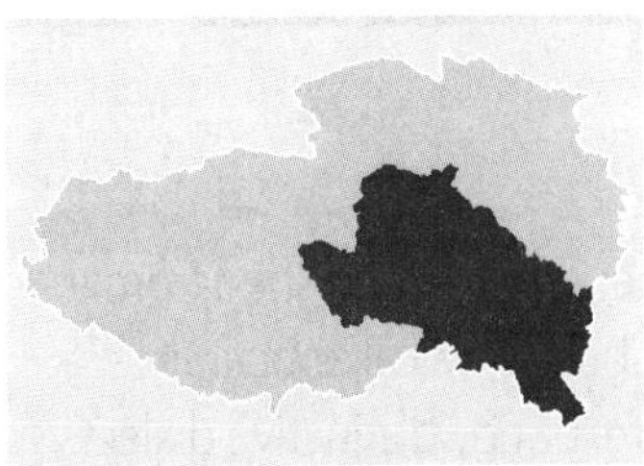

Footprint features

Introduction

The peoples of **Kham** (Eastern Tibet) are distinguished from other Tibetans not only by their robust physical appearance, colourful dress and braided coiffure, but by distinctive dialects and social customs. The terrain presents an amazing contrast to the landscape of the Brahmaputra valley and is characterized by extremely rugged mountains in parallel ranges extending from northwest to southeast, broken by deep forested gorges. The ranges are narrow and rocky with steep slopes, sharp ridges and high alpine pastures, while some peaks have spectacular glaciers. Eroded ravines and deep forested gorges of limestone and sandstone have been cut by the Salween, Mekong and Yangtze rivers and their numerous tributaries, hence the name traditionally given to the region of Kham: '**four rivers and six ranges**' (*chuzhi gangdruk*).

Nowadays this vast, fertile and most populated part of Tibet is divided for political and historical reasons between four Chinese provinces, comprising altogether 47 counties. The Khampa areas of the **Tibet Autonomous Region** include seven counties in Nakchu prefecture, 15 in Chamdo, and three in Nyangtri. The Khampa areas of **Yunnan province** include the three counties of Dechen Autonomous Prefecture; those of **Qinghai** include the six counties of Yushu Autonomous Prefecture; and those of **Sichuan** include 16 counties of Kandze Autonomous Prefecture, in addition to Mili Autonomous County.

The city of Chamdo at the heart of Kham is an important crossroads where Highway 214 from Kunming to Ziling intersects with the lateral highways 317 and 318, which connect Chengdu with Lhasa. The distance from Lhasa to Chamdo is 1,066 km via Nakchu; and 1,179 km via Kongpo. The distance from Chamdo to Chengdu is 1,272 km; from Chamdo to Kunming 1,789 km; and from Chamdo to Ziling 1,542 km.

Recommended itinerary: 8, 9, 10, 11 see page 20.

★ Don't miss...

1. **Lugu Lake** One of the world's few surviving matriarchal cultures can be seen in this remote southeastern corner of the plateau, page 455.
2. **Lhagang** If you cannot get to Lhasa, the sacred statue of Jowo Shakyamuni here is said to have the same blessings as the one housed in the Jokhang, page 477.
3. **Dzongsar** Visit the Yutok Medical Centre of Dr Lodro Phuntsok in the Mesho valley, and attend the formal debates at the monastic college, page 497.
4. **Derge** The cultural centre of Kham, a small trading town but more renowned for its monastery, temples and printing press, page 501.
5. **Dzogchen** A 17th-century monastery in a hidden glacial valley. For outstanding mountain panoramas hike to the lakes above the monastery, page 505.
6. **Jyekundo** One of the largest secular festivals of folk song, dance and equestrian skills is held here every year, in late July, page 529.

Background

Geography

The four great rivers of Kham, all of which rise on the Tibetan plateau, are the **Salween** (Tib Ngul-chu, Ch Nu jiang), the **Mekong** (Tib Da-chu, Ch Lancang jiang), the **Yangtze** (Tib Dri-chu, Ch Jinsha jiang), and the **Yalong** (Tib Dza-chu/Nya-chu, Ch Yalong jiang). The six highland ranges (*chuzhi gangdruk*) which form the watersheds for these river systems are the **Tsawagang** range (5,100-6,700 m) which includes the fabled snow peaks and glaciers of **Mount Kawa Karpo** (6,702 m) and which lies between the Salween and the Mekong; the **Markhamgang** range (Ch Ningjing Shan; 5,100-5,700 m) which lies between the Mekong and the Yangtze; the **Zelmogang** range (4,800-5,400 m) between the northern reaches of the Yangtze and Yalong; the **Poborgang** range (4,800-5,600 m) lies between the southern Yangtze and the lower Yalong; the **Mardzagang** (5,100-5,700 m) occupying the area between the upper Yalong and the Yellow River; and, lastly, the **Minyak Rabgang** range (4,800-7,750 m) including **Mount Minyak Gangkar** (7,756 m), the highest mountain in Kham, which lies between the lower Yalong and the Gyarong.

Climate

The climate is milder here than in more westerly parts of Tibet owing to the penetration of monsoon winds and rainfall from Southeast Asia, yet the great ruggedness of the terrain contributes to localized climatic diversity. Generally, there is little precipitation in winter (with the exception of the higher grasslands), and abundant rainfall in summer; the annual average varying from 500 to 1,000 mm.

Flora and fauna

In the more **arid areas** of Northwest Kham adjacent to the Jangtang Plateau, alpine steppes and meadows predominate on rock soil. Cobresia grows, along with rock jasmine, arenaria, rhubarb, gentian, buffalo pen, saussurea and astragalus. On lower mountain slopes are shrub thickets including rhododendron, willow, cinquefoil, spirea and juniper. Towards the southeast, the precipitation increases and the alpine steppes give way to forests. At 3,000-3,900 m there are balfour spruce, purple cone spruce and fir trees. On dry slopes the forests include juniper, oak and pine.

Within the **gorges** of Kham there are subalpine coniferous forests growing on podzolic soils. In the northeast these are characteristically mixed temperate and subtropical forests; and in the south and southwest mostly evergreen or laurel forests, with magnolia and michelia among others. There is great variation within these subalpine coniferous forests: ie fir in humid areas, spruce in dry areas; with numerous shrubs, grasses and mosses. In the far north gorges where winter is cold and dry there are mixed forests of oak and pine; and in the wetter southeast with rainfall exceeding 2,000 mm, there are fir, spruce, hemlock, lithocarpus, birch and poplar.

As for **fauna**: the high grasslands of the northwest are home to ungulates and rodents, especially the ubiquitous marmot and abra, and there are rare breeds of wild horse found in Nangchen. By contrast, the forested gorges of the southeast are known to have bears, badgers, lynxes, wild cats, otters, and, in some peripheral border areas, monkeys and giant pandas.

Traditional allegiances

The kingdoms and tribal confederations of East Tibet, whether nomadic or sedentary, have been shaped by this vast and formidable terrain. Since the disintegration of the Tibetan Empire following the demise of King Langdarma, for most of their history (with the notable exception of the Sakya period), they have fiercely maintained their independence from Lhasa, China and indeed from each other. In recent centuries, the most important states in Kham were the five kingdoms of **Chakla, Derge, Lingtsang, Nangchen**, and **Lhato**, ruled by hereditary kings (*gyelpo*), the five agricultural states of Trehor **Drango, Kangsar, Mazur, Trewo** and **Beri**, which were ruled by hereditary chieftains (*ponpo*), the nomadic clans of **Dzachuka, Nyarong, Sangen, Gonjo**, and **Khyungpo**, which were also ruled by hereditary chieftains; the southern states of **Batang, Litang, Markham, Tsawarong**, and **Powo** which were governed by Lhasa-appointed regents; and the western states of **Chamdo, Drayab** and **Riwoche** which, along with **Gyarong** and **Mili**, were governed by aristocratic lamas.

Festivals and power places

In Kham, religious and secular festivals have had great importance for local communities since earliest times. During the summer months preceding the harvest, the renowned horse festivals, such as those at **Jyekundo** and **Litang** are occasions for song, dance and sporting events, at which the boisterous Khampa crowds proudly display their local costume and traditions. Traders and spectators often travel throughout Kham from one region to the next, planning their travels to coincide with local festivals.

Pilgrimage is as important here as in Central Tibet. When Buddhism was established in the eighth century, Padmasambhava roamed throughout Kham and Amdo, concealing his *terma* teachings in many localities, and particularly in the following great 25 power places, which have primary and secondary affinities with either buddha-body, speech, mind, attributes or activities.

Kyadrak Senge Dzong in Dzachuka is the main site of **buddha-body**, and the five secondary sites are: Chijam Nyinda Puk in Dzachuka (body), Lotu Karma near Chamdo (speech), Nyen in the Yangtze valley (mind), Khala Rongo in Nangchen (attributes) and Hekar Drak (activities).

Gawalung in Po-me is the main site of **buddha-speech**, and the five secondary sites are: Mount Kawa Karpo in Dechen (body), Pema Shelri (speech), Nabun Dzong in Nangchen (mind), Yegyel Namka Dzong near Riwoche (attributes) and Chakdu Khawa Lungring near Nyarong (activities).

Dentik Shelgi Drak in Dowi is the main site of **buddha-mind**, and the five secondary sites are: Zhara Lhatse in Minyak (body), Warti Trak (speech), Dorje Drak in Jentsa (mind), Khandro Bumdzong in lower Nangchen (attributes), and Po-ne Drakar near Riwoche (activities).

Rudam Gangi Rawa at Mount Trori Dorje Ziltrom above Dzogchen is the main site of **buddha-attributes**, and the secondary sites are: Ngulda Podrang in Derge (body), Pema Shelphuk in Mesho (speech), Tsandra Rinchen Drak at Pelpung (mind), Dzongsho Deshek Dupa in Dzing (attributes), and Dzomtok Puseng Namdrak by the Yangtze (activities).

Katok Dorjeden is the main site of **buddha-activity**, and the five secondary sites are: Ngu in Pelyul (body), Tsangshi Dorje Trolo (speech), Kampo Kangra (mind), Hyelgi Trak (attributes), and Drakri Dorje Pungpa (activities).

Despite internal rivalries, the diverse states of Kham were broadly noted for their religious tolerance, at least until the 17th century. The Nyingma, Kagyu, Sakya and Geluk schools of Tibetan Buddhism were represented, alongside the adherents of Bon. Among areas of Kagyu influence, the strongest were **Nangchen** and **Derge**. For the Sakya school the most influential regions were **Jyekundo** and **Derge**, and for the Nyingmapa the **Zelmogang** and **Southern Derge** regions. Prior to the 17th century, the

 Gelukpa had their greatest centres at **Chamdo** and **Litang,** while the Bon tradition maintained an important presence in the **Khyungpo** region of the Upper Salween.

Mongolian sectarianism

A fundamental change occurred in the 17th century, however, and this is closely connected with the rise to political power of the Fifth Dalai Lama in Lhasa. The long civil wars waged between the supporters of the Kagyu and Geluk schools in Central and Western Tibet had some impact in the east. The zealous king Gushi Qan of the Qosot Mongolians sought to intervene on behalf of the Gelukpa faction by sending his armies against Donyo Dorje, the king of **Beri** who adhered to the Bon religion. That kingdom was subdued between 1639-1641, and the rich farming belt that extends from Rongpatsa to Drango was settled by Mongolian tribesmen, who forcibly converted and renamed a number of local Kagyu and Bon monasteries. They intermarried with the local population, and their descendants, known as **Trehor Khampa,** maintained the Gelukpa heritage, founding 13 great monasteries, such as **Kandze Gonpa** and **Dargye Gonpa** near Rongpatsa.

Meanwhile, the older established Gelukpa monasteries of **Chamdo** and **Litang** also expanded southwards during this period with Mongolian assistance, converting earlier Kagyu and Bon communities in **Drayab**, **Markham**, **Batang**, and **Chaktreng**, and even as far as **Dechen**, and **Gyeltang**. Eastwards, their influence extended to **Dartsedo** on the fringes of the Tibetan world.

This Gelukpa expansionism did not go unchallenged. The kingdoms of **Derge, Riwoche** and **Nangchen**, along with the inhospitable tribal confederations of **Nyarong** and **Khyungpo** successfully resisted, enabling their diverse spiritual heritages to flourish into the 20th century relatively unscathed. In **Jyekundo** and **Dzachuka**, the Gelukpa established a mode of coexistence alongside earlier Sakya, Nyingma and Kagyu enclaves.

Mongolian intervention in Tibetan politics had even more serious repercussions in the 18th century. In 1705-1706, the Manchu emperor of China Kangxi had supported the Qosot leader Lhazang Qan in his abduction of the Sixth Dalai Lama and murder of the regent Sangye Gyatso. The Dzungar Mongolians then intervened in 1717 to kill Lhazang and plunder Central Tibet. Although the Tibetan forces were eventually able to gain the upper hand, in 1720 the emperor despatched an army to vanquish the Dzungars and instate the Seventh Dalai Lama Kelsang Gyatso, who was conveniently in his custody. Following the death of Kangxi in 1721, the Manchu armies extended their campaign against the Qosot Mongolians in Amdo. In 1724 Amdo, Jyekundo and Nangchen were annexed to form the Kokonor Territory (Ch. Qinghai), and in 1727 the Manchus claimed the part of Kham that lies east of the Yangtze as their own protectorate. From 1728 they also posted two representatives in Lhasa.

Manchu Warlords and occupation

Despite these Manchu declarations of suzerainty over Amdo and the easternmost parts of Kham, in practice only a nominal authority was exercised. The reality of the situation was that the kingdoms and tribes of Eastern Tibet maintained their independence, as they had done for most of their history; and there were hardly any Chinese settlers outside the border zones. In the 19th century when the forces of **Nyarong** under **Gonpo Namgyel** emerged from their inhospitable ravines to conquer Trehor, Derge and Dzachuka, it was the Tibetan government of Lhasa which subdued the power of Nyarong in the campaign of 1863-1865.

Sichuan warlords, among them Chao Erh Feng, began to penetrate Kham from 1894, but official Chinese intervention in Khampa affairs was only sanctioned following the arrival of the Younghusband expedition in Lhasa (1904). In 1909, Chao Erh Feng implemented a 'forward policy,' which sought to carve out a new and governable Chinese province with 33 districts, which would be called **Xikang**. The proposed territory would encompass the entire region from **Gyamda** in Kongpo to **Dartsedo**. This 1909-1918 campaign, which devastated much of Kham, resulted in the eventual Chinese withdrawal from the region following the collapse of the Manchu Empire, despite British diplomatic efforts to maintain the artificial boundaries devised by the Manchu emperors. However, the conflict later resumed with the arrival in Kham of the PLA, following the rise to power of Mao Zedong in Beijing. The denigration of local traditions and imposition of communist land reforms which ensued from 1956 onwards were strongly resisted by militant Khampa guerrillas, who were outnumbered and eventually defeated by the occupying forces. The retribution exacted on Kham for its militancy resulted in the massacre and incarceration of many communities, some of the most influential figures in Khampa society— tribal chieftains and incarnate lamas among them. Later, during the Cultural Revolution, virtually all the great Buddhist artefacts of the region were destroyed. Only a few significant buildings, like the Parkhang at **Derge** and the Jokhang at **Lhagang** mercifully survived.

Further reading

Useful works on Kham include: Eric Teichman's *Travels of a Consular Official in Eastern Tibet*, Warren Smith's historical opus *Tibetan Nation: A History of Tibetan Nationalism and Sino-Tibetan Relations*, R A Stein's *Les Tribus Anciennes des Marches Sino-tibetaines*, the writings of the botanist Frank Kingdon Ward who travelled throughout Konpo and Southern Kham between 1913-1920, Steve Marshall and Suzette Cooke's *Tibet Outside the TAR* (on CD Rom),and the cartographic studies of Pieter Kestler. Among travelogues, the most readable include Andre Migot's *Tibetan Marches*, Chogyam Trungpa's autobiography *Born in Tibet*, and the works of the American evangelist Marion Duncan.

Ins and outs

Getting around

Since late 1998, the beautiful forests of eastern and southern Kham (Kandze and Dechen Prefectures) have been officially open to foreign tourism, and they are now highly accessible to independent travellers. Economic necessity forced a reappraisal of government policy following a ban on lumbering in those areas, which was belatedly introduced following the severe flooding of the lower Yangtze in 1998. Tourism is now regarded as a valid alternative means of generating economic development.

Unfortunately, the areas of Kham controlled by the Tibet Autonomous Region are still restricted and, for Chamdo prefecture at least, military permits are required, in addition to an alien travel permit issued by the police. Any traveller venturing towards Markham from Dechen or Batang, to Jomda from Derge, or to Chamdo Airport from Chengdu will require both documents. Permits are also required by those seeking to travel from Kermu (Ch. Golmud) in Amdo to Nakchu prefecture, or from Jyekundo southwards through Nangchen to Riwoche. Despite these restrictions, there are still a few adventurous individuals, travelling without permission, who somehow make their way to Lhasa. Organized group travel is possible on any of the routes once the necessary documents have been obtained. **NB** Some of these routes through Eastern Tibet are often impenetrable in winter when high passes are snow-bound, and in the rainy season (July-August) when mud slides can damage fragile road surfaces. The only paved roads in Kham are Highway 109 from Lhasa to Kermu via Nakchu, Highway 214 from Kunming to Dechen via Gyeltang and from Pomda Airport to Chamdo, Highway 318 from Chengdu via Dartsedo to Litang, and Highway 317 from Chengdu to Rongpatsa via Dartsedo and Kandze.

At present, there are three motorable roads leading from Lhasa to Chamdo in the heart of Kham: the **northern route**, which passes through Nakchu, Sok Dzong, Hor Bachen, Khyungpo Tengchen, and Riwoche; the **central route** via Driru, Pelbar and Lhorong; and the **southern route**, through Gyamda, Bayi, Po-me and Pasho. The northern route (Highway 317) is currently in greater use as it permits faster driving and is more reliable during the rainy season. The southern route (Highway 318) is subject to recurring landslides due to the glacial snow-melt and deep river gorges between Po-me and Lunang. The central route is more rugged, following the Salween gorge and linking also with the **old caravan trail** from Lhasa to Chamdo via Gyamda and Lhari. All three routes offer considerable variation in landscape and cultural attractions.

Lhasa to Chamdo: via Nakchu

The northern route, described in this section, comprises the counties of Nakchu, Sok Dzong, Hor Bachen, Khyungpo Tengchen, Riwoche, and Chamdo. In addition, two outlying counties: Amdo and Nyenrong, are also included. ***Recommended itineraries: 4, 5 and 7. See page 20.*** » *For Sleeping, Eating and other listings, see pages 424-427.*

Nakchu County ནག་ཆུ

→ *Population: 81,211. Area: 17,194 sq km. Colour map 6, grid C5.* 那曲县

Nakchu prefecture, traditionally known as **Jang Nakchuka**, is the name given to the high nomadic terrain of the East Jangtang Lakes and the Salween headwaters, average altitude 4,500 m. This is a vast wilderness region through which the Nak-chu, Shak-chu, and Sok-chu tributaries flow to form the **Salween** (Tib Nak-chu): a 2,784 km river rising in the Dangla range to the north and flowing into the Gulf of Martaban, south of Burma. The city of **Nakchu**, which has undergone unprecedented development within the last seven years, is the administrative capital of nine counties within the upper Salween basin, as well as having its own county-level bureaucracy. It is located on the excellent Highway 109 that runs from Lhasa to Lanzhou, 315 km northeast of Lhasa, near the headwaters of the Nak-chu tributary, from which it derives its name. The actual sources of the Nak-chu are at **Chutsen Narak** (Jukchu), north of the Brahmaputra-Salween watershed, and at **Galong** on the southern shore of the freshwater **Lake Tsonak** to the northwest. The distance from Damzhung to Nakchu city is 169 km, and from Nakchu to Draknak in Amdo county, 138 km along the highway.

Koluk and Lhoma

Heading northeast from Lhasa via Yangpachen and Damzhung, the recently widened Highway 109 enters Nakchu county 27 km beyond **Omatang**. The stupas of **Chorten Rango** lie just north of the county border. Passing through **Koluk** township after 14 km, the road rises slowly towards **Zangzhung La** pass (4,727 m), which forms the watershed between the Brahmaputra and Salween river systems, and after crossing this divide, it bypasses **Sangzhung** township on the west. The

Nakchu, Amdo & Nyenrong

road now crosses the Nak-chu southern source, and runs parallel to it. Light snowfall is a normal occurrence in this exposed and sparsely populated Jangtang region, even in summertime! The township of **Lhoma** straddles the highway, 66 km northeast of Koluk, and 17 km further on there is a turn-off on the right (east), which follows the Nak-chu through **Takring** and **Hor-me** townships in the direction of **Lhari,** on which see below, page 427.

Nakchu City → *Phone code: 0896. Altitude: 4,509 m.*

Continue along the highway for 10 km, and soon the city of Nakchu (4,509 m) comes into view, impressively large in its wilderness setting. Cross the Nakchu Zamchen bridge on the right (east), which leads off the highway into town.

Average temperature
10° mid-summer
-10° mid-winter
Oxygen content 61%

The phenomenal growth of this city is due to its important location on the highway, linking Ziling and Amdo with Central Tibet, and as the centre of trade for the entire nomadic region of North Tibet, which urban and farming communities refer to as **Hor**.Once the railway from Kermu to Lhasa, scheduled to open in 2008, is in business, Nakchu is likely to expand even more and become an important rail hub. There are strategic petrol stations, both civilian and military to the west of town, and to the south is the **Nakchu Race Course**, where an important horse festival is held each year, commencing on 10 August. More than 10,000 visitors from the Lhasa and Nakchu regions attend the events, which also provide an occasion for traditional barter and regional folk dances. The colourful appliqué tents, which surround the race track, some of them larger than houses, are particularly impressive.

Within the town the crossroads is the commercial centre. Here there are grocery, textile and electrical stores, as well as shops selling traditional crafts. Local industry is mostly a derivative of nomadic animal husbandry: dairy products and meat processing, and cashmere wool production (also including yak and sheep wool). The Chinese population is less pronounced in this high inhospitable climate than in other Tibetan cities. Muslim shopkeepers from the Ziling area have their own quarter.

There are two main temples in town, one Nyingma and the other Gelukpa, both of which are extremely active and well supported by the local community. Among them, **Zhabten Gonpa**, recently reconstructed and with outstanding murals, now houses 80 monks.

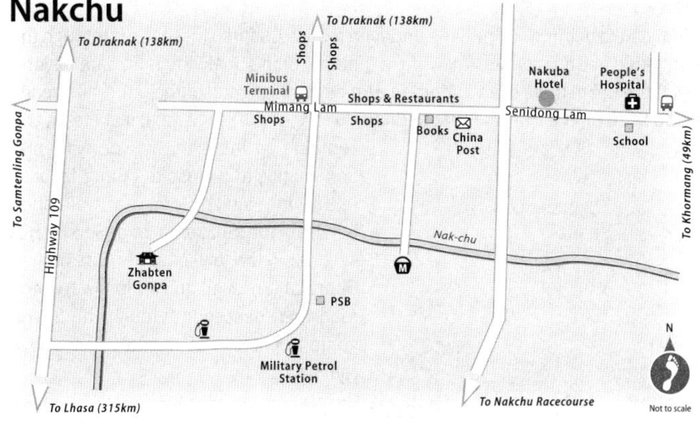

Amdo County ཨ་མདོ་ → *Population: 33,211. Area: 22,159 sq km.* 安多县

Highway 109 to Kermu and Ziling continues northwest from Nakchu, following the valley of its source tributary upstream to **Tsaring** (40 km), and thence to **Draknak**, the capital of Amdo county, which is located to the northeast of **Lake Tsonak**, the source of the Nak-chu branch of the Salween River. This town is 98 km from Tsaring on a side road, which leaves the highway after 81 km. At an altitude of 4,600 m, Draknak is even more inhospitable than Nakchu. Nonetheless, it is an important crossroads town, which is likely to expand when the railway opens.

From here, a westerly route cuts across the exposed saltpans and lakes of the **Jangtang Plateau** to **Senge Khabab**, near Mount Kailash (1,333 km). The paved highway runs north to cross the **Dang-La pass** (5,220 m), a watershed between the Salween and Yangtze headwaters, which also marks the present-day boundary between the Tibet Autonomous Region and Qinghai province. The Dangla mountains, where the highest peaks range from 5,700 to 6,300 m, are rich in minerals, including iron ore, coal, graphite, asbestos and soapstone. From Draknak to Dang La pass the distance is 106 km. Before reaching the pass, there is a turn-off on the west, 67 km from Draknak, which leads to the coal mines at **Tumen Dosol Terka**. The mines are located near the source of the **Trakara-chu**, a tributary of the **Tsakya Tsangpo** River, which drains internally into the salt Lake Serling. The lifestyle of the Draknak region is nomadic. Economic activity is centred around animal husbandry, as well as coal mining and salt-panning.

Nyenrong County སྙན་རོང་ → *Pop: 28,871. Area: 7,259 sq km.* 聂荣县

Nyenrong county is a large sparsely populated area to the south of the Dangla Range. It comprises both the sources of the **Shak-chu** and the **Sok-chu** tributaries of the Salween. The townships of Serkhang and Dzamar are to be found near the source of the Shak-chu, and those of Bezhung and Trawola around the source of the Sok-chu.

About 11 km along Highway 109 from Nakchu in the direction of Amdo, there is a turn-off on the right (north), which leads to **Serkhang**, the capital of Nyenrong county, 82 km distant. The watershed between the Nak-chu and Shak-chu is crossed at **Gyatsam La** pass, 38 km along this road. **Shakchuka** is the traditional name given to the barren upper reaches of the Shak-chu valley, which extends through both Nyenrong and Driru counties, as far as the confluence with the Nak-chu.

Sok County སོག་རྫོང་ → *Pop: 35,097. Area: 5,839 sq km. Colour map 6, grid C6.* 索县

From Shakchuka on Highway 317, the unpaved road to Chamdo first passes through the northern fringe of Driru county, following a tributary of the Shak-chu upstream beyond **Drilung.** After 22 km there is an important turn-off on the right (southeast), which leads to **Naksho Driru** on the **central route to Chamdo** (see below, page 427). If, instead, you continue on the highway, you will enter Sok county, and cross the **Gang La** pass (4,811 m), which forms a watershed between the Shak-chu and Sok-chu. A second slightly lower double pass named **Shara La** (4,744 m) quickly follows, as the road then descends through the Si-chu gorge to enter the Sok-chu valley above **Nyinpa** (72 km).

Sok

Sok Tsanden Zhol

Sok Tsanden Zhol, the county town (4,100 m), is located some 22 km upstream from Nyinpa within the Sok-chu valley. The terrain here is arid and barren. The lower reaches of the Sok-chu valley are administered from this town (whereas the upper reaches are within the neighbouring county of Hor Bachen). ▸▸ *For listings, see pages 424-427.*

Sok Tsanden Gonpa

As you drive into town from Nakchu and Shakchuka, you will notice across the river the hilltop Gelukpa monastery of **Sok Tsanden Gonpa**, which was founded by the Mongolian chieftain Gushi Qan Tendzin Chogyel during the 17th century. Prior to the civil war between Lhasa and Zhigatse, the region had been a stronghold of the Bon religion. The recently renovated temple is currently home to 200 monks though once it housed 600, and it has an impressive citadel-like façade, reminiscent of the Potala. It comprises the Lhakhang Marpo (Red Temple), the Rabselkhang, and the Lhakhang Karpo (White Temple). The ground floor of the **Lhakhang Marpo** contains a temple dedicated to Tsongkhapa. The main images are Shakyamuni flanked by his foremost students and the 16 Elders, along with 1,000 small Tsongkhapa images. The second floor houses the Gonkhang dedicated to Vajrabhairava and Shridevi; the Rinchen Lhakhang with images of the Thirty-five Confession Buddhas, Tara, Avalokiteshvara, Jowo Shakyamuni and Amitabha; and the Kangyur Lhakhang which contains the Lhasa edition of the Tibetan canon. Adjacent to the Gonkhang is the residence of the incumbent lama, Kangyur Rinpoche. In the 56 columned **Lhakhang Karpo**, there is a renowned sandalwood image of Avalokiteshvara, from which the monastery acquired its name ('tsanden' means sandalwood); and other images including Padmasambhava. The present sandalwood image is a replica of the damaged original which has been inserted within the heart of the new image. On the lowest level, there is a Mani Wheel chamber. **NB** Since 2001 access to this monastery has only been possible for foreigners with permits clearly indicating Sok Tsanden Gonpa.

Kabgye Lhakhang

Southwest of Sok Tsanden Gonpa, on the west side of the Sok-chu, within the old quarter of town, is the Nyingmapa temple known as **Kabgye Lhakhang**. This shrine was founded in 1169 by the renowned treasure-finder Nyangrel Nyima Ozer (1136-1204). Following its destruction by Gushi Qan's Mongolian army in the 17th century, it was restored by the *terton* Nyima Drakpa (1647-1710). There are 30 married *mantrins* now living around the temple, where the main spiritual practices include the Kabgye Deshek Dupa of Nyangrel Nyima Ozer, the *terma* teachings of Nyima Drakpa, the Lama Gongdu of Sangye Lingpa, and the Rigdzin Dupa of Jigme Lingpa. The temple is in need of further funds to complete its restoration.

Further downstream below Nyinpa, a trail leads towards the confluence of the Sok-chu and Salween at **Shamchu**. The townships in the southeast of the county include Chungpa and **Chamda**, where there are six cave hermitages associated with Padmasambhava. One of these, **Dorje Sherdzong**, has a cave temple complex. Rongpa township in the extreme east of the county will be described below with Hor Bachen, as it follows Hor Bachen on the motor road.

Bachen County སྦྲ་ཆེན

→ *Population: 36,963. Area: 13,738 sq km. Colour map 6, grid C6.* 巴青县

Bachen county, more properly known as **Hor Bachen**, comprises the upper reaches of the Sok-chu and its feeder rivers, the Bon-chu and Bachen-chu, all three of which converge above **Gurkhuk**. The county capital is located at **Tartang** in the Ye-chu valley, 37 km northeast of Sok Dzong on the Chamdo road, and a short distance beyond **Patsang Monastery** (Yeta).

Tartang

This area was formerly the centre of the **Hor Jyade** nomad camps, who successfully maintained their nomadic lifestyle and relative independence from Lhasa until the early 20th century. A large horse festival is held on the **Tartang** plain in summertime; and the Bon tradition survives, alongside a Gelukpa nunnery. The town has both civilian and military guesthouses, a petrol station, a few shops, and a small roadside restaurant cum tea house.

The townships within Bachen county are located in the upper reaches of the various feeder rivers: **Bonsok** on the Bon-chu, township on the Sok-chu, **Tsek-ne** on the Bachen-chu, and **Chang-me** on the Ye-chu.

Trekking North of Tartang Trekking routes lead up these river valleys to the **Dangla** watershed range, crossing the Salween-Yangtze watershed into present day Qinghai (see below, page 525). Among these **Trawo La** pass (4,930 m) leads directly from the Sok-chu valley, and **Tsek-ne La** (5,140 m) from the Bachen-chu valley.

East of Tartang

Continuing along Highway 317 to Chamdo, 44 km east of Tartang, at **Yangada**, the road crosses yet another tributary of the Salween, which flows downstream through Chungpa to its confluence above **Chamda**. There are a number of small Tibetan guesthouses and teahouses here. The road then cuts southeast via **Chak La** pass (4,502 m) into the **Rongpo Gyarubtang** region, where an important battle was fought between the Tibetan government forces and the Kuomintang in the early decades of this century.

Rongpo Gyarubtang

The township of **Rongpo Gyarubtang**, on the meandering Ri-chu tributary of the Salween, is 33 km beyond Chak La pass, at the base of the **Pugyel Gangri** snow range (6,328 m). There is a small guesthouse with a congenial attendant, but lacking in electricity. Southwest of town at **Sertram Drak**, there is a thriving Nyingmapa monastery; and accessible on a more remote but motorable trail is the Gelukpa residence of Zhiwalha, the second most important incarnation of Chamdo monastery. The road now ascends the high **Shel La** pass (4,830 m) on a spur of the Pugyel Gangri range. The forested alpine terrain of the middle Salween is visible to the southwest. On reaching the pass, 44 km from Rongpo, there is a spectacular view of the **Dangla** range to the northeast and the cragged **Tanyi Tawun** (Ch Tanlan Taweng) range to the southeast.

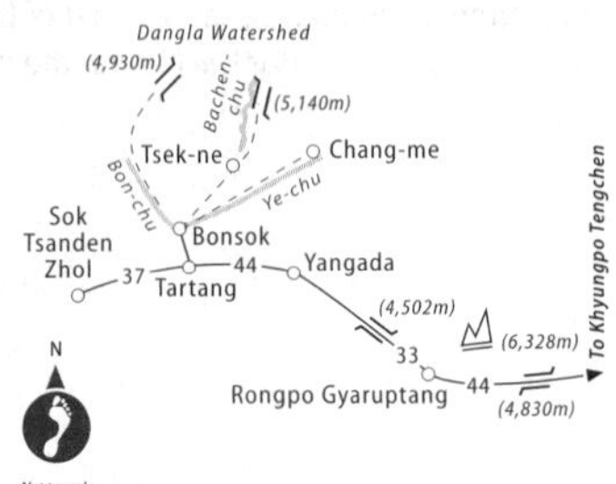

Tengchen County སྟེང་ཆེན

→ *Population: 61,979. Area: 11,175 sq km. Colour map 4, grid A1.* 丁青县

On the descent from Shel La pass, the highway enters the **Khyungpo** district of Kham, where the Bon tradition predominates. **Tengchen** county comprises the valleys of the south-flowing Ga-chu and Ru-chu tributaries of the Salween and those of their northwest-flowing feeder rivers, the Dak-chu and Kyilkhar-chu. The county capital is Khyungpo Tengchen, also known as **Gyamotang**, 271 km southeast of Sok Dzong, 98 km from Shel La pass, and 143 km northwest of Riwoche.

Routes from Shel La

About 18 km from Shel La pass, the Chamdo road cuts across the Ga-chu River at **Trido**. A trekking route leads off on the left (north) through the upper Ga-chu valley to **Gata** township, and the river's source southeast of **Mount Lagen Zhushab**. Another trekking route leads due south from Trido to the river's confluence with the Salween in **Lhorong** county (see below, page 429). The **highway**, however, cuts southeast from Trido, following a tributary of the Ga-chu upstream to Sertsa (35 km), where the Ru-chu also flows in from the north and the Dak-chu from the southeast.

Sertsa

This small township of Sertsa has several monasteries. Among them, the largest Bonpo monastery is **Sertsa Yongdzong**; and the largest Gelukpa monastery is **Sertsa Tashiling**. The latter is located across the **Tsuri La** pass (4,200 m) from Sertsa township, and on the right (south) side of the motor road. Originally a Kagyupa monastery, Tashiling was converted to the Gelukpa school by the armies of Gushi Qan in the 17th century. It also has affinities with the Nyingma school, as evidenced by its main chapel, which contains large images of Padmasambhava flanked by Shantaraksita and King Trisong Detsen. The traditions of this renovated monastery, which once housed 300 monks, are being revived under the guidance of Tulku Ngawang Zangpo, who presides over a group of 80 monks. Sertsa has a government compound with guesthouse and dining facilities, a motor repair shop, and a petrol station.

Tengchen → *Altitude: 3,750 m. Colour map 4, grid A1. For listings, see pages 424-427.*

Following the Dak-chu downstream from Sertsa, after 45 km the road reaches **Tengchen**, the county capital, situated in a wide cultivated valley, hemmed in by red sandstone hills. The old Tibetan village of **Tengchen Kha** and the county town of **Tengchen** face each other across the river, as if worlds apart.

The inhabitants of **Tengchen Kha** village are extremely hospitable, and display a remarkable sense of religious tolerance. At a Padmasambhava 10th day ceremony in

Tengchen County

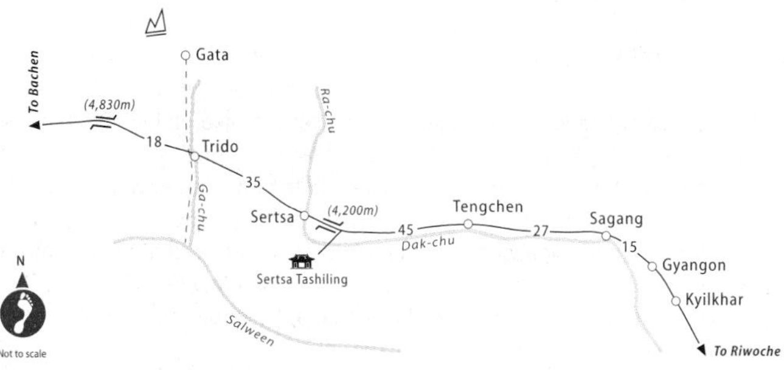

 1988 attended by the author, Nyingmapa *mantrins*, Gelukpa monks, and Bonpo practitioners participated together with an exemplary sympathy. A branch road to the northwest leads 25 km along the Zhe-chu valley to Zhezhung township.

Tengchen Monastery The region of Khyungpo, as its name suggests, is one long connected with the Bon tradition; for **Khyunglung** ('Garuda Valley') in Far West Tibet was an original Bon stronghold, and many later Bon communities also adopted this name. Most religious establishments in the region are Bon rather than Buddhist, and among them, there are two important monasteries situated side by side on the northern ridge, which overlooks the town: **Tengchen Monastery** and **Ritro Lhakhang**. The former, also called Namdak Pema Long-yang, was founded in 1110 by Sherab Gyeltsen and Monlam Gyeltsen who hailed from the 'White Lineage of the Chen family'. The third lineage-holder (ie the successor of those two) greatly expanded the community of practitioners around Tengchen and established the **Ritro Lhakhang** hermitage above the temple in 1180. The two monasteries have had long close connections with the Bon communities of **Yungdrungling** and **Menri** in West Tibet, and with those of the **Ngawa** region of Amdo.

Renovations began in 1986 under the guidance of Lama Sherab Gelek. Of the original vast complex of buildings, two chapels have been restored in each monastery. The **Ritro Lhakhang** comprises the **Serdung Chewa**, a chamber containing the reliquary of the second lineage-holder, Monlam Gyeltsen; and the **Serdung Chungwa**, containing the reliquaries of the six other early lineage-holders: Nyima Gyeltsen (I), Kunga Gyeltsen (III), Jinpa Gyeltsen (IV), Tsultrim Gyeltsen (V), Yungdrung Gyeltsen (VI), and Tsultrim Nyima (VII). **Tengchen Monastery** contains the **Nampar Gyelwa Lhakhang** (downstairs) and the **Residence of Lama Monlam** and the library (upstairs), which are finely decorated with frescoes of Bon divinities and mandalas. The **Ritro Lhakhang** also has an abbot's residential chamber, in its upper storey, where the murals depict scenes from the life of Shenrab, and a copy of the Bon *Kangyur* is housed. Formerly both monasteries had 300 monks each, but now the Tengchen Monastery has only 85 and the Ritro Lhakhang a mere 23.

Kyilkhar Lhakhang

Continuing along the main highway from Tengchen, the route follows the Dak-chu downstream through **Sagang** (27 km) and the valley of its feeder river, the Kyilkhar-chu, upstream through **Gyangon** (15 km). This region contains a number of large Bon monasteries perched on remote precipices, high above the motor road. Among them, **Tsedru Gonpa** is one of the largest and most active. At **Kyilkhar**, where the Kyilkhar-chu thrusts its way out of a long narrow red sandstone gorge, there is an impressively large mani stone mound and an important branch monastery of Chamdo Jampaling. Two temples have been restored in recent years and there are now 250 monks. Inside are fine murals and images depicting Shakyamuni, Tsongkhapa flanked by his foremost students, Green Tara, White Tara, and three meditational deities: Guhyasamaja, Carasamvara and Vajrabhairava.

Rotung Nyedren Gonpa

This monastery of the Karma Kagyu school, adjacent to Kyilkhar Lhakhang, is currently undergoing renovation. Images include Mahakarunika, flanked by Padmasambhava and Vajrakila; and there are tangkas depicting the Karmapas. Recently a Mani Lhakhang has been constructed. In the past there were some 600 monks at Rotung, but nowadays there are only 70 under the direction of Tsepak Lama. Beyond Rotung, the road bypasses the grassy knoll of Kharje and plunges into the **Kyilkhar gorge**. The red sandstone walls rise sharply on both banks of the river. Only in the summer months is there evidence of vegetation. A hydroelectric power station has been constructed at **Meru** within the gorge.

Riwoche County རི་བོ་ཆེ

→ *Population: 41,735. Area: 5,699 sq km. Colour map 4, grid A2.* 类乌齐县

Riwoche county extends from the **Dzekri La** pass (4,809 m), which forms the watershed between the Salween and Mekong river systems, as far as the **Zhopel La** or Trugu La pass (4,688 m), which divides the Dzi-chu and Ngom-chu tributaries of the Mekong. The county capital is located at Ratsaka, 143 km southeast of Tengchen and 105 km east of Chamdo.

Kharmardo

After passing through the Kyilkhar gorge, the highway to Riwoche and Chamdo crosses the **Dzekri La**, 66 km from Gyangon in Tengchen county. Then, descending abruptly into the **Kharmardo** valley, the terrain is utterly transformed. High altitude barren landscape is replaced by juniper and conifer forests, and rolling alpine meadows carpeted with blue gentian and white edelweiss. To the southeast large outcrops of red sandstone and white marble are strewn across the undulating slopes. After Kharmardo, the road drops due north into the lower Ke-chu valley at **Sibta**. A motorable side trail follows the Ke-chu upstream (northwest) from Sibta, reaching **Tramoling** after 55 km. The main road follows the Ke-chu downstream from Sibta to its confluence with the Dzi-chu at **Ratsaka** (35 km from Dzekri La pass).

Takzham Monastery

In the lower Ke-chu valley, some 20 km before Ratsaka, the road passes **Takzham Monastery** on the left. This was the residence of Takzham Nuden Dorje, an 18th-century treasure-finder who discovered various texts hidden by Yeshe Tsogyel including her own biography, and who held the lineages of Katok Monastery and Choje Lingpa. The main temple, constructed in Zangdok Pelri style, contains images of Padmasambhava, Amitayus, Vajrasattva and Shakyamuni, as well as several large prayer wheels replete with the mantras of Vajrasattva, Padmasambhava and Amitabha. The central throne bears a photograph of the present Takzham Rinpoche, who lives in Switzerland. The newly painted murals depict the Takzham lineage. Outside and to the left of the temple entrance there are sets of stupas symbolizing the deeds of the Buddha, both in traditional stone design and in the distinctive wooden style of Kham. A group of nomadic campers occupies the grassland behind the monastery.

Ratsaka (Riwoche county town) → *Altitude: 3,690 m. Colour map 4, grid A2.*

Entering the town of **Ratsaka** from the west, you first pass the turn-off to the north which crosses the Dzi-chu bridge, heading in the direction of Riwoche Tsuklakhang. The paved main street contains all the buildings of note: the Public Security Bureau and government buildings are at the west end, while the three hotels are at the east end. The largest general store is on the south side, to the west of the hotels, and the

Riwoche

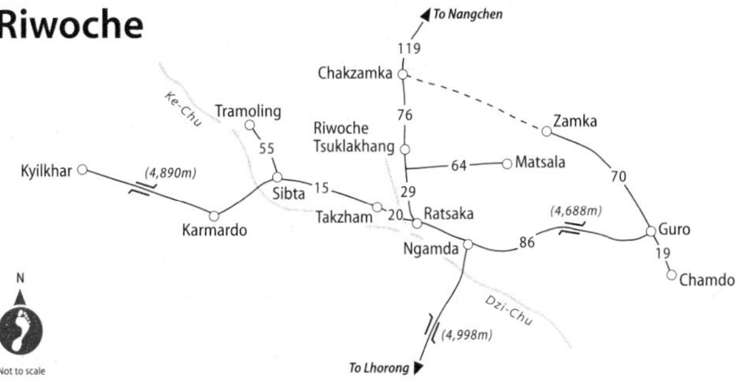

 Post Office is on the north side. Entertainment is minimal, being confined to open-air pool tables and a video parlour. » *For listings, see pages 424-427.*

Riwoche Tsuklakhang → *Colour map 4, grid A2*

Getting there If you wish to visit **Riwoche Tsuklakhang**, situated in the old Riwoche valley (which is the only reason for spending time in Ratsaka), you should first obtain clearance from the Public Security Bureau in town. Take the turn-off at the west end of the main street, which leads across the Dzi-chu Bridge, and then head north, following the Dzi-chu upstream on its west bank for 29 km. En route you will pass a turn-off on the right, across the river, which leads through a defile to the **Matsala Coal Mines**, located on a prominent spur of the **Tanyi Tawun** range, 64 km distant. It is on account of these peaks that the valley received the name Riwoche. Another detour leads west to **Tramoling**, where Kham's only deer breeding park is located. The track continues through **Nyinta**, and then opens out into a wide plain, where the resplendent Riwoche Tsuklakhang is visible in the distance.

History The great temple, known as **Riwoche Tsuklakhang**, was founded in 1276 by Sangye On, a student of Sangye Yarjon, the third lineage-holder and abbot of the Taklung branch of the Kagyu school. Following the death of Sangye Yarjon, who was interred at Taklung in a stupa reliquary alongside his two predecessors Taklung Tangpa Tashipel and Kuyalwa, Sangye On took charge of the mother monastery for some time, but then departed abruptly for Kham, leaving Taklung in the hands of Mangalaguru, in order to fulfil a prophecy to the effect that he should found an even greater branch of the monastery at Riwoche. As such Riwoche Tsuklakhang became the main branch of Taklung in Kham, and according to Go Lotsawa, author of the *Blue Annals*, it had the greatest reputation among Khampa monasteries, once housing as many as 2,000 monks. From the time of its foundation, the Taklung Kagyu school was considered to have upper and lower branches, the former being the original monastery at Taklung and the latter the Riwoche Tsuklakhang. The lineages associated with both are recounted in the religious history called *Chojung Ngo-tsar Gyatso*, written in 1648 by Ngawang Damcho Zangpo.

The temple The temple at Riwoche is physically imposing in the manner of the main temples at Samye and Sakya, with enormous tree trunk columns supporting its three storeys. It is painted in the distinctive black, white and red vertical stripes which are a hallmark of the Taklung lineage. In the early 15th century Tsongkhapa is known to have praised the community at the Tsuklakhang for their expertise in the meditation practices of Hevajra and other deities. The surrounding community of practitioners, married or monastic, adhered to both the Taklung Kagyu and the Nyingma lineages. The Nyingmapa element in Riwoche has been especially strong since the time of Jedrung Rinpoche (Trinle Jampa Jungne), who was the teacher of both the late Dudjom Rinpoche (1904-1987) and the late Kangyur Rinpoche (1888-1975).

The temple dwarfs the surrounding Riwoche village, which contains the government compound, the residences of Jedrung Rinpoche and Panchuk Rinpoche to the northeast, that of Zhabdrung Rinpoche to the east, and the quarters of the monastery's 500 monks which extend between them. It is well supported by those members of the local community who are engaged in the rebuilding project and in spiritual pursuits.

The three-storey temple has been undergoing restoration since 1985. The outer wall is surrounded by a pilgrims' walkway complete with rows of prayer-wheels on all four sides. The temple is entered from the east side. The **ground floor** comprises the assembly hall with enormous larger-than-life size images on all four walls, separated from the hall by wooden lattices. Proceeding clockwise from the left you will pass on the east wall: Maitreya, Aksobhya, Eleven-faced Avalokiteshvara, and Eight Stupas (symbolizing the deeds of the Buddha); then on the south wall: Shakyamuni, an original Vajrapani, Amitayus, Padmasambhava in the form of Nangsi Zilnon, the Eight Manifestations of Padmasambhava and another Shakyamuni. On the west wall, which is the **inner sanctum**, there are eight small stupas and assorted small statues, followed by the Buddhas of the Three Times and two images of Sangye Yarjon, flanked by two old Munindra images. On the north wall are: Shakyamuni, Sangye Yarjon, Sangye On, Sarvavid Vairocana, Dipamkara Buddha, Shakyamuni and

Riwoche Tsuklakhang

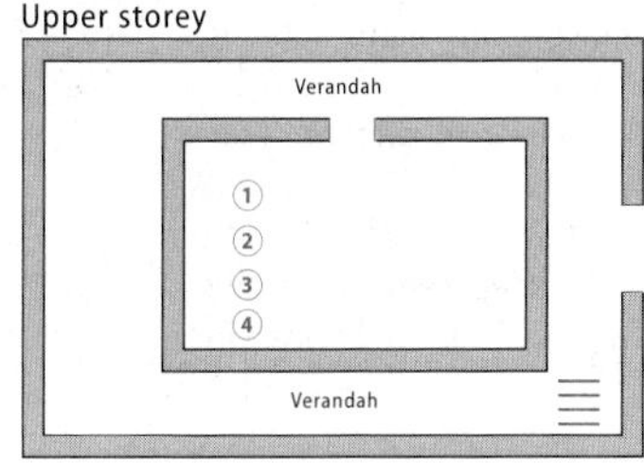

1 Amitayus
2 Sangye Yarjon
3 Stupa Reliquary
4 Panchuk Rinpoche

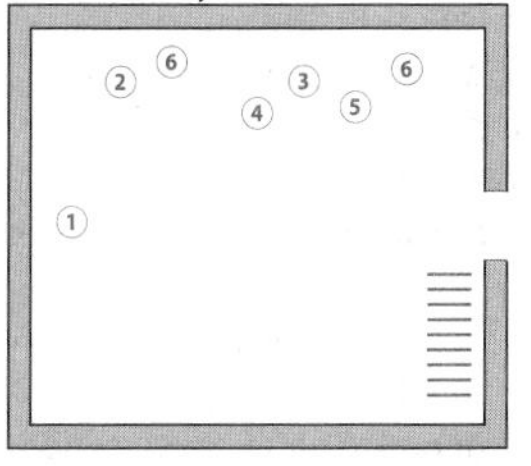

1 Padmasambhala
2 Ardokta with nagas
3 Buddha
4 Shariputra
5 Maudgalyayana
6 16 Elders

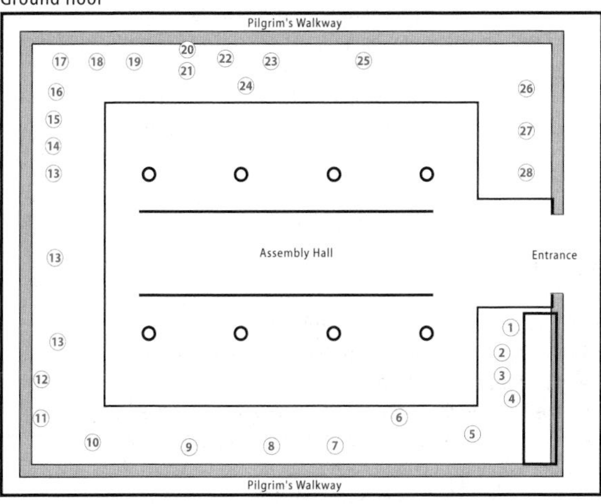

1 Maitreya
2 Aksobhya
3 11-faced Avalokiteshvara
4 8 Stupas
5 Shakyamuni
6 Vajrapani
7 Amitayus
8 Padmasambhava
9 8 Manifestations of Padmasambhava
10 Shakyamuni
11 8 Stupas (small)
12 Assorted small images
13 Buddhas of 3 Times
14 Munindra
15 Sangye Yarjon
16 Sangye Yarjon
17 Munindra
18 Sangye Yarjon
19 Sangye On
20 Derge Kangyur
21 Sarvavaid Vairocana
22 Dipamkara
23 Shakyamuni
24 Maitreya
25 Bhaisajyaguru
26 11-faced Avalokitesvara
27 Remati
28 Local Protector

Not to scale

Mekong River

The Mekong (Tib Da-chu, Ch Lancang jiang) is the world's 12th longest river, and the seventh longest in Asia, extending 4,350 km from its high altitude Ngom-chu and Dza-chu sources (4,900 m) in the Tangula Mountains of present-day Qinghai province, to its delta in Vietnam. The river has a total drainage area of 810,600 sq km. In its upper reaches, the Mekong flows through the deeply eroded narrow gorges of East Tibet and Yunnan for 1,955 km. Its waters have a distinctly greenish hue, except during the rainy season, when its flow is faster and turbid silt abruptly turns it reddish brown. Overall, the river has an annual sediment of 187 million tons. The lower reaches of the Mekong are wide, meandering for 2,390 km through the Khorat plateau of Thailand, the Annamese Cordillera, and Cambodia, from where it eventually enters South Vietnam to form a wide delta.

Bhaisajyaguru. Behind Sarvavid Vairocana is a full set of the Derge *Kangyur*. Lastly, on the east wall near the exit, you will pass Eleven-faced Avalokiteshvara and the protector deities including Remati. One thousand small statues of Padmasambhava surround these principal images.

The **middle storey**, which has recently undergone much restoration, contains images of Padmasambhava, Ardokta surrounded by *naga*-spirits, and Shakyamuni flanked by his foremost students and the 16 Elders. The murals here depict the Taklung lineage, the 100 Peaceful and Wrathful Deities, and 1,000 aspects of Amitayus. The **upper storey**, entered from the open rooftop gallery, contains images of Amitayus, the late Panchuk Rinpoche and Sangye Yarjon, as well as a reliquary of the late preceptor, Khenpo Pema Rangdrol, who was instrumental in maintaining the tradition through recent difficult times. It also houses the Derge *Kangyur*, 400 small images, and the riding saddle and sword of Ling Gesar, which are kept behind the beams. The rebuilding at Riwoche is currently supervised by Tendzin Tulku, Lama Orgyan, Mr Ngadra, who is a relative of the late Kangyur Rinpoche, and Kunga, the son of the present Jedrung Rinpoche. In Toronto, Canada, the Riwoche Society founded by Lama Sonam Topgyel has actively sought to promote the Riwoche lineage overseas and contributes to the various restoration projects.

Riwoche to Nangchen

From **Riwoche Tsuklakhang** the motorable road continues northwest for 76 km, following the Dzi-chu upstream, before cutting northeast to **Jikto** and descending to **Chakzamka** on the Ngom-chu branch of the Mekong. Here there is a small Gelukpa monastery called **Gozhi Tubden Dorjeling**. After crossing the river at Chakzamka, the road traverses the TAR-Qinghai border at **Shoknga** to enter the Nangchen district of Kham. Immediately above the border checkpoint is **Netengang**, the seat of the great Nyingmapa *terton* Chogyur Dechen Zhikpo Lingpa (1829-1870). For a description of the road from Nangchen to Riwoche, see page 525.

Chakzamka to Chamdo

From Chakzamka, there is also a trekking route which follows the Ngom-chu branch of the Mekong downstream to **Zamka** township. Below Zamka, the track becomes motorable as far as **Chamdo** (89 km). A turn-off on this road at **Zo** village, between Zamka and Sagang leads to the **Matsala Coal Mines**.

Riwoche to Chamdo

The highway from Ratsaka to Chamdo (105 km) follows the Dzi-chu downstream to the farming village of **Ngamda**, where a trail branches off to the southwest for Lhorong county via the **Yikdruk La** pass (4,998 m). There is an attractive Gelukpa monastery here, with a series of the eight stupas by its entrance.

At **Teda** the highway leaves the Dzi-chu valley and ascends **Zholpel La** or Trugu La pass (4,688 m), at the southern extremity of the high **Tanyi Tawun** range. The terrain beyond the pass is a spectacular fusion of alpine conifer and deciduous forest. If you cross in the summer or early autumn, the rich diversity of the forest hues never ceases to amaze. **Trugu Gonpa** of the Gelukpa school is located on a forested alpine crag, clearly visible on the descent. The road continues plunging deeply through this forest to emerge in the Ngom-chu valley at **Guro** (sometimes written Karu), an important neolithic site, 19 km above Chamdo, where pottery, bone artefacts and stone walls were excavated between 1978-1979.

Chamdo County ཆབ་མདོ

→ *Population: 89,570. Area: 9,800 sq km. Colour map 4, grid A2.* 昌都县

Chamdo (literally meaning 'river confluence') usually refers to the **city of Chamdo** (Chamdo Drongkhyer) which straddles the Mekong at the point where its Ngom-chu and Dza-chu branches converge. It may also refer to **Chamdo prefecture** (Chamdo Sa-khul), which is the administrative headquarters for 15 counties of Kham, extending from Tengchen to Jomda in the north and from Pasho to Tsakalho in the south. In addition, it may refer specifically to **Chamdo county** (Chamdo Dzong), a triangular-shaped wedge of territory which includes the upper reaches of these Mekong branch rivers and the Lhato and Menda areas, which lie respectively on the Ri-chu and Ke-chu tributaries of the Dza-chu. It is expected that the recent decision to give Lhato and Menda a separate county status will soon be implemented, when these areas will have their own county towns at **Topa** and **Sibda** respectively. At present, the county and prefectural capitals are located in Chamdo city, one of the largest conurbations of East Tibet.

Distances The distance from Chamdo to Lhasa is 1,066 km via Nakchu; and 1,179 km via Kongpo. The distance from Chamdo to Derge is 345 km; and to Kunming 1,789 km.

Chamdo City → *Altitude: 3,600 m. For listings, see pages 424-427.*

The city of Chamdo is located at a strategically important crossroad, where highways intersect and the Mekong headwaters converge. It is therefore a town of bridges – three crossing the Ngom-chu, three crossing the Dza-chu, and yet another spanning their combined waters. Although the expansion of the city in recent decades has been curtailed by the narrow ravines of the Mekong tributaries, which offer only limited space for construction, there is now an ambitious plan to widen the valley by building over the river confluence.

The Northern Approach Approaching Chamdo from Riwoche (105 km), you will reach the Ngom-chu (Mekong) valley at **Guro** and follow the west bank of that river downstream. Just north of town, the road crosses to the east bank, entering the city on **Gyelsung Lam** (Chotrika), between the Ngom-chu and the hilltop citadel of Kalden Jampaling Monastery. Passing large military garrisons, you drive down into **Ozer Lam** (Daratang) which forms a T-junction with **Dekyi Lam** (Sarkyelam/Zetsongsing), the original commercial heart of the city.

Dekyi Lam If, at this point, you turn right on **Dekyi Lam** to cross the newest suspension bridge over the Ngom-chu (alongside the old footbridge), you will quickly reach the administrative heart of the city on Zetotang Lam (Ch. Changdu Xi Lu). If you turn left, you will pass on the north side of the street the Xinhua Bookstore, the Chamdo City Government Buildings, the Commercial Hotel, the local police station; a number of tea houses and coffee shops, including the Derge Teahouse (upstairs), an open square, and the Agricultural Bank. Opposite on the south side there is a small cinema, the Gang-tse Nangma nightclub, the junction with Tromzikhang Lam, China Post and the Post Hotel.

Tromzikhang Lam This street which formerly contained the open-air Tibetan market, has recently been transformed into a wide terraced street of shops and department stores in pseudo-Khampa style (using modern building materials to

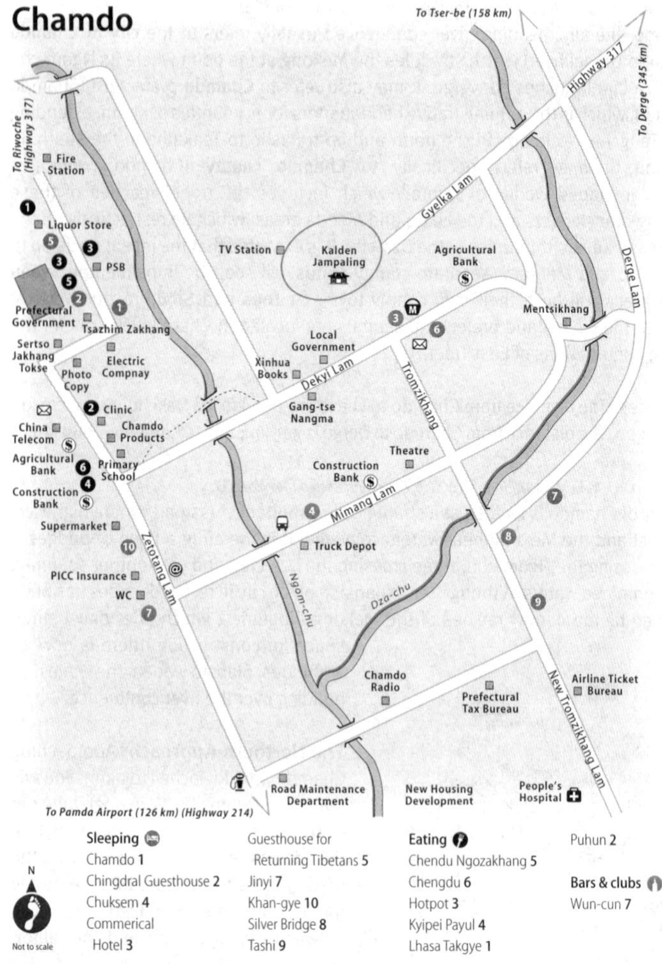

replicate the traditional horizontal red timbers and decorative windows). Descending a wide flight of steps through this new central market (Tromsazhung), you will emerge on to the lower section of Mimang Lam, near the bus station. This bizarrely innovative architecture has not dented the spirits of the Khampa traders, whose traditional merchandise is still displayed in barrows, as they ply their wares alongside the pretentious new stores. Look out for textiles, household artefacts, Tibetan books and the occasional trader who claims to possess antiques. The black-braided coiffure of the Chamdo men and the attractive costumes worn by both sexes contrast with the ill-fitting modern dress of many Chinese migrants – the men wearing oversize jackets with the label showing prominently on the outside of the sleeve and the girls made up like prostitutes!

Mimang Lam At the east end of Dekyi Lam, there is a T-junction, leading on to **Mimang Lam** (Gyelzam drong). Turning left you will now notice the Dza-chu River on the east (right), with Highway 317 (for Derge) winding its way across the hillside on the far bank. On the west (left) side, you will pass the **Chamdo Mentsikhang** before heading down to cross the upper **Dza-chu Suspension Bridge.** Just before the bridge, a lane on the left side of the road called Gyelka Lam (Barongka) leads steeply uphill to **Kalden Jampaling Monastery** and the sky-burial ground, passing the Armed Police Compound on the right.

If you turn right at the T-junction on Mimang Lam, mentioned above, the road forms a crescent that eventually connects with the lower Ngom-chu suspension bridge at the main bus station. Heading in this direction you will notice on the left (east) the turn-off for the middle Dza-chu suspension bridge, and on both sides of the road a number of small Sichuan and Muslim restaurants. Then, after the lower entrance to Tromzikhang Lam on the right, you will pass, on the same side, the Chamdo County Theatre, China Construction Bank, the Chuksem Hotel, and the Bus Station. Opposite, on the left, you will pass New Tromzikhang Lam, the Chamdo Truck Depot and the Transport Guesthouse. Thereafter the road crosses the lower Ngom-chu bridge, where it intersects with Zetotang Lam.

New Tromzikhang Lam Heading south on the newly built extension of Tromzikhang Lam, you will immediately cross the Dza-chu. The turn-off on the left is Highway 317 to Derge. On the corner there are two new hotels: the Silver Bridge (Ngulzam Dronkhang/ Yin Qiao) and the Jinyi (Lobso Dronkhang). Continuing south, you will then pass a turn-off on the right, that leads west across the combined waters of the Ngom-chu and Dza-chu via the **Tsatsatang Bridge**. Along here are the Prefectural Tax Bureau, Chamdo Radio and a large new housing development. Further south, you pass on the left an airline ticket office, a red light district, the Tashi Hotel, the Chamdo Stadium, and an army camp. Opposite on the right there is the People's Hospital.

Zetotang Lam (Ch. Changdu Xi Lu) can be reached by crossing any of the Ngom-chu bridges or the Tsatsatang Bridge. If you take the last of these crossings, you will notice the Chamdo Road Maintenance Department on the left and a petrol station. Turn left (downhill) here and head out of town on Highway 214 for Pomda Airport, Markham and Kunming, or turn right and head uphill for the Chamdo Hotel and the Prefectural Government Buildings.

Heading uphill, you will pass on the left the Wun-cun Bar, a public toilet, the PICC insurance company, the Kham-gye (Khang Sheng) Hotel, a modern supermarket, the Construction Bank, the Kyipei Payul Restaurant, the Chengdu Bar & Restaurant, the Agricultural Bank, China Telecom and a local post office. Opposite on the right, there is an internet café, a primary school, Chamdo Native Products, a clinic, a bookshop, the Puhun Restaurant, and a photocopy store. Directly opposite the Construction Bank there is a lane leading down to the riverside, where an old footbridge (**Chaktak Zampa**) spans the Ngom-chu. On both sides of Zetotang Lam there are new glass-fronted department stores and electrical stores.

Uphill from here, the road opens out into a square. The Chamdo Prefectural Government Buildings are located behind a high enclosure wall on the left, and alongside are a number of small upmarket restaurants and teahouses, among them the second-floor Sertso Jakhang Tok-se. Opposite on the right is the Chamdo Electric Company. The road bends twice at the square before turning north again. On the right (east) side you will pass in succession the Chamdo Hotel, the Public Security Bureau, a Sichuan hotpot restaurant and the fire station. On the corresponding left (west) side you will pass the Tsel-zhim Restaurant, the Mopei Restaurant, the Chengdu Ngozakhang Restaurant, a small hotpot restaurant, the Guesthouse for Returning Tibetans, a liquor store, the Lhasa Ta-gye Tibetan Restaurant, the Prefectural Court and a cinema.

If you head downhill on Zetotang Lam from **Tatsatang Bridge** on Highway 214, after 12 km you will reach the old Chamdo Cement Factory at Karub near **Chaka** township. The factory was recently relocated and expanded following the discovery of another neolithic site here. **Chamdo Airport** is also located on this highway, 126 km to the south, near Pomda.

History Neolithic excavations at **Guro** suggest that the Chamdo area was one of the earliest centres of population on the Tibetan plateau. Exhibits from Guro are on display in the Tibet National Museum at Lhasa. In **Drayab** county to the southeast there are rock carvings attributed to the royal dynastic period; and following he second diffusion of Buddhism the area became a stronghold for the Karma Kagyu tradition. The obvious strategic importance of the Mekong confluence at Chamdo combined with the relatively low altitude and the excellent climate to generate a considerable population density. The high ground above the monastery was chosen as the site for the construction of **Kalden Jampaling** during the 15th century; and ever since control of this area has been regarded as essential for the control of communications between Kham and Lhasa. From 1909-1918 Chamdo was occupied by the Chinese forces of Chao Erh Feng and General Peng, and later in 1950 the fall of Chamdo was a key event in the advance of the PLA into Tibet.

Kalden Jampaling Monastery

The great monastery of **Kalden Jampaling** was founded by Tsongkhapa's student Jangsem Sherab Zangpo between 1436-1444. It formerly had over 1,000 monks and ranked alongside Litang and Kandze among the largest Gelukpa establishments in Kham. However, it had greater prestige and influence insofar as it was the oldest Gelukpa monastery in the region. The development of Kalden Jampaling was maintained over the centuries by the successive incarnations of Pakpalha; whose father, Kuchor Tokden, had been an actual disciple of Tsongkhapa. The other important incarnate successions associated with the monastery were those of Phakpalha's own disciples Zhiwalha and Chakra Tulku.

The original monastery was destroyed in 1912-1913 by Chao Erh Feng, who had captured the town in 1909. After the Chinese retreat following the siege of Chamdo by the Tibetan army in 1917, the monastery was rebuilt, but it was again destroyed during the Cultural Revolution, along with a multitude of precious artefacts – 800-year-old tangkas among them.

During recent renovations, the site of the monastery, which formerly occupied the entire plateau above the town, has been considerably reduced in size. There are five major buildings on the north and east sides of the compound, which have now been restored: the **Gonkhang** (northwest), the **Jamkhang** (north), the **Labrang** (north), the **Dukhang** (northeast), and the **Lhakhang Nyingba** (east). The kitchen and the committee meeting rooms (*uyon lhenkhang*) are located between the Dukhang and the Lhakhang Nyingba, while two monastic residences for the monks who now number 800 have also been renovated to the rear and alongside the main complex. A stupa walkway encircling the whole complex enables pilgrims and townsfolk to circumambulate the monastery and the adjacent television antenna. It offers interesting panoramas of both the Ngom-chu and Dza-chu valleys.

Assembly Hall (Dukhang) The largest building at the monastery is the wide three-storey **Assembly Hall** (*dukhang*), on the right. The vestibule, approached via a broad flight of stairs, has murals depicting the Gelukpa protectors and the Four Guardian Kings, with a panel illustrating the monastic dress code on the left and a fine Wheel of Rebirth on the right. Inside, the wooden floor is well polished and oiled. The red columns and silk pendants lead to the central throne of the Dalai Lama, behind which, in the **inner sanctum**, is an exquisite image of Shakyamuni flanked by his foremost students Shariputra and Maudgalyayana. The altar below this image is in silver and inscribed with the words "Shakyamuni, supreme guide and matchless speaker". On both sides of this central image are statues representing the progenitors of the Gelukpa lineage. Those to the left include (L-R): Tokden Jamyang Lodro, Chakra Pandita, Phakpalha, Zhiwilha, Khenzur Chole Namgyel, Gyelse Darma Rinchen, Tsongkhapa and Khedrup Gelek Pelzang. The statues to the right include (L-R): Atisha with Dromtonpa and Ngok Lekpei Sherab, Purbuchok Ngawang Jampa, Gyelwa Kunga Dechen, Longdol Lama, Jangsem Sherab Zangpo (the founder of the monastery), and

Kalden Jampaling Monastery

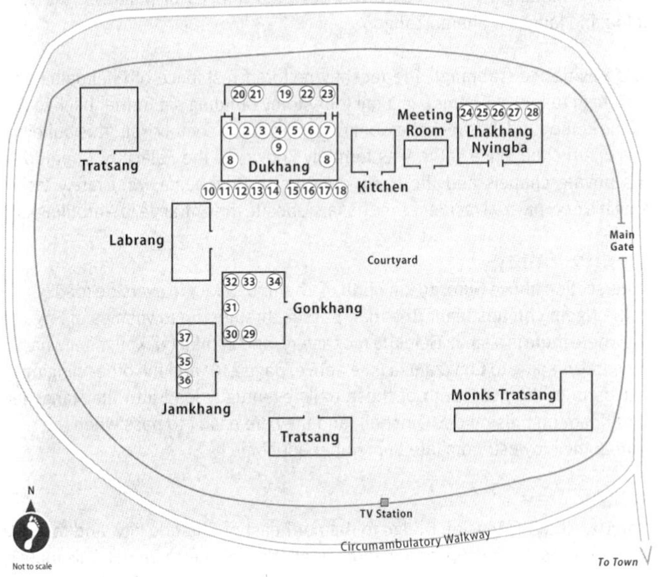

1 Sarvavid Vairocana
2 Hevajra
3 Kalacakra
4 Guhyasamaja
5 Vojrabhairava
6 Cakrasamvara
7 Amitayus
8 8 Medicine Buddhas
9 Throne of Dalai Lamas
10 Vinaya (mural)
11 Tseringma (mural)
12 Nechung Chokyong
13 Shridevi
14 Two Guardian Kings
15 Two Guardian Kings
16 Dudjom Dorje
17 Kongstun Demo
18 Wheel of Rebirth
19 Shakyamum flanked by foremost students
20 Phakpalha
21 Tsongkhapa
22 Atisha
23 Jangsem Sherab Zangpo
24 Vaishravana
25 Standing Manjughosa
26 4-armed Avalokiteshvara
27 Tsongkhapa and foremost students
28 Amitayus
29 Shridevi
30 Guhyajamaja
31 Bhairava
32 Dharmaraja
33 Tutor of Phakpalha
34 Remati
35 Maitreya
36 Phakpalha I
37 Jangsem Sherab Zangpo

 Chamdo Choyang. Other images within the inner sanctum include Maitreya and Amitayus (left) and Manjushri (right). The outer main hall contains images of Sarvavid Vairocana, Hevajra, Kalacakra, Guhyasamaja, Vajrabhairava, Cakrasamvara and Amitayus, while the murals depict the Eight Medicine Buddhas and the protector deities. **Upstairs** there is a shrine dedicated to Jowo Rinpoche, containing an image of Jowo Yizhin Norbu, flanked by Maitreya and Guhyasamaja. The body of the Jowo image is original but the head has recently been replaced. Smaller images of Pakpalha are interspersed with these. There is also an inner chamber on this level where the present Dalai Lama stayed in 1954 en route for Beijing.

Old Temple (Lhakhang Nyingba) To the right of the assembly hall and beyond the kitchen and the committee rooms is the old temple (**Lhakhang Nyingba**), which is at present used as a college for dialectics (*tsenyi tratsang*). Inside (from left to right) are images depicting Vaishravana, Manjushri (standing), Four-armed Avalokiteshvara, Tsongkhapa flanked by his foremost students, Eleven-headed Avalokiteshvara and Amitayus.

Protector Temple (Gonkhang) Situated to the left (northwest side) of the compound, the **Gonkhang** contains images of Bhairava flanked by Four-armed Mahakala and Dharmaraja on the inner wall, Kongtsun Demo, Shridevi, and Guhyasamaja on the west wall, and Remati and the tutor of Phakpalha on the east wall. Upstairs is the library.

Maitreya Temple (Jamkhang) Located to the rear of the protector temple, the newly constructed **Jamkhang** contains large well-sculpted images of Maitreya, the First Phakpalha and Jangsem Sherab Zangpo.

Master's Residence (Labrang) The recently restored residence of Phakpalha and the other main tulkus of Chamdo is a tall four-storey building set further back to the north of the compound, between the Gonkhang and the Assembly Hall. This building, under reconstruction since 1988, was formerly known as the Palace of Chamdo. It contains private chapels and the living quarters of Phakpalha, who rarely visits, preferring his new palatial residence in Lhasa, opposite the entrance to Norbulingka!

Ngom-chu Valley

At the intersection above Guro, 19 km north of Chamdo, take the riverside road which follows the Ngom-chu upstream. The road passes through the townships of **Sagang** (36 km), where there is a small Gelukpa monastery, and **Zamka** (34 km), after which it forks, one trail leading to **Chakzamka** (see above, page 416) and the other clinging to the west bank of the river. Both of these trails eventually lead into the Nangchen district of Kham (in present day Qinghai), and they are easier to pass when the river levels are at their lowest: from late September until March.

Dza-chu Valley

Cross the Dza-chu Suspension Bridge to the northeast of Chamdo city, and take the road which follows the river upstream (rather than the highway to Derge). This route is motorable for 158 km as far as **Tser-be**, passing through **Ridung** and **Kokhyam**, where the Ri-chu tributary flows into the Dza-chu from Lhato. Above Tser-be, a trekking trail continues following the river bank upstream to **Karma** township. En route, it passes through the important **Karma Gon**, the original Karma Kagyu monastery, which was founded in 1147 by the First Karmapa Dusum Khyenpa (1110-1193). Formerly, its 100-pillared Assembly Hall was one of the largest in Tibet, with 12 chapels and outstanding murals depicting the deeds of the Buddha and the history of the Karma Kagyu school. The inner sanctum contained enormous gilded brass images of the Buddhas of the Three Times. The central Shakyamuni image and the sandalwood throne were designed personally by the Eighth Karmapa. The buildings that remain display a unique synthesis of Tibetan, Naxi (Jang) and Chinese styles, indicative of the influence that this school exerted as far south as Lijiang. The reconstructed assembly hall contains the largest image of Maitreya in Chamdo prefecture.

Above Karma, the trail forks at the confluence of the Dza-chu and Ke-chu rivers, the former branch leading to **Nangchen** and the latter to **Zurmang Namgyeltse** – both in present-day Qinghai (see below, page 522).

Lhato

Getting there To reach **Lhato**, there is a new road from **Kokhyam**, but the older road follows the Drugu-chu downstream from **Topa** on the main Chamdo-Derge highway. To reach Topa from Chamdo, follow the Derge highway on the east bank of the Dza-chu, and drive through Tayer township, and across the **Tama La** pass (4,511 m), from where there are fine views of the city. The road is rutted and subsidence is commonplace in the rainy season. A second pass, **Jape La** (4,680 m) is then crossed, offering a clear vista of the ranges around Lhato and Nangchen (north) and around Drayab and Gonjo (south). Descending from this pass you arrive at Topa township, in the grasslands of the Drugu-chu valley. The distance from Chamdo to Topa is only 109 km, but the journey can take over five hours! To remedy this, the Dza-chu riverbank road from Chamdo is currently being paved and extended through Kokhyam to Topa, thereby avoiding these difficult passes. When completed in 2005 the journey from Chamdo via Topa to Derge will be considerably easier. ▸▸ *For listings, see pages 424-427.*

One of the five formerly independent kingdoms of Kham, **Lhato** comprises the river valley of the Ri-chu and those of its tributaries: the Drugu-chu and the A-chu. According to a recent directive, this area will soon be governed from Topa county town, independent of Chamdo county. The Ri-chu rises northeast of Lhato township, in the stunning limestone crags of the **Tanyi Tawun** range (5,082 m) which thrust upwards through the red sandstone landscape. It flows southeast to **Lhato**, where it is joined by the Drugu-chu, and then due west to converge with the Dza-chu at **Kokhyam**. The most important monastery in the upper Ri-chu valley is **Dzodzi Gon**.

The A-chu follows a parallel southeast course to enter the Drugu-chu, south of Lhato. In the nomadic grasslands of this **A-chu** valley, is the famous Drukpa Kagyu monastery of **Khampagar**, founded during the 18th century by the Fourth Khamtrul Chokyi Nyima under the inspiration of his great predecessor the Third Khamtrul Ngawang Kunga Tendzin (1680-1728). Formerly there were two temples here and over 300 monks, with 200 affiliated branches throughout this part of Kham. An important college was founded at Khampagar by the late Khamtrul Dongyud Nyima, who also established a vital branch monastery in exile at Tashijong, Northwest India.

Ke-chu Valley

Getting there Two trails lead to **Menda** from Chamdo – one via Lhato and Pangri; and the other following the Ke-chu downstream from its source near **Chunyido** and via **Sibda**. Sibda has recently been designated as the new county town from which the Ke-chu valley will soon be governed. Another approach, motorable by jeep, can be made from Zurmang Dutsitil in Qinghai province (see below, page 521).

Menda township is located in the extreme northeast of Chamdo county at the confluence of the Ke-chu and the Kyang-chu. The Ke-chu rises in southeast Lhato and flows northwest in an arc to Menda on the frontier of TAR and Qinghai, where its waters are swollen by the Kyang-chu, flowing south from **Zurmang Dutsitil** (see page 521). Southwest of Menda, the river is joined by the Tsi-chu, which flows south from **Zurmang Namgyeltse**, and the combined waters then converge with the Dza-chu branch of the Mekong above Karma Gon. The entire region bounded by the Tsi-chu and Ke-chu rivers, including Zurmang, is sometimes known as **Tsi-ke.** The landscape is typically nomadic, interspersed by these fast-flowing Mekong tributaries. Historically, the Karma Kagyu and the Nyingmapa traditions have both maintained a strong presence in Tsi-ke.

Sleeping

Nakchu City *p407, map p407*
C **Grassland Telecom Hotel**, T0896-3828888. Newly opened and comfortable, has doubles at ¥480 and triples at ¥280.
C **Nakchu Hotel**(Ch Naqu Fandian) on 262 Senidong Lam, T0896-3822424/3822463. A 3-storey building with 88 rooms, deluxe at ¥480, singles and doubles at ¥320-360 and 4-bed rooms at ¥30 per bed. Accommodation is adequate, but the attached bathrooms lack running hot water, which has to be supplied by thermos flasks. The hotel has its own shop, karaoke bar, and 2 restaurants.
E **Bus Station Hotel**, has doubles and triples at ¥50-60.
E **Western Hotel** (Ch Xibu Binguan), next door to the Nakchu Hotel. Doubles at ¥100-160, triples at ¥95, and 4-bed at ¥100.

Sok Tsanden Zhol *p409*
E **Bus Station Hotel** (Tib Soktreng Yulkor Khang), T08078-2261. Has 9 clean rooms with comfortable beds (¥60 per bed, ¥240 per 4-bed dorm).
E **Government Guesthouse**, has poor rooms, doubles at ¥100.
E **Huopi Guesthouse**, also has inferior accommodation, at ¥25-30 per bed.
E **Yigzam Guesthouse**, has clean rooms (¥30 per bed) adjoining a small compound.
NB Barking dogs are unavoidable at night.

Tengchen *p411*
E **Grain Department Guesthouse (Drurik Dronkhang)**, T0895-4592141. Has 4-bed rooms with sofas and wooden floors at ¥80-150.
E **Pengsheng Hotel**, T0895-4592662. Has new and clean rooms (doubles at ¥100), with public showers near the entrance (¥5).
E **Tengchen Government Guesthouse**, left of the square. Has doubles at ¥60, and triples (¥15 per bed, ¥45 per room).
E **Forestry Guesthouse**, next to the school below the motor road. Has very basic accommodation (¥25 per bed).

Ratsaka *p413*
E **Grain Department Guesthouse (Drurik Dronkhang)**, T0895-4502253, on the south side of the main street. Has 8 fairly comfortable rooms, at ¥60 per bed.
E **Post Hotel (Yikzam Dronkhang)**, has 4-bed rooms, at ¥120.
E **Riwoche Government Guesthouse (Sizhung Nelen Khang)**, T0895-4502257, on the north side of the street. Recently refurbished, with best rooms upstairs (range: ¥100-200), and simpler rooms below (¥15 per bed and ¥45 per room).

Chamdo City *p417, map p418*
C **Chamdo Hotel (Qamdo Hotel)**, 22 Zetotang Lam (Changdu Xi Lu), T0895-4825998, F0895-4821428. Has over 150 rooms on 4 floors (no elevator), some in the deluxe category recently refurbished with fine wooden floors and functional attached bathrooms (hot water in evenings), including doubles at ¥260, deluxe doubles at ¥320, triples at ¥300, and deluxe suites at ¥580. The hotel has a business centre, a chess room, ticketing services, a lobby hairdresser and beauty salon, a banquet hall, a seasonal outdoor BBQ Restaurant, and the Chafing Chinese Restaurant, which is decidedly overpriced. IDD and DDD calls can be made from the lobby using ICC phone cards.
D **Kham-gye Hotel (Khang Sheng Bin guan)**, Zetotang Lam, T0895-4823168. Has rooms (attached bath) including deluxe doubles at ¥160, single suites at ¥160, deluxe suites at ¥280, standard doubles at ¥80 and triples at ¥105. The hotel is new, comfortable and owned by the grain department.
E **Post Hotel (Draksi Dronkhang)**, T0895-4826925, Mimang Lam, above China Post. Has new rooms, superior twins at ¥100, and economy doubles at ¥80.
D **Silver Bridge Hotel (Ngulzam Dronkhang/ Yin Qiao Binguan)**, New Tromzikhang Lam, T0895-4827919. Has deluxe singles at ¥200, standard doubles at ¥100, and ordinary doubles at ¥80. The deluxe

and standard rooms have hot water morning and evening, and the ordinary rooms have no attached bath. Best rooms overlook the Ngom-chu and Dza-chu confluence.

Some of the following budget hotels may or may not be allowed to accept foreigners:
E **Chuksem Hotel**, Mimang Lam, T0895-4826919, next to bus station.
E **Commercial Hotel (Nyotsong Kungsi Dronkhang)**, Mimang Lam.
E **Guesthouse for Returning Tibetans**, Zetotang Lam, opposite PSB.
E **Jinyi Binguan (Lobso Dronkhang)**, New Tromzikhang Lam.
E **Jinsu Hotel (Serdang Nyemei Dronkhang)**, Mimang Lam, T0895-4823518.
E **Tashi Hotel**, New Tromzikhang Lam, T0895-4827545.

Topa *p423*
Topa has a number of small guesthouses.
Topa Wangtang Hotel, T0895-4512996. Has 10 clean and simple rooms at ¥10 per bed (¥20-40 per room), and a good restaurant with friendly staff.

Eating

Nakchu City *p407, map p407*
There are a number of small street restaurants near the Nakchu Hotel. Sichuan, Muslim and Tibetan food.

Sok Tsanden Zhol *p409*
There is a good Sichuan restaurant, northeast of the Government Guesthouse, on the main road, and a public bathhouse (open Wed, Sat and Sun).

Tengchen *p411*
For Sichuan cuisine, try the Dingqing Jiujia Restaurant, or the nearby restaurant and shop that are attached to the Tengchen Guesthouse.

Ratsaka *p413*
There are Sichuan-style restaurants and small shops on both sides of the street near hotels.

Chamdo City *p417, map p418*
There are many street restaurants of varying qualities in the upper and lower parts of town.

Simpler Chinese and Muslim restaurants are found near the bus station.
Chengdu Bar & Restaurant, Zetotang Lam. Sichuan hotpot.
Chengdu Ngozekhang, opposite the Chamdo Hotel. For excellent Sichuan dishes.
Derge Teahouse, on Dekyi Lam. For Tibetan and Chinese tea.
Kyipei Payul Restaurant, Zetotang Lam. For noodles.
Mopei Zakhang, opposite the Chamdo Hotel. For excellent Sichuan dishes.
Puhun Restaurant, for noodles
Sertso Jakhang Tok-se, next to the Prefectural Government Buildings on Zetotang Lam. For Tibetan and Chinese tea.

Bars and clubs

Chamdo City *p417, map p418*
Nangma, Dekyi Lam. Nightclub offering some relief from the tedium of this brave new world.
Wun-cun Bar, Zetotang Lam.

Entertainment

Tengchen *p411*
In the square outside the hotel compound gates, there are karaoke bars, pool tables, etc.

Chamdo City *p417, map p418*
The Sports Stadium is to the south of the city, on New Tromzikhang Lam. There are 2 cinemas, one on Zetotang Lam behind the Prefectural Court, and the other downtown on Dekyi Lam, and numerous video parlours.

Shopping

Chamdo City *p417, map p418*
Books
Xinhua Bookstore, Zetotang Lam and Dekyi Lam.

Handicrafts
For textiles, Khampa knives, metalwork, jewellery, and traditional religious or household artefacts, try the open-air market (Tromzikhang).

Modern goods
There are large glass-fronted department stores in Zetotang Lam, selling groceries, electrical goods, ready-to-wear clothes and so forth. Official currency exchange is impossible; but a few market traders will

accept payment in US dollars. It is best to change currency in Lhasa, Kunming or Chengdu long before reaching Chamdo.

Photography
Print film and processing are available at the department stores, and smaller electrical shops in town.

Stamps
Stamps and EMS express services are available at China Post on Dekyi Lam, and at the branch post office on Zetotang Lam.

Transport

Nakchu City *p407, map p407*
Routes from Nakchu From Nakchu, if you wish to continue travelling to **Amdo** and **Ziling** on Highway 109, retrace the route west out of town, and then turn north onto the highway. Those intending to take the northern route or central route to Chamdo should turn left (east) on exiting from the Nakchu Hotel, and drive along the dirt road (Highway 317). This leads out of town over the ridge, and across the Langlu La pass (4,300 m), through **Khormang** township, and via the Jangkhu La pass (4,700 m) to **Shakchuka**, where the motor road cuts across the Shak-chu valley. The Shak-chu flows southeast from its upper reaches in Nyenrong county to its confluence with the Nak-chu in Driru county. There are truck-stop and restaurant facilities at Shakchuka. Try the Zigong Fanguan for Sichuan cuisine. The distance from Nakchu to Khormang is 49 km, and from Khormang to Shakchuka township, another 49 km.
Bus Buses depart the South Bus Station daily for Lhasa (¥73) and Kermu (couchette, ¥150); and there are also infrequent services to Sok Dzong (¥55), Bachen (¥65), Driru (¥60), and Lhari (¥25).

Chamdo City *p417, map p418*
Most visitors to Chamdo, whether arriving from Lhasa, Nangchen, Kunming or Chengdu, will have their transportation organized by the travel services because military and police permit restrictions still apply.
Air Chamdo Airport, located in Pomda township, 126 km south of town, is reckoned to be the world's highest civilian airport. China South-west Airlines have connections to from **Chengdu** on Tue, Wed, Sat and Sun (1 hr 5 mins) at ¥750, and from **Lhasa** (55 mins) on Thu at ¥720. Taxis and landcruisers are available from the airport (range ¥60-100), and there is also an airport bus service (¥40).

Bus Public buses run from the main bus station on Mimang Lam to the following destinations: **Drayab** (0900 and 1600 daily at ¥25); **Riwoche** (1000 alternate days at ¥50); **Dzogang** (0800 daily at ¥65); **Jomda** (0700 weekly at ¥50); **Markham** (0800 weekly at ¥100); **Dechen** (0700 weekly at ¥170); **Chengdu** (1100 daily at ¥200-300); and **Lhasa** (on the 4th, 10th, 15th and 20th of each month at ¥240).

Car/jeep Long distance car and jeep transportation is more easily available from Lhasa, but occasionally through the Chamdo Transport Depot, opposite the bus station.

Taxi Operate within the town (¥5 flat rate).

Directory

Tengchen *p411*
Government buildings and public security bureau are located on a side road to the left, which adjoins the square near the Guesthouse entrance.

Chamdo City *p417, map p418*
Banks China Agricultural Bank, Dekyi Lam. China Construction Bank, Mimang Lam Subsidiary branch on Zetotang Lam. **NB** Foreign exchange is not yet available. Best to change money in Lhasa or Chengdu. **Hospitals** Peoples' Hospital, New Tromzikhang Lam, T0895-21745 (direct), T0895-22965 (inpatients), T0895-22947 (outpatients). Military Hospital. Chamdo Hospital of Tibetan Medicine, Mimang Lam.
Internet Internet Bar, on Lower Zetotang Lam. **Post offices** China Telecom, Zetotang Lam, adjacent to Chamdo Prefectural Government Buildings. Sells ICC cards for IDD and DDD calls. **Tour companies** Chamdo Travel Service, 24 Zetotang Lam, T0895-4821273, F0895-4821197. Chamdo Tourism Bureau, 20 Zetotang Lam, T0895-4821376,

F0895-4822009. **Useful addresses** Chamdo Prefectural Police and Public Security Bureau, Zetotang Lam near Chamdo Hotel, responsible for monitoring the movement of foreigners and will fine those whose military and police permits are out of order. Chamdo City Police, Dekyi Lam, opposite open-air market.

Lhasa to Chamdo: via Driru

The central route from Lhasa to Chamdo (1,316 km), which is rarely travelled on account of the difficult road surfaces, corresponds largely to the old caravan trail, which was followed by pilgrims and traders alike for centuries before the construction of the northern and southern highways. In its initial section, the route is identical to the northern highway, passing through ***Damzhung, Nakchu*** *and* ***Shachuka****. After* ***Drilung****, a branch road leaves the highway, cutting southeast to enter the main Salween gorge in Driru county. This is the ancient trading route, which passes through three present-day counties:* ***Driru****, which is administered from Nakchu, as well as* ***Pelbar*** *and* ***Lhorong****, which are administered from Chamdo.*

Driru County འབྲི་རུ → *Pop: 46,635. Area: 11,295 sq km. Map 6, grid C6.*

Leaving Highway 317 at the turn-off for Driru (see above), you will pass 比如县 through **Chaktse** township after 39 km, and then cross the **Dam-ne La** (5,013 m). The barren landscapes of the upper Salween tributaries now give way to a forested valley, passing through **Traring**, where the Ka-chu River comes in from the southwest to swell the combined waters of the Nak-chu and Shak-chu. **Naksho Driru**, the county capital, is located 16 km downstream in the Salween gorge. Timber is the main industry and logging trucks can frequently be seen plying the road between Driru and Nakchu. The region is characterized by small Gelukpa monasteries interspersed with those of the Bonpo, representing two distinct phases of religious propagation.

The south of the county is bordered by the snow peaks of the **Nyenchen Tangla** range, which forms a watershed between the Salween and the Brahmaputra. Approach roads lead into this region from Naksho Driru. One of the peaks, **Sepu Gangri**, has been filmed in the course of two recent expeditions led by Chris Bonington.

From Naksho Driru, there are two tracks leading towards **Pelbar** (see below, page 428). Of these, the southeast track is the motorable **central route to Chamdo**. It crosses **Zha La** pass (5,090 m) after 27 km, and descends via Sentsha (after 35 km), and Benkar (after 8 km), to join the Kyil-chu tributary of the Salween. It then heads due east to **Sateng** township in Pelbar county, 59 km distant, where the Kyil-chu converges with the Salween. The other track is a trekking route, which heads east from **Naksho Driru**, following the main Salween gorge, through **Bompen** and **Chamda**, and on downstream to Sateng. The forests of this middle Salween region are delightful but rarely visited on account of the treacherous road conditions.

Lhari County ལྷ་རི → *Pop: 25,083. Area: 7,483 sq km. Colour map 2, grid A6.* 嘉黎县

The remote county of Lhari comprises the upper reaches of the **Reting Tsangpo River** (which eventually flows into the Kyi-chu at Pondo) and the feeder rivers of the **Yi'ong Tsangpo** (which eventually joins with the Parlung Tsangpo to merge with the Brahmaputra northeast of Mount Gyala Pelri). This sparsely populated nomadic area holds strong allegiance to the Nyingmapa tradition, particularly the teachings of the treasure-finders Sangye Lingpa (14th century) and Nyima Drakpa. The county capital is located at **Takmaru** in the Yi'ong Tsangpo valley, which can be approached most easily from a turn-off on Highway 109 to the south of Nakchu, that leads via Artsa.

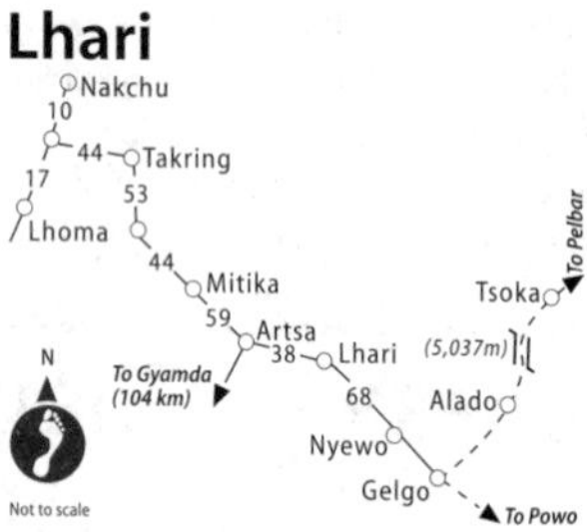

Lhari

Nakchu 10 44 Takring 17 53 Lhoma 44 Mitika 59 Artsa 38 Lhari 68 Nyewo Gelgo To Gyamda (104 km) (5,037m) Tsoka To Pelbar Alado To Powo N Not to scale

Ins and outs

About 10 km south of Nakchu on Highway 109, there is a motorable side road to the east, which follows the Nak-chu downstream to Taksar and then cuts across the **Shilok La** pass (5,100 m) and the **Apa La** pass (5,140 m) in quick succession to enter the upper Reting Tsangpo valley. At **Mitika**, the road crosses the Reting Tsango via the Miti Tsangpo Zamchen bridge, and then it ascends to cross another watershed to reach **Artsa**, on the banks of the Zhung-chu. Artsa is 202 km driving distance from Nakchu City, and the county capital is located at **Takmaru**, a further 38 km downstream from Artsa.

Trekking access

Trekking routes also lead to Artsa from Gyamda, Drigung and Reting. The trail from **Gyamda** (104 km) in the south, which is part of an old trade route linking Lhasa with Chamdo, is motorable for much of the way, as it follows the Nyang-chu upstream to its source, before crossing **Tro La** pass (4,890 m) to reach the scenic **Lake Artsa**. The latter trails follow the **Reting Tsangpo** upstream through the townships of **Sebrong**, **Drakar** and **Sangpa**.

Below Takmaru, the Zhung-chu merges with the Sung-chu (source above Lharigo), and thereafter is known as the **Nye-chu**. The road follows this river downstream for 68 km to **Nyewo** township. Below Nyewo, the Zha-chu tributary joins the river from the northeast at **Gelgo**, and their combined waters are then known as the **Yi'ong Tsangpo**. The motor road presently does not continue beyond this point; but trekking routes follow the Yi'ong Tsangpo downstream into **Po-me** county (see below, page 430) and the Zha-chu tributary upstream through **Alado** to the Brahmaputra-Salween divide.

Trekking

Taking the last mentioned trail, the Salween basin can be reached within four days' trek. From **Nyewo to Alado** the trail is particularly difficult and precipitous, passing through the gorge of the Zha-chu rapids. Above **Alado**, the trail through the upper Zha-chu valley becomes easier, passing Ngodroke township and the monasteries of **Arig** and **Namgyel**. Eventually it crosses the watershed pass of **Shargang La** (5,037 m) in the Nyenchen Tanglha range, and connects with the motorable Pelbar-Chamdo road at **Tsoka** in the Salween basin. On the ascent of Shargang La, there are wonderful views of the high 6,000 m peaks of this barrier range.

Pelbar County དཔལ་འབར

→ *Population: 30,441. Area: 8,641 sq km.*
Colour map 2, A6. 边坝县

Pelbar county is the thickly forested region of the middle Salween basin, extending from **Sateng** township in the northwest as far as **Rayul** in the northeast, and including the north- flowing tributaries of the Me-chu and the Gye-chu. In the southwest of the county the Nyenchen Tanglha watershed range forms a formidable barrier. The capital is located at **Domartang**, 177 km west of **Dzitoru** in Lhorong county.

The central route to Chamdo cuts southeast from Sateng, following the course of the Salween on a newly constructed 88-km road to **Domartang** in the Me-chu valley. The track is motorable but hard to traverse during the summer months. Trekking routes also reach the capital from Driru county (see above, page 427) and from **Tengchen** county (see above, page 411). At **Tsoka** , 4 km south of Domartang and below the village of **Orgyen Tamda**, where there was once an important Nyingmapa temple, another old trade route runs southwest through the Nyenchen Tanglha range. This track is not yet motorable. Crossing **Shargang La** pass (5,037 m), it eventually reaches **Alado** and **Nyewo** in **Lhari** county (see above).

The Chamdo road runs east from Tsoka, traversing the upper reaches of the Me-chu and Gye-chu tributaries. En route it passes through **Pelbar** township (27 km), and **Lhatse** township (3 km), each of which has a Gelukpa monastery. From Lhatse a southerly trekking route also crosses the watershed and follows the Jepu Tsangpo downstream to **Poto**.

Lhorong County ལྷོ་རོང་ → *Pop: 41,134. Area: 6,728 sq km.* 洛隆县

The county of Lhorong is (in Tibetan terms) a densely populated area of the middle Salween basin through which the river completes its east-flowing course and turns south in the direction of Tsawagang. The county capital is located at **Dzitoru**, 177 km from **Domartang** in Pelbar and 187 km west of the paved Highway 214, which links **Pomda Airport** with Chamdo.

There is a trekking route which follows the main Salween gorge downstream on the north bank from **Rayul** through Ngulsho and Shingrong townships, and thence to **Zhabye**. However, the main central highway runs further south from Lhatse and crosses the Dakwang-chu tributary to reach Shopado and Dzitoru after 117 km. **Shopado** was formerly the seat of the Martsang Kagyu school in Tibet, and its main monastery was extensive, with 12 chapels and over 200 monks at its height. At **Dzitoru**, the modern county capital, the Gelukpa tradition predominates, its monasteries for the most part being affiliated to Chamdo.

Trekking

A four-day trekking route follows the Dakwang-chu downstream from **Shopado** to its Salween confluence and thence via the Dak-chu valley on the north bank to **Khyungpo Tengchen** (see above, page 411). Another motorable 55-km side road from **Dzitoru** heads southeast, initially following the Malatso-chu tributary, and then cutting across a watershed pass to **Nakchok**. Below Nakchok, the southeast flowing tributaries: Dzi-chu, Pel-chu, and Dungtso-chu converge with the Salween, now itself plunging southwards.

Dzitoru to Chamdo

The main road from Dzitoru to Chamdo continues eastwards as far as old **Lhorong township** (36 km), and then crosses the Salween at Zhabye Zampa bridge. After **Mar-ri** (90 km from old Lhorong) it crosses the Salween/Yu-chu divide, and passes into the border area of Riwoche, Pasho and Drayab counties.

The 18th-century **Dolma Lhakhang**, the seat of Akong Rinpoche, who resides at Samye Ling in Scotland, is located at **Dolma-ne**, near **Chakdado** in the upper Yu-chu valley, 24 km beyond Mar-ri.

Further south within its vicinity at **Kulha Drak**, there is a Padmasambhava meditation cave known as Zangtal Yeshe Puk, and a Bonpo power place with many grottoes. Generally in Tsawagang, Kulha Drak is revered as the power place of buddha-body, Dolma-ne as the power place of buddha-speech and **Dorje Drilkar** as the power-place of buddha-mind. A trail crosses the **Yikdruk La** pass (4,998 m) to reach Riwoche; while a jeep track leads south to **Tangkar** township in Pasho county (42 km).

The main road follows the upper Yu-chu for 37 km as far as **Shayak** township (in Pasho county), where it connects with the southern route to Chamdo on the paved Highway 214. From **Shayak to Chamdo via Kyitang** the distance is 87 km.

Lhasa to Chamdo: via Powo

The southern route from Lhasa to Chamdo (Highway 318) is by all accounts the most scenic, and yet road conditions are often precarious, particularly in summer, when glacial melt and rainfall can cause havoc. Most drivers prefer to take the northern route via Nakchu and Riwoche. The southern route into Kham begins on the descent from Serkhyem La pass (4,515 m) in Nyangtri county, and traverses the present-day counties of Po-me and Pasho. The virgin forests and subtropical areas of low-lying Po-me county are unique on the Tibetan plateau. Trails also lead south from the highway into Pemako (Metok), one of Tibet's remote 'hidden lands' and largest wildlife reserves; and into Dzayul where the Lohit River winds its course through tribal areas to join the Brahmaputra in India. The counties of this region are administered from Nyangtri, with the exception of Pasho and Drayab, which are administered from Chamdo. The distance from Lhasa to Serkhyem La is 452 km (via Kongpo Gyamda), and from Serkyem La to Chamdo 653 km. ***Recommended itineraries: 4, 5 and 7. See page 20.*** » *For Sleeping, Eating and other listings, see pages 439-440.*

Po-me County སྤོ་སྨད་ → *Pop: 25,897. Area: 16,072 sq km. Colour map 4, B1.* 波密县

The **Powo** region, nowadays known as Po-me county, includes both **Upper Powo** (Poto) and **Lower Powo** (Po-me). The former comprises the valleys of the Poto-chu and its tributary, the Yarlung-chu, which converge below **Chumdo**. The latter comprises the lower reaches of the Yi'ong Tsangpo and Parlung Tsangpo rivers which converge above **Tang-me** to join the Rong-chu and the Brahmaputra in quick succession, northeast of **Mount Gyala Pelri**. The county capital is located at **Tramog**, 182 km beyond Serkhyem La pass in the lower gorge of the Parlung Tsangpo.

Po-me (Lower Powo) སྤོ་སྨད་

The southern highway descends through a series of switchbacks from **Serkhyem La** to reach the picturesque valley of **Lunang** (see above, page 249) and enter the flowering Rong-chu gorge. There are spectacular views of **Mount Namchak Barwa** (7,756 m) and **Mount Gyala Pelri** (7,150 m) to the east and northeast respectively, as the recently resurfaced road descends into thick forest, passing **Tongjuk** after 46 km, and then **Trulnang**, where there are simple truck station facilities. Below Trulnang, the road reaches its lowest point at **Taktra**, where the Rong-chu converges with the Parlung Tsangpo to flow into the

Brahmaputra gorges. Here, the moist subtropical forests resonate with the constant buzzing of cicadas.

The road surface now deteriorates, susceptible to mudslides in summertime, as it follows the Parlung Tsangpo upstream to its confluence with the Yi'ong Tsangpo.

An even rougher side road extends from this confluence to the northwest through the Yi'ong Tsangpo valley towards **Dra-ke** and **Nyewo** townships. Up here are the Yi'ong and Bencha tea plantations, where the rich yellow soil around the lakeshore of **Yi'ong tso** has been successfully cultivated.

After crossing the Yi'ong Tsangpo and climbing gradually from this confluence, the road conditions improve, following the east bank of the Parlung Tsangpo upstream in a southeast direction. At **Tang-me** (47 km from Tongjuk), there are a number of transport stations offering food and lodging. The best accommodation is found at the Tang-me Zakhang to the south of the road, which has triples at ¥10 per bed and doubles at ¥15 per bed. From the low-lying jungle settlement of Tang-me (1,700 m), the highway continues its gradual ascent, reaching **Kanam** (Khartak), the traditional seat of government in Powo, after 73 km. Here the dirt road surface gives way to a finely paved road.

Kanam The rulers of Kanam traditionally claimed descent from Prince Jatri Tsenpo, the younger son of Tibet's first 'mortal' king, Drigum Tsenpo, who fled here following the death of his father. Henceforth, the **Kanam Depa** was regarded as one of Tibet's princely states until the unification of the county was achieved by Songtsen Gampo in the seventh century. Special privileges were granted to the rulers of Kanam by the Yarlung Dynasty monarchs in recognition of their royal descent. The region maintained its independence from Lhasa in later centuries, despite the military intervention of 1834, which sought to quell civil unrest. Eventually, in 1928, Kanam was absorbed by the government of the Thirteenth Dalai Lama, and its ruler fled to India. In recent times, the most illustrious scion of the house of Kanam has been the late head of the Nyingmapa school, Dudjom Rinpoche (1904-1987).

At Kanam, the Khartak Zampa bridge crosses the Parlung Tsangpo to **Bakha**, where the Nyingmapa residence of Bakha Tulku is located. The main temple here has recently been reconstructed, but it remains an empty shell under the charge of a single caretaker and four monks. The present incumbent lives in the United States.

Trekking A trekking route leads southwest across the **Zholwa La** pass to the Brahmaputra gorge, and thence downstream to **Pemako** (see below, page 433).

Tramog Continuing southeast from Kanam, the highway crosses the entrance to the Poto-chu valley and reaches **Tramog** (2,743 m) the county capital after 16 km, set deep within the thickly forested gorge of the Parlung Tsangpo. Timber, not surprisingly, is the primary source of wealth and industry.

Po-me Drodon Gonpa

Getting there Cross the bridge to the southwest of town, which spans the Parlung Tsangpo and turn west on the far bank. At the next intersection turn left and head steeply uphill to the monastery.

The Nyingmapa monastery of **Po-me Drodon Gon** is located across the Parlung Tsangpo, overlooking the town from a hilltop promontory some 8 km distant. It is a branch of **Takzham Gonpa** near Riwoche (see above, page 413) and the present Takzham Tulku, who resides in Switzerland, has visited on two occasions. The assembly hall has a large inner sanctum, containing (L-R) images of Padmakara, Hayagriva, Four-armed Avalokiteshvara, Padmakara flanked by his consorts Mandarava and Yeshe Tsogyel, Shakyamuni flanked by Shariputra and Maudgalyayana, Amitabha, Takzham Nyingpo,

 Vajrapani, Green Tara and Maitreya. Within the hall there are two thrones, bearing photographs of the late Khenpo Jigpun and the present Takzham Tulku (left) and of Nyarong Rigzin Gyatso (right). The finely executed murals of the upper gallery depict (L-R): Takzham Nyingpo, Shakyamuni, Padmasambhava with his 25 disciples, Vajradhara and Chogyur Dechen Lingpa. Outside in the courtyard, there is a large Mani Wheel chapel. The monastery at present has 20 monks.

Gawalung The forested valleys of Po-me are intimately connected with Padmasambhava, and among them, the cave hermitage of Gawalung, in particular, is revered as the main pilgrimage site associated with buddha-speech throughout Kham. Gawalung is located 24 km southwest of the turn-off for Drodon Gonpa. The road is motorable except in spring and autumn, but not in summertime, when snowmelt swells the flow of a fast-flowing tributary. The great treasure-finders Sanggye Lingpa (1340-1396) and Dudul Dorje (1615-1672) meditated here and discovered treasures at **Pukmoche** and **Takdzong** respectively. Treasure-sites (*terkha*) of Dudul Dorje are to be found, additionally, in the environs of **Mount Namchak Barwa**.

Continuing beyond Gawalung, a cart road (accessible by tractor) crosses **Galung La** pass and heads south for 80 km towards **Pemako** (see below, page 433), at which point it is necessary to trek with porters.

Upstream from Tramog, another trail fords the Parlung Tsangpo and leads into Northeast Pemako via the **Chendruk La** pass.

Side valleys of the Parlung Tsangpo in Po-me Continuing upstream from Tramog and Khamog on the paved highway, the virgin forest is still dense, extending as far as the snow peaks and glaciers, which protect the hidden land of Pemako to the south. Here and there some trees have succumbed to disease, as evidenced by their reddened leaves and bare trunks. After 41 km, you will reach the entrance to the **Chodzong** valley at **Sumdzom,** where a small rebuilt temple stands alongside the ruins of a larger monastery. A motorable track, marked by a large cluster of prayer-flags, branches off here, following the Chodzong Tsangpo upstream for 42 km to **Dorje** township. From here, a trekking route leads across **Kudza La** pass to **Khangyul** in the Salween basin. At Sumdzom itself the paved highway once again becomes a dirt road.

Continuing eastwards from Sumdzom, the side valleys of the Moglung-chu, Yupuk-chu and Midpa-chu rivers are similarly accessible from the highway. Of these, the entrance to **Yupuk valley** is at the township of the same name, located some 34 km southeast of Sumdzom. Above Yupuk, the road continues following the Parlung Tsangpo upstream to its source at the magnificent glacial lake known as **Ngan Tso** (see below, page 436).

Poto (Upper Powo) སྤོ་སྟོད

Upper Powo comprises the valley of the Poto-chu, and those of its main tributaries: the Dong-chu (west) and Yarlung-chu (east), which converge at **Chumdo**.

Getting there From Kanam, leave the Parlung Tsangpo valley, and head north to Chumdo (23 km).

Dong-chu valley The **Dong-chu valley** is intimately associated with the activities of the treasure-finder Dudul Dorje. It was here that he discovered a Guidebook to the Secret Land of Pemako, and practices pertaining to the meditational deities Yamari and Bhairava. In the **Dechen Sangwa** cave in this same valley, he then discovered the text entitled *Gathering of the Entire Intention of the True Doctrine* (*Damcho Gongpa Yongdu*). Below the cave, at **Dechen Tang** he established his main residence.

Above Chumdo, the road follows the Dong-chu as far as **Shulmo** (29 km) and **Yuri** (9 km), before cutting northeast towards the **Zhartse La** pass for a further 30 km. From here, you can trek across the watershed to Lhorong county in the Salween basin. At **Yuri Gango**, there used to be a second temple founded by Dudul Dorje.

Metok County མེ་ཏོག → *Pop: 9,785. Area: 6,787 sq km. Colour map 4, grid B1.* 墨脱县

The **Pemako** region, one-third of which currently lies within Tibet and the remainder within the **Arunachal Pradesh** province of India, is the name given to the wild jungle terrain of the Brahmaputra valley, southeast of the foaming rapids formed where the river plunges 5,000 m through the gorge between the East Himalayan peaks of **Mount Namchak Barwa** and **Mount Gyala Pelri**. Pemako is exposed to the full force of the Assamese monsoon (over 300 cm per annum), and its altitude is low (4,500 to 600 m). The climate is hot, tropical and humid, and its virgin forests form one of the **largest wildlife preserves** on the Tibetan plateau. A haven for bears, wild cats, snakes, leeches, and countless species of insects, the region is even now extremely isolated. No proper motorable road yet links Pemako with the rest of the country. Most supplies are flown in by helicopter from **Nyangtri** to the county capital at **Metok**; and tractors sometimes negotiate the main trail from **Tramog** in Po-me, across the **Galung La** pass. The population is predominantly tribal, comprising the jungle-dwelling **Abor (Lhopa)**, who subsist as hunter-gatherers, and the **Monpa**, who also cultivate the land. Later influxes of Tibetan peoples from Kongpo and Powo have added to the population diversity, and the indigenous Abor have been pushed into peripheral border areas.

Despite the inhospitableness of the terrain, the Pemako region has long been regarded as one of the prime pilgrimage sites in Tibet. When Padmasambhava propagated Buddhism during the eighth century, he included Pemako at the head of a select number of 'hidden lands' (*beyul*), as an ideal environment for Buddhist practice in the future. Even now there are caves and *terma*-sites in Pemako associated with the great master and his 25 Tibetan disciples.

Later, during the 17th century, the treasure-finder Dudul Dorje discovered a pilgrims' guide to Pemako near his hermitage in Poto. Accordingly, the valley was identified as the abode of Vajravarahi, her head at **Mount Gangri Karpo** (northeast), her neck at **Mount Dorjeyang**, her navel at **Mount Rinchenpung**, and her breasts as **Mount Gongdu Podrang** and **Pemasiri**. The gateway to the 'hidden land' is located at **Pemakochung** in the Brahmaputra gorge (see above, page 241). It was only during the late 18th century, that Pemako was formally opened as a place of pilgrimage by Gampopa Orgyen Drodul Lingpa (b 1757), Choling Garwang Chime Dorje (b 1763), and Rikdzin Dorje Tok-me (1746-1797).

Pemako

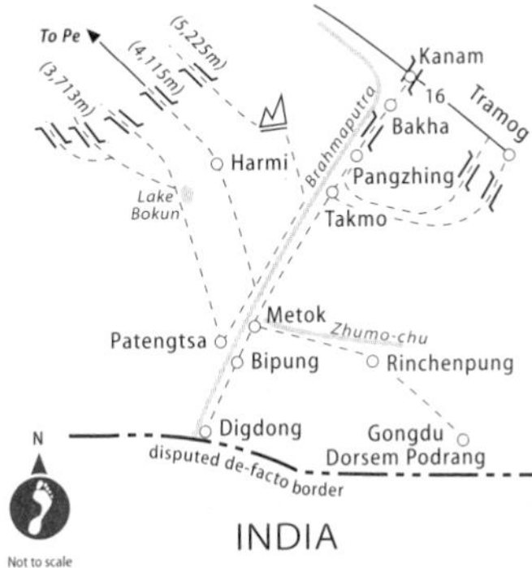

Trekking

Various trekking routes lead into Pemako. From Tramog the most important are via Galung La, Chendruk La, and Pokhung La passes, and from Kanam via Bakha and the Zhowa La pass. From Pe in Kongpo there are most direct trekking routes from Southern Tibet, via the Tamnyen La, the Deyang La (3,713 m), Buddha Tsepung La, Dozhong La (4,115 m) and Nam La (5,225 m). Of these latter passes, **Dozhong La** is the most direct, reaching Metok county town from Pe within four days. The best times to trek from Kongpo are in July or late

 September, but Pemako is a destination recommended only for pilgrims and explorers of great stamina and physical endurance. **NB** In addition to military and police permits, special documents for Pemako also have to be obtained from the Forestry Department in Lhasa.

Metok

Trek across **Zhowa La** pass from Kanam to reach the east bank of the Brahmaputra at **Pangzhing** township, and continue south to **Takmo**, where the Chendruk Tsangpo flows in from the east. The trekking routes from Tramog via Galung La and Chendruk La also converge here.

The main trail continues to follow the east bank of the river downstream to the county capital at Metok. A trail also follows the west bank from **Jarasa** down through **Muknak Gonpa**, to Dezhing township, and thence to **Metok**, which is at the low altitude of 760 m. A trail leads west from this riverside track towards **Mount Namchak Barwa**, and Dudjom Rinpoche's sacred *terma*-site known as **Phurparong**.

Zhumo Valley

From the confluence of the Brahmaputra and Zhumo-chu at Metok, follow the latter upstream to reach **Mount Zangdok Pelri**, and **Rinchenpung Monastery**, where there is a sacred image of Hayagriva. A three-day trek from Rinchenpung leads southeast to **Gongdu Dorsem Podrang** a wildlife sanctuary close to the de facto Indian border, consecrated to the meditational deity Vajrasattva.

Bipung

Bipung or Drepung township lies southwest of Metok on the east bank of the Brahmaputra. Within this township, at **Tirkhung**, is the birthplace of the late Dudjom Rinpoche (1904-1987), former head of the Nyingmapa school. Across on the west bank is the village of **Patengtsa**, from where a three-day trek leads to **Buddha Tsepung La** pass. The valley approaching the pass is the location of the fabled talismanic lake **Chime Dutsi Latso**, otherwise known as **Lake Bokun**, which is set against the backdrop of a sheer forested mountain, its slopes harbouring temples dedicated to Vajravarahi. Phukmoche, a meditation cave of Padmasambhava, is also located here.

A parallel valley leads via **Harmi** and across **Dozhong La** to Kongpo. South of Bipung the trail follows the Brahmaputra downstream, passing through **Digdong** village and thence directly to the de facto Indian border (closed and disputed). The river from this point on is known as the **Dihang**.

Dzayul County རྫ་ཡུལ

→ *Pop: 24,106. Area: 19,693 sq km. Colour map 4, B2.*

Dzayul county comprises the upper reaches of the Dzayul-chu (**Lohit**), which is fed by two main sources: the Zang-chu (east) and the Gangri Karpo-chu (west). These tributaries converge at Lower Dzayul township before flowing south into Arunachal Pradesh. Towards the southeast of the county, is the valley of the Kyita-chu (Burmese: Nmai), a major source of the 2,170 km long **Irrawaddy** River, which rises at the Languela glacier in Dzayul and enters Burma via Yunnan province.

Kyigang

The county capital of Dzayul is located at **Kyigang** (formerly known as **Sangak Chodzong**) in the Zang-chu valley, 258 km southeast of **Sumdzom**, and 172 km southeast of **Rawok**. Dzayul shares its southern borders with India (which controls one third of its territory), Burma, and Gongshan county of Yunnan. The sparse population is both Tibetan and tribal Lopa.

Getting there To reach Dzayul, leave the highway at **Rawok**, and drive southeast across **Demo La** pass. The road follows the Zang-chu tributary of the **Lohit** through **Goyul** township (92 km from Rawok), and thence downstream to **Drowa Gon** (63 km) and the county capital at **Kyigang** (17 km).

Lower Dzayul

After Kyigang, the river changes course southwest, and the motorable road follows it for 61 km as far as its confluence with the Gangri Karpo-chu at **Lower Dzayul township (Dzayul Rong-me)**.

Upper Dzayul

The Gangri Karpo-chu, which rises in the snow range of the same name in Northeast Pemako, passes through **Upper Dzayul** township (Dzayul Rongto) and eventually merges with the Zang-chu at Lower Dzayul township (Dzayul Rong-me). The only motorable stretch is between these townships (66 km), but there are also trekking routes leading northwest from Upper Dzayul to **Pemako** and southeast from Lower Dzayul to **Burma** and **India**.

Salween gorge

The extreme east of the county comprises the lower Salween gorge, from the villages of **Golak** township on the Ralung-chu tributary as far south as Tsawarong, on the east bank of the Salween. This area is described below, page 443, in the context of the **Kawa Karpo** pilgrimage circuit.

NB The Salween in this stretch is not motorable, but trekking routes follow the river downstream from Pasho county, through Golak to Tsawarong. Below Tsawarong, the trail continues downstream into Yunnan.

Pasho County དཔའ་ཤོད

→ Pop: 36,862. Area: 12,580 sq km. Colour map 4, B2.

八宿县

Pasho county, nowadays governed from Chamdo, occupies the Salween/ Brahamaputra watershed on the southern Highway 318. The county capital is located at Pema, 217 km from Tramog in Po-me and 92 km west of Pomda on the paved Chamdo-Kunming Highway.

Rawok

The southern highway from Po-me to Chamdo continues to follow the Parlung Tsangpo upstream to its source, passing through alpine forested landscape for

 127 km as far as **Rawok** township, where it enters Pasho county. The approach to Rawok is truly magnificent, as the road skirts the western and northern shores of the azure lake. ▸▸ *For listings, see pages 439-440.*

Ngan Tso (3,720 m). The lake, which is 26 km long and 2 km wide, is dramatically girded by forests and snow peaks, with the high **Languela glacier** visible on the horizon to the southeast.

Leaving town, the road forks, south-east for Dzayul and north for the Salween divide. A turn-off on the Dzayul road leads to the ruins of the Gelukpa **Shukden Gonpa**, which overlook the shore of neighbouring Rawok Lake. Instead, keep to the highway, which leads steeply uphill on its 23-km ascent of **Ngajuk La** pass (4,468 m). On the ascent, there are outstanding views of the Eastern Himalayan peaks to the southwest.

Pema (Pasho)

Crossing this pass, which forms a watershed between the Brahmaputra and Salween river systems, there are some small lakes, but the beautiful alpine forests quickly recede. The road follows the more arid Ling-chu valley downstream for 67 km to **Pema,** the county capital, located in the mid-Salween basin. En route it passes through **Chidar** township, skirts the hilltop ruins of **Tashitse Dzong** and bypasses **Rangbu Gonpa** to the north.

Pema (3,180 m) is a small one-street town at the heart of the Ling-chu valley. Approach roads are paved on both sides for several kilometres, but the town itself has little to offer except as an overnight stop. Outside town to the north, there are said to be some ancient rock inscriptions associated with Padmasambhava, but this will require further investigation. To the northwest of town the Gelukpa Monastery of **Neru Gonpa** contains a large image of Maitreya in its inner sanctum, and a throne of Phakpalha of Chamdo in its assembly hall. ▸▸ *For listings, see pages 439-440.*

Salween Bridge and Gama La

The paved highway continues to follow the Ling-chu downstream from Pema for 30 km, bypassing a turn-off on the right (south) which leads to **Lingka** township. The ruins of **Nera Gonsar** monastery are visible here. The dirt surface then returns as the road approaches the confluence of the Ling-chu with the Salween at **Po**. Here the highway enters a steep-walled canyon to cross the Salween via the high **Ngulchu Zampa** suspension bridge almost immediately. On the far side of the bridge, the highway tunnels through the bare canyon rocks and then, after **Teto** township, it rises steeply from the gorge through 180 switchbacks to scale the **Gama La** pass (4,839 m). This new road is a feat of engineering, funded by the prefectural government and subcontracted to local army units. Long channels of reinforced concrete have been constructed down the mountainside to divert the summer floods, and ensure that the road will stay open.

Pomda

The descent on the far side of the pass is much more gradual, leading down to the rolling grasslands of **Pomda** in the Yu-chu valley. Here, 92 km from Pema, the southern Highway 318 from Lhasa finally connects with the paved Highway 214 from Chamdo to Kunming. Pomda township (4,084 m) lies 13 km further upstream in the wide Yu-chu valley. It is an important crossroads for traffic heading west to Lhasa, north to Chamdo, and south to Yunnan or Sichuan. A small Gelukpa monastery, named **Pomda Sangak Dechen,** was founded here by Phakpalha Tongwa Donden as a branch of Chamdo. Destroyed by the Bonpo king of Beri in the 17th century, it was subsequently rebuilt by Phakpalha Gyelwa Gyatso. It had 70 monks, and was formerly the main attraction of the valley, prior to the construction of the highway. The assembly hall contains images of Shakyamuni flanked by Manjughosa, Maitreya and Tara, while the inner sanctum has Tsongkhapa with his foremost disciples.

The gently sloping grasslands of the Yu-chu valley (the principal tributary of the Salween) are located in the highlands of **Tsawagang**, north of the Tsawarong (Salween) gorges. **Chamdo Airport** (4,300 m), renowned as the world's highest civilian airport, lies 27 km north of Pomda and 126 km south of Chamdo. The spartan Bangda Airport Hotel has only a few doubles with attached bath at ¥ 240, and these are rarely available. Standard doubles and 4-bed rooms (¥160) have only outside toilet facilities, so this hotel is overpriced and not to be recommended.

Airport to Chamdo

From Pomda Airport the combined highway follows the Yu-chu valley upstream on an excellent paved road surface to **Shayag** (59 km). About 16 km along this road, there is a turn-off on the left (northwest) which connects with the central route to Lhasa via Shabye Zampa and **Lhorong** (see above, page 429). The main road then cuts east across **Larlha** pass (4,572 m), which is a watershed between the Mekong and Salween river systems. On the descent from the pass you will notice the **Dzi-chu** river cutting its way through from Riwoche in the northwest to converge with the Mekong. **Kyitang** (Jyitang) village lies beyond the pass, above the Mekong valley, in Drayab county. From here to Chamdo the distance is only 65 km via **Nyenlha** pass (3,465 m).

Drayab County བྲག་གཡབ → *Pop: 53,577. Area: 9,672 sq km.* 察雅县

Drayab county extends southeast from **Kyitang** on the Pomda-Chamdo highway through the valley of the Me-chu tributary of the Mekong and those of its small feeder rivers, including the Leb-chu and the Do-chu. The county capital is located at **Endun**, 42 km from the intersection, alongside one of the most important Gelukpa monasteries in Kham. The county is also renowned for its ancient rock carvings.

Kyitang

Kyitang township is distinguished by its sturdy houses with flat roofs and horizontal timbers: a typical feature of Khampa domestic architecture. It has a popular roadside Tibetan restaurant, serving wholesome dumplings, noodles and rice dishes. From Kyitang, the road crosses **Nyenlha** pass (3,465 m) and then descends into the Mekong gorge in the direction of Chamdo, quickly reaching the Drayab turn-off at the Me-chu confluence after 10 km.

Nyagre Rock Carvings and Images

In **Nyagre** district of Drayab county, there are ancient rock carvings and statues which suggest that this area had close connections with the Yarlung Dynasty kings of Tibet. At **Denma Drag** (now known as Rinda Dekyiling) there is a relief carving of Vairocana Buddha, said in the *Mani Kabum* to have been commissioned by Princess Wencheng in the seventh century. An important inscription suggests however that the image was actually fashioned in the time of King Tride Songtsen (r. 704-755).

Drayab Endun (Mother Monastery)

Driving through the Me-chu valley from the intersection, after 42 km, you will reach the county capital at **Endun**. In

1621, the First Drayab Kyabgon Ngupe Trakpa Gyatso (1572-1638) founded the Gelukpa monastery of **Drayab Tashi Chodzong** here, and unified the surrounding areas: three agricultural valleys including Nyag-re, and two outlying nomadic tracts. The original monastery became known as the **Magon** ('mother monastery') following the foundation of the **Bugon** ('son monastery') at Jamdun in 1640; and since that time Drayab county has comprised both the **Endun** area, under the authority of the Magon, and the **Jamdun** area under the authority of the Bugon.

Drayab Tashi Chodzong

The monastery rapidly became one of the most influential cultural centres of East Tibet, developing under the guidance of the nine successive Drayab Kyabgon incarnations (also known as Tulku Chetsang) and the successive incarnations of Sangye Tashi, who are known as the Tulku Chungtsang. The monastery housed over 1,000 monks. It was destroyed twice in the 20th century – once by Chao Erh Feng's forces and more recently by the Communists. Reconstruction is proceeding apace through the effort of the local populace and the development project initiated by the Ninth Drayab Kyabgon who resides in Germany.

Of its former 32 temples, which symbolized the 32-deity mandala of Guhyasamaja, a three-storey **Assembly Hall (Dukhang)** has been restored. On the ground level, the spacious **Jamkhang temple** contains images of the Ninth Drayab Kyabgon Loden Sherab, Ngok Lekpe Sherab, Atisha and the protector Ksetrapala, among others. The residence of the Kyabgon is on the third floor of this building. Below the monastery the restored **Drayab Gonkhang** contains images of Dorje Drakden, Dorje Shukden, Ksetrapala (six forms), and Dorje Yudronma, as well as fine murals depicting the 12 Tenma protectors.

Formerly the Magon monastery had 33 branches throughout Drayab county, including the nunnery of **Dolma Ritro** and **Evam Ritro** hermitages. Currently there are about 100 registered monks at the Magon, and approximately 900 unofficial monks.

Jamdun

Further south at Jamdun, there is a life-size stone image of Maitreya, said to have been the central image of a geomantic temple dating from the period of the royal dynasty. Formerly, it was flanked by smaller images of the Eight Bodhisattvas, Princess Wencheng and Minister Gar. In 1265, when Chogyel Phakpa visited Drayab, he identified the main image as Maitreya. Other authorities, such as Karma Chak-me, have stated that a Maitreya temple existed there during the royal dynastic period. At **Kyilechu Nyal**, there is a large stone image of Bhaisajyaguru, the medicine buddha; and at **Langrung-ne Tramo** there is a relief image of Avalokiteshvara, near a temple dedicated to the same deity.

Jamdun Bugon Monastery

Getting there Jamdun is reached by jeep from Endun, via **Rangdrub** township. The other outlying townships of the county, such as **Khora**, are accessible on horseback from Endun or Jamdun. **Wakhar** can however be reached by jeep from Endun (27 km). **Khargang** township is reached 14 km from Kyitang, following the Mekong valley downstream.

The Bugon ('son monastery'), properly known as **Jamdun Ganden Shedrub Chokhor**, was founded at Jamdun, near the ancient stone Maitreya image, by the Second Drayab Kyabgon Ngawang Sonam Lhundrub in 1640. Formerly it housed 1,300 monks and had some 19 branches within the county, including the **Jorkhe Ritro** hermitage, which was once one of the largest nunneries in Tibet, housing 700 nuns at its height. The Bugon was also destroyed twice in the 20th century, first by Chao Erh Feng and then by the Communists. Current rebuilding is under the direction of the Ninth Drayab Kyabgon.

Sleeping

Po-me Drodon Gonpa *p431*

E **Po-me Hotel**, has suites with attached bath (cold water only) at ¥80, and triples at ¥20-30 per bed.

E **Government Grain Department Guesthouse (Mangsi Nelenkhang)**, has doubles with attached bath at ¥25-50 and dormitory beds at ¥10.

E **Po-me Guesthouse**, located at the east end of town, has cheaper rooms.

E **Post Office Guesthouse**, T0894-5423284. Has doubles at ¥40 and singles at ¥50.

E **Transportation Guesthouse**, T0894-5422798, located at the west end of main street. Has singles at ¥60 and triples at ¥40 per bed (heated showers available).

Rawok *p435*

Pingan Guesthouse, near to Transport Guesthouse. Accommodation at this guesthouse is abysmal (¥15 per bed).

Transport Guesthouse, accommodation is poor (¥15 per bed).

There are many excellent campsites near the lake.

Pema *p436*

E **Fukang Hotel**, T0895-4562178. Has doubles at ¥60 and triples at ¥45.

E **Highway Maintenance Guesthouse**, has doubles at ¥80, singles at ¥50, dorm beds at ¥10-20, and hot showers at ¥6 .

E **Post Hotel**, T0895-4562378. Of recent construction, has doubles at ¥50 per room.

E **The Old Post Office Guesthouse**, adjacent to the new hotel, has simpler rooms: doubles at ¥30 and triples at ¥45.

Alternative accommodation may be found at:

Government Guesthouse, west end of town.

Meteorological Bureau Guesthouse, west end of town.

Nera Guesthouse, east end of town.

Drayab *p438*

The town of Drayab (Endun), which lies at 3,660 m, below the Magon Monastery, has simple guesthouse facilities.

Eating

Po-me *p431*

There are some Sichuan and Tibetan-style restaurants in town, among them the **Dzakalo Restaurant**, and small shops on both sides of the street near the hotels.

Rawok *p435*

The township has a number of small Sichuan-style restaurants catering to truck drivers, among which the **Dzayul Restaurant**, opposite the Transport Guesthouse, is the best.

Pema *p436*

There are a few simple Sichuan-style restaurants, the best probably being the **Tianlong** and **Post Hotel** restaurants.

Pomda *p436*

The township has Sichuan restaurant facilities and a transport station guesthouse, beloved by truck drivers. When the southern highway to Lhasa is blocked by landslides or snowmelt in summer, the trucks often remain stationary at Pomda for prolonged periods.

Shudu Fandian, on southwest corner of the township square. For the best Sichuan cuisine in town.

Next door to the Shudu Fandian there is a small Tibetan restaurant serving excellent fresh butter tea.

Drayab *p438*

There are 3 small Sichuan-style restaurants on the main street, and small grocery stores.

Transport

Po-me *p431*

A military **permit** and an alien travel permit issued by the public security bureau in Lhasa are both required for visiting Tramog and any sites within Po-me county. The police are particularly vigilant, and any foreigner arriving in town is required to register with them.

Po-me *p431*
China Telecom sells ICC cards, which can be used for IDD and DDD calls. **China Post** has EMS facilities.

Drayab *p438*
The government buildings and public security bureau are located within a compound at the end of the main street.

Chamdo to Kunming: descent of Yu-chu and Mekong Gorges

The motor route from Chamdo at the heart of Kham to Kunming in Southwest China follows the great waterways of East Tibet and the contours of the high ranges dividing them. The initial section runs along the west bank of the Mekong as far as Kyitang, and, after crossing Larlha pass (4,572 m), hugs the Yu-chu through the grasslands as far south as Dzogang county. Recrossing the Tsawagang range here via Dungda La pass (5,008 m), the road then plunges down to cross the Mekong at Drukha Zampa. Reaching the east bank, it abruptly rises through the Markhamgang range and forks, the eastern branch, known as Highway 318 leading to Batang (on which see below, page 463), and the southern branch, known as Highway 214, leading through Markham and Gartok. Taking the latter turning, the road eventually rejoins the Mekong at Lagyab Sho above Tasakalho, and follows its course downstream as far as Dechen county (in present day Yunnan). On this section there are spectacular views of the Kawa Karpo glaciers (6,740 m). From Dechen, it cuts southeast across the watershed to enter the Yangtze river system, crossing this mighty river twice: in Gyeltang and Jang Sadam (Lijiang) counties. Finally, the highway leaves the Tibetan area and re-enters the Mekong basin near Dali.

*Altogether, the highway traverses two counties which are administered from Chamdo (**Dzogang** and **Markham**), three which are administered from Gyeltang (**Dechen, Gyeltang** and **Balung**), and the **Jang Sadam** (Ch Lijiang) region, before heading south to **Dali** and east to **Kunming** City. The overall distance from Chamdo to Kunming is 1,789 km. **Recommended itinerary: 7. See page 20.***

__NB__ This itinerary can be reversed, and those who have entered Tibet from Kunming have often been impressed by the proximity offered by this approach. » *For Sleeping, Eating and other listings, see pages 458-462.*

Dzogang County མཛོ་སྒང

→ *Population: 42,276. Area: 12,320 sq km. Colour map 4, B2.* 左贡县

Tsawa Dzogang county comprises the valley of the Salween south of Pasho and those of its tributaries, the Le-chu and the Yu-chu (south of Pomda). The county capital is located at **Wamda**, 260 km from Chamdo and 168 km from Markham.

Upper Yu-chu

At the intersection 27 km south of **Pomda Airport**, take the left (east) road, which continues to run through the Yu-chu valley. Gradually the wide grasslands narrow, and the Yu-chu tapers into a forested gorge. After 29 km, you will pass on the left (east) a turn-off for **Meyul** township. The renovated Gelukpa monastery of **Temto** (founded as a branch of Drepung Loseling) is one of the most impressive among the 13 Gelukpa monasteries of this area. Notice the distinctive roadside stupas of the Yu-chu valley, which have a protective wooden pavilion to guard against rain.

Wamda

At Temto, 22 km south of the Meyul turn-off, there are two branch roads: one to the east leading to **Sayul** (50 km) and **Sanor** on the Mekong, and the other to the southwest leading to **Tobang** (22 km). Keeping to the main highway, continue south via Uyak to **Wamda**, the county capital, which is located on a spur (3,780 m) overlooking the Yu-chu, with a backdrop of forest. Timber is plentiful here and this is reflected in the local building construction.

The monastery of **Tsawa Dzogang Sangakling** was founded by Phakpalha of Chamdo, following the conversion of various local Bon monasteries to the Gelukpa tradition. Spend the night here at the Dzogang Government Guesthouse, which has 4-bed rooms (with electric blankets) at ¥35 per bed. The exceedingly long main street has a number of small shops and restaurants, government buildings, schools, and the inevitable karaoke bar, Tibetan-owned, and with a surprisingly sophisticated sound system. On the outskirts of town there is a petrol station.

Dungda La

South of Wamda, the road branches. Keep to the main road, which leaves the Yu-chu valley to ascend the watershed **Dungda La** pass (5,008 m) after 40 km, and enter Markham county.

Drakyol

If instead you continue along the riverside south of Wamda, the Yu-chu gorge deepens and a dirt road passable by jeep follows the river downstream for 92 km as far as **Drakyol** township, where there is a small Gelukpa monastery. Further south there is no vehicular access as the Yu-chu is abruptly forced to change course by the snow massives of the **Kawa Karpo Range**. The rapid river snakes back upon itself before flowing southwest into the Salween above **Tsawarong** (see below, page 447). It is, however, possible to trek south from Drakyol to Tsawarong, as the French adventurer Alexandra David-Neel did in reverse on her journey to Lhasa (1923). Upstream from this confluence are the remote Salween townships of **Kyil Lingka** (Trung Lingka) and **Zha Lingka**, which offer trekking access to Dzayul and to Pasho.

Dzogang & Markham

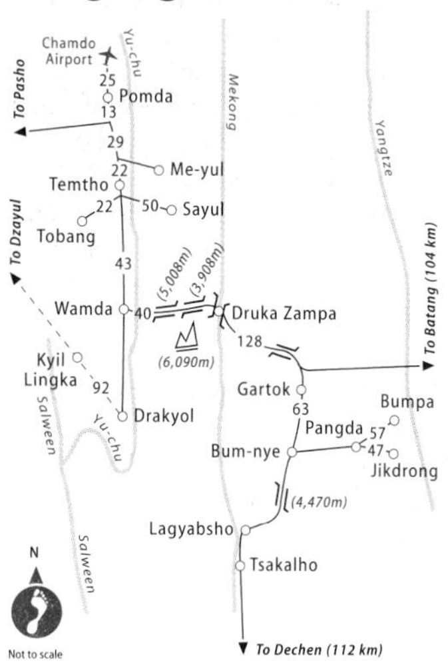

Markham County

སྨར་ཁམས → *Populaton: 71,533.*

Area: 12,258 sq km. Colour map 4, B3. 芒康县

Markham county is a prosperous and densely populated part of Kham, occupying the high ground (**Markhamgang**) between the Mekong and Yangtze rivers. The farm houses of Markham are for the most part large three-storey detached buildings of whitewashed adobe with ornate wooden lintels. Trade has been a significant factor in its economy, in that the county straddles the crossroads from Lhasa (via Chamdo or Pasho), Chengdu (via Batang), and Kunming (via Dechen). The capital is located at **Gartok**, 168 km from Wamda in Tsawa Dzogang, and 104 km from Batang.

Descent from Dungda La pass to the Mekong

Ascending the **Dungda La** pass (5,008 m) from Dzogang, the highway offers spectacular views of **Mount Dungri Karpo** (6,090 m) to the south. A second but lower pass **Joba La** (3,908 m) is quickly crossed after **Dempa**, and then the road zigzags down the barren sandstone ravine to **Druka Zampa** bridge, which spans the Mekong. Alongside the bridge there are simple guesthouse facilities and Sichuan-style restaurants. A gradual ascent on the east bank via **Rong-me** township leads across **Rongsho La** pass (4,060 m) into the alpine meadows of Markhamgang.

Gartok

The prosperity of the region is instantly apparent. Passing the turn-off for Batang, you soon reach **Gartok**. Its main attraction is the Gelukpa **monastery of Markham**, a beautiful yellow building containing in its inner sanctum a large impressive image of Maitreya, flanked by smaller images of Tsongkhapa and his students. Markham Monastery is affiliated to Drayab, see above, page 437. ➤➤ *For listings, see pages 458-462.*

South of Gartok

Following the highway south from Gartok, along the Drong-chu (Markham Kyilchu) valley, you will pass **Biru** village and 63 km south of Gartok, at **Bum-nye** a turn-off leads east across the river to the farming village of **Pangda**, home of Lhasa's famous merchant Pangdatsang. Motorable country roads link Pangda with **Bumpa** township (57 km) and Jikdrong township (47 km). The **Bum La** pass (4,115 m) above Bumpa was held by the Qing emperors as the boundary between independent Tibet and Chinese-occupied Tibet from the mid-18th century onwards (although this had little meaning on the ground at that time).

Staying on the highway, you soon cross **Hung La** pass (4,470 m), and the road re-enters the Mekong gorge through the Drong-chu valley at **Lagyabsho**, some 48 km north of Tsakalho. The descent into Tsakalho is impressive, overlooking the sheer ravine, and the road tunnels its way through precipitous cliffs.

A side road leads east from Lagyabsho for 54 km to reach the shores of the sacred **Mangtso Lake**, in the vicinity of which a wildlife reserve has recently been established. This is a good area for sightings of deer and waterfowl.

Tsakalho

Tsakalho (Ch Yenching) lies 914 m above the Mekong gorge, and the cliffs are so steep that the river cannot be seen from the town. Near the riverside are the commercial salt-pans which give Tsakalho its name. The altitude here is relatively low (3,109 m), and the climate is warm. Beware of mosquitos in summer. For centuries Tsakalho has been a staging post on the trading route from **Jang** (Lijiang) and Dechen to Lhasa, and it has recently acquired the status of a county town in its own right. In addition to the Tibetan Khampa population, there is a substantial **Jang (Naxi)** community. Tsakalho also possesses the only Catholic church within the Tibet Autonomous Region. South of town there is a checkpoint, 12 km below which the road crosses the present day frontier between the TAR and Yunnan province.

Getting there There are public buses to **Tsakalho** from **Markham** and **Dechen**, although the connections to Dechen cannot always be made in summertime when mudslides frequently damage the road. **NB** Military and police permit restrictions are applicable for foreign travellers heading north from Tsakhlho, but movement southwards to Dechen is now unrestricted. ➤➤ *For listings, see pages 458-462.*

Dechen County བདེ་ཆེན → *Pop: 60,000. Area: 7,164 sq km.* 德钦县

Dechen county, along with the adjacent counties of Gyeltang and Balung, nowadays forms part of the Dechen Tibetan Autonomous Prefecture, governed from Kunming. The county extends through the deep Mekong gorge south of Tsakalho and includes the **Kawa Karpo** range (also known as the Minling range; Ch Meili) which divides the Mekong from the Salween. Its eastern boundary is formed by the Yangtze. The county capital is located at Dechen town, also known traditionally as Jol or Atunzu, 112 km south of Tsakalho and 184 km northwest of Gyeltang.

The best seasons for driving from Tsakalho to Kunming are spring and autumn. In summer the road surface can be devastated by heavy landslides, necessitating a walk of over two days to reach **Dechen**. Pack animals can be hired in Tsakalho.

Hongshan

From Tsakalho, follow the east bank of the Mekong downstream for 40 km to **Hongshan** (locally pronounced Fuchang), where there is a hospitable roadside inn and the Markham County Naxi Guesthouse (beds at ¥7 per night). Continue downstream, crossing and recrossing the river, until reaching a point where the road rises high above the river and turns southeast for Dechen.

Mount Kawa Karpo

Across the gorge as you approach Dechen from Tsakalho and Hongshan, there are truly dramatic views of the Kawa Karpo glaciers. The astonishing main glacier of **Mount Kawa Karpo** deceives the eye, appearing to plunge downwards almost to the level of the Mekong in the gorge below. This mighty watershed range has 13 snow peaks forming a north-south alignment. Among them, Mount Kawa Karpo, the highest, is 6,740 m, and to its north is **Mount Dradul Wangchuk** (6,379 m). Immediately south of Kawa Karpo, there is a glacial protuberance known as **Phakpa Neten Chudruk**, and to its south **Mount Pawo Pamo** (6,000 m), followed in succession by the spectacular five-peaked crown of **Mount Gyelwa Rikngа** (5,471 m), **Mount Men Tsunmo** (6,055 m), and two lesser peaks known as **Chugen-je** and **Tsela Nyenpo**. Kawa Karpo itself is conceived as a male protector deity and Men Tsunmo as the corresponding female consort. The range is an important focal point for pilgrimage, revered as one of the 25 important meditation sites associated with Padmasambhava in Kham and Amdo. Specifically, this mountain range symbolizes the body-aspect of buddha-speech (see above, page 403). In the past its sanctuaries and hermitages have been a stronghold of the Nyingmapa school. Vairocana gave teachings on Dzogchen to his followers at Tsawarong, to the northwest of the range; and there are branches of **Katok Monastery** in its environs. The most renowned figure in this lineage was Kawakarpowa Namka Gyatso who, with his teacher Khedrup Yeshe Gyeltsen, expounded the Katok lineage throughout this extreme southern region of Kham.

Dechen & Gyeltang

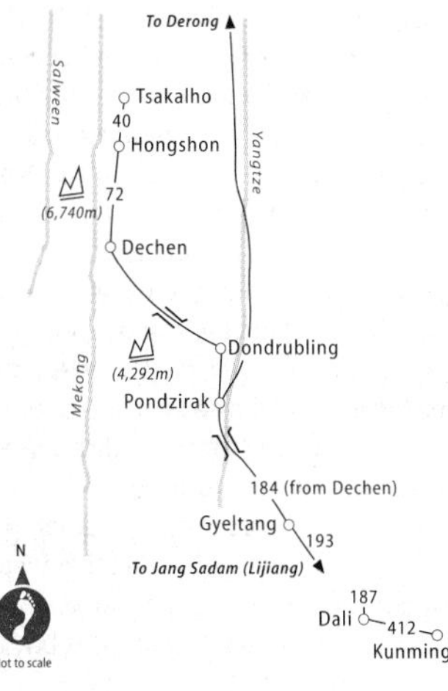

 Panoramas The best viewing platforms for the entire range are found on the ridge above the east bank of the Mekong, particularly at **Namka Tashi Lhakhang**, where the sunrise is most spectacular, and at **Chorten Gang**, a sacred stupa overlooking the Mekong gorge with the central glacier in the distance.

About 10 km north of Dechen and above the gorge you will reach **Namka Tashi Lhakhang** (Ch.Feilaisi). This temple complex ⓘ *admission ¥15*, was reconstructed in 1986 to commemorate the visit to Dechen of the late Tenth Panchen Lama. Inside, the images depict (L-R): Tsongkhapa with his foremost students, Jowo Shakyamuni, Padmasambhava in the upright form of Totrengtsel, and the protector deity Kawa Karpo. Above the door is a mural depicting the Lords of the Three Families, while those on the wall adjacent to the door portray the Nyingma protectors Rahula, Ekajati and Dorje Lekpa, along with Six-armed Mahakala and Mahakala in the form of Bernakchen. The left wall has murals of the meditational deities including Guhyasamaja, Cakrasamvara, and Vajrabhairava; while the right depicts the deities according to the Konchok Chidu revelation of Jatson Nyingpo. Slightly further north (at road marker 1854) there is an observation pavilion from which the sunrise on Mount Kawa Karpo may be witnessed. Adjacent to the pavilion is a monument dedicated to 17 members of a Sino-Japanese mountaineering expedition who died on Kawa Karpo in 1990.

Treks and pilgrimages There are two trekking circuits which pilgrims, experienced trekkers and botanists frequently undertake at Kawa Karpo: the **inner route** to the waterfall below Mount Gyelwa Riknga and the central Kawa Karpo glacier at Melong Gonpa; and the **outer route** which circumambulates the entire range. The sheep year, occurring once every 12 years (last in 2003 and next in 2015), is considered to be a special year for the Kawa Karpo pilgrimage.

The **inner route** **Day 1** Driving north from Dechen, you cross the Mekong at **Bachok Ne**, and climb south-west to reach the hot springs at **Shartang Chutsaka** (1,900 m, which is the starting point for the trek. **Day 2** Trekking for six hours (or riding on horseback for eight hours), you cross **Nakdzokto La** pass (3,900 m), before descending to **Lekbam** (locally pronounced Yibum, 3,600 m), and then climbing gradually to **Khandro Nesar** (4,390 m), the sacred abode of the dakini Yeshe Tsogyal, and **Orgyan Drupuk** (4,400 m), the cave hermitage of Padmasambhava. In the late afternoon you will reach the waterfall at **Babchu**, situated dramatically below the five-peaked snow-covered crown of **Mount Gyelwa Riknga** (5,471 m). **Day 3** Retracing the route to the hot springs, you then trek or ride northwards to **Melong** village (locally pronounced Miyam), from where a trail leads uphill through alpine meadows and forested terrain to the small temple of **Melong Gonpa Demchok Podrang**. **Day 4** After exploring the central Kawa Karpo glacier and visiting both the **Gon-me** and **Gon-to** temples, you head downhill to re-cross the Mekong at **Bachok Ne** en route for Dechen.

Melong Gonpa In the Mekong gorge north of Dechen (at road marker 1838) a motorable trail leaves the main road at 2,700 m, and descends to **Pandzara** village, where the headman Mr Tsering Dorje and his sons can arrange porterage if you wish to trek to Kawa Karpo. Since 1997 it has also been possible to drive nearly all the way to the glacier! After crossing the Mekong by a concrete bridge below the village at 2,215 m, the trail ascends a 45-degree gradient to reach Melong valley. Fording the **Melong-chu** river at 2,523 m, you then climb through the forest to reach **Melong Monastery**, located spectacularly below the glacier at 3,030 m. This monastery is also known as **Go-me Gonpa**, in contrast to **Go-to Gonpa**, which lies even higher up at the head of the valley.

Formerly Melong Gonpa had three temples, an outer shrine dedicated to Avalokiteshvara, an inner shrine dedicated to Cakrasamvara, and an upper shrine dedicated to Shakyamuni. The small renovated temple which is supervised by Jampa Pema Dondrub has large images (left to right) depicting Manjughosa, Padmasambhava, Jowo Shakyamuni, Four-armed Avalokiteshvara and Vajrasattva, along with smaller icons of Jowo Shakyamuni, Padmasambhava, Tara, Aksobhya,

Vajradhara and Vajrapani. Posters decorate the side walls, depicting calendrical charts on the left and the Eight Manifestations of Padmasambhava on the right. The portico has an inscription recounting the history of the monastery on the left and a large Mani Wheel on the right.

The **outer route** This is a very demanding circuit, which will tax even experienced and hardy trekkers, particularly during the long rainy season when high river levels and leeches make the going difficult. The rewards for pilgrims, botanists and trekkers are quite tangible: high passes (which are crossed without respite), diverse ecosystems, rich forests, high grasslands, close encounters with the rarely seen Salween gorge, and the scorching valley of Tsawarong.

The circuit covers a distance of approximately 200km, about 80 trekking hours altogether, and can be completed in 12 days. **Day 1**: Driving south from Dechen on the Balang (Ch. Weixi) road, you will reach **Yangkyi** (Ch. Yangzi, 2,000 m) after 2-3 hours. Here the Mekong is crossed, the motorable road comes to an end, and you enter the outer pilgrimage circuit around the sacred six peaks of Mount Kawa Karpo. A two-hour trek (6 km) leads uphill as far as **Drezhitang** village (Ch. Yongjiu, 2,480 m), where there is a small temple and a stone footprint of one of the Karmapas. **Day 2**: An eight-hour trek leads uphill to **Langjor Lhundrupteng** temple (under Lama Sonam Gyatso) and **Gongri** (3,130 m) before descending to **Chushak** (Ch. Qisua, 2,950 m), and following a ridge through charred forest and millet fields to **Lungnak-chu** bridge. Near Langjor there is a miraculous spring, reputedly brought forth by Vairocana, and the descent offers a distant view of Langdre village, from which Alexandra David-Neel once began her epic journey to Lhasa. The trail then follows the torrent upstream from the bridge through boulder-strewn marshland to the meadow camp at **Langshitang** (3,290 m). **Day 3**: Another eight-hour trek leads uphill to the watershed pass of **Do-ke La** (4,487m), which has been well known to botanists since Frank Kingdon Ward's expedition of 1913. On the switchback descent, there are excellent views of the

Mount Kawa-Karpo treks

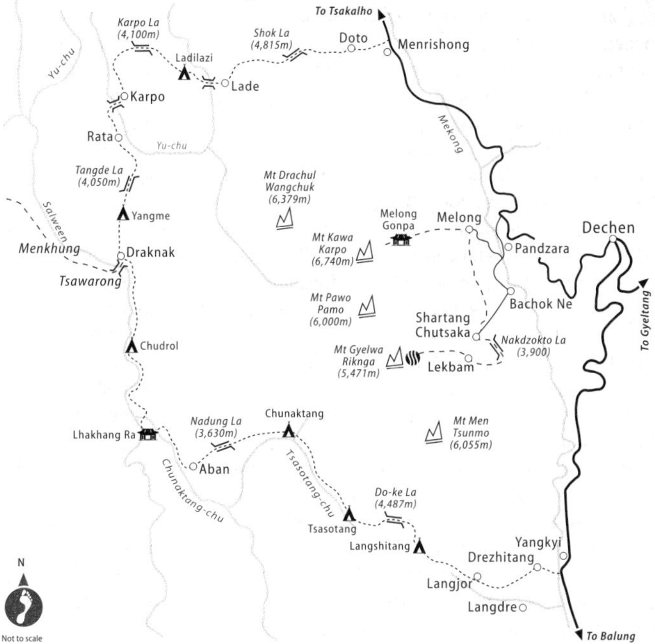

The Great Rivers National Park

In 1998, following two years of negotiation, an agreement was signed between Yunnan province and the US Nature Conservancy, with a view to establishing the Great Rivers National Park. Covering an area of 66,000 sq km (four times the size of Yellowstone National Park), this is claimed to be China's first world-class national park, extending from Shigu in the south to Tsakalho on the TAR border in the north, and from the Burmese border in the west to Lugu Lake in the east. As such, it will include the gorges of the Salween, Irrawady, Mekong and Yangtze, amalgamating several former national parks under the jurisdiction of Dechen Prefecture, Ninglang county and Lijiang. This vast region which is home to diverse ethnic groups, including the Khampa Tibetans, Naxi, Yi, Li, Nu, Moso, and Malimoso, has been described by the Royal Botanic gardens of Edinburgh as "one of the most significant resources of plant diversity in the northern temperate hemisphere". It sustains 10,000 of the 15,000 plant species found in Yunnan, including 60% of those used in traditional Chinese medicine and 75% of those used in Tibetan medicine. There are also more than 1000 species of bird, at least 30 endangered species of animal, including the snow leopard, the clouded leopard, the lesser panda and the Yunnan golden monkey. A single tiger was reportedly spotted in 1979! The four mountain ranges within the proposed park, including Mt Kawa Karpo and Mt Padma, contain more than 30 major peaks, several of which are above 6,000 m. It is hoped that the park, once established, will extend special protection to the biological and cultural diversity of the region.

glaciers to the south-east. Then, fording a river in the valley below, a gentle pathway leads through the forest to reach the **Tsasotang** meadow camp (3,600m). **Day 4**: A nine-hour trek which initially follows the **Tsasotang-chu** downstream on a narrow and sometimes precipitous trail, before climbing through **Dotri Sumdzom**, the scene of an important battle fought between the Tibetan army and Guomintang forces, to cross **Lho Asil La** pass. This prayer-flag bedecked ridge overlooks the confluence of the Tsasotang and Chunaktang rivers, which are both tributaries of the Salween. The trail then descends steeply through forested terrain as far as the campsite at **Chunaktang** clearing (Ch. Qunatong, 2,470m). **Day 5**: A six-hour trek leads uphill through forested terrain where **songrong mushrooms** are plentiful, to reach **Nadung La** pass (3,630 m). On a clear day there are fine views of Mount Kawa Karpo to the north-east and of **Dzayul** to the west. Warm air filters through from the distant Burmese hills, transforming the ecosystem, as rain forest gives way to banks of wild roses, honeysuckle and spruce. A three-hour descent through the spruce forest leads to the low-lying farming village of **Aban** (Ch Abin, 2,230 m), located within the Salween gorge. **Day 6**: Following the increasingly arid **Chunaktang** gorge downhill from Aban, after five hours you will reach the lower reaches of the valley, where there are ancient Buddhist rock inscriptions and carvings which depict the Thousand Buddhas, the Buddhas of the Three Times, and the Thirty-five Confession Buddhas. Some were effaced during the Cultural Revolution, and there is evidence here of mani stones having been used as paving stones. The temple of **Lhakhang Ra** overlooks the confluence of the Chunaktang-chu with the Salween (1,730 m) and contains images of Padamasambhava and a previous Karmapa. An adjacent Mani Lhakhang still preserves its ancient flagstones, and outside there is a fine stupa. On the rock face on the west bank of the Salween opposite, there is a large body imprint of

Padmasambhava, which has a circumambulatory pathway for pilgrims. The trail now follows the east bank of the Salween upstream through grey sandy terrain for two hours to reach the camp at **Chudrol** (1,830 m), where there are five wonderful bathing springs. **Day 7**: The trail cuts across the grey beaches of the Salween's east bank and narrow ledges of limestone shale, to reach the gully of **Draknak Seratang** in aptly named **Tsawarong**, where sweet cactus fruit grow and the temperature can exceed 108 degrees. Soon **Draknak** township, the capital of Tsawarong, comes into view and there are small shops here selling soft and cold drinks. There is a very small temple, containing an image of Padmsambhava, a copy of the Lhasa edition of the *Kangyur*, and a photograph of the late Khenpo Jigpun of Sertal. One-hour's trek inland from here there is the sacred meditation hermitage of **Gyelmo Taktse** where, in the eighth century, the great Dzogchen master Vairocana sought refuge when exiled from Lhasa. It was here that he transmitted the teachings of the Mental Class of Dzogchen (*sem-de*) to his foremost students, Sangton Yeshe Lama and Pangen Sangye Gonpo. At the **Wa Senge Cave**, three successive generations of Dzogchen masters who had received teachings from Vairocana attained the rainbow body. Leaving Draknak, a side road leads west across a footbridge spanning the Salween to reach **Menkhung** area, which is a focal point for botanists. The main trail rises to the northeast, where you have the option of camping near **Jena Dungkar** or of continuing uphill through **Lungpu**, to the excellent campsite at **Yangmo** gully (Ch. Shenmu, 2,640 m), adjacent to the small **Tsedor Gonpa**. **Day 8**: A six-hour trek leads sharply uphill to cross **Tangde La** pass (Ch. Tongdila, 4,050 m), which offers magnificent views of the Kawa Karpo range to the southeast, and the **Salween-Irrawady** divide to the west. The trail then descends on a rutted pathway to **Drakgo Lhakhang** and **Rata** village, from where the pristine waters of the **Yu-chu**, a major tributary of the Salween are crossed en route to **Karpo** village (2,330 m). **Day 9**: The longest trekking day on the circuit (over nine hours) leads directly uphill through spruce forest to cross the sacred **Karpo La** pass (4,100 m), where (in the right season) there are magnificent views of the Kawa Karpo range to the south. Mushroom gatherers are active in this area. The descent leads from the amphitheatre of the pass through boulder-strewn marshland to the campsite at **Ladilazi** (2,800 m), a forest farm nestling within the looping bend of the Yu-chu. **Day 10**: Trekking three hours downhill, the trail crosses the Yu-chu loop for the second time **at Ladilazi Dungkar bridge**, before climbing yet again to reach the campsite at **Lade** village (Ch Laide, 3,090 m). **Day 11**: Now the trail rises sharply through the meadows of **Menchok Pangzang**, where aromatic herbs and mushrooms abound. Higher up you emerge onto a tundra-covered saddle below the convex amphitheatre of **Shok La** pass (Ch Shuola, 4,815 m), which offers splendid views of **Mount Dradul Wangchuk** (6,379 m), the northernmost peak of the Kawa Karpo range. The pass itself forms a northern watershed between the Salween and Mekong basins. Descending from the pass, you enter the upper reaches of the **Doto-chu**, a tributary of the Mekong and camp below **Doto** hamlet (4,100 m) at a small forest farm (3,460 m). The trekking time on this day is over nine hours, but in the rainy season this campsite is unsuitable, necessitating a further two-hour trek to reach an appropriate clearing. **Day 12**: Continue the descent through the **Doto-chu** valley as far as its confluence with the **Do-me-chu**, where there is a roadside shrine containing a Karmapa stone handprint. In the rainy season the path will be submerged by the river in certain places. The valley gradually widens and the forest thins out at lower elevations, as the Mekong finally comes into view below. This last stage of the trek takes six hours to reach the motorable road at **Menrishong** (Ch. Meilishi, 2,150 m) from where you can drive the short distance into Dechen.

Dechen

(Ch Shenping/ Deqin) The hill station of Dechen (3,480 m) is located in a sheltered side valley high above the Mekong gorge, its slopes and climate strangely reminiscent of Darjiling in Northeast India. The original names of the town are **Jol** and **Atunzu**, but in the 17th century, the Fifth Dalai Lama renamed it and its environs Dechen ("supreme bliss"). The town has a population of approximately 9,700, of which the majority are still local Khampa.

The main street, leading uphill from the hotel towards the open market has a number of small Sichuan- and Yunnan-style restaurants. In the wet season, the local economy is centred on mushroom picking, since the **Songrong mushroom** which grows on the nearby river banks and in the forests is exported to Japan, where it is reckoned to have curative effects for the treatment of certain cancers and male impotence. The monasteries of this region traditionally belonged to both the Karma Kagyu and the Gelukpa schools.

Kawa Karpo Lhakhang In town, the recently constructed Kawa Karpo Lhakhang on Wenhua Lam, is a three-storey building containing fine murals. The walkway around the **ground floor chapel** has murals depicting the Eight Medicine Buddhas, the Twenty-one Taras, the Lords of the Three Enlightened Families and the Three Deities of Longevity. Within this chapel, there is a magnificent Wheel of Rebirth and other murals depicting the protector Kawa Karpo alongside Padmasambhava, and Cakrasamvara, flanked by Khecari, Begtse, Kurukulla and Acala. On the staircase leading to the middle floor, the murals depict the seven insignia of royal dominion, the eight auspicious symbols and other well known motifs. The walls of the **middle floor chapel** illustrate the Thirty-five Confession Buddhas, the Five Meditational Buddhas and Shakamuni, flanked by his two foremost disciples. On the staircase leading to the third storey, the murals depict Shambhala, Vajravidarana, Pratisaravidyarajni and some minor nature deities. The **top floor chapel**, unusually, has a large Mani Wheel at the centre, the surrounding murals depicting (L-R): Karmapa Dusum Khyenpa, Tangtong Gyelpo (south), Padmasambhava with Shantaraksita and Trisong Detsen, the Five Founders of Sakya, Marpa with Milarepa and Gampopa (west), and Drigung Jigten Gonpo, Tilopa, Naropa, followed by Atisha with Dromton and Ngok Lekpei Sherab (north).

The monastery of **Dechenling** is located on a high ridge, 4 km outside the town, overlooking the valley and the Mekong gorge. This is the residence of Samdhong Rinpoche, the principal of the Institute for Tibetan Higher Studies in Sarnath, India, who was recently elected as the prime minister of the Tibetan Government in Exile by the entire international Tibetan diaspora. The monastery itself is in a poor state of repair. A smaller temple, **Jomoling**, is located higher up the hillside, and in the valley belonw, in the direction of Yuling and Yangkyi, there is **Homgya Gonpa**, under the direction of Tropa Guru. *For listings, see pages 458-462.*

Dechen

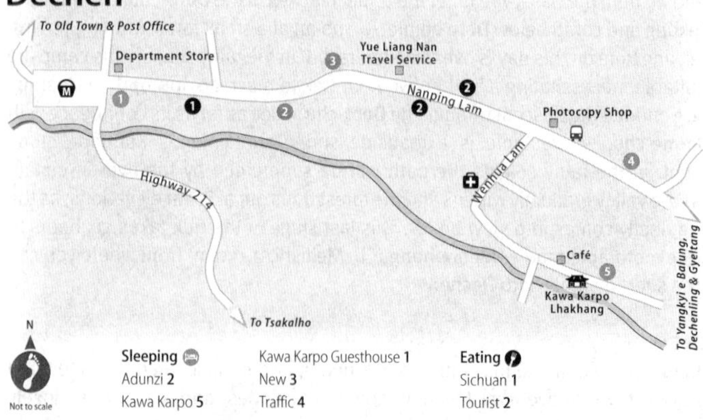

Mount Padma

From Dechen, Highway 214 heads southeast (a turn-off at Seji village leads down to Yulring and Yangkyi villages, from where one can undertake the 12-day outer circuit of Mount Kawa Karpo or trek north through Dzayul and Dzogang counties). It then passes the turn-off for Dechenling Monastery before crossing **Yak La** (4,230 m) which forms a watershed between the Mekong and the Yangtze. Just before the pass there are excellent views of Dechen town and, when skies are clear, the entire Kawa Karpo range extends in an unforgettable panorama from north to south. Reaching the pass, there is also a spectacular view of the snow peaks of **Mount Padma** (Ch Baima Shan; 4,292 m) to the south. This area is now an important forested nature reserve. Two loop roads descend from the pass at different elevations, ensuring the road will remain open in winter. On the descent towards the Yangtze basin, three smaller passes are crossed in succession (two at 4,260 m and one at 3,540 m). Then, you will reach the large Gelukpa monastery of **Ganden Dondrubling**.

Ganden Dondrubling

This Gelukpa establishment is the principal monastery within the county, founded by Kusho Dondrub during the 17th century. The **lower storey** has some recent but finely executed murals, depicting (L-R): the Twenty-one Taras (east), the Seven Generations of Past Buddhas (south) and the Eight Medicine Buddhas (north). Along the west wall are images of Tsongkhapa flanked by his foremost disciples and the eight mounted bodhisattvas, the reliquary stupa of Kusho Dondrub, and texts including the Lhasa edition of the *Kangyur*. The central throne bears photographs of the last three Panchen Lamas and the Dalai Lama. The **middle storey** contains the **Kangyur Lhakhang,** which has an impressive gilded copper image of Maitreya. The top storey houses a **Jokhang**, containing images of Jowo Shakyamuni flanked by his two disciples and the teaching thrones of Guru Ngadrak and Guru Dratang. The murals of the vestibule depict the Four Guarding Kings, cosmological charts, and the Wheel of Rebirth. Outside in the courtyard there is a statue in Chinese style depicting the 'laughing buddha', and a stele with faded inscriptions in Tibetan and Chinese. Formerly there were 456 monks at Dondrubling, but nowadays it is maintained by a mere 22 monks.

Pongdzirak

Downhill from Ganden Dondrubling, you will pass a charnel ground known as **Riknying Durtro**. Above the village of **Shukdzong**, the Yangtze comes into view, with the old Lhasa tea trail and the road to Derong in the distance. The road soon reaches the bustling town of Pondzirak (Ch Benzilan). Here there are plentiful Chinese restaurants, among which the Ga-ha Restaurant is recommended. Public buses also run daily for Gyeltang from the Duowen Luguan Hotel.

Below Pondzirak, a **branch road** crosses to the east bank of the Yangtze, and follows the river upstream to **Derong** county in present day Sichuan (see below, page 472). The **main road** continues south on the west bank for some distance before crossing the Yangtze and a southeast flowing tributary, at a point made famous by the Long March. From here, it proceeds through Gyeltang county.

Gyeltang County

→ *Pop: 130,000. Area: 11,869 sq km. Colour map 4, grid C4.* 中甸县

Gyeltang county is a densely populated area, bounded on the west, south, and east by the bending course of the Yangtze, and comprising the wide fertile plain of the Gyeltang-chu, a major tributary of the Yangtze. Both the county and prefectural capitals are located at **Gyeltangteng**. 184 km southeast of Dechen, and 193 km northwest of Lijiang. Nowadays only 40% of the county's population is estimated to be Tibetan. The remainder are Chinese, Naxi, Lisu, Yi, Bai and Pumi. The Gyeltang region prospered over the centuries since it commanded the trade routes between East Tibet and Burma, Yunnan and Northeast India. Brick tea from Yunnan, and the raw silk and cotton from British India were particularly valued. The summer horse festival of Gyeltang dates back to the 17th-century equestrian master Topden.

Napa Lake

Entering Gyeltang county from the north, the road ascends a pass, from where there is a turn-off leading west towards the east bank of the Yangzte. The main road then descends through **Nyezhi** village (Ch Nixi) to enter the wide Gyeltang-chu basin. The Gyeltang airstrip is visible in the distance. Descending into the Gyeltang plain from the northeast, the road skirts the east shore of the seasonal **Napa Lake**, which is occupied by nomads' camps. The marshlands of the **Napa Lake Nature Reserve** are a migratory home to the black-necked crane in winter. Large herds of yak are commonplace here, and the exposed plain has a number of windmills.

Gyeltangteng City

The large city of **Gyeltangteng** (Ch Zhongdian) lies at the heart of the Gyeltang-chu plain, at an altitude of 3,344 m. There is an airport here and another at Lijiang, four hours driving distance to the south. Nowadays, Gyeltangteng functions as the capital of the entire Dechen Autonomous Prefecture, a region of extraordinary biodiversity, which supports some 7,000 species of native plant including the blue poppy and other types of meconopsis, azaleas and 200 types of rhododendron. Many of these have medicinal uses. This discovery was made known to the outside world through the work of George Forrest of the Royal Botanic Gardens in Edinburgh; and in recent years this Scottish connection has been renewed when a conservation programme was implemented by the Dechen Forestry Bureau, in liaison with the Royal Botanic Gardens, Edinburgh and a US-based local entrepreneur. **NB** In consequence of the natural beauty of the region, the Dechen Tourism Bureau has been seriously marketing the prefecture as "Shangrila," turning the western mythology of Tibet on its head! Bewitched by this bizarre non-Tibetan utopia, the authorities even "officially" renamed Gyeltang as Shangrila in 2002. Nonetheless, I have continued to use the real name Gyeltang. ▸▸ *For listings, see pages 458-462.*

Orientation The architecture of the city is largely drab and uninspiring Chinese provincial style. Badly damaged by a major earthquake, which had its epicentre at neighbouring Lijiang in early 1996, the city was rapidly reconstructed, and all its streets have Chinese names. Entering the city from Dechen on **Zhongde Lu**, you will pass the Forestry Department on the left. Turn left at the intersection with **Jinxian Lu** for the Birong Hotel, Gangchen Nyima Hotel, the Prefectural Mentsikhang, the Tibetan Family Guesthouse and **Sungtseling Monastery** turn right at the next intersection on **Wenhua Lu** for the Teachers' Training College, the School of Hygiene, the Tibetan Institute of Performing Arts, a primary school, the Bilingual Middle School and Number One Middle School.

On the main road you will next reach the **Horseman Roundabout**, where you can turn left on to **Zhongxiang Lu** for Chaktreng and Chukar, or proceed straight ahead into town. On Zhongxiang Lu you will find the Xinhua Bookstore and the Prefectural Bus Station.

Heading into town on **Changzheng Lu**, you will first pass on the left the Dongba Cultural Park and after crossing the Na-chu river, the Prefectural People's Bank, the Nanyue Restaurant, the Wangda Hotel, the Hongda Hotel and the Agricultural Bank. Opposite on the right is **Huancheng Xilu** (leading to the Yuntong and Antong Hotels), followed by the National Tax Bureau, the Shunyuan Hotel, the Bita Hotel and the post office.

At this point **Xiangyang Lu** intersects on the left, leading to the Hydroelectric Bureau and a clinic. Continuing south on Changzheng Lu, you will pass on the right

Gyeltang

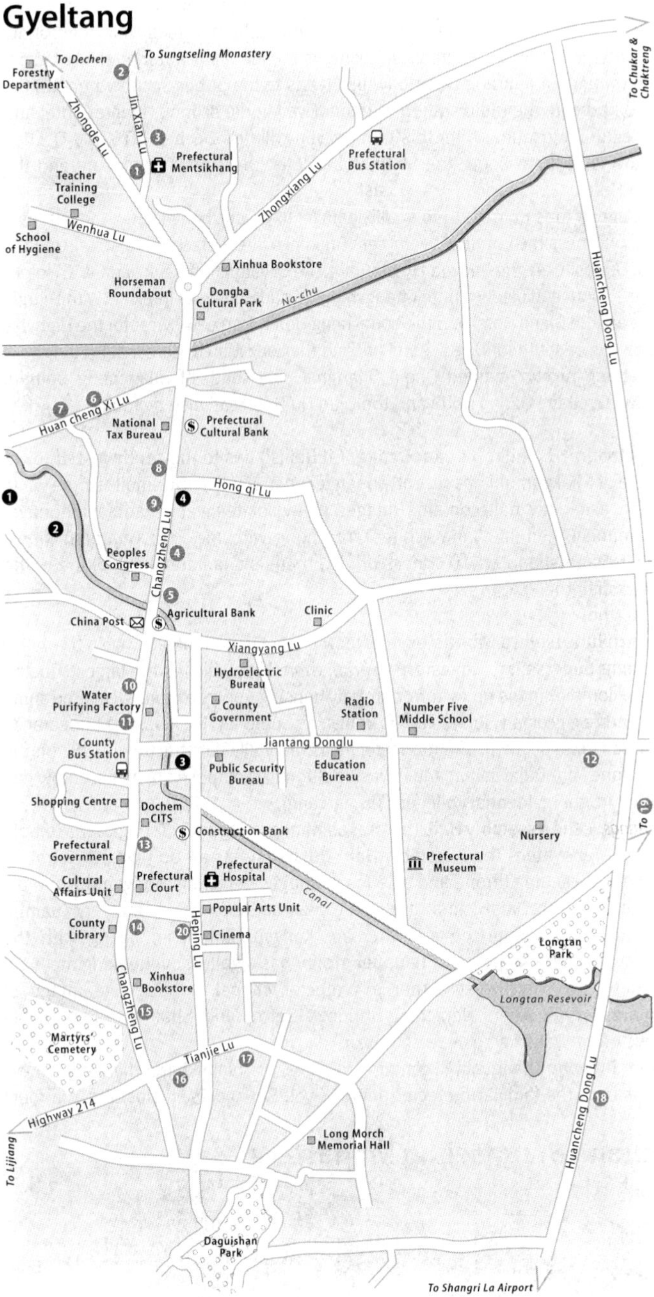

To Dechen
To Sungtseling Monastery
Forestry Department
Zhongde Lu
Jin Xian Lu
Prefectural Mentsikhang
Teacher Training College
Wenhua Lu
School of Hygiene
Zhongxiang Lu
Prefectural Bus Station
To Chukar & Chaktreng
Xinhua Bookstore
Horseman Roundabout
Dongba Cultural Park
Na-chu
Huancheng Dong Lu
Huan cheng Xi Lu
National Tax Bureau
Prefectural Cultural Bank
Hong qi Lu
Changzheng Lu
Peoples Congress
Agricultural Bank
China Post
Clinic
Xiangyang Lu
Hydroelectric Bureau
Water Purifying Factory
County Government
Radio Station
Number Five Middle School
Jiantang Donglu
County Bus Station
Public Security Bureau
Education Bureau
Shopping Centre
Dochem CITS
Construction Bank
Nursery
To 19
Prefectural Government
Prefectural Hospital
Prefectural Museum
Cultural Affairs Unit
Prefectural Court
Canal
Popular Arts Unit
County Library
Cinema
Heping Lu
Longtan Park
Longtan Resevoir
Xinhua Bookstore
Changzheng Lu
Martyrs' Cemetery
Tianjie Lu
Highway 214
To Lijiang
Long Morch Memorial Hall
Huancheng Dong Lu
Daguishan Park
To Shangri La Airport

Sleeping
Antong 7
Birong 1
Bita 9
CAAC Hotel 20
Dechen 13
Dianli 16
Gangchen Nyima 2
Guangyuan 10
Gyeltang Dzong 19
Hongda Garden 5
Huantai 12
Khampa 15
Qian Hu 18
Shambhala 14
Shunyhuan 8
Tibetan Family Guesthouse 3
Wangda 4
Xuelian 11
Yongsheng 17
Yuntong 6

Eating
Gaoyuan 3
Nanyue 4
Salong 1
Shunyong 2

Not to scale

the Guangyuan Hotel, the Xuelian Hotel, the County Bus Station, Shangrila Shopping Centre, the Prefectural Government Buildings, the Cultural Affairs Unit, the County Library and the Martyrs' Cemetery. Opposite on the left are a water purifying factory and the turning for **Jiantang Donglu** (which leads to the public security bureau, the education bureau, the radio station, Number Five Middle school, Huantai Hotel and the Prefectural Museum). After this turning, you will find Dechen CITS, the Dechen Hotel, the Prefectural Court, the Shambhala Hotel, the Xinhua Bookstore and the Khampa Hotel.

Heping Lu runs from north to south, parallel to Changzheng Lu. On the left (east side) you will pass the County Government Buildings, the Prefectural Hospital, and the cinema. Opposite are the Gaoyuan Restaurant, the Construction Bank and CAAC Hotel.

At the south end of town, both Changzheng Lu and Heping Lu intersect with **Tuanjie Lu**. Here are the Dianli Hotel and the Yongsheng Hotel. Turn southwest for the Highway 214 to Lijiang or south for Daguishan Park and the Long March Memorial Hall.

Gyeltang Airport, named Deqin Shangrila, lies south of **Huancheng Donglu**, where the Gyeltang Dzong Hotel and the Qian Hu Hotel can also be found.

Dokar Dzong The hilltop **Dokar Dzong** (Ch Beijisi) lies to the southwest of town. An image of Shakyamuni has recently been reconstructed in the small temple while the main assembly hall contains images of Avalokiteshvara, Padmasambhava, Shakyamuni, Green Tara and White Tara, along with the Four Guardian Kings. Nearby in **Daguishan Park** ⓘ *admission: ¥5*, there is a memorial exhibition to the Long March of the PLA.

Gyeltang Sungtseling Monastery By far the most important site within the valley is **Gyeltang Sungtseling Monastery** ⓘ *admission: ¥10*, which is the largest Tibetan Buddhist complex in the prefecture, currently housing 600-700 monks. Located some 8 km from the city on an isolated ridge, known as Guardian Hill, it has the appearance of a small monastic town. The monastery was originally constructed in 1681 on the advice of the Fifth Dalai Lama, and it was traditionally composed of an assembly hall flanked by eight residential colleges (khangtsang).

Recently, the **Assembly Hall**, the **Drayab Khangtsang** and a Tsongkhapa temple have been renovated. The Assembly Hall (Dukhang) has an 80-pillared chamber, containing a teaching throne and a series of images depicting Tsongkhapa and his students, the Fifth Dalai Lama, and three past lamas of the monastery (Sambo Rinpoche, Kensur Rinpoche and the late Kangyur Rinpoche), along with the reliquary of Sambo Rinpoche. The **upper storey** has a gallery overlooking the main hall, and in its northwest corner a protector chapel with a large image of Dharmaraja, and others depicting Shridevi, Sertro and Shukden. The private quarters of the Dalai Lama are also here.

The **Drayab Khangtsang** contains images of Tsongkhapa flanked by his students, and the familiar protector deities Gyel, Se, and Tsen. **Upstairs** is a room

Gyeltang Sungtseling Monastery

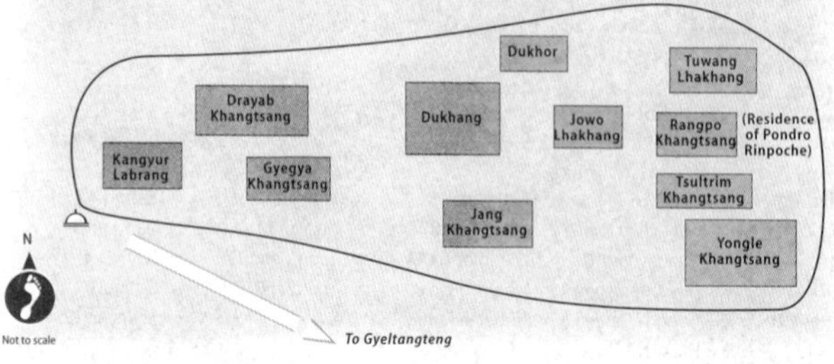

where seamstresses can occasionally be seen preparing brocade hangings and ceremonial dance costumes for use on the 29th day of the 11th lunar month.

The **Jang Khangtsang**, currently being refurbished by Kyapje Pondro Rinpoche and Ngawang Tropel, is seeking to raise US$9,000 for restoration work.

Rutapo and Rutamo Hills South of town, the protector hills of Rutapo and Rutamo rise above the Gyeltang Dzong Hotel. A four-hour walk leads across the flower-carpeted hills to **Rikngα Lhakhang**, where there are images of the Five Meditational Buddhas.

Routes and excursions from Gyeltangteng

There are four roads leading from Gyeltangteng city. One (already described) heads northwest towards **Dechen** county (184 km); a second runs northeast via **Geza** and the rich nomadic grasslands of **Zhakdo** and **Mikzur** to **Rakwa** (Wengshui) (156 km) on the present-day Sichuan border and thence a further 69 km to **Chaktreng** (see below, page 472); a third which is the **Kunming highway**, running south for 152 km to **Jang Sadam** (Lijiang); and a fourth heading southeast to **Chukar** and the Haba Gangri range.

Hongshan Mountains Heading northeast via Geza in the direction of the Chaktreng county border, a rough side road leads into the Hongshan Mountains (4,000 m), which are well known for their azaleas, rhododendrons, meadow and scree flowers.

Zhado and Beta Lakes If you take the last of these roads, heading southeast from town, there are turn-offs on the left leading to the pristine waters of Zhado Lake (Ch Shudu hai), the shores of which are famous for their alpine meadow flowers, and to the Beta Lake Nature Reserve and the Balgo Forest Nature Park. **Beta Lake** ⓘ *admission: ¥20, cabin accommodation: ¥30*, is the habitat of the rare species of Bitachunyu fish, and the reserve is a breeding ground for the white-lipped deer. From the forested shores of Jehra Lake (Ch Jisha hai), near Beta Lake, a trail leads through the meadows to the spectacular high alpine glacial lake of Yangdo Ubdutso, also known as Lhamo Dungtso.

Chukar ⓘ *Admission: ¥10*. The main southeast road comes to an end below Mount Haba Gangri (5,425 m) at the Chukar limestone platform (Ch Baishuitai), where the ridge formation resembles a terraced field or tiers of jade and silver. This is revered as the sacred birthplace of the Jang (Naxi) people. There are simple guesthouse facilities (¥15-20 per bed).

Tiger Leaping Gorge

The main Kunming highway running south from Gyeltangteng follows the west bank of the Shudu-chu or Yangpang Tsangpo, a tributary of the Yangtze, as far as its confluence below Mount Haba Gangri. Here, at the renowned Tiger Leaping Gorge (Tib Takchong Gak, Ch Hu Tiaoxia), the foaming Yangtze rapids cascade down a precipitous ravine at an angle of 75-80°. The spectacle is alluring for tourists but arrange to go with a local guide since rock slides and sheer cliffs are a hazard for the unprepared traveller.

At the south extremity of Gyeltang county the Yangtze makes a remarkable bend, flowing abruptly northeast as its torrents are channelled between the snow peaks of Haba Gangri and Yulong Shan (Mount Jade Dragon, 5,596 m).

Balung County འབའ་ལུང

→ *Population: 140,000. Area: 1,529 sq km. Colour map 4, grid C3.* 维西县

Occupying the Mekong gorge due south of Dechen county, Balung is a region of great ethnic diversity, the dominant group being the Li (Ch Lizu), intermingled with Jang

 (Naxi), Tibetan, and Chinese. Terraced farming is the mainstay of the economy here. The county capital is located at **Balung**, known in Naxi language as **Nyinak** and in Chinese as Baohezhen, in the extreme south of the county, 217 km from Dechen.

Heading south from Dechen, following the east bank of the Mekong, you will pass through **Yulring** township and **Yangkyi** village, where the outer trekking circuit around Mount Kawa Karpo begins. Road conditions are difficult in the rainy season. Below Yanmen on the west bank of the river at **Cizhong**, there is a prominent Protestant church (dated 1907). The road continues to follow the river downstream, passing through Badi and Yezhi, where the Naxi monastery of **Shuoguosi** (founded 1728) maintains the Karma Kagyu tradition. At Baijixun village, the road leaves the gorge, climbing inland to the county capital at Balung.

Balung is predominantly a Chinese town, interspersed with Tibetans, Naxi, and Lisu. The most important Buddhist site in the county is **Damozushidong**, a Karma Kagyu monastery constructed in 1662, which overlooks the Yangtze, 100 km to the northwest of the capital. According to tradition, there is a meditation cave here, associated with the Chan Buddhist master Bodhidharma.

Jang Sadam འཇང་ས་དམ → *Population: 1,100,000. Area: 19,594 sq km. Colour map 4, grid C4.*

Jang Sadam, known as Lijiang in Chinese, is the Tibetan name for the narrow peninsula bounded on three sides by the bend of the Yangtze River, to the southeast of Gyeltang. The ancient kingdom of Jang Sadam, where the population is predominantly **Naxi** (Tib Jang) was for 253 years of its history directly absorbed within the Tibetan Empire from the reign of King Songtsen Gampo onwards, ie from 649 until the disintegration which followed the assassination of Langdarma in 902. Thirteen successive kings of Jang, who ruled from **Bumishi**, were regarded with fraternal respect by the Tibetan monarchs in recognition of their ethnic affinity.

The Naxi are a Qiangic people, said to have migrated here from the northeast in antiquity. They speak two dialects and are divided into four distinctive clans, with a combined population of 250,000. The Dongba culture and religion which the Naxi maintain is a synthesis of indigenous polytheism, Tibetan Bon, Chinese Daoism, and Buddhism. The Dongba (meaning priest or sorceror) are the main carriers of the traditional culture. The scriptures of the Dongba comprise 20,000 extant volumes and rare scrolls preserved in the libraries of Yunnan, Nanjing, Beijing, Taiwan, the USA and Europe. These concern philosophy, history, religion, medicine, astronomy, folklore, literature and art. The Dongba script has some 1,400 ideographs and is considered to offer insights into the development of both Chinese traditional calligraphy and seal cutting. Contemporary research into this ancient culture has been internationally acclaimed, largely through the efforts of the Academy of Social Sciences in Lijiang county and particularly, Dr Xuan Ke (Tib name: Tsering Wangdu), a well-travelled Dongba ethnomusicologist who has turned his own family home at 11 Jishan Alley into a museum.

During the Yuan Dynasty (13th century), the capital of Jang was moved from Bumishi to **Lijiang** by Qubilai Qan; and Tibetan Buddhist influence on the indigenous Dongba culture of the Jang people gradually prevailed. The main beneficiaries of this early missionary activity were the Karma Kagyu and the Katokpa branch of the Nyingma school. During the Ming Dynasty, the authority of the successive kings of Jang Sadam was officially recognized; and their influence even spread north into the Dechen area of Kham and Mili. Presently, the majority of Jang (Naxi) people reside in the **Naxi Autonomous Prefecture** of Yunnan county, which has its capital at Lijiang, but there are also sizeable minority groups as far north as Tsakalho in Markham county of TAR.

Lijiang City → *Altitude: 2,000 m. Colour map 4, grid C4.*

The city of Lijiang, dramatically situated below the snow peak of Mount Yulong Shan (Jade Dragon, 5,596 m), was the setting for the award-winning television documentary series Beyond the Clouds. Despite its status as the Naxi capital and the vigorous promotion of the local culture by the former Naxi governor of Yunnan, the predominant influence here is clearly Chinese. The exceptions are the old narrow cobbled streets of the traditional market and evening Naxi music concerts which are an obvious attraction for visitors. During the winter of early 1996 the city was badly damaged by a severe earthquake, but the subsequent rebuilding has conformed to traditional Naxi architecture, and the city and its environs are now listed as a UNESCO world heritage site.

Bumishi (Baisha) Monastery Also known as **Liu Lidian Temple** in Chinese ('Coloured Glaze Temple'), the monastery of **Bumishi** stands at the site of the former capital of the Naxi Kingdom on the outskirts of Lijiang. The present building was constructed somewhat later between 1385-1619, in Chinese style. There are three successive halls, the **outermost** containing the temple office and a shop selling Naxi memorabilia. The second and third halls are particularly interesting because they contain original Tibetan-style frescoes. Within the **innermost hall** a central Buddha image has to its rear a series of outstanding murals depicting (left to right): Avalokiteshvara, Vajrasattva, Karmapa, Vajrasattva (again) and Vajrayogini. To the left near the entrance by contrast there are later Chinese-style paintings.

Tashi Gepel Gonpa The monastery of **Tashi Gepel** (Ch Yufeng Si), in the Lijiang countryside, has been reconstructed and is currently under the supervision of a Naxi caretaker, whose Tibetan name is Karma Chokyab. It contains images of Shakyamuni, flanked by his foremost students, as well as four-armed Avalokiteshvara and Tara.

Jade Dragon Mountain The graceful snow peak of **Yulong Shan** (Jade Dragon) has become an important alpine resort for Yunnan and Sichuan tourists. There is a **cable car** ⓘ *0800-1600, ¥162*, to the summit area (4,600 m) from Snowflower Village Hotel, and another **smaller cable car** ⓘ *Yunsongping, 0800-1600, ¥42*, runs between the Jade Dragon Villas (2,970 m) and the Spruce Meadow.

Shigu

The township of **Shigu**, located on the "first bend" of the Yangtze river, is built at the site of a 16th-century battle fought between Tibetan and Naxi forces, the outcome of which determined the southern boundary of the Tibetan world. A marble plaque shaped like a stone drum (*shigu*) commemorates this event. ▸▸ *For listings, see pages 458-462.*

Lugu Lake → *Colour map 4, grid C5*

Getting there To reach Lugu Lake from the south, drive from Lijiang to **Yongsheng** (101 km), and thence to **Ninglang** (107 km), which is the county capital, predominantly inhabited by Yi people. From Nyinlang to **Luoshui** at Lugu Lake the distance is 80 km. Public buses will charge ¥20 per person. On the way, four passes are crossed, the first at 2,460 m, after which the Yi territory is left behind, and the others respectively at 2,460 m, 2,760 m, and 3,240 m. Lugu Lake may also be reached from the northwest, by following a rough motorable trail from Tong-nyi (see below, page 472) in South Dabpa county, or from **Xichang** via **Yanyuan** and **South Mili** (see below). ▸▸ *For listings, see pages 458-462.*

Beautiful **Lugu Lake** straddles the present day frontier between Yunnan and Sichuan provinces. Its south shore lies within the Yi Autonomous County of **Ninglang**, and the north shore within the Tibetan Autonomous County of **Mili** (Ch Muli). The lake covers an area of 50 sq km and is 2,688 m above sea level. The average depth is 45 m and its transparency is as deep as 11 m. There are five islands and four peninsulas. It is possible to go by canoe from Luoshui village on the Yunnan side to Mukua village on the Sichuan side, via Liwubi Island (where there is a small Gelukpa monastery), and to trek around the lake shore, before returning to Luoshui (¥30 per person).

The local Tibeto-Burman people, known as Moxi, maintain the Tibetan Buddhist religion. In the past there were important monasteries constructed near its shores. Most of these were Gelukpa establishments: **Daming Gonpa**, or **Yardzong Gonpa**, **Shubi Gonpa**, **Ozer Gonpa** and **Galong Gonpa** (of which only the first two have been renovated), but the Sakya monastery of **Dzembu** was also noteworthy. The Buddhist traditions of Lugu have been documented by the local lama Lobzang Yeshe Rinpoche. However, the area is better known for its unique maintenance of an ancient matriarchal culture, in which property is handed down from mother to daughter, rather than from father to son. The maroon blouses and long white pleated skirts worn by the women and girls of Lugu Lake are indeed striking, while the boldness and confidence they display reveals the secure basis of their authority. The Ninglang region and Lugu Lake straddle a fault zone, and in 1998 an earthquake measuring 6.5 on the Richter scale severely damaged this pristine environment.

Mili County སྨི་ལི → *Pop: 124,000. Area: 12,573 sq km. Colour map 4, grid B5.* 木里

The county of **Mili** lies to the north of Lugu Lake, near the confluence of the Li-chu and the Yalong River. It may be approached from **Ninglang** county in Yunnan, or by road from **Xichang**, the capital of the Yi Autonomous Prefecture of Liangshan in South Sichuan. Mili traditionally had an 80% Tibetan population and 20% Jang (Naxi) population, but nowadays Yi and Han immigration has radically altered the ethnic composition of the region. In town (Altitude: 2,310 m), the Tibetan population now amounts to only 50%. Within the county as a whole there are three ethnic Tibetan concentrations. The majority (*yi-qu*) live in the north around old Mili Dzong at **Wachang**, 120 km from the county town. The second largest group (*er-qu*)

Lugu Lake

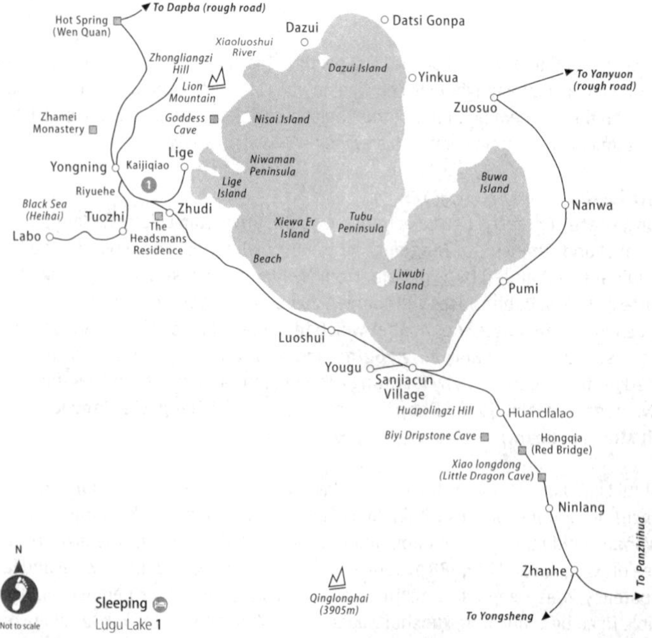

live in the town itself, and the smallest (*san-qu*) live at remote **Chabulang**, 180 km from town (via Wachang). ›› *For listings, see pages 458-462.*

Ins and outs

Getting there From **Ninglang** county town the Yunnan-Sichuan border is reached after 58 km on a rough road, which is in a state of disrepair, particularly during the summer rainy season. Avoid night travel since the local Yi people may ambush vehicles and extract money for safe passage! One pass (3,150 m) is crossed on the Yunnan side. After the provincial border, continue driving to the settlement of **Meiyu** (57 km), where there is a local school guesthouse. From Meiyu to **Mili** (92 km) the road crosses a 3,210 m pass, before which there is a turn-off for the easy highway leading to **Xichang** (162 km). Descending from the pass, the road enters a deep gorge, spanned by a high suspension bridge, which carries traffic into town. From Lugu Lake there is a more direct but rougher road, which reaches **Mili Gonpa** (Ch Muli Da Si), north of town, bypassing **De'ong Gonpa** of the Sakya school and a Bon monastery. It is also possible to trek from **Yongning** near Lugu Lake via **Wujiao** and **Xilinshan** to Mili (3-4 days).

Further north, there is road access to **Litang** county via **Lato** and **Chaksum**, and to **Dabpa** county via **Jiulong**, north of the three sacred snow peaks of **Dabpa Lhari**, which are named after the three bodhisattvas, Manjushri, Avalokiteshvara and Vajrapani, and are a focal point of pilgrimage for the inhabitants of Mili (see above).

History

Prior to the 16th century the ancient kingdom of Mili was a stronghold of the Karma Kagyu school. The influence of the kings of Jang Sadam who were patrons of the Karma Kagyu, and of Kampo Nenang monastery at Litang (which had been founded by the First Karmapa) was instrumental in shaping the early cultural development of Mili.

However, following the expansion of the Gelukpas into Kham during the 15th and 16th centuries, the Third Dalai Lama Sonam Gyatso oversaw the construction of a large Gelukpa monastery at Litang, and actively encouraged the propagation of his tradition further south in the Li-chu valley. Thus, in 1544, the Gelukpa temple of **Khe'ong Dewachen Sonam Dargyeling** was founded in Mili by Lama Dampa Neten Tsultrim Zangpo. Subsequently, the monastery of **Ganden Shedrub Namgyeling** was founded by Pakti Rabjampa Samten Zangpo in 1596. Through the efforts of their successors and their patrons, including Lama Peljor Gyatso and Khen Rinpoche Lobzang Tutob, the Geluk tradition became the dominant school in the region. In 1640 when Gushi Qan ended the kingdom of Beri, his armies subdued the Kagyu opposition to the Geluk dominance throughout the Litang valley and adjacent areas. Subsequently, Buddhist activity throughout Mili was uniformly sponsored by the Gelukpas of Lhasa and their Qing patrons.

Sights

At present in Mili county there are three main and 18 minor Gelukpa monasteries, of which 13 are currently undergoing restoration. The nearest to town is the small grassland monastery of **Dzikri Gonpa**. Among the three main ones, **Khe'ong Dewachen Sonam Dargyeling** is currently accessible from town on a poor road surface, near the Long Lake, about 3-4 hours distant. The reconstructed **Mili Gonpa**, also known as Ganden Shedrub Namgyeling, is 126 km from town on a better road surface, near Wachang township. The ruins of the old **Mili Dzong** and settlements are to be found here. Dormitory accommodation is available in Wachang at the Gucheng Hotel (¥7 per bed). **Warja Monastery** is even more remote in Chabulang township.

Dali → *Population: 500,000. Area: 1,062 sq km. Average temperature 15°. Average rainfall 1,176 mm.*

Those not wishing to fly directly from Gyeltang or Lijiang may travel by road to **Dali** and **Kunming**, capital of Yunnan province. **Dali**, 187 km from Lijiang, is situated on the west shore of **Lake Erhai**, at the crossroads leading from Kunming to Tibet (north) and Burma (east). Eighteen streams cascade from the 19 symmetrical peaks of the Canshan Range to the east shore of the lake and the climate is pleasant.

During the period of the Tang and Song dynasties, Dali was the capital of the **Nan Chao Kingdom**, which came into conflict with the Tibetan Empire of Songtsen Gampo and his successors. The celebrated **Three Pagodas (Sanda)** of Dali date from this era. Later during the Yuan period, Dali county fell under the authority of neighbouring Jang Sadam. Nowadays, the county is home to more than 20 ethnic minorities, including the Bai, Yi, and Hui.

From Dali, it is possible to take an excursion west to **Chicken Foot Mountain**, where according to the Chinese Buddhist tradition, Kashyapa the student of Shakyamuni Buddha passed away, his body being sealed within the mountain until the advent of Buddha Maitreya.

On to Kunming Kunming, the capital of Yunnan province, lies 412 km east of Dali by rail or road. For information on this gateway city, see below, page 727.

Sleeping

Gartok *p442*
E **Markham Guesthouse**, has suites at ¥60, doubles at ¥50, and inferior dormitory-style beds at ¥12 per person.

Tsakalho *p442*
E **Tsakalho Guesthouse (Yenching Xouzhen)**, T08082-2055. Has superior rooms at ¥40 per bed.

Dechen *p447, map p448*
C **Kawa Karpo Hotel (Taizi Mount Hotel)**, Wenhua Lu, T0887-8413188, F0887-8412688. Comfortable 3-star is the best in town with 30 double rooms (attached bath, hot water) at ¥300; 20 triples at ¥280, and suites at ¥480. The hotel has a Tibetan/Chinese restaurant with evening Khampa dancing, a 2nd floor dance hall with KTV, a small business centre, IDD and credit card facilities, and an in-house travel service under the management of Mr Yu Xiang Qian (Tibetan).
C **Adunzi Hotel**, Nanping Lu, T0887-8413398, F0887-8413388. The 2-star hotel has suites ¥388, doubles ¥218, triples ¥268, and economy rooms ¥20 per bed. The hotel has a restaurant, dance hall, bar and travel service.
C **New Hotel**, Nanping Lu. Comparable to the Adunzi in standard.
E **Kawa Karpo Guesthouse**, Nanping Lu. Has doubles at ¥120 and triples at ¥170.
E **Traffic Hotel**, Nanping Lu. Has doubles at ¥110 and triples at ¥160.
E **Government Guesthouse**, Nanping Lu. Simpler budget accommodation (¥40 per single room and ¥14 per bed in dormitory).

Gyeltangteng City *p450, map p451*
B **Guanguang Hotel**, Changzheng Lu, T0887-8230698, F0887-8229847. A 4-star hotel, currently the best in town, with doubles at ¥638, singles at ¥658, and suites at ¥1,508.
B **Huantai Hotel**, Jiantang Donglu, T0887-8229999. A 3-star hotel, has doubles at ¥420, triples at ¥520, and suites at ¥998.
B **Longfeng Hotel**, Heping Lu, T0887-8229788, F0887-8230558. Has doubles at ¥528, singles at ¥688, and suites at ¥1,680 or ¥1,880.
B **Salong Hotel**, Changzheng Lu, T0887-8232222, F0887-8231387. Has doubles at ¥480, and suites at ¥680.
B **Xinhua Dajiudian**, Changzheng Lu, T0887-8288088, F0887-8230938. Has doubles at ¥480, singles at ¥520, and suites at ¥1,180.
C **Antong Hotel**, Huancheng Xilu, T0887-8228241. This 2-star hotel is a 6-storey building with 96 rooms.
C **Birong Hotel**, Jinxian Lu, T0887-8228990, F0887-8228989. Has 28 doubles (¥200) and 2 triples (¥260) with specialist jewellery shops in the lobby.
C **Dechen Hotel (Ch Deqing Binguan)**, South Changzheng Lu, T0887-8227599. A 6-storey building with 110 doubles (¥380), 5 triples (¥420), 2 deluxe suites (¥1,280) and 40 economy doubles (¥280).

For an explanation of the sleeping and eating price codes used in this guide, see inside the front cover. Other relevant information is found in Essentials pages 44-46.

C Gyeltang Dzong Hotel (Ch Jentan Binguan), Huancheng Donglu, T0887-8223646, F0887-8223620. Situated below the Rutapo and Rutamo hills which traditionally protect the Gyeltangteng valley, under international management, with 54 rooms (¥300), and Metok Pema Restaurant serving Tibetan, Western, Chinese and Indian cuisine, cultural programmes highlighting botany and Tibetan medicine, and an in-house travel agency, T0887-82227493.
C Hongda Garden Hotel, Middle Changzheng Lu, T0887-8227788, F0887-8228499 (formerly known as the Beta Hotel). Has doubles at ¥268 and singles at ¥298, with business centre, lobby shops, lounge, and 2 restaurants (Tibetan and Chinese).
C Khampa Hotel (Ch Kang Beng Jiulou), South Changzheng Lu, T0887-822. Has 50 doubles (¥300) and 2 economy rooms (¥30 per bed).
C Qian Hu Hotel, Huancheng Donglu, T0887-8231111, F0887-8229688. Has doubles at ¥320, triples at ¥420, 4-bed dorms at ¥480, and ¥360.
C Shambhala Hotel, South Changzheng Lu. Has 76 doubles (¥200-280) and economy dorms (¥40 per bed).
C Tibet Hotel (Ch Yongsheng Luguan), Tuanjie Lu, T0887-8222448. With 22 doubles (¥280-320), 5 triples (¥360), and 28 dorms (communal showers) at ¥20-25 per bed.
D Yuntong Hotel, Huancheng Xilu, T0887-8228815. Has 24 standard doubles (¥200) and 8 economy doubles (¥100).
E Gangchen Nyima Hotel, Jinxian Lu, T0887-8228338, F0887-8223388. Has doubles at ¥90-100.
E Tibetan Family Guesthouse, Jinxian Lu, T0887-8223974. Has cheaper rooms for budget travellers.
E Xuelian Hotel, Changzheng Lu, T0887-8224000. Has 33 doubles (¥100), 11 triples (¥120), and 24 economy rooms (¥90).

Others, some of which may accept foreign guests:
Guangyuan Hotel, Changzheng Lu, T0887-8228885.
Hongda Hotel, North Changzheng Lu, T0887-8228585.
Shunyuan Hotel, Middle Changzheng Lu, T0887-8228189.
Wangda Hotel, North Changzheng Lu, T0887-8228152.

Lijiang *p455*

A Gongfang Hotel, Shangalila Ave, T0888-5788888. A 5-star hotel, has doubles and singles at ¥984, and suites at ¥3,280 (plus 15% service charge).
A Guanguang Hotel, Shangalila Ave, T0888-5160188. A 4-star hotel, has doubles at ¥728, singles at ¥708 and suites at ¥1,180-1,680 (plus 15% service charge).
B Grand Hotel, Xinyi St, Dayan, T0888-5128888, F0888-5127878. A 3-star hotel, has doubles at ¥498 (plus 15% service charge.
B Guyunsan Hotel, Shangalila Ave, T0888-5166966. Has doubles ¥528, triples ¥578, normal suites ¥580, and deluxe suites ¥1,980.
B Yulong Huayuan Hotel, 62 Jishan Lane, Xinyi Rd, Dayan Zhen, T0888-5182888. Has doubles at ¥680, singles at ¥740, and suites ¥1,480-2,680 (plus 15% service charge).
C Jiquanhui Hotel, Shiqiao, T0888-5103620. Has doubles at ¥250.
D Airport Hotel, Fuhui St, T0888-5120274. ¥180 per room.
D Guluwan Hotel, Xinda St, T0888-5121446, F0888-5121019. Standard rooms at ¥180-220.
D Lijiang Binguan, T0888-5121911. Has doubles at ¥200.
D Yu Quan Binguan, T0888-523927/5123925. Has doubles at ¥180.

NB There are also a number of newly built traditional style Naxi inns, among them:
Diyiwan Kezhan, T0888-5181688. ¥100 per room.
Dongba House, T/F0888-5175431. Tibetan run, ¥50-75 per room.
Sifang Kezhan, ¥60 per room.

Lugu Lake *p455*

Amenities for tourists have been improving in recent years; and local arrangements, including boating and horse riding, can be made through the **Lugu Lake Travel Agency** (head office at Ninglang), or the **Lugu Lake Girls' Travel Company**, T0888-5521169/5521999.
Musuo Yuan Mountain Lodge, Luoshui village. Best accommodation available, ¥18-36 per room, contact Mrs Tsering Lhamo.

Simpler lodge accommodation is available at Ligen village, on the northwest corner of the lake for ¥10 per bed.

Mili *p456*

E Muli County Guesthouse, T0834-6523730. ¥80 per room.

Dali *p457*
A Yaxing Hotel, Gucheng Nanlu, T0872-2670009. ¥840 per room.
B Manwan Hotel, Canglang Lu, Xiaguan, T0872-2188188. ¥540 per room.
B Shanyang Hotel, Yunling Ave, Xiaguan, T0872-2165188. ¥480 per room.
C Yangrenjie Kezhan, Gucheng. ¥200 per room.
D Dali Hotel, Fuxing Lu, T0872-2670368. Has superior accommodation at ¥220 per room, cheaper rooms at ¥110-150.
D Dali Travellers' Home, Gucheng. ¥160 per room.
D Honglongjing Hotel, Gucheng. ¥150 per room.
D Koreana Guesthouse, Gucheng, T0872-2665083. ¥150 per room.
D Red Camellia Hotel, Gucheng, T0872-2670423. ¥140-180 per room.
E Erhai Dragon Hotel, T0872-2125064. ¥100 per room, offers quieter lakeside accommodation.
E MCA Guesthouse, 700 Wenxiang Lu, T0872-2673666. ¥100 per room, or ¥20 per dorm bed.

Eating

Gartok *p442*
The town has a number of Sichuan-style restaurants.

Tsakalho *p442*
There are small Sichuan and Tibetan-style restaurants in the market, which is well worth a visit.

Dechen *p447, map p448*
The Sichuan Restaurant, located upstairs on Nanping Lu, overlooking the Nanping River. Good value.
Tourist Restaurant, on Nanping Lu, opposite the Kawa Karpo Hotel on Wenhua Lam. Serves reasonably-priced Chinese dishes.

There is a small upmarket café adjacent to the Kawa Karpo Hotel on Wenhua Lam.

Gyeltangteng City *p450, map p451*
Cheap Sichuan and Yunnan style restaurants are plentiful on Changzheng Lu, outside hotels.
Gaoyuan Restaurant, Heping Lu T0887-822926. The best outside restaurant, serves Yunnan, Sichuan, and Tibetan dishes.
Nanyue Restaurant, North Changzheng Lu, T0887-8229196. Another good option.
The Tibetan Art Café and Coffee Shop, has, as its name suggests, an English menu, and is popular with backpackers.

Lijiang *p455*
Alibaba Café, Mao Square. Caters to backpackers.
Mama Fu's, Xianfeng Lu. Western food.
Sakura Café, Yuhe Xilu. Serves Japanese and Korean dishes.

Those located close to the old Naxi quarter are also popular, especially **Dindin Friendly Café, Well Bistro, Simon Café, Blue Page**; all have English menus.

Lugu Lake *p455*
The Husi Tea House, T0888-5886089, www.chinainfo.net/husi. Has a good restaurant and local information desk.

Moxi traditional dances are performed in Luoshui in the evenings by arrangement (2100-2230).

Mili *p456*
Norgye Zakhang, recommended.

Dali *p457*
In the old town, there are many popular restaurants serving western and Japanese cuisine, among them **Marley's Café**, T0872-2676651, **Café de Jack, Tibetan Café**, T0872-2670188, **Taibailou**, T0872-2672112, **Old Wooden House**, and **Happy Café**.

Festivals and events

Gyeltangteng City *p450, map p451*
Feb/Mar: Tibetan New Year (Losar) is commemorated by a 15-day festival of prayers and religious dances at Ganden Sungtseling Monastery. In 2005 this will begin on 9 Feb.
May/Jun: Gyeltang Horse Festival; **1-4 Oct**: Traditional Folk Dances (Tibetan, Lisu and Yi).

Shopping

Dechen *p447, map p448*
There are a few interesting craft shops on both Nanping Lu and Wenhua Lu, selling local products including saddles, swords, azalea wood bowls and tsampa containers. The Department Store on the corner of

Wenhua Lu and Nanping Lu has modern and traditional items for sale. The vegetable markets are interesting, particularly during the Songrong mushroom-picking season.

Gyeltangteng City *p450, map p451*
Tibetan handicrafts are available at small shops on Changzheng Lu, particularly azalea wood bowls, silver ornaments, and embroidered covers which are made locally. The largest shopping precinct in town, for traditional and modern goods, is the Shangrila Shopping Centre, T0887-8228088.

Dali *p457*
Locally produced marble products, ornate boxes and batik are the specialities available at small shops in Gucheng. Avoid the bizarre clothing market unless you wish to be stereotyped as a throw-back to the 1960s!

Activities and tours

Dechen *p447, map p448*
Dechen Tourism Bureau, in the Kawa Karpo Hotel, T0887-8412408. Headed by Mr Tsering Nyima.
Dechen Travel Service, in the Kawa Karpo Hotel. Headed by Mr Yu Xiang Qian, offers expeditions to Mount Kawa Karpo.
Yue Liang Nan Travel Service, based in the old Meili Hotel on Nanping Lam. Caters mostly to domestic tourism. Day trips to Kawa Karpo glacier can be arranged (approximately ¥350 per vehicle from Dechen, ¥100 per horse from Melong village).

Gyeltangteng City *p450, map p451*
Dechen CITS, South Changzheng Lam, T0887-8225657, F0887-8222364.
Dechen Kawa Karpo Travel Service, Bita Hotel, T0887-8226620.
Jiaotong Travel Service, T0887-8223498.

Transport

Gartok *p442*
The public security bureau vigilantly inspects all military and alien travel permits.

Dechen *p447, map p448*
Bus
Public buses for **Gyeltang** (Ch Zhongdian) depart from the main bus station on Nanping Lam (3 daily, ¥33.50). Minibuses for **Tsakalho** depart in season from the area outside the open market.

Taxi
In town and the suburbs there is a taxi and auto-rickshaw service (range: ¥10-30).

Gyeltangteng City *p450, map p451*
Air
Gyeltang Airport, otherwise known as Deqin Shangrila has daily flights to **Kunming** (Yunnan Airlines, ¥560). There are also Wed and Sat flights to and from **Lhasa** (Air China Southwest, ¥1,250) and **Chengdu** (Air China Southwest, ¥1,160, via Kunming).

Bus
Long distance Buses depart the main bus station on Middle Changzheng Lu (T0887-8223501) for the following destinations: **Kunming** (5 daily, with couchettes, 1000-1800, 1 daily express 0900, ¥141); **Lijiang** (8 daily, 0700-1330, ¥30); **Dali** (12 daily, 0630-1100, ¥45 couchette ¥65); **Pondzirak** (Ch Benzilan – daily, 0650, ¥17); **Dechen** (3 daily, 0720, 0820, 0920, ¥33.50); **Balung** (Ch Weixi – 2 daily, 0650, 0700, ¥40); **Chaktreng** (Ch Xiangcheng – 1 daily, 0730, ¥53.50); **Derong** (1 daily, 0700, ¥37); **Chukar** (Ch Baishuitai – 2 daily, 0830, 1100). Please check the bus station for current schedule and prices: T0887-8222816/8222972.

Lijiang *p455*
Air
Lijiang Airport, 25 km east of the city, has daily flights to **Kunming** (¥ 450), **Shanghai** (¥2,090), and **Xishuangbanna** (except Thu, ¥620). Airport bus (¥10).

Bus
Long distance Buses depart the main bus station for the following destinations: **Kunming** (daily couchettes, 1430, 1700 and 1715, ¥115-24, express ¥155); **Gyeltang** (8 daily, 0710-1330, ¥29); **Dali** (10 daily, 0645-1410, ¥44); **Shigu** (1250, ¥7); and **Ninglang** (3 daily, 0710, 0800, 0900, ¥40).

Mili *p456*
Bus
Buses depart for the following destinations: **Xichang** (daily via Yanyuan, 0530, ¥40);

Wachang (yi-qu- 1 weekly, 0700, ¥25); and **Chabulang** (san-qu, 1 weekly, ¥25).

Dali *p457*

Air

Xiaguan Airport, 30 km east of Dali, has daily flights to Kunming (¥ 340) and Xishuangbanna (¥520).

Bus

Local Buses (number 4) run at 5-min intervals to **Xiaguan** (14 km).
Long distance Buses depart Xiaguan for **Kunming** (daily couchettes, ¥71, daytime express ¥54), and **Gyeltang** (daily, 0700, ¥40); and from Dali Gucheng for **Lijiang** (¥25-48).

Directory

Dechen *p447, map p448*

Post offices China Post on Zhongxin Lam, has EMS facilities and sells ICC cards for long distance and international phone calls, as well as postage stamps.

Gyeltangteng City *p450, map p451*

Banks China People's Bank, Changzheng Lu, changes foreign currency and gives cash advances on credit cards. Other banks include: China Agricultural Bank, Changzheng Lu and China Construction Bank, Heping Lu.
Hospitals Prefectural Hospital, South Changzheng Lu, T0887-8224273. Gyeltang Hospital of Tibetan Medicine, Jinxian Lu, T0887-8223974, is one of the largest in Tibet and a magnificent building.
Internet Gyeltangteng has over 30 internet bars, among which the biggest are Benteng Wanba, Heping Lu, Xueyuan Wanba, Xiangyang Lu, and Jinqiao Wanba, Xiangyang Lu. **Telephone** China Telecom, South Changzheng Lu, adjacent to Dechen Prefectural Government Buildings. Sells ICC cards for IDD and DDD calls. **Useful addresses** Police & public security, Jiantang Donglu, T0887-8223333.

Lijiang *p455*

Tourist offices Lijiang Culture Travel Service, T/F0888-5123462. Naxi Dongba Cultural Museum, Black Dragon Pool Park. Admission ¥2.

Mili *p456*

The main street has a post office, bank, bookshop, communist party office and public security bureau on the north side and the Mentsikhang traditional hospital on the south side.

Dali *p457*

Tourist offices Dali Travel Information, 34 Dali Huguo Rd, T0872-2671890. Dali CITS, T0872-2191967, F0872-2124902. Dali Chahua International Travel Service, T0872-2129504, F0872-2134427. Dali Merchants' International Travel Service, Cangshan Rd, Xiguan, Dali, T0872-2178619, F0871-2123292.

Chamdo to Chengdu: via Litang

There are two motor roads from Chamdo to Dartsedo and thence to Chengdu, the capital of Sichuan province. The northern route (Highway 317) which leads through Derge and Kandze will be described below, page 489. The first section of the southern route (Highway 318) via Batang and Litang follows the same road as the Chamdo-Kunming highway as far as the turn-off for Batang in Markham county (see above, page 442). The distance from Chamdo to the turn-off is 428 km. On reaching the turn-off do not head south into Gartok on the road to Tsakalho. Instead, take the left (east) turning which leads 72 km down to Druparong Zampa, the bridge spanning the Yangtze. Batang is a mere 32 km on the far side of the bridge. The distance from there to Dartsedo (Ch Kangding) is 497 km, and from Dartsedo to Chengdu 353 km. All the counties of Kham described in this section at present fall within the administration of the Kandze Autonomous Prefecture of Sichuan province. ***Recommended itineraries: 5, 10. See page 20.*** *»» For Sleeping, Eating and other listings, see pages 486-489.*

Batang County འབའ་ཐང་

→ *Population: 45,000. Area: 9,201 sq km. Altitude: 2,740 m. Colour map 4, grid B3.* 巴塘县

Batang lies 32 km northeast of the confluence of the Batang-chu with the Yangtze. It is an important town, spread out across the fertile and densely populated Batang-chu valley.

The earliest habitation is attributed to a legendary garuda bird (*jakhyung*) whose modern sculpted form can be seen in the town centre. For this reason, the town was originally known as Jakhyung. From the 16th century onwards the Gelukpa tradition established itself in the valley, and two monasteries were constructed, **Batang Chode** (Tsesum Gyashok Kapu Gon) and **Jakhyung Rito Pendeling Gon**. During the Sino-Tibetan wars of the early 20th century, the former was destroyed along with the castles of the Batang chieftains, and gradually repaired over the following decades. One of the Potala Palace's massive appliqué tangkas was offered to Batang following this reconstruction.

The low-lying prosperous Batang valley (2,740 m) was one of the few localities in Tibet which had a Chinese settlement prior to the 1950s. There were also American Protestant and French Catholic missions, which focused largely on medical and educational projects. The work of Shelton at the American mission was particularly respected by the Tibetans. Many Bapa (natives of Batang) acquired high bureaucratic positions following the Chinese occupation in consequence of their familiarity with the Chinese language and modern education.

Orientation

Nowadays, Batang resembles a modern provincial Chinese town. Entering Main Street from the Markham Road, you pass an important intersection at the west end. Head downhill for **Batang Chode** or the Hospital via the Grain Department, the Radio Station and Health Clinic, or uphill via the Primary School, Public Security Bureau, and local tax office to **Jakhyung Rito Pendeling**, which lies within the old part of town. Returning to the intersection, head due east along Main Street, passing a number of shops. The Post Office, Agricultural Bank and Batang Hotel are on the left, while the Jakhyung Monument, the Local Government Offices, Government Guesthouse and National Tax Office are on the right. A second intersection is then passed. Head downhill via the open market to the riverside, or continue due east on the Litang Road to reach the long distance bus and truck station.

Batang Chode

Renovated most recently in the aftermath of the Cultural Revolution, **Batang Chode** now has some 400 monks under the guidance of Kusho Jamda and Geshe Pema Gyeltsen. The complex is entered from the street through a high gateway, which leads into a spacious courtyard. Murals here depict the motif known as the 'Mongolian leading a tiger' (Sokpo Taktri). The monastic kitchen is to the left and the Tsuklakhang in the far left corner of the courtyard. The **assembly hall** has faded murals on the left wall and 1,000 small Amitayus images inscribed on the right. The **inner sanctum** has large images of Tsongkhapa flanked by his foremost students and murals depicting 1,000 forms of Shakyamuni. **Upstairs**, accessible by an external staircase, is the Jampa Lhakhang, containing a large image of Maitreya, which was constructed in 1994 by a sculptor from Dartsedo.

Batang County

Jakhyung Rito Pendeling → *For listings, see pages 462-473.*

This small temple, which nowadays houses the Batang County Buddhist Association, is a manifestly old building, located at the higher end of town, and approached via a steep stone staircase. There are only three monks residing here, but it contains, nonetheless, some original images. Beyond the portico, which has a Mani Wheel and a depiction of Green Tara, flanking the Four Guardian Kings, the temple has in its **inner sanctum** (left to right): Vajrayogini, Tsongkhapa with foremost students, Lakhor Lama, Shakyamuni flanked by his foremost students, Maitreya, 1,000-armed Avalokiteshvara, a small Padmasambhava, two small Tara images, a reliquary stupa, and the Collected Works of the Fourth Panchen Lama and Tsongkhapa. The left wall has old and faded murals, some of which appear to depict Tara and Amitabha.

Routes from Batang

A rough motorable trail follows the Yangtze upstream from the Batang-chu confluence into the gorge known as **Sangenrong** ('badlands'). The turn-off lies a few kilometres east of Batang on the Litang road. Passing through Sumdo township, the trail cuts across a pass before descending into a cultivated valley, where Sangen township is located, and crossing Meri La pass to eventually link up with the Kandze-Pelyul road. Feeder rivers, such as the Karda-chu and the O-chu swell the river's flow on both banks of the inhospitable gorge. Another rough but motorable trail follows the Yangtze downstream to Zang-me in Derong county (see below, page 472).

The **main highway** runs inland (northeast) from Batang, following the gorge of the Batang-chu upstream as far as **Taksho** (42 km). Not far from town the road forks. Avoid taking the lower road, which leads through a timber yard, and keep to the high road. At **Tsopugo**, there is a turn-off on the right leading uphill into the **Tsopu Nature Reserve**, where magnificent forests, snow peaks, ands hot springs can be explored in the environs of Tsopu Lake. It is said that visions of the Potala Palace in Lhasa can be seen reflected in its waters. There is a Padmasambhava cave here, and **Tsopu Monastery**, a branch of Dzogchen, is frequented by wild deer which fearlessly approach and are fed by the monks. Trekking routes lead from here to the watershed.

Continuing uphill from Tsopugo, you will pass through Lingshika, where there is a Katok branch monastery. A pass (3,450 m) is then crossed on the ascent and the tree-line left behind at 4,230 m (Km marker 3,222). Two glacial lakes are visible below

Batang

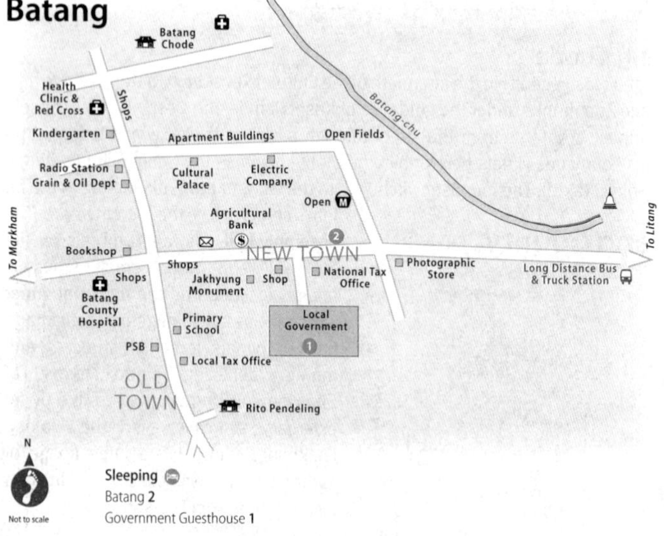

the road on the approach to the watershed pass (Ch Haizi Shan; 4,500 m) which divides the Batang-chu and Li-chu (crossed at Km marker 3,214), and is effectively the county border. The distance from Batang to Litang is 195 km, and there is one public bus each day, departing Batang at 0730.

Litang County ལི་ཐང་ → *Pop: 48,000. Area: 14,619. Colour map 4, grid B4.* 理塘县

Litang county occupies the high **Puborgang** range, which forms a watershed between the Yangtze around Batang and the lower Yalong basin (here called Nya-chu). The town of **Litang**, characterized by its large stone houses, lies near the source of the Li-chu tributary of the Yalong, and is one of the highest settlements in East Tibet (Altitude: 4,014 m). The distance from Litang tp Pundadrong in Nyachuka is 135 km, to Dabpa 152 km, and to Pelyul via Sangenrong 310 km. The county has 31 monasteries; and the annual seven-day Litang Horse Festival, which nowadays begins on 1st August, is a great colourful spectacle, attracting visitors from all parts of Kham and even from overseas.

Getting there Entering Litang county from Batang after the watershed pass (4,500 m), the meadows of the Puborgang range are carpeted in eidelweiss and gentian. At **Ronko** township (Km marker 3,184), there is a turn-off which leads up country to **Kampo Nenang** (see below). Then, the paved highway enters the high Litang plain around the headwaters of the Li-chu. A large rusting yellow dredging machine sifts the Li-chu's silt for gold (Km marker 3145). Making the gradual descent into Litang, a turn-off on the right, 11 km before the town, leads southeast to **Getse** (81 km), where there is an important branch of Katok Monastery.

Orientation Three roads converge at Litang: the west road from Batang, the east road from Pundadrong and the south road from Dabpa. Entering via the Batang Road, you will pass on the right a petrol station, a large enclosed stupa, which was consecrated in 2000, and an internet cafe. Opposite on the left there is a school, the Traffic Police Bureau and the Forestry Department. Shops line both sides of the road. Reaching a T-junction, turn left into Main Street, which leads uphill to the Government Buildings. On the left you will pass China Telecom, China Post, the Agricultural Bank, and on the right the Genyer Hotel, the Merchandise Monitoring Office, and the Nationalities' Shop (Mirik Tsongkhang). Then, at an intersection, dominated by a tapering monument named 'Pearl of the Grassland' (*tsatang-gi mutik*), you can turn left (west) for the public toilets, the Transportation Company and a CCP committee room, right (east) for the School of Agriculture and Animal Husbandry, the Litang Hospital and Middle School, or continue uphill towards the Government Buildings. Heading uphill, you will pass on the left (west), the cinema and karaoke club, a number of good cheap Sichuan restaurants, the Electricity Company, the County Guesthouse and the Public Order Standing Committee Office, while on the right (east) you will pass the High City Hotel, the Public Security Bureau and the law courts. At the top end of Main Street there is another T-junction, turn right (east) for the Conference Centre and the County Government Buildings, or left (west) for the Environment Bureau, and sharp right to continue uphill to Litang Chode Monastery.

Horse festivals

The horse festival (*ta-gyuk du-chen*) tradition in Central Tibet is said to trace its origins back to King Rabten Kunzang Phak of Gyantse in Western Tibet, who in 1408 organized a religious and secular festival in his grandfather's memory. It included wrestling, weightlifting, and horse racing, to which archery on horseback was added in 1447. However, the festival tradition in the Amdo and Kham areas of Eastern Tibet, where horses abound and horse riding remains a skill acquired at a tender age, may have had an even longer history. Most festivals, with the exception of Gyantse, which coincides with the fourth month of the lunar calendar, are held in the autumn when the grasslands begin to turn yellow and the harvest has been gathered in the villages. Among the sites in Central Tibet, which are renowned for their horse festivals, the Lhasa four-day event coinciding with the Great Prayer Festival (Monlam Chenmo) is not at present held; but those of Damzhung and Nakchu are still extremely popular. The Nakchu Festival is particularly grand, the 10-km site being covered with the blue appliqué tents of the riders, traders and locals. The Yak Race is the comic highlight of the event.

In East Tibet, horse festivals nowadays tend to be organized according to the western or modern Chinese calendar. For instance, the well known Jyekundo Festival begins on 25 July; and the Litang Festival on 1 August. In addition to racing, there are other equestrian events, with riders stooping from their galloping steeds to pick up kataks from the ground or twirling Tibetan muskets around their shoulders before shooting at a target on the ground. Tugs-of-war and weightlifting add to the spectacle – sometimes with strongarm monks from the local monasteries taking part; and there are folk song and dance troupes representing the different regions. A brisk trade is conducted amid the copious drinking of beer, chang, and hard liquor At Litang the standard festival programme is as follows: first day: opening ceremony, equestrian skills of five townships; second day: horse racing and trotting, equestrian skills; third day: folk songs and dances, fourth day: dance competition, fifth day: costume show and costume dance competition, sixth day: equestrian skills, local customs, closing ceremony .

Returning to the T-junction formed by the Batang Road and Main Street, continue east, passing on the left an open market, a large clothing store, the White Stupa Hotel, the Forestry Department Guesthouse and the White Crane Hotel. Opposite on the right are the Labour Guesthouse, the run-down Army Guesthouse, a clinic for the prevention of infectious diseases, the Chunglai Hotel and Restaurant, and the Bus Station. Continue east out of town on the Pundadrong Road (125 km), or turn right down a dirt road towards the Litang Festival Site and the Dabpa Road.

Kampo Nenang

The **Puborgang** area was traditionally a stronghold of the Karma Kagyu and Katokpa branch of the Nyingmapa. In 1165 the First Karmapa Dusum Khyenpa founded the monastery of **Kampo Nenang**, at a site where a large rock reputedly bears the letter KA whenever a new Karmapa appears in the world. He remained there until the age of 74 (ie 1184) and only in his later years did he go on to found the renowned **Karma Gon** monastery in Lhato (see above, page 422). Kampo Nenang is located in Ronko township, 80 km from Litang (one hour's drive) and one hour by horse from the

Litang-Batang road. Later in the 15th century, Khedrub Yeshe Gyeltsen, a local lama and prolific author, propagated the Katokpa tradition of the Nyingmapa here. Nyingmapas in Litang at the present day maintain strong contacts with the Nyingma monasteries of Nyarong and Sertal.

The Karma Kagyu tradition however was eclipsed in 1580 when the Third Dalai Lama Sonam Gyatso founded **Litang Chode**. An outstanding image of Jowo Shakyamuni was placed in its Tsuklakhang. Subsequently, in 1640, opposition to the expansion of the Gelukpa order in Litang was suppressed by the Mongolian armies of Gushi Qan, and, as an institution, the monastery quickly became the largest in Puborgang, and the dominant influence on local cultural life. Litang Chode rivals Chamdo and Kandze as the most influential Gelukpa monastery in Kham.

Litang Chode

Litang Chode, also known as **Ganden Tubchen Chokhorling**, was founded in 1580 by the Third Dalai Lama, and rebuilt recently in the aftermath of the Cultural Revolution, under the guidance of Litang Kyabgon Tulku Palden Dorje and Shodruk Tulku. The reconsecration was carried out in conjunction with the Litang Horse Festival in July, 1996. Entering the main gate from the town, there are four main buildings within the precincts of the monastery. The assembly hall known as **Jamchen Chokhorling** and the **Shakya Tubpa Podrang** occupy the centre, while the **Serkhang Nyingba** and **Lhakhang Karpo** temples are higher up the hill to the rear.

The door of the **Jamchen Chokhorling** is surmounted by murals depicting the lion, tiger and bear- headed protector deities (Sengdong, Takdong, and Domdong). Proceeding clockwise, the murals of the wall adjacent to the door depict Dharmaraja and the Four-armed and Six-armed forms of

Litang Chode

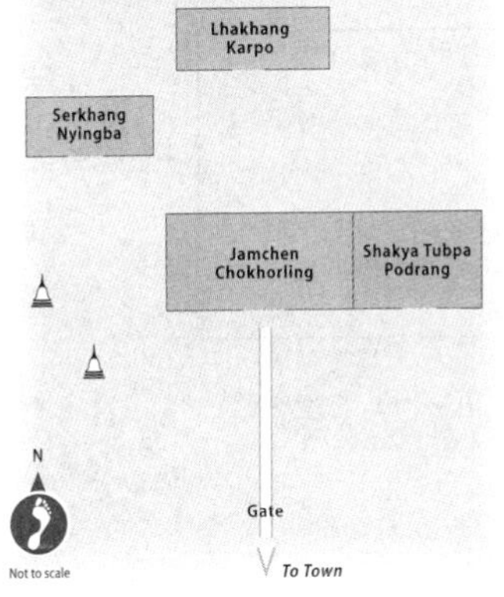

Jamchen Chokhorling

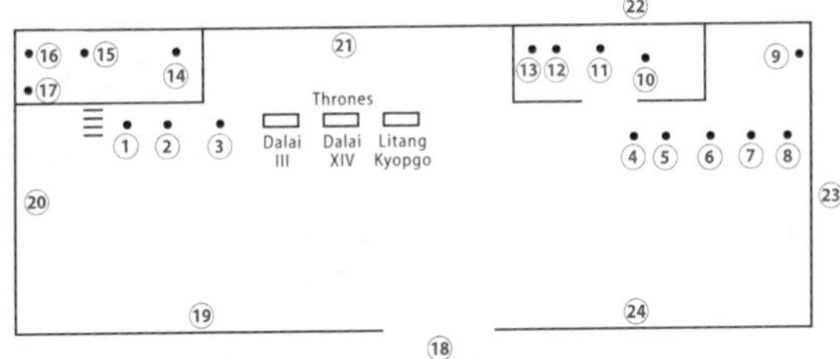

1 Manjughosa
2 Avalokiteshvara
3 Shakyamuni
4 Avalokiteshvara
5 Tsongkhapa
6 Maitreya
7 Tara
8 Sarasvati
9 Padmasambhava
10 Vajrapani Khorchen
11 4-arms Avalokiteshvara
12 Maitreya
13 Manjughosa
14 Senge Dongma
15 Dharmaraja
16 Shridevi
17 6-armed Mahakala
18 Murals of Sengdong, Takdong & Domdong above door
19 Murals of Dharmaraja with 4-armed & 6-armed Mahakala
20 Murals of 2-armed Mahakala, Asksobhya, Guhyasamaja, Cakrasamvara & Vajrabhairava
21 Murals 1000 Tsongkhapa
22 Murals of Buddhas of 3 Times
23 Murals of Manjughosa, Amitabho, Aksobhya, Cakrasamvara & Marici
24 Murals of Shridevi, Dorje Draxden Nechung Chokyong & Sertai

 Mahakala. Those of the left wall depict Two-armed Mahakala, Aksobhya, Guhyasamaja, Kalacakra, and Vajrabhairava. In the centre of the hall are thrones of the Third and Fourteenth Dalai Lamas and Litang Kyapgon. Behind are murals depicting 1,000 forms of Tsongkhapa. To the left of the thrones there are images depicting Manjughosa, Avalokiteshvara and Shakyamuni, and a protector shrine-room reached by a steep wooden staircase. It contains images of (left to right): Six-armed Mahakala, Shridevi, Dharmaraja, Senge Dongma and Shukden. To the right of the thrones are images depicting Tsongkhapa, Avalokiteshvara, Maitreya and Tara, while to their rear there is an **inner sanctum**, also approached via a wooden staircase. It contains images of (left to right): Manjughosa, Maitreya, Four-armed Avalokiteshvara and Vajrapani Khorchen, while its murals depict the Buddhas of the Three Times. Some 1,000 miniature images of Shakyamuni line the left wall, and 1,000 small Tsongkhapa statues fill the right wall. Continuing clockwise around the assembly hall, the right wall has images of Padmasambhava and Sarasvati, backed by murals depicting Manjughosa, Amitabha, Aksobhya, Cakrasamvara and Marici. Finally, the right wall adjacent to the door depicts the protectors Shridevi, Dorje Drakden, Nechung Chokyong and Sertri.

Shakya Tubpa Podrang

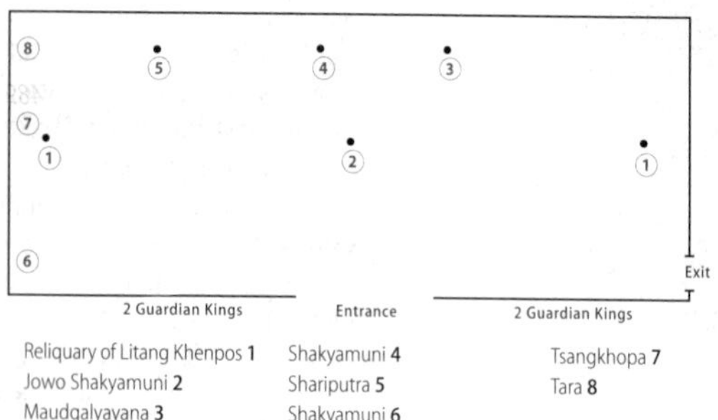

Reliquary of Litang Khenpos **1**
Jowo Shakyamuni **2**
Maudgalyayana **3**
Shakyamuni **4**
Shariputra **5**
Shakyamuni **6**
Tsangkhopa **7**
Tara **8**

Serkhang Nyingba

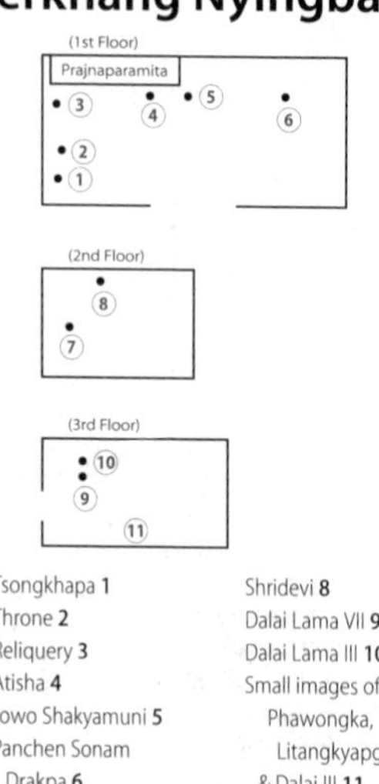

Tsongkhapa **1**
Throne **2**
Reliquery **3**
Atisha **4**
Jowo Shakyamuni **5**
Panchen Sonam Drakpa **6**
Reliquery of Litang Kyapgon **7**
Shridevi **8**
Dalai Lama VII **9**
Dalai Lama III **10**
Small images of Phawongka, Litangkyapgon & Dalai III **11**

Lhakhang Karpo

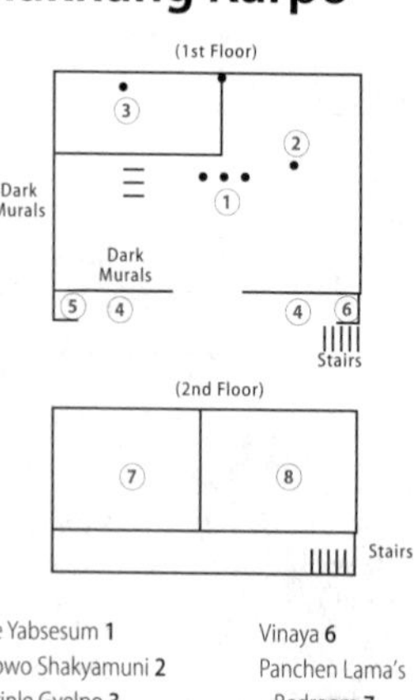

Je Yabsesum **1**
Jowo Shakyamuni **2**
Trinle Gyelpo **3**
Four Guardian Kings **4**
Wheel of Rebirth **5**
Vinaya **6**
Panchen Lama's Bedroom **7**
Panchen Lama's Day Room **8**

To the right of the assembly hall, the **Shakya Tubpa Podrang**, constructed on the site of the original 1580 temple, has an **outer vestibule** with murals depicting the Four Guardian Kings. **Inside**, there is a large central image of Jowo Shakyamuni backed by others depicting Shakyamuni and his foremost students, and flanked by the reliquary stupas of two former preceptors of Litang Chode. The murals of the left wall depict Shakaymuni, Tsongkhapa and Tara, each surrounded by 1,000 identical icons.

The **Serkhang Nyingba** is a three-storey building. On the **ground floor** there are images of (left to right): Tsongkhapa, Atisha, Jowo Shakyamuni and Panchen Sonam Drakpa. To the left there is a throne and a reliquary stupa, and against the innermost wall a full set of the 16 volumes of the *Shatasahasrika Prajnaparamita*. The **second floor** has an image of Shridevi and the reliquary stupa of Litang Kyapgon. The **third floor** has large images of the Third and Seventh Dalai Lamas, surrounded by smaller images of Phawangka, Litang Kyapgon, and the Third Dalai Lama.

The large **Lhakhang Karpo** (White Temple) has a **vestibule** with murals depicting the Four Guardian Kings, the Wheel of Rebirth and the Vinaya code of discipline for monks. **Inside** on the **ground floor** there are images of Jowo Shakyamuni and Tsongkhapa flanked by his foremost students. The murals are dark and obscure. An **inner sanctum** on the left, reached by a wooden staircase, contains an image of the protector Pehar in the form Trinle Gyelpo. On the **second floor** there are the bedroom and dayroom of the late Tenth Panchen Lama, the former containing a throne with photographs of the Ninth and Tenth Panchen Lamas, and the latter the robes of the Third Dalai Lama and the Tenth Panchen Lama, along with old original images of Amitayus, Avalokiteshvara and Shakyamuni. ▸▸ *For listings, see pages 486-489.*

East of Litang

From Litang, the paved highway leads east to **Pundadrong** in Nyakchuka county (135 km). There is a massive radar station on the way (approximately N 30°08', E 100°55').

South of Litang to Dabpa and Mili

A dirt road leads due south from Litang, following the Li-chu valley downstream through the grasslands to **Gyawa** (32 km). En route a 4,050 m pass is crossed, leading

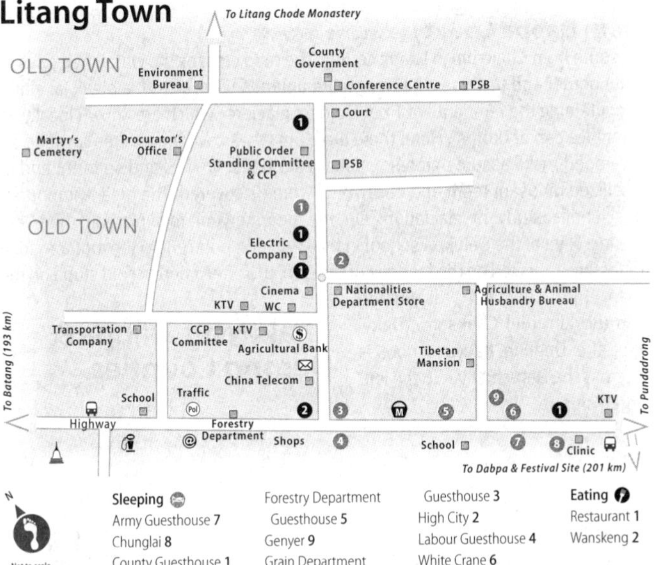

 into forested and craggy terrain. **Drakar Ritro**, a sacred abode of Padmasambhava, is located to the right (east) of the road here. This is revered as the most ancient pilgrimage site of the Litang area, and pilgrims will circumambulate the crags, where a natural stone impression of the Six-syllable Mantra of Avalokiteshvara can be seen above a cavity in the rock (*nego*) that marks the start of the 20-minute circuit. On the ascent pilgrims will pass the Zangdokpelri Cave of Padmasambhava, the narrow rock passage (*bardo trang*) through which they will crawl to gauge the extent of their past negative actions, and the prayer-flag strewn summit, from where the forested descent begins. From Gyawa, a side trail leads southeast to **Mola** (53 km), where the local monastery, **Wa Gon**, was converted to the Gelukpa tradition during the 17th century.

The main road runs due south across a 3,600 m pass to enter a wide north-flowing river valley. At **Chaksum** (15 km) it branches, the wider track leading southwest to **Dabpa**, and a second continuing due south for a further 73 km to **Lato**. At Lato the monastery of **Jangwar Lato Gon** can be visited. This was formerly a Karma Kagyu temple constructed by Karma Pakshi in the 12th century; but in the 17th century it was converted into a Gelukpa monastery by Serkong Onpo. From Lato, a trekking route leads south to **Mili** (see above, page 456).

Taking the **Dabpa** road from Chaksum, you leave the plain and ascend through a forested gorge (4,050 m) to re-cross the Yalong-Yangtze watershed (4,320 m) where there are a number of nomad encampments. Here, you will reach the border between Litang and Dabpa counties. The distance from Chaksum to Sumdo in Dabpa county is 80 km.

Dabpa County འདབ་པ

→ *Population: 28,000. Area: 5,870 sq km. Altitude: 3,735 m. Colour map 4, grid B4.* 稻城县

Dabpa county is a mountainous region in the south of Puborgang. The county town lies on the south bank of the Dab-chu (Ch Shuiluo he), a tributary of the Yangtze which rises in the Sangtobla uplands in the north of the county and flows south to merge with other Yangtze tributaries. In the south of the county there are the sacred snow peaks known as **Dabpa Lhari** or **Riksum Gonpo**, which are visited by pilgrims and mountaineers.

Northern Dabpa County → *Altitude: 3,600-5,000 m*

Heading south from **Chaksum** in Litang county, the road crosses the watershed pass at the county border and traverses the **Sangtobla uplands** (Ch Haizhu), a bleak lakeland plateau containing the remnants of Tibet's oldest glaciers , which are known locally as the 'ancient ice cap of Dabpa'. Here, there are 1,145 lakes covering an area of 3,200 sq km. The eroded rocks assume grotesque shapes – dogs, flowers and so forth; and in 1982 fossilized dinosaur teeth and eucalyptus were discovered. The area is important for the scientific study of glaciation. On the periphery of this plateau there are monasteries: **Niya** of the Gelukpa school in the east, and adjacent to the motor road, a Bon monastery is passed on the far bank of the Dab-chu after a derelict old stupa on the right. On the approach to **Sumdo** township (80 km from Chaksum), **Dekyi Gonpa** of the Drigung Kagyu school is visible across the Dab-chu river to the left. It has three stupas.

Sumdo

At Sumdo, there is a turn-off to the southwest which leads into Chaktreng county (67 km). The valley abounds in rhododendrons, buttercups, peonies

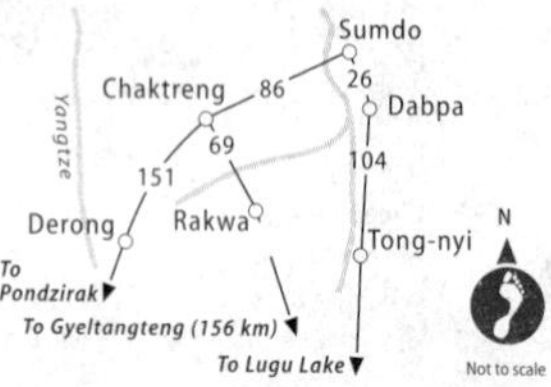

and daisies, and the village houses are of sturdy stone construction, as at Litang further north. The county capital lies 26 km downstream from Sumdo and 152 km south of Litang.

Heading into Dabpa town from Sumdo, most buildings are located on Main Street. On the left (east) you will pass the Public Security Bureau, the Electric Company, the Culture and Education Department, and the karaoke bar, while on the right (west) are the law courts, the local hospital, the open market, the tax office, the communist party offices, the dance hall and the bank. At the main intersection, turn left (east) for the Government Guesthouse and the road to Yangteng Gonpa, or continue due south on the Tong-nyi Road, passing the Government Buildings, the Post Office and the Daocheng Binguan.

Dabpa Yangteng Gonpa → *Altitude: 4,080 m*

Dabpa Yangteng Gon was originally a Kagyu monastery, converted to the Gelukpa school by Lodro Namgyel, a student of Jetsun Jampal Nyingpo in the 17th century. Formerly it housed 100,000 texts and many images including a Shakyamuni presented to the monastery by the Ninth Panchen Lama. As the most important of the 13 monasteries in Dabpa county, it was once even larger than Litang Chode. It is located on a hilltop approximately 20 km east of town above the east (Sanmo-Litang) road, and depending on weather conditions, it may be possible to drive uphill all the way. In recent decades, the most important lamas associated with Yangteng Gonpa have been Dzeme Tulku who resides in Paris and Gosok Rinpoche who is based in India. At present there are some 300-400 affiliated monks.

Within the reconstructed Tsuklakhang, the main images represent (L-R): Dharmaraja, the Buddhas of the Three Times and Hayagriva, in front of which are smaller images of (L-R): Lodro Namgyel, Phabongka and Tsongkhapa with his foremost students. A poster of Dorje Shukden is positioned in front of Hayagriva. Alongside the Tsuklakhang is a smaller recently renovated temple containing images of Dharmaraja, Tsongkhapa flanked by his foremost students, and Amitayus. In a corner recess there is a covered image of Dorje Shukden. Here, there are also photographs of the monastery's lineage holders alongside the present Fourteenth Dalai Lama, the Tenth Panchen Lama, and his communist-backed reincarnation. A Mani Wheel is located below the Labrang, which also functions as a tea room for visiting guests. ⏩ *For listings, see pages 486-489.*

Southern Dabpa County

in the rock (*nego*) that marks the start of the 20-minute circuit. On the ascent pilgrims will pass the Zangdokpelri Cave of Padmasambhava, the narrow rock passage (*bardo trang*) through which they will crawl to gauge the extent of their past negative actions, and the prayer-flag strewn summit, from where the forested descent begins. From Gyawa, a side trail leads southeast to **Mola** (53 km), where the local monastery, **Wa Gon**, was converted to the Gelukpa tradition during the 17th century.

Here, in South Dabpa county, the **Ngulso Range** (5,140 m) hugs the east bank of the **Tong-nyi Tsangpo** river. The larch forests of the mountain slopes in autumn are a fusion of red, yellow and green, while the river banks are broken by copses of trees and jagged rocks, against which the rushing torrent noisily cascades.

The Three Sacred Snow Peaks of Dabpa Lhari

Lying to the east of the Ngulso Range is the most important site in Dabpa: the triple peaked mountain sanctuary, generally known as **Rigsum Gonpo**, but given the special name of Dabpa Lhari by the Fifth Dalai Lama. **Mount Chenrezi** (6,032 m) lies to the north, **Mount Jampeyang** (5,958 m) to the south, and **Mount Chakna Dorje** (5,958 m) to the east. These perennial snow peaks, which face each other like the legs of a tripod, cover an area of 800 sq km and are focal points for pilgrimage from Litang, Dabpa and Mili. In front of each peak there is a limpid lake, poetically described as the mirrors in which the Lords of the Three Families shaved their hair. Wild goats, deer, monkeys and black bears thrive in this protected environment.

The motor road continues to follow the Tong-nyi Tsangpo south via **Tong-nyi** township, 104 km distant from Dabpa town, after which a rough motorable trail leads southeast to **Lugu Lake** on the Yunnan border (see above, page 455). There are currently plans to upgrade this road surface.

Chaktreng County ཕྱག་ཕྲེང → *Pop: 27,000. Area: 4,712 sq km.* 乡城县

Chaktreng county, in the middle reaches of the Chaktreng-chu valley, has been a staunchly partisan Gelukpa area since the 17th century when the local Kagyu monastery Gyazawei Gonpa was razed to the ground by the Mongol army of Gushi Qan. Pon Khandro, a local chieftain, subsequently constructed the Gelukpa monastery of Chaktreng Sampeling on the same site.

The inhabitants of Chaktreng vigorously resisted the Chinese occupation of Chao Erh Feng's army in the Batang area during the early decades of the present century.

Trijang Rinpoche, the late tutor of HH Dalai Lama XIV, was a native of Chaktreng, and many of his most devoted followers hail from this part of East Tibet and the adjacent areas of Drayab and Gyeltang.

Ins and outs

The road to Chaktreng from Sumdo in Dabpa county leaves the Dab-chu valley and crosses a grass-covered pass (4,560 m), at Km marker 138 (from Litang). It then descends through a deep forested gorge, penetrating the tree-line at 4,140 metres. The distance from Dabpa to Chaktreng is 112 km, and from Sumdo 86 km.

Chaktreng Town → *Altitude: 3,180 m*

The county town occupies a high ridge above the Chaktreng-chu gorge. The escarpment plunges steeply to the river banks below. On the long Main Street there are a number of small Sichuan restaurants, some of which now serve local fish, and there are two guesthouses towards the south end near the bus station. A turn-off on the right leads uphill to Chaktreng Monastery, which is under reconstruction. On the way you will pass the Government Buildings and the Primary School. » *For listings, see pages 486-489.*

Routes from Chaktreng Town

From Chaktreng there is a 69 kilometre drive due south to Rakwa (Ch Wengshui) on the Yunnan border, after which Gyeltangteng city (see above, page 450) is only a further 156 km distant.

Alternatively, drive west into Derong county. Heading south from the town, the road climbs through a richly forested gorge to cross a 4,080 m pass after 30 km. This marks the county border between Chaktreng and Derong.

Derong County སྡེ་རོང → *Pop: 24,000. Area: 2,244 sq km.* 得荣县

Derong county includes the east bank of the Yangtze south of Batang and the valley of the Ding-chu along with its tributaries. It is a region of deep gorges and steep dusty river banks. The county town, otherwise known as **Lower Zang (Zang-me)**, lies on the banks of the Ding-chu River, south of its confluence with the Mo-chu, and north of its confluence with the Mayi-chu. The distance from Chaktreng to Derong via **Zangang** is 151 km.

Ins and outs

Getting there After crossing the pass 30 km south of Chaktreng, which forms the county border, the road descends towards Zangang, via a 3,750 m ridge. Here, it divides, one trail leading north to the Yangtze and Batang (see above, page 464); and the other south to Zang-me, the county town, which sprawls along the banks of the Ding-chu in the Derong gorge. Taking the latter route, you will observe (at 2,880 m) many roadside stupas in classical Tibetan style and in simple mani-stone or sog-shing styles. A final pass (3,300 m) leads across a slate mountain into the county town.

Zang-me → *For listings, see pages 462-473.*

The road from Zangang leads into town on the east bank of the Ding-chu. The town hugs both banks of the river, which is spanned by three main bridges. Heading into town, you will pass on the left, the Forestry Department Guesthouse, the water and electricity company, the post office, the police station and law courts, a post-natal health clinic, the Derong Hospital and the primary school. Opposite the post office there is a small Tibetan Guesthouse overlooking the river. Across the upper bridge, on the west bank, there are the Government Buildings and a newly constructed Government Guesthouse. Heading downhill on the west bank you will pass the tax office, the bank, barber shops and grocery stores, the Tashi Tsongkhang, which sells Tibetan artefacts, the cinema, and the open market. Trekking routes lead across from the west bank of the Ding-chu into the Yangtze gorge where the monasteries of Derong county are mostly located.

Derong to Yunnan

Leaving Derong by the south road on the west bank of the Ding-chu, you will soon cross another bridge leading over to the east bank and continue following the course of this river downstream to its confluence with the Yangtze at **Gamdrong** (Ch Wakha) on the Yunnan border. Here at the provincial checkpoint, a suspension bridge crosses the Yangtze, and the road divides: one branch heading northwest to **Pondzirak** (Ch Benzilan) and **Dechen** (see above, page 443), and the other southeast to **Gyeltangteng** (see above, page 450).

Nyachuka County ཉག་ཆུ་ཁ → *Pop: 41,000. Area: 6,732 sq km.* 雅江县

The Yalong River (known as the Dzachu near its source and the Nya-chu in its middle reaches) emerges from the once impenetrable and inhospitable Nyarong gorge at **Pundadrong**, the capital of Nyachuka county, which broods over the eddying silted waters of the Yalong. The distance from Pundadrong to Litang (west) is 135 km, to Barshok in Nyarong county (north) 142 km, and to Dartsedo (east) 150 km.

Nyachuka & Gyezil

Litang to Pundadrong

Taking the paved highway 318 east from Litang, you cross a 4,258-m pass and after 17 km reach a fork. Here you can head left (north) on a dirt road for Barshok in Nyarong county, 165 km distant, or due east on the main road for Pundradrong. The side road ascends gradually through nomadic pastures to cross a 4,447-m pass, which can be snow-covered even in early summer. Descending into a forested valley, where the sturdy stone village houses have intricately carved lintels, you reach

 Chunda township, to cross a bridge over the Yalong and connect with the main road north from Pundadrong to Barshok.

If instead you keep to the highway, after 42 km you will pass through the verdant forested meadows around **Nub Golok** township (Ch Xi Golok), where a branch of Litang Chode named **Golok Gonsar** was founded in the 17th century by Ripa Sarampa. Hiku Nunnery is also passed on the right. Then, driving across two passes, the first (4,718 m) which is grass-covered, and the second named **Lama La** (4,412 m) which is forested, you reach the watershed between the Li-chu and Yalong. Here, there are spectacular views towards Nyarong (northeast) and the Batang-Litang divide (west). After a further 66 km the road descends into **Nyachuka,** where there are important monasteries such as **Odozangpo Gonpa** of the Sakya school.

Pundadrong

The administrative capital is located at **Pundadrong** in the Yalong gorge. The elegant timber dwellings of the old town rise in tiers above the south bank of the Yalong River, as it surges out of the high-cliffed Nyarong ravine. A strategically important bridge spans the river here, and it is well guarded. The roads leading down to the bridge are steep, but there are a number of Sichuan-style restaurants, and a guesthouse. ▸▸ *For listings, see pages 486-489.*

Orientation Entering the town from the Litang road, you will bypass a narrow dirt road which crosses the Yalong and follows the east bank upstream into Nyarong county, where it connects with the Litang-Barshok road (see below, page 536). From here, the paved road descends into the upper part of the town, where the government buildings, banks, Yajiang Hotel, and markets are located to the right (southeast). Heading downhill (left) you will then pass China Telecom, a military camp, the Forestry Department Guesthouse and a number of Sichuan-style restaurants including the Yajiang Fandian, before reaching the Yalong Suspension Bridge and the old Tibetan quarter.

Routes from Pundadrong

Four roads diverge at Pundadrong: west to Litang, north to Nyarong and Tawu, south to Bawolung, and east to Minyak and Dartsedo. Among these the north-south roads follow the course of the Yalong River (known here as the Nyak-chu). For a description of the northern roads to **Tawu** (121 km) and **Nyarong** county (142 km), which are important cultural areas for the Nyingmapa and the Bonpo, see below pages 536 and 540. The southern road to **Bawolung** is only motorable in its initial 39 km sector, as far as Lake Malangtso, where villages were devastated by a severe earthquake in 2000.

The paved highway, after crossing the suspension bridge, ascends the **Minyak Rabgang** highlands, which form the watershed between the Yalong and the Gyarong basins. En route you will bypass **Kabzhi Monastery**, which represents the Karma Kagyu tradition. The ascent becomes drier and dusty, and **Kabzhi La** pass (4,412 m) is eventually reached at Km marker 2,940. Then the road winds downhill to its intersection with the Dartsedo-Derge highway, 4 km north of Dzongzhab.

Dzongzhab

Dzongzhab township (Ch Xinduqao), 72 km east of Pundadrong, is an important transport station. The valley in which it lies straddles the intersection of four main roads: north to Tawu, Kandze and Derge, south to Gyezil, and east to Dartsedo. ▸▸ *For listings, see pages 486-489.*

Gyezil County བརྒྱད་ཟིལ → Pop: 51,000. Area: 7,478 sq km. 九龙县

Taking the southern route from Dzongzhab, you will arrive in **Gyezil** county, traditionally known as **Gyezur**. The road at first follows the Tung-chu (a tributary of the Yalong) upstream through South Minyak district. There are fine views of **Mount Minyak Gangkar** (7,556 m), the highest snow range in East Tibet. At **Rindrubtang**, 95 km south of Dzongzhab, the road forks, south to the county capital, 83 km distant, and east to **Lugba** (Ch Liuba), an important trail head for the Minyak Gangkar Base Camp.

Mount Minyak Gangkar → *See map next page.*

This is the highest peak of the **Minyak Rabgang** range (Ch Daxue), which covers an area of 290 sq km, with more than 20 peaks over 6,000 m and some 45 glaciers. In summer the mountain is shrouded in cloud, the air temperature sometimes falling to -20°, and most of the annual rainfall (800-900 mm) occurs between July and September. The precipitous granite ridges of the mountain's north-west, north-east, south-west and south-east faces have attracted mountaineering expeditions since 1878. The first ascent was made by an American team in 1932.

Climbing, pilgrimage circuit and trekking The optimum seasons for climbing are spring and autumn, and the 14-day **pilgrimage circuit** of the entire range is best undertaken in autumn. The clockwise circuit begins 14 km south of Dartsedo at **Laoyulin** (3,100 m), passing **Yagya Ge La** pass (3,990 m), **Mozhi**, **Hailuoguo Glacier**, **Dzumi** (3,600 m), **Gangkar Monastery** (3,830 m), **Gyezil Dzong** (the former summer palace of the Chakla kings) and **Gyezil La** pass (4,680 m). For trekkers, there are three main approaches to the range: from **Laoyulin** in the north, from **Lugba** in the southwest, and from **Mozhi** in the east. The first two are described here and the third under **Chakzamka** county (see below, page 484).

Laoyulin to Base Camp Drive south from Dartsedo for 14 km to **Laoyulin**, which lies to the west of the snow peak **Mount Tsechen Nyima** (6,089 m). Trek through the Gyezil-chu valley for three days (via Gesarlei, Banaklei and Nomad Camp) to reach **Bu-chu La** (4,940 m), in close proximity to the northernmost peaks of the range, **Rongyi Gangkar** (5,680 m) and **Gyezil Gangkar** (6,801 m). Then descend through the forested Bu-chu valley for three further days to join the pilgrimage circuit just south of **Gangkar Monastery** (3,830 m), which is dominated by the snow massif of **Minyak Gangkar** itself (7,556 m). This is a recently rebuilt monastery of the Karma Kagyu school with 20 monks and hermits. The assembly hall contains images of White Tara, and Marpa, flanked by Milarepa and Gampopa, and the present incumbent lama, the Sixth Gangkar Rinpoche, who is currently studying at Bir in India, under the guidance of Tai Situ Rinpoche. **Base Camp** is situated in a meadow above Gangkar Monastery at 4,390 m.

Lugba to Base Camp Lugba (3,640 m) can be reached by bus from Dartsedo or Litang via Rindrubtang and the Tung-chu valley. Monasteries in this area include **Giwakha Jampaling**, which was founded by Lama Gangringpa, a student of the Second Dalai Lama, and the smaller monasteries of **Sokpo**, **Nego**, **Tongku** and **Chukmo**, which appear to have been originally of Kagyupa provenance, and were later absorbed by the Sakya and Geluk traditions. Sokpo Monastery contains an impressively large image of Tangtong Gyelpo. A horse trail and two-day trekking route leads via Muju hamlet (3,840 m) and **Dzumi La** pass (4,660 m) to Gangkar Monastery.

Karpo

South of the Rindrubtang turn-off, the road enters the valley of the Dridzin-chu tributary of the Yalong, and follows it downstream. The administrative capital of Gyezil county is at **Karpo**, 83 km south of Rindrubtang and 176 km south of Dzongzhab. The town is located in the extreme southeast of the Tibetan plateau. The population here is predominantly **Yi** rather than Tibetan; and the road itself continues south from Karpo out of Tibetan territory into the **Liangshan** Yi Autonomous Prefecture.

Dardo County དར་མདོ → *Pop: 108,000. Area: 11,125 sq km.* 康定县

Present-day **Dardo** county broadly corresponds to the heart of the ancient **Chakla Kingdom,** which until the mid-20th century was governed by the Chakla Gyelpo from Dartsedo town. It therefore includes both the Minyak hinterland of the Tibetan plateau and the plunging gorge formed by the Gyetochu and Yakra-chu tributaries of the Gyarong. The administrative capital is at **Dartsedo,** 75 km from Dzongzhab (Xinduqiao) and 353 km from Chengdu. **NB** Minyak should not be confused with the medieval kingdom of Minyak (Ch Xixia), located in present-day Ningxia Province of China, which was founded in 1038 and destroyed by Genghiz Qan in 1227. The survivors of this kingdom are said to have fled into East Tibet, where they

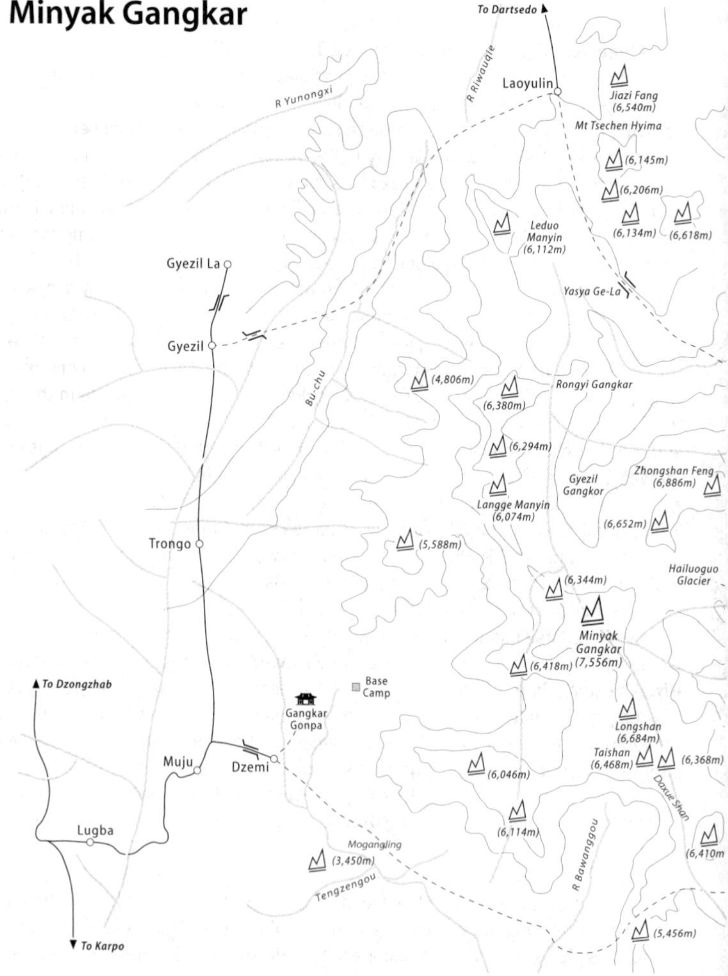

intermingled with the local populace in the west of Minyak Rabgang. Some say that the distinctive language of Tawu reflects this intermingling.

Lhagang → *For listings, see pages 462-473.*

At the intersection of highways 317 and 318, 4 km north of **Dzongzhab**, take the latter road, which passes through **Lhagang** in the Tung-chu valley after 37 km. Entering the main street from Dzongzhab, you will pass on the right (east) side a small Tibetan guesthouse, the bus station, and the handicraft centre. On the left (west), are the Government guesthouse, the local government buildings, a turn-off leading to the **Nyingmapa Shedra**, and **Lhagang Monastery** itself. In town, a large orphanage has recently been opened under the auspices of the New York-based Trace Foundation.

Lhagang Monastery

ⓘ *Admission: ¥10.*

At the north end of town surrounded by three hills symbolizing the bodhisattvas Manjushri, Avalokiteshvara and Vajrapani, is **Lhagang Monastery**, formally known as **Lhagang Gon Tongdrol Samdrubling Chode**. The chapel to the right of the Assembly Hall contains a revered Jowo Shakyamuni image named Semnyi Ngalso (popularly called Lhagang Jowo). According to legend, when Princess Wencheng travelled to Tibet, she stayed overnight here, and the Jowo Shakyamuni image which she brought as her dowry to Lhasa is said to have spoken out aloud, requesting to be left in that idyllic setting! Subsequently King Songtsen Gampo constructed 108 temples in the direction of China, the last being Lhagang. Later in the 12th century, the original temple was expanded into the form of a monastery by the Kagyupas, and from the 13th century onwards under the influence of Chogyel Phakpa it was gradually absorbed by the Sakyapa school, to which it still holds allegiance.

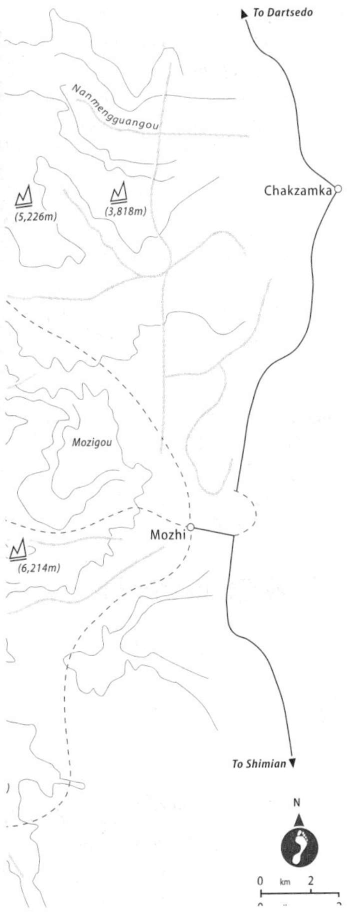

The renovated **Assembly Hall** in its **lower storey** contains images of the Buddhas of the Three Times, Manjughosa, three of the Five Founders of Sakya (Kunga Nyingpo, Sakya Pandita and Chogyel Phakpa), and a set of the Eight Stupas symbolizing the deeds of the Buddha. The murals depict Mahakala, Remati, Panjaranatha and Tara (adjacent to the door), the meditational deities of the Sakya school (left wall), and the Sakyapa lineage (right wall). In its **upper storey** there are reliquary stupas containing the remains of past teachers associated with the monastery – including Do Khyentse Yeshe Dorje.

The **Jokhang Chapel**, containing the sacred Jowo Semnyi Ngalso image, has an air of great sanctity. Pilgrims from Kham who have seen this image will sometimes say that the blessing resembles that of seeing the Lhasa Jowo image itself! The main image is flanked by others depicting (L) Thousand-armed Avalokiteshvara, Four-armed Avalokiteshvara, and Buddha (twice); and (R) the previous Sakya Trizin, Padmasambhava flanked by Shantaraksita and King Trisong Detsen, Vajrasattva and Tara; and (to the rear) the Sixteen Elders. The ancient murals of this chapel depict the deities of the four classes of tantra and the Sukhavati paradise of Amitabha. In 2002 this important chapel was extended, enabling new clay images to be installed along its side and rear walls. New murals have also been commissioned.

The newly reconstructed **Tuje Chenpo Lhakhang** to the left of the Assembly Hall contains a central image of Mahakarunika, and finely executed murals.

Behind the assembly hall compound, which is surrounded by a perimeter wall of prayer wheels, there is a large garden containing 124 stupas of various sizes. One ancient stupa housed here is said to vibrate of its own volition; and there are wonderful views of the snow peak of **Mount Zhara Lhatse** (5,820 m) on a clear day to the northeast. Alongside the entrance to Lhagang, there is a shop belonging to the monastery, which sells groceries and Tibetan artefacts.

Nyingmapa Shedra

On the left side of the road before reaching the monastery, there is a dirt road leading across the fields towards the Nyingmapa Shedra (college) run by Khenpo Chodrak. Here there are over 100 monks of the Nyingma tradition engaged in the study of classical philosophical texts. The small temple of the college has recently been expanded into a large Lhakhang, capable of accommodating an increased number of students. The view from the plain below the college dramatically overlooks the distant snow range of **Minyak Gangkar**.

Lhagang grasslands

The pastures to the north of the town are often the venue for horse festivals in the summer months. In summer 2000 the celebrations commemorating the 50th anniversary of the founding of the Kandze Autonomous Prefecture were held here, with distinctive tents and towers representing each of the prefectural counties.

Minyak Pelri Gonpa

A trail northwest from the college leads to **Minyak Pelri Gonpa**, a Nyingmapa monastery in a wonderful grassland setting, where the Northern Treasure (Jangter) tradition is maintained.

Mount Zhara Lhatse

Continuing northwest on the paved Highway 317, you will cross **Drepa La** (3,817 m), with the sacred snow peak of **Mount Zhara Lhatse** (5,820 m) visible to the northeast. This mountain (Ch Haitzu Shan) is revered as one of the 25 Padmasambhava sites in East Tibet, specifically representing the body aspect of buddha-mind. According to the ancient pre-Buddhist tradition, the mountain is regarded as an offspring of Nyenchen Tanglha. The beautiful lake **Zhara Yutso** is located on the northeast side of the mountain, and around it are

Dardo & Chakzamka

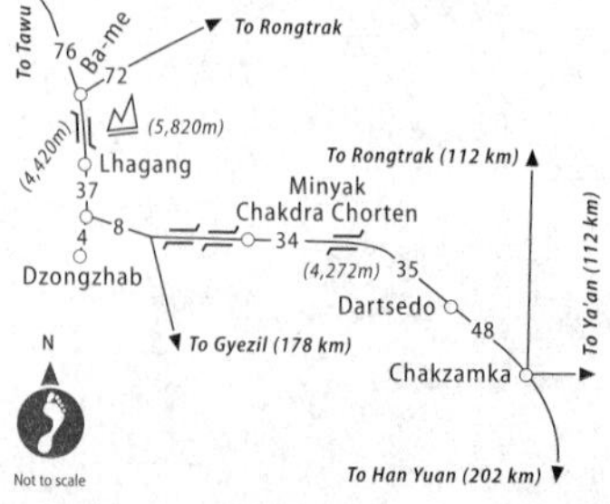

many meditation caves associated with Do Khyentse Yeshe Dorje (19th century). On the southwest side of the mountain, there are as many as 15 medicinal hot springs. The snow peak remains visible far to the north for those crossing the **Mejesumdo** uplands. The road through the **Mejesumdo** uplands to Garthar and Tawu will be described below, page 538.

Southeast to Dartsedo

Heading southeast from **Dzongzhab** (Xinduqiao), the highway branches after 8 km, the southern dirt track leading to **Gyezil** county (see above, page 475) and the paved road leading towards **Dartsedo**. Taking the latter, two minor passes are crossed, and the road enters a wide pasture, flanked by an avenue of poplars and willows. The farming villages of **Minyak** have distinctive detached three-storey stone mansions. At **Rilung Drongde** village there is a circular prayer flag formation wound around a central wooden axis, and some fine mani stone carvings. A new tourist restaurant has recently been opened here.

Minyak Chakdra Chorten

The main landmark in this part of East Minyak however is the enormous white stupa known as **Minyak Chakdra Chorten**, dedicated to the Eight Medicine Buddhas. The stupa stands beside the highway to the east of the village called Minyak Dem Drongde. The original stupa is attributed to Tangtong Gyelpo; but it has been renovated and reconsecrated several times, by great masters such as the late Tenth Panchen Lama. The adjacent Gelukpa monastery has a small temple depicting images of Shakyamuni and his foremost disciples. From here a motorable side trail leads south to **Rikuk Monastery** of the Sakya school.

The highway continues east to cross the **Gye La** pass (4,272 m), which the Chinese call Zheduo Shankou. This watershed, which divides the Yalong and the Gyarong basins, is 42 km east of Dzongzhab township and 33 km above Dartsedo.

Dartsedo དར་རྩེ་མདོ་ → *Altitude: 2,590 m*

The town of Dartsedo (Ch Kangding) lies deep within a gorge at the confluence of the Gyetochu and Yakra-chu tributaries which form the Dardo River. It was formerly the capital of the **Chakla** Kingdom – one of the five independent kingdoms of Kham, under the hereditary authority of the Chakla Gyelpo. The town prospered as the centre for the tea trade between Tibet and China. Traders would travel long distances, carrying herbal medicines from the Tibetan plateau to sell in exchange for the tea grown in the Ya'an region, which appealed to the Tibetan palate when blended with salt and butter. The main streets were flanked by large tea warehouses. Nowadays, the profitable tea trade continues, but the town has grown into a large city, containing the Kandze prefectural government as well as the local Dardo county administration. In the past Dartsedo always had the air of a frontier town where Chinese and Tibetans would intermingle. However, the Chinese element of the population has grown considerably in recent years, far outweighing the indigenous element. ▸▸ *For listings, see pages 486-489.*

Orientation Descending from the **Gye La** pass, the highway eventually reaches an intersection and a traffic checkpoint, with a military camp on the right (south). Opposite on the left there are a number of small karaoke bars and restaurants, the **Dartsedo Mentsikhang**, the entrance to **Dordrak Gonpa**, a cemetery, **Lamotse Monastery** and the county hospital. Reaching a T-junction, turn left and head downhill (northeast) into town on **Xiangyang Jie**. On the left you will pass the Economic Affairs Bureau, a loop road leading to the CCP school, the Communication Bureau, the County Court, the Public Security Bureau, the Armed Police Unit and **Dentok Riwo** Hill and the PLA Guesthouse.

At this point, Xiangyang Jie intersects with the parallel **Xinshishou Jie** on the right (east) and a wide street on the left (west), which crosses the Gyeto-chu for the Kangding Hotel. Continuing south on Xiangyang Jie, you will pass buildings on both sides which were rebuilt following a devastating flood in 1995, among them a Catholic Church, the Kalakaer Hotel and the Agricultural Bank.

Heading northeast from the intersection on **Xinshishou Jie**, you will pass on the right a small noodle restaurant, the Jinlu Hotel, a clinic, the Electricity Company and the Agricultural Bank, with a mosque on the left. Further down the lane you will find clothing shops, Xinhua Books, Shambhala Tibetan Handicrafts, a department store, the Trewongke Restaurant, a pharmacy, the Shuijiu Julo (Well Restaurant), and the vegetable and meat market. The lane rejoins Xiangyang Jie here in the open market area.

Reaching the open market area, Xiangyang Jie forks yet again, left (north) for **Xinshiqian Ave** and right (south) for Chakzamka. If you take the former road, you follow the south bank of the Dardo River downstream, passing the Guesthouse for

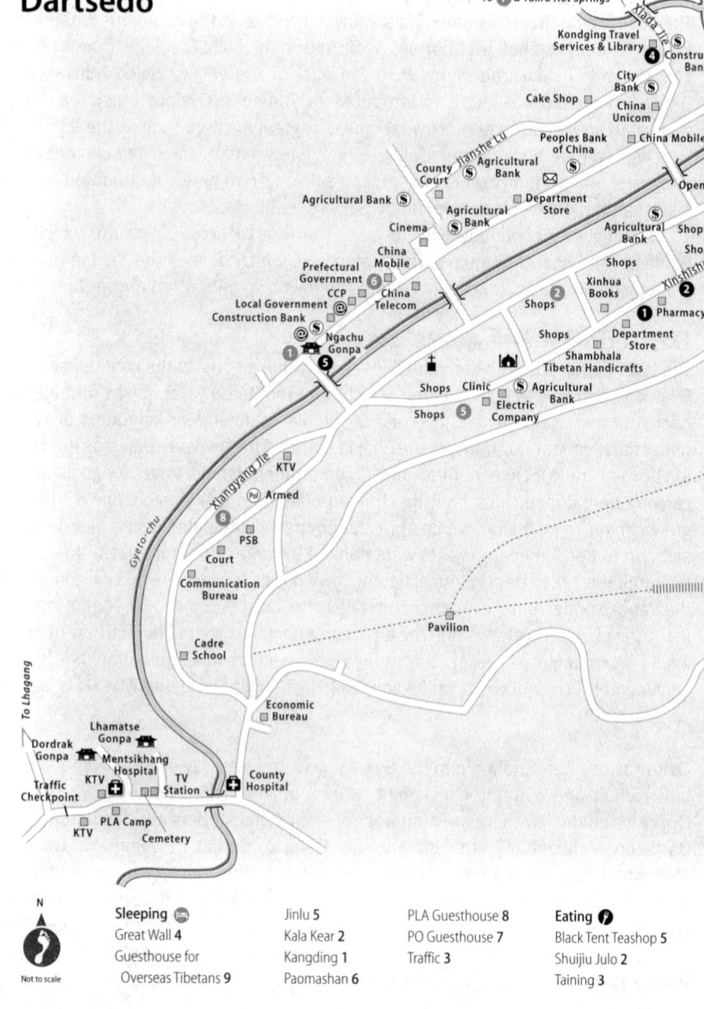

Overseas Tibetans and the Traffic Hotel. On the main road, you will pass small Tibetan shops, the Great Wall Hotel, the Taining Restaurant, the Traffic Police, the **ring road** for through traffic (Huangshan Donglu) and the Bus Station. At this point, the two roads reconnect, and head east, out of town in the direction of Chakzamka, passing the transport depot and a petrol station.

Returning to the intersection near the top end of Xiangyang Jie, if you cross the **Gyeto-chu**, you will reach the commercial and administrative heart of the city. On the right is the strikingly designed Black Tent Teashop, and **Ngachu Monastery**, with the Kangding Hotel in front and the Kandze News Agency down a lane to the left. Turn right here onto **Guangming Lu**, which runs parallel to the north bank of the Gyetochu. Down here you will find an internet café, the Construction Bank, the County Government Buildings, another internet café, the CCP HQ, the Prefectural Government Buildings, the Paomashan Hotel, China Mobile, and China Telecom. On the left, in **Renmin Square**, there is a large cinema and theatre. Downhill from the square on Guangming Lu, you will pass the Agricultural Bank, a department store, China Post, the People's Bank of China and China Mobile.

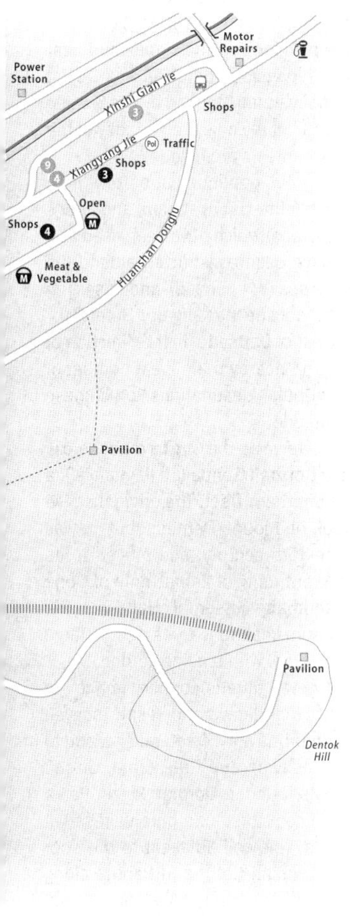

At the next crossroads on Guangming Lu, proceed straight ahead for the power station and a new hotel complex, or turn left onto **Xida Jie**, which parallels the west bank of the Yakra-chu. Along here are China Unicom, China Construction Bank, a large Tibetan Restaurant, the Kangding Travel Service, a library, the People's Hospital, the County Government, the PO Guesthouse and the Stadium. The road continues out of town for the **Yakra Hot Springs** and **Migotso Lake**. Alternatively take the branch road **Jianshe Lu**, which leads southwest towards the City Bank, the Agricultural Bank and the County Court.

There are several schools in town, including the **Tibetan Language University of East Tibet**, which moved here recently from Tawu. Mist permeates the steep walls of the valley, particularly in summertime, and in the winter icy conditions make the main street somewhat slippery.

Ngacho Monastery (Tenlo Gonsar)

Dartsedo formerly had seven monasteries – three Nyingma, two Sakya and two Geluk. Among these, the largest and best known was the Gelukpa monastery of **Ngacho Gonpa** (Ch Anjuesi), founded by Minyakpa Tenpel Nyima in 1654 as a branch of Drepung Losaling College. The monastery once had over 100 monks. In 1954 the present Dalai Lama stayed there en route to Beijing.

The monastery is located close to the Kangding Hotel and its striking roofs in Sino-Tibetan style are visible from the balconies of that building. The restored **Assembly Hall** contains large images of (L-R): Jowo Shakyamuni flanked by his foremost students (Shariputra and Maudgalyayana), of Padmasambhava flanked by his foremost consorts Mandarava and Yeshe Tsogyel, and of Tsongkhapa flanked by his foremost students (Gyeltsabje and Khedrubje). Other images to the right depict Avalokiteshvara in the form of Simhanada, Manjughosa, Vajrapani, White Tara, and Green Tara. On the side walls are images of the protector deities: Dorje Drakden (left) and Shridevi and Dorje Drakden (right). The **Maitreya Hall**, which once housed an enormous three-storey high image of Maitreya, has recently been renovated. It contains a central image of Maitreya, flanked by the bodhisattvas Manjughosa and Samantabhadra. A new **Mani Wheel** chapel lies to the left of the courtyard portico. At present, there are 18 monks here, most of them young novices. Kusho Dardo, the head lama, passed away some years ago at Nalanda in India.

Excursions Dentok Ri Hill (Ch Paomashan), which overlooks the town and is immortalized in the words of a popular Chinese song (Kangding Lu), is the sacred power place of the valley. There are Chinese-style pavilions on the slopes and near the summit **Dentok Gonpa** of the Gelukpa school, alongside Confucian and Daoist shrines. The assembly hall contains an image of Shakyamuni, flanked by the Sixteen Elders. The mountain is a focal point for pilgrims, particularly on the eighth day of the fourth lunar month, when horse races and sporting contests are held.

Yakra-chu hot springs ⓘ *1100-1800, admission: ¥6*. Continue out of town from the square on the east bank of the river following the **Yakra-chu** upstream, and after 4 km you will reach the Yakra-chu hot springs (Ch Erdaoqiao) which have been used as a medicinal spa for centuries. Private bathhouses have been constructed around the sulphurous pools. There is a small guesthouse at the spa (¥15 per bed), and buses run throughout the day from a bus stop on Guangming Lu, outside the Kangding Hotel (¥1).

Migotso Lake (Ch Mugecuo) lies 37 km northwest of Dartsedo, in the direction of **Mount Zhara Lhatse**. The lake is 4 sq km in area, and nearby there are a number of other diversely coloured lakes, which are now popular destinations for Chinese tourists. Buses run to **Yumu** near Migotso from Dartsedo.

Dordrak Gonpa (T0836-12828818) Northeast of town on the **Gye La** road there is an unobtrusive passageway on the right leading to **Dordrak Gonpa** (Ch Jinggangsi), a branch of the celebrated Dorje Drak monastery of Southern Tibet. The original Kagyu foundation dated 1272 was located at the foot of Mount Derntok, but it was established as a branch of Dorje Drak during the 16th century, and moved to its present location in the mid-17th century under the authority of Pema Trinle of Dorje Drak. There are four restored buildings here: the **Dukhang** (Assembly Hall), with the Jokhang to its left and the Gonkhang and Shakyamuni Lhakhang to its right. A large stupa rises to the right of the Shakyamuni Lhakhang, set within a fine garden.

Within the **Assembly Hall**, there is a new gilded copper image of Padmasambhava, flanked by his foremost consorts Mandarava and Yeshe Tsogyel. To the left there are further images of White Tara, Amitabha and Shantaraksita, and to the right King Trisong Detsen, Four-armed Avalokiteshvara and Green Tara. On the central throne there is an image of the monastery's founder, Dordrak Rigzin Pema Khyenrab. Of the original frescoes, only the magnificent torso of a blue Vajrasattva figure remains; but there are excellent new murals. The wall adjacent to the door depicts Padmasambhava, Nyenchen Tanglha and Ekajati (left), and Rahula along with the Five Aspects of Pehar (right). On the left wall are Four-armed Avalokiteshvara, Padmasambhava, flanked by Shantaraksita and King Trisong Detsen, and Amitayus flanked by Vijaya and White Tara, along with Hayagriva. The murals of the right wall depict Padmasambhava in the form of Tukdrub, Vajrakila, the Kabgye meditational deities, Tsedar and Four-armed Mahakala. Other outstanding new murals are found

Tibetan Tea

Tea has been an indispensable part of the Tibetan diet since the seventh century, and yet it has only recently been grown within the moist low-lying valleys of Dzayul and Pemako in the southwest of the country. Instead, the Tibetans have throughout their history relied upon imported tea from China. Following the arrival of the Chinese princesses Wencheng and Jincheng in imperial Tibet, it was soon realized that the drinking of tea acted as an antidote to the cold and dryness at high altitudes, as well as compensating to some extent for the absence of fruit and vegetables in the Tibetan diet. Nomads and villagers alike drink tea throughout their working day; and, like alcohol in other lands, tea has developed an important social dimension. Whenever Tibetans have guests or visit their relatives or friends, they will offer tea as a courtesy. A cup, once offered, will never be left empty, and will constantly be replenished. If you do not wish to drink it is best to leave the cup full and drain it at the time of departure!

Chinese potentates and emperors, realizing the significance of the tea trade for Tibet, would sometimes exert economic pressures, obliging the Tibetans to trade horses for tea or to pay exorbitant tea taxes to avoid the anguish of a tea embargo! The preferred traditional brand of tea is black, with thick twigs and leaves, which is imported from Ya'an in Sichuan and other border areas in the form of compressed bricks, packed inside long oblong bamboo cases, and transported by pack animals over immense distances. This tea is consumed either as a clear black tea (*ja-dang*) to which a pinch of salt is added, or as butter tea (*so-ja*), or more recently, due to Indian influence, as a sweet milk tea (*ja ngar-mo*). Butter tea is unique to Tibet and particularly well suited to the Tibetan climate. Contrary to popular belief, most people prefer fresh rather than rancid butter in their tea! The strained black tea is mixed with dri butter and salt in a wooden churn (*dong-ma*) and then poured into a kettle for heating and serving. Rounds of dri butter are packed and sewn into yak-skin cases (*mar-ril*) by nomad ladies for the village market and for their own use; and it is important that the supply should never run out! Tea churns made of pine or bamboo consist of an outer cylindrical tube tightly bound with brass hoops at both ends, and an inner wooden piston into which holes are drilled to enable the liquid and air to pass during churning. They come in various sizes: the largest over 1 m in height and 30 cm in diameter, and the smaller types 60 cm or 30 cm in height, with proportionate diameters. Butter tea may be consumed from a wooden bowl (which one would normally carry in one's pocket), or mixed with ground-roasted barley flour (tsampa) into a dough, which is the staple Tibetan meal.

Among the Muslim communities of Far East Tibet, the preferred brew is known as 'eight treasure' tea (Ch baboa cha). This is a delicious concoction of chun jian tea, crystal sugar, and dry fruits such as red jujube, apricot, raisin and gui yuan. Nowadays, Chinese jasmin tea is also popular; and drivers will carry a screw-top jar, filled to the brim with this thirst-quenching brew when crossing the dusty roads of the plateau. To be prepared, bring your own screw-top or jam jar!

 in the uppermost gallery, depicting the 25 Disciples of Padmasambhava and Zangdokpelri, and in the upper gallery depicting the liturgical cycle known as Lama Sangdu and the Fifth Dalai Lama (left) and Rigzin Godemchen (right). In 2003 the outer walls and supporting beams of this hall were renovated on account of dry rot.

The adjacent **Jokhang,** which once housed the canonical texts of the *Kangyur*, *Tangyur*, *Nyingma Gyubum* and commentaries, contains central images of Shakyamuni flanked by his foremost students and the Eight Bodhisattvas and Eight Medicine Buddhas. Along the side walls are images of the Sixteen Elders and the Dorjedrak lineage-holders, while the walls adjacent to the entrance have images of the Four Guardian Kings, Longchenpa and Tsongkhapa (left), and Milarepa with Sakya Pandita (right). The skylight murals depict the Twenty-five Disciples of Padmasambhava (left), Vajradhara with the Eighty-four Mahasiddhas (centre) and the Twenty-one Taras (right).

The **Gonkhang** has a central image of Mahottara Heruka flanked by Vajrapani and Vajrakila, and its side walls have images of the Dorjedrak protector deities. The **Shakyamuni Lhakhang** contains a remarkable white jade Reclining Buddha, flanked by Mahakarunika and Sitatapatra. The central image, weighting 10 tons, was brought from Burma in 1998, and is recognized as the first such image ever to be installed in a Tibetan Buddhist monastery.

The magnificent restoration at Dordrak Gonpa has been undertaken by Gyelse Rinpoche (Kusho Putruk), who is based in Chengdu. There are at present only 15 monks, in contrast to the 70-100 who once lived here. However a large number of additional monks' quarters have recently been reconstructed.

In front of Dordrak Gonpa, by the roadside, is the renovated Gelukpa monastery of **Lhamotse** (Ch Nanwusi), which contains images of Shakyamuni and Tsongkhapa, each with their foremost students. Originally this monastery was located on the hill top facing the town where the Dentok Stupa now stands, and it has been rebuilt on two subsequent occasions, most recently at its present site. Of the other former monasteries of Dartsedo, the **Dolma Lhakhang** is unrestored, and the **Sungmakhang**, which once contained an important image of Mahottara Heruka but has functioned in recent years as a guesthouse and a school, is soon to be restored.

Chakzamka County ལྕགས་ཟམ་ཁ

→ *Population: 77,000. Area: 1,570 sq km. Colour map 4, grid B5.* 泸定县

Chakzamka county is a picturesque area, bordering the Gyarong Ngul-chu river (Ch Dadu), with **Mount Minyak Gangkar** to the west and Mount **Ulak Riwo** (Erlang Shan) to the east. The old suspension bridge spanning the river at **Chakzamka** (Ch Luding) once marked the traditional boundary between the Tibetan ands Chinese worlds, although the population is almost entirely Chinese and Qiang at the present time. There are a number of medicinal hot springs (temperature range 52-92°C) within the county, not to mention the spectacular Hailuogou Glacier, which is reckoned to be the lowest in Asia (2,900 m). The distance from Dartsedo to the county capital is 49 km; and from here to Ya'an 165 km via the Erlang Tunnel.

Dartsedo to Chakzamka

Below Dartsedo, the paved highway 317 follows the Dardo-chu downstream to its confluence with the Gyarong Ngulchu (Ch Dadu) in **Chakzamka** county. Here, the road forks, a narrow branch on the left (north) following the rapids upstream to **Rongtrak** in Gyarong (see below, page 660). The main road bears right (south) and shortly thereafter crosses the Gyarong via a new bridge to reach the county town.

Chakzamka

Chakzamka (Ch Luding) is a small town hugging the Gyarong river banks. There are a number of small roadside restaurants of varying quality to the west of the river, and after crossing the bridge, you pass the vegetable and meat market, the bus station, and the old Luding Hotel, before reaching the entrance to the **Chakzam Footbridge** on the right. A side road leads uphill from here into the centre of the town, where there are several fish and hotpot restaurants, a cinema and administrative buildings. Continuing south from here, the main road forks, climbing east for the **Erlang Tunnel** (to Chengdu) or south, along the river bank. If you take the latter road, you will pass the Yagudu Hotel, the People's Hospital, and a leather factory, opposite which there is a motor bridge leading across continue to the west bank of the Gyarong and the Long March Memorial. The new Luding Qiao Hotel is located on the far bank, by the riverside. Further south on the east bank, you will reach the turn-off for Mozhi and Shimian.

Chakzam Footbridge

ⓘ *Admission ¥10.*

The old wooden suspension bridge, constructed in 1706, once marked the traditional frontier between Tibet and China. There is a Chinese-style temple on the west bank. Chinese tourists now flock here in great numbers in memory of a heroic episode in the Long March when the PLA was obliged to take the bridge from the Guomintang in order to secure its passage northeast to Yenan. There is a small museum and south of the bridge a tall but rather nondescript stone column commemorating the martyrs of that occasion. Walk across the bridge, which sways markedly towards the middle, and peer down through the slats of its walkway to observe the torrents of the Gyarong below!

Hailuogou Glacier Park and Minyak Gangkar Base Camp

From Chakzamka, tourist, trekking and mountaineering groups set out for Hailuogou Glacier and the eastern approaches of Mount Minyak Gangkar (see above, page 475). Drive 52 km from Chakzamka to Mozhi (Ch Moxi) village, which is the base camp for the **Hailuogou Glacier Park** ⓘ *admission: ¥70*. Public buses also run here from Dartsedo and Chakzamka. At Mozhi the park admission fee is collected by the Luding County Tourism Bureau. The Hailougou (Conch Ditch) Glacier is the longest of Mount Minyak Gangkar's five glaciers, more than 10 km in length, plunging steeply from snow-covered rocks through primeval forest, to an elevation of only 2,900 m. Here, the most spectacular sight is the great ice cataract, more than 1,000 m long and wide. Three tourist camps have been established along the way, offering log cabin accommodation. Camp I is at 1,960 m, Camp II at 2,620 m, and Camp III at 2,940 m. Recently the upmarket Glacier Hotel (Binchuan Binguan) was opened here. Two-way **horse riding trips** ⓘ *¥100-200 per person*, to the glacier are also available.

Only serious mountaineering and trekking parties venture beyond Hailougou. Most expeditions on the eastern face of Miyank Gangkar would spend 17 days on the ascent to the summit and the descent to Xinxing, before driving back to Mozhi. Expeditions are organized by the Sichuan Mountaineering Association in Chengdu. It is also possible for experienced and well-equipped trekkers to reach the East Base Camp by a two-day/twelve-hour trek via Daozaizhong or a one-day/six-hour trek from Xinxing.

Chakzamka to Chengdu (via Rongtrak, Ya'an, or Hanyuan)

There are three possible routes from Chakzamka to Chengdu, the capital of Sichuan province. The **northern route** follows the west bank of the Gyarong upstream to **Rongtrak** (112 km), where it crosses to the east bank and follows the Tsenlha-chu upstream to the large town of **Tsenlha** (58 km). The watershed pass known as **Balang Shan** (4,237 m) is crossed 79 km beyond Tsenlha, and thereafter, the road descends for 59 km into the **Wolong Panda Reserve**. Spend the night here, and drive the following morning to **Chengdu** via **Dujiangyan** (156 km).

Mount Emei Shan

An interesting detour to Emei which extends the journey to Chengdu by 1-2 days offers you an opportunity to visit the Chinese Buddhist shrines on Mount Emei Shan – one of the four sacred Buddhist mountains in China – which rises abruptly 2,600 m from the Sichuan plain. This peak (admission: ¥60) is dedicated to the bodhisattva Samantabhadra. It has 70 temples and is a veritable treasure-store of medicinal herbs. Altogether, more than 3,000 tropical and temperate plants grow on Emei, many of them having medicinal properties. At the base of the mountain, the Baoguo Temple actively espouses the Chinese Vajrayana tradition, and it has a well-kept guesthouse. The peak monastery may be reached on foot or by cable car; and at sunrise the diffracted light sometimes produces the distinctive aura effect known as the "precious light of the Buddha". It is possible to spend several days making a complete pilgrimage circuit of the mountain. The main temple of Wannian Si, with its life-size image of Samantabhadra riding an elephant, is particularly renowned. Stay in the foothills below Emei at the splendidly tranquil Hongzhushan Hotel, T0833-5525888, F0833-5525777 (superior doubles at ¥940, singles at ¥1500, suites at ¥2400). After Emei, don't forget to visit the Temple of the Great Buddha at Leshan-site of the world's largest stone Buddha image (71 m), which was carved between 719-803 during the Tang Dynasty. This statue is 18 m taller than the destroyed statues of Bamiyan in Afghanistan. In 2002 measures were undertaken to protect it from the effects of weathering and acid rain. The distance from Han Yuan to Emei is 237 km; and from Emei to Chengdu 296 km.

The **central route** is the most direct and by far the easiest. Drive east from Chakzamka on Highway 317, which reaches the entrance to the **Erlang Tunnel** on **Mount Ulak Riwo** (Ch Erlang Shan) after 29 km (This short stretch of highway was still under reconstruction in 2003, entailing long delays). The tunnel, opened in 1999, is 4,176 m long. Prior to its construction, vehicles had to cross the treacherous **Khakha Buddha La** pass (3,000 m), which rewardingly offers magnificent views of **Minyak Gangkar** (7,556 m) on a clear day. In the past, traders, pilgrims and adventurers who walked this ancient tea-trail from Ya'an to Dartsedo were constantly subjected to harassment by brigands. Nowadays, having negotiated the tunnel, Ya'an can be reached in 136 km, and the **Chenya Expressway** takes traffic rapidly from there down to Chengdu (139 km). **NB** This is a toll road, the first booth (¥6) at the exit of the tunnel, the second (¥6) near Ya'an, and the third (¥40) at the approach to Chengdu.

The **southern route** from Chakzamka to Ya'an initially follows the Gyarong downstream on its east bank to **Hanyuan** (202 km), crossing a 2,340 m pass from which Mount Minyak Gangkar is visible in the distance, before cutting northeast to **Ya'an** (220 km) and on to **Chengdu** (170 km). Both Han Yuan and Ya'an are large uninspiring towns, although the latter is more prosperous, with better accommodation and restaurants.

For information on the gateway city of Chengdu, see below, page 722.

Sleeping

Batang *p464, map p464*

D **Batang Hotel (Batang Bingun)**, T0836-5622436. At ¥108 per single, ¥144 per double, and ¥108 per triple, meals also available.

D **Government Guesthouse**, on the opposite side of the road tp the Batang Hotel. Has superior VIP accommodation and ordinary rooms.

E **Bus Station Guesthouse**, has simple dormitory beds at ¥10.
E **Jinhui Hotel**, T0836-5622700. Has doubles with attached bath at ¥70, and dorm beds at ¥10-20.

Litang Chode *p467, map p469*
E **Chunglai Hotel and Restaurant**, T0836-5322772. Has 10 triples at ¥45.
E **County Government Guesthouse**, T0836-5322787. Has doubles at ¥40, triples at ¥45, and 5-bed rooms at ¥125.
E **Forestry Department Guesthouse**, T0836-5323871. Has a few simple rooms.
D **Genyer Hotel (Genie Fandian)**, T0836-5322999. Newly built hotel, has doubles at ¥140.
E **Grain Department Guesthouse**, T0836-5322528. Has doubles and singles at ¥50, triples and 4-bed rooms at ¥60.
E **High City Hotel**, T0836-5322706. Singles at ¥50, doubles at ¥100-280, triples at ¥60, and suites at ¥400.
D **Monastery Guesthouse**, the best accommodation available, doubles at ¥160, triples at ¥120.
E **White Crane Hotel**, T0836-5322344. Doubles ¥50, singles ¥40, and triples ¥60.
E **White Stupa Hotel**, T0836-5323089. Has doubles at ¥50, and triples at ¥60.

NB Hotel prices will double during the 1st week of Aug when the Litang horse festival is held annually.

Dabpa *p471*
E **Blue Moon Valley Guesthouse**, T0836-5728751/5728760. Has doubles at ¥70 and triples at ¥105.
E **Government Guesthouse**, T0836-5728247. Has doubles at ¥100 and suites at ¥300, meals available.
E **Jinliang Hotel**, T0836-5728436. Doubles at ¥70 and triples at ¥105).

Chaktreng Town *p472*
C **Bamushan Hotel**, T0836-5822664. Has the best rooms in town, doubles at ¥240, triples at ¥180, and 4-bed rooms at ¥30 per bed.
E **Xiaxia Transport Station**, has 4-bed dorms at ¥10 per bed.

Zang-me *p473*
E **Forestry Department Guesthouse (Lin Yie)**, ¥20 per bed and ¥80 per room, meals available.
E **Government Guesthouse**, meals available.
E **Tibetan Guesthouse**, meals available.

Pundadrong *p474*
E **Yajiang Fandian**, T0836-5124004. The best option, nearer the bridge in the lower part of town, has 19 beds and an excellent restaurant serving hotpot and Sichuan dishes. Buses travelling between Dartsedo and Batang or Chaktreng will sometimes stop overnight here.
E **Yajiang Hotel**, adjacent to the public security bureau in the southeast of town. Best accommodation available, doubles at ¥50.

Dzongzhab *p474*
E **Kangding Xinduqiao Hongsheng Inn**, on the edge of town. There are a number of small guesthouses in Dzongzhab, but this is probably the best and quietest, ¥20 per double and ¥36 per 4-bed rooms. The downstairs restaurant offers wholesome Sichuan cuisine.

Lhagang *p477*
E **Government Guesthouse**, simple accommodation for ¥12 per bed.
E **Tibetan Guesthouse**, opposite the monastery. Privately run, ¥20 per bed.

Most visitors will prefer to camp beyond the monastery or stay at the Nyingmapa Shedra.

Dartsedo *p479, map p480*
C **Kala Kaer Hotel**, Xiangyang Jie, T836-2828888, F0836-2828777. Currently the best in town, with 40 superior twin rooms at ¥320, 6 suites at ¥560, and 30 economy rooms at ¥280.
C **Kangding Hotel**, 25 Guangming Lu, T0836-2833084, F0836-2833442. Has 120 rooms (north wing 3-star doubles at ¥288 and suites at ¥360; east wing doubles at ¥240, singles at ¥252, suites at ¥288, and triples at ¥188).
C **Paomashan Hotel**, Guangming Lu, T0836-2833110, F0836-2830134. Centrally located, with doubles at ¥240, suites at ¥312, and triples at ¥150.
C **Traffic Hotel (Jiatong Binguan)**, Xinshiqian Lu, T836-2822492/2836914, F0836-2821688. Has 54 excellent rooms

For an explanation of the sleeping and eating price codes used in this guide, see inside the front cover. Other relevant information is found in Essentials pages 44-46.

(doubles at ¥288, suites at ¥300, deluxe suites at ¥360, economy doubles at ¥80 and triples at ¥90).

D **Jinlu Hotel**, Xinshishou Jie, T0836-2834583, F0836-2834551. Doubles at ¥168, suites at ¥240, singles at ¥180, and triples at ¥105.

E **Great Wall Hotel**, Xiangyang Jie, T/F0836-2822837. Has doubles at ¥86, singles at ¥65, triples at ¥54, and economy rooms at ¥60.

Chakzamka *p485*

B **Luding Qiao Hotel**, Shaba, T0836-3123838, F0836-3133608. Has doubles at ¥480, suites at ¥680, deluxe suites at ¥2,800, and triples at ¥580, caters for upmarket Chinese tourist parties visiting the glacier.

D **Luding Hotel**, Yuanhe Lu, T/F0836-3122617. Has fan-cooled rooms, doubles at ¥140, singles at ¥150, and triples at ¥150.

Ya'an *p486*

C **Ya'an Hotel**, 121 Dong Dajie, T0835-2222826, F0835-2222806. A 2-star hotel which has 120 rooms, new building: doubles ¥380, suites ¥880, singles ¥480, and triples ¥980; old building: doubles ¥160-180, suites ¥580, singles ¥280, and 4-bed rooms ¥480.

C **Yudu Hotel**, 20 Tinjing Rd, T0835-2601999, F0835-2601993. A 3-star hotel with doubles ¥318, suites ¥680, and singles ¥198-238.

Eating

Litang *p467, map p469*

The best restaurant in town is currently that on the 2nd floor of the Genyer Hotel. There are also new glass-fronted restaurants near the White Crane Hotel, but the small Sichuan restaurants on the west side of Main Street are still good value.

Dzongzhab *p474*

There are several other Sichuan-style restaurants and a Tibetan teashop in this bustling market town.

Lhagang *p477*

There are a few small restaurants on the main street.

Dartsedo *p479, map p480*

Outside the hotels, the best include:

Black Tent Teashop, next to Ngacho Gonpa

Shuijiu Julo (Well Restaurant), Xinshishou Jie.

Three Friends' Fish Restaurant (San You Yu Zhuang), Xiangyang Jie, T0836-2822830.

Tibetan Restaurant, Xida Jie. Elegant design.

Trewongke (Old Drunk Pavilion) Restaurant.

Other downmarket restaurants can be found further downhill on Huanshan Donglu.

Entertainment

Dartsedo *p479, map p480*

The **People's Cinema** is located on the main square of the west bank of the river. Karaoke bars can be found on lower Xiangyang Jie, and throughout the city

Shopping

Dzongzhab *p474*

There are a number of stores on the main road, selling interesting Tibetan textiles and fabrics, as well as general supplies.

Dartsedo *p479, map p480*

Shambhala Tibetan Handicraft, store on Xinshishou Jie. Sells Khampa costumes for men and women, as well as leather belts, religious artefacts and interesting household goods.

Activities and tours

Dartsedo *p479, map p480*

Great Wall Hotel Travel Service, Xiangyang Jie, T0836-2822837.

Kandze Prefectural Tourism Bureau, Jiang Jun Bridge, T0836-2833777.

Kangding County Tourism Bureau, Xi Dajie, T0836-2822928.

Kangding Travel Service, in Tibetan Restaurant, Xida Jie, T0836-2834000, F0836-2831946.

Kangma Travel Service, in Paomashan Hotel, T0836-2832132.

Paomashan Travel Service, Jiang Jun Bridge, T0836-2233777.

Transport

Litang *p467, map p469*

Bus Depart for the following destinations: **Dartsedo** (daily, 0600, ¥76); **Batang** (3 buses weekly, 1200, ¥56); **Chaktreng** (3 buses weekly, 0700, ¥58), and **Dabpa** (Dartesdo-Dabpa bus, ¥43).

Dabpa *p471*

Air A new airport may soon be constructed at Dabpa, mainly for the promotion of tourism in the beautiful Dabpa Lhari region in the south of the county, which the local tourist bureau has equated with Shangrila, in an effort to rival neighbouring Gyeltang's equally spurious claim to this worthless title. Flights are expected to operate between Chengdu and Gyeltang.

Bus Depart for the following destinations: **Dartsedo** (daily, 0630-0700, ¥123); **Litang** (daily minibus, 0630-0700, ¥55); and **Chaktreng** (daily 0630-0700, ¥30).

Chaktreng Town *p472*

Bus Depart for the following destinations: **Dartsedo** (daily, 0630-0700, ¥137); **Litang** (daily, 1200, ¥58-68); **Sumdo** (daily minibus, ¥25-30) and **Gyeltang** (daily, 0600, ¥53-68).

Lhagang *p477*

Bus Public buses stop here en route for **Drango** or **Kandze** (westbound) or **Dartsedo** (eastbound). Taxis and public minibuses also run to the crossroads at Dzongzhab (¥20).

Dartsedo *p479, map p480*

Bus The bus station and petrol station lies at the lower end of town. Buses run throughout the prefecture but permit restrictions apply and tickets may not be sold to foreigners. Chengdu tickets are readily available.

Chengdu 0700, 0800, 0900, 1000 (¥99) (Ivico and Yaxing bus); 1300, 1400, 1500 (¥99) (couchettes). **Karpo** 0730 (¥71) (Yaxing bus). **Rongtrak** 0730, 0830 (¥34) (ordinary bus). **Pundadrong** 0700 (¥43) (Yaxing bus). **Litang** 0700 (¥79) (Yaxing bus). **Dabpa** 0700 (¥123) (Yaxing bus). **Chaktreng** 0730 (¥138) (Yaxing bus). **Batang** 0800 (¥138) (Yaxing bus). **Tawu** 0730 (¥43) (ordinary bus). **Drango** 0700, 0730 (¥79) (Ivico), ¥56 (ordinary bus). **Sertal** ex Drango. **Kandze** 0700 (¥104) (Yaxing bus). **Barshok** ex Kandze. **Derge** 0930 (even calendar days only) (¥164) (Yaxing bus). **Pelyul** 0830 (odd calendar days only) (¥194) (Yaxing bus). **Sershul** 0700 (even calendar days only) (¥147) (ordinary bus).

Directory

Dartsedo *p479, map p480*

Banks Bank of China, Xida Jie, has foreign exchange facilities, as do the larger tourist hotels. **Hospitals** People's Hospital, Xida Jie, Dartsedo Mentsikhang on Gye La road. **Internet** (¥25 per hr), found on Guangming Lu, near the Paomashan Hotel. **Telephones** China Telecom, sells ICC cards for IDD and DDD phone calls. China Post, has EMS facilities. The larger hotels all have business centres and IDD facilities. **Useful numbers** Visa extensions can be arranged at the Public Security Bureau, T0836-28114159 ext 6035.

Chamdo to Derge: the cultural heart of Kham

The northern route from Chamdo to Chengdu via Derge will be described in this and the following sections. The first part of the route follows unpaved highway 317 from Chamdo to Topa and then passes through Jomda to cross the Yangtze and enter either Derge or Pelyul. From Jomda there is also a side road leading south into Gonjo county. The distance from Chamdo to Derge is 345 km, and from Topa to Derge, 230 km. Of these five counties, Topa, which has already been described (see above, page 423), along with Jomda and Gonjo are currently administered from Chamdo prefecture, within the Tibet Autonomous Region; while Pelyul and Derge are administered from Dartsedo, within the Kandze Autonomous Prefecture of Sichuan Province. ***Recommended itineraries: 5, 8, 10. See page 20.*** ⏩ *For Sleeping, Eating and other listings, see page 509.*

Jomda County འཇོ་མདའ་ → *Pop: 66,212. Area: 13,384 sq km.* 江达县

Jomda county comprises the upper reaches of the Ri-chu around **Chunyido** and of the Ke-chu around **Sibda**, as well as the Do-chu (Tsang-chu valley) and its tributary, the Dzi-chu, which eventually flow into the Yangtze at **Bolo** in Gonjo county. In the extreme northeast of the county, **Denkhok Nubma** is more accessible by ferry and bridge from Denkhok on the Sichuan side of the border. The county capital is located at **Jomda**, still known locally as Derge Jomda in recognition of the fact that the kingdom of Derge once extended across the west bank of the Yangtze.

Ins and outs

Getting there To reach Jomda from Chamdo, first follow the Derge highway out of town on the east bank of the Dza-chu, and cross the **Tama La** (4,511 m) and **Jape La** (4,680 m) passes to arrive at **Topa** township in the grasslands of the Drugu-chu valley. The distance from Chamdo to Topa is 109 km, but this (and the driving time) will be reduced once the new paved road through the Dza-chu valley and Kokhyam has been completed. After Topa the highway crosses **Lazhi La** (4,450 m) and enters Jomda county at **Chunyido** township, where there are excellent camping grounds. The distance from Topa to Chunyido is 63 km, and from Lazhi La to Chunyido 40 km.

Dordzong and Dzigar

The main monastery in the Chunyido nomadic area is **Dordzong Gonpa** of the Drukpa Kagyu school. The present incumbent lama lives at Tashijong in India. From Chunyido near the source of the Ri-chu, the highway continues east to **Khargang**, crossing Gele La pass (4,352 m) en route and passing through **Tralso**, where there is a small Sakya Monastery. Khargang, on the banks of the Dzi-chu River, is 44 km from Chunyido. A motorable road follows this river upstream for 33 km to **Dzigar**, which is another stronghold of the Drukpa Kagyu school (a branch monastery has been established at Rewalsar in India through the efforts of Lama Wangdor and Dzigar Choktrul).

Trekking

A trekking route crosses Guru La from Dzigar to enter the Ke-chu valley, and head downstream to **Sibda**. Here there are important Kagyu monasteries: **Taklung Gon** and **Cho-ne Gon**. From Sibda, the trekking trail continues following the Ke-chu downstream to **Menda** area, where it merges with the Kyang-chu River of East Zurmang (see above, page 423 and below, page 521).

Jomda town

The highway runs east from Khargang, following the Dzi-chu downstream to the county capital (12 km). **Jomda** is a large town, sprawling along both banks of the river. The main industries are timber and cement. The town with its finely decorated log cabin houses has an air of prosperity, particularly during the harvest season. There are guesthouse and restaurant facilities, but none are particularly attractive; and the police are ever vigilant when foreigners pass through town. At **Troru Gonpa** of the Karma Kagyu school, there is a small Tibetan hospital which supplies herbal

medications throughout the county. The monastery is under the direction of the Eighth Lagen Tulku and Khenpo Tsenam, one of Tibet's foremost scholars and physicians who is based at the Tibet Medical University in Lhasa. After Jomda, the road descends to **Tangpu** (22 km), where the Dzi-chu river flows into the Do-chu.

A motorable side road runs north from Tangpu to **Terton** township (53 km), where there are a number of important Kagyu monasteries: **Dokhar Gon**, **Gonsar Gon**, and **Kyapje Gon**, among them. It is also possible to trek northeast from Terton township to **Denkhok Nubma** on the banks of the Yangtze.

Below Tangpu, the Do-chu is known as the Tsang-chu as far as its confluence with the Yangtze at **Bolo**. The road to Bolo from Tangpu (55 km) passes through **Kutse**, where many of the renowned Derge woodblocks were carved.

Wara Monastery

The highway continues east from Tangpu towards the **Nge La** pass (4,245 m). En route you will drive through the beautiful **Wara Gonpa** (3,444 m), a significant monastery of the Sakya school, which had its own woodblock edition of the *Kangyur*, prepared during the 20th century by Jamyang Khyentse Chokyi Lodro. The temple complex at Wara has undergone considerable restoration in recent years. The main **Assembly Hall** contains fine images of (L-R): Padmasambhava, Hevajra, Jowo Shakyamuni, Vajrabhairava and Vajrapani, while its side murals depict the meditational deities of the Sakya school. Outside in the courtyard, there is a covered walkway, decorated with murals depicting historical figures of the monastic succession and King Tenpa Tsering of Derge, along with the well known motifs – the Four Harmonious Brethren (Tunpa Punzhi), the Indian sadhu leading an elephant (Atsara Langtri) and the Mongolian chieftain leading a tiger (Sokpo Taktri). The adjacent **Yerne Lhakhang** (used during the summer rain retreat) has a central image of Shakyamuni Buddha. Further west, there is a large college complex (*shedra*) of recent construction.

Descending from Nge La pass, the road reaches **Kamtok** on the banks of the Yangtze. The distance from Tangpu to Kamtok is 63 km.

Trekking

Trek upstream through the Yangtze gorge to visit **Onpo-to** township, or cross the Yangtze to enter Derge county at **Kamtok Drukha Zamchen** bridge. The small village of Khamtok, overlooking the Yangtze, has a pilot school scheme and clinic, which were founded by the volunteer doctors and teachers of the Italian-based Asia Project.

Gonjo County གོ་འཇོ་ → *Population: 44,186. Area: 4,994 sq km.* 贡觉县

The county of Gonjo comprises the valleys of the south-flowing Ri-chu and north-flowing Mar-chu, which converge above **Akar**, and then flow due east to enter the Yangtze at **Motsa**. It also includes the valley of the Je-chu and adjacent rivers which flow into the Yangtze further southeast, opposite **Sangenrong** (the 'badlands'). The county capital is located at **Akar** on the Mar-chu. The distance from Chunyido to Akar is 82 km.

Akar

At **Tranak**, 3 km east of Chunyido, there is a turn-off on the south side of the road, which runs parallel to the course of the Ri-chu River. Driving along this road, you will cross a 4,064 m pass after 5 km, which leads into **Pelha Gon**, and a second pass, **Gyelpo La** (4,472 m) after 22 km. Descend into **Kyabal** township (12 km) and **Tsanda**, where a trail follows the Ri-chu upstream to the Nyingmapa monastery of **Nyakla Gonpa**. The motorable track continues downhill from Tsanda to the confluence of the Ri-chu and Mar-chu, and then rises again to reach **Akar**, the county town (40 km from Kyabal), also known nowadays as **Gonjo**. There are spartan guesthouse facilities at Akar.

You can continue driving southeast from Akar for 24 km as far as **Lhagyel** in the upper reaches of the Mar-chu, but beyond that point it is necessary to trek southeast to reach Lhato township.

Sangenrong

Beyond northeast Gonjo county, the township of **Bolo** (55 km drive from Tangpu) lies on the west bank of the Yangtze. The township of **Tsepa** is situated on the Tse-chu tributary of the Mar-chu. Further southeast, a trail crosses **Pel-yi La pass** (4,642 m) to enter the Je-chu valley. Passing through **Jangsum** and **Bumkye** townships, this trail follows the Je-chu downstream to its confluence with the Yangtze, opposite **Sangenrong** ('badlands'), a wild and traditionally lawless part of Kham. The people of Gonjo are regarded as barbarous, headstrong, and somewhat inhospitable, compared to the other inhabitants of Kham.

Pelyul County དཔལ་ཡུལ ལ → *Pop: 42,000. Area: 10,646 sq km.* 白玉县

At **Kamtok Drukha** two bridges span the swift-flowing waters of the Yangtze. The lower bridge is the original one constructed by the PLA during the occupation of Tibet in 1950. The other is the modern suspension bridge which carries all motor vehicles and pedestrians across the present day border between the Tibet Autonomous Region and Sichuan. Traditionally, the areas on both banks of the Yangtze belonged to the independent kingdom of **Derge**; and the peoples of Jomda and Pelyul often refer to themselves even now as inhabitants of Derge. Crossing to the east bank of the Yangtze (ie into the Kandze Prefecture of Sichuan Province), there are two motorable roads, one following the river upstream towards Derge (28 km), and the other following the river downstream to Pelyul. Taking the latter road, you will reach **Pelyul** after 87 km.

Pelyul county comprises the lateral valleys of the Horpo-chu and Ngu-chu tributaries of the Yangtze, which between their estuaries demarcate a dramatic section of the awesome gorge, where the river abruptly changes course from southeast to southwest and again to northwest within the distance of 39 km. Two outstanding Nyingmapa monasteries, Katok and Pelyul, are located within the county.

Horpo → *Colour map 4, grid A3*

Driving southwards down the east bank of the Yangtze on a narrow but passable by jeep road, after 34 km you pass the turn-off for Pelpung in the Pha-chu valley, and after a further 5 km you will traverse the estuary of the Mesho-chu. Continue south for a further 10 km to reach the confluence of the Horpo-chu and the Yangtze. **Horpo** township (3,170 m) is located a short distance upstream at a point where the Dzin-chu and Horpo-chu streams flow together. The township was formerly one of the 25 districts within the kingdom of Derge, and especially renowned in the past for the high quality of its metalwork. Foundries producing Khampa knives are still active here.

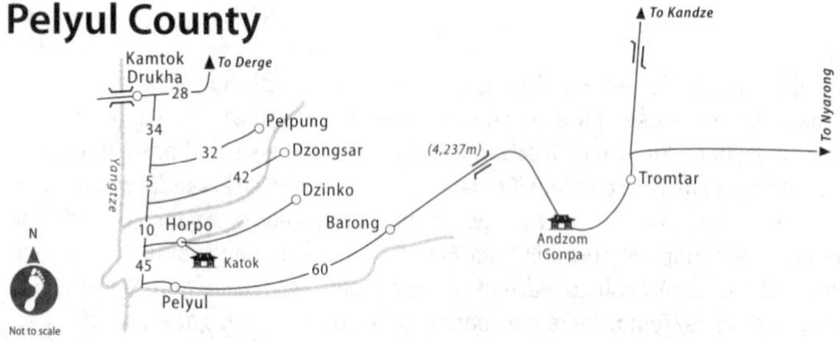

Yangtze River

This mighty river (6,300 km) is the longest in Asia and the third longest in the world. There are two main sources: the southern one, known as the Dam-chu (Ulan Muren) rises in the Dangla mountains at 5,486 m; and the northern source, known as the Chumar-chu, rises in the Kunluns. These converge above Chumarleb, and flow initially through a spacious lakeland valley. The Yangtze has eight principal tributaries, of which the Yalong, Gyarong, Minjiang, and Jialing all originate on the Tibetan plateau. The upper reaches of the river are inhabited by nomadic peoples, who are largely pastoralists, but also engaged in subsistence farming. South of the Bayankala range, the river forms a narrow gorge, 3-5 km deep in places, and with sheer river-bank peaks as high as 4,900 m. Some remote villages are located high up on the river banks. For over 350 km the river flows south through this gorge in close proximity to the Salween and Mekong (which are all within 25-40 km of each other). In winter when the water level is lowest the river is deep blue in colour; but in the rainy season when coffee-coloured alluvium is carried downstream at the rate of 430-500 million tons per annum, its rapid flow increases to more than 2,000 cu m per second.

On reaching the territory of the Jang (Naxi) peoples, at the southernmost outpost of Tibetan culture (now in Yunnan province), the river loops sharply northeast to touch the Sichuan border near Mili, and bends back upon itself (southwest), before turning east into Dukou. Here, at the confluence of the Yalong, the river widens to 396 m and increases to 9 m in depth. The other major tributaries – the Gyarong (Dadu) and the Zung-chu (Minjiang), which both rise in Amdo, converge together at Leshan in Sichuan province, before emptying into the Yangtze at Yibin.

Katok Dorjeden Monastery ཀཿཐོག་རྡོ་རྗེ་གདན

Getting there Katok Dorjeden Monastery (4,023 m) is some 853 m above Horpo on a hilltop resembling the shape of the Tibetan letter KA, or that of an 'eight-footed lion'. Until 1993 visitors to Katok were obliged to walk five hours or ride on horseback from Horpo. The tranquillity of the remote hilltop monastery was rarely disturbed. Now, following the construction of a jeep track, the monastery can be reached with ease in 20 minutes. However, there are still occasions when the road is damaged by flash floods, forcing travellers and pilgrims to resort to traditional horse power! In Horpo, there are two simple guesthouses, Sichuan-style restaurants, and a general store. Public buses stop here en route between Pelyul and Katok, and pack animals can be hired if one has to ride to Katok ⓘ *¥35-40 for a horse or donkey, although foreigners have been charged ¥80-100.*

History The monastery was founded in 1159 by Katok Dampa Deshek (1122-1192). Immediately below the site is a large boulder, in which a local Bon divinity is said to have been trapped at the time of the monastery's founding. According to legend, Tsangtongpa, the student and successor of Dampa Deshek, helped drag it along to the river bank below the valley where it can still be seen today.

Katok is revered as the main pilgrimage site of buddha-activity in Kham and is the oldest surviving monastery of the Nyingma school, excluding Samye and the temples constructed by the early kings. Dampa Deshek gave teachings continuously to students from all parts of East Tibet and his monastery acquired great prestige both for philosophical studies and meditation practice. It is known to have maintained certain rare lineages of teaching from the 12th century at times when they were lost in central Tibet.

The development of the monastery from its inception was guided by the 13 successors of Katokpa Dampa Deshek, by their students, and the 13 successors of Mokton Jampel Senge. In the 13th century Mani Rinchen of Katok, an associate of the treasure-finder Guru Chowang, constructed reliquaries for the remains of the first three Katokpa, and then flew across to an adjacent hilltop before vanishing into light. During the time of Jampabum, the Third Katokpa, 100,000 students are said to have flown on their robes to another adjacent hilltop, which thereafter became known as 'Cloth Hill'.

In the 16th century the monastery was expanded by Rigdzin Dudul Dorje, Longsel Nyingpo and Sonam Detsen. Sonam Detsen's successive incarnations, beginning with Drime Zhingkyong Gonpo, maintained the ancient lineage of Katok, and were ably assisted by great scholars of the calibre of Tsewang Norbu (1698-1755) and Gyurme Tsewang Chokdrub (late 18th/early 19th century). More recently, the monastery has been connected with respected figures such as the Second Katok Situ Chokyi Gyatso (1880-1925) and Khenpo Ngaga (1879-1941), as well as living meditation masters such as Chatrel Senge Dorje. In the early years of the 20th century the community of monks at Katok numbered only 400, but the hermitages above Katok (Ritsip, Bartro and Dechen Choling) continued to produce great masters of meditation. Consequently, the monastery has over 1,000 far-flung branches in Eastern Tibet and Central Tibet.

The site The track from Horpo to Katok crosses a wooden cantilever bridge over the Dzin-chu and proceeds through lush green countryside, initially on level ground alongside a newly built monastery guesthouse (T0836-8321699), but gradually rising to a steep ascent of 4,023 m. On reaching the hilltop, a track to the right leads round the contour of the hill to Katok. On the way it passes a cremation ground, the site from which a former lama, Katok Mani Rinchen, is said to have flown off into space, and the seven damaged stupas, which still contain relics of the founders of Katok.

Anyone viewing the majestic setting of Katok's red and white buildings which cover the peaceful mountain top can appreciate why the concept of 'sacred outlook' or 'pure visionary perception of the landscape' is so significant here. To the right of the hillside are rocks in the shape of Vajrasattva's vase, and of Vajrakila and the Kabgye deities, while to the left of the last of these rocks is the **Bartro** hermitage. Beyond and behind that retreat centre are the **Ritsip** and **Dechen Choling** hermitages. Behind the mountain on the circumambulatory trail, there are impressions in stone of Hayagriva and Simhavaktra, as well as a Padmasambhava footprint.

Two temples have been renovated in recent years, under the auspices of Moktse Tulku, Jamyang Tulku, Getse Tulku, and the present Drime Zhingkyong incarnation (who lives in Chengdu). Of these, the large **Assembly Hall (Dukhang)** is for the most part unimpressive, housing new clay images of (L-R): Longsal Nyingpo, Vajrasattva, Padmasambhava and Tara. A number of small bronze images, including one of Vajrasattva, are kept is a glass case, but most of the monastery's remaining precious artefacts have been locked away for security. In the course of its reconstruction all the original stones of the Assembly Hall were utilized and thus an original blessing was preserved.

The **Zangdokpelri Temple** is a magnificent and ornate structure overlooking the open courtyard, where **religious dances** (*cham*), based on the choreographic tradition of Guru Chowang's Lama Sangdu, are performed on the 10th day (Tsechu) of the sixth month of the lunar calendar, commemorating the birth of Padmasambhava. Large appliqué tangkas depicting Katokpa Dampa Deshek and Longsal Nyingpo (founder and restorer of Katok) are erected to the side of the amphitheatre. The dances take place over two days, initially with monks dressed in their normal robes, and on the second day with the elaborately costumed performers. A large image of

Padmakara is wheeled into the arena in a chariot, on either side of which four of his manifestations take their seats before performing a solo dance in turn. As the finale draws near, bandsmen in Manchurian garb fire gunpowder, deafening of hapless spectators, and human peacocks and snowlions prance around. Comic relief is provided at the most serious stages of the dance by a jester, dressed as an old man, and his stooges. At the conclusion of the dances, which are performed in the context of an elaborate *drubchen* ceremony, the Lama Sangdu empowerment is conferred on the congregation. If you decide to visit Katok at this time, the pageantry and colourful costumes of the dancers and spectators will forever haunt the memory. To visit Katok at other times of the year is to appreciate the tranquillity of this mountain-top bastion of Nyingmapa learning.

A new college (*shedra*) is currently under construction on the opposite side of the courtyard from the Zangdokpelri temple. There are over 180 resident monks and 300 affiliated monks, studying philosophical texts of the Nyingma tradition under senior students of the late Khenpo Jamyang, the author of a History of Katok Monastery.

Trekking

Returning to Horpo, you can drive south to Pelyul (45 km), north to Derge (77 km), or east to Dzinko (43 km). The drive to **Dzinko** follows the Dzin-chu upstream via Racha, from where one can trek across the Yangtze-Yalong watershed (4-6 days) to **Manigango** (see below, page 499), or into the adjacent Mesho-chu valley via Bayak La (3 days) to **Dzongsar** (see below, page 497).

Pelyul → *Colour map 4, grid A3. For listings, see page 509.*

Crossing the Horpo-chu near its confluence with the Yangtze, the motor road continues down the east bank as far as **Barna**, where it spans the Ngu-chu tributary, flowing in from the southeast. It then follows the latter upstream to **Pelyul** (Ch Baiyu), the county capital, 45 km from Horpo.

Pelyul (3,150 m) is a large and rapidly expanding town with a considerable Chinese population. Chinese traders and gold-miners fill the streets, alongside somewhat incongruous Khampa inhabitants. Slightly uphill, the **Hospital of Traditional Tibetan Medicine** and its college are presided over by Dr Phuntsok Rabten, who has struggled heroically to provide a service in great demand by the local Tibetan population.

Dominating the Ngu-chu valley, which is somewhat reminiscent of the Austrian Tyrol, the renovated **Pelyul Monastery** broods over the town on a verdant and picturesque hillside. The former tranquillity of the monastery will be hard to recapture since the sound of music and the radio broadcasts from the town permeate the hillside.

Pelyul Namgyel Jangchubling

Getting there Public buses run from Dartsedo via Kandze on odd calendar days (¥194). Taxis can also be hired in Derge.

History The monastery of Namgyel Jangchubling was founded at Pelyul in 1665 by the king of Derge, Lachen Jampa Phuntsok, who appointed Rigdzin Kunzang Sherab (1636-1699) as its first throne-holder. The location, sacred to the bodhisattva Vajrapani, had ancient associations with Garab Dorje, Padmasambhava and the latter's second generation disciple, Kyere Chokyong Wangpo. As such, it was an important power-place for the discovery of *termas*. Prior to the 17th century, the site also had Kagyu connections.

At Pelyul, the teaching cycles of the Nyingma school were maintained with a particular emphasis on the *terma*-tradition of Ratna Lingpa (1403-1471). The monastery was also inspired from its foundation by the visionary teachings of Namcho Migyur Dorje (1645-1667), who lived in nearby **Muksang** until his untimely death at the age of 23. Along with Katok, it played a major role in the dissemination of the Nyingma Kama (the oral teachings of the Nyingma school), and the wooden blocks for this collection of oral teachings (20 vols) along with the Collected Works of Namcho Mingyur Dorje were prepared and published here under the guidance of the eighth throne-holder, Orgyen Dongak Chokyi Nyima (1854-1906).

The temples of Pelyul were constructed on the slopes below the peak of Dzongnang and the ridge of Dago Osel Lhari. Among them the most important was the **Lhasarkhang** or **Chagrakhang**, constructed by Kunzang Sherab himself and containing a gilded copper image of Shakyamuni in the form of Jowo Yizhin Norbu, as well as frescoes of the Namcho deities. Stupas and reliquary halls housed the remains of past masters including those of Namcho Migyur Dorje. The **Dorsem Lhakhang** with its enormous image of Vajrasattva was constructed by the seventh throne-holder, Gyatrul Pema Dongak Tenzin (1830-1891), and the **Terdzokhang** or library by the eighth. The ridge-top temple of **Dago Osel Lhari** contained images, tangkas and frescoes of deities according to the Mahayoga and Anuyoga systems.

The expansion of Pelyul was supervised by 11 successive throne-holders, beginning with Rigdzin Kunzang Sherab and including the emanations of Drupwang Pema Norbu and Karma Kuchen. In past times the monastic population at Pelyul fluctuated greatly, but there were over 100 branches throughout East Tibet, the most important being the monastery of **Tarthang Dongak Shedrupling** in the Golok region of Amdo, which was founded in 1882 by the seventh throne-holder. A new branch of the monastery, **Namdroling**, was constructed in South India in 1963 under the guidance of the present throne holder, Pema Norbu Rinpoche III, who has served as the Head of the Nyingmapa School.

The site The monastery (3,261 m) is approached from the west end of town via the Hospital of Traditional Tibetan Medicine and a lane which leads sharply uphill through a timber yard. The reconstruction at Pelyul began in 1981. The new **Assembly Hall** (Dukhang) contains images of Padmasambhava flanked by Shantaraksita and King Trisong Detsen. The skylight murals are exquisitely crafted. In succession (left to right) they depict: (left wall) Karma Chakme, Rongzompa and Trisong Detsen; (inner wall): Namcho Mingyur Dorje, Longchen Rabjampa and Rigdzin Kunzang Sherab, and (right wall): Nubchen Sangye Yeshe, Ratnal Lungpa, and Jamyang Khyentse Wangpo.

Approximately 150 monks currently live in houses across the hillside, studying under the supervision of Tulku Tubten Pelzang and Chi-me Tulku, who are responsible for the reconstruction during the exile of Pema Norbu Rinpoche in India. Beside the new temple is a chapel containing four large Mani Wheels and a room containing the relics of Namcho Migyur Dorje. Hardly any of the wooden blocks mentioned above survive, and new blocks are expensive to make.

Higher up on the ridge, the ruined walls of the original massive two-storey temple are still prominent. On close inspection they reveal bullet-holes, as well as Marxist slogans in Chinese from the period of the Cultural Revolution. Above this ruin, on the northwest summit, is the newly restored hermitage of the late Dzongnang Rinpoche. The meditation retreat centre lies on the upper east side of the ridge.

Pelyul to Kandze road

Following the Ngu-chu valley upstream from Pelyul, the road passes through **Lingtang**, where a turn-off leads south through **Sangenrong** to connect with the Batang-Litang road (see above, page 464). Litang is 310 km from Pelyul. Uphill from Lingtang, the Kandze road passes through **Barong** (60 km from Pelyul), where forestry is the main industry; and **Zhang Chumdo**, where many small teams of Chinese gold prospectors can be seen spraying the hillside and panning the streams. Crossing the watershed pass (4,237 m), the road cuts southeast to **Adzom Gar**, a most influential monastery for the Longchen Nyingtik tradition, and **Tromtar**, where it forks, northeast towards Kandze (see page 532) and southeast to Nyarong (see below, page 535).

Taking the former road, you will pass through **Dorkho Gonpa** of the Sakya school (3,612 m). On this stretch, there are spectacular upland lakes and variegated grasslands of gentian, meconopsis and edelweiss. The final watershed pass cuts through the glacial **Kawalungring** range to enter the Yalong basin. The overall distance from Pelyul to Kandze is 222 km.

Derge County སྡེ་དགེ → *Pop: 65,000. Area: 11,711 sq km.* 德格县

Derge is often regarded as the cultural, if not the geographical, heart of Kham. Traditionally it is the name given to a large independent kingdom, which occupied until recent times present-day Jomda, Pelyul and Sershul counties, in addition to Derge county. The much diminished county of Derge now comprises only the valley of the Zi-chu tributary of the Yangtze, extending from its watershed in the **Tro La** range to its confluence with the Yangtze, the outlying grasslands of **Yilhun** and **Dzachuka** to the north and the valleys of **Pelpung**, **Pewar** and **Mesho** to the south. The county capital is located at **Derge Gonchen** in the Zi-chu valley – 28 km northeast from the Kamtok Drukha bridge, 345 km from Chamdo, and 120 km from Pelyul.

Dzongsar རྫོང་གསར → *Colour map 4, grid A3.*

About 10 km north of **Horpo** township, and 37 km south of the **Kamtok Drukha** bridge, on the east bank of the Yangtze, the road swerves into a ravine to span the estuary of the **Mesho-chu**. A derelict fortified machine-gun post beside the bridge bears witness to the vigorous resistance that was once maintained here by the Khampa Chuzhi Gangdruk organization against the Chinese occupation. Heading inland from the bridge, a new road (constructed in 1992 to facilitate the timber industry) follows the Mesho-chu upstream towards **Dzongsar**, criss-crossing the river and passing through a delightful forest, where bears and wild cats are even now said to roam. Some 30 km along this road, the gorge deepens and you will notice an escarpment with a plunging waterfall to the left. Some of the sheer rock cliffs would be a great attraction for rock climbers. After a further 12 km, the valley opens out into cultivated fields, and Dzongsar Monastery (3,690 m) appears on the ridge ahead, with the college and Mesho township below. Alongside the College for Buddhist Studies, which is the main building in the township, there are small shops, restaurants, a guesthouse where buses for Derge park overnight, a small clinic and a police station. The

Derge County

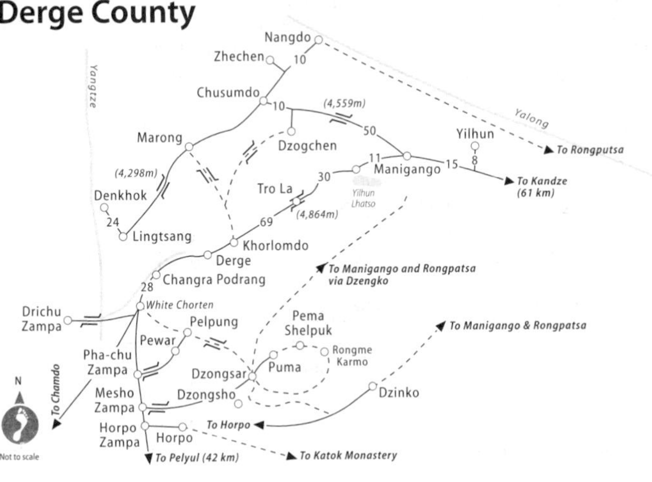

 township is at the centre of an important barley growing area, and traditional crafts (wood carving, ceramics and tangka painting) have also been maintained through the efforts of Dr Lodro Phuntsok .

Dzongsar Tashi Lhatse

This Sakya Monastery was founded in 1253 by Drogon Chogyel Pakpa, although there appear to have been older Nyingma and Kadampa establishments on the same site. The Sakya institution was maintained by the 24 successive Gangna Choje hierarchs and the 16 Ngari Choje preceptors. During the 19th century, the buildings were renovated and in 1871 a small temple was constructed on the sandy plains below the hillside by the eclectic master Jamyang Khyentse Wangpo (1820-1892). Later in 1918 a college, known as Dzongsar Khamje Shedra, was constructed alongside this temple by his incarnation, Dzongsar Khyentse Chokyi Lodro (1896-1959). These two were among the most prolific teachers and lineage-holders of the combined Sakya, Nyingma and Kagyu traditions in East Tibet. Under their inspirational guidance, Dzongsar became one of the most vital and active colleges in the whole of Tibet during the 19th and 20th centuries, with 23 far-flung branches. However, the entire complex was razed to the ground in 1959. The present Third Dzongsar Khyentse, Tubten Chokyi Gyatso, who is based in Bhutan, has travelled widely throughout the world and revisited his monastery on several occasions. To Tibetans he is the grandson of the great Nyingma master Dudjom Rinpoche, and himself the founder of affiliated colleges at Bir in Northwest India and in Bhutan, whereas in the international film world he is well known as a colleague of Bernardo Bertolucci and as the director of *The Cup*!

The renovated **Assembly Hall** of the monastery has been slowly refurbished since 1983. It contains tangkas depicting the life of Jamyang Khyentse Wangpo, and there are six chapels with some 150 monks. **Upstairs**, the most important chapel contains the reliquaries and images of Jamyang Khyentse Wangpo and his successor, along with an image of Vimalamitra, whose emanations they are said to have been. Regular ceremonies have been reinstated at Dzongsar in recent years, including the Dance of Vajrakila, held on 15th-16th and 25th-26th days of the ninth lunar month. Rebuilding at Dzongsar is in the capable hands of Dr Lodro Phuntsok who collects many of his medicinal herbs on the grasslands above the monastery. To promote Tibetan medicine and social welfare in the Mesho and Derge areas, he has established the Yuthok Yonten Gonpo Association (T0836-8223174). With the support of the late Panchen Lama, the college was re-established in 1986 with a six-year curriculum.

Dopu Valley

The tranquil alpine valley of **Dopu**, where glacial rivers flow from **Mount Rongme Ngadra** through forested copses and pristine meadows to swell the Mesho-chu, is an attractive area for trekkers and hikers. In its lower reaches there is a ruined hermitage, formerly associated with Dzongsar Monastery, but in the upper reaches there are no permanent buildings— only a few nomadic lean-tos and huts.

Getting there From Dzongsar the motor road continues uphill, passing through **Puma** township where there is a turn-off for Nezhi and Pema Shelpuk Cave after 8 km. Just beyond Puma the trail narrows – motor bikes can proceed further, but soon the trail is only suitable for walking or riding. The distance from here to Dopu is a further 10 km.

Pema Shelpuk and Rongme Karmo Taktsang

Four hours' trekking above Dzongsar will bring you to the **Pema Shelpuk cave** (4,510 m), which is a hermitage associated with Padmasambhava. This power-place is one of the 25 important pilgrimage sites in East Tibet, specifically representing the speech aspect of buddha-attributes. Here in the 19th century, the treasure-finder Chogyur Dechen Lingpa (1829-1870) discovered an important work entitled

Three Classes of the Great Perfection (*Dzogchen Desum*). In 1856 he constructed an active hermitage around the cave, with the co-operation of Jamyang Khyentse Wangpo, and a precious image of Padmasambhava in the form of Guru Dewachenpo ("supreme bliss") was installed there. The complex became a focal point for pilgrimage in the monkey and dragon years, but it was destroyed in 1959. Following its recent restoration, the chapel contains a new Padmasambhava image, and there are other rooms – a hermitage used by Jamyang Khyentse, a room for visiting hermits, and the caretaker's residence. Rock-carved mantras can be seen on the lower slopes of the pinnacle shaped rock. To reach the trailhead, drive north from Mesho township to **Nezhi**, where the motorable road comes to an end, and trek through hamlets and forest to reach the base of the prayer-flag strewn rock.

From Pema Shelpuk, another trekking trail crosses Dzonka La (4,790 m) and Hachung La (4,740 m) to reach the towering **Rong-me Karmo Taktsang** (4,430 m) in four hours. This 'tiger den' hermitage, once frequented by Padmasambhava, is also revered as a *terma*-site of Chogyur Dechen Lingpa. Here, too, Jamyang Khyentse Wangpo (1820-1892) and Jamgon Kongtrul Lodro Thaye (1813-1899) edited a Means for the Attainment of Dorje Drolo (Drolo Drubtab) and experienced portentous signs of successful practice, when two huge scorpions appeared in a vision. The scorpion is the hand-emblem of the deity Dorje Drolo. Mipham Rinpoche (1846-1912) also stayed here in retreat for 13 years, and his cave is accessible to visiting pilgrims, unlike the main cave, which is at present occupied by hermits affiliated to Dzongsar. Rong-me Karmo Taktsang can also be reached on foot from the lower reaches of the Rong-me valley on a seven-hour trek, starting from the motor road south of Mesho (Km marker 36). From the cave there is a further two-hour trek uphill to the sacred **Sengur Yutso** Lake (4,720 m), where Jamyang Khyentse Wangpo discovered *terma* texts. The trail continues above the lake to cross **Senge La** pass (4,880 m), leading towards Mount **Rong-me Ngadra** in the Trola Range.

Rupon Gonpa to Dagam Wangpuk Trek

From **Rupon**, a small Bon monastery in the Mesho valley about 12 km below Dzongsar, it is possible to trek uphill through the forest to **Rongkhanang** in three hours, and across **Redak La** (4,180 m) to **Chesa** in the upper Ting-chu valley in a further seven hours. Here the trail divides, one track following the gorge upstream to **Ngamongna Gonpa** of the Sakya school, and another heading downstream to **Komagen Monastery** (3,750 m), a Nyingmapa hermitage built alongside another Padmasambhava cave. **Dagam Wangpuk** cave is accessible on the west bank of the Ting-chu on this latter route. This is where, in the late 19th century, Jamgon Kongtrul discovered his Seven Line Sadhana, with the aid of Jamyang Khyentse Wangpo. From Komagen, a five-hour trek also leads south across a high ridge to reach **Dzongsho Deshek Dupa**. This rugged hermitage (4,270 m) overlooking the Dzin-chu valley is yet another of the 25 power places of Kham and Amdo, specifically representing the buddha-attributes. It has associations with both Jamyang Khyentse Wangpo and Chogyur Dechen Lingpa. Another six-hour trail leads east from Komagen to cross **Bayak La** (3,960 m) and reach **Dzinko** in the upper Dzin-chu valley, from where one can drive to **Horpo**.

Rupon Gonpa to Manigango Treks

The trekking routes from **Redak La** pass to **Manigango** take three days. One follows the steep walled Ting-chu gorge via the Bon monastery of Nenang upstream to cross the watershed at **Dzin La** pass (5,000 m), leading directly into the Dzenu-chu valley, while the other follows the Ngamongna-chu upstream past nomad encampments to **Zi-ne La** (4,880 m). The latter route is usually open when Dzin La is still blocked by snow in the late spring. From Zi-ne La, the trail descends to a long mani stone wall, before criss-crossing the fast-flowing Zhugo-chu on its descent past the stupas of **Dekyi Khangsar** towards Manigango. There are fine views of the snow peaks Akhu

Successive incarnations of Tai Situ

Tai Situ I	Kyechok Chokyi Gyeltsen (1377-1488)	Tai Situ VII	Mipham Trinle Rabten (1683-1698)
Tai Situ II	Tashi Namgyel (1450-1497)	Tai Situ VIII	Chokyi Jungne (1700-1774)
Tai Situ III	Tashi Peljor (1498-1541)	Tai Situ IX	Pema Nyinje Wangpo (1774-1853)
Tai Situ IV	Mitruk Chokyi Gocha (1542-1585)	Tai Situ X	Pema Kunzang Chogyel (1854-1885)
Tai Situ V	Norbu Sampe (1586-1657)	Tai Situ XI	Pema Wangchuk Gyelpo (1886-1852)
Tai Situ VI	Chokyi Gyeltsen Gelek Pelzangpo (1658-1682)	Tai Situ XII	Pema Dongak Nyinje Wangpo (b 1954)

Dzari to the east and Maho Dzari to the west; but it is virtually impossible to do this trek without riding a horse when fording the river. Another side trail leaves the Zhugo-chu valley, south of Dekyi Khangsar, to cross Pi La (4,800 m), bypassing the glacial Pi-tso and Dzin-tso lakes to reach the Dzenu-chu valley, where it links up with direct trail. The track then follows the Dzenu-chu downstream to its confluence with the Tro-chu near **Yilhun Lhatso** lake (see below, page 505). **NB** These trekking routes can easily be reversed.

Pewar Gonpa

If you head north from the entrance to the Mesho-chu valley, following the Yangtze upstream for 5 km, you will reach its confluence with the Pha-chu river. Here, a side road leaves the gorge, and heads through the Pha-chu valley to Pelpung. En route it passes a logging checkpoint and the cliff-hanging Pewar Gonpa (Ch. Baiyasi). To reach Pewar, take the trail that branches off from the Pelpung road, just beyond the cliffs. **Pewar Gonpa** is a Sakyapa monastery under the guidance of Pewar Rinpoche (Chime Dorje), who has contributed greatly to the resurgence of Tibetan culture in East Tibet. The monastery has recently been reconstructed and re-consecrated – its original murals conserved with the assistance of the US-based Kham Aid Project. There is a small shop in the hamlet at Pewar.

Pelpung Tubden Chokhorling Monastery → *Colour map 4, grid A3.*

The Pha-chu valley jeep trail leads northwest through a pine-clad ravine for 32 km to **Pelpung** (3,930 m), which is located on the knoll of a grassland valley, girded with pine-forest. The five-storey, red-walled assembly hall of **Pelpung Tubten Chokhorling,** founded in 1717 by the Eighth Tai Situ Chokyi Jungne, is the largest Kagyu establishment in Derge, and it rapidly became the most important study centre in East Tibet for the Kagyu tradition. Prior to its construction the previous seven incarnations bearing the name Tai Situ lived mostly at **Karma Gon Monastery** in Lhato (see above, page 422). The first of these had received the title from the Da Ming emperor in the 15th century. An important woodblock collection for the five anthologies of Jamgon Kongtrul, including the *Store of Precious Treasures (Rinchen Terdzo)* was housed here; but severely damaged in the 1960s. The building however was not destroyed, and new woodblocks have recently been prepared in Derge to replace the missing volumes. The refurbished hall, which has more than 100 small rooms and chapels, contains a large gilded copper image of Maitreya, flanked by Padmasambhava and Tara.

The **courtyard** gives access to residential buildings and to the reliquary chapel in which the mortal remains of previous Tai Situ incarnations are interred. The **labrang** (residence) of the present incumbent, whose base is at Bir in North India, has also been rebuilt, as has the once-celebrated **college** of Pelpung. Young lamas of the Karma Kagyu school, including the young Twelfth Trungpa Tulku, are being educated here.

Above Pelpung there is a rock with red markings, said to bear the footprint of a previous Karmapa. Further uphill, three hours walking distance from Pelpung, there is the Nyingma monastery of **Dordrak Gonpa.** The hermitage of **Tsandra Rinchen Drak**, a cave retreat established by the 19th-century master Jamgon Kongtrul, is also located 2-3 hours above Pelpung in the upper Pha-chu valley. This site is revered as one of the 25 power places of Kham and Amdo, specifically representing the buddha-mind aspect of buddha-attributes.

Facilities At Pelpung village, there is a clinic, a small school and a general store, but as yet no formal guesthouse.

Trekking access Pelpung can also be reached by trekking from the prominent **White Chorten** in the Yangtze gorge, 16 km below **Derge Gonchen**. The two-day trail leads through **Gongyeshin** (3,310 m) and **Shigar** villages, before crossing **Gotse La** pass (4,481 m), which leads downhill through forested alpine meadows to the upper Pha-chu valley. Another two-day trekking route leads west from **Pema Shelpuk** above Dzongsar, crossing **Ha La** pass (4,359 m) to reach the upper Pha-chu valley, below Pelpung.

Changra Podrang → *Colour map 4, grid A3*

A short distance north of the White Chorten which marks the beginning of the Pelpung trail, the unpaved highway 317 (from Jomda to Derge) leaves the Yangtze at its confluence with the Zi-chu, and follows the latter upstream through a prosperous farming belt. Here it passes below the ruins of **Changra Podrang**, the former summer palace of the kings of Derge, where a small temple (Changra Gonpa) has recently been restored. Dances enacting the epic deeds of Ling Gesar are performed here at a tented riverside camp each summer to mark the end of the monastic rain retreat.

Derge Gonchen → *Altitude: 3,292 m. Colour map 4, grid A3.*

Derge Gonchen was once the capital of the largest and most influential of the five kingdoms of Kham. The crafts of Derge, particularly in printing and metal work were renowned throughout Tibet. The independence of the kingdom was firmly maintained until 1865 and sporadically thereafter by its hereditary kings, who have been documented in J Kolmas, *A Genealogy of the Kings of Derge*. The town still has a majority Tibetan population; which is considerably increased in summertime when the **Rain Retreat Festival** attracts visitors from all parts of Kham.

Orientation

The buildings of Derge are located in a sharp-sided ravine, which abuts the Zi-chu valley. At present, it appears to have lost much of its former grandeur. Two bridges span the Zi-chu, connecting the Chamdo-Kandze highway on the west bank with the town on the east bank. Along the highway you will find the county bus stop and bus station, the Forestry Department Guesthouse, which has hot public showers, a number of restaurants, shops, bars, and two power stations, one at either end of the town.

The best view of the town is to be obtained from the cave of Tangtong Gyelpo, high up on the cliff-face across the Zi-chu. From this vantage point one can clearly discern the ruins of the royal palace and the reconstructed monastery of **Derge Gonchen** at the top end of Culture Street (Tib Rig-ne Lam; Ch Wenhua Jie). Further downhill on Culture

 Street, the Derge Middle School, the renowned **Derge Parkhang** and its guesthouse and bookshop are located, while further to the south (right), accessible via a narrow lane, is the old Tibetan quarter where the houses are clustered around the **Temple of Tangtong Gyelpo**. Below the Derge Parkhang is a large reconstructed stupa – originally founded by Dudul Dorje and later rebuilt by Jamyang Khyentse Wangpo.

Heading downhill from Culture Street, a turn-off on the right leads north towards the County Hall, the Government Buildings and the cinema. Continuing downhill you will pass a number of shops and general stores, and arrive at an intersection. Turn south (left) on to Sanitation Street (Ch Weisheng Jie) for the People's Hospital, the Tibetan Hospital, the petrol station and the PLA base. Turn north (right), on to Main Street (Ch Zheng Jie), for the Xinhua Bookstore, the Post Office, the Public Security Bureau, the Derge Hotel and the Festival Site. Alternatively, continue downhill on Commercial Street (Ch Shang Yie Jie) to the Chamdo-Kandze Highway on the west bank of the Zi-chu.

Derge Gonchen Monastery

ⓘ *Admission: ¥20.*

The monastery of **Derge Gonchen** was rapidly reconstructed between 1987 and 1988 following its devastation during the Cultural Revolution, the internal structures and windows being rebuilt around the shell of the outer walls which had largely survived. The **Assembly Hall** (Dukhang) with its high fluted columns is illuminated by windows on the upper level. It contains images of the Five Founders of Sakya and relics of the previous Dzongsar Khyentse Rinpoche. The murals depict

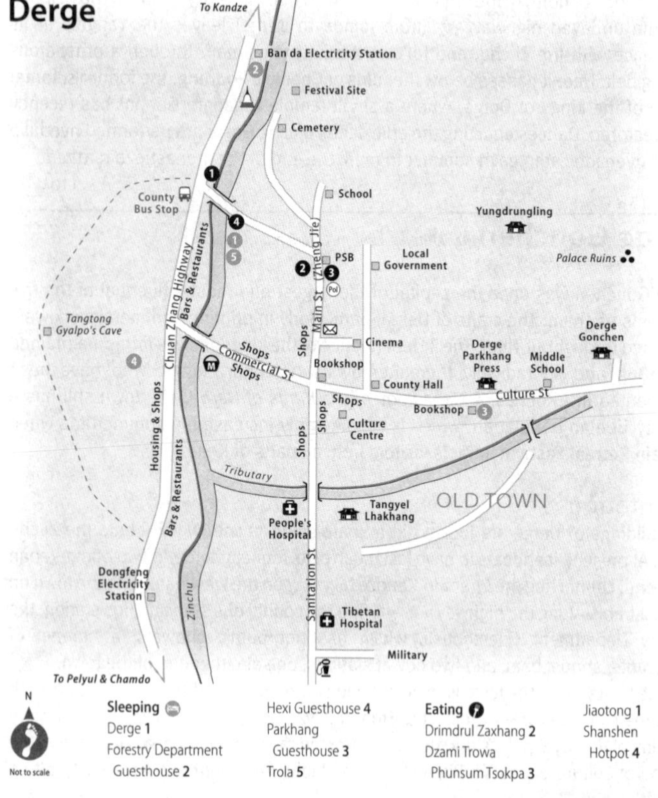

History of Derge

The Kings of Derge claimed descent from the ancient Gar family, the most illustrious representative of which was Songtsen Gampo's chief minister. Their early Bonpo religious affiliations appear to have been superseded first by the Nyingmapa, and then by Chogyel Pakpa and the Sakyapa who granted them authority in Kham.

In the 15th century, the 31st generation descendant, Lodro Tobden, moved his capital to the present site and constructed the royal palace. He also invited Tangtong Gyelpo to select an adjacent site for the new monastery of **Lhundrupteng** (or Derge Gonchen). Tangtong Gyelpo is said to have consecrated the site in 1448 while meditating in a cave high on the cliff-face across the Zi-chu River. The town has since had another temple dedicated to his memory. Lhundrupteng was eventually completed by the king Lachen Jampa Phuntsok in the mid-17th century. It became the most important centre for the Ngorpa order of the Sakya school in East Tibet and its branches were to extend throughout the kingdom from Khorlomdo and Dzongsar to Wara.

At Derge itself the monastic population was approximately 1700. In the 18th century the king Tenpa Tsering (1678-1738) brought Derge to the height of its power by conquering the outlying northern districts of **Dzachuka**. Under his auspices, the celebrated printery, **Derge Parkhang**, was founded in 1729, and eventually completed in 1750 during the reigns of his successors. Here, the Sakya scholar Zhuchen Tsultrim Rinchen produced his own edition of the *Kangyur* and *Tangyur*, generally regarded as the most accurate in Tibet. However, the massive collection of 217,000 xylograph blocks housed at the printery, carved in the style of the **Kutse school**, was also regarded as the most eclectic in Tibet. Works of the Nyingma, Kagyu and Geluk schools were printed alongside those of the Sakyapa, as were texts on non-Buddhist subjects, such as medicine, divination, history, grammar and biography. The eclecticism of the kingdom was also reflected in the scope given to non-Sakya traditions, particularly of the Nyingma and Kagyu schools, for their own development.

The kingdom which had survived the campaign of Gushi Qan in the 17th century finally succumbed to Gonpo Namgyel, the chieftain of Nyarong in 1863. However, the latter was defeated by the Tibetan army in 1865 and after an interim period of administration from Lhasa, independence was restored. Later, the armies of Chao Erh Feng occupied the kingdom and it remained in Chinese possession between 1909-1918.

Buddha in the form of Ardhokta and the meditational deities of the Sakya school. Towards the centre of the hall is prominently situated the grand throne of Sakya Trizin, the head of the Sakyapa school who currently resides at Rajpur in India. Behind it there are three **inner sanctums** approached by steep wooden staircases, which respectively contain enormous clay images of the Eight Manifestations of Padmasambhava, a gilded Jowo Shakyamuni, and Maitreya flanked by the eight standing bodhisattvas. The antechamber contains on its walls a painting of the deer and dharma-wheel motif alongside a list of all those who have made donations towards the rebuilding programme.

Derge Parkhang Printing Press

ⓘ *Guided tour: ¥50, including introductory pamphlet and VCD.*

The celebrated printing press of **Derge Parkhang** is a magnificent four-storey building with original frescoes that were blackened by smoke during the wanton destruction of the 1960s, but recently restored with painstaking care. Beyond the portico, there is an inner courtyard, giving access to the **temple** on the ground level, **the printing works** on the second and third levels, and **the rooftop chapels** on the fourth level. The temple contains original exquisite images of (L-R): the three emanations of Manjughosa, namely: Sakya Pandita, flanked by Tsongkhapa and Longchen Rabjampa; along with Four-armed Avalokiteshvara, Amitabha, Shakyamuni, Padmasambhava, Manjughosa, Tara, Pelpung Situ Chokyi Jungne, and King Tenpa Tsering. There is an old tangka depicting Milarepa and murals of the 1,000 Buddhas of the Aeon. Adjacent to the temple there is an atmospheric protector chapel, entered through a separate flight of stairs. **Upstairs**, is the precious collection of xylograph blocks, including the Derge editions of the *Kangyur*, *Tangyur*, *Nyingma Gyudbum* and other works, which are constantly in demand throughout the towns, villages and monasteries of Tibet. The entire printing process can be observed here: from the preparation of the paper and the ink to the carving of the woodblocks and the actual printing and collating of the various texts. The bookshop (open Monday to Saturday) is located in the south wing of the building opposite the Parkhang.

Tangyel Lhakhang

Surrounded by the timber and adobe residential houses of the Tibetan quarter, the **Tangyel Lhakhang** is dedicated to the memory of Tangtong Gyelpo, Tibet's multi-talented bridge-builder, dramatist, engineer and treasure-finder, who consecrated the site of the Gonchen Monastery in 1448. The temple, which was severely damaged during the 1960s, contains a fine characteristic image of this great figure – identified by his reddish brown complexion, white hair and white beard. There is also a large Mani Wheel in an adjacent building; and the elderly townspeople devote much time to the circumambulation of the entire complex. ▸▸ *For listings, see page 509.*

Upper Zi-chu Valley

The highway from Derge to Chengdu (927 km) begins by following the Zi-chu River upstream to its source in the Drida Zelmogang range. This is the name given to the highland region forming a watershed between the upper Yangtze and the upper Yalong. En route it passes through **Khorlomdo** and **Rida**, where there are small Sakyapa monasteries, and the **Kasado** gorge.

Khorlomdo, 28 km from Derge Gonchen, has an old copper image of Jowo Shakyamuni in its assembly hall, which is now maintained by some 50 monks. Two 3-4 day trekking routes lead from Khorlomdo to **Dzogchen** Monastery (see below), crossing the Trola Range via **Henak La** (4,950 m) and via **Le La** (4,390 m). The former passes in close proximity to **Mount Dorje Ziltrom** (5,816 m), which is one of the highest peaks of the Trola Range. The latter, which is the old trade route to Dzachuka, passes through **Galen Gonpa** (3,700 m), the seat of Namkhai Norbu, who resides in Italy and has established an international network of centres, known collectively as the Dzogchen Community.

The ascent to the watershed **Tro La** pass (4,864 m), 69 km northeast of Derge, is precipitous and switchback, gradually rising above the tree line into a world of jagged snow mountains. There are magnificent views of the Yangtze gorge to the southwest. On the far side of Tro La, the landscape is totally different, the enclosed forested valleys giving way to rugged open grassland. The crossroads town of **Manigango** is located in the grassland, 110 km from Derge, and 41 km from Tro La pass.

Yilhun

The grassland region to the northeast of Tro La pass is known as **Yilhun**. Here two rivers, the Tro-chu and Dzenu-chu, drain from the Trola Range to form the Yi-chu, a fast-flowing tributary of the Yalong. On the descent, take a turn-off on the right (south) to visit the sacred glacial lake of **Yilhun Lhatso** (Ch Xinluhai, 4110 m), situated some 30 km below the pass. This lake is one of the most beautiful in all Tibet – its shores bedecked with carved mani stones. The mountains and rocks surrounding the lake are said to assume the divine form of the Cakrasamvara mandala to those who have the pure vision to perceive them as such. The Yilhun Lhatso Nature Reserve (190 sq km), extending from the lakeshore as far as the jagged snow peaks of the Trola range to the south, is a natural habitat for 176 species of wild animals, including the red deer *cervus albirostris*, the snow-leopard, the argali, the red fox and various birds of prey. The flora of the reserve include distinctive azaleas, dragon spruce, cypresses and the snow lotus. There is a **toll barrier** ⓘ *¥20*, at the bridge and you must cross the Tro-chu on foot to get to the lake. If you have time, pitch a tent here, and explore the pilgrims' trail along the lake shore. A lakeside retreat house and pavilion have recently been constructed by one Lama Dorje, who has spent many years in retreat in this locality. **Trekking routes** also lead from the northern shore of the lake through the Dzenu-chu valley and across **Pi La** or **Dzin La**, in the direction of Dzongsar (see above, page 497). The nomads of these upper valleys supplement their income by collecting caterpillar fungus for Chinese medicinal consumption.

Manigango The bustling town of **Manigango** (3,960 m), 11 km below the lake, lies at the junction of three important roads. Derge lies 110 km to the southwest, Jyekundo 429 km to the northwest, and Kandze 84 km to the southeast. Despite its "wild west" ambience, in the grassland to the south, there is an active hermitage affiliated to Dzogchen Monastery, known as **Yazer Gon**, and, in town, opposite the bus stand, there is a small **Mani Lhakhang**. It was in this locale that Derge Yilhunpa Sonam Namgyel attained the rainbow body accomplishment in 1952. An interesting account of this event is described by Chogyam Trunpa in his autobiography *Born in Tibet*.

Some 23 km east of Manigango, a motorable road leaves the Kandze highway and the Yi-chu valley, via a side bridge and heads north to **Yilhun** township. Here, in August, there is a small but interesting horse festival, held on a wide plain below the local monastery and village.

Dzogchen Rudam Orgyen Samten Choling Monastery རྫོགས་ཆེན་དགོན་པ

Getting there From Manigango, take the northwest route for **Jyekundo**, and cross the Muri La pass (4,559 m). After 50 km, you will notice the hamlet of **Ganda** coming into view on the left (south) side of the road. Above it you will glimpse the **Mani Wheel Chapel** of Dzogchen Monastery on a ridge, protruding from a hidden valley to the southwest. Leave the highway here and drive across a stream, leading down to the hamlet, where there are a few grocery stores and a private guesthouse. The road then cuts across a low defile to enter the wonderful valley of **Rudam Kyitram**, where Dzogchen Monastery is located.

History of Dzogchen Monastery Dzogchen is recognized as the major pilgrimage site of buddha-attributes in East Tibet and as one of the largest monasteries of the Nyingma school in Kham. It lies at an elevation of 4,023 m, in the concealed valley of Rudam Kyitram, dominated to the southwest by the jagged snow peaks of Mount **Dorje Ziltrom** (5,816 m).

The monastery was founded in 1684-1685 on the advice of the the Fifth Dalai Lama, by the charismatic the First Dzogchen Pema Rigdzin (1625-1697), and it was subsequently maintained by his students, including Zhechen Rapjam Tenpei

 Gyeltsen, and by his successive incarnations. Among the latter, the Second Dzogchen Gyurme Tekchok Tenzin (1699-1758) is known to have inspired the king of Derge to construct the famous **Derge Parkhang**, the Third Dzogchen Ngedon Tenzin Zangpo (1759-1792) built 13 hermitages, colleges and mantra-wheels, the Fourth Dzogchen Migyur Namkei Dorje (b 1793) presided over the monastery when its greatest college was founded, and the Fifth Dzogchen Tubten Chokyi Dorje (1872-1935) increased its branches to over 200 throughout Kham, Amdo and Central Tibet. The mother monastery itself had a population of 1,000 monks. The Sixth Dzogchen Jikdrel Jangchub Dorje (1935-1959) died tragically during the resistance to the Chinese occupation of East Tibet, and his reliquary is even now revered in the main temple. The Seventh Dzogchen Rinpoche lives in Karnataka in South India, where he has constructed a branch of the monastery.

At Dzogchen Monastery, two great temples were constructed. The **larger** housed exquisite images of Shakyamuni, Vajradhara and Padmasambhava, alongside the reliquaries of the past emanations of Pema Rigdzin. The **smaller** to the northeast contained enormous images of Padmasambhava, Shantaraksita and King Trisong Detsen. In the early 19th century, a college was constructed below the monastery by Gyelse Zhenpen Thaye at a site consecrated by the ancient Nyingma lineage-holder Shrisimha. The college, known thereafter as **Shrisimha**, became renowned for the study of philosophy and Vajrayana until the mid-20th century. It attracted some of the greatest literati of East Tibet, such as Peltrul Rinpoche (1808-1887), Mipam Rinpoche (1846-1912) and Khenpo Zhenga (1871-1927), who wrote commentaries on 13 major texts.

Meditation hermitages The monastery was equally renowned for its meditation hermitages and the caves which were inhabited by hermits in the upper reaches of the Rudam Kyitram valley. Important figures such as Dodrub Trinle Ozer (1745-1821), Do Khyentse Yeshe Dorje (b 1800), Peltrul Rinpoche and Mipham Rinpoche passed many years in meditation in this region, the rocks of which are intimately connected with their visionary experiences. It was also here that Peltrul Rinpoche composed his great commentary on the preliminary practices of Buddhist meditation, the *Kunzang Lamei Zhelung* (translated into English under the title "Words of my Perfect Teacher").

The site The monastery is located on the north slopes of the Rudam Kyitram valley. The larger of the two temples which formerly housed the relics of past Dzogchen Rinpoches was restored in 2004. The **smaller** one, which has been rebuilt twice in recent years, contains impressively large images of Padmasambhava, King Trisong Detsen and Shantaraksita – the founders of the Nyingma tradition in Tibet. It has decorative columns at the entrance, protected by silk wrappings, and in its upper storey there is a chapel containing the relics of the Sixth Dzogchen Jikdrel Jangchub Dorje, who was killed in 1959. Religious dances are still held in the courtyard on the 10th day of the first month of the Tibetan calendar.

To the north of these temples is a **Mani Lhakhang**, and to the south are two lower elongated buildings on either side of an open courtyard. Approaching these from the temple, one passes the **Ngakhang** on the left and the **Podrang Khamsum Zilnon** on the right. The latter building, which once housed many chapels, contains in its upper storey the residence of Dzogchen Rinpoche, **Chime Drupei Gatsel**, a library, a printery, and a temporary residence where the present Dzogchen Rinpoche stayed during a recent visit. The hillside adjacent to these temples is covered with the log cabin cells of the monks, their horizontal timbers painted red in the Khampa style.

Below the monastery and to the right is the **Shrisimha college**, so called because this ancient yogin is said to have appeared in a vision to the college's founder and to have left an impression in a nearby rock. The buildings within the small campus have been restored by Tulku Kelzang, who has revitalized the college in collaboration with Khenpo Dazer and Khenpo Pentse. Accommodation may be available here, near the lama's house.

The Cave Hermitages Heading up the valley from the college towards the cave hermitages and the Dorje Ziltrom glacier, you first pass, in a clearing, a series of burial stones marking the graves of past monastic preceptors. Above and to the right as you ascend the valley is the ruined hermitage of the monastery where long regulated retreats were once held. Higher up the slope on the same side of the valley are firstly the cave-hermitage of Do Khyentse Yeshe Dorje (4,040 m), known as the **Tseringma cave** (either because he met the deity Tseringma here face to face, or because it reminded him of Tseringjong hermitage), and secondly that of Peltrul Rinpoche (4,190 m).

Continuing up the central part of the valley you reach an elevated area where there are well-constructed and active hermitages. On the hillside to the left, high up and across the rushing river is the cave-hermitage known as **Shinje Drupuk** (4,110 m) – a former retreat of Dodrub Jigme Trinle Ozer, containing a footprint of Yamantaka which gives the cave its name. Directly opposite the cave site on the right side of the valley is a rock into which the deity Palchen Dupa vanished after appearing in a vision to Dodrub Trinle Ozer. Below this cave is another, approached from the site where Peltrul Rinpoche first taught his celebrated text, Kunzang Lamei Zhelung. It contains the meditation-box of Peltrul Rinpoche and natural stone impressions of Yamantaka, which appeared while Dodrub Rinpoche was engaged in practice there. Still further down is a **cave of Mipam Rinpoche** containing original but damaged clay relief images of the 25 disciples of Padmasambhava.

From the top of these caves one has an excellent view to the north beyond Dzogchen Monastery to the **Kyadrak Senge Dzong** retreat (4,872 m) in Dzachuka, the major pilgrimage site representing buddha-body in Kham. There, Padmasambhava himself is reputed to have passed three months.

Above the valley in the Rudam Kangtro range are three sacred lakes, which can be reached in a single day's trek – **Shama Tso** (4,390 m), **Kama Tso** (4,600 m) and **Barma Tso** (4,880 m). On this circuit, there is a meditation cave where Padmasambhava made medicinal myrobalan.

Zhechen Tenyi Dargyeling Monastery ཞེ་ཆེན་དགོན་པ

Getting there Returning to the highway from Dzogchen, drive west for 10 km as far as the transport station at **Chusumdo** (Ch Sansaho). Here, a side road follows the Nang-chu tributary of the Yalong downstream to its confluence. Some 10 km along this road, you will reach **Zhechen Monastery** (3,780 m) on the left (west). This monastery, located in the Nang-chu valley, is situated in a defile between the **Bonri** and **Dolmari** hills (3,780 m). The site was chosen because on the slopes of Dolmari there were many sacred hermitages and caves associated with Padmasambhava, Yeshe Tsogyel, Vajravarahi and Tangtong Gyelpo.

History of Zhechen Monastery The monastery was founded in 1735 by the Second Zhechen Rabjam, Gyurme Kunzang Namgyel (1710-1769). His predecessor, the First Zhechen Rabjam Tenpei Gyeltsen (1654-1709), had been a student of the Fifth Dalai Lama and Dzogchen Pema Rigdzin. The seat was maintained by his successive emanations, including the Third Zhechen Rabjam Rigdzin Peljor Gyatso (1771-1809), who constructed the **Pema Choling** hermitage in 1794; and the Fourth Zhechen Rapjam Garwang Chokyi Gyeltsen, as well as by a succession of regents. In the time of the regent Gyeltsab Tendzin Chogyel, 100,000 students gathered from all four Buddhist traditions and also from the Bon to receive his teachings. In more recent years however, the resident population of the mother monastery included about 300 monks. The present Seventh Zhechen Rabjam, under the guidance of the late HH Dingo Khyentse Rinpoche, constructed a new flourishing branch of the monastery at Boudha in Nepal.

The monastery was known for its fine sculptures, tangkas and murals. Formerly there were two temples with major images of Shakyamuni and Padmasambhava, respectively representing the sutra and mantra traditions. There was also a famous image made of herbs, representing Terdak Lingpa, the founder of Mindroling. Alongside these images were eight reliquaries containing the remains of past Zhechen Rabjam emanations and their regents.

A prestigious college at Zhechen was founded in the early 20th century by the Third Gyeltsab Pema Namgyel (1871-1927), and it rapidly became known in Kham for the excellence of its study programme, largely through the efforts of the late Zhechen Kongtrul (d 1959) and the late Sixth Zhechen Rabjam (d 1959). Woodblocks were kept for the works of Karma Lingpa and for liturgical texts associated with Mindroling Monastery.

The site The hill to the right as one approaches from the Chusumdo-Nangdo road, is **Bonri** and the one to the left **Dolmari**. Of the former impressive structures on the slopes of Dolmari, nothing remains. Down below, two original buildings have now been reconstructed – the red-walled **assembly hall** and the white-walled **podrang** of Zhechen Rabjam. At present there are approximately 200-300 monks affiliated with Zhechen, some of whom live permanently at the site.

Above the temple is the ruined hermitage, and below and beyond the stream is the **college**, restored through the efforts of the late Lama Gyenpel. The main building of the college contains a shrine with a new Padmasambhava image and a gold-painted footprint of its founder, the Third Zhechen Gyeltsab.

Sacred caves Above the monastery on **Dolmari** are many sacred caves and hermitages associated with important historical figures and deities. Among them the following are most notable:

The **Kabgye Drupuk**, where Vajravarahi reputedly appeared in a rock during the meditations of Gyeltsab Gyurme Pema Namgyel. This cave was damaged during the Cultural Revolution, but the earth inside is held by pilgrims to be sacred.

The **Zangdok Pelri Drupuk** of Padmasambhava and Yeshe Tsogyel, where pilgrims go to gather natural medicinal nectar.

The **Khandro Bumgyi Drupuk**, which is adorned with a red and white stupa and a dark blue relief image of Tangtong Gyelpo.

The former **hermitage of Gyeltsab Tenzin Chogyel** and site of the destroyed hermitage of the previous Sixth Zhechen Rabjam.

The **Osel Drupuk** which has a naturally-produced image of the deity Rigdzin Dupa.

Zhechen to Nangdo

Some 10 km north of Zhechen, the Nang-chu flows into the Yalong at **Nangdo**. From here there are trekking routes following the Yalong downstream towards the farming settlements of **Rongpatsa**, and upstream into the sparse grasslands of **Sershul** county. The monasteries of **Drokda Gonpa** and **Samdrub Gonpa** are located downstream around the confluence of the Ding-chu with the Yalong, while **Peni Gonpa** and **Dzechen Gonpa** lie upstream.

Chusumdo to Denkhok

Another motorable trail leads southwest from Chusumdo to **Marong**, where Jamgon Kongtrul discovered *termas* in the 19th century. (A trekking route also leads from here across **Le La** pass to **Khorlomdo** near Derge, see above, page 504). The motorable trail then crosses the watershed **Latse Kare La** pass (4,298 m) and enters **Lingtsang**, one of the former independent kingdoms of East Tibet, where the Gyelpo (king) claimed descent from Tibet's epic hero Ling Gesar. A new temple-cum museum dedicated to Ling Gesar has been recently constructed here, but the most important site in Lingtsang is the large distinctively striped Sakya monastery called **Gotse Gon**.

Sleeping

Pelyul *p495*
C **Pelyul Hotel**, on south bank of the Ngu-chu, T0836-5922661. Recently refurbished, doubles at ¥280, singles at ¥150, triples at ¥300.

Derge *p504, map p502*
E **Derge Hotel**, adjacent to the Trola Hotel and shares the same compound. Has superior rooms upstairs (no attached bath, at ¥100) and hot shower cubicles in an outdoor compound.
E **Forestry Department Guesthouse**, poor but hot showers available here.
D **Trola Hotel**, T0836-8222167. The best in town, doubles with attached bath at ¥180, singles at ¥100, triples at ¥120, and suites at ¥888, and a good Sichuan-style restaurant.

Public showers can be found opposite the Post Office (open Wed, Sat and Sun).

Manigango *p505*
E **Qinghai Guesthouse**. Basic accommodation.
E **Sichuan Guesthouse**, has electric blankets on beds, and fairly good Sichuan-style food, long-frequented by truckers and bus drivers.
E **Sizhoudian Guesthouse**, opposite the Mani Lhakhang. Best accommodation in town, upstairs: ¥15-20 per bed, downstairs: ¥10 per bed), this guesthouse even has a telephone with a reliable IDD connection.

Eating

Pelyul *p495*
The main street, on the north bank of the Ngu-chu, has a number of smaller restaurants, serving both Tibetan and Sichuan cuisine.

Derge *p504, map p502*
Dondrub Zakhang, above the Derge Hotel, opposite the PSB.
Sichuan Jiatong Restaurant (Drimdrul Zakhang), Main Street, on the corner below the Trola Hotel.

Manigango *p505*
Tibetan Restaurant next door to Sizhoudian Guesthouse has become very popular.

Festivals and events

Derge Gonchen *p504, map p502*
Rain Retreat Festival, this monastic festival is an occasion for religious dances, depicting the purification of negativity by Shakyamuni over his successive past lives. The performance is held on the open plain by the Zi-chu River, adjacent to the Chinese Martyrs' Cemetery, beginning on the 1st day of the 7th lunar month (6 Sep, 2005). Colourful tents pitched on site for duration of festival.

Shopping

Pelyul *p495*
Several shops sell clothing, groceries, electrical goods, and luxury items.

Derge *p504, map p502*
Traditional Tibetan artefacts and antiques, including items of Derge metalwork, can be found in a small shop on the west side of Commercial Street. The **Xinhua Bookstore** is poorly stocked. Telephone cards and groceries are easily obtained.

Manigango *p505*
There are a number of shops here and a clean public toilet. Two small general stores outside the Sichuan Guesthouse also sell groceries, liquor, and a few household necessities.

Transport

Derge *p504, map p502*
Public transport rarely crosses the Yangtze and permit restrictions apply. A local tourism bureau has now been established in Derge, T0836-8223355.

Bus
Public buses run from **Derge** to **Dartsedo** (2 days, ¥164), stopping at **Kandze** (¥61) and **Drango** (¥83); and there are occasionally buses on the riverside road to **Pelyul** (¥30).

Taxi
Taxis run within the town and its outlying suburbs. For longer hauls, contact Sonam Dondrub, T0836-8222448.

Grasslands of Dzachuka, Jyekundo and Nangchen

The upper reaches of the Yalong, Yangtze and Mekong rivers in the extreme northwest of Kham flow through spacious grasslands, largely above the tree line. Here are some of the richest nomadic pastures in Tibet, and a surprisingly large number of monasteries, which minister to the spiritual needs of the nomadic population as well as to the inhabitants of the relatively few agricultural settlements. Driving across the watersheds of these mighty rivers, you will pass through seven counties, one of which (Sershul) is presently administered from Dartsedo (Sichuan), and the remaining six from Jyekundo (Qinghai). **Recommended itinerary: 8. See page 20.** *» For Sleeping, Eating and other listings, see pages 528-529.*

Sershul County གསེར་ཤུལ་ → *Pop: 63,000. Area: 20,477 sq km.* 石渠县

The rich nomadic pastures of **Sershul** extend through the upper reaches of the Yalong as far as the present day Sichuan-Qinghai provincial border. (The actual source of the Yalong lies across the border near **Domda**.) In the south of the county, across the watershed, there is the seventh-century geomantic temple of Langtang Dolma Lhakhang, which overlooks the Yangtze. The county capital is located at **Jumang**, in the Yalong valley, 139 km from Jyekundo, and 219 km from Manigango. There are 43 monasteries within Sershul, reflecting all the diverse traditions of Tibetan Buddhism and Bon.

Langtang Dolma Lhakhang

After 24 km, the rough motorable trail from **Lingtsang** descends through sharp ravines to reach the east bank of the Yangtze at Denma or **Denkhok**, where a wide cultivated barley plain opens out. The name Denma derives from General Tsegon Denma, a companion of the legendery Ling Gesar, who was born here. Nowadays it is divided into two main sectors – **Denkhok Nubma** lying within the jurisdiction of the Tibet Autonomous Region on the west bank of the Yangtze, and **Denkhok Sharma** within Sichuan province on the east bank.

Denkhok Nubma is a small village, lacking basic electricity. The large Gelukpa monastery of **Chunkor**, which had been founded by the fourth Ganden Tripa and is revered as the mother monastery of **Sershul Gonpa**, is located nearby on the west bank of the Yangtze, and there are bridges spanning the river here. The monastery, however, is isolated from other towns in the TAR, forcing those who eschew the horse to drive to Chamdo via Nangchen or Manigango! The Ninth Dalai Lama Lungtok Gyatso was born near Chunkor, and the monastery also maintained a close connection with the late Ling

Rinpoche, senior tutor to the present Dalai Lama. It presently has about 80 monks. A natural stone image of Tara (Dolma Rangjung), attributed in some sources to Princess Wencheng, is visible on the river bank when the water level is low.

Denkhok Sharma is a large township with its own post office, guesthouses, and market facilities. The geomantic temple, **Langtang Dolma Lhakhang**, is situated within the township, close to the Yangtze. This is revered as one of Songtsen Gampo's 12 major geomantic temples, specifically located on the right hand of the supine ogress. In the temple courtyard there is an obelisk commemorating the origins of this shrine, and a row of prayer wheels. The murals of the vestibule depict the Four Guardian Kings and on the inner wall adjacent to the door, the protector deities: Vaishravana, Four-armed Mahakala and Rahula (left), with Remati, Six-armed Mahakala and Dharmaraja (right). The main hall on the ground floor contains three central "speaking images" of Tara, which were reputedly installed here by Princess Wencheng, the Fifth Dalai Lama and Miwang Sonam Topgye. Along the left wall are the following images (L-R): Usnisavijaya, Cintamanicakra Tara, Jowo Shakyamuni, Sarvavid Vairocana, Vajrakila, Guhyasamaja, Vajrabhairava, Shantaraksita, Padmakara and King Trisong Detsen. An enlightenment stupa occupies the corner. Opposite, on the right wall, are images of (L-R): Ekajati, Vajrapani, Mahakarunika, Hayagriva, Khecari, Cakrasamvara, Tsongkhapa with his foremost students, Dawa Nyinje, Bhaisajyaguru and Nyima Nyingje. Nowadays the temple is maintained by the Gelukpas and there are 20 monks, under the guidance of Kusho Dechen, Kusho Rangdrol and Kusho Orgyen Dondrub. The upper halls and the four peripheral stupas have yet to be restored, and all rebuilding here is privately funded. Artists from Chunkor have undertaken much of the reconstruction.

Above Denkhok, there is a one-day trekking circuit around **Mount Senge Ngadzong**, where the Pema Ritro hermitage contains a stone handprint of Padmasambhava. Tulkus appear to have been born here in unusual concentrations. One family in particular gave birth to four prominent incarnations: the Sixteenth Karmapa, Zhamarpa, Dzogchen Ponlob and Tsechu Tulku!

Denkhok Sharma to Jyekundo

The rough road continues to undulate along the east bank of the Yangtze for 170 km to Jyekundo. The birthplace of the late Dingo Khyenste Rinpoche is passed near **Degon Gonpa** of the Gelukpa school, and various large Sakyapa monasteries, including **Damtok Gonpa**, are passed on both banks of the river. At **Manje** village there is a roadside Bon temple, and upstream from here is the Nyingmapa monastery of **Dzungo** which spectacularly overlooks the Yangtze from its hilltop pinnacle. It was here that the French traveller Andre Migot remained in retreat in the 1940s. The Bon tradition is once again prevalent around **Benda** and **Tsenda**, where a traffic checkpoint bars the road. After a further 10 km, the rough trail connects with the paved highway 214, linking Ziling with Jyekundo.

Denkhok Sharma to Jumang

Another rough but motorable trail leads 78 km inland from Denkhok Sharma, crossing the watershed (4,650 m) to **Jumang**, the capital of Sershul county. On the ascent, the ravine of **Drak Lhamo** has an important rock inscription concerning the activities of King Trisong Detsen, with relief images of the Three Deities of Longevity, which were attributed to Princess Jincheng. The forests of the gorge soon give way to the pass and the grasslands of the upper Yalong valley.

Chaktsa Gon

The main highway from Derge to Jyekundo enters Sershul county at the **Chusumdo** intersection (Ch Sansaho), initially heading northwest through the Nang-chu valley, before crossing a pass (4,350 m), which leads down through the **Magar Drokra** grassland. After passing the Gelukpa **Trugu Gonpa** on the left (36 km from Chusumdo), the road follows the Tra-chu downstream past the turn-off for **Ralung-kado** village on the right (42 km from Trugu Gonpa), and the Karma Kagyu monastery of **Chaktsa Gon** (locally pronounced Tsaktsa Gon) after a further 10 km.

Here, there is a turn-off on the right, which follows the Tra-chu downstream for 40 km as far as its confluence with the Yalong at **Tung** township. The Nyingmapa monastery of **Tashul** can be visited on this side road. At Tung township, the Ngoshi-chu tributary also flows into the Yalong from the northwest.

Junyung Mehor Sangak Choling

Keep to the highway at **Chaktsa Gon**, and the road will continue north to reach the south bank of the Yalong. There are magnificent expansive sunsets over the clear blue waters of the Yalong in this region. Following the Yalong upstream, after 38 km (at marker 186), you will arrive at **Rinyur Gonpa** (on the left) and, after a further 8 km, at **Junyung Forestry Department** (also on the left). **Junyung Mehor Sangak Choling** and its retreat hermitage, where the renowned Mipham Rinpoche (1846-1912) once studied and practised, is located on the slopes above. There are two reconstructed temples here: the larger has an image of Padmsambhava in the form of Guru Gyagarma and in its inner sanctum a silver image of Jowo Shakyamuni and a fine Vajrasattva, with the reliquary of Mipham Rinpoche to its right. The other temple contains images of Padmasambhava, flanked by Shantaraksita and King Trisong Detsen. Further to their right there is a large stupa and a Mani Wheel chapel (*korkhang*).

Uphill, alongside the retreat house, there is a rock with natural stone impressions of the syllables Om Arapacana Dhih, which are the mantra syllables of Manjughosa, the boshisattva of discernment. Dracocephalum (nodding dragonhead) herbs grow in abundance here. The re-established college at Junyung has 80 student monks under the guidance of Tulku Chojor, Khenpo Zangkyab and Khenpo Yongdul.

Arikdza Gonpa and Kabzhi

Two kilometres after Junyung, a motor bridge leads across the Yalong, before forking right to **Arikdza Gonpa** and left to **Gemang** and **Kabzhi**. Arikdza, where there are wonderful campsites, is an important branch of Dzogchen Monastery, under the guidance of Khenpo Pema Tsewang. **Gemang** is another significant branch of Dzogchen, and **Kabzhi**, in the Muge-chu valley, has active monasteries representing both the Gelukpa and *Longchen Nyingtik* traditions. From here, you can trek across the provincial border to reach the source of the Yalong at Domda in present-day Qinghai.

Bumsar and Bumnying

Beyond Junyung, the Omchung-chu flows into the Yalong from the south via **Bumsar** township. The Nyingma monastery of **Ponru Gonpa** is located in a lateral valley on its north bank. The highway continues following the Yalong upstream for a short distance, and then abruptly heads southwest, following the Om-chu tributary upstream to the large roadside Gelukpa monastery of **Bumnying Gonpa** , 19 km from Junyung, where there are 200 monks.

Jumang

Jumang (4,110 m), the county capital is in the Om-chu valley, 6 km south of Bumnying Gonpa. It has grown rapidly recently and is now the largest Chinese settlement northwest of Kandze. Here the nomadic peoples of the grasslands intermingle incongruously with Chinese immigrants. » *For listings, see pages 528-529.*

Orientation Entering town from the east, you will pass a petrol station, the Disabled People's Unit, and the People's Hospital on the left, with the county government buildings and a middle school on the right. Crossing a bridge which spans the Om-chu, you will reach a T-junction, where the Tashigar Hotel is situated at the head of Main Street. Heading west along Main Street, you will pass the Grain Department, the Armed Police Unit, the PLA Unit, the Agricultural Bank and a number of small shops on the left. Opposite on the right are the police station, China Post and a pharmacy. A turn-off on the left now leads south towards China Telecom, a small guesthouse, the vegetable market and the TV station. Continuing on Main Street you will pass the Kha-le Guesthouse and the Traffic Police Bureau, with the Communication Bureau, the Mentsikhang, the Transport Guesthouse, and a cemetery on the right. Towards the far end of town, a side road leads south for 78 km to Denkhok Sharma (see above), while the main road leads due west to Sershul Monastery (38 km).

Sershul Monastery

Getting there Leaving the capital, the road also leaves the Om-chu valley, and heads northwest, passing **Deongma** township after 18 km. The Nyingmapa monastery of **Dzakya Gonpa**, where there are only 50 monks, is located in the grassland far to the northwest.

Sershul Tekchen Dargyeling (4,054 m) is an important monastery of the Gelukpa school, located 20 km west of Deongma, on the right side of the road. This is currently the largest monastery in Sershul county, with 800 monks divided into six colleges, under the guidance of the youthful but charismatic Drukpa Rinpoche. The rain retreat festival held in August is a magnificent spectacle, attracting nomad communities from afar. The hills and grasslands around the monastery are sparse and spacious. The complex was originally founded as a branch of **Chunkor** (see above, page 510) but soon outgrew the latter. The recently restored buildings at Sershul, which are all in close proximity to the motor road, include the Tsokchen (assembly hall), the Jamkhang (Maitreya temple), the Gonkhang (protector temple), the Dewachen Lhakhang (Amitabha temple), the Mentsikhang (where Mipham Rinpoche's tradition is maintained), the college, a Mani Wheel chapel (containing three wheels constructed by the father of the present Drukpa Rinpoche) and a new guesthouse.

Tsokchen There are actually two assembly halls at Sershul, one (rarely used) which is said to be 300 years old, and an adjacent hall of recent construction. The latter has central images of Tsongkhapa with his foremost students and Padmasambhava with Shantaraksita and King Trisong Detsen, along with Begtse and Hayagriva. There are two inner sanctums, one containing larger images of Tsongkhapa with his students, and the other the Buddhas of the Three Times and the Lords of the Three Families. **Upstairs** there is a reliquary chamber, containing tooth relics of Shakyamuni Buddha, the robes of past Panchen and Dalai Lamas, 200 year-old sandalwood images, and other relics, some of which have associations with Tara and Cakrasamvara. Alongside this chapel there is a Gonkhang, containing a wooden sandalwood *gandi* from Nalanda in ancient India, and the residence of Drukpa Rinpoche.

Dewachen Lhakhang The 4-storey Dewachen Lhakhang is the most recent construction at Sershul, funded by Chinese patrons from Taiwan and Beijing. The ground floor has images of (L-R): Avalokiteshvara, Ksitigarbha, Amitabha, Vajradhara, Akashagarbha and Manjughosa. The second floor has corner chapels dedicated to the Eight Followers of Tsongkhapa and the Eight Manifestations of Padmasambhava, and residential apartments for the Dalai and Panchen Lamas. The third floor has corner chapels dedicated to the Twenty-one Taras, the Thirty-five Confession Buddhas, the various wealth deities including Vaishravana, Jambhala and Manibhadra, and a small administration office. The fourth floor has images of the Buddhas of the Five Families, flanked by Tara, Bhaisajyaguru, Shakyamuni, Amitabha and Manjughosa.

Sershul Gonpa to Zhiwu

The potholed and deeply rutted dirt road from Sershul Monastery to **Zhiwu** crosses **Ngamba La** pass (4,450 m), which divides the Yalong and Yangtze basins, as well as the present day provinces of Sichuan and Qinghai, after 24 km.

Trindu County ཁྲི་འདུ → *Pop: 40,558. Area: 9,717 sq km.* 称多县

Trindu county comprises the area around the southern source of the Yalong River, which now belongs to the Yushu Tibetan Autonomous Prefecture of Qinghai Province. The county capital is at **Druchung**, 24 km west of the Jyekundo-Ziling highway. Within the county, which has a rich nomadic heritage, there are at present 26 monasteries representative of all the major schools: Sakya, Kagyu, Geluk and Nyingma.

Zhiwu

Descending from the **Ngamba La** pass (4,450 m) after Sershul, the highway zigzags downhill for 36 km to the township of Zhiwu (Ch Xiwu), a low-lying (3,900 m) settlement straddling an important crossroads. Cultivated fields appear around Zhiwu, in contrast to the high grasslands of Dzachuka to the east. The climate is several degrees warmer. On the descent from the pass there are magnificent views of **Drogon Monastery**, clinging to the sheer cliff-face above the town, and painted in the distinctive Sakya colours. At the crossroads, a barrier blocks the road, indicating that you are about to drive from Sichuan into Qinghai. The road to the north (right) leads 777 km to Ziling, and the road to the south (left) leads 48 km to Jyekundo. Southwest of town, is the hilltop monastery of **Nyidzong** (founded 1580), which belongs to the Drigung Kagyu school and has a revered charnel ground alongside. ▸▸ *For listings, see pages 528-529.*

Drogon Puntsok Dargyeling The Sakyapa monastery known as **Drogon Puntsok Dargyeling** originally belonged to the Kadampa tradition, but was converted by Drogon Chogyel Phakpa in 1265 when he stayed here on his return journey from Mongolia to Lhasa. From his time until the present, there have been 18 lineage-holders, bearing the title Do-la. The previous incumbent, Do-la Jikme Chokyi Nyima, a son of the late HH Dudjom Rinpoche, and father of the present Dudjom Rinpoche, passed away in 1999. Do-la Jikme was recognized at the age of seven by the head of the Sakya school; and thereafter educated in Kham. Other teachers associated with Drogon Monastery include Gaden Wangchuk (Ga Tulku) and Ngakpa Ngoten. Currently there are about 70 monks here. The summer festival following the end of the rain retreat is a major event held in the plains below the monastery.

The **main temple** with 38 columns contains the reliquary stupa of the late Do-la Jikme, whose son and consort are overseeing the completion of his building projects at Zhiwu. It is planned to install two-storey images of Shakyamuni, Padmasambhava, and Maitreya in gilded bronze. The smaller **Tsuklakhang** with 16 columns contains a central image, encased in glass, depicting the previous Sakya Gongma, and the altar also has colour photographs of the present throne-holders of the Dolma and Phuntsok palaces of Sakya, who reside respectively at Rajpur in India and Seattle in the USA. Alongside these is a photograph of the present Dzongsar Khyentse, a nephew of Do-la Jikme, now resident in Bhutan and the West. To the left of Sakya Gongma are images of Shakyamuni and the Sixteen Elders, while to the right are an assortment of

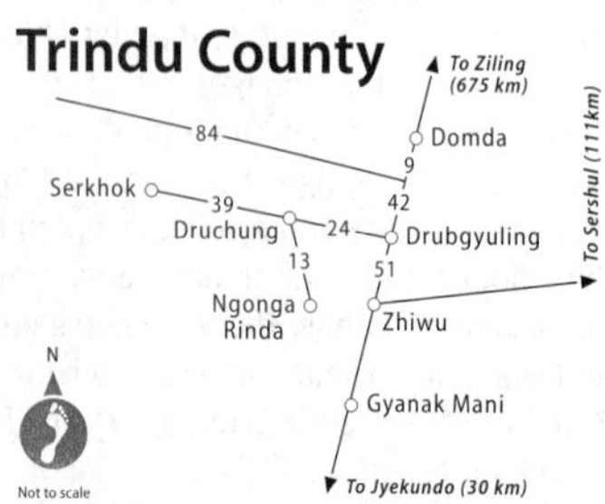

images, including Tara, Padmasambhava, and Vajrasattva. Below the central image of Sakya Gongma (in the same glass case) are a number of old images including Vajrasattva. Tangkas which decorate the side walls, including two very old ones depicting Two-armed Mahakala and Vajrabhairava. There are also new images, which have been brought from Chamdo, including one of Padmasambhava. On the left is a large Maitreya in a glass case.

Among other restored chapels at Drogon Monastery, visit the **Gonkhang**, containing images of Panjaranatha and the eight classes of spirits (Lhade-gye), the **Mani Wheel Chapel**, and the revered **Vajrayogini Temple**. Below the complex, to the right, is a series of the Eight Stupas symbolizing the major events in the life of the Buddha.

Northern Route from Zhiwu to Domda and Druchung

Heading north from Zhiwu, the paved Highway 214 reaches the Drigung Kagyu monastery of Drubgyuling Gonpa after 51 km. Here, a turn-off on the left (west) leads 24 km to the county capital at Druchung. Alternatively, you can continue north on the highway from Drubgyuling for 51 km to Domda (Ch Qingshuihe), near the northern source of the Yalong River. En route the road crosses **La-me Latse** (Ch Dayan Shan, 4,260 m), which forms a watershed between the Yangtze and Yalong basins. From Domda, the highway leaves Trindu county for Mato and Ziling (675 km).

Drubgyuling Gonpa Prior to the 13th century it is said there was a Nyingmapa temple at this site overlooking the trails to Druchung, Zhiwu and Domda. It appears to have been converted to the Drigung Kagyu cause by a Mongolian nobleman, after which it has always been considered as a branch of Drigungtil in Central Tibet. The **main temple** at Drubgyuling contains many new tangkas flanking a central appliqué which depicts Drigung Kyopa, with the protector deities below and Vajradhara above. There is a new image of Padmasambhava, as yet unpainted, and many small reliquary stupas. Within the **Gonkhang** there is a larger stupa inset with a photograph of the present Drigung Kyapgon, surrounded by the protector deities of the Drigung Kagyu lineage. There are two other buildings, one of which is the Labrang and the other the residence of Drubgyu Tulku (most senior of the five tulkus of this monastery). Currently there are 200 monks at Drubgyuling.

Druchung town The county town is small, and the community mostly pastoral farmers. In the vicinity of the town there are Sakyapa monasteries, such as **Karzang Peljor Gonpa**, which was built by Drogon Chogyel Phakpa's student Ame Dampa in 1268. Formerly a revered eighth-century Jowo Shakyamuni was housed in this monastery, but it was destroyed during the 1960s. There is, however, a small collection of original 15th-century images, costumes and a chair used by Drogon Chogyel Phakpa in person. **Gatri Dudongtre Samten Chokhorling** was also founded at the behest of Chogyel Phakpa in 1269 and is affiliated to Ngor Monastery of the Sakya school. The Karma Kagyu also have a presence near the town at **Zhedzong Gonpa** (founded 1727), as do the Drigung Kagyu at **Khamjok Gonpa**.

Sekhok Roads lead from Druchung, west to Sekhok (39 km) and southeast to Ngonga Rinda (13 km). Some 15 km south of Sekhok (Ch Saihe), there is a Drigung Kagyu monastery known as **Tashi Gonpa**, while further north in the direction of Gato there is a Mongolian monastery, **Pangshar Gon**, which still espouses the Sakya tradition, and at Trado (Ch Zhaduo), an influential branch of Sera called **Zerkar Gonpa** (originally founded in 1398).

Ngonga Rinda In this area, 13 km south of Druchung county town, the Gelukpa school have long established a strong presence. **Lab Gon Ganden Dongak Shedrubling** was founded in 1419 and its images were said to have contained the hair and garments of Tsongkhapa which he personally donated; and at nearby **Yawa Gonpa** there is a small Gelukpa nunnery affiliated to Lab Gon. Smaller Sakya and Nyingma monasteries also co-exist here, north and west of the Dri-chu (Yangtze).

Domda Gold panning is extensive in this area, where the town of Domda has grown up to service the truckers and bus companies which ply the highway from Ziling to Jyekundo. There are several Sichuan and Muslim-style restaurants. There are small Nyingmapa communities at **A-me Gonpa**, **Yangshar Gon** and **Kyewo Gon**, these last two being itinerant nomadic camps which are affiliated to Dzogchen.

Southern Route from Zhiwu to Yangtze Crossing

The highway from Zhiwu to Jyekundo heads south on an excellent paved surface, following the Zhiwuchi-chu downstream to its confluence with the Yangtze after 18 km. En route you will pass by trails leading to the small Kagyupa monasteries of **Bage Gonpa** and **Bambi Gonpa**. From the bridge over the Yangtze, which marks the county border, Jyekundo is only 30 km distant. A rough side road leaves the highway before the bridge, following the east bank of the Yangtze downstream to **Denkhok Sharma** (see above, page 511).

River Rafting on the Yangtze It is possible to raft on the Yangtze from the bridge, as far as the confluence of the Zi-chu, south of Derge over a five day period.

Jyekundo County སྐྱེ་དགུ་མདོ་

→ *Population: 76,218. Area: 13,784 sq km. Colour map 5, C1.* 玉树县

Jyekundo region in the northwest region of Kham, known locally as **Gawa**, occupies the upper reaches and source feeder rivers of the Yangtze. At the present day the city of Jyekundo is not only the county capital, but also the administrative capital of six counties belonging to the Yushu Tibetan Autonomous Prefecture of Qinghai Province. Here the predominant traditions are those of the Sakyapa and Kagyupa.

Ins and outs

Getting there Crossing the bridge over the Yangtze at **Druda**, 18 km south of Zhiwu, the paved Highway 214 reaches Jyekundo after 30 km.

Labda

Crossing the Yangtze bridge, you will notice a trail on the right (west) which follows the course of the Yangtze upstream for 35 km to **Labda** township. En route, you can visit the 13th-century **Tarlam Monastery** (4,000 m), the residence of Pende Rinpoche of the Ngorpa branch of the Sakya school, who currently lives in France. Other monasteries on that road include **Samdrub Gonpa** of the Sakya school (22 km further west), the 18th-century **Palchung A-me** which is affiliated to Katok, and **Gargon Dechenling** (30 km west of Labda), a 13th-century Drigung Kagyu foundation which has functioned as a branch of Sera since the 15th century, when Tsongkhapa presented offerings to the monastic community.

Domkar Lhundrub Dechen Sadon Chokhorling

This impressively large bastion of the Karma Kagyu school overlooks the highway, only 5 km east of Jyekundo. The monastery, which is is affiliated to Pelpung, has been in its present location since 1239. The original foundation is attributed to Pasang Tamdrin (1110-1193), and there is a branch temple in Jyekundo itself.

Gyanak Mani

At the beginning of the descent into Jyekundo valley, the road passes through **Gyanak Mani** – the largest field of mani stones in the whole of Tibet, approximately 1 sq km in area. Stop here to circumambulate the field and wander through the lanes between enormous piles of carved stones and prayer flags. Some stones are intricately inscribed with entire sections from the scriptures, and others have bas-relief images of certain meditational deities. According to one tradition, the original temple on this site was constructed in the late 13th century by Gyanak Tulku who came here from Chamdo on a return visit from China, although it has also been attributed to Tangtong Gyelpo. The field of stones bears witness to the faith of the Tibetan pilgrims who would travel along the trade routes from Ziling to Lhasa via Jyekundo and make offerings as an expression of their devotion. During the 1960s, many stones were removed for the construction of latrines, but the site has since been reconsecrated. Renovation here was supervised by the present incumbent lama, the Seventh Gyanak Tulku.

The **main temple** to the northeast of the site contains seven images, viz. (left to right): Doringpa, Shakyamuni, Avalokiteshvara, Padmasambhava, Vajrasattva, Green Tara and White Tara. There are also stone footprints and handprints of Doringpa. The Mani Wheel chapel called **Sengzer Dungkhar Chenpo**, reconstructed in 1987, has colour reproductions of the Indian Buddhist masters Vasubandu, Dignaga, Dharmakirti, Aryadeva and others. The wall on the left has an inscription listing the donors who provided funds for the rebuilding.

Above Gyanak Mani at **Lebkhok** there are rock carvings of Maitreya and rock inscriptions from the royal dynastic period, which have recently been documented.

Jyekundo སྐྱེ་དགུ་མདོ

Jyekundo (Ch Yushu), meaning 'confluence of all attributes or growth', is named after the town's illustrious hill top monastery, **Jyekundo Dondrubling**. In ancient times, the Bon religion was strong in the region. The earliest Buddhist contact appears to have coincided with the period of King Songtsen Gampo and his Chinese consort Princess Wencheng, who passed some time at nearby **Bida** (see below, page 520). In the 13th century a small monastery and nunnery of the Karma Kagyu school were established here, but in 1398 the site was cleared to make way for a Sakyapa monastery, the foundation of which was encouraged by Dagchen Sherab Gyatso of Sakya. It was claimed that Drogon Chogyel Phakpa himself had given teachings here en route for Mongolia.

The town of **Jyekundo** (3,700 m) quickly sprang up around the monastery as a trading centre, controlling the caravan trails between Ziling and Lhasa; and its traditional summer festival has for centuries attracted crowds of itinerant merchants and pilgrims. Teichman, travelling through Jyekundo in 1919, noticed all sorts of imported goods (tea, textiles, metalware, sugar etc) in the marketplace for sale at cheaper prices than in Dartsedo; and the products of Tibet's nomadic economy, hides, furs, wool, medicines, and so forth attracted the investment of Muslim traders and middlemen. In 1727 the area was nominally brought within the sphere of influence of the Kokonor Muslim territory; but prior to that it had held allegiance to the independent kingdom of Nangchen for centuries. Since 1951 the town has been the capital of Yushu Tibetan Autonomous Prefecture, comprising six counties with a total population of 237,000 and 121 monasteries; and it therefore has a two-tier bureaucracy. The town alone currently has a population of 37,000, and the street names are once again in Chinese. ▸▸ *For listings, see pages 528-529.*

Orientation

Following the Jyeku River upstream from its confluence with the Yangtze, you will soon reach Jyekundo, with **Dondrubling Monastery** on the hill to the northeast of town. Entering town on **Hongwei Lu**, you drive downhill past a number of motor repair shops to cross the Jyeku River. On the left there is the turn-off for **Dangdai Lu** (leading to the town-residence of the present Dudjom Rinpoche), a petrol station, and immediately opposite a dirt road that leads uphill to the monastery. Continuing along Hongwei Lu, you will pass the Tashi Restaurant and the Nationalities Hotel on the left and the TV Station, a small Tibetan restaurant, the vegetable market and the Foreign Trade Guesthouse on the right. At this point you reach the centre of the town, where Hongwei Lu intersects with Minzhu Lu (heading west to **Drito** county) and with Shengli Lu (heading south to **Nangchen**).

Along **Minzhu Lu** on the right you will find a department store, Xinhua Books, the Yushu Hotel, the County and Prefectural Government Buildings, the Customs Bureau, the Public Security Bureau, the PLA camp, the People's Bank, and a lane leading to a small temple, which is affiliated to **Domkar** (see above). Opposite on the left are an internet café, the Prefectural Tax Bureau, the Bank Hotel, China Telecom, China Post, the Post Hotel, a primary school, and (accessible through a narrow lane), the Gymnasium and the People's Hospital.

Heading south from the intersection on **Shengli Lu**, you will find on the right the Tibetan street market, and after the Peltang-chu bridge, the Snowland Printing House, a cigarette company, a branch post office, the Agricultural Bank, the Traffic Hotel, and the bus station. Over on the left you will pass the Traffic Police, a Muslim

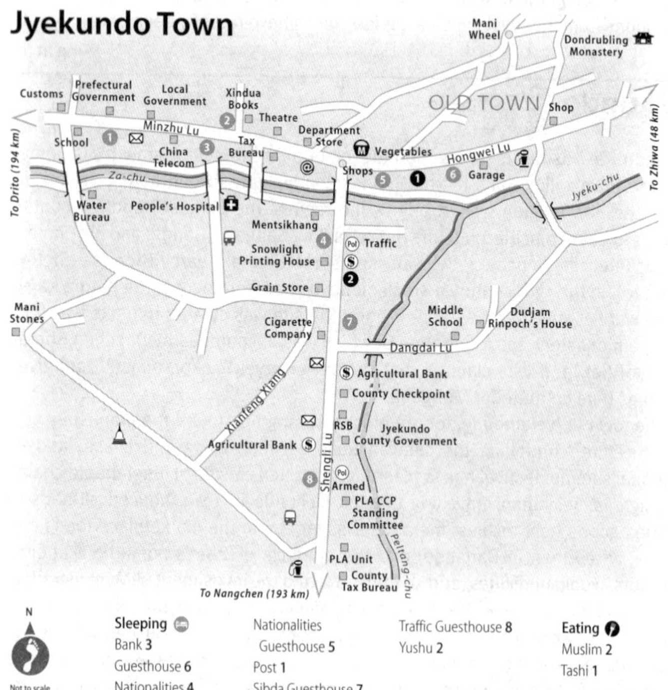

Restaurant, the Sibda Guesthouse, the County and Prefectural Courts, a PLA unit and the County Tax Bureau.

Jyekundo Dondrubling Monastery

Following the consecration of its site by Drogon Chogyel Phakpa who taught here, the monastery was gradually established in two phases: by Dagchen Sherab Gyatso of the Sakya school in 1398, and the Seventh Karmapa Chodrak Gyatso of the Kagyu school. The construction was finally completed by Dagchen Palden Chokyong of the Ngorpa suborder of the Sakyapa, to which it now holds allegiance. Until recently there were 16 temples and 1,000 monks. One of these was restored in 1977 and there are currently 140 monks.

The monastery has been visited over its history by illustrious pilgrims, such as the Mongolian prince Gaden Qan, and the Ninth Panchen Lama who passed away here in 1937.

The **lower storey** of the temple houses the Delhi edition of the *Kangyur*, a large image of Padmasambhava, and several smaller images including one of Dagchen Palden Chokyong. Murals depict the meditational deities and lineage-holders of the Ngorpa tradition; and there are tangkas on the side walls depicting Mahakala and Bhairava. Within its **inner sanctum**, there are images of the Buddhas of the Three Times, the central Shakyamuni being flanked by his foremost students and the Sixteen Elders. **Upstairs** is a small assembly hall, where rain retreat observances are held in summertime. Formerly, the monastery is said to have held one of the most revered representative objects of buddha-speech in Tibet, the **Chokorma** image, but this no longer survives.

A new protector shrine has recently been renovated to the west of the complex. It is dedicated to Panjaranatha, and has a number of macabre stuffed animals.

Dondrubling Dungkhor

Below, on the approach road to the monastery, there is a Mani Wheel chapel named **Dondrubling Dungkhor**, which was newly constructed in 1983 by one Tenkyong at the request of Dzongsar Khyentse Rinpoche. The chapel contains images of Avalokiteshvara, Padmasambhava and White Tara; several tangkas depicting Green Tara, and murals of Vajrasattva, Padmasambhava, Shantaraksita, King Trisong Detsen and Sachen Kunga Nyingpo. The mantras contained within the wheel include those of the deities Amitayus, Bhaisajyaguru, Vajrapani, Manjushri, Vajrasattva, Padmasambhava, and Sitatapatra; as well as the entire sutra texts of the *Bhadracaryapranidhanaraja* and the *Parinirvanasutra*. Outside the antechamber has paintings of the Four Guardian Kings and the Wheel of Rebirth, as well as a painting of Dondrubling Monastery as it once looked.

Trangu Monastery

Some 7 km south of Jyekundo, after a dam and artificial lake, the newly paved road passes **Trangu Monastery** on the left (east). This is the seat of the great contemporary Karma Kagyu scholar and lineage-holder Trangu Rinpoche, who is now based at Rumtek in Sikkim. Formerly there were two buildings, some 70 m apart, known as the lower and upper monasteries. The original foundation is attributed to the First Karmapa Dusum Khyenpa during the 12th century. The **lower monastery** has a renovated assembly hall containing exquisite gilded brass images of the Buddhas of the Three Times, flanked by murals depicting the 16 past Karmapas. The **upper monastery**, restored in 1998, has an image of Shakyamuni, flanked by the Thousand Buddhas, with Vajradhara in an alcove above. The excellent Repkong-style murals depict the Twelve Deeds of Shakyamuni. The outbuildings are still utilized as granaries by the neighbouring village.

Bida Nampar Nangdze Lhakhang

At **Peltang**, 19 km south of Jyekundo, the road branches: the left fork leading south towards **Nangchen** (174 km via Kela or 280 km via Zurmang) and the right leading west towards **Dzato** (237 km). If you take the former road, after 1 km a dirt track on the left (east) leads across streams to the **Bida gorge**. Here, surrounded by four sacred peaks, there are rock inscriptions, some revered as naturally produced, which proclaim the site's ancient association with King Songtsen Gampo and Princess Wencheng. According to one legend the princess stayed here for one month while en route for Lhasa and she is said to have had stone relief images of Vairocana flanked by the eight major bodhisattvas carved into the rocks. Subsequently, when the princess Jincheng passed through in 710, she made arrangements for a hall to be constructed, and this was enlarged in 730. According to another legend, the princess had a miscarriage here; and a temple was subsequently commissioned by Lochen Yeshe Yang and erected as a memorial during the reign of King Trisong Detsen.

The temple at Bida was traditionally maintained by the Drigung Kagyu school, but nowadays, it is in the care of monks from neighbouring Trangu Monastery. Outside there is a set of the Eight Stupas, constructed in 1998, and a stone plaque outlining the inventory and history of the temple. The anteroom contains images of the Four Guardian Kings alongside the First Tro-le Tulku, while the inner sanctum has large images of Vairocana and the Eight Bodhisattvas, along with several photographs of lineage-holders associated with Bida (The present Tro-le Tulku lives in Australia). The original images have been 'restored' in recent years. Among them, the central Vairocana, which some hold to be natural, is said to contain relics of Kashyapa Buddha and the remains of Princess Wencheng's deceased child.

Most of the **rock inscriptions** are located immediately behind the temple, and reached via a rear gate. The majority are in Tibetan but there are also some Chinese inscriptions among them. Some have been documented, although there are many unclear expressions. There is a footprint of Karma Pakshi in the rock above.

Another set of inscriptions representing verses from the well known Zangcho Monlam can be seen on a rock to the west, alongside a relief image of Shakyamuni. These are also revered as naturally occurring syllables! Above on the cliff face there are rock impressions of the 18 Buddhist hells. Another rock to the south of the gorge has a natural stupa impression, with an active hermitage above it.

Kyurak Gonpa

Kyurak Gonpa, near Bida, belongs to the Drigung Kagyu order, and nowadays has 20 monks. There are two temples: the Jokhang, rebuilt in 1988, contains an image of Jowo Shakyamuni and a photograph of Drigung Chetsang, who resides in India. The Dolma Lhakhang is somewhat smaller. To their rear is a cave hermitage of Padmasambhava, overhanging the temples. A narrow rock aperture through which pilgrims crawl to gauge their negativity is located next to the entrance.

Benchen Puntsok Dargyeling

Returning to the road from the Bida gorge, turn south and drive past a disused airstrip through a wide plain. A trail then turns off the road to the left (east) to **Benchen Puntsok Dargyeling**, facing into the plain against a backdrop of grassy knolls. This is a monastery of the Karma Kagyu school, the seat of Sangye Nyenpa Rinpoche and Chime Rinpoche. The monastery was originally located on the hill at Jyekundo, but moved to its present site in 1398 when Dondrubling was consecrated. Later, in 1797, the Thirteenth Karmapa passed away here. The **Assembly Hall** at Benchen has been restored in recent years, and there is a finely crafted row of eight stupas outside, symbolizing the eight major deeds of the Buddha. Within the assembly hall are the reliquaries of previous lamas and the thrones of the present incumbents, both of whom are in exile – in India and England respectively.

Zurmang Dutsitil Monastery ཟུར་མང་བདུད་རྩི་མཐིལ་ → *Colour map 4, A2.*

The village now known as **Xiao Zurmang** lies 120 km south of the Peltang intersection. The road crosses the snow-carpeted Ku La watershed pass which divides the Yangtze and Mekong basins, and a second lesser pass, before descending into the valley of the Kyang-chu, a fast-flowing stream which eventually merges with the Ke-chu at Menda (see above, page 423). A difficult motorable trail follows the river downstream for a further 35 km to reach Zurmang Dutsitil, on occasions fording it at places where bridges have been damaged by the summer rains. Notice that old carved mani stones have been used in places for road construction.

The monastery of **Zurmang Dutsitil** is located on high ground above the road to the right (west). Founded in the 15th century by the First Trungpa Kunga Gyeltsen, a close disciple of Trungpa Ma-se of the Karma Kagyu school, the monastery developed into an important meditation and study centre for the nomads and pastoralists of the Nangchen grasslands and surrounding areas. The site was expanded by his successors the Second, Third and Fourth Trungpas Kunga Zangpo, Kunga Osel and Kunga Namgyel respectively, the last of whom was renowned both for his meditation skills and prolific compositions. In the time of his successor, the Fifth Trungpa Tendzin Chogyel, the monastery reached the high point of its development. Exquisite murals depicting the lives of the Buddha were executed in gold line on a red background. In the time of the Seventh Trungpa Jampal Chogyel the site was plundered in 1643 by the Mongolian army of Gushi Qan, and the important lamas were briefly incarcerated. Reconstruction of the assembly hall, temples, and the founding of the Zurmang library were undertaken during the late 17th and early 18th century by the Eighth Trungpa Gyurme Tenpel, who was himself a reputable artist of the Karma Gadri school. His successors, the Ninth and Tenth Trungpas Karma Tenpel and Chokyi Nyima, ensured that the Karma Kagyu tradition was maintained and revitalized in this part of Tibet during a time of increasing strife as Muslim overlords from Kokonor rivalled the Tibetan government and Chinese warlords for control of the region. The Eleventh Trungpa Chokyi Gyatso (1939-1987) left Tibet in 1959 and established the **Samye Ling Monastery** in **Scotland**. Later, he founded the worldwide Buddhist organization known as **Dharmadhatu**. The present Twelfth Trungpa is now being educated at **Pelpung** Monastery, near Derge.

Little remains of the grandeur of this site, which not so long ago housed 300 monks. The main **assembly hall** is currently undergoing reconstruction. **Upstairs** are the residential quarters of the Trungpa Tulku and the Chetsang Tulku. There is an image of Four-armed Mahakala. Above the site is the retreat centre known as **Repuk Dorje Chodzong**, and a ruined fortress.

Below the monastery, the road, passable by jeep, continues southwest through pine forest for some 30 km, crossing the present-day Qinghai-TAR border, to reach **Menda** and the **Lhato** region of Kham (see above, page 423). Other monasteries in this area include **Dongtsang Gon** of the Sakya school, 4 km north of Xiao Zurmang township, which possesses a mask and conch shell donated by Drogon Chogyel Phakpa; and **Ladro Samdrub Lhaden Chokhorling** (8 km west of Xiao Zurmang township), which was founded by a student of the Fifth Karmapa during the 15th century.

Nangchen County ནང་ཆེན་ → *Pop: 60,578. Area: 15,014 sq km.* 囊谦县

Nangchen was formerly one of the five independent kingdoms of East Tibet. Its territory corresponds to the upper reaches of the five main Mekong feeder rivers: the Ngom-chu, Do-chu, Dza-chu, Tsi-chu and Kyang-chu. As such it includes the region of **Zurmang** in the east and **Nangchen** proper in the west (although the easterly parts of Zurmang in the Kyang-chu valley are now administered directly from Jyekundo). This area was able to maintain its Kagyupa heritage despite the onslaught of Gushi Qan's armies during the 17th century; and it may in fact have been spared the fate of Litang owing to the nomadic lifestyle of its inhabitants and the inhospitability of the terrain for settlement. Only in a few lower sheltered areas are cultivated fields to be seen; yet the rolling grasslands, dramatic limestone and sandstone cliffs, and pristine nature reserves combine to make Nangchen one of the most interesting and unspoilt parts of Kham. Currently it is estimated there are 78 monasteries within the county, of which some 70% are Kagyupa and the remainder Sakyapa, Nyingmapa and Gelukpa in descending order. The capital is at **Sharda**, 193 km from Jyekundo (via Ke La), 160 km from Zurmang Dutsitil, and 189 km from Riwoche.

Upper Tsi-chu

To reach Nangchen from Jyekundo by the more direct route, drive west from the **Peltang** intersection for 46 km to **Rato** (Ch Duolamakang), crossing the high **Zhung La** watershed pass (4,816 m). Then turn south, following the Tsi-chu downstream for 35 km to **Rabshi Lungsho Ganden Chokhorling**, one of the very few Gelukpa monasteries in Nangchen. This site is said to have been frequented by Lhalung Pelgyi Dorje during the ninth century when he fled to Amdo from Lhasa, having slain the evil king Langdarma. Subsequently, a temple was constructed by the Drigung Kagyupas, and later, during the 18th century, it was converted to the Gelukpa school with the encouragement of the Seventh Dalai Lama. The **Rabshi** area (Ch Xialaixue) also has Drukpa Kagyu communities at **Drukpa Gon** and **Ajung Gon**, who fled persecution in 16th-century Central Tibet, as well as smaller Sakyapa, Drigungpa and Nyingmapa temples.

Two paved roads lead from Rabshi: highway 214 crossing the Ke La (4,267 m) which divides the Tsi-chu from the Dza-chu, to arrive at **Kharda** in the Dza-chu valley (93 km), and another following the Tsi-chu downstream towards **Zurmang Namgyeltse** (73 km).

Zurmang Namgyeltse Monastery ཟུར་མང་རྣམ་རྒྱལ་རྩེ → *Colour map 4, A2.*

Getting there The monastery of **Zurmang Namgyeltse** lies 60 km west of Zurmang Dutsitil in the Tsi-chu valley. It may also be approached from the turn-off south of Rabshi, following the Tsi-chu downstream for 67 km to the **Tsi-chu bridge** (Ch Maozhuang Qiao). If you are travelling from Zurmang Dutsitil, follow the Kyang-chu back upstream in the direction of Xiao Zurmang for 15 km and then turn left (west) after the first pass. The road runs through rich pasturelands where the herds of yak and dri are particularly impressive; and crosses a second pass to enter a narrow gorge. Flowers and medicinal herbs abound in this area. Descending into the Tsi-chu valley, you will pass the Sakyapa monastery of **Dordu Gon**.

On reaching the Tsi-chu bridge, leave this trail (which heads downstream on the east bank for **Karma Gon** via Lintrang) and cross the river. The road then forks: upstream (to the right) for **Rabshi** (67 km) and downstream to the left for **Da Zurmang** township. The forested Tsi-chu valley is an important nature reserve and you will notice roadside signs prohibiting the killing of animals. Da Zurmang, also known as Maozhuang in Chinese, lies only 6 km from the bridge. Here are the grand ruins of the monastery known as Zurmang Namgyeltse.

Nangchen & Dzato Counties

The original foundation dates from the 15th century when Trungpa Ma-se, a disciple of the Fifth Karmapa constructed a 'many-cornered' (*zurmang*) meditation hut here. His disciples gathered in numbers and the local chieftain Adru Shelubum donated his castles (at both Namgyeltse and Dutsitil) to Trungpa Ma-se and his followers. The ruins of the large **assembly hall**, founded by the Fifth Trungpa Tendzin Chogyel, convey an impression of the former magnificence of the monastery. It once contained large images of the Buddha of the Three Times and over 40 images of the Karma Kagyu lineage-holders. Three colleges also once existed here: the **Dechen Dratsang** (450 monks) on the higher slopes, the **Lingpa Dratsang** (350 monks) on the lower slopes, and the **Lama Dratsang** (300 monks) adjacent to the assembly hall.

Nowadays there are between 100-200 monks affiliated to Zurmang Namgyeltse, and one temple has been reconstructed. It contains murals depicting Padmasambhava, Simhavaktra, Vajrayogini, Vajravarahi, Cakrasamvara, and various Kagyu lineage-holders including the Zhamarpas. Upstairs a chapel contains newly sculpted clay images of the 16 previous Karmapas.

At the township, near Zurmang Namgyeltse, there is another noteworthy monastery named **Ganden Gontsi Zurmang Ganden Tubten Ngelekling**, which was founded by a Nyingmapa lama in 1535 and later converted to the Gelukpa school in 1652 when the Fifth Dalai Lama passed through on his return from Beijing to Lhasa.

Zurmang Namgyeltse to Sharda

From Namgyeltse, the distance to Sharda (Nangchen county town) is 100 km. The road crosses the precipitous **Yi gu La pass** (5,000 m) – its difficult surface both narrow and gravel-covered. Drive slowly! This is the watershed between the Tsi-chu and Dza-chu rivers, and on the far side, the descent cuts across rolling meadows towards Kharda. Here you rejoin the direct Jyekundo-Nangchen road (highway 214) and enter the wide valley of the Dza-chu, the greatest of the Mekong source rivers. The tableland limestone crags of **Rakjangri** stand out across the sandbanks of the meandering river.

Rabshi to Sharda

Ke La If you take the highway from Rabshi into Nangchen, avoiding the turn-off to Zurmang Namgyeltse, the road crosses the Ke La watershed (4,267 m) between the Tsi-chu and Dza-chu rivers, and gradually descends to reach **Kharda** township after 93 km. This wilderness is a stronghold of the Barom Kagyu school, the most prestigious of its monasteries being **Kyodrak Gonpa**, where Tashi Rolpa, the student of Barom Darma Wangchuk, passed away in the 14th century, and the affiliated nunnery at **Metil Gegon**.

Sharda

After Kharda, the highway descends to **Sharda**, the county capital of Nangchen, after a further 13 km. Here, the Dza-chu river meanders around sandbanks and the tableland mountain known as **Rakjangri** dominates its west bank. This is a natural habitat and breeding ground of the macaque. Sharda comprises one long and broad main street, where dust and tumbleweed are blown in sporadic gusts. Formerly this town was the heart of the independent kingdom of Nangchen, to which the 25 clans of the Mekong grasslands held allegiance. The inhabitants of the town are largely engaged in trade, and you may find some interesting Tibetan artefacts here. There are some cultivated barley fields, but agriculture is generally less important to the economy than animal husbandry and lumbering. The horsemanship of Nangchen is particularly esteemed, and there are rare breeds of Nangchen horse, which have been noted by Michel Pessel in particular. ▸▸ *For listings, see pages 528-529.*

Excursions Some 6 km north of town, in the hills, there is an important Barom Kagyu nunnery at **Merchen Gegon Tashi Choling**. During the 1920s it was absorbed by the Drigungpas, and recently it has undergone reconstruction. Nearby is the Barom Kagyu monastery of **Dzamo Gon Tubten Metok Choling** which was founded by Lama Tashi Rolpa (1128-1201), and further to the northwest (15 km from town), there is a small Sakyapa monastery called **Nyayakyul Gonpa**.

Southwest of the county town near **Palme** village, there are 17th-century Drigung Kagyu monasteries named **Tekchen Evam Gatseling** and **Chibub Gonpa**, while to the southeast of town there is a Sakyapa presence at **Taksar Gonpa** and, 3 km from town, a Drukpa Kagyu presence at **Tashi Gatseling** (founded 1923). Also, **Go-che Gonpa** is an important branch of Yangpachen, the seat of the Zhamarpas in Central Tibet.

Roads from Sharda

From Sharda there is a road heading northwest for 46 km to Yeyondo (Ch Sigeton), from where trails lead to **Drokshok** (44 km) and west to **Dompa** (94 km) in the Ngom-chu valley. The highway, rough as it is, leads south to **Treltsa** township (9 km), where it forks: southeast for **Nyagla** (43 km) in the Dza-chu valley, and southwest across the mountains to **Chichu** (72 km) in the Ngom-chu valley. All these roads lead towards **Tengchen**, **Riwoche** and **Lhato** counties in the present-day Tibet Autonomous Region.

Drokshok

The most influential monastery in the vicinity of Drokshok township (Ch Zhuoxiao) is **Karma Dargyeling**, the seat of Beru Khyentse Rinpoche who has established branch monasteries in India and USA. The monastery here was founded in the 1950s by the previous Sixteenth Karmapa Rikpei Dorje. Other sites of interest in this region include **Tilyak Gonpa** (18th century) and **Nege Gegon** nunnery of the Karma Kagyu school, **Rabjor Gonpa** which maintains the Nedo lineage of Karma Chakme, and **Beru Lachen Gon**, a 13th-century Barom Kagyu centre.

Dompa

There are nine monasteries around Dompa township, the most significant being the 14th century **Tongnak Gonpa** which converted from the Barompa to the Karma Kagyu tradition, **Domyo Kalzang Gon** (Karma Kagyu), **Rela Gonpa** (Sakyapa), and further west towards the Tengchen county border, the Nyingmapa nunnery of **Dechen Ting Gegon**.

Tsashul

At Tsashul township (Ch Jienesai) on the east bank of the Ngom-chu, approached on a 63 km detour southwest from the Shadra-Yeyondo road, the Barom Kagyu tradition is present in strength. One of their monasteries, **Chiradzago Gonpa** (6 km west of the township), is revered as the place where Sachen Kunga Nyingpo, the first of the Five Founders of Sakya, passed away. Others have maintained their allegiance to the Drukpa Kagyu school at **Totrari Gonpa** and the Yelpa Kagyu school at **Tana Senge Gon**, which was founded in 1180 by Yeshe Tsekpa. Some 20 km downstream in the direction of Chichu, there is the largest nunnery of the Nyingma school in present day Qinghai province at **Gechak Gegon** (founded in 1893 by Gechak Tsangyang Gyatso).

Treltsa

Following the highway south from Sharda through the Dza-chu valley, you will reach the township of Treltsa after 9 km. Here, there are also influential Kagyu monasteries: **Tsechu Gonpa** of the Drukpa Kagyu school and **Gonzhab Gonpa**, founded in the 15th century by a student of the Seventh Karmapa Chodrak Gyatso, are both close to the township, while **Nedo Sangak Dechenling**, the main seat of Karma Chakme's student Nedo Karma Losung, lies 5 km east.

Nyagla

If you take the Dza-chu river road from Treltsa to Nyagla, you will reach **Lhato** county after 43 km. **Karma Gon**, the oldest of all the Karma Kagyu monasteries in Tibet, lies across the border (see above, page 422). Around Nyagla, on the **Qinghai** side of the border, there were three small monasteries affiliated to Zurmang Namgyeltse, of which **Trikso Gonpa** and **Jereda** have been rebuilt.

Chichu

From Nangchen, you can drive south to **Riwoche** (189 km) when the river levels are low. The road heads southwest from Treltsa, crossing the triple pass of **Tsedri La** (4,277 m) and **Churi Meri La** pass (4,504 m) which form the watershed between the Dza-chu and the Do-chu. Driving conditions have improved in the Do-chu gorge, but the road still precariously hugs the cliffs beside the swift flowing river. Leaving the Do-chu valley, the road soon descends to Chichu township on the east bank of the Ngom-chu. The distance from Treltsa to Chichu is 72 km.

Most of the monasteries around Chichu represent the Drukpa Kagyu school, which survived persecution in 16th- and 17th-century Central Tibet in these remote outposts. Among them are, **Jam-me Gon**, 30 km northeast of the township, **Chopuk Gon** (30 km west), and **Tsabzhi Gon**, which was eventually outgrown by its branch monastery at Tsechu Gonpa (see above). Exiles from Chichu established a thriving centre for Tibetan culture at Mainpath in Madhya Pradesh, India during the 1960s and 1970s, under the leadership of their chieftain, Namka Dorje. A new Tibetan school has recently been established at Chichu for young nomadic children through the efforts of the **Nangchen Children's Trust** ⓘ *Mukairn, Taynuilt, Argyll, Scotland PA35 1JN, T44-1866-822241.*

Nangchen to Riwoche

From Chichu, a rough road follows the east bank of the Ngom-chu downstream to the provincial border, crossing into Riwoche county above Shoknga (see above, page 416). In the hills above (approximately 80 km from Chichu), there is influential Nyingma monastery of **Neten Gang**, the seat of Chogyur Dechen Zhikpo Lingpa (1820-1870), which was founded in 1858. Currently there are some 50 monks here, and one small temple which survived the Cultural Revolution. Some two hours uphill from the monastery, there are sacred Padmasambhava meditation caves and terma-sites in the range known as **Yegyel Namkadzo**. This is the power place representing the attributes-aspect of buddha-speech in East Tibet, where this lama discovered important *terma*-texts and representative images of Padmasambhava. There are upper and lower circumambulatory routes around the range, both of which can be undertaken in a day (although this means that the lower route has to be partially driven).The overall distance from Sharda to Riwoche Tsuklakhang is 189 km.

Dzato County རྫ་སྟོད → *Pop: 36,333. Area: 33,127 sq km.* 杂多县

Dzato county is the area around the source of the Dza-chu tributary of the Mekong, far upstream from Nangchen. To reach Dzato, drive west from Peltang in the direction of Nangchen, but do not turn south at the **Rato** turn-off (46 km). Continue due west for a further 172 km, en route crossing the Tsi-chu valley to the north of **Mount Sharpu Karpur** (5,104 m), and entering the Dza-chu basin at **Chidza**. Apart from a few coal mining communities, this is a sparsely populated nomadic area. Nonetheless, there are 24 small monasteries within the county, mostly representing the Kagyu and Nyingma schools.

Chidza

In the hills above the Dza-chu, close to **Chidza** township (Ch Jiezha), there are five Karma Kagyu monasteries, including **Pelbeu Gon**, which originally belonged to the Barong Kagyu tradition. A small branch of Dzogchen monastery known as **Tubten Samdrub Gatseling** was also founded here by the First Dzogchen Pema Rigdzin in 1685. Below Chidza, the road descends to the banks of the Dza-chu, where in modern Angsai township, there are Nyingmapa monasteries affiliated to Pelyul, and Choling Gonpa, including **Chogyege Gon**, a nunnery which was founded in 1910 by Choling Rinpoche. At **Tobchu Gonpa** there are both Bon and Nyingmapa practitioners living alongside one another.

Dzato town

The county town, 60 km upstream from Chidza on the bank of the Dza-chu, is one of the most isolated on the plateau. Yet there are Drigung and Karma Kagyu monasteries which have survived here, including a 13th-century Barong Kagyu establishment at **Geuna Gon**, which converted to the Karma Kagyu school in 1673. To the west of town, there are trails leading south via Ato township, through the Dangla range, into the Tengchen, Bachen and Sok Dzong counties of the present day Tibet Autonomous Region (see above, pages 408-412).

River Rafting on the Mekong (Dza-chu) It is possible to raft on the Dza-chu from Dzato as far as Sharda in Nangchen (320 km) in three days.

To the source of the Mekong From Dzato county town, two roads diverge: northwest for 59 km to **Sangchen** (Ch Zhaqin) and southwest for 36 km to **Ato** township, which lies in the hills to the south of the Dza-chu river. The monasteries and nunneries in these remote parts are mostly tented camps, affiliated to the Drigung or Karma Kagyu, although the Nyingmapa and Gelukpa do have some representation at **Damzhung Terton** and **Tashi Lhapuk Gon** respectively. Continuing beyond Sangchen on the northwest road, you can drive as far as **Mukzhung** (Ch. Moyun), about 230 km from the county town. From here it is possible to trek or horse ride to the actual source of the Mekong and back again within eight or nine days.

Drito County འབྲི་སྟོད → *Pop: 23,447. Area: 78,945 sq km.* 治多县

Drito county is the area around the southern source of the Yangtze, the county capital being located at **Gyelje Podrang**, 194 km northwest of Jyekundo. To reach Drito, drive west from **Jyekundo** following the Za-chu tributary upstream and passing a grass seed escarpment on the road out of town. On a hill to the north there is a sky-burial site.

Ato Monastery

Above **Jalakda**, the road crosses a pass, and descends through an isolated area to **Lake Rongpo** and the township of **Gyelring**, 73 km from Jyekundo. En route, there is also a turn-off on the left, which leads south to the Karma Kagyu monastery of **Ato Gonpa**, the seat of Ato Rinpoche who now resides in England.

Rongpo Nature Reserve

In the vicinity of Lake Rongpo, the **Rongpo Nature Reserve** has the most important breeding site in present-day Qinghai province for the black-necked crane. There are about 100 birds (adults and chicks) within the reserve, where the marsh is up to 2 m deep in places. Other

protected species here include the ruddy sheldrake, the barheaded goose, the brown-headed gull, the redshank, and various types of wader and song bird. There is a small barracks-style guesthouse, where the wardens also live. The nests of the black-necked crane are protected for several days after hatching by the wardens who camp near the nests to ward off hostile nomads' dogs. A guide and photographic permit are available for ¥150 (officially per hour but generally per day!).

Gyelring

Northwest of the marshy lake, there is a mani stone wall and **Rongzhi Monastery** stands on a hilltop opposite **Gyelring** township. Gyelring itself is 73 km from Jyekundo, and there are two significant Gelukpa monasteries here. **Bumgon Chokle Gyelnamling**, 1 km east of the township, was originally a Bon temple, which converted to the Drigung Kagyu school in the 13th century, and subsequently in the 16th century to the Gelukpa school. A branch monastery, **Gyezang Gonpa**, was constructed in the township in 1957. At Gyelring the road forks: the main route heading northwest into Drito county, and a side road running north for 55 km towards **Hashul** (Ch Haxie) and **Anchong** townships, which are a stronghold of the Sakyapa and Karma Kagyu schools, exemplified by **Purang Sakya Gon** and **Nezang Gonpa** respectively.

Gyelje Podrang

Continuing on the main road from **Gyelring**, you will cross a pass to enter Drito county, and head downstream through the sparsely populated Jong-chu valley, where marmots, hares and pika abound. The Yelung-chu flows in from the southwest, and the valley opens out. There are horses in the pastures here and the eroded terrain is evidence of intensive grazing. **Damjong** township is 61 km northwest of Gyelring and southeast of the Jong-chu valley. **Drito** county town, known as **Gyelje Podrang**, lies above the confluence of this river and the Nechak-chu, 60 km further northwest. It is an unattractive town with a few compounds and a dozen shops. A gravel works depot is located by the riverside.

From Drito, there are routes leading west towards the southern source of the Yangtze in the Dangla range. These eventually link up with the road from Dzato at **Mukzhung** to head south across the range into **Bachen** and **Sok Dzong** counties of the Tibet Autonomous Region. About 19 km along this road from the county town there is a Gelukpa monastery known as **Gonsar Gonpa**, which currently has 150 monks.

A more frequently travelled road follows the Nechak-chu downstream to its confluence with the Yangtze, and the latter upstream to Chumarleb county, 45 km to the northwest.

Chumarleb County ཆུ་དམར་ལེབ

→ *Population: 21,582. Area: 43,123 sq km. Colour map 5, grid C1.* 曲麻莱县

The county of Chumarleb comprises the area around the northern source of the Yangtze, which flows in a southeast course from the Kunlun Mountains. The county capital is located at **Serpo Lungpa**, a new town 45 km from Drito and 270 km from Jyekundo (via Domda). Nowadays there are 12 monasteries within the county, of which at least five are itinerant Nyingmapa camps. At **Chizhi** (Ch Qiuzhi) village, 121 km north of the county town there is the Nyingmapa monastery of **Khorama Gonpa**, affiliated to Katok, while to the southeast of town there is a Gelukpa monastery at **Kyabdung Gonpa**.

The hills around Chumarleb have been heavily eroded by the itinerant 70,000 or 80,000 Chinese gold miners who come here during the summer months. The lawlessness of these prospectors is encouraged by the paucity of the police force assigned to monitor them. The town is larger than Drito, and is a centre for the wool and meat trade. Muslim traders come here on trucks to kill sheep; and there are a number of restaurants that have been opened in Chumarleb to serve these butchers and the itinerant mining population.

Formerly there were many herds of wild yak (drong), wild ass (kyang), and antelope in the Chumarleb River valley to the northwest of **Serpo Lungp**a, but now only a small number of herds remain. There is, however, another black-necked crane nature reserve to the northwest of the river.

A trail leads into the remote interior of the Yangtze source region to link up with the Lhasa-Kermu road near Toma.

NB This route is not passable in summer when the river levels are high, and at other times only in a four-wheel drive jeep with a high-axled support truck.

River Rafting on the Yangtze It is possible to raft on the Yangtze from Chumarleb, as far as the Zhimenda Bridge near Jyekundo (330 km) over a four day period.

Chumarleb to Domda

South of the town, there is a good motorable road which runs southeast for 199 km to **Domda** (Ch Qingshuihe), where it connects with the main Jyekundo-Ziling highway. Head east out of town and turn southeast at the road junction. After 16 km (at marker 174) a pass is crossed. To the south, between the road and the Yangtze there are some argali mountain sheep and gazelle. The road now passes through a gorge, where gold miners are encamped near **Bagon** township, 74 km from the pass (around marker 100). A four-hour trek west from Bagon leads for 9 km to **Ba Gonpa** of the Gelukpa school, where there are 100 monks, and thence to **Sharu Gonpa** (25 km from Bagon township), which is a branch of Zerkar, founded in 1447 by Choje Palden Gyatso.

Staying on the main road, after **Bagon** you climb steeply, crossing a pass after 16 km (marker 84), and then after 20 km, reaching a well-equipped government gold mine. Then, after 12 km (marker 42), the road crosses the south-flowing Gara-chu tributary of the Yangtze, before heading northeast up a lateral valley to **Trado** (Ch Zhaduo) township. The final watershed pass crosses the Yangtze-Yalong divide, offering fine views of the rounded peaks of the **Bayankala** range to the north. Thereafter the road descends to the main highway, and **Domda** township (Ch Qingshuihe) lies only 9 km to the north, near the northern source of the Yalong River.

Sleeping

Jumang *p512*
E **Tashigar Hotel**, the best in town, doubles at ¥25-30, triples at ¥15.

Zhiwu *p514*
E **Mirik Dronkhang**, at the north end of town, on the left. Tibetan family-run hotel. The best of these 2 hotels.
E **Transport Station Guesthouse**, at north end of town, down an alleyway on the right.

Jyekundo *p517, map p518*
D **Yushu Hotel**, Minzhu Lu, T0976-826999. This 5-storey hotel has the best accommodation in town, superior rooms with attached bath and economy rooms without, superior doubles at ¥120, superior singles at ¥350, superior triples at ¥460, suites at ¥691, economy doubles at ¥80, economy triples at ¥180, and 5-bed dorms at ¥160.
E **Bank Hotel (Yinhang Binguan)**, Minzhu Lu. Recently renamed as the Nanghang Guesthouse.
E **Post Hotel**, Shengli Lu, T0976-8825357. Has fine twin rooms at ¥100.
E **Traffic Hotel**, Shengli Lu, T0976-8822009. Has cheaper accommodation, at ¥40 (twin) and ¥45 (triple).

Sharda *p523*
E **Nangchen Guesthouse**, located in a compound on the east side of the main

For an explanation of the sleeping and eating price codes used in this guide, see inside the front cover. Other relevant information is found in Essentials pages 44-46.

street, near its middle section. Comfortable rooms and friendly maids.

Eating

Jumang *p512*
Tiemushe Restaurant, one of a number of small Sichuan-style restaurants.

Zhiwu *p514*
There are a number of small tea shops and restaurants near the crossroads, some serving excellent Muslim tea and lamb dishes.

Jyekundo *p517, map p518*
Snowland Restaurant.
Tashi Restaurant, Tibetan-run.
Yushu Hotel, the best and most expensive cuisine is found here.

The Muslim Restaurant, on Shengli Lu is another good choice.

There are many other small Sichuan and Muslim style restaurants clustered around the crossroads and near the open-air market.

Sharda *p523*
Outside the hotel, there are small restaurants, some of them Muslim-owned (distinguished by their green banners).

Entertainment

Jyekundo *p517, map p518*
The theatre and city cinema are located at the crossroads.

Festivals and events

Jyekundo *p517, map p518*
South of town, there is a wide plain – extending southwest from the confluence of the Dzi-chu and Peltang-chu rivers. Here, starting on each **25 Jul**, the **Jyekundo Horse Festival** is held. Throughout the last week of **Jul** and the 1st week of **Aug**, colourful appliqué tents are pitched across the plain, and a programme of horse riding events, and folk dancing attracts people from all corners of the prefecture and other parts of East Tibet, as far afield as Nakchu. Each year one of the 6 counties takes it in turn to organize the event, and approximately 60% of the budget (average ¥160,000) is provided by the prefectural government, the balance being provided by the organizing county. In 2001 all 6 counties held a joint festival to commemorate the 50th anniversary of the prefecture. In other years, however (such as 1996 and 1997) the festival has been cancelled owing to the severe winter snows which badly damaged the pastoral economy.

Shopping

Jyekundo *p517, map p518*
Books can be purchased at **Xinhua Bookstore**, immediately to the east of the hotel. South of the crossroads is the open air market. Look out here for Tibetan carpets, household and religious artefacts, as well as nomadic produce: hides, furs, chubas, fresh meat and butter, as well as imported Chinese goods.

Transport

Jumang *p512*
Bus
There are public buses running every other day to **Dartsedo** (¥147), stopping at **Kandze** (¥43), and a daily truck connects Jumang with **Zhiwu** (¥20 per person).

Jyekundo *p517, map p518*
Bus
Buses run from Jyekundo to **Ziling** (¥139 for couchette, ¥78 for seat); **Nangchen** (¥25), **Zhiwu** (¥9), **Trindu** (¥15), **Chumarleb** (¥39), and **Dzato** (¥35). The bus station is located south of the crossroads.

Directory

Jyekundo *p517, map p518*
Internet There is an internet café next to the Prefectural Tax Bureau on Minzhu Lu (¥25 per hr). **Telephone** China Post, Minzhu Lu, has an EMS service, and **China Telecom**, next door sells ICC cards for DDD and IDD calls. IDD calls can also be made from the Yushu Hotel.

Sharda *p523*
The Public Security Bureau is on the west side at the extreme south end of the main street.

Trehor and Nyarong: the Yalong valleys and gorges

The middle reaches of the Yalong and the valley of its main tributary, the Zhe-chu, together form the widest cultivated tract of land in Kham, sustaining a large sedentary population, as well as nomadic pastoralists on the high ground. Emerging from the Dzachuka region at Rongpatsa, the Yalong flows through this wide valley as far as Kandze, where the massive snow range of Kawalungring forces it to change course, cutting south through the Nyarong gorge to converge with the Yangtze at Dukou.

The Zhe-chu and its Nyi-chu tributary both rise in the Dzachuka area to the east of Sershul county, and flow southeast in parallel courses to converge at Drango, and then, after meandering through the pleasant Tawu valley, their combined waters flow south to merge with the Yalong above Nyachuka.

Prior to the 17th century, the ***Nyarong*** *valley was a stronghold of the Nyingma and Bon traditions, while the plains to the north were also important for the Sakya and Kagyupa. Further east the peoples of* ***Tawu****, who speak an extremely idiosyncratic dialect or language, may well be descended from the migrant Minyak (Xixia) population, following the destruction of their kingdom by Genghiz Qan in the 13th century. However, from 1638-1641 the Qosot Mongolian armies of Gushi Qan forcibly converted many of these Yalong settlements to the Gelukpa tradition, eventually defeating the Bonpo king of Beri in 1641. They then established the five Trehor states:* ***Beri****,* ***Kangsar****,* ***Mazur****,* ***Trewo*** *and* ***Drango****, which supported a large number of new Gelukpa institutions. Settling there, they intermarried with the local populace, from which time on the inhabitants have been known as the* ***Trehor Khampa****. Secular arts and crafts also flourished; and the renowned metal work of the region still exhibits many distinctive features – such as animal motifs – reminiscent of Scythian or Ordos bronzes.*

Nowadays this region includes four counties administered from Dartsedo namely ***Kandze*** *and* ***Nyarong*** *in the Yalong valley, and* ***Drango*** *and* ***Tawu*** *in the Zhe-chu valley.* ***Recommended itineraries: 5, 8, 10. See page 20.*** *»» For Sleeping, Eating and other listings, see pages 541-542.*

Kandze County དཀར་མཛེས → *Pop: 56,000. Area: 6,232 sq km.* 甘孜县

Kandze county extends from the lower Yi-chu valley and **Rongpatsa** township as far as the **Latseka** watershed pass (also known as **Dresel La**) in Trehor. The county capital is located at **Kandze** town, 94 km east of Manigango, and 158 km northwest of Tawu.

Yi-chu Valley

Following the Yi-chu downstream from **Manigango**, the highway passes the turn-off for Yilhun township after 15 km and continues along the south bank of the river through Trowo township. Sometimes in the rainy season the river level rises above that of the road! Soon the **Pak-tse Mani Wall** comes into view on the right (south), while, on the distant hilltop across the river, you can see the

Kandze & Nyarong

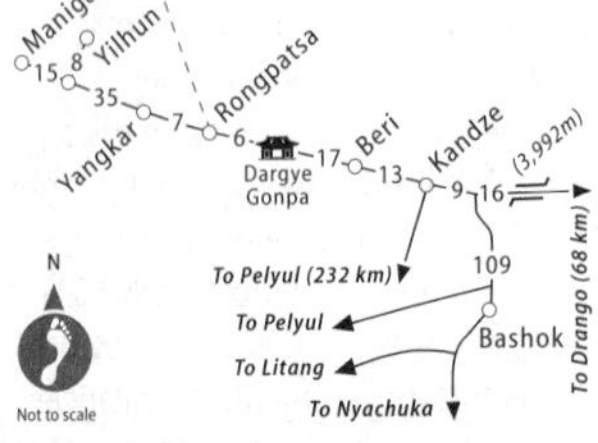

Nyaduka Retreat Hermitage, a branch of Dzogchen Monastery, bedecked in streaming red prayer flags. Thereafter the river cuts northeast to join the Yalong, while the road, now paved and smooth, continues due east to Rongpatsa.

Yangkar Dorje Phakmo

Some 50 km east of Manigango, the road passes on the left a cave containing an image of the deity Vajravarahi. The pathway leading down to the cave is adorned with prayer flags, but the cave itself lies across a stream and is only accessible in the dry season when the water level is low. This is the most important power place of the Rongpatsa valley.

Rongpatsa

Driving east from Yangkar, the road soon crosses an almost indiscernible pass to enter the wide fertile valley of **Rongpatsa**. Fields of golden barley extend on both sides from the first village of **Lawa** as far as the distant foothills. To the right (south) you will pass the side valley leading from **Dzinko** and **Horpo** (see above, page 492) and the village of **Lakhar**, where there is a small rebuilt monastery. Lakhar is the home village of Sogyel Rinpoche, who is based in France. The road continues through the valley to **Denma**, the main township in Rongpatsa (57 km east of Manigango), where there are a number of small grocery shops.

Just before town, a turn-off on the left leads towards a ridge overlooking the valley. Here you can visit **Bongen Gonpa**, a finely reconstructed temple in the midst of a flower garden, which is the seat of the late Kalu Rinpoche of the Kagyu and Shangpa Kagyu traditions. The ruins of the original temple still occupy the hillside far to the northeast. The present Kalu Rinpoche is currently being educated at Sonada in Darjiling, where his predecessor passed away.

Trekking

Trekking routes follow the Yalong upstream from Rongpatsa in the direction of **Dzachuka**, where there are many monasteries representing all the Buddhist traditions and the Bon. The largest Gelukpa Monastery in that vicinity is **Samdrub Gonpa**, a 17th-century foundation, which formerly had 700 monks, while the **Lingtsang Katok Gonpa** of the Nyingma school and **Ripu Gonpa** of the Sakya school are also prominent.

Dargye Gonpa

Leaving Denma, the road passes through **Yartsa** village, where there is a hot spring, and after 6 km runs through a tree-lined avenue to **Dargye Gonpa** in Khargang township. This monastery (3,536 m) which represents the Gelukpa school and was founded in 1642, is the oldest of all the 13 so-called Horpa monasteries established by the victorious Mongolian forces of Gushi Qan in the 17th century. Its traditional precedence continues, although it is smaller than Kandze Monastery.

The Ngakpa Tratsang has not yet been rebuilt, but the quality of reconstruction in the **Tsenyi Tratsang** (Dialectical College) is outstanding. The most impressive feature is its enormous three-storey **assembly hall**, approached from named gates in each of the building's four directions. Large teams of volunteer and commissioned craftsmen have been working on the reconstruction of the buildings since 1988. The **main hall** contains a throne of the Dalai Lama, flanked by images of the 16 Elders. Side murals depict scenes from the Avadanakalpalata, and Tara who protects from the eight fears. The murals adjacent to the entrance doorway depict the protectors and meditational deities: Guhyasamaja, Cakrasamvara, Vajrabhairava and Shridevi (L); and Dralha, Dharmaraja, Vaishravana, Avalokiteshvara and Manjughosa (R). The **inner sanctum** contains images of (L-R): Tsongkhapa, Maitreya, Sarvavid Vairocana, the Fourteenth Dalai Lama, Tsongkhapa, Atisha, Simhanada and Jowo Yizhin Norbu, all flanked by the Eight Standing Bodhisattvas and the Eight Medicine Buddhas, with Hayagriva and Vajrapani guarding the gate.

Upstairs, on the second floor, there is a Gonkhang containing images of (left to right): Shridevi, Modak, Six-armed Mahakala, Three-faced Vajrabhairava, Two-armed Mahakala, Four-armed Mahakala, Vaishravana, Jo-se, and the Five Aspects of Pehar.

Beri

Located 17 km east of Dargye Gonpa on the **Horko plain** (3,536 m), **Beri** was the capital of an important Bonpo Kingdom and the cultural centre of this part of Kham until the 17th century. The king of Beri, Donyo Dorje, was defeated by the armies of Gushi Qan between 1639-1641, and this event led to the formation of the Trehor states. At Beri, the Bon monastery was converted into a Gelukpa monastery, housing 100 monks.

The strategic importance of the town overlooking a narrow part of the Yalong valley, continued to be recognized. In 1918, it was occupied as the front line of defence by the Chinese army, and this subsequently attracted the animosity of the villagers around Dargye Gonpa, who held the Tibetan front line. In 1931 when Beri was assisted in its dispute with Dargye Gonpa by the Chinese governor of Sichuan, the Tibetan forces stationed at Derge came to the assistance of Dargye Gonpa and the attackers were thrust back to Kandze.

Approaching the Beri acropolis from Dargye, the reconstructed buildings of **Beri Gonpa**, where there are more than 200 Gelukpa monks, are visible from afar on the north bank of the Yalong. The river crossing is at **Shenkhang**, below the citadel on the south bank, which dominates the approaches through the valley from east and west. Here within a walled town are the ruins of **Beri Castle** and the renovated **Kablung Monastery**, where there are 50 monks. Kablung, which represents the Nyingma school, is a combined branch of both Katok and Dzogchen, the former tradition being maintained by Norbu Tulku and the latter by Babu Tulku. Extant murals at Kablung depict the *Longchen Nyingtig* tradition. Inland from Beri, towards the Kawalungring Range, is the power place of **O Tashi Pema Tsepel** at Lake Tashi Tso, which is frequented by pilgrims to the present day.

Kandze → *Altitude: 3,581 m*

Kandze (Ch Ganzi), the county capital, is a large provincial town located in the loess hills close to the banks of the Yalong, 13 km east of Beri and 9 km east of the Pelyul turn-off. Two of the five Hor states, Kangsar and Mazur, were formerly located above the gently sloping plain of Kandze; and since the construction of their castles in the 17th century, the town has been the largest and most important in the Trehor region. During the 1909-1918 war, the castles were occupied by Chinese garrisons; and today they lie in ruins below **Kandze Monastery**. Apart from this monastery and the historically important **Den Gonpa**, there were several other monasteries of note in the valley. These include Drakar, Nyatso, Khangmar, and Tsitso monasteries of the Gelukpa school; Dontok Monastery of the Sakya school, and Rirak Gonpa of the Kagyu school. Since 1950 the name Kandze has also been given to the Autonomous Prefecture administered from Dartsedo. ▸▸ *For listings, see pages 541-542.*

Orientation

At the entrance to town, a bridge spans the Yalong, carrying all traffic across to the north bank. The road then climbs to the north leaving the river, and winds downhill to the crossroads, which marks the town centre. The bus station and Golden Yak hotel lie to the right, near the crossroads.

The road to the left from the crossroads leads uphill towards the hilltop **Kandze Monastery**, passing en route a large number of shops, selling traditional Tibetan artefacts and modern Chinese or Indian goods. Further uphill (on the left) there are electrical stores, a photographic studio, China Telecom, the Post Office Hotel, and on the right a middle school. At the top of this road, you will pass residential town houses – their horizontal red timbers adorned with bright flower pots – and climb sharply to the monastery. Alternatively, you can take one of the bridges which span

Kandze

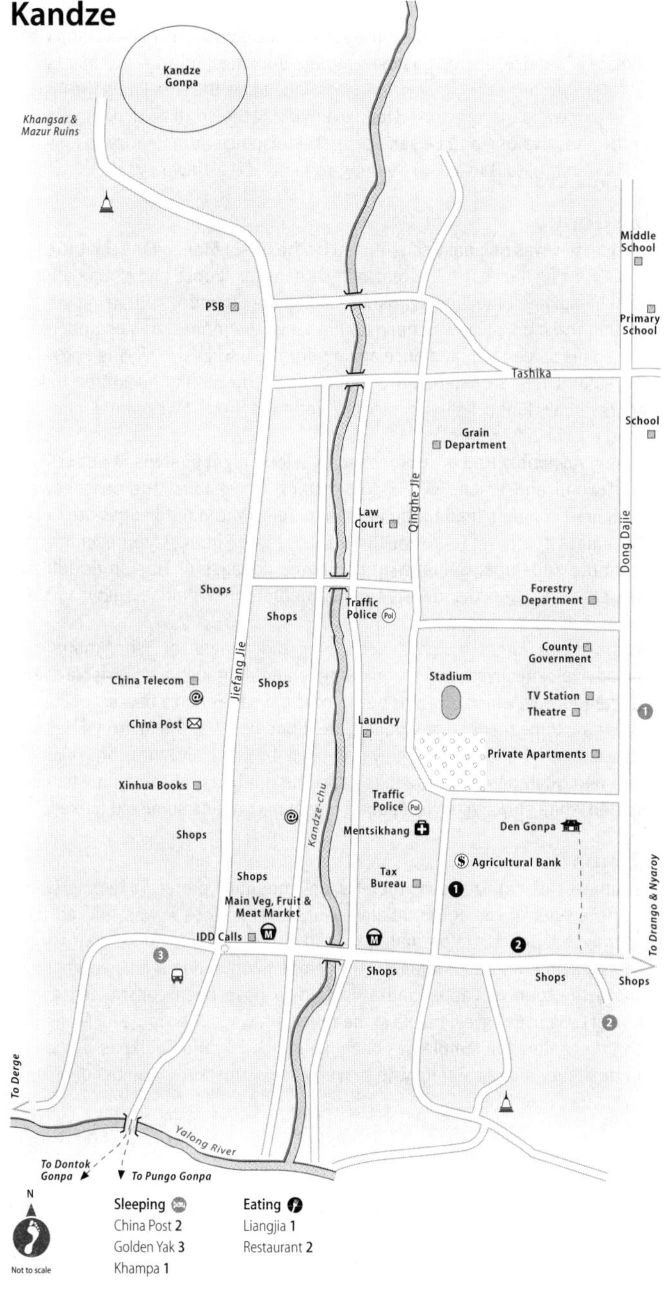

 the Kandze-chu to the right of this road. These lead across to a parallel residential street offering good photographic views of the monastery. Here there is a public park, the Agricultural Bank, the County Tax Bureau and the Liangjia Restaurant.

Returning downhill to the crossroads, if you go straight ahead, you will pass the Post Office, a few electrical stores, and the vegetable and meat market. There are some restaurants on this street also, and small shops selling Tibetan artefacts, including old carpets. After the market, a turning on the right leads to the new China Post Hotel, and a wide avenue on the left leads into the compound of **Den Gonpa**, the oldest temple of Kandze, and on past government buildings, private apartments, the Khampa Hotel and Kandze TV Station. If you continue along the street from the market you can head down to the large new stupa overlooking the north bank of the Yalong, or out of town for Nyarong and Latseka pass. The distance from Kandze to Pelyul is 232 km (via Tromtar), to Barshok in Nyarong 109 km, and to Tawu 158 km.

Kandze Gonpa

Kandze Monastery was originally constructed by the Qosot Mongolians circa 1642 on a hilltop overlooking their castles of Mazur and Khangsar. It once had a population of 1,500 monks, making it the largest in Kham alongside Chamdo; and the pilgrimage circuit around the monastery was nearly 8 km long. The monastery has undergone extensive repairs since 1981, and once again offers an impressive skyline above the town. Currently it has an estimated population of 700 monks and three tulkus, including Lamdrak Rinpoche who recently returned from Switzerland and has established a local girls' school.

The main **Assembly Hall** is approached by a long flight of steps. It is a striking building in wood and stone, with a golden roof. Downstairs, the passageways between the red columns lead to the **inner sanctum**, where the images are raised high within glass cabinets. There are three sets of three images, representing the founders of the Kadampa, Gelukpa and Nyingma lineages of Tibetan Buddhism. There are also fine tangkas depicting the meditational deities Guhyasamaja, Cakrasamvara and Yamantaka.

Upstairs are a *Kangyur* library containing old images of Tsongkhapa and Eleven-faced Avalokiteshvara and a **Gonkhang**, entered through a striking black and gold painted doorway, which contains new protector images and a new set of images representing the three meditational deities mentioned above. The **Maitreya Hall** has an enormous central image of Maitreya, flanked by Bhaisajyaguru, Shakyamuni, Dipamkara and Sitatapatra. On the hillside to the northeast of the monastery is a reconstructed white stupa. A newly opened museum contains some old tankas.

Den Gonpa

In the southeast of Kandze town there is an important protector temple which survived the events of the 1960s relatively unscathed since it was utilized as a granary during that period. Unfortunately the old murals here are now showing signs of recent weathering and deterioration. The temple, containing a revered image of Mahakala in the form of Panjaranatha, is said to have been constructed at the suggestion of Drogon Chogyel Phakpa in the 13th century while en route for Mongolia. Since the 17th century the temple has been maintained by the Gelukpas. There is a circumambulatory walkway replete with prayer wheels. Upstairs a number of original woodblocks are preserved.

Kandze to Latseka pass

The highway leaves Kandze and heads southeast, rejoining the course of the Yalong. The outlying Gelukpa monasteries of **Drakar**, Tangkor, **Khangmar** and **Tsitso**, and the Sakyapa monastery of **Dontok**, are all to be found in the hinterland. After 9 km, a side road leaves the highway on the right, following the river as it changes course to head into **Nyarong**. The highway itself veers steeply to the east, passing through the picturesque farming village of **Puyulung** (Ch Lozhling), and you can then see rising on the southeast horizon the snow peaks of **Kawalungring** (5,082 m), which conceal the entrance to Nyarong. About 16 km after the Nyarong turn-off, the road enters a nomadic grassland area, passes through the small **Sharchok** township, and reaches the high **Latseka** pass (3,992 m), which forms a watershed between the Yalong and Zhe-chu rivers.

Nyarong County ཉག་རོང་ → *Pop: 43,000. Area: 9,821 sq km.* 新龙县

Nyarong county is the name given to the traditional tribal area of **Upper Nyarong**, in contrast to that of **Lower Nyarong**, which is now under the jurisdiction of **Nyachuka** county. The Yalong River flows through both Upper Nyarong and Lower Nyarong on a southerly course towards its confluence with the Yangtze at **Dukou**. The county capital is located at **Barshok**, 109 km from Kandze.

The isolated Nyarong valley has always been a stronghold of the Nyingmapa school and the pre-Buddhist Bon tradition. During the 19th century, the chieftain of Nyarong, Gonpo Namgyel subdued most of Kham, unifying much of East Tibet under his command in the military campaigns of 1837-1863. He was eventually defeated in 1865 by the Tibetan government and forced to withdraw into the citadels of Nyarong, where he came to an untimely end.

Chakdu Kawalungring

Driving into Nyarong from Kandze, the dirt road leaves the paved highway, following the east bank of the Yalong downstream through a deep gorge. Snow peaks soon appear on both sides of the ravine, high above the road. After **Sha-de Gonpa**, the road reaches the entrance to the **Kawalungring wildlife sanctuary** on the left, 29 km from Kandze. A giant seed syllable A is engraved on the cliffs above the road. Continuing south into Nyarong, after a further 26 km you will reach **Da-ge Drongtok Gon**, an important branch of Katok Monastery. Another 14 km brings you to an intersection, where a motorable side road crosses the Yalong to link up with the Kandze-Pelyul road near **Tromtar** (see above, page 496). As the gorge narrows further, the river is spanned intermittently by wooden footbridges, leading to remote villages perched high on the ridges above. After a further 40 km, the road eventually reaches **Barshok**, the county capital, where it crosses to the west bank of the Yalong.

Barshok

The county capital, **Barshok**, lies at the heart of Nyarong (Ch Xinlong). This was formerly the residence of Nyarong Gonpo Namgyel who, in the 19th century, unified the upper and lower districts of Nyarong under his command and embarked on a military campaign against the neighbouring independent kingdoms and provinces of Kham. Trehor, Derge, Dzachuka, Lhato, Nangchen and Jyekundo all succumbed to his forces, as did Batang, Litang, Chaktreng and Gyeltang in the far south, and Chakla, Trokhyab and Tawu in the east. Only the intervention of the Tibetan government army in 1865 brought an end to this expansion; and Gonpo Namgyel was himself incinerated when the government forces set fire to his fortress. ▸▸ *For listings, see pages 541-542.*

Orientation The old town of Barshok (2,970 m) is located on the east bank of the Yalong, but the main road immediately crosses to the west bank, where the post office, forestry bureau and bus station are all located. From the post office crossroads, you can also head west to reach a parallel loop road where the government buildings, hospitals, bank, bookshop and various restaurants are all located.

Karzang Gonpa and Chakdu Gonpa

The road to **Pundadrong** follows the west bank of the Yalong south from Barshok. After 17 km, it crosses a narrow bridge, spanning a tributary. A narrow track veers right after the bridge, following the tributary upstream for 15 km to **Karzang Gonpa**. The road is difficult in summertime when its surface can be eroded by the lapping waters of an artificial lake (created by a quarry). Karzang Gonpa was once the residence of two outstanding 19th-century Buddhist masters: the treasure-finder Nyakla Pema Dudul (who was born at Shunlung, 17 km west of Barshok) and Lerab Lingpa, also known as Terton Sogyel (1856-1926), who was a close associate of the Thirteenth Dalai Lama. The former was one of the few lamas venerated personally by the warrior chieftain Nyarong Gonpo Namgyel! The community of monks and *mantrins* at Karzang is currently under the guidance of the charismatic Lama Rikdzin Gyatso, but it also has affiliation with **Larung Gar** in Sertal (see below, page 647).

A further 65 km drive on a rugged track leads to **Chakdu Gonpa**, the residence of the late Chakdu Rinpoche, who in his later years established thriving retreat centres in Oregon and Brazil. The most important power-place associated with Padmasambhava in the Nyarong valley is located above this monastery near the snowline at **Chakdu Kawalungring**. It represents the activity aspect of buddha-speech.

Barshok to Nyachuka

From Barshok there is a difficult motorable trail to Pundadrong, the capital of Nyachuka county in lower Nyarong, which straddles the Litang-Dardo highway. The road follows the Yalong downstream, crossing to the east bank and passing the Bon monastery of **Lhunpa** in Shaja township. A turn-off for **Chunda** and **Litang** is reached after 80 km (see above, page 465), but the direct route to **Pundadrong** (see above, page 474) continues to follow the east bank. There have been reports of banditry on this road even in recent years. An alternative route from **Tawu to Pundadrong**, following the Zhe-chu (Ch Xianshui) downstream, offers easier access to lower Nyarong.

Drango County བྲག་འགོ → *Pop: 39,000. Area: 4,764 sq km.* 炉霍县

Drango county comprises the valley of the Zhe-chu as far as its confluence with the Nyi-chu tributary, at the county town of the same name. The distance from Kandze to Drango is 93 km, and from Drango to Tawu 72 km.

Khasa Lake

On the descent from the watershed **Latseka Pass** (3,992 m), also called **Dresel La**, the paved highway passes through sparsely populated nomadic country, dotted with dark yak wool tents. Soon you will reach the recently rebuilt **Joro Gonpa**, a Gelukpa nunnery dating from 1642. Below the nunnery there is a magnificent panorama of an idyllic blue lake, which was once a thriving bird sanctuary. A farming village is located by the lakeside near the road.

Trewo

Below Khasa Lake, the road descends for 19 km to **Trewo** (3,612 m), where it meets up with the Zhe-chu valley. Trewo, like Khangsar and Mazur at Kandze, was one of the five Trehor kingdoms set up by the Qosot Mongolians in this part of Kham. Formerly it had a large citadel with impressive walls, which was the residence of the chieftain of Hor Trewo.

Drango County

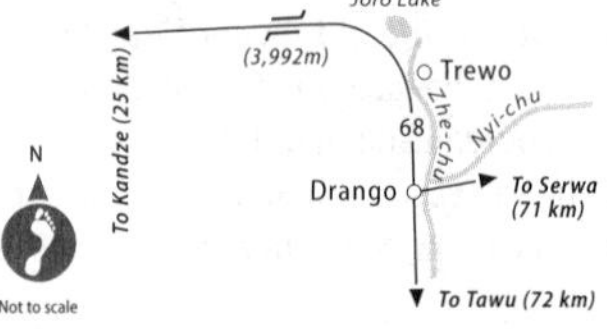

The golden roofed temple of **Trehor Gonpa** stands out against the flat-roofed earthen houses of the Tibetan village, clustered around the castle ruins and alongside new Chinese compounds. Across the river on the north bank of the Zhe-chu is the rebuilt temple of **Dzaleb Gonpa**.

Drango

As the name ('head of the rock') suggests, **Drango** is a strategic location on the mountain slope at the confluence of the Zhe-chu and Nyi-chu rivers. The castle of **Drango Dzong** formerly stood at this vantage point at an elevation of 3,475 m. Above it in the 17th century, the Gelukpa monastery of **Drango Gonpa** was constructed. At its high point, this monastery housed 1,000 monks, making it the largest in Kham east of Litang and Kandze. In 1863 Drango along with the other Trehor kingdoms and Derge was overwhelmed by the tribal forces of Nyarong Gonpo Namgyel. Then, in 1865 on the defeat of Gonpo Namgyel, the town became a protectorate of Lhasa. Subsequently, the Chinese settlement, **Luho Xian**, was founded in 1894 by Lu Ch'uan-lin who ended the succession of local chieftains. ▸▸ *For listings, see pages 541-542.*

Orientation Most buildings in Drango are newly constructed, the older town having been devastated by an earthquake in 1973. Entering the town from the west (49 km from Trewo), the main street runs past a prison, followed by a number of high-rise concrete buildings, including the Bank of China. Reaching the crossroads, which marks the town centre, there are two parallel streets running uphill, both filled with small shops and restaurants. At the upper end of the westernmost of these two streets, turn right and then left to enter the Drango Government Guesthouse compound. The Government Buildings are to its rear.

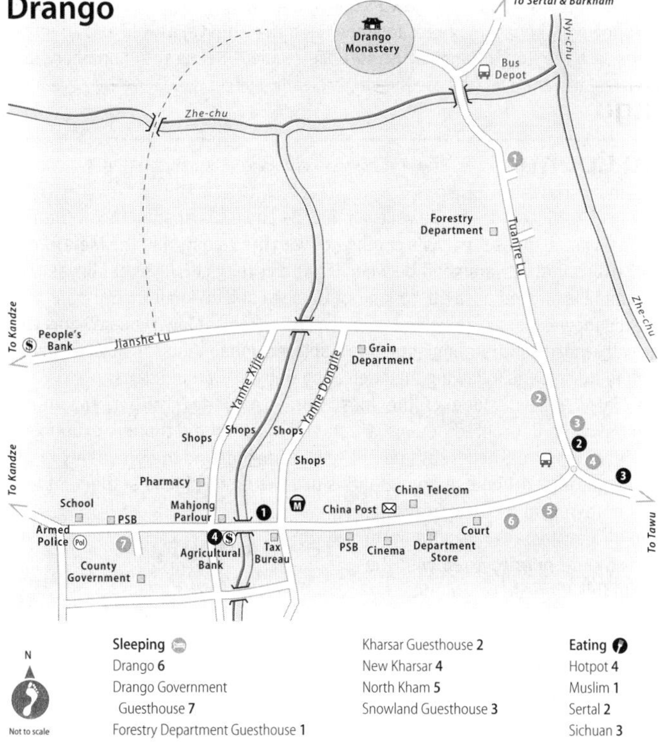

Outside the hotel, turn right and walk along the boulevard running along the upper end of the two parallel market streets. There are hotpot restaurants, several video parlours and karaoke bars. Head downhill on this main road, and you will pass the main commercial centre: glass-fronted shops selling textiles, ready-to-wear clothing, shoes etc, as well as China Telecom, the Agricultural Bank, the Public Security Bureau, the law courts, the Drango Hotel and the North Kham (Kang Bei) Hotel. The bus station and cinema are located at a roundabout at the bottom of this road – a barrier on the right pointing the way out of town in the direction of Tawu.

Turning right at the roundabout, head downhill to the bridge which spans the Zhe-chu River. This is the road leading north to **Serwa** (71 km) and thence to **Sertal** or **Dzamtang** (see below, pages 645 and 648). On the way you will pass the New Kharsar Hotel, the Snowland Hotel, and the Old Kharsar Guesthouse. Before reaching the bridge you will also pass a rundown Forestry Department Guesthouse on the right.

Drango Gonpa The monastery which gives the town its name is located across the river on the 'head of the rock' promontory. The **main hall** which has 63 pillars contains images of Tsongkhapa and his foremost students, Buddha in the form of Gyelwa Yizhin Norbu, and the Buddhas of the Five Families, with a teaching throne in front. Along the side walls are tapestries in Chengdu brocade depicting the 1,000 Buddhas of the Aeon, while adjacent to the door there are depictions of Six-armed Mahakala and the Thirty-five Confession Buddhas. The **inner sanctum** has images of Tsongkhapa and Jowo Shakyamuni, the latter crafted in India. On the **second floor**, there is a rear section containing the **Reliquary Chapel** of Geshe Yeshe Norbu and Geshe Kentsang, both former preceptors of Drango Monastery; the **Jamyang Lhakhang**, containing the reliquary of the late Umdze Jamyang who rebuilt Drango Monastery in recent years; and the private apartments of the Dalai Lama (as yet unused). The front section contains the **Dolma Lhakhang** and the **Guru Lhakhang**, which respectively house images of Tara and Padmasambhava, as well as a chamber where the late the Tenth Panchen Lama once resided. Below the monastery, the confluence of the Zhe-chu and the Nyi-chu is clearly visible.

Tawu County རྟའུ → *Population: 47,000. Area: 5,099 sq km.* 道孚县

The county of **Tawu** comprises the valley of the Zhe-chu (Ch Xianshui) below Drango, extending as far south as the river's confluence with the Yalong, and the **Mejesumdo** uplands, which form a watershed between it and the Tung-chu River of Minyak. The county capital is located at **Tawu**, 72 km from Drango and 76 km from Garthar.

The distinctive dialect spoken here (known in Tibetan as 'Tawu Lok-ke') may well accord with the legend stating that the displaced inhabitants of Xixia (Minyak) migrated to these parts following their defeat by Genghiz Qan in 1227.

The Tawu valley is one of the most attractive parts of Tibet, the neatly constructed white flat-roofed houses with their horizontal red timbers exuding an air of quiet prosperity. The low altitude of Tawu (3,125 m) and the prosperity of the valley have attracted Chinese immigrants since the first Chinese settlement was founded here in 1911 by Chao Erh Feng. Catholic and protestant missions were also based here prior to 1949 with the support of this Chinese community.

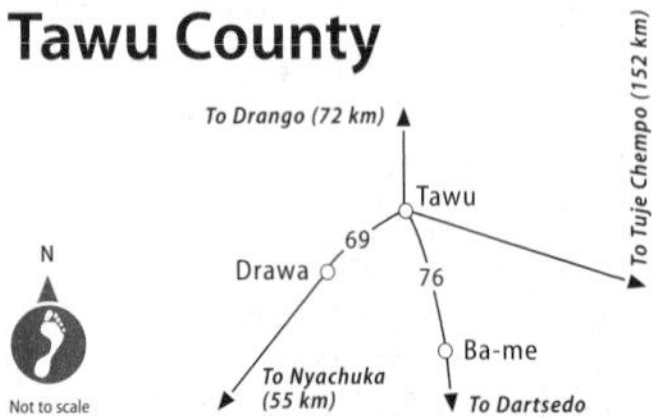

Tawu

Orientation Entering Tawu from Drango via the **Trongmi** goldfields (72 km), the road crosses to the north bank of the Zhe-chu and passes the Forestry Department Guesthouse at the west end of town. Above the main street, on the hillside to the northwest you will notice the white gravestones of the Chinese martyrs' cemetery and the renovated buildings of **Nyitso Gonpa.** ▸▸ *For listings, see pages 541-542.*

The town On both sides of the main street there are small Sichuan-style restaurants. Pass the compound on the right where the Tibetan Language University of East Tibet was based until recently, and on the left a lumber yard. The road forks here; the left branch (Jietang Xijie) leading towards Nyitso Gonpa, the government buildings, the post office, and courts; and the right branch (Jietang Xinjie) leading to the bus station and the main crossroads at the centre of the town.

Reaching the crossroads, a turning on the left (Jietang Nanjie) leads uphill to the Tawu Government Guesthouse, eventually connecting with Jietang Xijie opposite the law courts. General stores, grocery stores and vegetable sellers line the main street near the crossroads. Continue due east from the crossroads to head out of town in the directions of Garthar, southeast for Nyachuka and northeast for Barkham. A petrol station lies at the extreme east end of town.

Nyitso Gonpa

This restored Gelukpa monastery is the easternmost of the 13 major Trehor monasteries, founded in the 17th century by Mongolian force of arms. It has three buildings within its secure courtyard: a **Gonkhang**, containing images of the main Gelukpa protectors, a **Dungten**, containing the reliquary stupa of Ponlob Rinpoche, and a large two-storey assembly hall with kitchen attached. Among them, the **assembly hall** (Dukhang) has some fine murals illustrating scenes from the

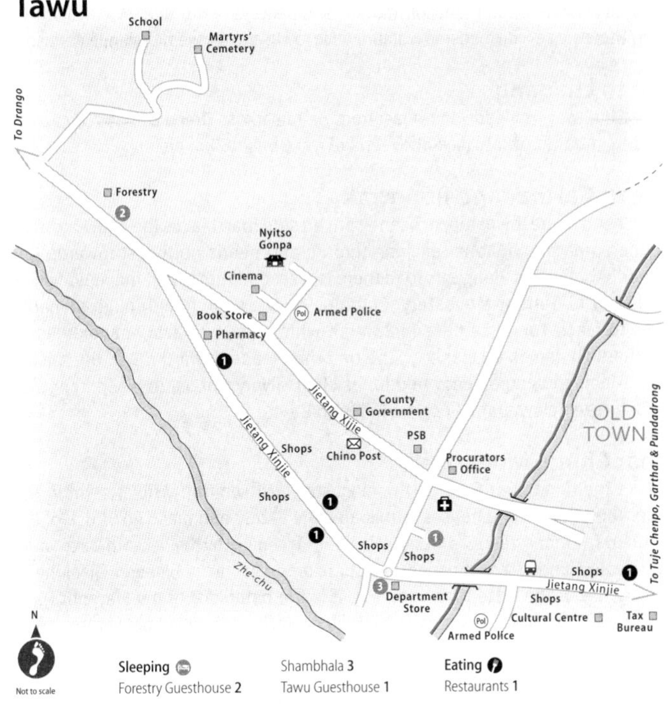

 Avadanakalpalata. On the ground floor the principal images depict Tsohgkhapa with his students and Padmasambhava. There are two inner sanctums – the one on the left has further images of Tsongkhapa and students, and the one on the right has images of Padmasambhava flanked by Shantaraksita and King Trisong Detsen, with the Sixteen Elders in their bas relief grottoes on either side. Upstairs there is a viewing gallery and the private apartment of the Dalai Lama. Nowadays there are 700 monks affiliated to the monastery.

Tawu to Nyachuka, Tu-je Chenpo, and Garthar

Three different roads lead east from Tawu, diverging beyond the petrol station at the edge of town. To the south, a dirt road (Tianjie Nanlu) crosses the Zhe-chu and follows its east bank downstream, leaving the Tawu valley at an enormous 30-m high white stupa. After 69 km this road passes through **Drawa**, where there is a small Gelukpa monastery, and continues on past the confluence of the Zhe-chu and the Yalong for a further 56 km to reach **Pundadrong** (see above, page 474).

A second dirt road (Tuanjie Beilu) leads north from the intersection. Leaving town, it abruptly crosses the watershed into **Gyarong** and follows a tributary of the Do-chu upstream for 152 km to **Tu-je Chenpo** (Ch Qanyiqao) in Chuchen county. Here there are roads east to **Barkham**, and west to **Dzamtang** or **Sertal** (see below, pages 648 and 645).

Lastly, the paved Highway 317 runs southeast from Tawu, ascending the richly forested watershed region of Mejesumdo, where there are wonderful picnic spots in view of **Mount Zhara Lhatse**. It then crosses the **Nedreheka La** pass (3,952 m) to enter the Minyak region of East Tibet at **Ba-me**. The distance from Tawu to Dartsedo via Ba-me is 240 km.

Ba-me township (Ch Qianning)

Ba-me is an important road junction, 76 km southeast of Tawu and 16 km north of Lhagang. There are several roadside restaurants in town, and a government guesthouse.

Ba-me to Lhagang

The paved highway 317 leads southeast from Ba-me across **Drepa La** pass (4,420 m) to **Lhagang** in Dardo county (see above, page 477), only 16 km distant.

Ba-me to Garthar and Rongtrak

At the east end of the township, a recently paved side road leaves the highway, next to a stone stupa and a stone teaching throne, and heads northeast towards the watershed. About 7 km along this road there is a second turn-off on the right, which leads directly to **Garthar Monastery**. Continue on the main trail through nomadic pastures to reach **Tongu La** pass (3,840 m), which offers amazing panoramas of Mount Zhara Lhatse on a clear day. The trail then leads down through the thickly forested Tongu-chu gorge, renowned for its clear silvery waters, to reach **Rongtrak** in Gyarong (see below, page 660), 72 km from Ba-me.

Garthar Chode Monastery

If you take the turn-off for Garthar, the monastery will soon be visible, 2 km in the distance. The village stone houses in this area are sturdy and make good use of the local timber. The monastery was founded in the 18th century by the Seventh Dalai Lama Kalzang Gyatso, and its construction was sponsored directly by Emperor Qianlong of the Qing Dynasty. The ridge to the southwest is the birthplace of the Eleventh Dalai Lama (b. 1838). On a clear day there are excellent views of Mount Zhara Lhatse.

The monastery compound is encircled by 108 stupas. Within the courtyard the buildings to the right are residential *tratsang* and the single structure on the left is the *labrang* residence of the Seventh Dalai Lama. There are two main buildings: a

Jamkhang to the left (which has images of Maitreya and various protector deities), and the **assembly hall** (*dukhang*), in front of which there is a stone tablet inscribed in Chinese and Manchu. The hall, which is entered from a small door on the right, has large images of Tsongkhapa with his students and Padmasambhava flanked by Shantaraksita and King Trisong Detsen, with Choje Showa on the right. The murals here depict symbols of long life and Manchurian power, as well as (L-R): Vaishravana, Mahamati, Sadaprarudita, Vajravidarana, the Sixteen Elders, Aksobhya and Sitatapatra. Within the inner sanctum there are enormous images of the Buddhas of the Three Times, flanked by a statue of Minyak Kyabgon Rinpoche, and a Qianlong bronze bell, inscribed with the legend "may it be heard forever"! The books housed here are the Derge edition of the *Tangyur*. **Upstairs**, there is a chapel dedicated to the Twenty-one Taras and three private apartments: for the Dalai Lama, the chief disciplinarian (*geko*) and the senior chant-master (*um-dze*). The turquoise tiled roof formerly had a gilded *gyabib*, similar to those at the Potala and Jokhang in Lhasa. At present there are 200 monks at Garthar. The main dance ceremonies are held on the 16th day of the first lunar month (when Maitreya circumambulates the monastery in a masked procession), and on the first to fourth days of the sixth lunar month, commemorating the original teachings of Buddhism by Shakyamuni. In 2005 these corresponded respectively to 24 February and 7-10 July.

Sleeping

Kandze *p532, map p533*

C **Khampa Hotel**, T0836-7523214. The best in town, with deluxe rooms at ¥488, singles at ¥388, standard twin rooms at ¥140, and triples at ¥188. There is a clean restaurant, where local officials like to hold banquets, and a washroom.

E **China Post Hotel**, T0836-9229811. Has doubles at ¥45, singles at ¥30, and triples at ¥45, with communal hot showers.

E **Golden Yak Hotel (Jinmaoniu Jiudian)**, above the Bus Station, T0836-7525188. Has doubles with attached bath at ¥160.

E **Hongyueliang Hotel**, T0836-4522676. Has doubles at ¥40, singles at ¥40, triples at ¥45, 4-bed rooms at ¥60.

Barshok *p535*

E Very simple dormitory accommodation is available at the **Bus Station Guesthouse**, the **Government Buildings**, and the **Forestry Department**.

Drango *p536, map p537*

E **Drango Government Guesthouse**, T0836-68367332. Best rooms on 2nd floor, as well as cheaper accommodation on 3rd floor (superior doubles at ¥80, suites at ¥120, and singles at ¥80, economy doubles at ¥30, triples at ¥36 and 4-bed rooms at ¥40).

E **Drango Hotel**, T0836-7322625. Has superior doubles at ¥100, superior triples at ¥90, and economy doubles, triples and singles at ¥50.

E **Forestry Department Guesthouse**, has very poor dormitory accommodation.

E **New Kharsar Hotel**, T0836-7323666. Has doubles at ¥35, triples at ¥54.

D **North Kham (Kang Bei) Hotel**, T0836-7322332. Has very clean double rooms at ¥140-160.

E **Old Kharsar Hotel**, has doubles at ¥30, singles at ¥26, triples at ¥30, 4-bed dorms at ¥40.

Tawu *p538, map p539*

D **Shambhala Hotel**. Has a macabre atmosphere with stuffed animals in the lobby. ¥120 per room.

D **Tawu Government Guesthouse**, Jietang Nanjie, T0836-7122486. Has the best accommodation in No 4 Bldg, as well as economy rooms in No 1 and No 2 Bldgs (superior suites at ¥150-280, economy doubles at ¥15-22 per bed, and economy triples at ¥13 per bed). The hotel restaurant is mediocre. Better to dine outside at the simple street restaurants, some of which serve good Sichuan fare.

For an explanation of the sleeping and eating price codes used in this guide, see inside the front cover. Other relevant information is found in Essentials pages 44-46.

E Forestry Department Guesthouse, also has simple rooms, but may not accept foreign guests.

Ba-me *p540*
Hong Taiyuan Hotel and Restaurant, T0836-7255168. The best food and cleanest lodgings between Dartsedo and Drango are to be found here. Traditionally constructed, privately owned by a Tibetan lady Mrs Pematso (9 rooms at ¥45 per room or ¥15 per bed). The exquisite family altar has images of Longchen Rabjampa, Sakya Pandita and Tsongkhapa, and there are special rooms reserved here for visiting lamas. The proprietor can also arrange 1-2 day-horse treks around the Garthar region. Down a lane opposite this hotel there is a public washroom with hot showers (¥5).

Eating

Kandze *p532, map p533*
Liangjia Restaurant, T0836-7522748. Good Sichuan dishes.
Xueyu Fandian, for good Sichuan dishes.
Several smaller restaurants are also to be found adjacent to the bus station, around the intersection, and in the market street. These invariably serve noodles and dumplings, as well as Sichuan and Muslim dishes. Small tea houses on the road up to Kandze monastery also sell delicious home-made bread.

Barshok *p535*
The Sichuan restaurants leave much to be desired – the best probably being the one located down a dingy staircase facing the county government buildings. The Focus Tea House and the Bus Station Restaurant are brighter and cleaner, but serve only snacks.

Drango *p536, map p537*
Drango Hotel Restaurant, probably the best in town, although the best hotpot is available at a 2nd-floor restaurant near the entrance to the Drango Government Guesthouse, opposite the Mahjong Parlour.
The guesthouses generally have a slow service and are more expensive than the small roadside restaurants and noodle bars, which serve Sichuan, Tibetan and Muslim cuisine. There is a good Tibetan restaurant upstairs near the crossroads, opposite the New Kharser Hotel.

Transport

Kandze *p532, map p533*
Bus
Buses leave Kandze for the following destinations: **Dartsedo** (daily, 0630, ¥102); **Chengdu** (daily, 0630, ¥200); **Nyarong** (daily, ¥35); **Yilhun** (daily, ¥24); **Derge** (odd days, 0800, ¥60); **Dzogchen** (odd days, ex Dartsedo, ¥45); **Chusumdo** (odd days, ex Dartsedo, ¥48); **Sershul** (odd days, ex Dartsedo, ¥90); **Pelyul** (even days, 0800, ¥89).

Barshok *p535*
Bus
Buses run from Barshok to **Kandze** (daily minibus, 0700, 1400, ¥22-23; with a deluxe bus on even days only, mornings, ¥30). Private buses very seldom run west to **Pelyul** or south to **Pundadrong** and **Litang**. They will drop you at Shaja township for ¥10.

Drango *p536, map p537*
Bus
Buses depart Drango for **Dartsedo** (daily deluxe, ¥85 and ordinary ¥59); **Chengdu** (daily deluxe, ¥127); and **Sertal** (daily, ¥46).

Tawu *p538, map p539*
Bus
There are daily public buses to **Drango** and **Kandze** (0600 and 1430), as well as to **Dartsedo** (0600).

Directory

Kandze *p532, map p533*
Internet There is an internet café next to China Telecom (¥30 per hr).
Telephones China Post has an EMS service, and **China Telecom** sells ICC cards for DDD and IDD calls.

Drango *p536, map p537*
Telephones China Post has an EMS service, and **China Telecom** sells ICC cards for DDD and IDD calls, as well as having an operator service for IDD calls.

Far East Tibet (Amdo and Gyarong)

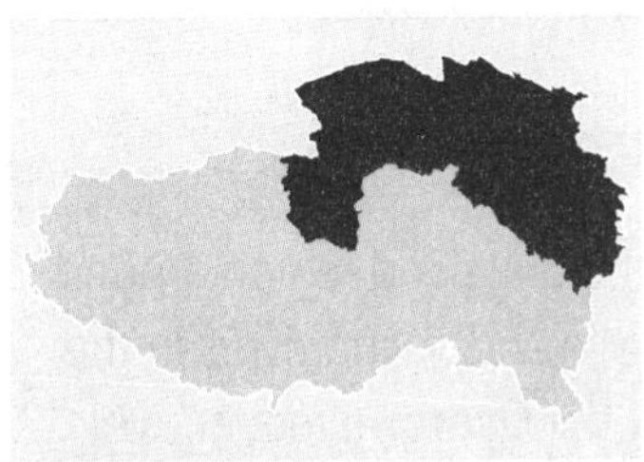

Footprint features

Introduction

Far East Tibet includes **Amdo** or the grassland region around the upper reaches of the Yellow, Min and Jialing rivers in the northeast and the deep gorges of the **Gyarong** feeder rivers, Ser-chu, Do-chu and Mar-chu further south. Amdo is the region in which the Tibetan population has been most exposed over the centuries to cultural contacts with neighbouring peoples: Tu, Salar, Mongolian, Hui, and Chinese; and this intermingling is reflected in the demographic composition of the grasslands. By contrast, the isolated Gyarong valleys remained aloof for centuries from all outside influences and their inhabitants were known for their expressed hostility towards intruders, whether Tibetan, Mongolian, Manchu or Chinese.

Recommende itinerary: 8, 9, 11, see page 20

★ Don't miss...

❶ **Lake Kokonor** At bird island on the western shore of Tibet's largest lake there is a thriving bird sanctuary for cormorants, bar-headed geese, black-necked cranes among others, page 560.

❷ **Tsong-chu Valley** Highly accessible from Ziling and Lanzhou are some of Amdo's most important historical sites: Martsangdrak, Kumbum Jampaling and Drotsang monastery, as well as the birthplace of the present Dalai Lama at Taktser.

❸ **Achung Namdzong** Take the ferry across the Yellow River to Khamra National Park and the soaring sandstone pinnacles of Achung Namdzong and fascinating temples, page 602.

❹ **Horgon** Ride horseback through the Amdo grasslands and work on the restoration of a revered wall of stone carved scriptures, page 612.

❺ **Tsogon Geden Choling Gon** A magnificent nine-storeyed temple, illustrating the entire history of Buddhism in Tibet, page 672.

❻ **Mewa Gonpa** A thriving monastic city of the Nyingma school, containing many temples, hermitages and a fine library, page 687.

Background

There are seven sections in the following description of Far East Tibet: the first details the route from **Lhasa to Ziling** (Xining) across the West Kokonor plateau; the second, third and fourth trace the old caravan trails and describe the densely populated valleys to the north, east, southeast and southwest of **Lake Kokonor**; the fifth and sixth follow the upper reaches of the Yellow River through **Golok** and the Gyarong feeder rivers through **Sertal** and **Ngawa** as far as **Rongtrak** and **Tsenlha**; and finally, the seventh follows the upper reaches of the Min and Jialing rivers from **Lanzhou to Chengdu** via **Labrang**, **Dzoge** and **Zungchuka** (Ch Songpan).

At present this entire region of Far East Tibet comprises 60 counties, of which 37 are within Qinghai province, eight within Gansu province, and the remainder in Sichuan (13 in the Ngawa Autonomous Prefecture and two in the Kandze Autonomous Prefecture).

Getting there

The nearest points of access are the large provincial capital cities: Chengdu, Lanzhou and Ziling.

History

Tibetan-speaking tribes played an important role in the formation of several Chinese dynasties in the northeast; but during the Tang Dynasty, the Tibetan Empire of the **Yarlung kings** consolidated its control over the whole region of Far East Tibet. Culturally, the peoples of the region have remained within the Tibetan orbit ever since, influenced by both the Bon and the Buddhist traditions. The unifying influence of Tibetan culture withstood the political fragmentation of the region which followed the collapse of the Yarlung Empire in the ninth century; and it was through contact with the Sakyapa and Kagyupa traditions in the grasslands that the Mongolian tribes of **Genghiz Qan** and his successors were brought within the fold of Tibetan Buddhism.

For some 500 years (13th-18th century) the Mongolian tribes dominated the grasslands, and following the conversion of **Altan Qan** to the Gelukpa school by **the Third Dalai Lama** in 1580, successive qans zealously sought to impose the acceptance of the Gelukpa order upon the diverse cultural traditions of the region. **Gushi Qan** of the Qosot Mongolians established his kingdom around Lake Kokonor, and in 1641 aided the Fifth Dalai Lama to establish a combined spirtual and temporal authority in Lhasa. His military campaigns directed against the Bonpo and Kagyupa monasteries of Kham in particular were extended into the Gyarong region during the 18th century by **Changkya Qutuktu Rolpei Dorje**, who targeted the Bonpo and Nyingmapa in particular. Despite these efforts, the traditions of the Bonpo, Nyingmapa and Jonangpa remain strong in Gyarong and neighbouring areas to the present day.

Following the pacification of the Mongolians by the Manchu emperor **Qianlong** in the 18th century, the political vacuum in the Amdo area was filled by the Muslims, who encroached southwest from Ziling towards Jyekundo, dominating the trade routes. From 1727 until the mid-20th century the towns of the grasslands and Tsong-chu valley were controlled by the **Ma** family who looked upon the Kokonor Territory as their own protectorate. Gradually their influence filtered south from Jyekundo into Nangchen, but the nomadic areas of Golok, Sertal and Gyarong always remained beyond their jurisdiction, in the hands of the local Tibetan populace. The present Dalai Lama was born in the Tsongkha Khar area of Amdo in 1935, firmly under the control of the Muslim warlord **Ma Pu-feng**. The Tibetan government had to pay a large ransom to ensure his release and safe passage to Lhasa. In 1950, Ma Pu-feng succumbed to the PLA, leaving most of Amdo in the hands of the Communists.

Yellow River

The **Yellow River**, known in Tibetan as **Ma-chu** and in Chinese as **Huang He**, is often regarded (in its lower reaches) as the cradle of Chinese civilization. The world's sixth longest river, it flows 5,464 km (1,167 km in Tibet) from its source in the Bayankala Mountains to its estuary in the East China Sea; and has a drainage area of 745,000 sq km (of which 77,249 km are within Tibet). From its source, the river flows east, traversing **Kyaring** and **Ngoring** Lakes, then turning westwards through a hairpin bend (*khug-pa*), it crosses the **Amnye Machen** range, and flows northwards from **Rabgya**, descending in a series of rapids (fall 2m per km) to **Lanzhou**. Two enormous navigable lakes have been created by hydroelectric dams at Lugyagak and Liujiaxia. From Lanzhou, the river flows east through Ningxia, Mongolia, and the Shanxi, Henan and Shandong provinces of mainland China. The river averages a flow of 1,530 cu m per second, an annual volume of 48.2 cu km, and an precipitation of 470 mm (mostly snow-melt in the upper reaches). It is the world's muddiest river, carrying 1.52 billion tons of silt per year.

Geography

The southern border of Amdo is divided from the Salween basin of West Kham by the **Dangla** Mountains, and from the Yangzte and Yalong basins of East Kham by the rolling **Bayankala** Mountains, which form a southeast spur of the Kunluns. In the northwest, the **Altyn Tagh** range divides the Tsaidam basin of Northwest Amdo from East Turkestan (Ch Xinjiang); and in the northeast the jagged **Chokle Namgyel** Mountains (Ch Qilian) divide the Kokonor basin of Northeast Amdo from the Gansu corridor and Mongolia. In the extreme east, the **Min**, **Longmen** and **Qionglai** mountains divide the Amdo grasslands and Gyarong gorges from the mainland Chinese parts of Sichuan and Gansu.

Other ranges internally demarcate the distinct regions of Amdo and Gyarong: the **Kunluns**, which divide the Jangtang Lakes and Yangtze headwaters from the Tsaidam basin; the **Amnye Machen** range which forms the bend of the Yellow River, dividing the nomadic tribes of Golok (south) from those of Banak (north); the **Nyenpo Yurtse** range dividing Golok from Gyarong; and the **Nanshan** range, which divides Kokonor from the Yellow River basin.

The terrain of Far East Tibet is characterized by its broad valleys, rolling hills and extensive flat tableland. However, there are considerable variations between the deserts of the **Tsaidam** and **Jangtang**, the rich grasslands of **Amdo**, and the forested gorges of **Gyarong**.

In the northwest of the region, the depression of the **Tsaidam** basin is extremely low. The northwesterly parts of the Tsaidam (2,700-3,000 m) are characterized by denuded plains of bedrock; while in the lower southeast part (2,600-2,700 m) there are thick Meso-Cenozoic deposits. The terrain therefore varies between gravel, sand and clay deserts, semi-desert tundra and salt wastelands.

The **Altyn Tagh** Mountains, which divide the northwest border of the Tsaidam from the Tarim basin of East Turkestan, extend over 805 km. The western hills are rugged and rocky, above 5,700 m with perennial snow peaks and glaciers. The central part of the range is lower at 4,000 m; but is higher in the northeast, 5,000 m. There are few rivers except in the southwest, and the central portion which adjoins the Tsaidam is arid and waterless.

The **Chokle Namgyel** (Qilian) range, dividing the Kokonor basin from the Gobi desert of Mongolia, runs from northwest to southeast at an average altitude of

5,100 m. Many rivers originate from its glaciated peaks, especially the Ruo Shui (known as Etzingol River in Mongolian) which flows northwards into Mongolia. Around 4,200 m there is high altitude pastureland. The area is rich in minerals including iron, chromium, copper, lead, zinc, gold and coal.

The **Nanshan** range, which divides the Kokonor basin from the Yellow River, has an average altitude of 4,000-5,000 m; the higher western peaks being glaciated and exceeding 6,000 m. There are a number of tectonic depressions on both sides of the range, the largest being that of Lake Kokonor to the north. In the lower eastern parts of the range, where the valleys are more open, humid and warm rain penetrates. Tributaries of the Yellow River rise to the south of the range.

In the south, the **Bayankala** range divides Amdo from Kham. The northwest peaks of this range lie south of Kyareng and Ngoreng lakes, at an average altitude of 4,600-5,100 m; and they are the source of the Yellow River. The central hills of the range are rounded and rolling. The most renowned peak in the southeast is **Mount Nyenpo Yurtse** (5,369 m), the sacred mountain of the Golok, which is surrounded by five lakes.

The **Amnye Machen** range, which forms the bend of the Yellow River, extends from higher northwest peaks to lower southeast peaks. This range, which is revered as the sacred abode of the protector deity Machen Pomra, has 21 major snow peaks: the three main ones are situated towards the northwest end. Mount Dradul Lungshok (6,154 m) is the northernmost peak, Mount Amnye Machen (6,282 m) is the central peak, and Mount Chenrezik (6,127 m) is the southernmost peak. The northern Golok foothills between the Bayankala and Amnyen Machen ranges average 4,200 m.

The **Min Shan** range, which demarcates the eastern extremity of the Amdo grasslands, forms the river basins of the Minjiang and Jialing, characterized by strata of red clay, red sandstone and gypsum. This part of the plateau is exposed to higher levels of rainfall, as much as 508 mm.

Flora and fauna

The upper reaches of the Yellow River are predominantly a region of grassy hills and marshlands; but they are not entirely without trees. Small patches of spruce and fir are often found on north-facing slopes, and their presence is important in maintaining the water tables, preventing soil erosion and protecting local ecosystems. The best quality grassland also contains a wide range of flowers and grasses, but sadly many areas are now becoming overgrazed, and exhibit only a limited diversity of species. Large wild animals have almost disappeared from this region, but smaller mammals such as the pika (abra), mole, vole, rabbit and marmot have proliferated in the absence of predators. Before 1950, this area did support some large herds of yak and sheep, but banditry was rife, and many sidevalleys were rarely used for grazing. The modern emphasis on animal husbandry, the new road network and changes in stock management techniques have led to increasingly intensive use of the grasslands and a deterioration in pasture quality.

Many of the marshes have shrunk in size, threatening the habitat of wading birds, including the well known black-necked crane. In a few places, the thin top-soil has been completely eroded by the action of wind and water, causing some of this rich grassland to turn into semi-desert. Around Lake Kokonor, the plateau vegetation includes tamarisk, haloxylon, feather grass, white willow, craxyweed, astragalus, gentian and allium. Spruce forests are found on the northern slopes of the Nanshan Mountains.

People

The Tibetan population of Amdo comprises the **Drok-ke**-speaking nomads of Banak, Golok and Ngawa; the **Rong-ke**-speaking towns of the Tsong-chu valley, and the **semi Drok-ke** (also called Rongma Drok-ke) speaking settlements of Repkong, Labrang, Luchu and Jo-ne areas. The development of Tibetan literary studies in Amdo has been successfully maintained in recent decades, with the result that the region even now produces a high percentage of scholars and literati writing in the Tibetan language. Non-Tibetan languages are also spoken within the Amdo area: particularly among the **Salar** Muslims of Dowi county, the **Tu** of Gonlung and Pari counties and the **Mongols** of Sogwo county. Further south, in the Gyarong gorges and the lower Min valley, there are Tibeto-Burman populations of the ancient **Qiangic** language group, including those who speak **Tawu-ke** (in Tawu and Rongtrak), **Gyarong-ke** (in Chuchen and Tsenlha), and **Qiang-ke** in Maowen.

The **Qiang** were forced into the mountain strongholds of the Gyarong and Min valleys by the Qin and Han Emperors following their unification of China in the pre-Christian era. Their **Qiang Long** stone culture is characterized by the construction of large stone watchtowers and sturdy stone dwellings, often containing white quartz rocks which were regarded as sacred artefacts.

The rich pastures of the Amdo grasslands sustain a larger nomadic population than any other part of Tibet. These nomads, including the **Golok** (south of Amnye Machen) and the **Banak** (north of Amnye Machen) have recently benefited economically from the reforms in China, but face a long-term threat to their future from environmental deterioration. The education system is basic at best, with Tibetans forced to study Chinese if they wish to advance in their chosen career. There are few employment opportunities in this region, so most children follow their parents and become nomadic pastoralists, while a few, mostly boys, join one of the numerous monasteries that have been rebuilt in recent years. Government funds have sometimes been allotted to help rebuild these monasteries, and such sites are given a quota of timber and building materials, as well as a construction team, usually composed of Chinese craftsmen. This official help however covers little more than the basic building, and the Tibetans are forced to look to the local communities for the cost of internal and external decoration, and the construction of monastic residences. As a result, most of these monasteries are little more than concrete sheds, only the timber entrance and porch roof supports being made in traditional style. In general, shrines and statues are poorly executed, but there is a small body of well-trained artists, centred at the excellent schools of painting in **Repkong** (see below, page 608). With the exception of the main temples in **Repkong**, **Labrang** and **Kumbum**, virtually all the original monasteries of Amdo were destroyed in the Maoist era, and the vast bulk of Amdo's artistic heritage has been lost.

The West Kokonor Plateau

The paved highway 109 from Lhasa crosses the border between the Tibet Autonomous Region and Qinghai at Dang La pass (5,220 m), 85 km north of Draknak in Amdo, and then runs through the Autonomous Prefecture of West Kokonor to Kermo (Ch Golmud) and Ziling. The West Kokonor area, so-called because it lies to the west of Lake Kokonor (Tib Tsongon), comprises the sparsely populated and spacious terrain of the Jangtang Lakes and the Tsaidam basin, as well as the source of the Yangtze River. There are eight counties within the prefecture, which is administered from Kermo, 837 km northeast of Nakchu and 782 km west of Ziling. The indigenous population of Mongolians, Tibetans and Kazakhs must nowadays contend with widespread Chinese immigration, both official and unofficial. One of the great concerns is the increase in the number of lawless and unaccountable Chinese gold prospectors. ***Recommended itinerary: 6. See page 20.*** ▸▸ *For Sleeping, Eating and other listings, see pages 558-559.*

South Kermo County ལྷོ་ཀེར་མོ

→ *Population: 49,939. Area: 44,278 sq km. Colour map 6, grid B4.* 南格尔木

The highway from Lhasa breaches the **Dangla Mountains** at Dang La pass (5,220 m), 85 km north of Draknak, where there is a memorial depicting Chinese soldiers. To the west of the pass, Mount Dangula (6,022 m) is clearly visible, and the higher Mount Longyala (6,104 m) soars to the east. The road then enters the Yangtze basin, following the Bu-chu tributary as far as its confluence with the Kar-chu at **Karchudram Babtsuk** (Ch Gaerquyan). En route it passes through Dangla Maktsuk after 19 km, and reaches the hot springs of Chutsen and **Toma** township (Ch Wenquan) after 54 km further. Toma has simple guesthouse facilities beside the road which are not recommended. The coal fires used here in the spring, autumn and winter months exude noxious fumes.

From Toma a seasonal side road leads southwest for 88 km to the crystal mines between the glaciers of Mount Jang-gyen Deuruk Gangri (6,548 m) and Mount Kolha Dardong (Ch Geladandong, 6,621 m) in the Dangla range. Here and around Lake Mirik Gyadram to the southwest are the main **southern sources of the Yangtze**: the Kar-chu and the Mar-chu (Ch Tuotuohe). Climbing expeditions to Mount Kolha Dardong are organized by the Qinghai Mountaineering Association in Ziling.

Continuing on the highway from Toma, you will reach **Yanshiping** after 25 km and **Marchudram Babtsuk** (Ch Tuotuohe) on the banks of the Mar-chu after 90 km. This last settlement has better guesthouse and restaurant facilities; and just to the north of town the road crosses the **first bridge over the Yangtze. NB** From here it is possible to explore the **source of the Yangtze**, driving for 250 km, and then trekking or riding on horseback for four days.

Northeast of Marchudram Babtsuk, the highway reaches the county border after 64 km; and then traverses the extreme northwest of Drito county (see above, page 526) to cross the Chumar River, the **northern source of the Yangtze** which rises in the Kunluns. The main settlement in the Chumar valley is **Chumarhe**, 141 km northeast of the border. To the west lie the Jangtang Lakes, and the road in places passes small isolated lakes dotted over a fairly barren plain. Occasionally gazelle and kyang (wild ass) can be seen from the road but wild yak, antelope and argali can only be found in the high plains to the west. At present this area is reached by bus from the Norbulingka Bus Station in Lhasa, but by 2008 there will be a new railway line, connecting Kermu with Lhasa. Expeditions to the sources of the Yangtze are organized by the Qinghai Mountaineering Association.

South Kermo County

To Kermo
Chumarhe
Yangtze
Drito Border
141
64
Yangtze
Marchudram Babsuk (Tuotuohe)
90
(6,548m)
Yanshiping
25
Toma
(6,621m)
88
54
Dongla Maktsuk
19
Dang La (5,220m)
85
Amdo
To Nakchu and Lhaso
N
Not to scale

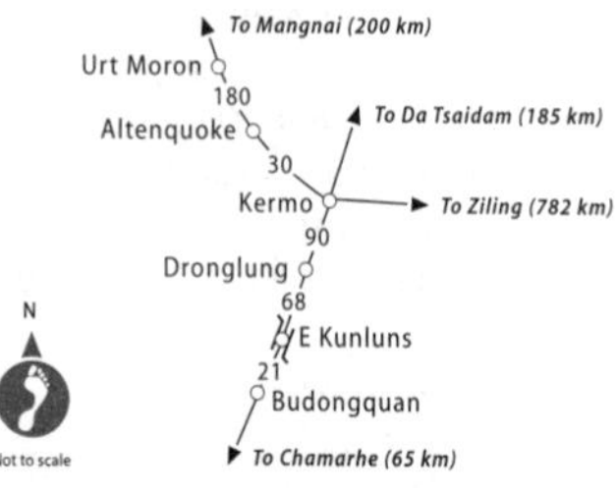

Kermo County ཀེར་མོ

→ *Population: 98,213. Area: 51,484 sq km. Colour map 6, grid B5.* 格尔木市

Kermo county lies between the Kunlun and Tsaidam Pendi ranges. Its rivers, which rise on the southern slopes of the Kunluns, flow into the salt lakes of the South Tsaidam. The county capital, **Kermo**, is located on the banks of the Kermo-chu at the Qinghai railway terminus. It is an important intersection, in that roads lead north to Gansu and northwest to Xinjiang provinces, as well as south to Lhasa and east to Ziling.

Eastern Kunluns

The highway from **Chumarhe** reaches **Budongquan** after 65 km and, leaving the Yangtze basin, crosses the pass through the Eastern Kunlun Mountains after a further 21 km. To the west lies the snow peak of **Mount Yuxu** (5,933 m), revered by Chinese Daoists as the abode of the celestial princess Yuxu, and to the east is **Mount Hohosai Kenmenho** (Ch Yuzhu, 6,178 m).

Geography Distinct from the Western Kunluns, which divide the Jangtang Plateau of Northwest Tibet from the Tarim basin of Central Asia (see above, page 547), the Eastern Kunluns are characterized by their high perennial snow line (5,700-6,000 m), low temperatures, aridness, strong winds, intense solar radiation and brief summers with rainfall under 100 mm. The mean July temperature in the higher parts of the range is less than 10°, and the nights can be bitterly cold. The winter is long with severe frosts and strong dust storms (minimum temperature -35°, and wind speed exceeding 20 m per second). The Kunlun landscape largely consists of rock desert and stagnant water pools.

Wildlife This is more plentiful here than in the Himalayas and other ranges which have been exploited more on account of their proximity to large centres of population. The ungulates of the Kunluns include the gazelle, wild ass, wild goat, wild yak, blue sheep and argali, while brown bears and wolves are also found in fewer numbers. Waterfowl are frequently seen on the saline lakes around the Kunluns during the migratory season.

The Qinghai Mountaineering Association organizes expeditions to the major peaks of the range, including **Mount Pukhala Ritse** (Ch Xinqing, 6,860 m), **Mount Achen Gangchen** (Ch Daxuefeng, 5,863 m), and **Mount Wuxuefeng** (5,804 m), all of which lie southwest of Kermo, towards the Xinjiang border.

Kermo

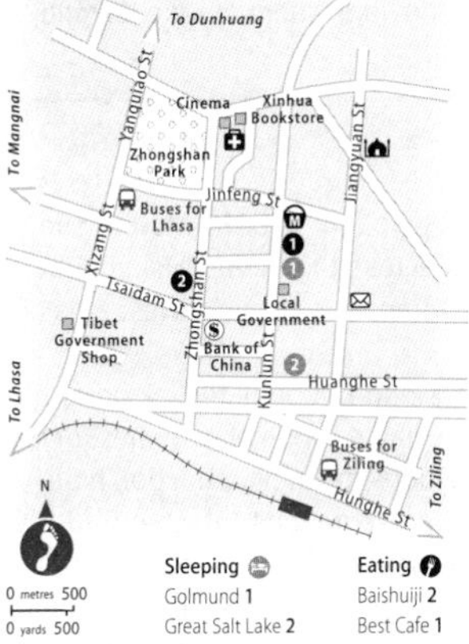

Dronglung

From the pass through the East Kunluns, the road descends into the valley known as **Dronglung** ('Wild Yak Valley') to its Tibetan herders (Mong Niaj Gol). The Kunlun foothills to the south of this valley are still home to the full range of Jangtang mammals in their upper reaches, despite the activities of professional hunters and itinerant gold miners. Here the temperature range is also extreme: averaging 25-28° in mid-summer, and -9° in mid-winter. After **Naij Tal** township (68 km from the pass), the highway leaves the spectacular plain of the Kunlun snow ranges and, below the Naij Gol River's confluence with the **Kermo-chu**, it descends through a gorge with a hydroelectric station to emerge after 90 km at Kermo city on the southern fringe of the Tsaidam desert.

Kermo City → *Altitude 2,800 m. Colour map 6, grid B6.*

Kermo (Ch Golmud) is a large new town which has developed in recent decades as a centre for potash mining, and (even more recently) oilrefining. Formerly there were barely a dozen houses here! The sprawling concrete buildings and barracks-style compounds line straight avenues, but there is little of interest in the city itself, its population largely consisting of Chinese immigrants. It is however an important transit point for visitors to Lhasa, Ziling or Dunhuang. » *For listings, see pages 558-559.*

Orientation Approaching the city on the paved highway 109 (from Lhasa via Nakchu), you will pass a turn-off on the right (Huanghe Street), which leads to the **railway station** and the **Ziling Bus Station**, and continues east out of town in the direction of Ziling. If you stay on the main road, you will head north onto **Xizang Street**, passing to the left the TAR government shops and the **Lhasa Bus Station.**

A second right turn leads from Xizang Street along **Tsaidam Street**. Take this turn-off and you will soon reach the intersections of **Zhongshan Street**, **Kunlun Street** and **Jiangyuan Street** in quick succession. The Agricultural Bank of China is located on the south side of Tsaidam Street after its intersection with Kunlun Street. On the east side of Kunlun Street itself you will find (in succession) the Best Café, the Municipal Government Buildings, the Golmud Hotel & Restaurant and the open-air market. Further along, on the opposite side, there is the People's Hospital. The Post Office is located on the corner of the Tsaidam Street and Jiangyuan Street intersection.

Returning to Xizang Street, if you head north, you will soon reach an important crossroad, from where you can head west out of town in the direction of **Mangnai** and the Xinjiang border, east via **Jinfeng Street** to the **downtown** area, or north via **Yanqiao Street**, out of town in the direction of **Dunhuang**. The cinema, Xinhua Bookstore and the Public Security Bureau are all located on Jinfeng Street.

Northern Routes from Kermo

From Kermo, you can drive due east to **Ziling** (782 km), via Dulan; or due north through the Tsaidam Pendi range to **Dunhuang** (524 km) via Lenghu and Aksay. A third and more difficult drive follows the 568-km road to **Mangya** on the Xinjiang border, but parts of this road are seasonal and sealed by the military. Alternatively, take the **train to Ziling**, which runs parallel to the Dunhuang road, before cutting east through Greater Tsaidam, Ulan and Tianjun counties and skirting the north shore of Lake Kokonor.

Mangnai District → *Population: 60,665. Area: 53,788 sq km. Colour map 6, grid A5.*

A road runs northwest from Kermo via **Altenqoke** (30 km) and **Urt Moron** (180 km), where there are borax mines. It then continues across the Kermo-Mangnai border, following a seasonal track for some 200 km as it traverses the northwest area of the **Tsaidam** desert.

The terrain here is low-lying, arid, waterless and unpopulated. Sand is blown southwest from the Mongolian plateau, and the climate is one of extremes: dry, cold and windy winters, followed by hot summers. Perhaps the main attraction here is the collection of a "thousand" natural stone representations of the Buddha in **Youyuanggou Valley**, which were formed by the erosion of the red malmstone of the Tertiary Period. The largest of these figures measures 700 m! The road surface improves around **Mangnai** (where highway 215 from neighbouring Lenghu district connects). The distance from here to the Xinjiang border is 159 km. En route you will pass to the north of Gasikule Lake, where there is a black-necked crane reserve.

Onwards to Xinjiang From the border, the road crosses the **Altyn Tagh** range to reach **Ruoqiang** in the Qaraqan valley of Xinjiang province, and thence Korla and **Urumqi**.

Greater Tsaidam County

→ *Population: 62,040. Area: 55,007 sq km. Colour map 6, grid A5.* 大柴旦

The main road north from Kermo (highway 215) follows the railway line through the **Tsaidam Pendi** range. En route it crosses a spectacularly long 32 km bridge of salt (Ch **Wangzhang**), which is the main scenic attraction around Kermo. The railway then cuts eastwards through south Tsaidam for **Ulan**, while the road heads north for the town of **Da Tsaidam** (185 km from Kermo). On reaching Da Tsaidam, you can turn right (southeast) on highway 315 for **Terlenka** (201 km) and **Ulan** (142 km), or continue north for a further 43 km to **Yuqia**, where highway 315 branches west towards **Mangnai** (351 km).

The only fertile tracts are those around Da Tsaidam and Xiao Tsaidam lakes, and further east at Hurleg and Toson lakes near Terlenka railway station. However, the oil industry has recently become a significant factor for the local economy, and there are currently plans to conduct Tsaidam natural gas and oil through new pipelines to Lanzhou in mainland China.

The complexity of the Tsaidam landscape has engendered great variation in climate, soil and vegetation. In general, there is a continental climate, the average rainfall being less than 100 mm (mostly in summer). The northwest is particularly arid and waterless. The winters are dry, cold and windy; while the summers are hot. Strong winds from the Mongolian plateau cover the region with sand. There are, however, some fertile tracts in the foothill and lakeside areas of this basin; while the southeast is a broad saline swamp formed by the rivers draining internally from the Kunluns. Only in the northeast, towards the East Nanshan mountains does the climate become milder.

Highway 215 from **Kermo** via Da Tsaidam **to Dunhuang** enters **Lenghu** district to the north of Yuqia. It passes through the unpopulated northern part of the Tsaidam desert, and after 112 km reaches the township of **Huahaizi**. From here it continues for 55 km to the Qinghai-Gansu provincial border at **Dangjin Shankou** pass, located in a defile between the Altyn Tagh and Chokle Namgyel ranges. The only oasis in these parts is the area close to the shores of **Lake Suhai**. This part of the Tsaidam is largely uninhabited, but there are occasional Kazakh settlements, related to those from neighbouring Aksay in Gansu. Recently some bizarre three-dimensional caves and cavities through the sandrock were discovered at the north-east corner of Lake Toson. It is possible to drive there and back from Terlenka in a single day (about 400 km).

Greater Tsaidam

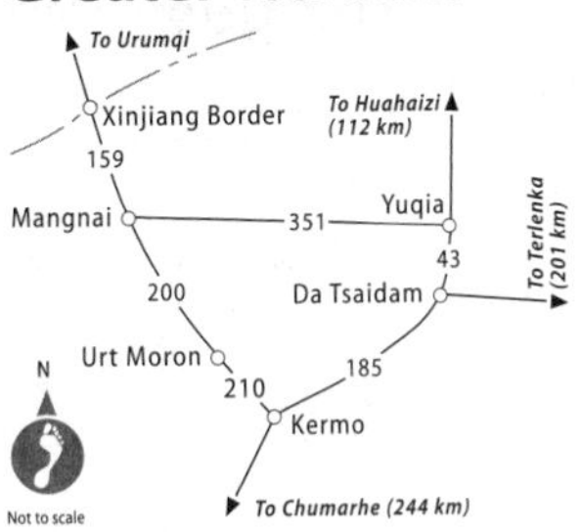

Lenghu District

Panchen Zhingde County པཎ་ཆེན་ཞིང་སྡེ

→ *Population: 54,138. Area: 53,518 sq km. Colour map 5, grid B2.* 都兰县

The paved highway 109 from Kermo to Ziling runs due east for 782 km. En route, it passes through **Panchen Zhingde** county, which has its capital at Dulan, 354 km from Kermo. The initial stretch of 250 km passes through the barren southeast fringe of the Tsaidam. Only occasional desert vegetation on low sand-dunes and stony desert breaks up the horizon as the road runs parallel to the Kunluns. Some 150 km after Kermo, a line of trees to the north marks **Nomahung**, one of the prison farms for which Qinghai is renowned, located near a prehistoric archaeological site.

Balung Hunting Ground

Leaving the desert, at Balung hamlet, there is a side road on the right (south), which leads south into the **Balung Hunting Reserve** of the Kunlun Mountains. Here, over a 127-sq-km area (average altitude: 4,200 m), the few remaining large mammals of the Tibetan plateau, including argali, gazelle, white-lipped deer, red deer, corsac foxes, wolves and marmots, can be shot for hefty fees (ranging from US$10,000 for a white-lipped deer to US$60 for a marmot). Hunting trips (definitely not recommended) are organized from mid-August until late-November, and from April until late-May. Organized hunting on this scale could be halted if ecologically sensitive wildlife tourism could be promoted successfully throughout the region. There is also a small Gelukpa monastery at Balung, which is regarded as a branch of Tashilhunpo. ▸▸ *For listings, see pages 558-559.*

Panchen Zhingde Monastery

After Balung, the highway passes through **Shang** (in Panchen Zhingde) (Ch Xiang Ride), where there are interesting stone carvings and cliff paintings. A major river cuts through the Kunlun range here, its two sources rising in Alag Lake and Dongi Tsona Lake to the south. This area is the ancestral home of several nomadic Tibetan groups at present living north of Lake Kokonor. These Shang Tibetans were forced northwards en masse into Mongolian territory during the 18th century, probably due to pressure from the Goloks. Now there are controversial plans to extend irrigation in Shang, with a view to moving non-Tibetan economic migrants here from impoverished parts of eastern Qinghai. The World Bank recently declined to participate in this project. **Panchen Zhingde**, a Gelukpa monastery affiliated to Tashilhunpo, under the patronage of local Mongolian herdsmen, is located close to the road. The original foundation is dated 1779, coinciding with the visit of the Sixth Panchen Palden Yeshe, who was en route for Beijing. In 1904 the Thirteenth Dalai Lama also stayed here on his return from Mongolia, where he had fled during the Younghusband Expedition. Further south, at **Guri**, a second hunting park can be visited. The local Nyingmapa monastery, **Guri Gonpa Samten Choling** (founded circa 1690) is 15 km southeast of Guri village. From **Lake Dongi Tsona** there is a route leading to **Tsogyenrawa** on the main Jyekundo-Ziling highway (see below, page 632).

Dulan

The county capital is located 60 km north of Panchen Zhingde, on the banks of the **Qagan Us** River. Situated in the southeast corner of the Tsaidam, where irrigated fields and tree plantations have brightened the marshy desert, it is a growing town, inhabited largely by Chinese and Muslims. In the hinterland there are Mongolian herdsmen; while

Panchen Zhingde County

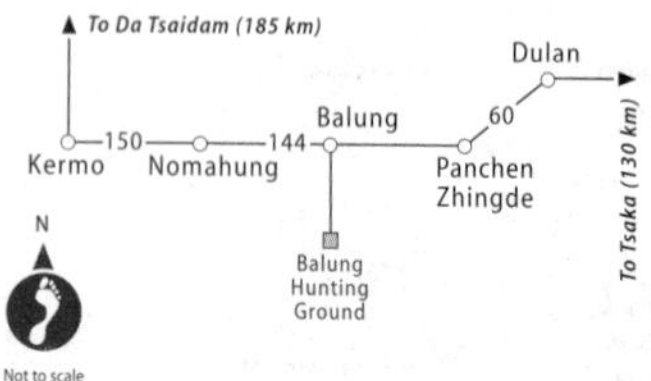

Tibetans inhabit the high mountains further south, where three monasteries are located: **Puntsok Dargyeling** and **Aten Tsamkhang** of the Gelukpa school, and **Lungmar Gonpa** which is maintained jointly by Gelukpa and Nyingmapa monks.

Ulan Sok County ཐུའུ་ལན

→ *Population: 100,594. Area: 32,959 sq km. Colour map 5, grid A2.* 乌兰县

The road and railway links from Da Tsaidam area to Ziling both pass through **Ulan Sok Dzong** county. At **Keluke Lake**, between the road and the railway tracks, there are large fish reserves. The only functioning monasteries in the west of the county are **Gormo Gonpa** and **Tenpa Pelgyeling** of the Gelukpa school, while those at **Tototala** are still in ruins. **Terlenka** (Ch Delingha), 56 km further east, where the road rejoins the railway track, is a burgeoning Chinese city, which has recently been granted a separate municipal status in Qinghai province.

Terlenka → *Population: 59,480*

Orientation Heading into town from the west, you reach **Dexin Street**, which is the main thoroughfare. Continue due east on Dexin Street, crossing the Bayan River, to reach the bus station and the railway station, and thereafter head out of town in the direction of **Ulan, Tianjun** and **Ziling**. A turn-off on the left (**Qingxin Street**) leads towards the Delingha Mosque, the Post Office, the City Government Buildings and the city, where there are department stores and the Nationalities Hotel (Minzu Fandian). A second turn-off on the left (**Kunlun Street**) leads north towards the Gansu border, while the hospitals and prefectural government offices are in the north of the city, between Kunlun Street and Tuanjie Street. ▸▸ *For listings, see pages 558-559.*

Ulan

Ulan, the county capital, lies 142 km southeast from Terlenka, at the next major intersection of the road and railway tracks. In this area there are several Mongolian settlements which have been hugely expanded by recent Chinese immigration. The important Mongolian monastery of **Ganden Sangak Yarpeling** was established 15 km to the northeast during the late 18th century by Konchok Tashi, a great grandson of Gushi Qan. Among its former treasures were a gold manuscript of the *Kangyur*, each volume reputedly weighing over 30 kg! The complex of buildings is marked by a large white stupa and a Mongolian-style invocation tower, which are visible from the motor road. The rebuilt assembly hall, which has Repkong-style murals depicting the main Gelukpa lineage-holders and meditational deities,

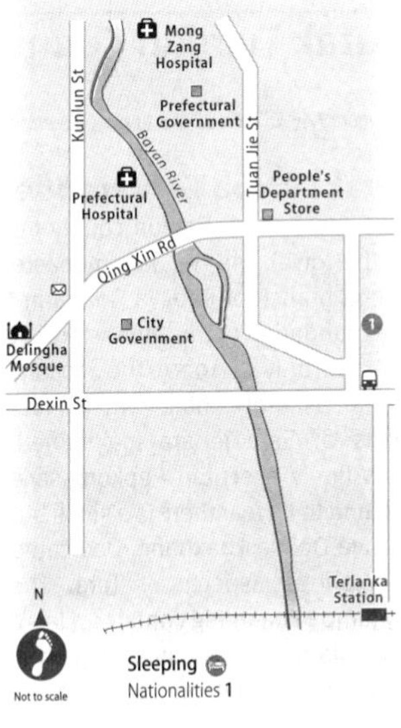

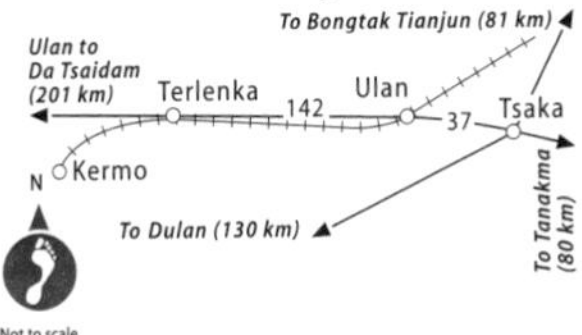

Tsaka Salt Lake

From Dulan, a pass leads northeast across the attractive Erla hills, to Wang Gaxun and the salt city of Tsaka (130 km). Tsaka is encased in salt; vast heaps of it cover the plain, buildings are encrusted, and it is even in the air you breathe. The lake offers spectacular mirages. There is a Mongolian festival here in spring connected with the small monastery in the northern hills. A network of trolley trains carries salt over the lake and a branch line (and road) lead northwest to Ulan on the Ziling-Kermo railway. Beyond Tsaka, the highway climbs southeast through a semi-desert landscape with spiky tuftgrass, into the grassy pastures of the Nanshan (South Kokonor) range. Mongolian tents and camels can typically be seen on this plain. After some 80 km you will reach the Chabcha county border, leaving the West Kokonor region behind.

nowadays houses 100 monks, who have also established a medical college to serve the local community.

Tsaka

From Ulan to **Tsaka**, on the northeast corner of **Tsaka Lake**, the distance is 37 km by road or rail. Some 8 km north of the township, there is a small branch monastery of Ganden Namgyeling, named **Ganden Gepeling,** which was founded in 1800 below Mount Changjie. West from Tsaka, there is also the monastery of **Pekhokho Gon Gendun Dekyiling**, which was originally founded as a tented encampment by the Fourth Panchen Lama, Lobzang Chokyi Gyeltsen (1570-1660). Further north in Ulan county, the Northeast Tsaidam desert is largely unpopulated, apart from a few nomadic groups in the upper reaches of the **Yangkang-chu** valley, and to the west of **Hara Lake**.

The road from Ulan via Tsaka eventually reconnects with the paved Highway 109 (linking Kermo with Ziling) and passes into Chabcha county (see below, pages 562 and 623), along the southern shore of Lake Kokonor.

Bongtak Tianjun County བོང་སྟག་ཐེམ་ཆེན་རྫོང་

→ *Population: 17,628. Area: 22,396 sq km. Colour map 5, grid A2.* 天峻县

Bongtak Gonpa Gendun Shedrubling

Heading into Bontak Tianjun county from Tsaka or Terlenka, you will pass (60 km before the town), the Gelukpa monastery of **Bongtak Gonpa Gendun Shedrubling,** which is a branch of Rabgya Gonpa in Golok (see below, page 636). Although the original foundation of this monastery is dated 1812, the complex was relocated to its present site only in 1920. The recently restored assembly hall, where the traditions of Sera Je are maintained, contains finely executed Repkong-style murals, and to its rear there is a small but impressive Dolma Lhakhang, dedicated to the various aspects of Tara. The nearby Jampa Lhakhang contains a large Maitreya, flanked by smaller images of Padmasambhava and Manjughosha.

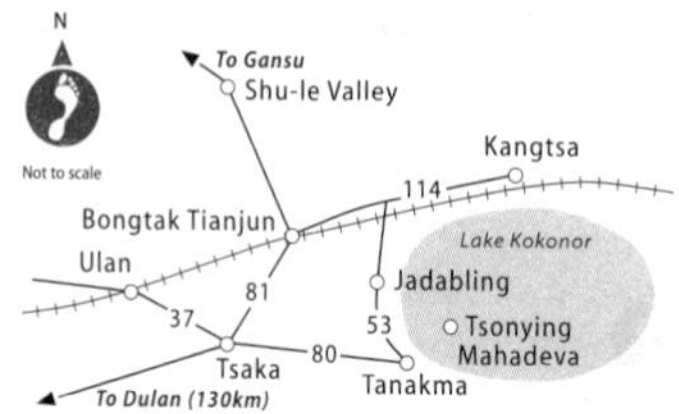

Bongtak Tianjun → *Altitude: 3,420 m. Colour map 5, grid A3*

This desolate town is located in a windswept plain where the Tsaidam tableland rolls gently down towards the west shore of Lake Kokonor. The town has grown in recent years with the development of the railway network. There is a wool and textile factory, processing the produce of the nomadic inhabitants of the Kokonor hinterland, who maintain large flocks of sheep as well as yaks. Despite its 'wild west' ambience, the town boasts guesthouses, schools, a hospital, cinema, TV station and assorted government buildings. » *For listings, see pages 558-559.*

Getting there A road link connects the town with **Tsaka**, 81 km to the southwest, and from Tianjun to **Kangtsa** on the north shore of Lake Kokonor, 114 km distance. On reaching the outskirts of town, the road crosses the railway tracks, and continues north in the direction of the Yangkang valley and the Gansu border. There are two turn-offs on the right, leading to the town centre. The first will bring you to the bus station, the railway station, and the Tianjun Government Guesthouse. Continue past the guesthouse, heading due east for Kangtsa. There are no monasteries in close proximity to the town, but further north there are Nyingmapa temples at **Mari Gonpa**, **Changho Ngakhang** and **Drakmar Gon Mindrol Dargyeling**, the last being affiliated to Dzogchen Monastery in Kham.

A jeep trail follows the **Yangkang** valley upstream from Bongtak Tianjun, and across the watershed into the Shu-le river basin. From here it runs northwest, past an area of sulphur mines, and through the **Shu-le Nanshan** branch of the Chokle Namgyel Mountains, into Gansu province. The flat gravel road east from Tianjun to **Kangtsa** (highway 315) bypasses a range of rolling hills to the south, where the snowline is low,

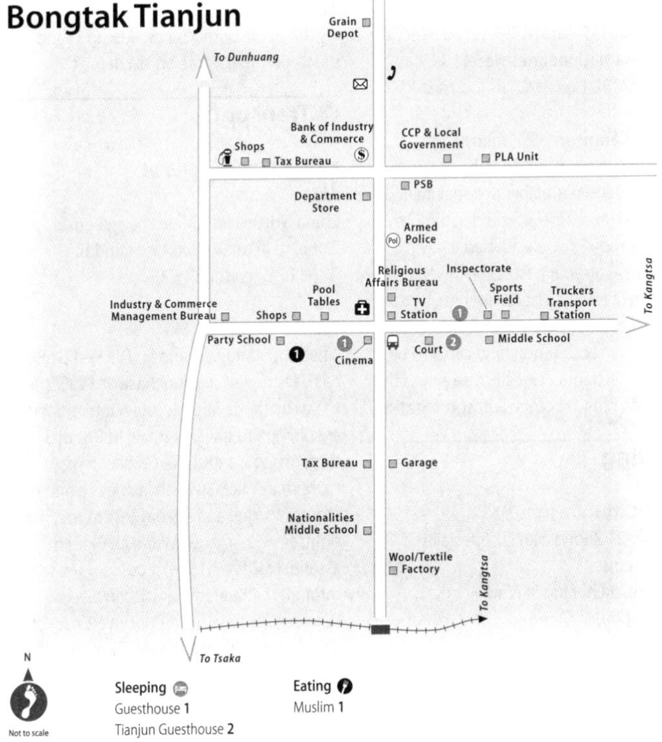

 even in May. Large flocks of sheep studiously avoid the railway tracks. After 19 km, it reaches the railway station near **Ping** township. Some 6 km to the northwest there is the small Nyingmapa monastery of **Tempung Ngakhang**, located north of the railway and south of the road. Continuing along the Kangtsa road, after 30 km, you will reach a long bridge spanning a seasonal river. From here, you pass into Kangtsa county.

Sleeping

Kermo City *p552, map p551*
C **Great Salt Lake Hotel**, 46 Huanghe Rd, T0979- 8448886, F0979-8448888. The best in town, with doubles at ¥360, singles at ¥600, and deluxe singles at ¥1,800.
C **Golmud Hotel (Golmud Binguan)**, 160 Kunlun Rd, T0979- 8412061, F0979-8412817. Has superior doubles at ¥300, standard doubles at ¥108, and guesthouse dormitories (triples at ¥28 per bed and six-beds rooms at ¥16 per bed). Public showers are available outside the hotel for budget travellers (¥3).

Balung Hunting Ground *p554*
E Accommodation is provided in Mongolian-style yurts and proper kitchen facilities including refrigeration are available.

Terlenka *p555, map p555*
E **Delingha Nationalities Hotel**, T0977-222781. Has standard rooms at ¥100.

Bongtak Tianjun *p557, map p557*
E **Tianjun Government Guesthouse**, T0977-266280. Reasonably well-maintained and heated rooms (no attached bathrooms) at ¥54 per room. You are advised to keep a watchful eye on your possessions. Even the spare tyre of a Toyota landcruiser can disappear overnight from the secure car park!

Alternative accommodation can also be found at the **Tianjun Guesthouse** across the road, and at the **Truckers' Transport Station**.

Eating

Kermo City *p552, map p551*
Baishuiji, 21 Zhongshan Lu. Speciality chicken soup.
Best Café, on Kunlun St (2nd Floor). Western food.
Golmud Hotel Restaurant, Kunlun St. Good and reasonably priced Chinese food.

Bongtak Tianjun *p557, map p557*
Tianjun Government Guesthouse, has the best restaurant in town, frequented nightly by Chinese and Tibetan government officials.

Outside, there are small Muslim and Tibetan street restaurants.

Entertainment

Kermo City *p552, map p551*
The only forms of entertainment are pool, karaoke, and tourist baiting!

Shopping

Kermo City *p552, map p551*
Try the open-air market on Kunlun St and the Department Store on Tsaidam St.

Transport

Kermo City *p552, map p551*

Air

China Northwest Airlines have regular flights to **Xi'an** (¥1,200) and **Qindao** (¥1,800), departure: 1300.

Bus

Tibet Bus Station, Xizang St, T0979-423688, has daily departures for **Lhasa** at 1400. The basic couchette fare is ¥300, but foreigners are obliged to travel in small groups of 5 through CITS, and should expect to pay more than ¥1,660 (which includes a hefty registration fee and a 3-day minimum Lhasa sightseeing package). Warm clothing is essential for the 1,150-km bus journey through the Kunluns, which can take between 28 and 35 hrs. Bus drivers may offer a discount for direct payment, but security

For an explanation of the sleeping and eating price codes used in this guide, see inside the front cover. Other relevant information is found in Essentials pages 44-46.

checkpoints have to be avoided en route. Returning 4WD landcruisers from Lhasa may also be available (¥600 per person, minimum group size 4-5), but the same security problems have to be encountered. The Main Bus Station, opposite the Kermo Railway Station, has daily bus departures for **Ziling** at 1600 (12 hrs), **Da Tsaidam** at 0800 (3 hrs), **Mangnai** at 1500 (12 hrs), and **Dunhuang** at 0800 and 1900 (¥80, 12 hrs).

Train

There are express and local services operating to **Ziling**. Train No K428 departs Kermo Railway Station at 1650 and will reach Ziling around 0511 the next morning. Train No. K5702 departs around 1840 and takes over 15 hrs, reaching Ziling around 1006 the following day. Pressurized express trains to **Nakchu** and **Lhasa** are scheduled to begin running in 2008 once the track has been laid, and will cover the journey in a single day.

Directory

Kermo City *p552, map p551*
Banks Agricultural Bank of China, Tsaidam St. **Hospitals** Golmud Hospital, 43 Kunlun Rd, T0979-412677. **Internet** There is an internet café next to the Agricultural Bank (¥15 per hr). **Telephones** China Post has an EMS service, and China Telecom sells ICC cards for DDD and IDD calls. IDD calls can also be made from the Golmud Hotel. **Tour companies** CITS, Golmud Branch, 160 Kunlun Rd, T0979-413003. **Useful addresses** Police and Public Security: Golmud City Police and Public Security Bureau, Tsaidam St. PSB Foreign Affairs Department, Jinfeng Street, for visa extensions.

North Kokonor and Tsongkha

This route follows the course of the Qinghai-Gansu railway, and its adjacent valleys. It includes the environs of Lake Kokonor, Tibet's largest lake, and the densely populated Tsong-chu valley, the main artery between the cities of Ziling and Lanzhou, where Tibetan, Mongolian, Muslim and Chinese traders have intermingled over the centuries. Also included are the lateral valleys of the Tsong-chu's south-flowing tributaries: Serkhok-chu, Julak-chu and Zhuanglang. ▸▸ *For Sleeping, Eating and other listings, see pages 587-593.*

History

A few city-states, ruled by Tibetans, had fleetingly existed in this area from the fourth century onwards, but it was not until the Yarlung Dynasty arose in Central Tibet during the seventh century that Tibetan power was consistently applied throughout the region. During the reign of Relpachen in 823 a peace treaty was signed between Tibet and China, demarcating the border at **Chorten Karpo**, near present day **Labrang** in Gansu.

When refugee monks from Central Tibet fled Lhasa following the persecution of Buddhism by King Langdarma, they settled in the Tsong-chu valley at **Ziling** and **Martsangdrak**, as well as at **Achung Namdzong** and **Dentik** further south. Here they transmitted the monastic lineage of Tibetan Buddhism to Lachen Gongpa Rabsel and ensured its continuity through to the present day.

The power vacuum, left in the wake of the Yarlung Empire's disintegration in the ninth century, was filled by the Tangut Kingdom of **Minyak** (Ch Xixia) which emerged towards the end of the 10th century, with its capital in the Ordos desert (modern Ningxia Province). Reaching its zenith in 1038 during the reign of King Si'u Gyelpo, the Tangut Kingdom ruled over Tibetans, Mongolians, Turks, Arabs and Chinese. During the 19th century, Russian explorers discovered relics and books from this little-known civilization, which Genghiz Qan and his armies completely obliterated in 1227. The surviving population are said to have fled to the Tawu and Minyak areas of Kham (on which see above, page 538).

The Mongolians ruled the area through princeling chieftains called the **Tu**, who were mostly of Mongolian and Arab descent; but who acquired Tibetan Buddhism under the influence of their Tibetan subjects. Important lamas of the Karma Kagyu and Sakya schools visited Amdo during this period and so, by the time of Tsongkhapa, several large monasteries and many small ones had been established in the Ziling valley and north of the Yellow River. Tsongkhapa himself was taught at the most important of these, **Jakhyung Gonpa**, but it is his birthplace, **Kumbum** in modern Rushar (Huangzhong) county, that later grew into one of the major monasteries of Tibet under both Mongolian and Manchu patronage.

Political power remained in the hands of Mongolian tribes who became zealous patrons of the Gelukpa school. During the 17th and 18th century, Gushi Qan of the Qosot Mongolians and Sonam Rabten of the Dzungars both launched sectarian assaults on Tibet. By the time the Mongol tribes were brought to heel by the Manchus in the mid-18th century, the Kokonor and Tsong-chu areas had fallen under the control of Muslim warlords; and so they remained until the Communist occupation of the mid-20th century. It is important to note that despite the variable political climate in Amdo, it was Tibetan culture that provided the common ground to these disparate populations.

Nowadays this region consists of 13 counties, of which 12 are in Qinghai and only one in Gansu. The former include all four counties of the Tibetan Autonomous Prefecture of North Kokonor and all eight counties of Ziling district, while the latter is the remote Pari autonomous county on the Zhuanglang River.

Recommended itineraries: 6 and 8. See page 20.

Kangtsa County ཀང་ཚ

→ *Population: 38,880. Area: 9,155 sq km. Colour map5, grid A3.* 刚察县

The county of Kangtsa occupies the area around the west and northwest shores of Lake Kokonor and its hinterland. The county capital, Kangtsa, which is part of the North Kokonor Tibetan Autonomous Prefecture, lies 114 km east of Bongtak Tianjun and 110 km northwest of Dabzhi, on the railway line and northern shore road to Ziling (highway 315).

Lake Kokonor

The largest lake on the Tibet plateau, 4,456 m in area, known in Mongolian as **Kokonor** and in Tibetan as **Tsongon** (Ch Qinghai, Eng Blue Lake), gives its name to the present-day province of Qinghai. In former times the wide open shores of this saline lake provided rich pastures for both Tibetan and Mongolian nomads. However, the 'vast and magnificent pasturage of Kokonor', where Abbé Huc reported 'vegetation so vigorous that the grass grows up to the stomachs of our camels' and where other visitors of old reported sightings of gazelle and Tibetan wild ass, has been sadly degraded by intensive grazing and a spread of cultivation near the lake shore. The fields of yellow rape in the summer attract numerous bee-keepers from the eastern provinces of China, and groups of hives are scattered all over the plains. At this time, most of the local Tibetans have moved their herds south into the mountains, but a few tents remain near the lake for the whole year. In August, a delicious yellow mushroom

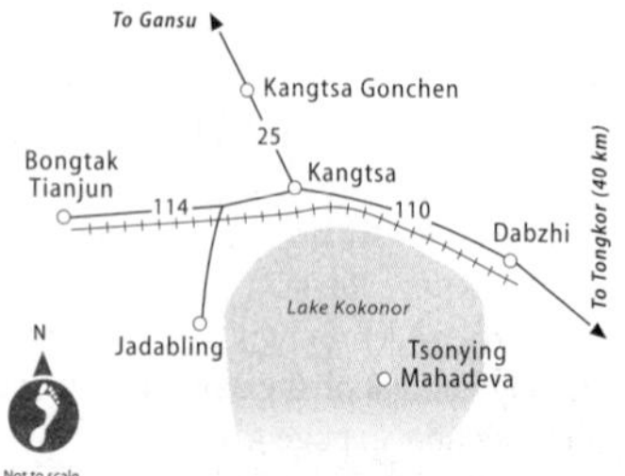

is sold to passing traffic by Tibetans at the roadside. Fish is also occasionally offered but the official fishing fleet, based at the southeast corner of the lake, takes the bulk of the 5,000 ton annual catch of scaleless carp. Nowadays, the shores of the lake and their environs are administered from four counties: Kangtsa in the west and northwest, Dabzhi in the northeast, Tongkor in the east, and Chabcha in the south.

Hetugang

Driving from Bongtak Tianjun, the gravel road enters Kangtsa county after 49 km. At **Kyimon** township, 6 km further, the road crosses south of the railway tracks, and gradually descends towards the northwest shore of Lake Kokonor. A trail leads north to the Nyingmapa monasteries of **Pontsang Gongma Gonpa** (10 km) and **Chuknor Gon Dongak Shedrub Dargyeling** (17 km), which is located at the foot of a table mountain, while another leads northeast (20 km) to **Rumang Gonpa**, a branch of distant Dzitsa Monastery in Bayan Khar county. After Kyimon, the blue atmospheric haze of the lake rises in the distance, contrasting with the barren landscape, and after 22 km the highway intersects with the road leading along the west shore, frequently criss-crossing the railway line en route. The west shore of the lake is known as **Hetugang** and here, there are two noteworthy sites: the **Bird Island Sanctuary** (Tib Jadabling, Ch Niao Dao), and the nearby Nyingmapa monastery of **Sato Kalden Tashi Chokhorling**.

Jadabling ⓘ *The sanctuary is open 0830-1730 daily, admission fee: ¥40 per person, payable at the Bird Sanctuary Management Office (Ch Guanlicu) in the Bird Island Hotel outside the park, and there is a further ¥2 charge for entry to the hatching room, though the best nesting sites are 16 km further along the peninsula.* The bird island sanctuary (Jadabling), known in Chinese as Niao Dao, is a national reserve located on a peninsula of the west shore of the lake, 29 km south of the Tianjun/Kangtsa highway and 53 km north of **Tanakma** (Ch Heimahe) in Chabcha county. It is also accessible by train from the rail head at **Sixin**. There are local inhabitants of Hetugang who can still recall the days when the site was a true island, but the waters of the lake have receded in recent decades, forming a narrow peninsula. In spring, more than 100,000 birds of 26 different species, including brown-headed gulls, fish gulls, speckle-headed wild geese, cormorants and red-spotted ducks, converge at this peninsula, their tumult reminiscent of a crowded sports stadium. April, May, June and early July are the best months for nesting

Lake Kokonor

Legends of Lake Kokonor

The island or Tsonying Mahedeva has several legendary origins. One, encountered by Abbé Huc, details how the lake was connected to Lhasa by an underground sea, which caused a temple being constructed there to constantly fall down. An old Mongolian shepherd carelessly gave away his secret to a passing lama and the sea flooded out as Kokonor. Another, recounted by Sven Hedin and Dr Rijnhart, recalls a great lama who dug up one white and one black root. He cut the black root, out of which the lake's water fortunately emerged. If he had cut the white root, the lake would have been full of milk and thus unsuitable for use as pastureland! In these legends the island forms the plug which dams the underground sea. In Chinese chronicles over 2,000 years the island is regarded as the breeding place of the fastest horses on earth: the dragon colts, which were born from mares released on the island. Throughout the centuries important lamas, such as Zhabkar Tsokdruk Rangdrol, have passed periods of time in retreat on Tsonying Mahadeva.

barheaded geese, gulls, terns and even an occasional black-necked crane. At nearby **Cormorant Island** (Ch Liuci Diao), a black rocky outcrop is home to nesting cormorants throughout the summer. ▸▸ *For listings, see pages 587-593.*

Sato Kalden Tashi Chokhorling Above the village of Jadabling and its tented camp, there is an important Nyingmapa monastery. **Sato Kalden Tashi Chokhorling** is a branch of Dzogchen Monastery (see above, page 505), originally founded in 1665 on a site sanctified by the Fifth Dalai Lama on his return journey to Lhasa from Beijing, where he had gone to visit the Manchu emperor, Shun Zhi. There are four stupas and four large temples, and a hillside where the rocks are carved with the syllables of the Vajra Guru mantra of Padmasambhava. Apart from the **Gonkhang**, dedicated to the foremost protectors of the Nyingma tradition, the main buildings are located to the left of the complex. Here, the restored **assembly hall** (area 300 sq m) contains images of Padmasambhava, Maitreya, Shakyamuni, Four-armed Avalokiteshvara and Padmapani. Adjacent to the assembly hall there is the **Menpa Tratsang**, dedicated to the medicine buddha Bhaisajyaguru, and the **Guru Lhakhang**, containing a large image of Padmakara, and murals depicting Aksobhya, Bhaisajyaguru, Tara, Mahakarunika, Sitatapatra, Shakyamuni Buddha and the 16 Elders. To its left is the residence of the monastery's presiding lamas and tulkus, its temple containing an image of Padmakara and excellent murals of the Peaceful and Wrathful Deities, Bhaisajyaguru and Zangdokpelri. Nowadays, there are 60-70 monks at Sato.

Hetugang to Tanakma

An excellent paved road leads from the bird sanctuary at Jadabling along the west shore of the lake to Tanakma. The road owes its construction to the patronage of an Australian visitor whose wife died in a car accident close to the sanctuary, some 15 years ago (her tomb is located within the grounds of the sanctuary). After 27 km, the road crosses a pass (3,240 m) and winds its way through excellent lakeside grazing pastures to Tanakma, 37 km distant, in Chabcha county (see page 623). Here, it links up with the Ziling-Lhasa highway 109, giving access to Tsaka and to the southern shore of Lake Kokonor.

Tanakma → *Altitude: 3,060 m*

Tanakma (Heimahe) is a modern roadside town on the southwest edge of Kokonor. From here, public buses run to Kermo on the highway to Lhasa, and directly to Ziling

(¥21, five hours). Tsaka (see above, page 556) lies 79 km to the west. Excellent grazing pastures sustain large herds of yak and sheep. Near the town, there are two small monasteries: the newly-founded Gelukpa Gonpa of **Lamoti**, two hours' walk away, and **Gyasho Benkhar**, also called Gyayi Ngotsar Tardrenling, founded by Jeu Neten Lobzang Nyima in the 16th century, which is several hours' walk to the southeast. About 35 km northwest of Tanakma is **Karsho Gonpa** of the Gelukpa school, which was founded by Tashi Gyatso. ⏩ *For listings, see pages 587-593.*

Southern Shore of Lake Kokonor

Driving along the southern shore of Lake Kokonor from Tanakma through rich grassland, after 49 km the road passes through the township of **Jiangxigou**. Accommodation is available at the Electric Company Hotel (Lokhang Dronkhang), and there are a few shops and Muslim restaurants alongside. The island of **Tsonying Mahadeva** now comes into view. In July and August the shore is carpeted with brilliant yellow rape flowers and the Kokonor range (Ch Nanshan), which once met the waters of the lake, divides the lowlands (3,240 m) from the Yellow River basin beyond. Some 14 km further east, at **Khyamri**, there is the Qinghai Tented Hotel (Tib Bagur Dronkhang).

Tsonying Mahadeva

There are several small Gelukpa and Nyingma monasteries in the hills around the lake, but the most important religious site is on a small island in the centre, known as **Tsonying Mahadeva**, the 'heart of the lake' (Ch Haixin Shan). This temple, founded on the ruins of a Tang dynasty fortress, destroyed in 748 by the Tibetan army, was inhabited by only a handful of monks. It used to be isolated for most of the year, since boats were not permitted on the lake. The monks could therefore only be reached during the three-month winter period when the lake froze sufficiently deeply for it to be safely crossed.

Nowadays, the island receives regular tour boats from the Qinghai Tented Hotel and is occasionally visited by fishing vessels. The tour-boat has a capacity of around 60 people and costs about ¥1,660 to hire for the day, so casual visitors must hope to be able to join a pre-existing tour. Barely an hour is spent on the hilly island, but the boat continues to other rocky outcrops where colonies of birds can be found.

Khyamri to Rikmon (Ch Daotonghe)

Driving 15 km east from Khyamri, the road reaches a fish farm and the Kokonor fishing fleet, which is stationed near the southeast corner of the lake. After a further 7 km, a turn-off leads 15 km north to the **Qinghai Farming Commune** on the east shore of the lake. The highway abruptly leaves Lake Kokonor for the **Rikmon** (Daotonghe) intersection, 28 km distant (see below, page 623). Northwest of Rikmon, close to the east shore of the lake, there are two small monasteries, the most significant being **Ganden Tashi Rabgyeling**, 15 km from Rikmon, which was originally a Mongolian tented monastery before becoming a branch of Jakhyung, under the guidance of the female incarnation Tulku Damdo Dolma. ⏩ *For listings, see pages 587-593.*

Kangtsa Town

Returning from the Jadabling Bird Sanctuary north to the intersection on Highway 315 (see above), turn right, and follow the railway line along the north shore of Lake Kokonor. The gravel road quickly turns to hard earth and mud, and the grazing pastures are of poorer quality. After 15 km, the road passes through **Tsokyil** township, from where the Nyingmapa monastery of **Jokor Gon Puntsok Namgyeling** and the Gelukpa monastery of **Khotse Gonpa** are accessible to the north. Both were founded in the 1930s and are currently under reconstruction. The villages after Tsokyil are bedecked with colourful prayer flags, as you negotiate the muddy road surface through to the county town. About 2 km before reaching town, a turn-off on the left leads inland to Kangtsa Gonchen, a branch of the Gelukpa monastery of Dzitsa in Bayan Khar county (see below, page 595). This impressive establishment, some 20 km inland, is considered to be the oldest monastery in the county.

Orientation Approaching the town from Tianjun (114 km distant) or the Bird Island Sanctuary (62 km), the road crosses the Kangtsa river, which flows south into Lake Kokonor. A turn-off on the right, just before the bridge, leads to Kangtsa railway station (10 km) and the Qinghai Agricultural Farm. After the bridge, you will pass (left) the petrol station, the leather factory and the tax bureau, and (right) Muslim restaurants, the bus station and the China Construction Bank. Then, reaching an intersection, turn left (north) for the road out of town to **Kangtsa Gonchen**, right (south) for **Dabzhi** county, or continue straight ahead for the Xinhua bookstore, the pharmacy or primary school. Taking the Gonchen Road, you will pass (left) the China Agricultural Bank, the Procurator's Office, and the Water Company, and (right) the post office, the armed police, the PSB and a health clinic. On the Dabzhi Road, you will pass (left) shops, the Nationalities' Trading Company, the China Agricultural Bank, the Department of Animal Husbandry, the TV and radio stations, the government buildings and the Nationalities' Middle School, while to the right are the Nationalities' Trade Building, the market, the County Peoples' Hospital, the Electric Company, a wool-washing factory and a newly opened restaurant.

Kangtsa Gonchen → *Altitude: 3,450 m*

Kangtsa Gonchen of the Gelukpa school, is located 25 km northwest of the town. Follow the east bank of the Kangtsa river upstream from town, to cross a pass (3,240 m). The surface is rough and broken by several streams, which have to be forded. After 10 km a stupa is passed above the river bank on the right, and the extensive buildings of **Kangtsa Gonchung** are visible on a distant ridge above the west bank. After a further 2 km, the small Gelukpa monastery of **Gyanyak Gonpa** comes into view in a side valley adjacent to Kangtsa Gonchung. Then, after 11 km, you will reach an intersection. Continue north for the **Chilen** region (see below, page 568) on an extremely rough surface, or turn right for Kangtsa Gonchen (2 km).

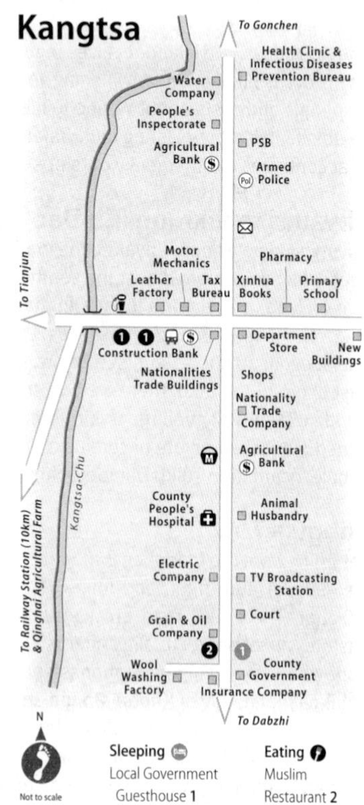

The monastery of **Kangtsa Gonchen Ganden Chopeling**, like its sister monasteries across the valley, is a branch of Dzitsa. The complex was originally founded in 1915 as a tented encampment, and the first adobe buildings were erected only in 1925. The restored **assembly hall**, approached through a cluster of stupas and Mani Wheels has a façade draped with blue and black yak hair canopies. Its portico has images of the Four Guardian Kings and an inscription outlining the history of the monastery. The central images are of Tsongkhapa and Shakyamuni, flanked by their students and the volumes of the Buddhist canon, along with Vajrasattva, Vajrapani, Padmasambhava, Maitreya, Hayagriva and local lamas. The central throne has photographs of the Fourteenth Dalai Lama and the Tenth Panchen Lama, while the murals, in Repkong style, depict (left) Shridevi, Tara, Sarvavid Vairocana, Mahakarunika and Guhyasamaja; and (right) Lama Chopa, Shakyamuni, Bhaisajyaguru (twice) and Six-armed Mahakala. To the left of the assembly hall, which currently houses 80 monks, there is the **Dukar Lhakhang**, containing a large image of Sitatapatra, and the residence of Alak Shenyen.

Kangtsa to Dabzhi

The highway from Kangtsa to Dabzhi (122 km) runs some distance north of the lake, which is no longer visible. A pass (3,300 m) is crossed after 3 km, and several motorable trails lead down to the lakeside. The roadside fields are increasingly cultivated in these parts. **Har-ge** township soon comes into view, 28 km from Kangtsa. From here trails lead north for 16 km to the ruined Gelukpa monastery of **Pontsang Zholma Gon** and northeast for 16 km to **Tashi Chokhorling**, another Gelukpa establishment, which is now undergoing reconstruction. After Har-ge, the road crosses the railway line and soon, after 7 km, enters Dabzhi county.

Dabzhi County མདའ་གཞི

→ *Population: 31,287. Area: 4,195 sq km. Colour map 5, grid A3.* 海晏县

The county of Dabzhi (Ch Haiyan) occupies the northeast shore of Lake Kokonor and the Tsong-chu River, which flows through the area traditionally known as Tsongkha via Ziling city to its confluence with the Yellow River near Lanzhou, rises in its hinterland.

The county capital is **Haiyan** (Sanjiaocheng), 122 km southeast of Kangtsa and 40 km northwest of Tongkor (Ch Huangyuan). Only 13 km inland from Haiyan, at **Nubtso** (Ch Xihai) the ghost town of China's defunct nuclear bomb factory was transformed in 1996 into the administrative capital of the North Kokonor Tibetan Autonomous Prefecture, formerly located at Mongyon.

Har-ge to Haiyan

Entering Dabzhi county from Kangtsa, the road crosses a long bridge, and after 10 km reaches an important intersection. Both roads lead to Ziling! The southern approach (152 km) passes through the county town of Haiyan and the northern one is an excellent paved road (146 km), which appears on no published maps because it passes through Nubtso, the first manufacturing plant of China's nuclear arsenal. Taking the longer route, a second intersection is reached after 11 km. Turn north for the mining town of **Reshui** in upper Kangtsa (68 km) or continue southeast for 65 km to reach Haiyan town.

On the shorter route, you quickly cross a pass (3,240 m) and descend to the shore of **Lake Tsochung Norbu** (Ch Ga hai). After skirting the north shore of this lake for 28 km, another pass (3,270 m) bedecked with prayer flags is crossed, and on the descent you can see to the right the ruins of the Gelukpa monastery of **Ngod Ariktang**, which was built by Rushokpa to fulfil a prophecy made by the Third Dalai Lama Sonam Gyatso during the 16th century. Some 4 km south of **Qinghaihu** village, near the northeast shore of the Lake Kokonor there is the Gelukpa monastery of **Lamo Gartok Kuntu Deweiling**, a branch of Lamo Dechen Monastery in Jentsa county (see below, page 600). The foundation of

Dabzhi County

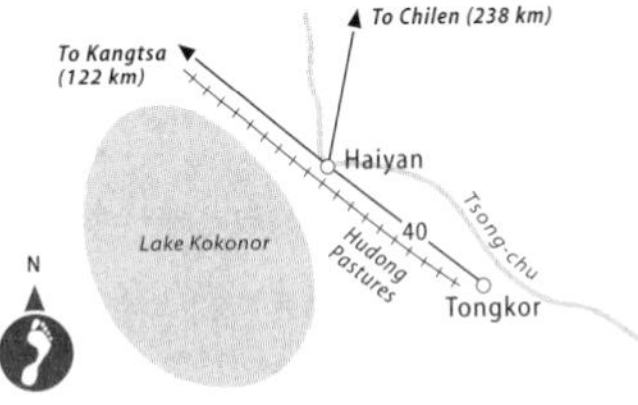

 this monastery is attributed to the Fifth Lamo Zhabdrung Karpo Nomonqan (1660-1728), who established a tented encampment here following a tribal migration from the Jentsa area. In 1916, the Seventh Zhabdrung Karpo (1873-1927) erected the first adobe buildings, and the complex that can be visited at the present day was reconstructed from 1981 onwards. The assembly hall, housing 100 monks, contains impressive bronze images of Shakyamuni, Maitreya, Manjughosa and Tara, and exquisite Repkong-style murals. Alongside there is a Dungten Lhakhang, containing the reliquary stupa of the seventh Zhabdrung Karpo. The **Hudong** pastures by the lake shore provide excellent grazing for nomadic livestock. Adjoining Lamo Gartok, there is also a newly established Gelukpa monastery, called **Dabzhi Gonsar Namgyeling**, yet another branch of Lamo Dechen, which was relocated in 1987 from a monastery of the same name in the **Bayan** township of neighbouring Tongkor county.

Bridges now carry the railway line back and forth across the road. A brick kiln factory is passed on the left, followed by two intersections, only 1 km apart. Take the left turn on both occasions, and you will arrive immediately in Haiyan town.

Haiyan → *Altitude: 3,000 m*

Entering from the main Kangtsa-Ziling road (highway 315), you will pass on the right government tax buildings, the Haiyan Guesthouse and the County Peoples' Hospital. On the left, after the PLA barracks, there is a turn-off leading into **Market Street** where banks, the Nationalities Trade Company and the Xinhua Bookstore are located, alongside a number of well stocked fruit and vegetable stalls. A second turn-off on the left leads to the PSB, the post office, the local government, more banks, restaurants and the Peace Hotel (Ch Hoping Fandian).

Nubtso → *For listings, see pages 587-593.*

If you turn right at the intersection before Haiyan town, you will enter the valley between the hills which Chinese inhabitants have named Reclining Buddha and Dragon peaks, and after 13 km you will reach **Nubtso** (Ch Xihai), a large surreal town of Soviet-style factories and residential buildings which was constructed during the 1950s as a manufacturing plant for China's first nuclear arsenal. The town (Altitude: 3,090 m) was apparently constructed on the site of an ancient Han Dynasty military garrison, although the 18th-century Gelukpa monastery of Machak Gon Ganden Puntsoling had to be destroyed to make way for a factory. The monks have more recently been relocated at Lamo Gartok. In 1996 this ghost town with its excellent infrastructure of paved roads was officially opened, though conspicuously absent from the maps, and it was given the status of prefectural capital of North Kokonor.

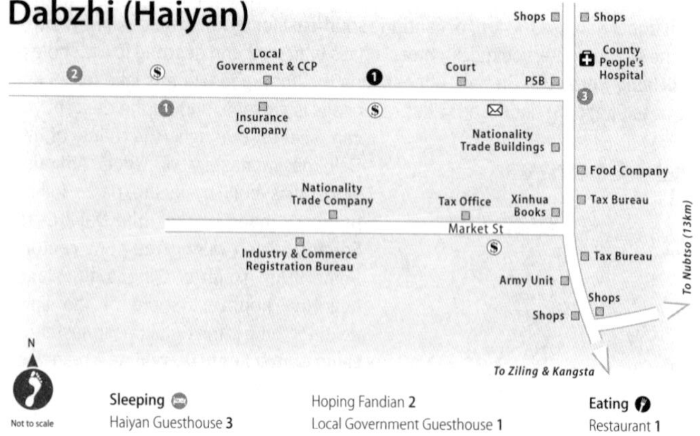

Entering Nubtso from Haiyan, you will pass on the right a race track, where the North Kokonor inaugural horse festival was held in 1997. Continue north along this road for the mining town of **Reshui**, 92 km distant, or turn left into **Main Street**. Here, on the right are the bus station, the PSB and prefectural government buildings, while on the left you will pass a monument dedicated to China's first nuclear arsenal, the market, the National Security Bureau and the library. Reaching a crossroads, you can continue straight ahead for the Communist Party building, the Government Dining Hall, the Peoples' Hospital, Sanitation Dept and Tibetan Hospital; or else turn right for the North Kokonor Hotel (Heibei Binguan). Near this hotel there is a large park, dominated by a horse sculpture commemorating the national unity of China, and beyond the park there is the Cultural Palace and a number of banks, restaurants and cinemas. Nonetheless, the population is small, and the broad, well-paved streets, flanked by Soviet-style buildings, still have the air of a desolate ghost town. One can easily imagine them filled with the throngs of factory workers who were sent here to manufacture the bomb. Radiating out from the town into the hinterland there is a complex network of paved roads, some leading to factory buildings, others into solid rock, or underground bunkers! Industrial workers, engineers and scientists were once bussed from nondescript apartment buildings to their respective work sites, but tight security ensured that very few personnel had access to the whole labyrinth.

Dabzhi to Reshui and Chilen

The road north from Nubtso to **Reshui** (98 km) initially passes through the outlying factories of this former nuclear manufacturing zone. Air raid shelters are now used as donkey stables. After 25 km, it crosses a pass (3,390 m), on both sides of which there are excellent grasslands for sheep. Descending from the pass, after 9 km an intersection is reached. Turn left for Haiyan town, continue straight ahead for Kangtsa, or turn right for Reshui. Heading towards Reshui, the road re-enters Kangtsa county, and begins its gradual ascent towards the **Chokle Namgyel** (Chilen) range. Many trucks pass by, weighed down with coal from the Reshui mines, and after 45 km the paved surface gives way to the old familiar dirt road. The distant snowline now comes into view, and the Reshui branch railway line is crossed on the way into town. After following this dirt road for 16 km, you will arrive at **Reshui** (Altitude: 3,510 m), a drab mining town, where several side roads lead directly to the pits. Continuing uphill, north out of town, after 10 km the road surface becomes extremely rough. An intersection now looms: turn left for the Jiangcu coal mine (97 km) or right for Chilen (104 km). Taking the latter route, you drive through pastures where yaks are grazing, and a pass (3,810 m) is crossed after 4 km, leading downhill for 17 km to the upper reaches of the Julak-chu. Crossing the river, the road forks yet again, a rough track

Nubtso Tsojang Prefectural Town (Xihai Zhen)

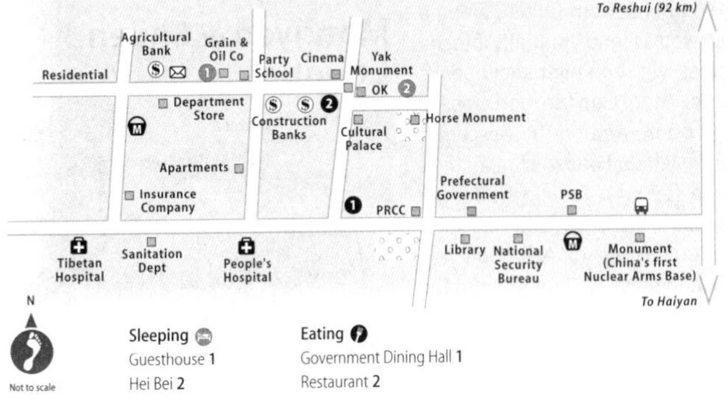

 heading north-east for Chilen (82 km) and a better surface leading east to **Mo-le** township (10 km). The Chilen road follows a tributary of the Julak-chu upstream into the Chokle Namgyel range, crossing five passes and frozen streams. The highest of these passes (4,050 m) forms a watershed between the Julak-chu and a tributary of the Rui Shui, which flows northwards through Gansu and Inner Mongolia. The snowline is low, and the road is often impassable, even in April.

Chilen County → *Population: 44,964. Area: 13,575 sq km.* 祁连县

Chilen county lies across the watershed, deep within the Chokle Namgyel range, and is administered nowadays from Nubtso, within the North Kokonor Autonomous Prefecture. This is a culturally diverse region, and prior to 1958 there were six Gelukpa monasteries in the county, which have all been permitted to reopen in recent years. The largest and most renowned among them is Arik Gon Ganden Chopeling. The county town, which derives its name from the Chinese name for the Chokle Namgyel Mountains, is 170 km northwest of Mongyon, and 212 km from Nubtso. Buses also run from Ziling to this remote border area.

Chilen has been identified with the ancient kingdom of **Bhatahor**, from which the Tibetan imperial armies acquired Shingjachen, a sacred bird-image of the protector deity Pehar, during the eighth century.

Reshui to Chilen

After crossing the watershed from Reshui (see above), the road enters a deep glacial gorge. The tree line begins at 3,360 m after 16 km, and soon red sandstone cliffs appear, but the upper reaches of the valley are still dominated by the snow peaks of the **West Chokle Namgyel**. Nomadic Tibetan groups pitch their tents amid the evergreens. After a further 11 km the first village is passed, with a small Chinese-style mosque. Then, following the river downstream, after 5 km, the road reaches an intersection at the outskirts of **Chilen** town. Turn left for the defunct monastery of **Huangzangsi** (8 km), which is now a mosque, or left for the town, which is only 2 km distant.

Chilen → *Altitude: 2,760 m*

Chilen town is a picturesque alpine settlement, overlooked by the high snow peaks of the West Chokle Namgyel range. A bridge spans a small tributary of the Hei River and leads into the long main street. Here, there are shops, banks, guesthouses and the bus station, as well as the usual government buildings, police station and hospitals. The population is predominantly Muslim, but there are also Mongolians, Tibetans and Chinese traders in the marketplace. ➤➤ *For listings, see pages 587-593.*

Arik Gonchen

Heading southeast from Chilen, along a dusty road, you ascend gradually into the alpine forest, with the high snow peaks to the south. After 11 km the road crosses a pass (3,000 m) and on the descent it divides. Turn left for **Ebao** (52 km) or right for **Xiaobao** (18 km). Taking the former road, the valley soon widens and after 7 km the monastery of **Arik Gonchen Ganden Chopeling** is reached on the high ground to the left. This isolated Gelukpa monastery was constructed during the 17th century by the Arik

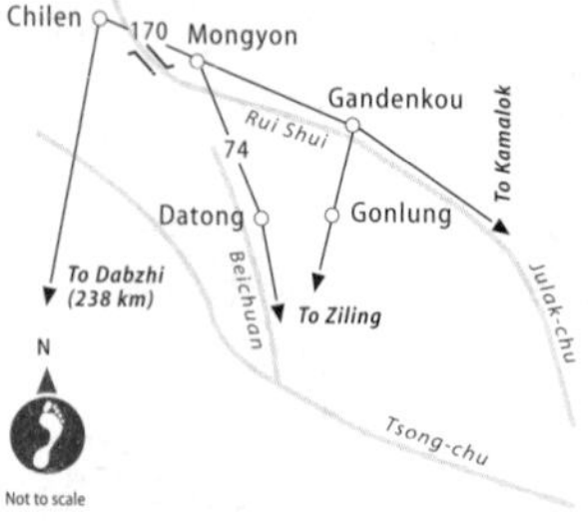

Mongolians of Sogwo county (Henan), to commemorate the site where both the Third and Fifth Dalai Lamas had stayed. There is a protector shrine room and to its rear, through an ornate gateway, an **assembly hall** with a trilingual inscription above the door. Inside, the throne has photographs of the late Tenth Panchen Lama and Lama Gari, who currently presides over the monastery's 40 monks from his residence at Nubtso. The murals, which are in Repkong style, depict (left): Amnye Nyizang, Shridevi, Vaishravana, Mahakarunika, Sarvavid Vairocana, Tara and Guhyasamaja; along with (right): Shakyamuni, Lama Chopa, the Thirty-five Confession Buddhas, Bhaisajyaguru, two local protectors, Dharmaraja and Dorje Lekpa. Along the innermost wall are reliquaries containing the remains of Arik Dorje Chang of Repkong and other lamas, as well as a full set of the *Kangyur*, and images of Vajrabhairava, Shakyamuni, Manjughosa, and Vajrasattva in union with consort.

Ebao

After Arik, the road continues to follow the north side of the West Chokle Namgyel range through excellent grazing pastures which sustain large herds of yak. A small temple and the ruins of **Demang Ganden Samtenling** monastery (founded 1940s) are passed on the left. Ebao township, dominated by a bizarre mock castle, is eventually reached after 45 km. Here the road intersects with the paved Highway 227. Head north for Zhangye and **Dunhuang** in Gansu, or south for **Mongyon** and Ziling. Taking the latter route, the valley soon narrows into a gorge, with snow peaks rising both to the south and the north. The watershed pass (3,720 m) is reached 24 km after Ebao, and at this point the road enters Mongyon county.

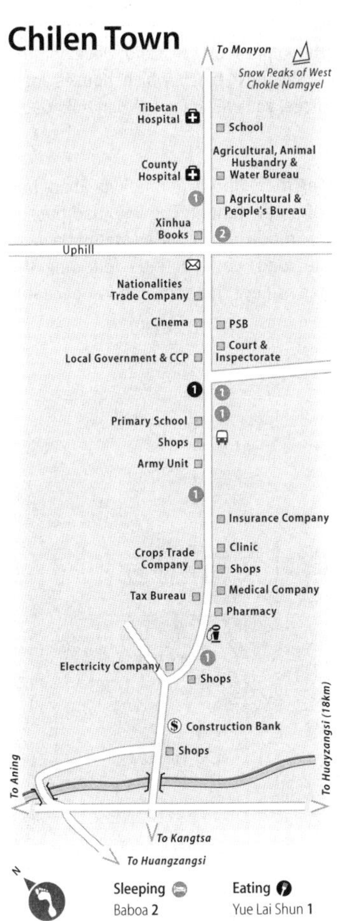

Mongyon Hui Autonomous County

མོང་ཡོན → *Population: 147,849.*

Area: 5,497 sq km. Colour map 5, grid A4.

Mongyon county occupies the mid-reaches of the **Julak-chu**, which converges with the Tsong-chu at Minhe, after flowing through a gorge between the East Chokle Namgyel range to the north and Mount Dawa to the south. Further north lie the Gansu corridor and Mongolia, so this is truly the northeast extremity of Amdo. Until 1996, Mongyon functioned as the prefectural capital of North Kokonor. The county town is located 74 km north of Datong in **Serkhok**, and is largely populated by Muslims. There are, however, isolated Gelukpa monasteries further southeast, on or near the north bank of the Julak-chu.

Ebao to Mongyon

Crossing the watershed from Ebao in Chilen county, the road re-enters the Julak-chu valley. The streams here are frozen, even in May, but the road surface is excellent. Gold-dredging machines can be seen at work in this area. A second pass (3,420 m) is crossed after 25 km, and the only inhabitants of this snowbound terrain are a few groups of hardy Tibetan nomads. On its descent the road enters the Julak-chu valley, following the north bank of the river down to **Qingshizui** township (32 km), where it forks: the highway on the right leading to **Ziling** (132 km) and the branch road to the left leading into **Mongyon** (20 km). The highway has been considerably shortened by the construction of a long tunnel bored through the watershed range. Taking the potholed branch road into Mongyon, you cross to the south bank of the Julak-chu.

Mongyon Town → *Altitude: 2,880 m.* *For listings, see pages 587-593.*

The county town is still coming to terms with its much diminished status, following the recent move of the prefectural government to Nubtso. Many large official buildings appear to be empty and unused. Entering **Main Street** from the northwest, you will pass two guesthouses and the bus station, before reaching a roundabout. Continuing on Main Street, the Mongyon Hotel is on the left with the post office and Chinese Medicine Hospital on the right. Turning right or left at the next crossroads, you will find some good inexpensive Muslim restaurants, alongside the offices of the Gold Development Company. If you continue straight ahead, via the next block which houses local government buildings, banks and insurance offices, you will reach the Serkhok road.

Mongyon to Kamalok

Three roads lead from Mongyon to Ziling. Among them, the high road (via **Ebao**) has recently reopened, following the completion of a new tunnel. The low road passes through **Gonlung** (see below, page 580), and the middle road crosses **Mount Dawa** to reach the **Serkhok** valley. Taking the middle road, you continue following the Julak-chu downstream through a well-cultivated valley. The snowline is noticeably

Mongyon Town

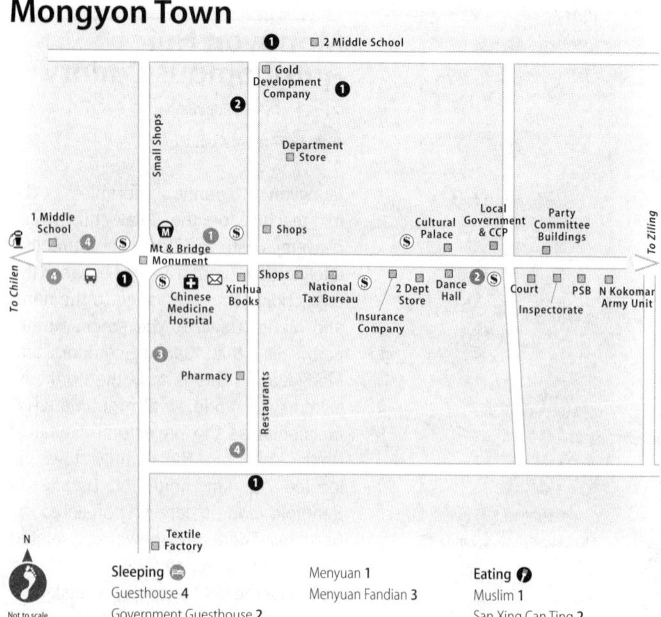

low on both the East Chokle Namgyel range to the north and Mount Dawa to the south. After 18 km, the road reaches an intersection at **Shengli**. Continue heading southeast for **Julak** (Ch Minhe) and **Gonlung**, or turn right for **Serkhok**.

If you continue in the direction of Julak, after 28 km you will reach the T-junction at Serkhok-chu Bridge. Turn right (south) for Julak and Gonlung or left (north) to reach **Semnyi** (Xianmi) township. Taking the latter option, you may wish to visit the Gelukpa monasteries of **Drugu Gon Ganden Chokhorling** (founded in 1644 by Dondrub Gyatso of Serkhok), **Semnyi Gon Ganden Dargyeling**, which was founded in 1623 by Lhari Khenchen Tseten Dondrub, a monk from Yerpa near Lhasa, and **Bengyu Gon Mindrol Tosam Dargyeling**, which was founded circa 1607-1682. If you turn right (south) at the bridge, you will pass the turn-off for Gonlung (see below, page 580) after 69 km at Gandenkou. The Kamalok county border lies some 42 km southeast of here in the lower Julak-chu valley.

Mongyon to Serkhok via Mount Dawa

Taking the middle route to **Ziling** from Mongyon, you leave the Mongyon-Julak road at the **Shengli** intersection, crossing the **Julak-chu** (Altitude: 2,700 m), and then following the course of a tributary upstream through Muslim villages and verdant hills towards the snowline. On the ascent of Mount Dawa, there are wonderful views of the jagged East Chokle Namgyel peaks to the north and the Gansu corridor beyond. Three passes are crossed in quick succession, but ice and snow can make driving hazardous. The snowline is reached at 3,120 m and the watershed at **Dawa La** pass (3,960 m), 25 km from the intersection, is frequently shrouded in mist and swept by hailstones.

Serkhok County གསེར་ཁོག

→ *Population: 426,417. Area: 2,945 sq km. Colour map 5, grid A4.* 大通县

The **Serkhok** valley (Ch Beichuan) extends from the watershed pass on Mount Dawa to the river's confluence with the Tsong-chu at Ziling. The county capital, **Datong**, is an industrial city, situated 39 km north of Ziling. Formerly, there were eight Gelukpa monasteries in Serkhok, of which three have been reopened in recent years. The largest and most renowned among them is **Tsenpo Gon**. **Minyag Hermitage** is under the authority of Kumbum Jampaling, while **Ganden Rinchenling** is a branch of Gonlung Monastery.

Upper Serkhok Valley

The descent into the **Serkhok-chu** valley from **Dawa La** pass is on a treacherous muddy road surface. Nomads can be seen herding sheep across the hillsides. Gradually, the tree-line appears, followed by small hamlets and cultivated fields. Then, some 23 km below the pass, the dirt road comes to an abrupt end, and Highway 227 is rejoined, leading down to **Datong** and **Ziling**.

Serkhok County

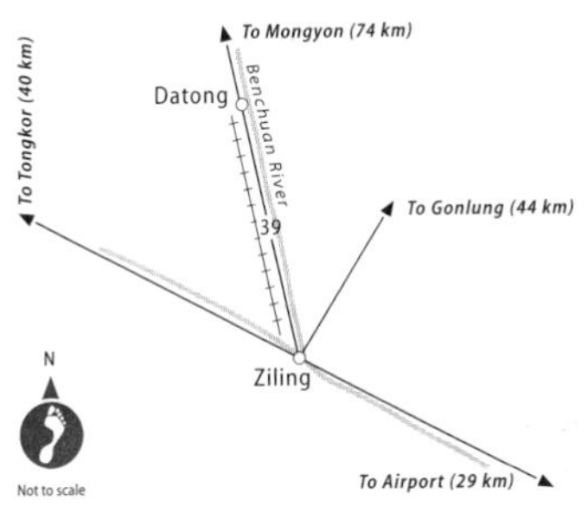

Tsenpo Gon

The principal monastery of Serkhok is **Tsenpo Gon Ganden Damcholing** (Ch Guanhuasi), which was founded in 1649 by Tsenpo Dondrub Gyatso, an abbot of Gonlung. Later, it became the seat of the Mindrol Nomenqan incarnations, who were influential in Lhasa and Beijing. In 1724 the complex was destroyed by Chinese forces on the grounds that it had supported the Mongolian prince

Lobzang Tendzin, but restoration was completed within the next decade. The site is located 32 km below Dawa La pass and 6 km below Zhanghua township, along a narrow track to the west of the road. Only two temples still stand within its courtyard: the **Jokhang**, which has elegant door panels and a Chinese inscription donated by Emperor Qianlong above the door, and the **Protector Shrine** (Gonkhang). The former contains images of Tsongkhapa with his students, Jowo Shakyamuni, Jowo Ramoche, Amitayus, Maitreya and Mahakarunika, as well as an inscription and seal given by the Ninth Panchen Lama, while the murals depict the 1,000 Buddhas of the Aeon, the hidden land of Shambhala, and the main peaceful deities of the Gelukpa tradition. Behind the Jokhang, there are extensive ruins. To its left, the smaller Gonkhang houses images of Dorje Drakden and several local protectors. Currently there are 30 monks and two incarnate lamas at Tsenpo Gon, which appears as a highly sinicized enclave within a Muslim-dominated valley.

Datong

The large city of **Datong** lies only 19 km south of Tsenpo Gon, in the lower reaches of the valley. This is a polluted, heavy industrial zone, with a large aluminium smelting plant, cement factory and power station. To the east of town, on **Mount Laoye Shan** (Old Grandfather Mountain), the Flower Song Festival (Ch Huarhui) is held by the **Tu** nationality each year on the sixth day of the sixth lunar month (11 July, 2005). Song, dance and serious drinking take place against the backdrop of a brisk trade fair. Driving south from Datong, the road crosses the Ziling-Datong railway line after 5 km, and from here the provincial capital is only 28 km distant.

Tongkor County སྟོང་སྐོར → *Pop: 133,607. Area: 1,293 sq km.* 湟源县

The county of **Tongkor**, which occupies the upper reaches of the Tsong-chu valley and the east shore of Lake Kokonor, nowadays belongs to the East Kokonor Prefecture, governed from Ziling. The county capital, **Tongkor**, is 40 km equidistant between Dabzhi in the northwest and Ziling City in the southeast.

Dabzhi to Tongkor

The road from Haiyan town in Dabzhi to Tongkor follows the banks of the **Tsong-chu** downstream. It passes through **Bayan** township, where two monasteries were once sited. **Gonpa Soma** is now derelict, its monks having been relocated at Dabzhi Gonsar Namgyeling (see above, page 566). **Dratsang Gon Ganden Chokhorling**, which was built to commemorate the visit of the Third Dalai Lama in 1578, formerly housed the sword and armour of the Mongolian king Gushi Qan and a precious trilingual *Kangyur*. It is an important monastery for the Mongolian tribes of the Kokonor region, who used to hold their assemblies here, and it has undergone reconstruction since 1984. Driving on from Bayan, after 15 km, you will reach **Tongkor**, where highways 109 and 315 converge. The ruins of **Ladrol-ne Gonpa** and **Rali Hermitage** are passed en route near **Dahua** township.

Tongkor Town

For centuries, this has been an important trading post for the Mongolians and Tibetans of Kokonor. Abbé Huc joined a large caravan to Lhasa here in the 1860s, and noted how, even then, the Chinese were 'encroaching on the desert, building houses, and bringing into

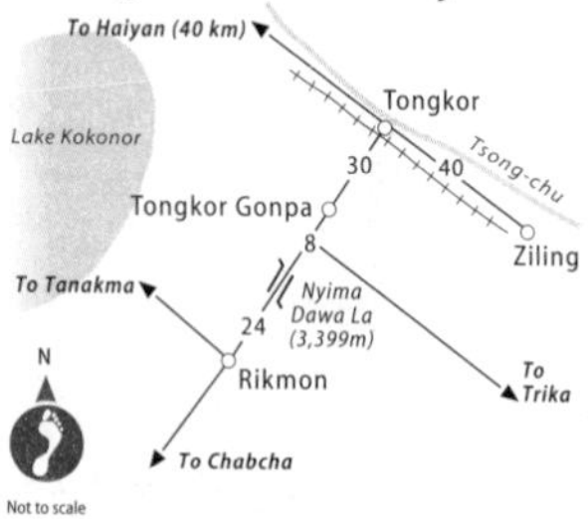

cultivation portions of the land of grass'. Some 30 years later, Dr Susie Rijnhart witnessed the second major Muslim rebellion when almost 10,000 Muslims were massacred in the town by a combined force of local Tibetans and the Chinese army sent from Lanzhou. Just to the northwest of town are the ruins of **Ganden Tengyeling** (Ch Cinghosi), which was founded as a branch of Tongkor Monastery in 1783.

Tongkor Gonpa

Following Highway 109 southwest from town, you will pass through several small Chinese farming villages. Then, about 30 km from the town, you will reach the ruins of **Tongkor Gonpa, Ganden Chokhorling**, which was founded by the Fourth Tongkor, Dogyu Gyatso in 1648. This was formerly the largest monastery in the county – its land had been given by the Mongolian Gushi Qan himself – and despite its destruction in 1724, it quickly revived, and acquired a high reputation for the study and practice of the tantras. An American visitor, WW Rockhill, noted that it housed 500 monks at the end of the 19th century. Two buildings have recently been restored here: an assembly hall containing gilded clay images of the Buddhas of the Three Times, flanked by Amitayus and Bhaisajyaguru, and a Jokhang which exhibits some original architectural features. A few kilometres further on, the tarmac road splits, with the west branch leading over the famous **Nyima Dawa La** ('sun-moon') pass, and the east branch leading to **Trika** county (see below, page 616).

Nyima Dawa La Pass

The **Nyima Dawa La** pass (Ch Riyueting, 3,399 m), situated 38 km south of Tongkor, was made famous when Princess Wencheng, en route for Tibet to marry King Songtsen Gampo in the seventh century, looked in a magic mirror with a sun-moon design, which was supposed to show her family home in Changan (modern Xi'an). On seeing only her own reflection, the princess smashed the mirror in despair. The river near the pass, unusually flowing from east to west, is said to be formed from the princess's tears as she continued on her journey to meet Songsten Gampo. Nowadays, two small concrete temples have been constructed on the pass, and the murals are modern, depicting nomad life and the royal couple. A Flower Song Festival (Ch Huarhui) is held here every summer around the sixth day of the sixth lunar month (11 July, 2005). On the far side of the pass, the road descends into Chabcha county (see below, page 624).

Tongkor to Ziling

Driving east from Tongkor, the combined highway follows the north bank of the Tsang-chu downstream to Ziling. On this 40-km stretch, it bypasses the Chinese townships of **Zhama, Duoba, Hezui** and **Mafang**.

Ziling City ཟི་ལིང་

→ *Population: 1,764,205. Area: 430 sq km. Colour map 5, grid A4.*

Ziling (Ch Xining) is the capital of Qinghai province, located at 2,200 m on the edge of the Tibetan plateau in a wide section of the **Tsong-chu** valley, where the **Serkhok-chu** (Ch Beichuan) flows in from the northwest. The valley floors are a well irrigated patchwork of fields and trees but the hills nearby are barren, affording only poor grazing. Most heavy industry is located further north in Serkhok (Ch Datong), which also possesses a coal mine, but Ziling itself is largely a residential and market town, with expanding boundaries that will soon absorb the surrounding counties, such as Rushar, Tongkor and Tsongkha Khar. The population of Ziling is mostly Muslim (25%), Chinese, Mongolian or Tu, and very few Tibetans live in the town itself. It

Average temperature in Jan: -7°, minimum -27°
Average temperature In Jul: 18°, maximum 34°
Annual precipitation: 366 mm (mostly in summer), llittle winter precipitation

 has, however, become an important centre for Tibetan Studies. The Tibetan Nationalities' College, the Tsongon Publishing House and the Gesar Research Institute are in the vanguard of this movement. » *For listings, see pages 587-593.*

Ins and outs

Getting there The distance from Ziling to Tongkor is 40 km, to Repkong 185 km, to Gonlung (Huzhu) 41 km, to Serkhok (Datong) 39 km, and to Lanzhou 280 km. See Transport, page , for further details.

History

The city developed through trade between China and Persia, linking with the famous Silk Route to the north. Buddhist pilgrims such as Fa Xian passed this way en route for India, and both the Han and Northern Wei Dynasties sponsored the construction of Chinese-style Buddhist and Daoist temples. Tibetan influence increased following the consolidation of the Yarlung Empire in the seventh century, and during the ninth century it was here that the three ordained monks from Central Tibet passed away, having fled the persecution of the apostate king Langdarma. Later, there were influxes of Mongolian, Tu and Muslim groups. Muslim migrants from Central Asia gradually became the dominant sector of the population; and from 1860 onwards, successive uprisings among the Muslims resulted in the destruction of many old settlements in the region. Even Kumbum Monastery itself was badly damaged. The Chinese, calling on their Tu and Tibetan allies, managed to suppress each insurrection with great loss of life, and for decades Muslims were not allowed to reside within the walled city of Ziling. However, by the 1930s, Muslim warlords, in agreement with the Nationalists, once again controlled the entire valley down to the Yellow River.

The Tibetans, to whom the region is known as Tsongkha, largely continued to govern their own affairs, but were forced to allow Muslim trade as far south as

Ziling

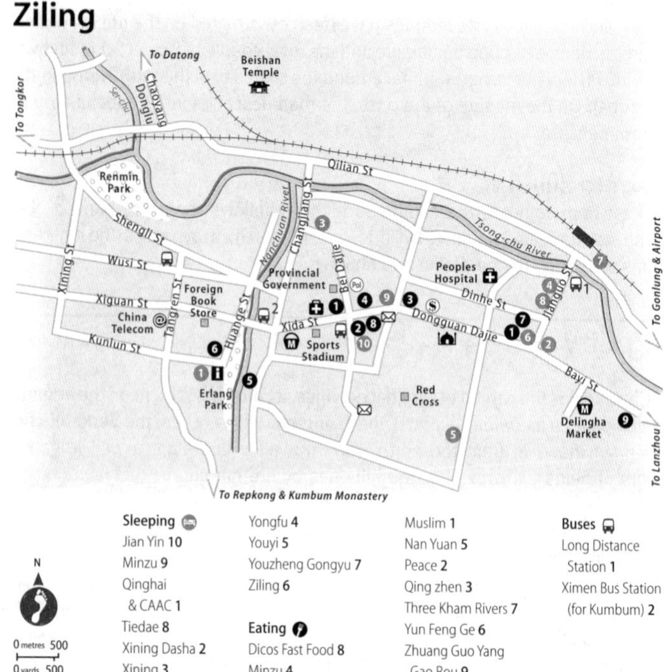

Sleeping
Jian Yin 10
Minzu 9
Qinghai & CAAC 1
Tiedae 8
Xining Dasha 2
Xining 3
Yongfu 4
Youyi 5
Youzheng Gongyu 7
Ziling 6

Eating
Dicos Fast Food 8
Minzu 4
Muslim 1
Nan Yuan 5
Peace 2
Qing zhen 3
Three Kham Rivers 7
Yun Feng Ge 6
Zhuang Guo Yang Gao Rou 9

Buses
Long Distance Station 1
Ximen Bus Station (for Kumbum) 2

Jyekundo. The Mongolians were concentrated in outlying parts of Kokonor, Tsaidam and the Kunlun mountains, and were organized into banners or districts, which owed only nominal allegiance to the Ziling amban and Muslim government. In recent years there has been an increasing influx of Chinese immigrants from Nanjing in Southeast China.

Sights

Approaching Ziling city from Tongkor (Ch Huangyuan), the road, known as **Qilian Street**, follows the railway and the Tsong-chu River (Ch Huangshui) on the north bank and crosses the Beichuan tributary, just upstream from its confluence with the Tsong-chu. **Renmin Park** (Ziling) lies to the south overlooking the confluence. Soon the road passes a turn-off (**Chaoyang Donglu**) which heads north out of town for Serkhok and the Datong branch railway. The Daoist temple of **Beishan** is located 45 minutes' walking distance up the mountainside to the north of the road. Continue east along Qilian Street, following the north bank of the Tsong-chu, to reach the main **Xining Railway Station**.

Four bridges span the Tsong-chu in the city: the westernmost bridge leads into the west part of town. Here, Xinning Street, Tongren Street and Huanghe Street all run north-south and the lateral roads known as Shengli Street, Wusi Street, Xiguan Street and Kunlun Street bisect them on an east-west axis. **Tongren Street**, in particular, leads south out of town in the direction of Repkong. **Huanghe Street** runs parallel to the west bank of the north-flowing Nanchuan River. **Ertong Park** in the south of the city can be reached via either Tongren Street or Huanghe Street. The city's best hotel, Qinghai Hotel, is located beside the grounds of the park.

Four bridges span the Nanchuan River, leading into the commercial and administrative heart of Ziling. All of them link up with **Changjiang Street** on the east bank of the Nanchuan, which extends all the way from Qilian Street (on the north bank of the Tsong-chu) to the south end of town. The **West Gate Bus Station** (Ximen) (for buses to Kumbum) is located on this street.

At the city centre is the **Da Shizi** (Great Cross) intersection, alongside the Xining Sports' Stadium and the provincial government buildings. The old city which lies to the east of Changjiang Street, contains the municipality buildings, the open-air market (one of the most interesting in China) and the **Post Office**.

The municipality buildings on **Xida Street** (west of Da Shizi) in particular, were constructed on the site of a 13th-century Buddhist temple, built to commemorate the place where Mar Shakyamuni and his two colleagues maintained the Tibetan monastic tradition and finally passed away during the persecution of Buddhism in Central Tibet by Langdarma. Formerly it contained exquisite images of the three great monks. The temple, known in Chinese as **Dafusi**, was levelled to make way for the government offices, but one small section was rebuilt in the mid-1980s, and further rebuilding is being carried out at the site. It is only a few hundred metres west of the main Post Office. None of the other three Tibetan Buddhist temples of Ziling now survive. Among these, Hongjuesi, which was founded in 1390, and Jintasi, which was a branch of Kumbum Jampaling, were formerly located further south on **Hongjuesi Street**, while the Tu nationality monastery of Cangjinsi, founded in 1412, was situated to the west of **Nanda Street**.

North from the main Post Office on Beida Street lies the **Public Security Bureau** and at the head of the same road, the Xining Hotel.

The **Bank of China** lies further east on Dongguan Street in the Muslim quarter. The **Great Mosque**, built originally in the 14th century, is one of the largest in the region; and there are a number of excellent small Muslim restaurants. From here, follow **Jianguo Street** northeast to cross the Tsong-chu at the entrance to the main **Xining Railway Station**. The long-distance bus station is located just before the bridge on the right (east) side of the road. The Yongfu Hotel is on the opposite side of the road.

 There is also an interesting Tibetan quarter (shops, hotels and restaurants), occupying the lanes that lead off from Jianguo Street in front of the railway station. From the railway station follow Qilian Street out of town (north) in the direction of Gonlung (Huzhu) county; or follow Bayi Street southeast in the direction of Lanzhou.

The Qinghai Institute for Nationalities has an interesting exhibition hall, and the Qinhgai Provincial Museum houses some of the province's greatest archaeological treasures, including ancient Persian and Chinese artefacts, as well as Buddhist manuscripts.

Rushar County རུ་ཤར → *Pop: 455,980. Area: 2,488 sq km.* 湟中县

The county of Rushar (Ch Huangzhong) lies 26 km southwest of Ziling city; only a 40 minute bus ride away. The county capital, **Huangzhong**, is a town dominated by Muslim traders, and much of the countryside around consists of Chinese farming villages. Prior to 1950 there were 29 Tibetan monasteries, temples and hermitages of the Gelukpa school within Rushar, the largest and best known being **Kumbum Jampaling**. Nowadays three of these have reopened with official permission, and eight have done so privately. Among them, **Ame Zhidak Lhakhang** lies 1 km south of Kumbum, **Chesho Ritro Samtenling**, a small branch of Kumbum Jampaling, lies 28 km southeast of the county town, while to the northwest are **Zurgyi Chokhang** (18 km) which contains revered relics of Tsongkhapa, **Lasar Gonchung** (27 km), and **Sertok Gon** (43 km).

Huangzhong

Approaching the town from Ziling, you will find the local hospital, bank, post office and China Telecom outlet all on the left side with the government buildings and the Xinhua bookstore on the right. Turning uphill towards the monastery, you will pass the public security bureau, a taxi stand, and many small restaurants and shops, selling Tibetan artefacts and metal fittings for temple roofs. A short flight of steps leads up to an open square, with the monastery to the south and the Tsongkha Hotel immediately to the east.

Kumbum Jampaling Monastery

History At **Rushar Drongdal**, the county boasts the most renowned monastery in Tsongkha, and one of the greatest in all Tibet: that of **Kumbum Jampaling** (Ch Taersi), which was founded in 1560 to commemorate the birthplace of Tsongkhapa by Rinchen Tsondru Gyeltsen. The monastery is built around the tree that marks his actual birthplace, where Tsongkhapa's mother, Shingza Acho, had herself built a stupa (kumbum) in 1379. Later, in 1583, the Third Dalai Lama Sonam Gyatso stayed here, and encouraged Rinchen Tsondru Gyeltsen to build a Maitreya Temple (**Jampa Lhakhang**), after which the site became known as Kumbum Jampaling. Over subsequent centuries, the monastery developed into a large complex, 41 ha in area.

Kumbum has been sacked and rebuilt several times in its history, particularly during the Muslim rebellion of 1860, when hundreds of monks died protecting the main chapels. It has recently undergone major restoration work, which was finished in 1997. Only half of the monks in Kumbum are Tibetan, and most of these come from the Kokonor region or areas to the south of the Yellow River, while Mongolian, Tu and a few Chinese make up the remainder of the monastery's 400

Ziling & Rushar

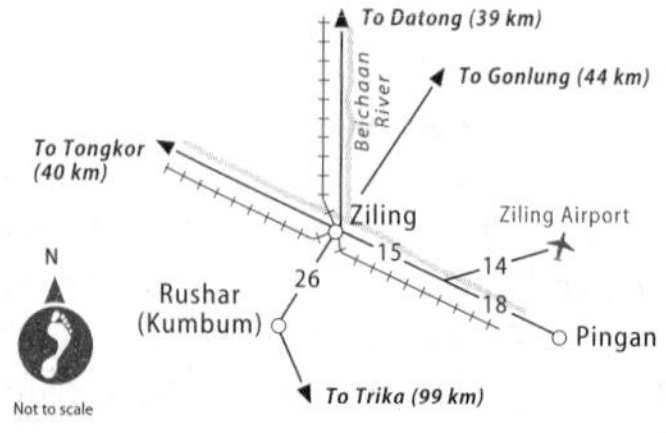

monks. Despite the obvious sanctity and grandeur of the complex at Kumbum, the monastery at times has the sad air of a museum, and this is enhanced by the arrival of strident Chinese tourists from Ziling, Lanzhou and other urban areas.

The site As one approaches the monastery from the square in front, there are a large number of souvenir stalls selling a range of Tibetan jewellery, both old and new, as well as tangkas and other religious artefacts. By the side of the road you will pass the **Chorten Gobzhi** (1), which is a large stupa with four gates. Then, at the entrance to the monastery are the **Chorten Degye** (2), the eight stupas symbolizing the deeds of the Buddha. The originals were destroyed during the Cultural Revolution, the present set having been reconstructed in the early 1980s. The ticket office and a small guesthouse, known as **Nelenkhang Kakun Gon** (5) are located beside the stupas, and the entrance fee for the following nine main temples and halls is for ¥36.

Kumbum Jampaling Monastery

1 Chorten Gobzhi
2 Chorten Degye
3 Champa Dratsang
4 Minyak Garwa
5 Nelenkhang Kakun Gon (ticket office)
6 Gomangwei Gyencho Zhengsa
7 Tsenkhang Chenmo
8 Dukhor Chorten
9 Zhabten Lhakhang
10 Labrang Tse Tashi Khangsar
11 Patrik Garwa
12 Gonkya Garwa
13 Sertok Garwa
14 Parkhang
15 Chichen (admin)
16 Menpa Dratsang
17 Jokhang
18 Serdong Chenmo
19 Jamkhang
20 Tsokchen Dukhang
21 Jamyang Kunzik Lhakang
22 Thamche Khyenpei Lhakhang
23 Dukhor Dratsang
24 Chesho Garwa
25 Gyupa Dratsang
26 Jetsunpei Gyencho Zhengsa
27 Yarcho Chora
28 Akya Garwa
29 Gonkhang
30 Dukhor Lolang Kyilkhor

Main temples The gold-tiled **Tsenkhang Chenmo** (7), constructed in 1692 and rebuilt in 1802, is a protector chapel dedicated to the five aspects of the protector deity Pehar known as Gyelpo Kunga. The **Zhabten Lhakhang** (9), which was completed in 1717 and consecrated by the Seventh Dalai Lama, contains images of Shakyamuni Buddha with his foremost disciples, along with the Sixteen Elders. The **Jokhang** (17), constructed in 1604, has an exquisite image of Shakyamuni in bodhisattva form, inlaid with pearls and gems, as well as the reliquary of its founder, Ozer Gyatso; and the adjacent **Gonkhang** (29), dated 1594, has images of Tsongkhapa and Yamantaka.

The most sacred temples are those at the heart of the complex: the **Serdong Chenmo** (18) was originally built by Tsongkhapa's mother in 1379 on the spot where a sandalwood tree is said to have sprung from the ground where Tsongkhapa's placenta fell at the time of his birth. The walls are covered with aquamarine tiles, and the central gold image of the master, which overlooks the branches of the original tree, is housed in the upper storey below a gilded roof. Adjacent to it is the **Jamkhang** (19), the temple dedicated to Maitreya, containing an image of Maitreya at the age of 12 and the reliquary stupa of Rinchen Tsondru Gyeltsen, which dates from 1583.

The lavish grand assembly hall, **Tsokchen Dukhang** (20), was originally constructed in 1611, but rebuilt in 1776 and again in 1912. The present building has a spacious outer courtyard, and a vast hall with 166 pillars with ornate yellow dragon motifs, and murals depicting the 1,000 Buddhas of the Aeon. The volumes of the Tibetan canon are stacked up on the side walls. The **Jamyang Kunzik Lhakhang** (21) is an elongated building with a Chinese-style roof, dating from 1592. In the centre of its shrine are large images depicting the bodhisattvas Manjughosa, Avalokiteshvara and peaceful Vajrapani; while to the right are Buddha in the form of Simhanada, flanked by Sitatapatra and Sarasvati; and to the left, Tsongkhapa flanked by his students and the great scholars of ancient India known as the 'Six Ornaments and Two Supreme Ones'. The protector Dharmaraja stands guard at the side. Afternoon debates are held in the large courtyard outside this temple. Lastly, the **Thamche Khyenpei Lhakhang** (22) contains a reliquary stupa of the Third Dalai Lama (not to be confused with his principal reliquary at Drepung in Lhasa).

The colleges In addition to those temples there are four colleges: **Champa Dratsang** (3) is for the study of religious dancing. **Menpa Dratsang** (16), the medical college, was built in 1757 and contains images of Tsongkhapa, Bhaisajyaguru and Shakyamuni, along with a three-dimensional mandala of the Eight Medicine Buddhas. **Gyupa Dratsang** (25), the tantric college, dating from 1649, contains images of Shakyamuni and Maitreya, the meditational deities Guhyasamaja, Cakrasamvara and Bhairava, and murals depicting the 1,000 Buddhas of the Aeon. Finally, **Dukhor Dratsang** (23) for the study of Kalacakra-based astrology and esoteric practices, founded in 1817, contains images of Kalacakra, Shakyamuni and Avalokiteshvara, as well as some fine old tangkas.

Residential buildings The building known as **Labrang Tse Tashi Khangsar** (10) is the residence of the presiding abbot of Kumbum; and it was where the Fifth Dalai Lama and the Sixth Panchen Lama stayed during their historic visits. The original structure dates from 1650 and it was further renovated in 1687.

There are six other residential buildings, each associated with one of the great incarnating lamas of the monastery. The largest is that of the Tulku Akya (**Akya Garwa**; 28), followed by those of Tulku Chesho (**Chesho Garwa**; 24), Tulku Minyak (**Minyak Garwa**; 4), Tulku Patrik (**Patrik Garwa**; 11), Tulku Sertok (**Sertok Garwa**; 13), and the monastic supervisor (**Gonkya Garwa**; 12). Among them, Tulku Akya recently sought political asylum in the United States. Next to the residence of Tulku Akya is the **Dukhor Lolang Kyilkhor** (30), containing a 40-cubit sized three-dimensional mandala of the meditational deity Kalacakra, which was built in 1987 by Gyabak Lobzang Tenpei Gyeltsen to mark the beginning of the 17th 60-year year cycle.

Other buildings Other buildings include the **Parkhang** (14) where woodblock editions of the Tibetan Canon and the Collected Works of Tsongkhapa are housed; the hillside **Yarcho Chora** (27) or 'summer debating courtyard', the **Dukhor Chorten** (8), the general administrative office known as **Chichen** (15), and two small rooms for moulding *tormas* and so-called 'butter-sculptures' – the **Gomangwei Gyencho Zhengsa** (6) and the **Jetsunpei Gyencho Zhengsa** (26).

Tsongkha Khar County ཙོང་ཁ་མཁར

→ *Population: 112,196. Area: 671 sq km. Colour map 5, grid A5.* 平安县

Tsongkha Khar (Pingan) county occupies the banks of the Tsong-chu river and their hinterland southeast of Ziling. The capital is located at **Pingan** (Altitude: 2,070 m), 33 km from Ziling, and 29 km northwest of Ledu in Drotsang county. The Ziling-Lanzhou highway follows the Tsong-chu downstream, parallel to the railway line. To the east of the city, it becomes a toll road, which forks after 5 km: north for **Ziling Airport** (14 km) and east for Pingan (18 km). Continuing towards Pingan, after 1 km, you will pass on the right (south) the Xiha Du Jia Cun bungalows (no attached bathrooms). Pingan town lies 3 km further along this road. There are five Gelukpa monasteries within the county, one of which, **Martsangdrak Gonpa**, originally dates from the ninth century.

Taktser and Sanhe

Getting there Just before entering Pingan, a turn-off leads southwest for 18 km to **Sanhe** township. After passing through Sanhe, turn right at the fork. Then, on reaching Shihuiyao hamlet after a further 15 km, cross a small bridge to the right which leads uphill through barley fields for 5 km to Taktser (Ch Hongaisi).

The birthplace of the present Dalai Lama is located in **Taktser** (Ch Hongaisi), 38 km southwest of Pingan, above a stupa marking the site where his predecessor had passed some time in retreat, ensuring the auspicious coincidence for his subsequent rebirth in that locale. The house, which was rebuilt in the early 1950s and completely reconstructed in 1986, consists of an outer courtyard and an inner two-storey building. The courtyard, now functioning as a school, has a small restored chamber on the right, where the Dalai Lama was actually born. Downstairs in the main building, there is a sitting room where old family photographs adorn the walls. His Holiness actually stayed here for a brief visit in 1955, and the property is maintained by his nephew, a local school teacher named Gonpo Tashi. Upstairs there is a fine household shrine.

Below Mount Amnye Gyeli, some 28 km southwest of Pingan and also within Sanhe township, there is the **Shadzong Hermitage** where relics of the Chinese pilgrim Fa Xian were once housed. Fa Xian passed through Sanhe en route for India in 399 AD. Later, in 1359, the Fourth Karmapa Rolpei Dorje visited the site and conferred the *upasaka* vows on Tsongkhapa here. There are also small branches of Kumbum Jampaling and Labrang located in the neighbouring townships.

Pingan

Entering **Pingan** from Ziling, you will pass a turn-off on the left (north) which leads across the Tsong-chu river for Gonlung Monastery (see below, page 581). The historic red-walled temple of **Martsangdrak** is visible high against the cliff-face on the north bank. Continuing along the highway, you will pass restaurants and the Bank of China, opposite which a side road leads south for Jentsa, Dowi, Linxia (211 km) and Labrang. Facing an open square at the town centre are the bus station and the railway station, along with other banks and the Pingan Guesthouse. Then, reaching the crossroads at the east end of town, you can turn right (south) for the East Kokonor Prefectural Government Buildings and the Haidong Hotel, or continue on the highway in the direction of **Lanzhou** (195 km). ▸▸ *For listings, see pages 587-593.*

Tsongkha Khar

Martsangdrak Gonpa

When, during the ninth century, Buddhism was persecuted in Central Tibet by the king Langdarma, the three monks Mar Shakyamuni, Tsang Rapsel and Yo-ge Jung fled to Amdo where they maintained the monastic lineage intact for the sake of posterity. They lived for some time at Martsangdrak and passed away at Ziling. During their sojourn, they ordained **Lachen Gongpa Rapsel** (892-975), who was later to transfer the lineage of Buddhist monasticism back to 10 monks from Central Tibet. Lachen himself passed away at Martsangdrak and his mortal remains are enshrined here.

To reach the site, turn left (north) to cross the Tsong-chu on the Gonlung road, and after a second smaller bridge, turn right along a narrow but motorable track towards a large stupa. High above, the temple sits precariously on the ledge of a steep red cliff, which is in danger of subsidence due to heavy rainfall. A Maitreya image guards the approach to the complex, warding off the flooding waters of the Tsong-chu with his defiant hand-gesture. There are two chambers: the upper one housing the embalmed remains of Lachen Gongpa Rapsel and the lower one a shrine with images of the three Tibetan monks and their two fellow Chinese monks who formed the quorum to ordain Lachen during the early 10th century. Alongside these are images of Lhalung Peldor, the yogin who assassinated the apostate king Langdarma before fleeing to Amdo, and Makakarunika, the compassionate bodhisattva. Nowadays, the temple is under the management of Gonlung Monastery.

Martsangdrak is known in Chinese as Baimasi ('White Horse' temple) either because in 1584 the Third Dalai Lama's riding horse died here, or else because it was the earliest Tibetan Buddhist temple in Amdo, just as the famed White Horse Monastery in Henan was the earliest Buddhist monastery in China.

Pingan to Ledu

Leaving Pingan on the highway, the road criss-crosses the railway line, passing through more intensively cultivated fields. After 13 km, a turn-off on the right (south) leads to **Xiaying** township, while the highway continues on to **Ledu** (19 km).

Gonlung County དགོན་ལུང

➔ *Population: 370,606. Area: 3,133 sq km. Colour map 5, grid A4.* 互助土族自治县

Gonlung county (Huzhu) lies 44 km northeast of Ziling in a minor side valley of the Tsong-chu River. Here the **Tu** people, who are of Turkic origin but practitioners of

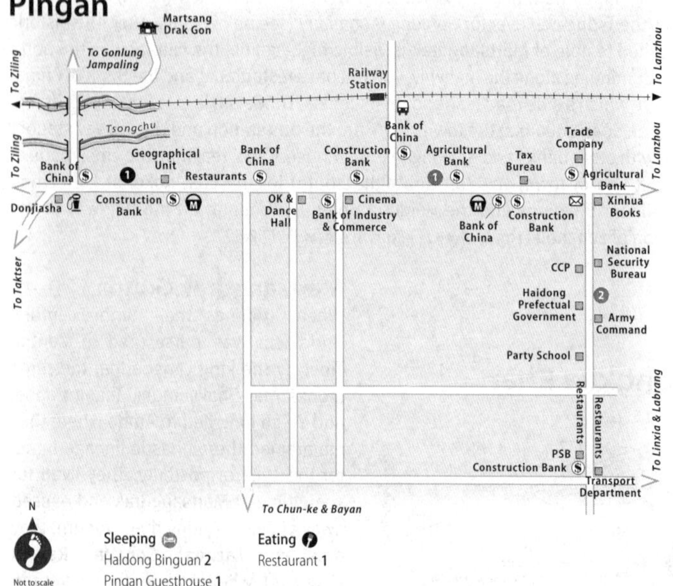

Tibetan Buddhism, are to be found in one of their greatest concentrations. Most wear Chinese clothes, but occasionally Tu women in distinctively striped dresses can be seen in the villages. The county capital is located at **Huzhu**, 54 km north of Pingan town and 60 km south of Gandenkou on the Mongyon/Minhe road. Traditionally, there were 14 Tibetan and Tu monasteries within the county, of which two were Nyingmapa and the remainder all Gelukpa.

Pingan to Gonlung

Driving from Pingan in Tsongkha Khar county, you will pass a turn-off on the right for Martsangdrak Gon (see above, page 579), and continue north through a prosperous valley where there are plentiful beehives and the best potatoes grown in the Ziling area. The villages in the lower reaches are all Chinese. After 25 km, the road forks, right (6 km) for **Sangdu** and left (28 km) for Huzhu town. Taking the former, you will reach **Chozang** hermitage of the Gelukpa school and **Kata Lhakhang** of the Nyingma school, which are 4 km east of Sangdu township. Following the latter road north towards **Huzhu**, after 1 km, a branch road leads east for 6 km to the renowned Gelukpa monastery of Gonlung Jampaling.

Gonlung Jampaling → *Altitude: 2,850 m*

Gonlung Jampaling is the most influential monastery north of the Tsong-chu river. The picturesque and lightly forested valley of Gonlung was visited in 1584 by the Third Dalai Lama and in 1602 the Fourth Dalai Lama Yonten Gyatso passed through en route for Lhasa. Subsequently, in 1604, the monastery was founded by Gyelse Donyo Chokyi Gyatso and supported thereafter by 13 Tu and Tibetan clans. Later, the Second Changkya, Ngawang Lobzang Chokden (1642-1714), revered as the incarnation of Jamchen Choje Shakya Yeshe (founder of **Sera Monastery** at Lhasa) was invited here by the Manchu emperor, and constructed a number of temples. His incarnation was the Third Changkya Rolpei Dorje (1717-1786), the sectarian author and zealot who waged war against the kingdoms of Gyarong (on which see below, page 656). The monastery was destroyed by the Manchus in 1724 during the suppression of Lhazang Qan, but rebuilt officially in 1732. During this period, the most influential scholars of Gonlung were Sumpa Yeshe (1704-1787), the Second Tuken Ngawang Chokyi Gyatso (1680-1736), and the latter's erudite incarnation, the Third Tuken Lobzang Chokyi Nyima (1737-1802), who wrote a widely studied treatise entitled Crystal Mirror of Buddhist Philosophical Systems (Drubta Shelgyi Melong) at Gonlung in 1801.

The monastery, which has some 49 branches, presently houses 300 monks of Tu, Tibetan and Mongolian origin. Nowadays there are two important tulkus: the Ninth Tuken, who has recently been educated at Labrang Monastery, and the Ninth Yonten Sumpa, who lives in Ziling.

The monastery stretches over the north ridge of the valley, and there are 11 main buildings. To the left of the car park and the reception building there is a hall for religious dancing and a stupa, while to its left there is the **Gyupa Tratsang**, containing images of the meditational deities Guhyasamaja, Cakrasamvara and Vajrabhairava. Heading up hill from

Gonlung County

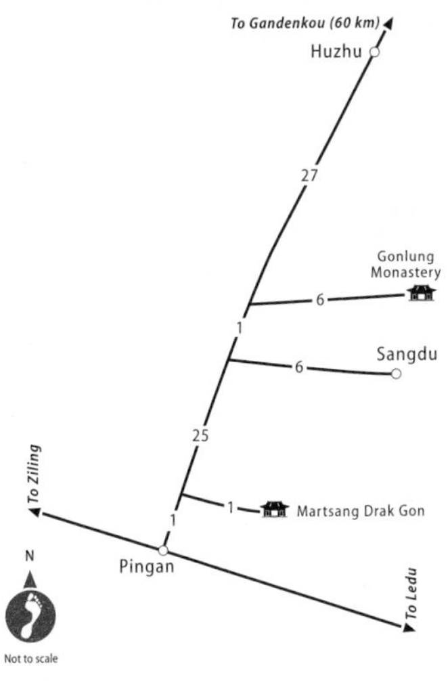

 here, you will pass (R) the **residence of Tuken** and (L) the **residence of Changkya**. The former has an image of the Eighth Tuken, the throne of the present lineage-holder the Ninth Tuken, and a fine mural depicting the complete Tuken lineage. Further uphill, there is the **Assembly Hall** (Dukhang), a building of 108 pillars with a central throne holding a portrait of the previous Changkya, who died in Taiwan. To its rear there are images (L-R) of Jowo Shakyamuni, Tubpa Chokhorma, Tara, Tsongkhapa with his students, the Buddhas of the Three Times, Vajrasattva, Amitabha and Vajradhara. Behind the Assembly Hall, and higher up the ridge, there is the **Jampa Lhakhang**, containing a precious image known as Jampa Yelogma, along with small images of the Sixteen Elders, the 1,000 Buddhas of the Aeon and the eight bodhisattvas. Climbing further, you will reach the **Zhidak Lhakhang**, a protector shrine built by the Second Changkya, and his adjacent tomb, which lies within a walled garden. Towards the top the ridge, there is the **Gyelsekhang**, with an image of Maitreya, the **Tuken Hermitage** (Tuken Zimchung) and the **Sumpa Hermitage** (Sumpa Zimchung), the last of which contains an image of Atisha. About 2 km distant from Gonlung is the **Gyelse Hermitage**, affiliated to the monastery, while there are other branches in the valley at **Sangdu** and **Denma** townships.

An important ceremony is held at Gonlung Monastery during the **prayer festival** of the New Year (February, 2005); while masked dances are held during the first, third and fourth months of the lunar calendar.

Huzhu Town and Chubzang

The burgeoning county town of **Huzhu** lies 33 km north of Gonlung Monastery. In nearby **Bazha** township there is the Gelukpa monastery of **Kanchen Gon**, which was founded in 1654 by a student of the Fourth Panchen Lobzang Chokyi Gyeltsen. To the northwest of Bazha (3.5 km), there is also a small Nyingma monastery called **Kanchung Gon** which was founded during the 1930s. About 20 km north of town, on the plain of **Bumlung Tashithang**, there is yet another influential Gelukpa monastery known as **Chubzang Ganden Migyurling**, which was founded in 1649 by Chubzang Lalebpa Namgyel Peljor (1578-1651), who hailed from Tolung near Lhasa. Like Gonlung, this establishment was destroyed in 1724 and subsequently rebuilt in 1765 and refurbished in 1887. Its branches extend as far as Trika and Ulan Sok counties.

Gonlung Jampaling

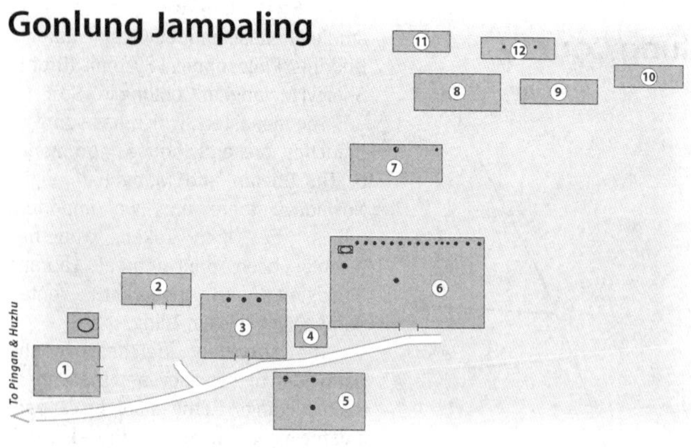

1 Chamra (hall for religious dancing)
2 Reception
3 Gyupa Tratsang
4 Changkya Tsang
5 Tuken Tsang
6 Dukhang (Assembly Hall)
7 Jampa Lhakhang
8 Zhidak Lhakhang
9 Tomb of Changkya II
10 Gyelsekhang
11 Tuken Zimchung
12 Sumpa Zimchung

Drotsang County གྲོ་ཚང

→ *Population: 291,159. Area: 2,520 sq km. Colour map 5, grid A5.* 乐都县

Drotsang county comprises the section of the Tsong-chu downstream from Tsongkha Khar, and its lateral valleys to the north and south, where **Drotsang Monastery** is located. This region was formerly known as **Neu-be**. Traditionally, the county had 31 Tibetan monasteries or temples, representing the Gelukpa school, and of these Drotsang is still the most important. Now eight have been officially reopened and four have privately reopened. The county town, Ledu, lies 32 km southeast of Pingan and 47 km northwest of Minhe in Kamalok.

Ledu → *Altitude: 2,010 m*

Driving southeast from the Xiaying intersection in Tsongkha Khar into Drotsang county, after 5 km a branch road leads across to the north bank of the Tsong-chu for 15 km to reach the old market of Ledu town. Instead, if you continue on the highway, after 8 km, a turn-off leading south to **Fengdu** will be reached. The county capital is only 6 km distant at this point. ▸▸ *For listings, see pages 587-593.*

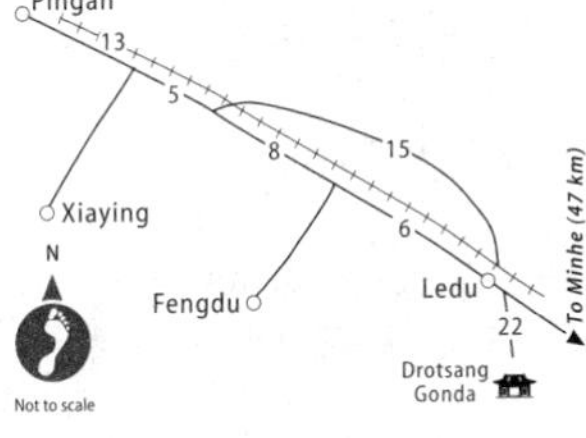

Ledu is a rapidly growing Chinese market town, situated on both banks of the river. No street signs at all appear to be written in Tibetan! Entering town, you will pass the People's Park and the South Bus Station on the left, and a petrol station, carpet factory and the Ledu Hotel on the right. Here, a side road leads across the Tsong-chu through a banking and commercial street towards the old market and the Ledu bus and railway

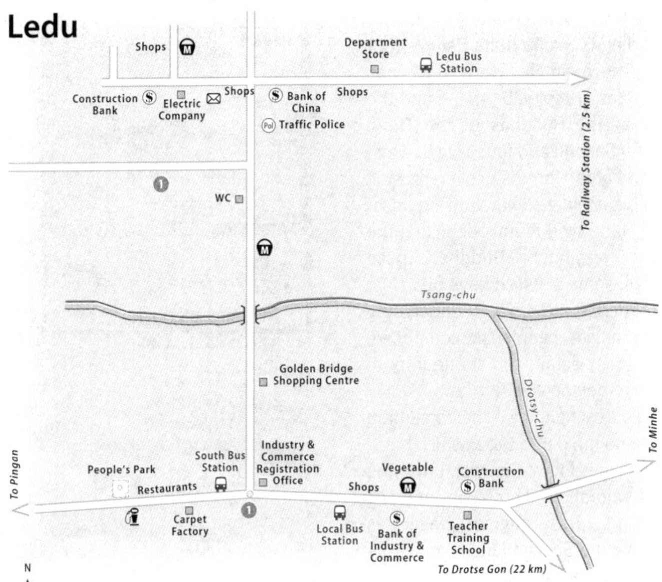

Sleeping
Guesthouse 2
Ledu 1

stations. If you continue along the highway, you will pass the local bus station and a teacher training school on the right, after which a side road leads inland to **Drotsang Monastery**, following the Drotsang-chu tributary upstream.

In the north of the county, the largest monastery is **Tongshak Tashi Choling**, a branch of Gonlung, founded in the 17th century by Gendun Lodro on the site of an earlier Kagyupa monastery. The complex which once held 300 monks, has been rebuilt since 1981.

Drotsang Monastery

ⓘ *Admission: ¥15.*

Drotsang Monastery (Ch Qutansi), formally known as Drotsang Lhakhang Gautamde Gegye Dechenling, is located 25 km from the intersection at the east end of Ledu town. A generally well paved road with occasional potholes leads gradually uphill through the farming villages of the Drotsang valley. After 14 km, it bypasses a dam and an artificial lake. The monastery is located 11 km further on in **Drotsang** township (Qutan; Altitude: 2,430 m). This remarkably symmetrical complex of temples in Sino-Tibetan style, 10,000 sq m in area, dates from 1392 and originally belonged to the Karma Kagyu school. It was founded by Samlo Lama Sangye Tashi and funded by his patron, the Ming emperor Zhu Yuan Zhang. Although the temple has the air of a museum, it is worthy of a visit since it does contain original images and unique murals. Entering the front gate, there are two tablet pavilions, containing inscriptions dating back to the Ming emperors Zhu Gaozhi (1425) and Zhu Zhanji (r. 1426-1435). Beyond these pavilions, four main halls are entered in succession, in typical Chinese temple design. These are known respectively as the **Vairocana Hall** (Ch Jing Gang), the **Vajradhara Hall** (Ch Qutansi), the **Amitabha Hall** (Ch Bao Guang) and the **National Protection Hall** (Ch Longguo). Flanking the Amitabha Hall are two small assembly halls and surrounding the Vajradhara Hall are four stupas. The perimeter wall, which has two temples (a protector shrine and the **Temple of the Buddhas of the Three Times,** Ch Sanshi) and four drum towers, is remarkable for its covered side corridors decorated with 400 sq m of spectacularly vivid murals depicting the life of Shakyamuni Buddha. These paintings, some of which have been lost and others are now undergoing restoration, are ingeniously composed, full of vibrant detail, and subtle in both colour and perspective.

The oldest building is the Vajradhara Hall (170 sq m), dated 1392, which has a central image of Jowo Shakyamuni in the form of Vajradhara, known as Drotsang Dorjechang. This original image is flanked by the Sixteen Elders, while the murals of the hall are in Tibetan style and relatively unscathed. The Amitabha or Middle Hall (400 sq m), dated 1418,

Drotsang Gonpa

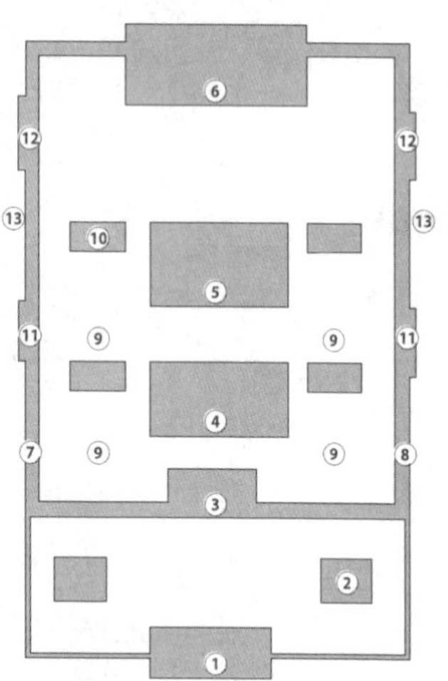

1 Front Gate
2 Tablet Pavilion
3 Vairocana Hall
4 Gautama/Vajradhara Hall
5 Amitabha Hall
6 National Protection Hall
7 Protector Temple
8 Hall of Buddhas of the Three Times
9 Stupas
10 Small Hall of Scripture
11 Small Bell-Drum Tower
12 Big Bell -Drum Tower
13 Side Corridor

contains four marble seats inscribed with characters from the Yongle period. The Great Hall (912 sq m), dated 1427, has a large stone throne, once occupied by images of Maitreya. Later, in 1564 the complex was refurbished as a Gelukpa monastery by Sherab Chokden (Drepung Samlo Rabjampa), in accordance with a prediction made by the Third Dalai Lama. Three tulkus were recognized here, and 17 branches developed throughout Drotsang and adjacent counties. However, the influence of the monastery sharply declined during the late 17th century for political reasons.

The hermitage of Drotsang known as **Tashilhunpo** lies 9 km from the temple in the remote uplands. It was founded in 1619 as a branch monastery at the behest of the Third Dalai Lama who had visited the site in 1583. However, it soon came to rival and eclipse the mother monastery in size and wealth. Also, 5 km southwest of nearby **Zhongba** township, there is the historic hermitage of **Pula Yangdzong**, where the ninth-century monks Mar Shakyamuni and Tsang Rabsel sought refuge from persecution in Central Tibet.

Kamalok County བཀའ་མ་ལོག

→ *Population: 373,964. Area: 1,681 sq km. Colour map 5, grid B5.* 民和县

Kamalok county lies 48 km downstream from Drotsang on the border of present day Qinghai and Gansu provinces. **Minhe**, the new county town, which is situated near the confluence of the Tsong-chu and the **Julak-chu** tributary (Ch Datong he), is 47 km southeast of Ledu and 121 km from Lanzhou. Traditionally, the county had 61 Tibetan monasteries or temples, most of them in the lower **Julak** valley, but the vast majority of these were small, with a mere handful of monks. In recent years, some 55 have been rebuilt, approximately half with official permission and half funded privately. All of them are Gelukpa (circa 16th-19th centuries), and many house monks of Tu nationality.

Minhe → *Altitude: 1,830 m*

The road from Ledu to **Minhe** town continues following the Tsong-chu downstream. After 10 km, a turn-off leads right (south) for **Yahongying**. The hills in this section of the valley are of grass-covered red sandstone. After 15 km, the highway crosses to the north bank, while the railway line is on the south bank. The valley narrows here, and the hills are barren. The **Songzhi** intersection, 12 km further downstream, marks the beginning of the polluted Minhe industrial zone. The monastery of **Lenhate Ganden Nechu Pelgyeling** (founded 1694), which is the most influential in Julak county, overlooks the north bank of the Tsong-chu at this point. Many of the small temples and monasteries of the county are affiliated to it.

The county capital itself is located 2 km off the highway. It is a large and growing town with a considerable Muslim and Tu population, rendered unattractive by a large ferrochrome smelting plant. Local landmarks include a hill top temple with a stupa at its base and a mosque.

In the far south of the county, in the vicinity of **Chuangkou** township, 64 km from town, there are several monasteries and shrines. These include **Shangparsi Samten Dargyeling**, 35 km to the southwest of Chuangkou, which was

Kamalok & Pari Counties

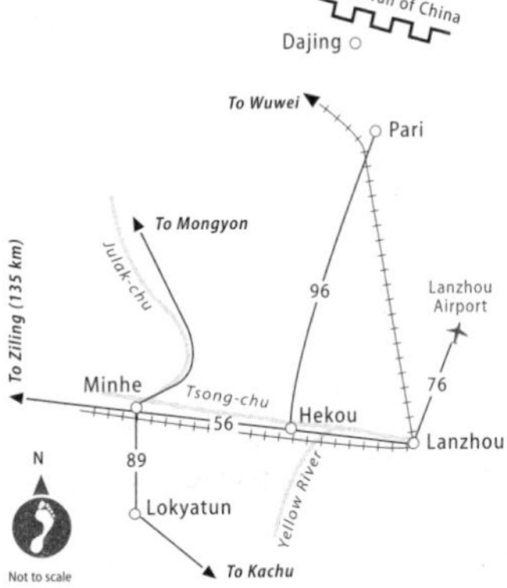

 founded by Tsongkhapa's student Jamyang Choje Shakya Yeshe while en route for Beijing, and later renovated in 1895. Some 3 km south of **Gankou** township, there is another major monastery, known as **Khataka Gonpa**, which was founded by Tsongkhapa's student Sonam Zangpo, and subsequently visited by the Third Dalai Lama.

Another road leads southeast from Minhe to cross the Yellow River at **Lokyatun** (Ch Guanting, 89 km via Gushan and Maying), and then to reach the **Sang-chu** river valley at **Kachu** (Hanjiaji), southwest of Linxia in Gansu province.

Liuwan

North of the highway, at **Liuwan** cemetery, 1,600 tombs and 30,000 relics have been excavated, including a celebrated clay pot with dancing figurines, which is regarded as a national treasure. This is the largest of many archaeological sites, which have been opened in the Qinghai area. A detailed report was published in 1980, including extensive illustrations of the unearthed pottery.

Pari County དཔའ་རིས

→ *Population: 228,400. Area: 6,633 sq km. Colour map 5, grid B6.* 天祝藏族自治县

After Kamalok, the highway crosses the present Qinghai-Gansu border en route for Lanzhou. At **Hekou** (78 km from Minhe town), it passes the confluence of the Tsong-chu and Yellow rivers (Altitude: 1,650 m), and from there it is just a short drive into the city on a toll road. From Hekou, there is also a side road which heads due north, following the **Zhuanglang** tributary upstream for 96 km to **Pari** (Ch Tianzhu). This autonomous county is the furthest outpost of Tibetan habitation in Northeast Amdo, and lies not far to the south of Dajing on the **Great Wall of China**. It is also accessible via the Lanzhou-Wuwei railway line, but unlike neighbouring Ziling and Labrang districts it is not yet classed as an open area. Alien travel permit restrictions still apply.

The Pari region has been occupied by Tibetan tribes since the period of the Yarlung Dynasty. The most important historical site in this region is the monastery of **Chorten Tang Tashi Dargyeling**, which is situated 95 km to the west of the county town in Tiantang village. This was originally a Bon monastery, constructed during the period 806-820. Subsequently, during the 11th century the Amdowa Tibetan tribe known in Chinese as Liangzhou Liugu conquered the region. When Sakya Pandita passed through en route for Mongolia in 1274, the Sakyapa monastery of **Chorten Tang** was built upon the earlier Bon foundation. Later still, when visited by the Fourth Karmapa Rolpei Dorje in 1360, the monastery was converted to the Karma Kagyu school, and following its destruction by Mongolian tribes it finally resurfaced as a Gelukpa establishment. In subsequent centuries the monastery was maintained by the Tibetans and the Tu, who, as at Gonlung, are present in large numbers here. Nowadays, the site is accessible by bus from the county town, about 4-5 hours to the east, and also by bus from Huzhu in Gonlung. There are restored **temples** ⓘ *admission: ¥3*, dedicated to Shakyamuni and Kalacakra, as well as a restored assembly hall, and a newly constructed Milarepa-style tower.

Prior to 1958 there were over 800 monks in Pari, but nowadays there are no more than 70 affiliated to the eight temples or monasteries, which have recently been reopened. Apart from Chorten Tang, the most important of these is **Gonsar Tosam Dargyeling**, 11 km west of the county town. This Kagyupa foundation was converted into a Gelukpa monastery during the 17th century, and still houses precious artefacts, including an ivory image of Avalokiteshvara presented by the Seventh Dalai Lama and a costume worn by the Sixth Dalai Lama. The monastery of **Taklung Gon Ganden Choling** originally, as its name suggests, represented the Taklung Kagyu school since its founding by Lobzang Tenpa Chokyi Nyima during the late 14th century. However, it too was subsequently converted to the Gelukpa tradition. **Pari Rabgye Gonpa** (Ch Huacangsi) is a small monastery located within the county town itself. Originally a 14th-century Kagyu foundation, it was converted to the Gelukpa school in the 17th century and rebuilt in 1981.

Sleeping

Jadabling *p561*
D **Bird Island Hotel**, T0984-7652447. Newly refurbished superior rooms are now available (¥220 per standard), and there are also triples (¥30 per bed) and 4-bed rooms (¥25 per bed).

Tanakma *p562*
E **Drolsu Dronkhang Guesthouse** in town.
E **Traffic Guesthouse**, Tsaka Rd.

Khyamri *p563*
C **Qinghai Tented Hotel**, T0974-513520/513874. Constructed on the site of former military camp Number 151, this complex has been transformed over recent years into a tourist resort and theme park. Entered through an ornate gateway with the inscription 'Turquoise Mirror' (Yu'i Melong), the hotel is even now laid out as a camp. There are rooms in mock Tibetan-tent style at ¥290, standard rooms at ¥232, and inferior rooms at ¥207 a night. Facilities include a dining hall, dance floor and jetty giving access to Tsonying Mahadeva island. Tourists are encouraged to visit the local nomad tents to have some experience of the daily life and the typical nomadic diet of curd, mutton, butter tea, and barley-ale (chang). Horse and camel riding activities are provided, as well as boating and shooting. Khyamri village, outside the hotel, has Muslim restaurants and jewellery shops. Most travellers will avoid this theme park, opting instead for more authentic encounters with the nomads of the grasslands.

Nubtso *p566, map p567*
E **North Kokonor Hotel**, T0970-642648. Standard rooms, with attached bathrooms, but no hot running water, at ¥80 per room. There are cheaper rooms, ranging from ¥8-¥25 per bed, and suites or VIP rooms (also without hot running water!), ranging from ¥120-¥888.

Chilen *p568, map p569*
D **Baboa Hotel**, T0970-672547. Standard doubles at ¥176-196, deluxe singles at ¥396, economy doubles at ¥40-60, triples at ¥54, and 4-bed dorms at ¥52.

There are also 4 guesthouses in town.

Mongyon *p570, map p570*
E **Menyuan Hotel**, T0970-612226. Has single rooms at ¥120, doubles at ¥84, and triples at ¥105.

There are also 3 guesthouses located on Main St.

Ziling *p573, map p574*
C **Jian Yin Hotel**, 55 Xida Jie, T0971-8261885/8; F0971-8261515. This 3-star hotel is one of the best in town, with comfortable doubles at ¥328-398, and a revolving roof-top restaurant.
C **Qinghai Hotel (Qinghai Binguan)**, 158 Huanghe Rd, T0971-6144888, F0971-6144145. A decaying 3-star hotel with 395 rooms (doubles at ¥180-¥468, and suites at ¥688-¥6,800), but some distance from city centre in Erlang Park. There is a good Chinese restaurant on the 2nd floor, and a lobby bar cum coffee shop. The CAAC airline office is located on the 1st Floor. Also tour agencies, excellent shopping arcades, a business centre, hairdressing and massage service. The karaoke bar and dance hall are located to the rear on the ground floor.
C **Xining Hotel**, located 5 km west of the railway station, T0971-8458701; F0971-8450798. A 3-star hotel, Russian-style building with double rooms (range: ¥240-280), and triples (¥35 per bed). The hotel restaurant does an excellent hotpot.
E **Youzheng Gongyu Hotel**, 138 Huzhu Lu, near railway station, T0971-8149484. Has dormitory accommodation at ¥16-24, and singles at ¥46.
D **Xining Mansion (Xining Dasha)**, corner of Jianguo St and Dongguan Dajie,

For an explanation of the sleeping and eating price codes used in this guide, see inside the front cover. Other relevant information is found in Essentials pages 44-46.

T0971-8149991. In Muslim quarter, 10 mins' walking distance from railway station, has standard rooms (range: ¥132-¥168), singles (range: ¥181-239), and triples (¥165 per room).

E **Yongfu Hotel**, on Jianguo St near railway station. Is the best value, double rooms at ¥50, with attached bathrooms and good hot water supply, and a coffee shop.

The small Tibetan-run guesthouses outside the railway station may not be allowed to accept foreigners.

Rushar Drongdal *p576*

B **Tsongkha Hotel (Taersi Binguan)**, T0972-236761-8888, F0972-233900. Under the Hong Kong management of Silk Road Hotels, which has doubles at ¥360-680, and Tibetan-style rooms at ¥450-880 (extra bed ¥120), the hotel has a fine restaurant, with good Tibetan-style dumplings, although the small Tibetan and Muslim restaurants below the steps are significantly cheaper.

Pingan *p579, map p580*

D **Haidong Hotel**, T0972-613516/6135. Has doubles at ¥120.

There are also 2 guesthouses located on Main St, but most visitors will prefer to stay in Ziling.

Ledu *p583, map p583*

D **Ledu Hotel**, T0972-631028. Has economy doubles at ¥80, triples at ¥75, standard doubles at ¥120, suites at ¥380, and deluxe doubles and triples at ¥480 and ¥680 respectively.

Minhe *p585*

D **Minhe Hotel**, 38 Chuan Kou Zhen Xin Cheng St, T0972-522149. Has standard rooms at ¥164, suites at ¥204, and triples at ¥186, although a 100% mark-up may be charged to foreigners.

Pari *p586*

E **Tianzhu Government Guesthouse**, has doubles at ¥50 and dormitory accommodation at ¥7-20 per bed.

Smaller guesthouses charge less but may not be permitted to accept foreigners.

Eating

Jadabling *p561*

Bird Island Hotel Restaurant, offers good quality Chinese food, and in the village there is an abundant supply of fresh fish (Ch Huangyu) for sale.

Tanakma *p562*

There are a number of small Muslim restaurants and shops.

Nubtso *p566, map p567*

Try the street restaurants, adjacent to the park.

Chilen *p568, map p569*

Yue Lai Shun Restaurant, T09846-672368, Main Street. Appears to be the best and newest restaurant, offering local seafood and standard Chinese and Muslim dishes

Mongyon *p570, map p570*

San Xing Can Ting Restaurant, situated behind the Menyuan Hotel. For Chinese food.

Sample the local Muslim dishes at one of the many small Muslim eateries.

Ziling *p573, map p574*

Dicos, adjacent to the Jian Yin Hotel. Burgers and western-style fast food.

Muslim Restaurant, on the corner of Jianguo St and Dongguan Dajie, for excellent Muslim food.

Peace Restaurant, for good inexpensive Chinese food.

Three Kham Rivers Restaurant, in the Tibetan quarter. For Tibetan momos and delicious curd.

Wenhua Jie Meishi Cheng, there are a number of plush restaurants offering a wide range of high-class cuisine, including seafood, Korean barbecue, and spicy Hunan dishes.

Yun Feng Ge, opposite the Qinghai Hotel entrance. Really excellent, offering Cantonese dimsum as well as northern Chinese cuisine.

Zhuang Guo Yang Gao Rou, restaurant opposite the petrol station on the Pingan road. For local mutton specialities.

Further down Huanghe Rd, there are a number of bars and small restaurants. The restaurant of the Xining Hotel offers an excellent Mongolian hotpot.

Festivals at Kumbum Jampaling (2005)

Festival	Starting time	2005
Masked Dance of Dharmaraja	1230	22 Feb
Butter Sculpture Display	1730	23 Feb
Marked Dance of Mahacakra	1200	14 May, 22 Oct
Buddha's Nirvana (Saga Dawa): Masked dances and display of Buddha Tangka	0800	22 May
Dharmacakra Day: Masked dances and display of Buddha Tangka	0800	13 Jul
Descent from Tusita Day: Masked dance of Hayagriva		24 Oct

Ziling also has many simple street restaurants, of which the cheapest are in the open air market area.

West Gate Bus Station has food and there are also kebab stalls in the Muslim quarter.

For noodle dishes, try the restaurant run by the Yongfu Hotel, near the railway station.

For local mutton specialities, try one of the large fashionable Muslim restaurants in the town centre, such as the large establishment opposite the Jian Yin Hotel.

Minhe *p585*
There are many small Muslim restaurants in town and by the highway.

Pari *p586*
Most of the small roadside restaurants are Sichuan or Muslim in style.

Entertainment

Ziling *p573, map p574*
Ziling has the usual nightlife of provincial or frontier towns. The main forms of entertainment are karaoke, disco, bathing and sauna complexes and cinema – all located in the central area near Da Shizi, by the riverside, or in the major hotels. In all, the city has more than 7 theatres and cinemas.

Festivals and events

Ziling *p573, map 574*
The Spring Festival (Ch Chunjie) is held on the 1st day of the 1st month of the lunar calendar (**9 Feb 2005**); and the Flower Song Festival (Ch Huarhui) on the 6th day of the 6th month (**11 Jul 2005**). For the 2005 dates of certain traditional Tibetan festivals, see above and Essentials, page 46.

Rushar Drongdal *p576*
Festivals and important ceremonies are still held here, notably the Great Prayer Festival during the first month of the lunar calendar, the masked dances held in the 4th, 7th and 9th months; the Dharmacakra anniversary (4th day of the 6th month); and the Anniversary of Tsongkhapa (25th day of the 10th month), followed by the Dance of Hayagriva (26th day).

Huzhu *p582*
The Lantern Festival, including local song and dance performances, will be held in Huzhu on the 15th day of the 1st lunar month (**23 Feb 2005**). The Broad Bean Festival, in which local costumes and embroidery are exhibited in conjunction with local opera and folk art performances, and the consumption of the local delicacy, broad beans, will be held on the 2nd day of the 2nd lunar month (**11 Mar 2005**). The Flower Song festival (Haurhui) will be held at Wufeng temple in Gonlung county from the 6th day of the 6th lunar month (**11 Jul 2005**). Other song and dance fairs of the Tu nationality are held within the county at Songshuiwan and Weiyuan in **Jul**, and at Tuguan in **Aug**.

Ledu *p583, map p583*
The Lantern Festival is held annually in Ledu, on the 15th day of the 1st lunar month (**23 Feb 2005**).

Qinghai and Gansu Provincial railway schedules

Train No	Depart	Time	Arrival	Time	Hard	Soft
653	Lanzhou	0818	Ziling	1117	¥33	¥50
655	Lanzhou	1526	Ziling	1825	¥33	¥50
654	Ziling	1152	Lanzhou	1451	¥33	¥50
656	Ziling	1941	Lanzhou	2240	¥33	¥50
K423	Yinchuan	2205	Ziling	+1133	¥128	¥200
K424	Ziling	1847	Yinchuan	+0700	¥128	¥200
T151	Beijing	1528	Ziling	+2039	¥430	¥658
T152	Ziling	0818	Beijing	+1320	¥430	¥658
K5701	Ziling	1918	Kermo	+1055	¥122	¥193
K5702	Kermo	1840	Ziling	+1006	¥122	¥193
K427	Lanzhou	2110	Kermo	+13.28	¥78	¥150
K428	Kermo	1650	Lanzhou	+0838	¥78	¥150

Fares to intermediate stations: Ziling-Bongtak Tianjun ¥63 (hard), ¥93 (soft); Ziling-Dabzhi ¥47 (hard), ¥66 (soft).

Drotsang Monastery *p584, map p584*
In addition to the Buddhist festivals held during the 1st and 4th months of the lunar calendar, a secular **Flower Song Fair** (Ch Huarhui) is also held here on the 6th day of the 6th lunar month, which in 2005 corresponds to **11 Jul**.

Shopping

Ziling *p573, map p574*
The large open air market near the West Gate Bus Station on Changjiang St, has handicraft stalls selling crystal salt carvings and Kunlun jade products, bookshops, traditional medicines, dried fruit, babao tea, and meat and vegetables, as well as textiles of great variety. The roads that intersect at Da Shizi also have interesting shops; among them Xinhua Bookstore which has a good Tibetan section. **NB** Pickpockets are rampant! For luxury items, including the hugely popular yak wool sweaters made in the Repkong area, try the shopping arcade in the Qinghai Hotel. A visit to the carpet factory is also worthwhile.

Photography
Film and processing available at photographic shops in town and in larger the hotels.

Stamps
Stamps are available at **GPO** on Dongda St, and also at the reception counters or shops in the major hotels.

Activities and tours

Ziling *p573, map p574*
Mountaineering
Qinghai Mountaineering Association, 7 Tiyuxiang, Xining 810000, T0971-8238877, F0971-8238933. There are 2 good camping stores in town.
Toread Camping Equipment (Tanlu Zhe), 59 Xiguan Dajie, T0971-6141132. Sells a large variety of tents, sleeping bags, rucksacks, and trekking gear.

Tour companies
Beijing Longmen International Tours, A9 Daquideng Lane, Meishuguan Houjie East District, Beijing, T010-84010085, F010-64012180.
China International Travel Service: Ziling Branch (CITS), 156 Huanghe Rd, T0971-6143950, F0971-6131080/8238721.
Qinghai International Sports Travel Service (QIST), 1 Shan Shaan Tai, Xining 810000, T0971-8238877, F0971-8238933.
Qinghai Tibet Adventures, 13 Beidajie, Xining, T0971-8245548, F0971-8212641.

Transport

Jadabling *p561*
Group tours depart from the lobby of the Qinghai Hotel in Ziling around 0600 and return in the evening around 2100 (¥120 for the day

Qinghai Regional long distance bus schedule from Ziling bus station

Destination	Schedule	Information	Price
Mangra (Guinan)	0830-0930	2 buses daily	¥34 ¥39 (minibus)
Kawasumdo (Tongde)	0800-0830	2 buses daily	¥41.30
Tawu (Maqen)	0845	1 bus daily	¥51 ¥60 (minibus)
Sogwo (Henan)	0715	1 bus daily	¥30.90
Repkong (Tongren)	0730-1200	7 buses daily	¥26 ¥30 (minibus)
Jentsa (Jianza)	0845-1530	3 buses daily	¥14 ¥16 (minibus)
Chilen (Qilian)	0815-0930	2 buses daily	¥26.00
Linxia	0730-0830	3 buses daily	¥30 ¥34 (minibus)
Tso (Hezuo)	0715	1 bus daily	¥32.80
Monyon (Menyuan)	0745-1300	5 buses daily	¥37 ¥42 (minibus)
Zhangye	0730-0845	2 buses daily	¥39 ¥43 (minibus)
Wuwei	0715-0900	2 buses daily	¥35.00
Lijiaxia	0720-1615	30 buses daily	¥11.80
Lanzhou	0800-1600	14 buses daily	¥29 ¥36 (minibus)
Bongtak Tianjun	0730	1 bus every other day	¥40 ¥46 (minibus)
Lhasa	1600	1 bus daily	¥340.00
Terlenka (Delingha)	0915	1 bus every other day	¥55 ¥64 (minibus) ¥90 (couchette)
Da Tsaidam	0715	1 bus every other day	¥69.40
Panchen Zhingde (Dulan)	1730	1 bus daily	¥45 ¥52 (minibus)
Ulan	0745	1 bus every other day	¥40 ¥47 (minibus)
Kermo (Golmud)	1600	3 buses daily	¥82 ¥94 (minibus)
Chumarleb (Qumalai)	1600	3 buses daily	¥100 ¥117
Chabcha (Gonghe)	0800	2 buses daily	¥16 ¥18 (minibus)
Tsigortang (Xinghai)	0955		¥29 ¥33 (minibus)
Darlag (Dari)	1015	2nd, 5th, 8th, 12th and 15th of each month	¥68 ¥79 (minibus)
Mato (Madoi)	0930	18th, 22nd, 25th and 28th of each month	¥89 (couchette)
Jyekundo (Yushu)	1100-1300	2 buses daily	¥155 (couchette)
Dunhuang			¥107 ¥112 ¥185 (couchette)

trip or ¥240 for a 2-day trip). Few public buses run from Tanakma, and a taxi costs at least ¥50.

Mongyon *p570, map p570*
Public buses run from **Ziling** via Datong into the Mongyon area.

Ziling *p573, map p574*
Air
There are daily flights to **Beijing** as well as flights to **Chengdu** (on Tue to Sun inclusive), **Guangzhou** (on Tue, Thu and Sat), **Lhasa** (Mon, Wed, Fri and Sun), and **Urumqi** (on Mon-Thu inclusive and Sat). The airport is 29 km east of town on the north bank of the Tsong-chu River. Taxis: ¥50, shuttle bus: ¥10. **NB** Foreigners bound for Lhasa will require a Tibet Entry Permit, without which the flight ticket cannot be purchased.

Lanzhou West Bus Station Schedule

Destination	Time	Price
Labrang (Xiahe)	0730, 0830	¥32 ¥44 (minibus)
Luchu	0830	¥42
Cho-ne	0630	¥34.50 (foreigners not allowed)
Lintan	0730	¥41
Ganlho Dzong (Hezhuo)	0730-1230 (every 30 mins)	¥32 (standard), ¥43.80 (Iveco)
Tewo	0830, 1400	¥82 (Iveco), ¥92 (couchette)
Drukchu	0700	¥49.50
Ziling	0700-1700 (regularly)	¥26.50
Linxia	0830-11.30 (hourly)	¥26.50

Bus

Buses run throughout Qinghai province to and from **Kermo** (Golmud), **Repkong**, **Lanzhou**, **Mato** and the **Xinjiang border**. **Local** Buses leave from the West Gate (Ximen) Bus Station. **Long distance** Ziling long-distance bus station information office: T0971-8149690. Buses leave from the Main Bus Station near the railway station (see schedule), and in addition there are frequent buses departing throughout the day for all county towns in East Kokonor prefecture, including **Tongkor**, **Rushar**, **Serkhok**, **Gonlung**, **Tsongkha Khar**, **Drotsang** and **Minhe**.

Minibuses and landcruisers can be hired (with driver) from CITS. Some bus fares from Ziling: **Tsongkha Khar** (Pingan) ¥4.10; **Gonlung** (Huzhu) ¥4.80; **Drotsang** (Ledu) ¥6.70; **Dowi** (Xunhua) ¥16.50; **Minhe** ¥12-¥14; **Tongkor** (Huangyuan) ¥5.50; **Bayan Khar** (Hualong) ¥13-¥15; **Rikmon** (Daotonghe) ¥10.50; **Tanakma** (Hemahe) ¥21; **Tsaka** (Chaka) ¥28.30; **Shang** (Xiang Ride) ¥47; **Nomahung** (Nuomuhong) ¥102.60; **Kangtsa** (Gangca) ¥19.10; **Longyang Xia Dam** ¥14.60; **Padma** (Baima) ¥81; **Trika** (Guide) ¥12.50; **Tsogyenrawa** (Huashixia) ¥63.30; **Dabzhi** (Haiyan) ¥20-¥23; and **Zhiwu** (Xiewu) ¥117. For other destinations, please consult the table.

Taxi

Call T0971-6142393 for information.

Train

There are frequent train connections to **Lanzhou** (4 hrs); as well as to **Beijing**, **Shanghai**, **Qingdao**, **Xi'an**, and **Kermo** (both evening express, and morning local services). Railway station automatic answerphone: T0971-8149970.

Pari *p586*

Bus

Buses depart for **Lanzhou** (3 hrs, ¥11) and **Tashi Dargyeling** (4-5 hrs, 94 km, ¥8). There are also daily departures for **Huzhu** in Gonlung and **Kumbum Jampaling** in Rushar.

Train

Trains bound for Wu Wei to Lanzhou depart from Huacangsi station.

Directory

Ziling *p573, map p574*

Airline offices Minghang Flight Ticket Centre, 85/1, Bayi St, T0971-8174616. Books flights to Kermo, Xi'an, Chengdu, Chongqing, Guangzhou, Beijing, Shanghai, Shenyang, Urumqi and Wuhan. CAAC, Qinghai Hotel, 1st Flr, also has a flight booking service. Airport information: 0971-8174612 ext 2091. **Banks** Bank of China, Dongguan Dajie. Open (1000-1200 and 1500-1700, Mon-Fri) and Bank of China, Da Shizi (open 1000-1500) have foreign exchange facilities and will advance cash on credit cards. Foreign exchange is also available at the Qinghai Hotel, Jian Yin

Hotel, and Xining Hotel, while credit card payments are accepted at the Qinghai and Jian Yin hotels. **Hospitals** Peoples' Hospital, Gonghe St. Shengzhong Hospital, Qiyi St, Emergency T0971-120. **Post offices** General Post Office, Beida St (open daily: 0830-1730), has EMS and IDD services. China Telecom, Tongren St, has internet facilities on 2nd floor. Postal facilities, fax and internet also available in major hotels. **Tourist offices** Qinghai Tourist Corporation (QTC), Qinghai Hotel, 156 Huanghe Rd, T0971-6143711, F0971-8238721. **Useful addresses** Police and Public Security: Foreigners' Registration Office, Beida St (open 0930-1230, and 1530-1730) for visa extensions. Lost or stolen property: T110. Automatic weather forecast: T0971-6145121. Traffic accident unit: T0971-6146027. Directory enquiries: T0971-114 (city), T0971-113 (long distance).

The Yellow River Bend: Repkong and Sogwo

There are three routes from Ziling to the Golok region in Southern Amdo: one via Tsongkha Khar, Bayan Khar or Jentsa, and Repkong; a second via Rushar and Trika; and a third via Chabcha and Mato. The first is described in this section, and the others in the following section.

The ethnic mix to the north and east of ***Repkong*** *is the most complex in Amdo. The Xionglu, distant relatives of the Sodgians, once ruled here, in constant conflict with neighbouring Han China, after which came the Tuyunhun (Tib Azha), the Qiang, and then, during the seventh to the ninth centuries, the Tibetans. The Tangut state of Xixia and the Mongolian Empire ruled this area in turn during the 10th-14th centuries. There were, additionally, pockets of Hor or Uighur tribes of Turkic origin, who had been dispersed along the oases of the Silk Road very early, and from the eighth century Arabs and Persians. Hui Muslims, who are mostly of Turkic origin, and the Salar, a distinct tribe exiled from Samarkand, also settled here. The earlier conquering armies had a tendency to disband at the end of their campaigns, frequently displacing the locals.*

After the Ming emperors of China had rescinded the ancient imperial policy of 'using barbarians to rule barbarians', colonial settlements were gradually established in the grasslands, and the agricultural Chinese began to push back the nomadic tribes. Many outlying groups of Amdowa Tibetans became isolated from the rest of the Tibetan population by these large settlements, and at the start of the 20th century in a few regions Tibetans were becoming a minority. To complicate matters, some Tibetans converted to Islam, often at the point of a sword, and racial intermarriage was commonplace.

The route described in this section comprises six counties, of which three now belong to the South Yellow River Tibetan Autonomous Prefecture (Jentsa, Repkong and Tsekok), two (Bayan Khar and Dowi) are administered directly from Ziling, and one (Sogwo) is a Mongolian Autonomous Prefecture in its own right. **Recommended itineraries: 6, 8, 9, 11. See page 20.** ▸▸ *For Sleeping, Eating and other listings, see pages 614-616.*

Bayan Khar County བ་ཡན་མཁར

→ *Population: 229,049. Area: 2,732 sq km. Colour map 5, grid B5.* 化隆回族自治县

From **Pingan** town, a branch road leads south from the Ziling-Lanzhou highway. Leaving the Tsong-chu valley it crosses into **Bayan Khar** (Hualong) county, where virtually half the population is Muslim. Nonetheless, some 50,000 Tibetans also live here, the third highest concentration of Tibetans in Qinghai. Most of these Tibetans are in villages far to the east and west of the county, with the town itself being predominantly Hui and Han. The county capital, known as **Hualong**, lies 84 km southeast of Pingan, on a south-flowing tributary of the Yellow River, or 56 km from Dowi and 58 km from Jentsa. In the northeast of the county, there is also an important north-flowing tributary of the Tsong-chu. There used to be 44 temples or monasteries within the county, the most historically important being **Jakhyung** and **Dentik**. Twenty-seven of these survived the Cultural Revolution, having been used as granaries and storerooms. At present, the county has 34 monasteries, four of which are Nyingmapa and the remainder Gelukpa.

Jakhyung Shedrubling Monastery → *Colour map 5, grid B5*

Getting there The southern road from Pingan bypasses a stupa on the right and the Jimbu Restaurant (where Hu Yao Ban once dined), before crossing the watershed **Lambar La** pass (Altitude: 3,210 m) on Mount Chingsha, which marks the county border. Entering Bayan Khar county, the road then passes through **Zawa** (Ch Quanzhuang) township (39 km), from where a paved road leads directly to **Dongma Bridge** over the Yellow River, and a rough side road heads west to **Chapu** and **Zhongshen** (Ch Xiongxian) villages. Both Jakhyung and Dzitsa monasteries are accessible south of this branch road, which, after Zhongshen, links up with the Ziling-Trika road (see below, page 616).

The site The monastery of **Jakhyung Shedrubling** lies to the south of the Zawa-Zhongshen road on a ridge overlooking the Yellow River, 19 km beyond Zawa or 10 km from Chapu. This is one of the most historic and renowned Gelukpa monasteries of Amdo, founded in 1349 by Lama Dondrub Rinchen, the teacher of Tsongkhapa. The attractive monastery is situated in a small forest zone, popular with Chinese picnickers from Ziling at weekends. Small tractors wait for passengers at the turn-off, and will charge about ¥15 for the trip to the monastery.

Prior to the Gelukpa foundation, an earlier monastery had been established on the same site by the Second Karmapa, Karmapakshi in the 12th century. Later, following the incumbency of Lama Dondrub Rinchen, the monastery was listed, along with Serkhok, Chubzang and Gonlung, as one of the 'four great monasteries of the north', a phrase used in Amdo to signify the oldest and most significant Gelukpa institutions of the region. It was here in 1363 that Tsongkhapa became ordained as a renunciate, and studied until leaving Amdo for Lhasa at the age of 16. The small forest on the eastern slope of the ridge on which Jakhyung lies is said to be formed from his hair, and is included on the two-hour circumambulation of the monastery. There are currently about 500 monks and 10 reconstructed temples. The large **assembly hall** is brand new and unimpressive, but the small temples to the rear have more character. Among them, a green-glazed brick **Jampa Lhakhang** houses images of Shakyamuni, Maitreya and Tsongkhapa; while the **Serkhang** has a reliquary stupa containing the mortal remains of Lama Dondrub Rinchen, flanked by large images of Jowo Shakyamuni, Maitreya and Manjughosa.

From Jakhyung, a two-hour walk heads steeply down through the barren 'badlands' to the north bank of the Yellow River.

Bayan Khar & Jentsa Counties

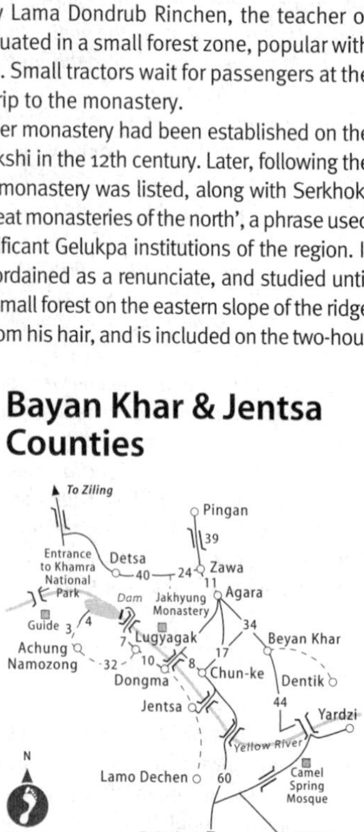

Dzitsa Tashi Choding Monastery → *Colour map 5, grid B4*

There are two Gelukpa monasteries to the northwest of Dzitsa township, some 40 km beyond Jakhyung along the spur road. The lower one, **Dzitsa Gonpa**, is a branch of Jakhyung, founded by Lama Wangchuk (fl. 17th century). The upper one, known as **Dzitsa Tashi Choding**, is a well-respected Gelukpa monastery that was founded in 1903 by the Fourth Sharma Pandita Gendun Tendzin Gyatso. It has two temples, the larger with a stupa and statue of the founder, along with modern images depicting Jowo Shakyamuni, Atisha and Tsongkhapa, and mural panels created by artists from Repkong. The smaller holds a large Avalokiteshvara, a small Manjughosa and a White Tara. There are currently four lamas and about 300 monks, many of whom come from far afield, drawn by the quality of teaching here. Further up the valley en route to **Trika** (Ch Guide) is a patch of coniferous forest that must have once covered much of the Lhamori mountain and the small hermitage of **Zhongshen Ritro**, connected to Kumbum, which was originally a 13th-century Sakyapa foundation.

Jintsamani

Returning to the main road from Jakhyung, turn southeast and after 11 km there is a major fork at **Agara** (Ch Laqutan). The southwest branch leads directly to **Chun-ke** on the north bank of the Yellow River, from where bridges cross to Lugyagak, Jentsa and Repkong; and the southeast branch to **Dowi** (Xunhua) after first bypassing Hualong county town. Taking the former, you will soon reach the temple complex of **Jintsamani** in Ngotsoto township (Ch Ansodo), which is located alongside a mineral water plant. The original buildings were founded by Tsongkhapa's teacher and affiliated to Jakhyung. More recently, in the early 20th century, a large water-powered prayer wheel dedicated to the deity Cintamanicakra Tara was constructed here. Now there are three water-powered wheels in the **main hall**, the central one containing the remnants of the original (destroyed during the Cultural Revolution). The main hall also has images of Jowo Shakyamuni, Tara, and (unusually) Shantaraksita flanked by Padmasambhava and King Trisong Detsen. The naïve but delicate side murals depict the Sixteen Elders, and on the right there is a fresco showing the temple as it once looked. The ceiling is high, elegantly carved and decorated. To the left of the main hall, a **Jokhang** temple is currently under construction.

Bayan and Dehinglang → *Colour map 5, grid B5*

If you take the southeast fork from Agara, you will pass through **Ertang**, where **Gechuk Gonpa**, a branch of Lamo Dechen is located, and after 17 km you will reach another intersection, where a turn-off on the right (south) leads downhill to **Bayan** and **Dehinglang** townships. The few monasteries along this road are mostly branches of Jakhyung, although **Ngosa Gon**, 8 km southeast of Dehinglang, is affiliated to Lamo Dechen. If, instead, you take the left fork, you will soon reach the turn-off for **Hualong** (32 km from Agara). The town lies only 2 km to the east of the road.

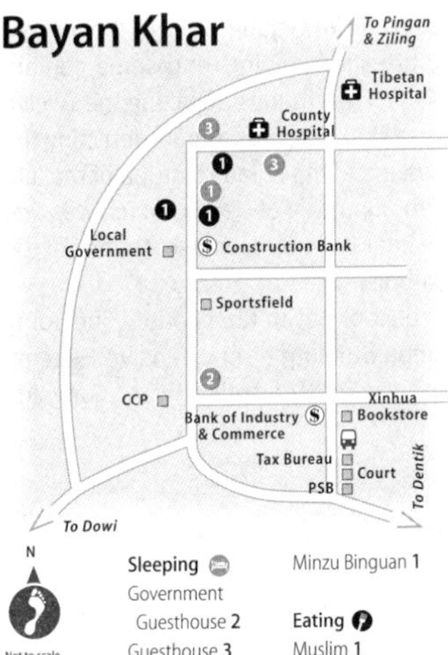

Hualong County Town

→ *Colour map 5, grid B5*

Entering Main Street from the north, you will pass the Tibetan Hospital on the left. A turn-off on the right leads to the County Hospital, the Nationalities' Hotel (Minzu Binguan), the government buildings, and a number of small Muslim restaurants. Continuing south on Main Street you will pass the post office, bank and tax office, along with the bus station, court and police station. At the south end of Main Street, the road forks. Turn left (east) for **Dentik** (63 km), or southwest for **Dowi** (58 km). » *For listings, see pages 614-616.*

Hualong to Dentik

Heading east from Hualong, the road passes through **Shidachang** and **Chuma** townships, where the monasteries are mostly affiliated to **Lenhate Gonpa** in neighbouring Kamalok (see above, page 585). However, south of **Jinyuan** (45 km east of Hualong), on the approach to Dentik, you will pass the 17th-century **Drakargya Ngakhang**, which is the largest Nyingmapa monastery in the county, and its retreat hermitage at **Khorpa Ngakhang**.

Dentik → *Colour map 5, grid B5*

Getting there Driving south from Jinyuan, the motor road comes to an end at the village of Korba, one hour's walking distance from Dentik. Traffic is very infrequent and if you have no transport, it may be easier to access the site on foot from Dowi (see below, page 597).

Some 63 km from Hualong town and 18 km due south of Jinyuan township, there is the most important pilgrimage site and power-place in all of Amdo. **Dentik Sheldrak** (Sheldrak/Shelgyi Bamgon), also known as **Dentik Shelgyi Bamgon**, has been revered since the time of Padmasambhava as the foremost power-place associated with buddha-mind throughout Kham and Amdo. Later, it was here that Mar Shakyamuni and his colleagues first accepted Lachen Gongpa Rabsel (892-975) as their student, thereby saving the monastic tradition for the sake of posterity. It was in Dentik that Lu-me and the 10 men of Utsang received ordination from Lachen, enabling them to revive monastic Buddhism on their eventual return to Lhasa. Lachen himself is said to have built the first monastery here, and the site was subsequently visited by successive generations of Tibetan pilgrims over the centuries, including the Third Dalai Lama.

The monastery is spread along the floor of a small side valley with two simple temples and a number of caves and sacred springs. One of the caves is associated with Lachen Gongpa Rabsel, while Lhalung Pelgyi Dorje, the monk who assassinated Langdarma with an arrow, also spent his last years here although, because of the crime he had committed he refused to take part in the ordination of Lachen Gongpa Rabsel. It contains images of Mar Shakyamuni, Tsang Rabsel and Yo Gejung. Most of the original pre-1958 buildings (approximately 200 rooms) are still standing, and some contain undamaged images. Among them, the assembly hall has murals depicting the Twelve Deeds of Shakyamuni Buddha, and the Rabdragpa Lhakhang has murals depicting the life of Prince Vassantara, an image of Cakrasamvara and the reliquary stupa of the late Tseten Zhabdrung. The hermitage of **Yangtik Ritro**, 1 km east of Dentik, which was first opened by the Third Dalai Lama in 1583, contains natural stone representations of the eight bodhisattvas and the eight auspicious symbols.

There are several other monasteries in the east of Bayan Khar county, including two which represent the Bon tradition, and **Jampa Bumling** – an extensive Gelukpa establishment, which was founded by Rinchen Gyatso in the 16th century alongside an earlier Maitreya temple.

Hualong to Dowi

Heading south from the Hualong intersection on the Pingan-Dowi road, you will cross a pass (2,400 m) after 4 km, followed by an artificial lake to the east. The descent leads for 32 km down to **Kado** township, and eventually reaches the north bank of the Yellow River at **Kado Tashi Chodzong** (Ch Gando), where it crosses over into Dowi county (44 km). This monastery is a branch of Labrang, founded in 1791, when the Second Jamyang Zhepa Konchok Jikme Wangpo passed away here.

Dowi County རྫོ་སྦིས

→ *Population: 111,027. Area: 2,132 sq km. Colour map 5, grid B5.* 循化撒拉族自治县

The county capital of Dowi, traditionally known in Tibetan as Yardzi or Dowi Khar and in Chinese as Xunhua, lies on the south bank of the Yellow River, 56 km southeast of Hualong, and 113 km west of Linxia. Since the 14th century the county has been predominantly inhabited by the **Salar**, a very tight-knit band of Central Asian Muslims. A legendary camel carried bags of earth from their Samarkand home, which were matched with earth around a nearby spring, and the tribe's long migration came to an end. The camel appropriately turned to stone!

By the 19th century, the Salar had absorbed several villages north of the Yellow River, but they were badly defeated by the Chinese armies during the intermittent Muslim wars. The county town is quite large, but surrounded by fields, some open and others enclosed by mud walls, where fruit trees are cultivated.

Despite the Salars' overwhelming dominance in the agriculturally rich valleys of lower Dowi, the Tibetans continue to occupy the upper valleys, and several important monasteries can be visited. Prior to 1958 there were altogether 33 Tibetan shrines or monasteries within the county, the most important being **Bimdo Gonpa** and **Gori Gonpa**.

Yardzi → *Altitude: 1,920 m. For listings, see pages 614-616.*

Crossing the bridge over the Yellow River which leads into Dowi county from Bayan Khar, after 5 km you will reach the Camel Spring Mosque at Lutuo. This is where the stone camel, talisman of the Salar people, is to be seen. The highway to Repkong, Labrang and Linxia continues south from the mosque, bypassing the town, while a branch road leads left (east), 5 km into town.

Taking the latter road, you will pass on the right the Abdul and Chenglai restaurants and the West Gate Market, while on the left you will pass the Tianchi Hotel (Tianchi Fandian), banks and government buildings. The bus station is next to the Traffic Guesthouse, towards the south end of town. Although the town has excellent Muslim restaurants, the sanitation of the hotels leaves much to be desired.

Dowi to Dentik

A small bridge leads northeast across the Yellow River from Xunhua town in the direction of **Dentik** (see above, page 596), but the journey has to be made on foot and will take eight hours. On crossing the river, leave the motor road, and take a footpath which heads directly uphill for five hours through a narrow rocky gorge, climbing steeply along a series of ridges, 610 m above the valley. This trail eventually descends for three hours into a narrow side valley where Dentik is located.

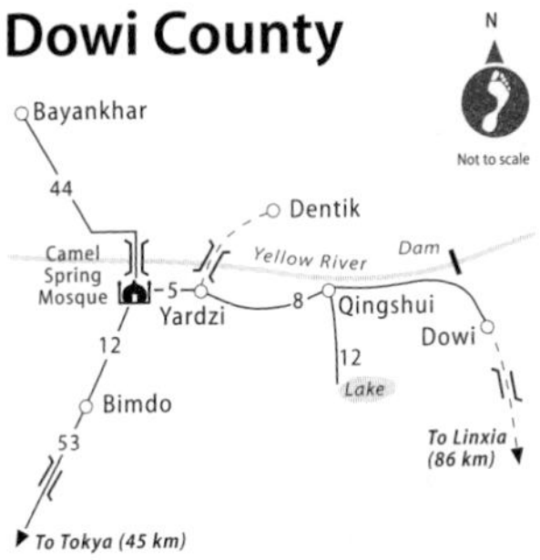

Dowi County

N
Not to scale
Bayankhar
44
Camel Spring Mosque
5
Yardzi
Dentik
Yellow River
Dam
8
Qingshui
Dowi
12
Lake
12
Bimdo
53
To Linxia (86 km)
To Tokya (45 km)

Dowi to Linxia

Mengda Tianchi Lake If you take the southeast road from Yardzi, which initially follows the Yellow River downstream, and then crosses the mountains, you will reach **Linxia** after 86 km. Some 8 km due east of Yardzi on this road at **Qingshui**, three trails diverge, east for the small dam on the

Qinghai-Gansu border (17 km), southeast for Linxia, or southwest to **Mengda Tianchi Lake**. The last of these cuts through a lateral gorge for 12 km to reach the lake, which is revered by Tibetans who view it as a talismanic power-place. It is now a nature reserve, although its woods are still extensively used by the last Salar village. There is a guesthouse before the lake, which hires out horses for the four-hour trail through the craggy mountain gorge to the lakeside.

Heading southeast towards Linxia from the Qingshui intersection, after 22 km, the road passes through **Dowi** township. In this vicinity, there are 13 monasteries, the most important being **Gori Dratsang Ganden Pelgyeling**. This was originally a Sakyapa establishment, founded in the 13th century by Lama Samten Rinchen, which converted to the Gelukpa school during the 17th century. It contains the impressive reliquary chapel of the late Sherab Gyatso (1883-1968) – a native of Dowi – with clay images of Tsongkhapa and Maitreya flanking the central stupa. Most of the small monasteries around Dowi are affiliated to Gori. The exceptions are **Sechang Gar** which is a small branch of Labrang, **Dabma Gon**, which is a 19th-century Nyingmapa nunnery 8 km northwest of the township, and **Changshar Gar**, 9 km southeast of the township, which was founded in 1626. Among these, Dabma Gon is easily identified by the adjacent **Dowi Chorten**, which dominates the surrounding landscape.

After Dowi, the road crosses the rugged watershed at **Dargye La** pass (3,540 m), which forms the current Qinghai-Gansu border. On the ascent, there is a side trail that leads after a few hours' walking to the oracle lake of **Dargye Yumtso**. After crossing the pass, the paved road descends through Muslim villages to reach the large towns of **Kachu** (Ch Hanjiaji) and Linxia. On the descent to Kachu, amid this overwhelming Muslim presence, you will notice one significant Tibetan monastery at **Gangshun Gon**, and the impressive stupa at **Chorten Rangma**. The latter has a small community of nuns, founded during the 15th century by Nakjin Rangron.

Dowi to Repkong

At the Camel Spring Mosque of Lutuo, 5 km west of Yardzi, you can head north across the Yellow River to Hualong and Pingan (see above, page 579), or southwest for 57 km to **Lanja Bridge**, where roads diverge for **Repkong** via Tokya (16 km) and **Labrang** (78 km). The southwest road climbs gradually from Lutuo for 12 km to reach **Bimdo** village

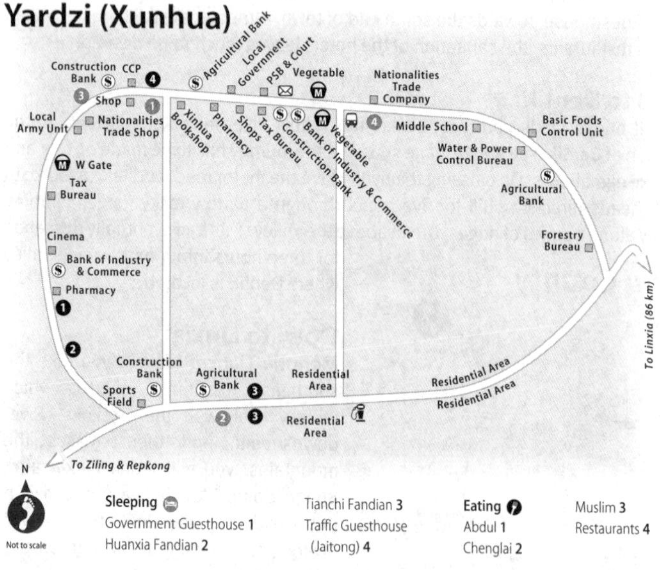

(Altitude: 2,280 m), which is the most important Tibetan settlement in Dowi, and the birthplace of the late Tenth Panchen Lama.

Bimdo

Entering **Bimdo** (locally pronounced Wimdo), on the right (west) there is an impressive large building in classical Tibetan style with sloping white walls and architrave of red potentilla wood. This is a Tibetan primary school, which was funded by Tibetan residents of India. A stupa is passed on the left (east) and soon, on the right (west) you will reach a well preserved farmhouse, which was the **birthplace of late Tenth Panchen Lama.** The building takes the form of an open courtyard, surrounded by wood-panelled rooms with packed-mud roofs, typical of Amdo hamlets. Downstairs are the residential quarters, still occupied by the late Panchen Lama's mother and brother. Upstairs, there is a spacious chapel, attended by caretaker monks. A footpath leads over a spur, one hour's walk from here to **Bimdo Gonchen Tashi Chokhorling**. This monastery was founded in 1402 by Lama Kashiwa Sherab Gyeltsen, a student of Tsongkhapa, on the site of an earlier Sakyapa monastery. Bimdo Gonchen later became one of the most influential Gelukpa establishments in central Amdo, renowned for the rigour of its academic programme. The complex was rebuilt quite lavishly in the late 1980s but has not yet regained its religious atmosphere and former importance.

Around Bimdo, there are six other monasteries, including **Kyilkhor Sangak Choding**, a branch of Labrang founded in 1777, and a Bonpo power-place at **Wangtsangma**.

Karing

Higher up, in the mountains northwest of Bimdo, at **Karing**, there were formerly 11 monasteries, of which the Gelukpa **Lungyontang Hermitage**, **Bitang Lakhagar**, and **Ronpo Yershong** have all been rebuilt, along with the Nyingma temples at **Dampoche Ngakhang** and **Rato Ngakhang**.

Kangtsa and Lanja Bridge

After Bimdo, the recently repaved road continues to follow a tributary of the Yellow River upstream for 8 km to the watershed. On the descent, after 10 km, you will pass through **Kangtsa**, where there is a small 17th-century Gelukpa monastery of the same name, and after a further 22 km you will reach the **Lanja Bridge** intersection, where the Repkong and Labrang roads diverge (see below, page 605).

Jentsa County གཅན་ཚ → *Population: 49,158. Area: 1,601 sq km.* 尖扎县

Jentsa county straddles the Yellow River, between Trika to the west, and Bayan Khar and Repkong to the east. The county town is situated 18 km southwest of Chun-ke and 58 km from Hualong, overlooking the south bank of the river. Though small and largely Tibetan, it has seen much encroachment from Muslim traders in recent years. There used to be 18 Tibetan monasteries in the county, the most important being **Lamo Dechen** of the Gelukpa school and **Achung Namdzong** of the Nyingmapa school.

Hualong to Chun-ke township

From the Agara intersection, 34 km northwest of Hualong, you can head north into Pingan (see above, page 579), or south towards the Yellow River. **Chun-ke** (Ch Qunke) township (Altitude: 2,040 m) lies 18 km due south of the intersection on the north bank of the Yellow River. Many of the small quiet hamlets passed on the descent are now inhabited by Muslims, and each has its own village mosque. Tibetan monasteries were destroyed by Muslim zealots here as recently as 1952 (Gomzhi Gonpa). Chun-ke, however, has an air of activity; for three busy roads lead across the

 Yellow River from here in different directions: west to Lugyagak (Ch Lijiaxia), southeast to Jentsa town and east to Rongpo Gyakhar in Repkong. Slightly south of Chun-ke, and overlooking the north bank of the Yellow River is the monastery of **Andarchagen Kharnang**, where a large image of Maitreya was recently rebuilt.

Jentsa town → *Altitude: 2,040 m*

To reach the county town, turn east at the Chun-ke T-junction, and after 16 km on an excellent paved road surface which follows the north bank of the Yellow River, you will arrive at a turn-off which heads south across the river to **Jentsa**, 2 km distant. (The main road continues east into Repkong, reaching **Rongpo Gyakhar** after 62 km.) Crossing the bridge into town, you will pass a cinema and shops on the right and the bus station on the left, before reaching an intersection, dominated by a monument bearing the inscribed legend Tashidelek! Turn left here and head south for **Lamo Dechen Monastery**, or right (west) to the centre, where there are banks, government buildings and the Jentsa Guesthouse where the local tourism bureau is based. Then, turn south for **Kowa Gonpa** or head due west, following the river bank upstream to **Magur Namgyeling** monastery. » *For listings, see pages 614-616.*

Lamo Dechen Monastery

Lamo Dechen Chokhorling, with around 250 monks, is the largest monastery of Jentsa county, located high on a ridge about 25 km, south of town near **Lengke** township, and approached on a soft earth surface which can be treacherous during the rainy season. The monastery is sited amidst high altitude Tibetan farming villages with some nearby patches of original forest.

The monastery was founded by the Third Lamo Ngawang Lobzang Tenpei Gyeltsen (1660-1728) in 1682. Although it subsequently developed into the largest monastery in the county, **Magur Namgyeling** which was founded by his predecessor the Second Lamo Lodro Gyatso (1610-1659) is still revered as its mother monastery. Gradually Lamo Dechen's influence increased throughout the region, until at its zenith there were 40 affiliated branch monasteries, extending as far as Dabzhi on the northeast shore of Lake Kokonor, and as many as 51 recognized tulkus, presiding over the main temple complex of two assembly halls and 26 additional shrines.

The principal line of incarnations here is that of the Lamo succession. The first of the line was Zhabdrung Karpo (fl. late 16th century) from Lamo Rinchengang in Central Tibet, who is formally known by the title First Lamo Tsoknyi Gyatso. The line was extended retrospectively to include the great Kadampa masters Chengawa Tsultrim Bar (1038-1103), Lama Dampa Sonam Gyeltsen (1312-1375) and Chengawa Lodro Gyeltsen (1402-1472). His successors were scions of the Tumed and Arik Mongolian clans, who had occupied much of Amdo since the military campaigns of Gushi Qan, namely: the Second Lamo Lodro Gyatso (1610-1659) who established Magur Namgyeling; the Third Lamo Ngawang Lobzang Tenpei Gyeltsen (1660-1728) who was recognized by the Fifth Dalai Lama; the Fourth Lamo Lobzang Tendzin Gelek Gyeltsen (1729-1796); the Fifth Lamo Pende Wangchuk Khetsun Gyatso (1797-1831); the Sixth Lamo Ngawang Chokdrub Tenpei Gyeltsen (1832-1872); the Seventh Lamo Tendzin Norbu Pelzangpo (1873-1927); the Eighth Lamo Lobzang Lungrik Tenpei Gyatso (1928-1981), who was also known as Alak Sharak; and the present incumbent, the Ninth Lamo Lobzang Tendzin Chokyi Gyeltsen, who is currently being educated at the **Dabzhi Gonsar** branch monastery (see above, page 566).

Although there are six newly constructed temples and one assembly hall at Lamo Dechen, they are all extremely basic, with the Repkong mural panels as the main point of interest. In the vicinity of **Dangshun** township which is passed on the way to Lamo Dechen, there are two affiliated monasteries at **Gyertang Ritro** and **Trika Gonpa**. Also, at **Angla** township, 12 km south of town, there is the **Nangra Serkhang**, which was founded in 1341 by Dondrub Rinchen before he went on to establish the more illustrious Jakhyung Shedrubling (see above, page 594). Some original buildings in Sino-Tibetan style have been preserved here.

Magur Namgyeling

The monastery of **Magur Namgyeling**, also known as **Gurgon**, is located 5 km north of Jentsa town, on a ridge overlooking the south bank of the Yellow River. The original foundation is attributed to Zhabdrung Karpo who received an injunction from the Third Dalai Lama, but it appears to have been rebuilt by his incarnation the Second Lamo Lodro Gyatso in 1646, and to have been refurbished in later centuries following periodic damage inflicted by the flooding waters of the Yellow River. Nowadays, there are 40 monks at Gurgon. Two buildings now stand: the newly constructed **assembly hall** (Dukhang) and a magnificent **Jokhang temple**, which survived the Cultural Revolution unscathed when it was used as a granary. The former contains images of Tsongkhapa, Alak Sharak and his reliquary, and Repkong murals depicting (left): Shridevi, Vaishravana, Vajrapani, Kalacakra, Guhyasamaja, Cakrasamvara and Vajrabhairava, and also (right): the paradises of Abhirati, Sukhavati and Sudarshana, along with Sarvavid Vairocana, Six-armed Mahakala and Dharmaraja. In the vestibule, there is an inscription outlining the Lamo incarnate lineage. The **protector temple** to the rear is still incomplete, but above its entrance there are fine murals depicting Tsongkhapa, the Gurgon lineage, the 16 Elders and the 35 Confession Buddhas. To the west of the courtyard stands the undamaged **Jokhang temple**. Inside there are images of the Buddhas of the Three Times, flanked by the eight standing bodhisattvas, with Songtsen Gampo near the door. Murals also depict the Six Ornaments and Two Supreme Masters of Ancient India (left) and the 10 teachers of Tsongkhapa (right).

Kowa Gon and Ngagrong Gon

There are several smaller monasteries in Jentsa county, most of them set high up the side valley between Lugyagak and Jentsa. These can be accessed on a hill-road, which connects the bridge at **Dongma** with the county town. Some 4 km west of town, there is the **Lo Dorjedrak cave**, where Lhalung Pelgyi Dorje stayed in retreat after his assassination of the Tibetan king Langdarma in the ninth century. Nearby is the mountain hermitage of **Bumkhang Ja'oma**, which is said to have been founded in the 13th century by Sakya Pandita, and which contains relics of the Nyingma treasure-finder Sangye Lingpa and the bow used by Lhalung Pelgyi Dorje to slay Langdarma. Then, 10 km west of modern **Cuozhou** township, there is the monastery of **Kowa Gonsar**, founded in the 14th century by the Sakyapa master Kowa Shinglu Jangchub Osel, who acted as a quorum member when Tsongkhapa was ordained at Jakhyung. The monastery moved firmly into the Gelukpa sphere during the lifetime of Kowa Kachu Chokyi Gyatso (1571-1635), who had affiliations also with Drepung and Kumbum Jampaling. The Gelukpa monastery of **Ngangrong Tashi Chopeling** (founded 1738), lies 5 km further southwest from here.

Sangdrok Gon and Dzongang Gon

Continuing northwest on the hill road, a turn-off on the left leads inland to modern **Jiajia** township and **Sangdrok Dechenling**, another 14th-century Sakyapa monastery which was absorbed by the Gelukpas of Lamo Dechen. Then, just 5 km south of Lugyagak there is the Gelukpa institution of **Gawu Dzongnang**, which houses a fine set of old tangkas. All of these smaller monasteries in Jentsa county have 50-100 monks each.

Lugyagak

If you drive west from the Chun-ke intersection on the north bank of the Yellow River, you will cross to the south bank at **Dongma** after 8 km and reach **Lugyagak**, after a further 10 km. Just before entering town the Gelukpa monastery of **Jakhyung** (see above, page 594) comes into view on the opposite north bank. Lugyagak, also known in Tibetan as **Ngagyagak** (Ch Lijiaxia), is a rapidly growing town located alongside the largest hydroelectric construction project on the Tibetan plateau. The dam at Lugyakag is 155 m high and 411 m long, creating a 320-sq km reservoir lake. From here it is possible to visit the **Khamra National Park** (Ch Kanbula) and the historically important monasteries and caves of **Achung Namdzong.** » *For listings, see pages 614-616.*

Khamra National Park and Achung Namdzong → *Colour map 5, grid B4.*

ⓘ *Admission: ¥10.*

Getting there Khamra National Park is accessible by road on a 32-km detour to the south. The easier option is to drive 7 km to the jetty on the shore of the vast artificial lake created by the dam, and cross by ferry boat (4 km). The road from the town to the jetty recrosses the Yellow River just below the dam, offering a close view of this ambitious construction project in progress, and then traverses a pass (2,220 m) before descending to the lakeside. There are several large boats moored at the jetty (¥300 per boat) and the crossing of the lake itself will take about 15 minutes. On reaching the southeast shore, jeeps are available (¥43 return) to negotiate the rough 4-km track uphill to the Gate of the Khamra National Park (Ch Kanbula). The road divides here, with the right fork heading into the protected forest area of the National Park, and the left heading up to Achung Namdzong. It is estimated that when the lake is full, the water level will rise a further 30 m, enabling the ferry boats to moor alongside the gate.

Khamra National Park (Ch Kanbula) is a spectacularly forested region to the south of the Yellow river, covering an area of 152.5 sq km. The forest is named after the homeland of the Nub clan who moved here from Central Tibet via Kham. Approximately 80% of the park is virgin forest. Some 276 species of plants and trees have been identified, including pine, cypress and birch. However, the park is characterized by its extraordinary peaks, many of which rise abruptly from the verdant valley floor in the form of bare red rock pinnacles. The central peak is known as **Namdzong** (approximately 2,000 m) and around it, spread throughout the park, there are 18 identifiable peaks. Among these, the highest group of six are revered as the snow-white abodes of the gods (ie Gopodzong, Nepodzong, Bashingdzong, Trichdzong, Jomodzong and Ngadzong); the middle group of six are known as the red-rock abodes of the haunting spirits (ie Razhudzong, Gonpodzong, Lamtrengdzong, Tadzong, Degyedzong and Lugdzong); while the lowest group of six are known as the verdant abodes of the serpentine water spirits (ie Mukpodzong, Nordzong, Shadzong, Radzong, Sermodzong and Zordzong). The name Achung Namdzong is an amalgam of Mount Namka and the hill blocking its approach, which is said to resemble the Tibetan letter "a-chung"; while the term "dzong" here implies that the peaks are citadel hermitages for meditation.

Achung Namdzong → *Colour map 5, grid B4*

The historically important site of **Malho Dorje Drakra Achung Namdzong** is located inside the Khamra National Park. During the eighth century this sacred abode was entrusted by Padmasambhava to the protector deity Mesang, and it was revered as one of the 25 important power-places of Kham and Amdo, specifically symbolizing the mind aspect of buddha-mind. Later, when Buddhism was persecuted in Central Tibet by the king Langdarma, the three wise monks, Tsang Rabsel of Chuwori, Mar Shakyamuni of Tolung and Yo-ge Jung of Bodong fled via Qarloq to Amdo, where they initially stayed for 20 years in the cave hermitage of Achung Namdzong. Lhalung Pelgyi Dorje followed them here, after his assassination of Langdarma, and the meditation hermitage on the adjacent Ugdzong Hill, known as Shamalung, is said to contain the remains of his robe. It was here, and in other power-places of Amdo, such as Dentik, that the monastic lineage was preserved from persecution and eventually restored intact to Central Tibet by their disciples and successors. In later centuries,

Achung Namdzong was visited by important lamas, including Zhabkar Tsokdruk Rangdrol who likened the red-rock terrain to a red ruby. Four monasteries (Sangak Tengyeling, Dzatro Dorjeling, Tashi Namgyeling, and Samten Chopeling) were built around Namdzong, along with the 13 residences of the great lamas who lived here. Lama Gurong Tsan, the chief Nyingmapa master of the region, whose aged mother also lives here, has overseen the construction, but funds are now short and the temples still require interior decoration.

Samten Chopeling

Overlooking the gateway to the Khamra National Park, the nunnery of **Samten Chopeling** occupies the flat tableland of **Chorten Tang** on Jomodzong Hill. Tibetan Buddhist nuns lived here since 1710, during the lifetime of the famed meditation teacher Yeshe Drolma. The actual monastery was founded in 1870 by Gurong Natsok Rangdrol, and the ornate roof of the assembly hall was added by Gurong Orgyan Jikdrel Choying Dorje in 1899. Samten Chopeling quickly became the most important nunnery of the Nyingma school in Amdo, visited by great Dzogchen masters of Kham and Amdo alike. The present reconstructed buildings, which date from 1979, were completed due to the efforts of Gurong Gyelse, Lama Drolo, Tulku Pema Namdrol and Ani Rigzin who presides over some 200 nuns. The approach to the nunnery is marked by a large stupa and a set of the eight stupas symbolizing the major events in the life of Shakyamuni Buddha. It contains images of Padmakara, flanked by his two consorts, along with Manjughosa and Tara. The murals, in Repkong style, depict (left): the 35 Confession Buddhas, Shakyamuni with the 16 Elders and the Longchen Nyingtig lineage, and (right): Sarvavid Vairocana, Sitatapatra and Ekajati.

Tashi Namgyeling

About 2 km up valley from the nunnery on the **Tashitang** tableland, there is a small Gelukpa temple, named **Tashi Namgyeling**. This establishment was founded in 1794 by Kapukpa Pandita Lobzang Dondrub, and subsequently rebuilt in 1809 and 1821. The present structure dates from the 1980s, and there are only a few monks in residence. The assembly hall contains images of Tsongkhapa with his students, the reliquary of Serkhang Rinpoche Lobzang Tendzin Gyatso, and murals depicting the 35 Confession Buddhas, Vaishravana, Shakyamuni with the 16 Elders, Khecari, Sarvavid Vairocana, and the life story of Milarepa.

Sangak Tengyeling

The original Nyingma temples were constructed on the table hill of **Namtar Tang** in conjunction with the adjacent mountain hermitages of Lhalung Pelgyi Dorje and the three wise monks. Later, in 1814, a large temple was founded here by Palchen Namka Jikme, and in 1848 it was refurbished by Gurong Natsok Rangdrol. In 1898, Gurong Orgyan Jikdrel Choying Dorje extended the complex of buildings and added a golden spire to the roof. During the 19th century and early 20th century, the monastery was visited by most of the great Nyingma lamas of Kham, and had the reputation for being the most active teaching and meditation centre of the Nyingma school in Amdo, with some 25 branches under its authority. From 1932 onwards the lineage has been maintained by Gurong Gyelse and his successors, and the present buildings date from 1981 onwards. There are about 100 monks and a variable number of long-haired *mantrins* (Tib. *ngakpa*). The *mantrins* at Sangak Tengyeling are generally older men who have received some religious instruction in the past, and take a limited number of Vinaya vows in conjunction with their bodhisattva and mantra vows. Most are married farmers or, less frequently, nomads, and one who lives nearby acts as the caretaker.

Sangak Tengyeling is rare amongst the monasteries of Amdo for the high quality of its construction, particularly the woodwork, which is excellent. There are two main temples: the **Dolma Lhakhang** and the **Assembly Hall** (Dukhang). The former contains large images of Padmakara flanked by his two consorts, along with Manjughosa, Shakyamuni with his foremost students, the Lords of the Three Enlightened Families and Tara, along with 1,000 smaller images of Tara. There is a throne bearing a portrait of the Fourth Gurong, the current incumbent who resides in Jentsa county town, and fine murals depicting (left): Amritakundalin, Vaishravana, Zangdokpelri, and the Nyingtig lineage, and (right): Sukhavati, the Kabgye meditational deities, Gonpo Maning, Ekajati, Rahula and Dorje Lekpa. The balcony has images of Longchen Rabjampa, Padmasambhava and Zhabkar Tsokdruk Rangdrol, while towards the roof there are murals depicting the 35 Confession Buddhas and the Nyingma lineage.

The **Assembly Hall** contains images of Padmakara with his two foremost consorts, along with Manjughosa and Tara, and the volumes of the *Kangyur* and *Tangyur*. The murals here depict (left): Amritakundalin, Kabgye, Vajrakila, the Lords of the Three Enlightened Families and Sukhavati, and (right): Vajrasattva with consort, Khorwa Yongdul, Bhaisajyaguru, Guru Drakpo and Hayagriva. The balcony has images of the Eight Manifestations of Padmasambhava, and the eight stupas symbolizing events in the life of Shakyamuni Buddha.

Dzatro Dorjeling

The reliquary temple of Gurong Choying Dorje was originally founded in 1913, and named **Dzatro Dorjeling** in 1923. It functioned as an important hermitage for Nyingma practice until its destruction during the Cultural Revolution. In 1993 it was relocated at **Namdzong Tse**, the summit of Mount Namka, near the caves of the three wise monks. Within the caves, which are spectacularly located on a ledge near the summit of Namkadzong Tse, there are traces of original murals to be seen. This site is accessible by a steep track on the north side, which should not be attempted during or just after heavy rain.

Below Sangak Tengyeling, there is the residence of Lama Drolo, which has a finely constructed Mani Lhakhang. There are images of Amitayus, White Tara and Vijaya, tangkas depicting Vajrakila and Zangdokpelri, and nine large water-powered prayer wheels.

Repkong County རེབ་གོང་

→ *Population: 75,038. Area: 3,353 sq km. Colour map 5, grid B5.* 同仁县

Central Amdo, the region south of Tsongkha, contains a large proportion of the Tibetan population of Amdo. Farmers and nomads are spread through the verdant valleys and plains, and there are many monasteries dotted around the region. **Repkong**, just south of the Yellow River, can in many ways be considered the heart of Amdo. Its principal monastery predates Labrang and Kumbum by several centuries, and the county itself possesses 36 smaller monasteries, mostly of the Gelukpa school, although there are also important Nyingmapa and Bon hermitages here.

The main river of Repkong is the Gu-chu, which flows north to converge with the Yellow River below Lamo Dechen. The 'nine side valleys' that make up the Gu-chu basin vary from rolling grasslands, which support the camps of nomadic, through forested gorges, to an agricultural zone near the county town itself. The ethnic mix is also fascinating, for there are four villages inhabited by thoroughly Tibetanized Tu people in the valley, while to the east lies Dowi (Xunhua), home of the Muslim Salar, to the north the Hui enclave of Bayan Khar (Hualong) and to the south Sogwo (Ch Henan), a Mongolian autonomous county.

The capital, **Rongpo Gyakhar**, is both the administrative centre for Repkong county and for the entire South Yellow River Prefecture. The distance to the capital from Jadir in Tsekok is 97 km, from Jentsa 64 km, from Yardzi 67 km, and from Labrang 115 km.

Lower Gu-chu Valley

Driving east from the Chun-ke intersection on the north bank of the Yellow River (see above, page 599), you will bypass the turn-off for Jentsa town after 16 km, and continue on to cross the Yellow River near an ancient water-burial site, and then head south into the Gu-chu valley. Rongpo Gyakhar lies 62 km from the Jentsa turn-off. Driving into the valley, there are branch monasteries of Rongpo Gonchen close to the road at **Rongpo Gon Chopeling** (18th century) and **Tashikyil** (founded 1625-1648). The road follows the spectacular Gu-chu gorges upstream, and gradually the valley broadens into a fertile plain, dotted with villages and monasteries, that stretches all the way to Rongpo Gyakhar, the county and prefectural capital. About 22 km south of the bridge, a side road cuts southwest for 25 km to **Yershong Gon**, another branch of Rongpo Gonchen. Continuing south on the main road, after 5 km you will reach **Mepa** township, in the vicinity of which there are three monasteries, the most significant being **Yiga Chodzinling**, which was converted from the Nyingmapa to the Gelukpa tradition in 1685. Some 5 km south of Mepa, the road intersects with the highway from Dowi and Labrang (see above) at **Tokya** (Ch Bao'an) 16 km north of the county capital.

Tokya Tashi Chopeling

Tokya (locally pronounced Toja) is nowadays the site of a large aluminium smelting plant, which contributes heavily to pollution in the lower Gu-chu valley. Formerly it was more important for its monastery, **Tokya Tashi Chopeling**, which is located in a side valley to the south, on a cliff at the approach to a vast cave network. The extensive caves (about 20 km from Tokya) are rumoured to link up with the cave at Drakar near Labrang after an eight-day journey through an underground pothole. There is a natural cave temple dedicated to Cakrasamvara here, and it is one of the 'eight places of spiritual attainment' sited around the Gu-chu valley. A roadside stupa marks the approach to the caves.

Yarma Tashikyil

The road to Labrang climbs for 12 km from the Dowi turn-off at **Lanja Bridge** (see above, page 599), leaving the Gu-chu valley, and entering a beautiful red sandstone gorge, which is forested in its upper reaches. Here, it reaches the township of **Zhongpang Chi** (Ch Shuangpengxi), a farming village with two temples, one of which (20 minutes' walk north of the road) marks the birthplace of Zhabkar Tsokdruk Rangdrol (1781-1851). The Gendun Chopel Memorial Middle School was founded here recently with generous French funding. Driving 6 km uphill from the township, you will reach a clearing on the left, from where a trekking trail leads sharply uphill towards the ridge of the valley. The climb takes approximately 50 minutes, and leads to a flat tableland where the monastery of **Yarma Tashikyil**, an important hermitage of the Nyingma tradition, maintained by a strong community of monks and *mantrins*, is located. On the approach to the monastery, you will pass three stupas, built by Zhabkar Tsokdruk Rangdrol in person, and the empty spot where the

Repkong County

 house of Gendun Chopel, one of Tibet's greatest 20th-century writers, once stood. The temple itself has images of Padmakara flanked by Shantaraksita and King Trisong Detsen, with Vajrasattva to the left and the volumes of the *Kangyur* and *Tangyur* on the side walls. Murals depict (left): Ekajati, Guru Drakpo, Zangdokpelri and Vajrasattva with consort, and (right): Dompa Trungri, Hayagriva, Tara, White Jambhala and Shridevi. The gallery has images of the Third Zhabkar, Shakyamuni with his foremost students and Atisha with his foremost students. The murals below the roof depict the 84 Mahasiddhas.

From the vantage point of Yarma Tashikyil, there are wide panoramic views of the Repkong region with the snow peak of **Mount Amnye Nyenri** (4,298 m) to the left. Zhabkar spent many years teaching here, and his stone chairs are still enclosed in ancient groves. There is a small government compound truckstop at **Zhongpang Chi**, where it may be possible to stay. The youthful incumbent, the Fourth Zhabkar is being educated at Rongpo Gyakhar.

Gartse Gonpa

Continuing through the heavily logged gorge from Zhongpang township and crossing a spur, the road ascends 12 km to the attractive **Gartse Gonpa**. This is revered as one of the eight foremost places of spiritual attainment in Repkong, and it currently has 140 monks. There is a Jokhang temple, a protector temple, and an assembly hall (Tsokchen Dukhang), all decorated in the Labrang style. Within the **assembly hall**, there are images of Tsongkhapa with his foremost students, along with images of Alak Gangzang, Shar Kalden Gyatso, the Fifth Jamyang Zhepa (b. 1916) and Alak Sertsang, as well as murals depicting (left): Shridevi, Vaishravana, White Tara, Green Tara, Amitabha, Sarvavid Vairocana and Vajrabhairava, and (right): Vajrapani, Hayagriva, Sitatapatra, Tsegyel, Six-armed Mahakala and Dharmaraja.

After Gartse, the road traverses a broad grassy plain beside **Mount Amnye Nyemri**, and continues 6 km to the watershed pass (3,600 m) which marks the current provincial frontier between Qinghai and Gansu. From here, Labrang (see page 666) in Sangchu county is only 48 km distant (via Kangya and Drakar Gonpa). A more indirect trekking route continues southeast across the plain from Gartse to **Dowa** (42 km), and thence to Labrang via Sangke. A branch of Rongpo Gonchen, named **Dowa Dongak Dargyeling**, was also established at remote Dowa.

Rongpo Gyakhar → *For listings, see pages 614-616.*

The town is not well developed as a tourist destination, but this is slowly changing following the completion in the late 1990s of the high-rise Huangnan Hotel, at the top of Zhongshan Rd, and the China Telecom Hotel. The open air market, entered by a passageway opposite the old Huangnan Hotel is well worth a visit.

Orientation Entering town from the Tokya intersection, you will pass the bus station on the left and reach a roundabout where the Agricultural Bank of China is located. Head south (left) for the Prefectural Hospital, the County Government Buildings, Rongpo Gyakhar Monastery and the road to Sogwo; right (north) for the Recreational Park, the Mentsikhang, the Finance Department and Construction Bank; or straight ahead (west) for Zhongshan Rd (Main Street), entering through an ornate Dragon Gate.

On the left (south) side of **Zhongshan Road** you will find a bookstore, the Construction Bank, the Ga-de Market, the Old Huangnan Hotel and an internet café. Opposite on the right (north) are China Telecom, the Telecom Hotel, China Post, a library, the New Century Restaurant, the Yinzhen Hotel, a cinema, the Ga-de Market, the Dakar Restaurant and the Cadre School.

At the west end of **Zhongshan Road** you will reach another roundabout, dominated by the high-rise New Huangnan Hotel. Turn left (south) for the law courts, assorted middle schools and the Agricultural Bank, or right (north) for the Public

Security Bureau, Prefectural Government Buildings, department stores and insurance buildings. Reaching yet another roundabout, turn right (east) for the People's Bank, the Cultural Art Museum, the Gymnasium and the Mentsikhang; or continue straight ahead (north) out of town for Gomar Gonpa.

Rongpo Gonchen Monastery ⓘ *Admission: ¥18.* Rongpo Gonchen, the principal monastery of Repkong, lies in the southern part of town. The original buildings were constructed in 1301 and developed by the Sakyapa master Samten Rinchen, whose grandfather had been an emissary of Drogon Chogyel Phakpa. Later, it was reconstituted as a Gelukpa monastery by Shar Kalden Gyatso (1607-1677). The complex currently has nine temples and around 400 monks; headed by the important incarnate lamas of Rongpo. The principal tulku, the Eighth Rongpo Kyabgon, is now in his early 20s. The previous incumbent passed away in 1978.

There are 35 branch monasteries, most of them in Repkong county, and these are often associated with the other lamas affiliated to the mother monastery: Alak Re Yerchung, Alak Kutso, Alak Rongwo, Alak Tson-de, and so on. The main north-south road runs between the monastery and a small cliff below which is the old village, complete with Chinese temple and a mosque, on the banks of the Gu-chu.

At its high point, Rongpo Gonchen had four major colleges, including a meditation hermitage called **Drubdra Nechok Tashikyil**. The others were the dialectical college known as **Dratsang Tosam Namgyeling**, which was founded by

Rongpo Gyakhar

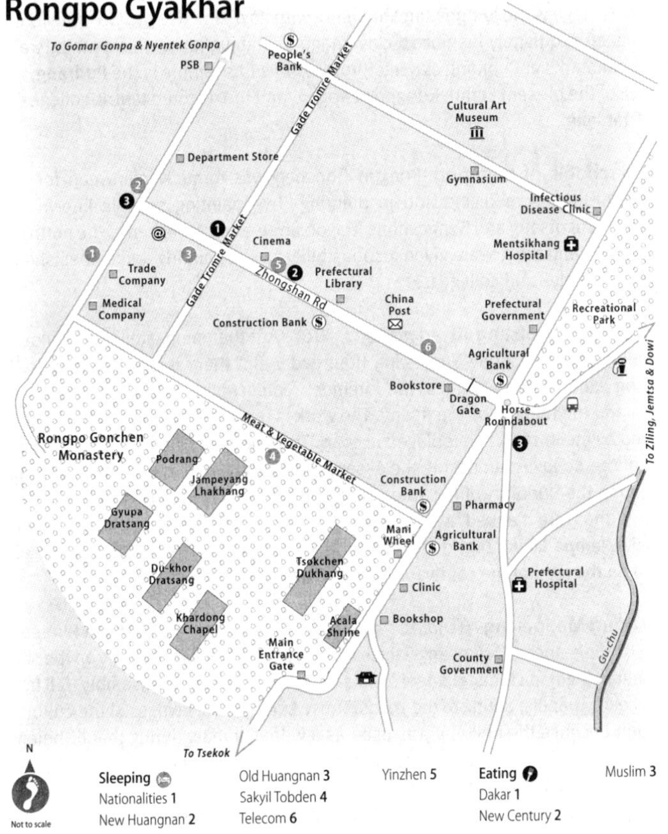

 Shar Kalden Gyatso in 1630; the tantric college known as **Gyudra Sangchen Chokyi Bangzo**, which was founded by the Second Shartsang Ngawang Trinle Gyatso (1678-1739); and the Kalacakra college known as **Dudra Sangak Dargyeling**, which was founded in 1773 by the Third Shartsang Gendun Trinle Rabgye (1740-1794).

Among the recently renovated buildings at Rongpo Gonchen, the **Great Assembly Hall (Tsokchen Dukhang)** is close to the main road, behind a shrine dedicated to the gate-keeper Acala (containing an enormous image of this sword-wielding deity). The main entrance of the monastery is located some distance further south, through a chapel gateway decorated with modern murals. The interior of the Great Assembly Hall is vast, supported by 164 columns, and refurbishment is currently in progress. The porch contains some interesting murals, which depict the ubiquitous Four Guardian Kings, the dress code for monks and, in addition, the local protector deities of Amdo, known as Amnye Machen and Amnye Jakhyung. Inside the hall there are many images, including an impressive Shakyamuni Buddha and a gilded copper Tsongkhapa, 11 m in height.

To the south and slightly uphill from the Great Assembly Hall is the **Khardong Chapel**, containing the reliquary stupa of the Seventh Rongpo Kyapgon Shartsang (1916-1978). The renovated **Kalacakra College (Dukhor Dratsang)** lies behind it, and contains some beautiful new murals executed by the master artist, Kharsham Gyal, in the Repkong style. There are new images of the kings of Shambhala, and a few old tangkas, notably a large Tsongkhapa and a depiction of Tsongkhapa flanked by his followers (Je Yabsesum). One of the statues depicts Shar Kalden Gyatso, who established the Gelukpa tradition here in the 17th century. Far to the right of the Kalacakra College is the **Jampeyang Lhakhang** with its distinctive *gyabib*-style roof. It contains an exquisitely fashioned clay image of Manjughosa, which exhibits all the best hallmarks of Repkong clay sculpture. Above this temple is the **Podrang**, or residence of the present Eighth Rongpo Kyapgon, and the restored tantric college or **Gyupa Dratsang**.

Painting schools of Repkong Rongpo Gonchen was formerly renowned for its expertise in Tibetan medicine and in painting. Two painting schools known as Sengeshong Yagotsang and Sengeshong Magotsang were established to the north of the monastery and these were given responsibility for the painting and embellishing of different temples and colleges.

Sengeshong Yagotsang ⓘ *Admission: ¥10*. At the monastery of Palden Chokhorling in Sengeshong Yagotsang (founded 1385) there is an **Assembly Hall** containing exquisite clay statues, the foremost representing the Seventh Repkong Kyapgon and the founder of Yagotsang. The work is recent, the original having been destroyed by fire in 1946 and replaced in 1949. Texts housed here include the Derge edition of the *Kangyur*. Alongside the assembly hall to the left is a **Jokhang temple** dedicated to the Buddhas of the Three Times, in which the enormous figures of the three buddhas are flanked by the eight standing bodhisattvas. The new and impressive **Jampa Lhakhang**, dedicated to Maitreya, can be entered from a raised platform on the right of the courtyard. It has some outstanding murals.

Sengeshong Magotsang ⓘ *Admission: ¥10*. At the monastery of **Gendun Puntsok Choling** in Sengeshong Magotsang, which was founded in the 17th century on the site of a former Nyingmapa temple), there are currently 150 monks. The **Assembly Hall** has original ceiling panels, dating to the 1910s. These survived the ravages of the Cultural Revolution because the building was used as a wheat granary during that turbulent period. Three of its wall panels are also original: one on the left depicting the thousand buddhas of the aeon and two on the right that depict Vajrabhairava and Mahakala. To the left there is a **Jampa Lhakhang,** containing enormous and

Sengeshong art schools

Slightly north of the town, the two renowned painting schools of Repkong, known as Sengeshong Yagotsang and Sengeshong Magotsang, are located within their unique idyllic village settings. Almost every house is an artist's studio, and in recent years four artists have become celebrities in their own right: the late Shawu Tsering of Sengeshong Yagotsang, the late Gyatso of Sengeshong Magotsang, Kunzang (who lives across the Gu-chu river) and Jigme (also deceased). Their works are on display in the Repkong Art Centre of the Huangnan Tibetan Nationality Autonomous Prefecture in town. More importantly, their work is represented in the exquisitely decorated temples of Sengeshong Yagotsang and Magotsang monasteries.

The Repkong school of art, known as Wutun to the Chinese, was established by the 15th century and, by the 18th century, it had spread to cover much of Amdo, as indeed it does today. Almost all of the work executed here over the centuries was lost, unseen by the outside world, during the destruction of Amdo's monasteries in the Cultural Revolution; but due to the dedication of a few elderly masters the tradition is now being carefully handed down to the next generation. The style broadly follows that of Central Tibet, but the infusion of cultures generated by contact with the Mongolians, Tu and neighbouring Chinese makes the work distinctive. This is reflected in the ethnic origins of the people of Sengeshong themselves, who are said to have come from Western Tibet and to have intermingled over the centuries with neighbouring communities.

outstanding clay images: Maitreya, flanked by Manjushri (twice), Mahakarunika and Tsongkhapa. The image of Manjushri to the left is upright, as is that of Mahakarunika to the right. The central Maitreya is the masterpiece of the recently deceased artist and sculptor Gyatso. To the left of the courtyard, within its own enclosure wall, there is a **Tsongkhapa Lhakhang**, containing a central image of Tsongkhapa, surrounded by 1,000 miniature images of Manjughosa. Two panels in its portico have murals depicting the guardian kings, painted with pigments compounded from gold, silver and other precious substances.

Surrounding the temple complexes at both Yagotsang and Magotsang, are a number of artists' studios, where modern paintings produced by the monks and laity are on sale.

Middle Gu-chu Valley

Nyentok Gonpa On the valley floor north of Repkong are the Gelukpa monasteries of **Nyentok** ⓘ *admission ¥10*, and **Gomar**, both traditionally inhabited by Tu rather than Tibetan monks (although at Gomar most are at present of Tibetan origin). Nyentok, which was founded between 1740 and 1794, is small and close to town. There are a few original structures which survived the Cultural Revolution here, including the assembly hall (*dukhang*), and some impressive older murals depicting the Twelve Deeds of Shakyamuni adorn the walls of the **Jampa Lhakhang**, which also contains a newly sculpted 13-m Maitreya image.

Gomar Gonpa ⓘ *Admission: ¥20*. Gomar is 5 km further north and much more impressive. The three-storey **Jampa Lhakhang** built in 1741 by Alak Yeshe Jang still stands. There are also newly built temples, all of a much higher artistic and architectural standard than the normal concrete and brick, and a colourful seven-tiered stupa, constructed in 1990, with walk-in chapels on successive levels dedicated to the meditational deities of the four classes of tantra. The top of the stupa offers an excellent view of the valley. On a raised platform behind the stupa, there is a **Dukhor Lhakhang**, with new but incomplete wall panels, dedicated to the meditational deity Kalacakra. In conjunction with the New Year celebrations, an enormous tangka (20 m by 40 m) will be displayed at Gomar, followed by masked dances, on the 10th-11th days of the first lunar month (18-19 February 2005).

From **Rongpo Gyakhar**, a branch road extends northwest for 10 km to **Shadrang Gon Puntsok Choling**, which was built by Tsongkhapa's teacher Dondrub Rinchen in 1341 before he founded **Jakhyung Monastery**. En route, at **Dangpozhi Magon Tubten Chokhorling**, 4 km from town, the original foundation is attributed to one of Lhalung Pelgyi Dorje's students (10th century). Another branch road runs southeast from town towards **Tsagyel Tarpaling**, 25 km to southeast, and thence to **Dechen Ritro** hermitage.

Upper Gu-chu Valley

Jangkya Due south of Rongpo Gyakhar, the main road continues to follow the Gu-chu upstream, into the broad grassy plains of Tobden, Tsekok and Sogwo. **Jangkya** is the first village, 7 km out of town, and it has a tiny Nyingmapa temple. A few original Repkong wall hangings are preserved here, reputedly thanks to their being hidden on **Mount Amnye Mori** behind the village during the 1960s. The valley to the east contains the affiliated **Janglung Khyung Gonpa**, also of the Nyingmapa school, which once housed 125 monks, and a small Gelukpa monastery, named **Janglung Garsar Ganden Chopeling**.

Chukhol Khartse Gonpa Further south, at **Chukhol Khartse Gonpa**, 18 km from town, there are sacred hot springs, and a small hotel complex. **Dardzom Gonpa**, a 17th-century branch of Rongpo Gonchen, lies higher, above the valley at some distance from the road, giving unparalleled views and a tantalizing glimpse of **Mount Amnye Jakhyung**, the most sacred mountain of Central Amdo, in the distance to the west. There are many other significant hills and mountains in the vicinity of Rongpo Gyakhar, including **Mount Amnye Taklung** to the southeast, and almost every village will have its arrow shrines on a nearby hill, which are visited annually.

Chuku Also in the Upper Gu-chu region, near **Chuku** township, there are old Nyingmapa hermitages at **Kodegon Dzogchen Namgyeling** and **Muselgar**, the former having been an original 13th-century Kadampa foundation, and the latter affiliated to Katok.

After Chuku, the road continues climbing through partially forested hills to cross the watershed pass known as **Wanbu Lhatse** (3,500 m), where it enters the county of **Tsekok**, 20 km above Chuku township. The distance from the county border to Jadir town in Tsekok is only 62 km.

Tsekok County རྩེ་ཁོག

→ *Population: 53,249. Area: 6,858 sq km. Colour map 5, grid B4.* 泽库县

The county of Tsekok is a broad grassland which extends through the upper reaches of the Tse-chu, north of the sharp bend in the Yellow River. The county town is known as **Jadir.** Within Tsekok county, Nyingmapa and Gelukpa nomadic communities have co-existed since the 15th century. At present there are 13 monasteries, of which six are Nyingmapa, and the remainder mostly affiliated to Rongpo Gonchen in Repkong.

Ins and outs

Getting there Buses heading south to Sogwo from Rongpo Gyakhar or Kawasumdo will stop briefly at Jadir, which has no bus station of its own. Services are infrequent, and most foreign visitors will have their own transportation. The distance from Rongpo Gyakhar in Repkong to Jadir is 98 km, from Jadir to Henan in Sogwo county, 39 km, and from Jadir to Tungte in Kawasumdo 111 km.

Repkong to Jadir

The recently asphalted road to Jadir leads across the watershed into a forested area, where, around Tobden township, there are three monasteries of note: **Karashong Gon** was founded as a branch of Labrang in the 1950s. **Karong Sangchen Gatsel Choling** is a large Nyingmapa monastery, founded in 1944 by Lama Tsering Dondrub; and **Dzongmar Tashi Choling** is an 18th-century branch of Rongpo Gonchen. The township of **Tobden** (Ch Duofudun), 25 km down valley, is little more than a restaurant and checkpost on the grasslands, and the distance from here to Jadir in the upper Tse-chu valley is only 37 km.

Jadir → *For listings, see pages 614-616.*

Jadir itself has an air of the Wild West. Nomads in shaggy sheepskin coats typical of Amdo ride into town on yaks or horses to shop, play pool, and sell a sheep or yakskin. There are two intersecting roads. Entering from the north you will pass the local middle school, the bank, the Jinxin Restaurant, and a department store, before reaching the crossroads, where public buses stop. Turn north (right) for the hospital, armed police, and the northern road to Hor township; south (left) for Sogwo county, or proceed straight ahead (west) on Main Street for the livestock markets, the government buildings, the guesthouse, cinema, Mentsikhang clinic, China Post and the law courts. At the west end of the street, alongside a mound of prayer flags and a stupa, the road turns southwest for Hor township and Kawasumdo county.

South of Jadir

Heading south from Jadir on the main road to Horgon, a turn-off veers left across the grassland, before descending into the Tse-chu valley. Along this road, about 3 km from town, the small Nyingmapa temple of **Sonak Tersar** will be passed, on the descent towards the riverbank. Slightly further, the Gelukpa monastery of **Sonak Geden Tashi Choling**, 4 km south of town, lies on the north bank of the meandering Tse-chu. It was originally a tented monastery, its first adobe buildings being constructed by Tendzin Gyatso (1616-1687), and it is affiliated to Repkong, under the authority of Khenchen Tsang. The complex is extensive: the Assembly Hall with a Tsongkhapa Lhakhang (cum library) to the left and a Gonkhang and Labrang behind, now houses 86 monks. The assembly hall has Gelukpa murals in the Repkong style, but its images interestingly depict Padmasambhava, Shakyamuni and Tara. There are excellent campsites along the flowering riverbank.

Beyond the ridge to the south, there is another small Gelukpa monastery, named **Tukchen Yonden Dargyeling**, which is also affiliated to Rongpo Gonchen. One of its temples is built of stone, all too rare in modern Amdo, and decorated with Repkong-style tangkas which depict Tara, Bhaisajyaguru, Avalokiteshvara, Sitatapatra, Tsongkhapa and the protectress Shridevi, alongside the standard set of images. At **Chakor** township, 10 km southeast of town on a branch road, the Gelukpa monastery of **Gartse Gonpa** is located on the north bank of the Tse-chu.

East of Jadir

Heading east from Jadir town on a branch road to the northeast, you will reach **Chisa** (Ch Xibusha) township after 8 km. In the hills above Chisa, there is the Gelukpa monastery of **Chisa Drubde Gecheling**, formerly a tented camp, where the first adobe temples were constructed in 1936 by Chisa Lodro Gyatso (d. 1957). A small Nyingmapa hermitage known as **Chisa Ngakhang** was founded nearby in 1950 by Rekong Tulku. The motorable trail continues into the hills from Chisa as far as **Dokar Ngakhang**, where there is a small Nyingma hermitage dating from 1955. Some 20 km further north in a remote area of **Dorjedzong**, there is a Gelukpa hermitage affiliated to Rongpo Gonchen, and the **Dzikar Caves** containing a natural stone image of Maitreya.

Hor township

Two roads lead west from Jadir to Horgon, a northerly road (90 km which is now being asphalted, and a south-westerly route (72 km) which is unpaved and rough. Taking the latter route, some 2 km before reaching **Hor** township, where the roads converge, there is a Nyingmapa monastery known as **Terton Chogar**, located in a sheltered ravine. Buses will stop in the township en route for Kawasumdo, and there are simple guesthouse facilities.

Terton Chogar Gonpa → *Altitude 3,450 m*

This monastery, also known as Hor Gon Tekchok Tashiling (Ch Herisi), was originally a tented camp. The first solid buildings were constructed by the First Terton Rinpoche in 1831, and the monastery, considered a branch of Dodrubchen, was moved to its present location in the early decades of the 20th century. The local community, now under the guidance of the Fourth Alak Tulku and the young Fifth Terton Rinpoche, comprises around 90 *mantrins* and monks of the Nyingma school. The most senior *mantrin* Rakha Gomchen, now spends much of his time in retreat, and the master stone mason Gonpo Tsetan lives nearby.

In front of the monastery, there is a series of the eight stupas symbolizing the deeds of Shakyamuni Buddha, and *mantras* painted on rocks. The first compound contains the **residences** of Alak Tulku and Tulku Loyang of Dodrubchen, and the recently restored **assembly hall,** where the *mantrins* hold their ceremonies. The latter has Repkong-style murals depicting Longchenpa, the Kabgye meditational deities and the *Longchen Nyingtig* lineage. There is a central image of Padmasambhava, flanked by Palchen Dupa and Yumka Dechen Gyelmo, and an appliqué and mural panel depicting Padmasambhava and his 25 disciples. An adjacent compound contains the main assembly hall for monks (**Dukhang**) and a recently consecrated **Guru Lhakhang**, which has a large central image of Padmasambhava flanked by Shantaraksita and King Trisong Detsen, surrounded by 1,000 miniature representations of Padmasambhava. Other images here include Longchenpa and Jigme Lingpa. The murals depict the Nyingtig Tsokchen and the Eight Manifestations of Padmasambhava (Guru Tsengye). Within the assembly hall are stored a number of woodblocks for the *Collected Works of Terton Rinpoche*, *The Words of My Perfect Teacher*, and the *Life of Padmasambhava*.

Festivals Four major religious dances are performed at Horgon: Vajrakilaya during the first month of the lunar calendar, Peaceful and Wrathful Deities (Zhitro) during the fourth month, Tsechu, dedicated to Padmasambhava, during the seventh month, and the Kabgye Deities (performed by the *mantrins* alone) on the 29th day of the 12th month.

On the hilltop above the monastery, there is an extraordinarily long wall of mani stones, totalling some 600 m in length, which was engraved with two full revised versions of the *Kangyur*, and at its extremity a small mound, holding the engraved texts of the *Tangyur* – amounting to almost 200 million syllables! Alongside these used to be 2,000 flagstones, intricately engraved with Buddhist icons and meditational deities. This outstanding creation, which has few rivals in Tibet, was undertaken by local monks and itinerant artisans between 1923 and 1951. The wall was badly damaged during the Cultural Revolution of the late 1960s and early 1970s, and despite more recent repairs, it is now in a dilapidated condition. In some sections the supporting dykes urgently require strengthening or buttressing, while a large number of elegantly engraved icons and texts have been fractured. In October 2002 a restoration plan was initiated, and it is envisaged that a completely new stone *Kangyur* will be carved in the coming years.

Trekking In addition to the two motorable routes from Jadir to Hor, it is also possible to trek or ride across the grasslands in two days, starting in the **Donketang** valley, and crossing the double pass of **Kachu La** to reach **Egong** and **Yalo Drak** Hermitage (associated with the charismatic Trodo Rinpoche). From here a tractor route crosses three ridges to reach the monastery.

Hor to Kawasumdo

Two roads diverge at Hor township, southwest on a rough trail for 40 km to Kawasumdo (Ch Tongde) and northwest for 11 km to join the paved highway at **Bongya**, from where you can drive through the grasslands southwest into Kawasumdo (44 km) and **Golok** (via Rabgya), or northeast to **Mangra** and **Trika** (see below, page 617). At **Bongya**, there is an eclectic community in which Nyingma, Geluk and Bon monks all participate, and at **A-me Gur**, there is a sacred image from Sakya which was originally offered to Repkong by an emissary of Chogyel Phakpa during the 13th century, and later brought here by the nomads of the grassland.

Sogwo Prefecture སོག་པོ

→ *Population: 30,134. Area: 6,072 sq km. Colour map 5, grid B4.* 河南蒙古族自治县

Getting there Buses run daily to Henan, the county capital, from Ziling (via Rongpo Gyakhar) and from Linxia (via Tso). There are also buses running on alternate days from Kawasumdo and from Labrang (via Tso).

Sogwo prefecture is a region where the dominant population is ethnically Mongolian, but so thoroughly integrated with the Amdowa, that only a few distinctive cultural traits remain. The yurt, the round felt tent of the Mongolians, is found in abundance here, and slight differences in dress and jewellery can be detected. The best sheepskin coats, for which this region is famous, (Tib chuba) are made from the skins of blue sheep. All four monasteries within the prefecture are Gelukpa.

Henan

Henan is located on the north bank of the Tse-chu, 39 km southeast of Jadir in Tsekok. Entering the town from the northwest (from Tsekok), you will first pass the Meteorological Department, the Tibeto-Mongolian Hospital, a cinema, the bus station, a middle school, the public security bureau, the livestock market, and the Zeyang Hotel. Reaching the crossroads, turn left (north) for the government buildings, government guesthouse, and cemetery; right (south) to cross the Tse-chu en route for Taklung Shingza, Luchu and Linxia; or straight ahead (east) for China Post and Telecom, an armed police unit, the county hospital and Lakha Gonpa.

The small monastery of **Lakha Gon Ganden Shedrub Dargyeling** overlooks the town 2 km to the east. It was founded in 1924 at the request of the Ninth Panchen Lama by the Fifth Lakha Tulku Lobzang Sonam Gyatso (1846-1926), and expanded by his successor the Sixth Lakha Tulku Lobzang Jinpa Tubten Gyatso (1926-1969). The current incumbent the Seventh Lakha Tulku has supervised reconstruction in recent years, although it is said that some artefacts did survive the Cultural Revolution. The monastery is affiliated to **Tsang-gar Gonpa** near Rabgya (see below, page 622).

Some 31 km southwest of Henan town, below Mount Dongwu and facing the Tse-chu river, there is the Mongolian monastery of **Chogar Tashi Chodzong** (Ch Qugesi), which was founded by the mother of a local chieftain in 1937. The monastery has been considered a branch of Labrang since 1948.

Southern Sogwo

The main road south from Henan crosses the Tse-chu and then forks, due south for 75 km to **Taklung Shingza** on the north bank of the Yellow River, and southeast for 61 km to **Serlung** and thence to **Luchu** in present-day Gansu province. The former road is a difficult but motorable trail.

Taklung Shingza Gon

Taklung Shingza Monastery (Ch Xiangza), also known as Tashi Delekyil, was founded on the north bank of the Yellow River in 1905 by Shingza Lobzang Chokyi Gyatso, and it is affiliated to Labrang. Originally it was a tented camp, the first solid adobe buildings dating only from 1930. These grasslands are particularly well known for their beautiful riding horses. Rough unreliable trails lead upstream to **Rabgya** (and from there to Machen in Golok) and downstream for 40 km through marshland and gorges to **Machu** in present-day Gansu province.

Southeast Sogwo

The main road running south-east from Henan to Serlung is better, and public buses can be seen making their way across the provincial border as far as Luchu, Tso and Linxia. The eastern grasslands on this route are as good as they get in Amdo, but the density of livestock is high and several species of pika (abra) burrow extensively under the terrain. They prefer not to use steeper land, rough shrub or marshlands, so the extension of pastures and drainage of marshes suit them well. As the last remaining mammal predators are eliminated by hunting they, along with the marmot, have often prospered. Several birds of prey, led by the steppe eagle and the huge lammergeier vulture, as well as songbirds, inhabit the steppe for most of the year, nesting in deserted holes and roosting on telephone poles. At **Serlung**, 61 km southeast of Henan, the monastery of **Datsengon Tashi Gandenling** overlooks the banks of the upper Luchu. A branch of Labrang, its foundation dates to 1924, and it actually marks the end of Mongolian territory.

Serlung to Luchu

The shrub-covered hills between Serlung and Luchu contain a disputed border, one of many among the present-day provincial, prefectural, or county borders throughout the plateau. The distance from Serlung to Luchu is only 48 km, following the upper reaches of the Luchu downstream. For a description of the Luchu valley, see below, page 674.

Sleeping

Hualong *p595, map p595*
D **Nationalities Hotel (Minzu Binguan)**, T0972-712128. Has singles and triples at ¥120 and doubles at ¥50.

There are also 3 guesthouses in town.

Yardzi *p597, map p598*
D **Tianchi Fandian (Minzu Binguan)**, T0972-813068. Has standard rooms.
Government Guesthouse, T0972-814959. Has suites at ¥70-¥80, standard rooms at ¥25 per bed, triples at ¥12 per bed, and 4-bedded rooms at ¥8 per bed, foreigners have to pay a 100% surcharge.
Huanxia Fandian, located on the bypass road.

Jentsa *p600*
E **Jentsa Government Guesthouse**, T0973-732503. Has en suite doubles at ¥80, economy doubles at ¥44, triples at ¥120.

Lugyagak *p601*
E **Lijiaxia Hotel**, T0973-42888. Has excellent double rooms at ¥94, but in 2002 it was temporarily closed pending resolution of a financial dispute.
Mirik Dronkhang one of a few other small guesthouses in town.

Rongpo Gyakhar *p606, map p607*
D **New Huangnan Hotel**, T0973-725655, F0973-722293. Opened in 1997, is already decaying, but it does have a sauna (doubles at ¥156-200, singles at ¥68-90, and suites at ¥345-580).
D **Old Huangnan Hotel**, T0973-722684/722293. Also known as the Tongren County Guesthouse, has a range of rooms (superior doubles at ¥180) and dormitory accommodation from ¥20 per bed. There is a good 2nd floor Chinese restaurant, and a cheaper one on the ground floor (sharing the same kitchen).
D **Telecom Hotel (Dianxing Binguan)**, 2 Zhongshan Rd, T0973-726888/555, F0973-721555. Currently has the best rooms in town, with attached bath (doubles at ¥136, suites at ¥260, dorms at ¥68 per bed), and a lively bowling alley downstairs,
D **Yinzhen Hotel**, T0973-725776. Smaller hotel, with suites at ¥176, singles at ¥60 and triples at ¥90.

Jadir *p611*
Tsekhok Hotel, Main St, T0973-8752224. Has clean doubles at ¥76 (¥38 per bed).

Henan *p613*
Zeyang Hotel, with its Mongolian dome, has the best rooms in town (doubles at ¥40, triples at ¥45, and 4-bed dorms at ¥38).

Eating

Hualong *p595, map p595*
The Muslim noodle restaurants adjacent to the Nationalities' Hotel are the best in town. Alternatively, try the small restaurants situated by the highway outside town.

Yardzi *p597, map p598*
Abdul Restaurant, T0972-812305. The best cuisine in town, grilled lamb dishes are particularly good here.
Chenglai Restaurant, has wholesome food served in setting of traditional solar courtyard.

Jentsa *p600*
There is a newly constructed Sichuan restaurant at the crossroads, which has the best and cleanest food in town.

Lugyagak *p601*
Lijiaxia Hotel, undoubtedly the best cuisine on offer in town.

There are many small restaurants catering to dam workers and engineers.

Rongpo Gyakhar *p606, map p607*
The Hotpot Restaurant, north of Recreational Park. Good.

As with most Amdo towns, there are mostly Muslim noodle restaurants, and a few more upmarket Chinese ones, of which the **New Century Restaurant**, **Dakar Restaurant** and **Taishan Restaurant**, on Zhongshan Rd, T0973-724504, are all recommended.

Jadir *p611*
The town has several Muslim noodle restaurants, and the **Jinxin Chinese Restaurant**.

Henan *p613*
The local restaurants are surprisingly all Muslim.

Festivals and events

Rongpo Gyakhar *p606, map p607*
The shamanic tradition is still important in Repkong, not only among the outlying Bon monasteries, but even among Buddhist communities. A **local festival** is held in the Gomar and Nyentok area, from the 16th to the 25th days of the 6th month of the lunar calendar (**30 Jul-8 Aug 2005**). The highpoint of the ceremonies, to which tourists are beginning to flock to see naked youths piercing their cheeks with needles, and sword-swallowing prowess, lasts for about 3 days.

For an explanation of the sleeping and eating price codes used in this guide, see inside the front cover. Other relevant information is found in Essentials pages 44-46.

Rongpo Gonchen *p607*
Ceremonies, including the unveiling of a large tangka, debates and religious dances, will be held during the 1st month of the lunar calendar on **16 -19 Feb 2005**.

Sengeshong Yagotsang *p608*
Ceremonies, including the unveiling of a large tangka and masked dances, will be held here during the New Year celebrations on the 5-7 days of the 1st lunar month (**13-15 Feb 2005**).

Sengeshong Magotsang *p608*
A masked dance of *torma* exorcism, preceding the New Year celebrations, will be held here on **7 Feb 2005**. The actual new year ceremonies take place on the 8th-10th days of the 1st lunar month (**16-18 Feb 2005**).

Transport

Hualong *p595, map p595*
Bus
Bus routes link this town with **Ziling**, **Jentsa**, and **Rongpo Gyakhar**.

Rongpo Gyakhar *p606, map p607*
Bus
There are public buses running to **Ziling**, **Yardzi**, **Sogwo**, **Tsekok**, **Labrang**, **Lugyagak** and **Linxia**.

Directory

Rongpo Gyakhar *p606, map p607*
Internet Available alongside the Old Huangnan Hotel and at the business centre of the New Huangnan Hotel. **Post offices** China Post, Zhongshan Rd, has EMS services. China Telecom, next door has IDD facilities.

Ziling to Mato: South Kokonor and Yellow River Basin

The second and third routes from Ziling to the Golok area of Southern Amdo are described in this section. The second runs from Ziling via Rushar through Trika and Kawasumdo to cross the Yellow River at Rabgya Gonpa. The third (Highway 214) runs from Ziling via Tongkor and Nyima Dawa La pass to Rikmon (Ch Daotonghe) and thence via Chabcha to Tsigortang and Mato. This entire area, presently administered within the Tibetan Autonomous Prefecture of South Kokonor, comprises five counties: Trika, Mangra, Kawasumdo, Chabcha and Tsigortang. ***Recommended itineraries: 8, 9, 11. See page 20.*** ▸▸ *For Sleeping, Eating and other listings, see pages 629-630.*

Trika County ཁྲི་ཀ

→ *Population: 94,290. Area: 3,408 sq km. Colour map 5, grid B4.* 贵德县

Trika is the traditional name for the region straddling the banks of the Yellow River, west of Jentsa. The county capital, also known as Trika (Ch Guide) is located 117 km south of Ziling, and 55 km northeast of Guinan in Mangra. Within the county there are approximately 56 monasteries, of which 33 represent the Gelukpa school, 20 the Nyingmapa, and three the Bon tradition. Regular buses

Trika County

leave Ziling for Trika, taking the Kumbum road for 18 km and then heading south across the **Lhamori** mountains, which comprise three prominent craggy black peaks on the watershed of the Yellow River. The pass (Altitude: 3,750 m), where snow can fall even in May, is 16 km from Rushar. Just 17 km down from the pass, a rough road heads east to Dzitsa monastery and **Bayan Khar** (see above, page 595), but the main road continues south through a few small Muslim and Tibetan villages, including **Garang** and **Akong**, to the Yellow River, 43 km below the watershed. The final stretch is through some very barren rusty brown hills – typical Yellow River scenery.

Garang

Garang township, just 10 km after the turn-off for Dzitsa, has a high concentration of Nyingmapa monasteries. Among them, **Yutsa Ngakhang** is within the township, while the biggest, **Karju Damkazhar Ngakhang Namdrol Pemaling**, lies 3 km to the southwest. **Sumbha Ngakhang**, 22 km south of the township, faces towards the Yellow River, while **Akong Ngakhang** overlooks the north bank. In addition, one of the largest Gelukpa monasteries of Trika is located 1.5 km northwest of the township at **Chorten Ki Ganden Tashi Dargyeling**. This is a branch of Kumbum Jampaling, founded in 1706.

Horkya

After Garang, the road follows the north bank of the Yellow River upstream. Narrow strips of cultivated land flank the tree-lined road, but the steep canyon walls of the Yellow River at this point are pale yellow, reminiscent of the North African Mahgreb. Some 13 km further on, at **Horkya** township, a rough side road heads west in the direction of Chabcha and Tongkor counties via Lhakhangtang, while the highway crosses to the south bank, where West Trika town (Ch Hexi) is only 2 km distant. At Horkya, on the north bank of the Yellow River, there is the Gelukpa monastery of **Horkya Dratsang Samtenling**, which was founded by the First Minyak Tulku Losel Dargye. A small Nyingmapa temple, **Horkya Ngakhang** is located nearby within the village. About 8 km north from here, **Go-me Do-re Dratsang**, founded in the 16th century by Do-re Tulku Rongkor, was reopened in 1983, and alongside it is the Nyingmapa temple of **Do-re Ngakhang**.

Lhakhangtang

Lhakhangtang (Ch Luohantang) township, 26 km west of the bridge in the direction of Tongkor, has three Gelukpa and four Nyingmapa monasteries within its jurisdiction. The Nyingmapa temples are all located close to the township, the largest being **Lhakhangtang Wangchen Drupei Gatsel**, which currently has 70 monks. Among the Gelukpa establishments, which lie further north, the most noteworthy is **Dechen Gon Sangak Rabgyeling**, a branch of Labrang.

Trika Town → *Altitude: 2,280 m. For listings, see pages 629-630.*

The county town of Trika, generally known in Chinese as Guide, is 2 km south of the bridge and 117 km from Ziling. Trika is a fairly large town spread along the south bank of the Yellow River, where it has absorbed several farming villages. The village houses of this region have high outer walls enclosing a courtyard where fruit trees or vegetables grow, and a single-storey house built of mud brick. Tibetans account for 32% of the population, but only a few live in the town itself, which is predominantly Chinese and Muslim. In fact, the town has had a Chinese presence since 1376 when a Ming garrison was established. The city walls, which still stand, were built in 1380, enclosing Daoist temples within them. Trika is a town of two distinct halves, separated by the waters of the Trika-chu, which flows into the Yellow River here. West Trika (Ch Hexi) has guesthouses, banks and a larger volume of through traffic, whereas Central and East Trika (Ch Heyin and Hedong) have parks, government buildings, guesthouses, a hospital, bus station, opera theatre, mosque and an old Daoist temple called Yihuangsi.

Formerly the most important site in town was the ancient stupa, founded by Tibetan kings during the ninth century, and gilded in 1806 by Tsewang Tenpei Nyima. The stupa, which did not survive the Cultural Revolution, was 30 m high with a five-tier base. A new replica was subsequently constructed in 1989-1990. Alongside the original, the First Minyak Tulku Losel Dargye (1675-1753) founded the Gelukpa monastery of **Minyak Dratsang Tashi Chopeling**. The complex was further developed by the Fifth Minyak Tulku Tsultrim Tenpei Nyima (1755-1817), who obtained funding from Mongolia. Nowadays, the greatest attraction of Trika is the large number of medicinal hot springs, which have been documented for over 600 years. These are particularly recommended in the treatment of muscular and stomach disorders.

Eastern Trika

Heading east of the county town, after 2 km, you will reach the rebuilt **Jojo Lhakhang**. This temple was originally constructed in the 13th century, and funded by Sakya Pandita in person who visited the Great Stupa en route for Mongolia, and donated a set of pearls offered to him by Godan Qan. Nearby, there are also Nyingmapa temples at **Kepa Ngakhang**, **Gongpa Ngakhang** and **Mepa Ngakhang**, while **Gongwa Dratsang** of the Gelukpa school is now regarded as a branch of Tashilhunpo, although it was originally constructed by the Sakyapa lama Kunga Kechuwa (1387-1446) who amalgamated two separate temples here.

Southern Trika

The greatest concentration of monasteries in Trika is found in modern **Dongkou** township, 16 km south of the county town. It is in the upper valleys around here that most Tibetans can be found, and there are numerous small monasteries, mostly Gelukpa but including five Nyingma temples and even a Bon presence. Among them, the most renowned are **Rabza Dratsang Samten Choling**, 5 km northwest of the township, which is an 18th-century branch of Lamo Dechen in neighbouring Jentsa county, and **Rongzhi Dratsang**, in the same locale, which was reopened in 1986. Other branches of Lamo Dechen are found here: **Gyabtsa Dratsang** (2 km southwest of the township), **Drom Dratsang** (a few kilometres southeast), and **Nyedrubde Lhundrub Chodzong** (7.5 km southeast). The Nyingmapa temples include **Lingtsa Ngakhang**, founded in 1939, and **Lanju Gongma Ngakhang**, which has a 700-year history. Further south of Dongkou, at **Changmu** township, there are branches of Lamo Dechen and of Bimdo Gonpa in Dowi (see above, page 599).

Southwest Trika

Heading southwest from town in the direction of Mangra, the main road passes through a thick belt of planted trees and then through a stony desert stretching towards the distant Mount **Amnye Jakhyung**. After 10 km, a turn-off on the right leads to the Health Spa Hotel, where it is possible to stay in a guesthouse, at a range of prices, with a piping hot mineral bath in every bathroom. Continuing on the highway, after 2 km you will reach the Gelukpa monastery of **Rungan Dratsang Dekyi Puntsok Choling** (Ch Riansi). Here, there are only a few monks, mostly from Mangra, and two temples with a stupa outside. The older temple contains images of Tsongkhapa with his foremost students along the inner wall, and images of Shridevi, Vaishravana, Six-armed Mahakala, the eight bodhisattvas and eight Medicine Buddhas along the left wall, while a photograph of Alak Gergya of Kumbum Jampaling, and volumes of the *Kangyur*, *Tangur* and the *Collected Works of Tsongkhapa* occupy the right inner corner. The murals, executed by artists from Kumbum, comprise (left to right): Shridevi, Vaishravana, Six-armed Mahakala, Vajrabhairava, Sukhavati, Tara, 35 Confession Buddhas, Tara, Atisha, Lama Chopa, Eight Medicine Buddhas, Sitatapatra, Shakyamuni with the 16 Elders, Amitayus, Sarvavid Vairocana, Hayagriva, Dampa Karnak and Dharmaraja. The other temple is of recent construction and it has a distinguished *gyabib*-style roof, with a stele in its courtyard.

Leaving **Puntsok Choling**, the stony desert gradually recedes and grass-covered hills appear, with large herds of yak grazing on the higher slopes. The road climbs to reach a watershed pass (3,360 m), 30 km from Puntsok Choling, within the green hills of the Amnye Jakhyung range. This demarcates the border between Trika and Mangra counties. The distance from Trika to Mangra is 55 km.

Mangra County མང་ར → *Population: 65,474. Area: 5,585 sq km.* 贵南县

Mangra county occupies the bend of the Yellow River, southwest of Trika and southeast of the dam and hydro-electric power plant at **Longyang Xia**. Here, the Mangra-chu tributary flows west towards its confluence with the Yellow River. The northern part of the county is barren, sandy desert, while south of the Mangra-chu, towards the low mountain range that divides it from Kawasumdo, there is some lush grassland. Prior to 1958 there were 19 monasteries and temples within the county, including one Gelukpa nunnery and one Nyingmapa centre. Of these, approximately 13 have been rebuilt and two (Ati Gon and Rungan Dratsang) allocated to neighbouring Trika county. The county town lies 144 km from Trika and 96 km from Kawasumdo, and until recently it was the only county in this prefecture still closed to foreigners.

Gomayin

After crossing the watershed pass of the Amnye Jakhyung range, the road from Trika descends through a windswept plain where sheep and goats graze freely. At **Gomayin**, a rapidly growing township 15 km below the pass, there is a major intersection, from where the main road heads south towards Mangra and Kawasumdo, and northeast to Trika and Ziling. Lesser but motorable trails also head west in the direction of Longyang Xia Dam, and southeast to reach the Gelukpa monastery of **Ati Gon Samtenling** after 35 km. This is a branch of Lamo Dechen, which may also be accessed directly from Trika on a southerly trail (37 km). In its vicinity, there are three other Gelukpa monasteries, of which **Wanshul Gon Shedrub Rinchenling**, founded in 1895 by Wangshul Lobzang Tashi Gyatso, is also a branch of Lamo Dechen. Some 13 km northwest from Gomayin, in the direction of the dam, there is a small Gelukpa temple at **Kharngon Garka**, constructed in the 1940s.

Gomayin to Mangra

Continuing south, the main road gradually climbs through sandy hills and desert landscape to reach the grasslands and pass (Altitude: 3,765 m) after 31 km. The descent on an excellent paved surface traverses wide open grassland, which extends towards the horizon. Strong winds blow from the Amnye Jakhyung range to the southeast. About 22 km below the pass, the two southerly roads from Gomayin converge at another intersection, from where you can also head west to Mangra town or southwest to Kawasumdo. If you take the former option, you will pass **Shengdor** township after 15 km, where a trail leads 19 km northeast to **Wanshul Garka** monastery, and reach the county town after a further 19 km. The terrain here is arid, but for narrow strips of cultivation close to the dirt road.

Mangra town → *Altitude: 3,090 m*

Mangra town (Ch Guinan), consists of one main street with two intersections. Entering from the east, you will pass the bus station and post office on the left, and a guesthouse, hospital and banks on the right. Then, continuing along Main Street, after the first intersection, you will pass the Government Guesthouse and clothing market on the left and the government buildings on the right. Three roads radiate outwards from the west end of Main Street, southwest to **Tarshul Monastery**, due west to **Atsok Gon**, and northwest to the police station, cinema and **Lutsang Gonpa**, which is the only monastery within the town, 3 km distant. » *For listings, see pages 629-630.*

Lutsang Gonpa This monastery, also known as **Shedrub Gepeling**, currently has 150 monks. It was founded in 1889 by the Fourth Alak Nyenzang Lobzang Chokyi Nyima, whose present incarnation, the Sixth Alak Nyenzang is in his 20s. The reconstructed **Assembly Hall** (Tsokchen) has 56 pillars, and it has been redecorated by sculptors from mainland China and artists from Repkong. The central images are of Tsongkhapa and his foremost students, to their left is a photograph of the present the Eleventh Panchen Lama, Gendun Chokyi Nyima, and to their rear the volumes of the *Kangyur* and *Tangyur*. The murals here depict (left): Shridevi, Vaishravana, Tara, Sarvavid Vairocana and Vajrabhairava; and (right): Vajrapani, Mahakarunika, Sitatapatra, and Dharmaraja. The **Jampa Lhakhang** to its rear contains a large image of Maitreya, flanked by smaller images of the Fourteenth Dalai Lama and the Tenth Panchen Lama. The volumes of the Kangyur are to the left, along with encased images of Shakyamuni and his students flanked by the six ornaments and two supreme masters of ancient India. The *Tangyur* is stacked along the right wall, along with encased images of Tsongkhapa and his foremost students, with the 35 Confession Buddhas.

Mangra township

Heading west from Mangra, a turn-off leads north to old **Mangra** township after 16 km. The township lies 15 km along this side road, on the banks of the Mangra-chu. Here, the **Podu Garka** temple, affiliated to Bimdo Gonpa in Dowi, can be visited, along with the Nyingmapa monastery of **Turol Ngakhang** (9 km west). About 19 km northwest of the township, there is the monastery of **To-le Gon Namgyel Puntsoling**, a branch of Lamo Dechen, founded in 1916, which was recently moved to this location following the construction of the Longyang Xia Dam.

Tarshul Gonpa

Continuing due west from the intersection south of Mangra township, you will pass through **Tarshul** township after 16 km. Southeast of here (approximately 25 km from the county town), there is the Gelukpa monastery of **Tarshul Gonpa Namdak Trimdenling**, pleasantly located in the grassy hills. There are approximately 80 monks here, under the guidance of the charismatic First Alak Yongdzin Lobzang Khedrub Gyatso (b. 1908), now in his mid-90s, who founded the monastery in 1935 with the support of Tarshul Tulku Gelek Wangchen Choying Gyatso. Previously, a tented monastery had been founded here in 1671 by the First Tarshul Tulku Choying Gyatso. Alak Yongdzin is revered by many as the best lama in Mangra and one of the most learned in all of Amdo. He himself was formerly a tutor at Labrang, although his own monastery is affiliated to Lamo Dechen. Near Tarshul, there are the ruins of the Gelukpa nunnery of **Maril Jomo Tsamkhang** and the **Chubzang Tsamkhang**, a branch of Labrang founded in the early 19th century by the Third Jamyang Zhepa.

Mangra to Tsigortang

A rough road extends west from Guinan via Tarshul township and after 63 km crosses the Yellow River at Atsok Gonpa. From **Atsok Gonpa**, two roads connect with the main Ziling-Jyekundo highway in Tsigortang county (see below, page 625). Another rough road cuts northwest, crossing the Yellow River at Kyikyug to arrive in Chabcha county.

Mangra & Kawasumdo Counties

Mangra to Kawasumdo

Returning to the paved highway 34 km east of Mangra, you can turn northeast for Trika (110 km) or southwest for Kawasumdo (62 km). Taking the latter road, you drive quickly and easily through lush grasslands to cross a pass (Altitude: 3,480 m) after 15 km, and reach the county border.

Kawasumdo County ཀ་བ་སུམ་མདོ

→ *Population: 48,269. Area: 5,331 sq km. Colour map 5, grid B4.* 同德县

Kawasumdo is the traditional name given to the grasslands in the bend of the Yellow River to the south of Mangra. As the name suggests, it lies at the junction of three main routes: northeast to Trika and Ziling, west to Tsigortang and Chabcha, and south to Tsekok and Machen. There are 14 monasteries in the county, of which 10 are Gelukpa and four Nyingmapa. The county capital (Ch Tongde) is in a sheltered defile, 96 km from Mangra, 102 km from Tsigortang, and 111 km from Jadir in Tsekok.

North Kawasumdo

The paved highway descends from the pass on the Mangra-Kawasumdo county border through rolling green hills and rich wide open pastures which now sustain large herds of yak. The grasslands are dotted with nomads' tents, and in summer there are occasional grassland festivals, when scores of tents, including tented monasteries, are pitched together. After 12 km, a dirt road branches to the southeast in the direction of Jadir (82 km), and then after a further 13 km, it forks again at a petrol station, the highway leading south to Rabgya Gonpa and Tawo in Machen county (180 km), and a bumpy gravel road heading west into the county town. A smoother dirt road, which bypasses the petrol station from the south, runs parallel to the gravel road for most of the 22 km-drive into town, criss-crossing it occasionally. This offers a much better driving surface than the gravel.

Kawasumdo Town → *Altitude: 3,180 m*

The county town (Ch Tongde) is located in the Ba-chu gorge below the level of the surrounding tableland, affording some protection from the strong winds. There is one long main street, which forks at the west end. Entering from the east (Mangra, Trika or Jadir), you will pass on the right a petrol station, the martyrs' cemetery, assorted banks, a Tibetan hospital, government buildings and the Government Guesthouse, while on the left you will pass the Traffic Guesthouse, the bus station, market, banks, post office, bookstore and cinema. The local middle school and armed police unit are located in a lane to the north. At the west end of Main Street, you can head south on a rough trail for **Gumang** township and **Serlak Gonpa** or northwest for Tsigortang, crossing the Yellow River. ▸▸ *For listings, see pages 629-630.*

Gumang

Gumang township can be reached after a six-hour trek over a pass to the southwest, or more easily by returning to the intersection 22 km east of the county town and driving southwest for 15 km, after which a dirt road leads west for 20 km to Gumang. On the way you will pass through **Serlak Gon Ganden Puntsok Tengyeling**, the largest monastery in North Kawasumdo. Affiliated to Sera Monastery at Lhasa, it was founded during the 17th century at the bidding of the Fifth Panchen Lama by two monastic preceptors from Sera and Tashilhunpo. Currently, there are around 180 monks here, headed by Do-me Rinpoche. The small brick and concrete temple of **Gochen Dzong Gon** lies 15 km east of Serlak, and is visible from the main road across a small river. Also, 12 km southeast of Gumang, there is a Nyingmapa hermitage at **Drakto Tsamkhang**.

Southern Kawasumdo

From the intersection 22 km east of the county town, you can drive northeast to Mangra and Trika, or continue south towards Rabgya Gonpa and Machen county. Taking the latter road, which is smooth and fast, you continue heading south through the rich flat grasslands. Motorable dirt roads cross the highway after 8 km and again (for Gumang and Serlak) after 7 km. Heading further south, the terrain soon becomes hilly, prayer flags are suspended across the road, and a clinic serving road maintenance workers is passed on the left (east). Climbing gradually, three passes are crossed in succession. The first of these, **Amo La**, is crossed after 23 km, and this is followed by **Khyimda La** pass (4,024 m) after a further 12 km, as the road traverses the snow range to the north of the Yellow River (beyond this is the third, as yet unnamed pass). On the descent into the valley of the Serchung Nang-chu, which flows due south into the Yellow River, there are grasslands where caterpillar fungus abounds. After 5 km, a rough track leaves the highway, heading east through a broad side valley and crossing a southerly pass to reach **Hedong** township and **Tsang-gar Gonpa**, about 20 km from the main road. Buses heading to and from Machen will stop at the turn off (Hebei).

Tsang-gar Gonpa **Tsang-gar Dondrub Rabtenling** (Ch Shizangsi) was founded in 1765 by Tsang Pandita, a local monk who had affiliations with Tashilhunpo. In 1941 the monastery was destroyed by the Muslim warlord Ma Bufang, and the monks were forced to flee east into the Sangke grasslands near Labrang. Subsequently, the original site was reclaimed and the monastery reopened in 1981. Currently, it is the largest monastery in the county, housing over 400 monks. The complex includes two assembly halls, three temples, and three colleges, although some of these buildings, such as the larger assembly hall, have not yet been fully decorated. The Jokhang, situated behind the assembly hall, is an original structure, containing new images of Shakyamuni flanked by the eight standing bodhisattvas. Beautiful Repkong panels decorate its side walls. The Gyupa Tratsang contains in its upper storey a protector chapel dedicated to Gochen, a local deity. Lastly, the Khangsar Labrang has a temple dedicated to Tsongkhapa, surrounded by 1,000 smaller images of the master and fine Repkong-style murals. Many of the monks are Sogwo Arik, a Mongolian clan who are mainly concentrated in Sogwo Prefecture to the east and Chilen county, north of Lake Kokonor.

The descent to Rabgya

In order to avoid the steep gorges as the tributaries plunge sharply towards the Yellow River, the main road crosses several small ridges before descending to **Rabgya Gonpa**, 137 km from Kawasumdo (and 371 km from Ziling). About 22 km after the turn-off for Tsang-gar Gonpa, the road enters a red-rock canyon, interspersed with good grazing pastures and forested copses. **Majang** township (Altitude: 3,360 m) lies 4 km within the canyon, and there are a number of inexpensive roadside Muslim restaurants here. Four ridges, the highest at 3,630 m, are crossed before the road finally descends into full view of the Yellow River. The distance from Majang township to Rabgya Gonpa is 33 km. Below Rabgya, there is a bridge crossing the Yellow River, which leads from Rabgya to Tawo, the capital of Machen county, 43 km to the south. There is a small Muslim-run truckstop near the bridge, where it is possible to stay. Although Rabgya is on the north bank of the river, it technically falls within the Machen county of Golok, for which reason it is described below, page 636.

Kawasumdo to Tsigortang

Heading west from Kawasumdo county town, after 1 km, the road forks, the southern trail leading across a bridge which spans the Ba-chu in the direction of Gumang, and the western trail following the river downstream towards its confluence with the Yellow River. Taking the latter, the gorge gradually opens out into a wide cultivated valley, and the road becomes a tree-lined avenue. After 15 km, a side road crosses the Ba-chu to the south bank, where it follows the course of an aqueduct. The main road, however, continues on the north bank, passing through a series of small farming villages, such as **Bagu**, where the houses have typical courtyards and adobe perimeter walls. Some 24 km west of town, the road bypasses **Sumdo Gon**, a branch of the Gelukpa monastery of Drakar Tredzong (see below, page 626), which was founded in 1925.

After Bagu township, the road cuts northwest for 27 km to reach the suspension bridge (2,760 m) spanning the Yellow River and enter Tsigortang county (see below, page 625). In this area there are a number of small shrines and monasteries, the most important being **Shartsang Rigzin Jigme Kalzangling**, a branch of Kowa Gon in Jentsa, which was founded in 1945, and the Nyingmapa hermitage at **Togen Nagar**, founded in 1935.

Chabcha County ཆབ་ཆ

→ *Population: 123,631. Area: 16,313 sq km. Colour map 5, grid B3.* 共和县

The third route from Ziling to Golok, follows Highway 214 southwest from the city, through Tongkor county and **Nyima Dawa La** pass (see above, page 573), to enter Chabcha county. **Chabcha** (Ch Gonghe) occupies the exposed basin between Lake Kokonor and the Yellow River. As such, it includes the southern shore of Lake Kokonor as far west as Tanakma, and the plain through which Highway 214 cuts its way southwest towards Mato and Jyekundo. The county capital is located at Chabcha town, 143 km from Ziling, and 350 km northeast of Mato in Golok. There are 21 monasteries within the county, 10 of which are Gelukpa, eight Nyingmapa, two Bonpo, and one, **Sokpo Gon**, which is both Gelukpa and Nyingmapa.

Rikmon intersection

Descending from Nyima Dawa La pass, at **Rikmon** (Ch Daotonghe), 102 km from Ziling, two roads diverge. Head west for **Lake Kokonor**, **Kermo** and **Lhasa** on Highway 109; or alternatively, head southwest for Chabcha, Jyekundo and Kunming on Highway 214. The former route via Tanakma and Tsaka has already been described (see above, page 562).

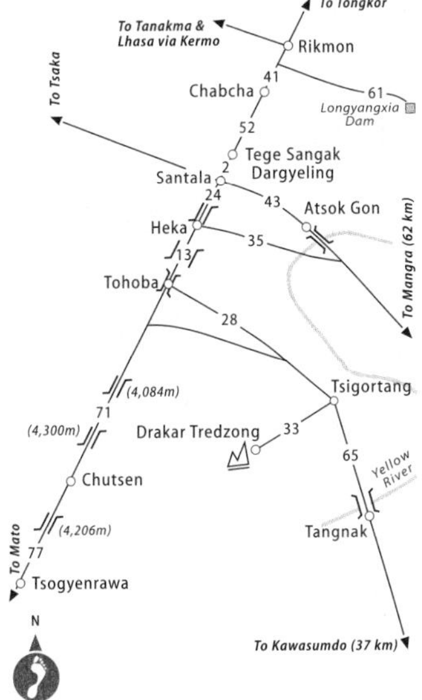

Longyang Xia Dam

→ *Colour map 5, grid B4*

Heading southwest from Rikmon, the highway crosses a pass, known in Chinese as Liu Shankou (3,580 m), and then descends through the rolling green hills of the South Kokonor range. About 18 km south of Rikmon, a dirt turn-off on the left leads east for 61 km to the Longyang Xia Dam on the Yellow River. This is one of China's largest dams but the reservoir has silted up fast under the heavy sediment load of the river. A smaller reservoir dam to the west of Chabcha burst in 1993 due to an earthquake, killing over 200 people. Earthquakes are common in this region, and a powerful one also struck in the mid-1980s. Monasteries in this area are largely Nyingmapa, including the 13th-century **Tingkya Sangak Choling**, which subsequently became a branch of Zhechen (see page 507), and **Tsotolung Ngakhang**, which had to be moved to its present location when the dam was constructed. Continuing southwest on the highway, you will cross three passes in quick succession, the highest at 3,210 m, to arrive at the county town, 41 km from Rikmon.

Chabcha → *Altitude: 2,940 m. Colour map 5, grid B4.*

Chabcha is a surprisingly large modern town on the fringe of an exposed arid steppe, and nowadays it functions as the administrative capital of the entire South Kokonor Prefecture. Entering from the northeast, a bypass takes through traffic around the town en route for Mato and Jyekundo. If you turn left at the petrol station, you will pass on the left a memorial temple and stupa dedicated to King Songtsen Gampo, which was constructed recently by the Tenth Panchen Lama. The road curves past the South

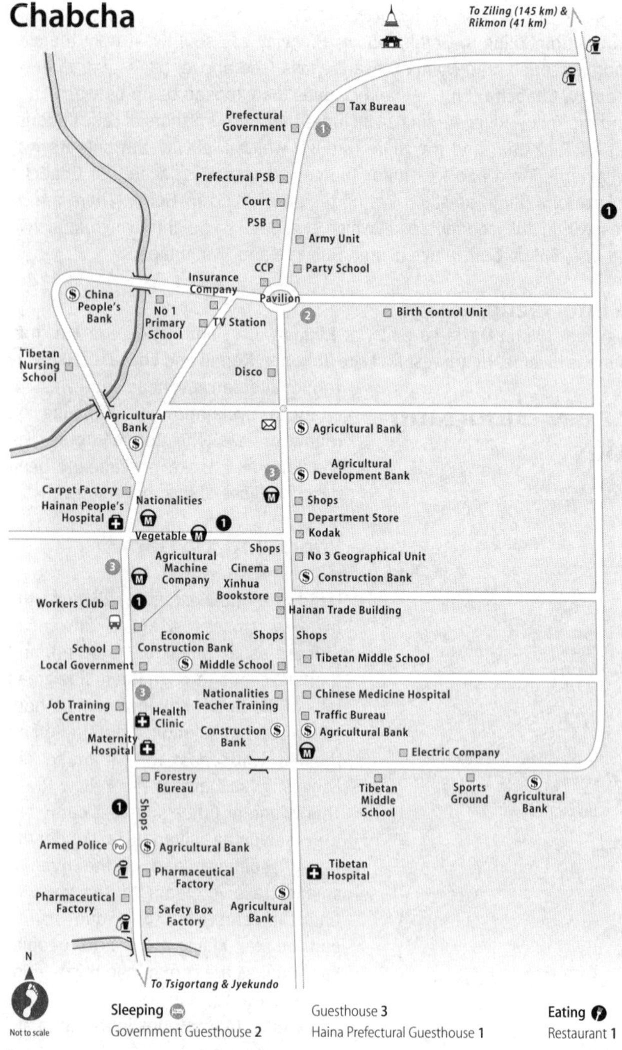

Kokonor Prefectural Government Buildings and the Hainan Hotel to reach a roundabout, dominated by the police and Communist Party buildings. Three roads diverge here. Turn left (west) across a bridge for the Tibetan Nursing school, the carpet factory, the Hainan People's Hospital, the bus station, and some smaller guesthouses. Turn right (east) for the Government Guesthouse, the Birth Control Unit and the bypass, or continue straight ahead (south) on Main Street, where you will find the post office, supermarkets, department stores, street markets, cinemas, schools, banks and the hospitals of both Chinese and Tibetan traditional medicine.

North of Chabcha there are several monasteries which can be visited, including **Gonpa Soma** of the Gelukpa school (founded 1902), **Kyildong Ngakhang** of the Nyingma school (founded 1942), and at **Gandi** township, 13 km northwest of town, **Khyamru Gon Tashi Gepeling**, a branch of Labrang founded in 1813 by the Third Jamyang Zhepa, which is the biggest monastery within the county. The latter has a fine Jampeyang Lhakhang, containing images of Manjughosa flanked by Maitreya and Tara, and excellently executed Repkong-style murals. Some 6 km south of Chabcha there is another important Gelukpa centre at **Sachuk Sangak Tengyeling** (founded in 1943). ▸▸ *For listings, see pages 629-630.*

Santala → *Colour map 5, grid B3*

Driving southwest from Chabcha, the highway climbs gradually through the plains to reach the **Santala** intersection after 54 km. En route it is intersected by tall electricity pylons, connected to the power station at Longyangxia Dam. About 2 km before Santala, there is a small Nyingmapa temple called **Tege Sangak Dargyeling**, located to the right (west) of the road. The building, founded only in 1984, is of an excellent construction, surrounded by large heavy prayer wheels on three sides. Its central image of Padmasambhava is flanked by Repkong-style murals, appropriate to the Nyingma tradition. There are 20 monks here under the guidance of Lama Kham Kunkhyab. On the horizon some 40 km to the west, one can clearly discern the fault line formed where the Yellow River gorge meets the high tableland plateau. The blue haze of the river filters into the atmosphere. At Santala, four roads diverge. Turn right (northwest) for Tsaka (see above, page 556), left (southeast) for Atsok Gonpa and Mangra (105 km), or continue southwest on the paved highway for Mato (296 km). At this point the highway enters Tsigortang county.

Tsigortang County ཚྭ་གོར་ཐང་

→ *Population: 57,610. Area: 11,621 sq km. Colour map 5, grid B3.* 兴海县

The county of Tsigortang (Ch Xinghai) occupies the tableland west of the bend of the Yellow River, formed by the Amnye Machen range. The county capital is 65 km southeast of the Santala intersection on a branch road, which leaves the highway at the Tohoba bridge. The town is also accessible from Kawasumdo, 102 km to the southeast. Altogether, there are 14 monasteries within the county: nine Gelukpa, four Nyingmapa and one Kagyupa.

Atsok Gon

From the Santala crossroads, you can head southeast for 43 km on a dirt road to **Atsok Gon**, where a bridge crosses the Yellow River to enter Mangra county (see above, page 619). This bridge may also be reached from Heka, 24 km further along the highway, over a rougher 35-km stretch. **Atsok Gon Dechen Chokhorling** is a small but important Gelukpa monastery, located some 2 km south of the bridge which spans the Yellow River into Mangra county. It has an impressively sited set of the eight stupas symbolizing the deeds of Shakyamuni Buddha, and several old tangkas. The monastic community here was founded in 1889 and currently numbers 70.

Heka

From Santala, the paved Highway 214 continues southwest for **Heka** (24 km), crossing four passes (range 3,180-3,300 m) on the way. Heka township (Altitude: 3,330) is a busy road junction for truckers and there are several Muslim restaurants and shops. The attraction here, and in similar roadside towns throughout Amdo, lies in the local Tibetans who frequently visit to purchase supplies from the Chinese, Hui and Salar shopkeepers. Northwest of Heka, there are small Nyingma monasteries at **Yulung Drakar** (3 km), **Cholung Ngakhang** (26 km), and **Tsidung Ngakhang** (26 km), all of which have only a few monks or *mantrins*. From the Heka intersection, there is also a branch road leading 35 km southeast to Atsok Gon.

Leaving Heka, the highway crosses a higher pass (3,900 m) on **Mount Heka** after 6 km, and then descends to the Tohoba bridge after a further 7 km, where a well paved side road branches off the highway to the left, heading 28 km for the county town.

Tsigortang town → *For listings, see pages 629-630.*

Turning off the highway at the Tohoba bridge, the side road crosses a pass (3,450 m) after 10 km, and reaches the town after a further 18 km on an excellent paved surface. **Tsigortang** (Ch Xinghai) is large, surprisingly attractive and situated near the scenic power-place of **Drakar Tredzong**. The surrounding tableland is intermittently broken by the deeply eroded gorges of its Yellow River tributaries. Entering town from the Chabcha side (north), you will pass on the left the local government guesthouse and tax bureau, while on the right are the carpet factory, the Xiashuidian Guesthouse and various commercial buildings. Reaching the crossroads, turn left for the police station, the People's Hospital, and the road to Kawasumdo (Ch Tungte), right for the Xinghai Hotel and the road to Drakar Tredzong, or continue straight ahead (south) for the Allah Restaurant, the bus station, cinema, market and the road to **Chutsen** (Ch Wenquan).

Drakar Tredzong

Drakar Tredzong, the celebrated 'white monkey fortress' is classed along with Dentik and Achung Namdzong, as one of the three most important sacred sites in Amdo. A high 5,000-m peak with thickly forested slopes and abundant wildlife, it is located only 33 km southwest of the county town, but transport is irregular. Heading west out of town, a grass-covered motorable track leaves the main dirt road after 3 km heading west. Take this trail, and after 7 km, descend from the high tableland plateau into a steep arid gorge, which extends downhill for 4 km. Then, ford the river and follow another tributary upstream for 6 km to regain the tableland (Altitude: 3,390 m). Drakar Tredzong peak now comes into view. The approach on foot is impressive, crossing a

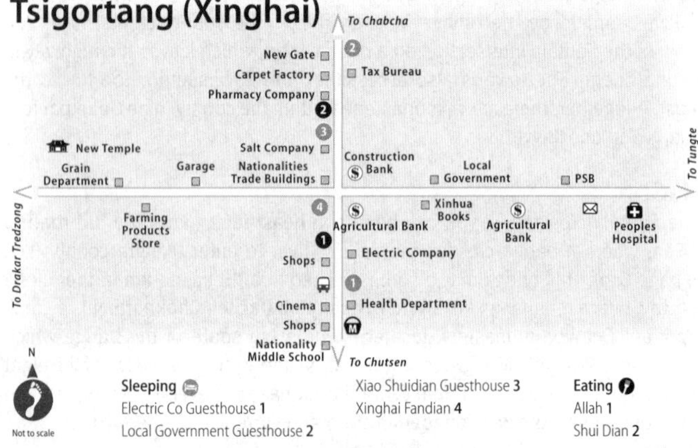

final 3,606-m pass, and for the last 6 km the trail joins the pilgrims' route, which is one of the most renowned in Amdo. Aromatic herbs and incense permeate the air.

Tosam Yonten Dargyeling The large Gelukpa monastery of **Tosam Yonten Dargyeling**, located on the south side of the mountain, was constructed in 1923 by Arik Tsang (1888-1959) of Rongpo Gonchen,and its present youthful incumbent the Fourth Arik Tsang, who lives in town, currently presides over 400 monks, although it is capable of holding 1,000. Approaching the entrance to the monastery, on the left there is a large stone wall where a ceremonial tangka is displayed on the 14th day of the first lunar month, and on the right, a fine set of the eight stupas representing major events in the life of Shakyamuni Buddha. The residential buildings are located to the left of the entrance. The courtyard is entered via a steep flight of stone stairs, and inside there are three buildings: the Assembly Hall in front, and the Jampa Lhakhang and Gonkhang to the left. The **Assembly Hall** is particularly impressive. It has 100 carpeted pillars, Repkong-style murals, and the reliquary stupa of the Third Arik Tsang. The main gilded images represent (L-R): Acala, Sitatapatra, Acala, the Second Arik Tsang, Padmasambhava, Shar Kalden Gyatso of Repkong, the Third Arik Tsang, Manjughosa, Vajrapani and Avalokiteshvara. The throne bears a photograph of the Third Arik Tsang. The murals on the ground floor depict (L): Shridevi, Six-armed Mahakala, Cakrasamvara, 21 Taras, Vairocana, Bhaisajyaguru, Guhyasamaja and Kalacakra, and (R): Vajrapani, Hevajra, 35 Confession Buddhas, Sukhavati, Abhirati, Mahakarunika, and Dorje Lekpa. **Upstairs**, alongside the residence of the Fourth Arik Tsang and the large tangka banner, there are images replicating those of the ground floor, while the murals include the Lama Chopa refuge tree, Padmasambhava and the Tenth Panchen Lama. Within the **Jampa Lhakhang**, there is a large 8-m Maitreya image, flanked by Aksobhya, Amitabha and Shakyamuni, along with tangkas depicting the Lords of the Three Enlightened Families and the Three Deities of Longevity, while the murals depict the 16 Elders, the Eight Medicine Buddhas, Sukhavati and Abhirati.

Pilgrimage circuit of Drakar Tredzong **Tosam Yonten Dargyeling** is one of the so-called 18 sacred sites of Drakar Tredzong. Others, which can all be seen on the five-hour pilgrimage circuit around the mountain, include a natural image of Tara said to cure infertility (**Dolma Bujin**), the rock impressions of Ling Gesar's horse; a stone image of Avalokiteshvara which is said to have saved the life of an old native inhabitant of Arik; a renowned charnel ground associated with Vajrasana in India; a passageway through which pilgrims squeeze to test their karma in the face of the Lord of Death (**Chogyel Nang**); a hermitage of Yeshe Tsogyel (**Khandro Tsokhang**); a cave where Padmasambhava meditated (**Yamatarkhung**); and the site where he tamed the hostile spirits (**Dresin Tulsa**); a medicinal spring (**menchu**); the entrance to the sacred abode (**nego**) where there are stone footprints of Padmasambhava and many mani stones; a natural pillar of crystal in a bottomless cave; the auspicious pass (**Tashi La**) where Tsongkhapa gave wondrous teachings; the place where Tsongkhapa rested; a cave containing a wish-granting 'cow'; the vase and begging bowl of Padmasambhava; and the deep cave (**Dorje Puklam**) at the centre of a natural amphitheatre where Padmasambhava hurled his vajra into the air to create a natural skylight in the cave-roof.

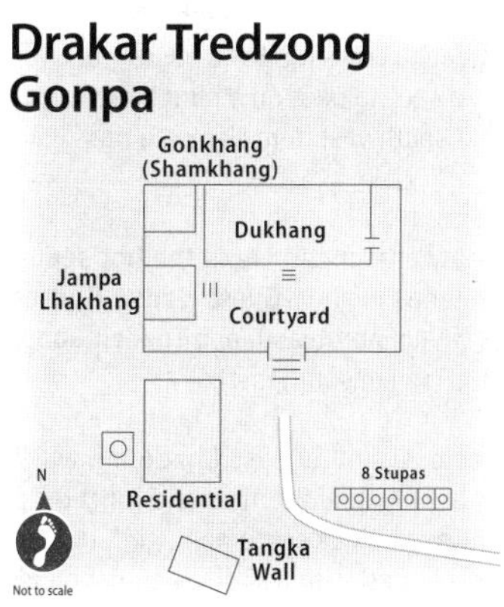

Drakar Tredzong: abode of solitude

The attractions of Drakar Tredzong for the meditator are summarized in the following verse by Zhabkar Tsokdruk Rangdrol:

"Ema! The Trakar Dredzong mountain
Is as beautiful as a heap of precious white crystals.
It is a supreme abode of solitude
Blessed by Padmakara, the Lord of the Victorious Ones.
There are countless miraculously arisen images of deities,
The refuge of all beings, men and gods.
Almost all the practitioners who, after
renouncing the world,
Meditated in this place, attained realisation"

M Ricard (transl) *The Life of Shabkar*

A number of active retreat hermitages are also found on the mountain, as well as a small camp of Nyingma nuns. Formerly there were also 400 Nyingmapa monks at Drakar Tredzong.

Tsigortang to Kawasumdo

Heading east from Tsigortang town, the road cuts across the tableland plateau, descending steeply over 300 m on two occasions to ford tributaries of the Yellow River, and climbing back to the high plateau. On the tableland itself driving is easier on the dirt road which runs parallel to the gravel road surface. After 53 km, the road finally begins its descent towards the Yellow River canyon. There are magnificent views of its confluence with the Ba-chu below. A power station is passed on the left and the suspension bridge at **Tangnak** is eventually crossed after a further 12 km. This marks the border between Tsigortang and Kawasumdo counties (see above, page 622). The overall distance from Tsigortang to Kawasumdo is 102 km.

Tsigortang to Chutsen

A rough trail leads south for 9 km from Tsigortang to **Daheba** township, and then cuts across the grassland towards **Chutsen** (Ch Wenquan), on the highway.

Tohoba to Tsogyenrawa

Continuing southwest on Highway 214 from the intersection at Tohoba bridge (see above, page 626), you eventually leave the plateau to cross **Ngalo La** pass (4,084 m), known in Chinese as Waka Sankou, followed by a second pass on **Mount Erlan** (4,300 m). The township of **Chutsen** (3,400 m) is 71 km southwest from Ngalo La pass.

Chutsen and Tsogyenrawa

The town functions as a truck stop, and the only attraction here is the hot spring, which is yet to be developed. Outlying monasteries include **Gyesa Dzitsa Gonsar**, which is a branch of Jakhyung founded in 1938 (18 km northeast), and **Tokden Gonpa** of the Kagyu school, which was founded in 1887 (12 km southeast).

From Chutsen, the paved highway continues across another pass (4,206 m), which leads into the basin of a small lake and over a stony plain to the road junction at **Tsogyenrawa** (Ch Huashixia, 77 km). Tsogyenrawa is a bleak settlement, girded to the southwest by a high rocky amphitheatre of diverse hues, with two dingy guesthouses and noodle restaurants. There is a small tented Nyingma monastery at **Tsorik Chogar**, 24 km to the southwest of Tsogyenrawa, but the main interest is the proximity of Golok. The various routes from here into Amnye Machen, Central Golok, and Mato in Upper Golok are all described in the following section.

Sleeping

Trika *p617*
D **Hotsprings Hotel (Wenquan Binguan)**, T0974-18553234. Has the best rooms in town on 3rd floor (doubles at ¥120, suites at ¥240, and dormitory beds at ¥14), each room has a private bath and shower with 24-hr piping hot mineral water (average temperature 76°), IDD and fax facilities are available at reception.
E **Gyelnyer Dronkhang** in East Trika. Cheaper.
E **Hexi Guesthouse** in West Trika. Cheaper.

Mangra *p619*
E **Bus Station Guesthouse**, an alternative option to the Government Guesthouse.
E **Government Guesthouse**, the best, though very basic, dormitory accommodation at ¥14 per bed.

Kawasumdo *p621*
E **Tongde Government Guesthouse**, T0974-591759. Has singles and doubles at ¥70, triples at ¥60, newly decorated suites at ¥168 (Tibetan style) and ¥128 (Chinese style).
E **Traffic Guesthouse**, cheaper.

Chabcha *p624, map p624*
E **Hainan Prefectural Government Hotel**, T0974-512773. Suites and doubles at ¥50-90, triples at ¥18 per bed, and hot showers at ¥2.50.

Cheaper accommodation is available at the other guesthouses in town.

Tsigortang *p626, map p626*
D **Xinghai Fandian** T0974-581385. Has the best rooms in town (singles at ¥120, doubles at ¥80, and suites at ¥120).
E **Xiao Shuidian Guesthouse**, T0974-581271. Has superior doubles at ¥24 per bed, and standard rooms at ¥20 per bed (without attached bathroom).
E **Electric Company Guesthouse**, cheap.

Chutsen *p628*
E Small truckers' guesthouse (¥12 per bed) and a few roadside noodle restaurants.

Eating

Trika *p617*
There are many small Muslim noodle restaurants in town, but the best food is found at the **Hotsprings Hotel**.

Mangra *p619*
Chongqing Restaurant, Main St. The best and cleanest place to eat in town.

Kawasumdo *p621*
The best is a Sichuan noodle restaurant, near the Tibetan Hospital on north side of Main St.

Chabcha *p624, map p624*
Try the upmarket Sichuan restaurant, located on the 2nd Floor of a building to the north of the vegetable market. Most downtown restaurants are Muslim-owned.

Tsigortang *p626, map p626*
Allah's Restaurant, has the best Muslim food in town.
Shuidian Dajiujian, has the best Sichuan fare.

Transport

Trika *p617*
Bus
Buses run daily to and from **Ziling** and **Chabcha**, and intermittently to and from **Mangra**.

Mangra *p619*
Bus
Buses run daily to and from **Chabcha**, **Trika** and **Ziling**, and on alternate days to and from **Kawasumdo**.

For an explanation of the sleeping and eating price codes used in this guide, see inside the front cover. Other relevant information is found in Essentials pages 44-46.

Kawasumdo *p621*

Bus

There are daily buses to and from **Ziling** and **Machen**, and connections on alternate days with **Chabcha**, **Tsigortang** and **Tsekok**.

Chabcha *p624, map p624*

Bus

There are regular daily buses on the highway linking Chabcha with **Ziling** (4 hrs), **Trika**, **Tanakma**, **Kawasumdo** and **Jyekundo**, with less frequent services to and from **Mangra**, **Trika**, and **Darlag**.

Tsigortang *p626, map p626*

Bus

There are regular daily buses linking Tsigortang with **Ziling** (7-8 hrs), **Trika**, **Heka**, **Chutsen** and **Kawasumdo**.

Car

It is possible to hire a 4WD vehicle for Drakar Tredzong (¥200 round trip).

Golok-Sertal and Ngawa: Amnye Machen Range and the Gyarong Headwaters

The Bayankala and Amnye Machen ranges of Amdo demarcate the upper reaches of the Yellow River, homeland of the Golok; while the Mardzagang range forms a watershed between the Yellow River and the three main sources of the Gyarong: the Ser-chu, Do-chu, and Mar-chu. This entire region is the domain of independently minded nomadic peoples who have maintained their distinctive cultural traditions for centuries.

Four of the six counties currently included in the Golok Tibetan Autonomous Prefecture of Qinghai occupy the valley of the Yellow River, whereas the other two, Padma and Jigdril along with those of Sertal, Dzamtang and Ngawa, all lie within the gorges and valleys of the Gyarong source rivers. Nowadays the counties of the Golok Tibetan Autonomous Prefecture are administered from Machen, Sertal from Dartsedo (in the Kandze Tibetan Autonomous Prefecture), and the last two from Barkham, within the Ngawa Tibetan Autonomous Prefecture of Sichuan province. ***Recommended itineraries: 9, 11 (also 8). See page 20.*** *» For Sleeping, Eating and other listings, see pages 653-655.*

Mato County མ་སྟོད

→ *Population: 10,803. Area: 25,263 sq km. Colour map 5, grid B2.* 玛多县

This county, also known as **Machuka**, contains the source of the Yellow River, and lies north of the Bayankala watershed. There are a few small Nyingma shrines and monasteries, of which the largest and most influential is **Horkor Gon**. The county town, **Mato**, lies 331 km northeast of Jyekundo and 494 km southwest of Ziling.

Bayankala Watershed

Approaching Mato from Kham (ie from Jyekundo or Sershul via Zhiwu, on which see above, page 515), Highway 214 gradually ascends through the rolling swamplands of the upper Yalong to cross **Trawo La pass** (5,082 m) in the Bayankhala Range, 61 km beyond **Domda** (Ch Qingshuihe). On the approach to the pass there are fine views of the rolling humps of the Bayankala range to the east of the road, and yellow poppies are commonplace. After crossing this watershed, a bleak expanse of high altitude lakeland unfolds. The road descends gradually passing en route a blue stone obelisk at **Chungonlung** after 29 km, and groups of nomads' tents at **Lungen** (Ch Yeniugdo) after 51 km. Foxes are a common sight by the roadside. Soon small lakes appear close to the road on the left and right; and there is a charnel ground marked by prayer-flags. At **Yematen**, a turn-off on the right leads southeast to Machu township (Ch Huanghe) and **Horkor Gon Shedrub Dargyeling** (69 km), an important branch of Dzogchen, which was founded in 1927 by the Fifth Dzogchen Rinpoche Tubten Chokyi Dorje. Then, skirting a larger lake on the left, the highway enters the valley of the Yellow River. It soon crosses the **first bridge over the Yellow River** (Ch Huanghe Daqiao) and after a further 5 km arrives at **Mato** town (70 km from Lungen).

Mato Town → *Altitude: 4,300 m. For listings, see pages 653-655.*

Mato is a high altitude town, where snow is not uncommon in summertime! Entering the town from the southwest, a bypass leads directly ahead and beyond, to continue in the direction of Ziling. A turn-off on the left leads into the centre of town. There are two main streets forming a T-junction. Heading north towards the junction, you will pass on the left the Bus Station, the Grain Department, a general store and the Chengdu Restaurant, with the Muslim Restaurant and the bank on the right. At the head of this road, commanding the T-junction, is the Mato Theatre/Cinema. Turn left for the Xinhua Bookstore, the Tax Bureau, the Government Guesthouse, the County Government Buildings, the PLA camp, the Public Security Bureau, the Prison and the dirt road to Lake Ngoring Tso; or turn right for China Post & Telecom, the Education Bureau, the Agricultural Bank, the Mato Hospital, the Nationalities School and yet another PLA camp. The open air market has an interesting selection of nomadic produce and Golok-style clothing. The town itself is small, but its bus station and market are important for the locals.

Ngoring and Kyaring Lakes

Mato county has several marshy plains dotted with tiny lakes and meandering rivers which provide good grasslands for the many nomads around the source of the Yellow River. There are, however, two particularly large lakes, known as **Kyaring Tso** and **Ngoring Tso**, through which the Yellow River itself flows. To reach these lakes, take the jeep dirt road from Mato which follows the Yellow River upstream, for 57 km to Ngoring Tso, the closer of the two lakes (area 618 sq km, average depth 17 m). There is a bird sanctuary at the southwest corner of Kyaring Lake (area 526 sq km, average depth 9 m), where swans, gulls, wild geese and ducks can be seen nesting. Both lakes provide a rich fishing ground for Chinese immigrants. Tibetans, even in these remote parts, are reluctant to eat fish.

On a hilltop (4,610 m) between the lakes there is a very small reconstructed monastery, **Tsowar Kartse Doka**, said to mark the unknown site of **Kartse Palace**, which, according to old Chinese sources, is where Songsten Gampo met and married Princess Wencheng. It contains the mortal remains of Mani Lama, who passed away at Jyekundo in the late 1950s, and is maintained by Nyingmapa and Gelukpa monks, despite having been built originally by a Bon lama. A hilltop monument to the west has a monument, said to mark the source of the Yellow River, but this is a symbolic approximation.

Mato County

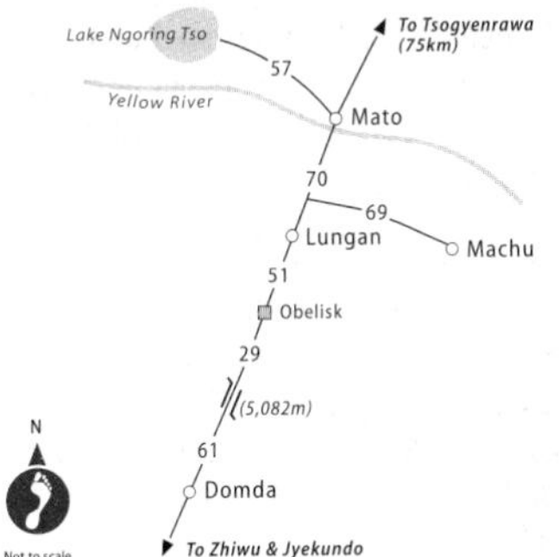

To the source of the Yellow River

The region west of the lakes is in places very marshy and an excellent breeding ground for many of the plateau's bird species, including the rare black-necked crane. It leads through the 'plain of stars' (Ch Xingsuhai) towards **Mount Yakra Tatse** (5,442 m), near the hamlet of **Dzomo Manang**, which is just inside Chumarleb county (see above, page 527). This area, known as **Machuka**, contains the actual source of the Yellow River, where Mato township is located. The driving distance from Mato county town to Mato township is 210 km, and it is possible to drive a further 90 km towards the source, before trekking for two further days.

Rafting on the Yellow River

It is possible to raft on the Yellow River from Kyaring Lake to Darlag (360 km) over a five-day period; and also further downstream from Darlag through the river bends to Trika (470 km) in 13 days.

Tsogyenrawa → *Colour map 5, grid B3*

Highway 214 from Mato to Ziling cuts northeast through a fairly flat plain, following a tributary of the Yellow River upstream for 75 km to cross **Dungye La** pass and reach the gorge of **Tsogyenrawa** (Ch Huashixia, 4,039 m). On the approach to Tsogyenrawa (see above, page 628), a large lake named **Tongi Tsonak** comes into view to the left of the road.

Four roads converge at Tsogyenrawa: a side road leading northwest to Lake Tongi Tsonak and the **Panchen Zhingde** area (on which see above, page 554); another jeep track leading east for 45 km to **Tawo Zholma** village on the Amnye Machen circuit; the main paved highway leading northeast to **Ziling** or southwest to **Mato**, and a wide gravel road, which leads southeast into **Machen** and **Darlag** counties. Tsogyenrawa marks the extremity of the Golok penetration. Further north from here, the nomads belong to the Banak group rather than the Golok.

Machen County རྨ་ཆེན

→ *Population: 35,439. Area: 16,625 sq km. Colour map 4, grid B4.* 玛沁县

The **Amnye Machen** range, which forms the large bend of the Yellow River, is the ancestral homeland of the **Golok**; and the sacred abode of the protector deity, **Machen Pomra**, revered by Bonpo and Buddhists alike. As recently as 1949 there had been reports suggesting that the highest peak of this isolated range exceeded the height of Mount Everest; and it was only during the 1950s and 1960s that the height was fixed at 6,282 m. The county of Machen includes the entire pilgrims' circuit around the range. The county capital is located at **Tawo** (Machen), 209 km from **Tsogyenrawa** (Ch Huashixia) and 68 km from **Rabgya Monastery** on the banks of the Yellow River (see below, page 636).

Amnye Machen Circuit ཨ་མྱེ་རྨ་ཆེན

The traditional starting point for the Bon and Buddhist pilgrims, who all circumambulate the range in a clockwise direction, is the **Chorten Karpo** near **Chuwarna** (Ch Xueshan) village; although most pilgrims at present set out from **Tawo Zholma** village, 45 km due east of Tsogyenrawa. On the rough road approaching this village, the Amnye Machen range comes into sight in the distance. There are wonderful sunsets to be seen here.

Tawo Zholma (Ch Xiao Dawu) is a pastoral commune with hardly more than 100 inhabitants of whom nearly half are children attending the local primary school. Most of the pastoralists are of Banak origin, but a transient workforce from Labrang area, and even far-off Shanxi in mainland China, contributes to the ethnic mix. Pack animals for the circuit of the mountain (approximately 180 km) can be arranged in this village. Nowadays it is even possible to drive around the range (when key bridges are not washed out). For this reason, trekkers will often prefer to drive closer into the range to Halong and other points from where the inner valleys can be peacefully explored on foot.

Guri Gonpa Fording the **Zhochen-chu** (Ch Qushian) below the village, the trail leads 5 km to **Guri Gonpa**, a branch of Dzogchen and Dodrub Chode of the Nyingma school, which until recently was the seat of the late Thubten Tsering, a charismatic lama descended from Lhalung Peldor, who was also a contemporary of Dodrupchen Rinpoche and a qualified Dzogchen master in his own right. It was he who founded the original tented camp at the beginning of the 20th century, and who supervised the temple's construction from 1985 onwards. The local community in the monastery and surrounding village numbers approximately 100. There are a few monks, but the majority of practitioners here are *mantrins*.

The complex comprises three main buildings, in addition to the lama's residence. Among these, the **main temple** contains excellent new images of Padmasambhava, Shantaraksita and King Trisong Detsen, as well as White Tara, Green Tara, Vairocana, Vajrasattva, Four-armed Avalokiteshvara, Eleven-faced Avalokiteshvara, Machen Pomra and Tangtong Gyelpo. The vestibule has a large Mani Wheel chapel in addition to the murals depicting the four guardian kings.

To the left of the temple is a **Reliquary Chapel** containing the consecrated remains of Lama Gyatso (d 1987) and Lama Thubten Tsering. It also has images of Padmasambhava and of the three deities symbolizing longevity: Amitayus, White Tara and Vijaya. The **Gonkhang**, situated behind the lama's residence, contains a revered central image of Ling Gesar, the hero of Tibetan epic poetry who has many associations with Amnye Machen. Its murals depict (left) Tangtong Gyelpo, and (right) Machen Pomra, complete with retinue. In the **lama's residence** there are images of Padmasambhava, Jigme Lingpa and Tangtong Gyelpo. Texts are kept here which describe both the Buddhist and Bon pilgrimage guides to Amnye Machen.

Approaching the Snow Peaks The trail climbs steadily from the plain of **Drentatang** below the monastery, following the **Niwagu** River upstream. A large *latse* bedecked with mantra-engraved stones and colourful prayer flags is passed before crossing **Drado Wangchuk La** pass (4,005 m). A trail of steeper gradient then ascends the high **Drakdo Latse Chogon** pass (4,328 m), close to the glaciers. The walk from the monastery to this pass takes eight hours. A ridge above the pass leads towards the glaciers and the icy **Tso Karpo** ('white lake'), otherwise known as **Drodu Nyaka** (4,600 m). Slightly below the pass, on the south side, there is a field of protuberant glaciers, known as **Rigar Tongka** or **Rigar Tongjung**. This is revered as a sacred site symbolic of the 1,000 Buddhas of the Aeon, or of the Sixteen Elders. Camps of Golok nomads are to be found in this vicinity in summertime.

The view of the main peaks of the range is genuinely impressive from this vantage point. The highest of the 14 peaks forming the range are **Dradul Lungshok** (6,154 m), the northernmost peak, which lies close to the trail across the Rigar Tongjung glacier field. The next peak is the dome-shaped **Mount Amnye Machen** itself (6,282 m), followed by the pyramid-shaped **Mount Chenrezig** (6,127 m), down the valley towards Chuwarna.

Machen County

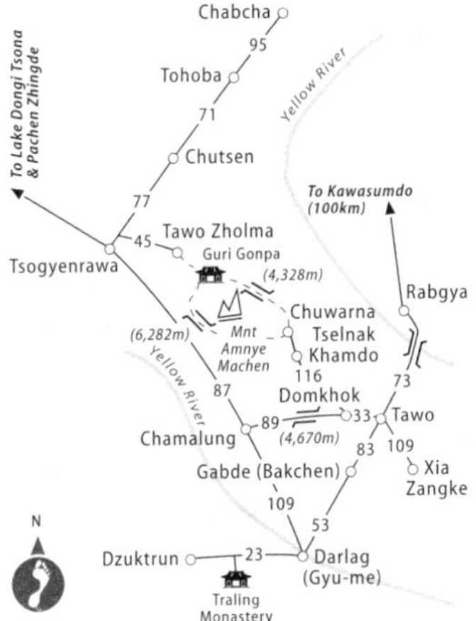

Pilgrimage

Throughout the Buddhist world, pilgrimage is an important means of affirming the faith of devotees and above all of accumulating merit (*punya*) and virtuous actions (*kushala*), without which progress to enlightenment or buddhahood would not be possible. In Tibet, pilgrimage (*ne-khor*) has assumed a significant social role, and there is a distinct genre of literature, the pilgrimage guidebook (*ne-yig*), which describes both the historical background and development of any given site, as well as the manner in which its rocks and contours are to be viewed from the perspective of 'pure vision'. The peaks, stones, and rivulets of the most sacred sites are properly viewed as deities or consecrated objects in their own right.

While travelling through remote areas of Tibet, you will occasionally come upon remarkable individuals who are in the course of prostrating themselves hundreds or even thousands of kilometres, all the way from their local villages to Lhasa, the most magnetic of Tibet's pilgrimage places. Often elected by village communities to undertake the pilgrimage, their journey may take several years to complete. Such pilgrims frequently wear leather aprons, knee and hand pads to protect their bodies from the rough road surfaces, and they may travel in a group, accompanied by an assistant who will arrange food and shelter on their behalf. On reaching the goal of their pilgrimage, the sacred image of Jowo Rinpoche in Lhasa, they will make offerings, and then return home by motor vehicle.

The act of prostration (*phyag-tshal*) is generally combined with the recitation of the refuge prayer (*kyab-dro*), through which the Buddhist meditator or practitioner reduces pride, generates humility, and becomes confident in the goals and methods of Buddhism. Outside the Jokhang temple in Lhasa, the flagstones have been worn smooth by centuries of prostrations. Inside, pilgrims will add lumps of butter to the lamps as they proceed from one shrine to the next in a clockwise sequence, occasionally also making monetary offerings, or attaching some metallic or precious object to the wire mesh of a shrine as an act of simple devotion.

This movement of pilgrims around the countryside and its great Buddhist shrines (ne-khor) is nowadays contrasted with the movement of tourists around the very same buildings and locations (ta-khor). If you wish to be taken as a pilgrim rather than a tourist, invariably generating more respect or courtesy, it will be best to assert your status as a 'pilgrim' (ne-khor-wa) rather than a 'tourist' (ta-khor-wa)!

Descending from the pass through the **Zhideka** valley, after three hours the side valley of the **Yekhok-chu** joins the circuit from the north. The trail then descends through flower-carpeted grassland to the junction of the **Halong-chu** valley, where a trekking route leads northwest towards the **Amnye Machen Base Camp** (4,600 m). It will only be possible to drive around the mountain if the bridge at Halong is intact. Crossing the Halong-chu can even be difficult on horseback during the summer when the water level is high. Gazelles can frequently be seen in these parts, and there is a sky-burial terrace. Deep within the Halong-chu valley near the rocks of **Phawang Serka** and **Phawang Hekar**, there is the **Terdak Phawang Drubzhi**, containing the *termas* of Ling Gesar, the warrior king of Tibetan epic poetry, who is said to have hidden his sword here, pledging one day to retrieve it. Even closer to the mountain are the **Ser Tso** ('golden lake') and **Ngon Tso** ('blue lake').

Eastern Part of the Circuit From the Halong-chu junction to the **Chorten Karpo** at **Chuwarna** (Ch Xueshan) village it is an easy six-hour trek. Here, the **Yonkhok-chu** (Ch Qiemuqu) flows from the southwest to join the Yekhok-chu, thereby forming the **Tshab-chu**, which flows east into the Yellow River. At **Chuwarna** (Ch Xueshan) village there are small shops and a motorable track. The recently rebuilt **Zangdokpelri Temple** at Chuwarna contains fine Repkong murals depicting the Eight Manifestations of Padmasambhava, Sukhavati and Shakyamuni Buddha, and on the ground floor there is a lifelike image of the late Lama Thubten Tsering of Guri Gonpa. A new Chinese-style temple has also been built here, adjacent to a large white stupa (Chorten Karpo), which is itself surrounded by a wall of Mani Wheels. Beyond the stupa, there is a long stone dyke, known as **Gonying Mani Lhartse**, inscribed with the mantra of the meditational deity Vajrakila. Traditionally, this is the starting point of the circuit for many pilgrims.

Follow the motor road for four hours from Chorten Karpo, passing several nomads' houses set among sparse juniper woods in the hills around. At **Tselnak Khamdo**, the road leaves the circuit, and cuts southeast for 149 km to **Tawo** (Machen), the capital of the Golok region. Prayer flags and stone cairns bedeck the trees and the trail along this section of road.

Southern Part of the Circuit Continuing on to the southwest sector of the pilgrims' circuit, the trail passes the entrance to the **Halong Langri-chu** valley, which leads north towards the Base Camp, and then gradually ascends the **Yonkhok-chu** valley, to eventually reach the **Tamchok Gongkha la** pass after about seven hours. The broad saddle of the pass stretches for a further 10 km (three hours). In summer this area is a carpet of wild flowers set against the imposing snow peaks and many nomads establish camps here. After the saddle there is a curious rock formation in the middle of the valley called **Mowatowa**, which houses several meditation caves, including that of the great Nyingmapa meditation master Zhabkar Tsokdruk Rangdrol (1781-1851). The variegated cliffs of **Goku Chenmo** are said to mark the entrance to the 'palace' of the protector **Machen Pomra**.

Some four hours later, the trail reaches the **Dolma Gur-chu** spring, which marks the final part of the circuit. Rather than follow the gorge of the Zhochen-chu, the path heads over a spur, where Ling Gesar once tethered his horse, and then descends back down to **Guri Gonpa**, about five hours away.

Practicalities The best months to make this circuit are May/June and September/October, avoiding the summer rains and the biting cold of winter. A tent and sleeping bag are essential as well as a good supply of food, for apart from being offered tea, tsampa and yoghurt by the occasional nomad, there is no chance of restocking. It is advisable to allow about nine days for the full circuit.

Chuwarna to Tawo

If you leave the Amnye Machen circuit at **Tselnak Khamdo**, below Chuwarna (see above, page 635), the road undulates through grass-covered hills, crossing three passes (the second over 4,000 m), before reaching **Domkhok** after 116 km. Here the trail merges with a paved road from Tsogyenrawa and Chamalung to **Tawo**. The county capital, Tawo, is only 33 km east of Domkhok in the Tshab-chu valley, and two further passes are crossed en route.

Tawo (Machen) Town → *For listings, see pages 653-655.*

The Golok capital at **Tawo** once conjured the archetypal image of the Wild West! Prior to the 1960s when a concerted policy was adopted to settle the nomadic Golok and Banak populations of Amdo, Tawo was just a small hamlet. Now high-rise buildings of glass and concrete are beginning to transform the skyline. Many Tibetans live and work in he town, which also has itinerant traders and work-unit appointees who come during the seasonable months, for in winter temperatures of -20° are common. Most of the Tibetan nomad families currently have a small disposable income and Tawo, situated on a tributary of the Tshab-chu, is a natural gathering place.

Orientation Entering the town from the northwest on Danwei Lu (Unity Rd), you will pass on the left (east) a frozen meat factory, the Machen Power Station, the Economic Bureau and the Agricultural Bank, with the Mentsikhang, the Cadre School, a construction company, the Machen Tax Bureau, the Golok Agricultural Bank, the Cultural Theatre, Machen County Government and an army unit opposite. Reaching a crossroads where there are a number of Tibetan-run shops with interesting nomadic artefacts for sale, continue straight ahead, passing on the left (east) the Construction Hotel, the Golok Nationalities School, the CCP Standing Committee, a cinema and China Post. Opposite on the right (west) are the Prefectural Hospital, the Gymnasium, Xinhua Bookstore and the Agricultural Bank.

Reaching a second crossroads, turn right for the open market, left for the Geoseismic Bureau, the Middle School and the Muslim Restaurant, or straight ahead for China Telecom, China Mobile, the Nomad Hotel, the Bus Station, the Construction Bank and the Prefectural Government Buildings. After a third major crossroads, you will pass on the left a pharmacy, the Sihayan Restaurant, the Golok PLA Camp and the People's Bank. Opposite on the right are the Machen Trade Guesthouse, the Grain Department, the Armed Police Unit, the Scientific Research Hotel, the Public Security Bureau, the National Security Bureau, the Snow Mountain Hotel and the Traffic Police. From here, you can head out of town to a junction where the road forks, northeast to Kawasumdo and Trika or south for Gabde and Darlag.

Roads from Tawo

Various roads diverge at Tawo: west for 122 km to **Chamalung** (Ch Temahe) on the Tsogyenrawa-Darlag road; northwest for 155 km to **Chuwarna** (Ch Xueshan) on the Amnye Machen pilgrimage circuit; northeast for 73 km to **Rabgya Monastery** on the banks of the Yellow River; southwest for 83 km to **Gabde**; and southeast for 109 km to **Tsangkor Zholma** (Ch Xia Zangke) on the Yellow River. Heading southeast on the last of these roads, there is a small monastery affiliated to Dzogchen called **Tokden Gon Dongak Shedrubling**, 210 km from town.

Rabgya Monastery → *Altitude: 3,090 m*

Taking the paved northeast road, you cross **Heto La** (4,234 m) and a second lower pass (4,204 m) to enter a lightly forested red-rock canyon. This leads down to the long bridge spanning the Yellow River at **Khyungon**. This is a small township, with a number of grocery shops, restaurants and DDD phone connections. Crossing the bridge, the road turns east for 2 km to reach Rabgya. **Rabgya** (locally pronounced Rabja) is a small enclave on the north bank of the Yellow River (3,050 m) belonging to Machen rather than Kawasumdo county. There are a few roadside stalls and an independent boys' school, which has 70 pupils and 11 teachers.

Rabgya Monastery (formally known as **Tashi Kundeling**), is an important branch of Sera monastery, founded on the advice of the Seventh Dalai Lama in 1769 by a Mongolian from Kokonor named Arik Geshe (1726-1803). Even today there are several monks from the Sogwo Mongolian prefecture just to the east. The second preceptor of the monastery, Shingza Pandita Lobzang Dargye (1753-1824), is regarded as an incarnation of Tsongkhapa's mother, Shingza Acho, and his subsequent incarnations have presided over the monastery.

The complex has been substantially rebuilt during the last 13 years, and reconstruction continues even now. However, a few old artefacts did survive, including a handful of pillar carpets in the main prayer hall and a set of tangkas. The architecture of the modern temples is functional but unimaginative, except for the artwork, which is in the wonderful Repkong style. Approaching the main entrance of the **Assembly Hall** (Tsenkhangling), marked by two ornate stone lions, there is a large stupa and the **Menpa Dratsang** to the left, with an unrestored residential building to its rear, and to the right the **Dukhor Lhakhang**. Higher up the hillside is the newly built **Dungten Lhakhang**, containing the reliquary of the late Je Serkhangpa of Rabgya. The college of Rabgya lies 1 km east, adjacent to the motor road.

The **Assembly Hall** which has a trilingual inscription above the door, contains 64 carpeted pillars and an original flagstone floor. The **inner sanctum** contains (left to right): images of Amitabha, Arik Geshe, the Buddhas of the Three Times, Tara and Aksobhya, along with the volumes of the *Kangyur*. The **main hall** has truly wonderful murals executed in silver, which depict Shakyamuni surrounded by the 1,000 Buddhas of the Aeon, as well as Padmasambhava flanked by the masters of the Kadampa and Kagyupa lineages, and Tsongkhapa surrounded by his students. The hall still holds an air of antiquity. Outside in the courtyard, the newly executed murals are the work of master artists from Jentsa and Repkong.

The **Menpa Dratsang** contains a throne bearing the portrait of Alak Yongdzin of Tarshul in Kawasumdo (see above, page 621), and images of the Eight Medicine Buddhas and the Lords of the Three Enlightened Families. The murals here depict (left to right): Mahakala, Sitatapatra, Havagriva, Eight Medicine Buddhas, Amitabha, Aksobhya, Mahakarunika, Uchusmakrodha and Simhavaktra.

The broad cliff behind Rabgya is known as **Mount Khyung-ngon** (Blue Garuda) and the walk to the hilltop shrine (3,570 m) passes several smaller shrines and caves, giving a good view of the Yellow River.

Chamalang

To reach the main Jyekundo-Ziling highway from **Machen**, take the west road out of town and on reaching **Domkhok** (Ch Dongqingguo) after 33 km, do not turn northwest for Chuwarna and Amnye Machen. Instead, turn southwest across the **Dramani La** pass (4,760 m) for **Chamalung** (Ch Temahe), reaching that township after 89 km. **Trangmar Chogar**, a small Nyingma monastery, is located here to the west of the township.

Then head northwest over a shallow pass, which can be muddy in summer and snow-bound in winter, to arrive at **Tsogyenrawa** (87 km). This road runs parallel to the southern and western sectors of the Amnye Machen circuit. Alternatively, from Chamalung, you can head southeast towards **Darlag**, passing through **Dangzhung** (Ch Dangxiang), where a small monastery, **Dangzhung Makar Chogar**, holds simultaneous allegiance to Katok and Rabgya!

Gabde County དགའ་བདེ

→ *Population: 23,314. Area: 6,554 sq km. Colour map 5, grid C4.* 甘德县

Gabde county lies in Central Golok to the south of the Amnye Machen range and within the bend of the Yellow River. It is an important breeding area for the black-necked crane. The county capital is located at **Bakchen** (Ch Gabde) on the Shi-ke-chu, a southeast flowing tributary of the Yellow River. There are seven monasteries within the county, including some representing the rare Jonangpa school.

Ins and outs

Getting there Bakchen is 83 km southwest of the prefectural capital **Tawo** (Machen), and 53 km from **Darlag**, but it can also be approached from Tsogyenrawa on the Jyekundo-Ziling highway. A turn-off at Tsogyenrawa leads southeast through Chamalung (87 km), and **Jang-gegye** (91 km) in the direction of Darlag. Turn northeast at Jang-gegye to reach Bakchen after 35 km.

Bakchen

Bakchen (locally pronounced Wakchen), is one of the smaller county towns in the Golok Prefecture. Its government buildings, guesthouses (¥24 per bed), hospital and cinema are all located on the west bank of the Shi-ke-chu river, but the town and its approach roads are now undergoing rapid reconstruction. Most restaurants are Muslim, but Sichuan cuisine can be found at the Jinhai Restaurant.

Eastern Gabde

Towards the end of the 19th century, the Jonangpa lamas of Dzamtang (see below, page 650) began to establish branches within the Gabde region of **Golok**. Three monasteries were constructed here to represent that unique lineage of Tibetan Buddhism. Among them, **Lungkya Gonpa** is located 23 km from town on a bumpy road, on the south bank of the Shike-chu. Affiliated to Dzamtang Tsangpa Gon, the monastery is developing under the guidance of the charismatic bearded figure Tulku Pema Namgyal. Its **assembly hall**, where electricity is now installed, has images of Dolpopa, Shakyamuni and Taranatha in its inner sanctum, and interesting Repkong-style murals that reflect this unusual tradition. The **Jamkhang**, above and to the right, is an active retreat hermitage. Currently there are some 200-300 monks at Lungkya, but the monastery is not easy to reach in the summer months when vehicles have to drive through the deep river on the final approach.

Further downstream, some 45 km from the town, is **Washul Lama Chogar**, the largest Nyingmapa community of Gabde, which was founded in the 19th century as a branch of Dzogchen. Its large assembly hall, known as Dechen Podrang, contains 4-5-m images of Shakyamuni and Padmasambhava, murals depicting the Drupa Kabgye meditational deities, and the protectors of the Nyingmapa tradition. Other buildings of interest here include the Dukar Lhakhang and the Dzogchen Lhakhang.

Another Jonangpa monastery. **Tashi Choling**, 75 km east of town is affiliated to Dzamtang Chode, while **Trayaklung Gon**, which is the largest monastery within the county is a branch of Lungkya Gonpa, founded by a Jonangpa monk from Sertal. The last of these is located near Jiangqian, in a side valley southeast of Qingzhen on the Gabde-Machen road, about 15 km before the Yellow River. The head lama here is Tashi Gyatso, currently living in New York.

Southern Gabde

A little used side road leads southeast from Bachen to the north bank of the Yellow River at **Sharo Gonpa** (Ch Xiagongma). Here, the Gelukpa monastery of **Sharo** is noted for its strict discipline and excellent teachings. The monastery, which was founded in 1922 as a branch of Rabgya, is situated on the ridge north of the Yellow River, 46 km down-valley from the county town.

Western Gabde

Heading southwest from Bakchen in the direction of Darlag county, you will pass the large Nyingmapa monastery of **Dongyu Dokha Gon** on the right side of the road after 12 km. There is a large assembly hall, rebuilt among the residential hermitages, and an impressive mani wall.

Darlag County དར་ལག → *Population: 24,030. Area: 14,351 sq km.* 达日县

Darlag county straddles the Yellow River due south of the Amnye Machen range in Golok, and extends further south as far as the Mardzagang watersheds, which separate the Yellow River basin from the Ser-chu, Do-chu and Mar-chu tributaries of the Gyarong. The county capital is located at **Gyu-me** on the banks of the Yellow River. The distance from Gyu-me to Gabde is 53 km, to Tawo in Machen 118 km; to Tsogyenrawa 196 km, to Padma 168 km, and to Jigdril 261 km. There are currently 10 monasteries within the county, eight of which are Nyingmapa.

Southwest of Dongyu Dokha Gon in Gabde, the road reaches the north bank of the meandering Yellow River, passing through beautiful open countryside, on the approach to Gyu-me. The road from **Chamalung** joins up here, and there is a long-term plan to construct a railway through this broad valley. Crossing the long bridge over the Yellow River, you will arrive at the county capital.

Gyu-me Town → *Altitude: 3,993 m*

Gyu-me (locally pronounced Ju-me) has two long and wide intersecting streets. Entering the town, you will pass the turn-off for Padma county on the left, and then reach the bus station and its noisy guesthouse. On reaching the market, turn south for the government buildings, schools, Government Guesthouse, Telecom Hotel, department store, and the road to Traling Gonpa. A side road extends between the guesthouse and the hotel towards the Darlag County Hospital. ›› *For listings, see pages 653-655.*

Traling Monastery The Nyingmapa monastery of **Traling Gon Tashi Chodenling**, which is the largest and best known in the county, is situated 11 km west of town in the direction of **Dzuktrun** (Ch Jianshe), and a further 4 km along a side road. For much of the journey the road follows the Yellow River upstream through rich pasture lands. This monastery, which has over 300 monks, was founded in 1895, and is affiliated to Katok in Kham. It has been visited by Moktse Tulku of Katok, who in recent years has been responsible for the reconstruction of the mother monastery (see above, page 494). Within the **main temple** there are large cast images of Shakyamuni and Padmasambhava, and old tangkas representing the Eight Manifestations of Padmasambhava, as well as the **reliquary stupa** containing the remains of the previous Lingtrul Rinpoche. The present incumbent, also called Ya Tulku, currently lives in Vancouver. In his absence, monastic affairs including reconstruction are in the hands of Tulku Taknyi and Khenpo Peljor.

Above the monastery is a renowned **charnel ground** (*durtro*), to which corpses will be brought for dismemberment and sky burial from all parts of Golok. Here there is a raised platform above the circular dismemberment stones, and on its rear wall there are individually framed paintings of the Hundred Peaceful and Wrathful Deities, who appear to the deceased following death and before rebirth.

Gesar Lhakhang

Returning to the intersection 4 km below Traling, if you turn west in the direction of Dzuktrun, after 4 further km, you will reach a turn-off on the left leading to the already prominent **Gesar Lhakhang** – a temple dedicated to the memory of the warrior hero Ling Gesar and his retainers, who had many associations with the Darlag and Sertal areas.

Trails from Dzuktrun to Dzachuka

Dzuktrun lies 23 km west of Gyu-me, and after crossing a bridge, two roads diverge here: southwest to **Sangruma** (50 km) on the Khanglong-chu and **Taktok** on the Yellow River (40 km); and southeast for 123 km to **Ponkor Gongma** (Ch Xiahongke) on the Darlag-chu. **Sangruma Gonpa** is affiliated to Traling Gon, while **Taktok Gonpa** was founded in 1890. The Bayankala watersheds are crossed on both these roads. From Sangruma you can trek southwest to **Arikdza Gonpa** and the Yalong River (see above, page 512).

Dzuktrun to Ponkor Gongma

This road is the main northern approach to Sertal, which crosses the Qinghai-Sichuan border, 17 km beyond Ponkor Gongma. The initial stretch from the bridge at Dzuktrun has an excellent dirt surface and the driving is fast for 80 km as far as **Mapa**, where there is a small Mani Lhakhang and a roadside restaurant. However, road conditions quickly deteriorate over the next stretch of 43 km – a deeply rutted trail leading across the **Bayankala watershed** (4,800 m) before descending through a pristine forested valley with several nomadic encampments to the small township of **Ponkor Gongma** (4,100 m). There is a small family-run guesthouse and restaurant by the roadside here, and, further downstream to the right of the road, a local monastery, founded in 1920, which is affiliated to Katok.

Ponkor Gongma to Ponkor Ogma

Continuing down the valley from Ponkor Gongma, you will reach **Wara Drubde Gon**, a branch of Katok, where the Gesar Lhakhang contains splendid statues of the warrior king and his 30 retainers, along with a likeness of the late Kharchu Tulku. Further downstream, is the small settlement of **Ponkor Ogma**, 21 km from Ponkor Gongma, where a bridge spans the provincial border between Qinghai and Sichuan. The distance from here to Gogentang, capital of Sertal, is 159 km, and for a description of this road, see page 645.

South of Gyu-me

Taking the main road southeast from **Gyu-me**, you will pass through the valley of the **Gyu-chu**, a tributary of the Yellow River, reaching **Ozer** (Ch Wesai) after 21 km, and **Dernang Gonpa** after a further 39 km. **Dungchung Gonpa** at Ozer is a small Nyingmapa monastery, founded in 1940 as a tented camp, while **Dernang** is a branch of Katok, founded in 1910. Continuing south from Dernang, you will cross the watershed (4,465 m) between the Gyu-chu and the Mar-chu tributary of the Gyarong. At **Mangdrang**, 46 km further southeast, where the small **Budon Gonpa** is a branch of Katok, the road forks, leading southeast into Padma county and northeast into Jigdril county.

Jigdril County གཅིག་སྒྲིལ

→ *Population: 17,986. Area: 7,963 sq km. Colour map 5, grid C4.* 久治县

Jigdril county, at the southeast extremity of Golok, occupies the watershed between the Yellow River basin and the Nga-chu tributary of the Gyarong. The county capital is located at **Drukchen Sumdo**, 155 km from Mangdrang, and 75 km from Ngawa.

Tarthang Monastery

དར་ཐང་དགོན་པ

From **Mangdrang**, where the road branches, take the left fork which heads east over an occasionally snowy pass. In the distance there are views of the Nyenpo Yurtse mountain range. Reaching **Warje** village after 22 km, the road divides again, east for Sogruma and south for Tarthang. Taking the latter, you

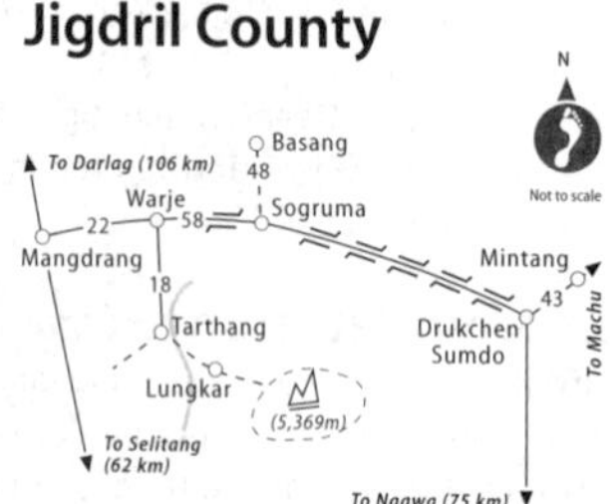

will enter a side valley which follows the **Mar-chu** downstream. After travelling along this rough road for 18 km (sometimes it is impassable in the rainy season), you will arrive at **Tarthang Monastery** (Ch Baiyu), which is the largest in the county.

History This monastery, properly known as **Tarthang Dongak Shedrub Dargyeling**, was founded in 1857 or 1882 by Gyatrul Rinpoche, Pema Dongak Tendzin (1830-1891), the seventh throne-holder of the great Nyingmapa monastery of Pelyul in Kham. It quickly became the largest and most influential branch of Pelyul in the entire Golok-Sertal area, with 1,210 monks and 30 incarnate lamas, headed by the Pelyul Choktrul incarnation, who presently lives in Nepal. Among the other important figures connected with this monastery in recent times, special mention should be made of Lama Kunga or Tarthang Tulku, who has established a Nyingma institute and publishing centre (Dharma Publishing) in California. In addition, the charismatic tulku Garwang Nyima is at present responsible for the reconstruction and revitalization of the monastery, which houses over 1,000 monks.

The complex The **Great Assembly Hall (Tsokchen)** has 140 pillars, and contains large cast images of Jowo Shakyamuni, Padmasambhava and Amitabha. There are important murals in the Repkong style, the work of the master artist Kalzang, which focus on the meditational deities of the Nyingma lineage.

Alongside the assembly hall, there are two other buildings, the **Serdung Lhakhang**, containing the reliquary stupas of the previous Pelyul Choktrul and of two former monastic preceptors of Tarthang and the **Teaching Hall (Dukhang)**, with Repkong-style murals which depict the *terma* visions of the Nyingma school, such as the Peaceful and Wrathful Deities according to Karma Lingpa's *Tibetan Book of the Dead*. In front of this complex of buildings there is a **wall of prayer wheels**, over 2 km in length; and beyond that, further down the valley, there is a new **Buddhist Studies College (Shedra)**, sponsored by Tarthang Tulku in the United States.

After the college and close to the road, there is the magnificent **Zangdok Pelri Lhakhang**. On its **ground floor** there are cast images of the Eight Manifestations of Padmasambhava (made by Chamdo artisans) and clay images of the Twenty-five Disciples of Padmasambhava (made by the Repkong artist Kalzang). The surrounding corridors depict scenes from the Biography of Padmasambhava (*Pema Katang*). On the **second floor**, there are images of the Lords of the Three Enlightened Families (ie Manjughosa, Avalokiteshvara and Vajrapani), along with Tara and Acala. Amitabha is the central image on the **third floor**.

Behind the Zangdok Pelri Lhakhang, there is another temple known as the **Phurba Lhakhang**, dedicated to the meditational deity Vajrakila. Here, the central image depicting Vajrakumara is made of wood and its facial features of clay. To the right of the last two temples and close to the road, there is the residence of Tarthang Tulku (now in the United States) and his sisters.

The township lies beyond the monastery lower down the Mar-chu valley. It contains a small guesthouse run by a Tibetan medical practitioner and his family (¥10 per bed).

From Tarthang, it is possible to trek further, following the Mar-chu downstream into Padma county.

Mount Nyenpo Yurtse

From Tarthang Monastery, the trail continues southeast to **Lungkar Gonpa**, a branch of Rabgya founded in 1785, where there are over 200 monks. It then leads to the western edge of **Mount Nyenpo Yurtse** (5,933 m), the principal holy mountain of southern Golok, which is revered as the birthplace of the Golok tribes. The range has 14 peaks over 5,000 m, and the 10-15 day outer pilgrimage circuit is much harder than that at Mount Amnye Machen. A shorter six-day inner circuit can also be undertaken, starting from the Base

 Camp, 80 km driving distance from Drukchen Sumdo. The steep snow-capped ridges of the mountain are surrounded by marshland and glacial lakes, such as **Tsochen** and **Tsochung** which feed streams flowing north into the Yellow River, or **Tso Nagma** and **Nojin Tso**, which feed streams flowing south into the headwaters of the Gyarong. The **Base Camp** is located at 4,000 m, and climbing expeditions are organized by the Qinghai Mountaineering Association. On the south side of the mountain there are three hot springs and a nature reserve for the macaque.

Drukchen Sumdo (Jigdril) Town → *Colour map 5, grid C5*

After **Warje**, where the hermitage of **Yakra Nagar** dates from the 1940s, another steep pass leads to Sogruma (58 km). Just 8 km before reaching this township, the Jonangpa monastery of **Chamda Gonpa** is visible on the left of the road. A trail leads northwest from here for 48 km to **Basang** (Ch Wasai), where there are branch monasteries of Zhechen, Katok and Pelyul. The main road turns southeast from Sogruma, crossing five more major passes, which offer increasingly spectacular views of Mount Nyenpo Yurtse's glaciers. After traversing the glacial rivers, which flow northwards from this sacred mountain, the road eventually reaches **Drukchen Sumdo**, the county capital of Southeast Golok.

Essentials The town has a population of only a few thousand, but there are comfortable guesthouse facilities (with wooden floors and electric heaters), and a fine Sichuan-style restaurant with a chef who once worked at the Jinjiang Hotel in Chengdu! There are no public buses connecting this town with other county towns in Qinghai, but there is a daily service crossing the provincial border to and from Ngawa. **NB** Permit restrictions may apply here since neighbouring Ngawa county is still regarded as a tightly-closed enclave in Sichuan.

Taklung Gonpa → *Colour map 5, grid C5*

Located just to the south of Drukchen Sumdo town, and on a side road, this Nyingma monastery is a branch of Pelyul, under the supervision of Dampuk Rinpoche who has dedicated his recent years to its reconstruction. There is an Assembly Hall, a Zangdok Pelri-style temple, a Potala-style temple, named after the residence of Avalokiteshvara on Mount Potalaka, a protector chapel (Gonkhang) and a large Tara stupa.

The road to Ngawa

A poorly serviced road heads south across the watershed to **Ngawa** (75 km) in the Nga-chu valley, while another with even less traffic heads northeast for 43 km to **Mintang** (Ch Mantang) from where it crosses the Yellow River twice en route to Machu in present day Gansu. Along the Ngawa road, apart from Taklung, there are two other small monasteries: **Khangsar** (Nyingma) and **Nyinyu** (Jonangpa and Gelukpa combined).

Padma County པད་མ → *Population: 22,503. Area: 6,437 sq km.* 班玛县

Padma county (locally pronounced Parma) is one of the most beautiful parts of Tibet. It lies south of the watershed range that divides the rolling grasslands of the Yellow River basin from the forested gorges of Gyarong. Specifically it occupies the upper reaches of the Mar-chu and Do-chu rivers. The county capital is located at **Selitang** on the Mar-chu, 168 km southeast of Darlag, 217 km southwest of Jigdril, and 202 km northwest of Ngawa. There are 23 monasteries scattered throughout the valleys of the county, 20 of which are Nyingmapa establishments, and the remainder Kagyupa and Jonangpa.

Do Gongma Gonpa → *Colour map 5, grid C3*

Crossing the watershed from **Mangdrang** (see above, page 640), after 26 km the road reaches **Do Gongma Gonpa** in the valley of the **Kyilho-chu**, a tributary of the Mar-chu. This important monastery is a branch of Katok, founded in 1840, with over 200 affiliated monks. Outside the temple by the river bank, there is a fine set of stupas symbolizing the deeds of Shakyamuni Buddha. Nearby, there is also another branch of Katok, called **Wemda Gonpa**, which was founded in 1830 and expanded in 1942.

Padma Bum

At Do Gongma Gonpa, there are four large stupas and a soaring nine-storey tower, marking the entrance to the **Padma Bum** region. A side trail leads southwest from here, into the upper reaches of the Do-chu valley. Trekking routes also give access to this region from Ozer and Dernang Gonpa on the north side of the watershed (see above, page 640). It is possible to drive along the side road from Do Gongma Gon for 17 km as far as **Makehe** township, where **Pangyu Gon**, yet another branch of Katok, is located. From here trails lead to the birthplace of Do Khyentse at **Wangchen Drok Gon** and the spectacularly located **Tsimda Gonchen**.

Upper Do-chu Region

At Makehe, a rough motorable road leads west across the watershed into the upper Do-chu valley, where trails diverge: northwest to Daka, southwest to Dodrub Chode (27 km), and west towards **Mapa** (Ch Maba) in the valley of the Darlag-chu. Apart from **Langwu Gon** in Mapa, which is a Jonangpa branch of Dzamtang Tsangpa Gon, the entire region is a stronghold of the Nyingmapa. The most important establishments here are **Nyagen Gonpa**, affiliated to Zhechen in Kham (70 km from the county town), which was founded in 1904, and **Dodrub Chode** (Ch Zhiqinsi), 107 km from the county town, which holds allegiance to Dzogchen and maintains the tradition of Rigdzin Jigme Lingpa.

Dodrub Chode Monastery

The upper reaches of the Do-chu valley are rich in gold and there is a major mine 8 km south of the village of **Dankar**, where **Kharnang Gonpa** (founded 1840), an active, reconstructed Nyingmapa monastery with some 150 monks, may be visited. The nomads of this region appear wild and unkempt with most men having long hair and heavy silver earrings. There is a trekking route and a rough jeep trail leading down the valley to Dodrub Chode.

History This monastery, properly known as **Tsangchen Ngodrub Pelbarling**, was founded by the Second Dodrub Chen Jigme Phuntsok Jungne in the mid-19th century when the monks of its mother monastery, **Yarlung Pemako** in Sertal, fled north to escape the marauding army of Nyarong Gonpo Namgyel (see above, page 404). An older tented monastery had been founded here in 1527 but destroyed by Mongolian forces during the civil war. At Dodrub Chode the tradition which is maintained is that of the 18th-century treasure-finder Jigme Lingpa, whose *Longchen Nyingtig* cycle is widely practised throughout Tibet. Jigme Lingpa's disciples the First Dodrubchen Jigme Trinle Ozer (1745-1821) and Jigme Gyelwei Nyugu returned to their native Kham after receiving these teachings from the master in person, and they founded the monasteries of **Dzagya** in

Padma County

 Dzachuka and **Drodon Lhundrub** at Sukchen Tago in the Do valley. Dzagya was where the great Paltrul Rinpoche (1808-1887) studied under Jigme Gyelwei Nyugu. Dodrubchen then went on to found **Tseringjong Monastery** at Yarlung Pemako (also called **Pemako Tsasum Khandroling**) in neighbouring Sertal. It was his successor, the Second Dodrubchen Jigme Puntsok Jungne, who moved the monastic community to its present location in Padma county, seeking to avoid the Nyarong disturbances, and building anew on the site of an ancient 13th-century Sakyapa monastery (once visited by Drogon Chogyel Phakpa).

Subsequently, the new monastery was developed and expanded by the Third Dodrubchen Tenpei Nyima (1865-1926), the son of the great treasure-finder Dudjom Lingpa (1835-1904). He was a renowned scholar who built the great temples of **Dodrub Chode**, and established a non-sectarian college as well as a meditation hermitage. The woodblocks for his published works were formerly housed here. In all, the monastery had 13 incarnate lamas and 250 monks until the 1950s. Recent reconstruction at Dodrubchen is largely due to the activity of Tulku Loyang. The present the Fourth Dodrubchen Rinpoche, Thubten Trinle Pelzangpo (b 1927), resides at the Chorten Monastery in Gangtok, Sikkim; and he has also established a Buddhist Temple in Massachusetts.

From Dodrub Chode, a seasonal jeep track heads south to **Nyenlung** in Sertal county, and thence to Gogentang (65 km from Nyenlung).

Selitang

Selitang, the county capital, lies 62 km below **Mangdrang**, in the upper Mar-chu valley. It is a small garden town, pleasantly situated amidst coniferous forest, which is being exploited for timber. Before entering the town from the northwest, a side road leads northeast to **Tarthang Monastery**, following the Mar-chu upstream. Main Street has the usual array of government buildings, restaurants and KTV outlets, and there are two newish hotels adjacent to the post office. ›› *For listings, see pages 653-655.*

Jangritang Gonpa

Jangritang Gonpa is a Nyingmapa establishment, founded by Khenpo Ngaga as a branch of Katok in 1937. The monastery is only 4 km southeast of town and its towering Zangdok Pelri-style temple can be clearly seen from the town. The three storeys of the temple, which are partly original, are dedicated respectively to Padmasambhava, Avalokiteshvara and Amitabha – the three buddha-bodies. The impressive hilltop building is encircled by a spacious ring of some 100 stupas and three high mani stone walls, which are a focal point for pilgrims.

Mar-chu Gorge

Heading south from Selitang, the Mar-chu plunges through virgin forest, one of the most spectacular locations in all Tibet. The road runs parallel to the river, passing the villages of **Yartang** (30 km), **Bengen** and **Tinta** (35 km), before crossing the current Qinghai-Sichuan border to enter Ngawa county.

Along this road, you will pass the Jonangpa monastery of **Ekyonggya Gonpa** after 10 km. This was originally a Nyingmapa site, founded by Lama Trinle Namgyel in 1367. Later, in 1716, it converted to the Jonangpa school under the authority of Lama Ngawang Tendzin Namgyel (1691-1738). The reconstructed assembly hall contains murals and statues representative of the Jonangpa tradition, along with the reliquary stupa of Tulku Sangye Dorje (d. 1984). An adjacent Serdungkhang contains the reliquary stupa of Lama Shel Drukpa and some original bronzes. Three remarkable 30-m stupas, originally dating from 1856, have also been renovated within the complex. Their *harmikas* have painted eyes, somewhat reminiscent of those at the great stupas of Boudha and Svayambhu in Nepal.

Some 20 km further south, around **Yartang** and **Bengen**, there are several branch monasteries of Pelyul and Katok, including **Butsa Gon** (founded 1887), **Tralo Gonpa** (founded 1849), and **Raya Gonpa** (founded 1650). An isolated Kagyupa monastery also survives here, 58 km south of Selitang at **Gyude Gonpa**, which was founded at the behest of the Eighth Karmapa Mikyo Dorje in 1520. The monastery is impressively set within a narrow agricultural belt between the forested canyon and the rushing waters of the Mar-chu, spanned by an iron chain suspension bridge. Finally, before crossing the county border into Ngawa, at **Tinta** there are branch monasteries of Pelyul: **Dhida Gon** and **Getse Gon**, both of which were founded in the early decades of this century.

The capital of **Ngawa**, is 108 km northeast of the border in present-day Sichuan, but foreigners should know that permit restrictions still apply. After crossing the border, the road continues following the Mar-chu downstream to its confluence with the Dzi-chu at **Khok-po** (see below, page 651), before following the latter upstream for 55 km to Ngawa.

Sertal County གསེར་ཐལ

→ Population: 36,000. Area: 7,454 sq km. Colour map 5, grid C4. 色达县

Sertal county occupies the valley of the Ser-chu, a major source river of the Gyarong, which drains the grasslands from the northwest and, as in neighbouring Dzamtang, its southern portions are quite densely forested. Since these hills are less steep than the gorges downstream, they have been heavily logged, and until the recently imposed ban on logging, many convoys of trucks could be seen transporting lumber to Chengdu. The Pelyul branch of the Nyingmapa school predominates in Sertal county and there are several small monasteries in the villages and on the grasslands further north. The county capital is located at **Gogentang**, within present-day Kandze prefecture, 159 km southeast of the Qinghai-Sichuan border. The distance from Gogentang to Dzamtang is 152 km, to Nyenlung 65 km, and to Drango 149 km.

Ins and outs

Getting there The easiest access is from the south by road from Drango (see page 536) or Barkham (see below, page 658). However, there are two northern motorable tracks leading into Sertal county from Golok. The first, which is a seasonal road, crosses from **Dodrub Chode** into **Nyenlung** township, and thence downstream to Gogentang. The second is the main motor road from **Ponkor Ogma** to Gogentang via **Nyichu**.

Ponkor Ogma to Nyichu

After crossing the Bayankala watershed north of **Ponkor Ogma**, and the Qinghai-Sichuan border (see above, page 640), the road leaves the river valley and veers steeply over a 4,000-m pass, before descending into the caterpillar infested Nyi-chu valley. Here it descends gradually through the settlement of **Nyito**, where Pogo Gonpa, a branch of Pelyul is located, and **Kekang** hamlet to reach **Nyichu**, about 88 km from the border.

Nyichu and Khenleb

At **Nyichu**, there are two Nyingma monasteries of note: **Zhichen Kharmar Sang-me Gon** is a branch of Katok, with over 1,000 monks. Beru Rinpoche, the head lama, currently resides in Nepal. He is the father of the present head of the Drukpa Kagyu school. The smaller monastery of **Taklung Gon** is located nearby. About 9 km further southeast is the small **Khenleb Gonpa**, a branch of Pelyul, in Khenleb township.

Dartsang and Ser

After Khenleb the road climbs steeply to the east, crossing another pass (4,050 m), before heading down to a junction. Turn left here for **Dartsang Gonpa**, the main seat of Dudjom Lingpa (1835-1904), which is now accessible by vehicle, or right, past a road workers' unit, before climbing yet again to reach **Ser**. The distance from Khenleb to Ser is about 20 km. In and around the township of Ser, which is only 42 km from the county capital at Gogentang, there are a number of monasteries – nearly all branches of Pelyul. Among them, **Raktrom Jampaling** has a Zangdok Pelri-style temple under reconstruction. Smaller monasteries in the vicinity of Ser township include **Jekar Luklha Gon** in Sholeb (450 monks), **Sangsang Dradra Gon** (100 monks), **Tashul Barmi Gon**, **Tashul Ogmi Gon**, **Washul Pon Gonsum**, and **A'u Sera Gon**.

Yarlung Pemako

From Ser, the road undulates for 31 km on its descent to **Yarlung Pemako**. This monastery, only 11 km north of the county capital, was founded by the First Dodrubchen on his return from Central Tibet, and therefore follows the tradition of Rigdzin Jigme Lingpa. The **Guru Lhakhang** at Yarlung Pemako is situated below the motor road. It contains a large image of Padmakara above floor level, with assorted images of Vajrasattva, Shakyamuni and other figures beneath. The murals in Repkong style are kept covered for protection, and the side walls also have 1,000 small icons of Shakyamuni and Padmasambhava. The **assembly hall** (Dukhang) is located above the motor road, alongside the **Mani Lhakhang** and a set of the eight stupas symbolizing the deeds of Shakyamuni Buddha. The incumbent lama, Yarlung Dodrubchen, who has supervised the reconstruction since 1984, generally resides at Gogentang, and there are 100 monks. Nearby, there are smaller branches of Pelyul at **Serto Gonpo Drongrir Nego Gon** and **Ser Shorok Gon**, where there are fewer than 200 and 300 monks respectively.

Singsing Dungkar Gon

Singsing Dungkar Gon is one of the largest monasteries in the county, with 300-400 monks (it once had over 1,000 monks). The complex is well situated on a hilltop, overlooking Gogentang to the south. Below the monastery at the base of the hill there is a nine-storey tower and a Mani Lhakhang. The steep ascent leads to the large assembly hall and a more impressive **Zangdok Pelri Lhakhang**, which was reconstructed in 1998. The images are all sculpted by Chamdo artisans and the frescoes painted by Repkong artists. On the ground floor there are finely sculpted images of Padmakara flanked by his foremost consorts, with his Eight Manifestations and eight teachers to the sides. There is also a large photograph of Lama Chokyi Gyatso, who currently presides over the monastery. The murals depict symbols of longlife and Avalokiteshvara (left), Tara (right), and the 84 Mahasiddhas and Padmasambhava with his 25 Disciples adjacent to the door. The middle floor has a Four-armed Avalokiteshvara flanked by the eight Medicine Buddhas, and the top floor has a central Amitabha, surrounded by the eight standing bodhisattvas. The volumes of the *Kangyur*, *Tangyur* and *Nyingma Gyudbum* line the walls.

Gogentang

Gogentang (altitude: 3,690 m), the county capital of Sertal, is 11 km east of Yarlung Pemako. The approach road from the north is currently undergoing reconstruction, but those driving in from the south will clearly observe the town's major landmark, the large 50-m white stupa, known as **Gogen Chorten**, rising in the manner of a beacon or lighthouse in the distant grassland. Like the well known stupa in Gyantse (see above, page 272), this also contains multiple chapels within it. On the ground floor these consist of Jowo Rinpoche (south), Vajrakila (east), Padmasambhava (north) and Shakyamuni Buddha (west). A small monastery, named **Ser Gogen Chorten Gon**, lies alongside the stupa.

Entering the town from the north, you will pass on the left the Forestry Department, the Sertal Animal Husbandry Bureau and the Agricultural Bank, with the bus station opposite. At the Golden Horse Roundabout, which marks the town centre, you can turn left (east) for the open market and the County Government Guesthouse, right (west) for China Post, or straight ahead for the CCP offices, the police and fire brigade, the bookstore, the cinema, restaurants, a primary school and the sports stadium. Towards the western end of Main Street there is a turning on the right (west) leading to the Traffic Hotel, and further down on the left, a turn-off for the private residence of Yarlung Dodrubchen Rinpoche. The enormous Gogen Chorten, which is visible in all directions for a great distance, dominates the west end of town. Opposite it there is a large cluster of prayer flags. » *For listings, see pages 653-655.*

Nyenlung

From Gogentang, a poor seasonal road leads north over the grasslands via **Nyenlung** (65 km) to **Dodrub Chode** in Padma county (see above, page 643), but it receives very little traffic. The monasteries of **Nyenlung Gon** and **Bochung Rusal Me Gon** are located here.

Larung Gar

The main road follows the Ser-chu downstream from Gogentang to an important intersection at **Serwa**, above its confluence with the Do-chu. **NB** In the summer months this road can be cut off by the flooding waters of the Ser-chu.

About 15 km along this road, you will reach the turn-off on the left for **Larung Gar**, until recently the largest active monastery on the Tibetan plateau with 8,000-10,000 log cabin hermitages and lean-tos covering the slopes of a secluded side valley. This Nyingmapa hermitage was originally founded by Dudjom Lingpa in the late 19th century, but it owes its recent revival to the late charismatic lama, Khenpo Jikpun (also recognized as Terton Sogyel, the incarnation of Lerab Lingpa), who is the spiritual teacher of thousands of monks and nuns of both Tibetan and ethnic Chinese origin. The main buildings at Larung Gar are on three levels: the lowest containing an assortment of small temples and concrete structures. The main **assembly hall** and the famous **monastic college** (*shedra*) of Larung Gar are at the mid-level, and the hilltop is dominated by two spectacular chapels: the three-dimensional **Gyutrul Lhakhang**, and the **Tonpei Dekhang** (containing a large Reclining Buddha). Khenpo Jikpun was well known for obtaining the 'bird-dogs' of Tibet, a tiny dog which is reputably found in the nest of cliff-nesting birds, and has the power to detect poison in food! He presented one to the Dalai Lama on a previous visit to India. He also travelled widely in Europe and North America. However, in 2001 the Communist authorities in Chengdu ordered a clampdown on the spiritual activities at Larung Gar, fearing the influence that Tibetan Buddhism has increasingly acquired with ethnic Chinese Buddhists. Many monks and nuns were forcefully evicted in August of 2002, their hermitages destroyed in a petulant display of official paranoia. Subsequently Khenpo Jigpun passed away at a Chinese military hospital in Chengdu on 7 January, 2004.

Nubzur

Nubzur (Ch Loro) township lies further along the motor road, 27 km southeast of Gogentang. Here, the principal monastery is **Ser Nubzur Gon**, which was the original seat of Khenpo Jikpun before he moved to Larung Gar.

Serwa and Lhartse Sangak Tenpeling → *Colour map 4, grid C4*

On the gradual descent into Serwa, the road passes through many small picturesque agricultural villages, where the high-walled farm houses are distinguished by their top storeys, made of wood, which overhang the two lower storeys, generally made of stone. Passing through **Horshe** township after 13 km, where the monastery of **Horshe Gon** is a branch of Pelyul, the road follows the Ser-chu downstream via **Sheldrub** (16 km), and **Yango** (10 km), before reaching Serwa township (12 km). This important crossroads village, where roads lead south to Drango and east to Barkham, has a large guesthouse, small shops, a post office and restaurants. The monastery of **Serlha Tsechu Jar Gon** is also located here.

Taking the east road from Serwa which leads to Dzamtang and Barkham, you will pass through **Gyasho** after 9 km, and **Golatang** after 20 km. Barley is cultivated in these lower reaches of the Ser-chu; and before reaching the wooden barrier which demarcates the border between Kandze and Ngawa prefectures, you will pass by a **Mantra Wheel Chapel (Dungkor)** containing the mantras of Padmasambhava, a white stupa containing an image of Padmasambhava, and 13 km from Serwa, the Pelyul branch monastery of **Lhartse Sangak Tenpeling**, which has a high tower replica of **Sekhar Gutok** (see above, page 220), the tower of Milarepa. The tower was rebuilt by the late Tenth Panchen Lama. The monastery is located above this tower on the ridge. The road then passes into Dzamtang county.

Likhok and Tsang-chu Valleys

Taking the south road from Serwa, you will reach Drango after 71 km. A verdant pass crosses the watershed (4,115 m) between the Ser-chu and Nyi-chu rivers after 17 km. The nomads of this area are tough and not particularly hospitable to strangers. Sometimes they will block the road with logs and extract protection money from passing drivers! At **Nyipa**, a branch road on the left leads sharply northeast into the **Likhok** and **Tsang-chu** valleys. There are many Nyingmapa monasteries in this area, including **Rahor Gonpa**, in Tsangto township, a branch of Dzogchen which is the seat of Rahor Khenpo Thubten, now resident in Switzerland; and **Khaordong Monastery**, the Jangter seat of the late Lama Chime Rigdzin who also resided in Europe for many years. Other Nyingmapa monasteries in this small enclave include: **Shukgang Gon**, **Tsangda Gon**, **Senge Dzong** (a branch of Katok in Tsang-me township), **Sago Gon**, **Domang Gon**, **Dicham Gon**, **Jangang Gon** and **Gochen Gon**. From Nyipa the road crosses another watershed pass (3,990 m) to reach Drango (see above, page 536).

Dzamtang County ཛམ་ཐང

→ *Population: 32,000. Area: 7,650 sq km. Colour map 4, grid A4.* 壤塘县

Dzamtang county occupies the valley of the Do-chu, from the grasslands and gorges of its mid-reaches, through its confluence with the Ser-chu, and as far as its confluence with the Mar-chu, at which point it becomes known as the **Gyarong** (Ch Dadu) River. It also includes the valley of the north-flowing Dzi-chu, a tributary of the Mar-chu. The county capital is located at **Dzamtang**, 152 km from Gogentang, 213 km from Barkham, and 155 km from Drango.

Access

Driving into Dzamtang county from Sertal or Drango, a wooden barrier marks the modern border between Kandze and Ngawa prefectures. The road surface immediately improves, indicative of the affluence that Ngawa prefecture has acquired through the exploitation of its natural resources, particularly the mass tourism introduced at Dzitsa Degu (see below, page 694). At the confluence of the Ser-chu and Do-chu rivers, 39 km beyond Serwa, the road crosses the high **Dzago**

Bridge over the Do-chu, and there is a turn off on the left, which follows the Do-chu upstream through a precipitous gorge. In the summer season this road can become impassable due to the damage caused by the swollen river banks. Turn left for Dzamtang (45 km), or continue due east for Barkham (159 km). The distance from this intersection to Drango is 110 km.

Drukje and Sirin Khar Gon

If you head north through the Do-chu gorge, you will pass **Drukje** township after 18 km and reach **Dzamtang**, the county capital, after a further 27 km. By the roadside near Drukje, there is the monastery of **Sirin Khar Gon**, a recent branch of the Karma Kagyu school, with intricately designed temples, three nine-storey towers and a stupa cluster, founded apparently in 1954. Among the reconstructed temples here, the **Riknyi Lhakhang** contains an unusual white jade Shakyamuni, flanked by Vajradhara and Avalokiteshvara. The **Kamtsang Lhakhang** contains a central image of Marpa, flanked by Milarepa and Gampopa. The **assembly hall** has large images of Shakyamuni, Mahakarunika, aspects of Tara and historical figures associated with the Karma Kagyu tradition. The adjacent **Zangdok Pelri Lhakhang** is flanked by two of the high towers – the one to the left known as **Jingkhar**. Its uppermost floor is empty, and the lower eight storeys respectively feature images of Samantabhadra, Jowo Shakyamuni, Amitabha, Manjughosa, Milarepa, Serte Rinpoche, Marpa and Vajradhara. A markedly older tower, next to the assembly hall, has a different arrangement on its eight lower floors: Avalokiteshvara, Aksobhya, Shakyamuni, Jowo Rinpoche, Marpa, the Eight Bodhisattvas and Padmasambhava, along with Shantaraksita and King Trisong Detsen.

Dzamtang Town → *For listings, see pages 653-655.*

The county town (3,200 m), where police will vigilantly inspect travel permits (Dzamtang is still a closed county), is drab and uninspiring with a high Chinese population. Entering town from the south, the road crosses to the west bank of the Do-chu, passing rows of shops and concrete apartment buildings. The Public Security Bureau and Forestry Department Guesthouse are on the left. Reaching a T-junction, turn left for the National Tax Bureau (which houses the best restaurant in town) and the road to Doto, or right for the County Government Buildings, the Government Guesthouse, the hospital, cinema, bookstore, bus station and the road to Dzongda.

Yutok

The road bifurcates at Dzamtang, the left branch heading northwest through the Do-chu valley to **Doto** (32 km) and **Yutok** (24 km); and the right branch heading northeast across the watershed (3,870 m) to **Nada** (28 km) and **Dzongda** (18 km) in the Dzi-chu valley. Around Yutok, the Nyingmapa monasteries of **Do Shukchung Gon** and **Do Yutok Gon** each have about 500 monks. A trail leads from Yutok via Shukchung to **Dodrub Chode** (see above, page 643) across the Qinghai border.

Dzamtang

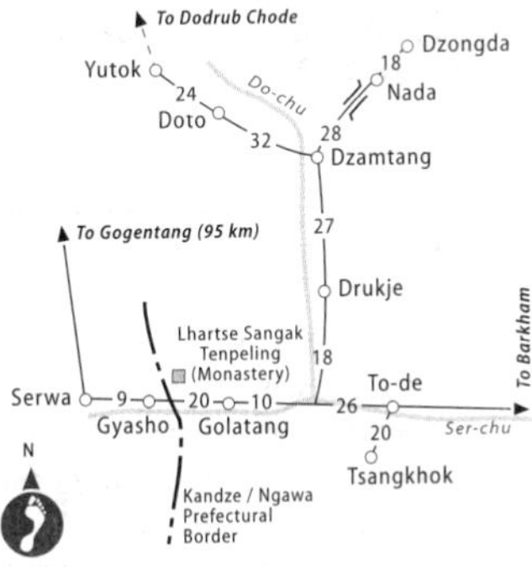

Dzi-chu Valley

Driving northeast into the Dzi-chu valley, quite suddenly the forested gorges with their stone and wooded houses blend into open grasslands inhabited by yak herding nomads. From here, the road descends gradually into the Mar-chu valley, where it forks, north across the Sichuan-Qinghai border into Padma county (see above, page 642), or east for Ngawa. In the higher grasslands of the Dzi-chu valley, there are some minor Nyingma monasteries, including **Dzika-me Akye Gon**, and most of these are affiliated to Dodrub Chode (see above, page 643). More influential and historically important, however, are the three main monasteries of the Jonangpa school, clustered together in a plain below the holy peak of Dzambhala, which gives the Dzamtang region its name. Among them, **Dzamtang Chode Gonpa** was founded by Drung Kazhi Rinchenpel of Gyarong circa 1378. The neighbouring **Tsechu Gon** was founded by his student Tsechu Ratnakirti in the 15th century, and **Dzamtang Tsangpa Gon** was established in 1717 by Ngawang Tendzin Namgyel of Tsang, whose uncle had been an actual student of Taranatha.

Prior to the arrival of Drung Kazhi Rinchenpel, the Dzamthang area had been a stronghold of the Bon religion. The Jonangpa ascendancy was secured by Ming imperial patronage when Rinchenpel visited Beijing in 1419, and his successors, including Gyelwa Zangpo (1419-1493) and Gyelwa Senge (1508-1568), further developed these ties. When friction developed between the Jonangpa and Gelukpa orders in Western Tibet, ostensibly based on their diverse philosophical interpretations of the nature of emptiness, the strength of the Jonangpa in Dzamtang provided a sanctuary against the prevailing trend of persecution. The order flourished here, particularly under the guidance of Ngawang Tendzin Namgyel, so that his foundation, Dzamtang Tsangpa Gon, quickly became the largest of the three adjoining monasteries, with over 2,000 monks. The original foundation, Dzamtang Chode Gon, had 300 monks, while Tsechu Gon, the smallest, had only 100.

Among the temples which can be visited at the present day, Andreas Gruschke in his *Cultural Monuments of Tibet's Outer Provinces*, Vol. 2, reports that there are four original three-storey buildings which survive, including the Gangsha Lhakhang, the Gongma Lhakhang and the main assembly hall (dated 1834). The last of these contains a 6-m Shakyamuni image, along with statues of Dolpopa Sherab Gyeltsen, Taranatha, and the reliquary stupas of important Jonangpa masters, along with 5,300 volumes of Buddhist scriptures. Other buildings of note include the Parkhang, containing woodblocks for the *Collected Works of Dolpopa and Taranatha*, the Lolang Lhakhang, containing a three-dimensional mandala of Kalacakra, the Gonkhang, which exhibits some surviving early murals, and the Drubkhang, where three-year meditation retreats are practised. Tsechu Gon is noted for its large stupa containing multiple chapels.

Lower Do-chu Valley

Heading east from the confluence of the Do-chu and Ser-chu at the Dzago Bridge (2,896 m) mentioned above, the road follows the combined waters of these Gyarong feeder rivers downstream for 122 km as far as their confluence with the Mar-chu. On this route through the gorges, there are only a very few small roadside settlements. After 26 km, the road passes through **To-de** (2,743 m), where a side road leads southwest to **Tsangkhok** (20 km), and after a further 40 km it leaves Dzamtang for Chuchen and Barkham counties (see pages 656-658).

Ngawa County ང་བ → *Population: 60,000. Area: 8,776 sq km.* 阿坝县

Ngawa county, named after the Nga-chu tributary of the Mar-chu, which flows south from **Mount Nyenpo Yurtse**, is an area where nomadic groups and long-established settled communities intermingle. The villages are characterized by large detached adobe farming houses with tapering walls and windows all on one side of the building! Agricultural produce is limited to valley floors and alluvial fans, where fields of barley, rapeseed and beans are planted, but it is animal husbandry and forestry that provide the principal economic outputs. Ngawa has also thrived on trade for centuries, and its inhabitants even now frequently undertake business trips to Chengdu and Lhasa. Several antique stores in Chengdu are owned by traders from Ngawa. The capital is located at **Ngawa** town (Ch Aba); 75 km from Jigdril, 254 km from Barkham, and 157 km from Mewa (Ch Hong Yuan).

Upper Ngawa (Ngawa To)

Two roads approach Ngawa from Golok, one following the Mar-chu downstream from Padma, across the Qinghai-Sichuan border, as far as **Khokpo**, where a side road leaves the Mar-chu and heads northeast across a 3,640-m pass for 55 km to Ngawa town (total distance 192 km). The other follows the Nga-chu downstream from Jigdril on the southeast side of Mount Nyenpo Yurtse, via **Ngato** (total distance 75 km). The road from Dzamtang to Ngawa through the Dzi-chu valley (see page 649) connects with the former on the Sichuan side of the border.

The monasteries of Upper Ngawa (Ngato) include **Tsinang Gon** of the Jonang school, and Gelukpa institutions such as **Tsegon Sangchen Tashiling** (founded by Khenchen Ngawang Drakpa), and **Ziwei Ritro Ganden Tashi Choling**. Just before reaching the town, the road leaves a narrow gorge marked by a vast stone cairn in the open hills that lead up towards the sacred Mount Nyenpo Yurtse, just visible in the distance. Some 15 km northeast of town is **Gomang Gonpa**, formally known as Gomang Gar Ganden Labsum Zungjuk Dechenling. This is a branch of Labrang Tashikyil, housing 600 monks. Its assembly hall contains central images of Jowo Shakyamuni, Mahakarunika, Tsongkhapa and the first five Jamyang Zhepas of Labrang. Most of the Nyingma monasteries of Ngawa are smaller and located in this northern part of the county. ▸▸ *For listings, see pages 653-655.*

Middle Ngawa (Ngawa Barma)

The town of **Ngawa** itself (population approximately 20,000) has grown extensively in recent years. Despite its typical mix of Chinese compounds, department stores, simple shops and a remote location, it is a vitally important and thriving trading town, with scenic hill top panoramas. In common with most of Amdo, gold is a predominant local product, and large numbers of itinerant Chinese workers visit the area to pan for gold in summer. As in Dzamtang and Sertal, the forested hills on the upper reaches of the Nga-chu tributaries have proved easier to log than the gorges further south, and many hillsides were stripped bare prior to the 1998 ban on logging. There is little evidence of replanting except beside the roads of the valley floor, and the denuded slopes are soon covered with herds of yaks and sheep, making regeneration almost impossible. The Public Security Bureau are over-vigilant and may restrict one's movements, even when all travel permits are in order. Even Chinese visitors fashionably dressed like Hong Kong people have been sent packing! The town has an interesting leather goods factory and a teacher training college.

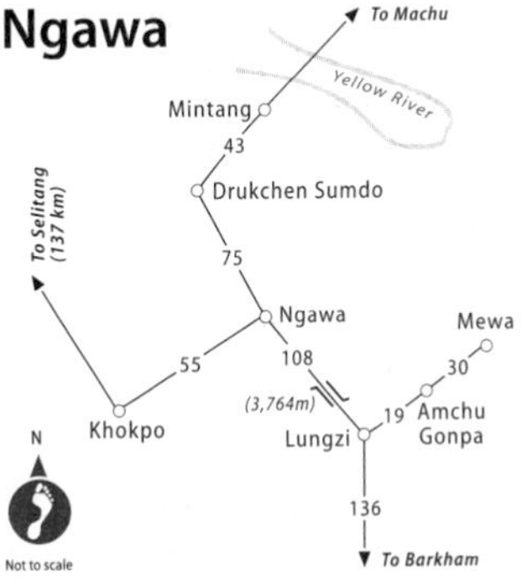

Orientation

As elsewhere, the streets all have Chinese names. Entering town from the northwest (ie from Jigdril) on **Qiantang Xijie**, you will first pass Kirti Gonpa on the left (north), followed by the Agricultural Bank, the Mentsikhang, the Ngawa Public Security Bureau, the Xinhua Bookstore and the Grassland Hotel. Opposite the entrance to Kirti Gonpa, on the right (south) there is a turn-off for Padma and Dzamtang counties, followed by many small restaurants, including the Tashi Khangsar, and the Traffic Hotel. Reaching a crossroads, where the side roads (**Dajie jie**) lead into residential quarters, continue straight ahead, passing on the left the Carpet Factory, primary school and bus station with small restaurants opposite. Next, a turn-off on the right (**Dekang Lu**) leads south towards the China Post and China Telecom, and the Aba Government Guesthouse. Down this side road you will reach the intersection with Deji Lu and the Commercial Committee Hospital. Or continue straight ahead on the main street for the Women and Children's Hospital, the Tibetan Middle School, the Road Maintenance Bureau and the southern route to Setenling Gonpa, Nangzhik Gonpa, Mewa and Barkham.

On **Deji Lu**, which is parallel to the main street, you will find the County Government Buildings, the County Court, the Cultural Bureau, the Cinema and the Agricultural Bank.

Kirti Gonpa

The hills around the town are dotted with more than 30 monasteries of the Nyingma, Sakya, Geluk and Jonang schools of Buddhism, as well as major Bon institutions. The largest monastery, Kirti Gonpa, properly known as **Kirti Kalari Gon Tashi Lhundrub**, is located on the northwestern edge of town. It was founded in 1472 by Rongpa Chenakpa, a disciple of Tsongkhapa; and established as a branch of the original Kirti Monastery at Taktsang Lhamo (see below, page 675) in 1693. By 1840 it had outgrown its mother monastery, and now houses approximately 2,500 monks. The head lama Kirti Tsenzhab Rinpoche currently lives in India. At its entrance is a huge 35-m stupa, known as the **Dudul Chorten**, one of the largest in Amdo, which contains multiple chapels on successive floors, respectively dedicated to Shakyamuni Buddha, Mahakarunika, the Three Deities of Longevity, Tsongkhapa, and Sitatapatra.

Then, passing a small guesthouse on the right, the entrance pathway leads into a large courtyard, where the large imposing **Tsokchen** (assembly hall) is located immediately in front, with the **Labrang** (palace) of Kirti Rinpoche and the **Tsenyi Dratsang** (Dialectical College) to the left. The **Dukar Lhakhang**, dedicated to Sitatapatra, and the **Dukhor Dratsang** (Kalacakra college) are on the right. A passageway leads behind the courtyard on the right to the **Gyupa Dratsang** (Tantric College). The restored murals and images at Kirti display a high standard of craftsmanship. The assembly hall contains an 8-m image of Maitreya, flanked by Jowo Shakyamuni and Kirti Lobzang Chungla. New year ceremonies, including the display of a large tangka and masked dances, are performed here annually during the first lunar month. In 2005 these events will take place on 21-22 February.

Other Gelukpa monasteries near the town include **Khashi Ritro Tashi Gepeling, Dongkhu Gon Yulgyel Samtenling** and **Namkyak Ritro Namdakling**, the last having been founded by a student of the Seventh Dalai Lama, named Gyakhe Lama.

Nangzhik Gonpa

The Bon monasteries of **Nangzhik** (locally pronounced Narshi) and **Topgyel** lie just northeast of town. Both represent the so-called 'old Bon' tradition, which remains aloof from the 19th-century ecumenical movement, according to which the traditions and practices of masters such as Sharza Tashi Gyeltshen moved closer to those of the various Buddhist traditions. **Nangzhik Gonpa** is the larger of the two, and its monks are well versed in dialectics, composition and the decorative arts. The monastery was founded in 1107 by Nangzhik Lodro Gyeltsen, and relocated at its present site in 1754. The central images of the assembly hall depict Nampar Gyelwa, flanked by Kunzang Gyelwa Gyatso and Ngangzhik Tonpa Chenpo. A sacred round dance is performed here, in conjunction with the new year ceremonies, next scheduled for 23-24 Feb, 2005.

Setenling Gonpa

The Jonangpa tradition is also represented close to town at **Setenling Gonpa**, which was established by Namnang Dorje, and reconstituted in the late 19th century by

Droge Yonten Gyatso. There are 800 affiliated monks, some currently practising retreat in Dzamtang under the guidance of Sangye Dorje. The head lama here is Thubten Dorje Hwon Rinpoche. The restored **Assembly Hall** contains new tangkas and images of Kunkhyen Dolpopa, Jetsun Kunga Drolchok, Taranatha, Namnang Dorje and the deities Cakrasamvara and Kalacakra. The large 6-m central image depicts Maitreya, and in a glass case there are 1,000 small images of Dolpopa, along with others depicting Padmasambhava, Maitreya and others. Relics include the boot of Taranatha. There are various collections of texts including the *Kangyur* from Derge and *The Collected Works of Taranatha* (28 vols). Woodblocks for the Six Yogas of Niguma are also preserved here.

The **Gonkhang** has a central image of Mahakala in the 'tiger-riding form' Takkiraja; while the **meditation hermitage** has images of Dolpopa, Taranatha, Namnang Dorje and the meditational deity Vajrakila. In the **lama's residence**, there is a Jokhang Chapel with fine images, tangkas and books, including one tangka depicting Taranatha surrounded by the so-called Rinjung Gyatsa deities.

Lower Ngawa (Nga-me)

The 108 km descent from Ngawa town to **Lungzi** (Ch Longriwa) crosses six passes, offering fine views (north) of Mount Nyenpo Yurtse and (south) of the deforested hillsides towards Barkham. Only the first 12 km are currently paved. Gelukpa monasteries in this area include **Tsakho Gon Ganden Dargyeling**. The highest of the passes on this route (3,810 m) is the main watershed dividing the Mar-chu/Nga-chu basin from the Yellow River basin, 56 km south of the town. Crossing this pass, on a hillside just north of the road, is the Gelukpa monastery of **Darchen**, with around 200 monks.

Amchok Tsenyi Gonpa

Further on, about 40 km from the pass, the monastery of Amchok Tsenyi Gonpa (Ch Anqu Chalisi) comes into view in the distant valley floor far below. At the **Lungzi** (Ch Longriwa) intersection, the road converges with Highway 213, which has an excellent paved surface leading south into **Barkham** county (136 km) and northeast through the meandering Ger-chu grasslands for 49 km to **Mewa** (Ch Hongyuan). If you take the latter route, after 19 km you will reach the turn-off for **Amchok Tsenyi Gonpa** (50 km distant in the grassland). This is a particularly large Gelukpa monastery, which was established through the gradual conversion of an ancient Bon site in 1823 by the Second Amchok Konchok Tenpei Gyeltsen. During the incumbency of the Third Amchok (1911-1934), the monastery was enlarged, forming two distinct complexes: the **Tsenyi Lhakhang** for the study of dialectics and the **Tenyi Lhakhang** for the study of sutra and tantra. Altogether there are 900-1,000 monks, under the occasional guidance of the Fourth Amchok Rinpoche, who returns regularly from his residence in exile. The main assembly hall contains a remarkable image of Avalokiteshvara, which is said to have moved its arms and exude nectar in public!

Sleeping

Mato *p631*

D Mato Government Guesthouse, T0975-345081. Doubles at ¥140, triples at ¥210, has coal fire heaters.

E PLA Guesthouse (Huangyeyan Bingzhan), cheaper accommodation may be found here.

Tawo *p635*

E Nomad Hotel, cheaper.

E Scientific Research Hotel, cheaper.

D Snow Mountain Hotel (Xueshan Binguan), T0975-382142. Has best, though rapidly ageing rooms, doubles at ¥200, plus ¥6 tax, triples at ¥50 per bed, reception desk receive IDD calls.

For an explanation of the sleeping and eating price codes used in this guide, see inside the front cover. Other relevant information is found in Essentials pages 44-46.

Gyu-me *p639*
E **Bus Station Guesthouse (Dari Qichezhan Lushe)**, cheaper, grimy, has doubles at ¥26.
E **Government Guesthouse**, opposite the Telecom Hotel. Cavernous.
E **Telecom Hotel**, the best rooms are on the 3rd floor, has comfortable triples at ¥90.

NB Street lighting in the town leaves much to be desired, and the unsuspecting traveller could well mistake an open roadside drainage channel for a pavement!

Selitang *p644*
E **Changjiang Daxia**, nearby the Huangjin Daxia Hotel, slightly cheaper.
E **Huangjin Daxia Hotel**, the best rooms in town, doubles at ¥70, triples at ¥60, and singles at ¥40.

Older guesthouses should be avoided.

Gogentang *p646*
E **County Government Guesthouse**, T0836-8522120. Cheaper but much poorer accommodation available, doubles at ¥40 and triples at ¥45.
E **The Traffic Hotel**, T0836-8522967. Has the best accommodation in town, doubles at ¥80, triples at ¥90, and 4-bed dorms at ¥80; electric blankets, Chinese have 50% discount.

Dzamtang *p649*
E **Forestry Department Guesthouse**, poorer rooms, doubles at ¥30, triples at ¥45.
E **Government Guesthouse**, simple accommodation, no attached bathroom, doubles and triples at ¥30.

Ngawa *p651*
E **Aba Government Guesthouse**, T0837-2482268. The best in town, deluxe doubles and singles at ¥80, deluxe triples at ¥120, economy doubles at ¥40, triples at ¥54, and 4-bed dorms at ¥40-60.
E **Grassland Hotel**, T0837-2483997. A good alternative, close to Kirti Gonpa, doubles at ¥40, triples at ¥45 and 4-bed dorms at ¥60.

Eating

Mato *p631*
The guesthouse restaurants are uninspiring, and inferior to the **Chengdu Restaurant**.

Tawo *p635*
There are a few Muslim and Chinese-style restaurants, apart from the hotel restaurant, the best perhaps being the **Sihayan Restaurant**.

Gyu-me *p639*
There are 2 good Sichuan and Muslim style restaurants. Most restaurants clustered around the market area are Muslim-owned.

Selitang *p644*
The town has both Muslim and plentiful Sichuan-style cuisine.

Gogentang *p646*
Hongmei Restaurant, located on east side of Main St, between CCP offices and primary school. One of best Sichuan eateries in town.
Ruyi Restaurant, near Hongmei Restaurant. One of the best Sichuan eateries in town.

Dzamtang *p649*
Suiwuju Zhigong Shitang (Tax Bureau Dining Room), the best in town.

There are a number of small noodle and dumpling breakfast restaurants located on the main street.

Ngawa *p651*
Tashi Khangsar Restaurant, next to the Traffic Hotel.

The town also has several other Sichuan-style restaurants, and there is a varied nightlife with lively karaoke bars and discos.

Transport

Mato *p631*
Bus
The only buses stopping here are those running between **Ziling** and **Jyekundo**. Trucks will occasionally pick up travellers at the busy intersection on the highway.

Machuka *p632*
If you try to reach the lakes without pre-arranged transportation, it may still be possible to hire a 4WD vehicle from the County Government in Mato.

Tawo *p635*
Daily couchette service runs between **Ziling** and Tawo, and also daily bus connections with **Kawasumdo**, **Gabde** and **Darlag**.

Travel services **Amdo and Kham Travel Service**, T0975-383438, F0975-383431, have an office in the Snow Mountain Hotel. The tourism co-ordinator for Amnye Machen is Mr Tsechik.

Rabgya Monastery *p636*

Bus

Public buses heading to and from **Tawo** in **Machen** may stop here.

Bakchen *p638*

Bus

Daily buses connect Bakchen with neighbouring **Tawo** and **Darlag**.

Gyu-me *p639*

Bus

There are daily minibuses to and from **Tawo**, and infrequent connections with **Ziling** and **Padma**.

Raft

It is possible to raft on the Yellow River from Gyu-me through the river bends to **Trika** (470 km) in 13 days.

Selitang *p644*

Bus

Public buses run here infrequently from **Ziling** via Darlag.

Gogentang *p646*

Bus

Public buses depart Gogentang Bus Station for **Drango** (daily, ¥45), for **Chengdu** (20 per month, ¥121 by Yaxing, ¥136 with couchettes), and for **Ponkor** (regularly, ¥40).

Dzamtang *p649*

Bus

Public buses connect Dzamtang daily with **Barkham** and **Chengdu**; and with **Ngawa** on the 2nd, 5th, 8th, 12th, 15th, 18th, 22nd, 25th and 28th of each month.

Ngawa *p651*

Bus

Buses depart Ngawa daily for **Chengdu** (0600, ¥73), **Machu** (0530, ¥35), and **Jigdril** (0830, 1530, ¥18). Services also run on odd calendar days to **Tso** (0600, ¥75) and **Linxia** (0530, ¥89), on even days to **Barkham** (0600, ¥34) and on the 2nd, 5th, 8th, 12th, 15th, 18th, 22nd, 25th and 28th of each month to **Dzamtang** (0530, ¥29).

Gyarong Gorges རྒྱལ་རོང

South of Ngawa, in the precipitous rugged gorges of Trokhyab, the source rivers of the Gyarong converge. This is the beginning of the Gyarong region, which extends through the lower reaches of this river valley as far as Chakzamka, and includes the lateral valleys of the Tsenlha-chu and Somang-chu, as well as the upper reaches of the Trosung-chu. This section, outlining the Gyarong gorge and its adjacent valleys, comprises five present-day counties: ***Chuchen, Barkham, Rongtrak, Tsenlha*** *and* ***Tashiling****, of which only Rongtrak falls within the Kandze prefecture – the others all being within the Ngawa prefecture. Chakzamka has already been described (see above, page 476).* ***Recommended itinerary: 9 (also 5). See page 20.*** *►► For Sleeping, Eating and other listings, see page 664.*

History

In Gyarong, the indigenous population speak a distinctively archaic Qiangic dialect called **Gyarong-ke**, and they have maintained their unique way of life and culture for centuries. Until 1949, the tribes of Gyarong were organized into **18 petty kingdoms**. Among them, the **northern group** includes Trokhyab (Zhousejia), Dzongak (Songang), Barkham, Choktse (Zhoukeji), Somang (Suomo), Zida, Tsakhok (Li dzong/Zagunao), Gyelkha and Wasi. These are all located around the Do-chu/Somang-chu confluence and in the upper Trosung-chu valley.

The **central group** comprises Rabten (Chuchen/Jinchuan), Badi, Pawang (Chuchen), Geshitra, Rongtrak and Dardo (Chakla), which are all located in or around the main Gyarong valley; and the **south-eastern group** includes Tsenlha, Dawei, Hva-hva (Hanniu) and Dronba (Muping), which are all located in the Tsenlha valley and the mountains further south.

Traditionally, **Trokyab**, **Rabden**, **Tsenlha** and **Dardo** were the most influential among these 18 kingdoms, which kept the powerful Sino-Manchu armies of Emperor Qianlong at bay for 10 years during the 18th century. Nowadays, both Barkham and Dardo are prefectural capitals, responsible for the administration of those parts of Kham, Amdo and Gyarong presently under the control of Sichuan province.

Chuchen County ཆུ་ཆེན

→ *Population: 69,000. Colour map 4, grid A5.* 金川县

Chuchen county lies deep in the awesome and unwelcoming Gyarong gorge. Formerly known as **Rabden**, it was at times the most powerful of all the Gyarong kingdoms, and its king was a vigorous proponent of the Bon religion. At **Yungdrung Lhading**, 15 km south of Rabden, there was the largest and most important Bonpo monastery in this part of Tibet. Between 1746-1749 and 1771-1776 the Sino-Manchu armies of Emperor Qianlong (1736-1795) marched into Gyarong, sustained by the messianic zeal of the Gonlung lama Changkya Qutuqtu Rolpei Dorje (1717-1786) who sought to convert the Bon and other communities of Gyarong to the Gelukpa school by force of arms. The tenacious resistance of the Gyarong people owed much to the isolation of the terrain and to their skill at constructing fortified towers – a tradition indicative of their Qiang ancestry. The imperial forces were driven back in disgrace across the **Balang Shan** pass (see below page 663) before eventually returning to destroy the Bon monastery with their Portuguese cannons, and achieving a partial conversion to the Gelukpa cause. The present county capital is located at **Chuchen** (Ch Jinchuan), also known as Rabden, 46 km south of Tro-ye and 84 km north of Rongtrak.

Ga-ne and Tuje Chenpo Gon

Entering Chuchen county from Dzamtang (see above, page 648), on an excellent paved road, you will first pass through **Ga-ne** township (2,590 m), where a bridge spans the river and a side road leads south to **Tawu** (see above, page 538) in Kham. On the far bank of the Do-chu at Ga-ne, there is a **Mani Wheel Chapel**.

Continuing downstream from Ga-ne for 13 km, the road passes through **Tuje Chenpo** township (Ch Guanyinqiao), where there are several small shops and restaurants. Another motorable bridge cuts south across the river here, leading above

Chuchen County

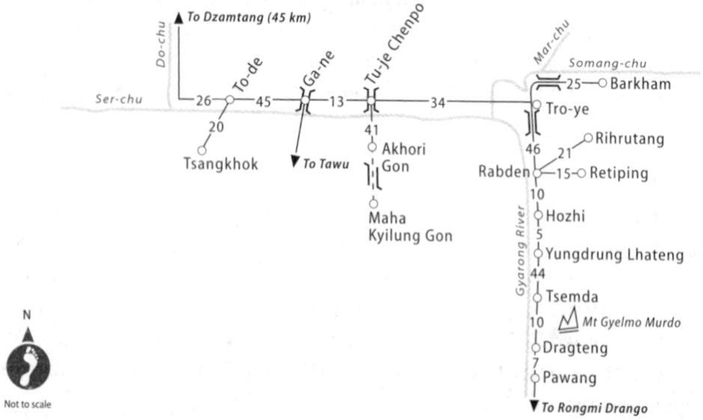

the town (one and a half hours' walking distance) to the reconstructed Nyingmapa monastery of **Tuje Chenpo Gon**. This impressive site formerly had over 300 monks (now 70), and is revered as one of the major power-places in Gyarong. The winding path uphill is dotted with small roadside shrines where pilgrims leave old bits of clothes, tufts of wool from their sheep and broken jewellery. Within the town on the south bank of the river there are two small guesthouses, among which the Tashidelek (upstairs above a restaurant) has better rooms. Opposite it is the Snowland Tea House (open for breakfast).

The side road from Tuje Chenpo leads southwards to **Akhori Gon** (41 km), a branch of Dzogchen monastery. Across the pass from here (in Rongtrak county), is **Maha Kyilung Gon**, the seat of Zenkar Rinpoche, the incarnation of Do Khyentse Yeshe Dorje. The present incumbent is currently based in Canada and the United States.

Trokhyab

Following the main road downstream for 4 km from Tuje Chenpo, you will arrive at **Trokhyab**, once one of the most powerful of the 18 ancient kingdoms of Gyarong, but nowadays having the appearance of a small country village. Some houses have the Tibetan syllable 'Tro' (written khro) inscribed on the doors!

Rabden Town

Some 34 km further east at **Tro-ye**, the road reaches the confluence of the Do-chu and Mar-chu rivers (2,073 m). Just before the confluence a suspension bridge carries traffic across to the south bank of the Do-chu, from where it enters the Gyarong gorge, following this mighty river downstream for 46 km to Rabden, the county capital of Chuchen. En route it passes through the impressive hillside Bon villages of **Drukzur** (Ch Xiazhai) and **Chingnying** where the boulders are carved with the Bon mantra: OM MATRI MUYE SALI DU. The gorge here is one of the most precipitous in Tibet.

Rabden, one of the ancient Gyarong kingdoms, is still a small county town with simple guesthouse and Sichuan restaurant facilities, and a nearby hot springs. The town and county are currently closed to foreigners, so permit restrictions still apply. Public buses run daily to and from Rongtrak and to and from Chengdu via Barkham.

Side roads lead northeast from the town for 21 km to **Rihruntang** (via Kalingka), and for 15 km to **Retiping** (via Wenlin).

Yungdrung Lhading

Further south, the road passes **Hozhi** after 10 km; and then, after **Dosum**, it reaches the site of the Bon monastery of **Yungdrung Lhading** (near Kharatang). Following the subjugation of Chuchen and the destruction of this monastery by the forces of Qianlong, a Gelukpa monastery named **Tenpel Gonpa** (Ch Guangfasi) was constructed here in 1776, and developed with funds directly from the imperial coffers. Its golden roofs were among the most lavish in Tibet. The wealthy monastery was destroyed during the 1960s and has subsequently been reclaimed by the Bonpos, who have once again resurrected Yundrung Lhading.

Anying and Tsemda

From here, the road follows the river south. Tall fortified towers are commonplace on both banks of the river, particularly at strategic confluences. Passing through **Anying**, the road reaches the town of **Tsemda** (59 km south of Chuchen), and from here it crosses the modern prefectural boundary to enter Rongtrak county (see below, page 660).

Barkham County འབར་ཁམས

→ *Population: 54,000. Area: 7,327 sq km. Colour map 4, grid A5.* 马尔康县

Barkham county is the northern limit of the Gyarong region and the language here (considered a branch of the archaic Qangic group of Tibeto-Burman) is almost unintelligible to the Amdowa populations further north and the Khampa peoples to the west. The dress is also distinctive. Most of the women wear multi-coloured embroidered headscarfs and elaborate belts and aprons. Fewer men wear the traditional felt tunic, which is quite distinct from the Tibetan chuba or bulky sheepskin coat. The vast majority of men now wear Chinese clothes, and only a small number in traditional costume can be observed in the market. There are almost 40 monasteries in the county, representing the Nyingma, Geluk, Sakya, Jonang and Bon traditions, several of them in attractive mountain locations. The county capital of Barkham also functions as the capital of the entire Ngawa Prefecture.

If instead of crossing the bridge that leads to Rabden (see above, page 657), you continue to follow the west bank of the Mar-chu upstream from its confluence with the Do-chu, you will reach a second sturdy suspension bridge which leads across to the east bank. Following the Mar-chu upstream on a well paved road, you soon enter the Somang-chu gorge and Barkham county, reaching the county capital after 55 km.

Mar-chu Region

Alternatively, from the confluence of the Mar-chu and Somang-chu, you can follow the former upstream on a dirt side road, which leads to **Tsedun Sobdun Gonpa** – the largest Gelukpa monastery in the county, and Khangsar; as well as Jonangpa monasteries such as **Dzago**, **Bala**, and **Tashigang**, all of which are in the Mar-chu gorge and its side valleys. The Gelukpa monastery of **Datsang**, located above **Sar Dzong** on a west-flowing tributary of the Mar-chu, is also accessible by this route. There are fine views from here of **Mount Shukgopuk** (4,906 m) to the southwest. Unfortunately, the road does not continue upriver to the junction of the Mar-chu and Nga-chu. Visitors and pilgrims to Ngawa are therefore forced to go back to Barkham and head for Ngawa via the Somang valley.

Barkham City → *Population: 25,000. For listings, see page 664.*

Getting there Heading upstream through the Somang-chu gorge to Barkham city, you will pass through several of the ancient Gyarong kingdoms: **Dzonggak** lies 10 km east of the turn-off, **Barkham** (15 km further east), **Choktse** (9 km further east), and **Somang** (38 km further east). Of these Barkham, which was once one of the smaller of the ancient kingdoms, is now a large city full of high-rise apartment buildings. As the capital of both Barkham county and Ngawa Prefecture, the city is now comparable to Dartsedo in its importance. See Transport, page 664, for further details.

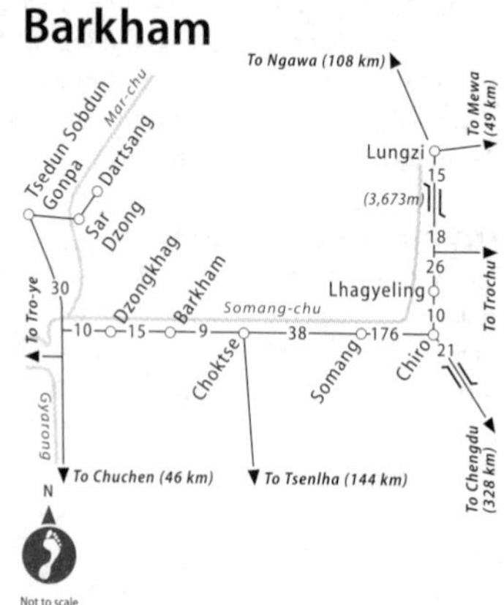

The steep-sided valley of the fast-flowing Somang-chu, in its lower reaches denuded of its original forest, constricts the town into a long thin corridor. Much of the town is composed of administrative buildings and compounds of uninspired design (large high-rise concrete

apartments), but nearby the traditional three-storey Gyarong village houses are still constructed of solid masonry. Alluvial fans on the valley floor and gentler slopes high above the river provide some rich agricultural land and terraced fields, irrigated by cleverly contoured canals which surround the small hamlets throughout this area.

Orientation Entering the city from the west, you will pass through the old town, with a clinic, primary school and branch post office on the right. A side road on the left now leads to the Martyrs' Cemetery, while the main street passes a cycle rickshaw stand, the Tax Bureau, the Agricultural Bank and a small police station on the left. Now the road forks at the Linye Hotel. Turn left for China Telecom, China Post, the Maerkang Hotel, the Barkham Hotel and the Stadium, or right for the bus station, the County Public Security Bureau and the main bridge, which leads across the Somang-chu to the County Government Buildings, the County Court and an outlet for forestry products.

Continuing along the main street, you will next reach a roundabout. Turn sharp left for the Construction Bank, the Agricultural Bank and the Barkham Hotel, second left for the Prefectural Government Buildings and the Prefectural Public Security Bureau, or straight ahead for the Shambhala Restaurant and a second motor bridge that leads across the Somang-chu to the Bank of China, PICC, the National Tax Bureau, Ngawa TV and Radio Station, and China Telecom. After passing this bridge, the main road leads out of town in the directions of Ngawa and Chengdu.

Local monasteries

The small Gelukpa monastery of **Barkham Dargyeling** which overlooks the town is little more than a concrete shed, with about 30 attendant monks. **Gyidruk Gonpa** of the Nyingma school is located some three hours' climb southwest of town. It offers spectacular valley views, although the building and its contents are also disappointing artistically.

Upper Somang Valley

From Barkham the paved road continues to follow the Somang-chu gorge upstream, passing the ancient kingdom of **Choktse** after 9 km. Here there is a turn-off to the south which crosses a pass and then follows the Tsenlha River (Ch Xiaojin) downstream for 144 km to Tsenlha county (see page 661). In these parts the gorge is well forested and magnificent in early summer. This is where, according to one tradition, the great translator Vairocana meditated and transmitted the Dzogchen teachings during his exile from Central Tibet in the eighth century.

Passing **Somang**, another of these ancient Gyarong kingdoms, after 47 km, you will then reach after 8 further km the major intersection with Highway 213 at **Chiro** (Ch Shuamalukou). Chiro is 65 km from Barkham. Turn southeast on the highway for **Tashiling** (Lixian), **Lungu** (Wenchuan) and **Chengdu** (326 km) or north, following the Somang-chu upstream to the watershed area, and on to **Mewa or Ngawa**.

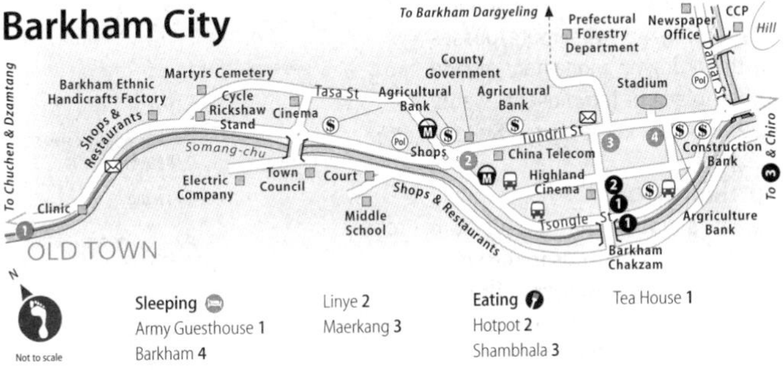

Taking the latter, the terrain becomes increasingly arid and rugged, as the highway enters Mewa county, cutting through a narrow gorge for 10 km to emerge at **Lhagyeling**. This important Gelukpa monastery once specialized in gold-printed texts, and is one of the oldest in Amdo. After a further 26 km, there is a turn-off on the right (east) which leads to **Trochu** (Ch Hei shui) county. Snow peaks are visible in the distance. Continuing on the highway for a further 18 km, you will cross the watershed between the Gyarong and Yellow River basins (3,673 m), and then after 15 km reach **Lungzi** (Longriwa) in the wide open Amdo grasslands. From here you can detour northwest for 108 km to Ngawa (see above, page 650), or continue on the highway, northeast through the Ger-chu plain to Mewa (Hongyuan).

Rongtrak County རོང་བྲག

→ *Population: 57,000. Area: 6,887 sq km. Colour map 4, grid A5.* 丹巴县

Rongtrak county occupies the Gyarong gorge further south from Chuchen. Here the rapids are strong and the sound of rushing waters all-pervasive. The most important pilgrimage centre and power-place is **Mount Gyelmo Murdo,** from which the Gyarong region gets its name. Gyarong is a contraction of Gyelmo Tsawarong. This mountain of solid quartz which once reputedly had mantra syllables inscribed in the rock crystal, has sadly been fully exploited for its minerals. The county capital is located at **Rongmi Drango**, 84 km south of Chuchen and 112 km north of Chakzamka.

Dragteng and Pawang

From **Tsemda** in Chuchen county (see above, page 657), the road runs due south, passing the sacred **Mount Gyelmo Murdo** on the east bank of the Gyarong. Two of the ancient Gyarong kingdoms are passed along this stretch – **Dragteng** after 10 km, and **Pawang** after 7 km. At **Dragteng** there are two major monasteries: the Gelukpa monastery of **Phuntsoling** and a large Bonpo monastery, which was once the principle shrine of the Dragteng kings. Near **Pawang** there is another 18th-century Gelukpa monastery and the **Bumzhi Hermitage**, associated with the great translator Vairocana, who is said to have built 100,000 stupas here during the eighth century.

Geshitra

Continuing south from Pawang, after 3 km, a branch road on the northwest leads over a high pass to **Geshitra**, another of the ancient Gyarong kingdoms, 44 km distant. In Lower Geshitra there is the Gelukpa monastery of **Yangra Gon** and the Bon monastery of **Chadolo Gon**. Middle Geshitra has a large Bon monastery named **Taksum Gonpa** (at Cherba township) and a ruined Jangter monastery of the Nyingma school. In Upper Geshitra there is a Bon monastery named **Halo Gonpa**. Two trails lead from here to **Maha Kyilung Gon,** the seat of Zenkar Rinpoche, incarnation of Do Khyentse Yeshe Dorje (see above, page 657). The first crosses high passes and a hot springs, while the second, the easier route, passes through the Nyingma monastery of **Odu Gonpa,** birthplace of the present Gyatrul Rinpoche who lives in the United States.

Rongtrak County

Rongmi Drango

Some 4 km south of the turn-off from Geshitra, the road descends to the small county town of **Rongmi Drango** (1,950 m), at the confluence of the Gyarong and Tsenlha rivers. Tall

18th-century fortifications dominate the landscape of this ancient Gyarong Kingdom. **Mount Lateng**, opposite on the south bank of the Tsenlha-chu, has three monasteries, situated one above the other on the hillside. The lowest of these is Gelukpa, the second is Nyingma, and the third is **Norbupuk Hermitage**, located at the site of Vairocana's eighth-century cave, where a *drubchu* stream attributed to that great master remains ice-cold even in summer. ➡ *For listings, see page 664.*

Rongmi Drango to Garthar and Chakzamka

A long bridge spans the Gyarong, which is particularly wide at Rongmi Drango. Crossing to the west bank, you can head south, following the river downstream to Chakzamka (112 km), upstream to Rabden (on the road just described), or southwest on a side road which follows the Tong-gu-chu tributary upstream and across the watershed to **Garthar** (74 km, see above, page 540). The last of these was formerly the main motor road to Garthar and Tawu prior to the construction of the paved road across **Gye La** from Dartsedo (see above, page 479). On its ascent the old road passes through **Tong-gu** township, where there is a fine old temple with a Chinese-style roof.

On the main Chakzamka road from Rongmi Drango, you will pass through **Sokpa** (5 km), where there is a small Bon monastery named **Taktse Gon**, **Gudzong** (20 km), and two small villages (at road markers 85 and 28), which once functioned as labour camps during the Cultural Revolution. The low-lying county of Chakzamka (1,829 m) has already been described (see above, page 484).

Rongmi Drango to Tsenlha

Alternatively, if you cross to the east bank of the Gyarong, where the county town is located, you can follow the Tsenlha-chu upstream to reach the capital of Tsenlha county after 58 km.

Tsenlha County བཙན་ལྷ་ ➡ *Population: 77,000. Area: 5,074 sq km.* 小金县

Tsenlha county occupies the valley of the Gyarong river's main tributary, the Tsenlha-chu (Ch Xiaojin), which nowadays lies within Ngawa prefecture. The population here is mixed Tibetan and Qiang, and both the Bon and Gelukpa traditions have co-existed since the 18th century. The county capital is located at **Drongdal Mezhing**, 58 km northeast of Rongtrak, 143 km south of Barkham, and 146 km west of the Wolong Panda Reserve.

Dronang and Tselung ➡ *Colour map 4, grid A5*

Taking the newly paved road from Rongmi Drango to Tsenlha (Ch Xiaojin), you pass through villages that were devastated by recent flooding, before crossing the Tsenlha-chu, and following this river upstream on its south bank. After 8 km, you will reach **Dronang**, where another motorable bridge spans the river, and there are two

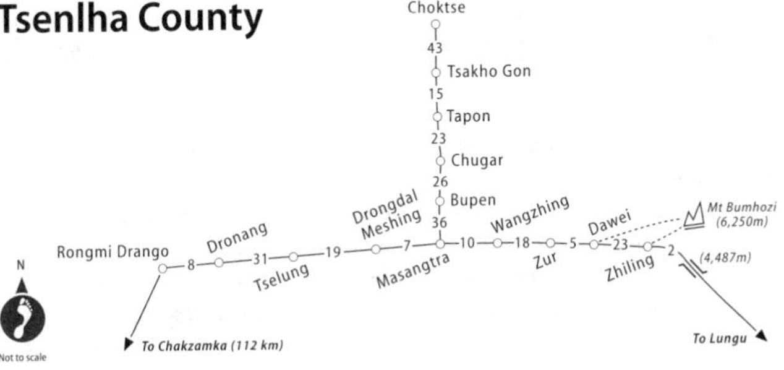

 small monasteries, **Langchen Gonpa** of the Gelukpa school and a small Jangter monastery of the Nyingma school, as well as a hot spring. The Tsenlha valley is renowned for its apples, pears, walnuts and red chilli peppers. Continuing on to **Tselung** (31 km), where the road crosses the prefectural border, you will reach the county capital after a further 19 km.

Drongdal Mezhing Town → *Colour map 4, grid A5*

Drongdal Mezhing (Ch Xiaojin) is a picturesque town, located on the steep slopes of the Tsenlha valley, below its confluence with the Bupen-chu. Even the government buildings have been built in pagoda style and the local municipality has taken over the old Catholic Church. Traditionally one of the important kingdoms of Gyarong, with an impressive cliff-face temple, Tsenlha entered the mythology of Chinese 20th-century history as the place where the participants of the Long March met up with the Fourth Front Army on 21 June 1935. Nowadays the population has a considerable Han majority. Some 11 km south of Tsenlha a side road leads to **Huanniu**, one of the minor kingdoms of ancient Gyarong. ▸▸ *For listings, see page 664.*

Bupen-chu Valley

Heading east from Drongdal Mezhing, after 7 km, the road crosses the Menda Bridge (Ch Menda Qiao) at **Masangtra**, where the two tributaries of the Tsenlha-chu converge: the Bupen-chu flowing from the north and the Wangzhing-chu flowing from the east. A dirt side road follows the Bupen-chu upstream and across the watershed to **Choktse** and thence to **Barkham** (see above, page 658). On this road you will pass **Bupen** (36 km), **Chugar** (26 km), **Tapon** (23 km) and **Tsakho Gon**, the seat of Tsongkhapa's great student Tsakho Ngawang Drakpa (15 km). However, this branch road appears to get much less traffic than the main route through the Wangzhing-chu A signpost at Menda Bridge indicates that it is 63 km from Rongtrak and 134 km from Barkham.

Wangzhing-chu Valley

Following the Wangzhing-chu tributary upstream, the road passes through **Wangzhing** township after 10 km and **Zhokdi** after 5 km. Here there is a prominent pagoda and the **Warihe Admanwa Watchtower** beside the road. A turn-off leads north from here for 12 km to Kyo-me (locally pronounced Jo-me, Ch Jiesi). Continuing on the main road, you pass **Zur** after 13 km and, after a further 3 km, a branch road that heads south for 104 km to Baoxing en route for Ya'an. **Dawei**, one of the old Gyarong kingdoms, lies 3 km further up the main valley, and there is a trekking route from Dawei through **Shuangqiao Gully** that gives access to **Mount Bumozhi** (Ch Siguniang, 6,250 m). The lateral valleys here are extremely mountainous, with raging rivers flowing through steep-sided gorges. Only a few still contain patches of original forest. Many of the villages, often with small Gelukpa or Bonpo temples, are on the flatter slopes, high above the road and are only visible on account of the numerous tall watchtowers found beside nearly every settlement. The village houses of the mixed Tibetan and Qiang population who inhabit this region are characteristically made of stone, their small windows decorated with swastikas, and their roofs surmounted with stacks of sacred quartz from Mount Gyelmo Murdo (see above, page 660).

Mount Bumozhi → *For listings, see page 664.*

From Dawei, the road climbs more sharply, winding its way towards **Balang Shan** pass (4,458 m). On the ascent, after 23 km, you pass through the tourist village of **Zhilung** (Ch Rilong), which is the main trailhead for visitors to the **Mount Bumozhi** (Ch Siguniang) National Park. The trail leaves the road at the Siguniang Mountain Hotel, and cuts through the central **Changping Gully** to the snow range. Another trekking trail leads from Zhilung through the parallel **Haizi Gully** to the **Guozhuang Flats**, from where high altitude lakes and the four "girl-like" peaks can be observed in close proximity.

Balang Shan

The main road eventually reaches the pass, 25 km above Zhilung. Balang Shan is often shrouded in mist, obscuring the view of the snow peaks of Mount Bumozhi to the north, and it is not difficult to visualize the demoralized armies of Qianlong retreating across Balang Shan watershed in disarray. But when the mists do clear, there are excellent viewing platforms for the panorama of snow peaks.

After crossing the pass, the road enters **Lungu** (Ch Wenchuan) county, reaching Shawan in the **Wolong Panda Reserve** (see below, page 699) after 59 km.

Tashiling County བཀྲ་ཤིས་གླིང

→ *Population: 44,000. Area: 4,569 sq km. Colour map 4, grid A6.* 理县

The county of **Tashiling** occupies the valley of the Troksung-chu, a tributary of the Minjiang, which rises south of the Trakar Shankou (Partridge Pass) watershed below Chiro in Barkham county (see above, page 658). Four of the ancient Gyarong kingdoms are located in this valley. The county capital is located at **Li Dzong**, 186 km southeast of Barkham (via Chiro) and 56 km southwest of Lungu (Wenchuan).

Trosung-chu Valley

Getting there From the intersection at **Chiro**, 65 km east of Barkham, the paved Highway 213 heads north for Lhagyeling, Ngawa and the grasslands of Mewa within the Ger-chu valley (a tributary of the Yellow River); and south across the Gyarong-Minjiang watershed to Chengdu (326 km). On the southbound section, there is a plan to bore a tunnel through the mountains that will, on its completion, considerably reduce the driving distance between Chengdu and Barkham. Until then traffic has to cross **Trakar Shankou pass** (4,110 m), 21 km south of Chiro. After the watershed, the highway enters the long valley of the Trosung-chu, a major tributary of the Minjiang, passing **Hrenchopa** (15 km), **Teu Rampa** (18 km), and **Nyaglo** (9 km), where the attractive Nyaglo Lungpa valley extends to the northeast. Then, after a further 23 km, it reaches **Hrapa**, the site of the ancient Zida Kingdom of Gyarong, and **Phudu** (27 km).

Li Dzong At this point the highway changes direction, as it climbs northeast for 15 km to reach to **Li Dzong**, the county capital. The countryside around Li Dzong is famous for its spectacularly variegated autumn leaves. The village stone houses are typical of the Tibeto-Qiang culture. The main monastery is **Tashiling** of the Gelukpa school. Across the south bank of the Trosung-chu from Li Dzong are the remnants of the ancient Gyarong Kingdom of **Tsakhok** (Ch Zagunao).

Essentials In town, there are simple guesthouse and restaurant facilities. Public buses run daily to and from Chengdu and Wenchuan.

After Li Dzong, the highway leads 23 km northeast to **Zhutreng** (Ch Xuecheng), where the Gyarong kingdoms of **Gyelkha** and **Wasi** were. A side road branches northwest from here for 27 km to Shuko.

Then, after descending through **Tonghua** (9 km), **Lungchin** (9 km), Highway 213 finally converges, after 15 km, with the main road from Zungchu (Ch Songpan) at Wenchuan (see below, page 698), where the Trosung-chu flows into the Minjiang.

Sleeping

Barkham *p658, map p659*
D **Barkham Hotel (Maerkang Binguan)**, T0837-2822726. Upmarket, has best rooms in town, attached bath, 24-hr hot water, with superior doubles ¥120, suites ¥380, economy doubles ¥80-120, and triples ¥90.
E **Linye Hotel (Linye Binguan)**, T0837-2822725. Smaller, has doubles ¥100-120 and suites ¥180.
Maerkang Hotel (Maerkang Fandian), T0837-2823001. Smaller, has superior doubles ¥80, economy doubles ¥30-45, and triples ¥40-60.

Rongmi Drango *p660*
E **Government Guesthouse**, T0836-3523612. Has restaurant facilities and a noisy nightclub, doubles at ¥50, singles at ¥80, and economy singles without attached bath at ¥60.

Drongdal Mezhing *p662*
E **Telecom Hotel**, T0837-2782888, F0837-2782250. Best in town, has standard twin rooms with attached bath at ¥100.
E **Xiaojin Government Zhaodaisuo**, 3 Zhengfu Jie. Double rooms ¥25 per bed.

Zhilung *p662*
There are a few tourist hotels in the rapidly developing complex at Zhilung.
D **Jinkun Hotel**, T0837-2791088. Deluxe twin rooms ¥198, standard twin rooms ¥120.

Eating

Barkham *p658, map p659*
The city has many Sichuan-style restaurants. **Hotpot Restaurant**, located on a lane behind the Maerkang Hotel, opposite the Highland Cinema. The best outside the Barkham Hotel, palatial 2-storey restaurant.

Drongdal Mezhing *p662*
The restaurants here are not particularly good – a few simple Sichuan eateries can be found near the main roundabout in town.

Shopping

Barkham *p658, map p659*
The city has several industries: handicrafts, Tibetan medicines, matches and wooden furniture. Look out for the **Minority Handicrafts Shop** (Ch Minzu Yongpin Shangdian), for traditional products. **Xinhua Bookstore**, for interesting books on the region.

Entertainment

Barkham *p658, map p659*
A cinema and sports stadium provide local entertainment, along with the usual turgid nightlife.

Transport

Barkham *p658, map p659*
Bus
Public buses run daily from the main bus station to **Chengdu** (0540, 0600, ¥60), **Sertal** (0600, ¥56), **Ngawa** (0540, ¥34.50), **Tu-je Chenpo** (0800, ¥12.50) and **Rabden** (0830, ¥13). Minibus services also run to **Tsenlha**, **Lungu** and **Dzoge**.

Rongmi Drango *p660*
Bus
Buses run daily to and from **Dartsedo** and **Chengdu** via Chakzamka.

Drongdal Mezhing *p662*
Bus
There are public buses running to and from **Chengdu** and **Rongtrak**.

Directory

Barkham *p658, map p659*
Internet (¥20 per hr) are available at China Telecom. **Telephones** China Telecom, sell ICC cards for IDD and DDD calls, which can be made from certain public phone booths or from the Barkham Hotel. China Post, have an EMS service

For an explanation of the sleeping and eating price codes used in this guide, see inside the front cover. Other relevant information is found in Essentials pages 44-46.

Labrang to Chengdu: the Upper Minjiang and Jialing Valleys

The paved Highway 213 from Lanzhou to Chengdu passes through some of Amdo's richest grasslands, giving access to magnificent nature parks, interspersed with areas of high Chinese population density. The basins of the Yellow River, the Jialing, and the Minjiang are crossed and re-crossed by the network of roads, which cover this most easterly region of the Tibetan plateau. Fourteen counties are visited, the first seven of them currently in the Ganlho Tibetan Autonomous Prefecture of Gansu, and the others in the Ngawa Tibetan Autonomous Prefecture of Sichuan. ***Recommended itineraries: 11 (also 6, 8, 9). See page 20.*** » *For Sleeping, Eating and other listings, see pages 700-706*

Binglingsi

Leaving the gateway city of Lanzhou, you can drive west through **Yongjing** county, where the major attraction is the **Binglingsi Cave** complex. Here there are 183 Buddhist grottoes containing 694 statues and many terracotta sculptures and frescoes. The oldest date from the proto-Tibetan Western Qin Dynasty (385-431), and the greatest period of development occurred during the Tang Dynasty. The largest image is a 27-m seated Maitreya. During the Yuan and Ming dynasties, the site was strongly influenced by the aesthetics of Tibetan Buddhism, and there is an extant temple dating from this period.

Getting there The caves are situated in a 60-m high ravine beside the **Liujiaxia** reservoir on the Yellow River, and are accessible by boat. An average return trip from Lanzhou to Binglingsi takes 12 hours, of which half the time is spent in the boat. Boats depart from the reservoir, 30 minutes' walk above Yongjing county town. A round trip will cost around ¥60 per person or ¥400 for a speed boat. Package tours arranged in Lanzhou can cost ¥250-300 per person (group size three or four), and entrance charges to certain groups of caves are extra (as much as ¥300 for caves that are generally kept locked)! It is easy to link up with other Chinese or foreign tour groups at the lake, but the local bus from Lanzhou only goes twice a day. Alternatively, stay overnight at Lidian Hotel in Yongjing (¥80 per double with attached bathroom), or the Huanghe Hotel (¥60 per room), and continue by bus from Liujaxia to Linxia the next day (4 hours 30 minutes)

Linxia → *Colour map 5, grid B5. For listings, see pages 700-706.*

If you decide to drive directly from Lanzhou to Linxia (approximately four hours), you will take Highway 213 which leads through a recently constructed 1½-km tunnel, providing easy access to Linxia, and avoiding the former route which entailed crossing the reservoir by ferry boat. The direct route links up with the older road north of Linxia, after passing through the fertile loess-covered hills of **Dongxiang** county. The drive is interesting, climbing through high terraces of lilybulbs and small villages, each with its distinctive mosque.

Linxia (Tib Kachu Khar), located in the lower valley of the Sang-chu (Ch Daxia), is an extensive county town renowned for its hundreds of mosques and as a trading centre throughout the centuries. It is currently accorded priority development as a Special Economic Zone. The main attraction here is the Ma Bufeng Memorial Garden (Gong Yuan). Brick carving among the Hui community has a long history here, and the houses are well decorated with flowers. The population pressure is obvious – the markets and bus stations are crowded, and it is hard to keep up with the pace of construction.

Linxia to Dowi

At **Kachu** (Ch Hanjiaji), 20 km southwest of Linxia on Highway 213, a side road heads northwest over **Dargye La** pass for 80 km to **Dowi** (see above, page 597). The main highway, however, continues southwest from Kachu, following the Sang-chu upstream to Sangchu county, into the mountains of Central Amdo.

Sangchu County བསང་ཆུ

→ *Population: 70,800. Area: 8,562 sq km. Colour map 5, grid B5.* 夏河县

Sangchu county, as its name suggests, occupies the grasslands around the upper reaches of the Sang-chu (Ch Daxia) river. The county capital is located at **Labrang** (Ch Xiahe), 280 km from Lanzhou, and it is easily accessible from Lanzhou via Linxia on Highway 213. The Tibetan population of the county is nowadays estimated at 45% and there are six Tibetan monasteries along with 29 lesser shrines, the most important being **Labrang Tashikyil**, the largest monastery in Amdo, which dwarfs all the others, and is located to the west of the town.

The winter here is severe, with temperatures falling to -20°, but in the short spring season the hillsides bloom, providing excellent hill walks or horse riding, and summer is very pleasant despite the rain. Autumn is cool and clear, and in this season the minor dirt roads of Central Amdo are more comfortable for travelling.

Chorten Karpo

Driving southwest from Linxia, at Km marker 201 an ornamental gateway bridges the highway, indicating that you are leaving the Muslim for the Tibetan area. Then, 6 km further on, a large stupa comes into view, maintained by a small adjacent monastery, which has 30 monks. This is considered by some to be the restored **Chorten Karpo**, commemorating the site where an original white stupa and stele in two languages were erected in 823 to mark the official frontier between Tibet and China, as determined by a peace treaty approved by the Tibetan monarch Relpachen.

Upper Sang-chu Valley

At **Wandotang**, 71 km from Linxia, the road to Labrang leaves the highway, heading due west through the upper reaches of the Sang-chu, while the highway itself continues south to **Tso** (see below, page 675). Taking the branch road, you will reach Labrang (Ch Xiahe) after 36 km, on a new route that avoids the former crossing of **Da-me La** pass (3,698 m). In this steep gorge, there are a few houses, with small Gelukpa monasteries (such as Tsaktsak Gonpa and Kirti Gonlag), interspersed among the hamlets. Among them the most noteworthy is **Terlung Yiga Chodzinling**, founded on the site of a former Drigung Kagyu temple in 1760, which long sought to distance itself from Labrang, its dominant neighbour.

Labrang → *Altitude: 2,920 m*

The county town of Labrang (Ch Xiahe) sprawls along the banks of the Sang-chu, for over 2 km, and is predominantly Hui Muslim at the east end and Tibetan at the west end. In all, the town is well developed for tourism with several hotels, guesthouses, restaurants and souvenir stalls.

» *For listings, see pages 700-706.*

Orientation Entering from the east, you first pass a turn-off on the right that leads southwest to Repkong across the present-day Gansu-Qinghai border. There is a petrol station near this intersection, and the distances given here are 221 km to Lanzhou, 28 km to Kangya (locally pronounced Ganja), and 5 km to Labrang. Continuing into town you will find the bus station, the Public Security Bureau, the County Government Buildings, the Daxia Hotel and the Post Hotel on the right, with China Telecom on the left. Soon two roads diverge: **Gonpa Lam** (Ch Renmin Xijie) continuing due west for the entrance to Labrang Monastery and **Rigdra Lam** bypassing the monastery to the south en route for the Labrang Hotel and the Sangke grasslands. Continuing along **Gonpa Lam**, you will pass on the left the White Conch Hotel, the Gangkar Nechok Hotel & Restaurant, the Everest Restaurant, the Overseas Tibetan Hotel, Tibetan bookshops and the Tara Guesthouse, after which a lane runs down towards Rigdra Lam. Opposite on the right is the Serkhar Hotel, and on both sides of the street there are many shops selling Tibetan and Muslim curios and carpets. Continuing west on Gonpa Lam, you will pass the Tibetan Restaurant on the left and, after crossing a small bridge, the health clinic, the Snowland Restaurant, Labrang Monastery Guesthouse and the Mentsikhang. Now, on the right the walls of Labrang Monastery appear, the debating hall (Sokshing Chora), the School of Buddhist Studies (Nangten Lobdra) and the Main Gate (Zhung-go). From here, Gonpa Lam continues due west until reaching a large two-storey restaurant at the west end, beyond the precincts of the monastery. Here, it turns sharply to the left (south), past a Tibetan school, to cross the Sang-chu river and rejoin Rigdra Lam.

Rigdra Lam, heading south from the White Conch Hotel, crosses the Sang-chu and turns abruptly west, passing on the right the residential buildings of Alak Dema Sertri and the late Gontang Rinpoche, and the spectacular Gongtang Chorten, accessed via a motorable bridge (Gongtang zam). It then passes to the right the Labrang Metal Press, before rejoining Gonpa Lam south of another bridge, which spans the Sang-chu.

On the left (south) side of Rigdra Lam, there is a hilltop offering a panoramic view of the entire complex of buildings at Labrang. Continuing west from the junction, you will soon reach the turn-off on the right for the Labrang Hotel, or else continue out of town, southwest into the Sangke grasslands. Development west of the monastery is restricted, leaving the splendid Labrang Hotel attractively isolated in the midst of fields and hamlets. Cycle rickshaws and taxis operate along the tarmac road, and on the 40-minute walk to the hotel, you can detour north along a muddy track to visit the Nyingma Gonpa and Labrang nunnery.

Labrang Town (Xiahe)

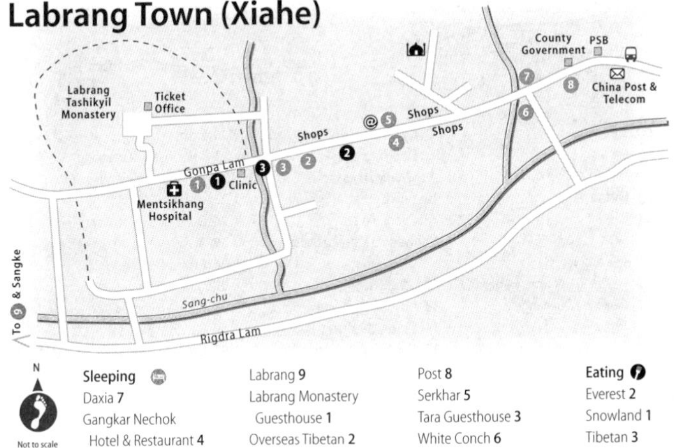

Sleeping			Eating
Daxia 7	Labrang 9	Post 8	Everest 2
Gangkar Nechok Hotel & Restaurant 4	Labrang Monastery Guesthouse 1	Serkhar 5	Snowland 1
	Overseas Tibetan 2	Tara Guesthouse 3	Tibetan 3
		White Conch 6	

Labrang Tashikyil Monastery བླ་བྲང་བཀྲ་ཤིས་འཁྱིལ → *Altitude: 2,820 m*

ⓘ *Guided tours of the monastery (the only means of access) are available ¥25 per person (for foreigners) and ¥15 per person for Chinese nationals, from the ticket office (closed from noon until 1400), ¥5 per person for the printing press, and at ¥5 per person for the Gontang Chorten. The supervisor, Konchok Gyatso, was a close aide of the late Gontang Rinpoche. Internal photography is generally prohibited, except in the museum.*

History **Labrang Tashikyil** is one of six great Gelukpa monasteries in Tibet and, although 90 damaged temples have yet to be restored, it is amongst the handful anywhere in Tibet that survived the Cultural Revolution relatively intact. It was founded in 1709 by the First Jamyang Zhepa Ngawang Tsondru (1648-1721), who was revered as an emanation of Tsongkhapa's teacher Umapa Pawo Dorje. Within the Gelukpa hierarchy, the incarnations of Jamyang Zhepa are superseded only by the Dalai Panchen Lamas. During his studies in Lhasa, where he was a contemporary of Desi Sangye Gyatso, he received his title 'Jamyang Zhepa' (laughing Manjughosa), when a statue of Manjughosa (Jamyang) laughed at his prostrations. Returning to his homeland, he then founded the most powerful monastery in Amdo, under the patronage of Chahan Tendzin Ponjunang, a prince of the Qosot Mongolians.

Main buildings The great temples and colleges of Labrang Tashikyil were constructed by Jamyang Zhepa and his successors. He himself founded the **Tsokchen Dukhang Tosamling** (3) or assembly hall in 1709, the **Gyume Dratsang** (9) or lower tantric college in 1716, the **Sokshing Chora** (12) or college of dialectics, and the **Jokhang temple** (1), containing a much revered Jowo Rinpoche image (flanked by 108 others) in 1718.

His successor, the Second Jamyang Zhepa Konchok Jigme Wangpo (1728-1791) founded the **Dukhor Dratsang Evam Chogarling** (10) for the study of Kalacakra chronology and astrology in 1763. Then, in 1784 he instituted the medical college, **Menpa Dratsang Sorik Zhenpenling** (7), which has a fine image

Labrang Tashikyil Monastery

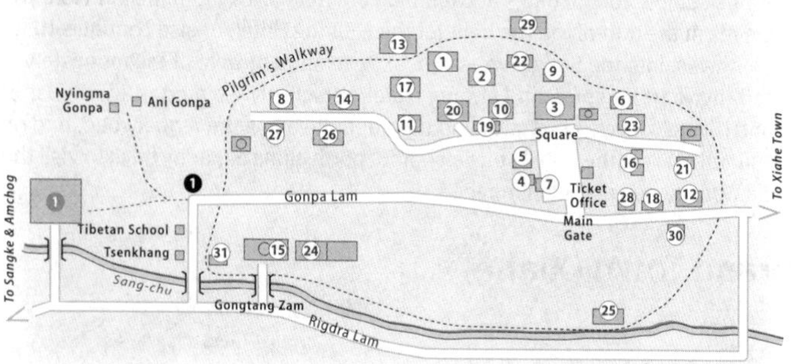

Sleeping
1 Labrang

Eating
1 Restaurant

1 Jokhang Temple
2 Serkhang Chenmo Tsegaling
3 Tsokchen Dukhang Tosamling
4 Jamyang Lhakhang
5 Dedenling Senge Ngaro
6 Je Rinpoche Lhakhang
7 Menpa Dratsang Sorik Zhenpenling
8 Gyuto Dratsang Sangchen Dorjeling
9 Gyume Dratsang
10 Dukhar Dratsang Evam Chogarling
11 Kyedor Dratsang Sangak Dargyeling
12 Sokshing Chora
13 Dukhar Lhakhang
14 Dolkar Lhakhang
15 Gongtang Chorten
16 2 Printing Presses
17 Deyang Podrang
18 Cham Jangsa
19 Labrang Museum
20 Dolma Lhakhang
21 Tuje Chenpo Lhakhang
22 Zhabten Lhakhang
23 Library
24 Gongtang tsang Nangchen
25 Alak Dewa Sertri Nangchen
26 Alak tsang Nangchen
27 Gongma tsang Nangchen
28 Nangten Lobdra (School of Buddhist Studies)
29 Gyume Tsamkhang
30 Mentsikhang
31 Metal Press

of Aksobhya Buddha and is currently the most active of Labrang's colleges. Towards the end of his life, in 1788, he founded the monastery's most renowned temple, the **Serkhang Chenmo** (2), also known as Tsegaling, which contains an eight-storey-high cross-legged image of Maitreya, murals of the three deities of longevity (Amitayus, White Tara and Vijaya) as well as side images of the Eight Bodhisattvas and Tsongkhapa. The gilded roof, which gives the temple its name, was donated in 1884 by Karpotsang Rinpoche of Chone Monastery.

The tradition was maintained by his successors, the Third Jamyang Zhepa Kyabchok Jigme Gyatsode (b 1792) and the Fourth Jamyang Zhepa Kalzang Thupten Wangchuk (b 1855). The latter founded the **Kyedor Dratsang Sangak Dargyeling** (11) for the practice of the Hevajra meditational cycle in 1879. It contains images of Hevajra flanked by Guhyasamaja, Kalacakra, Cakrasamvara and Vajrapani in the form of Chakdor Khorchen, as well as Maitreya. The **Gyuto Dratsang Sangchen Dorjeling** (8) or Upper Tantric College, containing a large bronze Maitreya as its centrepiece, was built by the Fifth Jamyang Zhepa Je Tenpei Gyeltsen Pelzangpo (b 1916), in 1928, as was the **Dolkar Lhakhang** (14) in 1940.

Other temples and buildings Other important temples at Labrang include **Jamyang Lhakhang** (4), which was founded in 1928 and has a large 7-m image of Manjughosa in gilded copper, flanked by Maitreya and White Manjushri; the **Dedenling** (5) temple, dedicated to Sukhavati buddhafield and containing an enormous 13-m image of Avalokiteshvara in the form of Simhanada, which was completed in 1809; **Je Rinpoche Lhakhang** (6), which was reconstructed in 1929 and contains images of Tsongkhapa and Kharsapani; **Dukhar Lhakhang** (13), dedicated to Sitatapatra, the still closed **Dolma Lhakhang** (20), which is dedicated to Tara, **Tujechenpo Lhakhang** (21), dedicated to Mahakarunika, **Zhabten Lhakhang** (22), and the **library** (23).

There are also two printing presses (16): one for woodblocks and the other for texts printed in movable type. The former contains the Collected Works of Tsongkhapa and those of his closest students. The residence of the Jamyang Zhepas called **Deyang Podrang** (17), the **Cham Jangsa** or religious dancing school (18), and the **Labrang Museum and Butter-Sculpture Collections** (19) are also worth a visit. The entire complex can be circumambulated by pilgrims in a 3-km circuit.

Recent renovations at Labrang At its high point Labrang Tashikyil Monastery housed 4,000 monks, and when the Fifth Jamyang Zhepa passed away in 1947 there were 300 *geshes*, 3,000 monks and 50-100 incarnate lamas. The present incumbent, the Sixth Jamyang Zhepa, who lives in Lanzhou, presides over a much depleted monastery where there are barely more than 1,000 monks, of whom half are engaged in the study of dialectics and the rest in tantric meditation practice. In April 1985 the **Assembly Hall** (Dukhang) was destroyed by fire, and the renovated hall (3), which can now be visited, was consecrated only in 1990. It contains a central image of Maitreya, with images of Tsongkhapa, the Eight Bodhisattvas, and Shakyamuni with his two foremost students to the left, and the five stupa reliquaries of the previous Jamyang Zhepa incarnations to the right, along with their respective images. The hall itself has 140 pillars and 1,000 small buddha images.

The restored **Gongtang Chorten** (15) is one of the most recent buildings in the complex. Funded by a Chinese American devotee and consecrated in 1992 by the late Gongtang Rinpoche, its **ground floor** contains resplendent images of Sarvavid Vairocana, Manjughosa, Maitreya and an exquisite reclining white jade Buddha from Burma. There are 21,000 volumes of texts incorporated within the structure. On the **second floor** there is an image of Amitabha, along with the 1,000 buddhas of the aeon. The gallery offers a wonderful view of the murals downstairs, which depict the diversity of the Buddhist lineages in Tibet. On the **uppermost level** there is an inscription bearing the name of the sponsor.

School of Buddhist Studies Outside the main gate of the monastery, there is an important **School of Buddhist Studies** (Nangten Lobdra), where some of the great contemporary teachers of Labrang, such as Geshe Gendun Gyatso and Geshe Jamyang Gyatso continue to teach.

Festivals at Labrang The major festivals of the Buddhist calendar are observed at Labrang. During the Great Prayer Festival, reminiscent of the identical ceremonies held at Lhasa on the 13th day of the first lunar month, a large (30 by 20 m) appliqué tangka is displayed on the **Tangka Wall** on the south bank of the Sang-chu River, opposite the monastery. This is followed on the 14th by religious masked dances, on the 15th or full moon day by *torma* (butter sculpture) offerings, and on the 16th by the procession of a Maitreya image around the monastery (see table page 704). In 2005 these ceremonies are scheduled for 21-24 Feb.

Sangke Grasslands

Getting there The Sangke grasslands are some 31 km southwest of the Labrang Hotel, just before the watershed pass at the head of the Sang-chu valley, on a road that is now being paved. The distance from the grasslands to Amchog Gonpa is 32 km.

The open **Sangke** grasslands, where large horse racing festivals are held, are located 14 km southwest of Labrang. The main festival falls in the seventh month of the lunar calendar and is a highly organized display of sports in which teams of Tibetans from settlements far and near participate, each wearing their distinctive dress. A rough road leads over to **Amchog Gonpa** from Sangke's huge open grassy bowl and a large crowd attends, swelled by Chinese and western photographers. White tents mushroom on the hills and a great deal of beer is drunk. In recent years a number of formal tented camps have been built for the use of Chinese tourists, who can ride horses in a controlled environment. The Labrang Hotel also has a traditional tented camp here on the grasslands, enabling tourists to sample the nomadic life.

Ngakpa Dratsang

If you head west from Labrang Monastery to **Sakar** village, passing the pathway which circumambulates the monastery and the turn-off for the Labrang Hotel, you will soon reach **Ngakpa Dratsang**.

This hermitage and college is the seat of the late Lama Gonpo Tseten, who passed many years teaching in India and the United States. It is maintained by Nyingmapa *mantrins* following the *Longchen Nyingtik* tradition of Rigdzin Jigme Lingpa (see above, page 643). Above Sakar, at the **Ritrogong** hermitage, there are meditation caves associated with Shar Kalden Gyatso, the founder of Rongpo Gyakhar in Repkong, and with the First Jamyang Zhepa, the founder of Labrang.

Trekking

There is a five-day trek from Sakar to **Rongpo Gyakhar** in Repkong (see above, page 606). The trail crosses two passes that lead into the grassland pastures of the Serchen-chu valley, before cutting south of Mount Amnye Nyemri and crossing **Chubzang La** (4,010 m) to enter the Gu-chu valley above Gyelwo township.

Kangya Drakar Gonpa

Getting there Buses leave Labrang daily for the 115-km (six hours) journey to **Rongpo Gyakhar** in Repkong although during heavy summer rain the muddy track near the pass can be hard to traverse. From the intersection, 5 km east of town, a winding road gradually climbs for 7 km to cross the **Naring La** watershed (3,360 m) leading into the **Tsilung** valley. There are several small villages on both sides of the pass, and rich grazing pastures, with a panoramic view of the distant snow range of Mount Amnye Nyemri.

Kangya The township of **Kangya** (locally pronounced Kanja) lies 19 km beyond the pass in a nomadic area, and on the approach you can observe a complex of caves, visible on the limestone cliff face, as far as 17 km northeast. From here the main road continues across the provincial border into present-day Qinghai, but there is a turn-off leading 9 km northeast through **Karnang** (said to be an ancient Minyak village) as far as **Kangya Drakar Gonpa**.

This monastery, nestling below the cliff, is supervised by the female incarnation Gongri Khandroma, and is affiliated to Labrang, where the present incumbent resides in town. The original foundations are attributed to Shar Kalden Gyatso of Rongpo Gonchen (see above, page 607). Around 30 minutes' walk above the monastery, you will reach **Nekhang**, the principal cavern where there are subterranean pools dedicated to Vajravarahi. The vast fractured pothole at Nekhang is said to have legendary underground connections to caves in the Repkong and Sogwo areas (see above, page 593).

Trekking There are three distinct circuits of the 4,636-m mountain peak at Kangya. The longest, passing several lakes starts from the monastery but requires camping equipment for one night at least. There is a small Bon temple on the opposite mountainside.

From Kangya, the road crosses two higher passes, the second (3,600 m) after 20 km, with a cairn of mani stones marking the current Gansu-Qinghai provincial frontier. In these upper grasslands marmots can be seen in great numbers. A recently paved road then descends to **Gartse, Yarma Tashikyil** and **Rongpo Gyakhar** (see above, page 606).

Amchog Gonpa

Getting there Amchog can be reached directly from Labrang by driving 59 km southeast through the **Sangke grasslands** on a rough seasonal road, and across the watershed pass (3,570 m) which lies at the head of the Sang-chu valley. Four small Tibetan villages are passed en route, but the grasslands here are largely the preserve of nomads, marmots and wild hares. A longer but better road (Highway 213) leads 107 km from Labrang via Wangdotang, **Pongartang** village, and across a pass to the prefectural capital of **Tso** or Ganlho Dzong (Ch Hezuoshen), from where it traverses a 3,048-m pass to reach Amchog.

The Gelukpa monastery of **Amchog Demotang Ganden Chokhorling** (2,835 m) is an important branch of Labrang, located in the grasslands further southeast. The monastery was founded in 1760 by the Second Jamyang Zhepa, and the recently reconstructed complex has two temples, a large stone wall where tangkas are ceremonially displayed and a long mani wall. The **Dukhang** (Assembly Hall) contains images of Guhyasamaja, Tsongkhapa and Cakrasamvara and, within the **inner sanctum**, an image of Maitreya flanked by Alak Yongdzin of Amchog, the First and Fourth Jamyang Zhepas, and the reliquary of Alak Yongdzin. The murals of the main hall depict (L-R): Vaishravana, Tsegyal, six-armed Mahakala, Guhyasamaja, Vajrabhairava, Cakrasamvara, Kalacakra, Sitatapatra, Nechung Chokyong, Shridevi, four-armed Mahakala and Dharmaraja. Amchog is an active monastery, with much local support among the nomads and villagers of the grasslands, and currently houses 300 monks. It should not be confused with **Amchok Tsenyi Gonpa** (see above, page 653). This Amchog means "ear", while the other, situated in the grasslands below Ngawa, means "supreme syllable A".

Roads from Amchog

Three roads lead from Amchog: north to **Labrang** (59 km), south to **Luchu** (43 km), and northeast to **Tso** (34 km). Taking the last of these you will pass through **Bora Gonpa** after 13 km, to the right (east) of the highway. Yet another branch of Labrang, Bora was founded in 1757. After a further 6 km a side road leaves the highway at **Dzatsa**, heading northwest for the **Sangke grasslands**, while the main road crosses a pass (3,240 m) and cuts through the hills to the prefectural capital, 15 km distant.

Tso → *Altitude: 2,895 m. Colour map 5, grid B5.*

Tso (Ch Hezuoshen) is a large city of recent development, 36 km south of **Wandotang** (the turn-off for Labrang) on Highway 213, and 34 km northeast of Amchog. Nowadays it functions as the prefectural capital of Southern Gansu, for which reason it is also called Ganlho Dzong. » *For listings, see pages 700-706.*

Orientation

Entering the city from the north (ie Lanzhou or Labrang side), you will pass the monastery of **Tsogon Geden Choling** and the Geology and Mining Bureau on the right. A turn-off next to the private bus station and petrol station then leads west, enabling through traffic to avoid the city en route for Luchu (southwest) or Lintan (southeast). Along this ring road (Highway 213), you will pass the People's Hospital, the Hezhuo Mosque and the Tibetan clinic.

If, instead, you continue straight ahead into town, you will enter the busy thoroughfare of **Tengzhi Street**, where there are shops, banks, government buildings, and tax offices, as well as restaurants and hotels. On the left you will pass the Tibetan Hospital (Mentsikhang), the Bayi Hotel, the Ganlho market, the Jinling Dajiudian Hotel, the Minzu and the Gansu Hotels, while the main bus station is on the right. After the first roundabout, you will pass the Xinhua bookstore, an insurance company and a pharmacy on the left, with the cinema and police station on the right. The next two blocks are lined by an avenue of trees which divides the road from its cycle lanes. Here, on the left are the post office, and the local government buildings. Then, after the Yak Roundabout, you will pass the Communist Party offices, Tibetan middle and primary schools, and the Muslim Wengsan restaurant on the left, with the Ganlho Hotel and assorted schools on the right. Crossing a bridge, the road forks at the south end of town, heading southeast for Lintan (78 km), or southwest for Luchu (81 km).

Tsogon Geden Choling

ⓘ *The ticket office is located outside the main gate, admission: ¥2.*

The local monastery, **Tsogon Geden Choling** on the outskirts of town has a nine-storey tower replica of Sekhar Gutok (see above, page 220), which dominates the skyline. The original foundation of this monastery is dated 1673 and an inspirational self-originated image of Milarepa, which had been offered by Shar Kalden Gyatso of Repkong to the local lama Gyeltsen Senge (the 53rd Ganden Tripa) was installed in 1678. The complex was first renovated as a nine-storey building in 1888 by Lobzang Dargye, himself revered an incarnation of Milarepa, and it survived until its destruction during the Cultural Revolution (1967). The newly constructed tower, funded by local resources as well as by donations from Mongolia and Tibetan exiles in India, was built between 1988 and 1994. It ranks among the greatest modern temples of Tibet for its exquisite design and art. The perimeter wall is surmounted by 1,500 brick stupas and the building itself is surrounded by 130 large prayer wheels.

Inside, the well-carpeted **ground floor** contains images of the principal bodhisattvas, accomplished masters and ancient kings of Tibet. The central images are of Maitreya, Manjughosa and Vajrapani, flanked on the left by Machik Labdron, Padampa Sangye, Tangtong Gyelpo, Tsangnyon Heruka, Dacharuwa, Ralotsawa, Nyimadzin, the Three Deities of Longevity, White Tara, Bhaisajyaguru, Shakyamuni, Milarepa and Mahakarunika. To the right of the central images are: Tonmi Sambhota, Relpachen,

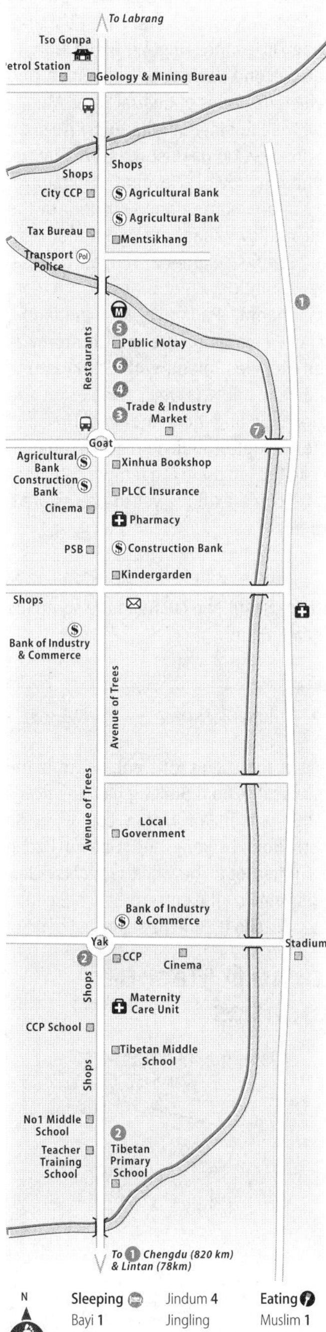

Trisong Detsen, Tride Tsukten, Nyatri Tsenpo, Bhrikuti, Wencheng, Songtsen Gampo, Rudracakra, Simhanada, Jowo Shakyamuni, Aksobhya, Prajnaparamita, Green Tara and Sitatapatra.

On the **second storey**, there are images depicting the historic figures associated with the New Translation Schools of the Kadampa, Sakyapa and Gelukpa orders. The central images depict Atisha and Tsongkhapa, flanked by their foremost respective students, along with Remdawa, Lhodrak Namka Gyeltsen, Umpapa Pawo Dorje, Sherab Senge, Drakpa Gyeltsen, the First, Fifth and Fourteenth Dalai Lamas, the Fourth, Ninth and Tenth Panchen Lamas, the eight foremost students of Tsongkhapa, Potowa, Chengawa Tsultrim Bar, Puchungwa, Tsang Rabsel, Yo Gejung, Mar Shakyamuni, Lachen Gongpa Rabsel, Shakyashri, the Five Founders of Sakya and the five major throneholders of Ganden including Gyeltsen Senge, Dzopa Aten Tenpa Gyeltsen, Sera Jetsun Chogyen, the First Rongpo Shar Kalden Gyatso and the Seventh Rongpo Shar, Kirti Tenpa Rabgye, Kirti Lobzang Trinle, the First and Sixth Jamyang Zhepas, the Sixth Gungtang, the successive emanations of Drubchen Choying Dorje, Sherab Chokden and other lamas affiliated to Tsogon Monastery.

The images from the third to eighth stories upwards are all fashioned from wood, and each storey also contains 1,000 small images of Milarepa. Among them, the **third storey** is dedicated to the lineage masters of the Nyingmapa school, with Padmasabhava, Shantaraksita and King Trisong Detsen in the centre, flanked by Mandarava, Yeshe Tsogyel, the Eight Manifestations of Padmasambhava, Vairotsana, Garab Dorje, Vimalamitra, Terdak Lingpa, the Fourth Rigzin Pema Trinle, Jikme Lingpa, Longchen Rabjampa, Minling Terchen, Hayagriva, Vajrakila and other meditational deities, along with Zangdok Pelri. The **fourth storey** is dedicated to the assembled deities of the lower tantras: the Lords of the Three Enlightened Families, flanked by Vairocana, Amitabha and Amoghapasha; as well as to the ancient Indian masters

 Asanga, Vasubandhu, Dignaga and Dharmakirti. The **fifth storey** is dedicated to the lineage holders of the Kagyupa school, and above all to Marpa, Milarepa and Gampopa, each flanked by their foremost students, along with the First Karmapa, Phakmodrupa, Tokden Darma Wangchuk, Zhang Drogonpo, Drigung Jikten Gonpo, Taklung Tangpa, Lingrepa, Tsangpa Gyare, the Second Karmapa, Gotsangpa and Dakpo Gomtsul, who all founded the great Kagyu monasteries of Central Tibet. Murals here and on the floor immediately above depict the life-story of Milarepa. The **sixth floor** is dedicated to the deities of the Ngok transmission of Unsurpassed Tantras, including Guhyasamaja, Cakrasamvara, Vajrabhairava, Hevajra, Nairatmya, Mahamaya, Caturvajrapitha, Jnaneshvara and Vajrapanjara; along with four of the eight bodhisattvas. The **seventh storey** is dedicated to Vajradhara and the ancient Indian lineage holders of the Unsurpassed Tantras, namely: Tilopa, Naropa, Indrabhuti, Saraha, Nagarjuna, Aryadeva, Shantideva, Candrakirti, Luipa, Ganthapada, Krisnacarin, Lalitavajra, Amoghabhadra, Padmavajra, Jalandaripa, Guhyaka, Maitripa, Dombipa, Kurmikapada and Vijayapada. The **eighth storey** is dedicated to Buddhas of the Five Enlightened Families, along with Shakyamuni, Kurukulla, Uchusmakrodha, Acala, Avalokiteshvara and Maitreya. Finally, at the centre of the **ninth storey**, there is a large tangka depicting the mandala of Hevajra.

Outside, to the right there is the Protector Temple, dedicated to Tseringma, Cimara and the Twelve Tenma Goddesses, while to the left there is a temple in honour of Jambhala. The other destroyed temples in the complex have yet to be restored. Nowadays, there are 200 monks in residence here.

Roads from Ganlho Dzong

Highway 213 connects with **Lanzhou** to the north (258 km) and **Luchu** to the south (81 km), while a lesser road cuts southeast for **Lintan** (78 km).

Luchu County ཀླུ་ཆུ → *Population: 30,700. Area: 4,253 sq km.* 碌曲县

The county of **Luchu** occupies the upper reaches of the Luchu (Ch Tao), which is the principal tributary of the Yellow River in Ganlho prefecture, from **Serlung** near the river's source (on the Qinghai frontier) through to the borders of **Lintan** county in its mid-reaches. The grassland roads leading south from Labrang and Ganlho Dzong converge at **Amchog**, 43 km north of Luchu town. Further south, beyond the Luchu valley, Highway 213 extends for 95 km as far as **Taktsang Lhamo** on the present Gansu-Sichuan border. Here, important roads diverge: southwest to **Machu** (71 km) near the first bend of the Yellow River, south to Dzoge (90 km) on the highway, and southeast across the watershed to **Tewo** (90 km). Formerly, there were eight monasteries within the county, of which the two most important have been reconstructed.

Luchu Dzong and around

The pleasant county town of **Luchu** lies 43 km south of the nomadic pastures of Amchog and in the sheltered Luchu valley (2,957 m). En route you will pass through **Nyimalung** village where there are interesting stone houses and the turn-off for the **Kotse** grassland, before crossing a 3,200-m pass. The 106-km drive from Labrang takes approximately three hours.

Formerly Luchu was a stronghold of the Bon tradition, and a major Bonpo monastery survived here until its final conversion by the Gelukpa in 1688, at which time it was renamed **Gegon Ganden Phuntsoling** by Lobzang Dondrub, the lord of neighbouring Cho-ne. The town's tranquil setting, 4 km off the highway, and the mild climate add to its attractions. The population is even now largely Tibetan. On Main Street you will find the Mentsikhang Hospital, the Luchu Hotel, the County Government Buildings, China Post & Telecom and the Bus Station. A T-junction leads south from Main Street to cross the Luchu, leading into the old quarter of town, and if you continue along Main Street, past the police station, you will find the road for Shitsang Gonpa.

Side roads from Luchu A side road from Luchu leads upstream from a junction just north of the town for 45 km through a rugged and wide range of hills to **Serlung** on the edge of the Sogwo region (see above, page 613). The exact provincial border is marked differently on maps published in Qinghai and Gansu provinces.

Yet another side road heads downstream, following the north bank of the Luchu to **Ala** and then via Mapusola to **Lintan** (185 km). The reconstructed Gelukpa monastery of **Shitsang Ganden Chokhorling** is located along this road, 13 km down-valley from Luchu. It is a branch of Labrang, founded in 1839 by the Third Dewatsang Jamyang Tubten Nyima. The new assembly hall contains fine murals and images of the First Jamyang Zhepa, Jowo Shakyamuni, Tsongkhapa, and the first seven Dewatsang incarnations. The inner sanctum is dominated by a 6-m wooden image of Maitreya. Currently the complex is maintained by the Eighth Dewatsang.

South from Luchu Heading south from Luchu, the paved highway leaves the Luchu valley and crosses the watershed (3,414 m) between the Luchu and Yellow River, eventually reaching the rugged mountain terrain of **Taktsang Lhamo** after 95 km. About 10 km out of town on this section of the road there are superb views of the **Dzichen** range to the southwest, which hides the Yellow River from view. Three further passes are crossed in close proximity, the highest (4,054 m) offering a vista of verdant and cragged terrain as the Dzichen range draws near. Then, at Lake **Drangto Tso**, 79 km south of Luchu (at marker 414), there is a dirt trail on the west (right) which leads into the range towards the source of the Luchu.

Taktsang Lhamo → *For listings, see pages 700-706.*

About 19 km further south (at marker 433), a spectacular mountain view heralds the valley of the **Druk-chu** (Ch Bailong), which stretches from the cliffs of Taksang Lhamo at its source through Tewo and Drukchu counties to converge with the Jialing River in **Guangyuan**, Sichuan. The highway veers left (east) for Dzoge only 4 km north of **Taktsang Lhamo**.

Continuing south into the hilly township of Taktsang Lhamo, two major monasteries can be visited. **Kirti Namgyel Dechenling** (locally called Gerda Gonpa) is the higher of the two, currently falling within Sichuan province, while neighbouring **Sertang Gonpa**, more formally known as **Ganden Shedrub Pekar Drolweiling**, is under the jurisdiction of Gansu. Although Taktsang Lhamo (Ch Langmusi) itself is the name traditionally given to the cave-shrine beside the higher monastery, nowadays it is applied to both monasteries and the township which they share.

Kirti Namgyel Dechenling

A tiger's den popularly associated with Padmasambhva, was visited by Kirti Tenpa Rabgye in the 15th century and frequented by generations of later meditation masters such as Tola Ngawang Palzang, who offered his hermitage to Kirti Tenpei Gyeltsen (1712-1771). The latter founded the monastery of Kirti Namgyel Dechenling in 1731, and it was gradually developed by his successive incarnations, The restored assembly hall of the present day houses some 700 monks, and it contains the teaching throne of the

Eleventh Kirti Rinpoche, who generally resides in India. The impressive inner sanctum has large images of Maitreya, Tsongkhapa and Manjughosa. The labrang residence of Kirti Rinpoche has also been carefully rebuilt and the architecture of the whole monastery is of a higher standard than most new Amdowa monasteries.

Sertang Gonpa

Sertang Gonpa, which currently has 300 monks, is situated slightly below Kirti Namgyel Dechenling to the southeast. The present complex of buildings, some of which survived the Cultural Revolution, was founded in 1748 by Gyeltsen Senge, the 53rd throne-holder of Ganden, who had been sent to propagate the Gelukpa teachings in his native Amdo by the Seventh Dalai Lama. The monastery was subsequently enlarged by the Fourth Sertri Lobzang Tendzin Senge (1877-1939), so that eventually four colleges developed for the study of dialectics, medicine, Kalacakra and tantra. The **Assembly Hall** (Dukhang) here contains gilded clay images of Shakyamuni and Tsongkhapa, each flanked by their foremost students, along with the 16 Elders, the six ornaments and two supreme masters of Ancient India, the Three Deities of Longevity, and the preferred meditational deities of the Gelukpa school. The **Trichen Lhakhang** to its left contains the teaching throne of Sertri Rinpoche, and there are other impressive buildings to the rear, including the **Protector Temple** (**Gonkhang**) and the residence of Alak Chetsang.

Roads from Takstang Lhamo

The dirt motor road from Taktsang Lhamo to **Machu** (71 km, see below) heads west from a turn-off opposite the post office. Alternatively, for **Tewo** and **Dzoge**, drive north for 4 km to rejoin the highway. After a further 8 km, the road forks, the highway running south for Dzoge and a paved branch road leading to Tewo in the upper Druk-chu valley.

Machu County མ་ཆུ → *Population: 40,100. Area: 10,249 sq km.* 玛曲县

Machu county is traditionally regarded as the southeast extremity of Golok, although nowadays it falls within Gansu province. Its hinterland contains almost all of the Yellow River's first bend as it makes its 'southerly' curve through Amdo. Much of the terrain is flat, marshy grassland, but a spine of mountains runs down to **Sogtsang** monastery, at the apex of the bend. The county capital, recently opened to outsiders, is located at **Dzoge Nyima**, 71 km west of Taktsang Lhamo, 22 km southeast of the Sogwo border, and 143 km northwest of Dzoge. Prior to 1958 there were eight monasteries in the county, all holding allegiance to Labrang. These were originally tented monasteries, and they subsequently remained small in scale since the nomadic population of the region were constantly moving from one pasture to the next. The riding horses raised by the nomads here are highly prized throughout Amdo.

Lake Drangto Tso

Some 23 km north of Taktsang Lhamo and 79 km south of Luchu, a dirt road leads west from Highway 213 into Machu county. About 3 km along this side road, at **Lake Drangto Tso** (Ch Gahe), there is a small bird sanctuary.

Takstang Lhamo to Machu

The main road into Machu heads directly west from the high watershed at Taktsang Lhamo on the Sichuan side of the current provincial border. It undulates through the rugged **Amnye Lhago** range, rising to 3,540 m before reaching the flat grasslands. After 29 km, a turn-off leaves the road, heading south on an equally rough and potholed surface for Dzoge. The main road continues through the grassland, passing **Mazhi** (Ch Maizhi) village and then crossing the border to re-enter **Gansu**. On the way into town, it passes Dashui Military Farm (21 km from town) and a gold mining complex.

Dzoge Nyima → *Altitude: 3,480 m*

The capital, **Dzoge Nyima,** is a fairly large town, located 5 km north of the Yellow River. Entering from the east, you will pass the Tibetan Hospital on the right, after which a turn-off on the left leads 5 km southwest to the bridge over the Yellow River. Continuing on **Main Street**, you will pass on the left the Government Guesthouse, the Primary School and tax office, while on the right are the Agricultural Bank, a number of small restaurants and shops, and the Gangjong Hotel. Then a turn-off on the right leads northwest towards the border of Sogwo county (22 km). Taking this road, you will pass on the left the People's Hospital, and on the right the Tashi Dronkhang Hotel (Ch Ji Xiong Fandian), and the Mirik Dronkhang Hotel, followed by the police station and the county government buildings. A gate spans the road marking the limits of town. Beyond it, on the left, a side road winds its way uphill to **Dzoge Nyima Monastery**, 2 km distant.

Returning to the intersection on Main Street, continue heading west and you will pass on the left the bus station, the Gangri Dronkhang Hotel, the open market, and another turning on the left, which leads down to the Yellow River. On the right, there are banks and government buildings. » *For listings, see pages 700-706.*

Dzoge Nyima Gonpa The monastery of **Dzoge Nyima**, which currently has 90 monks, is located on high ground above the town, offering a distant panoramic view of the first bend of the Yellow River. It is a branch of Labrang, founded by the Second Jamyang Zhepa Konchok Jikme Wangpo (1728-1791). The **Dukhang** (**Assembly Hall**), decorated in Repkong style, contains images of (left to right): Tsongkhapa, the Second Jamyang Zhepa, Avalokiteshvara, Maitreya and Vajrapani, along with a stone footprint of the Second Jamyang Zhepa, and the volumes of the *Kangyur* and the Collected Works of Jamyang Zhepa. The murals here depict (left to right): Six-armed Mahakala, Hayagriva, Cakrasamvara, Vajrabhairava, Bhaisajyaguru, Guhyasamaja, Kalacakra, Sarvavid Vairocana and Dharmaraja. Other temples located to the rear of the Assembly Hall include the **Tamdrin Lhakhang** on the right, dedicated to Hayagriva, and the **Gongtang Zimchung** on the left, which is the residence of the late Gongtang Rinpoche and contains a natural stone mani inscription.

West of the Yellow River

Crossing the Yellow River from Dzoge Nyima (5 km) two roads diverge at **Duku**: southwest to **Wawentsang** (Ch Awantsang, 54 km), from where a trail leads across the lower part of the Yellow River bend to Jigdril county in Golok (see above, page 640), and southeast via a PLA breeding station for Golok riding horses to cross the Yellow River north of **Chukama** (Ch Gihama), and enter **Ngawa** county (see above, page 650). A number of small Gelukpa monasteries have been reconstructed in these outlying parts, including **Mura Gon.**

Dzoge Nyima

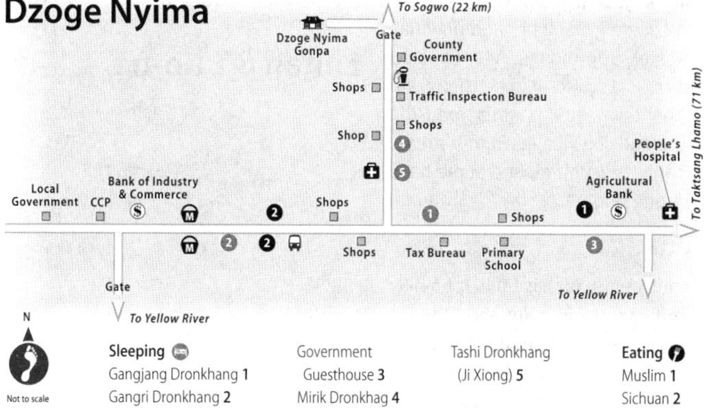

Sleeping
Gangjang Dronkhang **1**
Gangri Dronkhang **2**
Government Guesthouse **3**
Mirik Dronkhag **4**
Tashi Dronkhang (Ji Xiong) **5**

Eating
Muslim **1**
Sichuan **2**

Lintan County ལིན་ཐན

→ *Population: 146,400. Area: 1,399 sq km. Colour map 5, grid B5.* 临潭县

The fertile counties of **Lintan** and **Cho-ne** in the mid-reaches of the Luchu valley can be reached from Lanzhou (via Linfa on Highway 212 and Kangle), from Drukchu (via Minxian on Highway 212), from Tewo on a rough hill road, or from Lanzhou and Labrang via Tso on Highway 213. The Tibetans of this area claim descent from the disbanded Tibetan army of the Yarlung kings, which occupied the region in the eighth and ninth centuries. The county town of **Lintan**, set some kilometres back from the Luchu river, lies 29 km northwest of Cho-ne and 78 km southeast of Tso.

Tashigar Monastery

Head southeast from Tso (see above, page 672), through rugged grassland. After 12 km the road passes the monastery of **Tashigar** on the right (south). It is affiliated to Labrang and follows the tradition of Jamyang Zhepa, despite having been founded prior to Labrang, by Lama Tri Gompa, almost 300 years ago. There is a large complex of buildings here, among which the Kungarawa monastic residential building to the left and the Assembly Hall to the right are the most prominent. The **assembly hall** contains images of (left to right): Manjughosa, Guhyasamaja, Jowo Shakyamuni, the First to Sixth Jamyang Zhepa (encased in glass along with orange and white aspects of Manjughosa), Tara and Sarvavid Vairocana. An **inner sanctum** to the rear contains (left to right): the reliquaries of Lama Tri Gompa and another local lama, and images of Mahakarunika, Maitreya and Sitatapatra. The **murals** of the **Assembly Hall** depict (left to right): Tsegyal, Hayagriva, Sarvavid Vairocana, Vajrapani, Vajrabhairava, Guhyasamaja, Hevajra, Kalacakra, Cakrasamvara, Sitatapatra, Nechung, Shridevi, Mahakala and Dharmaraja. The volumes of the *Kangyur* are stacked along the right wall, and the central throne carries photographs of the present the Fourteenth Dalai Lama and the Sixth Jamyang Zhepa. Currently, there are 80 monks at Tashigar.

Tashigar to Lintan Dzong

A road sign at Tashigar indicates the following distances: Lintan (66 km), Tso (12 km), Labrang (60 km), and Linxia (117 km). Continuing southeast through the scrublands, the road traverses five small Tibetan villages before crossing two passes, the second of which (3,300 m) is 32 km from Tashigar. The descent leads after 9 km to an open plain and an intersection, where a branch road cuts south to **Mezho** village (15 km) and over the hills to Tewo county (see below, page 681). During the period of the Yarlung Empire, a major battle was waged here between the Tibetan and Chinese armies. Further southeast (15 km northwest of town), there is the Gelukpa monastery of **Gyakhar Gon Shedrub Dargeling**, which was founded during the 18th century by the First Gyakhar Gongma Lobzang Damcho, and now has approximately 100 monks. After Gyakhar Gon you cross a 2,880-m pass, then 6 km before the town you pass a roadside stupa. The outlying villages in this stretch are primarily agricultural, and some have public phone booths.

Lintan town → *Altitude: 2,790 m*

The county town, which is built upon hilly terrain, has a large Muslim and Chinese population. Few Tibetans are in evidence. Entering the top or west end of town (from Tso), the road forks:

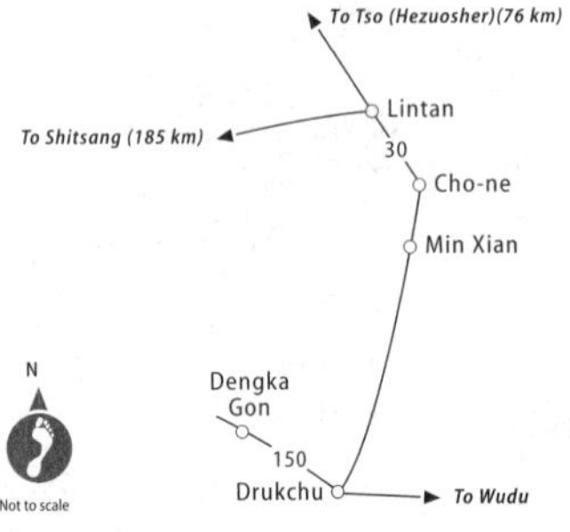

northwest to outlying villages and southeast downhill to the downtown area. Taking the latter road, you will pass on both sides of the road banks, Muslim restaurants and shops. The Minzu Fiandian and the cinema are on the left. At the first of two crossroads, turn left for the Lintan Mosque and the road to Kanle/Linfa, or continue downhill through the commercial part of town, passing the post office on the left and the Lintan Guesthouse on the right. Then, at the second crossroads, turn right for the trail leading down to the north bank of the Luchu (a Christian church is located at this corner), or left for the local government buildings and the bus station. Then, continuing downhill, you will head out of town in the direction of Cho-ne. Lintan town itself has little of interest, and visitors generally pass through en route for Cho-ne, 29 km to the southeast on the north bank of the Luchu.

Yerwa Gon Samdrubling

Heading southeast from town, the road crosses two passes (2,880 m) to reach the Cho-ne intersection after 24 km. From the high ground there are excellent views of the range to the southwest which forms the watershed between the Yellow River and the Jialing. If, instead of turning south for Cho-ne (only 6 km distant), you traverse a third pass (2,850 m), you descend via a Chinese fort to **Yerwa Samdrubling**, 5 km northeast of the intersection. Approached via a large earthen stupa, this monastery, constructed in Sino-Tibetan style, was originally a Sakyapa foundation. It has been dated 1146, or else classed among the 108 border temples constructed by Qubilai Qan (13th century) to atone for his war crimes. The monastery has been reopened since 1985 and there are 12 monks.

Lintan to Minxian

After Yerwa Gon, the road climbs again to cross another pass (2,940 m), leading down to another intersection. The landscape is one of green terraced fields and red soil. Here, you can turn left (north) for Xiliguan (77 km) or southeast, crossing yet another pass (2,865 m) to reach the border of Lintan and Minxian counties after a further 19 km. Leaving the Tibetan ethnic area behind, the road then crosses a 3,000-m pass and follows a tributary downstream to its confluence with the Luchu at Minxian, 40 km from the pass. On this descent, the villages are entirely Muslim and Chinese, some with small mosques and temples. The only Tibetan landmark is a ruined stupa in Tibetan style, which lies just above the confluence of the two rivers, indicating the easternmost limit of Tibetan penetration at the height of the Yarlung Dynasty.

Minxian

Cross the Luchu via the Yefu Qiao bridge to enter the largely Muslim city of **Minxian** (2,340 m), where the road links up with Highway 212. Head north on the highway for Linfa and Lanzhou, or south, across the watershed, for Drukchu county (137 km). This road is described below, page 683. ▸▸ *For listings, see pages 700-706.*

Cho-ne County ཅོ་ནེ → *Population: 100,400. Area: 4,954 sq km.* 卓尼县

Cho-ne county straddles the banks of the Luchu in its mid-reaches. The county town, which is on the north bank, is renowned for its ancient monastery, and across the river there are lateral valleys where there used to be branches of Cho-ne. Presently there are only six monasteries in the county, all of them Gelukpa.

Cho-ne town → *Altitude: 2,610 m. Colour map 5, grid B6.*

The **town of Cho-ne**, adjacent to the monastery, is fairly large, 374 sq km in area, with a predominantly non-Tibetan population. Entering town from the Lintan intersection, 5 km to the north, the road descends towards the bank of the Luchu. After a bridge, which spans a small tributary, a turn-off on the left leads into Main Street. As you drive downhill on Main Street, you will pass on the left the Cho-ne Printing press, the Bank of Industry and Commerce, and the Xinhua Bookstore, while on the right are the People's Bank, the Commercial Guesthouse, and a turn-off leading to the local government buildings and police station. At the foot of the hill, the road meets the north bank of the river, where it forms a T-junction with the riverbank road. Turn left here (east) for the bus station and bridge spanning the Luchu, or right (west) for access to the monastery.

Cho-ne Gonchen

Cho-ne Gonchen Ganden Shedrubling was originally a Sakyapa monastery, founded by Drogon Chogyel Phakpa and his patron Qubilai Qan in 1269. Subsequently, it was converted to the Gelukpa tradition in 1459 by Choje Rinchen Lhunpo. The colleges at Cho-ne were established in the 18th century by Kunkyen Jigme Wangpo: the school of dialectics (**Tsenyi Dratsang**) in 1714, and the tantric college (**Gyupa Dratsang**) in 1729. The monastery was renowned for its woodblock collection of the *Kangyur* and *Tangyur*, prepared in 1773. Printed copies of this collection are still extant, in the United States and elsewhere, although the woodblocks have been irreparably damaged.

At the entrance to the complex there is a Chinese pavilion, containing a stele inscribed in Tibetan and Chinese which commemorates the history of the monastery and its expansion with Manchu patronage during the 18th century. Within the precincts, there are six original grand buildings, only one of which is in ruins (to the left). The Dukhang (Assembly Hall) is in the centre, and the Gyupa Dratsang to the right, while to their rear are the Tsenyi Dratsang, the Debating Garden (Chora), the Taknyi Lhakhang, dedicated to Hevajra, and the Sariwa Lhakhang.

Among them, the **Assembly Hall** contains large images of Tsongkhapa with his students, flanked by Mahakarunika and four-armed Avalokiteshvara (left) and Manjughosa (right). Within the **inner sanctum**, there are large images of Jowo Shakyamuni and Maitreya with 1,000 small images of Tsongkhapa, a library and two stacked editions of the *Kangyur*. The Repkong-style murals depict the meditational deities and lineage-holders of the Gelukpa school.

To the right of the Assembly Hall, the **Gyupa Dratsang** contains images (left to right) of Padmasambhava, Jowo Shakyamuni, Vajrabhairava, Tsongkhapa with his students, Maitreya, Guhyasamaja and Cakrasamvara. The murals, also in Repkong style, depict the tantra lineage of the Gelukpa school. Presently, there are only 120 monks at the monastery, which means that, despite its scale, former prestige, and grandeur, it cannot avoid having the air of a ghost town.

South Bank of the Luchu

Some 31 km west of Cho-ne on the south bank of the Luchu, at Ka-che township, there is the monastery of **Marnyung Jampaling**, which was founded in 1405 and is currently under reconstruction. In 1962 this site was transferred from Cho-ne to Lintan county. Closer to the county town, there are other branch monasteries of Cho-ne Gon, notably: **Nakdo Gon** (founded 1676), **Kyage Gon** (founded 1587), and **Showa Khedrubling** (founded 1685 at the behest of the Fifth Dalai Lama). Only **Ganden Tashi Sambrubling** at **Azitang**, founded in 1789, is affiliated to Labrang.

Cho-ne Monastery

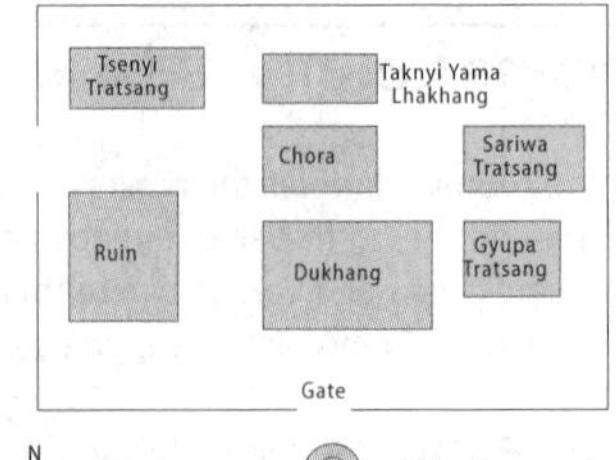

Tewo County ཐེ་བོ་ → *Pop: 54,400. Area: 4,927 sq km.* 迭部县

Tewo county occupies the upper reaches of the Druk-chu, a major tributary of the Jialing, which rises near the watershed at **Taktsang Lhamo**, and flows into the Jialing 18 km below **Drukchu** town. This valley is the eastern extremity of Amdo and most of the population is highly sinicized. Nonetheless, it is a scenic and historic route, visiting pockets of Amdowa who trace their ancestry back to border armies from the time of the Tibetan kings. Formerly the Sakyapa school had a strong presence in these parts, but since the 18th century, most Buddhist monasteries have espoused the Gelukpa order. The exceptions are those of the ancient Bon tradition which have survived in remote corners of the Druk-chu valley. The county capital is located at **Dengka Gon** (Ch Tebo), 90 km southeast of Taktsang Lhamo and 157 km northwest of Drukchu town at the lower end of the valley.

Taktsang Lhamo to Tewo

As an alternative to going due south on the highway through the grasslands from Taktsang Lhamo to Dzoge, it is possible to detour through the forested counties of **Tewo** and **Drukchu** within the valley of the Druk-chu (Ch Bailong), a tributary of the Jialing. To enter the Druk-chu ('white dragon') valley, turn right (east) at the road junction 4 km north of Taktsang Lhamo, and then left (southeast) after 8 km at the Tewo/Dzoge fork. Beehives are plentiful in this area, and in season you will be able to buy fresh honey at the roadside.

The first section of this road currently falls within the borders of Dzoge county in Sichuan province. The township of **Khoser**, located at the fork, has a Ngawa Prefectural Tibetan Language Middle School and a small Gelukpa monastery. Here, the tree line begins and a hot spring is passed on the left. There is also some evidence of roadside cultivation, usually of wheat and beans. Some other small Gelukpa monasteries can be visited on this stretch, including **Keri Gon, Trinpa Gon** and **Bompo Gon**, and there is a turn-off on the right which leads south to the Bon monastery of **Tatsa Gon**. Eventually, at Marker 175, the county border is crossed and the road now re-enters **Gansu**, on a better paved surface.

Dengka Gon town (Tewo Dzong) → *Altitude: 2,370 m. Colour map 5, grid B5.*

The county town at **Dengka Gon** lies only 8 km southeast of the provincial border, and deep within the forested gorge of the Druk-chu. The town is a narrow strip of urban development, hugging the north bank of the river. Entering from Taktsang Lhamo (west), you will pass on the left side of **Main Street,** the tax office, the forestry department, the Nationalities Market, government buildings, the Tewo Hotel, Xinhua Bookstore, police station, Peoples' Hospital, Yohou Hotel and the Tibetan Middle School. On the right side of Main Street, close to the river, you will pass the Tibetan Hospital, the Grain Department Guesthouse, the Tewo Dronkhang, the post office, cultural bureau, sports hall, assorted banks and schools and the bus station. Two small bridges span the Druk-chu, leading to outlying lateral valleys on the south side; and in this vicinity, there is the hermitage of **Tratsang Ritro**, which was founded by a lama named Tewo Rabjampa Palden Senge.

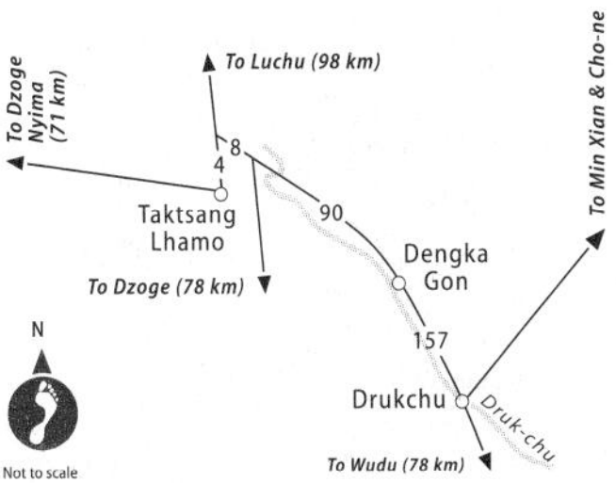

Pal-she Dengka Gon The monastery of **Pal-she Dengka Gon**, which gives the town its name, lies 2.5 km northwest. Its foundation is originally attributed to Pakshi Rolpa, a student of Drogon Chogyel Phakpa in the 13th century, and later it converted to the Gelukpa tradition. In 1982 this monastery was reopened, and it currently supports 100 monks.

Tewo to Lintan

About 5 km northwest of town, at a turn-off on the right (north), a side road leaves the Druk-chu valley, for **Lintan** (91 km), via **Yiwa, Niba**, and **Jango** (Gyakhar Gon). This rough trail crosses the hills forming the watershed between the Yellow and Jialing river systems, and there are some peaks exceeding 4,000 m.

Tewo to Drukchu

Some 10 km southeast of town, the Bon monastery of **Tsotsang Gon** lies on a ridge to the north of the road. This complex was reconstructed in 1990, amalgamating within it three local Bon monasteries. There are currently 40 monks, who uphold the Khyungpo Tengchen lineage. The foremost image within the main hall is that of Shenrab Miwoche, while the murals, in Repkong style, depict Namka Gyelmo, Drenpa Namka, Shenrab Miwoche, and protector deities such as Machen Pomra.

Continuing down valley, the rapids of the Druk-chu begin in earnest 18 km below town at the Drukchu Dam. A power station is located 7 km below the dam, and 7 km further on at Khapa village there is the hill-top Gelukpa monastery of **Tashi Dagye Gon**. The undecorated newly constructed assembly hall contains images of Tsongkhapa and students, flanked by Maitreya, Manjughosa and 1,000 small images of Tsongkhapa. A full set of the *Kangyur* is kept here. Below Tashi Dagye Gon, the road surface suddenly becomes rough, and the gorge deepens. A turn-off on the left (3 km after Tashi Dagye) leads for 20 km to **Gyeli Gon** of the Bon tradition. Continuing on the main road, you will pass another recently completed dam. The cliffs here are red and white and the river bed is strewn with large rocks in the same colours. About 20 km below the gorge in **Maya** township, there is the monastery of **Wangtsang Gon Tashi Puntsoling**, an 18th-century branch of Cho-ne, which has 32 monks. Then, after a further 15 km, a paved road branches off on the left, heading for **Minxian** (Marker 86). Keeping right, and continuing uphill on the rough dirt road, you will reach **Tsenyi Gon** of the Gelukpa school after 3 km. There are 45 monks here, and the assembly hall is large. Continuing along this road, you will reach the county border after 18 km, and enter the territory of **Drukchu**.

Drukchu County འབྲུག་ཆུ

→ Population: 134,300. Area: 2,972 sq km. Colour map 5, grid C6. 舟曲县

Drukchu county is the name given to the lower reaches of the Druk-chu river around its confluence with the Yao tributary, where the terrain ranges from 3,000-4,000 m. The Tibetan population of Drukchu is now confined to rural areas. The county capital

Drukchu Town

The forest dwellers of Drukchu

Formerly this was the wealthiest part of the prefecture because it was an important forest region with a reserve of 156 million cu m of wood. The local people had lived by lumbering generation after generation and, at the same time, taken care of the forest which sustained them, so that it never deteriorated and provided a beautiful green environment with scenic waters and roaming pandas. The forest dwellers of Drukchu had a higher living standard than the peasants and nomads. However, great changes have occurred since the establishment of the Bailong Forest Administration Bureau in 1966, and the immigration of 10,000-20,000 lumber workers and their families from Manchuria and Sichuan. These alien people have no affinity toward this heavily wooded region. They have actively cut down trees but have no intention of replanting. Consequently, the hills on both sides of the Druk-chu are denuded, and the ecological system endangered. The Tibetan inhabitants are gradually being marginalized and impoverished – all that is left for them is the cultivation of mountain barley. Since the 1950s, the area of forest has shrunk by 30% and the reserve of timber reduced by 25% due to overfelling. The sand in the river water has increased by 60%, and the water flow volume has reduced by 8%, resulting in increased flooding and drought.

is located 157 km southeast of Dengka Gon in Tewo, 137 km south of Minxian, and 78 km northwest of Wudu.

Tewo to Drukchu

The dirt road from Tewo enters Drukchu county at Km Marker 65, ie 46 km above the town of Drukchu. The descent into town is disappointing. The hills are largely deforested, and there is some evidence of inbreeding among the population. The narrow river banks are cultivated in places, but the only cultural sites of note appear to be two small village temples at **Nyiga** and **Peltsang**, located 10 and 32 km above the town respectively.

Drukchu town → *Altitude: 1,380 m*

Entering the town from the northwest, the **Main Street** leads downhill towards a T-junction on the north bank of the river. On the left, you will pass a small guesthouse, the Workers' Hospital, the Forestry Department Guesthouse, assorted banks, the bus station and the vegetable market, while on the right there are only a few shops, and a lane leading down to the bridge which spans the Druk-chu here. After the T-junction, you will pass on the left a restaurant, the local government buildings and the local transport company, while on the right are the traffic police, the Zhengda Hotel, a small dance hall and a Muslim restaurant.

Drukchu to Minxian and Wudu

From Drukchu, you can continue following the river road downstream to its confluence with the smaller Yao River at **Lianhekou**. Here, the road unites with Highway 212, which can be followed downstream to **Wudu** (59 km), or upstream through the Yao valley to the watershed (2,550 m) and thence to **Minxian** in the Luchu valley (118 km), from which the Tibetan areas of **Lintan** and **Cho-ne** can be reached (see above, page 678).

Dzoge County མཛོད་དགེ

→ *Population: 65,000. Area: 11,226 sq km. Colour map 5, grid C5.*

The county of Dzoge lies south of the craggy **Amnye Lhago** range (Ch Erlong Shan), which in parts forms the provincial divide between present-day Gansu and Sichuan. It is an area of high grassland, corresponding to the valley of the Me-chu, a tributary of the Yellow River, which rises in the Minshan range and flows northwest to converge with the Yellow River below Machu. The county capital is located at **Taktsha Gondrong**, in the mid-reaches of the Me-chu valley, 90 km south of Taktsang Lhamo (via **Zhakdom**), 140 km northeast of Hongyuan, and 174 km northwest of Zungchu. There are altogether 80 monasteries in Dzoge county, of which only three are Sakya and five Bonpo; the remainder are all Gelukpa. Among them, the best known (but not the largest) is **Dzoge Gonsar Ganden Rabgyeling**.

Northern Dzoge

In the extreme north of the county, there are important lateral roads which carry traffic from Taktsang Lhamo along the south fringe of the Amnye Lhago range to Machu in Gansu, and also to Tewo in the Drukchu valley. These routes have already been described (pages 676 and 681). The main road, Highway 213 continues south from Taktsang Lhamo, following the Me-chu upstream to Dzoge. After 20 km, another dirt road converges from the west. This turn-off leads southwest to the banks of the Me-chu from where motorable trails lead northwest to Machu (48 km via Mazhi), and southwest to Tangkor (77 km) in the Ger-chu valley. Continuing south on the highway, you will reach Taktsha Gondrong after 58 km, crossing one pass (3,480 m) en route.

Some small remaining clumps of forest are visible on the steeper hills, but the landscape is still primarily grassland, and the terrain around **Taktsha Gondrong** consists of high windswept marshland and open grasslands (3,292 m), with an abundance of medicinal herbs. The horizon is dotted with nomad camps ringed by piles of yak-dung. The topsoil is thin and grazing land is intensively used, which has resulted in severe wind and water erosion in several areas. Everywhere there are molehills and the small holes made by pika, a voracious herbivore, which have added to the deterioration of the grasslands.

Taktsha Gondrong → *For listings, see pages 700-706.*

The land around **Taktsha Gondrong** (Ch Roergai) is classic yak-herding country: shaggy-haired nomads, dressed in little more than filthy sheepskin chubas edged with fur, ride into town to barter skins or shoot pool in the market square, and fights are commonplace. Muslims from Gansu visit regularly to buy wool and carcasses, which they transport northwards on ancient Chinese lorries, some of them settling to run the noodle restaurants and tea houses, which are found all over northern Amdo. Most of the Chinese here are administrators or shopkeepers selling a range of cheap nylon and plastic goods, and it is evident that few enjoy their stay. There are local industries based on the traditional nomadic produce: especially milk powder-processing and meat-canning factories; while at **Chukcho** near town there is an international joint-venture gold mining development project.

Orientation Entering town from Taktsang Lhamo (northwest) on the highway, turn left at the T-junction, or else continue southwest towards Mewa, bypassing the town. If you turn left, you will pass on the left the Tibetan Medical College (Mentsikhang) and the Agriculture and

Dzoge County

Animal Husbandry Guesthouse, while on the right there is the Forestry Department and a number of small restaurants. At the next intersection, turn left onto **Main Street** or continue east towards the Education Bureau and the bus station, close to the banks of the Me-chu. On the left side of Main Street you will pass the cinema, Xinhua Bookstore, the post office, the Dzoge Hotel, the County Government Guesthouse, the Communist Party offices and the police station, while on the right are banks, small restaurants and the County People's Hospital. At the far end of Main Street, turn left for Dzoge Gonsar monastery or right, heading out of town in the direction of Zungchu.

Mentsikhang The town is most famous for its hospital of traditional medicine. This **Mentsikhang** is a teaching hospital with a four-year study course run by Lopon Tenko, a former pupil of Geshe Lobzang Palden of Labrang who died in 1963 at the age of 88. The medicinal compounding room, the grinding machine, the dispensary and the library are all open to visitors. On average the hospital treats 80 patients each day, mostly for stomach and liver ailments, as well as arthritis and bronchitis.

Dzoge Gonsar Ganden Rabgyeling The Gelukpa monastery of Dzoge Gonsar Ganden Rabgyeling was founded in 1798, the site having been offered by Konchok Rabten, the chieftain of neighbouring **Mewa** (Ch Hongyuan). Currently there are more than 100 monks here. Entering the precincts of the monastery via an ornate gateway and a large white stupa, the residential buildings (Labrang) are on the right, while the Protector Temple (Gonkhang), Medical College (Menpa Dratsang), Mani Wheel chapel, and **Assembly Hall** (Dukhang) are to the left. Among them, the assembly hall has images of Shakyamuni,

Taktsha Gondrong

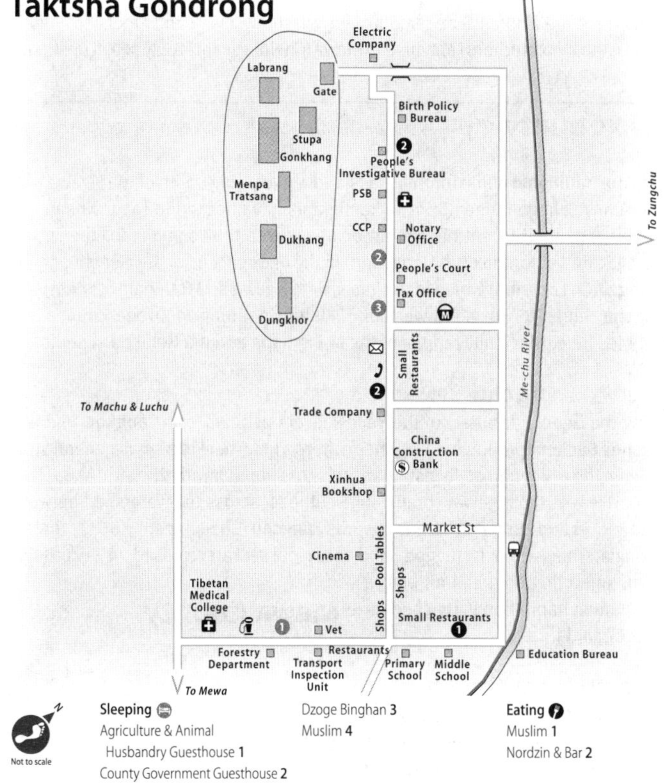

 Tsongkhapa and Maitreya. In the **Gonkhang** there is a Four-armed Mahakala, while the **Mani Wheel Chapel (Dungkhor)** was constructed in 1988. The monastery has an important medical college (Menpa Dratsang), under the guidance of Akhu Puntsok.

Minshan Region

Crossing the bridge to the east of town, you pass through pastures where sheep and goats graze in large numbers, and after 25 km the road forks, its branches following the tributaries of the Me-chu upstream to **Bozo** (33 km) in the Minshan range, and **Choje Nangwa** (20 km) in the grasslands. The former leads deep into the Minshan range, and gives access to **Dzitsa Degu** in Nampel county (see below page 694). The latter road is a rough pot-holed surface, which passes the monastery at Choje Nangwa and stockaded villages and crosses two passes (3,600 m and 3,570 m) to enter a disputed grassland region. Here, the nomads of Mewa, Dzoge and Zungchu have resumed their age-old dispute concerning ownership of these border grasslands. Every year there are fatalities as marauding nomadic groups assault their neighbours. Taking the latter road, after 107 km, you will reach the intersection of the three border roads at **Garita** (Ch Galitai). Turn northwest for **Bachen** (115 km) in the Ger-chu valley (see below, page 689), or southeast for **Zungchu** (62 km), in the upper valley of the Zung-chu (Ch Min) river.

Ger-chu Valley

Leaving the county town on Highway 213, you head southwest from the bypass west of town, and gradually climb through the grasslands, leaving the Me-chu valley behind en route for **Tangkor** (57 km). Here, the highway enters the valley of the Ger-chu, a north-flowing tributary of the Yellow River, which merges with the latter at nearby **Sogtsang Gonpa**. This is beehive country and the monastery is visible just to the north of the road. There are also ancient camouflaged village dwellings, their roofs covered in grass and earth for protection. From here to **Mewa** (Ch Hongyuan) is only 76 km upstream.

Mewa County རྨེ་བ → *Population: 36,000. Area: 7,328 sq km.* 红原县

Mewa is the traditional name for this grassland region, lying south of the Ngawa hills and the Amnye Lhago range. Chinese immigrants have flocked to the towns in this area, buoyed by their recent historic associations with the Long March. The county capital is located at **Kakhok** (Ch Hongyuan) in the mid-reaches of the Ger-chu, 59 km from **Lungzi** (Ch Longriba) which is the gateway to Ngawa and Barkham, 177 km west of **Zungchu**, and 136 km southwest of Taktsha Gondrong in Dzoge county. The monasteries here principally represent the Nyingmapa and the Gelukpa schools.

Bachen to Zungchu

Following the Ger-chu tributary of the Yellow River upstream from **Tangkor**, Highway 213 reaches **Bachen** (pronounced Wachen) after 33 km. There is a small general store here, alongside a Sichuan-style restaurant, which is popular with truckers. At Bachen, a side road leaves the highway, branching southeast across the watershed between the Yellow River and Zung-chu basins towards **Zungchu** (Ch Songpan), 186 km distant via Changla. The terrain is rugged, and three passes are crossed in succession (3,570 m, 3,360 m, and 3,450 m) before the first human habitation is reached en route for **Changla**.

Razhitang Mani Khorlo

Continuing on the highway, southwest from Bachen, the Ger-chu valley flattens out, and by pools beside the meandering

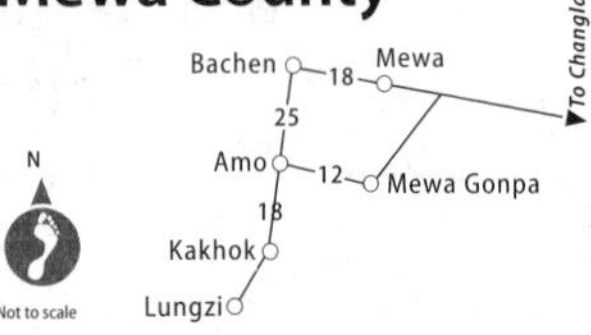

river black-necked cranes can occasionally be seen nesting in summer. At the restored **Razhitang Mani Khorlo**, 2 km south of Bachen, there is a small Gelukpa monastery under the guidance of Zhabtra Rinpoche, with a teaching throne of the late Tenth Panchen Lama.

Mewa Gonpa

At **Amo** (Ch Amu), 25 km southwest of Bachen, a motorable dirt track (marked by stupas and prayer flags to the right of the road) branches east, just before a bridge. It follows the Amo-chu tributary upstream in the direction of the **Mu-ge** grasslands for 25 km, before looping northeast to rejoin the Bachen-Zungchu road mentioned above.

About 18 km along this road, you can visit **Mewa Gonpa**, formally known as **Dargye Jamchen Chokhorling**, which is the largest monastery in the county and the largest of all the Nyingmapa monasteries following the Longchen Nyingtik tradition. The complex was originally founded in 1646 and the Longchen Nyingtig lineage was first established here by the First Do Rinpoche in the 19th century. The monastery has branches throughout Amdo and even one at Patlikhul in Northwest India, founded by the exiled Khenpo Thubten. The site is most impressive – the monastic buildings cover the hills overlooking the north bank of the Amo-chu, and they are encircled by a stupa wall with three main gateways. Among them, the large assembly is surrounded by log cabin hermitages, with the Labrang (residence) of the incumbent lama Tulku Jamyang Sherab Gyeltsen on the slopes above, and the Drubkhang (hermitage) further to the east.

The **assembly hall** ⓘ *admission: ¥10*, is a three-storey building, with a spacious open grass court in front, where masked dances are performed on the 10th day of the 7th lunar month (commemorating the birth of Padmasambhava). Inside there is seating space for the assembled community of over 1,300 monks. The hall, which faces south, is generally entered from a side door on the east. Notice the wonderful Repkong-style murals of the **ground floor**, which depict in succession (L-R): the Twelve Deeds of Shakyamuni, Vajrakila, Kabgye and the Nyingtik Tsokchen (all in the southeast corner) and, after the main door, Vajrasattva, Sriheruka, Padmasambhava with the 84 Mahasiddhas and Manjughosa (all in the southwest corner). The murals of the west wall depict The Twelve Deeds of Shakyamuni (two panels), followed by the Dzogchen progenitors Vimalamitra, Jnanasutra, Manjushrimitra and Pramohavajra – each surrounded by 100 small buddha images. In the northwest corner there are murals depicting Shakyamuni surrounded by the 16 Elders and Padmsambhava with his Twenty-five Disciples. Opposite on the east wall the mural panels depict the preferred teaching cycles of Karling Zhitro, Rigdzin Dupa, Palchen Dupa, Yumka Dechen Gyelmo, Guru Drakpo, Rigsum Gonpo, Sampa Lhundrub and Lama Sangdrub. At the centre of the hall is the teaching throne, and behind it is the **inner sanctum**, accessed from an antechamber with murals illustrating Tara and the Buddhas of the Three Times. The principal gilded copper images are all installed here (L-R): Padmasambhava, Vimalamitra, Manjughosa in the form of "lion of speech", Jowo Shakyamuni, Padmakara, Maitreya, Amitayus, Longchenpa and Jigme Lingpa, with smaller statues of the First Do Rinpoche and Do Khyentse Yeshe Dorje in front, alongside a stone footprint of the present incumbent Tulku Jamyang Sherab Gyeltsen.

Upstairs on the **second floor**, the west wall holds the glass-encased reliquary stupas of Khenpo Norgye, Khenpo Tsewang Rigdzin, Do Rinpoche Zilnon Gyepe Dorje, and Do Rinpoche Thubten Jangchub Gyeltsen. Among them, Khenpo Tsewang Rigdzin is widely recognized to have attained the "rainbow body" (*jalu*) through Dzogchen practice. The same glass case also contains a stone handprint attributed to Jamyang Sherab Gyeltsen. On the north wall are important texts including several Guhyagarbha commentaries, while the east wall has images depicting the main Nyingmapa protector deities: Gonpo Maning, Rahula, Ekajati, Vajrasadhu, Cimara and Dorje Yudronma. The throne in this chapel supports a large photograph of the previous Panchen Lama who sanctioned the rebuilding of the monastery from 1982 onwards.

On the **third floor**, there is a library and a series of images depicting (L-R): Vajrasattva, King Trisong Detsen, Manjushrimitra, Pramovajra, Guhyapati, Vajradhara, Shakyamuni, Samantabhadra in union, Shantaraksita, Amitabha, Manjughosa, Peaceful Vajrapani, Avalokiteshvara, Cintamanicakra Tara and Maitreya.

The **Drubkhang** (hermitage) is another large three-storey building, recently reconstructed alongside an active three-year retreat hermitage. On the ground floor there are splendid images of Padmakara flanked by Shantaraksita and King Trisong Detsen, a mountain of books from floor to ceiling along the north wall, and murals which depict the three roots of Longchen Nyingtig and the Gyutrul Zhitro. On the second floor, there is a gallery overlooking the hall below, with an elongated chapel to its south. The same design is repeated on the third floor.

The latest project at Mewa Gonpa is the as yet unfinished construction of a giant **World Peace Stupa**.

Gongtang Temple

Returning to the highway, and heading south towards the county town, you will notice that the marshy plains support several nomadic encampments. There are numerous Gelukpa and Nyingmapa monasteries, such as **Regur**, but these are little more than concrete sheds whose most attractive feature is the decorative field of prayer-flags beside them. Approaching the town, just above a little village to the west, is the small **Gongtang Lhakhang**, the summer residence of the late Gongtang Rinpoche of Labrang, whose lineage is traced back to Je Gongtangba (1762-1823).

Kakhok

The burgeoning county town of **Kakhok** (Ch Hongyuan, altitude 3,360 m) is located on the highway, 18 km south of Amo and only 2 km south of Gongtang Dargyeling, at Km Marker 647. Here Chinese settlers have established themselves in great numbers, alongside the indigenous nomadic population, but it is still not uncommon to see horses and yaks tethered in front of shop doorways. The name Hongyuan ('red plain') refers to the comparatively recent associations of the county with the Long March, and the original settlement here appears to have had the local names Kakhok and Khyungchu (pronounced Shungchu). ▸▸ *For listings, see pages 700-706.*

Orientation Entering the town from the northeast (ie from Dzoge or Mewa Gonpa on the highway), you will first pass a number of motor repair shops, the Muslim Restaurant, the Delek Guesthouse and several clothing stores, before reaching a crossroads. Turn right (northwest) through an alleyway of simple restaurants to cross the Ger-chu en route for Gongtang Lhakhang, continue straight ahead (southwest) on the highway for Ngawa and Barkham, or turn left into the downtown area.

On the right (south) side of Main Street you will find the Bus Station, Dekyi Tibetan Restaurant, shops selling Tibetan artefacts, the Hongmao Hotel, the Yellow River Restaurant, the Amchok Tsenyi Gonpa Hotel & Shop, a lane leading to the Old Hongyuan Guesthouse and the National Tax Bureau. Opposite on the left (north) side of the street are the County Tax Bureau, the Dolmaling Guesthouse, a supermarket, the Red Grassland Restaurant, a lane leading to the open market and the Traffic Bureau Guesthouse. Towards the far end of Main Street, another turning leads right to China Post, China Mobile (which has an internet café upstairs), the TV Station, hospital, stadium, middle school, education bureau and the police station. A corresponding turning on the left leads to a meat-processing factory. At the extremity of Main Street there is the Mentsikhang Hospital.

From Mewa, the highway leads southwest to the **Lungzi** intersection (49 km) where it divides: a branch road heading northwest to **Amchok Tsenyi Gonpa** and Ngawa and the highway itself continuing south to Barkham (see above, page 658).

Zungchu County ཟུང་ཆུ

→ *Population: 68,000. Area: 6,517 sq km. Colour map 5, grid C6.* 松潘县

Zungchu (Ch Songpan) county occupies the upper valley of the Zung-chu (Ch Minjiang) river, from its source in the Minshan range to the deep gorges north of Maowen county in the south. The county capital is located at **Zungchu** (Ch Songpan), 177 km southwest of Mewa, 174 km south of Dzoge, and 142 km north of Maowen. The region is a stronghold of the Bon tradition, although there are also some Gelukpa monasteries.

Grassland Watershed

Roads lead south into Zungchu county from Kakhok in Mewa via Bachen (see above, page 686) and from Dzoge via Choje Nangwa (see above, page 686). The latter heads south through disputed grassland terrain, while the former leaves Highway 213 and the Ger-chu valley at **Bachen** (90 km south of Dzoge and 43 km north of Kakhok), and crosses rugged grasslands towards the source of the Me-chu, after which it converges with the Dzoge road at the **Garita** intersection.

The first part of the road from Bachen passes through classic Amdo country: low hills, broad grassy valleys and meandering rivers with patches of marsh. Black yak-hair tents, typical of all Tibetan nomads, are abundant here, and the rich grazing land supports vast herds of yak and many sheep and goats. Much of the milk produced in this region is collected in large churns and taken by truck to Mewa, Dzoge and other centres where it is processed into powdered milk. The remainder is used by the nomads to make butter, cheese and yoghurt, some of which is sold or bartered for tsampa, wheat, tea and salt, the principal constituents of the Tibetan diet.

Dechen Chokhorling

About 70 km from Bachen, the road passes through **Serdutang**, where there is an attractive Nyingmapa monastery, known as **Dechen Chokhorling**. This is a branch of far-off Dzogchen Monastery in Dzachuka (see above, page 505), and it also has a particular affinity with the lineage of Chogyur Dechen Lingpa, whose image and reliquary stupa are housed here. The main hall additionally has central images of Padmakara flanked by various buddhas and bodhisattvas and the reliquary stupa of Khenpo Norten. The murals, once again in Repkong style, illustrate the teaching cycles of Kabgye and Vajrapani in the form of Drekpa Kundrol. Outside in the grounds of the monastery there is a Mani Wheel chapel. Currently 103 monks are affiliated to Dechen Chokhorling.

Garita Intersection

Some 55 km from Serdutang, after crossing watershed passes between the Yellow River and Zung-chu (Minjiang) basins, the cross country roads from Dzoge and Mewa converge at Garita (Ch Galitai), Winding its way down from the high grasslands through **Pangzang** village, the road enters the forested Zung-chu valley at Aling (Ch Chuanzhusi), 46 km southeast of Garita.

Zungchu & Nampel Counties

Aling → *Altitude: 2,880 m*

Aling, on the banks of the Zung-chu, is a rapidly growing crossroads town, where many large Chinese tour groups visiting Dzitsa Degu and Sertso will now chose to stay overnight. The attractive timber houses with carved gables, seen here for the first time, are typical of many Zungchu villages. Formerly, there was a monastery at Aling, as the Chinese name still suggests. This was destroyed during the Second World War when the Japanese airforce bombed a Guomintang airstrip slightly north of town. A smaller monastery, known as **Tsotso Gon**, has however been rebuilt. There is also a 45-m memorial tower dedicated to Long March veterans, who passed through in 1934. From Aling, you can follow the Zung-chu valley upstream to visit **Nampel** (Nanping) county and the **Dzitsa Degu** (Ch Jiuzhaigou) **National Park** (128 km), or cross the Minshan range to reach the **Sertso National Park** (56 km). Alternatively, you may continue downstream to reach the county town after 16 km.

Sertso National Park (Ch Huanglong)

ⓘ*Admission: ¥80.*

Getting there Public buses do not generally run from Zungchu to Sertso Park, and hitchhiking it is difficult. The best option is to join an organized tour group from Chengdu, Zungchu or even Aling.

From **Zungchu** town, there is also a horse trail and trekking route to **Sertso**, which follows a tributary of the Minjiang upstream through **Dongna** to **Rongkok**, where you can visit **Rongpa** monastery of the Sakyapa school and **Sebo** monastery of the Gelukpa school. En route are small villages with Bonpo temples, such as **Rinpung** and **Kharchung**.

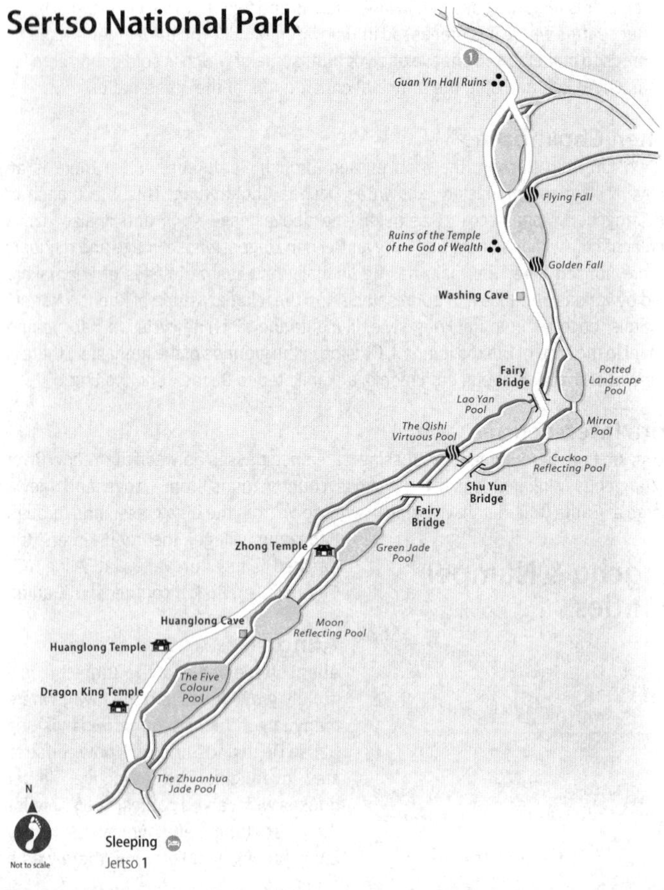

Crossing the Zung-chu (Minjiang) river at Aling, the road forks after 2 km: northeast towards Dzitsa Degu, following the Zung-chu upstream to its source, and due east, across the Minshan watershed to **Sertso National Park** (Tib Sertso Rangjung Sungkyong Sakul). Taking the latter route, which was once followed by the PLA during the Long March (a monument has been erected here), to the right you will pass the Bon monastery of **Lingpo Gon**, situated below the road on the right. Two passes are crossed on this winding hill road, the second, known in Chinese as Xue Bading Shankou (4,420 m), being in the heart of the Minshan range, near the holy Bon mountain called **Mount Shar Dungri** (5,588 m), which is the main peak of the Minshan range. After crossing the watershed, the road descends to the **entrance of the park** at Sertso village on the road to **Pingwu**. From Sertso, the distance is 56 km to Aling and 114 km to Pingwu.

The park, a steep valley which extends for 9 km, was established as a nature reserve in 1983. It contains a series of variegated lakes suffused with minerals and algae, and (according to one tradition) received its name from the yellowish karst limestone formations which cover the terrain. Visitors should be aware, however, that the lower pools, close to the entrance, are dry until July, which is the best month here. The trail from the entrance leads past a series of small lakes and steep coniferous forests to an impressive alpine meadow (1,080 m), with numerous rhododendron species, at the eastern foot of **Mount Shar Dungri**. The climb takes approximately one and a half hours, and there are local guides available to escort groups or individual travellers to the summit. The lakes and pools have been given fanciful names: Flying Fall, Golden Fall, Potted Landscape Pool, Cuckoo-Reflecting Colourful Pool, Green Jade Colourful Pool, and Zhuanhua Jade Pool, which is the highest. Reaching the meadow, there are three small reconstructed Chinese temples which can be visited in turn: Zhongsi, Huanglongsi and Longwangsi, all of which have Tibetan shrines in front, where juniper is burnt and *lungta* (Tibetan printed prayers) are scattered. Among them the most famous is **Huanglongsi** (Tib Sertso Gon), a Daoist temple with one resident Chinese monk, where local Tibetan and Qiang peoples of the Bon tradition gather during a summer festival, held over a three-day period from the 15th day of the sixth lunar month.

Several protected species, including the red panda, golden monkey, takin and water deer are supposedly found in the Sertso National Park, but in such small numbers that they are unlikely to be seen by the casual visitor. The park has become a popular destination, particularly for Chinese tourists, and it is possible to stay at the upmarket Sertso Hotel (Sercuo Fandian), near the entrance, which has doubles at ¥100 and triples at ¥90. Cheaper guesthouse accommodation is also available, and there are restaurants close to the car park.

Source of the Min River

From the new **Jiuzhaigou Airport** or the intersection 2 km east of Aling, if you turn north for **Dzitsa Degu National Park** (85 km), the road follows the east bank of the Zung-chu (Minjiang) upstream towards its source in the Minshan hills. At **Tsangla** village, there are gold mines, attested by the extravagant house of the wealthiest local prospector, and across the river from here there is the unused Guomintang airstrip, which was bombed by Japanese planes during the Second World War. Continuing further upstream, there is a Bon monastery at **Nangzhi**, and several affiliated nearby temples, notably **Lenri** and **Kyang**, the last having been founded by Kyang Lobzang Gyatso.

Gamil Gonpa

Further north, just before reaching the source of the Zung-chu, the road passes through the village of **Shadri**, below the sacred **Mount Jadur**. The largest Bon monastery of the region, known as **Gamil Gonchen** or Pal Shenten Dechenling, is located by the roadside, and has an enormous prayer wheel at its entrance. The monastery was founded some 600 years ago by Rinchen Gyeltsen of the Khyung family, and so it is affiliated to Tengchen Monastery in Kham. Currently there are 450 monks and one tulku in residence. The complex has an Assembly Hall (Dukhang), and three colleges: Tsenyi Dratsang (Dialectics), Gyupa Dratsang (Tantric), and Dongak (Scriptural). The **Tsenyi Dratsang** has images of Shenrab Miwoche flanked by the fierce deities Takla Mebar and Welse Ngampa, while in the main hall of the **Dukhang** there are images of Shenrab Miwoche, Sherab Nampar Gyelwa and Sherab Chamma. A **stupa reliquary** here contains the remains of Khenpo Tendzin Dargye. Since it is beside the main road to **Dzitsa Degu National Park** (Ch Jiuzhaigou), Gamil Gonpa receives many Chinese tour buses, and has consequently assumed a very commercial ambience, although most visitors stay only a short while.

After Shadri, the road crosses the Zung-chu river near its source, and crosses the watershed to enter Nampel county (see below, page 694).

Zungchu Town

Driving south from Aling (Ch Chuanzhusi) township, the main road immediately becomes a proper highway with **toll gates** ⓘ*¥30 per landcruiser*, and follows the east bank of the Zung-chu downstream for 16 km to **Zungchu** (Ch Songpan), the county capital. Zungchu has long been an important trading town for Tibetans, Qiang, Chinese and Muslims. Much of the tea trade for Amdo was centred here, with wool, furs, musk, medicinal herbs and gold also providing important markets. The old city walls can still be seen, and the extensive market area still attracts a wide selection of visitors from the hills. The Zung-chu river runs through the town, until recently carrying an abundance of logs downstream in defiance of the posters urging conservation and restraint. The population is diverse but predominantly Muslim, and worshippers can frequently be seen at **Qingzhen Si Mosque** near the north end of town. All the streets have Chinese names.

Entering the city from Aling, you will first pass the Tianma Hotel, and after crossing the Zung-chu, you will find the North Bus Station, the Sunriver Hotel and a smaller private bus station on the right (west). Opposite on the corner are Happy Trails Horse Treks, and Shunjiang Horse Treks. At this point, before reaching the North Gate, a ring road (Weicheng Lu) follows the old city wall round towards the East Gate, passing the Linyu Hotel and the Agricultural Bureau, and then loops round to rejoin the main road south of the South Gate, passing the Songpan Hotel on the way.

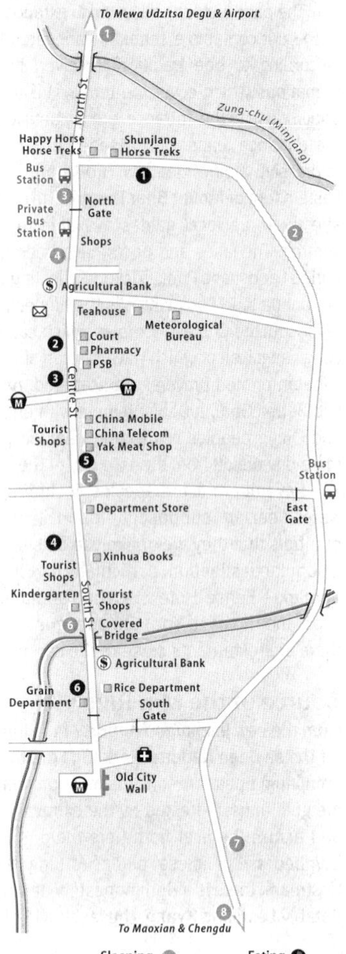

Sleeping
Defunct Songpan 6
Linye 2
New Huanglang 8
Old Huanglong 5
Songpan 7
Songzhou 4
Sunriver 3
Tianma 1

Eating
Cake Shop 5
English Menu 6
Shingyue Muslim 4
Weizhen 2
Xinxin 1
Yuan Pancake House 3

If, instead, you continue into town through the North Gate you will reach **North Street** (Bei Lu). Here on the left you will find the Songzhou Hotel, China Post (with a fax bureau), the Weizhen Restaurant and the Yulan Pancake House, with the Xinxin Restaurant, the Government Guesthouse, the Meteorological Bureau Teahouse (down a lane), the County Court and the Public Security Bureau opposite on the left. Both sides of the street have Tibetan curio shops catering for tourists. At this point, an open vegetable market bisects North Street on both sides. Continuing straight ahead, you will pass on the left China Mobile, China Telecom, a dry yak-meat shop, a cake shop and the Huanglong Hotel.

Reaching the main crossroads at the town centre, turn right (west) for the cinema and entertainment centre, standing where the ruins of the West Gate (destroyed by Japanese bombs in the Second World War) once stood. Turn left (east) towards the East Gate, where the County Government Buildings, banks and East Bus Station are located; or continue straight ahead on to Middle Street (Zhong Lu).

If at this point you continue on to **Middle Street**, you will find the Shingyue Muslim Restaurant on the left, with a large department store and Xinhua Bookstore opposite on the right. Further tourist shops lead towards the elegant old covered bridge that spans the Zung-chu, bisecting the town. Crossing the bridge, you will notice the Qingzhen Si Mosque on a forested ridge to the west.

After the bridge, you reach **South Street** (Nan Jie), passing the Agricultural Bank on the left, a small restaurant with an English menu on the right, and a lane which leads east to the County Hospital and west to the Mosque. Now you will pass through the South Gate, adjacent to the old market, where the main thoroughfare rejoins the ring road near the new Hualong Hotel, and continues following the steep gorge of the Zung-chu downstream towards Maowen county.

Zungchu is rapidly becoming an important tourist centre for domestic and foreign visitors; and in summer, dozens of minibuses leave daily for the national parks. It is also possible to hire horses and guides for trips into the mountains, lasting up to a week, but be sure you understand the itinerary, what services (eg food and accommodation) are included, and that you see the horses before parting with any money.

Horse Treks **Happy Horse Treks** ⓘ *T0837-7231064*, where the proprietor has an English spouse, offer 3-4 day all-inclusive horse trekking packages to Sertso National Park ⓘ *¥320 per person*, Shar Dungri Glacier (Ch Xuebao Bingchuan) ⓘ *¥330 per person*, and to Muni Gully ⓘ *¥320*. **Shunjiang Horse Treks**, immediately next door, offer similar packages.

Nyenyul Valley

To the west of town, a steep climb and descent leads into the picturesque **Nyenyul** valley, which can also be approached by road from a turn-off at **Anhong** township, 33 km south of Zungchu. Here, there are several Bonpo temples, including the important **Gyagar Mandi**, which is built on an Indian model, and the Sakya monastery of **Jara**. **Muni Gulley** (Ch Mounigou) to the west of Nyenyul has its own scenic lakes, hot springs, and a famous waterfall called **Zhaga Purbu**, which are increasingly visited by tourists on horse treks from Zungchu. Here, as at Sertso, the lakes have been given fanciful Chinese names: Ginseng Lake, Hundred Flower Lake, Wild Duck Lake, and so on.

Zung-chu Gorge

Heading south from Zungchu and Anhong, the main road follows the east bank of the Zung-chu downstream, passing through **Pada** (Ch Pata), **Dongna**, and **Zhenjiangquan** after 45 km. The village houses on this stretch are constructed of plain timber and accompanied by wooden frames where barley is dried during the harvest season before threshing. Some 27 km further south, it passes through **Tungping** (Ch Taiping), a lumber control checkpoint, after which it climbs along the upper ridge of the increasingly deep Zung-chu gorge to reach the roadside monument at Diexihaici, commemorating the

 2,000 inhabitants of a Qiang village which vanished from the face of the earth during the 1938 earthquake, when a large lake formed on the Zung-chu below. The lake is clearly visible from the high road. Descending to **Jiaochangba**, the road reaches a turn-off on the right, which leads 21 km to **Songpingkou** village in the Yungping valley. Continuing south on the main road, you will then cross two 2,400 m ridges, before arriving at **Hrihakon** (Ch Lianghekou), 107 km south of the county town, where an important branch road spans the river, giving access to the Zhangdu-chu valley, and connecting with the neighbouring Metsa valley in Tro-chu county (see below, page 697). South of Hrihakon, the main road soon passes the confluence of the Zung-chu and Tro-chu rivers to enter Maowen county, only 29 km north of Mao Xian town.

Nampel County རྣམ་འཕེལ → *Population: 58,000. Area: 6,175 sq km.* 南坪县

The county of Nampel occupies the upper reaches of the Baishui and Fujiang tributaries of the Jialing River, from their watershed in the Minshan range towards Wudu in mainland China. This region, once a stronghold of the Bon religion, has become culturally threadbare in recent years, despite its worldwide fame as the setting of the Dzitsa Degu National Park, an area of outstanding natural beauty. The county town of Nampel is located at **Nanping** town on the Baishui, 142 km northeast of Zungchu, 61 km northwest of Wen Xian in Gansu, and 132 km northeast of Pingwu in Sichuan.

Dzitsa Degu National Park (Jiuzhaigou) → *For listings, see pages 700-706.*

Named after its nine largest settlements, this national park is one of the most beautiful areas of the Tibetan plateau and a recognized World Heritage Site. **Dzitsa Degu** is a Y-shaped forested ravine, 30 km long, within the Minshan range. Numerous mineral-tinted pools and lakes, connected by small waterfalls, line the valley bottom, while the forest extends to the snow peaks above. The total area of the park is 720 sq km, and its altitude is in the range of 2,000-3,100 m. The park is rich is flora including wild roses, clematis, honeysuckle, violet, wild ginger, and above all rhododendron; and in recent years it has been developed as the major tourist destination of northern Sichuan.

Getting there By air **Air China Southwest** and **Sichuan Airlines** run several daily flights from Chengdu to the new Jiuzhaigou Airport, northeast of Aling (¥470). There are also occasional helicopter flights from Guangyuan in northeast Sichuan directly to the helipad at the park.

By road After Gamil Gonpa, the road from Zungchu and Aling (see above, page 689) reaches **Tatsang** near the source of the Zung-chu, and crosses the **Gang Gutok La** pass (3,510 m) in the Minshan range, which form the watershed between the Zung-chu (Minjiang) and Jialing basins. There are fine views of the snow peaks of the sacred Bon mountain, **Shar Dungri**, to the south. On the descent from the pass to Chukar, the excellent paved road cuts through juniper forests, passing **Dzole**, the first scenic spot in Dzitsa Degu to have been discovered and opened by local inhabitants. On the right there is a school and a crystal trinket factory, both funded by a Taiwanese entrepreneur. **Dartse Gonpa** of the Bon tradition is then passed on the left. This is one of only two monasteries in the area, and currently there are 91 monks, studying under a *khenpo* from Menri near Zhigatse. From here the road descends to **Chukar** at the entrance to the Dzitsa Degu National Park. See Transport, page 705, for further details.

Chukar Chukar (2,100 m), 42 km west of the county town, has undergone considerable development in recent years since it lies at the gateway to the park, and is the focal point for the vast legions of Chinese and Taiwanese tourists who come here by bus and air from Chengdu. It has several hotels and guesthouses, restaurants and a heliport, 3.5 km to the south. The ticket office is located at **Penpo** (Goukou) where the Fujiang River makes a hairpin bend. Admission: ¥208 per person. It is also possible to hire a horse and local guide: ¥350 per day.

Tsaru Village Entering the park, after 6 km, the road forks at **Tsaru** village. Tsaru has the only monastery located within the grounds of the park, **Rabwen Gonpa Tashi Puntsoling** of the Bon religion. The buildings were restored eight years ago, having been damaged by fire, and the main temple now has a large image of Shenrab Miwoche, surrounded by 1,000 small identical images. At present there are 67 monks at Rabwen Gon.

Mangsolde Village From Tsaru, the road continues following the west bank of the Fujiang River, on the far bank of which a number of scenic lakes are passed: Dumtsa Tso (Reed Lake), Tsozhi Nangchu (Four-Lake Waterfall), Mebar Tso (Burning Lake),

Dzitsa Degu Valley

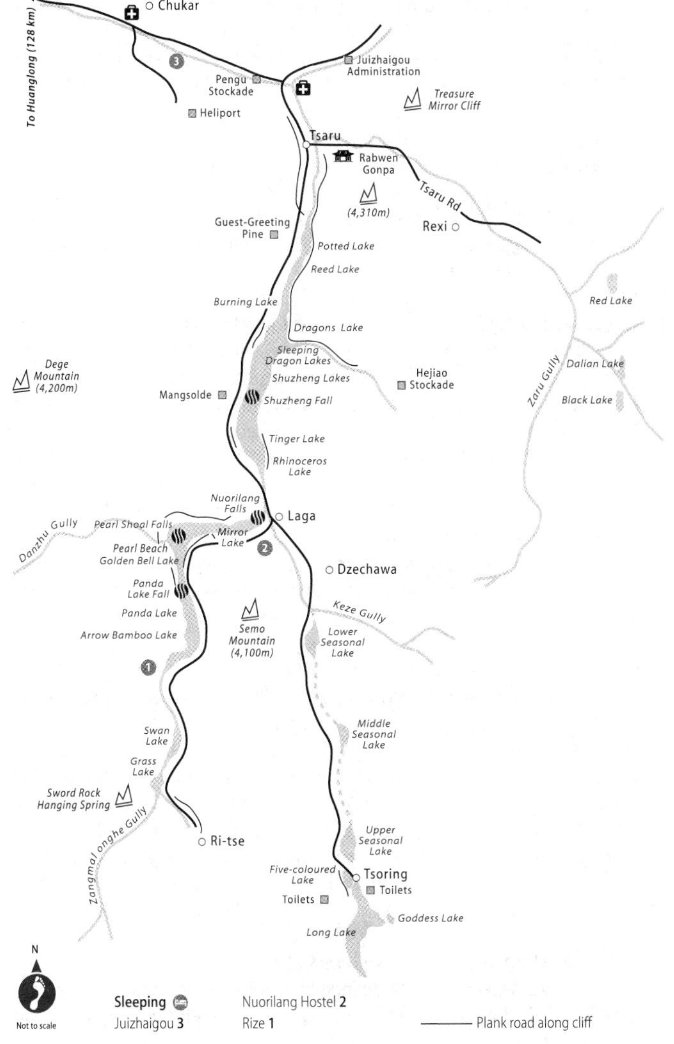

 Takchen Tso (Tiger Lake), and Seru Tso (Rhino Lake). **Mangsolde** village (Ch Shuzheng) lies 11 km upstream from the park entrance, and there are a number of tourist handicraft shops, small tea houses and restaurants, one of which (uphill from the car park) is smartly decorated in Tibetan style. About 3 km after Mangsolde, at **Laga**, the road forks below **Mount Senmo** (4,100 m): southeast for Tsoring (18 km), and southwest for Ri-tse and Domei Naktsal (17 km). Nurilang Guesthouse, just west of this intersection is a focal point for many visitors to Dzitsa Degu since buses run inside the grounds of the park, several times a day, from the entrance as far as this road junction. It takes about three hours to walk from the entrance to Laga (14 km). From the guesthouse, there are two public buses per day running back and forth (southwest) to **Ri-tse** (17 km), and a more infrequent public bus service to **Tsoring Lake** (18 km) in the southeast. Most of the buses operating within the park are private tour buses from Chengdu, which will not pick up individual travellers.

Dzechawa Gully Taking the left gulley from the Laga intersection, the road passes through **Dzechawa** village and three seasonal lakes on the left, before reaching **Doknga Tso** (Five-coloured Lake). It is said that the seasonal lakes have been ruined in consequence of the ecological imbalance caused by mass tourism in Dzitsa Degu. A steep flight of stone steps leads down to the shore of Doknga Tso, where yellow, blue, green and white hues are reflected through the clear calm waters, and submerged ancient tree trunks are sharply discerned. The motor road ends after 18 km at **Tsoring** (Long Lake), which is the park's largest lake (Altitude: 3,150 m). Another flight of steep stone steps leads down to the lake shore, where local Tibetans are waiting with their docile yaks to dress eager Chinese tourists in Tibetan garb for their personalized yak-riding photographs. The clear blue waters of the lake reveal all their secrets, including a pattern of submerged trees.

Ri-tse Gully From the Laga intersection buses run for 17 km, as far as **Domei Naktsal** (Primeval Forest) in the upper reaches of the southwest gully. This is undoubtedly the most spectacular section of the park. To the right of the road you will pass the resplendent **Shel Tso** (Mirror Lake) and the **Mutik Chu** (Pearl Shoal Waterfall), where white surf cascades over the white boulders of the Fujiang River, approached at their base via a long wooden bridge and stone staircase. Further on, **Gyila Domgyi Tso** (Panda Lake) has, at its southeast corner, shoals of fish which are fed by passing tourists, while **Tso Mukdachen** (Arrow Bamboo Lake), **Tso Ngangpachen** (Swan Lake), and **Tsa Tso** (Grass Lake) were formerly part of the giant panda's natural habitat. The motor road comes to an end at **Domei Naktsal**, the primeval forest (2,970 m), where horses are available to transport tourists uphill through the woods at ¥30 per person.

Nanping

The county town, **Nanping**, is located 42 km from Chukar at the entrance to the Dzitsa Degu National Park, in the valley of the Baishui river. The Tibetan population is small, and for the most part representative of the Bon tradition. There are guesthouse and restaurant facilities, although most visitors will proceed directly to Dzitsa Degu.

From Nanping, a rough motorable road heads upstream through the Baishui valley to the northwest extremity of the Minshan range, and thence through the grasslands to **Bozo** in Dzoge county (see above, page 684). The main road, however, follows the Baishui downstream for 61 km to **Wen Xian** in Gansu province, from where there are connections to **Pingwu** and **Wudu**. Buses run from these cities to connect with the Chengdu-Lanzhou railway line.

Tangjiahe National Park → *Colour map 5, grid C5*

Although Dzitsa Degu is still notionally a panda park, most of the few remaining giant pandas are found further southwest at the junction of Pingwu, Nampel, and

Qingchuan counties, especially in the **Tangjiahe National Park**. This represents the westernmost penetration of Tibetan influence. But nowadays this tiny Tibetan population is isolated in the mountain regions, greatly outnumbered by Chinese and Muslim settlements lower down.

Maowen County མའོ་ཝུན

→ *Population: 104,000. Area: 4,373 sq km. Colour map 5, grid C6.* 茂汶羌族自治县

Maowen is the county inhabited by the Qiang nationality, who are believed to be descendants of ancient Tibetan tribes that ranged widely across the extreme north and east of the plateau before and during the period of the Tibetan kings.

The Qiang women still proudly wear their national dress: long brightly coloured (often blue) slit dresses, with blue or black trousers underneath, and intricately embroidered collars adorned with heavy amber jewellery. Most wear a black or white turban, or a decorative headscarf.

The Qiang are renowned for their stone buildings and watchtowers, a culture which they share with the apparently related Qiangic peoples of East Tibet, such as those of Gyarong, and of Tawu and Minyak in Kham. Nowadays they are principally agriculturalists, with wheat and maize as their main crops, with a few domestic animals stabled in large courtyards or the ground floor of their three-storey stone and timber houses. A large number of these houses have been rebuilt in the last 15 years, and most window and door frames are painted in bright colours with traditional designs.

Higher up, above the treeline on alpine meadows, yak, sheep and goats are pastured by mixed populations of Qiang and Tibetan nomads living in traditional black yak wool tents.

Mao Xian town → *Altitude: 1,590 m. Colour map 4, grid A6.*

South of the Zung-chu's confluence with the Tro-chu at **Hrihakon** (see above, page 697), the road from the north begins to criss-cross the river on its 28 km descent into **Mao Xian** county town. Here, the waters of the Zung-chu are silvery in colour and the mountains are rich repositories of quartz and other minerals. The local people grow Sichuan pepper bushes (*hua jao*) and keep bee hives by the roadside. The town itself, which lies 142 km south of Zungchu and 55 km north of Wenchuan, has a population of 60,000 – mostly Muslim and Qiang. The open market is active, although the Qiang Handicrafts Shop on Main Street is disappointing. From Mao Xian a branch road leads northeast to **Beichuan** (199 km). » *For listings, see pages 700-706.*

Maowen, Trochu & Lungu Counties

Trochu County ཁྲོ་ཆུ

→ *Population: 57,000. Area: 2,952 sq km. Colour map 4, grid A6.* 黑水县

At **Hrihakon** (Ch Lianghekou), 28 km north of Mao Xian town, where the Tro-chu (Ch Heishui) River flows into the Zung-chu, there is a road branching off the Maowen-Zungchu highway, which follows the Tro-chu upstream. To reach **Trochu** county, head west up this side valley, passing through Pichi, Serkyu, Gagu and Shiwar Kazi. The county capital, also known as **Trochu**, is 98 km from the junction at Hrapa, on a tributary of the Tro-chu. Until the recent ban, many logs were floated downstream, continuing evidence of the massive deforestation which has halved the area's forest cover since 1950. Oddly enough the county is still closed to foreign travellers and permit restrictions apply, despite its close proximity to Chengdu.

Muge-chu Valley

Some 26 km before reaching the county capital, the road forks: the west branch leading to the capital and the north branch continuing to climb north through the Tro-chu gorge to **Tsimule**. At Tsimule, two valleys converge: the Muge-chu valley (west) and the Tsagi-chu valley (east). Taking the former, the road (69 km) passes through **Chunak**, the Bonpo monastery of **Yungdrung Gon**, **Muge** and **Norwa**. **Muge Gonpa** in particular is an important Gelukpa institution, and was visited by Mao Zedong during the Long March.

Tsagi-chu Valley

The east branch runs north to **Mechu**, where a jeep loop road heads southeast through the Tungping valley to rejoin the Zungchu-Maowen highway at **Jiaochangba** (30 km). Further north of Mechu, the road through the Tsagi-chu valley continues for 41 km, via **Natsi** and **Tsege**. These valleys are characterized by small village temples, all recently rebuilt and mostly of Bonpo origin. There are also a few very small Gelukpa temples, usually attended by a single caretaker or a handful of monks, and which only come to life during village festivals.

Lungu County ལུ་ང་དཀུ → *Pop: 112,000. Area: 3,537 sq km.* 汶川县

From Maowen the main road to Chengdu continues to follow the steep Zung-chu gorge downstream into **Lungu**. This is a traditional Tibetan name for the area around Wenchuan town and the confluence of the Trosung-chu with the Zung-chu. The Chinese name Wenchuan means Wen River, which is an ancient local name for the Zung-chu (Minjiang) River. Although there are patches of forest left on the steeper slopes, most of the mountains were deforested long ago and now exhibit a rich and varied selection of shrubs and wild flowers. Apple trees now grow by the roadside. The road lies only a few hundred metres above the raging river, and in many places is prone to landslides, particularly in early summer. Precarious bamboo and pulley-type suspension bridges span the chasm at intervals, and these are nonchalantly crossed by the locals.

Wenchuan → *Altitude: 1,326 m. For listings, see pages 700-706.*

The county capital, **Wenchuan**, is located 55 km southwest of Mao Xian at a point where the Troksung-chu flows in from the west. The attractive setting and colourful village markets are memorable, but the town is obscured by palls of dust arising from extensive construction projects on the Minjiang, and pollution caused by heavy industry. Wenchuan is architecturally uninspiring. More importantly, it is a gateway to Ngawa and the Gyarong region.

An important bridge (Wei Zhou Da Qiao) crosses the Zung-chu at Wenchuan, where the road from Zungchu converges with Highway 213, linking Lanzhou with Chengdu, via Tashiling (Li Xian), Nyaglo and Barkham (244 km) (see above, page 658). Most villages in this area are situated on flatter ground high above the road, and a few possess the tall stone watchtowers characteristic of the regional Qiang culture.

Xiasuo Qiao

The highway from Wenchuan to Chengdu continues following the course of the Zung-chu (Minjiang) southwards through a newly constructed road tunnel. After 30 km it reaches a bridge called Xiasuo Qiuao, which gives access to the last Qiang village, located on a hill-top promontory above the west bank of the river. The

The giant pandas of Wolong

This nature reserve (2,000 sq km) has acquired international renown as the principal breeding ground for the Giant Panda, an endangered species whose natural habitat in now confined to a few forested areas of Sichuan, Gansu and Shaanxi provinces. Established in 1983, under the auspices of the World Wildlife Fund, the Hetaoping breeding station within the reserve monitors the greatest concentration of the panda population (latest Chinese reckoning is about 1600), but their survival is constantly under threat due to rampant deforestation and the peculiarity of their diet. The arrow bamboo and umbrella bamboo on which they depend have a 50/60 year cycle, at the end of which many pandas die due to starvation.

Apart from the pandas, there are almost 100 species of animals, 230 species of birds, and 4,000 species of plants within the reserve; and the Wolong Museum of Natural History at Shawan (Wolong town) is well worth a visit. Here, the Wolong Nature Reserve Administration Office runs the comfy Panda Inn, T0837-6246628, F0837-6246614, which has doubles at ¥300, singles at ¥200, and deluxe suites at ¥668. An older bungalow-style guesthouse is cheaper (range: ¥25-50 per bed). To reach Shawan from Balang Shan pass, the road follows the Pitiao River, a tributary of the Minjiang, downstream for 59 km. From Shawan to the east entrance of the reserve the distance is 45 km, and from there to Chengdu only 136 km. In the northwest of the reserve near Mount Bumozhi (Ch Siguniang) there are trekking and camping facilities. The local population is a mix of Tibetan and Qiang.

watchtower and stone houses of this village have been well maintained, and the inhabitants have kept their local cottage industries.

Wolong Panda Reserve

Some 29 km south of the Xiasuo Qiao bridge, the road reaches **Yenzhing** (Ch. Yingxu), where the Pitiao River flows in from the Wolong Panda Reserve.

Wolong lies 45 km to the west of Yenzhing, and 59 km east of the **Balang Shan** pass, which leads into Tsenlha county (see above, page 663).

Guan Xian → *Colour map 4, grid A6*

After the turn-off for Wolong at Yenzhing, the road leaves Lungu (Wenchuan) county and Tibetan world for that of mainland China. It bypasses a dam and power station on the Zung-chu, crosses the Yinxiu Yenzhou hills, and descends to **Xuankou** village, where there is an 18th-century stone tower.

Qingcheng Shan

Just 23 km south of the Yenzhing, on the outskirts of the city of **Dujiangyan**, a turn-off leads 15 km uphill to the Daoist holy mountain, **Qingcheng Qian Shan** and the adjacent Buddhist holy mountain of **Qingcheng Hou Shan**. Both sites are worth visiting. The four hours' ascent of Qingcheng Qian Shan (Front Mountain) passes several temples and caves which once housed over 500 Daoist monks. Historically, the most important temple here is Tianshi Dong, revered as a major source of the Daoist religion. It is possible to sleep at **Shangqing Gong Temple** and rise early to see dawn at the summit (*Admission fee: ¥25*). At nearby Qingchen Hou Shan (Back Mountain), there is a two-day pilgrimage circuit of Buddhist shrines and caves, the most memorable sites being the scenic White Cloud Temple, Goddess of Mercy Cave, and the double waterfall passed on the descent. Stay overnight at **Youyi Cun** village (*Admission fee: ¥25*).

Dujiangyan

The county town, **Dujiangyan**, is only 55 km northwest of Chengdu. Here there is an important irrigation system which has been in use since the Han Dynasty (256 BC). The then governor of Chengdu, Li Bing, constructed a weir in the Minjiang River in order to split the river into two channels, diverting much of its flow through the irrigation network of the Chengdu Plain (6,500 sq km). This reduced the annual summer flooding of the valley, and, from that time on, Chengdu became a significant farming region. Models and inscriptions here commemorate Li Bing and his son. The nearby **Two Princes Temple (Erwangmiao)** was built in their honour, and there is also a Daoist temple (**Fulongguan**) commanding the weir.

Dujiangyan to Chengdu

At Dujiangyan, a toll expressway takes traffic towards Chengdu, 55 km distant. In **Pixian** county along this road, the Tibetan *Kangyur-Tangyur* Collation Project have their offices.

Sleeping

Linxia *p665*
E **Huaqiao Fandian**, less expensive, doubles cost ¥60.
D **Linxia Hotel**, T0930-6212207. The best in town, where the price range is ¥120-880.

Labrang *p666, map p667*
C **Labrang Hotel**, lies at the extreme west end of town, beyond the monastery, T0941-7121849, F0941-7121328. Charming hotel, formerly the Summer Palace of Jamyang Zhepa, it has been renovated as a Tibetan-style hotel with some modern comforts, set within its own tranquil grounds. There are 36 3-star chalets constructed in concrete in the style of an ornate Tibetan tented camp (¥360 per room), 61 standard rooms with attached bath (¥280 per night), economy doubles at ¥120 and triples at ¥60. The hotel has restaurants, a bar, dance hall, business centre, shop and laundry service.
C **Gangkar Nechok Hotel (Shuijing Shanzhuang)**, T0941-7121878. Has superior doubles at ¥120 and triples at ¥90.
C **Gansu Silk Road Travel**, office. Unfortunately, the complex is somewhat run down and hot water is not yet available round the clock. Better to stay at one of the other hotels in town.
D **Overseas Tibetan Hotel (Hua Qiao Fandian)**, 77 Gonpa Lam, T0941-7122642, othotel@public.lz.gs.cn. Has clean and very well maintained rooms, doubles with attached bath at ¥160 or ¥200, singles at ¥100 or ¥180, doubles without bath at ¥80, and 4-bed rooms at ¥60 or ¥80. The rooms have some authentic Tibetan decoration, and discounts are available during the low season. The hotel has its own internet and IDD/DDD phone services, the **Everest Café** (serving authentic Nepalese cuisine, as well as Chinese and continental dishes), a laundry service, bicycle and taxi hire, currency exchange facility, and local tour agency.
D **Post Hotel (Youdian Binguan)**, T0941-7123625, F0941-7121101. Has doubles at ¥160, suites at ¥380, and triples at ¥135.
D **Serkhar Hotel (Jinlin Binguan)**, T0941-7122305, F0941-7123125. Now one of the best in town, with superior doubles at ¥180, suites at ¥400, economy doubles and triples at ¥120 (¥40-60 per bed).
C **White Conch Hotel** (Baihailuo Fandian), T0941-7122486. Has 35 standard rooms at ¥250 (with attached bath) and ¥100 per bed, or without attached bath at ¥70 per bed, and triples at ¥50 per bed.

For an explanation of the sleeping and eating price codes used in this guide, see inside the front cover. Other relevant information is found in Essentials pages 44-46.

ELabrang Monastery Guesthouse, which has beds for ¥10 per night (no showers).
ETara Guesthouse, T0941-7121274. Has Tibetan-style doubles at ¥40-50, and 4-bed dorms at ¥20 per bed.

The Muslim commercial end of town (east) has less appealing hotels:
EDaxia Hotel, T0941-7121546, the best of these hotels, has doubles at ¥82, and dorms at ¥21 per bed, the **Xinhua Hotel**, the **Waterworks Hostel**, and the **Minzu Hotel**.

Tso *p672, map p673*

D**Jindun Hotel**, 60 Tengzhi St, T0941-8211135. Standard rooms at ¥130, suites at ¥220, and triples at ¥90.

Other accommodation is available at the many cheaper hotels on Tengzhi St, including the Gansu Hotel, the Minzu Hotel, the Bayi Hotel and the Gannan Hezuoshi Fandian, T0941-8213186, which has doubles at ¥40-60 and triples at ¥45.

Luchu *p674*

E**Bus Station Guesthouse**, showers are available.
D**Luchu Hotel**, the best rooms in town, doubles at ¥120, dorm beds at ¥25.

Taktsang Lhamo *p675*

Taktsang Lhamo can provide basic food and accommodation and the area has already become a popular stopover for travellers between Dzoge and Labrang.
E**Langmusi Binguan**, has dormitory accommodation from ¥10 per bed and ¥15 (with showers).
E**Langmusi Fandian**, has triples at ¥45 per room (evening showers available).

Dzoge Nyima *p677, map p677*

E**Tashi Dronkhang**, has newly constructed standard rooms at ¥17-¥18 per bed, and triples at ¥7 per bed.

More expensive rooms are available elsewhere, including: **Machu Government Guesthouse**, T0941-6121466.

Minxian *p679*

E**Minxian Garden Hotel (Huayuan Fandian)**, T0932-7723509. Comfortable standard rooms at ¥50, and suites at ¥120, with attached bathrooms and hot running water.

Dengka Gon *p681*

E**Tewo Hotel (Tebo Fandian)**, T09415-622155. Has singles at ¥46, comfortable doubles at ¥52 (no attached bathrooms), and triples at ¥63, with clean communal toilets and washrooms (hot showers: ¥2).

Taktsha Gondrong *p684, map p685*

E**County Government Guesthouse**, T0837-2298234. Has superior doubles at ¥80, singles at ¥60, and triples at ¥90 (electric heaters and electric blankets are provided).
E**Dzoge Grain Department Hotel (Roergai Liangju Binguan)**, T0837-2298360. Has doubles at ¥50, triples at ¥66, suites at ¥60, and cheaper rooms on the 2nd and 3rd floors (¥9-¥22 per bed). Foreigners pay ¥25 surcharge.

Kakhok *p686*

D**Hongmao Hotel**, T0837-2662044. Currently the best in town, with superior doubles at ¥180-280 and economy doubles at ¥60-160.
D**Old Hongyuan Guesthouse** is under reconstruction and will soon reopen with better rooms.

Cheaper alternatives are available at the Bus Station Guesthouse and the Dolmaling Guesthouse.

Aling *p689*

A**Chuanzhusi Hotel**, T0837-7242222, F0837-7242333, has the best accommodation in town, with standard twin rooms at ¥680.
C**Chunda Yinyuan Hotel (Chuanzhusi Yinyuan Fandian)**, T0837-7242166, has doubles at ¥280, triples at ¥200, and suites at ¥600 per room.
E**Gobin Dajiudian**, T0837-7242188, F0837-7242247, has 49 standard rooms ¥120, 9 deluxe rooms ¥120, and 9 triples ¥150, with Chinese restaurant and massage service.
E**Golden Scenery Hotel (Jinjing Dajiudian)**, T0837-7242262, has 140 standard rooms ¥80, 40 deluxe rooms ¥120, and 10 triples ¥120, also with in-house Chinese restaurant and massage service. Cheaper accommodation is available at the Tibetan run **Chunda Dronkhang**.

Zungchu *p692, map p692*
A The New Hualong Hotel (Hualong Shanzhuang), T0837-7242505. 147 deluxe rooms (doubles at ¥900), is further south and out of town but decidedly in this category.
A Tianma Hotel, T0837-7233168, F0837-7233188. Is currently the best, though a little far from the market, deluxe doubles at ¥780, deluxe suites at ¥880, economy doubles at ¥220, and triples at ¥180.
B Sunriver Hotel (Taiyanghe Dajiudian), T0837-7232888, F0837-7232719. Has doubles at ¥680, suites at ¥1,100, singles at ¥280, and triples at ¥300.
C Songpan Government Guesthouse, T0837-7231458. Has superior rooms at ¥388 (domestic rate) and ¥428 (foreign rate), but this is poor value for money.
C Huanglong Hotel, T0837-7232618. Has superior doubles at ¥260, triples at ¥380, and singles at ¥180, as well as economy doubles at ¥120, triples at ¥160, and 4-bed dorms at ¥200.
C Songpan Hotel (Songpan Binguan), on the ring road. Has doubles at ¥260-360.
C Songzhou Hotel, T0837-7232371. Has superior doubles at ¥280-340, and economy doubles at 120-180.
D Xinxin Restaurant, a cheaper hotel which also has some dormitory rooms.

Another cheaper option is the older building attached to the Songzhou Hotel, where there are dorm beds at ¥25.

Dzitsa Degu *p694*
Inside the park
D Lotus Leaf Guesthouse (Heyezai Guesthouse) at Mangsolde village. Doubles at ¥140 and triples at ¥100-¥110.
D Nuorilang Guesthouse, at Laga. Has double rooms with attached bath at ¥120, and there are 3 restaurants.
E Minzufeng Hostel, Tibetan-run, minimal facilities but inexpensive.
E Rhinoceros Lake Lodgings (Xiniu Hai Shishudian), minimal facilities but inexpensive.
E Ri-tse Guesthouse, minimal facilities but inexpensive.

Outside the park
AL Jiuzhaigou International Hotel, T0837-7739988, F0837-7606558. The first 5-star hotel on the Tibetan plateau, with 556 rooms (doubles at ¥1,000, singles at ¥1,600), 10 restaurants serving Chinese and Continental cuisine, business centre, function rooms, fitness and recreation centre, ticketing service, bookstore and bank.
AL Jiuzhaigou Tiantang Hotel, T0837-7789999. A new 5-star hotel located 61 km from the airport on the approach to the newly opened Shenxianchi scenic area, with deluxe single and double rooms (¥1,480, with electric furnace heating, ¥1,280 without electric furnace heating). The hotel has a sports-stadium style roof that opens out, and within the lobby biosphere there are ancient trees and rare plants growing. Package trip tickets into the Shenxianchi gulley are sold here (¥398 per person).
A CTS Hotel, T0837-7734988. New hotel, doubles at ¥1,000.
A Gesang Hotel, T0837-7734958, F0837-7734489. A 4-star hotel with 272 rooms (doubles at ¥680-880 and suites at ¥1,680-2,380), with 2 restaurants, bars, function rooms, business and recreation centres and sauna.
A Jinlong Yugang Hotel, T0837-7511668.
A New Jiuzhaigou Hotel, T0837-7520719, F0837-7540704. A 4-star hotel with 319 rooms (doubles at ¥780).
A Tanzhong Hotel, T0837-7734399. Has doubles at ¥800.
B Jiuzhaigou Hotel, T0837-7734023, F0837-7734024. A 3-star hotel, with 112 rooms (superior double in A Wing at ¥840, suites at ¥1,500, superior double in B Wing at ¥600 per room, and standard double in A Wing at ¥320). The hotel also has Chinese and Western restaurants, café, full recreational services, and Tibetan camp fire parties at which freshly roasted mutton and chang are offered to Chinese tourists (¥1,400 for a group less than 5).
C Jiuzhai Villa, T0837-7734041, F0837-7734046. With 70 rooms (doubles at ¥240).
C Jiuzhaigou Sangzhuang Hotel.
C Linxiagyuan Hotel, T08494-234030. Has 57 rooms at ¥240 per standard, ¥280 per triple (with attached bathroom).

Mao Xian *p697*
B Guibinlou Hotel, T0837-7425825, F0837-7425830. The best in town, which has 200 rooms (doubles at ¥680, singles at ¥580, and economy doubles at ¥498).

B Linye Hotel, has deluxe suites at ¥580, superior doubles in the west and south wings at ¥465-498, and economy doubles at ¥120.
B Maoxian Hotel, T0837-7422699, F0837-7421168. Has deluxe doubles at ¥400-580, deluxe suites at ¥680, triples at ¥380, and economy doubles at ¥260.
C Qianglin Hotel, T0837-7421437, F0837-7422999.
E Renmin Guesthouse, near the crossroads. Has rooms at ¥25 per bed.

Wenchuan *p698*

C New International Travel Hotel, on the south side of town, T0837-6224866. The best hotel for those obliged to stay overnight here, has doubles at ¥360, singles at ¥480, and deluxe suites at ¥1,180.

On the north side, the best options are the **Telecom Hotel**, **Jiangwei Hotel**, or the quieter **Shan Zhuang Hotel**.

Cheaper rooms are also available at the **Wenchuan County Government Guesthouse**, where there are beds at ¥25.

Dujiangyan *p700*

D Flying Crane Villa (Huo Xiang Shanzhuang), T028-7288006, F028-7288032. A 2-star hotel.
Gold Leaf Hotel (Jinye Binguan), T028-7119999. Comfortable hotel, has superior doubles at ¥580-680, singles at ¥580, suites at ¥980, and economy rooms at ¥220.

Eating

Linxia *p665*

The restaurants in town are overwhelmingly Muslim – those at the **Linxia** and **Haihe** hotels are quite good.

Labrang *p666, map p667*

Everest Cafe, attached to the Overseas Tibetan Hotel. For Tibetan, Indian, and Continental dishes, very popular.
Labrang Hotel, good but expensive Tibetan food prepared here.
Xiahe Henyuan Restaurant, adjacent to the Post Hotel, T0941-7121179. The best Chinese cuisine in town.

The cheaper options for Tibetan cuisine are the **Snowland Restaurant** and the **Tibetan Restaurant**.

Tso *p672, map p673*

Wengsan Restaurant, on the east side of Tengzhi St. Muslim.

Luchu *p674*

The town has both Sichuan and Muslim style restaurants.

Taktsang Lhamo *p675*

Roadside restaurants have English menus, offering Italian spaghetti and American apple pie! Try **Leisha's Café**, or the **Langmusi Restaurant**.

Dzoge Nyima *p677, map p677*

Try the Muslim noodle restaurant on Main St, opposite the Machu Government Guesthouse.

Minxian *p679*

The hotel has an excellent restaurant. Alternatively, try the many small Muslim noodle restaurants in town.

Dengka Gon *p681*

Muslim Restaurant, adjacent to the Tewo Hotel. Appears to have the best food on offer, large.

Taktsha Gondrong *p684, map p685*

Nordzin Restaurant and Bar, Main St, opposite the police station.
Muslim noodle restaurant.

Cheaper menus are on offer opposite the post office.

Kakhok *p686*

Yellow River Restaurant, has the best Sichuan and local cuisine.

Alternatively try the **Red Grassland Restaurant**, or the **Dekyi Tibetan Restaurant**. The lane next to the open market also has an evening hotpot restaurant, and breakfast noodle/ dumpling eateries.

Aling *p689*

Try the hotel restaurants for Sichuan cuisine, or the roadside Muslim restaurants and tea houses.

Zungchu *p692, map p692*

Shingyue Restaurant, one of several restaurants in town which serve Muslim and Sichuan cuisine. Recommended.
Weizhen Restaurant, another good

Festivals at Labrang Tashikhyil Monastery

Festival dates in 2005

Freeing of Animals from Death	16 Feb
Display of Buddha Tangka	21 Feb
Masked Dance	22 Feb
Butter Sculpture Display	23 Feb
Maitreya Procession	24 Feb
Anniversary of the First Jamyang Zhepa	14 Mar
Feast Offering Ceremony	22 May
Enlightenment Anniversary	23 Jun
Mountain Festival	7-13 Jul
Dharmacakra Day	10 Jul
Prayers and Debates	31 Jul-14 Aug
Milarepa Drama	12 Aug
Horse Races	17 Aug
Descent from Tusita	24 Oct
Masked dances	31 Oct
Anniversary of Tsongkhapa	19 Nov

restaurant serving Muslim and Sichuan cuisine. Recommended.
Xinxin Restaurant, has English menus catering for backpackers, moderately good.
Yulan Pancake House, best known restaurant in town which has English menus catering for backpackers.

Dzitsa Degu *p694*
Outside the park:
Try the hotel restaurants for Sichuan cuisine, or the roadside Muslim noodle restaurants and tea houses.
Yifengyuan Restaurant, recommended.
Inside the park:
There are Tibetan-style restaurants at Mangsolde and Dzechawa villages, but they are not particularly cheap, being geared to the tourist market.

Mao Xian *p697*
Shan Tsawan, the most interesting restaurant on the outskirts of town, run by the Qiang Tourism Department. Guests will be welcomed by resonant *gyalings* (oboes) and gunpowder fire as they approach the dining room, and during the meal athletic Qiang waitresses will vigorously bounce unsuspecting tourists bound for Dzitsa Degu up and down into the air, as they sing their traditional songs.

Wenchuan *p698*
Yutian Restaurant, T0837-7554289. Roadside restaurant, Sichuan cuisine.

Festivals and events

Taktsha Gondrong *p684, map p685*
Small grassland festivals are held in Dzoge county throughout the summer with horse and yak races, weightlifting and traditional dances. The monastery puts up a small tented temple and numerous visitors bring tents in which a great deal of alcohol is consumed.

Shopping

Labrang *p666, map p667*
Tibetan carpets and curios may be a good buy here, including clothing, textiles, boots, religious artefacts and household items. Some traders and shopkeepers have returned from exile in India over recent years.

Activities and tours

Dzitsa Degu *p694*
Tour companies
Jiuzhaigou International Travel Service, Room 207 Hualong Hotel, 18 Yingmenkou St, Chengdu, T028-87778699, F028-87778696. Offers package tours to

Dzitsa Degu National Park by bus, via Zungchu and Pingwu.

Transport

Linxia *p665*

Bus

Public buses run at 30-min intervals from Lanzhou bus station to Linxia throughout the day, and there are onward buses from Linxia to **Labrang** (2 hrs), **Tso** (over 3 hrs), **Dowi** and **Repkong** (via Kachu), and Ziling. Once in Linxia, local travel arrangements can also be made by the **Linxia Travel Company**, T0930-6213480/79/82.

Labrang *p666, map p667*

Bus

Daily public buses run to and from **Lanzhou**, **Linxia**, and **Repkong**. To reach Labrang by bus from Lanzhou be prepared for a 6-hr journey, departing at 0730 and stopping over for lunch at Linxia.

Tso *p672, map p673*

Bus

The main bus station is an important hub for passengers heading north to **Lanzhou**, and into the Tibetan areas of **Labrang**, **Luchu**, **Lintan**, and **Dzoge**. There is also a private bus station, which runs frequent minibuses to **Linxia** and **Labrang**. Foreign insurance can be purchased directly at the bus stations.

Luchu *p674*

Bus

Public buses connect Luchu daily with **Tso**, **Machu**, **Taktsang Lhamo**, **Dzoge**, **Tewo** and **Drukchu**, and also with **Henan** in Sogwo.

Taktsang Lhamo *p675*

Bus

Buses running between **Tso** and **Machu** will stop here, but through buses to **Dzoge** and **Tewo** only stop on the highway, 4 km north of town.

Dzoge Nyima *p677, map p677*

Bus

Public buses link Dzoge Nyima with **Tso** and **Henan**.

Taktsha Gondrong *p684, map p685*

Bus

Regular public buses connect Dzoge with **Mewa**, **Ngawa**, **Barkham**, **Zungchu**, **Chengdu**, **Tso** and **Linxia**.

Kakhok *p686*

Bus

There are daily morning departures from the Bus Station for **Chengdu** (¥65.70), **Zungchu** (¥28), **Wenchuan** (¥47), **Barkham** (¥25-27), **Ngawa** (¥21-23), **Linxia** (¥69-76), **Tso** (¥55-61), **Taktsang Lhamo** (¥30-32), and **Dzoge** (¥19-21).

Aling *p689*

Air

Jiuzhaigou Airport, located only 2 km to the northeast of Aling in the Zung-chu valley, opened in 2004, and both Air China Southwest and Sichuan Airlines operate daily flights to and from **Chengdu** (¥470).

Bus

Tour buses run frequently to **Zungchu** and **Chengdu** (south), **Sertso National Park** (east) and **Dzitsa Degu National Park** (northeast).

Zungchu *p692, map p692*

Bus

Public buses run from Zungchu to **Chengdu** (0600, ¥51), **Dzoge** (0700, ¥36), and **Dzitsa Degu** (1330, ¥25).

Dzitsa Degu *p694*

Bus

There are daily bus connections with Chengdu, via Aling and Zungchu. Packages from ¥250 per person (excluding park entrance fee, meals and accommodation) are available through travel services in Chengdu. A shuttle bus and taxi service is also available from Jiuzhaigou Airport in the Zung-chu valley.

Directory

Labrang *p666, map p667*

Internet Internet facilities are found in the major hotels, including the Overseas Tibetan Hotel. **Telephones** China Telecom, sells ICC cards for IDD calls, which can also be easily made from public operator-run booths in the main street. Some of the hotels also purport to have IDD and fax services, but they may not work well in practice. China Post, has an efficient EMS service. **Travel agents** China-Xiahe Labrang Travel Service, 74 Gompa Lam, T0941-7125168, under Tibetan management, offers tours of the Labrang and adjacent areas.

Taktsang Lhamo *p675*

The township has a small post office and a Tibetan language primary school.

Gateway Cities

Footprint features

Kathmandu

→ *IDD: +977, Phone code: (0)1, Population: 737,000.*

*The **Kathmandu Valley**, which is the cultural and political heart of Nepal, offers overland access via the Arniko Highway and Kodari to Western Tibet (see page 255), or trekking via Simikot to Far West Tibet (see page 347). In addition, a third land route is now being planned and this will eventually link Kyirong with Kathmandu via the Trishuli valley (see page 326). Air China Southwest has connecting flights between Kathmandu and Gongkar Airport on Tuesday and Saturday during the tourist season and on Saturday during the off-season. In addition it is possible to take a helicopter from Nepalganj, via Simikot (customs/immigration post) to Hilsa Bridge on the Purang border of Far West Tibet.*

After a long period of isolation throughout the 19th and early 20th centuries (which followed Nepal's unification in the late 17th century), Kathmandu has rapidly become an international centre for tourism. The first surfaced road to reach Kathmandu, from Raxaul Bazar, was only completed in 1956. In recent years Kathmandu has also become one of the important gateway cities for travel to and from Tibet.

The three medieval cities of the valley, Patan, Bhaktapur and Kathmandu itself, are rich in history and tradition. Here mention will only be made of those sites within the valley, which have a particular relevance for Tibetans and the Tibetan Buddhist world.

▸▸ *For Sleeping, Eating and other listings, see pages 716-721.*

Buddhist Kathmandu

Makhan Tole in downtown Kathmandu marks the start of the ancient trade route to Tibet and is lined with interesting temples and shops. Further west, almost halfway between Indra Chowk and **Asan**, is the **Sveta Matsyendranath Mandir** (or Jana Bahal), one of the most venerated Buddhist shrines in Kathmandu. It has a two-tiered bronze roof and two brass lions guard the entrance. The courtyard is filled with small shrines, carved pillars and statues. The white-faced image inside the elaborately carved shrine is **Padmapani Avalokiteshvara**, in the form of the compassionate and benevolent divinity Matsyendra (Tib Phakpa Jamali). There are an astonishing 108 paintings of Avalokiteshvara throughout the temple.

The **Svayambhunath Stupa** (Tib Phakpa Shangku) is revered as the oldest site of Buddhist worship in Kathmandu. It is a major landmark, towering above **Padmachala Hill**, 175 m above the valley and 3 km west of the city centre. According to legend, the hill and stupa occupy the site where the Buddha of the previous aeon, Vipashyin, threw a lotus seed into the lake which then filled the valley, causing it to bloom and radiate with a 'self-arising' luminosity, identified with that of the primordial Buddha, Vajradhara. The bodhisatva Manjushri is believed to have made this lotus-light accessible to worshippers by using his sword to cleave a watercourse for the rivers of the valley, and thereby draining the lake. Newar Buddhists hold that the primordial Buddha Vajradhara is even now embodied in the timber axis of the stupa.

The earliest historical associations of the site are linked to **Vrishadeva**, the patriarch of the Licchavi Dynasty, who is said to have built the first shrine, perhaps using a pre-existing projecting stone. Later inscriptions attribute the stupa's construction to his great-grandson King **Manadeva I** (c. 450 AD) and its reconstruction to the Indian master **Shantikara**, a contemporary of King **Amshuvarman**. It became a focal point for Indian pilgrims and was frequented by Padmasambhava, Atisha and others. By 1234 it had become an important centre of Buddhist learning, with close ties to Tibet. In 1349 Muslim troops from Bengal ravaged the shrine, but it was soon rebuilt with its now familiar tall spire. In 1614 additions and renovations were made by the Sixth Zhamarpa during the reign of Pratap Malla. Access from Kathmandu was improved with the construction of a long stairway and a bridge across the Vishnumati. Pratap Malla also added two new temple spires and a large vajra placed in front of the stupa. Later repairs were carried

Kathmandu

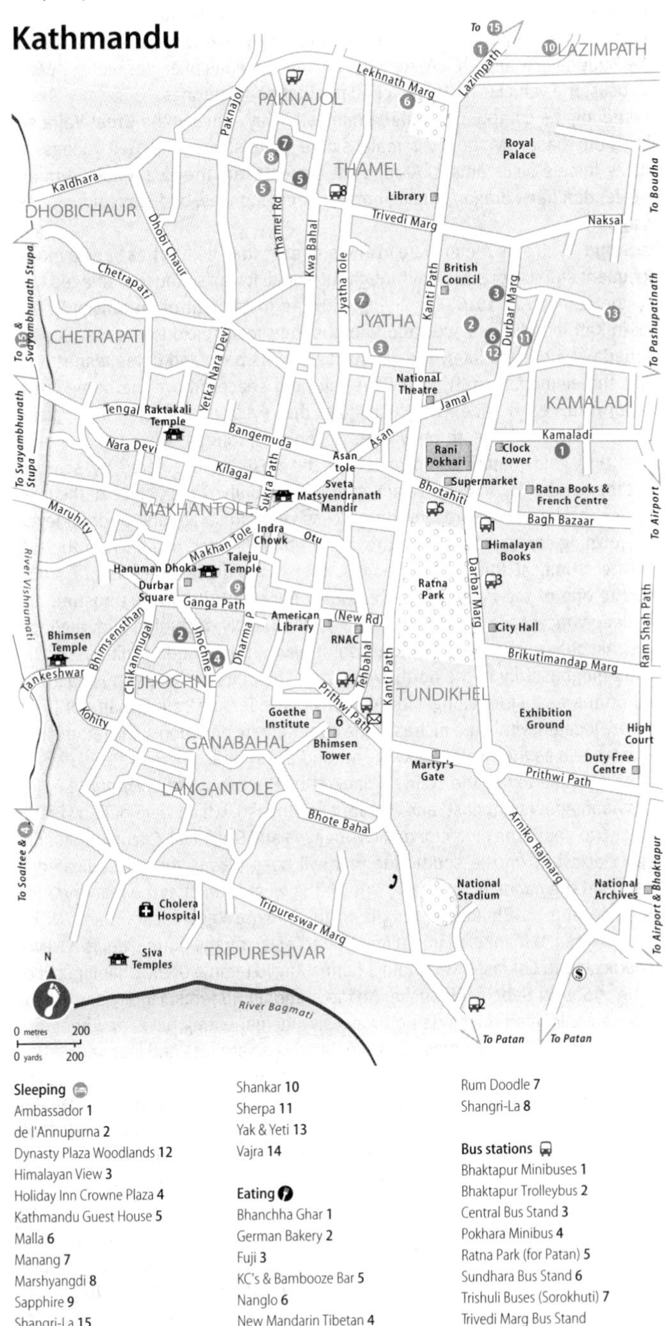

Sleeping
Ambassador **1**
de l'Annupurna **2**
Dynasty Plaza Woodlands **12**
Himalayan View **3**
Holiday Inn Crowne Plaza **4**
Kathmandu Guest House **5**
Malla **6**
Manang **7**
Marshyangdi **8**
Sapphire **9**
Shangri-La **15**
Shankar **10**
Sherpa **11**
Yak & Yeti **13**
Vajra **14**

Eating
Bhanchha Ghar **1**
German Bakery **2**
Fuji **3**
KC's & Bambooze Bar **5**
Nanglo **6**
New Mandarin Tibetan **4**
Rum Doodle **7**
Shangri-La **8**

Bus stations
Bhaktapur Minibuses **1**
Bhaktapur Trolleybus **2**
Central Bus Stand **3**
Pokhara Minibus **4**
Ratna Park (for Patan) **5**
Sundhara Bus Stand **6**
Trishuli Buses (Sorokhuti) **7**
Trivedi Marg Bus Stand

 out by Katok Tsewang Norbu (1750), the Seventh Pawo Rinpoche (1758), and the Shah kings (1825 and 1983).

The Eastern Stairway The climb up the 400 stone steps is more impressive than the modern road. At the bottom are three painted images symbolizing the Three Precious Jewels of Buddhism, which were erected in 1637 by Pratap Malla and his son, Lakshmandra Singh Malla. A large **footprint** in the stone is said to be that of either the Buddha or Manjushri. At regular intervals are pairs of eagles, lions, horses and peacocks, the vehicles of the peaceful meditational buddhas.

On entering the compound from the main stairway, you see the **Great Vajra** set upon its drum base, symbolizing male skilful means, and the **Bell** alongside, symbolizing female discernment. Around the pedestal are the 12 animals from the Tibetan calendar: hare, dragon, snake, horse, sheep, monkey, bird, dog, pig, mouse, ox, and tiger.

The Stupa With a diameter of 20 m and standing 10 m high, it has been a model for subsequent stupas constructed throughout Nepal. It was seriously damaged by a storm in the summer of 1816, coinciding with the instalment of an official British Resident in Kathmandu, an association not lost on the suspicious Nepalis. Repairs were carried out a decade later. The various tiers of its base and dome respectively symbolize the elements: earth, water, fire, air, and space. Above the dome is the square *harmika*, each side of which has the eyes of the Buddha, gazing compassionately from beneath heavy black eyebrows, fringed by a curtain of blue, green, red and gold material. The shape of the nose is considered by some to represent the number '1' in Nepali script, symbolizing unity. The 13 steps of the spire surmounting the *harmika* represent the successive bodhisattva and buddha levels and the crowning canopy represents the goal of buddhahood. On each of the four sides of the stupa, at the cardinal points, there is a niche containing a shrine dedicated to one of the meditational buddhas, each with its distinct posture and gesture, deeply recessed and barely visible within a richly decorated gilded copper repousse. Aksobhya is in the east, Ratnasambhava in the south, Amitabha in the west, and Amoghasiddhi in the north. Vairocana, the deity in the centre, is actually depicted on the east side, along with Aksobhya. The female counterparts of these buddhas are located within the niches of the intermediate directions. The faithful turn the prayer-wheels as they walk clockwise around the shrine.

The vajra at the top of the stairs is flanked by the two white *shikhara* temples, known as Anantapur (southeast) and Pratapur (northeast), which were built by Pratap Malla in 1646 to house the protector deities Bhairava and Bhairavai. Circumambulating the stupa clockwise, on the south side you will pass Newar shrines dedicated to Vasudhara and the *nagas* (rebuilt in 1983). On the west side, after the rear entrance, there is a museum, a Bhutanese temple of the Drukpa Kagyu school, and Newar temples dedicated to Manjushri and Ajima Hariti. Lastly, on the north side, is a Newar temple dedicated to Cakrasamvara, and a Karma Kagyu temple of the Zhamar school, built in the 1960s by Sabchu Rinpoche. An International Buddhist Library and Pilgrim Guest House are located on a side pathway. On a neighbouring hill is another stupa dedicated to Sarasvati, the goddess of discriminative awareness and learning.

Heading northeast from the **Goshala** intersection to the west of Kathmandu, you will pass through **Chabahil** where there is a small but elegant stupa known as **Dhanju Chaitya**. Believed to pre-date the Bodhnath stupa, its construction has been attributed to King Dharmadeva who also contributed to the early growth of Pashupati. During Licchavi times, Chabahil was a village at the crossroads of a major trade route between India and Tibet. Ashoka's daughter, **Charamuti**, is said to have lived here and, with her husband Devapala, founded two monasteries. Some sources also credit her with construction of the stupa itself, which is occasionally still known locally as **Charamuti**. Buddhist monks were based here during the early ninth century. The stupa was rebuilt during the seventh century and again renovated during the 17th century, and stands over 12 m high. Images of four meditational buddhas are found on each of the four sides around the stupa; and on the northern side, there is a 3½-m statue of Buddha in the earth-touching gesture (bhumisparshamudra). It is said that the copper gilt in which the stupa was originally plated was removed and sold by the Mallas to raise funds for their ultimately futile defence of the valley against the invading Gorkha forces.

About 1 km east of Chabahil, the **Bodhnath Stupa** (Tib Chorten Jarung Khashor) is 38 m high and 100 m in circumference, and looms above the road dominating the ancient trade route between Kathmandu and Lhasa. It is the largest stupa in Nepal and is revered by both Tibetan and Newar Buddhists.

Origins Tibetans believe the stupa to contain the bone relics of the past Buddha Kashyapa and to have been built by a lowly poultry keeper and widow named **Jadzimo**. Wishing to utilize her meagre resources as an offering to the Buddha, Jadzimo sought and received permission from the king to begin construction. When they saw what was being built, the local nobility became jealous and resentful that such a great stupa was being constructed by one of such humble social standing. They demanded that the king order its immediate destruction, but the good-hearted monarch refused with the words 'Jarung Kashor' ('The permission given shall not be revoked') from which comes the stupa's Tibetan name, Chorten Jarung Kashor. Jadzimo's sons are said to have been subsequently reborn as King Trisong Dtesen, Shantaraksita, and Padmasambhava, who together established Buddhism in eighth-century Tibet, while the widow herself is said to have attained buddhahood and is known as the protectress Pramohadevi.

Newar chronicles, in contrast, hold the stupa to have been constructed by the Licchavi king **Manadeva** in the latter half of the fifth century AD in order to atone for his crime of patricide. The stupa's Newari name, Khasti Chaitya (Dewdrop Stupa), comes from the drought that accompanied its construction when workers put out cloths at night to be able to drink the dewdrops which accumulated.

The structure was subsequently restored (some sources say reconstructed) by the Nyingmapa lama Shakya Zangpo in the early 16th century. Later, following the 1852 treaty between Nepal and the Manchus, which ended the Tibeto-Nepalese border wars, the custodianship of Boudha was granted in 1859 to a Chinese delegate whose descendants, known as the **Chini Lama** (Tib Gya Lama), continued until recently to hold a privileged position in local affairs.

By its sheer size, the Bodhnath stupa may seem even more impressive than that at Svayambhunath. It too has a hemispherical dome, symbolic of emptiness, topped by a square *harmika* painted on each side with the eyes of the Buddha symbolizing awareness, above which rises the spire with its 13 steps leading up to the canopy, which symbolizes the goal of Buddhahood. However, it is now almost hidden from distant view by the surrounding buildings, which create an attractive courtyard effect for the stupa itself.

Around the octagonal three-tiered base of the stupa there is a brick wall with 147 niches and 108 images of the meditational buddhas, inset behind copper prayer-wheels. Each section of the wall holds four to five such prayer-wheels. The main entrance to the stupa is on the south side, and the principal shrine dedicated to the female protectress Ajima/Hariti on the west. Around the stupa there is a pilgrim's circuit which is densely thronged in the early mornings and evenings by local Tibetan residents and by pilgrims from far-flung parts of the Himalayan region and beyond. Numerous shrines, bookstores and handicraft shops surround the circuit, the speciality being Newar silverware cast by the cire perdue ('lost wax') process.

In recent years Boudha, once a remote village, has become a densely populated suburb of Kathmandu. There is a particularly high concentration of Tibetans here, alongside the older Newar and Tamang communities, and this is reflected in the prolific temple building in which the various Tibetan traditions have engaged since the late 1960s. These shrines and monasteries are too numerous to describe here, but a few of the most important among them can be mentioned, some with well structured **teaching programmes**.

The only temple of importance on the south side of the main road is **Orgyen Dongak Choling**, the seat of the late Dudjom Rinpoche, a charismatic meditation master and scholarly head of the Nyingmapa school, whose mortal remains are interred here in a stupa. Those located to the **west** of the stupa include **Jamchen Monastery** (Sakya; under the guidance of Chogyel Trichen), **Sharpa Monastery** and Trulzhik Rinpoche's Monastery (both Nyingma), **Tsechen Shedrubling** (Kagyu), and **Shelkar Chode** (Geluk).

Heading **northwest** of the stupa, the following are the most important: **Tharlam Monastery** (Sakya), **Karnying Shedrubling** (Karma Kagyu; under the guidance of Chokyi Nyima Rinpoche), **Zhechen Tenyi Dargyeling** (Nyingma; under the guidance of the late Dilgo Khyentse Rinpoche and Zhechen Rabjam Rinpoche); Bairo Khyentse Rinpoche's monastery (Kagyu), and **Marpa House** (Kagyu; under the guidance of Khenpo Tsultrim Gyatso).

Close to the stupa on the **north** side are: **Dabsang Monastery** (Kagyu), **Trangu Tashi Choling** (Kagyu), and **Kyirong Samtenling** (Geluk).

To the **east** are: **Tashi Migyur Dorje Gyeltsen Ling** (Sakya; under Tarik Tulku), **Dezhung Monastery** (Sakya), **Leksheling** (Sakya/Kagyu; under Karma Trinle Rinpoche), **Thubten Ngedon Shedrubling** (Kagyu), and **Karma Chokhor Tekchen Leksheling** (Kagyu).

Further **north** on or near Mahankal Road are: **Mahayana Prakash Pelyul Dharmalaya** (Nyingma; under Penor Rinpoche), **To Pullahari** (Kagyu; under Jamgon Kongtrul Rinpoche), **International Buddhist Academy** (Sakya; under Khenpo Abe), and the **Drukpa Kagyu Monastery** (under Tsoknyi Rinpoche). Mahankal Road extends **northeast** to **Kopan Monastery** (Geluk; under Lama Zopa and Lama Yeshe), and **Ngagi Gonpa** (Kagyu; under Tulku Chokyi Nyima). To the extreme east of Boudha, on the north side of the main road, is **Chubsang Monastery** (Geluk; under Tsibri Chubzang Rinpoche).

The delightful three-storeyed **Vajrayogini Mandir** at **Sangku**, built by King Prakash Malla who was responsible for many of the buildings and monuments standing in Kathmandu's Durbar Square, commands magnificent views of the valley. The uppermost roof is said to be of gold, while the two lower roofs are gilded copper. The struts of all three roofs are lavishly carved with depictions of various deities and mythical animal figures. The main entrance of richly engraved copper is guarded by two large and brightly coloured stone lions. Just below and on plinths on either side of the steps are two smaller metallic lions. The current temple structure dates from the 17th century, but it is widely believed that the location was used as a place of worship even during Licchavi times.

Buddhist Patan

Patan (also known as Lalitpur) is steeped in Buddhist history, tradition and legend, stretching back as far as the disputed visit of the great emperor Ashoka in the third century BC. More than half of the city's population is Buddhist. Many of the temples and *bahals* are open to visitors, their monks happy to explain their traditions and to show the exquisite craftsmanship which decorates some of the buildings.

The remains of four **Ashokan stupas** are located approximately at the cardinal points delineating the ancient boundaries of Patan. Among them, the best preserved is the **Northern Stupa** (**Bahai Thura**), which lies north of Patan's Durbar Square, on the road towards the bridge to Southeast Kathmandu. A lotus-shaped adornment supports the *kalasa* pinnacle above the spire's 13 steps, and a group of *chaityas* form part of the circumference wall at the base of the stupa. A natural spring, active only during the monsoon, is said to exist on one side. A small shrine dedicated to Sarasvati stands on the northern side. The exterior of the stupa has recently been renovated. The **Eastern Stupa** (**Bhate Thura**) is the most remote and lies beyond the Ring Road to the southeast of Durbar Square at Imadole. Four *chaityas* are fitted into the brick perimeter wall at the cardinal points and a small stone structure, the remains of the pinnacle, projects from the top of the grassy hillock. The stupa is a landmark of sorts, but outwardly is otherwise undistinguished and attracts few visitors. The **Southern Stupa** (**Lagan Thura**) is the largest of the four and situated by a lotus pond just to the east of the main road leading south from Durbar Square, giving its name to this Lagankhel area of Patan. Protruding from the top of the stupa is a small hemispherical stone edifice painted with the eyes of Buddha, replacing an earlier wooden structure, and supporting a compact spire representing the 13 stages on the path to enlightenment. The circumference wall is interesting for its inset hewn images of Buddha. A stone mandala, representing the 'palace' of the meditational deity, stands beside the eastern *chaitya*, while the western *chaitya* has a shrine containing images of Amitabha. Lastly, the **Western Stupa** (**Pulchowk Thura**) is situated in Pulchowk, about 1 km along the main Mangal Bazar road heading west from Durbar Square. It is a large mound topped by a stone structure painted with the eyes of Buddha and with four *chaityas* in the base. This is where the annual Boro Jatra festival of Rato Matsyendranath begins its procession.

The **Golden Temple** (Hiranyavarna Mahavihara), also known as Kwa Bahal and Suvarna Mahavihara, is two minutes' walk north of Durbar Square, and its fabulous craftsmanship and lavish decoration should not be missed. Though first documented in 1409, it was renovated by the 11th century King Bhaskaradeva. It was presumably constructed some time before then – some sources say by a local trader in gratitude for the wealth he had accumulated in Tibet.

Behind the inconspicuous entrance (look for the street sign) guarded by a pair of decorative stone lions, the complex is surprisingly compact. The central courtyard contains a small but spectacular shrine dedicated to Svayambhunath. Mythical, griffin-like creatures stand on pillars at its four corners, and each side has wooden lattice windows. The golden pagoda roof is brightly polished and four *nagas* combine to support the *kalasa* at its pinnacle. On one side is a rack of prayer-wheels. This shrine is a late addition and, because it is no longer possible to view the fine façade of the main temple from across the courtyard, is considered by some purists to have diminished the earlier aesthetic appeal of the complex. The courtyard, circumambulated in a clockwise direction, is surrounded on three sides by lines of prayer-wheels which form the inner enclosure of a continuous verandah.

A large bell hangs beneath a gilded canopy near the entrance to the main temple, while above the entrance is a series of 12 carved images of Shakyamuni Buddha. On either side, the eyes of the Buddha are engraved into the bronze border and two richly decorated elephants stand guard. The temple itself is a marvellous three-storeyed pagoda building with each roof covered in copper whose colour gives the temple its popular name. Small statues of birds in flight are attached to the corners of each roof, while bells hang along the length of their rims. Latticed window screens and carved roof struts are found on the first two floors. The 13 steps forming the pinnacle represent the Buddhist stages on the path to enlightenment. Two bronze lions carrying the goddess Tara flank the entrance to the sanctum, which has a frieze depicting the life of Shakyamuni Buddha where a strong Hindu component of some images indicate the extent of religious cross-fertilization in the valley.

Heading southwest from Durbar Square in Patan, you will reach **Rato Matsyendranath Mandir**. The construction of the original temple is attributed to Narendradeva in 1408, though the present temple dates from 1673. It is venerated as an abode of the Bungamati Matsyendranath, also called Karunamaya Avalokiteshvara or, in Tibetan, Bukham Lokeshvara. Legend has it that when

 Gorakhnath, a disciple of Karunamaya, visited Kathmandu, he was not shown due respect. In his anger he cursed the people and consequently they suffered drought and famine lasting 12 years. When Karunamaya learnt of this, he told Gorakhnath to pardon the people and lift the curse; this was done and rain poured down. In honour of Karunamaya's kindness, King Narendra Deva built this temple and instigated the annual chariot race. The alternative residence of Rato Matsyendranath (where the image is installed during the six winter months) is at **Bungamati**, 5 km from Patan. Every 12 years (next in 2015) the whole village takes part as the image is carried on a huge chariot in a journey which can take weeks.

A number of pillars supporting statues of various creatures related to the Tibetan calendar stand in front of the elaborately decorated main north entrance, and to the left a large bell hangs from a Tibetan-style shaft. The revered image, made of sandalwood and clay, is repainted in red (hence *rato*) before each annual chariot race, and is further embellished with jewellery and garlands. The courtyard is filled with sculptures of animals including horses, lions and bulls. For several weeks from April onwards (in the month of Vaisakh), the deity is trundled through the streets of Patan in an enormous chariot. This culminates in the Boro Jatra festival, strategically timed prior to the onset of the monsoon, when the chariot reaches Jawalakhel. The lower roof of the temple is tiled, while the upper two are overlayed with copper. Carvings on the struts of each roof depict various deities with lesser beings placed deferentially at their feet.

To the southeast of Durbar Square, and along a southwest leading alleyway, is the 16th-century *shikhara*-style **Mahabouddha Mandir**, dedicated to the thousand buddhas of the auspicious aeon (Tib Sangye Tongsta) whose names are enumerated in the Bhadrakalpikasutra. Among these, Shakyamuna Buddha was the fourth, and the next to appear in the world will be Maitreya. Tightly hemmed in by surrounding buildings, the terracotta and tile building is difficult to locate. It is somewhat reminiscent of the great Mahabodhi Temple at Bodhgaya in India, and its construction was probably completed in 1585 by Pandit Abhaya Raja during the reign of Mahendra Malla. This is a masterpiece of terracotta and each of the 9,000 or so bricks is said to carry an image of the Buddha, and the face of Buddha is portrayed on blocks of the *shikhara* structure. In the centre is a gold image of the Buddha, which, some sources maintain, was brought here from Bodhgaya. Surrounding the shrine are numerous friezes depicting scenes from the Buddha's life, while the many oil lamps here are lit also in honour of Mayadevi. A narrow staircase leads to the upper part. Although it was completely destroyed in the 1934 earthquake, it has been rebuilt exactly like the original. The temple is surrounded by Newar Buddhist craft shops, most of them selling images of Buddhist deities fashioned in the renowned cire perdue ('lost wax') process.

About 100 m south of the Mahabouddha Mandir, the **Rudravarna Mahavihara** (also known as Oku Bahal, or Bankali Rudravarna Mahavihara) is one of the oldest in Patan. The use of the site for religious purposes probably dates back to the early Malla period and some of the fixtures of the present building are said to be from the 13th century. The main temple rises from the centre of the monastery buildings. The tiled lower roof of the two-storeyed pagoda temple is topped by five decorative stupas and small statues of peacocks, and the copper upper roof has beams trimmed with images of antigods. Above the richly adorned entrance are bronze friezes with various Buddhist representations, including Mayadevi. Inside the rectangular complex are courtyards alive with reflections of the culture of Patan, with bronze and stone statues of elephants, peacocks, Garudas and (remarkably many) lions, as well as mirrors, woodcarvings, bells, vajras, minor deities and a statue of the Rana prime minister responsible for rebuilding much of Kathmandu after the earthquake, Juddha Shamsher. The courtyard also contains a central statue of the Buddha and a line of oil lamps.

The area of Southeast Patan known as **Jawalakhel** is renowned for its large Tibetan community and the **Tibetan Refugee Camp**, now occupied by only the poorest of the exiles. This camp, along with those in Pokhara and at Bodhnath, was one of three major camps established by the Red Cross to accommodate the influx of Tibetans from the early 1950s, and over time it has developed from a transit camp into a focus for the manufacture of **handicrafts** and **carpets**. With further help from the Swiss Association for Technical Assistance, the production of Tibetan carpets blossomed, growing so rapidly that by the early 1990s carpet export accounted for more than half of Nepal's total export earnings. You can watch all stages of their production, from the dyeing and spinning of yarns to the weaving and final trimming. Such carpets can be bought directly from their makers in Patan, Jawalakhel, Boudha, Jorbati, or Bhaktapur, or from any of the numerous shops in Thamel, Indra Chowk and Durbar Marg, which stock a wide range of sizes, designs and qualities.

Buddhist Bhaktapur

The front entrance to the **Sammakrit Vihara** is guarded by two *vyalas*, or lion-like statues and the expansive metal door frame is ornately engraved. Inside is a modern statue of the Buddha. The surrounding walls have attractive representations of episodes of his life and were commissioned by a group of Buddhist monks from Thailand. The **Jetvarna Vihara** has a raised platform on which two small *chaityas*, or shrines, stand. Two *vyalas* are placed at the front corners. The pagoda-like shrines contain images of Shakyamuni and Avalokiteshvara. Squeezed between the two is a small white *chaitya* and behind it stands an ornamental pillar.

On the northern side of the road, the **Lokeshvara Vihara** is probably the city's most attractive Buddhist structure and its only three-storeyed pagoda temple. In front of the entrance, a Buddha statue is surrounded by several smaller *chaityas* and other objects. Two large bells are installed on either side of the main doorway, which is also guarded by stone lions.

Located on a side street just southwest of Dattatraya Square, the small **Mangal Dharma Deep Vihara** is memorable only for its ornately attired image of Dipamkara Buddha.

Chobar and Pharping

The village of **Chobhar** stands on a hill on the west side of the Bagmati River, 4 km from the Patan Ring Road. The village is dominated by a three-tiered **Adinath Lokeshvara Mandir**, which was built in the 15th century and renovated in 1640. The inner sanctum contains an image of Anadadi Lokeshvara (replacing the original Phakpa Wati image which was taken to Tibet). The roof of the temple is of gilded copper and the copper *torana* above the entrance to the shrine has six engraved images of the Buddha.

At the picturesque **Chobhar Gorge** the Bagmati River narrows to cut its way through the rocky hills. The gorge has an important place in Newari Buddhist lore. Legend recounts how the bodhisatva Manjushri, wishing to make the sacred lotus-flame of Svayambhu accessible to devotees, drained the huge lake that was the Kathmandu Valley of its waters by renting the hills to the south with his flaming sword of discriminative awareness (prajna). He thus created the Chobhar Gorge and a fertile valley fit for human habitation. A further 2 km south of Chobhar is **Taudaha Lake,** the only residue of the valley's original lake and mythical repository of the *nagas* released during Manjushri's draining of the valley.

At **Pharping** (Tib. Yanglesho), 11 km beyond Chobar, alongside a Vaisnavite temple known as **Shekha Narayana Mandir,** which lies below a steep limestone cliff, there is a sacred cave revered by Tibetan Buddhists as the place where Padmasambhava realized the Mahamudra teachings. It has an as yet 'unopened' *terma* in its rock walls. Adjacent to the temple, and approached via a flight of steps is the **Buddhist Monastery** under the guidance of Chatrel Rinpoche Sangye Dorje, one of the greatest living masters of the Nyingma school who maintains the Katok and Longchen Nyintig traditions, among others.

On a ridge a few hundred metres to the south, there is an ancient Newari pagoda dedicated to **Phamting Vajrayogini**. This 17th-century temple is one of the four main Vajrayogini sites of the valley. Higher up the hillside, there is the **Asura Cave**, where Padmasambhava attained realizations by propitiating the meditational deity Vajrakila combined with Yangdak Heruka. There are several Tibetan Buddhist temples and monasteries which have been constructed on the hillside around and below this cave in recent decades and which principally represent the Nyingma and Kagyu traditions. Among them are those under the guidance of Zatrul Rinpoche and Lama Ralo. An exquisite 'self arising' rock image of Tara, which was not so long ago exposed to the elements, has now been incorporated within a large temple complex.

Kirtipur and Nagarjuna Ban

The hilltop stupa at **Chilancho Vihara** in **Kirtipur** is widely attributed to the emperor Ashoka, like those at Patan (although the earliest recorded references are dated 1509). The stupa is 11 m high and above the dome 13 circular brass steps lead to the *chatra*. A bamboo structure supports an additional umbrella above the stupa. At the cardinal points around the base are smaller *chaityas* and between these are other shrines, some containing images of the meditational buddhas and various depictions of Tara. A bell, installed here in 1755, is suspended on one side.

Nagarjuna Forest (Tib Langru Lungten) Overlooking **Balaju** garden, 5 km northwest of the city, and covering Nagarjuna Hill (2,188 m) to the north of the Ichangu Narayana Mandir is the delightful forest reserve of **Nagarjuna Ban** (ban = forest) and **Rani Ban** ('Queen's Forest'). The wide expanse of forest is virtually unspoiled by the latter-day urbanization of Kathmandu and provides a natural habitat for a range of wildlife, including deer, pheasant, leopard and wild pigs. There are some lovely walks through tracts of rhododendron and oak, and the higher you climb the better are the views of both Kathmandu and the Himalayas to the north. Woodcutting is prohibited and penalties are strictly enforced. The hill is reputedly named after the Indian Buddhist master Nagarjuna, who is said to have lived in the caves inside the hill. According to the Tibetan tradition this hill was where the Buddha delivered the Prophetic Declaration of Goshringa (although other sources locate this peak in Khotan). The hilltop stupa of **Jamachu** marks the site of this sermon. Legend also has it that prayers for rain made from here are particularly efficacious. The stupa is a simple white structure standing on an exposed windswept stone platform, and numerous prayer-flags are attached to it. An observation tower at the summit offers excellent panoramic views of the Himalayan range to the north.

Sleeping

AL Dwarika's Kathmandu Village, Batisputali, near Pashupatinath, T4470770, F4472328. Singles at US$135 plus tax, and doubles at US$ 155 plus tax. Elegance combined with traditional Newar architecture.

AL Himalaya Hotel, Patan, T5523900, F5523909. Singles at US$110 plus tax and doubles at US$120 plus tax.

A Hotel de l'Annapurna, Durbar Marg, T4221711, F4225236. Rooms for walk-in guests at US$60 per room, while pre-booked singles are US$135 plus tax, and pre-booked doubles US$145 plus tax.

AL Hyatt Regency, Bodhnath, T4491234, F4490033. Currently has the best deluxe rooms in the city, with views overlooking the Bodhnath Stupa. All rooms are currently on offer at US$140.

AL Malla, Lekhnath Marg near the Royal Palace, T4410620, F4418382. Singles at US$120 plus tax and doubles at US$156.

AL Palace, Lazimpath, T4410151, F4412691. Singles at US$135 plus tax and doubles at US$155 plus tax.

AL Shangri La, Lazimpath, T4412999, F4414184. Singles at US$120 plus tax and doubles at US$150 plus tax.

AL Sherpa, Durbar Marg, T4227000, F4222026. Singles at US$105 plus tax and doubles at US $115 plus tax.

AL Soaltee Holiday Inn Crowne Plaza, Tahachal, T4272555, F4272205. Singles at US$180 plus tax, and doubles at US$190 plus tax.

AL Yak and Yeti, Durbar Marg, T44248999, F4227782. All rooms currently priced at US$185 plus tax. Popular meeting place with fine gardens and restaurants.

A Harati, Chetrapati, T4257907, F4223329. Singles at US$55 plus tax and doubles at US$65 plus tax.

A Manang, T4410993, F4415821. Singles at US$55 plus tax and doubles at US$65 plus tax.

A Marshyangdi, Chetrapati, 4414105, F4410008. Singles at US$60 plus tax and doubles at US$70 plus tax.

A Summit, Patan, T5521810, F5523737. Singles at US$65 plus tax and doubles at US$75 plus tax.

B Dynasty Plaza Woodlands, Durbar Marg, T4220623, F4223083. All rooms US$40.

B Vajra, Bijeshwari, T4224719, F4271695. US$33-61 plus tax. Cultural events are regularly held in the Great Pagoda Room and Naga Theatre.

C Classic, New Rd, T4222630, F4224889. All rooms at US$20 plus tax.

C Hotel Utse, Jyatha, T4226946, F4226945. Excellent value for money, with singles at US$15 plus tax and doubles at US$21 plus tax.

C Kathmandu Guest House, Thamel, T4700632, F4700133. A famous back-packing institution, with singles at US$17 plus tax and doubles at US$20 plus tax.

C Norbu Sangpo, Bodhnath, T4477301, F4488357. Singles at US$15 plus tax and doubles at US$20 plus tax.

C Sapphire, Shukrapath, New Rd, T4223636. Offers all rooms at US$20 plus tax.

D Hotel Tashi Delek, Bodhnath, T4250189. Singles at US$12 plus tax and doubles at US$14 plus tax.

D Mandap, Paknajol, T4413321, F4419734. Singles at US$10 plus tax and doubles at US$12 plus tax.

D Mustang Holiday Inn, Paknajol, T/F4249507, has singles at US$10 plus tax and doubles at US$15 plus tax.

D Potala Guest House, Chetrapati, T4220467, has singles at US$4 plus tax and doubles at US$11 plus tax.

E Earth House, Paknajol, T4418197, has singles at US$3.5 and doubles at US$5.5.

E Pheasant Guest House, Thamel, T4417415. Singles at Nrs 100 plus tax and doubles at Nrs 150 plus tax.

E Potala, Thamel, T4416680, F4419317. Singles at Nrs 125 plus tax and doubles at Nrs 200 plus tax.

E Villa Everest, Paknajol, T4413471, F4423558. Singles at US$10 plus tax and doubles at US$12 plus tax.

Eating

Many of the large hotels have excellent restaurants, such as the **Chimney Restaurant** at the Yak and Yeti, the **Rox Restaurant and Bar** at the Hyatt Regency, **Cozy Garden** at the Hotel Marshyangdi, the Jewels of Manang at the Manang Hotel, and **Gurkha Grill** at the Soaltee Holiday Inn. Some simpler hotels also offer fine multi-cuisine, such as the **Utse Restaurant and Bar**, Jyatha, T4253417, which was founded in 1971 and is one of the oldest well-known restaurants in Thamel. In addition, the following speciality restaurants are also recommended.

Indian

Third Eye Thamel, T4260160.

Nepali/Tibetan: **Bhanccha Ghar**, Kamaladi, T4225172. **Dechenling** Thamel, T4225195. **Nanglo Bakery and Café** Durbar Marg,

For an explanation of the sleeping and eating price codes used in this guide, see inside the front cover. Other relevant information is found in Essentials pages 44-46.

T4222636. Nepalese Kitchen, Thamel, T4260965. **Thamel House**, Thamel, T4410388.

Chinese

China Town Lazimpath, T5547453.

Continental

Bakery Cafe, Jawalakhel, T5522949.
Delima Garden Café, Paknajol, T4430717.
Everest Steak House, Chetrapati, T4260471.
Four Seasons, Thamel, T4412135.
German Bakery, Jhochen, T4433626.
Gourmet Vienna, Thamel, T4419183.
Helena's, Thamel, T412135.
KC's Restaurant and Bambooze Bar, Thamel, T4416911.
Kilroy's of Kathmandu, Thamel, T4250441.
K-Too Beer and Steak House, Thamel, T4433043.
Le Bistro, Thamel, T4411170.
Rum Doodle, Paknajol, T4414336.

Thai

Ying Yang Restaurant, Thamel, T4425510.

Japanese

Aji No Silk Road, Thamel Chowk, T4258178.

Mexican

1905 Boardwalk, Kantipath, T4225272.
New Orleans Café, Thamel, T4418197.
Northfield Café & Jesse James Bar, Thamel, T4424884.

English

Old Spam's Space, Thamel, T4412713.

Italian

Fire & Ice, Thamel, T4250210. La Dolce Vita, Thamel, T4419612.
Pradhan's San Francisco Pizza Restaurant, Thamel, T4427391, Roadhouse Café, Thamel, T4260187.

Vegetarian

Paradise Restaurant, Jhochen, T4240602.
Skala, Thamel, T4223155.

Activities and tours

Tour companies

NB Check all tickets, travel documents, etc, carefully.

Thamel area

Basanta Adventure, PO Box 8110, Thamel, Kathmandu, Nepal, T0997-1-423417, www.basantaadventure.com. All the treks and tours are designed to promote eco-tourism. Specialized service for customized trekking expeditions and cultural tours in all regions of Nepal.
Wayfarers, T0997-1-229110, F0997-1-245875, wayfarer@mos.com.np. 50 m south of Le Bistro restaurant, which is efficient and accepts credit cards, with a branch in Pokhara.

Around Durbar Marg

Everest Express, T0997-1-220759, F0997-1-226795.
Himalayan Travels, T0997-1-223045, F0997-1-224001.
Modern Travels, near Yak and Yeti Hotel, T0997-1-244357, F0997-1-242388. Natraj, Ghantaghar, T0997-1-222014.
Nepal Kamaz Tours, T0997-1-241811, F0997-1-223370.
President, T0997-1-220245, F0997-1-221180.
Shambhala, T225166, F227229. Specialists in Bhutan.
Team Tours, T0997-1-227057, F0997-1-243561.
Connections to Central Asia and Russia:
World Travels.
Indian Airlines reservations, T0997-1-226275, F0997-1-226088.
Yeti, T0997-1-221234.

Tridevi Marg

Sita World Travel, T0997-1-418363, F0997-1-227557, sitaktm@sitanep.mos.com.np.
Swiss Travels, T0997-1-412964, F0997-1-423336. Has branch in Pokhara.
Tibet Travel and Tours, T0997-1-231130, F0997-1-228986. Organizes package tours to Lhasa.
Ying Yang Travels, T0997-1-423358, F0997-1-421701. Specializes in ornithological and topographical expeditions throughout the Himalayas.

Elsewhere

Great Escapes Trekking, T0997-1-418951, F0997-1-411533.
Holy Land Travels, Bodhnath, T0997-1-479019, F0997-1-478592.
Kathmandu Travel and Tours, Tripureshvar,

T0997-1-222511, F0997-1-471379.
Marco Polo, Kamal Pokharai, T0997-1-414192.
Namaste, Maitighar, Ramshah Path, T0997-1-227484, F0997-1-226590.
Nepal Travel Agency, Ramshah Path, T0997-1-413188, F0997-1-420203.
Paramount Nepal Tours, Lazimpath, T/F0997-1-415078.
Pashupati Travels, Kantipath, T0997-1-248598, F0997-1-224695.

Transport

Air

Flights to Kathmandu

Qatar Airways (www.qatarairways.com) have daily flights from **London** and **Munich** via **Doha**. Gulf Air (www.gulfairco.com) have flights from **London**, **Paris**, **Frankfurt**, **Milan** and **Rome** connecting through **Abu Dhabi** on Monday, Wednesday and Saturday, while Aeroflot and Austrian Airlines both have flights from European cities on Thursday connecting via **Moscow** and **Vienna** respectively. For travellers from Europe, Southern Africa, and the east coast of North America there are also onward connecting flights from **Delhi** (on RNAC or Indian Airlines), **Karachi** (PIA), **Dhaka** (Biman), and **Bangkok** (Thai Air and RNAC). For those originating in **Australia**, **New Zealand** and the **west coast of the United States** there are onward connecting flights from **Hong Kong** (RNAC), Singapore (Singapore Airlines and RNAC). **Bangkok** (Thai Air and RNAC), **Osaka** (RNAC), and **Shanghai** (RNAC). For reservations and price information, contact the relevant airline website.

Flights from Kathmandu

For domestic airline and helicopter routes, as well as domestic bus schedule information, please refer to the detailed listings in Footprint Nepal Handbook (second edition). The following airlines have offices in Kathmandu: Aeroflot Russian Airlines (SU), Kamaladi, T4227399; Biman Bangladesh Airlines (BG), Kamal Pokhari, T4434740; Air China Southwest (CA), Lazimpath, T4440651, F4419778; Gulf Air, Hattisar T4228288; Druk Air (KB), Durbar Marg, T4225166, F4227229; Indian Airlines (IC), Hattisar, T4429468. **Ticket sales** At World Travels, Durbar Marg, T4226275, F4226088; Pakistan International Airlines (PK), Durbar Marg, T4439324; Qatar Airways (Q7), Kantipath T4267701; Royal Nepal Airlines (RA), New Road T4220757, F4225348; Singapore Airlines (SQ), Durbar Marg, T4226582, F4226795; Thai Airways (TG), Durbar Marg, T4224917, F4221130.

The following airlines not flying to Kathmandu also have offices or representatives here where you can make reservations, amend or confirm flights: Air France, Durbar Marg T4248059; American Airlines, Kamaladi T4268563. Delta Airlines, Durbar Marg T4223233; Air India, Kantipath T4211730; British Airways, Durbar Marg T4222266; Malaysian Airlines, Heritage Plaza T4247215; Cathay Pacific, Kamaladi T4225111; Dragon Air, Durbar Marg T4223502; Japan Airlines, Durbar Marg T4222838; Korean Airlines, Kantipath T4252048; Kuwait Air, Kantipath T4249887; Lauda Air, Kamaladi T4223331; Northwest Airlines, Lekhnath Marg T4418387; Philippine Airlines, Kamaladi T4218332; Qantas, Durbar Marg T4224956; Royal Brunei Airlines, Kamaladi T4437193; Saudi Arabian Airlines, Kathmandu Plaza T4246453; Martin Air, Heritage Plaza T4247215.

Directory

Banks

Normal banking hours are 1000-1400 Sun-Thur, 1000-1230 Fri, closed Sat. **NB** Keep your exchange certificates which are required to change money back when you leave. The main branch of Standard Chartered Bank is on Kantipath, with a Thamel branch, T4233128, F4228692. 100m south of Le Bistro restaurant, Mastercard and Visa withdrawals, telegraphic money transfer, open 1000-1600, Sun-Fri, closed Sat. Most of Thamel's various authorized money changers are open daily, 0800-2000. **On Kantipath** Nepal Bank, T4227375. Sat 0930-1230, closed Sun. Nabil Bank, T4227181. **On Durbar Marg** Nepal Investment Bank, T4228229. State Bank of India, T4225326. **On New Rd** Everest Bank, T4222230. Nepal Bank, T4229696. Open daily, 0800-1900. Himalayan Bank, T4224787. Open Sun-Fri 0800-2000, closed Sat. Rastra Banijya Bank, T5538103. At

Mangal Bazar.

Credit cards American Express, T4226172. Has an office in Jamal, between Durbar Marg and Kantipath. Also deals with Amex TC enquiries and travel services. Open 0800-2000 Sun-Fri, 0930-1600 Sat. Mastercard and Visa are at Alpine Travel, T4225020, on Durbar Marg, 0800-2000 Sun-Fri, 0930-1600 Sat.

Telephone

Kathmandu area code 1 (01 if dialling from within Nepal). Dozens of public call offices have sprung up in Thamel and throughout Kathmandu and offer international direct dialling & faxing (Rs 50-200 per minute, depending on international zone), as well as email facilities (Rs 40 per hour). The Central Telegraph Office at Tripureshvar, 200m south of the GPO has an international telephone service counter open 24 hrs and is a little cheaper than the private bureaux, but charges a minimum of 3 mins, even if answer phone. Phone calls, telex and fax messages may be sent. For international calls, T186, domestic information T197, and domestic trunk calls T186.

Post offices

Open 1000-1430 Sun-Thur, 1000-1230 Fri, closed Sat. **GPO**: at Sundhara, near Bhimsen Tower. Open Sun-Thur 1000-1700, Fri 1000-1500, closed Sat. **NB** Make sure that cards and letters are franked in your presence. There is a small post office in Durbar Square, often overlooked by visitors and therefore quicker. Major hotels sell stamps and have letter boxes. **Poste Restante** at the GPO (not efficient for forwarding mail), and a philately counter. The American Express office on Jamal has a poste restante service for cardholders. **NB** Have your mail addressed with your surname in capitals and underlined. Bring your passport for identification. **Courier and Freight Services**: DHL, T4264259, F4220215, Kamaladi. United Parcel Service T4476851, F4225915, Putali Sadak; TNT International Express T4240453.

Embassies and consulates

Australia, T4371678, Bansbari. *Austria, T4410891, Hattisar. Bangladesh, T4414943, Maharajganj. *Belgium, T4228925, Durbar Marg. *Canada, T4415193, Lazimpath. China, T4411740, Baluwatar. Denmark, T4413010, Baluwatar. Egypt, T5524844, Pulchowk, Patan. Finland, T4471221, Lazimpath. France, T4418034, Lazimpath. Germany, T4416832, Gyanesvara. *Greece, T4233113, Tripuresvara. *Hungary, T5525015, Pulchowk, Patan. India, T4414990, Lainchaur. Israel, T4411811, Lazimpath. Italy, T4412280, Baluwatar. Japan, T4426680, off Durbar Marg. North Korea, T5521855, Jhamsikhel, Patan. South Korea, T4270172, Tahachal. *Maldives, T4223045, Durbar Marg. *Mexico, T4412971, Pani Pokhari, Lazimpath. *Netherlands, T5523444, Kumaripati, Patan. Pakistan, T4411421, Pani Pokhari, Lazimpath. *Philippines, T4474409, Shinamangal. *Poland, T4221101, Ganabahal; Russia, T4412155, Baluwatar. *Spain, T4472328, Batisputali. Sri Lanka, T4417406, Baluwatar. *Sweden, T4220939, Kicha Pokhari. *Switzerland, T5523468, Jawalakhel, Patan. Thailand, T4420410, Bansbari. *Turkey, T4232711, Bijuli Bazar. United Kingdom, T4411590, Lainchaur. USA, T4411179, Pani Pokhari, Lazimpath. (*Consular service.)

Hospitals and medical services

If you fall ill, there are numerous **pharmacies** throughout Kathmandu where you can buy medicines without prescription. If you require a stool, blood or urine **test**, it is advisable to get this done at a reputable clinic. Results are usually ready the same day or by the following morning. For vaccinations, lab tests, health information and surgical or GP consultations, the Himalayan International Clinic, T4216197, F4220143, is in Chetrapati. This is a private clinic aiming to provide Western standards of care and travel medicine. Government hospitals include the Bir Hospital, T4226963, on Kantipath near the Tundikhel. The Japanese assisted Teaching Hospital, T4412808, and the Kanti Hospital, T4411550, are both in Maharajaganj. If you fall sick whilst **trekking** and require evacuation, the Himalayan Rescue Association (T4440293) can advise on helicopter rescue. This is expensive and requires proof of sufficient insurance or a written guarantee of full payment. **NB** Remember to keep receipts for insurance claims. The HRA office is 100m west of the old Immigration Office on Tridevi Marg (T419755). Open 1000-1700, Sun-Fri, closed Sat.

Tourist offices

There are two government tourist information offices in Kathmandu, one at the airport (T4470537), the other just off Basantpur Square (T4220818). Open 0900-1700 Sun-Thur, 0900-1500 Fri, closed Sat. The Department of Tourism headquarters (T4256909) has recently been relocated to Exhibition Rd, alongside the bus station, and it also has a supply of leaflets. Open Sun-Thur 1100-1600, Fri 1100-1500, Sat closed. There are a number of free magazines for tourists which carry interesting articles on various aspects of Nepali life as well as maps and compendious lists of useful and useless phone numbers. Titles include Adventure Nepal, Image Nepal, Nepal Visitor and Travellers Nepal and are available at the airport and in good travel agents.

Useful information

NGOs For information about NGOs based in Kathmandu, contact the Social Welfare Council, Lekhnath Marg, Kathmandu, T4418111, F4410279. A booklet, NGO Profile, listing the activities and contact addresses of 42 NGOs is published by IUCN and USAID, and is available from the KEEP office in Thamel.

Useful numbers

Emergency, T100. Police, T4226999. Tourist Police (Babar Mahal) T4211293. Fire T101. Ambulance, Bishal Bazar T4211121. Nepal Chamber T4230213; Bhimsenthan T4211959. Red Cross (Brikhuti Mandap), T4228094.

Government Offices Nepal Tourism Board and Information Service, Babar Mahal, T4256909. Immigration Office, Bhrikuti Mandap, T4222453. Kathmandu Municipality, Dharma Path, T4221280. Ministry of Tourism and Civil Aviation, Singha Durbar, T4211286.

Chengdu

→ *IDD: +86, Phone code: (0)28, Population: 10,140,000.*

The city of Chengdu is the main gateway for travellers visiting Eastern Tibet through the Erlang Tunnel (see page 486); and there are also overland routes to Barkham in Gyarong (see page 658), and Zungchu in Amdo (see page 692). Chengdu is directly connected by air with Lhasa, Chamdo, Gyeltang, Ziling and Dzitsa Degu National Park. As the capital of China's most populous province, Sichuan, Chengdu also has the advantage of being well connected to the outside world.

The city lies on the Jinjiang (Brocade River), a major tributary of the Zung-chu (Ch Minjiang), which flows southwards from Amdo to converge with the Gyarong at Leshan. During the Eastern Han Dynasty, it was formerly known as Jincheng (Brocade City); and during the Five Dynasties period, it was one of the capitals of China. Later in the 13th century, the Mongolian city of Chengdu was visited by Marco Polo. Nothing remains,

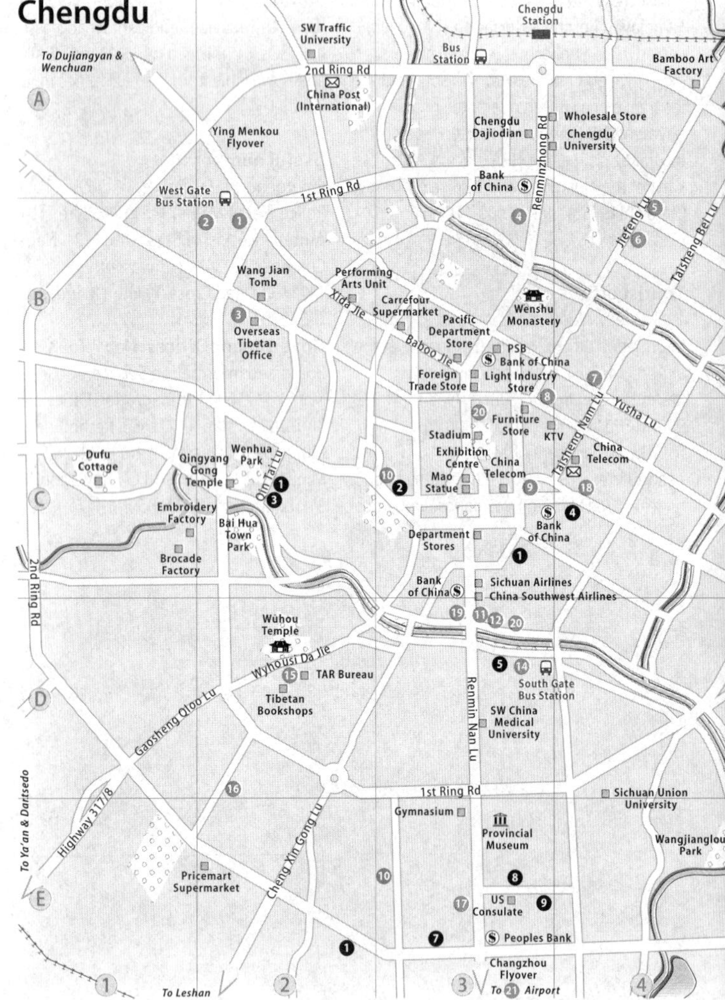

however, of the old Tatar city walls and towers. The narrow streets of the old town rarely preserve their quaint traditional-style wooden houses, except for the old quarter in West Chengdu, and the former Ming Dynasty imperial palace was destroyed and replaced by a grotesque concrete building, known as the Long-life Exhibition Hall (Ch Wang Sui Zhan Lan Guan), in front of which is one of China's largest statues of Mao Zedong.

As far as East Tibet is concerned, Chengdu is a city of great importance, in that the 19 counties of Kandze Autonomous Prefecture, the 13 counties of Ngawa Autonomous Prefecture; and the Mili Tibetan Autonomous County are all administered from here. Political and civil offices dealing with the affairs of East Tibet are hence located here; as are the head offices of the Sichuan Nationalities Publishing House and the Southwest China Nationalities Institute. ▸▸ *For Sleeping, Eating, and other listings, see pages 724-727.*

Sights

Central Chengdu is the commercial hub of the city, concentrated around the Renmin Road intersection, where the Ming Dynasty palace once stood. There are a number of five-star and four-star hotels, and good Sichuan restaurants. The Sichuan Nationalities Publishing House is located behind the Minshan Hotel on South Renmin Road, alongside a number of antique shops, some of which belong to traders from Ngawa. Also on South Renmin Road is the Sichuan Provincial Museum.

East Chengdu is the industrial sector of the city and largely of no interest to the casual visitor. However, in the southeast, the Wan Jiang Pavilion Park (River View Park) contains three Qing Dynasty buildings and a rare collection of 110 species of bamboo (including the 'mottled' and 'human face' varieties).

Most sites of cultural importance are to be found in the west of the city. Here, the Dufu Caotang contains the thatched cottage of the Tang Dynasty poet Du Fu (712-770). Du Fu was an impoverished nobleman from Shaoling near Xi'an; but as a poet he is regarded as the archetypal Confucian moralist. His difficult prose style contrasts with the libertine Daoist style of his contemporary, Li Bai (701-762). A Song Dynasty temple complex, reconstructed most recently during the Qing period, contains a stone tablet, a clay statue of Du Fu, and an exhibition with drawings and photographs illustrating his life and works.

Other temples can also be visited in West Chengdu: The Wuhou Temple is dedicated to Zhu Geliang, who appears as the greatest military strategist in the Chinese classic novel Romance of the Three Kingdoms. Nearby are the shops owned by Khampa and Ngawa traders, adjacent to the Kandze Hotel (Garze Binguan) and the TAR Government Guesthouse. The Qing Yang Gong is a Daoist temple, the original foundation of which is attributed to the ancient Zhou Dynasty, but most recently rebuilt between 1667-1671.

Near the West Gate Bus Station, there are shops owned by Ngawa traders and the **Ngawa Hotel**Ⓓ *Aba Binguan, T7768957*. Further west, in Pi Xian satellite county, on the road to Dujunyan, the important Kangyur-Tangyur Collation Project has its headquarters.

Near Zhongbei in South Chengdu there is a US Consulate, the combined campus of Sichuan University and Science University and a number of computer stores. It is here that the largest concentration of expatriates is to be found in the city. The Southwest China Nationalities Institute is also located nearby on First Ring Road (West Section).

In the north of Chengdu, the most important site is the Wenshu Monastery on Renmin Bei Road, an impressively large and active Chinese Buddhist temple, dedicated to Manjughosa, which contains a precious bone relic of Shakyamuni Buddha. On the site there is also an extraordinary vegetarian restaurant where the texture and shape of the food are prepared so as to resemble meat and eggs! Further northwest on the outskirts of town the Panda Research Institute is well worth a visit, rather than the Chengdu Zoo, which is also in the north of the city.

About 22 km north of Chengdu in the countryside is the Baoguangsi (Blazing Jewel Temple), which was founded during the Tang Dynasty. The Lohan Hall houses 500 *arhat* images from the Qing period, among the best of traditional Chinese sculpture.

Sleeping

AL **Holiday Inn Crown Plaza**, 31 Zongfu St, T028-86786666, F028-86786599. 5-star, 33 floors, 433 rooms (doubles and singles at ¥1623, suites at ¥3054), business centre, and the best western buffet in town.

AL **Jinjiang Hotel**, 80 Section II, Renmin Nan Lu, T028-85582222, F028-5582348. 5-star (recently refurbished), has 520 rooms (doubles and singles at ¥1105, suites at ¥1817) with Garden Korean BBQ, Fontaine Blue Bar, Louvre Garden, and Garden Grillroom.

AL **Sheraton Lido**, 15 Section 1, Renmin Zhong Lu, T028-86768999, F028-86768267. 5-star, high-rise (doubles and singles at ¥1432, suites at ¥3654),

AL **Sofitel Wamda Hotel**, 15 Bingjiang Zhong Lu, T028-66918899, F028-86666333. Has the newest deluxe rooms in the city, with twins and singles at ¥1,500 and suites from ¥2,000. Excellent location alongside the Jinjiang River.

A **Amara Hotel**, Taisheng Lu, T028-86922233, F028-86948796. 4-star (doubles and singles at ¥880, suites at ¥2360).

A **Chengdu Huayuan Hotel**, 8 Daye Lu, T028-86663388, F028-86655672. 4-star, 22 floors, 250 rooms (doubles at ¥800, singles at ¥770, suites at ¥1430).

A **Greenland Hotel**, 99 Zhongleici Xilu, T028-82938899, F028-82933633. 4-star, 41 floors, 200 rooms (doubles and singles at ¥946, suites at ¥2200).

A **Minshan Hotel**, 55 Section II, Renmin Nan Lu, T028-85583333, F028-85582154. 4-star high-rise hotel with 21 floors and 432 rooms (doubles and singles at ¥880, suites at ¥1540) with popular 2nd floor Cantonese restaurant.

A **Tianren Grand Hotel**, 18 Sandongqiao Lu, T028-87731111, F028-87717777. 4-star, 7 floors (doubles at ¥738).

A **Tibet Hotel** (Xizang Fandian), 10 Renmin Bei Lu, T028-83183388, F028-83185678. 3-star, 17 floors, 426 rooms (doubles at ¥858, singles at ¥570, suites at ¥1032).

A **Yinhe Dynasty Hotel**, 99 Xiaxi Shun Lu, T028-86618888, F028-86741351. 4-star, 26 floors, 348 rooms (doubles at ¥1210, singles at ¥1463, suites at ¥2199), with excellent Guangdong-style restaurant.

B **Babao Grand Hotel**, T028-85704101, F028-85702556. 3-star (doubles at ¥420, singles at ¥580, suites at ¥460).

B **Chengdu Hotel**, Shudu Dadao Dong Yi Duan, T028-84448888, F028-84432083. 3-star, 11 storeys (doubles at ¥460, singles at ¥580, suites at ¥950).

B **Lhasa Hotel**, 88 Xiaojia He St, 4 Ring Rd (South), T028-85198998, F028-85174397. 3-star (doubles and singles at ¥380, suites at ¥880).

B **National Hotel**, T028-87750888, F028-87768685. 3-star (doubles at ¥400, singles at ¥580, suites at ¥1180).

B **Sunjoy Inn (Xinzu Binguan)**, Renmin Nanlu

(Section 4), T028-85563388, F028-85571660. 3-star, 7 floors, 189 rooms (doubles at ¥400, singles at ¥450, suites at ¥860).

B **Xinliang Hotel**, 53 Shangdong Ave, T028-86739999, F028-86739333. 3-star, high-rise, 274 rooms (doubles and singles at ¥515, suites at ¥1980).

C **Angel Hotel**, 10 Dianxin Nanjie, T028-85422050, F028-85422794. Has 162 rooms (doubles ¥380, singles ¥320, suites ¥600).

C **Giant Dragon Hotel**, Chengdu Airport, T028-85704101, F028-85702556. (Doubles at ¥420, singles at ¥580, suites at ¥780).

C **Traffic Hotel (Jiatong Fandian)**, 6 Ninjiang Zhong Lu, T028-85451017, F028-85452777. Is the backpackers' favourite, with 7 floors, 122 rooms (doubles at ¥260, triples at ¥160-240.

C **Rongchen Hotel**, 130 Shaanxi jie, T028-86112933, F028-86135532. Centrally located (doubles ¥320, singles ¥260, suites ¥380).

C **Sam's Backpacker Guesthouse**, behind Rongchen Fandian, T028-86122529, F028-86135532. (Doubles ¥260, dorm beds ¥35-70).

D **Wanguan Hotel**, Chengdu Airport, T/F028-85703803.

Eating

Chengdu is famous for its spicy Sichuan cuisine. There are many excellent Sichuan restaurants throughout the city.

Banana Leaf (Jiaoye Fandian), T028-86133230, next door to the mosque on Xiyu Jie. Thai cuisine.

Beijing Gaoya Restaurant, on Zhongfu Jie, opposite the Holiday Inn. Serves Peking duck.

Chen Ma Po Dou Fu Restaurant, has many branches, including one outside the Daoist temple of Qing Yang Gong. Try the spicy bean-curd dishes.

Fiesta Thai, adjacent to the Traffic Hotel. Thai cuisine.

Furong Guo, near the Minshan Hotel. Good hotpot restaurant

Gingko (Yinxing) Restaurant, Ninjiang Zhong Lu, near the Traffic Hotel. Has The best and most expensive Sichuan cuisine in town.

Huang Cheng Lao Ma Restaurant, branches in Qintai Rd and South Section, Second Ring Rd. Offers the best Sichuan hotpot in the city.

Tandoor Restaurant, Sunjoy Hotel, 34 Section IV, Renmin Nanlu, T028-5551958. For amazingly good Indian cuisine

Wenjun Restaurant, Qintai Rd. Elegant, good for Sichuan dishes.

Western Home, 10 Lingshiguan Lu, T028-5216226. Western food and pizza in particular.

Yinxing Zaocha Restaurant, in the Binjiang Hotel, opposite the Jinjiang Hotel. Delicious Guangdong-style dimsum.

Chengdu also has many **KFC** and **MacDonalds** fast food outlets.

Bars and clubs

There are many bars throughout the city.

Pojong Ozer (Tibetan Bar and Restaurant), Ninjiang Zhong Lu, near the Traffic Hotel. Has an unusual Tibetan cabaret and monastic decor on the outside.

Half Dozen (Ban Da), Fangcaojie, Yueling. Chengdu's most popular pub, with the best live music performances in town.

Bands also at the **Amara** and **Sheraton**.

Chengdu West Gate bus station timetable

Destination	Departure Time	Price
Wolong	0700, 0840, 1140	¥19.50-21.50
Wenchuan	0700, 0830, 1000, 1130, 1200, 1330, 1400, 1600	¥20.50-22.50
Tashiling	0720, 1030, 1310	¥27.50-30
Maowen	0720, 1410	¥26.50-29
Trochu	0630, 0700, 0730	¥42.50-46
Tsenlha	0630	¥39.50-43
Rongtrak	0630, 0700	¥71-105 (deluxe)
Chuchen	06.30, 0640	¥66.50-73
Zungchu	0700	¥45-49
Hongyuan	0730	¥62-67.50 (deluxe)
Barkham	0630, 0700	¥55-60 (deluxe)
Ngawa	0630	¥69-75.50
Nanping	0840	¥91
Dzitsa Degu	0840	¥91
Dzoge	0730, 0800	¥80-87.50 (deluxe)
Sertal	0800	¥99-135
Dzamtang	0700	¥84.50-92.50
Chengdu: South Bus Station		
Ya'an	0730-1830	¥28-33
Chakzamka	0700, 0800, 0900, 1000	¥95 (a/c)
Dartsedo	0700, 0800, 0900, 1000	¥97 (a/c)
Tawu	0800	¥155
Kandze	0800	¥198
Litang	0800	¥173
Dabpa	0800	¥216 (a/c, Yaxing bus)
Batang	0800	¥229
Emei	0700-1800	¥28-33

Activities and tours

Tour companies

Chengdu Travel Service, 18 Qingnian Lu, T028-6275858, F028-667482.

China International Travel Service, 65 S Renmin Rd (Section 2), T028-6679186, F028-6672970.

Holyland Travel, Traffic Hotel, 6 Ninjiang Zhong Lu, T028-5440553, F028-5436433.

KhamTrek & Culture Co Ltd, 252 Shunji Mansion, Chengdu, PR China, T+86-28-86510838, khamtrek@yahoo.com. A specialist company organizing trips including trekking, hiking, overland and culture for individuals or groups in Kham, and Buddhist stone carving in Sichuan; co-ordinate throughout China.

Sichuan Mountaineering Association, 1 Xiatian Erlu, T028-5588047, F028-5588042.

Car hire T028-86260303/ 02. Open 24 hrs.

Trans Himalaya Tibet Expeditions,1 North Shuangqing Road, Bldg 2, Apartment 2A, Chengdu, 610072. T/F028-82984421, or 13540484871.

Transport

Air

Flights to Chengdu Both Dragon Air and Air China Southwest have daily flights from **Hong Kong**, while the latter also have daily flights from **Beijing**, **Guangzhou**, **Shanghai**, and **Xi'an**, as well as flights from **Bangkok** on Thu-Mon inclusive, from **Singapore** on Tue and Sat, and from **Seoul** on Mon. Thai Airways also operate daily flights from **Bangkok**. Air China Southwest (www.cswa.com) have offices in **Bangkok**: Shingpa Buli 38/1, Supola, T00662-6621940, in **Hong Kong**: Room 2008, 20/F Yingjun Centre, 23 Gangwan Rd, Wanchai, T0852-25286989, in **Singapore**: 61 Stamford Rd, #01-06 Stamford Court, T0065-3339566, in **Beijing**: 15 West Changan Ave, T010-66017579, in **Guangzhou**: 103 Zhanqian St, T020-86220156, and in **Shanghai**: 150 S. Maoming St, T021-64333355. **Dragon Air** (www.dragonair.com) is at 11 Tung Fai Rd, Lantau, Hong Kong, T00852-31933193.

Flights from Chengdu Dragon Air and China Southwest Airlines have daily flights to **Hong Kong**, while the latter also has daily flights to **Lhasa**, **Beijing**, **Kunming**, **Lanzhou**, **Guangzhou**, **Shanghai**, and **Xi'an**, as well as flights to **Chamdo** on Mon, Wed, Sat and Sun, to **Ziling** (all days except Mon and Wed), to **Bangkok** on Thu-Mon inclusive, to **Singapore** on Mon and Fri, and to **Seoul** on Mon. Thai Airways fly to **Bangkok** daily.

Directory

Airline offices Air China Southwest, 15 Renmin Nan Rd (Section Two), T8008866666 (freephone), T028-6668080 (information and delivery service), T028-5703060 (at airport). Dragonair, 65 Renmin Nan Rd (Section Two), T028-6679186 ext 363. Chengdu Central Ticketing Centre, T028-5190111. Yunnan Air, T028-6712822, F028-6712833. Discount offers are widely available (but not for Lhasa or Chamdo). Try Airline Ticketing Delivery Centre, T028-3555558 (which offers a 24-hr delivery service), Mingzhu Air Ticket Delivery Centre, T028-7787628, or Xinyu Ticket Delivery Centre, T028-6748781. **Medical services** Global Doctors, Bangkok Garden, 21 Renmin Nan Rd, Section 4, T028-85226058.

Kunming

→ *IDD: +86, Phone code: (0)871, Population: 4,810,000.*

Kunming in Southwest China provides access by land to the Gyeltang and Dechen areas of Southern Kham (see pages 447-453) and from there through Western Kham to Central Tibet. There are also direct air links with Gyeltang and Lhasa. The city is easily reached from Bangkok, Hanoi and other cities in Southeast Asia.

Kunming is a large modern city, with a remarkably relaxed and open society, and a pleasant climate that varies little from winter to summer. As the capital of China's most ethnically diverse province, Kunming has a cross-cultural ambience. There are different national exhibitions and the various styles of cuisine on offer include Bai, Dai and Wu. Three important Buddhist sites are located in and around the city: Huating Si in the western hills; Qongzu Si, which contains images of the 500 Elders; and **Yuantong Si**, *which is the largest monastery within the city. However, most first-time visitors to Kunming will prefer to take a day trip to the* **Stone Forest** *(Shilin), where there are bizarre limestone pillar formations and narrow passageways.*

Sleeping

AL Bank Hotel, T0871-3158888. 5-star (¥1145, plus 15% service charge), has excellent 4/F Japanese restaurant.

AL Hai Yi Hotel, T0871-5386688. (¥1037, plus 15% service charge).

AL Holiday Inn, 25 Dong Feng East Rd, T0871-3130623, F0871-3165888. 252 rooms (¥1320 per standard), 3 restaurants serving Chinese, Japanese, and Western cuisine, lobby lounge, disco/karaoke, swimming pool, sauna and massage centre, health and fitness centre, shopping arcade, and business centre.

AL Jiahua Westin Plaza, T0871-3562828. (Doubles at ¥1162, suites at ¥1660, executive suites at ¥1826, plus 15% service charge), has excellent American-style restaurant and upmarket discotheque.

A Golden Dragon Hotel, 575 Beijing Rd,

For an explanation of the sleeping and eating price codes used in this guide, see inside the front cover. Other relevant information is found in Essentials pages 44-46.

T0871-3133015, F0871-3131082. 4-star, 17 storeys, 290 rooms with attached bath (doubles at ¥730, singles at ¥996, surcharge 15%), 3 restaurants (Lobby Lounge for snacks, Yunnan Kitchen Chinese Restaurant for Chinese, and Czarina for international cuisine), room service available, swimming pool, fitness centre, shopping arcade, hairdresser, karaoke, airline offices, and business centre.

A **King World**, 28 Beijing Rd, T0871-3138888, F0871-3131910. 320 rooms with attached bathrooms (¥1020 per double, ¥950 per single, surcharge 15%), a revolving rooftop restaurant, Peony Banquet Hall, Rose Garden Restaurant, Magnolia function room, business centre and discotheque.

A **Kunming Hotel**, 145 Dong Feng Dong Lu, T0871-3169877, F0871-3138220. 12 floors and spacious rooms (¥996 per standard and single, surcharge 15%), 5 restaurants, bar, shopping arcades, beauty parlour, gym, sauna, mahjong room, travel centre, business centre.

A/B **Green Lake Hotel**, 6 Cuihu Nanlu, T0871-5158888, F0871-5153286. 306 rooms with attached bathrooms (new building: ¥863 per standard, ¥780 per single, and old building: ¥290 per standard, ¥340 per single, surcharge 15%), Chinese restaurant, Meldevere coffee shop, Mezzo Bar, business centre, and beauty parlour.

C **Kunming Airport Hotel**, T0871-7176965. Diverse rooms (¥300 with a/c, ¥208-282 without a/c, ¥206 per single, ¥257 per triple).

D **Kunming Camellia Hotel**, 15 E Dongfeng Rd, T0871-3161204, F0871-3162918. (Doubles at ¥150-240, and 4 or 7-bed dormitories at ¥33 per bed).

C **Red River Hotel (Honghe Binguan)**, 124 Chuncheng Rd, T0871-3515666, F0871-3515668. (¥298 per standard double, ¥338 per superior, ¥358 per single, ¥388 per executive room, and ¥860 per deluxe suite).

D **Bolan Hotel**, T0871-3162118. (¥248 per double).

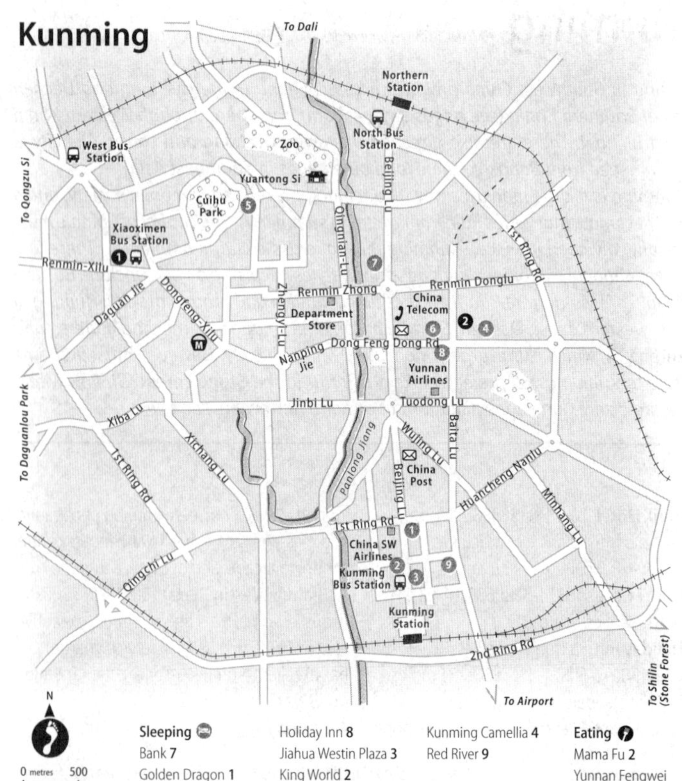

Yunnan bus station timetable

Kunming to:	Frequency	Cost
Dali	0730-2100 (every 30 minutes)	¥65-104
Lijiang	0830, 0930, 1300, 1700, 1800, 2030	¥119-152
Gyeltangteng	1730, 1830	¥142 (couchettes)
Ninglang (Lugu Lake)	1630 (every other day)	¥114.50
Ji Jiaoshan (Chicken-Foot Mountain)	1730, 1830, 1900	¥69.50

E **Jixie Hotel**, Baita Lu, T0871-3127606. (¥96 per room).

Eating

Kunming has a number of specialist restaurants offering ethnic cuisine. Among them, the Dai and Wa restaurants are particularly renowned.

Liao Zhi Qing Dai Restaurant, adjacent to the Green Lake Park (Cuihu Gongyuan).

North Star Restaurant, T0871-4176898. Includes a cultural performance.

Yunnan Fengwei Kuaican, opposite Walmart on Renmin Xilu. Yunnan dishes, including mixian noodles.

For western food, outside the big hotels, there are many restaurants of varying quality.

Mama Fu's Restaurant, near the Jixie Hotel.

Pizza da Rocco, near the Bird & Flower Market, T0871-3627951. Offers excellent Italian home cooking in a Qing period house.

Wei's Place-La Piazzetta located in an alleyway off Tuodong Lu.

Activities and tours

Tour agencies

Yunnan Exploration & Amusement Travel, 1/F Building B (North), 73 Renmin West Rd, T5312283, F0871-5312324.

Yunnan Overseas Travel Corporation, 154 E Dongfeng Rd, Kunming, T0971-3188905, F0086871-3132508.

Yunnan Panda International Travel, 31 Beijing Rd, T3532222, F0871-3530988.

Transport

Air

Flights to Kunming Both Yunnan Airways and Thai Airways (www.thaiair.com) have daily flights from **Bangkok**, and the former also operates flights from **Hong Kong**, **Beijing**, **Guangzhou**, and **Shanghai** daily, from **Singapore** on Mon, Wed and Fri, from **Kuala Lumpur** on Wed, and from **Vientiane** on Thu. Air China have flights from **Rangoon** on Wed and Sun. Thai Airways also have a flight from **Chiang Mai** on Thu and Sun.

Flights from Kunming Yunnan Airways and Thai Airways have daily flights to **Bangkok**, and the former also have daily flights to **Hong Kong**, **Beijing**, **Guangzhou**, and **Shanghai**, as well as to **Singapore** on Mon, Wed and Fri, to **Kuala Lumpur** on Wed, and **Vientiane** on Thu. Air China Southwest fly to **Gyeltang** and **Lhasa** on Sat. Air China have flights to **Rangoon** on Wed and Sun. Thai Airways also have a flight to **Chiang Mai** on Thu and Sun.

Train

The railway station has connections to **Hanoi** in Vietnam, but these have been temporarily suspended in 2003.

Bus

Yunnan Provincial Bus Station, has scheduled departures for **Dali**, **Lijiang**, **Gyeltangteng**, **Jijiaoshan** (Chicken-Foot Mountain), **Ninglang** and **Lugu Lake**.

Directory

Tourist offices Yunnan Provincial Tourism Bureau, Huancheng Nanlou St, Kunming, T0871-3132895.

Lanzhou

→ *Altitude: 1,600 m. IDD: +86. Phone code: (0)931. Colour map 5, grid A5.*

Lanzhou is an important starting point for travellers visiting Far East Tibet. It is the hub of the communications network for China's Northwestern provinces, and most travellers to Amdo in Tibet or the Silk Road in Xinjiang will begin their journeys here. The main roads into Amdo lead west through the Tsong-chu valley to Ziling (see page 573), and southwest to Labrang (see page 666) and Tso (see page 672). Two areas of Amdo currently fall within the administration of Gansu province, with their centre of government at Lanzhou: the Ganlho Tibetan Autonomous Prefecture and the Pari Tibetan Autonomous County.

Lanzhou is a large elongated industrial town set on the edge of the Tibetan plateau and Ordos desert. Many of the nearby hills are covered in thick deposits of loess, which can be very fertile where irrigated. However, the area around Lanzhou receives little rain, and many parts of Gansu are constantly challenged by desert encroachment.

Orientation

Lanzhou itself sprawls along the south bank of the Yellow River, and grew in importance after the construction of the first bridge in 1385. During the present century, the advent of the railways brought heavy industry to Lanzhou and the urban population rapidly increased.

The West Railway Station and the West Bus Station (for buses to Labrang) are located at the northwest end of town, and nearby are the Gansu Provincial Museum, and the Friendship Hotel. The Main Railway Station is to the southwest of the main shopping area, and connected to it by Pinglian Street (where the Post Office is

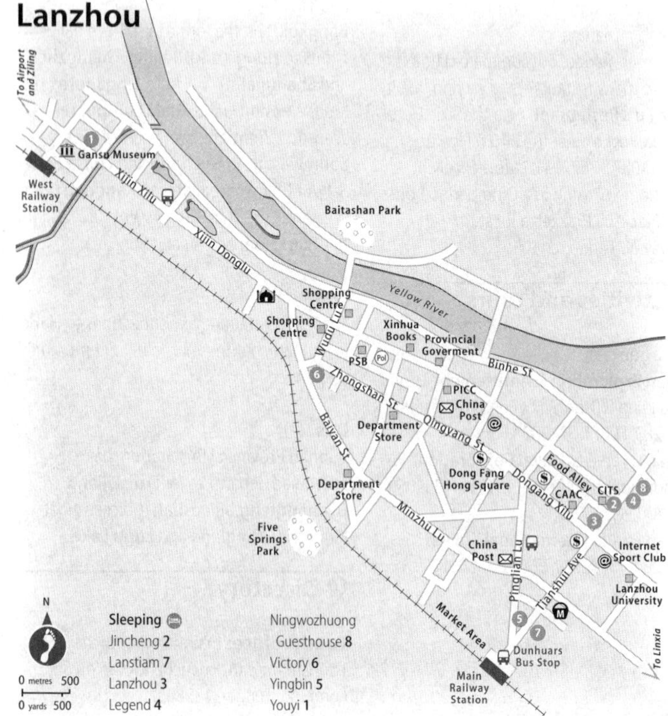

located) and Tianshui Avenue. Most hotels are clustered in the area around the Xuguan Traffic Circle on Tianshui Avenue, notably the Lanzhou Legend Hotel, the Lanzhou Fandian, the Jingcheng Hotel, and the Ningwozhuang Guesthouse. CITS and CAAC are conveniently here also. The Xi Min Xiang (Food Alley), off Tianshui Avenue, has a number of teahouses, fruit stalls and small restaurants. Across Central Square on Qingyang Street you will find the Bank of China and the Public Security Bureau.

Museums

The **Gansu Provincial Museum** ⓘ *near Friendship Hotel, 0900-1200 and 1430-1700, closed Sun and Mon, ¥15*, has an interesting collection of artefacts from the Silk Road, including neolithic painted pottery.

Sleeping

A **Lanzhou Legend Hotel (Lanzhou Feitian)**, 599 Tianshui Ave, T0931-8882876, F0931-8887876. 4-star, opposite Lanzhou University. This is the best and most modern hotel in Lanzhou with standard rooms at ¥800, deluxe rooms at ¥860, and suites ranging from ¥1,800 upwards, plus 15% surcharge.

B **International Hotel (Guoji Dajiudian)**, T0931-8457188, F0931-8457288. 3-star, with doubles at ¥488, and suites at ¥588-¥888 (35% discount available).

B **Jincheng Hotel (Jincheng Fandian)**, 363 Tianshui Ave, T0931-8811377, F0931-8418438. 3-star hotel, with 136 rooms, temporarily closed for refurbishment.

B **Lanzhou Fandian**, 434 Dongangxilu St, T0931-8416321, F0931-8416808. Large 1950s Russian-style building with 80 double rooms ¥480 (with attached bath), single rooms ¥288 (with attached bath), and suites ¥680-880.

B **New Century Hotel (Xinshiji Jiudian)**, T0931-8615888, F0931-8619133. 3-star, singles ¥428, doubles ¥480, triples ¥368, and suites ¥680-¥1,580 (35% discount available).

C **Friendship Hotel (Youyi Fandian)**, 16 Xijin St, T0931-2333051, F0931-2330304. 3-star, has 43 double rooms at ¥168-¥380, triples at ¥228, and suites at ¥288-¥660. The hotel has postal and shopping facilities.

C **Ningwozhuang Hotel**, 366 Tianshui Ave, T0931-8265888, F0931-8271379. Splendid garden hotel, once reserved for cadres, doubles ¥180-¥480, suites ¥560-¥1,280.

C **Victory Hotel (Shengli Fandian)**, 133 Zhongshan St, T0931-8465221, F0931-8461531. 168 double rooms at ¥180-¥280, and triples with attached bath at ¥153, and without attached bath at ¥93, and suites at ¥320-¥380.

D **Yingbin Hotel**, has doubles at ¥120.

E **Lanzhou Mansions (Lanzhou Dasha)**, opposite railway station, T0931-8417210, F0931-8417177. Has triples at ¥31 per bed, and doubles at ¥100-120, but very noisy.

Eating

Among the major hotels, the Lanzhou Legend and the Jincheng have both Chinese and Western menus, and the Friendship Hotel has inexpensive set meals. For local street food, try the restaurants on Xi Min Xiang lane behind the Jincheng Hotel, around the Main Railway Station or in the lane due east of the Bank of China. Local Muslim specialities include assorted noodle and lamb dishes.

Activities and tours

Tour companies

Gansu CITS, 361 Tianshui Ave, T0931-8826181/8861333, F0931-8418556.

Gansu Silk Road Travel, T0931-8414498/8416638, F0931-8418457/8414589.

Transport

Air

Flights to Lanzhou China Northwest Airlines have daily flights from **Beijing**, **Dunhuang**, **Jiayuguan**, **Guangzhou**, **Urumqi**, and **Xi'an**. The airline is based in Lanzhou (www.cnwa.com, T0086-931-8821964).

Flights from Lanzhou There are daily flights to **Beijing**, **Chengdu**, **Dunhuang**,

For an explanation of the sleeping and eating price codes used in this guide, see inside the front cover. Other relevant information is found in Essentials pages 44-46.

Guangzhou, **Shanghai**, **Urumqi**, and **Xi'an**. Also less frequent flights to **Chongqing**, **Guilin**, **Wuhan**, **Nanjing**, **Kunming**, and **Hangzhou**. The airport is 2 hrs' drive (88 km) from the city itself, up a northern valley, and the journey down to the Yellow River reveals typical small farms in the loess hills. CAAC shuttle buses are available (¥25 per person). Taxi Service, T0931-2667211, T13893304700 (mobile).

Bus *See also schedule p592.*

Buses run from the West Bus Station to **Linxia**, **Labrang**, and **Ganlho Dzong** (Hezuo), as well as **Wuwei**; and from the East Bus Station to more remote destinations in Shaanxi and Ningxia provinces. **NB** Foreigners travelling by public bus must pay local travel insurance through the Public Insurance Company of China, 150 Qingyang St, T0931-8416422 ext 114 (approx ¥25 for 30 days), or from travel services directly.

Train

There are train connections from **Xi'an** to Lanzhou (K119, d. 1805, a. +0651) at ¥175 (hard sleeper) and ¥264 (soft sleeper). The outbound train (K120) departs Lanzhou at 1711 and arrives Xi'an at +0630. 2 trains daily connect Lanzhou with **Ziling** and 1 with **Kermu**. There are also frequent train connections to **Urumqi**, **Beijing**, and **Chengdu**. Railway tickets and information: T0931-16090902.

Directory

Airline offices Jing Lan Flight Centre, 8 Qinan St, T0931-8831184. CAAC, 46 Dongang

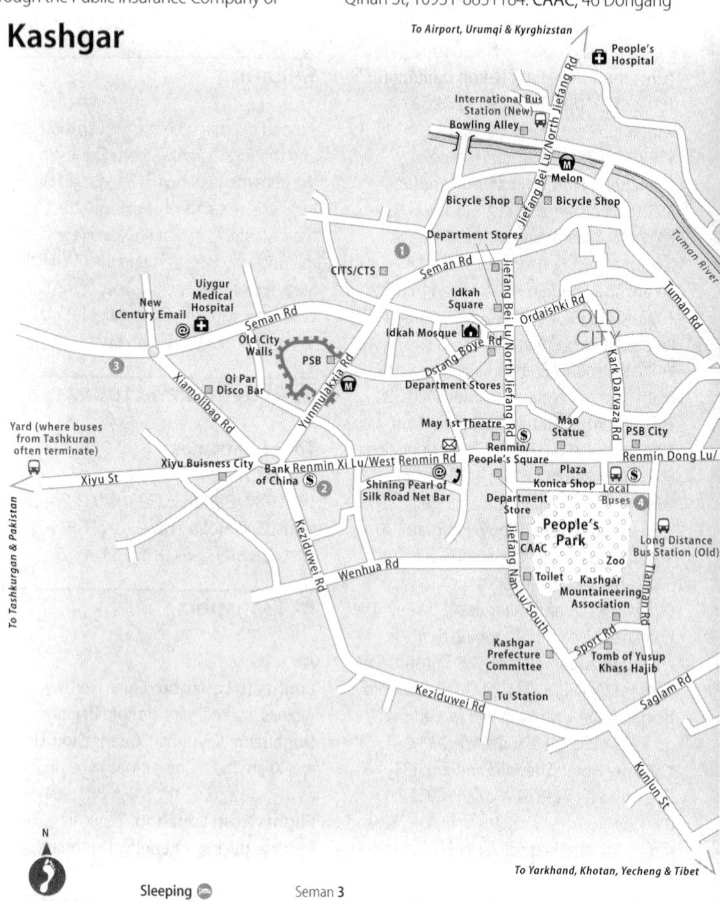

Xilu, T0931-821964/828174. Airline Ticket Centre: T0931-8821964. **Banks** Bank of China, Tianshui Ave, exchange facilities, cash advances on credit cards (open: Mon-Fri 1000-1200, 1430-1700, and Sat 1000-1600). **Post offices** General Post Office: Pingliang St (open 0800-1900), has parcel wrapping and EMS services. Postal facilities also available in major hotels. **Telephones** China Telecom, on Qingyang St, has IDD and internet facilities, although travellers prefer the Internet Sport Club to the left of Lanzhou University (¥4 per hr). **Useful addresses** Police and Public Security: Gansu Province Foreigners Registration Office, 38 Qingyang St, T0931-8827961, ext 8820 for visa extensions (open: Mon-Fri 0900-1130, and 1500-1700). Lanzhou City Foreigners Registration Office, 132 Wudu St.

Kashgar

→ *IDD: +86. Phone code: (0)998. Population: 320,000.*

Kashgar is the most remote of the five neighbouring gateway cities, connecting East Turkestan (the Chinese province of Xinjiang) by road with Northern and Far West Tibet. It is a large conurbation, undergoing rapid development, but parts of the old Uighur city have remained intact. Almost everything is sold in the markets, including Tibetan jewellery and prayer wheels.

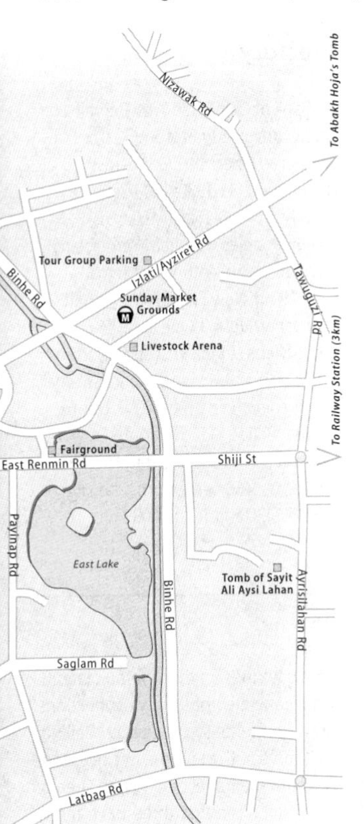

Sleeping

C **Seman Hotel** (the former Russian Consulate), 170 Seman Lu, T282-2147. Has superior rooms at ¥400, suites at ¥600, economy doubles at ¥120-280, and dormitory accommodation at ¥20-30 per person.

C **Kashgar-Gilgit International Hotel** (Youyi Binguan), T282-4173, F282-3842. High-rise hotel with doubles at ¥280 and suites at ¥700.

C **Kashgar Hotel**, T261-4954, F261-4679. Has 200 rooms with doubles at ¥200-250, and 4-bed rooms at ¥200.

D **Qianhai Binguan**, 48 West Renmin Lu, T282-2922. Has doubles (with a/c) at ¥240 and suites at ¥500.

D **Chini Bagh Hotel** (Qiniwake Binguan), formerly the British Consulate, 93 Seman Lu, T282-2084, F282-3842. Has single/double rooms at ¥120-180, and larger rooms at ¥25 per bed.

E **Tiannan Fandian**, near Bus Station. Has doubles at ¥30-90 per bed.

Noor Bish Guesthouse, T282 3092, has simple rooms at ¥10-20.

Eating

Uighur

Noor Look Kebab House, 285 Seman Lu.
Yuhuayuan Restaurant, Chini Bagh Gate.

Chinese

Taoyuan Canguan.
Or try the top-range hotel restaurants.

Transport

Air

Flights to Kashgar Xijiang Airlines have daily flights from **Urumqi**, and Urumqi itself is connected with **Moscow** (Tue and Fri), **Bishkek** (Tue and Fri), **Almaty** (Mon and Fri), **Tashkent** (Wed and Sat), **Hong Kong** (Sat), **Beijing** (daily), **Xi'an** (daily), **Guangzhou** (daily) and **Shanghai** (daily). The airline has its head office at 46 Yingbon Rd, Urumqi, T0086-991-3802472.
Flights from Kashgar There are daily flights to **Urumqi**, from where international flights operate as far as **Almaty**, **Bishkek**, **Moscow**, **Islamabad**, **Tashkent** and **Sharjah**, as well as major domestic destinations.

Bus

There are daily a/c buses to **Urumqi**, and public buses over the Khunjerab pass leading into **Pakistan**.

Jeep

Foreigners are not at present permitted to use public transport to the Torugart Pass on the Kyrgyz border. Those wishing to enter Kyrgyzstan by road have to hire a jeep (about US$450) to reach the border and have a pre-arranged vehicle to rendezvous at the pass for the transfer to **Bishkek** (another US$500). Exit permits can be arranged for land travel into **Pakistan** or **Kyrgyzstan** through the Kashgar Mountaineering Association, 45 Tiyu Lu, T282-3680, F282-2957, and at John's Information and Café (open summer months only), next to the Seman Hotel, T/F282-4186. **Expect to spend up to 1 week making these arrangements. NB** Visas for Pakistan and Kyrgyzstan are required but not obtainable in Kashgar.

Train

There is a direct rail link between Kashgar and **Urumqi**, and a direct international rail link between Urumqi and **Almaty**.

Directory

Banks Bank of China, 239 West Renmin Lu, will change foreign currency and TCs, or provide cash advances on credit cards. Opening hours: 0930-1330; 1600-2000 (weekdays) and 1100-1500 (weekends). **Hospitals** Peoples Hospital, North Jiefang Lu. **Internet** New Century, 243 Seman Lu (rate: ¥30 per hr). New Era, Chini Bagh Gate (rate: ¥30 per hr). John's Café (rate: ¥40 per hr). **Post offices** China Post and Telecom, 40 West Renmin Lu provide IDD and EMS mail services. Opening hours 1000-2000. **Useful addresses** Police, 111, Yunmulakexia Lu, issue visa extensions and also travel permits for closed areas (¥50 per person). Opening hours: 0930-1330 and 1600-2000.

Other gateway cities

Lijiang and Dali in Yunnan may also be regarded as gateway cities for the Tibetan plateau, and both have daily connections with Kunming, while Lijiang also has daily connections with Shanghai. Following the recent introduction of regular flights to Lhasa from Beijing, Shanghai, Guangzhou, Chongqing and Xi'an on Air China Southwest, these cities, too, are increasingly being seen as gateways to Tibet. They offer the traveller who has already obtained a Tibet entry permit greater choice of access since the first three have many direct connections with Europe, the United States and Australia, while the last two have connections with Seoul, and Chongqing is also connected with Bangkok and Nagoya.

For an explanation of the sleeping and eating price codes used in this guide, see inside the front cover. Other relevant information is found in Essentials pages 44-46.

Background

Footprint features

Introduction

Isolated by formidable mountain barriers, the peoples of the Tibetan plateau uniquely carried a sophisticated, traditional culture into the 20th century. The allure of Tibet's pristine high-altitude environment and profound Buddhist heritage attracted intrepid travellers and explorers from Europe, India, and America throughout the 19th and early 20th centuries. Many faced great physical and mental hardships in their journeys to Lhasa and elsewhere; and some tragically lost their lives without reaching their goal. The Tibetans actively discouraged such contacts and, with the exception of a few far-sighted intellectuals and lamas, no-one inside Tibet realized the implications that Tibet's self-imposed isolation would come to have in the latter half of the 20th century.

Following the Chinese occupation of the plateau and the abortive Tibetan uprising of 1959, the country was plunged into the long dark night of the Cultural Revolution. Then, quite unexpectedly, in the early 1980s, Tibet opened its doors to the outside world as a tourist destination.

Although there are still restrictions imposed on individual travel in certain parts of Tibet for socio-political reasons, ensuring that only the well-healed traveller can afford to undertake full-scale guaranteed itineraries, bureaucracy has not deterred the adventurous hardy backpacker who can often be seen trudging through remote parts of the country, following in the footsteps of his or her illustrious predecessors.

History

Legend

The Tibetan Buddhist historical work known as the Mani Kabum mentions both the drying up of the Tibetan lakelands and the legendary origins of the Tibetan race. The first Tibetans are said to have been the offspring of a monkey emanation of Avalokiteshvara (the patron deity of Tibet) – representing compassion and sensitivity – who mated with an ogress of the rocks, symbolizing the harshness of the Tibetan environment, at Zodang Gongpori Cave above Tsetang in Southern Tibet. They gave birth to six children, indicative of six types of sentient being, which later multiplied to 400, divided into four large tribes and two smaller groups. Gradually the monkeys evolved into humans, displaying both their paternal compassion and maternal aggression.

Other Bonpo (pre-Buddhist) legends, found in the Lang Poti Seru, trace the origin of the early tribes not to the monkey descendants of Avalokiteshvara, but to sub-human or primitive groups. Here, O-de Gung-gyel intermarries with various types of spirit – a lhamo, a nyenmo, a mumo, and a lumo, thereby giving birth to the Tibetan kings, demons, and human beings.

Meanwhile, there are other legends referring to the 10 groups of primeval non-human beings who held sway over Tibet prior to the dominion of the Tibetan monkey-tribes. Appearing in succession these were: Nojin Nagpo of Zangyul Gyen-me (who used bows and arrows), Dud of Dudyul Kharak Rong-gu (using battle axes), Sin of Sinpo Nagpo Guyul (using animal bone slings and catapults), Lha of Lhayul Gung-tang (using sharp swords), Mu-gyel (using lassoes with hooks and black magic rituals), canyon-dwelling Dre (using bolos with rocks attached), the Masang brothers of Bod (using armour and shields), the Lu of Bo-kham Ling-gu (using metamorphosis), the Gyelpo of Dempotse, and the 18 classes of bewitcher-demons or Gongpo (using guile but squandering good fortune). Subsequently, the monkey descendants of Zodang Gongpori emerged, perhaps indicating a shift from the primitive human culture of the Old Stone Age to a more advanced neolithic culture.

Archaeology

There has been no systematic archaeological survey of the Tibetan plateau, but the evidence that does emerge from the disparate excavated sites suggests that Tibet was inhabited during the Old Stone Age (2 million years ago-10,000 years ago). Crude pebble choppers have been unearthed at Kukushili, flake tools at Dingri, and stone scrapers, knives, drills, and axes at Lake Xiaochaili in the Tsaidam – the last dated to 33,000 BC. There are also primitive cave and 'nest' dwellings in Kongpo, Powo, Lhartse, Yamdrok, and the Jangtang Plateau.

A number of finely chipped blades from the Middle Stone Age (10,000 years ago) have been excavated at Serling Lake, Nyalam, Chamdo and Nakchu, indicating the prevalence of a hunting culture. Nonetheless, there are also indications of early farming communities in eastern areas: at the neolithic settlement of **Guro** north of Chamdo, dated 3,500 BC, where the remains of two-storey dwellings partitioned, as now, into human habitation upstairs and animal barns downstairs, have been discovered, along with stone artefacts, pottery and bone needles. Similar sites containing stone artefacts and pottery shards have been located in Nyangtri (discovered 1958/1975), and above all in Amdo, where the authorities of Qinghai and

 Gansu have funded a number of archaeological digs. Among them are the farming villages of Ma-chia-yao and Pan-shan in Cho-ne, respectively dated 3,000 BC and 2,500 BC; the village of Ma-ch'ang to the east of Lake Kokonor dated 2,000 BC; and the sites in the Sang-chu and Luchu valleys dated 1,850 BC. Evidence suggests that the yak became a domesticated animal around 2,500 BC and that there was an early interdependence between the hunting, nomadic and farming lifestyles.

Megalithic sites

Megaliths, generally dated 3,000-1,000 BC, have been discovered at Reting, Sakya, Shab Geding, Zhide Khar, Jiu near Lake Manasarovar, and Dangra Lake in the Jangtang. Sometimes these stones have an obvious formation: at Pang-gong Lake in Far West Tibet there are 18 parallel rows of standing stones with circles at end of each row; while at Saga there is a large grey stone slab surrounded by pillars of white quartz. Unusually shaped and coloured stones are found also in Kongpo, Powo, and Tsari.

The early Tibetan Clans

Tibetan historians refer to either four or six distinct Tibetan clans, which claimed descent from the legendary monkey and ogress. They comprise the Se clan, the Mu clan, the Dong clan, and the Tong clan (collectively known as the Ruchen Zhi). Sometimes, the Ba and Da clans are added to these. As the power of the 'non-human' rulers declined, the indigenous tribes took control of the land, eventually forming 12 kingdoms and 40 principalities. The 12 kingdoms were: Chimyul Drushul, Zhangzhung, Nyangdo Chongkar, Nubyul Lingu, Nyangro Shambo, Gyiri Jongdon, Ngamsho Tranar, Olphu Pangkhar, Simrong Lamogong, Kongyul Drena, Nyangyul Namsum, and Dakyul Druzhi. Only three of the 40 principalities are now known: Drokmo Namsum, Gyemo Yuldruk, and Semo Druzhi. These kingdoms and principalities are reckoned to have predated the first king of the Yarlung Dynasty (third/fourth centuries BC), and some, notably Zhangzhung in Far West Tibet, maintained their independence from around 3,000 BC (according to Bon sources) until their absorption by Songtsen Gampo in the seventh century.

Some sources associate the four original clans with four important Tibetan cultures of antiquity: the Dong with that of Minyak (Far East Tibet and Ningxia), the Tong with Sumpa (Jangtang), the Mu with Zhangzhung (Far West Tibet), and the Se with Azha (Lake Kokonor). Among the aristocratic family names of Tibet, those of Lang, Gar, Khyungpo, and Khon are said to have been descendants of the Se clan. Illustrious descendants of this clan include Amnye Jangchub Drekhol, who was the teacher of the epic warrior Ling Gesar, the ruling houses of Sakya and Phakmodru, Gar Tongtsen (the minister of Songtsen Gampo) and the Derge royal family, the great yogin Milarepa and Khungpo Neljor. By contrast, the Ba family, which assumed important military and civil positions during the period of the Yarlung Dynasty, claims descent from the Dong clan. Its members include Marpa, Phakmodrupa and Drigungpa who were all seminal figures in the development of the Kagyu school of Buddhism. The Kyura and Nyura families of Drigung and Mindroling respectively claim descent from the Tong clan, as do the Achakdru of Golok. Lastly, the ruling house of Zhangzhung in Far West Tibet claimed descent from the Mu clan, as attested in important Bonpo historical works.

Qiang Tribes

Chinese annals suggest that the Qiang or Ti tribes inhabiting the western periphery of the Chinese Empire were of Tibetan extraction. These tribes were established by 1,500 BC west of the Shang settlements near Chang-an (modern Xi'an), from where they would raid the farming communities. By 500 BC the Qiang were organizing themselves into agricultural and cattle-rearing societies, gradually developing into 150 sub-tribes, along the easternmost borderlands of the Tibetan plateau. They are said to have constituted a significant percentage of the region's population during the Zhou and Qin dynasties. Around the fifth century (CE) the Qiang tribe known as the Tang-hsiang (perhaps identified with the Dong clan) appear to have subdivided into western and northern groups, which Chinese sources identify respectively with the Tibetan (Ch T'u-fan) tribes (dominant from the seventh century) and the Tanguts (dominant in Xixia during the 11th century). Remnants of the Qiang tribes are found today around Maowen, and in those parts of East Tibet where the so-called Qiangic languages are spoken. Some sources suggest that it was an intermingling of Qiang tribes with the Yueh-chih and Hsiung-nu in the northeast (c 175-115 BC) which gave rise to the tall aquiline Tibetans of the northeast, who are distinct from the short Mongoloid type of western and southern origin.

The Yarlung Dynasty

The chronology of early Tibet is not easily determined with any degree of certainty. There are sources suggesting that by 781 BC the primitive groups mentioned above had been supplanted by the descendants of the four clans, and that until 247 BC the 12 kingdoms and 40 principalities formed by those clans held sway alone.

Seven Heavenly Kings called Tri

The first king of the Yarlung Dynasty, Nyatri Tsenpo (1) is said to have had divine origin and to have been immortal – ascending to the heavens on a sky-cord (*mu*) at the appointed time for his passing. Other sources suggest an Indian origin for the royal family – the lord Rupati who fled North India during the Pandava wars, and who is said to be descended from the mountain-dwelling Shakya clan, or the Licchavi clan of Nepal – connecting him with the family line of Shakyamuni Buddha. Alighting on **Mount Lhari Yangto** in Kongpo, he proceeded to **Mount Lhari Rolpa** in Yarlung around 247 BC (the time of Ashoka) and thence to **Tsentang Gozhi** where he encountered the local Tibetan tribes who made him their king. Carried shoulder-high, he was borne to the site of the **Yumbu Lagang** palace, which he himself constructed. Utilizing magical weaponry and powers, Nyatri Tsenpo defeated the shaman Oyong Gyelwa of Sumpa and the ruler of Nub.

The first seven kings of this Yarlung Dynasty, circa 247-100 BC, including Nyatri Tsenpo himself, are known as the 'seven heavenly kings called Tri', in that they all passed away in the celestial manner, without the need for tombs. Nyatri's successors were: Mutri (2), Dingtri (3), Sotri (4), Mertri (5), Daktri (6), and Sibtri (7). Towards the end of this period, the Silk Road was opened to the north of Tibet.

Two Celestial Kings called Teng

Sibtri's son, Drigum Tsenpo (8), is said to have fallen under the influence of the Iranian shaman Azha of Gurnavatra; who persuaded the king to adopt the fatalist line suggested by his own name 'sword-slain'. Deceived by his royal horse keeper Longam, the king accidentally cut his own sky-cord in a contest of swordmanship. Bereft of his divine powers the king was then killed by Longam's arrow, and thus had the dubious distinction of becoming the first mortal king of the Yarlung Dynasty. The king's three sons, Chatri, Nyatri and Shatri fled to the Powo area of Southeast Tibet, while the king's body was sent downstream to Kongpo in a copper casket, and Longam usurped the throne. Chatri later regained the throne in battle with Longam and adopted the name Pude Gungyel (9), after which he built the **Chingwa Taktse Castle** in Chongye.

Pude Gungyel's ministers, including his own nephew Rulakye who had helped him regain the throne, are accredited with the introduction of charcoal, smelting, metalwork, bridge-building, and agriculture. The rituals of the Bon shamans of Zhangzhung also gained prominence during this period on account of their elaborate funerary rites. Henceforth, the mortal kings of Tibet would be buried in locations such as the **Chongye tombs**. Drigum Tsenpo and his son Pude Gungyel, collectively known as the 'two celestial kings called Teng', reigned approximately from 100 BC-50 BC, making them contemporaries of Han Wu Ti (140-85 BC).

Six Earthly Kings called Lek

The six 'earthly kings called Lek' like their predecessors, mortal or otherwise, continued to marry into 'non-human' or rarefied aristocratic lines only. Pude Gungyel's son Esho Lek (10) was the first in this line, followed by his son, Desho Lek (11), the latter's son Tisho Lek (12); and so on through Gongru Lek (13), Drongzher Lek (14), and Isho Lek (15). Their castles were all located in and around Chongye Taktse; and their tombs were located on adjacent rocky peaks or foothills. During this period (c 50 BC-100 CE) farm animals were domesticated, and irrigation and taxation developed.

Eight Middle Kings called De

The eight 'middle kings called De' (c 100-300 AD) are little known, apart from their burial sites at river banks. They were: Za Namzin De (16), De Trulnam Zhungtsen (17), Senolnam De (18), Senolpo De (19), De Nolnam (20), De Nolpo (21), De Gyelpo (22), and De Tringtsen (23). Tibetan trade prospered with the neighbouring Shu Han Dynasty (221-263 AD), which had its capital at Chengdu. Large trade marts were established in the Kokonor region, and Tibetan horses were highly valued.

Five Linking Kings called Tsen

The 'five linking kings called Tsen' are significant in that it was during their reigns (c 300-493 AD) that the kings of Tibet first married among their Tibetan subjects. The ancient title lha-se ('divine prince') was now replaced with the title tsenpo ('king'/'potentate'). The first in this line was Tore Longtsen (24); followed by Trhitsun Nam (25), Trhidra Pungtsen (26), Trhi Tokje Toktsen (27), and Lhatotori Nyentsen (28). The important ministers during this period hailed from the Tonmi, Nub and Gar clans, and the rich heritage of Tibetan folklore was established through the activities of the Bon priests known as Shen, the bards who narrated epic tales (*drung*), and singers of enigmatic riddles (*de'u*).

During the reign of the last of these kings, Lhatotori Nyentsen (374-493), Buddhism was introduced to Tibet. According to legend, in 433 certain Buddhist sutras including the *Karandavyuha* (dedicated to Tibet's patron deity Avalokiteshvara) landed on the palace roof at Yumbu Lagang, along with a mould engraving of the six-syllabled mantra of Avalokiteshvara and other sacred objects, but these were given the name **'awesome secret'** because no-one could understand their meaning. Lhatotori was rejuvenated and lived to the ripe old age of 120. His tomb is said to be at Dartang near the Chongye River, though others say he vanished into space.

More sober historians, such as Nelpa Pandita, assert that these texts were brought to Tibet by Buddharaksita and Tilise of Khotan. It appears from this and other sources, such as Fa-hien's records of Buddhism in Central Asia (dated 400 AD), that Lhatotori's discovery of Buddhism was predated by Buddhist contacts in East Tibet, where the Tibetan P'u (Fu) family formed the ruling house during the Earlier Chin Dynasty (351-394). The secessionist Later Chin Dynasty (384-417), also Tibetan, offered patronage to the renowned Buddhist scholar Kumarajiva, and its rulers were well acquainted with Buddhism.

Meantime, an administrator of the P'u family named Lu Kuang was sent to Xinjiang where he ruled over a mixed Tibetan and Turkic population (T'u yu-hun), and founded the later Liang Dynasty (386-403) on the trade routes to the west.

The kings of this period were contemporaries of the Toba Wei emperors in China and the Gupta Empire in India.

Four Ancestors of the Religious Kings

The four immediate ancestors of the great religious kings of Tibet (493-629) were: Lhatotori's son Trhinyen Zung-tsen (29), Drong Nyendeu (30), Mulong or Takri Nyenzik (31), and Namri Songtsen (32). During these reigns the principal ministerial families were those of Shudpu, Nyen, Nyang, Be, and Tsepong. Lhatotori's son was the first king to be entombed in the **Dongkar** valley, east of Chongye. His consort gave birth to a blind son named Mulong, whose sight was subsequently restored by a Bonpo doctor from Azha. Taking the name Takri Nyenzik, the new king reoccupied the ancestral castle at Chingwa Taktse, and seized control of about half of the 12 ancient kingdoms that constituted Tibet. Following his untimely death circa 560, the task of conquering Tri Pangsum, the usurper king of the **Kyi-chu** valley, fell to his son Namri Songtsen. The usurper was successfully expelled to the north and the newly acquired territory named **Phenyul**. Namri Songtsen established an important political network of aristocratic families. He promoted the horse and salt trade; and secured diplomatic relations with the Toba Wei Dynasty (386-534), with the Turkish Khanates established by the sons of Bumin Khagan in Mongolia and Dzungaria, and finally with the Sui Dynasty which reunified China in 589. Following the Sui Emperor's annihilation of the T'u yu-un (c 600), the Tibetans of the Yarlung Dynasty (known in Chinese as T'u-fan) expanded into the northeastern borderlands to fill the vacuum. In 629, the king was poisoned by discontented nobles.

The Tibetan Empire and the Nine Religious Kings

It is not surprising that the unification of Tibet and its imperial expansion should have coincided with the adoption of Buddhism as the dominant civilizing influence in Tibetan life. This is the age of the nine great religious kings (629-841) and the most powerful political figures in the whole course of Tibetan history, namely: Songtsen Gampo (33), Gungsong Gungtsen (34), Mangsong Mangtsen (35), Dusong Mangpoje (36), Tride Tsukten or Me'agtsom (37), Trisong Detsen (38), Mune Tsepo (39); Tride Songtsen, also known as Mutik Tsenpo or Senalek Jinyon (40), and Tri Relpachen (41).

When Songtsen Gampo (617-650) acceded to the throne in 629, he conquered the far Western kingdom of Zhangzhung and successfully unified the whole of Tibet for the fist time in its recorded history. **Lhasa** became the capital of this grand empire, and the original **Potala Palace** was constructed as his foremost residence. In the course of establishing his empire, Songtsen Gampo came into contact with the Buddhist traditions of India, Khotan, and China, and quickly immersed himself in spiritual pursuits, reportedly under the influence of his foreign queens Bhrikuti, the daughter of Amshuvarman, king of Nepal; and Wencheng, daughter of Tang Tai Zong, Emperor of China. These queens are said to have brought as their dowry the two foremost images of Buddha Shakyamuni – one in the form of Aksobhya, which Bhrikuti introduced from Nepal and one in the bodhisattva form known as Jowo Rinpoche, which was introduced from China.

The king constructed a series of geomantic temples at important power-places across the length and breadth of the land, and these are revered as the earliest Buddhist temples of Tibet. He sent his able minister Tonmi Sambhota to India where the Uchen (capital letter) script was developed from an Indian prototype to form the Tibetan language. According to some Tibetan sources, in later years the king abdicated in favour first of his son and later in favour of his grandson; passing his final years in spiritual retreat. His tomb is the celebrated **Banso Marpo** in the Chongye valley (although other traditions claim that he was interred in the Jokhang).

The years immediately following Songtsen Gampo's unification of Tibet saw engagement in wide-ranging military campaigns. From 665-692 the Yarlung kings controlled the Central Asian oases and cities, and this Tibetan influence is reflected in the manuscripts and paintings preserved in the **Dunhuang** caves, which have been dated 650-747. Conflict with Tang China began in 670 and by 680 the Tibetan army

Taming the Ogress: the geomantic temples of Tibet

When the Tang princess Wencheng arrived in Tibet, she introduced Chinese divination texts including the so-called Portang scrolls. According to the ancient Chinese model of government, spheres of influence were based on six concentric zones, namely: an imperial centre, a royal domain zone, a princes' domain, a pacification zone, a zone of allied barbarians, and a zone of cultureless savagery. The Tibetan geomantic temples were laid out according to four of these zones, corresponding to the imperial centre, the royal domain zone, the pacification zone, and that of the allied barbarians. Just as China was conceived of as a supine turtle, so the Tibetan terrain was seen as a supine ogress or demoness, and geomantic temples were to be constructed at focal points on her body: the **Jokhang** temple at the heart, the four 'district controlling' temples (**runon**) on her shoulders and hips, the four 'border taming' temples (**tadul**) on her elbows and knees, and the four 'further taming' temples (**yangdul**) on her hands and feet.

According to literary sources such as the Mani Kabum, Buton, Longdol Lama, and Drukpa Pekar, the four 'district controlling' temples are: **Tradruk** (left shoulder), **Katsel** (right shoulder), **Yeru Tsangdram** (right hip), and **Rulak Drompagyang** (left hip). These same authors list the four 'border taming' temples as: **Khomting** (left elbow), **Buchu** (right elbow), **Jang Traduntse** (near Saga, right knee); and **Mon Bumtang** (left knee); while the four further taming temples are listed as: **Jang Tsangpa Lungnon** (left hand), **Den Langtang Dronma** (right hand), **Mangyul Jamtrin** (right foot), and **Paro Kyerchu** (left foot).

Other authors such as Sakya Sonam Gyeltsen, Pawo Tsuklag and the Fifth Dalai Lama list the 'district controlling' temples as: **Langtang Dronma**, **Kyerchu**, **Tselrik Sherab Dronma**, and **Jang Tsangpa Lungnon**; the four 'border taming' temples as: **Uru Katsel**, **Lhodrak Khomthing**, **Den Langtang Dronma**, and **Yeru Tsangtram**; and the four 'further taming' temples as: **Lhodrak Khomting**, **Kongpo Buchu**, **Mangyul Jamtrin**, and **Jang Traduntse**. These are the central temples among the 108 reputedly built in this period throughout Tibet.

had advanced as far southeast as the **Nan-chao** Kingdom (modern Dali in Yunnan province). King Tride Tsukten (r.704-755) constructed a number of Buddhist shrines, including the temple of **Drakmar Keru**, and by 737 had extended his imperial influence westwards into **Brusha** (the Burushaski region of Gilgit).

In 730, Tride Tsukten's Tibetan consort Nanamza gave birth to a son – Trisong Detsen, perhaps the greatest of all the Tibetan kings, in whose reign Buddhism was formally established as the state religion. In the early years of his reign (755-797) Trisong Detsen sent his armies against Tang China, eventually occupying the imperial capital **Xi'an** in 763. The **Zhol pillar** was erected at Lhasa to commemorate this event. Increasingly, the king sought to promote Buddhism, and he invited the Indian preceptor Shantaraksita to found the country's first monastery at **Samye.** Owing to obstacles instigated by hostile non-Buddhist forces, the king accepted Shantaraksita's advice and invited Padmasambhava, the foremost exponent of the tantras and the Dzogchen meditative tradition in India, to participate in the establishing of Buddhism. Padmasambhava bound the hostile demons of Tibet under an oath of allegiance to Buddhism, enabling the monastery's construction to be completed and the first monks to be ordained.

The king then instituted a methodical translation programme for the rendering of Sanskrit and Chinese Buddhist texts in Tibet. Intelligent children were sent to India to be trained as translators, and their prolific work ranks among the greatest literary endeavours of all time. Meanwhile Padmasambhava, Vimalamitra, and other accomplished masters of the Indian tantric traditions imparted their meditative instructions and lineages to the custodianship of their Tibetan disciples in remote but spectacularly located mountain caves, including **Chimphu**, **Sheldrak**, **Kharchu**, **Drak Yangdzong**, **Monka Senge Dzong**. In this way their Tibetan followers were brought to spiritual maturity and attained profound understanding of the nature of mind and the nature of phenomenal reality. Chinese Buddhist influence receded to some extent in the aftermath of the great debate held at Samye in 792 between Kamalasila of the Indian tradition and Hoshang Mo-ho-yen of the Chinese tradition.

The establishment of Buddhism as the state religion of Tibet, commemorated by an inscribed pillar at the entrance to Samye Monastery, was a threshold of enormous significance, in that the demilitarisation of Tibet can be traced back to that event. The great empire forged by the religious kings gradually began to recede.

Their successors all acted as lavish patrons of Buddhism, sometimes at the expense of the older Bon tradition and the status of Tibet's ancient aristocratic families. This trend reached its zenith during the reign of Tri Relpachen (r 813-841), who had each monk supported by seven households of his subjects. Among Tri Relpachen's many achievements, the most important one politically was the peace treaty agreed with China in 823; which clearly defined the Sino-Tibetan border at **Chorten Karpo** in the Sang-chu valley of Amdo. Obelisks were erected there and in Lhasa to commemorate this momentous event, the one in Lhasa surviving intact until today. The strong Buddhist sympathies of the king attracted an inevitable backlash on the part of disgruntled Bon and aristocratic groups. This resulted in his assassination at the hands of his elder brother, the apostate Langdarma Udumtsen in 841; and with this act, the period of the great religious kings came to an abrupt end.

Persecution of Buddhism and disintegration of Empire

When Langdarma (42) came to power following the assassination of his brother, the Bonpo suddenly found themselves once more in the ascendancy. Old scores against the Buddhists were settled and a widespread persecution ensued. The monasteries and temples were desecrated or closed down and Buddhist practice was driven underground. Practitioners of the tantras survived only in Central Tibet, whether in their remote mountain retreats or by living their lives incognito in small village communities. The monastic tradition was only able to survive in the remote northeast of Amdo, at **Dentik** and **Achung Namdzong**, because three far-sighted monks transmitted the Vinaya lineage to Lachen Gongpa Rabsel, ensuring that the lineage of monastic ordination would continue unbroken for the benefit of posterity.

Langdarma's severe persecution of Buddhism was itself brought to an abrupt end in 846, when he was assassinated by the Buddhist master Lhalung Pelgyi Dorje, a black-hatted and black-clothed figure, who shot the apostate king with an arrow and fled in disguise by reversing his clothes to reveal their white lining! This act is commemorated in the famous black hat dance (*shanak*). Lhalung Pelgyi Dorje eventually reached the safety of **Achung Namdzong** in Amdo where he remained in penance for the rest of his life.

The succession to the throne was then disputed by Langdarma's two sons, Tride Yumten, the son of his senior consort, and Namde Osung, the son of his junior consort. Osung gained control of Lhasa while Yumten moved to Yarlung, and this event marked the beginning of the disintegration of the royal dynasty and, correspondingly Tibet's political unity (869). Dunhuang had already been lost to the Tibetan empire by 848, and the line of 42 kings which began with Nyatri Tsenpo had come to an end, leaving Tibet without central authority for over 300 years.

The later diffusion of Buddhism

While anarchy prevailed in much of Central Tibet, the kingdoms of **Tsongkha** (c 900-1100) and **Xixia** (990-1227) maintained the Buddhist heritage in the remote northeastern parts of Amdo and the adjacent province of Ningxia. Around 953 or 978, Lu-me and his fellow monks from Utsang brought the monastic ordination back from Amdo to Central Tibet, having received it from Lachen Gongpa Rabsel. They embarked upon an extensive temple-building programme in the Kyi-chu and Brahmaputra valleys, which laid the basis for the later diffusion of Buddhism.

Further west, descendants of the royal family had effectively maintained the traditional royal sponsorship of Buddhism. The kingdom of **Guge** had been established on trade routes with North and Northwest India along the canyons of the upper Sutlej River. Among the most important kings were Yeshe-o (947-1024) who was a fifth generation descendant of Langdarma, and his nephew Jangchub-o (984-1078). They were both patrons of Rinchen Zangpo (958-1055), the great translator of the later diffusion, and Atisha (982-1054), the renowned Bengali Buddhist master. It was Atisha who reinforced the ethical discipline of the gradual path to enlightenment and its compassionate ideals, rather than the practices of the tantras, which apparently had been dangerously misapplied by some corrupt practitioners.

During this period, Tibetan translators once again began travelling to India to study Sanskrit and receive teachings in the various aspects of the Indian Buddhist tradition. The texts which they brought back to Tibet were naturally those in vogue in 11th century India, in contrast to those previously introduced during the eighth century by Padmasambhava and his followers. Consequently a distinction was recognized between the 'old translations' of the early period and the 'new translations' of the later period. Among this new wave of translators were Rinchen Zangpo and Ngok Lotsawa who represented the **Kadampa** tradition (associated with Atisha), Drokmi Lotsawa (992-1074) who represented the **Sakyapa** tradition (of Gayadhara and Virupa), and Marpa Lotsawa (1012-1097) who represented the **Kagyupa** tradition (of Tilopa and Naropa). By contrast the practitioners of the earlier teachings became known as the **Nyingmapa**, and among them, during this period was the outstanding translator Rongzom Pandita (11th century).

The foundation of large temples and monasteries soon followed: **Toling** in 996, **Zhalu** in 1040, **Reting** in 1054; **Sakya** in 1073, **Ukpalung** in the 11th century, **Katok** in 1159, and the Kagyu monasteries of **Daklha Gampo, Kampo Nenang, Karma Gon, Tsurphu, Densatil, Drigung, Taklung**, and **Ralung** – all in the 12th century.

Sakyapa Administration (1235-1349)

A new sense of militancy was introduced into Tibetan life during the 13th century when, in common with most peoples of Asia, the Tibetans had to come to terms with the phenomenal rise to power of the Mongolians who, unified by Genghiz Qan (r 1189-1227) swept across Asia, combining great horsemanship and mobility with astute strategy. In 1206 the Mongolians reached Tibet, and suzerainty was offered to **Sakya**. In order to avoid the fate of Xixia, the Tangut Kingdom, which was annihilated in 1227, the Tibetans decided to accommodate themselves to Mongolian aspirations by filling a unique role – that of spiritual advisors seeking imperial patronage. Consequently, after the Mongolian general Dorta Nakpo had sacked **Reting** and other northern monasteries in

1240, Sakya Pandita (1182-1251) proceeded to **Lake Kokonor** in 1244 to meet Guyug and Godan, the son and grandson of Genghiz Qan, accompanied by his nephew, Drogon Chogyel Phakpa (1235-1280). A 'patron-priest relationship' was established and Godan transferred the hegemony of Tibet to Sakya Pandita in 1249.

Later, in 1253, Prince Qubilai once again offered this hegemony to his new advisor, Drogon Chogyel Phakpa. Central Tibet (Utsang) was divided into four horns (ru) and 13 myriarchies (trikhor). Among these, the horn of **Uru** was centred at **Ramoche** in Lhasa with Olka Shukpa Pundun to the east, Mala Lagyu to the south, Zhu Nyemo to the west, and Drakyi Langma Gurpub to the north, including the myriarchies of Gyama, Drigung, and Shalpa. The horn of **Yoru** was centred at **Tradruk**, with Kongpo Drena in the east, Shawuk Tago in the south, Kharak Gangtse in the west, and Mala Lagyu in the north, including the myriarchies of Tangpoche, Pangpoche, Phakdru, and Yabzang. The horn of **Yeru** in Tsang was centred on **Namling** in Shang, with Drakyi Langma Gurpub in the east, Nyangang Yagpo'i Na in the south, Jemalagu in the west, and Smriti Chunak in the north, including the myriarchies of Chumik, Shang, and Zhalu. Lastly, the horn of **Rulak** was centred in **Drekyi Durwana**, with Jamnatra in the east, Belpo Langna in the south, Kem Yagmik in the west, and Jema Langon in the north, including the myriarchies of South Lhato, North Lhato, and Gurmo. Although the Mongolians sought to govern Tibet and actually held a census there in 1268 and 1287, power remained effectively in the hands of the Sakyapas.

Drogon Chogyel Phakpa thus became the most powerful Tibetan ruler since the assassination of Tri Relpachen in 841. Although the tribal confederations and kingdoms of East Tibet maintained a degree of independence, the power of Sakya even extended deeply into Kham and Amdo. When Qubilai Qan subsequently invaded China and established the Yuan Dynasty (1260-1368), Phakpa was given the rank of Tishri, imperial preceptor, and remained in **Dadu**, the imperial capital of Qubilai Qan (Beijing), where he devised a script for the Mongolian language, based on the Tibetan script. This script (Hor-yig) is still in use today for decorative purposes, especially among the Tu peoples of Amdo. Executive decisions on the ground were made by the Ponchen, or administrator, who was appointed to head the 13 myriarchies. Ponchen Shakya Zangpo (r 1265-1268) and Ponchen Kunga Zangpo (r 1268-1280) held this office during the lifetime of Phakpa; and following the latter's death in 1280, Dharmapala (r 1280-1287) was appointed as imperial preceptor and Shang Tsun as Ponchen. Later, following the lifetime of the imperial preceptor Danyi Zangpo Pal (r 1305-1322), the ruling house of Sakya split into four branches, two of which – the Phuntsok Palace and the Dolma Palace, took turns at holding supreme authority in Tibet. Actual power was however exercised by the successive Ponchen.

Some of the other Buddhist non-Sakya traditions inside Tibet did not accept this situation with ease: Emperor Mongke had been the patron of Karma Pakshi until his death in 1260; while the Drigungpa were backed by Hulegu of the Ilkhan Dynasty (1258-1335) – a brother of Qubilai Qan, who launched an abortive attack on Sakya in 1285. This resulted in the burning of **Drigung** and its sacred artefacts in 1290. Later, in 1350, during the reign of Sonam Gyeltsen and his Ponchen, Gawa Zangpo, power was usurped by one of the myriarchs, Tai Situ Jangchub Gyeltsen of Phakmodru. The power of the Sakyapa rulers rose and fell in proportion to the rise and fall in the power of the Mongolian qans in China.

Phakmodrupa Administration (1350-1435)

The Tibetan nationalist movement which wrested power from the Mongol-backed Sakyapas in 1350 was headed by Jangchub Gyeltsen (r 1350-1371), the myriarch of Phakmodru, and based at **Nedong** in Southern Tibet. On acquiring supreme power in Tibet, he and his successors assumed the title gongma ('king'). His power was belatedly recognized by the Mongolian emperors, who additionally conferred the title Tai Situ upon him. Jangchub Gyeltsen reorganized the myriarchy system into a system of dzong or regional fortresses, which persisted down to the 20th century. Dzongpon officials, such as Rabten Kunzang Phak at Gyantse, came to hold considerable autonomy under this administration. During this period the rulers of Tibet firmly backed the Kagyupa school of Tibetan Buddhism, but it also coincided with the rise of the indigenous Gelukpa tradition. Jangchub Gyeltsen's successors were Sakya Gyeltsen (1372-1384), Drakpa Jangchub (1385-1390), Sonam Drakpa (1391-1408), Drakpa Gyeltsen (1409-1434), Sangye Gyeltsen (1435-1439), Drakpa Jungne (1440-1468), Kunga Lekpa (1469-1473), Rinchen Dorje (1474-1513), Chenga Ngagi Wangpo (1514-1564), Ngawang Tashi Drakpa (1565-1578), and Drowei Gonpo (1579-1617). The power of the later *gongma* was gradually eclipsed by the house of Ringpung in Tsang, until by 1478 the position had little more than nominal or titular significance.

Rinpung Administration (1478-1565)

The Rinpung princes first came to prominence during the reign of the Phakmodrupa king Drakpa Gyeltsen (r 1409-1434), who appointed Namka Gyeltsen as lord of the **Rinpung** estates and governor of Sakya and Chumik. In 1435, his relation Rinpung Norbu Zangpo seized power from Phakmodru in Tsang, gradually bringing to an end the influence of Nedong in that region. His son Donyo Dorje in 1478 finally inflicted a decisive defeat on the kings of Phakmodru, and became the most powerful ruler in Tibet. He was a principal patron of the Zhamarpa branch of the Karma Kagyu school. The family's power was eventually eclipsed in 1565 by Zhingzhakpa Tseten Dorje of the Samdrubtse fiefdom at Zhigatse.

Tsangpa Administration (1565-1642)

The princes of **Samdrubtse** (modern Zhigatse) became powerful patrons of the Karma Kagyu school, particularly following the foundation of the Zhamarpa's residence at Yangpachen. In 1565, the power of the Rinpungpas was usurped by Karma Tseten (Zhingshakpa Tseten Dorje) of the Nyak family. He made **Zhigatse** the capital of Tibet. In religious affairs, he adopted a sectarian posture, which favoured the Karma Kagyu school at the expense of others. When he persecuted the Northern Treasures (Jangter) community of the Nyingmapa school, he is said to have been ritually slain in 1599 by Jangdak Tashi Topgyel; but the son who succeeded him, Karma Tensung Wangpo, maintained the same policy. He forged an alliance with the Chogthu Mongolians and captured Lhasa and Phenyul in 1605. On his death (1611), he was succeeded by his son, Karma Phuntsok Namgyel, who, in 1613, established a new 15-point legal system for Tibet. His imposing castle at Zhigatse is said to have been a prototype for the present Potala Palace at Lhasa.

In 1616 he forced Zhabdrung Ngawang Namgyel to flee **Ralung** Monastery for Bhutan, and following the latter's establishment there of a theocratic Drukpa state, the kings of Tsang engaged in a series of unsuccessful military campaigns against Bhutan. In 1618 he also established a Karma Kagyu Monastery, known as **Tashi Zilnon**, on the hill above Tashilhunpo, and once again sent Mongolian armies against Lhasa.

Following his death in 1621, he was succeeded by his son, Karma Tenkyong Wangpo (1604-1642). From 1635-1642 much of Tibet was plunged into civil war, the power of the Tsangpa kings of Zhigatse and their Chogthu allies being challenged by the Gelukpas of Lhasa, backed by the powerful Mongolian armies of Gushi Qan. Mongolian forces sacked Zhigatse in 1635, and eventually occupied the city in 1642, slaying Karma Tenkyong. Ever since then Lhasa has functioned as the capital of Tibet.

Depa Zhung (1642-1959)

From the 13th century onwards, the hierarchies of a number of Buddhist schools – the Sakyapas, the Drigungpas, the Karmapas and later, the Gelukpas – vied for political control of the country, relying upon the military power of Mongolian princes, with whom they established a 'patron-priest relationship'. The most famous of these princes were Godan, Qubilai Qan, Altan Qan, Arsalang, and Gushi Qan. While these schools managed to gain control of the country in succeeding centuries and established their capitals at Sakya, Nedong, Zhigatse and Lhasa, none of them exercised temporal authority over the whole of the Tibetan plateau in the manner of the early kings. The remote kingdoms and tribal confederations of East Tibet, whether nomadic or settled, fiercely maintained their independence and permitted a high degree of eclecticism in religious expression. The willingness of Tibetan potentates to involve Mongolian princes in Tibetan political life also had serious consequences for the nation's integrity.

In 1639-1641, during the prolonged civil war between Zhigatse and Lhasa with their partisan religious affiliations, the Qosot Mongolians decisively intervened on the side of Lhasa, enabling the Fifth Dalai Lama to establish political power for the Gelukpa school.

Reconstruction of the **Potala Palace**, symbol of Songtsen Gampo's seventh century imperial power, was undertaken by the Fifth Dalai Lama and the regent Desi Sangye Gyatso; and this building once again became the outstanding symbol of the Tibetan national identity. The new Lhasa administration gradually extended its influence over many parts of East Tibet through the agency of Gushi Qan's Mongolian armies, imposing a religious and political order that was often at variance with the local traditions. Kagyu monasteries suffered in particular, and many were converted to the Gelukpa order. Nonetheless, this was the first period since the early kings in which a strong national identity and political cohesion could develop. The Dalai Lama soon became an all-embracing national figurehead, representing not only the Gelukpa school but the aspirations of all the other traditions. As the embodiment of Avalokiteshvara, the patron bodhisattva of Tibet, his compassion permeated the land and provided a compassionate stabilizing influence in times of strife.

The predecessors of the Fifth Dalai Lama had been important figures for the early development of the Gelukpa school. The First Dalai Lama (1391-1474) had been a close disciple of Tsongkhapa, founder of the order, and he himself had established **Tashilhunpo** monastery in Zhigatse in 1447. His mortal remains are interred in a stupa within that monastery. His successors were based at **Drepung** to the northwest of Lhasa, and the Ganden Palace of Drepung remained their private residence and political power base until the construction of the Potala. The stupas containing the embalmed remains of the Second, Third and Fourth Dalai Lamas are housed at Drepung. Among them, the Third Dalai Lama Sonam Gyatso (1543-1588) travelled to Mongolia where he became spiritual advisor to Altan Qan, king of the Mongolians, and received the Mongol title Dalai Lama, 'ocean of wisdom'. Subsequently he was reborn as the grandson of Altan Qan. The Fourth Dalai Lama Yonten Gyatso is therefore the only Dalai Lama to have been born a Mongol rather than a Tibetan. From that time onwards, the backing of the Mongol armies was secured, and victory over Zhigatse in the civil war guaranteed.

The regents of the Dalai Lamas and external intrigues

The successive Dalai Lamas who ruled Tibet from the Potala Palace were assisted by powerful regents. During the time of the Fifth Dalai Lama, there were four regents: Sonam Rabten (1642-1658), Trinle Gyatso (1660-1668), Lobzang Tutob (1669-1674), and Sangye Gyatso (1679-1705) – the last of whom was a prolific scholar in the fields of Tibetan medicine, astrology and history. He concealed the death of the Fifth Dalai Lama in 1682 in the interests of national stability, but was himself tragically killed by the Mongolian prince Lhazang Qan who interfered to depose the libertine poet the Sixth Dalai Lama in 1706. Lhazang was later slain by the invading Dzungarwa armies of the Mongolian prince Sonam Rabten in 1717; and it was the turmoil caused by this invasion that prompted Kangxi, the Manchu emperor of China to become embroiled in Tibetan politics. Ostensibly supporting the Mongolian faction of Lhazang Qan, which had abducted the Sixth Dalai Lama and murdered the regent in Lhasa, and opposing that of the Dzungarwa, which had invaded Lhasa in response to that abduction, the Manchu armies effectively put an end to Mongolian influence on Tibetan affairs.

In 1720, during the regency of Taktsewa (1717-1720), the Manchus installed the Seventh Dalai Lama, who was in their custody. **Amdo** and **Nangchen** were annexed by the new **Kokonor territory** in 1724, and in 1727 the Manchus claimed much of Kham, east of the Yangtze as their own protectorate.

The next 150 years saw periodic intervention by the Manchus in the affairs of the Lhasa government, assisting it in its wars with Nepal and intriguing against it by ensuring that few Dalai Lamas ever reached the age of majority. This was the age when powerful regents and Manchu ambassadors (*amban*) held sway during the infancy and childhood of the Dalai Lamas. Some such as Miwang Sonam Topgyel (1728-1747) were highly regarded for their political acumen and secular stance; while others connived against the young Dalai Lamas within their charge.

During the lifetime of the Seventh Dalai Lama alone there were four important regents: Taktsewa (1717-1720), Khangyel (1720-1727), Miwang Sonam Topgyel (1728-1747), and Gyurme Namgyel (1747-1750). During the lifetime of the Eighth Dalai Lama, there were three main regents, Delek Gyatso (1757-1777), Ngawang Tsultrim (1777-1791) and Tenpei Gonpo (1791-1810). The next four Dalai Lamas all passed away prematurely before reaching the age of majority. During this period the following regents held sway: Jigme Gyatso (1811-1819), Jampal Tsultrim (1819-1844), the Seventh Panchen Lama Tenpei Nyima (1844-1845), Ngawang Yeshe Tsultrim (1845-1862), Wangchuk Gyelpo (1862-1864), and Khyenrab Wangchuk (1864-1873). Despite the unilateral machinations of the Manchus, which were designed to divide Tibet and weaken the rule of the Dalai Lamas, it is important to note that the Tibetans still controlled their own affairs and that apart from a diplomatic legation in Lhasa there was only a minimal Chinese presence on the Tibetan plateau, even in those supposedly partitioned eastern regions.

The Dalai Lamas of Tibet

Dalai Lama I	Gendun Drupa (1391-1474)
Dalai Lama II	Gendun Gyatso (1475-1542)
Dalai Lama III	Sonam Gyatso (1543-1588)
Dalai Lama IV	Yonten Gyatso (1589-1616)
Dalai Lama V	Ngawang Lobzang Gyatso (1617-1682)
Dalai Lama VI	Tsangyang Gyatso (1683- ?)
Dalai Lama VII	Kalzang Gyatso (1708-1757)
Dalai Lama VIII	Jampal Gyatso (1758-1804)
Dalai Lama IX	Lungtok Gyatso (1805-1815)
Dalai Lama X	Tsultrim Gyatso (1816-1837)
Dalai Lama XI	Khedrub Gyatso (1838-1855)
Dalai Lama XII	Trinle Gyatso (1856-1875)
Dalai Lama XIII	Tubten Gyatso (1876-1933)
Dalai Lama XIV	Tendzin Gyatso (b 1934)

This 19th-century pattern of regency power continued for a while during the childhood of the Thirteenth Dalai Lama, when Tatshak Jedrung Ngawang Palden (1875-1886) and Trinle Rabgye (1886-1895) held power, but the Dalai Lama himself soon took control and gained respect, not only for his spiritual status, but as the first Dalai Lama since the Great Fifth to hold genuine political power. Later regents during his lifetime, such as Lobzang Gyeltsen (1906-1909) and Tsemonling (1910-1934) acted more as the instruments of his policy. However, from the late 19th century onwards, Sichuan warlords (wary of the declining power of the Manchu Dynasty and of the enhanced power of Lhasa in the region,) began to intervene and establish military garrisons in East Tibet.

Global political concerns had a dramatic impact upon Tibet during the reign of the Thirteenth Dalai Lama. The Younghusband expedition from British India in 1904 forced the Dalai Lama to flee to Mongolia; and precipitated a new Chinese 'forward policy' in Tibet. The warlords Chao Erh-feng and Liu Wen-hui in their aggressive campaigns of 1909-1918 and 1928-1933 respectively attacked East Tibet, seeking to carve out a new Chinese province, which they would call Xikang (West Kham). The Dalai Lama again fled into exile, this time to Calcutta (1910) and the ill-equipped Tibetan forces bitterly resisted the invaders. In 1912-1913 all Chinese were expelled from Lhasa and the Dalai Lama began a period of internal reform and external independence from China. However, he was unable to change the deeply ingrained conservatism and xenophobia of the monastic and aristocratic hierarchy. Despite his warnings of what might befall the Tibetan nation if they did not adapt to modern conditions, Tibet continued in blind isolation from the world forces swirling about it. The 13th Dalai Lama died in 1933.

The present Fourteenth Dalai Lama was born in 1934 at **Taktser** in Amdo, an area then under the control of the Muslim warlord Ma Pufeng; and he could only be brought to Lhasa on payment of a ransom. During his childhood and formative years, political events were in the hands of the regents Reting (1934-1940), Takdra (1941-1951), and Lukhangwa Tsewang Rabten (1951/1952).

Chinese Administration (1951-)

In 1933, during the Long March, when the PLA forces under Mao Zedong fled northwards to escape the blockade of the Guomintang at Guangzhou and establish their northern stronghold in remote Yenan, they passed through Eastern Tibet, crossing the Yangtze in **Gyeltang**, the Gyarong at **Chakzamka**, and the Amdo grasslands in **Zungchu** and **Mewa**. Consequently, when Mao assumed power in 1949, these eastern areas were speedily occupied. Then, in 1951, while the world was preoccupied with Sino-American conflict in the Korean War, the PLA crossed the Yangtze to enter the areas of Tibet still controlled by the Dewa Zhung in **Lhasa**. The Tibetan army was hopelessly outnumbered, and the remainder of the country swiftly occupied by the Chinese communist forces. That same year, the Tibetan government in Lhasa was obliged to sign a 17-point agreement, outlining the policies for the 'peaceful integration of Tibet' into the 'motherland'.

Once occupied, Greater Tibet came to be divided between four Chinese provinces and one "autonomous region", administered, on the Soviet model, as autonomous prefectures and counties. The Ngawa and Kandze areas were initially designated as autonomous regions in their own right in 1949 and 1950, but they were both subsequently absorbed into Sichuan province as autonomous prefectures in 1953 and 1955 respectively. Most of Amdo, including Golok, and the Jyekundo autonomous prefecture of Kham had been fully integrated into Qinghai Province by 1951, following the suppression of Ma Pufeng's forces. Then in 1953, the Ganlho area of Amdo was formally incorporated as an autonomous prefecture of Gansu, and the Dechen area of Kham into Yunnan. The lands newly seized from the Dewa Zhung in 1951 remained under military rule and were not formally renamed the Tibetan Autonomous Region until 1965.

Early Western contacts with Tibet

1603	Portuguese merchant d'Almeida in Ladakh
1624-1632	Jesuit missionaries d'Andrade, Cabral and Cacella in Guge and Tsang
1661	Missionaries Grueber and d'Orville visit Lhasa from China
1707-1745	Capuchins in Lhasa; d'Ascoli and de Toursdella Penna and da Fano compile Tibetan dictionary
1715-1717	Jesuit cartographers survey Tibet
1716-1733	Jesuit Desideri in Lhasa
1774-1775	George Bogle of British East India Co visits Zhigatse
1783-1792	Samuel Turner's trade mission from British India
1811	Thomas Manning visits Lhasa
1823	Csoma de Koros in Zangskar
1846	Lazarist fathers Huc and Gabet visit Lhasa from Amdo
1879-1880	Przevalski visits Amdo, Kham, and Tsaidam
1885-1886	Carey from British India visits Tsaidam and Dunhuang
1889-1890	Bonvalot visits Amdo and Kham via Lop Nor
1890	De Rhins and Grenard travel to Namtso
1895	Sven Hedin in Jangtang
1896	Wellby and Malcolm travel to Kokonor and Kunlun and thence to Kashmir
1900-1906	Hedin in West Tibet
1900	Koslov in Kokonor, Tsaidam and South Amdo
1904	Francis Younghusband leads a British military force to Lhasa
1906-1907	Stein and Pelliot in Dunhuang
1906-1948	British Trade Mission in Gyantse and Lhasa

In this context it should be known that the word 'autonomous' is something of a euphemism. Although the "autonomy" of Tibet was constitutionally guaranteed, unwelcome social reforms and land collectivisation, which reached their height in 1956, soon degenerated into a full-fledged assault on Tibetan traditions. In 1959 an apparent attempt to kidnap the Dalai Lama by Communist generals in Lhasa triggered a spontaneous revolt by the Tibetan people against the occupation. The PLA ruthlessly suppressed the Lhasa uprising, resulting in the exodus of over 100,000 refugees to India, Nepal and Bhutan. Following the formal establishment of the Tibetan Autonomous Region in 1965, all official Chinese references to "Tibet" have referred to this truncated region alone, the other parts having already been divided between Qinghai, Gansu, Sichuan, and Yunnan.

During the dark years of suppression and the insanity of the Cultural Revolution (1966-1977) which immediately followed, systematic attempts were made to obliterate Tibetan culture. Thousands of monasteries were destroyed, along with their precious artefacts and vast libraries of great literary works. Some sources suggest that as many as one million Tibetans died in consequence of these events, whether directly through war and persecution, or indirectly through famine and material hardships. Accusations of genocide against the People's Republic of China were upheld by the International Commission of Jurists at The Hague.

Yet Tibetans, both inside and outside Tibet, never lost their strong sense of national identity, and at every opportunity they have striven to preserve and restore their precious culture. Under the guidance of the Dalai Lama in India a Tibetan Government-in-exile was established, and developed broadly upon democratic principles. The great centres of Buddhist learning were transplanted in the refugee settlements of Nepal and India and many important Buddhist masters who followed the Dalai Lama into exile have since established worldwide communities of Buddhist practitioners, holding allegiance to one or another of the schools of Tibetan Buddhism.

In 1989 HH Dalai Lama XIV was awarded the Nobel Peace Prize in recognition of his role as an international statesman of the Gandhian persuasion. Since 1983 His Holiness has abandoned the goal of Tibetan independence, despite the opposition of movements such as the exiled Tibetan Youth Congress, and instead he has been seeking a new deal for a reunified Greater Tibet within a modern democratic Chinese state. The Chinese administration was slow to react, and even now continue to portray him as a separatist, ignoring consistent statements to the contrary. However, informal talks did resume in 2002, after a hiatus of more than 20 years, and representatives of the Dalai Lama have been able to revisit parts of Tibet and meet with certain government officials. The hope on the Tibetan side is that some common ground can be found between more liberal elements of the current Chinese administration and moderate Tibetans. However, an official white paper published in Beijing on 23rd May 2004 appears to have ruled out a compromise Hong Kong type solution. More informal talks are expected to be held in the summer and autumn of 2004, but it is as yet unclear whether a breakthrough can achieved. In the meantime, observers will note that until a genuine political solution to the problems engendered by occupation can be found, the signs of internal dissension and discontent within the country known to the world at large as 'Tibet' are unlikely to diminish.

Tibetan Government in exile

In the aftermath of the suppression of the Lhasa Uprising in 1959, HH the Fourteenth Dalai Lama fled into exile, followed by some 80,000 Tibetan refugees, who sought sanctuary in India, Nepal, Bhutan and Sikkim. By 1970 there were some 100,000 Tibetan refugees dispersed throughout 45 settlements – extending from North India through Madhya Pradesh and Orissa, to Karnataka in the south. The Dalai Lama first settled in Mussoorie, but soon moved to Dharamsala, where the Government-in-exile was established.

In exile the Tibetan Government was reorganized according to modern democratic principles. Elections were called in 1960 for the establishment of a new body known as the Commission of People's Deputies; and in 1963 a draft Constitution of Tibet was promulgated, combining the aspirations of Buddhism with the needs of modern government. This constitution was eventually published in Tibetan in 1991, and in 2001 the head of government, Samdhong Rinpoche, was directly elected by the Tibetan diaspora for a five-year term.

The Government-in-exile administers all matters pertaining to Tibetans in exile, including the re-establishment, preservation and development of Tibetan culture and education, and, internationally, it leads the struggle for the restoration of Tibet's freedom. The Tibetan community in exile functions in accordance with the Charter for Tibetans in exile and is administered by the Head of Government and his Kashag (Council of Ministers), which is accountable to the Assembly of Tibetan People's Deputies (a democratically elected parliament). The Tibetan Supreme Justice Commission is an independent judiciary body.

The bureaucracy of the Central Tibetan Administration (CTA) comprises four autonomous commissions – Election, Public Service, Planning and Audit; seven departments – Religion & Culture, Home Affairs, Education, Information and International Relations, Security and Health.

The CTA mainly through the assistance of the Government of India and various international voluntary organizations, has successfully rehabilitated Tibetan refugees in 14 major and eight minor agricultural centres, 21 agro-industrial settlements and 10 handicraft centres throughout India and Nepal. There are also 83 Tibetan schools in India, Nepal, and Bhutan, with an approximate 26,000 children currently enrolled.

More than 117 monasteries have been re-established in exile; also a number of institutions including the Tibetan Medical and Astrological Institute; the Library of Tibetan Works and Archives, the Tibetan Institute of Performing Arts, the Centre for Tibetan Arts and Crafts – all based in Dharamsala, the Central Institute for Higher Tibetan Studies in Sarnath, and Tibet House in New Delhi. These institutions help to preserve and promote the ancient Tibetan heritage and culture, whilst enhancing the cultural life of the exiled community.

The CTA also maintains Offices of Tibet in New Delhi, New York, Zurich, Tokyo, London, Brussels, Kathmandu, Geneva, Moscow, Budapest, Paris, Canberra, Washington DC, and Taipei. These Offices of Tibet are the official agencies representing the HH Dalai Lama and the Tibetan Government-in-exile.

Modern Tibet

Statistics

Official name Bod. **Capital** Lhasa. **National flag** **Tibetan** (currently illegal): white snow mountain extending from lower corners to centre, with two snow-lions supporting a gemstone (symbolic of Buddhism) and *gakhyil* (symbolic of prosperity), and a yellow sun which rises behind the summit, emanating alternate red and blue rays of light (representing 12 traditional regions of Tibet) which reach the upper borders; bound on three edges with a yellow border (symbolic of Buddhism binding the cultural life of Tibet while remaining open to other religions) with one edge of the flag open. **Chinese**: the red flag of the People's Republic of China with one large yellow star representing the Chinese Communist Party, and four minor stars representing the peasants, industrial workers, intellectuals and military. **Official languages** Tibetan, Chinese. **Key statistics** 2001 National Census: 10,859,279 (including Ziling urban area), of which approximately 48% are Tibetan, 45% Han and Hui, and 7% minority nationalities (including Monpa, Lhopa, Qiang, Jang, Mongolian, Salar, Tu, Khazak, and Sarik). Area: 2,089,100 sq km (including Ziling urban area). Population density: 3.403 per sq km. Birth rate: 30:1,000. Death rate: 14:1,000. Life expectancy: 62. Literacy: 40%. Land use: forested 11.2 million ha, nomadic pasture 167 million acres (TAR only), agriculture 550,000 acres (TAR only). GNP per capita (approximate): US$200. Religion: Buddhist 57%, Atheist 32%, Muslim 8%, Bon 3%.

Government

Despite the current division of the Tibetan plateau into an autonomous region and several autonomous prefectures or counties, in most areas supreme authority still lies in the hands of the Communist Party and the PLA rather than in the civilian administration, many members of which appear to act as a rubber-stamp for decisions made elsewhere. There are numerous working committees and consultative bodies beneath the Communist Party right down to local village level, which has all engendered an in-built bias towards conservatism and a reluctance to embrace change.

Following the opening of China to the outside world and Premier Hu Yaobang's ground-breaking visit to Lhasa in 1981, when he publicly acknowledged past policy mistakes, the plateau was gradually prepared for tourism and international scrutiny. Delegations from Dharamsala in India even visited Tibet, but no effective dialogue was initiated as a means of resolving the situation; and even now no Tibetan has ever been appointed to any top position. The civil unrest that resurfaced in Lhasa from 1987 brought about the imposition of martial law and renewed restrictions on internal and foreign travel. Thereafter, in the TAR, successive party secretaries including Hu Jintao and Chen Kaiyuan adopted a rigid approach, designed to suppress pro-independence sympathizers at the expense of economic development. However, with the appointment of Guo Jinlong as the new party secretary in 2000, there have been modest indications of modernisation and economic development.

This trend has been even more noticeable in those parts of Tibet controlled by other Chinese provinces, particularly in Dechen, where successive governors of Yunnan have actively embraced development. The Tibetan prefectures of Qinghai, Gansu and Sichuan have all been formally declared as "open" areas (but for a few counties that remain "closed"). Yet issues of human rights and repression continue to surface, even in these provinces. In 2001 Tibetan and Chinese monks were evicted from Larung Gar Monastery in Sertal; an indication that the authorities will continue acting against traditional Tibetan culture and Buddhist values, in the absurd belief that the populace can be won over solely by economic development.

Economy

Urban Economy The economy of Tibet has undergone considerable reform in the last few years, though not to the same extent as in mainland China. The infrastructure of the country is still hampered by roads often washed away in the rainy season. Nonetheless some efforts have been made to extend the paved road network across the plateau. Even more significant for economic development is the construction of the Kermu-Lhasa Railway (due for completion in 2007) and the opening of new airports: Chamdo, Gyeltang and Dzitsa Degu are already functioning; others at Senge Khabab and Nyangtri will soon follow. These improved transportation links are already transforming the face of Tibet's towns and cities, which increasingly resemble Chinese provincial towns in their architecture and ambience as they sustain a growing influx of Chinese settlers. Urban development is underwritten by the numerous branches of the Bank of Industry and Commerce, China Construction Bank and China Agricultural Bank, present in all the county towns of the Tibetan Plateau. At the same time, telecommunications have improved, so that it is now possible to make international and trunk calls from virtually any county town, and mobile phones are widely used. The changing urban street plans published in this very guidebook – showing the banks and factories – are a barometer of this development. However, such changes tend to be confined to urban areas alone, and generally benefit educated Chinese immigrants and shopkeepers rather than the economically dispossessed Tibetan population.

The plateau is still conspicuously lacking an industrial infrastructure, although there are cement factories, smelting works, food processing factories, tea plantations, hydroelectric dams and mines. Ambitious irrigation schemes in Amdo and Tsang, and cross-county oil and gas pipelines linking the Tsaidam with mainland China have been opposed by international pressure groups on the grounds that they will bring an even greater influx of Chinese settlers and do nothing for the locals. Perhaps the best short-term hope is that the activities of the Lhasa-based **Tibet Development Fund**, and similar organisations which are encouraged to promote foreign investment in the economy, in education and in health, will focus more directly on sustainable development in the interest of the indigenous population. NGOs working in these fields in diverse areas of the plateau, such as the New York-based Trace Foundation, already have this ethos in mind. Yet it is equally clear that economic development will not be successfully achieved at the expense of Tibet's traditional culture, or indeed without a long-term resolution of the Tibetan situation.

 Rural economy The rural economy has changed little. There are greenhouses in the suburbs supplying vegetables to the urban communities, but most farmers are engaged in subsistence agriculture. Highland barley is the crop, supplemented in certain areas by wheat, peas, buckwheat and broad beans, and in more sheltered valleys by rape seed, potato, turnip, apple and walnut. Rice and cotton grow in the warmer parts of Southern Tibet. Nomadic groups are often better off, in that their livestock sustains the dairy and meat processing industry, as well as cashmere wool and leather production, and in season the caterpillar fungus trade on the grasslands can also be quite lucrative.

Importance to China Despite the often-proclaimed expense of Chinese investment in Tibet, the advantages to China of Tibet's occupation are indeed great – providing space for China's burgeoning population and enormous exploitable resources – particularly in water, timber, livestock, herbal medications and minerals. As the source of East and South Asia's greatest rivers, the Tibetan plateau has an enormous hydro-electric and geothermal potential which even now has hardly been exploited. There are large reserves of natural gas, and the landlocked lakes are rich in borax, salt, mirabilite, and soda. The mining of gold, copper, iron, coal, chromite, mica and sulphur has become widespread; and unregistered economic migrants from China have created serious law and order problems in the remote mining areas of East and Northeast Tibet. Oilfields have been opened in the Tsaidam basin of Northern Tibet.

The forests of Tibet have provided particularly rich pickings. Even prior to 1911, Sichuan had begun to export Chakla timber to China. Then between 1950 and 1998 many of the great virgin forests, extending eastwards from Kongpo to Gyarong, were severely depleted, as a constant stream of truck convoys freighted their lumber to Chengdu throughout the day and night. Tawu became an important centre for the lumber industry and the hillsides from Drango to Riwoche and Kongpo are still scarred and devastated, despite the ban on logging which was introduced throughout Kandze Prefecture in 1998.

The wildlife of East Tibet which once flourished is severely depleted and some species are on the verge of extinction, while only a few nature reserves, in Qinghai and the Ngari & Jangtang areas of the TAR appear to have taken the idea of conservation on board seriously. The lure of highly prized furs, including that of the Chiru antelope, valuable medications such as bear bile, musk, and caterpillar fungus often proves to be irresistible to the illegal hunter.

Economic life and minority nationalities The national minorities within Tibet have their own traditional economy: the **Monpa** grow rice, maize, buckwheat, barley, wheat, soya and sesame. The **Lhopa** largely follow their traditional barter-based economy, in which animal products and hides are traded for salt, wool, tools, clothing and tea. The **Qiang** of Far East Tibet produce herbal medications such as caterpillar fungus, while their lands are rich in oil, coal, crystal, mica and plaster. The **Jang** (Naxi) of Southeast Tibet live in a region of plentiful rainfall (average 2,700 mm), which sustains cash crops of rice, maize, wheat, potatoes, beans, hemp and cotton, and minerals such as gold, silver, copper, aluminium and manganese. The **Salars** of Dowi in Northeast Amdo grow barley, wheat, buckwheat and potatoes, with secondary occupations in stock-breeding, lumbering, wool-weaving and salt production. There is also a well-developed fruit-growing sector, including pears, apricots, grapes, jujube, apples, walnuts and red peppers.

Tourism

This sector of the economy has been developed since the mid-1980s and reached its highpoint in 1987 prior to the recent political movement in Lhasa. Even so, the development of tourism infrastructure is still a priority, and the plateau's first 5-star hotel opened at Dzitsa Degu only in 2001. Dzitsa Degu (with Labrang, Kumbum and Gyeltang) is one of the very few destinations on the plateau already developed for mass tourism. As of February 2004, Dechen, Ganlho and Kandze prefectures are completely open to unrestricted travel, as is Ngawa Prefecture (with the exception of Chuchen, Dzamtang, Ngawa and Trochu counties), and Qinghai (with the exception of Nangchen and Gabde counties). A special entry permit is still required for travel to the Tibetan Autonomous Region, and an alien travel permit (ATP) is prerequisite for internal travel there, regardless of the destination. In addition, a further permit issued by the Southwest Military Command is also required for travel to all destinations in Chamdo Prefecture. All these documents can be obtained through the various international organisations that organise travel on the Tibetan plateau. See the Information for visitors, page 32 for details.

Culture

People

The racial origins of the Tibetans are little known and still remain a matter of scientific speculation. Ethnologists, whose opinions vary and disagree, have distinguished **two main racial types**— one tall with long limbs and heads, and often distinctive aquiline features; and another of shorter stature, with high cheekbones and round heads. The former type, found mainly among the northern and eastern nomads of Kham and Amdo, like the modern Turkic and Mongolian peoples, is considered to be descended from a tall dolicocephalous race of great antiquity. The latter, inhabiting mostly the central and western parts of the country, as well as the Himalayan valleys of Northern Nepal and Bhutan, is regarded as a descendant of the Proto-Chinese of the Paroean group from which the modern Hans, Thais and Burmese are also descended.

However, this hypothesis appears oversimplified. There is evidence of great ethnic and linguistic diversity within the tribal confederations of Eastern Tibet, probably as a result of the process of intermingling with the neighbouring peoples and minority nationalities. The Tibetans themselves, according to legend, trace their ancestry to the union of an intelligent monkey emanation of Avalokiteshvara and a demonic ogress and, for their part, the Chinese have always considered the Tibetans to be racially distinct.

Population

Greater Tibet (Area: 2,108,700 sq km) is one of the mostly sparsely populated regions on earth with an estimated 10,859,279 people (2001 census, including the Ziling urban area). Modern census figures are complicated, owing to the current partition of Tibet into five diverse Chinese provinces, but even conservative Chinese publications have given the overall ethnic Tibetan population at over 5 million, suggesting that they comprise about 48% of the plateau's population. Tibetans in exile and a number of Tibetologists, who hold these figures to be underestimated, both on account of the non-registration of many nomadic peoples and the large number of refugees and ethnic Tibetans now in neighbouring countries, such as India, have assumed the total Tibetan population to be closer to six million. Of the remainder (maximum 52%), the majority (approximately 45%) are accounted for by the recent rapid influx of Chinese from Sichuan and other provinces of mainland China into urban areas of Tibet and the more gradual demographic movement of Hui Muslims from the Ziling region. **NB** These figures do not take into account the large transient Chinese population in Tibet (including the army), who are mostly registered in other provinces of mainland China.

Among the two larger groups, the Tibetans include within their numbers the **Topa** of the highland region (Far West Tibet); the **Tsangpa** of West Tibet, the **Upa** of Central Tibet, the **Horpa** of North Tibet, the **Khampa** of East Tibet, the **Amdowa** of Northeast Tibet, and the **Gyarongwa** of Far East Tibet. In all these areas, there are both sedentary communities (*rongpa*) and nomadic groups (*drokpa*).

The situation differs in the remote border areas where smaller nationalities have lived for centuries. These minorities, comprising approximately 7% of the total population, include peoples closely related to the Tibetans, such as the **Monpas** (8,496) and **Lhopas** (2,980) – who inhabit Metok and the adjacent counties of the extreme south; the **Qiang** (104,000) of Maowen and adjacent counties in the extreme east; and the **Jang** (Naxi; 281,503) and Li of Jang Sadam (Lijiang) who also inhabit the adjacent Tibetan counties of Markham, Dechen, Gyeltang, Balung, and Mili in the extreme southeast. Other nationalities found in the extreme northeast are of Mongolian or Turkic origin: some 25,000 of China's **Kazakhs** inhabit West Kokonor. Some 96,996 **Salars** inhabit Dowi (Xunhua Salar AC) and Gannan; and the 215,500 **Tu** are mostly found in Huzhu Tu AC and in the upper reaches of the Tsong-chu and Datong valleys. **Mongolian** populations, numbering approximately 9,1360, are confined to certain parts of West Kokonor and Sogwo AC.

Language

The Tibetan language is classified as one of the 23 Tibeto-Burman languages spoken within of present-day China, the others including Yi, Bai, Hani, Liau, Lahu, Jang (Naxi), and Qiang. But dialects of Tibetan are in fact spoken in six present-day countries, including China, Burma, India, Bhutan, Nepal and Pakistan, corresponding to the extent of the ancient Tibetan empire. A useful geographical survey of the Tibetan language can be found in the introductory pages of Philip Denwood's *Tibetan*. There are great variations in dialect from Ladakh in the Far West to the Golok, Gyarong and Gyeltang dialects of the east. With remarkable differences in pronunciation and vocabulary, these dialects have sometimes been taken for distinct languages in their own right.

Broadly speaking, the Tibetan language comprises the Utsang, Kham and Amdo groups of dialects. The first of these includes the **U-ke** spoken in Lhasa and Lhokha, the **Tsang-ke** spoken around Zhigatse and Gyantse, the **To-ke** spoken in the highland areas and Ngari (Far West), and the **Sharpa-ke** spoken by the peoples of the Northeast Nepal border. **Kham dialects** include those of Nangchen and Jyekundo in the north, Nakchu in the west, Dechen and Mili in the south, and Chamdo, Drayab, Batang, Derge, and other areas in the east. **Amdo dialects** include **drokpa-ke**, spoken by the nomads of Golok, and the adjacent areas of Sertal, Dzamtang, and Ngawa; **Rongpa-ke**, spoken by the settled farming communities of Tsongkha, Bayan Khar (Hualong) and Dowi (Xunhua); and the dialects spoken by the **semi-nomadic** people in Repkong, Labrang, and Luchu areas.

In general, the Tibetan language has constructed its specialized Buddhist vocabulary under Indian influence, while freely borrowing from Chinese commonplace words of everyday usage – food, drink, clothing. Tibetan writing has never made use of ideograms (the origins of the petroglyphs of Rutok and the Jangtang have not yet been properly investigated). The standard block-lettered script derives from the seventh-century Ranjana script of North India, and the more cursive handwriting script, it has been suggested, may have an even older origin in the Northwest Indian Vartula script.

National language The great disparity in pronunciation and vocabulary between the various Tibetan dialects creates many problems of communication, even for native Tibetan speakers. Nowadays, Tibetans from Amdo and Lhasa often find it easier to converse in Chinese rather than Tibetan, so that the former has become something of a lingua franca for Tibetans inside Tibet. The Tibetan Government-in-exile has for many years now been promoting the ideal of a standard form of Tibetan in its schools; and even within Tibet the need for a national Tibetan language is well understood, even if it seems a remote goal. By contrast, the written language has remained remarkably constant since the orthographic revisions of the ninth century.

Tibetan language is an important medium of instruction in primary schools and, to a lesser extent, in middle schools. Higher education almost invariably is imparted in Chinese, and there are very few scientific textbooks published in Tibetan. Nevertheless, some efforts have been made to establish a wide-ranging technical terminology for modern scientific subjects. For Tibetan words and phrases, see page 845.

Chinese speakers include those of the east and southeast who speak Sichuan dialect and those of the northeast who speak Putonghua (standard Mandarin) or Ziling dialect. Very few Chinese living or working in Tibet have attempted to master the Tibetan language, most assuming that the indigenous peoples will have to accommodate themselves to communicate with the newcomers who control the urban economy. This is undoubtedly the prevailing trend among the young in particular, and in parts of East Tibet it has become commonplace to see educated Tibetans adopt Chinese names in order to secure their own advancement. The greatest fear confronting the Tibetan people is not the prospect of another persecution or cultural revolution so much as being outnumbered by an influx of Chinese immigrants in their own land. After all, there are obvious precedents in Manchuria and Inner Mongolia.

Daily life

Social customs and life Tibetan daily life and social customs have for centuries been highly influenced by Buddhism. Whenever child-naming rituals, wedding ceremonies or funerals are held, it is important that an auspicious day is chosen.

The **Tibetan calendar** is based on the 60-year cycle of the Kalacakra Tantra (rather than the century of the western system). Each of the years within a 60-year cycle has its own distinctive name according to the Kalacakra Tantra, and a derivative name formed by combining the 12 animals and five elements of Chinese divination. Each cycle thus begins with the fire hare year and ends with the fire tiger year. At present we are in the 17th cycle counting from the year 1027 when this system was introduced to Tibet. Auspicious days within the lunar calendar may fall on the 15th or 30th days of any month, which are associated with Shakyamuni Buddha, or on the eighth (Medicine Buddha Day), the 10th (Padmasambhava Day), or 25th (Dakini Day). Specific events, such as the Buddha's first promulgation of the Buddhist teachings, are commemorated on set days of the year (ie the fourth day of the sixth month). In addition to such general auspicious days, there are also those which may be specific to a given individual, determined on the basis of the time of birth.

During all the important ceremonies of daily life, the offering of auspicious white scarves along with tea or barley ale and tsampa (roasted barley flour), is a prerequisite.

Naming ceremonies consequent on the birth of a child follow the Buddhist naming system rather than the western patronymic system. Surnames are rarely found, with the exception of aristocratic families who add their clan name as a prefix to their given Buddhist names. Weddings are generally arranged by the parents of the bride and groom, taking into account important issues such as compatibility of birth-sign, social class, and absence of consanguinity. Gifts are mutually exchanged – the 'milk price' being paid by the groom's family and the 'dowry' by the bride's family.

 Funeral ceremonies assume varied forms: sky burial being the most common and compassionate form of corpse disposal in Central Tibet and West Tibet, and cremation an equally popular method in East Tibet where wood is more plentiful. The former entails the dismembering of the body and distributing it to celestial vultures. Important lamas may be cremated or embalmed within stupa reliquaries. Lesser persons may be given water burial (particularly in the fast-flowing gorges of the southeast), or earth burial. The latter, which carried high prestige during the Bon period when the early Chongye tombs were constructed, gradually came to have inferior associations from the Buddhist perspective.

Diet The traditional staple diet of the Tibetans is somewhat bland, consisting of butter tea, tsampa (roasted barley flour), dried meat, barley ale (chang), and dairy products – milk, curd, and cheese. Many nomadic families still survive on this diet alone today; whereas urban communities also have rice, noodles, millet and a wide range of fresh vegetables and pulses.

Animal husbandry is still the main occupation of rural and nomadic communities, while subsistence farming is possible only in the low-lying valleys. Although Tibetans have traditionally displayed a compassionate Buddhist attitude to all forms of wildlife, the eating of meat is widespread (both out of choice and necessity) in view of the fact that, until very recently, the country was not known for its abundance of vegetables.

National dress

The inhabitants of different parts of the Tibetan plateau may be recognized by their distinctive dress, notwithstanding the ubiquitous Chinese clothing which is all too prevalent nowadays. Both men and women wear the **chuba**, a long-sleeved gown, tied at the waist with a sash. Farmers often wear sleeveless chubas and nomads sheepskin chubas. Local designs are distinctive, among them the black smock design of Kongpo, the otter-skin bordered chuba of Amdo, the shorter length but longer sleeved chuba of Kham, the brocade-bordered black tunic of Tsang and To.

Head-wear is also distinctive: the coiffure of both men and women indicating the part of the country from which they come. For example, Khampa men with black hair braids generally come from Chamdo and those with red braids from Derge or Kandze (ie east of the Yangtze). Brocade hats lined with fur are popular in Central Tibet while stetsons or Bolivian-style bowlers are widely used in East Tibet. In general Tibetans wear subdued colours, but there are areas of East Tibet in particular where maroons and shocking pinks are preferred, above all on festival days.

Jewellery Both men and women wear jewellery, the most highly prized stone being the uniquely Tibetan **zi** (banded agate or chalcedony). Ornaments of gold, silver, coral, turquoise, amber, beryl, and ivory are also worn, but none compare in value to the *zi* stone.

Tibetan houses

These vary in their design and material from one part of the country to the next. In Central Tibet and West Tibet, village houses are flat-roofed and made of adobe, in Kongpo and adjacent areas, they are made with wooden shingles and decorative features, reminiscent of Bhutanese architecture, in Kham horizontal timbers painted red with intricate window-sills are typical, and in Minyak, Litang or Gyarong the sturdy

Ceremonial scarfs

During the 13th century, Drogon Chogyel Phakpa, advisor to Emperor Qubilai Qan, introduced the custom of offering ceremonial scarfs (*katak*) on special occasions. This practice subsequently became the principal means of expressing courtesy, greetings, or respect in Tibet. Often the scarfs are presented to spiritual masters or sacred images, to the victors of sporting contests or divas of theatrical performances, or to dignitaries when being granted an audience, making a petition, or receiving tidings. Commonly, kataks are also offered to those about to embark on a long journey, and to new-born babies, newly weds, or deceased persons.

Simple ceremonial scarfs are made of loosely woven cotton, and superior scarfs of silk. The shorter ones may be 1-1½ m long, and the longer up to 7 m in length! Most are white in colour, indicative of purity, but blue, yellow, red, and green scarfs are not unknown. Generally five-coloured scarfs are offered only to Buddha-images, or else wrapped around a ceremonial arrow (*dadar*), used in longevity empowerments (*tsewang*) and marriage ceremonies. Most are plain, but some may be inscribed with the words 'good auspices' (*tashidelek*), or designed with the 'eight auspicious symbols' (*tashi da-gye*), the motif of the Great Wall of China, and so forth.

stone houses of Qiangic construction are commonplace. Perhaps the most beautiful village and small town architecture is to be seen in the Tawu area of East Tibet, where the building technique combines the horizontal red timber construction with pristine whitewashed adobe and finely carved windows. In general, village houses have a lower floor for animals and an upper floor for human habitation. Shuttered windows with a trefoil arch shape are colourfully painted. Electricity is now commonplace in towns and cities, but in the countryside oil lamps are still in use. The nomadic communities throughout Tibet live in large sturdy tents (*ba*) made of black yak tweed.

Minority groups

Among the smaller minority groups within Tibet, the **Monpa** inhabit the counties of Metok, Nyangtri, and Tsona. Their customs, religion and culture are fully integrated with those of the Tibetans through long-standing political, economic and marital links. Many speak Tibetan in addition to their own dialects. Both men and women wear robes with aprons, black yak-hair caps, and soft-soled leather boots with red and black stripes. Women wear white aprons, earrings, rings and bracelets. In subtropical Metok women and men both wear jackets – the women with long striped skirts. The slash and burn method of agriculture is practised here, and the staple diet consists of rice, maize, millet, buckwheat and chilli pepper, in addition to tsampa and tea. Hunting is still important in these areas where the virgin forest is dense, and species of wild boar, bears, foxes and langurs are to be found. Monpa houses are made of wood with bamboo/thatched roofs.

The **Lhopa** of Menling, Metok, Lhuntse, and Nang counties are largely forest dwelling hunter-gatherers and fishermen. Few of them speak Tibetan; and intermarriage is rare. The standard dress is a sleeveless buttonless knee-length smock of black sheep's-wool with a helmet-like hat made of bearskin or bamboo/rattan laced with bearskin, and no shoes. Men wear bamboo earrings and necklaces, and carry bows and arrows, while the women wear silver or brass earrings,

Ba and Gur: Tibetan tents

There are basically two types of Tibetan tent: the black yak tweed tent (*ba*) used as a dwelling by the nomads, and the white canvas tent with blue appliqué (*gur*) used by villagers and townspeople for picnics and recreation. The former are dotted around the high grasslands and pastures where the nomads tend their herds of yak and flocks of sheep. They are made of a coarse yak wool tweed, which is capable of withstanding wind, rain, and snow; and the design has changed little in centuries. There is a central tent pole, from which the four corners are pegged out in a rectangle and a low inner wall of earth and clumps of grass constructed on three sides. The door flap may be kept open or closed. The stove is in the centre of the tent, with a ventilation opening immediately above – the size of the opening being controlled by pulley ropes. The nomads occupy the high ground in the spring and summer; and by mid-autumn, they begin their age-old transhumance, exchanging the snow-bound pastures for the comparatively well sheltered dwellings of the lower valleys. During the 1960s efforts were made to settle the nomads permanently in camps, but they have now reverted to their original lifestyle. A few of the permanent camps are still used as a winter residence for the elderly and the young. Alongside the black tents, there are sometimes small white tepee-style tents to be seen. These are occasionally used for storage, but often for the daughter of a nomadic family while entertaining suitors.

The picnic tents of the townspeople are used during the festival season. Some are very large and ornate, with decorative blue appliqué designs, depicting the eight auspicious symbols (*tashi da-gye*) and other signs. The horse festivals of Gyantse and Damzhung, and those of Kham (eg at Jyekundo and Nakchu) provide an ideal opportunity for visitors to see the large variety of Tibetan picnic tents in use. Also, in Lhasa, there is a tent factory producing decorative tents and awnings to order.

bracelets, necklaces and ornate waist belts. The staple diet is a dumpling made of maize or millet, as well as rice and buckwheat, in addition to tsampa, potatoes, buttered tea and chilli peppers.

In Far East Tibet, the **Qiang** and related groups occupy fertile land and good mountain pastures. The adjacent forests are home to the giant panda, langur, and flying fox. Men and women wear long blue gowns over trousers with sheepskin jackets. The women have laced collars and sharp-pointed embroidered shoes, embroidered waistbands, and earrings. The staples are millet, barley, potatoes, wheat, buckwheat; and they have finely constructed stone blockhouses, two/three storeys high.

In Southeast Tibet the **Jang** or **Naxi** inhabit the Lijiang area and adjacent counties in Dechen, Markham and Mili. Here, the women wear wide-sleeved gowns with jackets and long trousers with an ornate waistband. The men tend to wear standard Chinese clothing. Naxi society is mostly patriarchal, but a few matriarchal elements survive in Yongining (Yunnan) and Yanyuan (Sichuan) counties. There, the children live with the mother and women comprise the main labour force.

In the extreme northwest of Amdo, there are **Kazakhs** inhabiting the West Kokonor prefecture. These Turkic-speaking peoples have a distinctive vocabulary assimilated from Chinese, Uighur, and Mongolian. The written language is based on Arabic. Most Kazakhs are engaged in nomadic animal husbandry, dwelling in yurts (*yu*) during the spring, summer and autumn. The men wear loose long-sleeved furs and skin garments, with sheepskin shawls or camel-hair lined overcoats in winter, and sheepskin trousers.

The women wear red dresses with cotton padded coats in winter, and white shawls embroidered with red and yellow designs. Dairy products such as milk dough, milk skin, cheese, and butter are plentiful. The diet also includes butter tea, mutton stewed in water without salt, smoked meat, horse sausage, fermented mare's milk, and sweets made of rice or wheat. Kazakh society is Muslim and patriarchal, while both monogamous and polygamous types of marriage are found.

In Dowi (Xunhua) county of Amdo, the **Salar** people of Turkic origin have lived since their arrival from Samarkhand during the Mongolian period (1271-1368). Theirs is a strict Muslim society and the women are rarely permitted to appear in public. Predominantly a farming community, the Salar grow barley, wheat, buckwheat and potatoes, with secondary stock-breeding, lumbering, wool-weaving and salt production.

The **Tu** peoples of Gonglung and Pari (Tianzhu) counties in the northeast extremity of Amdo are said to be Chahan Mongolians descended from the army of the Mongol general Gerilite, who intermarried with indigenous Turkic nomads (Horpa) during the time of Genghiz Qan. Later, they again intermingled with other Mongol groups who settled in those areas during the Ming period. Their language belongs to Mongolian branch of Altaic family and the script devised for the Mongol language by Drogon Chogyel Phakpa is still in use among them for certain literary purposes. Both men and women wear shirts with finely embroidered collars and bright colours. Traditionally livestock breeders, the Tu adapted to farming from the 13th century onwards, and became converts to the Gelukpa school of Tibetan Buddhism.

The **Hui Muslim** community inhabit much of Amdo and the northeast. They are predominantly Chinese-speaking urban dwellers, but maintain their distinctive religion, names, and (sometimes) dress. In Central Tibet they are often known as Zilingpa; and have a reputation for unscrupulous trading.

Mongols inhabit the West Kokonor and Sogwo areas of Amdo. They wear fur coats in winter and loose chubas in summer, generally red, yellow or dark blue in colour, with a green or red waistband, knee-length boots, and conical hats (in winter) or silk/cloth turbans (in summer). The girls have hair parted in the middle, with agate, coral and turquoise ornaments. Mongolian peoples are renowned for their excellent horsemanship and archery. Their staple diet consists of beef, mutton, dairy products, and tea; and they live in felt yurts. Both traditional shamanism and Buddhism are practised.

Art

Tibetan painting and sculpture date from the seventh century, coinciding with the unification of Tibet by King Songtsen Gampo and the gradual absorption of Buddhism from the neighbouring cultures of India, Nepal, China, and Central Asia. Apart from the petroglyphs of **Rutok** and the **Jangtang**, which have not yet been accurately dated, there is little evidence of Tibetan art prior to the seventh century. The earliest surviving examples so fully absorbed the impact of the surrounding artistic traditions that it is difficult to discern pre-Buddhist elements, should an earlier, purely indigenous tradition be found to exist.

Tibetan painting finds three principal expressions: manuscript illumination (*peri*), mural painting (*debri*), and cloth-painted scrolls (*tangka*), each inexorably linked to the goals and practices of Buddhism and Bon. Appliqué tangkas and sand-painted mandalas also evolved as by-products. Sculpted images of deities and historical figures are mostly produced in metal, clay or stucco, and to a lesser extent in wood, stone, or even butter. In theory, Tibetan works of art serve primarily as icons, intermediaries between man and divinity, a function underscored by the indigenous term 'tongdrol' (liberation by seeing the deity). In conjunction with ritual, a painting or a sculpted image houses a deity consecrated for purposes of worship, offering, meditative visualisation, and spiritual communication.

Among the various stylistic influences which have been observed in the art of Tibet, the oldest strand seems to be that of **Newar Nepal** (and Guptan India) as seen in the oldest door frames and pillars of the Jokhang temple in Lhasa. Early Central Asian or Khotanese influence has been discerned in the extant images of Drakmar Keru Lhakhang, Yemar and Dratang – the last of these also containing murals indicative of the Pala style of Bengal (eighth to 12th century). **Kashmiri art styles** are noticeable at Toling in the Guge Kingdom of Far West Tibet, and at the later murals of nearby Tsaparang which survived the Cultural Revolution. Other examples can be found at Tabo and Alchi in the adjacent Indian areas of Spiti and Ladakh. During the period of Mongolian influence, the monasteries of Sakya and Zhalu were lavishly decorated by Newar artists from Nepal. Subsequent indigenous developments included the 15th-century **Lato** style (eg the murals of Chung Riwoche stupa), the **Gyantse** style (of Kumbum and Pelkor Chode), the fluid **Khyenri** style named after the Sakyapa artist Jamyang Khyentse Wangchuk, the **Uri** style of Lhasa, which became the prevalent style from the 17th century onwards, the exquisite **Repkong** style of Amdo, and the **Karma Gadri** style of Kham which incorporated landscape elements and perspective from Chinese art, and later exerted considerable influence on the mainstream Central Tibetan style.

Crafts

Traditional handicrafts are made largely for the indigenous market rather than the tourist trade. They include the ubiquitous wooden churns (*dongmo*) used for making butter tea. The best birchwood bowls (sometimes inlaid with silver or pewter) are said to come from **Dechen.** Jade or agate bowls are made in **Rinpung** and **Chongye.** Knifes and daggers with ornately carved scabbards are a speciality in **Horpo**. Engraved amulet boxes, or gold and silverware engraved with motifs such as the Eight Auspicious Symbols, and other intricate metalwork objects come from **Derge** and **Zhigatse**. The best gilded copper and cast-metal Buddhist images are made in **Chamdo**, while clay sculptures and painted scrolls from **Repkong** are particularly renowned. Tibetan carpets and rugs are world famous, the best indigenous factory outlets being at **Gyantse**, **Zhigatse** and **Kandze**. Elegantly carved mani stones are available in and around **Jyekundo**. Ornate appliqué tents, brocade work, tailoring and stuffed mattresses with decorative covers are best in **Lhasa**. The making of hand-crafted wooden household furniture, including shrines, cabinets, and tables – all with decorative panelling, is an art continued to the present day by the carpenters of **Zhigatse** and **Lhasa**. Tibetan secular musical instruments, especially the lute (*dranyen*), are best in the **Lhartse** area. Striped aprons are woven in the village houses of **Chidezhol**, and bamboo artefacts in the southern counties of **Nyangtri**, **Menling**, **Metok**, and **Dzayul**. Brass fixtures for temple roofs are made in **Rushar**. Blankets, which may be finely woven, striped or shaggy, are woven in **Amdo**; and throughout the nomadic regions, pastoral artefacts, such as the yak hair sling and the sheepskin bellows, are easily found.

Music and dance

Song and dance have always been an important vehicle for social contact in Tibet. Apart from the epics of **Ling Gesar**, there are free-form mountain and nomadic ballads; lyric poems such as the Hundred Thousand Songs of Milarepa; and regional folk-songs from **To, Batang**, Kham and so forth. The song-gathering festivals of **Amdo**, known as Huarhui in Chinese, are held annually on the sixth day of the sixth lunar month. Such folk songs often have a thematic character: there are wedding songs,

Woodblock printing

The technique of woodblock or xylographic printing (*shingpar*) which was developed in Tang China predates the invention of movable type in Western Europe. A copy of the world's earliest extant printed book, the Chinese translation of the Diamond Cutter Sutra (*Vajracchedikasutra*), dated 868, is preserved in the British Museum in London. This technique was slow to reach Tibet, where from the introduction of the written script by Tonmi Sambhota in the seventh century until the intervention of the Manchu emperors in Tibetan affairs during the 18th, the vast Buddhist literature – both translated and indigenous – was recorded in manuscript form only. Some precious manuscript versions of the Buddhist Canon inscribed in gold ink (*sertri*) or silver ink (*ngultri*) on black paper have survived; and the general custom of utilizing red ink for canonical works and black ink for non-canonical commentaries persists even now. The oldest woodblock edition of the Tibetan canon, prepared in China by the Ming Emperor Yongle no longer exists (although one printed copy has been preserved in Sera Monastery).

During the 18th century, woodblock versions of the Kangyur and Tangyur – the compilations forming the Buddhist Canon, were commissioned at Nartang near Zhigatse, at Zhol Parkhang in Lhasa, at Derge in Kham, at Cho-ne in Amdo, and at Beijing. The letters are carved in reverse in oblong blocks of wood, and the paper, cut to size, is printed by impressing it with a roller against the inked surface of the woodblock. There are several teams, each of two persons, often monks, who work together, rhythmically printing multiple copies of a single page. The pages of the book (*pe-cha*) are then collated and the edges dyed red or yellow, in accordance with tradition. The pages are not bound but kept loose leaf, and wrapped in a cloth book cover (*pe-re*). This printing technique came to permeate most of the Tibetan plateau; and many small monasteries had their own distinctive woodblock collections, often reflecting their own traditions. Today, the largest woodblock collections are housed at Derge, Cho-ne, Lhasa, Labrang Tashikyil, and Kumbum. Copies of the Buddhist Canon and related works are once again being actively distributed throughout the plateau in this time-honoured method.

The storage of woodblocks of course requires a large amount of space. By contrast, the techniques of modern printing, including movable type, photo-offset, and computer typesetting are now in vogue, and the various nationalities' publishing houses of the TAR, Sichuan, Qinghai, and Gansu are particularly active in the printing and distribution of conveniently bound copies of classical and modern works of Tibetan literature at affordable prices.

labour songs, round dance songs, archery songs, drinking songs, love songs (such as those composed by the Sixth Dalai Lama), and songs in the form of repartee or playful rejoinders. These generally use simple language, which evokes an immediate mood or imagery, and employs both metaphor and hidden analogy. Modern songs are continually being written and performed in this traditional style, utilizing the sophisticated technology of the recording studio. Tibetan pop singers, such as Datron, Yangchen Dolma, Kalzang Chodron, and Tseten Dolma, are well known both inside and outside Tibet.

Songs are frequently accompanied by folk dances. Among the most popular are the round dances known as *gor-zhe* in **Lhasa**, **Tsang** and **Lhokha**, and as *gor-dong* in **Chamdo** area. Men and women form two concentric circles around a bonfire, singing alternate choruses, while stamping their feet to keep the rhythm. There are other distinctive dances, such as the drum dance of **Lhokha**, the bell-and-drum dance of **Chamdo** and **Kongpo**, the tap dance of the **highland** region (*to-zhe*), and the synchronized labour songs of **Tsang** (*le-zhe*). For a brief description of the religious dances (*cham*), which are distinct from these, see above, page 494.

The first **opera** troupe in Tibet was founded in the **Ngamring** area during the 15th century by Tangtong Gyelpo, the celebrated bridge-builder who may be regarded as the Leonardo da Vinci of Tibet. By the 17th century opera (*dogar*) had become an art form in its own right. A stylistic distinction developed between the traditional **White Masked Sect** and the innovative **Blue Masked Sect**. The former, which included troupes such as the Bingdungpa from **Chongye**, the Nangzipa from **Tolung**, and the Tashi Zholpa from **Nedong**, were gradually supplanted by the more sophisticated exponents of the latter style, such as those of Gyelkar, based at **Rinpung**, Shangpa and Jungpa, both based at **Namling**, and Kyormolung, based at **Lhasa**. Nowadays there are numerous troupes throughout the country, and the best time to see their performances is during the Zhoton festival in Norbulingka at Lhasa during the month of August.

Literature

The Tibetan language is the source of one of the world's greatest and most prolific literary heritages, rivalling those of China, India, Greece or Rome. Although most works are of a Buddhist nature, the secular tradition of poetry and drama continues to flourish. The epic poems of **Ling Gesar** are more voluminous than the great Mahabharata of ancient India – some 72 volumes having already been edited and published in Tibet by the provincial publishing houses and the Chinese Academy of Social Sciences. Three million copies of these texts have been distributed throughout the Tibetan world! The development of secular Tibetan literature has also been given a new impetus by the **Amnye Machen Institute**, recently established at Dharamsala in Northwest India to promote the work of contemporary Tibetan writers.

The classical literature, which remains highly popular at the present day, includes the canonical texts of Buddhism and their indigenous Tibetan commentaries – amounting to hundreds of thousands of volumes; as well as the great works on the traditional sciences – grammar, medicine, logic, art, astrology, poetics, prosody, synonymics, and drama. Religious histories, biographies and hagiographies provide an important frame of reference for the adherents of the various Buddhist schools and the Bon tradition. The works are too numerous to detail or even summarise here, but mention should be made of the great canonical compilations.

The Buddhist tantras translated into Tibetan during the early diffusion of Buddhism are contained in the Nyingma Gyudbum, the best known edition of which is preserved in woodblock form at the Derge Parkhang in Kham. The later translations of the tantras, as well as some earlier translations of both sutras and tantras, are contained in the 104-volume Kangyur, compiled in the 14th century by Buton Rinchendrub (1290-1364). Most extant commentaries of Indian origin are contained in a companion anthology, the 185-volume Tangyur, which he also compiled. There are several extant manuscript versions of these canonical texts – most of them housed in the great monasteries around Lhasa, but seven woodblock editions of the Kangyur survive, along with four of the Tangyur. At present these are being collated and republished in a new master edition by the Kangyur-Tangyur Collation Project in Chengdu.

Religion

Tibetan religious traditions may conveniently be considered in three categories – animism, Bon and Buddhism. The first concerns the control of animistic forces by bards and storytellers, and the second emphasizes the purity of space, funerary rituals, and certain meditative practices, which may have originated in either Zoroastrianism or Kashmiri Buddhism; and the third is the means of liberation from the sufferings of cyclic existence as propounded in ancient India by Shakyamuni Buddha.

Animism and the 'Religion of Humans'

The earliest form of Tibetan religion, which RA Stein has termed the 'nameless religion', is a type of animism based upon the worship of the elements and mountain deities. Incense offerings would be made to appease local mountain spirits, and 'wind-horse' (*lungta*) prayer flags or cairns were placed on prominent passes to ensure good auspices. Solemn declarations of truth (*dentsik*) and oaths would be made in the presence of local deities, to invoke good fortune (*gyang-khug*); and talismanic objects or places (*la-ne*) were revered as life-supporting forces. Enemies or hostile forces could then be overpowered by drawing in their life-supporting talisman in a ceremony known as *la-guk*.

The so-called 'religion of humans' (*mi-cho*) which evolved out of this early animism relied upon storytellers (*drung*) and singers of riddles (*de'u*) or epic poems to provide an ethical framework for social behaviour. According to a late 14th-century chronicle, the religion of humans had nine aspects, represented in the body of a lion – the right foot symbolizes tales of the world's origin; the left foot symbolizes tales of the appearance of living beings; the hindquarters symbolize tales of the divisions of the earth; the right hand symbolizes tales of the genealogy of rulers; the left hand those of subjects; the middle finger those concerning the origin of Buddhism; the neck those of the tribes holding allegiance to each ruler, the head those concerning patrilinear and matrilinear lines of descent, and the tail symbolizing paeans of joy.

Bon

The religion of Tazik (Persia) which was introduced into the Zhangzhung Kingdom of Far West Tibet and thence into Central Tibet during the period of the early kings is generally considered to have evolved in three distinct phases, known as 'revealed Bon' (*dol-bon*), 'deviant Bon' (*khyar-bon*) and 'transformed Bon' (*gyur-bon*). The original importance that Bon held for the Tibetan kings probably lay in its elaborate funerary rites and veneration of space. The earliest kings of Tibet are said to have been immortals who would descend from and ascend into the heavens on a sky-cord (*mu*); but following the death of Drigum Tsenpo, the mortal kings increasingly focused upon funerary rites and rituals for the averting of death through 'ransom' (*lud*).

The **'revealed Bon'** refers to those rituals which were prevalent in Tibet from the time of Drigum Tsenpo until the time of King Lhatotori Nyentsen. The **'deviant Bon'** included a new wave of rituals and practices derived from Zhangzhung and Brusha in Far West Tibet; and the **'transformed Bon'** refers to the synthesis which developed following the introduction of Buddhism to Tibet and its establishment as the state religion. Contemporary research into the earliest ritual and philosophical texts of Bon has been galvanized by the work of Professor Norbu in Italy. However, the Bon orders which have survived until the present are thoroughly imbued with Buddhist imagery and symbolism; and they have evolved their own parallel literature to counterbalance that of the Buddhists, ranging from exoteric teachings on ethics to highly esoteric teachings on the Great Perfection (*Dzogchen*).

Since the late 19th century there have been two camps: the traditionalists who claim to reject all contacts with other Buddhist schools (as at **Menri** in Tsang and **Nangzhik** in Ngawa), and the modernists who accept the ecumenical approach followed in Kham towards the turn of the 20th century by Jamgon Kongtrul, Zharza Tashi Gyeltsen, and others. Certain parts of Tibet remain strongholds of this tradition, notably the Shang valley in West Tibet, the **Bonri** area of Kongpo, the **Jangtang** lakelands, the **Tengchen** area of Kham, the **Ngawa**, **Repkong** and **Zungchu** areas of Amdo, and **Gyarong**.

In exile the principal Bon community is based at **Solon** in Himachal Pradesh, India.

Buddhism

Brief introduction

Buddhism evolved from the teachings of Siddhartha Gautama of the Shakya clan (known as the Buddha, the 'Awakened One'), who lived in northern India in the sixth or fifth century BC. The Buddha's teachings are rooted in a compelling existential observation: despite the efforts of all people to find happiness and avoid pain, their lives are filled with suffering and dissatisfaction. However, the Buddha did not stop there. He recognized the causes of suffering to be the dissonant mental states – delusion, attachment, aversion, pride and envy, and realized that it is possible to free oneself permanently from such sufferings through a rigorous and well-structured training in ethics, meditation and insight, which leads to a profound understanding of the way things really are that is, enlightenment.

The Buddha was born a prince and had known great opulence but had also experienced great deprivations when he renounced his life of luxury to seek salvation through ascetic practice. He concluded that both sensual indulgence and physical deprivations are hindrances to spiritual evolution. He taught the Middle Way, a salvific path which was initially interpreted to mean isolation from the normal distractions of daily life by living in communities devoted to the pursuit of spiritual liberation, which were disciplined but did not involve extreme deprivation. These communities, consisting of both monks and nuns, preserved and put into practice the Buddhist teachings. Initially, the teachings were preserved through an oral transmission, but by the first century BC were increasingly committed to written form. Unlike the world's other leading religious traditions, Buddhism does not rely on a single literary source (eg the Bible, Koran, or Talmud), but on a vast, rich, sophisticated literary corpus. The preservation of Buddhism brought literacy to hundreds of millions in Asia.

Buddhism's path to salvation depended largely on the individual's own efforts. Its emphasis on self-reliance and non-violence appealed to the merchant class in India, and thus it spread along trade routes – north through Central Asia, into China and then into the Far East, Korea and Japan. It also spread south to Sri Lanka and Southeast Asia: Burma, Thailand, Indo-China, and Indonesia. Later, Nepal and Tibet embraced Buddhism at the zenith of its development in India, and it was this tradition which eventually came to permeate Mongolia, Manchuria and Kalmukya. In recent years Buddhism has also found adherents in the West.

A Buddhist is one who takes refuge in the **Three Precious Jewels** (*Triratna*): Buddha, Dharma (his teachings), and Sangha (the monastic community). Beyond this, Buddhism has evolved remarkably different practices to bring about liberation, its teachings having been interpreted and reinterpreted by commentators in each new generation and in each cultural milieu. Buddhism's brilliance lies in its universality – its compelling existential appeal and, crucially, its efficacy. Historically it has appealed to peasants and to kings, to philosophers and to the illiterate, to prostitutes and murderers, and to those already close to sainthood. And though it was not its primary intention, Buddhism has transformed the cultures in its path – imbuing them with its ideals of universal compassion and profound insight.

Buddhist teachings

The Buddhist teachings are broadly said to have developed in three distinct phases: (1) the sutra, vinaya and abhidharma texts (ie Tripitaka) of the **Lesser Vehicle** (**Hinayana**), which were upheld by the four great monastic orders founded in different parts of India by Katayayana, Rahula, Upali, and Kashyapa; (2) the sutra teachings of the **Greater Vehicle** (**Mahayana**), which were maintained by the followers of Nagarjuna and Asanga; and (3) the tantras or esoteric teachings of the **Indestructible Vehicle** (**Vajrayana**), which were transmitted by accomplished masters such as Manjushrimitra, Indrabhuti, and Padmasambhava. These different vehicles have their distinctive points of emphasis: the **Lesser Vehicle** holding that obscurations and defilements are eliminated by renunciation; the **Greater Vehicle** holding that enlightenment can be cultivated through compassion and insight which comprehends the emptiness underlying all phenomena, including those obscurations; and the **Indestructible Vehicle** holding that all obscurations are originally pure and transmutable into their pristine nature.

A primary distinction is made between the **sutra** texts which emphasize the gradual or causal approach to enlightenment; and the **tantras** with their emphasis on the immediate or resultant approach.

Tibetan Buddhism

Among all the Buddhist countries of Asia, the highest developments of Indian Buddhism were preserved in Tibet. This was due partly to geographical proximity, partly to temporal considerations, and partly to the aptitude which the Tibetans themselves displayed for the diversity of Indian Buddhist traditions. The sparse population, the slow measured pace of daily life and an almost anarchical disdain for political involvement have encouraged the spiritual cultivation of Buddhism to such an extent that it came to permeate the entire culture.

All schools of Buddhism in Tibet maintain the monastic discipline of the **vinaya**, the graduated spiritual practices and philosophical systems based on the **sutras** and their commentaries, the shastras, and the esoteric meditative practices associated with the **tantras**. Different schools developed in different periods of Tibetan history, each derived from distinctive lineages or transmissions of Indian Buddhism.

The oldest, the Nyingmapa, are associated with the early dissemination of Buddhism during the period of the Yarlung Dynasty. The Sakyapa and the Kagyupa, along with the Kadampa, appeared in the 11th century on the basis of later developments in Indian Buddhism. The Gelukpa originated in Tibet during the 14th century, but can claim descent from the others, particularly the Kadampa and the Sakyapa. Each of these schools has had its great teachers and personalities over the centuries. Each has held political power at one time or another and each continues to exert influence in different parts of the country. Witness, for example, the strength of the Sakyapa in **Derge** and **Jyekundo**, the Kagyupa in **Tolung** and **Nangchen**, the Gelukpa in **Lhasa**, **Zhigatse**, **Chamdo** and **Tsongkha,** or the Nyingmapa in **Lhokha**, **Derge**, and **Golok-Sertal**.

NB The Mongolian and Chinese custom of referring to the major schools of Tibetan Buddhism by the colours of the ceremonial hats worn by their monks has been avoided in this book because it is an absurd oversimplification, containing a number of anomalies, as the late Tseten Zhabdrung clearly pointed out some years ago in an article in *China Tibetology*.

The Wheel of Existence

The Wheel of Existence (Skt *bhavacakra*, Tib *sidpei khorlo*), sometimes known as the wheel of life or the wheel of the rebirth process, is a motif widely depicted among the vestibule murals of Tibetan temples. Its graphic visual imagery symbolizes the modes of suffering endured by sentient beings of the six realms along with the causes of their sufferings, which generate a perpetual cycle of mundane rebirths. The wheel is firmly held in the jaws and clutches of Yama Dharmaraja, the lord of death who presides over all cyclic existence. It comprises four concentric rings, the outermost one representing the **twelve successive links of dependent origination** (Skt *pratitya-samutpada*, Tib *tendrel*) through which all forms of mundane existence come into being. The fundamental ignorance (1), propensities (2) and consciousness (3) which are the successive resonances of a past life continue to project their effects in a subsequent life in the following sequence: name and form (4), sensory activity fields (5), contact (6), sensation (7), attachment (8), grasping (9), and rebirth process (10), which in turn actualize birth (11) along with old age and death (12). The **second ring** depicts the actual sufferings endured by the gods (13), antigods (14), humans (15), animals (16), tormented spirits (17) and hell-bound beings (18), who are respectively dominated by pride, envy, diverse defilements, delusion, attachment, and hatred; along with the corresponding Six Sages who manifest in order to demonstrate the paths leading to liberation from cyclic existence. The **third ring** indicates the dynamic of the rebirth process (19): an upward momentum through the three higher modes of rebirth (gods, antigods and humans) and a downward spiral through the three lower destinies (animals, tormented spirits and hell-bound beings). The **innermost ring** (20) depicts the three primary defilements or dissonant mental states underlying the entire cycle, namely: the delusion, attachment and hatred, which are self-perpetuating. It is important to remember that, in the Buddhist view, the sufferings endured by the six realms of sentient existence are never considered to be eternal. Indeed the impermanence of all conditioned phenomena may be observed from moment to moment, as well as from death to rebirth. The wheel serves to remind its observer of the nature and causes of suffering and of the remedial actions to be followed in order to attain liberation from cyclic existence.

Nyingmapa

The Nyingmapa school maintains the teachings introduced into Tibet by Shantaraksita, Padmasambhava, Vimalamitra and their contemporaries during the eighth century. The entire range of the Buddhist teachings are graded by the Nyingmapa according to nine hierarchical vehicles, starting from the exoteric sutras of the Lesser Vehicle and the Greater Vehicle and continuing through the classes of Outer Tantras to those of the Inner Tantras. It is the Inner Tantras known as Mahayoga, Anuyoga and Atiyoga (or Dzogchen) which are the teachings of the Nyingmapa par excellence.

Following the establishment of Buddhism in Tibet by King Trisong Detsen, the Nyingma literature was systematically translated into Tibetan at **Samye** Monastery. The tradition survived the persecution of Langdarma thanks to the activities of yogins such as Lhalung Pelgyi Dorje, Nyak Jnanakumara and Nubchen Sangye Yeshe; and the monks who preserved the Vinaya lineage in Amdo. When Buddhism was restored

in Central Tibet, the unbroken oral tradition of the Nyingmapa flourished at **Ukpalung** in Tsang under the guidance of the Zur family, and the *terma* traditions (comprising teachings concealed in the past by Padmasambhava and his followers to be revealed for the benefit of future generations) developed their own local allegiances throughout the country. The most outstanding scholar and promulgator of this tradition was Longchen Rabjampa (1308-1363). The six main monasteries of the Nyingma school, each of which has hundreds of branches throughout the land, are: **Katok**, founded in 1159 by Katokpa Dampa Deshek (1122-1192); **Dorje Drak**, founded in 1632 by the Third Rigdzin Ngagi Wangpo (1580-1639); **Mindroling** founded in 1670 by Rigdzin Terdak Lingpa (1646-1714); **Pelyul**, founded in 1665 by Rigdzin Kunzang Sherab (1636-1698); **Dzokchen**, founded in 1685 by Dzogchen Pema Rigdzin (1625-1697); and **Zhechen**, founded in 1735 by the Second Zhechen Rabjam Gyurme Kunzang Namgyel.

Kagyupa

The Kagyupa school maintains the lineages of the Indian masters Tilopa, Naropa, and Maitripa, which emphasize the perfection stage of meditation (sampannakrama) and the practice of the Great Seal (Mahamudra). These were introduced to Tibet by Marpa Lo-tsawa (1012-1096) and Zhang Tselpa (1122-1193). Marpa, who lived in the **Lhodrak**

Sky Burial

The Tibetan custom of 'sky burial' in which corpses are dismembered and fed to vultures has attracted mixed feelings of revulsion, fear, and awe among outside observers. Yet it is important that the custom is seen properly in context. Firstly, 'sky-burial' is not the only means of disposing of the dead in Tibet; but it is the most popular.

Following the moment of death, the body of the deceased should be left untouched for three days, during which time an officiating lama should perform the transference of consciousness (*pho-wa*) which emancipates the consciousness (*nam-she*) of the deceased into a buddha-field or pure land; or else whisper advice into the ear of the deceased, informing him or her of the nature of the inner radiance experienced in the first of the successive intermediate states (*bar-do*) to be experienced after death. If the body is touched at all, it should be touched at the crown of the head, because the anterior fontanelle is the optimum point of exit for the consciousness. Touching the body elsewhere could result in the consciousness exiting from a lower unfavourable orifice. Relatives are encouraged neither to laugh and shout, nor to weep and cry during the period when the deceased's consciousness traverses the intermediate states. After three days, the officiating lama should continue offering advice to the deceased over the following seven weeks, during which the consciousness may attain liberation from rebirth, or assume a subsequent rebirth. On the last day of each of the seven weeks special prayers are recited and offerings made, culminating in the final ceremony. The purpose is to accumulate merit on behalf of the deceased, and to ensure his or her future well-being, to which end a special tangka or image may be commissioned.

The disposal of the body is generally regarded as a separate, lesser matter. 'Sky-burial' in which the corpse is dismembered, the inner organs removed, the flesh cut into shreds, and the bones crushed and mixed with tsampa-flour, before being fed to the vultures, is said to offer great merit. The vultures, who frequent the most popular 'sky-burial' sites and are summoned by an offering of incense, are revered as birds of purity, subsisting only on corpses and casting their droppings onto high mountain peaks. There are several well known charnel grounds (*durtro*) on the plateau, including those at Sera and Drigung in Central Tibet; and Traling Monastery in Golok. Corpses may be carried long distances for dismemberment at one of the preferred sites.

Alternative forms of funeral are also current. 'Water burial' is regarded as a pure but inferior method of disposal in that fish are traditionally protected by the Buddhist community. 'Earth burial' is less frequently used, but preferred by the Chinese and Muslim communities. Traditionally earth burial was in vogue in Tibet during the period of the Yarlung Dynasty, when massive tumuli were constructed in Chongye and elsewhere. However, later it came to be regarded as a lower form of burial reserved for robbers, murderers, and plague victims. Cremation is utilized in parts of Eastern Tibet where wood is more plentiful; and particularly for lamas and aristocrats. Lastly, the embalmed mortal remains of certain great lamas may be interred within a reliquary stupa, or 'golden reliquary' (*serdung*), as an object of offering for the sake of posterity.

area bordering Bhutan, had four main disciples including the renowned yogin Milarepa (1040-1123), who passed many years in retreat in the mountain caves of **Labchi**, and adjacent Himalayan valleys. Milarepa is one of a select group of Tibetan masters revered for their attainment of enlightenment or buddhahood within a single lifetime. His biography and songs are classic texts, available in English translation, but it was his principal student, Gampopa (1079-1153), who founded the first monastery of that school at **Daklha Gampo** in the early 12th century. Gampopa's principal students Phakmodrupa Dorje Gyelpo (1110-1170) and the First Karmapa Dusum Khyenpa (1110-1193) respectively founded the influential monasteries of **Densatil** and **Tsurphu**. The former was the source of the eight minor Kagyu schools, including those of **Drigung** (founded by Drigung Kyopa, 1143-1217), **Taklung** (founded by Taklung Tangpa Tashipel, 1142-1210), and **Druk** (founded by Lingje Repa, 1128-1188). Later, in 1717 the great monastery of **Pelpung** was founded in East Tibet by Situ Chokyi Jungne.

Kadampa

When the Bengali master Atisha (982-1054) reintroduced the teachings of the gradual path to enlightenment into Tibet in 1042, he transmitted the doctrines of his teacher Dharmakirti of **Sumatra**, which focused on the cultivation of compassion and the propitiation of the deities Tara, Avalokiteshvara, Acala and Shakyamuni Buddha. His disciples included Ngok Lotsawa (1059-1109) and Dromton Gyelwei Jungne (1004-1064) who respectively founded the important monasteries of **Sangphu Neutok** and **Reting**. During the early 15th century this tradition was absorbed within the indigenous Gelukpa school.

Sakyapa

The Sakyapa tradition represents a unique synthesis of early eighth century Buddhism and the later diffusion of the 11th century. The members of the Khon family had been adherents of Buddhism since the time of Khon Luiwangpo Sungwa, a student of Padmasambhava. Then, in 1073, his descendant Khon Konchok Gyelpo, who had received teachings of the new tradition from Drokmi Lotsawa, founded the **Gorum** temple at **Sakya**. His order therefore came to emphasize the ancient teachings on Vajrakila, as well as the new teachings on Hevajra, Cakrasamvara, and the esoteric instruction known as the Path and its Fruit. The monastery was initially developed and expanded by the so-called five founders of Sakya: Sachen Kunga Nyingpo (1092-1158), Jetsun Sonam Tsemo (1142-1182), Drakpa Gyeltsen (1147-1216), Sakya Pandita (1182-1251), and Drogon Chogyel Phakpa (1235-1280). The last mentioned built the **Lhakhang Chenmo** (1268) and secured the patronage of the Mongolian Empire, to establish a network of monasteries and temples throughout Central and East Tibet, comprising **Gongkar Chode**, **Jyekundo**, **Zhiwu**, **Dzongsar**, and **Lhagang**, to name but a few. After the death of the Sakya hierarch Danyi Zangpo Pal (r 1305-1322), the ruling house of Sakya split into two main branches – the Phuntsok Palace and the Dolma Palace, which have until the present shared their authority on a rotational basis.

Other important sub-schools of Sakya also developed. Among them, **Ngor** was founded in 1429 by Ngorchen Kunga Zangpo, **Nalendra** in 1435 by Rongton Sheja Kunzik, **Derge Lhundrupteng** in 1448 by Tangtong Gyelpo; **Tanak Tubten Namgyeling** monastery in 1478 by Gorampa Sonam Senge; and **Dra Drangmochen** during the early 16th century by Tsarchen Losel Gyatso, who was a student of the great Doringpa.

Gelukpa

The Gelukpa school maintains the teachings and lineage of Je Tsongkhapa (1357-1419), who established a uniquely indigenous tradition on the basis of his Sakyapa and Kadampa background. Born in the **Tsongkha** valley of Amdo, he moved to Central Tibet and founded the monastery of **Ganden** in 1409. He instituted the

Stupas

The stupa (Tib *chorten*) is a receptacle of offerings, symbolizing the buddha-mind, and the 'actual reality' (*dharmata*) or 'emptiness' (*shunyata*) behind the phenomenal appearance of the buddha-body in the world. When Shakyamuni Buddha passed away, poignantly offering his disciples a final instruction on the impermanence of conditioned phenomena, the funerary relics were interred in eight stupas, symbolic of that underlying reality, and distributed among the princes of the eight kingdoms which were his devotees: Kushinagara, Magadha, Vaishali, Kapilavastu, Calakalpa, Ramagrama, Visnudvipa, and Papa. Later, the practice of erecting such stupas as repositories of offerings at crossroads and geomantic sites became popular in ancient India, particularly among some of the Mahasanghika schools. Emperor Ashoka is credited with the multiplication of the original buddha-relics, which he reputedly inserted into 84,000 stupas constructed throughout the far-flung reaches of his Mauryan Empire and adjacent kingdoms. Some of these are said to survive to the present day, at Patan in Nepal and elsewhere.

The original stupas appear to have had a central axis, with an outer dome shape, forming a bulbous container where the relics were interred. Books and sacred artefacts would also be inserted. As a ubiquitous Buddhist monument, the stupa has taken on a diversity of forms throughout Southeast Asia, China, Japan, and other places in the Buddhist world. The later stupas of Tibetan and Nepalese design came to have five characteristic parts: a squarish plinth or base, a rounded dome, an oblong *harmika*, a tiered triangular spire, and a *bindu*-shaped finial, respectively symbolizing the five elements: earth, water, fire, air, and space. Tibetan stupas also adopted eight distinct motifs, which together form a set, indicative of the eight principal deeds of Shakyamuni Buddha: his birth, victory over cyclic existence, enlightenment, teaching, descent from Tusita, resolution of schism, performance of miracles, and final nirvana. Such sets can be seen throughout the Tibetan plateau: for example, at Kumbum in Amdo, Zhiwu and Takzham in Kham, and at Chorten Rang-go north of Damzhung in Central Tibet. The original purpose of the stupa was never forgotten, and in Tibet the custom of cremating important lamas in a temporary funerary stupa (*purdung*), or of interring their embalmed bodies within a reliquary stupa (*dungten*) or 'golden reliquary stupa' (*serdung*) is still widely practised. The golden reliquaries of the Potala Palace, in which past Dalai Lamas are interred, are particularly renowned.

Great Prayer Festival at Lhasa, and propagated his important treatises on the sutra and tantra traditions in and around the Tibetan capital. Two of his foremost students, Jamyang Choje Tashi Palden and Jamchen Choje Shakya Yeshe, respectively founded **Drepung** (1416) and **Sera** (1419); while others such as Gyeltsab Je and Khedrup Je, became the prime teachers of the new Gelukpa order. The latter was retrospectively recognized as the First Panchen Lama. Another of Tsongkhapa's students was the First Dalai Lama Gendun Drupa, who founded **Tashilhunpo** at Zhigatse in 1447.

The successive emanations of the Dalai and Panchen Lamas enhanced the prestige of the Gelukpa school, which swiftly gained allegiances among the Mongolian forces of the northeast. Following the civil wars of the 17th century, many Kagyu monasteries were converted to the Gelukpa tradition, and the regent Sangye Gyatso compiled his Yellow Beryl (Vaidurya Serpo) history of the Gelukpa tradition.

The six greatest monasteries of the Gelukpa school are those of **Ganden**, **Drepung**, and **Sera**, in addition to **Tashilhunpo**, **Kumbum Jampaling**, and **Labrang Tashikhyil** in Amdo. Along with **Chamdo**, **Litang**, **Dargye**, **Kandze** and many other important centres, these became important institutions for the study of dialectics and the serious practice of the sutras and tantras.

Others

The lineages of certain minor Buddhist traditions have also survived intact – among them the **Zhiche** ('pacification') and **Chodyul** ('object of cutting') which were expounded by the South Indian yogin Padampa Sangye and his female Tibetan disciple Machik Labdron (1031-1126). The rituals of the latter are particularly popular among adherents of the Nyingma and Kagyu traditions.

The **Jonangpa** tradition was founded at Jonang in Tsang by Kunpang Tu-je Tsondru (b 1243), and widely propagated through the writings of its great exponents: Dolpopa Sherab Gyeltsen (1292-1361), Jetsun Kunga Drolchok (1507-1566), and Taranatha (1575-1634). Its teachings combined an in-depth knowledge of the Kalacakra Tantra and other tantra texts of the new translation period, with a distinctive view concerning the nature of the emptiness (shunyata) which, according to Buddhism, underlies all phenomena. The Jonangpa differentiated between mundane phenomena which are regarded as being 'inherently empty' and the attributes of the Buddha which are regarded as being 'extraneously empty' of mundane impurities. The school was persecuted – ostensibly for holding this view – during the 17th century and its adherents have only survived in remote parts of **Dzamtang**, **Gabde**, and **Ngawa** in the Amdo area, where there are many Jonangpa monasteries.

The **Zhalupa** tradition is that associated with **Zhalu** monastery in Tsang and particularly with Buton Rinchendrub (1290-1364) who was one of Tibet's most prolific authors and the compiler of the modern Tibetan canon – known as the Kangyur and Tangyur. The **Bodong** tradition was founded, also in Tsang, by Bodong Cho-le Namgyel, who wrote 132 volumes of texts on all the subjects of classical science including Buddhism. Lastly, the **Shangpa Kagyu** lineage was based on the tantric teachings that the yogin Khyungpo Neljor (b 978) received from the Indian yogini Niguma, and the masters Maitripa and Sukhasiddhi.

Buddhism today

The Buddhist traditions permeated the social life of Tibet until the destruction of the country's 6,000 monasteries during the suppression of the 1959 Tibetan uprising and the Cultural Revolution. Only a few temples and shrines of historic importance survived intact, along with a small number of temples which were used as granaries. Since the demise of the Gang of Four heroic efforts have been made by the people to restore the buildings, which represent their Buddhist heritage, with or without the support of the government. More difficult is the reintroduction of systematic Buddhist learning and meditation practice. Many of the great Tibetan masters who reside in exile have returned home for visits to encourage a Buddhist renaissance; but some authorities often continue to react with suspicion and misunderstanding. This is particularly noticeable at **Larung Gar** in Sertal (which was recently "downsized" on account of the high number of ethnic Chinese students it attracts), and in the **Lhasa** area, where the political indoctrination of monks and nuns continues unabated. The political winds are themselves constantly subject to change. The hard-line attitude against government employees who overtly support monasticism or even maintain their traditional household shrines were somewhat relaxed in Lhasa during 2001, but in a system lacking proper accountability and transparency, any glimmer of progress can be reversed without forewarning.

Islam

The Muslim community of Tibet includes the descendants of medieval converts and merchants from **Ladakh**; as well as more recent migrants from the **Ziling** area. In Lhasa, there are mosques, such as **Gyel Lhakhang**, and Muslim cemeteries. In Northeast Amdo there are counties such as Bayan Khar (Hualong) and Dowi (Xunhua), where the Hui and Salar Muslim communities are predominant.

Religious and secular festivals

Religious festivals are important events throughout the Tibetan Buddhist world – commemorating the deeds of the Buddha, or those of the great masters of the past associated with one tradition or another.

Secular festivals include the traditional new year (Losar) festival, the summer horse-festivals held throughout the country between the fifth and seventh months of the lunar calendar, and the more recent national festivals adopted from the Chinese calendar.

The following are the main festivals observed according to the traditional calendar:

	M	**D**
Losar, Tibetan New Year	1	1
Monlam, the Great Prayer Festival	1	1
Day of Offerings	1	15
Enlightenment of Buddha	4	15
World Incense Day	5	15
Dharmacakra Day	6	4
Birth of Padmasambhava	6	10
Yoghurt Festival	6	29
Rain Retreating Festival	7	1
Bathing Festival	7	27
Damzhung Horse Festival	7	30
Ongkor Festival	8	1
Descent from the God Realms	9	22
Anniversary of Tsongkhapa	10	25

M = Month; D = Day

Land and environment

Location

The Tibetan plateau and the adjacent Sino-Tibetan border ranges (latitude: 39-27°N; longitude: 78-104°E), which have sometimes been poetically described as the 'roof of the world' or the 'third pole', form an enormous land-locked region in Central Asia, 2,100,000 sq km in area. The region is bordered on the west by India, on the north and northwest by Xinjiang (Chinese Turkestan), on the northeast, east and southeast by mainland China, and on the south by India, Nepal, Bhutan and Burma. As the highest land mass on the planet and the source of virtually all the important waterways of South and East Asia, this plateau has considerable importance within the biosphere. The indigenous name for Tibet is **Bod** or **Bod-Kham**; the English name being derived from the Mongolian Thubet, the Chinese Tufan, and the Arabic Tubbat.

Readers should note that the Tibetan world generally transcends current political borders. It includes the peripheral mountain areas to the south, which are defined by the Karakorum and Himalayan ranges: Gilgit and Baltistan (now in Pakistan); Ladakh,

Lahoul, Spiti, Kinnaur, Tehri-Garwal, Kumaon, Sikkim, and Arunachal (now in India); Manang, Dolpo, Mustang, Langtang, Helambu, and Khumbhu (now in Nepal); and the mountainous areas of Bhutan. These peripheral areas, where the cultures of the Tibetan world and the Indian subcontinent converge, have at one time or another been considered Tibetan territory and their cultures, languages, and ethnic composition are still predominantly Tibetan. The formidable terrain and its communication difficulties have ensured, however, that the plateau has rarely been politically united in the course of its history. The defining characteristics of the region are made, rather, on the basis of topography, ethnicity, language and religion, which together form the distinct Tibetan cultural milieu.

Provinces and terrain

Traditionally, Tibet is divided into three provinces (Tib *cholkha sum*): **Utsang** extends from Ngari in the Upper Indus and Sutlej valleys through the Brahmaputra basin as far as Sokla Kyawo in the Upper Salween. **Kham** extends eastwards from Sokla Kyawo across the Mekong and Yangtze towards the source of the Yellow River. **Amdo** extends further eastwards from the source of the Yellow River and Golok to Chorten Karpo on the Sang-chu, and through the Minjiang basin to Drukchu. To these should be added **Gyarong**, which extends southwards from Sertal, Dzamtang and Ngawa through the deep gorge of the Gyarong Ngulchu.

Currently, Tibet is administratively divided between the **Tibetan Autonomous Region** (1,106,780 sq km) of China, and four other Chinese provinces – Qinghai, Gansu, Sichuan, and Yunnan. Of these latter provinces, the plateau incorporates virtually the entire land-mass of **Qinghai** (676,851 sq km, excluding Ziling district), the **Ganlho Autonomous Prefecture** and **Pari (Tianzhu) Autonomous County** (44,323 sq km) of Gansu province, the **Kandze** and **Ngawa Autonomous Prefectures** of West Sichuan (240,154 sq km), and the **Dechen Autonomous Prefecture** of Northeast Yunnan (20, 562 sq km). Taken as a whole, the Tibetan plateau occupies about a quarter of China's territory.

Terrain

There are great variations in the elevation of the plateau, which generally tilts from northwest to southeast. The southern gorges can be as low as 1,700 m and the higher Himalayan massifs exceed 8,000 m. The main geographical zones are: the Northern Plain (**Jangtang**) which is sparsely populated by nomadic herdsmen, the arid far Western highlands (**Ngari**) which are the source of the Indus, Sutlej, and Karnali rivers, the central agricultural valleys of the Brahmaputra basin around Lhasa, Tsetang and Zhigatse (**Utsang**), and the more densely populated alpine gorges and grasslands of the east (**Kham and Amdo**), through which the Salween, Mekong, Yangtze, and Yellow River all flow.

Origins of Tibet's landscape

Most of the Tibetan plateau is considered to have formed the bed of the **Neo-tethys Ocean**, which was destroyed some 210-50 million years ago as the Indian sub-continental plate moved to throw up the mountains of the Himalayan region. This however is a comparatively recent geological event, and it is predated in the peripheral north and east of the plateau, where the oldest rocks are Precambrian granite, known to be about one billion years old. The geological correlation of these earlier strata has been complicated by subsequent neo-tectonic development.

During the **Palaeozoic** era (570-245 million years ago) the **Kunlun ranges** of Tibet's northern frontier, which are largely composed of Cambrian and Triassic granites, granodiorites, and andesites, began accumulating along the southern margin of the Tarim Basin. This developing mountain range continued westwards into the Pamirs and the Hindu Kush. Then, during the **Mesozoic** era (245-66.4 million

Geological history of the Tibetan Plateau

Precambrian
4,000-2,500 mya (million years ago): oldest stable continental rock.
660 mya: oldest Tibetan rock
Palaeozoic
500 mya: Gondwanaland included India and Southern Tibet.
Earliest South Tibetan fossils suggest latitude of modern Australia.
400/300 mya: Pangaea (fourth) supercontinent forms; and Old Tethys Sea contracts.
300 mya: formation of Kunlun, Pamir, and Altyn Tagh ranges.
Mezozoic
200 mya: fusion of Jangtang plain and Indochina with Asia, along two connecting zones of the Salween and Yangtze respectively. Consequent rising of plateau from seabed.
140 mya: India separates from Africa.
100 mya: tectonic pressure raises Gangtise and Nyenchen Tanglha ranges.
Cenozoic
45 mya: Himalayas begin to form as India fully collides with Asia, subducting the Neo-Tethys sea.
20 mya: older Himalayan rock thrusts upward through younger strata over 2,000 km central fault.
15-10 mya: Himalayas at 3,000 m; plateau at 1,000 m.
2 mya: rapid uplift of plateau and Himalayas along main boundary fault.
Pleistocene Epoch
1 mya: Himalayas at 4,500 m; plateau at 3,000 m.
10,000 ya: Himalayas at 6,000 m; plateau at 4,700 m.

years ago), the **Jangtang** plain of North Tibet became separated from the Southern Tibet block by an ocean; evidence of this can be found in the Dangla mountains of Northern Tibet. Further movement involving the break-up of the southern supercontinent 'Pangaea' produced the granite **Gangtise**, **Nyenchen Tanglha**, and **Karakorum ranges** (180-100 million years ago).

The formation of the Tibetan plateau as we know it occurred during the **Cenozoic** period (66.4 million years ago – onwards). The original collision of the drifting Indian subcontinent with Eurasia is considered to have taken place some 2,000 km to the south of the present Indus-Brahmaputra watershed. Since then, 800 km of this continental crust have been contracted to form the Himalayas – the world's highest mountain range and the largest concentration of continental crust on earth (69 km thick in places). Further south, the collision created the Gangetic basin. The massive plateau even now continues to extend upwards and outwards under its own weight, as the Indian sub-continental plate moves ever northwards at a speed of about 6.1 cm per year.

Earthquake and geothermal activity

The entire region is subject to intense geological activity. Satellite photos reveal widespread thrust fault zones throughout the plateau; deep fault zones in the Himalayas, the Jangtang Plain, and the river gorges of East Tibet; as well as strike-slip fault zones in the Kunlun and Altyn Tagh ranges, and in the Yalong, Yangtze, and Yellow River valleys. From 1870-2001 over 52 major earthquakes (measuring over six on the Richter scale) have occurred along these fault lines.

Over the plateau as a whole, there are more than 600 geothermal areas including hot springs, geysers and hydrothermal explosions. The majority of these are found in the region between the southern Himalayan watershed and the northern Gangtise/ Nyenchen Tanglha watersheds.

Mountain ranges

Two principal mountain belts extend eastwards in a pincer-like manner from the **Pamir knot**. To the north, the ranges stretch through the **Kunluns** to the **Altyn Tagh** and **Chole Namgyel** mountains. In the south, they extend through the **Karakorums** and **Himalayas**, and thence southeast to the **Arakan** mountains of Burma. These frontier ranges are imposingly high, with the highest individual peaks rising above 7,000-8,000 m. Their gentle interior slopes and precipitous exterior slopes have ensured the geographic isolation of the region and its unique terrain. The **plateau** extending between these two formidable mountain barriers is located between 3,990-5,000 m above sea level; and its surface is a complex combination of ranges and plains, generally tilting from northwest to southeast. The permanent snow-line averages 4,510-5,000 m; and may reach 6,400 m in the Himalayan areas.

Karakorum mountains

The Karakorum mountains (Ch Kala Kunlun Shan) extend southeast from the borders of **Afghanistan** for 800 km as far as the **Pang-gong** Tibet range and **Chang Chenmo Ladakh** ranges. Approximately 240 km wide, and characterized by craggy peaks with steep slopes and ravine-like transverse valleys, the Karakorums form a watershed between the **Indus River** to the south and the **Tarim Basin** in the north. The average elevation is 6,100 m, and there are four peaks which rise above 7,925 m, the highest being **K2** at 8,611 m.

The Karakorum glaciers, along with those of the Himalayas, are renowned for their immensity.

Himalayan mountains

The world's highest mountain range comprises 110 peaks above 7,300 m, and more than 10 above 8,000 m, the highest and best known being **Mount Everest** (8,848 m; 29,029 ft). The Himalayas extend 2,450 km from **Mount Nanga Parbat** (8,126 m) in the extreme west to **Mount Namchak Barwa** (7,756 m) in the extreme east (total area: 594,400 sq km).

The range is a drainage area for 19 major rivers, the greatest of which – the **Indus, Sutlej**, **Karnali**, and **Brahmaputra**, rise to the north, before flowing through gorges between 1,524-4,877 m deep and 10-48 km wide. Some of the world's most impressive glaciers, including the 32-km Gangotri Glacier and the Kumbhu Glacier feed their tributaries.

Kunlun mountains

The **Kunlun** mountains forming Tibet's northern frontier extend 2,000 km from the **Pamirs** in the west to the **Bayankala** and **Amnye Machen** mountains in the east. The range rarely exceeds 200 km in its width. The southern slopes, which rise only 1,500 m above the plateau, are contrasted with the steep northern slopes, which form a massive rampart as they are approached from the Tarim basin and its low-lying oases of **Khotan, Keriya** and **Qarqan**, only 900-1,500 m above sea level.

The highest peaks are located in the West Kunluns, eg **Mount Muztagh** (7,723 m), **Mount Keriya** (7,120 m), **Mount Kongur** (7,719 m), and **Mount Muztagh Ata** (7,546 m). The Central and East Kunluns are lower, including the parallel ranges of the Kukushili (some peaks above 6,300 m) and the Bayankala, characterized by their flat dome-shaped peaks and gently broken slopes. The region has long been subject to erosion, causing large sand dunes, and producing steppe and desert soils with low organic content. The high degree of evaporation has produced frequent saline depressions and largely undeveloped river systems.

The Himalaya: highest peaks in the world

The main Himalayan range, known as the Inner or Great Himalayas, runs parallel by two minor latitudinal ranges to the south, the southernmost being the sub-Himalayan or Outer Himalayan range of the Shiwaliks (274-760 m); followed by the Lesser Himalayas (4,600 m, valleys at 900 m) of Kashmir and Central Nepal. The Great Himalayas comprise nine of the 14 highest peaks in the world. The most prominent peaks are (from west to east): Nanga Parbat in Azad Kashmir (8,126 m), Gangotri (6,726 m), Kamet (7,756 m), and Nanda Devi (7,817 m) all in Northwest India, Nemo Nanyi (Gurla Mandhata, 7,728 m) in Far West Tibet, Dhaulagiri (8,172 m), Annapurna (8,078 m), Manaslu (8,160 m), and Himal Chuli (7,898 m), all in West Nepal; Ganesh Himal (7,411 m), Langtang (7,250 m), and Shishapangma (Gosainathan, 8,012 m) all bordering Central Nepal and West Tibet; Jowo Tseringma (Gauri Shangkar, 7,148 m), Jowo Guru (Menlungtse, 7,181 m), Jowo Oyuk (8,153 m), Jomolangma (Everest, 8,848 m), Lhotse (8,501 m), and Makalu (8,463 m), all bordering East Nepal and West Tibet; Kangchendzonga (8,598 m), Jomolhari (7,313 m), and Kulha Kangri (7,554 m) all of which border Sikkim or Bhutan and South Tibet; and finally Phulahari (7,410 m) and Namchak Barwa (7,756 m), which divide Arunachal Pradesh from Southern Tibet.

Main features of the plateau

Hemmed in by those formidable mountain barriers, in the western part of the plateau high plains predominate; while in the eastern part there is a predominance of ranges and deep gorges.

In the north are the **Northern Plateau (Jangtang)** and the **Tsaidam basin**. Both are hemmed in by mountain ranges with individual peaks which rise above 6,000 m but, in general, their soft and smooth outlines tend not to dominate the surrounding landscape.

By contrast, the eastern sandstone ranges are deeply eroded, forming deep ravines and forested gorges. These include the eastern peaks of the **Nyenchen Tanglha** range dividing the Brahmaputra from the Salween; the **Gaoligong Mountains** on the Burmese border, dividing the Irrawaddy from the Salween; the **Tshawagang** uplands and **Kawa Karpo** range (Ch Taniantaweng, Hengduan and Nushan), dividing the Salween from the Mekong; the **Markhamgang** uplands (Ch Ningjing and Yunling), dividing the Mekong from the Yangtze; the **Drida Zelmogang** and **Puburgang** uplands including the Tro La (Ch Cholashan) and **Kawalungring** (Ch Shaluli) ranges, which divide the Yangtze from the Yalong; the **Minyak Rabgang** uplands (Ch Daxue) dividing the Yalong from the Gyarong; the **Mardzagang** uplands along with the **Bayankala** and **Amnye Machen** ranges, dividing the Yangtze, Yalong, and Gyarong from the Yellow River and the **Minshan** range at the eastern extremity of the plateau, which divides the Yellow River from the upper Yangtze tributaries, the Minjiang and Jialing.

Soil

The far Western and Northern highland regions are largely covered with detrital desert; while the deeply-cut mountain ranges of the frontiers and east are subject in places to extensive glaciation or erosion. The **high-altitude plateau** in the far west and north sustains light brown or grey soils containing detritus and stony fragments, sandy wind-blown soils that form a thin surface layer above gravel or shingle. Here, the vegetation is extremely sparse, and the amount of humus reduced, increasing the content of unbleached mineral salts, and intensifying the upward flow of salt solutions to the surface.

In the south, the upper reaches of the **Indus** and **Brahmaputra** form deep marginal depressions running parallel to the frontier Himalayan range. This is a region of immature subsidence in which thick accumulations of earlier marine sediments and later continental deposits washed down from the mountains have been transformed into sandy deserts flanked by lateral valleys of alluvial deposits, enabling specialized agriculture to flourish in sheltered lower elevations.

South of this river system, the **Himalayas** have the most complex variety of vegetation and soil types. On a vertical axis, low-lying forested areas or desert steppe give way to alpine meadow or mountain tundra, and thence to detritus, snow and glaciation. Soil tends to be thicker on the north-facing slopes, which support dense forests at lower altitudes and grasslands at higher altitudes. Rich alluvial soil has been deposited by south-flowing tributaries onto the **Gangetic** plain of India.

Further east and northeast erosion has exposed the sandstone rocks, producing more fertile soils: the reddish alluvium of the **Mekong** and **Yangtze** gorges, the dark humus of the **Amdo** grasslands, and the thick loess deposits around the upper reaches of the **Yellow** River. Generally, the major threats to agriculture in the region are the increasing erosion and salinization of the soil, caused in the short-term by human deforestation, and on the geological scale by plate tectonics.

Minerals

Geological surveys suggest that the Tibetan plateau is extremely rich in its accumulation of ores within the folded zone – from the **Karakorums** in the Far West through the **Himalayas** to the **Kawa Karpo** ranges – due to intrusions of granites and igneous rock. Such deposits include ores of copper, iron, lead and zinc, as well as antimony, arsenic, molybdenum, borax, sulphur, coal, bauxite, mica, gypsum and sapphire. Throughout the plateau, many alluvial and vein deposits of gold are to be found.

Around **Lhasa** there is hard coal and alabaster; while magnetite is common in the eastern **Brahmaputra** valley.

Further north, in the **Dangla** range, iron ore, hard coal, graphite, asbestos and soapstone have been mined.

The **Northern Plain/Jangtang** has an almost unlimited reserve of salts: borax, gypsum, common salt, quartz and soda.

The **Chole Namgyel** mountains on the extreme northeast frontier of the plateau contain iron, chromium, copper, lead, zinc, gold and coal from the Carboniferous and Jurassic ages.

The **Tsaidam** depression is known for its Jurassic coal and oil, which are deposited within Lower Tertiary sandstone.

Rivers

The land-locked Tibetan plateau is the primary source of the water supply for most of Central, East and South Asia. **Internal drainage** is rare, being almost invariably confined to the short rivers and saline lakes of the Northern Plateau (Jangtang) and the Lake Kokonor region of the northeast.

Those rivers originating in Tibet which drain into the **Pacific Ocean** include the **Yellow** River (Tib Machu; Ch Huang Ho), the **Yangtze** (Tib Drichu; Ch Jinsha), and the **Mekong** (Tib Dachu; Ch Lancang); along with important tributaries of the **Yangtze**, namely the **Yalong** (Tib Dzachu/Nyachu), **Gyarong** (Ch Dadu), **Min** (Tib Zungchu), and **Jialing**.

Those rivers which drain into the **Indian Ocean** are the **Salween** (Tib Gyelmo Ngulchu; Ch Nujiang), **Irrawaddy** (Burmese Nmai Hka), **Brahmaputra** (Tib Tsangpo; Ch Zangbo), **Sutlej** (Tib Langchen Tsangpo), **Indus** (Tib Senge Tsangpo), and certain **Gangetic feeder rivers** including the **Karnali** (Tib Mabcha Tsangpo), **Trishuli** (Tib Kyirong Tsangpo), **Sunkosi** (Tib Matsang Tsangpo), and **Arun** (Tib Bum-chu).

Other tributaries of the Ganges and Brahmaputra have their sources further south in Nepal and Bhutan. Among these, important **Gangetic tributaries** include the Chamlia, Seti, Bheti, and Kali-Gandaki, while those of the **Brahmaputra** include the Wang-chu, the Puna Tsang-chu, the Mangde-chu and the Bumtang-chu.

Lakes

Many inland lakes have been formed on the plateau by the filling of geological basins, from volcanic debris, silting and glacial retreat. Dehydration, however, suggests that many lakes of the Northern Plain were once part of the headwaters of the Salween and the Yangtze. Some smaller lakes were once connected to larger lakes (eg Rakshas Tal to Manasarovar, and Zigetang to Serling). The process of salination is more prominent in the northern lakes; the deep blue colour being due to paucity of silt and the intense sunlight. In general, the lakes of the plateau are important sources of minerals, including mirabilite, gypsum, borax, magnesium, potassium, lithium, strontium, uranium. Among the largest are: **Kokonor** (97 km across), **Ngoring** and **Kyaring** (40 km across), **Namtso** and **Serling** (81 km across), **Dangra** (64 km long), **Yamdrok** (64 km across), **Manasarovar** (24 km across and 73 m deep), **Rakshas Tal** (24 km long), and **Pang-gong** (48 km by 113 km).

Climate

The climate of the plateau, conditioned by the terrain, is generally severe, dry, and continental, with strong winds, low humidity, a rarefied atmosphere, and a great fluctuation in temperatures. The region is exposed to unimpeded arctic air from the north; while the southern tropical and equatorial air masses barely penetrate the Himalayan barrier into Central Asia. The contrast between the strong heat in summer months and the chill in winter produces sharp seasonal variations in atmospheric circulation.

In winter, the polar continental air mass originating in Siberia dominates East and Central Asia, forming a persistent high-pressure anticyclone over Tibet. Cold dry air therefore moves eastward and southward out of the continent during the winter; and the plateau experiences cold but calm weather, with less snowfall than one might expect. This pattern is occasionally interspersed by cyclonic storms moving eastwards from the Mediterranean, which give rise to short periods of low pressure, bringing snow to the higher ranges. By contrast, **in summertime,** the heat caused by the dry and dusty continental wind creates a low-pressure area, which contributes to the onset of the monsoon rains in South Asia. Nearly all the plateau's precipitation (average 460 mm) falls in summer, and in specific areas.

The higher western and northern regions are less exposed to this monsoon weather pattern than the lower regions to the east and south. Thus, the former characteristically endure frost for all but 45 days per annum, along with severe salt accumulation and strong winds.

In the **Kunlun** mountains to the north, where strong winds, dry dusty heat, and frosty conditions predominate, the annual precipitation averages only 50-100 mm; and the temperature fluctuates between extremes: 25-28°C (foothills, in mid-summer) and -9°C (foothills, in mid-winter); 10°C (higher slopes, in mid-summer) and -35°C (higher slopes, in mid-winter).

Further west, in the **Karakorum** Mountains, the climate is characterized by rarefied air, intense solar radiation, and strong winds. Precipitation (100 mm per annum) is largely confined to high-altitude snow-fields above 4,900 m, and to immense glaciers, which plunge down the southern slopes from 4,700-2,900 m, and the northern slopes from 6,000-3,500 m.

In the **Jangtang** plateau, rainfall is less than 100 mm. July temperatures fluctuate from 30°C in daytime to -15°C at night. Winter temperatures may drop to -35°C. Snow evaporates due to dryness, and wind speed exceeds 20 m per second, causing severe dust storms.

Further south, in the **Himalayas**, a series of dramatic well defined vertical climatic zones presents considerable variation in temperature and environment. The formidable mountain barrier obstructs the passage of cold continental air southwards and equally impedes the passage of warm monsoon air northwards, so that, on the southern side, precipitation varies from 1,530 mm in West Nepal to 3,060 mm in parts of Bhutan. By contrast, on the northwest slopes (around Ladakh) the figure drops to 765-153 m, and in Tibet proper to even less. Winter precipitation is heavier in the West Himalayas, which are more exposed to weather patterns from West Asia, than in the East Himalayas; but this is reversed in summer when the east is directly exposed to southwest monsoon currents.

Different climatic zones are clearly defined on the southern slopes of the Himalayas, varying from the sub-equatorial and tropical climates of the foothills at the lowest level to the snowy climate of the peaks. The degree of exposure is also significant – the sunny southern slopes differing from the shady northern ones, and windward slopes exposed to moist ocean winds differing from leeward slopes. The barrier effect is most pronounced in areas where rain-bearing monsoon winds have a constant direction. Temperatures vary accordingly, so that the average pre-monsoon temperature is 11°C at 1,945 m, -8°C at 5,029 m, and -22°C at 5,944 m.

The **gorges of Eastern Tibet** are much more accessible to south and southeast Asian weather patterns. Here there is marked contrast between perennially snow-capped peaks, the temperate zone (1,800-3,400 m), and the mild weather prevailing in the valleys below, some of which in the southernmost part of **Kham** are subject to a sultry heat and high level of humidity. Annual precipitation is around 51 cm; and there is heavy snowfall in the mountain uplands during winter.

Flora and fauna

Prehistoric flora and fauna

The ancient environment of the plateau can be known from the fossils discovered in recent decades. These suggest a very different landscape from the one we have today. Marine fossils, including trilobites and brachiopods, characteristic of those found on ocean beds, have been dated to 500 million years ago (mya). Marine plant fossils (dated 400-300 mya) suggest there was once warm water over northern Tibet and cold water over southern Tibet. In the **Chamdo** area, fossils of tropical plants, giant horsetail plants, and the changdusaurus (2.7 m high and 6.1 m long) have been dated to 200-150 mya, as has the ichthyosaur fossil (9.1 m long), discovered at **Nyalam** in the Himalayas. Later fossils (dated 100 mya) suggest that swampland was gradually replaced by tropical plants and broadleaf forests, which still covered much of the **Tsaidam**, the **Kunluns**, and **Jangtang** as late as 25 mya.

Gradually (10-5 mya), those forests became drier grasslands as the temperature dropped, leaving only the subtropical eastern gorges and moister Himalayas forested. The plateau was frequented by gazelles, giraffes, deer, rhinos, wild cats, hyenas, three-toed horses, and rodents.

During the **Ice Age** (3 mya-14,000 ya), the dry cold steppe increased and the forests decreased, causing Central Asian animals, such as cattle, sheep, goats; marmots, kiang and wild yak to reach the Tibetan plateau, and other animals such as the badger, hyena, tiger, horse, porcupine, elephant, panda, and leopard to migrate southeast to warmer climates. Glaciation reached its maximum during this period, with some glaciers being 130 km long in **Kham**, 20-30 km long on **Kailash**, and 40 km long in the **Himalayas**! After a subsequent period of interglacial warming (14,000 ya – 1,000 BC) during which forests again increased, the **New Ice Age** (1,000 BC) brought a harsher climate, drier lakes and fewer forests. Unfortunately, there are no surviving vegetation relics from previous geological eras due to the relative youth of the plateau and the subsequent glaciation of the Quaternary Age, which destroyed the pre-glacial vegetation.

Vegetation

The present species of flora found on the plateau appeared in the wake of the retreating glaciers and are related through migration to the neighbouring desert flora of Central Asia and the mesophyte flora of East Asia. The vegetation of the region, like its climate, reflects the diversity of the topography.

The very high altitude, dryness and complex land forms create a local climatic zone on the Tibetan plateau which runs counter to the worldwide pattern. Thus, the south is more heavily forested than the north, which is mostly rocky desert; the southeast is more densely forested than the central parts, and the northeast is grassland. Mountain ranges also exhibit their own vegetation and vertical climatic zones, from tropical forest through deciduous forest to grassland, pine forest, alpine scrub, and barren rock. However this pattern is broken in the southeast where mountain zones divide forest and meadowland; and on the plateau where steppe and desert prevail.

In the north and west, where there is a predominance of cold alpine desert, the soil cover is shallow and only perennial hardy frost-resistant plants with roots reaching the bedrock survive. The arid climate of the **Jangtang** plateau is devoid of trees and larger plant forms and supports only grasses and a scattered vegetation of salt-tolerant bushes and artemisia plants. The environment of the **Kunluns** is one of stark and barren desert rock and stagnant pools. More variation is found in the **Karakorums**, where the lower river valleys (below 3,000 m) abound in willow, poplar and oleander; the lower slopes in artemisia, and the upper slopes in juniper.

Himalayan flora are divided according to four complex vertical zones: the **tropical foothills** of the East and Central Himalayas (180-730 m), which are covered in evergreens such as mesua ferrea, oak, chestnut, alder, and pandanus furcatus; the **subtropical zone** (900-1,400 m) in which are found deciduous sal trees, steppe forest, and steppe thorn; the **temperate zone** (1,400-3,350 m) in which grow pine, cedar, spruce, oak, and birch; and the **alpine zone** (3,350-4,450 m) where juniper, rhododendron, flowering plants, moss and lichen grow.

A richer plant life is found in the river valleys and low-lying gorges of **Southern** and **Southeast Tibet**, where the humidity level is higher. Here, there are willows, poplars, conifers, teak, rhododendron, oak, birch, elm, bamboo, tamarisk, sugar cane and tea.

On the mountain slopes dominating the **gorges** of **East Tibet** are rich virgin forests, abounding in spruce, fir, larch, juniper, pine, and medicinal herbs. The **grasslands of Amdo** and the **uplands of Kham** support grasses such as cobresia and sedge, which provide fodder and pasture for livestock.

Regional variations occur within the vertical climatic zones of **Kham**. For example, in the **Yangtze**, **Yalong** and **Gyarong gorges** of Eastern Kham, below 600 m grow cypress, palm, bamboo, citrus fruits; from 600-1,500 m evergreens and oaks; from 1,500-2,400 m mixed conifers; from 2,600-3,500 m sub-alpine coniferous forests; and from 3,500-4,880 m alpine shrub and meadow. Further south in the **lower Salween** and **Mekong gorges** of **Dechen** county, the vertical zones have a more pronounced subtropical vegetation: below 1,830 m there is conifer forest, from 1,830-3,350 m an abundance of azaleas, rhododendrons, camellias, roses, and primroses and from 3,350-4,570 m fir, bamboo, dwarf juniper, and flowering herbs.

In general, therefore, a transition is clearly observable from the grassy-shrub landscapes of the uplands, through the sub-alpine coniferous forests, to the forest landscapes of the warmly temperate and subtropical belts.

Yak, Dri, Drong, Dzo: The Highland cattle of Tibet

No creature exemplifies the uniqueness of the Tibetan plateau like the yak. From whichever of the gateway cities you approach Tibet: Kathmandu, Chengdu, Kunming, Lanzhou, or Kashgar, the initial appearance of the yak at altitudes of 8,000-9,000 ft indicates that you have arrived within the ethnic Tibetan area. For the Tibetan people and the yak are inseparable. Hardy, stubborn, frisky, and apparently clumsy (though deceptively agile on precipitous rugged terrain), this 'grunting ox' (*Bos grunniens*) comes in many shapes and sizes: the male of the species is known as the yak, and the female as the dri. These animals have been domesticated and tended by Tibetan nomads for thousands of years, along, subsequently, with the hybrid dzo (a cross between a bull and a dri), which has become an ideal ploughing animal in Tibetan farming villages. By contrast, the wild yak (*drong*), like the American bison, once roamed the grasslands of Northern and Eastern Tibet in large herds, but their numbers have been severely depleted during the last few decades, falling prey to Chinese hunters and modern weaponry.

Since antiquity, the yak has been used as a pack animal and is rarely ridden in the manner of a horse. Prior to the construction of motorable roads, yak caravans were the principal means of freight transportation, and they still are in many remote parts of the country. Though slow, they are untiringly capable of carrying loads of over 50 kg across 5,000 m passes, and they withstand temperatures of -30°C. For the nomads who rear the yak, this creature is the source of their wealth and livelihood. The flesh provides meat (*tsak-sha*), which may be cooked or freeze dried; the milk of the dri provides butter (*mar*) and cheese (*chura*). Some Amdo towns now have meat and dairy processing factories supplied by the local nomadic communities. The hide is used for the high Tibetan boots, clothing, and traditional coracle construction. The soft inner hair (*ku-lu*) is now used for the production of high quality sweaters, particularly in the Repkong area of Amdo, and these are exported worldwide. The coarse outer hair (*tsid-pa*) is spun by the nomads themselves and used for making their black yak-wool tents, known in Tibetan as *ba*.

Wildlife

Over 530 species of birds, 190 species of mammals, more than 40 species of reptiles, 30 species of amphibians, and 2,300 species of insects are found in the region as a whole.

In general it is said that **East Himalayan** fauna have an affinity with those of the Chinese and Indo-Chinese region, whereas **West Himalayan** fauna are more closely related to Turkmenian and Mediterranean fauna. In the **far west** and **North**, there are many hoofed mammals (ungulates), who thrive in this open habitat, and rodents. In the **Kunlun** ranges these include gazelle, wild ass, wild goat, wild yak, blue sheep, urial, ibex, brown bear, and wolf.

The **saline lakes** of the **Jangtang Plateau** are home to varieties of waterfowl during the seasonal migrations. In the **Karakorums**, the urial, wild yak, ibex, and wild ass are found; while birds of prey such as the lammergeier, griffon, and golden eagle are commonplace.

In the **Himalayan** region, **above the tree-line**, there are a number of localised species adapted to cold, such as the snow leopard, brown bear, red panda and yak. The **lower forests** are home to the black bear, clouded leopard and terai langur; and the **southern**

foothills are frequented by the rhino, musk deer, and elephant. There are distinctive varieties of fish, such as the glyptothorax, and reptiles, such as the japalura lizard, the blind snake (typhlops), and unusual species of insects, such as the troides butterfly. Over 800 species of birds have been identified, including the magpie, titmouse, chough, thrush, redstart, lammergeier, kite, vulture, and snow partridge.

The deep valleys of **Southeast Tibet**, which are exposed to the moist humidity of the monsoon, support dense forests with a plethora of animals and birds. Here leopard, bear, wild boar, wild goat, langur, lynx, jackal, wild dog, and spotted cat are found. Distinctive species such as the lesser panda and ling yang antelope are still found in the **Gyarong** region. In the high **grasslands of Amdo** and the **Kham uplands** there are brown bears, wild and bighorn sheep, mountain antelope, musk deer, wild ass, wild yak, snakes, scorpions, and mountain lizards. Waterfowl are abundant in the lakes of **East and Northeast Tibet**, as are fish, frogs, crabs, otters, and turtles. Birds include the hoopoe, hawk, mynah, gull, crane, shellduck, teal, owl and magpie.

Wildlife reserves

Among the current administrative divisions of Tibet, **Qinghai** province in the northeast has advanced furthest in the establishment of wildlife reserves (in Nangchen, Drito, and Amnye Machen). Then, in 1993, the TAR established the world's second largest reserve in the **Jangtang** region, where much interest has been generated by the work of Dr George Schaller. More recently, the Great Rivers National Park, covering an area of 66,000 sq km was established in the Dechen Prefecture of Yunnan Province. Details on these reserves will be found above, in the relevant chapters.

Books

Guidebooks

The present guidebook is still the only one which comprehensively describes the whole of the Tibetan plateau in detail, including the highly accessible gorges of Kham and grasslands of Amdo. Others include:

Batchelor, S *The Tibet Guide* (Wisdom, 2nd edition 1997). Good on monasteries of Central and Western Tibet.

Dowman, K *The Power Places of Central Tibet* (RKP, 1988). Translation with commentary on Jamyang Khyentse Wangpo's 19th-century pilgrimage guide to Central Tibet.

McCue, G *Trekking in Tibet* (Cordee, 2nd edition 2000). The best introduction to scenic trekking areas of the plateau.

Contemporary fiction

Dorje, Rinjing *Tales of Uncle Tompa* (Barrytown, 1998). A collection of amusing, scandalous and profane tales with a remarkable sexual candour.

Norbu, J *The Mandala of Sherlock Holmes* (Bloomsbury, 2003). Recounts the adventures of Sherlock Holmes in Tibet following his disappearance at the Reichenbach Falls.

Tailing, W *The Secret of the House of Tesur* (China Tibetology Publishing, 1999). Recounts life in a noble Tibetan family, pre 1950.

Travelogues

Bacot, J *Le Tibet Revolte* (Hachette, 1912). Records the turbulent events in Southeast Tibet during the aggressive campaigns of the warlord Chao Erfeng,

Bell, C *Portrait of The Dalai Lama* (Collins, 1946). A unique record of the life and times of the Thirteenth Dalai Lama following the collapse of the Qing dynasty in China.

de Poncheville, M *Sept Femmes au Tibet* (Albin Michel, 1990). Entertaining and informative account of a filming expedition through Eastern Tibet in the months following the events of Tiananmen Square.

Ford, R *Captured in Tibet* (Pan, 1958). First-hand account of the PLA assault on Chamdo in 1951.

French, P *Tibet Tibet* (Knopf, 2003). Impressions of a recent traveller in Tibet

Marshall, S & Cooke, S *Tibet outside the TAR* (CD Rom, 1996). A detailed illustrated account of Tibetan areas now incorporated

within Sichuan, Yunnan, Qinghai and Gansu.
Migot, A *Tibetan Marches* (Penguin, 1957). A classic account of travel and pilgrimage in Kham during the 1940s.
Harrer, H *Seven Years in Tibet* (Tarcher Reprint, 1997). Recounts the hazardous journey of two Austrian POWs who fled British India in the 1940s, crossing the Jangtang to reach Lhasa, where they were well received.
Teichman, E *Travels of a Consular Official in Eastern Tibet* (Cambridge University Press, 1922, Davis, 1953). An important account of diplomatic travels through Kham in the aftermath of the Chao Erfeng invasion and the Tibetan resurgence between 1911-1920.

Pilgrimage travel

Dowman, K *The Sacred Life of Tibet* (Thorsons, 1997). Account of the importance of pilgrimage and the inner spiritual dimension of Tibet.
Namgyel, Zangpo *Sacred Grounds* (Snowlion, 2001). An analysis of Tibetan sacred geography, focusing on the Pelpung area of Derge county.
Snelling, J *The Sacred Mountain* (Books Britain, 1990). A history of pilgrimage to Mount Kailash – the sacred axis mundi of Buddhism, Bon, Hinduism and Jainism.

Biography and autobiography

Douglas, K & Bays, G (trans.) *The Life and Liberation of Padmasambhava* (Dharma Publishing (1978). The extraordinary career of Padmasambhava who introduced the highest Buddhist teachings into Tibet from India during the eighth century.
HH Dalai Lama *My Land and My People* (Warner Reprint, 1997). Original autobiography of HH Dalai Lama, recounting his early years.
HH Dalai Lama *Freedom In Exile* (Harper, 1991). The later autobiography recounting early years in Tibet and later years in exile.
Gyatso, J (trans) *Apparitions of the Self* (Princeton, 1999). The inspirational autobiography of Jigme Lingpa, an 18th-century visionary and yogin whose teachings are actively practised in the present day.
Lhalungpa, L (trans) *The Life of Milarepa* (Dutton, 1977). A classic account of the austere meditative path through which an extreme evildoer is transformed into an enlightened being within a single lifetime.
Ricard, M (trans) *The Life of Shabkar* (Suny, 1994). The biography and mystical poetry of a travelling pilgrim from Far East Tibet.
Trungpa, T *Born in Tibet* (Unwin, 1979). Autobiography of the early formative years in Tibet of the first Tibetan lama to establish a foothold in the west.

History

Avedon, J *In Exile from the Land of Snows* (Wisdom 1986). Recounts Tibet's 20th-century tragedy, as the intelligentsia flee into exile and the depredations of the Cultural Revolution ensue.
Beckwith, C *The Tibetan Empire in Central Asia* (Princeton, 1987). Fascinating account of Tibet's Yarlung Dynasty who established an eighth- and ninth-century imperial domain far exceeding the confines of the plateau.
Goldstein, M *History of Modern Tibet 1939-1951* (University of California Press, 1989). A detailed account of the events leading to the collapse of independent Tibet and the subsequent Chinese occupation.
Richardson, H *High Peaks, Pure Earth* (Serindia, 1998). An insightful series of essays on early and medieval Tibetan history by a remarkable Tibetologist.
Richardson, H *Tibet and its History* (Shambhala, 1984). Classic telling of Tibet's history.
Shakabpa, TWD *Tibet: A Political History* (Potala, 1984). An authoritative history of Tibet from the Tibetan perspective.
Shakya, T *The Dragon in the Land of Snows* (Columbia University Press, 1999). Documents the recent events of Tibetan history following the Chinese occupation.
Smith, W *A History of Tibetan Nationalism and Sino-Tibetan Relations* (Westview, 1996). Focuses on the conflicts between Tibet and China in the early 20th century.
Stein, RA *Tibetan Civilization* (Faber, 1972). A classic synopsis of Tibetan culture from ancient times.
Vitali, R *The Kingdoms of Guge Pu-hrang* (Dharamsala, 1996). An important contribution documenting the survival of the Tibetan monarchy in Far West Tibet from the 10th century onwards.

Nature, grasslands and wildlife

Goldstein, M, & Beall, C *Nomads of Western Tibet* (UCP, 1990). An account of nomadic life in Tsang and the Jangtang areas of Tsochen,
Kingdon Ward, F *Mystery Rivers of Tibet* (Cadogan, 1986). A fascinating account of an early 20th-century British botanist's exploration

of the Kawa Karpo area of Southeast Tibet.

Nakamura, T *East of the Himalayas* (Japanese Alpine Club, May, 2003). Beautiful publication, fine photographs depicting ranges of Kham.

Rock, J *The Amnye Machen and Adjacent Regions* (SOR, 1956). Anthropological account of Golok people and their natural environment.

Rowell, G *Mountains of the Middle Kingdom* (Sierra Club Books, 1983). A pictorial record of the Amdo mountain ranges.

Schaller, G *Wildlife and Nomads of the Chang Tang Reserve* (Abrams, 1997). The only major study of nomads and wildlife in the Tibet's northern lakeland wilderness.

Cultural heritage, art and architecture

Gruschke, A *Amdo* (2 vols, White Lotus, 2001). Detailed illustrated record of Amdo monasteries.

Singer, J & Denwood, P (eds) *Tibetan Art: Towards a Definition of Style* (Laurence King, 1997). A collection of essays analysing diverse aspects of Tibetan painting, sculpture and architecture.

Snellgrove, D, & Richardson, H *Cultural History of Tibet* (Weidenfeld and Nicholson, 1968). Well known account of Tibetan civilization, written during Cultural Revolution.

Tucci, G *To Lhasa and Beyond* (Instituto Poligrafico dello Stato, 1956). A highly readable account of the explorations in Central and Southern Tibet by one of Europe's pioneering Tibetologists.

Tibetan medicine, astrology, divination

Cornu, P *Tibetan Astrology* (Shambhala, 1997). A practical integrated guide to Tibetan astrology and divination.

Dorje, G *Tibetan Elemental Divination Paintings* (Eskenazi & Fogg, 2001). Analysis and documentation of an important 18th-century illustrated manuscript on elemental divination.

Parfionovitch, Y, Dorje, G, and Mayer, F (eds) *Tibetan Medical Paintings* (Serindia, 1992). Analysis and documentation of an 18th-century series of paintings illustrating the course of Tibetan medicine.

Tibetan language and dictionaries

Beyer, S *The Classical Tibetan Language* (SUNY, 1992). An analysis of the historical development of the Tibetan language.

Denwood, P *Tibetan* (John Benjamins, 1999). An authoritative work on the structure of the Tibetan language.

Goldstein, M *The New Tibetan-English Dictionary of Modern Tibetan* (UCP, 2001). Best dictionary of colloquial Tibetan available.

Gyurme, K, Tournade, N & Stoddard, H *Le Clair Mirroir* (Prajna, 1992). Well-presented exposition of Tibetan grammar, including examples and exercises.

Buddhism and Bon

Chogyay Trichen *The History of the Sakya Tradition* (Ganesha, 1983). A brief account of the early history of Sakya and the emergence of its influential Ngorpa and Tsharpa branches.

Douglas and White *Karmapa: the Black Hat Lama of Tibet* (Luzac, 1976). An account of the history of the Karma Kagyu school.

Karmay, S *The Treasury of Good Sayings: a Tibetan History of Bon* (OUP, 1972). A 19th-century traditional history of the Bon religion.

Kvaerne, P *The Bon Religion of Tibet* (Serindia, 1995). An illustrated guide to the Bon religion and its iconography.

Pabongka Rinpoche *Liberation in the Palm of Your Hand* (Wisdom, 1991). Graduated path to enlightenment, as followed by the Gelukpa.

Paltrul Rinpoche *The Words of My Perfect Teacher* (Harper Collins, 1994). The standard work on the preliminary meditative practices of Tibetan Buddhism.

Powers, J *Introduction to Tibetan Buddhism* (Snowlion, 1995). A clear outline of the nuances of Tibetan Buddhism for beginners.

Snellgrove, D *Indo-Tibetan Buddhism* (Serindia, 1987). A scholarly account of the origins of early Tantric Buddhism in India and its transmission into Tibet.

Thondup, T *Buddhist Civilization in Tibet* (RKP, 1987). A synopsis of all the major Buddhist and secular sciences that were imported from ancient India into Tibet.

Tucci, G *The Religions of Tibet* (Berkeley, 1980). An overview of the various traditions of Tibetan Buddhism.

Williams, P *Mahayana Buddhism* (RKP, 1989). A clear account of the development of classical Mahayana Buddhism in ancient India and its early transmission to Central and East Asia.

Willis, J *Enlightened Beings: Life Stories from the Ganden Tradition* (Wisdom, 1995). Series of inspirational biographies illustrating and outlining ideal career of a monastic renunciate.

Footnotes

An iconographic guide to Tibetan Buddhism

It is impossible to visit Tibet without being overwhelmed by religious imagery. The sheer scale is breathtaking – the Potala Palace in Lhasa alone has 1,000 rooms, housing approximately 200,000 images. It will help both your understanding and enjoyment if you can recognize some of these images.

This guide contains the names of the deities or images most frequently depicted in the Buddhist temples and monasteries of Tibet. Illustrations of some of these are also appended. It is important to remember that, with the probable exception of images representing the ancient historic kings of Tibet, the others are not regarded as concrete or inherently existing beings in the Judeo- Christian or even in the Hindu sense. Rather, the deities are revered as pure expressions of buddha-mind, who are to be visualized in the course of meditation in their pure light forms: a coalescence of pure appearance and emptiness. Through such meditations, blessings are obtained from the teachers of the past; spiritual accomplishments are matured through the meditational deities, enlightened activities are engaged in through the agency of the dakinis, and spiritual development is safe-guarded by the protector deities. These therefore are the four main classes of image to be observed in Tibetan shrines. Among them, the images representing the spiritual teachers of the past are exemplified by Buddha Shakyamuni, Padmasambhava and Tsongkhapa; those representing the meditational deities by Vajrakumara, Cakrasamvara and Kalacakra; those representing dakinis or female agents of enlightened activity by Vajravarahi; and the protector deities by Mahakala, Shridevi, and so forth.

Temples: what to expect

Most temples have an entrance portico replete with murals depicting the Four Guardian Kings of the four directions and the Wheel of Rebirth (*bhavacakra*) on the outer wall. Within the main gate, there are often images of the gatekeepers Vajrapani (east) and Hayagriva (west), watching over the portals, while the murals of the inner wall nearest the gate depict the protector deities. The central hall, which is of variable size (depending on the number of columns), contains the rows of seats which are occupied by the monastic body during ritual ceremonies, with the thrones or elevated seats of the main lamas furthest from the gate. Proceeding clockwise around the hall, the side-walls may well depict scenes from the life of Buddha Shakyamuni, or other historical figures. Eventually you will reach the innermost wall (facing the gate and beyond the thrones), against which the rows of clay or gilded copper images, sacred scriptures, and reliquary stupas are positioned. These will vary according to the tradition which the temple or monastery represents, although images of the Buddhas of the Three Times are commonly depicted here. There may additionally be an inner sanctum containing the most precious images housed within the temple, with its own circumambulatory pathway. In front of the images, offerings will be arrayed, including water-offering bowls, butter lamps and torma-offering cakes, while donations will be left by the faithful as a meritorious action.

The guide

Acala (Tib Miyowa) one of the 10 wrathful kings (dashakrodha), forming a peripheral group of meditational deities in certain mandalas.

Akashagarbha (Tib Namkei Nyingpo) one of the eight major bodhisattvas, yellow in colour, symbolizing the buddha's sense of smell and holding a sword which cuts through dissonant emotions. See **Icon 36**.

Aksobhya (Tib Mikyopa) one of the five peaceful meditational buddhas forming the buddha-body of perfect resource (*sambhogakaya*), collectively known as the Buddhas of the Five Families. Aksobhya is blue in colour, symbolizing the purity of form and the mirror-like clarity of buddha-mind. He holds a vajra to symbolize that emptiness and compassion are without duality. See **Icon 4**.

Amitabha (Tib Opame) one of the five peaceful meditational buddhas forming the buddha-body of perfect resource (*sambhogakaya*), collectively known as the Buddhas of the Five Families. Amitabha is red in colour, symbolizing the purity of perception and the discerning aspect of buddha-mind. He holds a lotus to symbolize the purification of attachment and the altruistic intention. See **Icon 6**.

Amitayus (Tib Tsepame) a meditational deity with nine aspects, who is included among the Three Deities of Longevity, red in colour, and holding a vase full of the nectar of immortality. See **Icon 45**.

Amoghasiddhi (Tib Donyo Drupa) one of the five peaceful meditational buddhas forming the buddha-body of perfect resource (*sambhogakaya*), collectively known as the Buddhas of the Five Families. Amoghasiddhi is green in colour, symbolizing the purity of habitual tendencies and the activity aspect of buddha-mind. He holds a sword to symbolize the cutting off of dissonant emotions through buddha-activity. See **Icon 7**.

Amritakundalin (Tib Dutsi Kyilwa) one of the gatekeepers of the mandalas of meditational deities, dark-green in colour, symbolizing the inherent purity of sensory contact, and holding a crossed-vajra which subdues egotism.

Apchi a doctrinal protectress of the Drigung Kagyu school, who assumes both peaceful and wrathful forms.

Atisha (Tib Jowoje) a saintly Buddhist master from Bengal (982-1054), who introduced the Kadampa teachings into Tibet. See **Icon 93**.

Avalokiteshvara (Tib Chenrezik) one of the eight major bodhisattvas and the patron deity of Tibet, white in colour, symbolizing the buddha's compassion and sense of taste, and holding a lotus untainted by flaws. There are various forms of this most popular bodhisattva: the 11-faced 1,000-armed form known as Mahakarunika (Tu-je Chenpo, Zhal Chu-chikpa, **Icon 42**), the four-armed form (Chenrezik Chak Zhipa, **Icon 39**), a two-armed form known as Khasarpani (**Icon 44**), the lion-riding form called Simhanada (**Icon 43**), the soothing form called Mind at Rest (Semnyi Ngalso), or Jowo Lokeshvara, and the standing form called Padmapani, the last of which is usually red in colour (**Icon 33**).

Begtse a sword-wielding form of the protector deity **Mahakala**.

Bhairava (Tib Jikje) a wrathful bull-headed meditational deity (in Buddhism), or a wrathful counterpart of Shiva (in Hinduism).

Bhaisajyaguru (Tib Sangye Menla) the central buddha of medicine, otherwise called Vaiduryaprabharaja, who is blue in colour, holding a bowl containing the panacea myrobalan. See **Icon 12**.

Bodongpa Chokle Namgyel (1375-1451) one of Tibet's most prolific writers, the author of approximately 100 treatises, a product of the Bodong E college, who established his own distinctive school of Buddhism in Tibet.

Brahma (Tib Tsangpa) a four-faced protector deity associated with the world system of form (in Buddhism), the creator divinity (in Hinduism).

Buddha Shakyamuni (Tib Shakya Tupa) the historical Buddha (sixth to fifth centuries BC), known prior to his attainment of buddhahood as Siddhartha or Gautama, who is also revered as the fourth of the thousand buddhas of this aeon. He is depicted in diverse forms, seated, standing, or reclining (at the point of his decease), and with diverse hand-gestures (symbolizing past merits, generosity, meditation, teaching, fearlessness and so forth). The Jowo form depicts him as a bodhisattva prior to his attainment of buddhahood, and the form Munindra depicts him as he appears among the devas. See **Icon 9**.

Buddhas of the Five Families (Skt Pancajina/Tib Gyelwa Riknga) the five buddhas of the buddha-body of perfect resource (*sambhogakaya*; **Icons 3-7**). See listed separately **Aksobhya, Amitabha, Amoghasiddhi, Ratnasambhava**, and **Vairocana**.

Buddhas of the Three Times (Tib Dusum Sangye) see listed separately the Buddha of the past **Dipamkara (Icon 8)**, the Buddha of the present **Shakyamuni (Icon 9)**, and the Buddha of the future **Maitreya (Icon 10)**.

Buton Rinchendrub (1290-1364) compiler of the Buddhist canon, and major scholar within the Zhalupa tradition of Tibetan Buddhism. See **Icon 109**.

Cakrasamvara (Tib Khorlo Demchok) a four-faced 12-armed wrathful meditational deity, blue in colour, in union with his consort Vajravarahi, trampling upon Bhairava and Kali, and thus representing the Buddhist transmutation of the mundane Hindu divinity Shiva and his consort. See **Icon 54**.

Changkya Qutuqtu III Rolpei Dorje (1717-86) a holder of high office in Manchu China, who was responsible for escorting Dalai Lama VII to Lhasa, and for the prolonged military campaigns against the Bonpo in Gyarong.

Chenrezi Semnyi Ngalso see under Avalokiteshvara.

Cimara (Tib Tsimara) wrathful protector deity of Samye Monastery, and foremost of the *tsen* class of doctrinal protectors, greenish red in colour.

Cintamani(cakra) Tara see under **Tara**.

Dalai Lama (Tib Gyelwa Rinpoche) revered as the human embodiment of Avalokiteshvara, the patron deity of Tibet who symbolizes compassion, the successive Dalai Lamas (see page 748) have, since the mid-17th century, assumed both spiritual and temporal authority in Tibet. Among them, the most significant have probably been

Dalai Lama III Sonam Gyatso (1543-88; **Icon 116**), Dalai Lama V Ngawang Lobzang Gyatso (1617-82; **Icon 118**), Dalai Lama VI Tsangyang Gyatso (1683-1706; **Icon 120**), Dalai Lama VII Kalzang Gyatso (1708-57), Dalai Lama XIII Tupten Gyatso (1876-1933; **Icon 121**), and the present Dalai Lama XIV (b 1934; **Icon 122**).

Damsi a group of nine sibling demons who have violated their commitments and are said to endanger infant children.

Dashakrodha kings (Tib Trowo Chu) a group of 10 peripheral meditational deities known as the 10 wrathful kings, comprising Usnisacakravartin, Prajnantaka, Yamantaka, Vighnantaka, Padmantaka, Mahabala, Takkiraja, Shumbharaja, Acala, and Niladanda.

Desi Sangye Gyatso (1677-1705) an important regent of Tibet and author of seminal commentaries on medicine, astrology, religious history, and other subjects. See **Icon 119**.

Dharmaraja (Tib Chogyel) see **Yama Dharmaraja**.

Dharmatala one of two peripheral figures, sometimes classed alongside the group of **sixteen elders**. He is described as a layman (*upasaka*) who looked after the 16 elders during their visit to China.

Dipamkara Buddha (Tib Sangye Marmedze) the third buddha of this aeon, also known as Kashyapa Buddha, who was the one immediately preceding Shakyamuni. See **Icon 8**.

Dolpopa Sherab Gyeltsen (1292-1361) the most influential scholar of the Jonangpa school, who was a pre-eminent master of the tantras and an exponent of the *zhentong* philosophy. See **Icon 110**.

Dorje Drakden a doctrinal protector in the retinue of Pehar, who possesses the medium of Nechung, the state oracle of Tibet.

Dorje Drolo a wrathful tiger-riding form of Padmasambhava (Icon 91). See under **Eight Manifestations of Padmasambhava**.

Dorje Lekpa a goat-riding doctrinal protector of the Dzogchen teachings, wearing a wide-brimmed hat, who was bound under an oath of allegiance to Buddhism by Padmasambhava in the Oyuk district of Western Tibet.

Dorje Yudronma a doctrinal protectress of Menmo class, with whom the Nyingmapa master Longchen Rabjampa is said to have had a particular affinity. See **Icon 62**.

Drigungpa Jikten Gonpo (1143-1217) one of the foremost students of Phakmodrupa and founder of the Drigung Kagyu school, based at Drigung Til Monastery. See **Icon 101**.

Dromtonpa Gyelwei Jungne (1004-64) the foremost Tibetan student of Atisha and founder of Reting Monastery. See **Icon 94**.

Drubpa Kabgye the eight wrathful meditational deities of the Nyingma school, viz: Yamantaka, Hayagriva, Shriheruka, Vajramrita, Vajrakila, Matarah, Lokastotrapuja, and Vajramanrabhiru.

Drukchen the title of the successive heads of the Drukpa Kagyu school, for an enumeration of whom, see page 266.

Dzogchen Pema Rigdzin (1625-97) the founder of Dzogchen Monastery in Kham.

Eight Awareness-holders (Skt astavidyadhara/Tib Rigdzin gye) the eight Indian lineage-holders of the eight transmitted precepts of Mahayoga, who are said to have been contemporaries of Padmasambhava, namely: Manjushrimitra, Nagarjuna, Humkara, Vimalamitra, Prabhahasti, Dhanasamskrita, Rambuguhya-Devacandra, and Shantigarbha.

Eight Bodhisattvas (Tib Nyese gye) the eight major bodhisattvas, standing figures who are often depicted flanking images of Shakyamuni Buddha. See listed separately: **Manjushri (Icon 31), Vajrapani (Icon 32), Avalokiteshvara (Icon 33), Ksitigarbha (Icon 34), Nivaranaviskambhin (Icon 35), Akashagarbha (Icon 36), Maitreya (Icon 37), and Samantabhadra (Icon 38).**

Eight Classes of Spirits (Tib lhade gye) a series of lesser spirits or demons, who are to be appeased or coerced by means of ritual offerings.

Eight Deities of the Transmitted Precepts see Drubpa Kabgye.

Eight Manifestations of Padmasambhava (Tib Guru tsen gye) the eight principal forms assumed by Padmakara at different phases of his career, namely: **Saroruhavajra** (birth; **Icon 84**), **Padma Gyelpo** (kingship; **Icon 85**), **Shakya Senge** (ordination; **Icon 86**), **Loden Chokse** (mastery of the teachings; **Icon 87**), **Padmasambhava** (establishment of Buddhism in Tibet; **Icon 88**), **Nyima Ozer** (subjugation of demons; **Icon 89**), **Senge Dradrok** (subjugation of non-Buddhists; **Icon 90**), and **Dorje Drolo** (concealment of terma; **Icon 91**).

Eight Medicine Buddhas (Tib Menla deshek gye) the successive buddhas revered as the precursors of Buddhist medicine, viz: Sunamaparikirtana, Svaraghosaraja, Suvarnabhadravimala, Ashokottama, Dharmakirtisagaraghosa, Abhijnanaraja, Shakyaketu, and Bhaisajyaguru. For an illustration of the last of these, who is also the central medicine buddha, see **Icon 12**.

Eight Taras who Protect from Fear (Tib Dolma Jikpa Gye Kyobma) a group of female divinities, who offer protection from eight specific types of fear, viz: Manasimhabhayatrana (pride and lions), Mohahastibhayatrana (delusion and elephants), Dvesagniprashamani (hatred and fire), Irsyasarpavisapaharani (envy and poisonous snakes), Kudristicoropadravanivarani (wrong view and thieves), Ghoramatsaryashrinkhalamocani (avarice and fetters), Ragaughavegavartashosani (attachment and rivers), and Samshayapishacabhayatrana (doubt and carnivorous demons). See also under Tara.

Eighty-four Mahasiddhas (Tib Drubtob Gyachu Gyezhi) a group of 84 tantric masters of ancient India, for the life-stories of which, see J Robinson, *Buddhas Lions*.

Ekajati (Tib Ralchikma) an important protectress of the Dzogchen teachings, characteristically depicted with a single hair-knot, a single eye and a single breast.

Five Founders of Sakya (Tib Gongma Nga) the successors of Khon Konchok Gyelpo who founded Sakya in 1073, viz: Sachen Kunga Nyingpo (1092-1158; **Icon 104**), Sonam Tsemo (1142-82; **Icon 105**), Drakpa Gyeltsen (1147-1216; **Icon 106**), Sakya Pandita Kunga Gyeltsen (1182-1251; **Icon 107**), and Drogon Chogyel Phakpa (1235-80; **Icon 108**).

Four Guardian Kings (Skt Caturmaharajaika/Tib Gyelchen Zhi) the guardian kings of the four directions, whose martial forms are frequently depicted on the walls of a temple portico, viz: Dhritarastra (east), Virudhaka (south), Virupaksa (west), and Vaishravana (north). **Icons 123-126**.

Gampopa (1079-1153) the student of Milarepa and source of the four major and eight minor Kagyu schools. See **Icon 98**.

Ganesh (Skt Ganapati or Vinayaka/Tib Tsokdak) the elephant-headed offspring of Shiva (in Hinduism), an obstacle-causing or obstacle-removing protector deity (in Buddhism).

Genyen a group of 21 aboriginal divinities, most of whom are identified with snow peaks.

Gonpo Maning (Skt Mahapandaka Mahakala) a spear-wielding two-armed form of the protector deity Mahakala. See **Icon 58**.

Guhyasamaja (Tib Sangwa Dupa) a six-armed seated meditational deity, two forms of which are recognized: Aksobhyavajra (according to the Arya tradition) and Manjuvajra (according to the Buddhajnanapada tradition). The former is light-blue in colour, embraced by the consort Sparshavajra, and has three faces, symbolizing the transmutation of the three poisons: delusion, attachment, and hatred. See **Icon 51**.

Guru Chowang (1212-70) a great treasure-finder of the Nyingma school.

Gyelpo Ku-nga the five aspects of the important protector deity Pehar, known respectively as the kings of body, speech, mind, attributes, and activities. See **Icons 63-67**.

Hayagriva (Tib Tamdrin) a wrathful horse-headed meditational deity of the Nyingma school who is generally red in colour, symbolic of buddha-speech, and included among the Drubpa Kabgye. He also appears as a gatekeeper in certain mandalas, and, as the renowned tamer of the egotistical demon Rudra, is frequently positioned (along with Vajrapani) at the entrance of a temple.

Hevajra (Tib Kyedorje) a wrathful counterpart of the meditational deity Aksobhya, deep-blue in colour, who is depicted in a dancing posture, with two, four, six, or 16 arms, and in union with the consort Nairatmya. See **Icon 56**.

Huashang one of two peripheral figures, sometimes classed alongside the group of **sixteen elders**. He is described as a monk (Ch hoshang) who looked after the 16 elders during their visit to China.

Hundred Peaceful and Wrathful Deities (Tib Zhitro Lhatsok, Dampa Rikgya) the assembly of the 42 peaceful deities and 58 wrathful deities, according to the *Guhyagarbha Tantra*, the basis for the visionary account of the *Tibetan Book of the Dead*.

Jambhala (Tib Dzambhala) a protector deity of wealth, yellow in colour, frequently depicted holding a gemstone.

Jamchen Choje Shakya Yeshe a student of Tsongkhapa, who founded Sera Monastery in 1419.

Jampa see **Maitreya**.

Jamyang Choje Tashi Palden a student of Tsongkhapa, who founded Drepung Monastery in 1416.

Je Yabsesum the collective name given to Tsongkhapa (1357-1419) and his two foremost students, Gyeltsabje Darma Rinchen (1364-1431) and Khedrubje Gelek Pelzang (1385-1438), who were the first throne-holders of Ganden Monastery and thus the founders of the Gelukpa school. The last of these was also retrospectively recognized as Panchen Lama I. See **Icons 113-115**.

Jikme Lingpa (1730-98) an important Nyingmapa yogin who revealed the highly influential teaching-cycle known as the *Innermost Spirituality of Longchenpa (Longchen Nyingtig)*.

Jowo see **Jowo Shakyamuni**.

Jowo Lokeshvara see under **Avalokiteshvara**.

Jowo Shakyamuni a form of Buddha Shakyamuni, as a bodhisattva, prior to his attainment of buddhahood.

Kalachakra (Tib Dukhor, Dukyi Khorlo) a wrathful meditational deity, blue in colour, with four faces and 12 upper arms and 24 lower arms, embraced by the consort Vishvamata, symbolizing the transmutation of the wheel of time. See **Icon 53**.

Karmapa the oldest succession of incarnating lamas in Tibet, embodying Avalokiteshvara's compassion and presiding over the Karma Kagyu school. For a listing of the 17 Karmapas from Karmapa I Dusum Khyenpa on, see page 141. See also **Icon 99**.

Katokpa the title assumed by the first 13 hierarchs of Katok Monastery in East Tibet, founded by Katokpa I Dampa Deshek in 1159.

Khasarpani see under **Avalokiteshvara**.

Ksitigarbha (Tib Sayi Nyingpo) one of the eight major bodhisattvas, white in colour, symbolizing the buddha's eyes, and holding a sprouting gemstone of pristine cognition. See **Icon 34**.

Kubera (Tib Tadak Kubera) a protector deity of wealth, known as the 'lord of horses', black in colour, brandishing a sword and holding a jewel-spitting mongoose.

Kurukulla (Tib Rikchema) a red coloured female meditational deity in dancing posture, holding a flowery bow and arrow, symbolizing her charisma to fascinate and overpower even hostile forces.

Lokeshvara (Tib Jikten Wangchuk) an abbreviation of **Avalokiteshvara**.

Longchen Rabjampa (1308-63) pre-eminent scholar, treasure-finder, and systematizer of the Nyingma tradition. See **Icon 111**.

Longdol Lama Ngawang Lobzang (1719-95) an erudite encyclopaedist, who was a student of Dalai Lama VII and teacher of Jamyang Zhepa II Konchok Jikme Wangpo.

Lords of the Three Enlightened Families (Tib Riksum Gonpo) the three main bodhisattvas associated with the early Mahayana transmissions, namely

Manjughosa symbolizing discriminative awareness; Avalokiteshvara symbolizing compassion; and Vajrapani symbolizing power. See **Icons 39-41**.

Machen Pomra protector deity embodied in the snow peaks of the Amnye Machen range; one of the **Twelve Subterranean Goddesses**.

Mahakala (Tib Nagpo Chenpo) a class of supramundane protector deities, 75 aspects of which are recognized. Among these, the most widespread are Four-armed Mahakala (Skt Caturbhujamahakala; **Icon 57**); Six-armed Mahakala (Skt Sadbhujamahakala), Gonpo Maning (Skt Mahapandaka Mahakala; **Icon 58**), Tiger-riding Mahakala (Tib Gonpo Takzhon), Begtse, and Panjaranatha (Tib Gonpo Gur; **Icon 59**), the last of which is preferred among the Sakyapa.

Mahakarunika (Tib Tu-je Chenpo) see under **Avalokiteshvara**.

Mahottara Heruka (Tib Chemchok Heruka) the wrathful counterpart of the primordial buddha Samantabhadra, is dark-brown, with three faces symbolizing the three approaches to liberation, six arms symbolizing the six perfections, and four legs symbolizing the four supports for miraculous ability, trampling upon Mahedeva and Umadevi.

Maitreya (Tib Jampa) one of the eight major bodhisattvas (**Icon 37**) and the future buddha (**Icon 10**), whitish-yellow in colour, symbolizing the buddha's loving kindness and sight, and holding an orange bush which dispels the fever of dissonant emotions.

Manjughosa (Tib Jampeyang, Jamyang) one of the eight major bodhisattvas (**Icon 31**) who is depicted upright, whitish-green in colour and holding a lily, which symbolizes the renunciation of dissonant emotions. In a more familiar seated posture, he is one of the lords of the three enlightened families (**Icon 40**), orange in colour, symbolizing the buddha's discriminative awareness and tongue, and holding a sword which cuts through obscurations and a book of discriminative awareness. Other important forms include Manjushri Vadisimha, Manjushri Kumarabhuta, White Manjushri, and the five aspects which appeared in the visions of Tsongkhapa.

Manjushri (Tib Jampel) see **Manjughosa**.

Manjuvajra (Tib Jampei Dorje) a form of the meditational deity Guhyasamaja, according to the tradition of Buddhajnanapada.

Marici (Tib Ozerchenma) the red goddess of the dawn, who is propitiated for the removal of obstacles.

Marpa (1012-96) Marpa Chokyi Wangchuk, the student of Naropa and first Tibetan exponent of the Karma Kagyu lineage, whose disciples included Milarepa. See **Icon 96**.

Matsyendranath an aspect of Avalokiteshvara ('lord of fish') which is revered in Nepal, the white form known as Jamali being enshrined in Asan, and the red form, Bukham, in Patan.

Maudgalyayana (Tib Maudgal bu) one of the two foremost students of Shakyamuni, who passed away before the Buddha's parinirvana. See **Icon 14**.

Milarepa (1040-1123/1052-1135) the great yogin and ascetic poet of the Kagyu lineage, who was the student of Marpa and teacher of Gampopa. See **Icon 97**.

 Nairatmya (Tib Dakmema) female consort of the meditational deity Hevajra, symbolizing selflessness or emptiness.

Ngok Lotsawa Lekpei Sherab founder of the Kadampa monastery of Sangpu Neutok and a major student of the 11th century Bengali master Atisha.

Ngorchen Kunga Zangpo (b 1382) who founded the monastery of Ngor Evam Chode in 1429, giving rise to the influential Ngorpa branch of the Sakya school.

Nivaranaviskambhin (Tib Dripa Namsel) one of the eight major bodhisattvas, reddish-yellow in colour, symbolizing the buddha's ears, and holding a wheel of gems because he teaches the Buddhist doctrine. See **Icon 35**.

Nyangrel Nyima Ozer (1136-1204) a major treasure-finder (terton) of the Nyingma school.

Nyatri Tsenpo the first king of the Yarlung Dynasty. See **Icon 77**.

Nyenchen Tanglha the protector deity embodying the mountain range of the same name, which forms a watershed between the Brahmaputra and the Salween. The main peak looms over Lake Namtso Chukmo.

Padmakara (Tib Pema Jungne) the form assumed by Padmasambhava at the time when he and his consort Mandarava were burnt at the stake in Zahor, but miraculously transformed their pyre into a lake. See **Icon 81**.

Padmapani see under **Avalokiteshvara**.

Padmasambhava the form assumed by Padmasambhava (ie Guru Rinpoche) while establishing Buddhism in Tibet. See **Icon 88**.

Panchen Lama the emanations of the Buddha Amitabha, ranking among Tibet's foremost incarnate successions. Among them, Panchen Lama IV Chokyi Gyeltsen (1567-1662; **Icon 117**) was an important teacher of Dalai Lama V.

Panjaranatha (Tib Gonpo Gur) see under **Mahakala**.

Paramadya (Tib Palchok Dangpo) a major meditational deity of the Yogatantra and Mahyoga class.

Pehar an important protector deity within the Nyingma and Geluk traditions. See also **Gyelpo Ku-nga**.

Pelpung Situ the incarnations of Tai Situpa, including Situ VIII Chokyi Jungne who, in 1727, founded the largest Karma Kagyu monastery at Pelpung within the kingdom of Derge. For a full enumeration of the Tai Situpas, see page 500.

Pema Totrengtsal the form assumed by Padmasambhava while manifesting as the meditational deity Vajrakumara to subdue the demons of the Kathmandu valley at Yanglesho (Pharping).

Phadampa Sangye the 11th-12th century South Indian yogin who propagated the Chodyul and Zhiche teachings in the highland region of Western Tibet.

Phakmodrupa Dorje Gyelpo (1110-70) student of Gampopa and progenitor of the eight lesser branches of the Kagyu school, including the Drigungpa, Taklungpa and Drukpa branches. See **Icon 100**.

Phakpalha the title of the principal incarnate lama of Chamdo Jampaling Monastery in Kham, which was founded between 1436-44 by Jangsem Sherab Zangpo.

Prajnaparamita (Tib Yum Chenmo) the female meditational deity embodying the perfection of discriminative awareness, golden yellow in colour, and holding emblems such as the book, sword, lotus, vajra and rosary, which are indicative of supreme insight. See **Icon 48**.

Rahula (Tib Za) an important protector deity within the Nyingma school, depicted as a dark brown or black multi-headed semi-human semi-serpentine figure. See **Icon 61**.

Ratnasambhava (Tib Rinchen Jungne) one of the five peaceful meditational buddhas forming the buddha-body of perfect resource (*sambhogakaya*), collectively known as the Buddhas of the Five Families. Ratnasambhava is yellow in colour, symbolizing the purity of sensations or feelings and the equanimity or sameness of buddha-mind. He holds a gemstone to symbolize that his enlightened attributes are spontaneously present and that he fulfils the hopes of all beings. See **Icon 5**.

Rechungpa (1084-1161) a yogin who was one of Milarepa's foremost students.

Remati (Tib Magzorma) an aspect of the protectress Shridevi, who rides a mule and holds a sickle or a sandalwood club and a blood-filled skull. She is propitiated in order to overwhelm internal passions and outer disruptions due to warfare.

Remdawa Zhonu Lodro (1349-1412) a great exponent of the Madhyamaka philosophy within the Sakya tradition, who became one of Tsongkhapa's most significant teachers.

Rigdzin Ngagi Wangpo (1580-1639) the third successive emanation of Rikdzin Godemchen, founder of the Northern Treasures (Jangter) tradition of the Nyingma school. In 1632 he established the monastery of Dorje Drak in Southern Tibet.

Rinchen Zangpo (958-1055) the great translator and contemporary of Atisha whose centre of activity was in Far-west Tibet and the adjacent areas of Spiti and Ladakh.

Sakya Pandita see under **Five Founders of Sakya**.

Samantabhadra (Tib Kuntu Zangpo) the male or subjective aspect of the primordial buddha-body of actual reality (*dharmakaya*), blue in colour, symbolizing the ground of buddha-mind or luminosity. See **Icon 1**.

Samantabhadra (bodhisattva) (Tib Jangsem Kuntu Zangpo) one of the eight major bodhisattvas, reddish-green in colour, symbolizing the buddha's nose, and holding a corn-ear of gemstones because he fulfils the hopes of beings. See **Icon 38**.

Samantabhadri (Tib Kuntu Zangmo) the female or objective aspect of the primordial buddha-body of actual reality (*dharmakaya*), blue in colour, symbolizing the ground of phenomenal appearances or emptiness. See **Icon 1**.

Samayatara (Tib Damtsik Dolma) a wrathful female meditational deity, consort of the Buddha Amoghasiddhi.

Sarvavid Vairocana (Tib Kunrik Nampar Nangze) see under **Vairocana**.

Seven Generations of Past Buddhas (Tib Sangye Rabdun) the seven buddhas of the immediate past, in sequence: Vipashyin (**Icon 11**), Shikhin, Vishvabhuk, Krakucchanda, Kanakamuni, Kashyapa, and Shakyamuni.

Shakyamuni see **Buddha Shakyamuni**.

Shakyamuni Aksobhyavajra (Tib Shakya Tupa Mikyo Dorsem) the aspect of Shakyamuni Buddha depicted in the Ramoche Jowo image, which was originally brought to Tibet from Nepal by Princess Bhrikuti in the seventh century.

Shakyashri (1127-1225) the great Kashmiri scholar who visited Tibet in his later years, influencing all traditions.

Shantaraksita (Tib Zhiwei Tso/Khenpo Bodhisattva) a monastic preceptor of Zahor, who officiated at Nalanda Monastery prior to his arrival in Tibet at the invitation of King Trisong Detsen. He ordained the first seven trial monks in Tibet and was responsible for the construction of Samye Monastery, which he modelled on Odantapuri Monastery in Magadha. See **Icon 82**.

Shariputra (Tib Shari-bu) one of the two foremost students of Shakyamuni, who passed away before the Buddha's parinirvana. See **Icon 13**.

Shridevi (Tib Palden Lhamo) a major protectress and female counterpart of Mahakala, who has both peaceful and wrathful forms, the latter being a ferocious three-eyed form, dark-blue in colour, and riding a mule. Remati (see above) is included among her aspects. See **Icon 60**.

Simhanada (Tib Senge Ngaro) see under Avalokiteshvara.

Simhavaktra (Tib Senge Dongma) a lion-headed meditational deity, who is the female aspect of Padmasambhava, dark blue in colour and holding a vajra-chopper and skull cup, which symbolize that she dispels obstacles to enlightened activity.

Sitatapatra (Tib Dukar) a female umbrella-wielding meditational deity, depicted with a thousand arms, who is propitiated in order to remove obstacles.

Six Ornaments (Tib Gyen Druk) the six great Buddhist commentators of ancient India, viz: Nagarjuna and Aryadeva who developed the Madhyamaka philosophy; the brothers Asanga and Vasubandhu who developed the Yogacara, Cittamatra, and Vaibhasika philosophies; and Dignaga and Dharmakirti who developed a systematic Buddhist logic. See **Icons 69-74**.

Six Sages of the Six Realms (Tib Tupa Druk) six buddha aspects said to appear respectively in the six realms of existence in order to teach the way to liberation from sufferings, respectively: Munindra (among the gods), Vemacitra (among the antigods), Shakyamuni (among humans), Simha (among animals), Jvalamukha (among tormented spirits), and Yama Dharmaraja (among the hells).

Six-armed Mahakala (Tib Gonpo Chak Drukpa) see under **Mahakala**.

Sixteen Elders (Tib Neten Chudruk) a group of elders (*sthavira*) and contemporaries of Shakyamuni Buddha, who were traditionally assigned to promote the Buddhist teachings in the world throughout time, and who have been particularly venerated in Chinese Buddhism, where they are known as arhats (Ch lohan). See **Icons 15-30**.

Songtsen Gampo the seventh century unifying king of Tibet who made Lhasa the capital of his newly emergent nation and espoused the Buddhist teachings, revered thereafter as an emanation of the compassionate bodhisattva Avalokiteshvara. See **Icon 79**.

Taklung Tangpa Tashipel (1142-1210) a foremost student of Phakmodrupa Dorje Gyelpo, who founded the Taklung Kagyu sub-school and the monastery of the same name in 1178. See **Icon 102**.

Tangtong Gyelpo (1385-1464) the Leonardo of Tibet, renowned as a mystic, revealer of treasure-doctrines, engineer, master bridge-builder, and the inventor of Tibetan opera. See **Icon 112**.

Tara (Tib Dolma) a female meditational deity, who is identified with compassion and enlightened activity. There are aspects of Tara which specifically offer protection from worldly tragedies and fear of the elements (see above, **Eight Taras who Protect from Fear**), and an enumeration of 21 aspects of Tara is well-documented. Among these the most popular are Green Tara (Tib Doljang; **Icon 49**), who is mainly associated with protection, and White Tara (Tib Dolkar; **Icon 46**), who is associated with longevity. In addition, the form known as Cintamani (cakra) Tara is a meditational deity of the Unsurpassed Yogatantra class.

Terdak Lingpa (1646-1714) a great treasure-finder who revitalized the Nyingmapa tradition and founded Mindroling Monastery in 1670.

Thirty-five Confession Buddhas (Tib Tungshagi Lha Songa) a group of 35 buddhas associated with the specific practice of purifying non-virtuous habits, in which the names of each are invoked in turn (usually in conjunction with physical prostrations).

Thousand buddhas of the aeon (Tib Sangye Tongtsa) the thousand buddhas of the present aeon, whose names are enumerated in the *Bhadrakalpikasutra*. Among these Shakyamuni Buddha was the fourth, and the next to appear in the world will be Maitreya.

Three Ancestral Religious Kings (Tib Chogyel Mepo Namsum) the three foremost Buddhist kings of ancient Tibet, namely Songtsen Gampo who unified the country and espoused Buddhism in the seventh century (**Icon 79**), Trisong Detsen who established the spiritual practices and monastic ordinations of Buddhism in the eighth century (**Icon 83**), and Tri Ralpachen who sought to end Tibetan militarism and lavishly sponsored Buddhist activity in the ninth century (**Icon 92**).

Three Deities of Longevity (Tib Tselha Namsum) see respectively **Amitayus** (**Icon 45**), **White Tara** (**Icon 46**), and **Vijaya** (**Icon 47**).

Thubpa Gangchentso see under **Vairocana**.

Thubwang (Skt Munindra) see **Buddha Shakyamuni**.

Tiger-riding Mahakala (Tib Gonpo Takzhon) see under **Mahakala**.

Tonmi Sambhota the seventh century inventor of the Tibetan capital letter script (*uchen*). See **Icon 80**.

Trailokyavijaya (Tib Khamsum Namgyel) a peripheral deity, sometimes assuming a peaceful guise alongside the eight standing bodhisattvas, and sometimes in a wrathful form alongside the Dashakrodha kings.

Tri Ralpachen see under **Three Ancestral Religious Kings.**

Trisong Detsen see under **Three Ancestral Religious Kings.**

Tsangpa Gya-re Yeshe Dorje (1161-1211) the first Drukchen (head of the Drukpa Kagyu school). See **Icon 103**. For a full enumeration of the Drukchen emanations, see above, page 266.

Tsering Che-nga five female protector deities associated with the snow peaks of the Everest Range, viz: Miyowa Zangma, Tingi Zhelzangma, Tashi Tseringma, Drozangma, and Drinzangma.

Tseringma see under **Tsering Che-nga.**

Tsongkhapa (and his foremost students) see **Je Yabsesum.**

Tuken Lobzang Chokyi Nyima (1737-1802) the incarnation of Tuken Ngawang Choki Gyatso of Gonlung Jampaling Monastery in Amdo. In 1801 he wrote the *Crystal Mirror of Philosophical Systems*.

Twelve Subterranean Goddesses (Tib Tenma Chunyi) a group of 12 protector goddesses of the earth, who are associated with specific mountain localities, such as Kongtsun Demo, the protectress of Kongpo; and Machen Pomra, the protectress of the Amnye Machen range.

Twelve Tenma see **Twelve Subterranean Goddesses.**

Twenty-five Tibetan Disciples (Tib Jewang Nyernga) the Tibetan disciples of Padmasambhava, including King Trisong Detsen, Yeshe Tsogyel, Vairotsana, Nubchen Sangye Yeshe, Nyak Jnanakumara, and so forth.

Twenty-one Taras (Tib Dolma Nyishu Tsachik) see under Tara.

Two Gatekeepers (Tib gokyong nyi) in most temples the gates are guarded on the inner side by large images of Hayagriva (west) and Vajrapani or Acala (east).

Two Supreme Ones (Tib Chok Nyi) the ancient Indian Vinaya masters, Gunaprabha and Shakyaprabha, who are sometimes classed alongside the Six Ornaments. See **Icons 75-76.** Note that some traditions identify Nagarjuna and Asanga as the Two Supreme Ones and, instead, place the Vinaya masters among the Six Ornaments.

Ucchusmakrodha (Tib Trowo Metsek) a wrathful aspect of the meditational deity Hayagriva, in which form the spirit of rampant egotism (Rudra) is tamed.

Usnisavijaya (Tib Tsuktor Namgyel) a three-headed multi-armed wrathful deity, who is the first and foremost of the **Dashakrodha kings.**

Vairocana (Tib Nampar Nangze) one of the five peaceful meditational buddhas forming the buddha-body of perfect resource (*sambhogakaya*), collectively known as the Buddhas of the Five Families. Vairocana is white in colour, symbolizing the purity of consciousness and the emptiness of buddha-mind. He holds a wheel to symbolize that his teachings cut through the net of dissonant emotions. See **Icon 3**. Among other aspects of Vairocana are the four-faced form Sarvavid Vairocana (Tib Kunrik Nampar Nangze; **Icon 50**) in which all the peripheral buddhas are embodied, and Muni Himamahasagara (Tib Thubpa Gangchentso), in and around whose body all world systems are said to evolve.

Vairotsana one of the 25 disciples of Padmasambhava, revered as a major translator of Sanskrit texts and a lineage holder of the Dzogchen tradition.

Vaishravana (Tib Nam-mang To-se) the guardian king of the northern direction, who, like Jambhala and Manibhadra, is associated with wealth, and wields a banner and a jewel-spitting mongoose in his hands.

Vajradhara (Tib Dorje Chang) an aspect of the buddha-body of actual reality (*dharmakaya*), appearing in a luminous form complete with the insignia of the buddha-body of perfect resource (*sambhogakaya*). He is dark blue in colour, seated, holding a vajra and bell in his crossed hands. See **Icon 2**.

Vajrakila (Tib Dorje Phurba) a wrathful meditational deity of the Nyingma and Sakya schools in particular, and one of the **Drubpa Kabgye**. He is depicted dark-blue in colour, with three faces, and six arms, and wielding a ritual dagger (*kila/phurba*) which cuts through obstacles to enlightened activity.

Vajrakumara (Tib Dorje Zhonu) an aspect of the meditational deity Vajrakila. See **Icon 52**.

Vajrapani (Tib Chakna Dorje) one of the eight major bodhisattvas and one of the lords of the three enlightened families, blue in colour, symbolizing the buddha's power and sense of hearing, and holding a vajra because he has subjugated sufferings. There are various forms of this bodhisattva, among which the standing peaceful form (**Icon 32**), and the two-armed wrathful form, raising a vajra in the right hand and a noose in the left (**Icon 41**) are most frequently depicted.

Vajrasattva (Tib Dorje Sempa) an aspect of **Aksobhya** (**Icon 4**) who may appear in a blue form or a white form, holding a vajra in his right hand and a bell in the left, symbolizing purification and the indestructible reality of skilful means and emptiness.

Vajrasattva Yab-yum (Tib Dorsem Yabyum) the meditational deity **Vajrasattva** in union with his female consort.

Vajravarahi (Tib Dorje Phagmo) a female meditational deity who is the consort of Cakrasamvara, generally red in colour and with the emblem of the sow's head above her own. See **Icon 55**.

Vajravidarana (Tib Dorje Namjom) a peaceful meditational deity, seated and holding a crossed-vajra to the heart with the right hand and a bell in the left.

Vajrayogini (Tib Dorje Neljorma) a female meditational deity, red in colour and with a semi-wrathful facial expression. There are several aspects, including the one known as Kecari, the practices of which are associated mainly with the Kagyu school.

Vijaya (Tib Namgyelma) an eight-armed three-headed meditational deity, who is one of the **Three Deities of Longevity**, white in colour and holding a small buddha-image in her upper right hand. Statues of Vijaya are often inserted within Victory Stupas. See **Icon 47**.

Vimalamitra (Tib Drime Drakpa) a Kashmiri master and contemporary of Padmasambhava who introduced his own transmission of Dzogchen in Tibet, and was responsible for disseminating the *Guhyagarbha Tantra*.

Virupa one of the Eighty-four Mahasiddhas of ancient India who was a progenitor of the profound instructions set down in the *Path and Fruit* teachings of the Sakya school.

Yama Dharmaraja (Tib Shinje Chogyel) a proctector deity favoured by the Geluk school, dark blue in colour and bull-headed, and brandishing a club and a snare. He is identified with Yama, the 'lord of death'. See **Icon 68**.

Yamantaka (Tib Zhinje-zhed) a wrathful meditational deity, with red, black and bull-headed aspects who functions as the opponent of the forces of death. Practices associated with Yamantaka are important in the Nyingma and Geluk schools.

Yamari (Tib Zhinje) see **Yamantaka**.

Yangdak Heruka (Skt Shriheruka) a wrathful meditational deity associated with buddha-mind, from the Nyingma cycle known as the **Drubpa Kabgye**.

Yeshe Tsogyel one of the foremost disciples and female consorts of Padmasambhava, formerly the wife of King Trisong Detsen.

Yutok Yonten Gonpo (1127-1203) renowned exponent of Tibetan medicine.

Zhamarpa the title given to the successive emanations of Zhamarpa Tokden Drakpa Senge (1283-1349), a student of Karmapa III. The monastery of Yangpachen in Damzhung county later became their principal seat.

1 **Samantabdhara** with **Samantabhadri** (Tib. *Kunzang Yabyum*)

2 **Vajradhara** (Tib. *Dorje Chang)*

3 Buddhas of the Five Families: **Vairocana** (Tib. *Nampar Nangze*)

4 Buddhas of the Five Families: **Aksobhya-Vajrasattva** (Tib. *Mikyopa Dorje Sempa*)

5 Buddhas of the Five Families: **Ratnasambhava** (Tib. *Rinchen Jungne*)

6 Buddhas of the Five Families: **Amitabha** (Tib. *Opame*)

7 Buddhas of the Five Families: **Amoghasiddhi** (Tib. *Donyo Drupa*)

8 Buddhas of the Three Times: **Dipamkara** (Tib. *Marmedze*)

9 Buddhas of the Three Times: **Shakyamuni** (Tib. *Shakya Tupa*)

10 Buddhas of the Three Times: **Maitreya** (Tib. *Jampa*)

11 **Vipashyin** (Tib. *Namzik*), first of the Seven Generations of Past Buddhas (*Sangye Rabdun*)

12 **Bhaisajyaguru** (Tib. *Sangye Menla*), foremost of the Eight Medicine Buddhas (*Menla Deshek Gye*)

13 **Shariputra** (Tib. *Shari-bu*)

14 **Maudgalyayana** (Tib. Maudgal-bu)

15 Sixteen Elders: **Angaja** (Tib. *Yanlak Jung*)

16 Sixteen Elders: **Bakula** (Tib. *Bakula*)

17 Sixteen Elders: **Ajita** (Tib. *Mapampa*)

18 Sixteen Elders: **Rahula** (Tib. *Drachendzin*)

19 Sixteen Elders: **Vanavasin** (Tib. *Naknane*)

20 Sixteen Elders: **Cudapanthaka** (Tib. *Lamtrenten*)

21 Sixteen Elders: **Kalika** (Tib. *Duden*)

22 Sixteen Elders: **Bharadvaja** (Tib. *Bharadvadza*)

23 Sixteen Elders: **Vajriputra** (Tib. *Dorje Moyibu*)

24 Sixteen Elders: **Panthaka** (Tib. *Lamten*)

25 Sixteen Elders: **Bhadra** (Tib. *Zangpo*)

26 Sixteen Elders: **Nagasena** (Tib. *Luyide*)

27 Sixteen Elders: **Kanakavatsa** (Tib. *Serbe'u*)

28 Sixteen Elders: **Gopaka** (Tib. *Beche*)

29 Sixteen Elders: **Kanaka Bharadvaja** (Tib. *Serchen*)

30 Sixteen Elders: **Abheda** (Tib. *Michedpa*)

31 Eight Bodhisattvas: **Manjushri** (Tib. *Jampal*)

32 Eight Bodhisattvas: **Vajrapani** (Tib. *Chakna Dorje*)

33 Eight Bodhisattvas: **Avalokiteshvara** (Tib. *Chenrezik*)

34 Eight Bodhisattvas: **Ksitigarbha** (Tib. *Sayi Nyingpo*)

35 Eight Bodhisattvas: **Nivaranaviskambhin** (Tib. *Dripa Namsel*)

36 Eight Bodhisattvas: **Akashagarbha** (Tib. *Namkei Nyingpo*)

37 Eight Bodhisattvas: **Maitreya** (Tib. *Jampa*)

38 Eight Bodhisattvas: **Samantabhadra** (Tib. *Kuntu Zangpo*)

39 Lords of the Three Enlightened Families: **Four-armed Avalokiteshvara** (Tib. *Chenrezik Chakzhipa*)

40 Lords of the Three Enlightened Families: **Manjughosa** (Tib. *Jampeyang*)

41 Lords of the Three Enlightened Families: **Vajrapani** (Tib. *Chakna Dorje*)

42 Aspects of Avalokiteshvara: **Eleven-faced/ Thousand-armed Mahakarunika** (*Zhal Chuchikpa*)

43 Aspects of Avalokiteshvara: **Simhanada** (Tib. *Senge Ngaro*)

44 Aspects of Avalokiteshvara: **Kharsapani** (Tib. *Kharsapani*)

45 Three Deities of Longevity: **Amitayus** (Tib. *Tsepame*)

46 Three Deities of Longevity: **White Tara** (Tib. *Dolkar*)

47 Three Deities of Longevity: **Vijaya** (Tib. *Namgyelma*)

48 Meditational Deities: **Prajnaparamita** (Tib. *Yum Chenmo*)

49 Meditational Deities: **Green Tara** (*Droljang*)

50 Meditational Deities: **Sarvavid Vairocana** (Tib. *Kunrik Nampar Nangze*)

51 Meditational Deities: **Guhyasamaja** (Tib. *Sangwa Dupa*)

52 Meditational Deities: **Vajrakumara** (Tib. *Dorje Zhonu*)

53 Meditational Deities: **Kalacakra** (Tib. *Dungkor*)

54 Meditational Deities: **Cakrasamvara** (Tib. *Khorlo Dompa*)

55 Meditational Deities: **Vajravarahi** (Tib. *Dorje Pamo*)

56 Meditational Deities: **Hevajra** (Tib. *Kye Dorje*)

57 Protector Deities: **Four-armed Mahakala** (Tib. *Gonpo Chak Zhipa*)

58 Protector Deities: **Mahapandaka Mahakala** (Tib. *Gonpo Maning*)

59 Protector Deities: **Panjaranatha** (Tib. *Gonpo Gur*)

60 Protector Deities: **Shrivi** (Tib. *Palden Lhamo*)

61 Protector Deities: **Rahula** (Tib. *Za*)

62 Protector Deities: **Dorje Yudronma**

63 Five Aspects of Pehar: **Kuyi Gyelpo**

64 Five Aspects of Pehar: **Sung-gi Gyelpo**

65 Five Aspects of Pehar: **Tukyi Gyelpo**

66 Five Aspects of Pehar: **Yonten-gyi Gyelpo**

67 Five Aspects of Pehar: **Trinle Gyelpo**

68 **Dharmaraja** (Tib. *Damchen Chogyel*)

69 Six Ornaments and Two Supreme Ones: **Nagarjuna** (Tib. *Phakpa Ludrub*)

70 Six Ornaments and Two Supreme Ones: **Aryadeva** (Tib. *Phakpa Lha*)

71 Six Ornaments and Two Supreme Ones: **Asanga** (Tib. *Thok-me*)

72 Six Ornaments and Two Supreme Ones: **Vasubandhu** (Tib. *Yiknyen*)

73 Six Ornaments and Two Supreme Ones: **Dignaga** (Tib. *Choklang*)

74 Six Ornaments and Two Supreme Ones: **Dharmakirti** (*Chodrak*)

75 Six Ornaments and Two Supreme Ones: **Gunaprabha** (*Yonten-o*)

76 Six Ornaments and Two Supreme Ones: **Shakyapraha** (*Shakya-o*)

77 Three Early Tibetan Kings: **Nyatri Tsenpo**

78 Three Early Tibetan Kings: **Lhatotori Nyentsen**

79 Three Early Tibetan Kings: **Songtsen Gampo**

80 **Tonmi Sambhota**

81 Founders of the Nyingma School: **Padmakara** (Tib. *Pema Jungne*)

82 Founders of the Nyingma School: **Shantaraksita** (Tib. *Khenpo Bodhisattva/ Zhiwatso*)

83 Founders of the Nyingma School: **King Trisong Detsen**

84 Eight Manifestations of Padmasambhava: **Saroruhavajra** (*Tsokye Dorje Chang*)

85 Eight Manifestations of Padmasambhava: **Pema Gyelpo**

86 Eight Manifestations of Padmasambhava: **Shakya Senge**

87 Eight Manifestations of Padmasambhava: **Loden Chokse**

88 Eight Manifestations of Padmasambhava: **Padmasambhava**

89 Eight Manifestations of Padmasambhava: **Nyima Ozer**

90 Eight Manifestations of Padmasambhava: **Senge Dradrok**

91 Eight Manifestations of Padmasambhava: **Dorje Drolo**

92 **King Ralpachen**

93 Founders of Kadampa School: **Atisha** (Tib. *Jowoje*)

94 Founders of Kadampa School: **Dromtonpa**

95 Founders of Kadampa School: **Ngok Lekpei Sherab**

96 Founders of Kagyu School: **Marpa**

97 Founders of Kagyu School: **Milarepa**

98 Founders of Kagyu School: **Gampopa**

99 Founders of Kagyu School: **Karmapa I, Dusum Khyenpa**

100 Founders of Kagyu School: **Phakmodrupa Dorje Gyelpo**

101 Founders of Kagyu School: **Drigungpa Jikten Gonpo**

102 Founders of Kagyu School: **Taklung Tangpa Tashipel**

103 Founders of Kagyu School: **Tsangpa Gya-re Yeshe Dorje**

104 Five Founders of Sakya: **Kunga Nyingpo**

105 Five Founders of Sakya: **Sonam Tsemo**

106 Five Founders of Sakya: **Drakpa Gyeltsen**

107 Five Founders of Sakya: **Sakya Pandita**

108 Five Founders of Sakya: **Drogon Chogyel Phakpa**

109 **Buton Rinchen Drub**

110 **Dolpopa Sherab Gyeltsen**

111 **Longchen Rabjampa**

112 **Tangtong Gyelpo**

113 Founders of Gelukpa School: **Tsongkhapa**

114 Founders of Gelukpa School: **Gyeltsab Darma Rinchen**

115 Founders of Gelukpa School: **Khedrubje Gelekpel**

116 Masters of the Gelukpa Tradition: **Dalai Lama III Sonam Gyatso**

117 Panchen Lama IV, Lobzang Chogyen

118 Dalai Lama V, Ngawang Lobzang Gyatso

119 Desi Sangye Gyatso

120 Dalai Lama VI, Rigdzin Tsangyang Gyatso

121 Dalai Lama XIII, Tubten Gyatso

122 Dalai Lama XIV, Tendzin Gyatso

123 Dhritarastra, Guardian King of the East

124 Virudhaka, Guardian King of the South

125 Virupaksa, Guardian King of the West

126 Vaishravana, Guardian King of the North

Tibetan and Chinese place names

A

Tibetan	Chinese
Aban (Dzayul)	Abin
Achen Gangchen (ri)	Daxuefeng Shen
Achung Namdzong (Jentsa)	Aqiong Nanzong
Agara (Bayan Khar)	Laqutan
Akar (capital of Gonjo)	Gonjo
Aling (Zungchu)	Chuanzhisi
Amchog Ganden Chokhorling (Sangchu)	Amuquhu Si
Amchok Tsenyi Dratsang (Ngawa)	Chali Si
Amdo (dzong)	Amdo (xian)
Amdo (region)	Andu
Amnye Lhago (ri)	Erlang Shan
Amnye Machen (ri)	Animaqing Shan
Arik Gonchen Ganden Chopeling (Chilen)	Arou Da Si
Artsa (Lhari)	Azha
Ato Gonpa (Drito)	Anchong Si
Atsok Gon Dechen Chokhorling (Tsigortang)	Achuhu Si
Atunzu (capital of Dechen)	Diqing

B

Bachen (dzong)	Baqing (xian)
Bachen (Mewa)	Waqie
Bagon (Chumarleb)	Bagan
Bakchen (capital of Gabde)	Gande
Balung (dzong)	Weixi (xian)
Balung (Nyinak, capital of Balung)	Baohezhen
Balung (Panchen Zhingde)	Balong
Barkham (dzong)	Maerkang
Barong (Pelyul)	Barong
Barshok (capital of Nyarong)	Xinlong
Baryang (Drongpa)	Paryang
Batang (dzong)	Batang (xian)
Batang Chode (Batang)	Batang Si
Bayan (Tongkor)	Bayan
Bayan Khar (dzong)	Hualong (xian)
Bayankala (ri)	Bayan Har Shan
Bayi (drongkhyer)	Bayi (shiqu)
Benchen Puntsok Dargyeling (Jyekundo)	Bianqin Si
Beri (Kandze)	Baili
Beta Tso (tso)	Bita Hai
Bida Nampar Nangze Lhakhang (Jyekundo)	Darirulai Futang
Bimdo Gonchen (Dowi)	Wendu Si
Bipung (Metok)	Beibeng
Bodong Gonpa (Lhartse)	Podongai Si
Bolo (Gonjo)	Boluo
Bongen Gonpa (Kandze)	Baige Si

Tibetan	Chinese
Bongtak Gonpa Gendun Shedrubling	Ahandalai Si
Bongtak Tianjun (dzong)	Tianjun (xian)
Bonsok (Bachen)	Bensuo
Bora Gonpa (Sangchu)	Bola Si
Bozo (Dzoge)	Baozuo
Buchu Tergyi Lhakhang (Nyangtri)	Bujiu Si
Bum-chu	Peng Qu
Bumishi Gonpa (Lijiang)	Liu Lidian Si
Bumling Lhakhang (Yongjing)	Biling Si
Bumozhi (ri)	Siguniang Feng

C

Tibetan	Chinese
Chabcha (dzong)	Gonghe (xian)
Chakpori, Lhasa	Yaowang Shan
Chakri Gonpa (Padma)	Jiangritang Si
Chaktreng (dzong)	Xiangcheng (xian)
Chaktreng Sampeling (Chaktreng)	Xiangcheng Si
Chakzamka (dzong)	Luding (xian)
Chakzamka (Riwoche)	Jiasangka
Chamalung (Machen)	Temahe
Chamdo (dzong)	Changdu (xian)
Chemnak Gonpa (Menling)	Qiangna Si
Chichu (Nangchen)	Jiqu
Chidza (Dzato)	Jiezha qu
Chilen (dzong)	Qilian (xian)
Chimphu (Dranang)	Qinpu Miao
Chisa (Tsekok)	Xibusha
Chitu Kungaling Gon (Dabpa)	Gonggaling Si
Chogar Tashi Chodzong (Sogwo)	Quge Si
Choje Nangwa (Dzoge)	Qiouji
Chokhorgyel Gonpa (Gyatsa)	Qiongguojie Si
Chokle Namgyel (ri)	Qilian Shan
Chomolangma (Mt Everest)	Qomolangma Feng
Cho-ne (dzong)	Jone (xian)
Zhuoni Chongye (dzong)	Qonggyai (xian)
Chorten Nyima (Tingkye)	Qudian Nima Shankou
Chorten Tang Tashi Dargyeling (Pari)	Tiantang Si
Chozam (Nang)	Quzang
Chubzang Ganden Migyurling (Gonlung)	Quezang Si
Chuchen (dzong)	Jinchuan (xian)
Chukama (Machu)	Gihama
Chukar (Gyeltang)	Baishui
Chukhol Khartse Gonpa (Repkong)	Qukuhu Guashize Si
Chumarhe (Lho Kermo)	Qumar Heyan
Chumarleb (dzong)	Qumarleb (xian)
Chumdo (Po-me)	Qunduo
Chung Riwoche (Ngamring)	Qiong Riwuqe
Chunke (Jentsa)	Qunke
Chunyido (Chamdo)	Qunyido Qingnidong
Chushar (capital of Lhartse)	Lhaze Lazi
Chushul (dzong)	Quxu (xian)
Chusum (dzong)	Qusum (xian)

Tibetan	Chinese
Chusumdo (Derge)	Sanchakou
Chutsen (Tsigortang)	Wenquan
Chuwarna (Machen)	Xueshan
Chuwori (ri)Quwori Feng	

D

Dabma Gon (Dowi)	Danma Nigu Si
Dabpa (dzong)	Daocheng (xian)
Dabpa Lhari (ri)	Daocheng Sheng Feng
Dabpa Yangteng Gon	Xiongden Si
Dabzhi (dzong)	Haiyan (xian)
Dabzhi Gonsar Namgyeling (Dabzhi)	Xin Si
Da-chu (Mekong)	Langcang Jiang
Daklha Gampo Gonpa (Gyatsa)	Talaganbo Si
Damjong (Drito)	Danrong
Damzhung (dzong)	Damxung (xian) Dangxiong
Dang La (Lho Kermo)	Tangoula Shankou
Dangra Yutso (tso)	Tangra Yumco
Darchen (Purang)	Daoqin
Dardrong (town, Nyemo)	Nyemo
Dargye Gonpa (Kandze)	Dajin Si
Dargyeling (Saga)	Dajilin
Darlag (dzong)	Dari (xian)
Dartang Gonpa (Jigdril)	Baiyu Si
Dartsedo (dzong)	Kangding (xian)
Dawadzong (Tsamda)	Dabazong
Dechen (dzong)	Deqen (xian)
Dechen Dzong (capital of Taktse)	Dagze
Dechenling Gonpa (Dechen)	Tongtaling Si
Dekyiling (Rinpung)	Dejilin
Den Gonpa (Kandze)	Degongbu Fufadian
Dengka Gon (capital of Tewo)	Tebo
Denkhok Nubma (Jomda)	Xi Dengke
Denkhok Sharma (Sershul)	Luoxu
Densatil Gonpa (Zangri)	Dengsati Si
Dentik Sheldrak Gonpa (Bayan Khar)	Dandou Si
Derge (dzong)	Dege (xian)
Derge Gonchen (capital of Derge)	Dege Goinqen
Derge Gonchen Monastery (Derge)	Dege Gengqing Si
Derge Parkhang (Derge)	Dege Yinjingyuan
Derong (dzong)	Derong (xian)
Detsa Tashi Choding (Bayan Khar)	Zhizha Shang Si
Dingri (dzong)	Dingri (xian)
Dingri Gangkar (Dingri)	Lao Dingri
Do Gongma Gonpa (Padma)	Duogongma Si
Do Martang (capital of Pelbar)	Banbar
Do Yutok Gon (Dzamtang)	Yutuo Si
Dodrub Chode (Padma)	Zhiqin Si
Dogon Puntsok Dargyeling (Trindu)	Duogan Si
Dolma Lhakhang (Lhorong)	Zhuoma Simiao
Domar (Rutok)	Duoma
Domda (Chumarleb)	Qingshuihe

Tibetan	Chinese
Domkhok (Machen)	Dongqingguo
Dompa (Nangchen)	Domba
Dorje Drak Gonpa (Gongkar)	Duoji Zha Si
Dowa Dzong (capital of Lhodrak)	Lhozhag
Dowi (dzong)	Xunhua (xian)
Drak Yerpa (Taktse)	Yeba Si
Drakar Tredzong Gonpa (Tsigortang)	Saizong Si
Draknak (capital of Amdo)	Amdo
Draksum Tso (tso)	Basong Co
Drakya Drubgyu Tengyeling (Gegye)	Zhajia Gongba Si
Drakyol (Dzogang)	Zhayu
Dram (Nyalam)	Zhangmu
Dranang (dzong)	Zhanang (xian)
Drango (dzong)	Luhuo (xian)
Drango Gonpa (Drango)	Luhuo Si
Dratang Gonpa (Dranang)	Zhatang Si
Dratsang Gon Ganden Chokhorling (Tongkor)	Zhazang Si
Drawa (Tawu)	Jiawa
Drayab (dzong)	Zhagyab (xian)
Drepung, Lhasa	Zhebeng Si
Dri-chu (Yangtze)	Jinsha Jiang
Drigung (township, Meldro)	Zhikong (qu)
Drigung Til Gonpa (Meldro)	Zhikong Si
Driru (dzong)	Biru (xian)
Drito (dzong)	Zhidoi (xian)
Drokshok (Nangchen)	Zhuxiao qu
Dromo (dzong)	Yadong (xian)
Drongdal Mezhing (capital of Tsenlha)	Xiaojin
Dronglung (Kermo)	Naij Tal
Drongpa (dzong)	Zhongba (xian)
Drongpa Tradun (Drongpa)	Zhongba Zhabdun
Drongtse Gonpa (Gyantse)	Zhongzi Si
Drotsang (dzong)	Ledu
Drotsang Gonpa (Drotsang)	Qutan Si
Drubgyuling Gonpa (Trindu)	Zhujie Si
Druchung (capital of Trindu)	Chindu
Drugu Gon Ganden Chokhorling (Monyon)	Zhugu Si
Drukchen Sumdo (capital of Jigdril)	Jigzhi
Drukchu (dzong)	Zhugqu (xian)
Drukzur (Chuchen)	Xiazhai
Drumpa (capital of Gyatsa)	Gyaca
Dungdor (capital of Menling) **Mailing**	Milin
Dungkar (Tsamda)	Dongga
Dza-chu (Yalong)	Yalong Jiang
Dza-chu	Za Qu
Dzamtang (dzong)	Zamtang (xian)
Dzamtang Tsangpa Gon (Dzamtang)	Rangtang Da Si
Dzarongpu Gonpa (Dingri)	Rongbu Si
Dzato (dzong)	Zadoi (xian)
Dzayul (dzong)	Zayu (xian)
Dzigar Gonpa (Jomda)	Ziga Si
Dzitoru (capital of Lhorong)	Lhorong

Tibetan	Chinese
Dzitsa Degu (Nampel)	Jiuzhaigou
Dzogang (dzong)	Zogang (xian)
Dzogchen Rudam Samten Choling (Derge)	Zhuqing Si
Dzoge (dzong)	Ruoergai (xian)
Dzoge Nyima (capital of Machu)	Maqu
Dzongka (capital of Kyirong)	Gyirong
Dzongsar Tashi Lhatse Gonpa (Derge)	Zongsa Si
Dzongzhab (Nyachuka)	Xinduqiao
Dzuktrun (Darlag)	Jianshe

E

Ekyonggya Gonpa (Padma)	Ashijian Jiagong Si
Endun (capital of Drayab)	Zhagyab
Endun Gonpa (Drayab)	Yanduo Si
Eyul Lhagyari (capital of Chusum)	Qusum

G

Gabde (dzong)	Gande (xian)
Gampa (dzong)	Gamba (xian)
Gampa La	Ganbala Shankou
Gampazhol (capital of Gampa)	Gamba
Ganden Chokhorling (Tongkor)	Dongke'er Si
Ganden Chungkor (capital of Lhundrub)	Lhunzhub
Ganden Namgyeling (Taktse)	Gadan Si
Ganden Sangak Yarpeling (Ulan)	Dulan Si
Ganden Shedrubling (Cho-ne)	Zhuoni Si
Ganden Tengyeling (Tongkor)	Chingho Si
Gandrong (Derong)	Wakha
Gang Rinpoche (Mt Kailash)	Gangrenboqi Feng
Gangkar Gonpa (Gyezil)	Gonga Si
Ganlho Dzong (Sangchu)	Hezuoshen
Garita (Dzoge)	Galitai
Garthar Gonpa (Dartsedo)	Qianning Si
Gartok (capital of Markham)	Markam
Gartse Gonpa (Repkong)	Guoshize Si
Gawalung (Po-me)	Galong
Gegye (dzong)	Geji (xian)
Gemang Gonpa (Sershul)	Gemong Si
Gertse (dzong)	Gaize (xian)
Geshitra (Rongtrak)	Geshizha
Gogentang (capital of Sertal)	Sertar
Gomar Gonpa (Repkong)	Guomari Si
Gomayin (Mangra)	Guomaying
Gongkar (dzong)	Gonggar (xian)
Gonjo (dzong)	Gonjo (xian)
Gonlung (dzong)	Huzhu (xian)
Gonlung Jampaling (Gonlung)	Youning Si
Gonsar Ganden Rabgyeling (Dzoge)	Dazha Si
Gori Dratsang (Dowi)	Gulei Si
Gumang (Kawasumdo)	Gumang
Gungtang (Kyirong)	Gongdang

Tibetan	Chinese
Guri Gonpa (Machen)	Geri Si
Guro (Chamdo)	Eluo
Gurugyam Gonpa (Senge Tsangpo)	Guoerjian Gongba Si
Gyakhar Gon Shedrub Dagyeling (Lintan)	Jiangke Si
Gyala Pelri (ri)	Jiala Beidie Feng
Gyama (Meldro)	Jiama Si
Gyamda (dzong)	Gongbogyamda (xian)
Gyamotang (capital of Tengchen)	Dengqing
Gyanak Mani (Jyekundo)	Jiana Mani
Gyangon (Tengchen)	Jue'en
Gyantse (dzong) Gyangze (xian)	Jiangzi
Gyarong Ngul-chu	Dadu He
Gyatsa (dzong)	Gyaca (xian)
Gyatso (Namling)	Jiacuo
Gyelje Podrang (capital of drito)	Zhidoi
Gyeltang (dzong)	Zhongdian (xian)
Gyeltangteng (capital of Gyeltang)	Zhongdian
Gyezil (dzong)	Jiulong (xian)
Gyu-me (capital of Darlag)	Dari

H

Haba Gangri (ri)	Haba Xueshan
Hashul (Drito)	Haxie
Heka (Tsigortang)	Heka
Hohsai Kenmenho (ri)	Yuzhu Shan
Hongshan (Dechen)	Fuqang
Hor Gon Terton Chogar (Tsekok)	Heri Si
Horkor Gon Shedrub Dargyeling (Mato)	Huoke Si
Horkya Dratsang Samtenling (Trika)	Huo'erjia Si
Horpo (Pelyul)	Hepo
Horshe Gonpa (Sertal)	Huoxi Si
Hrihakon (Zungchu)	Lianghekou

J

Jadabling (Kangtsa)	Niao Dao
Jadir (of Tsekok)	Zekog
Jakhyung Shedrubling (Bayan Khar)	Xiaqiong Si
Jamchen Zhol (capital of Rinpung)	Rinbung
Jamdun (Drayab)	Xiangdui Si
Jang	Naxi
Jang Sadam	Lijiang
Jangtang (region)	Qiang Tang
Jentsa (dzong)	Jainca (xian)
Jigdril (dzong)	Jigzhi (xian)
Jintsamani (Bayan Khar)	Jianzha Mani Jingtang
Jiu Gonpa (Purang)	Qiwu Gongba Si
Jokhang, Lhasa	Da Zhao Si
Jomda (dzong)	Jomda (xian)
Jonang Puntsoling (Lhartse)	Pengcuolin Si
Joro Gonpa (Drango)	Jueri Si
Julak (Kamalok)	Minhe

Tibetan	Chinese
Julak-chu	Datong He
Jumang (capital of Sershul)	Sexu
Jyekundo (dzong)	Yushu (xian)
Jyekundo Dondrubling (Jyekundo)	Jiegu Si

K

Kachu Khar	Linxia
Kachu (Linxia)	Hanjiaji
Kachu (Sangchu)	Hanjiaji
Kado (Bayan Khar)	Gando
Kakhok (capital of Mewa)	Hongyuan
Kalden Jampaling (Chamdo)	Changdu Si
Kamalok (dzong)	Minhe (xian)
Kamtok (Jomda)	Gangtuo
Kanam (Po-me)	Galang
Kandze (dzong)	Ganzi (xian)
Kandze Gonpa (Kandze)	Ganzi Si
Kangtsa (dzong)	Gangca (xian)
Kangtsa Gonchen (Kangtsa)	Gangca Da Si
Karchudram Babtsuk (Lho Kermo)	Gaerquyan
Karma Gon (Chamdo)	Gama Si
Karong Sangchen Gatsel Choling (Tsekok)	Garang Si
Karpo (capital of Gyezil)	Jiulong
Karpo (Dzayul)	Gebu
Karzang Gonpa (Nyarong)	Hexi Si
Karzang Peljor Gonpa (Trindu)	Gazang Si
Katok Dorjeden Gonpa (Pelyul)	Gaduo Si
Katsel Gonpa (Meldro)	Gacai Si
Kawa Karpo (ri)	Meili Xueshan
Kawasumdo (dzong)	Tongde (xian)
Kengya Drakar Gonpa (Sangchu)	Baishiya Si
Kermo (dzong)	Golmud (xian)
Kham (region)	Kang
Khampagar Gon (Chamdo)	Kangba Gon
Khamra (Jentsa)	Kanbula
Khangmar (dzong)	Kangmar (xian)
Kharda (Nangchen)	Kanda
Khargang (Jomda)	Kagong
Kharmardo (Riwoche)	Kamaduo
Khasa Tso (tso)	Kasha Cuo
Khataka Gonpa (Kamalok)	Kadiga Si
Khomting Lhakhang (Lhodrak)	Lakang Si
Khorlomdo (Derge)	Keluodong Si
Khorzhak Lhakhang (Purang)	Kejia Si
Khyamru Gon Tashi Gepeling (Chabcha)	Qianbulu Si
Khyunglung (Tsamda)	Qulong
Kongtsun Demo (Menling)	Gongzun Dimu
Kowa Gon (Jentsa)	Guwa Si
Kumbum Jampaling (Rushar)	Taer Si
Kutse (Jomda)	Gucai
Kyakyaru (capital of Saga)	Saga
Kyaring Tso	Gyaring Hu

Tibetan	Chinese
Kyichu (river)	Lasa He
Kyigang (capital of Dzayul)	Zayu
Kyirong (dzong)	Gyirong (xian)
Kyirong (township)	Gyirong qu
Kyitang (capital of Lhuntse)	Lhunze
Kyo-me (Tsenlha)	Jiesi

L

Tibetan	Chinese
Labrang Tashikyil Gonpa (Sangchu)	Labuleng Si
Laka Gon Ganden Shedrub Dargyeling (Sogwo)	Laka Si
Lamaling (Nyangtri)	Lamaling Si
Lamo Dechen Gonpa (Jentsa)	Deqian Si
Lamo Gartok Kuntu Deweiling (Dabzhi)	Baifo Si
Lang (capital of Nang) **Nang**	Lang
Langkor Lhakhang (Dingri)	Langguo Si
Langtang Dolma Lhakhang (Sershul)	Longtang Zhuoma Si
Langtang Gonpa (Lhundrub)	Langtang Si
Lapchi Gang (Dingri)	Laqi Xuelin
Larung Gar Gonpa (Sertal)	Larong Wuming Foxueyuan
Lekbam (Dechen)	Yibeng
Lenhate Ganden Nechu Pelgyeling (Kamalok)	Lianhuatai Si
Lhagang Gonpa (Dartsedo)	Tagong Si
Lhagyeling Gonpa (Barkham)	Shuajing Si
Lhakhangtang Gonpa (Trika)	Luohantang Si
Lhalung Gonpa (Lhodrak)	Lalong Si
Lhamo Latso (tso)	Lamei Lacuo
Lhari (dzong)	Lhari (xian)
Lhartse (dzong) **Lhaze** (xian)	Lazi
Lhasa (drongkhyer)	Lasa (shiqu)
Lhato (Chamdo)	Laduo
Lho Taklung (Nakartse)	Daglung
Lhodrak (dzong)	Lhozhag (xian)
Lhokha (region)	Shannan
Lhorong (dzong)	Lhorong (xian)
Lhorong (township)	Lhorong qu
Lhundrub (dzong) **Lhunzhub** (xian)	Linzhou
Lhuntse (dzong)	Lhunze (xian)
Likhok (Drango)	Luokema
Lintan (dzong)	Lintan (xian)
Litang (dzong)	Litang (xian)
Litang Chode (Litang)	Litang Si
Liyul (Khotan)	Hetian
Lokyatun (Kamalok)	Guanting
Luchu (dzong)	Luqu (xian)
Lugba (Dartsedo)	Liuba
Lugu Tso (tso)	Lugu Hu
Lugyagak (Jentsa)	Lijiaxia
Lumaringpo (capital of Gertse)	Gaize
Lunang (Nyangtri)	Nulang
Lungen (Mato)	Yeniugdo

Tibetan	Chinese
Lungkar (Drongpa)	Longe'er
Lungkya Gonpa (Gabde)	Longshijia Si
Lungu (dzong)	Wenchuan (xian)
Lungzi (Ngawa)	Longriwa
Lutsang Gon Shedrub Gepeling (Mangra)	Nucang Si

M

Machen (dzong)	Maqen (xian)
Machu (dzong)	Maqu (xian)
Ma-chu (Yellow River)	Huang He
Magur Namgyeling (Jentsa)	Gunu Si
Mangra (dzong)	Guinan (xian)
Mangra (township)	Mangra qu
Manigango (Derge)	Maniganggo
Maowen (dzong)	Maowen (xian)
Mapam tso (tso, Manasarovar)	Mapang Yongcuo
Marchudram Babtsuk (Lho Kermo)	Tuotuohe
Markham (dzong)	Markam (xian)
Marnyung Jampaling (Lintan)	Manao Si
Martsangdrak Gonpa (Tsongkha Khar)	Baima Si
Mato (dzong)	Maduo (xian)
Mayum La (Drongpa)	Mayum La
Meldro Gungkar (dzong)	Maizhokunggar (xian)/Mozhu Gongka
Melong Gonpa (Dechen)	Meili Si
Menda (Chamdo)	Mianda
Mendong (capital of Tsochen)	Coqen
Mendong Gonpa (Tsochen)	Maindong Si
Menling (dzong)	Mailing (xian)/Milin
Metok (dzong, Pemako)	Medoq (xian)
Mewa (dzong)	Hongyuan (xian)
Mewa Gonpa (Mewa)	Wanxiang Dabei Falun Si?
Mikmar (Gertse)	Mami
Mili (dzong)	Muli (xian)
Mili Gonpa (Mili)	Muli Da Si
Minyak Dratsang Tashi Chopeling (Trika)	Miena Si
Minyak Gangkar (ri)	Gonga Shan
Minyak Rabgang (ritro)	Da Xue
Mitika (Lhari)	Maidika
Mola (Litang)	Mula
Mongyon (dzong)	Menyuan (xian)
Mozhi (Chakzamka)	Moxi
Mt Nemo Nanyi (Purang)	Namu Nani Feng
Muni (Zungchu)	Mounigou

N

Nakartse (dzong) **Nagarze** (xian)	Langkazi
Nakchok (Lhorong)	Lajiu
Nakchu (dzong)	Naqu (xian)
Nak-chu (Salween)	Nu Jiang
Naksho Driru (capital of Driru)	Biru
Naktsang (capital of Shentsa)	Xainza

Tibetan	Chinese
Nalanda Gonpa (Lhundrub)	Nalinchai Si
Namchak Barwa (ri)	Nanjiabawa Feng
Namka Ngoshi (capital of Tolung Dechen)	Dolungdeqen
Namling (dzong)	Namling (xian)
Nampel (dzong)	Nanping (xian)
Namru (capital of Palgon)	Baigoin
Namtso Chukmo (tso)	Nam Co
Nang (dzong) **Nang** (xian)	Lang
Nangchen (dzong)	Nangqen (xian)
Napuk (capital of Gegye)	Geji
Nartang Gonpa (Zhigatse)	Nadang Si
Narzhik Gonpa (Ngawa)	Langyi Si
Nechung Gonpa, Lhasa	Laiqiong Si
Nedong (dzong)	Nedong (xian)
Nenying Gonpa (Khangmar)	Nanni Si
Nezhi Zhitro Lhakhang (Tso-me)	Naixi Si
Ngamda (Riwoche)	Enda
Ngamring (dzong)	Ngamring (xian)
Ngapo Zampa (capital of Gyamda)	Gongbogyamda
Ngari (region)	Ali
Ngawa (dzong)	Aba (xian)
Ngen Tso (tso)	Ranwu Cuo
Ngom-chu	Ngom Qu
Ngor Evam Choden Gonpa (Zhigatse)	E Si
Ngoring Tso	Ngoring Hu
Ngotsoto (Bayan Khar)	Ansoduo
Nojin Gangzang (ri)	Ningjin Gangsang Feng
Norbu Khyungtse (Panam)	Luobu Qiongzi
Norbulingka, Lhasa	Luobu Linka
Nub Golok (Nyachuka)	Xi Golok
Nubtso (Dabzhi)	Xihai
Nyachuka (dzong)	Yajiang (xian)
Nyakla Gonpa (Gonjo)	Nina Gongba
Nyalam (dzong)	Nielamu (xian)
Nyang-chu (chu)	Niyang Qu
Nyang-chu	Nianchu He
Nyangtri (dzong)	Nyingzhi (xian)
Nyarong (dzong)	Xinlong (xian)
Nyelung (Sertal)	Nianlong
Nyemo (dzong)	Nyemo (xian)
Nyenchen Tanglha (ri)	Nianqing Tangla Shan
Nyenrong (dzong)	Nyainrong (xian)
Nyentok Gonpa (Repkong)	Nianduhu Si
Nyenyul (Zungchu)	Reyun
Nyetang Dolma Lhakhang (Chushul)	Nietang Si
Nyewo (Lhari)	Niwu
Nyichu (Sertal)	Niqu
Nyima Dawa La (Tongkor)	Ri Yue Shankou
Nyipu Shugseb Gonpa (Chushul)	Xou Se Nigu Si
Nyitso Gonpa (Tawu)	Lingque Si

O

Tibetan	Chinese
Ode Gungyel (ri)	Wodaigongjie Feng
Olka Taktse (Zangri)	Wokazong
Oma (Gegye)	Oma
Orgyen Mindroling Gonpa (Dranang)	Minzhulin Si
Oyuk Jara Gon (Namling)	Wuyu Si

P

Padma (dzong)	Baima (xian)
Padma Gangri (ri)	Baima Shan
Palgon (dzong)	Baigoin (xian)
Pal-she Dengka Gon (Tewo)	Baxi Dianga Si
Panam (dzong)	Bainang (xian)
Panchen Zhingde (dzong)	Dulan (xian)
Panchen Zhingde Gonpa	Xiangride Si
Pang-gong tso (tso)	Banggong Cuo
Pari (dzong)	Tianzhu (xian)
Parlung Tsangpo (chu)	Palong Zangbu
Pasho (dzong)	Baxoi (xian)
Pekhokho Gon Gendun Delkiling (Ulan)	Beikeke Si
Pelbar (dzong)	Banbar (xian)
Pelkhor Chode Gonpa (Gyantse)	Baiju Si
Pelkhu Tso (tso)	Paiku Co
Pelpung Tubden Chokhorling (Derge)	Babang Si
Pelri Gonpa (Chongye)	Bairi Si
Pelyul (dzong)	Baiyu (xian)
Pelyul Namgyel Jangchubling (Pelyul)	Baiyu Si
Pema (capital of Pasho)	Baxoi
Phakpa Wati Lhakhang (Kyirong)	Paba Si
Phari (Dromo)	Pagri
Phodo Dzong (township, Lhundrub)	Pangduo/ Lhunzhub (qu)
Phuma Yutso (tso)	Pumo Yongcuo
Pomda (Pasho)	Bamda
Po-me (dzong)	Bomi (xian)
Pondzirak (Dechen)	Benzilan
Ponkor (Darlag)	Xiahongke
Potala, Lhasa	Budala Gong
Pukhala Ritse (ri)	Xinqing Shan
Pundadrong (capital of Nyachuka)	Yajiang
Purang (dzong)	Bulan (xian)
Purok Gangri (ri)	Puruo Gangri Feng

R

Rabden (capital of Chuchen)	Jinchuan
Rabgya Gonpa (Machen)	Lajia Si
Rabshi (Nangchen)	Xialaixue
Rabza Dratsang Samten Choling (Trika)	Lazha Si
Raga Tsangpo (chu)	Rega Zangbu
Rakwa (Chaktreng)	Wengshui
Ralung Gonpa (Gyantse)	Relong Si

Tibetan	Chinese
Ramoche, Lhasa	Xiao Zhao Si
Rato (Nangchen)	Duolamakang
Rato Gonpa (Chushul)	Redui Si
Ratsaka (capital of Riwoche) **Riwoqe**	Leiwuqi
Rawame (capital of Gongkar)	Gonggar
Rawok (Dzayul)	Ranwu
Repkong (dzong)	Tongren (xian)
Reting Gonpa (Lhundrub)	Rezheng Si
Rikmon (Chabcha)	Daotonghe
Ringon (capital of Namling)	Namling
Rinpung (dzong)	Rinbung (xian)
Ritang (Lhuntse)	Ridang
Riwoche (dzong) **Riwoqe** (xian)	Leiwuqi
Riwoche Tsuklakhang (Riwoche)	Leiwuqi Si
Rong Jamchen Gonpa (Rinpung)	Rong Daci Si
Rongmi Drango (capital of Rongtrak)	Danba
Rongpatsa (Kandze)	Rongbacha
Rongpo Gonchen (Repkong)	Longwu Si
Rongpo Gyakhar (capital of Repkong)	Tongren
Rongpo Gyaruptang (Sog)	Jilutong
Rongpo tso (tso, Drito)	Longbao He
Rongshar (Dingri)	Rongxia
Rongtrak (dzong)	Danba (xian)
Rungan Dratsang (Trika)	Rian Si
Rushar (dzong)	Huangzhong (xian)
Rutok (dzong)	Rutog (xian)

S

Tibetan	Chinese
Saga (dzong)	Saga (xian)
Sagang (Chamdo)	Shagong
Sagang (Tengchen)	Shagong
Sakya (dzong)	Sagya (xian)
Sakya Gonpa (Sakya)	Sajia Si
Samding Gonpa (Nakartse)	Sangding Nigu Si
Samdrub Gonpa (Kandze)	Sangzhu Si
Samten Chopeling (Jentsa)	Nanzong Nigu Si
Samye Gonpa (Dranang)	Sangye Si
Sangak Choling Gonpa (Lhuntse)	Sananqulin Si/Sangngagqoling
Sangak Tengyeling (Jentsa)	Aqiong Nanzong Si
Sangchen (Dzato)	Zhaqin qu
Sangchu (dzong)	Xiahe (xian)
Sangruma Gonpa (Darlag)	Sangrima Si
Sardzong (Barkham)	Chabao
Sateng (Driru)	Sadeng
Sateng (Pelbar)	Sadeng
Sato Kalden Tashi Chokhorling (Kangtsa)	Shatuo Si
Se (Sakya)	Sai
Sekhar Gutok (Lhodrak)	Seka Guduo Si
Selitang (capital of Padma)	Baima
Semnyi Gon Ganden Dargyeling	Xianlai Si
Senge Tsangpo (capital of Senge Tsangpo)	Ali
Senge Tsangpo (chu, Indus)	Shiquan He

Tibetan	Chinese
Senge Tsangpo (dzong)	Shiquanhe (xian)
Sengeshong Magotsang (Repkong)	Wutun Xia Si
Sengeshong Yagotsang (Repkong)	Wutun Shang Si
Sepu Gangri (ri)	Sangpu Gangla Feng
Sera Thekchenling, Lhasa	Sela Si
Serkhang (capital of Nyenrong)	Nyainrong
Serkhok (dzong)	Datong (xian)
Serkhok (Trindu)	Saihe
Serkhok-chu	Beichuan Shui
Serlak Gonpa (Kawasumdo)	Sailihe Si
Serling Tso (tso)	Siling Cuo
Serlung Datsengon Tashi Gandenling (Sogwo)	Dacan Si
Serpo Lungpa (capital of Chumarleb)	Qumarleb
Sershul (dzong)	Sexu (xian)
Sershul Gonpa (Sershul)	Sexu Si
Sertal (dzong)	Sertar (xian)
Sertsa (Tengchen)	Sezha
Sertso (Zungchu)	Huanglong
Sertso Gon (Zungchu)	Huanglong Si
Setenling Gonpa (Ngawa)	Saige Si
Shab Geding (Sakya)	Xiabu Jiding
Shadzong Gonpa (Tsongkha Khar)	Xiazong Si
Shang (Panchen Zhingde)	Xiangride
Shang Zabulung (Namling)	Xiang Shapulong
Shar Dungri (ri)	Xue Baoding Feng
Sharda (capital of Nangchen)	Nangqen
Sharo Gonpa (Gabde)	Xiarihu Si
Sharsingma (capital of Dromo)	Yadong
Shelkar (capital of Dingri)	Xin Dingri
Shentsa (dzong)	Xainza (xian)
Shishapangma (ri)	Xixabangma Feng
Shitsang Ganden Chokhorling (Luchu)	Xicang Si
Shkachuka (Driru)	Xagquka
Shopado (Lhorong)	Suobanduo
Sinikhar Gonpa (Dzamtang)	Zengke Si
Sog (dzong) **Sog** (xian)	Suo
Sogwo (dzong)	Henan (xian)
Sok Tsanden Gon (Sog)	Sog (Suo) Zengdeng Si
Sok Tsanden Zhol (capital of Sog)	Sogxian/Suoxian
Somang (Barkham)	Semang
Sumdo (Dabpa)	Sangdui
Sumdzom (Po-me)	Songzong
Sungtseling Gonpa (Gyeltang)	Gadan Songzanlin Si

T

Takchong Gak (Tiger Leaping Gorge)	Hu Tiaxia
Taklung Gon Ganden Choling (Pari)	Dalong Si
Taklung Gonpa (Jigdril)	Duohelong Si
Taklung Gonpa (Lhundrub)	Dalong Si
Taklung Shingza Gonpa (Sogwo)	Xiangzha Si
Takmaru (capital of Lhari)	Lhari

Tibetan	Chinese
Taktsang Lhamo Sertang Gonpa (Luchu)	Langmu Si
Taktse (dzong) **Dagze** (xian)	Dazi
Taktser (Tsongkha Khar)	Hongaisi
Taktsha Gondrong (capital of Dzoge)	Ruoergai
Tamzhol (capital of Tso-me)	Comei
Tanakma (Chabcha)	Heimahe
Tangkor (Dzoge)	Tanggor
Tanyi Tawun (ri)	Tanlan Taweng (shan)
Tarlam Gonpa (Jyekundo)	Tanglong Si
Tarshul Gonpa (Mangra)	Taxiu Si
Tartang (capital of Bachen)	Baqing
Tashi Gepel Gonpa (Lijiang)	Yufeng Si
Tashi Namgyeling (Jentsa)	Gabu Si
Tashigang (Senge Tsangpo)	Zhaxigang
Tashigar Gonpa (Lintan)	Chadao'er Si
Tashilhunpo Gonpa (Zhigatse)	Zhaxilhunbo Si
Tashiling (dzong)	Li (xian)
Tashitse (Pasho)	Zhaxize
Tawo (capital of Machen)	Maqen
Tawo Zholma (Machen)	Xiao Dawu
Tawu (dzong)	Daofu (xian)
Tege Sangak Dargyeling (Chabcha)	Tiegai Si
Temahe (Machen)	Qamalung
Temto Gonpa (Dzogang)	Tiantuo Si
Tengchen (dzong)	Dengqing (xian)
Terlenka (Ulan)	Delingha (shiqu)
Tewo (dzong)	Tebo (xian)
Tim Guru Drupuk (Menling)	Pai Miao
Tingkye (dzong)	Dingjie (xian)
Tiyak (Tsamda)	Diya
Tobden (Tsekok)	Duofudun
Tokya (Repkong)	Bao'an
Tokya Tashi Chopeling (Repkong)	Woke Si
Toling (capital of Tsamda)	Zanda
Tolung Dechen (dzong)	Dolungdeqen (xian)/Duilong Deqing
Toma (Lho Kermo)	Wenquan
Tongkor (dzong)	Huangyuan (xian)
Topa (Chamdo)	Tuoba
Tosam Dargyeling (Pari)	Dongda Si
Trado (Chumarleb)	Zhaduo
Tradruk Lhakhang (Nedong)	Changzhu Si
Tradruka (Namling)	Dazhuka
Traling Gonpa (Darlag)	Chalang Si
Tramog (capital of Po-me)	Bomi
Trangu Gonpa (Jyekundo)	Changu Si
Trayaklung Gonpa (Gabde)	Qiayilong Si
Trewo Gonpa (Drango)	Zhuwo Si
Trigu Tso (tso)	Chigu Cuo
Trika (dzong)	Guide (xian)
Trindu (dzong)	Chindu (xian)
Trochu (dzong)	Heishui (xian)
Trola (ri)	Que'er Shan
Trugu Gonpa (Riwoche)	Zhuge Si

Tibetan	Chinese
Tsaka (Gegye)	Yanba
Tsaka (Ulan)	Chaka
Tsakalho (Markham)	Yanjing
Tsakhok (Tashiling)	Zagunao
Tsakya Tsangpo (chu)	Zhajia Zangbu
Tsamda (dzong)	Zanda (xian)
Tsang (region)	Houzang
Tsang-gar Dondrub Rabtenling (Kawasumdo)	Shizang Si
Tsaparang (Tsamda)	Zhaburang
Tsari	Zari
Tsari Mikhyimdun (Nang)	Zari qu
Tsashul (Nangchen)	Jienesai qu
Tsawarong (Dzayul)	Chawalong
Tsechu Gonpa (Nangchen)	Caijiu Si
Tsekok (dzong)	Zekog (xian)
Tsenlha (dzong)	Xiaojin (xian)
Tsenpo Gon Ganden Damcholing (Serkhok)	Guanghui Si
Tsetang (drongkhyer)	Zedang
Tsigortang (dzong)	Xinghai
Tsike (district)	Zigai
Tso Ngon (Lake Kokonor)	Qinghai
Tsochen (dzong)	Coqen (xian)
Tsochung Norbu (tso)	Gahai
Tsogon Geden Choling (Sangchu)	Hezuo Si
Tsogyenrawa (Mato)	Huashixia
Tso-me (dzong)	Comei (xian)
Tsona (dzong)	Cona (xian)
Tsong-chu	Huang Shui
Tsongdu (capital of Nyalam)	Nielamu
Tsongkha Khar (dzong)	Pingan (xian)
Tsonyi (Shentsa)	Shuang Hu
Tsonying Mahadeva (Kangtsa)	Haixin Shan
Tsowar Kartse Doka (Mato)	Cuowa Gashize Duoka Si
Tsurphu Gonpa (Tolung Dechen)	Chubu Si
Tu-je Chenpo (Chuchen)	Guanyinqao
Tu-je Chenpo (Chuchen)	Guanyinqiao
Tungping (Zungchu)	Taiping
Tupten Yangpachen Gonpa (Tolung Dechen)	Yangbajing Si

U

Ulak Riwo (Chakzamka)	Erlang Shan
Ulan Sok (dzong)	Ulan (xian)

W

Wamda (capital of Dzogang)	Zogang
Wandotang (Sangchu)	Wangatan
Wangden (Panam)	Wangdain
Wangtsang Gon Tashi Puntsoling (Tewo)	Wangcang Si

Tibetan	Chinese
Wanshul Garka Gonpa (Mangra)	Wangxiuga Si
Wara Gonpa (Jomda)	Wala Si
Wawentsang (Machu)	Awantsang

Y

Yamdrok Yutso (tso)	Yangzhuo Yongcuo
Yangkar Dorje Phakmo (Kandze)	Yage Si
Yardzi (capital of Dowi)	Xunhua
Yarlha Shampo (ri)	Yala Xiangbo Feng
Yarlung Pemako Gonpa (Sertal)	Yalong Si
Yarlung Tsangpo (river)	Yalu Zangbo Jiang
Yarma Tashikyil Gonpa (Repkong)	Yama Zhaxiqi Si
Yazer Gonpa (Derge)	Yaori Si
Yemalung (Dranang)	Yamalong Miao
Yrwa Samdrubling (Lintan)	oujia Si
Yeyondo (Nangchen)	Sigeton
Yi-ong Tsangpo (chu)	Yigong Zangbu
Yilhun Lhatso (tso)	Xinluhai
Yumbu Lagang (Nedong)	Yongbu Lagang
Yungdrung Gonpa (Trochu)	Yongzong Geng Si
Yungdrung Lhateng Gonpa (Chuchen)	Guangfu Si

Z

Zang-me (capital of Derong)	Derong
Zangri (dzong)	Sangri (xian)
Zangri Kharmar (Zangri)	Sangri Kangma Si
Zangzang (Ngamring)	Sangsang
Zar Gonpa (Tingkye)	Saer Si
Zawa (Bayan Khar)	Quanzhuang
Zhabten Gonpa (Nakchu)	Naqu Si
Zhado Tso (tso)	Shudu Hai
Zhalu Gonpa (Zhigatse)	Xialu Si
Zhara Lhartse (ri)	Haitzu Shan
Zhe Geding (capital of Zhetongmon)	Xaitongmoin
Zhechen Tenyi Dargyeling (Derge)	Seqing Si
Zhe-chu	Xianshui
Zhetongmon (dzong)	Xaitongmoin (xian)
Zhigatse (dzong) **Xigaze** (xian)	Rikezi
Zhilung (Tsenlha)	Rilong
Zhiwu (Trindu)	Xiwu
Zholsar (capital of Tsona)	Cona
Zhongpang Chi (Repkong)	Shuangpengxi
Zhoto Tidro Gonpa (Meldro)	Dezhong Nigu Si
Zhungba (Gegye)	Xiongba
Zhutreng (Tashiling)	Xuechang
Tibetan	**Chinese**
Ziling (drongkhyer)	Xining (shiqu)
Zungchu (dzong)	Songpan (xian)
Zung-chu	Min Jiang
Zurmang Dutsitil Gonpa (Jyekundo)	Sumang Deziti Si
Zurmang Namgyeltse Gonpa (Nangchen)	Sumang Langjieze Si

Glossary

A

abhidharma A class of Buddhist literature pertaining to phenomenology, psychology, and cosmology

All-surpassing Realisation (*thogal*) A meditative technique within the Esoteric Instructional Class of Atiyoga, the highest teachings of the Nyingma school, through which the buddha-body of form (*rupakaya*) is manifestly realized

amban A Manchu ambassador of the imperial Qing dynasty

Anuttarayogatantra The unsurpassed yogatantras, which focus on important tantric subject matters, such as 'inner radiance' and 'illusory body'

Anuyoga The eighth of the nine vehicles of Buddhism according to the Nyingma school, in which the perfection stage of meditation (*sampannakrama*) is emphasized

apsara Offering goddess, celestial nymph

argali (*Ovis ammon Hodgsoni Blyth*) A type of wild sheep

Arpacana Mantra The mantra of the bodhisattva Manjughosa (*Om Arapacana Dhih*), the recitation of which generates discriminative awareness (*prajna*) and intelligence

Atiyoga The ninth of the nine vehicles of Buddhism according to the Nyingma school, in which the resultant three buddha-bodies (*trikaya*) are effortlessly perfected, and the generation and perfection stages of meditation are both effortlessly present

Avatamsakasutra The title of the longest Mahayana sutra (excluding the Prajnaparamita literature)

B

bahal A Newari temple

bangrim The terraced steps of a stupa, symbolising the bodhisattva and buddha levels

beyul A hidden land conducive to meditation and spiritual life, of which there are several in the Hiamlayan region, such as Pemako in southeast Tibet, and Khenpajong in northeast Bhutan

Bhadracaryapranidhanaraja The title of an important aspirational prayer which is part of the **Avatamsakasutra**

bharal A species of blue sheep (Tib nawa; Pseudois nayaur Hodg)

bindu The finial of a stupa, symbolising the buddha-body of actual reality (*dharmakaya*). The term also refers to the generative fluids of human physiology (according to Tibetan medicine and tantra), and to the seminal points of light appearing in the practice of **All- Surpassing Realisation**

bodhicitta (Tib jangchub sem) The enlightened mind which altruistically acts in the interest of all beings, combining discriminative awareness with compassion

bodhicitta vow The aspiration to attain full enlightenment or buddhahood for the benefit of all beings

bodhisattva (Tib Jangchub Sempa) A spiritual trainee who has generated the altruistic mind of enlightenment (*bodhicitta*) and is on the path to full buddhahood, remaining in the world in order to eliminate the sufferings of others. Ten successive bodhisattva levels (*bhumi*) are recognized

Bodongpa An adherent of the Bodong tradition, stemming from Bodong Chokle Namgyel

body of light The rainbow body of great transformation, in which the impure material body is transformed into one of light, through the practice of the **All-Surpassing Realisation**

Bon An ancient spiritual tradition, predating the advent of Buddhism in Tibet, which is considered by scholars to be of Zoroastrian or Kashmiri Buddhist origin, but which has, over centuries, assimilated many aspects of indigenous Tibetan religion and Buddhism

border-taming temple (Tib Tadul Lhakhang) A class of stabilising geomantic temples, reputedly constructed by King Songtsen Gampo in the border regions of Tibet

bumpa The bulbous dome of a stupa

C

calm abiding (Skt shatipathana, Tib zhi-ne) A state of mind characterized by the stabilisation of attention on an internal object of observation, conjoined with the calming of external distractions to the mind

Caryatantra The name of a class of tantra and the fifth of the nine vehicles according to the Nyingma school. Equal emphasis is placed on internal meditation and external rituals

caterpillar fungus (*Cordiceps sinensis*) A medicinal plant used in the treatment of general debility and kidney disease

cave hermitage (Tib zimpuk/ grubpuk) A remotely located mountain cave utilized as a hermitage for meditative retreats

chaitya A chapel within a large temple, also used as a synonym for **stupa**

cham Religious dance

chang Barley ale or fortified wine (occasionally made of other grains)

charnel ground A sky burial site, where human corpses are dismembered and compassionately fed to vultures

Chod (yul) A meditative rite ('Object of Cutting') in which the egotistical obscurations at the root of all delusions and sufferings are compassionately visualized as a feast-offering on behalf of unfortunate spirits or ghosts, often frequenting **charnel grounds**

chorten See **stupa**

Chosi Nyiden The name given to the combined spiritual and temporal form of government maintained in Tibet from 1641 to 1951, and in Bhutan until 1902

chu river

chuba Tibetan national dress, tied at the waist with a sash. For men it takes the form of a long-sleeved coat, and for women a long dress, with or without sleeves, which may be shaped or shapeless

chulen The practice of subsisting upon nutritious elixirs and vitamins extracted from Glossary
herbs and minerals, undertaken for reasons of health or as a spiritual practice

D

dadar An arrow employed in longevity empowerments, marriage and fertility rites, and during harvest festivals

de'u Enigmatic riddle of the Bon tradition

debri Mural paintings, frescoes

desi The title of the regents of the Dalai lamas (in Tibet) and of the Zhabdrungs (in Bhutan), who often wielded considerable political power, particularly during the minority years of the incarnation under their charge

dharma (Tib cho) The theory and practice of the Buddhist doctrine, including its texts and transmissions

discriminative awareness (Skt prajna/Tib sherab) The faculty of intelligence inherent within the minds of all beings, which enables them to examine the characterisrtics of things and events, thus making it possible to make judgements and deliberations

district-controlling temple (Tib Runon Lhakhang) a class of stabilising geomantic temples, reputedly constructed by King Songtsen Gampo in Central Tibet, forming an inner ring around the central Jokhang temple

dogar Tibetan opera

Drepung Zhoton the Yoghurt festival held at Drepung one day prior to the start of the operatic Yoghurt festival of Norbulingka

dri fermale of the yak (*Bos grunniens*)

Drigungpa An adherent of the Drigung sub-order of the Kagyu school of Tibetan Buddhism

drokpa nomad

dronglhan urban districts

drubchu A sacred spring, said to have been brought forth from the ground through the meditative prowess of one of Tibet's great Buddhist masters

drubkhang Meditation hermitage

Drubtab Gyatsa ('Hundred Means for Attainment') A cycle of short meditative practices contained in the Kangyur, which were translated into Tibetan by Bari Lotsawa

Drukpa Kagyupa An adherent of the Drukpa sub-order of the Kagyu school of Tibetan Buddhism, which predominates in Bhutan

drung story

dukhang The assembly hall of a large monastery, in which the monks affiliated to the various colleges will congregate

Dzogchen Great Perfection, a synonym for **Atiyoga**

dzong County (administrative unit in Tibet), fortress, castle

E

eight attributes of pure water coolness, sweetness, lightness, softness, clearness, soothing quality, pleasantness and wholesomeness

eight auspicious symbols (Tib tashi tagye) umbrella, fish, conch, eternal knot, vase, wheel, and victory-banner, and flower

eight stupas symbolising the major events of the Buddha's life Eight styles of stupa reliquary, respectively symbolising the Buddha's birth, victory over cyclic existence, enlightenment, teaching, descent from Tusita (after teaching his late mother), resolution of schism, performance of miracles, and final nirvana

empowerment (Skt abhiseka/Tib wangkur) A ritual performed by a Buddhist master, which is an essential prerequisite, empowering prospective trainees into the practice of tantra by activating the potential inherent in their mental continuum

emptiness (Skt shunyata/Tib tongpanyi) The absence of inherent existence and self-identity with respect to all phenomena, the ultimate reality underlying all phenomenal appearances

enlightened mind See **bodhicitta**

enlightenment stupa (Tib jangchub chorten) One of the eight types of stupa, this one symbolising the Buddha's enlightenment

eternal knot (Skt srivatsa/Tib palbe'u) One of the **eight auspicious symbols**, and one of the 32 major marks of a buddha's body, sometimes rendered in English as 'heart-orb' since it is found at the heart of the Buddha

extensive lineage of conduct The transmission of Mahayana Buddhism which Asanga received in ancient India from Maitreya, and which emphasizes the elaborate conduct and spiritual development of the bodhisattva, in contrast to the 'profound lineage of view', which Nagarjuna received from Manjughosa

extraneous emptiness (Tib zhentong) The view that buddha-attributes are extraneously empty of mundane impurities and dualities, but not intrinsically empty in a nihilistic sense

F

Father Class of Unsurpassed Yogatantras One of the three subdivisions of the Unsurpassed Yogatantras (*Anuttarayogatantra*), according to the later schools of Tibetan Buddhism, exemplified by tantra-texts, such as the Guhyasamaja and Yamari

four classes of tantra See respectively: **Kriyatantra**, **Caryatantra**, **Yogatantra** and **Anuttarayogatantra**

four harmonious brethren (Tib tunpa punzhi) An artistic motif symbolising fraternal unity and respect for seniority, in which a partridge, rabbit, monkey, and elephant assist each other to pluck fruits from a tree

G

gakhyil A gemstone emblem comprising two or three segments

Ganden Tripa Title given to the head of the Gelukpa school of Tibetan Buddhism

gandharva (Tib driza) Denizens of space or celestian musicians who subsist on odours

garuda A mythological bird normally depicted with an owl-like sharp beak, often holding a snake, and with large powerful wings. In Buddhism, it is the mount of Vajrapani, symbolising the transmutative power that purifies certain malevolent influences and pestilence.

Gelukpa An indigenous school of Tibetan Buddhism, founded in the 14th century by Tsongkhapa, which, from the 17th century onwards, came to dominate the spiritual life of Tibet and Mongolia

generation stage of meditation (Skt utpattikrama/Tib kye-rim) The creative stage of meditation in which mundane forms, sounds, and thoughts are gradually meditated upon as natural expressions of deities, mantras, and buddha-mind

geshe (Skt kalyanamitra) Spiritual benefactor (of the Kadampa tradition), philosophical degree of a scholar-monk, a scholar-monk holding the geshe degree

gesture of calling the earth as a witness to past merits (*bhumisparshamudra*) The hand-gesture of the Buddha utilized during the subjugation of Mara through which he touched the ground, calling the goddess of the earth (*Sthavira*) to bear witness to his past merits

gomang chorten A multi-chapelled walk-in stupa

gomchen Experienced meditator

gongma king

Great Prayer Festival (Tib Monlam Chenmo) A festival held in Lhasa during the first month of the lunar calendar, instituted by Tsongkhapa in 1409

Great Seal (Skt mahamudra/Tib chakya chenpo) The realisation of emptiness as the ultimate nature of reality (according to the sutras), and the supreme accomplishment of buddhahood according to the tantras). The term also refers to the dynamic meditative techniques through which these goals are achieved

Greater Vehicle (Skt Mahayana/Tib Tekpa Chenpo) The system or vehicle of Buddhism prevailing in Tibet, Mongolia, China, Korea, and Japan, emphasising the attainment of complete liberation of all sentient beings from obscurations and sufferings (rather than the goal of the Lesser Vehicle which is more self-centred and lacks a full understanding of emptiness). The Greater Vehicle includes teachings based on both sutra-texts and tantra-texts

Guge style The artistic style prevalent in Far West Tibet (Ngari) and adjacent areas of northwest India (Ladakh, Spiti), exhibiting Kashmiri influence

gyaphib A Chinese-style pavilion roof

gyelpo losar Official Tibetan New Year, held at the beginning of the first month of the lunar calendar, which normally falls within February or early March

H

harmika The square section of a stupa, above the dome, on which eyes are sometimes depicted

I

incarnation (Tib yangsi) The human form taken by an incarnate lama (*tulku*) following his decease in a previous life

Industructible Vehicle (Skt Vajrayana/Tib Dorje Tekpa) The aspect of the **Greater Vehicle** emphasising the fruitional tantra teachings and meditative techniques concerning the unbroken mental continuum from ignorance to enlightenment. It includes the vehicles of **Kriyatantra**, **Caryatantra**, **Yogatantra**, **Anuttarayogatantra**, **Mahayoga**, **Anuyoga** and **Atiyoga**

Inner Tantra The three inner classes of tantra. See under **Mahayoga**, **Anuyoga** and **Atiyoga**

Innermost Spirituality of Vimalamitra (*Bima Nyingthig*) The title of a collection of esoteric instructions belonging to the **man-ngag-de** (esoteric instructional) class of **Atiyoga**, which were introduced to Tibet from India by Vimalamitra during the early 9th century, and later redacted by Longchen Rabjampa in the 14th century

J

Jatakamala A stylised account of the Buddha's past lives as a bodhisattva, in Sanskrit verse, composed by Ashvaghosa, and translated into Tibetan

Jonangpa An adherent of the Jonang school of Tibetan Buddhism

K

kadam (-style) stupa A small rounded stupa, the design of which is said to have been introduced into Tibet by Atisha during the 11th century

Kadampa An adherent of the Kadam school of Tibetan Buddhism, founded by Atisha in the 11th century

Kagyupa An adherent of the Kagyu school of Tibetan Buddhism, founded in Tibet by Marpa during the 11th century

Kangyur An anthology of the translated scriptures of the sutras and tantras, the compilation of which is attributed to Buton Rinchendrub

Karma Gadri A school of art, which evolved in Kham, integrating Tibetan iconography with Chinese landscape themes and perspective

Karma Kagyu A sub-order of the Kagyu school, founded by Karmapa I during the 12th century

kashag The official name of the pre-1959 Tibetan cabinet

khang A house or building and sometimes an abbreviation for lhakhang (temple)

khatvanga A hand-emblem, held by Padmasambhava and several wrathful deities, comprising a staff skewered with a stack of three dry skulls and surmounted by an iron trident

Khyenri A school of painting associated with the 16th century master Jamyang Khyentse Wangchuk

kira The waistband of a Tibetan or Bhutanese **chuba**

Kriyatantra The name of a class of tantra and the fourth of the nine vehicles according to the Nyingma school. Greater emphasis is placed on external rituals than on internal meditation

kumbum A stupa containing many thousands of images, and often multiple chapels, sometimes known as 'Tashi Gomang' stupa

kunzang khorlo (Skt sarvatobhadra) A type of geometric poetry in the shape of a wheel, the lines of which read in all directions

kyang The Asiatic wild ass (*Equus hemionus Pallas*)

L

la Mountain pass

la-do A stone assuming the function of a life-supporting talisman (*la-ne*)

la-guk A rite for summoning or drawing in the life-supporting energy or talisman of another

la-shing A tree assuming the function of a life-supporting talisman (*la-ne*)

labrang The residence of an incarnate lama within a monastery

lam road

Lama Chodpa A text on the practice of guruyoga ('union with the guru'), written by Panchen Lama IV

lama Spiritual teacher (Skt guru)

Lamdre A unique collection of meditative practices related to the meditational deity Hevajra, which are pre-eminent in the Sakya school, outlining the entire theory and practice of the **Greater Vehicle**

lamrim (Skt pathakrama) The graduated path to enlightenment, and the texts expounding this path

Lato style A localized and less cosmopolitan style of Tibetan panting, associated with sites in the highland region of Western Tibet

latse Top of a mountain pass, the cairn of prayer flags adorning a mountain pass

Lesser Vehicle (Skt Hinayana/Tib Tekmen) The system or vehicle of Buddhism prevalent in Sri Lanka, Thailand and Burma, emphasising the four truths and related teachings through which an individual seeks his own salvation, rather than the elimination of others' sufferings

lhakhang Buddhist temple

lhamo Female deity (Skt devi)

life-supporting talisman (Tib la-ne) An object imbued with a sympathetic energy force, said to sustain the life of its owner

Ling Gesar The legendary warrior king, who is the hero of Tibetan epic poetry

losar Tibetan New Year

lumo Female naga-spirit (Skt nagini)

lung-gom A set of meditative practices in which the vital energy (lung) of the body, including the respiratory cycle, is controlled and regulated

lungta Tibetan mantras printed on cloth for use as prayer flags, which are activated by the power of the wind, or on paper as an offering to local mountain divinities, in which case they are tossed into the air on a mountain pass

M

Madhyamaka The philosophical system of Mahayana Buddhism based on the Middle Way, which seeks to comprehend, either by means of syllogistic reasoning or by reductio ad absurdum, the emptiness or absence of inherent existence with respect to all phenomena. A distinction is drawn between the ultimate truth, or emptiness, and the relative truth in which all appearances exist conventionally

Mahamudra See **Great Seal**

Mahayoga The name of a class of tantra and the seventh of the nine vehicles according to the Nyingma school, emphasising the generation stage of meditation (*utpattikrama*)

man-ngagde (Skt upadeshavarga) The innermost class of instructions according to **Atiyoga**

mandala (Tib kyilkhor) A symbolic two or three dimensional representation of the palace of a given meditational deity, which is of crucial importance during the generation stage of meditation

mani (-stone) wall A wall adorned with stone tablets engraved with the mantras of the deity Avalokiteshvara, embodiment of compassion

Mani Kabum The title of an early Tibetan historical work, said to have been concealed as a terma-text by King Songtsen Gampo in the 7th century, and to have been rediscovered during the 12th century by three distinct treasure-finders (*terton*)

mani prayer-wheel (Tib dungkhor) A large prayer wheel containing mantras of the deity Avalokiteshvara, embodiment of compassion

mantra (Tib ngak) A means of protecting the mind from mundane influences through the recitation of incantations associated with various meditational deities, thereby transforming mundane speech into buddha-speech. Mantra also occurs as a synonym for tantra

mantra vows The various commitments maintained by those who have been empowered to practice the tantras

mantrin (Tib ngakpa) A practitioner of the mantras, who may live as a lay householder rather than a renunciate monk

-me The lower part of a valley

meditational deity (Skt istadevata/Tib yidam) A peaceful or wrathful manifestation of buddha-mind, which becomes the object of a meditator's attention, as he or she seeks to cultivate experientially specific buddha-attributes by merging inseparably with that deity

momo A Tibetan dumpling

monk (Skt bhiksu/Tib gelong) One who maintains the full range of monastic vows as designated in the Vinaya texts

Mother Class of Unsurpassed Yogatantras One of the three subdivisions of the Unsurpassed Yogatantras (*Anuttarayogatantra*), according to the later schools of Tibetan Buddhism, exemplified by tantra-texts, such as the Cakrasamvara and Hevajra

Mt Potalaka Abode of the deity Avalokiteshvara, said in some sources to be located in South India

mu A 'sky-cord' of light on which the ancient 'immortal' kings of Tibet were said to leave this world at the time of their succession

mumo A female mu spirit, said to cause dropsy

muntsam Meditation retreat in darkness

N

naga A powerful water spirit which may take the form of a serpent or semi-human form similar to a mermaid/man

Nagaraja King of naga spirits

Namchu Wangden A series of vertically stacked letters symbolising elemental power and buddha-attributes

Namgyel Chorten See **Victory Stupa**

nectar (Skt amrita/Tib dutsi) The ambrosia of the gods which grants immortality, metaphorically identified with the Buddhist teachings

New Translation Schools (*Sarmapa*) Those maintaining the Buddhsit teachings which were introduced into Tibet from India from the late 10th century onwards, and which are contrasted with the Nyingma school, representing the earlier dissemination of Buddhism. The New Translation Schools include those of the **Kadampa**, **Kagyupa**, **Sakyapa**, **Jonangpa and Zhalupa**

ngakpa See **mantrin**

nine (hierarchical) vehicles (Skt navayana/Tib tekpa rimpa gu) According to the Nyingma school of Tibetan Buddhism, these comprise the three vehicles of pious attendants (*shravaka*), hermit buddhas (*pratyekabuddha*) and bodhisattvas, which are all based on the sutras; as well as the six vehicles of Kriyatantra, Caryatantra, Yogatantra, Mahayoga, Anuyoga, and Atiyoga, which are all based on the tantras. Each of these is entered separately in this glossary

Northern Treasures (Tib jangter) The terma tradition derived from Rigdzin Godemchen's 14th century discoveries in the Zangzang area of Northern Tibet

Nyang Chojung Taranatha's history of the Nyang-chu valley

nyenmo A plague-inducing demoness of the soil

Nyingma Gyudbum The anthology of the Collected Tantras of the Nyingmapa, most of which were translated into Tibetan during 8th-9th centuries and kept unrevised in their original format

Nyingma Kama The anthology of the oral teachings or transmitted precepts of the Nyingma school, accumulated over the centuries

Nyingmapa An adherent of the Nyingma school of Tibetan Buddhism, founded in Tibet by Shantaraksita, Padmasambhava, King Trisong Detsen, and Vimalamitra

nyung-ne A purificatory fast (*upavasa*)

O

offering mandala A symbolic representation of the entire universe, which is mentally offered to an object of refuge,

such as the Buddha or one's spiritual teacher
Outer Tantra The three outer classes of tantra. See under **Kriyatantra**, **Caryatantra** and **Yogatantra**

P

pagoda A distinctive style of multi-storeyed tower, temple or stupa
Pala style Bengali style of Buddhist art
pandita Scholar, a Buddhist scholar of ancient India
Parinirvanasutra The sutra expounding the events surrounding the Buddha's decease
Path and Fruit See **Lamdre**
penma (*Potentilla fructicosa*) A type of twig used in the construction of the corbels of certain Tibetan buildings for aesthetic reasons, and to provide a form of ventilation
perfection stage of meditation (Skt sampannakrama/Tib dzog-rim) The techniques for controlling the movement of vital energy (*vayu*) and **bindu** within the central channel of the body through which inner radiance (*prabhasvara*) and coemergent pristine cognition (*sahajajnana*) are realized. It is contrasted with the **generation stage of meditation**
Phakmodrupa The dynasty of Tibetan kings who ruled Tibet from Nedong during the 14th-15th centuries
phurba A ritual dagger, which is the hand-emblem of the meditational deity Vajrakila/Vajrakumara, penetrating the obscurations of mundane existence
pilgrim's circuit (Tib khorlam) A circumambulatory walkway around a shrine or temple, along which pilgrims will walk in a clockwise direction
place of attainment (Tib drub-ne) A sacred power-place where great spiritual masters of the past meditated and attained their realizations
Prajnaparamita A class of Mahayana literature focussing on the bodhisattva paths which cultivate the 'perfection of discriminative awareness'
prayer flag A flag printed with sacred mantra syllables and prayers, the power of which is activated by the wind
prayer wheel A large fixed wheel (*dungkhor*) or small hand-held wheel (*tu-je chenpo*), containing sacred mantra-syllables or prayers, the power of which is activated by the spinning motion of the wheel
profound lineage of view The transmission of Mahayana Buddhism which Nagarjuna received in ancient India from Manjughosa, and which emphasizes the profound view of emptiness, in contrast to the 'extensive lineage of conduct', which Asanga received from Maitreya
protecter shrine (*gonkhang*) A temple or chapel dedicated to the class of protector deities (Skt dharmapala/Tib chokyong)
puja Offering ceremony

Q

qan A Mongol chieftain or king
qutuqtu The Mongol equivalent of **tulku** ('incarnate lama')

R

rainbow body (*ja-lu*) The buddha-body of great transformation, in which the impure material body is transformed into one of light, through the practice of the **All-Surpassing Realisation**
Ranjana (*lantsa*) The medieval Sanskrit script of Newari Buddhism from which the Tibetan capital letter script (*u-chen*) is said to have been derived
Ratnakuta An important section of the Mahayana sutras, which, along with the Prajnaparamita literature, largely represent the second promulgation of the Buddhist teachings
reliquary (*dung-ten*) A stupa containing buddha-relics or the relics/embalmed remains of a great spiritual master
residential college/unit (*khangtsang*) The residential quarters of a large monastic college, often inhabited by monks from one specific region of the country
Ringpungpa The dynasty of Tibetan princes who usurped the power of the Phakmodrupa kings during the late 15th century and ruled much of Tibet from Rinpung in Tsang, until they themselves were usurped by the kings of Tsang, based in Zhigatse
ritual dagger See **phurba**
rongpa villager
runon See **district controlling temple**

S

sacred outlook (*dak-nang*) The pure vision through which all phenomenal appearances, including rocks and topographical features, may assume the forms of deities

Sakyapa An adherent of the Sakya school of Tibetan Buddhism, founded by Gayadhara, Drokmi, and Khon Konchok Gyelpo in the 11th century

sand mandala A two-dimensional representation of the palace of a given meditational deity, made of finely ground coloured powders or sands

sangha The Buddhist monastic community (Tib gendun)

self-arising (object/image) (*rang-jung*) A naturally produced object or image, emerging of its own accord from stone, wood, and the like, in which great sanctity is placed

self-arising seed-syllable A (*A rang-jung*) a 'naturally produced' seed-syllable A, indicative of **emptiness**

self-arising terma stone (*rangjung terdo*) A 'naturally produced' stone, said to have been discovered as **terma**

serdung A reliquary stupa made of gold

Seven Trial Monks The first Tibetan monks ordained in the 8th century by Shantaraksita

sexagenary year cycle (*rab-jung*) The cycle of 60 years on which Tibetan chronology is based (rather than centuries). This system was originally adopted in Tibet from the Kalacakra Tantra, and each year of the sixty years was later given a distinctive name combining one of the 12 animals and one of the five elements of the Chinese system

Shambhala A mysterious hidden land, often identified with Central Asia, where the Kalackra Tantra was disseminated, and from where, it is said, messianic kings will emerge during the next millennium to subdue tyrannical empires on earth

Shangpa Kagyu A branch of the Kagyu school which originated from the Tibetan yogin Khyungpo Naljor of Shang rather than Marpa

shastra A treatise or commentary elucidating points of scripture or science (Tib ten-cho)

shen A type of Bon priest

sign of accomplishment A sign or intimation of success in spiritual practice

six-syllable mantra The mantra of the bodhisattva Avalokiteshvara (*Om Mani Padme Hum*), the syllables of which respectively generate com- passion for the sufferings endured by gods, antigods, humans, animals, ghosts, and denizens of the hells

sky-burial site (*dutro*) See **charnel ground**

sok-shing The central pillar of a building or the wooden axis inside an image, which acts as a life-support

sonam losar The agricultural new year, held one month prior to the official new year (in Bhutan and parts of Tibet)

stone footprint The imprint of the foot of a great spiritual master of the past, left in stone as a sign of yogic prowess

stupa (Tib chorten) The most well-known type of sacred monument in the Buddhist world, symbolising the buddha-body of reality (*dharmakaya*), and holding the relics of the Buddha or some great spiritual master.

Sukhavati The buddha-field of Amitabha, the meditational buddha of the west

supine ogress An anthropomorphic description of the dangerous terrain of the Tibetan landscape, which King Songtsen Gampo tamed by constructing a series of geomantic temples

sutra (Tib do) The discourses of the Buddha, belonging to either the **Lesser Vehicle** or the **Greater Vehicle**, which were delivered by Shakyamuni Buddha, and which expound the causal path to enlightenment in a didactic manner, in contrast to the **tantras**

Sutra of the Auspicious Aeon (*Bhadrakalpikasutra*) The title of a sutra enumerating the thousand budhas of this 'auspicious aeon', of whom Shakyamuni was the fourth and Maitreya will be the fifth

swastika (Tib yungdrung) A Buddhist symbol of good auspices, included among the thirty-two excellent major marks of a buddha's body. The inverse swastika is also a Bon symbol

syllable A The seed-syllable inherent in all syllables, which is indicative of **emptiness**

T

tadul See **border taming temple**

talismanic object/place (*la-ne*) See **life-supporting talisman**

tangka Tibetan painted scroll

tangka wall (*goku*) A large wall located within the grounds of a monastery, on which large applique tangkas are hung during specific festivals
Tengyur An anthology of the translated scriptures of the Indian treatises on Buddhism and classical sciences, the compilation of which is attributed to Buton Rinchendrub
tantra The continuum from ignorance to enlightenment
tantra-text (Tib gyud) Canonical texts delivered by the buddhas, which emphasize the resultant approach to buddhahood, in contrast to the causal or didactic approach of the **sutras**
teaching gesture (*dharmacakramudra*) The hand-gesture of the Buddha utilized during the teaching of the Buddhist doctrine
terma (Skt nidhi) The texts and sacred objects formerly concealed at geomantic power-places on the Tibetan landscape during the 7th-9th centuries, in the manner of a time capsule, which were later revealed in subsequent centuries by the treasure-finders (*terton*) appointed to discover them. Other termas, known as gong-ter, are revealed directly from the nature of buddha-mind
thread-cross (Tib do) A wooden framed structure crossed with many layers of coloured threads, used as a device for trapping and exorcising evil forces or demons
three approaches to liberation (Tib namtar gosum) As expounded in the **Greater Vehicle**, these are: emptiness, aspirationlessness and signlessness
three buddha-bodies (*trikaya*) The buddha-body of actual reality (*dharmakaya*) or emptiness underlying all phenomena; the buddha-body of perfect resource (*sambhogakaya*) whose light-forms appear in meditation to advanced level bodhisattvas; and the buddha-body of emanation (*nirmanakaya*) which manifests materially in the world to guide living beings from suffering
three roots (Skt trimula/Tib tsawa sum) The spiritual teacher (*lama*) who confers blessing, the meditational deity (*yidam*) who confers spiritual accomplishments, and the dakini (*khandroma*) who embodies enlightened activity
three world systems (*tridhatu*) Those of desire, form and formlessness
three-dimensional palace (*vimana*) The celestial palace of a given meditational deity
thukpa soup, noodle soup
Tishri The title of imperial preceptor to the Mongol Yuan emperors
-to The upper reaches of a valley
tongdrol Liberation by sight, an object conferring liberation by sight
torana Stucco halo of an image, arched pediment above a gateway
torma (Skt bali) Ritual offering-cake
tratsang A college within a large monastery
treasure chest (Tib terdrom) Container in which terma are concealed and from which they are subsequently discovered
treasure See **terma**
treasure-finder (Tib terton) The prophesied discoverer of a terma-text or terma-object
treasure-site (Tib terka) Locations in which terma are concealed and discovered
tsampa The staple Tibetan food consisting of ground and roasted barley flour, which is mixed with tea as a dough
tsha-tsha Miniature votive terracotta image, sometimes inserted within a stupa
Tsechu The tenth day of the lunar month, associated with the activities of Padmasambhava, and on which feast-offering ceremonies are held. These may assume the form of grand religious dance performances, for which reason, in Bhutan, the term refers to **cham** festivals
tsewang Longevity **empowerment**
tshe-chu Water-of-life spring
tsuklakhang large temple (Skt vihara)
tulku Incarnate lama, emanation, buddha-body of emanation (*nirmanakaya*)
tummo The name of a yogic practice of the perfection stage of meditation in which an inner heat is generated within the body to burn away all obscurations and generate the coemergence of bliss and emptiness
Tusita A low-level paradise within the world-system of desire (*kamadhatu*) where the future buddha Maitreya is presently said to reside
Twelve Deeds of Shakyamuni The 12 principal sequential acts in the Buddha's life, viz: residence in Tusita paradise, conception, birth, study, marriage, renunciation,

asceticism, reaching the point of enlightenment, vanquishing demonic obstacles, perfect enlightenment, teaching and final nirvana at the time of death

U

Uchen The Tibetan capital letter script
udumbara lotus A huge mythical lotus, said to blossom once every 500 years

V

vajra (Tib dorje) The indestructible reality of buddhahood, a sceptre-like ritual object symbolizing this indestructible reality, or skilful means
vajra and bell (*vajragantha*) A set of ritual implements, respectively symbolising skilful means and discriminative awareness
Vajra Guru mantra The mantra of Pasmasambhava (*Om Ah Hum Vajra Guru Padma Siddhi Hum*)
vajradhatu (Tib dorje ying) The indestructible expanse of reality
Vartula The Indic script from which the cursive Tibetan U-me script is said to be derived
Victory/Vijaya Stupa (Tib namgyel chorten) One of the eight types of stupa, this one symbolising the Buddha's victory over mundane influences
vihara A large Buddhist temple
Vinaya (Tib dulwa) The rules of Buddhist monastic discipline, the texts outlining these rules

W

wheel and deer emblem A motif symbolizing the deer park at Risipatana (*Sarnath*) where the Buddha gave his first teaching, turning the doctrinal wheel in a deer park
wheel of rebirth (Skt bhavacakra/Tib sidpei khorlo) A motif depicting the sufferings of the various classes of sentient beings within cyclic existence and the causal processes which give rise to their rebirth
wind-horse See **lungta**

Y

yaksa A type of malevolent mountain spirit
yangdul lhakhang The remote group of 'further taming' geomantic temples, reputedly constructed by King Songtsen Gampo, outside the line of the 'border-taming temples'
Yogatantra The name of a class of tantra and the sixth of the nine vehicles according to the Nyingma school. Greater emphasis is placed on internal meditation than upon external rituals
Yoghurt festival See **Zhoton**
yogin (Tib neljorpa) A male practitioner engaged in intensive meditative practices
yogini (Tib neljorma) A female practitioner engaged in intensive meditative practices

Z

Zangdok Pelri style A mode of temple construction symbolising the three-storeyed palace of Padmasambhava
Zhalupa An adherent of the Zhalu tradition, associated with Zhalu Monastery (founded 1040)
Zhidag A type of local divinity
Zhije The meditative technique of 'pacification' introduced to Tibet by Phadampa Sangye
Zhoton The Yoghurt operatic festival, held at Norbulingka in Lhasa in August
zi A species of etched agate or banded chalcedony, highly valued in Tibet
Zikpa Ngaden Tsongkhapa's five visions of diverse aspects of Manjushri

Tibetan phrasebook

There is no scope here for a detailed presentation of the Tibetan language, and the following publications will be useful: Stephan Beyer, *The Classical Tibetan Language* (SUNY, 1992); Philip Denwood, *Tibetan* (John Benjamins, 1999); *Kesang Gyurme* (trans. Nicholas Tournade and Heather Stoddard) and *Le Clair Mirroir* (Prajna, 1992).

The basic word order of the Tibetan language is Subject- Object- Verb, but vocabulary, pronunciation and even syntax may considerably from one dialect to the next. Please note that a final 'e' is never silent, but pronounced in the manner of the French é. 'Ph' is never pronounced like an English 'f', but like a 'p' with strong aspiration. Among the important regional variants, you should be aware that in some parts of the country, 'ky' or 'khy' may be pronounced as 'ch', 'gy' as 'j', 'b' as 'w', 'dr' as 'b', and 'ny' as 'hmy'. Also suffixes may be elided, and the basic vowel sounds may change, so that 'u' becomes 'i', etc.

Basic vocabulary

Welcome	Tashidelek or Chapenang (Central Tibet) Kha-a-te (Kham) Ke-demo (Amdo)
Goodbye	Kalepeb (if staying), Kaleshuk (if going) (Central Tibet) Yakpo Songa or Yamo (Kham) Demo che-a (Amdo).
Thank you	Tu-je-che or Tu-je-nang
Excuse me	Gongta
Please	...Nang Roknang (at end of sentence)
(honorific suffix)	...La (added to personal names for polite address)

Nga	I	**Gangdra**	how
Ngatso	we	**Gatse**	how much
Kherang	you	**Gare Chena**	why
Kherang-tso	you (plural)	**Di**	this
Khong	he/she	**De**	that
Khong-tso	they	**Ditso**	these
Su	who	**Detso**	those
Suyi	whose	**Phagi**	over there
Su-la	for/to whom	**Yagi**	up there
Ga-re, Gang	what	**Magi**	down there
Ga-wa	where	**La**	to, in, at, for
Ga-ne	from where	(Oblique particle used following noun)	
Gadu	when		

Useful nouns

Buildings

Ba	Nomad tent	**Desa or Nang**	residence
Chokhang	household shrine	**Dratsang**	monastic college

Dronkhang hotel
Dukhang assembly hall
Dumra garden
Gar Camp
Gonkhang protector chapel
Gonpa or Gon monastery
Gora yard
Gur picnic tent
Jakhang teahouse
Khangpa house
Lekhung office
Lhakhang temple
Lingkha park
Lobdra school
Nelenkhang guesthouse
Ritro mountain hermitage
Tsamkhang meditation hermitage
Tsangkhang inner sanctum
Tsongkhang shop
Zakhang restaurant

Food and drink

Khalak or Shelak food (Central Tibet)
Zama food (Kham/Amdo)
Tungya drink
Tsampa roasted barley
Tu barley cheesecake
Tukpa noodle soup
Momo steamed dumplings
Go-te fried dumplings
Dre rice
Dro wheat
Ba-le bread (Central Tibet)
Ko-re bread (Amdo)
Sha meat
Lug-sha lamb
Tsak-sha yak meat
Ba-sha beef
Nya-sha fish
Ja-sha chicken
Phag-sha pork
Gyuma blood sausages
Gonga eggs
Shamdre rice with meat
Tse vegetables
Lapu radish
Gonga lapu carrot
Shokhog potato
Tsong onion
Tsa salt
Sipen chilli
Jemakara, Chini or Baitang sugar
Oma milk
Mar butter
Chura cheese
Zho yoghurt
Tara buttermilk
Ja tea
Bocha or Socha butter tea
Jadang black salted tea
Chintrang green tea
Café Coffee
Bi-ra or Pijiu Beer
Chang barley wine
Arak hard liquor
Num oil
Sanum kerosene
Porwa bowl, cup
Derma plate
Kuaitsi chopsticks

Travel

Jang north
Lho south
Nub west
Shar east
U or Kyil centre
Namtang airport
Mekor Tsatsuk train station
Chititrang bus station (Chinese)
Namdru airplane
Mekor train
Langkor truck
Mota or Gadi vehicle
Gonggong Chiti bus (Chinese)
Piao ticket (Chinese)
Pass-se ticket
Shoktri 4WD vehicle
Khelma pack animal
Yak yak
Bon-gu donkey
Ta horse
Nekor pilgrimage
Nekorwa pilgrim
Ne sacred place
Khora circumambulation
Yulkhor/Takhor tourism
Yulkhorwa/Takhorwa tourist

Dronpo	guest
Newo	host
Dru	boat
Drukha	ferry
Lam	road, street
Lamka	road, trail)

Terrain

Ri	mountain
Gangri	snow mountain
Tso	lake
Chu	river/ water
Tsangpo	river
Zampa	bridge
Tang	plain
Jetang	desert
Drakpuk	cave
Drupuk	meditation cave
Kyakrom	glacier
Chutsen	hotsprings
Lungpa	valley
Risul	ravine
Ri-tse	summit
Saptra	map
Metok	flower
Shingdong	tree
La	mountain pass
Gyelkhab	country
Rangkyongjong	autonomous region
Shingchen	province
Sakhul	prefecture
Drongkhyer	city
Dzong	county town
Shang	township
Drongseb	village
Rongpa	villager
Shingkha	arable field
Shingpa	farmer
Drokpa	nomad
Pang	grassland, meadow
Shingnak	forest)

Weather

Charpa	rain
Sera	hail
Gang	snow
Mukpa	fog, mist
Tala	dust
Lhakpa or Lung	wind
Kyapak	ice
Nyima	sun
Trinpa	cloud
Sadip	mudslide, landslide
Sayo	earthquake)

Countries

Bo or Bokham	Tibet
Gyanak	China
Gyakar	India
Balyul	Nepal
Drejong	Sikkim
Drukyul/Lhomon	Bhutan
Sogpo	Mongolia
Meiguo or Ari	USA
Yinguo or Inji	UK
Faguo/Firenzi	France
Deguo/Jarmani	Germany
Sulien	Russia
Thaiguo	Thailand
Myandian	Burma
Riben	Japan

People

Mi	human being, man
Kyepa	man
Bu-me	woman
Phugu	child
Bu	son
Bumo	daughter
Ama-la	mother
Pha-la	father
Pho-la	grandfather
Mo-la	grandmother
Akhu	paternal uncle
Azhang	maternal uncle
Ani	aunt
Tsawo	nephew
Tsamo	niece
Punja	relative
Jola	older brother
Ola	younger sibling
Kunda	spouse, hon.
Choga	husband
Kyemen/Dero	wife
Gyen-la	sir
Acha-la	madam
Rinpoche	precious incarnation

Lama spiritual teacher, guru
Ngakpa mantrin
Neljorpa yogin
Gelong fully ordained monk
Drapa monk in general
Gomchen hermit
Ani nun in general
Leka work
Lechepa official
Gongan police, Chinese
Magmi soldier
Menpa or Amchi doctor
Gegen teacher
Drokpo friend
Drawo enemy)

Body parts

Lu body
Tra hair
Go head
Mik eye
Amchog ear
Kha mouth
So teeth
Lagpa arm
Kangpa leg)

Numbers

Cardinals

Chik one
Nyi two
Sum three
Zhi four
Nga five
Druk six
Dun seven
Gye eight
Gu nine
Chu ten
Chu-chik eleven
Nyishu twenty
Nyishu Tsa-chik twenty-one
Sumchu thirty
Sumchu Sochik thirty-one
Zhibchu forty
Zhibchu Zhechik forty-one
Ngabchu fifty
Ngabchu Ngachik fifty-one
Drukchu sixty
Drukchu Rechik sixty-one
Dunchu seventy
Dunchu Donchik seventy-one
Gyebchu eighty
Gyebchu Gyechik eighty-one
Guchu ninety
Guchu Guchik ninety-one
Gyatampa one hundred
Nyigya two hundred
Ton one thousand
Tri ten thousand
Bum hundred thousand
Saya million

Ordinals

Dangpo first
Nyipa second
Sumpa third etc.

Money, weights and measures

Gongjin kilo (Chinese)
Gyama half kilo
Gongli kilometre (Chinese)
Mi metres
To-tse altitude
Rintung distance
Gormo Yuan
Meyuan US dollar (Chinese)
Yingpan GBP (Chinese)
Gyakar Gormo Indian Rupee
Ngulkhang bank
Ngul Jewo Gyabsa currency exchange
Gong price

Useful adjectives

These usually follow the noun. Eg. *Lhakhang marpo* = Red Temple.

Ngonpo	light blue	**Tsangma**	clean
Tingkha	azure blue	**Sarpa**	new
Karpo	white	**Nyingba**	old
Serpo	yellow	**Lelawo**	easy
Marpo	red	**Kale Kapo**	difficult
Jangkhu	Green	**Jokpo**	fast
Nagpo	black	**Ga-le**	slow
Chenpo	big	**Kyipo**	happy
Chungchung	small	**sad**	Kyowa
Dringwa	average	**Gong Chenpo**	expensive
Ringbo	tall	**Gong Dewo**	cheap
Tungtung	short	**Dewo**	well
Ta Ringbo	far	**Mi Dewo**	unwell
Ta Nyebo	near	**Yepa**	right
Dzewa	beautiful	**Yonpa**	left
Nying Jewo	pretty	**Tsa-ba**	hot
Tsokpa	dirty	**Drangmo**	cold

Useful verbs

Most Tibetan verbs have four tenses; present, past, future and imperative, but there is also a large number of phrasal verbs, formed by attaching an auxiliary verb (such as *gyab-pa* (to strike), *tong-wa* (to send) or *che-pa* (to do/make) to a noun. The verb will usually come at the end of a clause or sentence, following the object. Here is a short list of some commonly used verbs:

To come

yong ba	present
yong ba	past
yong ba	future
shog!	Imperative

To go

dro wa	present
chin-pa	past
dro-wa	future
song!	Imperative

To go (hon.)

peb pa	present
peb-pa	past
peb-pa	future
peb!	Imperative

To arrive

leb pa	present
leb-pa	past
leb-pa	future

To sit

do-pa	present
de-pa	past
de-pa	future
do	imperative

To sit (hon.)

zhuk-pa	present
zhuk-pa	past
zhuk-pa	future
zhuk!	Imperative

To sleep

yal-wa	present
nyal-wa	past
nyal-wa	future
nyol!	Imperative

To eat

za-wa	present
ze-pa	past
za-wa	future
zo!	Imperative

To drink

tung-wa	present
tung-pa	past
tung-pa	future
tung!	Imperative

To do/ work

ched-pa	present
che-wa	past
ye-wa	future
che!	Imperative

To make

zo-wa	present
zo-pa	past
zo-wa	future
zo!	Imperative

To offer

bul-wa	present
phul-wa	past
bul-wa	future
phul!	Imperative

To meditate

gompa	present
gom-pa	past
gom-pa	future
gom!	imperative

Auxiliary verbs

Modern Central Tibetan also has nine auxiliary verbs that are commonly added to verbal stems. These are:

yin (to be) and its negative form **min**. This is used in simple statements.
eg: **Nga bo-pa yin** — I am Tibetan

re (to be) and its negative form **ma-re**. This is used in generic statements.
eg. **Ja di zhimpo re** — This tea is delicious [so they say!]

dug (to be) and its negative form **mindug**. This is used in assertive statements.
eg. **Ja di zhimpo dug** — This tea is delicious [I know it to be so!]

yo (to have) and its negative form **me**.
eg. **Nga la deb mangpo yo** — I have many books.

yong (to come) and its negative form **mi yong**. This is used in future statements.
eg. **Nge der leb yong** — I will come there.

jung (to have happened) and its negative form **ma-jung**. This is used in past statements
eg. **Nyima shar jung** — The sun rose.

song (to have gone) and its negative form **ma-song**. This is used in past statements
eg. **Nge ha go song.** — I understand.

zhak (to have certainly..) and its negative form **mindug**. This is used in past statements.
eg. **Kherang champa gyab zhak** — You have caught a cold.

nyong (to have experienced) and its negative form **ma-nyong**. This is used in past statements.
eg. **Khong lhasa la peb ma nyong** — He has never been to Lhasa.

Useful phrases

Meeting a stranger

What is your name?	Kherang ming-la ga-re zer gyi dug?
My name is Yonten.	Ngei ming yonten yin.
Which country are you from?	Kherang phayul ga-ne yin.
I am from India.	Nga gyakar ne yin.
How old are you?	Kherang lo gatse re.
I am fifty-six.	Nga ngabchu ngadruk yin.
Are you married?	Kherang changsa gyab songe?
Yes I am.	Nge changsa gyab tsar song.
I have three children.	Phu-gu sum yo.
Do you like Tibet?	Kherang Bo-la ga-gi dug-ge?
Yes, I do.	La dug.

Shopping

How much is that painting?	Tangkha di gong gatse re?
Six hundred Renminbi.	Gormo drug gya.
Its too expensive for me.	Nga la gong che tra gi re.
Please reduce the price.	Gong mar chag rok nang.
Can you pay five hundred?	Ngabgya ter tub gyi re we?
OK!	La re.

Travelling

Yesterday I went to Toling Monastery.	Khasang nga toling gonpa la chin ba yin.
I visited the Red Temple.	Lhakhang marpo zhal song.
Tomorrow I will leave for Tsaparang.	Sang nyin nga tsaparang la dro gi yin.
Can I buy a bus ticket to Kermo here.	Kermo gyi gonggong chiti piao dir nyo thub sa re we

Eating

Where is the Snowland Restaurant?	Gangjong zakhang gawa dug
It is on the east side on Mentsikhang Rd.	Mentsikhang lam gi shar chok la yo
Do you serve vegetarian dumplings?	Sha me wei momo tsong gi du ge
Where is the toilet?	Sangcho gawa dug.

Health

I have altitude sickness.	Nga la sa-to-wei natsa pok song.
Where is the hospital?	Menkhang ga-wa yo-re.
Where is the pharmacy?	Men tsongsa ga-wa yo-re.

Telling the time

What time is it?	Chutso ga-tse re
It is two thirty.	Chutso nyi dang cheka re
When will the train leave Kermo?	Mekor Kermo ne chutso gadu ton gyi re.
At ten to eight.	Chutso gyepa zin pa la garma chu la ton gyi re.

Index

D

M

Footnotes Index

U

V

W

X

Y

Z

Acknowledgements

This third edition of *Footprint Tibet* continues to build upon the earlier editions, reflecting the many changes that have taken place throughout the Tibetan plateau over the last five years. Thanks are due to the following organisations and individuals who have contributed directly to the present work. Footprint Handbooks sponsored fieldwork expeditions in 1995, 1998 and 2001, and the dedicated editorial team at Footprint continue to ensure that the work is user friendly, while maintaining a high standard of accuracy. Trans Himalaya have sponsored forty-three of my expeditions and visits to the plateau from 1989-2003 and their wide-ranging network of informants on the ground supplies a continuous stream of data on Utsang, Kham and Amdo. From 1985-1987, Abercrombie and Kent of Hong Kong sponsored my first seven trips to Tibet, for which I shall always be grateful. The British Academy funded my first expedition to Kham in 1987 through its Stein Arnold Exploration Award, which was followed in 1988 by a filming expedition organised by F Productions of Paris. The late Brian Beresford penned some inspirational passages describing the Kailash pilgrimage for the first edition and these have been retained. Michael Farmer's computer generated maps of Tibet, prepared for the first edition, have been expanded and reproduced in colour with enhanced topographical features by Kevin Feeney. Iconographic line drawings are reproduced from Dr Lokesh Chandra's Buddhist Iconography (Aditya Prakashan, New Delhi, 1988). The primary Tibetan language publications that I consulted while writing the historical sections of the text are too numerous to mention here. Tibetan script was included with the assistance of Chris & Yeshe Fynn, and Chinese script was supplied by Kelzang Drukdra and my wife Xiaohong, who also transcribed and translated a number of Chinese source materials. The the new dates for lunar festivals in 2005 was supplied by Tendzin Phuntsok of the Beijing Nationalities Publishing House.

Thanks are also due to the following friends, colleagues and readers who have made specific observations or provided additional information. For Utsang: Mr G. T. Sonam, Mr Sonam Puntsok, Mr Jigme Wangchuk, Ms Dawa Dolma, the late Tsewang Sidhar, Dorje Dolma, Weisi Pelyang, Khorolowa Rigzin, Samten, Tashi, Clive & Ann Dickinson, Debbie Ashencaen, Keeley Wilson, Andy Evans, Martin Landy, Louise Panton, J. Kleinwachter, John Ackerley, Charles Danzker, Graeme Brock, Cynthia Wu, Kalzang Dawa, Tsering Wangyel, Tobjor, and Thupten Yeshe. For Ngari: Douglas Kremer, Gavin Sacks, Sally-Ann Rudd, Peter Hammond, Tess Burrows, Michael Jantzen, Dr Andre Herold, Wolfgang Groh, Michael Wood, and J. Kleinwachter. For Kham: Professor Tubten Nyima (Zenkar Rinpoche), Sonam Tendzin, Fu Qing, Stephane Sednaoui, Ma Jie Yu, Luo Man, Claude Letort, Uttara Sacks, Barbara Horsecraft, Liu Hong Xia, Virginia Mintz, David Mills, Lynda Green, Karma, Stein Roed, and Jason Patent. For Amdo & Gyarong: Bradely Rowe, Duker Tsering, Guo Yan Hua, Lin Haitao, Rinchen Tsering, Pema Gyatso, Wan Fu, Hua Qing, Ashish Vashisht, Jan Govaert, and Wang Binxi. General: Mrs K.Y. Takla, Mr Tendzin Phuntsok Atisha, Mr Tsering Tashi, Dr Jane Casey, Mr Topgyel, David Hunter, the late Dr Michael Aris, Orgyan Dorje, Torty Conner, Annie Wang, Peter Fry, Basant Bajracharya and Gavin Talbott.

The health section was written by Dr Charlie Easmon MBBS MRCP MSc Public Health DTM&H DoccMed, Director of Travel Screening Services (www.travelscreening.co.uk).

Credits

Footprint credits

Editor: Sarah Thorowgood
Assistant editors: Emma Bryers, Stephanie Egerton
Map editor: Sarah Sorensen
Picture editors: Robert Lunn, Kevin Feeney

Publisher: Patrick Dawson
Editorial: Alan Murphy, Sophie Blacksell, Claire Boobbyer, Felicity Laughton, Laura Dixon, Nicola Jones
Cartography: Robert Lunn, Claire Benison, Kevin Feeney, Angus Dawson, Shane Feeney, Melissa Lin, Peter Cracknell
Series development: Rachel Fielding
Design: Mytton Williams and Rosemary Dawson (brand)
Advertising: Debbie Wylde
Finance and administration: Sharon Hughes, Elizabeth Taylor, Lindsay Dytham

Photography credits

Front cover: Richard Powers (Temple ceiling)
Inside: Richard Powers and Ben Winston (page 10 and No 5 page 12)
Back cover: Richard Powers (Prayer flags in landscape)

Print

Manufactured in Italy by LegoPrint
Pulp from sustainable forests

Footprint feedback

We try as hard as we can to make each Footprint guide as up to date as possible but, of course, things always change. If you want to let us know about your experiences – good, bad or ugly – then don't delay, go to **www.footprintbooks.com** and send in your comments.

Publishing information

Footprint Tibet
3rd edition

October 2004
ISBN 1 903471 30 3
CIP DATA: A catalogue record for this book is available from the British Library

Published by Footprint

6 Riverside Court
Lower Bristol Road
Bath BA2 3DZ, UK
T +44 (0)1225 469141
F +44 (0)1225 469461
discover@footprintbooks.com
www.footprintbooks.com

Distributed in the USA by

Publishers Group West

Neither the black and white nor colour maps are intended to have any political significance.

Every effort has been made to ensure that the facts in this guidebook are accurate. However, travellers should still obtain advice from consulates, airlines etc about travel and visa requirements before travelling. The authors and publishers cannot accept responsibility for any loss, injury or inconvenience however caused.

Map index

Map symbols

Administration

- Capital city
- Other city/town

- International border
- Regional border
- Disputed border

Roads and travel

- Main road (National highway)
- Unpaved or *ripio* (gravel) road
- 4WD track
- Footpath
- Railway with station
- Airport
- Bus station
- Metro station
- Cable car
- Funicular
- Ferry

Water features

- River, canal
- Lake, ocean
- Seasonal marshland
- Beach, sand bank
- Waterfall

Topographical features

- Contours (approx)
- Mountain
- Volcano
- Mountain pass
- Escarpment
- Gorge
- Glacier
- Salt flat
- Rocks

Cities and towns

- Main through route
- Main street
- Minor street
- Pedestrianized street
- Tunnel
- One way street
- Steps
- Bridge
- Fortified wall
- Park, garden, stadium
- Sleeping
- Eating
- Bars & clubs
- Entertainment
- cp Casa particular
- Building
- Sight
- Cathedral, church
- Buddhist temple / monastery
- Hindu temple
- Meru
- Mosque
- Stupa
- Synagogue
- Tourist office
- Museum
- Post office
- Police
- Bank
- Internet
- Telephone
- Market
- Hospital
- Parking
- Petrol
- Golf
- A Detail map
- A Related map

Other symbols

- Archaeological site
- National park, wildlife reserve
- Viewing point
- Campsite
- Refuge, lodge
- Castle
- Diving
- Deciduous/coniferous/palm trees
- Hide
- Vineyard
- Distillery
- Shipwreck
- Historic battlefield

Counties & regions of the Tibetan Plateau

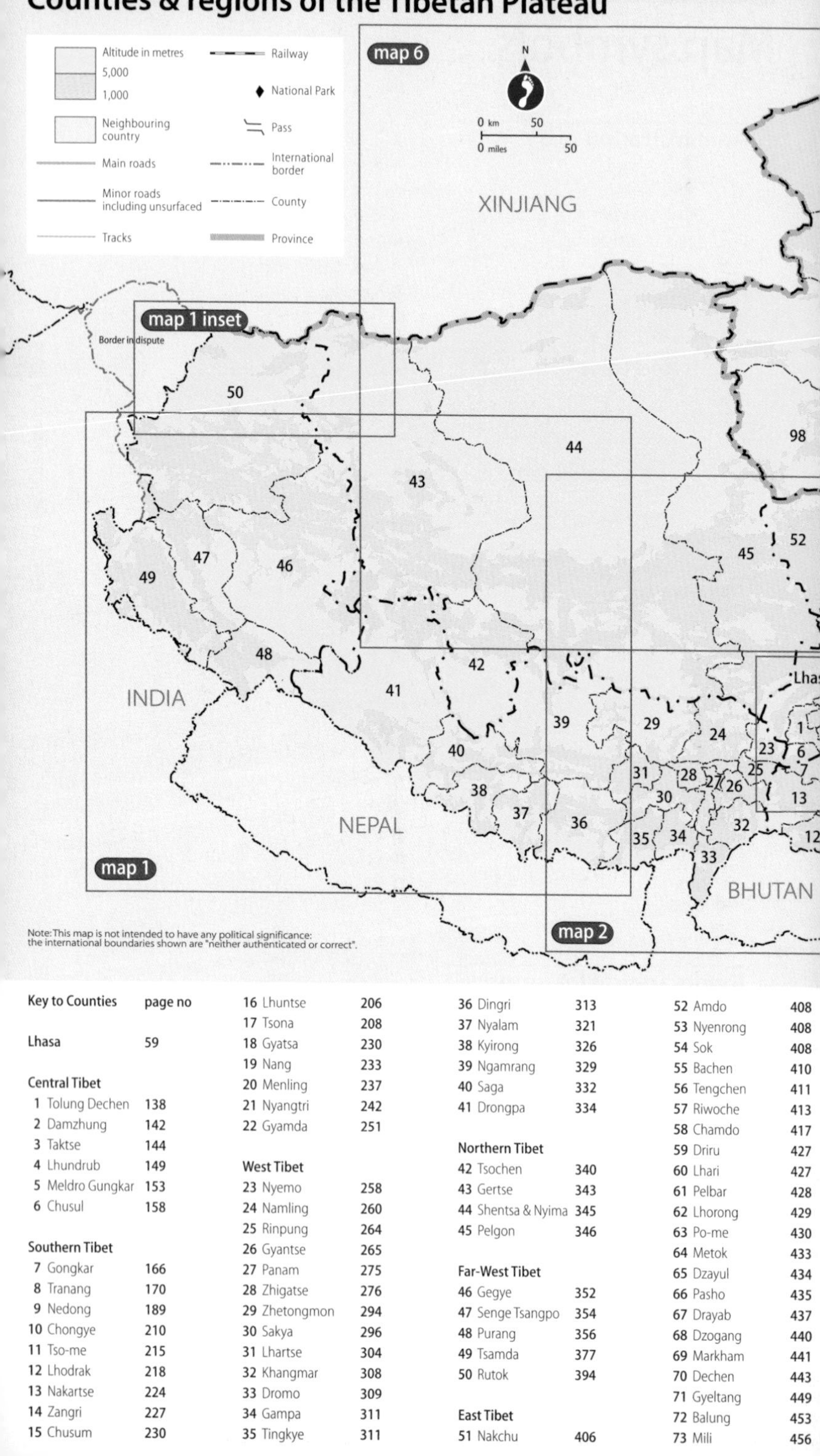

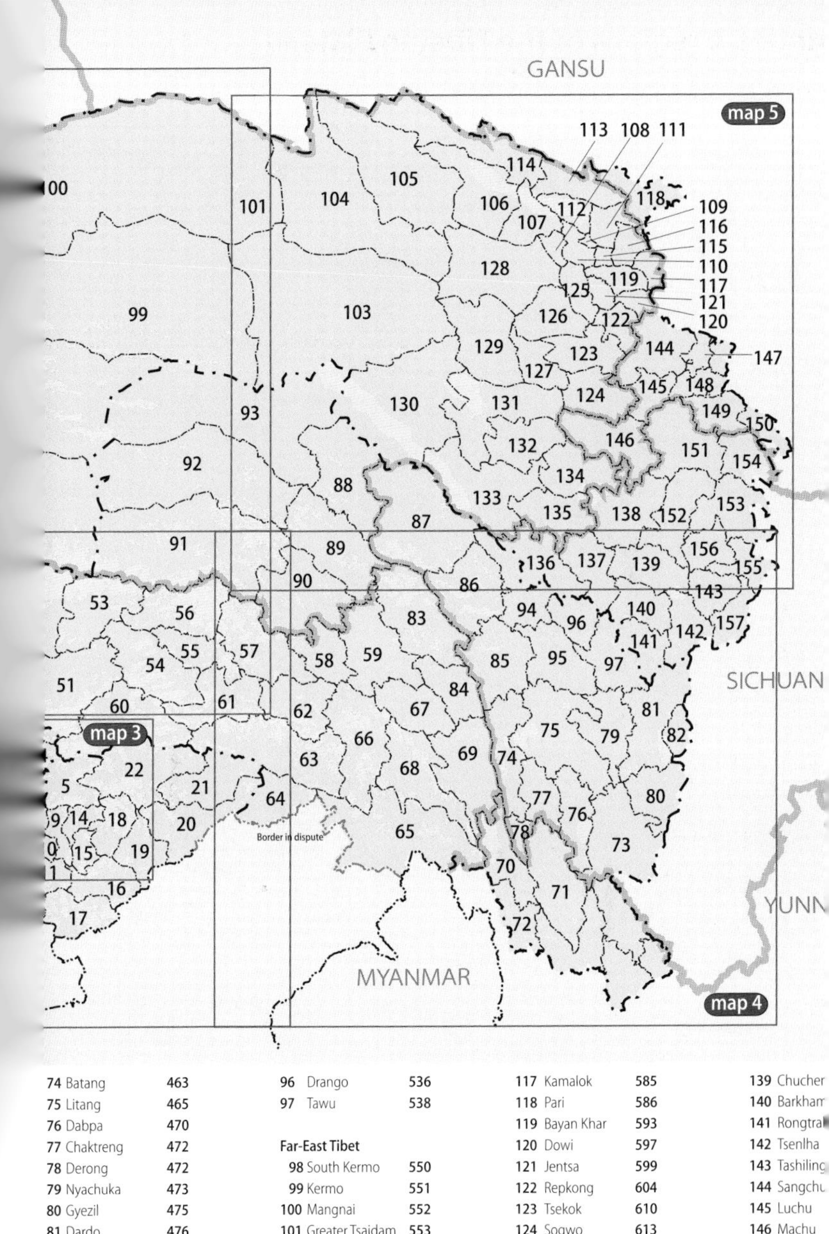
GANSU
map 5
SICHUAN
YUNN
MYANMAR
map 4
map 3
Border in dispute

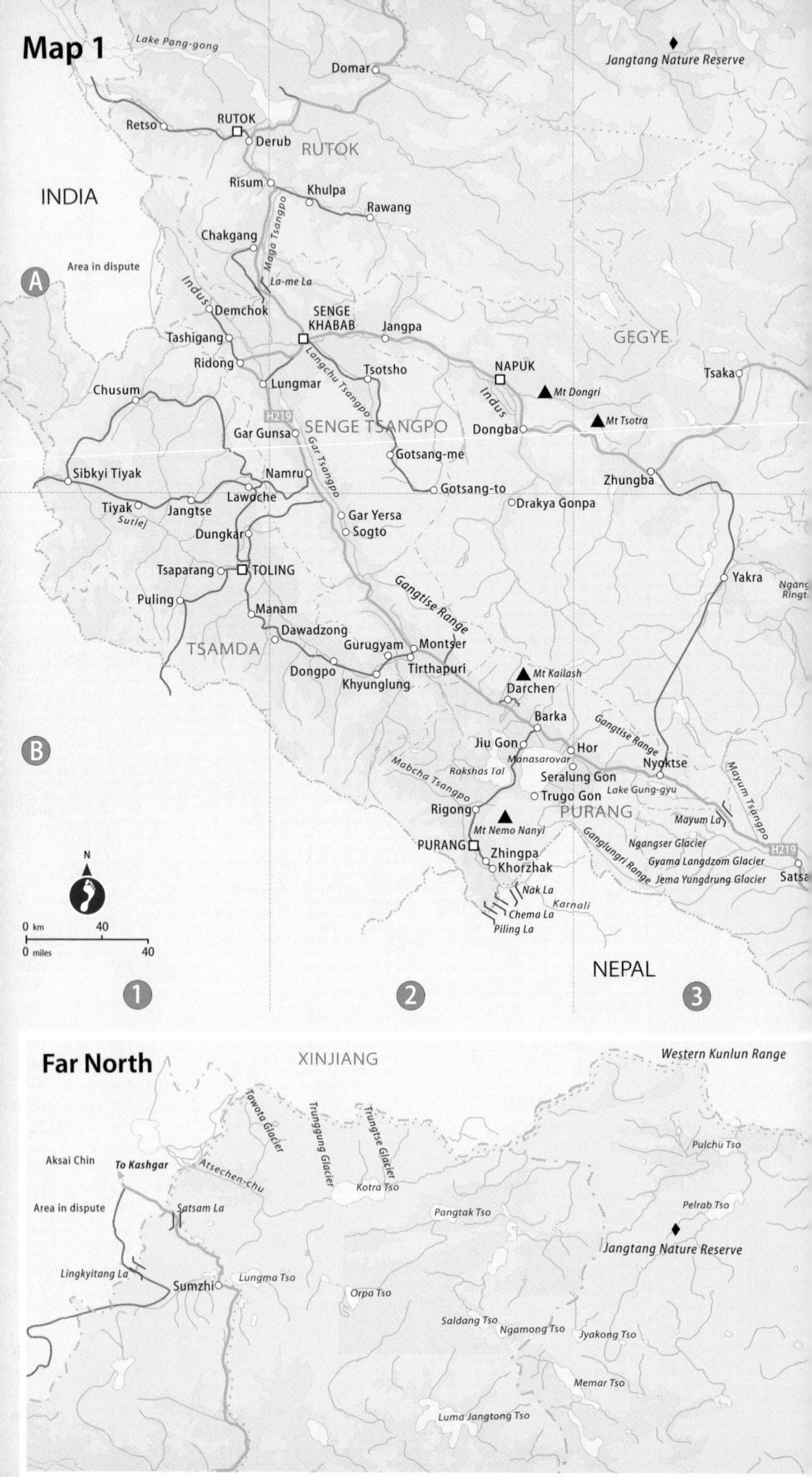

Map 1
Lake Pang-gong
Domar
Jangtang Nature Reserve
Retso
RUTOK
Derub
RUTOK
Risum
Khulpa
Rawang
INDIA
Chakgang
Maga Tsangpo
Area in dispute
A
La-me La
Indus
Demchok
SENGE KHABAB
Jangpa
GEGYE
Tashigang
Ridong
Langchu Tsangpo
Tsotsho
NAPUK
Tsaka
Lungmar
Mt Dongri
Chusum
Indus
H219
SENGE TSANGPO
Mt Tsotra
Gar Gunsa
Dongba
Gar Tsangpo
Gotsang-me
Sibkyi Tiyak
Namru
Zhungba
Lawoche
Gotsang-to
Tiyak
Jangtse
Drakya Gonpa
Sutlej
Gar Yersa
Dungkar
Sogto
Tsaparang
TOLING
Yakra
Puling
Gangtise Range
Manam
Dawadzong
TSAMDA
Gurugyam
Montser
Tirthapuri
Dongpo
Khyunglung
Mt Kailash
Darchen
Barka
B
Jiu Gon
Gangtise Range
Hor
Manasarovar
Mabcha Tsangpo
Rakshas Tal
Nyoktse
Seralung Gon
Mayum Tsangpo
Trugo Gon
Lake Gung-gyu
Rigong
PURANG
Mt Nemo Nanyi
Mayum La
PURANG
Ganglungri Range
Ngangser Glacier
H219
Zhingpa
Khorzhak
Gyama Langdzom Glacier
Jema Yungdrung Glacier
Nak La
Karnali
Chema La
Piling La
N
0 km 40
0 miles 40
NEPAL
1
2
3
Far North
XINJIANG
Western Kunlun Range
Tawota Glacier
Trunggung Glacier
Trungtse Glacier
Pulchu Tso
Aksai Chin
To Kashgar
Atsechen-chu
Kotra Tso
Area in dispute
Satsam La
Pangtak Tso
Pelrab Tso
Jangtang Nature Reserve
Lingkyitang La
Sumzhi
Lungma Tso
Orpa Tso
Saldang Tso
Ngamong Tso
Jyakong Tso
Memar Tso
Luma Jangtong Tso

Lugu
GERTSE
SHENTS
Mikpa Tsangpo
Khangtok
LUMA RINGPO
Tsa-tso
Marme
Dungtso
Boktsang
Drangyer Salt Field
Dawazhung
Dawa-tso
Tseri
Map 6
Taro-tso
MENDONG
Ombu
Dangra Yutso
Gyakok
Lungkar
Tashi Namtso
Balung-tso
Ribzhi
Kering-tso
DRONGPA
Khanghreng
Serzhing
Yutra
Tangori
Me La
Sanglung
Tso-me
TSOCHEN
Gyesar-tso
Zhuru-tso
Baryang
Gacho
Tsha-tse
Tserka
Tatok-chu
Tsa-chu
Kyibuk
Taklung-chu
Longpo Gangri
Rukyok Tsangpo
Soge La
Yur-chu
Takyel-tso
Map 2
Penchi
DRONGPA TRADUN
NGAMRING
Amchok-tso
Kang-lhe
H219
Lhaktsang
Kyibuk
Raga Tsangpo
Men-chu
Dargyeling
Lektse Tsongra
Dargye Tsangpo
SAGA
Raga
Gyedo
Zangzang
Drak Gyawu
Rila
Trazang
Sharpa La
Zhungru
KYAKYARU
Chung Riwoche
Gekha
Tengar
Takts
Lowo Matang
Brahmaputra
Yakpo
Trhango
Drepa
Matho
Gungtang
KYIRONG
DZONGKA
Legyun
Drakri
Gungtang La
Gongmo
Zurtso
DINGRI
Pelkhu Tso
Men-chu
Gungtang
Orma
Da-chu
Gurtso
Gya La
Nakdo-chu
Kyirong Tsangpo
Longda
Gemar
Bum-chu
SHELKA
Rud
Serlung
Gungtang Ritse (Manaslu)
Okla
Drotang
Tsamda
Dingri
Tse
Kyirong
NYALAM
Langkor
Padruk
Matsang
Ganesh Himal
Shishapangma
Kyarak
Langtang
Rizur Zampa
Dorje Lakpa
Chuzang
Dzarong-pu
TSONGDU
Lapchi Gang
Rongshar
Bumo Ritse
Everest (Jomolangm
Jowo Oyuk
Dram
Kodari
Drubden
Nangpa La
Lhots
Jowo Menlungtse
Jowo Tseringma
KATHMANDU
4
5
6

Map 2

Map 1
Map 6
see map 3
NYIMA
SHENTSA
PALGON
NAMLING
ZHETONGMON
LHARTSE
SAKYA
DINGRI
TINGKYE
GAMPA
DROMO
KHANGMAR
RINPUNG
NYEMO
TOLUNG DECHEN
SIKKIM
BHUTAN
Tsonyi
Yibuk Tsaka
Yakgen Tsa-Tso
Tsakya Tsangpo
NYIMA
Taktse-tso
Uru-tso
SerlingTso
Dayul
Kyewa
Kanglung
Ombu
Dangra Yutso
Zhung-me
NAMRU
Drowa
Ngangtse-tso
Gyakok
Kering-tso
NAKTSANG
Poche
Ringa Drok
Tashidor
Namtso Chukmo
Batsa
DAMCHU
Nyenchen Tanglha
Tso-me
Laga La
Nyangri
Pula
Lhabupu
Yangpachen
Somo Gangtse
Tserka
Tatok-chu
Delek
Chungdra
Sanak-chu
Yagmo
Drakla
Zhe Lapu Kangri
Namoche
Ridu
Gyatso
Trangto
Zabulung
Markyang
Kumalungpa Gangri
Mu Khangsar
Sanakda
Tong
Khampalho
Tanakpu
RINGON
Shang
Lhabu
Oyuk
Rikdzom
Jarasa
Menri
Dojo
Dongkar
ZHAB GEDING
Emagang
Tobgyel
Gangri Pelkye
DARDRONG
CHUSHUL
Sinpo
Chowok
Lingo
Trazang
NGAMRING
Gekha
Jonang
Bodong
Shab Geding
ZHIGATSE
Phungpo Riwoche
Gadong
JAMCHEN ZHOL
RAWA
Yakpo Gangri
H219
Nartang
H318
Kharto
Matho
CHUSHAR
Chumik
Zhalu
PANAM
Drongtse
Nojin Gangzang
NAKARTSE
Dorjang Sangwari
Samdrub
Tsesum
Ngor
Yamdrok Yutso
Drakri
Bulhari
Mangpu
SAKYA
Lazhung
Se
Wangden
GYANTSE
Lungmar
Lolo-chu
Mula
Kyilkhar
Nenying
Gyetong Soksum
Jangzang Lhomo
Lhago Gangri
Yago
Netsi
Phuma Jangtang
SHELKAR
Bum-chu
Pelbar
Dramtso
Mabja
Gamru
Phuma Yutso
Tu
Monda Kangri
Jigkyob Zampa
KHANGMAR
Nyeru
Tse
Trakar-chu
Chusum
Talma
Monda La
Lhalung
Padruk
Tsogo
TINGKYE DZONG
Gurma
Mangdza
Tre La
Monda
Kuru
Chugo
Tingkye
Mende
GAMPAZHOL
Kala
Wakye La
Kulha Kangri
Pemaling Lake
Nyarori
Dzarong-pu
Zar
Muk
Chorten Nyima
Dochentso
Yak La
Langdo
Kharda
Tarchen Drokri
Tashi
Bumo Ritse
Everest (Jomolangma)
Rabka
Jewo Gonpa
Chorten Nyima
Longpo Gyeldong
Duna
Monla Karchung La
Lhotse
Makalu
Drentang
Jangson
Tengkar
Jomolhari
Kangchendzonga
Phari Dzong
Rabka La
Yang-magang La
Tremo La
Khambu-me
Amo-chu
THIMPHU
SHARSINGMA
Paro
GANGTOK
Dorin
N
0 km 40
0 miles 40
A
B
C
1
2
3

DZATO
TENGCHEN
NYENRONG
BACHEN
NAKCHU
SOK
LHARI
GYAMDA
NYANGTRI
MENLING
MELDRO GUNGKAR
ZANGRI
GYATSA
NANG
CHUSUM
LHUNTSE
TSO-ME
TSONA
INDIA
Dangla Maktsuk
Dang La
DRAKNAK
SERKHANG
NAKCHU
SOK
TARTANG
NAKSHO DRIRU
DO MARTANG
TAKMARU
NGAPO
BAYI
MELDRO GUNGKAR
DECHEN DZONG
TSETANG
EYUL LHAGYARI
DRUMPA
LANG
CHONGYE
KYITANG
TAMZHOL
ZHOLSHAR
DUNGDOR
Tawang
De - facto Border
Map 4
4
5
6

Map 3
Namtso Chukmo
Lhachen La
DAMZHUNG
Omata
Dechen
Bo-chu
Dam-chu
H317
DAMCHUKA
A
Nyenchen Tanglha
Nyingdrong
Nyingdrong-chu
Rong-chu
PHODO DZONG
Taklung
Pha-chu
Ngarna
Yangpachen
Chak La
TOLUNG DECHEN
Yangpachen Gon
Lhundrub Dzong
Jomo Gangtse
Dechen
Yangra
Phenpo
Nalanda
Shogu La
Mar
Phenpo-chu
H317
Gyedar
Pempogo La
Nenang
Tsurphu
Yerpa
B
Kumalungpa Gangri
Nakar
NAMKA NGOZHI
LHASA
DECHE DZONG
H318
Kyormolung
TAKTS
Zhagong La
Lushon
Sagang
Sangda
Nyetang
NYEMO
Rato
Drak Yangdzong
Angang
Gangri Pelkye
Nam
Shugseb
CHUSUL
DARDRONG
Ton
CHUSHUL
H318
Sinpori
Dorje Drak
Zurkh
Dagar
RAWA-ME
DRATAN
Chuwori
Chedezhol
Kharak
Sa-me
Jampaling
Mindroli
Zhung Treshing
GONGKAR
Gampa La
Namgyel Zhol
Dingpoche
DRANANG
Rong Chutsen
Yarzik
Peldi
Donang Sangwari
Derong
C
H318
NAKARTSE
Samding
Tab
Nojin Gangzang
Yongpado
Chungkha Mori
Lango
Yamdrok Yutso
Khari La
Gyetong Soksum
Jangzang Lhomo
Lho Taklung
Pagyutso
Zhamda
Ling
NAKARTSE
1
2
3

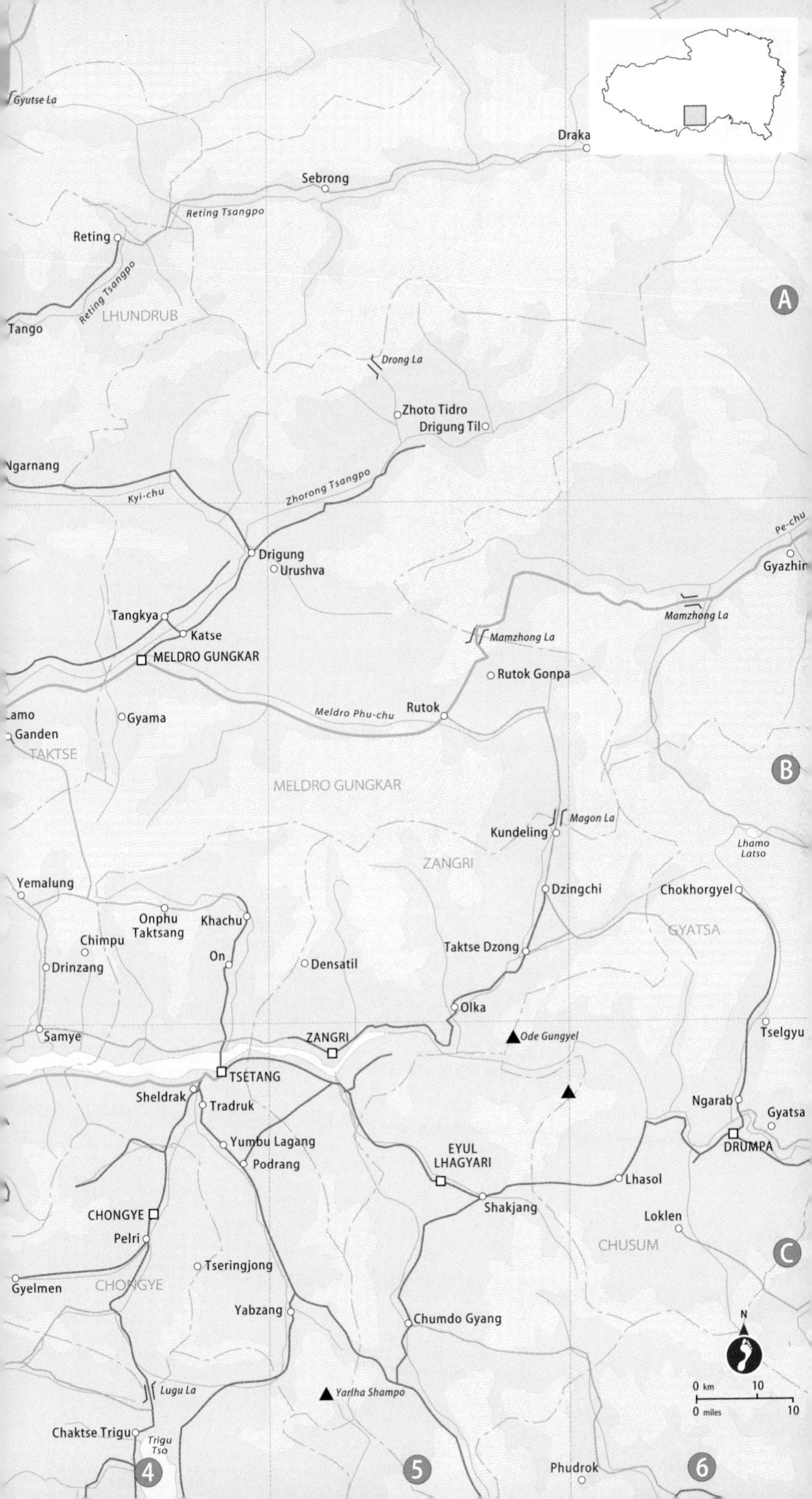

Gyutse La
Draka
Sebrong
Reting Tsangpo
Reting
Reting Tsangpo
LHUNDRUB
Tango
A
Drong La
Zhoto Tidro
Drigung Til
Ngarnang
Kyi-chu
Zhorong Tsangpo
Drigung
Urushva
Pe-chu
Gyazhin
Mamzhong La
Mamzhong La
Tangkya
Katse
MELDRO GUNGKAR
Rutok Gonpa
Lamo
Gyama
Meldro Phu-chu
Rutok
Ganden
TAKTSE
B
MELDRO GUNGKAR
Magon La
Kundeling
Lhamo Latso
ZANGRI
Yemalung
Dzingchi
Chokhorgyel
GYATSA
Onphu Taktsang
Khachu
Chimpu
Taktse Dzong
On
Drinzang
Densatil
Olka
Samye
ZANGRI
Ode Gungyel
Tselgyu
TSETANG
Sheldrak
Tradruk
Ngarab
Gyatsa
Yumbu Lagang
Podrang
EYUL LHAGYARI
DRUMPA
Lhasol
CHONGYE
Shakjang
Loklen
Pelri
CHUSUM
C
Tseringjong
Gyelmen
CHONGYE
Yabzang
Chumdo Gyang
N
Lugu La
Yarlha Shampo
0 km 10
0 miles 10
Chaktse Trigu
Trigu Tso
4
5
Phudrok
6

Map 4
Rato
Peltang
Bida
Zhung La
Sharpu Karpur
Benchen
Yangtze
Tsatsha Gon
Ralung-kado
Langtang
Dolma
Drenda
Druka
Rashi
Ke La
Ku La
Xiao
Zurmang
Denkhok
Trugu Gon
Peni Gon
DERGE
Lingtsang
Dzungo
Nangdo
Zhechen
Drokshok
Yigu La
Tsi-chu
Marong
Chusumdo
Dzogchen
Drokda
Yeyondo
Map 5
Dordu Gon
Dompa
NANGCHEN
SHARDA
Kharda
Zurmang
Zurmang
Muri La
Manigango
Dza-chu
Namgyeltse
Khorlomdo
Sa-chu
Ngom-chu
Menda
Sibda
Terton
Tro La
Yilhun
Tsashul
Nyagla
Gonsar
Kyapje
DERGE
Netengang
Tsedri La
Karma
Changra
Shokngu
Ke-chu
Dokhar
Ngom-chu
Pangri
Wara
Pelpung
Dzongsar
A
Ru-chu
Chakzamka
Dzodzi
Dzigar
Raka
Gata
Jikto
Tser-be
JOMDA
JOMDA
Horpo
Zamka
Lhato
Kutse
Trido
Sertso
CHAMDO
H317
Katok
Tashilin
Dak-chu
Ke-chu
Dzi-chu
Khampagar
Chunyido
PELYUL
Riwoche
Ridung
Topa
Bolo
TENGCHEN
RIWOCHE
Pelha
Barong
Takzham
DRIRU
H317
Guro
Ngu-chu
Sagang
Kyilkha
RATSAKA
CHAMDO
Nyakla
Kyabal
Motsa
Tsanda
Rayul
Meru
Ngamda
Tsepa
Gye-chu
AKAR
GONJO
Mar-ri
Khora
Shingrong
Zhabye
Chakdado
Wakhar
Rinda
Mar-chu
Ngulsho
Kyitang
ENDUN
Lhagyel
Gu-nye La
Shopado
DZITORU
Shayak
Obum
Jamdun
Jangsum
Lhorong
LHORONG
Lhato
Me-chu
Mekong
Yu-chu
Bumkye
Tangkar
Nakchok
PASHO
DRAYAB
Dzi-chu
Jepu Tsangpo
Pel-chu
Karda-chu
Jom-chu
Pomda
B
Yuri
Meyul
Sayul
MARKHAM
Map 2
Khangyul
PEMA
Po
Shulmo
Sanor
BATANG
Kudza Lhari
Tashitse
Lingka
Tang-me
Mekong
BATANG
Taktra
Chumdo
Kala
Temto
H318
Pelung
Chidar
Tobang
GARTOK
PO-ME
Tongjuk
Kanam
Ling-chu
Gyala Pelri
Tondem
TRAMOG
Uyak
Rong-me
Bakha
H318
Sumdzom
Bum La
Gokdem
WAMDA
Gyala
Pemakochung
Parlung Tsangpo
Pangda
Namchak Barwa
Yupuk
Ngajuk La
DZOGANG
Denpa
Bir
Bumpa
Kyilkar
Jarasa
Bum-nye
Rawok
Kyil Lingka
Timpei
Takmo
Shingki
Ngan Tso
Zha Lingka
Dungri Karpo
Jikdrong
Pe
Dozhong La
Gangri Karpo
Hung La
Harmi
Chendruk
Demo La
Drakyol
Deyang La
METOK
Zangdok Pelri
Goyul
Ralung-chu
Tsakhalho
Bongpori
Digdong
Yang-gyab La
Zang-chu
Golak
Bipung
Ngadra La
Gangri Karpo-chu
DZAYUL
Salween
Gongdu Dorsem Podrang
Wapuk
DECHEN
Drowa Gon
Hongchang
Dzayul Rong-to
Meili
KYIGANG
Tsawarong
Dungjang
Menkhung
Kawa Karpo
Pedma
Dupu-chu
Kyita-chu
Dzayul Rong-me
De-facto border
Nmai
Lohit
Irrawaddy
INDIA
C
BURMA
N
0 km 40
0 miles 40
1
2
3

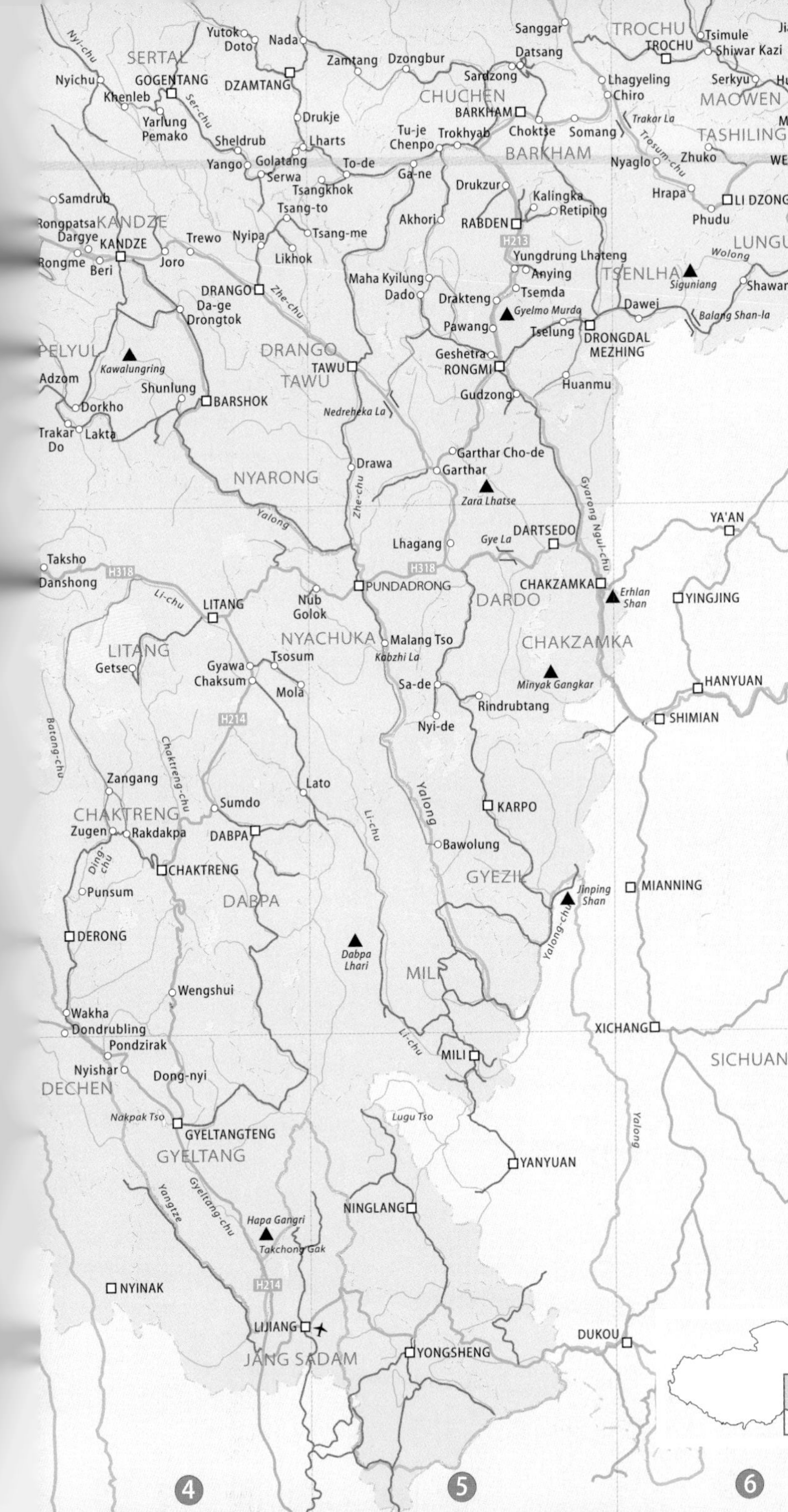

Yutok
Doto
Nada
SERTAL
Nyi-chu
Nyichu
GOGENTANG
DZAMTANG
Khenleb
Yarlung
Pemako
Ser-chu
Drukje
Sheldrub
Lharts
Yango
Golatang
Serwa
To-de
Tsangkhok
Zamtang
Dzongbur
Sanggar
Datsang
Sardzong
CHUCHEN
BARKHAM
Tu-je
Chenpo
Trokhyab
Choktse
Somang
BARKHAM
Ga-ne
Drukzur
Kalingka
Retiping
TROCHU
TROCHU
Tsimule
Shiwar Kazi
Lhagyeling
Chiro
Serkyu
MAOWEN
Trakar La
Trosum-chu
TASHILING
Nyaglo
Zhuko
Hrapa
LI DZONG
Phudu
LUNGU
Wolong
TSENLHA
Siguniang
Shawan
Balang Shan-la
Samdrub
Rongpatsa
KANDZE
Dargye
KANDZE
Rongme
Beri
Trewo
Joro
Nyipa
Tsang-to
Tsang-me
Likhok
Akhori
RABDEN
H213
Yungdrung Lhateng
Anying
Tsemda
Maha Kyilung
Dado
Drakteng
Gyelmo Murdo
Pawang
Tselung
Dawei
DRONGDAL
MEZHING
DRANGO
Zhe-chu
Da-ge
Drongtok
PELYUL
Kawalungring
Adzom
Shunlung
BARSHOK
Dorkho
Trakar
Do
Lakta
DRANGO
TAWU
TAWU
Nedreheka La
Geshetra
RONGMI
Gudzong
Huanmu
Drawa
Garthar Cho-de
Garthar
Zara Lhatse
NYARONG
Yalong
Zhe-chu
Gyarong Ngul-chu
Lhagang
Gye La
DARTSEDO
YA'AN
Taksho
Danshong
H318
H318
PUNDADRONG
CHAKZAMKA
Erhlan
Shan
YINGJING
Li-chu
LITANG
Nub
Golok
DARDO
NYACHUKA
Malang Tso
Kabzhi La
CHAKZAMKA
LITANG
Getse
Gyawa
Chaksum
Tsosum
Mola
Sa-de
Minyak Gangkar
Rindrubtang
HANYUAN
SHIMIAN
Nyi-de
H214
Batang-chu
Chaktreng-chu
Zangang
Lato
Sumdo
Li-chu
Yalong
KARPO
CHAKTRENG
Zugen
Rakdakpa
DABPA
Ding-chu
Bawolung
CHAKTRENG
Punsum
DABPA
GYEZIL
Jinping
Shan
MIANNING
Yalong-chu
DERONG
Dabpa
Lhari
MILI
Wengshui
Wakha
Dondrubling
Pondzirak
Li-chu
MILI
XICHANG
SICHUAN
Nyishar
Dong-nyi
DECHEN
Lugu Tso
Nakpak Tso
GYELTANGTENG
GYELTANG
Yalong
YANYUAN
Yangtze
Gyeltang-chu
Hapa Gangri
Takchong Gak
NINGLANG
NYINAK
H214
LIJIANG
JANG SADAM
YONGSHENG
DUKOU
4
5
6

Map 5

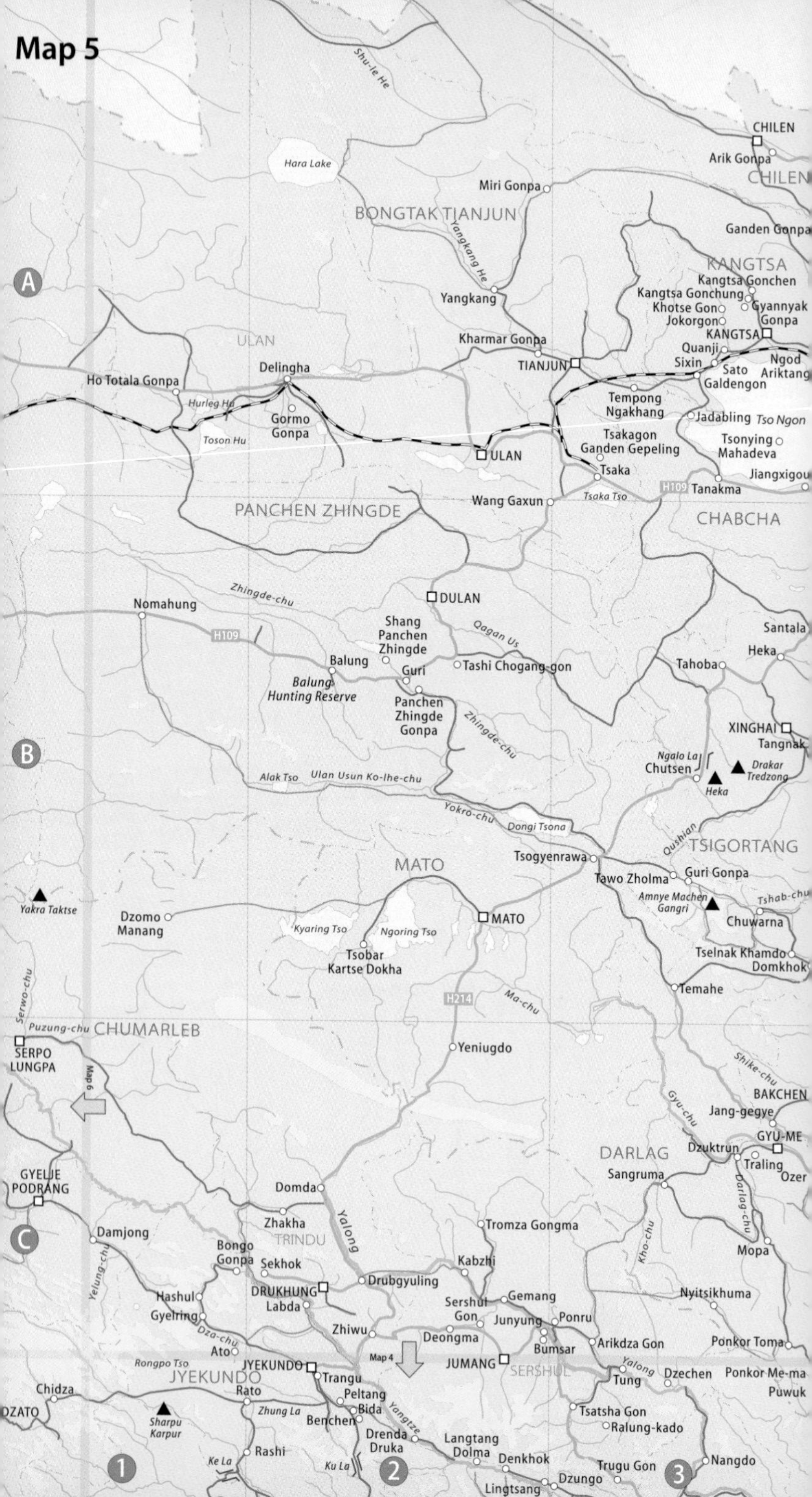

Shu-le He
Hara Lake
BONGTAK TIANJUN
Yangkang He
Yangkang
Miri Gonpa
CHILEN
Arik Gonpa
CHILEN
Ganden Gonpa
KANGTSA
Kangtsa Gonchen
Kangtsa Gonchung
Khotse Gon
Gyannyak Gonpa
Jokorgon
KANGTSA
Quanji
Sixin
Ngod Ariktang
Sato Galdengon
ULAN
Kharmar Gonpa
TIANJUN
Delingha
Ho Totala Gonpa
Hurleg Hu
Gormo Gonpa
Toson Hu
ULAN
Tempong Ngakhang
Jadabling
Tso Ngon
Tsakagon Ganden Gepeling
Tsonying Mahadeva
Tsaka
Jiangxigou
H109
Tanakma
Wang Gaxun
Tsaka Tso
PANCHEN ZHINGDE
CHABCHA
Zhingde-chu
DULAN
Nomahung
H109
Shang Panchen Zhingde
Qagan Us
Santala
Heka
Balung
Guri
Tashi Chogang-gon
Tahoba
Balung Hunting Reserve
Panchen Zhingde Gonpa
Zhingde-chu
XINGHAI
Tangnak
Ngalo La
Chutsen
Drakar Tredzong
Heka
Alak Tso
Ulan Usun Ko-lhe-chu
Yokro-chu
Dongi Tsona
Qushian
TSIGORTANG
Tsogyenrawa
MATO
Tawo Zholma
Guri Gonpa
Amnye Machen Gangri
Tshab-chu
Yakra Taktse
Dzomo Manang
MATO
Kyaring Tso
Ngoring Tso
Chuwarna
Tsobar Kartse Dokha
Tselnak Khamdo
Domkhok
Temahe
H214
Ma-chu
Serwo-chu
Puzung-chu
CHUMARLEB
SERPO LUNGPA
Yeniugdo
Map 6
Shike-chu
BAKCHEN
Gyu-chu
Jang-gegye
GYU-ME
Dzuktrun
DARLAG
Traling
Ozer
Sangruma
Darlag-chu
GYELJE PODRANG
Domda
Zhakha
Yalong
Tromza Gongma
Damjong
TRINDU
Kho-chu
Mopa
Bongo Gonpa
Sekhok
Kabzhi
Yelung-chu
DRUKHUNG
Drubgyuling
Labda
Hashul
Nyitsikhuma
Sershul Gon
Gemang
Gyelring
Junyung
Ponru
Dza-chu
Zhiwu
Deongma
Arikdza Gon
Ponkor Toma
Ato
Bumsar
Rongpo Tso
JYEKUNDO
Map 4
JUMANG
SERSHUL
Yalong
JYEKUNDO
Trangu
Tung
Dzechen
Ponkor Me-ma
Chidza
Rato
Peltang
Puwuk
DZATO
Sharpu Karpur
Zhung La
Bida
Yangtze
Tsatsha Gon
Benchen
Ralung-kado
Drenda Druka
Langtang Dolma
Rashi
Ke La
Ku La
Denkhok
Trugu Gon
Nangdo
Lingtsang
Dzungo

GANSU
N
0 km 40
0 miles 40
A
B
C
4
5
6
MONGYON
MENYUAN
Semnyi Gon
Julak-chu
Drugugon
PARI
TIANZHU
Kanchen Gonpa
H227
SERKHOK
Chubzang Gon
DATONG
GONLUNG
DABZHI
HAIYAN
Lamo
Gartok
ZILING
DROTSANG
Lokar Gon
TONGKOR
Tsong-chu
PINGAN
LEDU
Zhuanglang He
H214
RUSHAR
Taktse
HUANGZHONG
Tongkor Gon
Kumbum
Drotsang
MINHE
KAMALOK
LANZHOU
Daotanghe
Zawa
Detsa
Jentsa Nyinta
BAYAN KHAR
YONGJING XIAN
CHABCHA
Akong
Jakhyung
Dentik
Tingkya Gon
Kyikug
GUIDE
Achung
JENTSA
Kado
XUNHUA
Liujiaxia Reservoir
Longyang Xia
HUALONG
Gori Dratsang
DONGXIANG
LINXIA
MANGRA
TRIKA
Lhamo
DOWI
HANJIAJI
Tashiky
Gartse
Sengeshong
Drakar
Sang-chu
RONGPO
GUINAN
Ganja
H213
Amnye Jakhyung
Khartse
Tarshul
Dzongmer
REPKONG
Wandotang
Xiahe
Labrang
Sangke
Tobden
Karong
GANLHO DZONG
LINTAN
TONGDE
Ba-chu
Hor
Gu-chu
SANGCHU
JADIR
Amchog
Mapusola
Gyagar Gon
Serlak Gon
TSEKOK
Chokor Gartse
LINTAN DZONG
CHO-NE
Nyimalung
HENAN
Kotse
LUCHU
Ala
Lu-chu
KAWASUMDO
Tsang-gar Gon
Tse-chu
Shitsang
CHO-NE
Hin Xian
Chogar
SOGWO
Serlung
Rabgya Gonpa
LUCHU
TEWO
Drangto Tso
TAWO
MACHEN
DENGKA GON
Taklung Shingza
Taktsang Lhamo
Zhakdom
Ma-chu (Yellow River)
Druk-chu
DRUKCHU
DZOGE NYIMA
Jiangian
Me-chu
DRUKCHU
Qingzhen
MACHU
GABDE
DZOGE
Awantsang
TAKTSHA
NAMPEL
Mentang
Benyul
Bozo
Shike-chu
NANPING
Tatsang
Chukar
Sogtsang
Choje Nangwa
JIGDRIL
Tangkor
Dzitsa Degu National Park
Gyu-chu
Sogruma
DRUKCHEN SUMDO
Taklung
Ger-chu
Tangjiahe National Park
Dernang
Nyenpo Yurtse
Bachen
Mangdrang
Warje
Mewa Gonpa
Lungkar
Pangzang
Chungda
Sertso
Tarthang
Mar-chu
NGAWA
Amokok
Dodrup Chode
Ngato
Aling
Shan Dungri
Sertso National Park
Do Gongma Gon
NGAWA
HONGYUAN
Norwa
ZUNGCHU
ADMA
Nga-chu
Nyenyul
MEWA
Dankar
SELITANG
Jangritang
Muge
Pata
Amchok
Dongna
Do-chu
Yartang
Tsege
Jimkar
Dze-chu
Yungdrung
artsang
Tinta
Khokpo
Zhenjiangquan
Lungzi
Mechu
Nyenlung
Dodrub Gon
Ser-chu
Yutok
Dzongda
TROCHU
Sanggar
Nyi-chu
Tsimule
Jiaochangba
Doto
Nada
SERTAL
TROCHU
Shiwar Kazi
Zamtang
Datsang
Nyichu
GOGENTANG
Sardzong
Lhagyeling
Serkyu
Hualong
DZAMTANG
Dzongbur
Khenleb
CHUCHEN
BARKHAM
Chiro
MAOWEN
MAOWEN
Yarlung Pemako
Choktse
Somang
Drukje

Map 6
A
N
0 km 40
0 miles 40
XINJIANG
Muztag
Western Kunlun Range
B
Rola Gangri
PALGON
Map 1
Norlha Gan
Purok Gangri
SHENTSA
Dongzoldong Tso
Lugu
GERTSE
Tsonyi
Jangtang Nature Reserve
Mikpa Tsangpo
C
Khangtok
LUMA RINGPO
Tsa-tso
Marme
Tongtso
Taktse-tso
Nyima
Boktsang
Uru-tso
Kyewa
Zhung-me
Drangyer Salt Field
Kanglung
Ombu
1
Dawazhung
Dawa-tso
Tseri
2
Dangra Yutso
Kering-tso
3